Shojo Beat

STROBE EDGE

Vol. 9

Story & Art by
Io Sakisaka

STROBE EDGE

Volume 9
CONTENTS

Chapter 31 3
Chapter 32 51
Chapter 33 95
Chapter 34 147

Story Thus Far

Ninako is a down-to-earth high school girl who's in love for the first time—with Ren, the most popular boy in her grade. Even though she knows he has a girlfriend, she can't deny her feelings for him and tells him. She's not surprised when he turns her down and asks if they can still be friends.

Ren's friend from middle school, Ando, is attracted to Ninako and confesses his love for her, but she turns him down. Meanwhile, Ren and his girlfriend, Mayuka, realize their feelings for each other have changed, and they break up.

Now in their second year, Ninako, Ren and Ando are all in the same homeroom. Ando's ex-girlfriend, Mao, enters their school. She tells Ninako why Ren and Ando are not as close as they used to be. Ninako tries to give up on her love for Ren because she fears that if she tells Ren her feelings for him, the two boys could become even more distant. Not knowing any of this, Ren finally acknowledges his feelings for Ninako. He starts to feel uneasy, however, when he sees Ninako being friendly with upperclassman Toda outside of cheer practice...

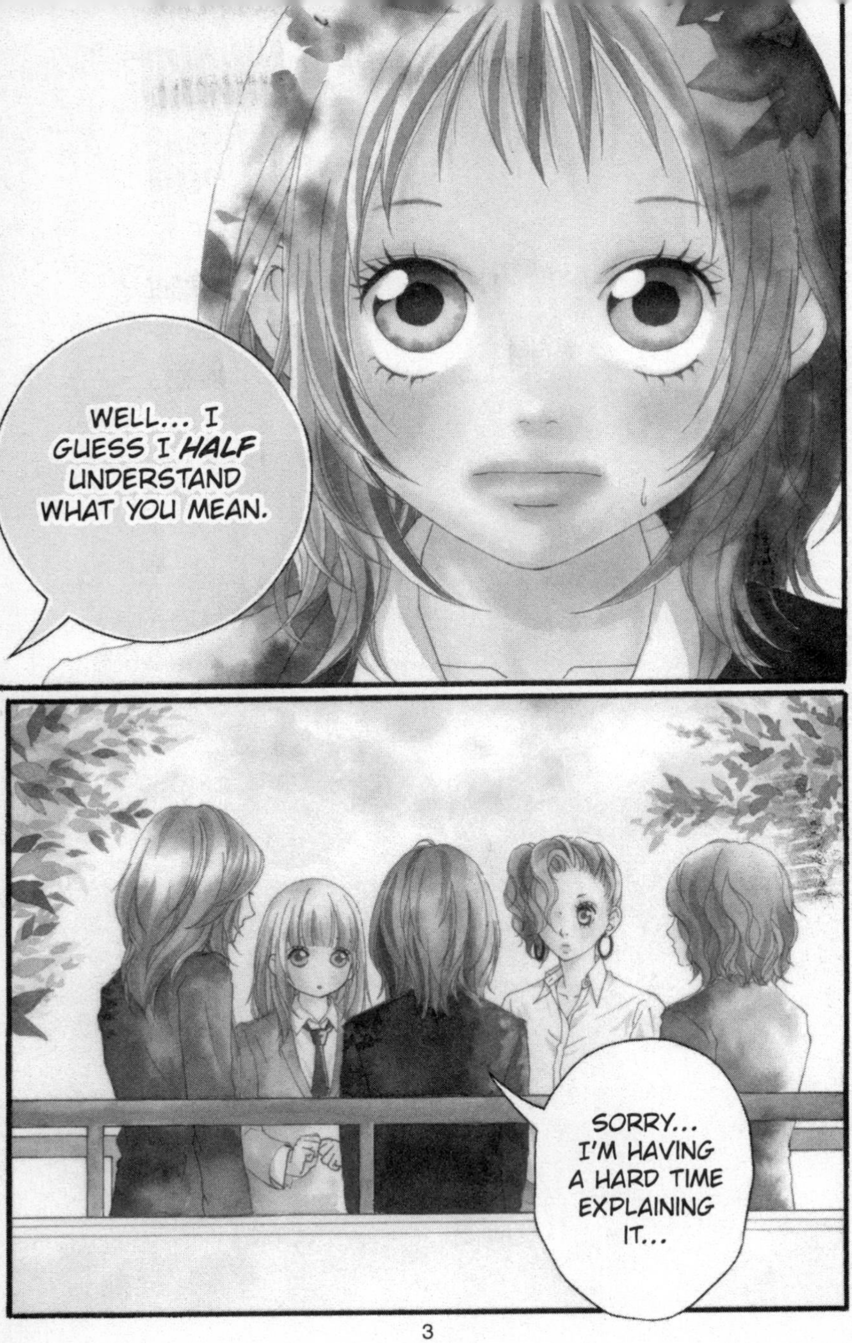
WELL... I GUESS I HALF UNDERSTAND WHAT YOU MEAN.
SORRY... I'M HAVING A HARD TIME EXPLAINING IT...

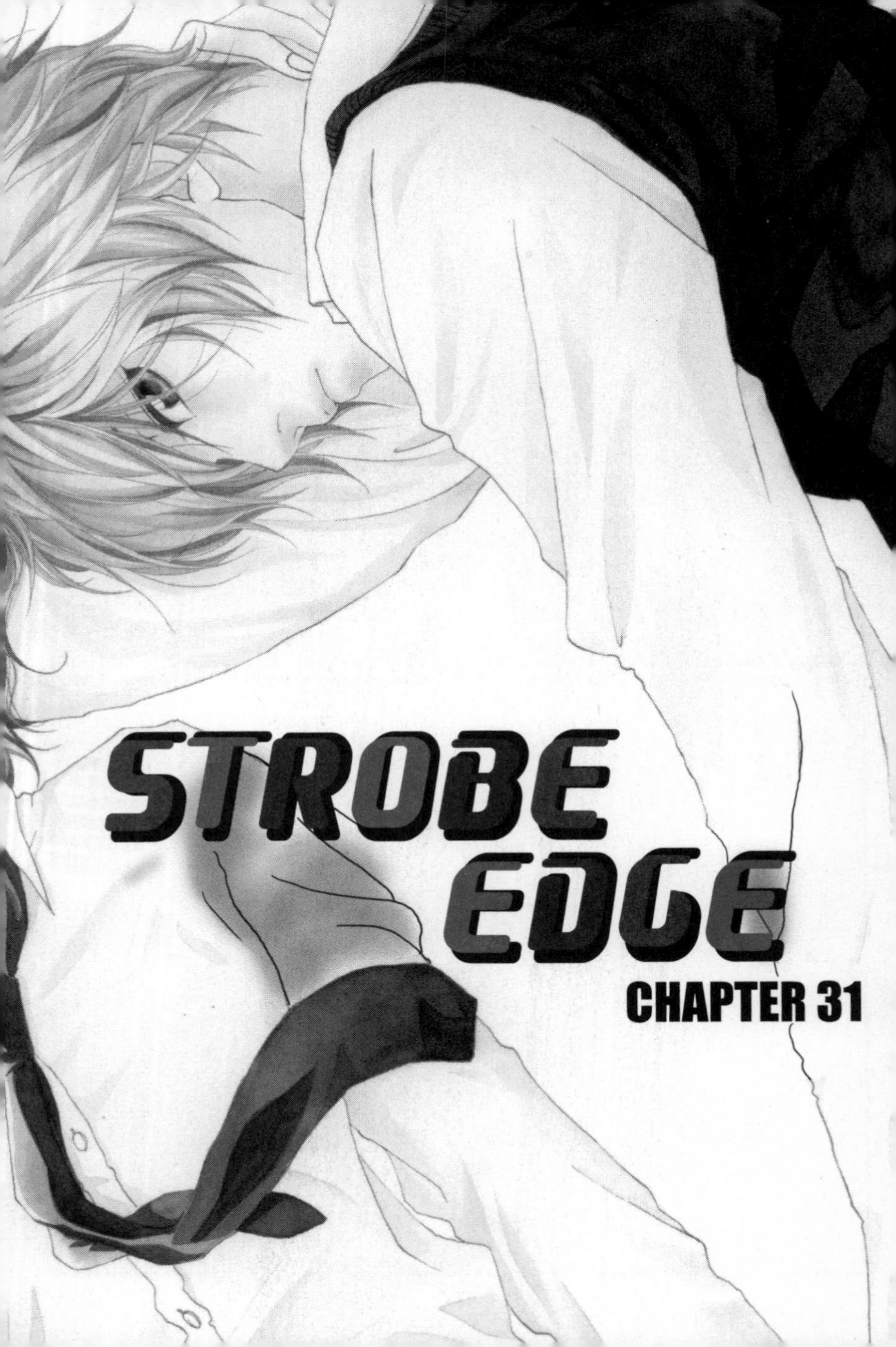
STROBE EDGE
CHAPTER 31

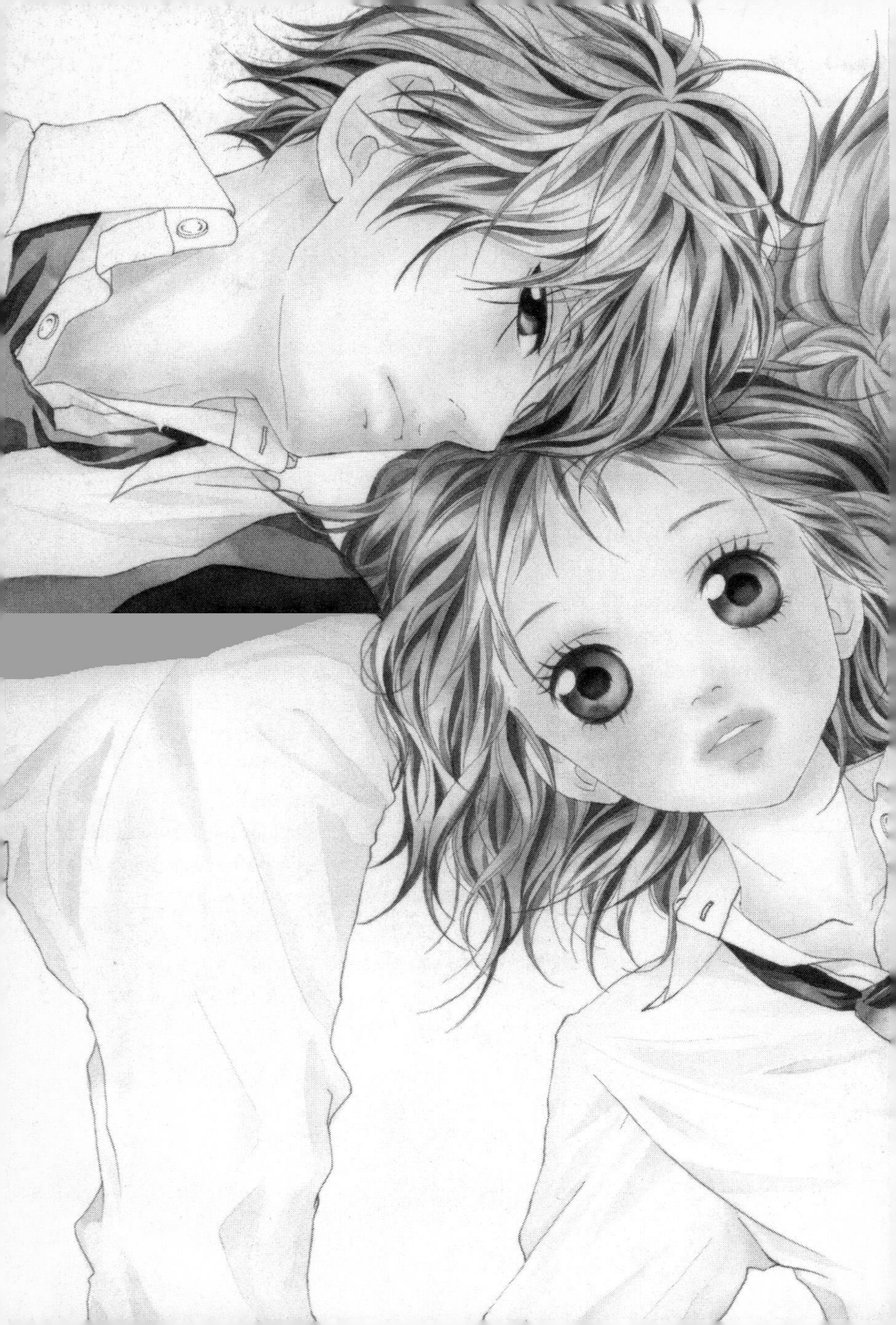

I FEEL BETTER NOW THAT I'VE TOLD YOU GUYS.

...HAVE UNTANGLED A LITTLE BIT NOW!

HAVING FRIENDS IS AMAZING.

I WAS THINKING IN CIRCLES BEFORE.

ALL MY JUMBLED FEEL-INGS...

BEING ABLE TO TELL THEM MY FEELINGS...

I'M SO GLAD I CAN DO THAT.

HAVING EVERYONE HERE...

"SOMETIMES YOU'VE GOTTA SPEAK UP BECAUSE SOMETHING'S IMPORTANT."

I NEED TO THANK TODA TOO...

THE TRAIN IS ARRIVING AT PLATFORM 2.

2

HEY, LOOK.

THERE'S TODA!

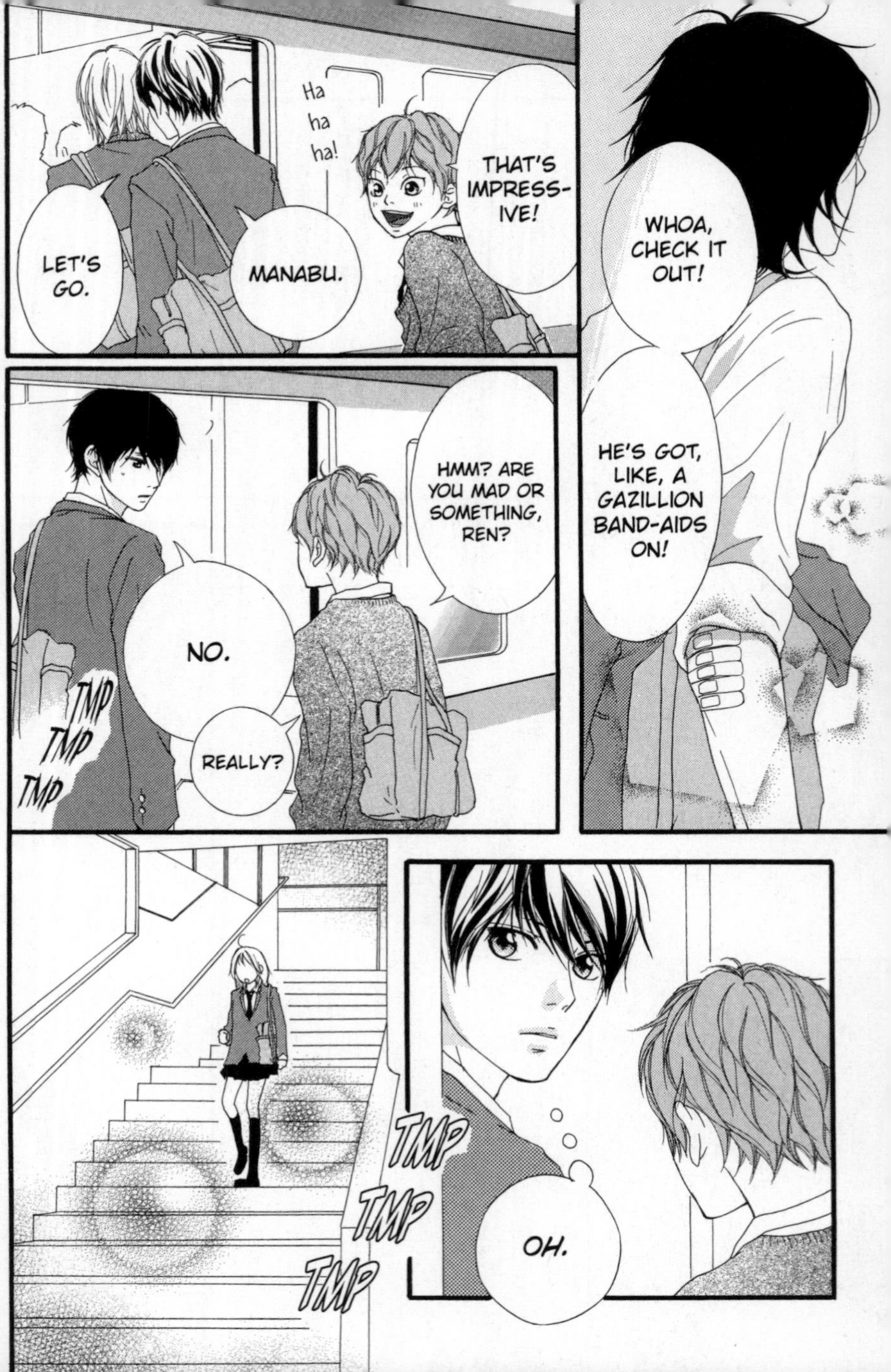
WHOA, CHECK IT OUT!
HE'S GOT, LIKE, A GAZILLION BAND-AIDS ON!
THAT'S IMPRESS-IVE!
Ha ha ha!
MANABU.
LET'S GO.
HMM? ARE YOU MAD OR SOMETHING, REN?
NO.
REALLY?
TMP TMP TMP
OH.
TMP TMP TMP

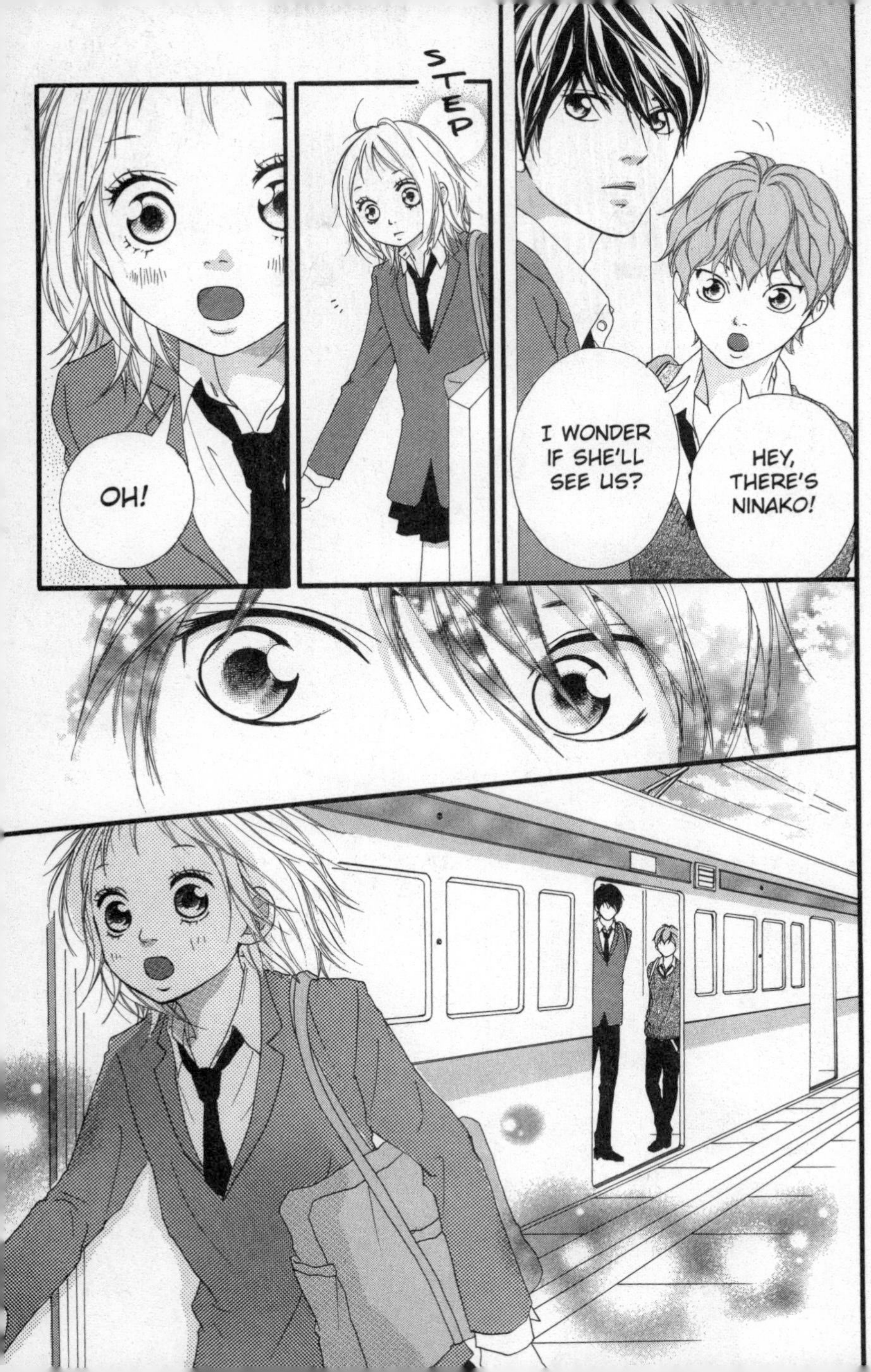

HEY, THERE'S NINAKO!
I WONDER IF SHE'LL SEE US?
STEP
OH!

I HAVE TO THANK TODA FOR HIS HELP!

HUH? REN-?

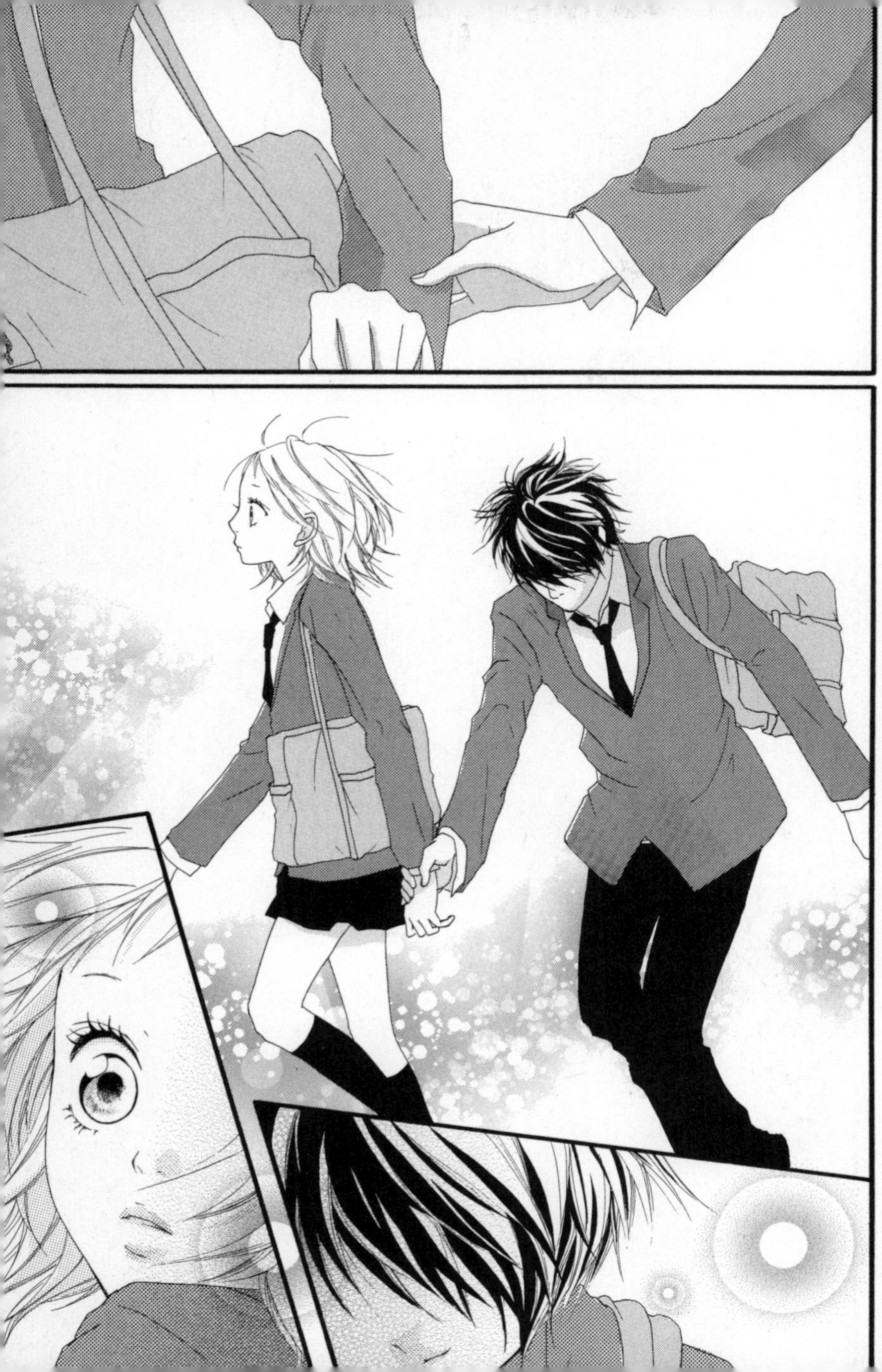

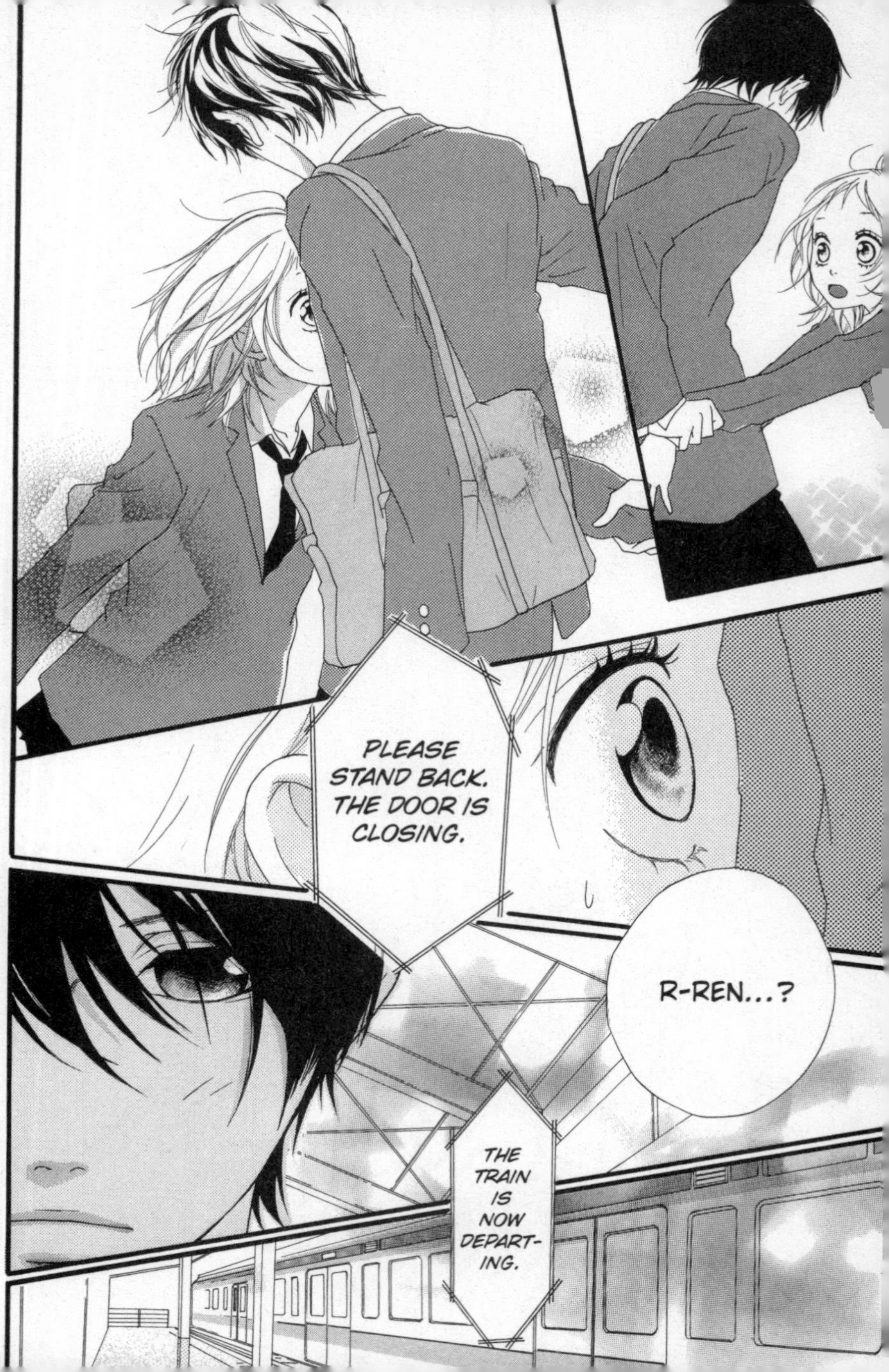
PLEASE STAND BACK. THE DOOR IS CLOSING.
R-REN...?
THE TRAIN IS NOW DEPART-ING.

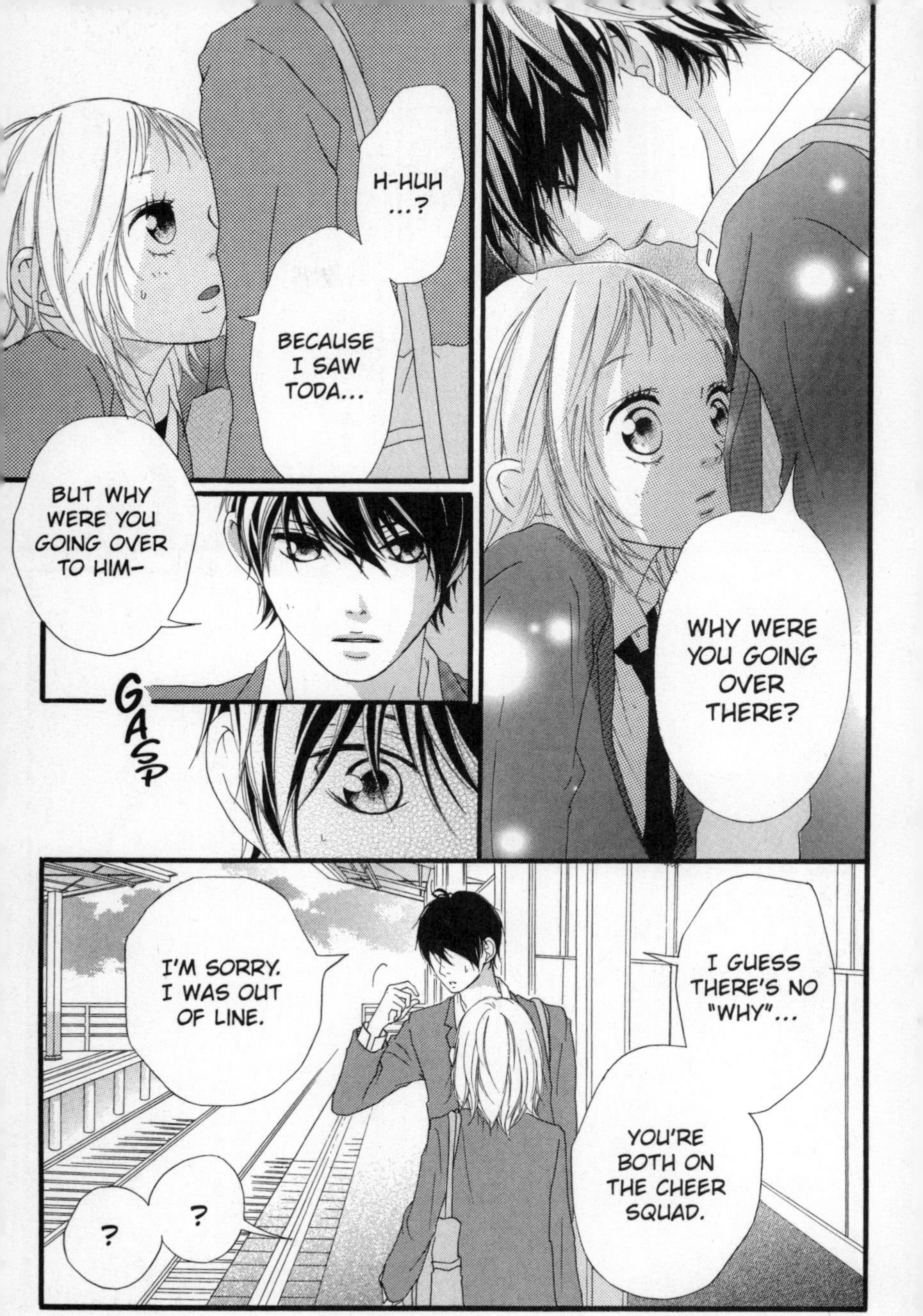
WHY WERE YOU GOING OVER THERE?
H-HUH ...?
BECAUSE I SAW TODA...
BUT WHY WERE YOU GOING OVER TO HIM-
GASP
I GUESS THERE'S NO "WHY"...
YOU'RE BOTH ON THE CHEER SQUAD.
I'M SORRY. I WAS OUT OF LINE.
? ?

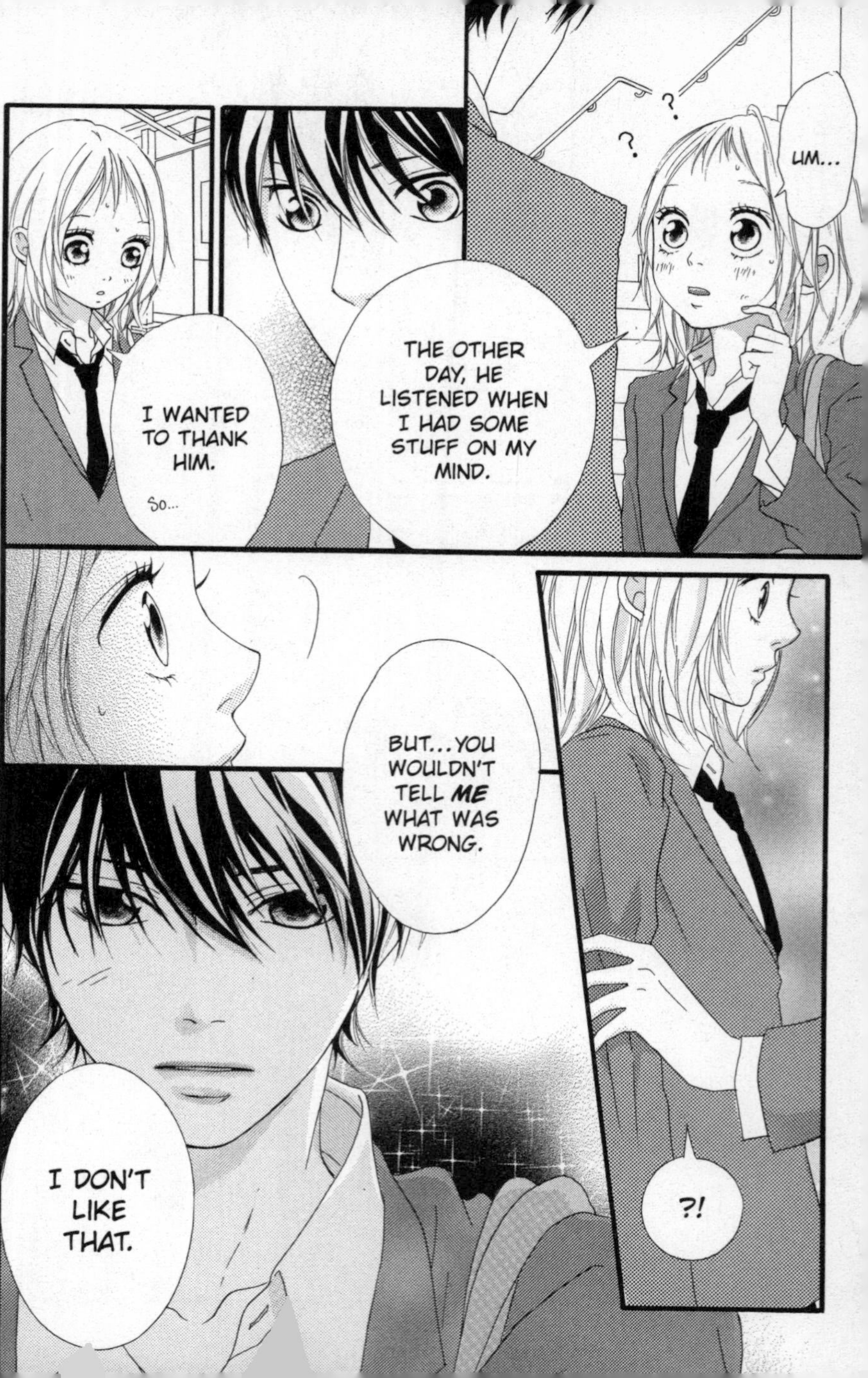
? ?
UM...
THE OTHER DAY, HE LISTENED WHEN I HAD SOME STUFF ON MY MIND.
I WANTED TO THANK HIM.
So...
BUT...YOU WOULDN'T TELL *ME* WHAT WAS WRONG.
I DON'T LIKE THAT.
?!

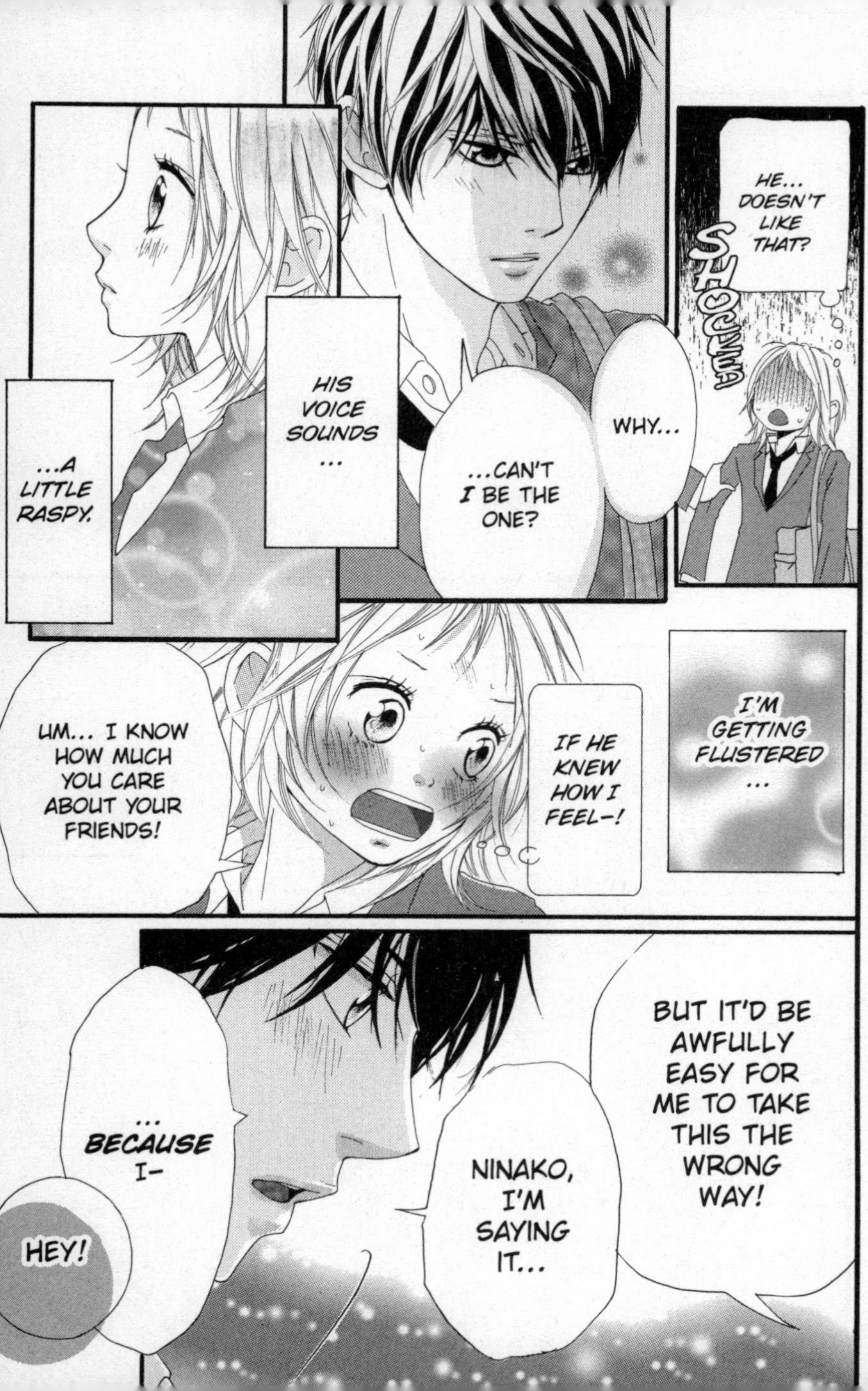
HE... DOESN'T LIKE THAT?
WHY...
...CAN'T I BE THE ONE?
HIS VOICE SOUNDS ...
...A LITTLE RASPY.
I'M GETTING FLUSTERED ...
IF HE KNEW HOW I FEEL-!
UM... I KNOW HOW MUCH YOU CARE ABOUT YOUR FRIENDS!
BUT IT'D BE AWFULLY EASY FOR ME TO TAKE THIS THE WRONG WAY!
NINAKO, I'M SAYING IT...
... BECAUSE I-
HEY!

HI.

?!

MANABU!

AUTOMATICALLY FOLLOWED REN OFF THE TRAIN

Mm.

You know how it is...

So that's what happened!

I see...

OH, THAT'S ME.

RIGHT! TIME TO GET OFF.

SHIN SAKUDA.

SHIN SAKUDA.

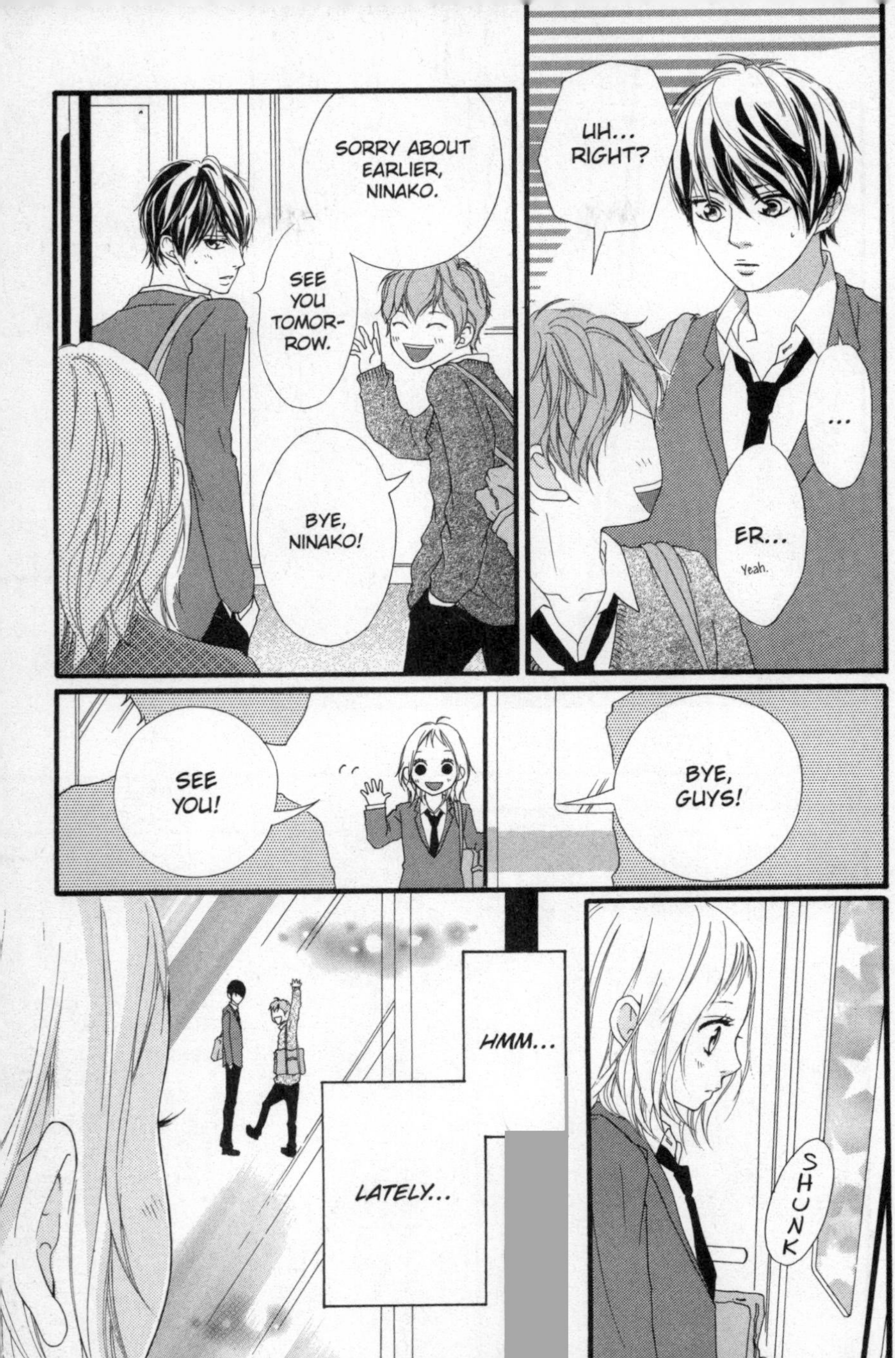
UH... RIGHT?
...
ER...
Yeah.
SORRY ABOUT EARLIER, NINAKO.
SEE YOU TOMOR-ROW.
BYE, NINAKO!
BYE, GUYS!
SEE YOU!
SHUNK
HMM...
LATELY...

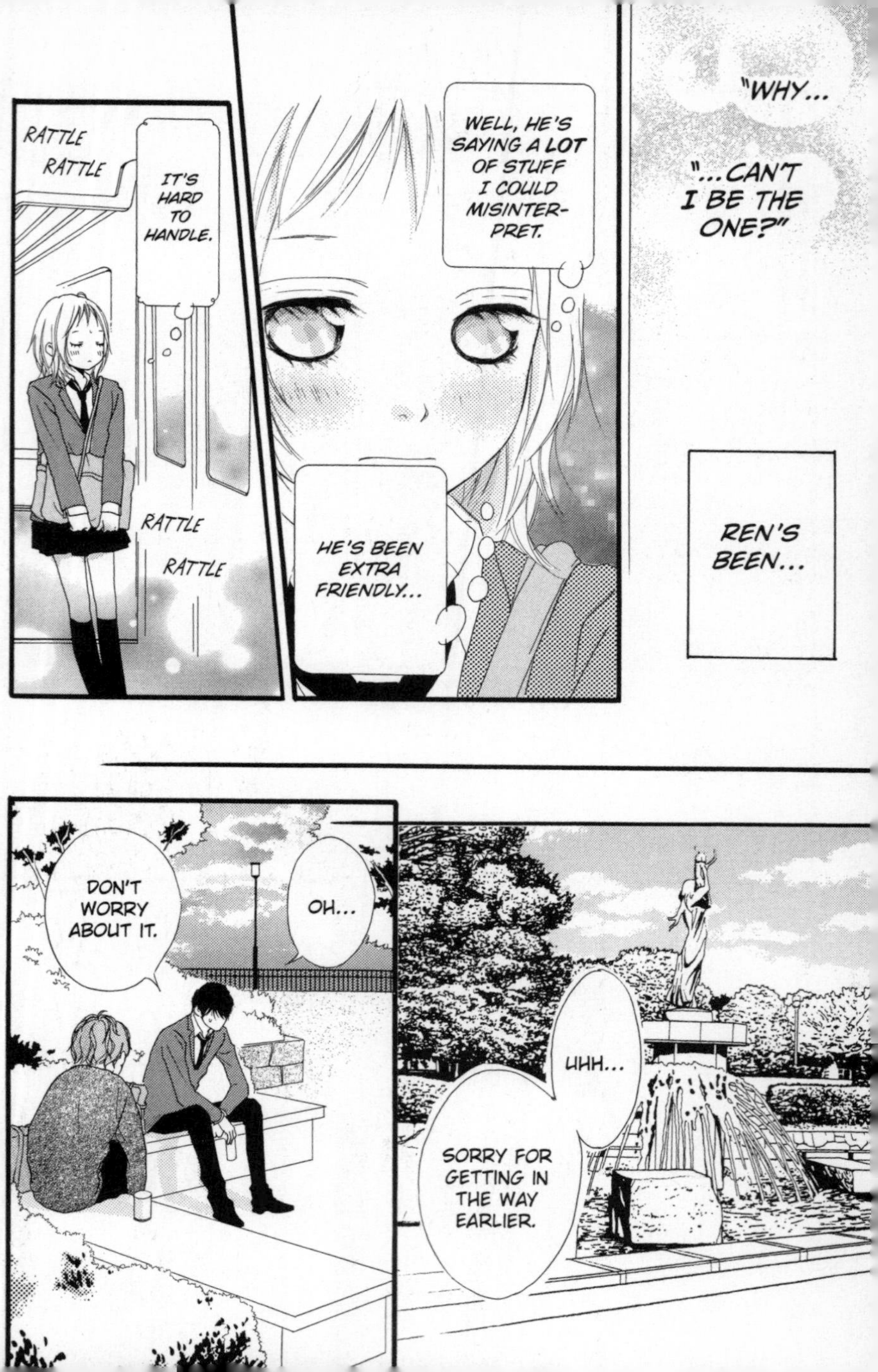
"WHY...
"...CAN'T I BE THE ONE?"
REN'S BEEN...
HE'S BEEN EXTRA FRIENDLY...
WELL, HE'S SAYING A LOT OF STUFF I COULD MISINTER-PRET.
IT'S HARD TO HANDLE.
RATTLE RATTLE
RATTLE RATTLE
UHH...
SORRY FOR GETTING IN THE WAY EARLIER.
OH...
DON'T WORRY ABOUT IT.

Guess what, guess what! There's going to be a drama CD of *Strobe Edge!* Yay! There will be two discs, and the first one goes on sale on 8/25.

So the other day, I went to a recording session for the CD. The actors all had such gorgeous voices. It was like a dream having them voice the *Strobe Edge* characters. It's a really impressive cast!

There's one scene in particular you should listen to at least a hundred times! It's from volume 3 of the manga, when they're studying in the library, and Ren says he loves math.

Another personal favorite is the school festival scene! It felt exactly as if I were at a real festival at a local school, with a really fun atmosphere. It was so funny! I laughed the whole time.

I'm so happy to see my work take shape in a form other than manga, and this is all because of you readers who enjoy the series! Thank you so much. I'm very blessed.

And! Guess what else! There's also going to be a novelization of *Strobe Edge,* and again, it'll be two volumes. You'll be able to take it to school! I'm so lucky...!

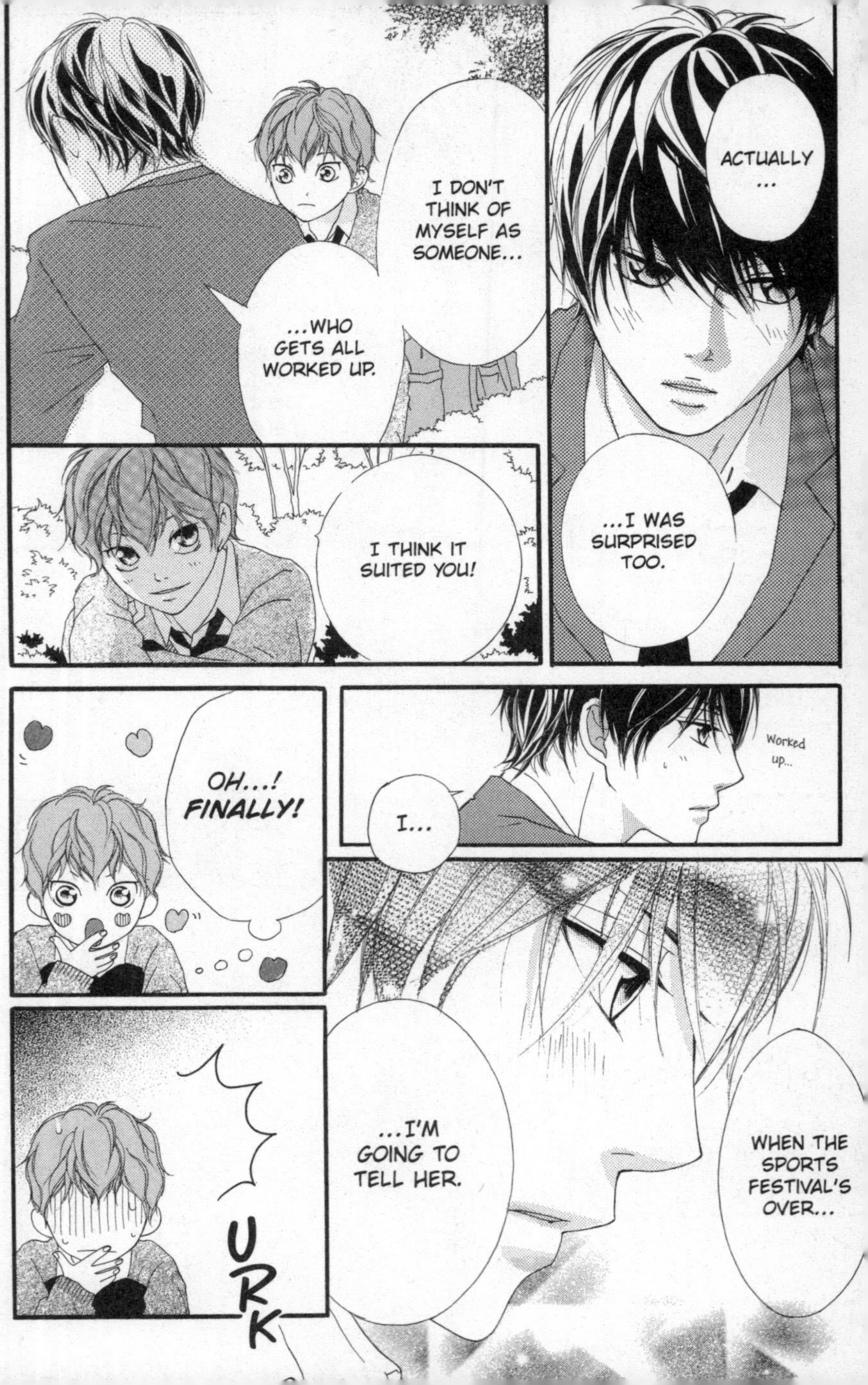
ACTUALLY ...
...I WAS SURPRISED TOO.
I DON'T THINK OF MYSELF AS SOMEONE...
...WHO GETS ALL WORKED UP.
I THINK IT SUITED YOU!
Worked up...
I...
OH...! FINALLY!
WHEN THE SPORTS FESTIVAL'S OVER...
...I'M GOING TO TELL HER.
URK

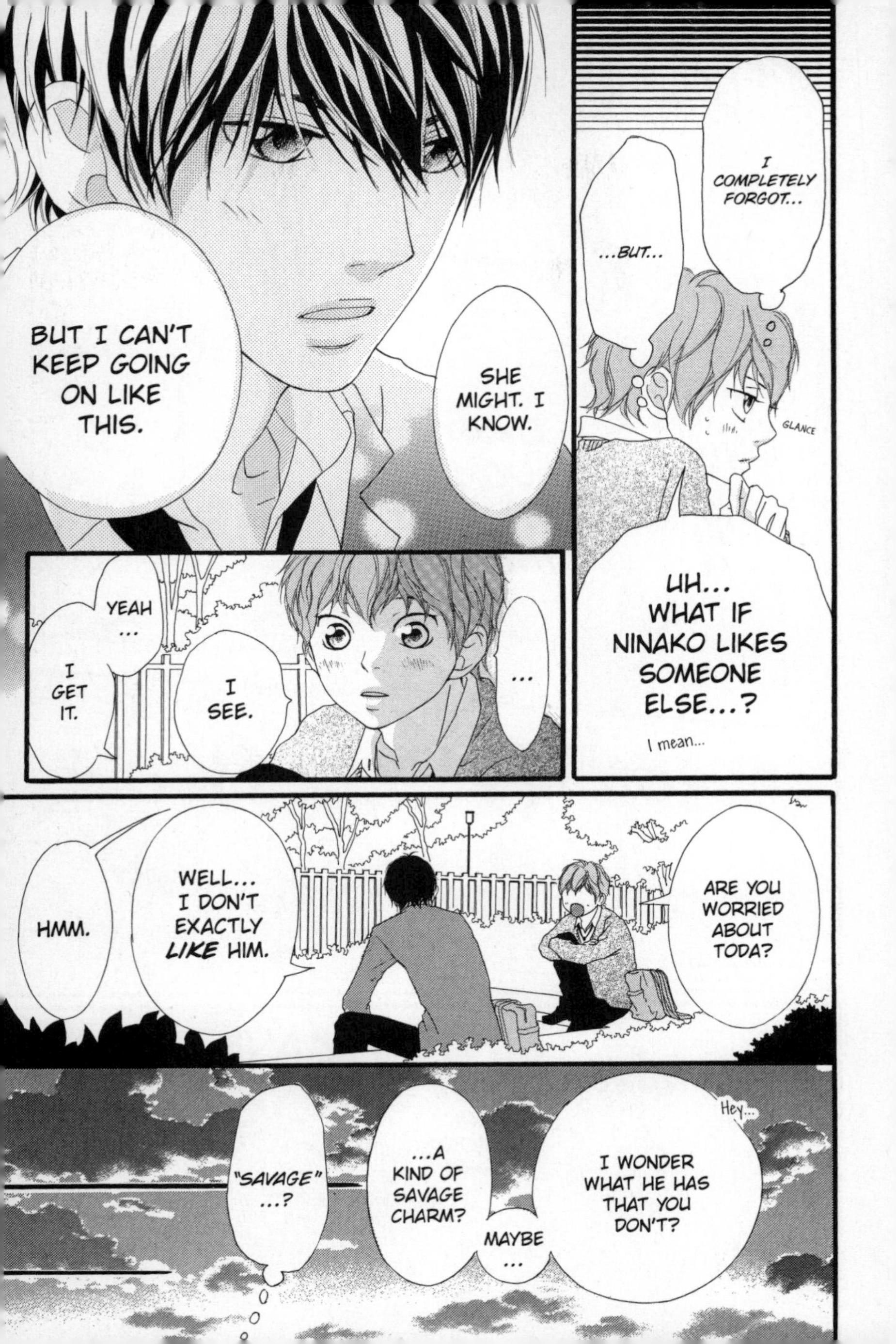
I COMPLETELY FORGOT...
...BUT...
GLANCE
UH... WHAT IF NINAKO LIKES SOMEONE ELSE...?
I mean...
SHE MIGHT. I KNOW.
BUT I CAN'T KEEP GOING ON LIKE THIS.
...
I SEE.
YEAH... I GET IT.
ARE YOU WORRIED ABOUT TODA?
WELL... I DON'T EXACTLY *LIKE* HIM.
HMM.
Hey...
I WONDER WHAT HE HAS THAT YOU DON'T?
MAYBE...
...A KIND OF SAVAGE CHARM?
"SAVAGE"...?

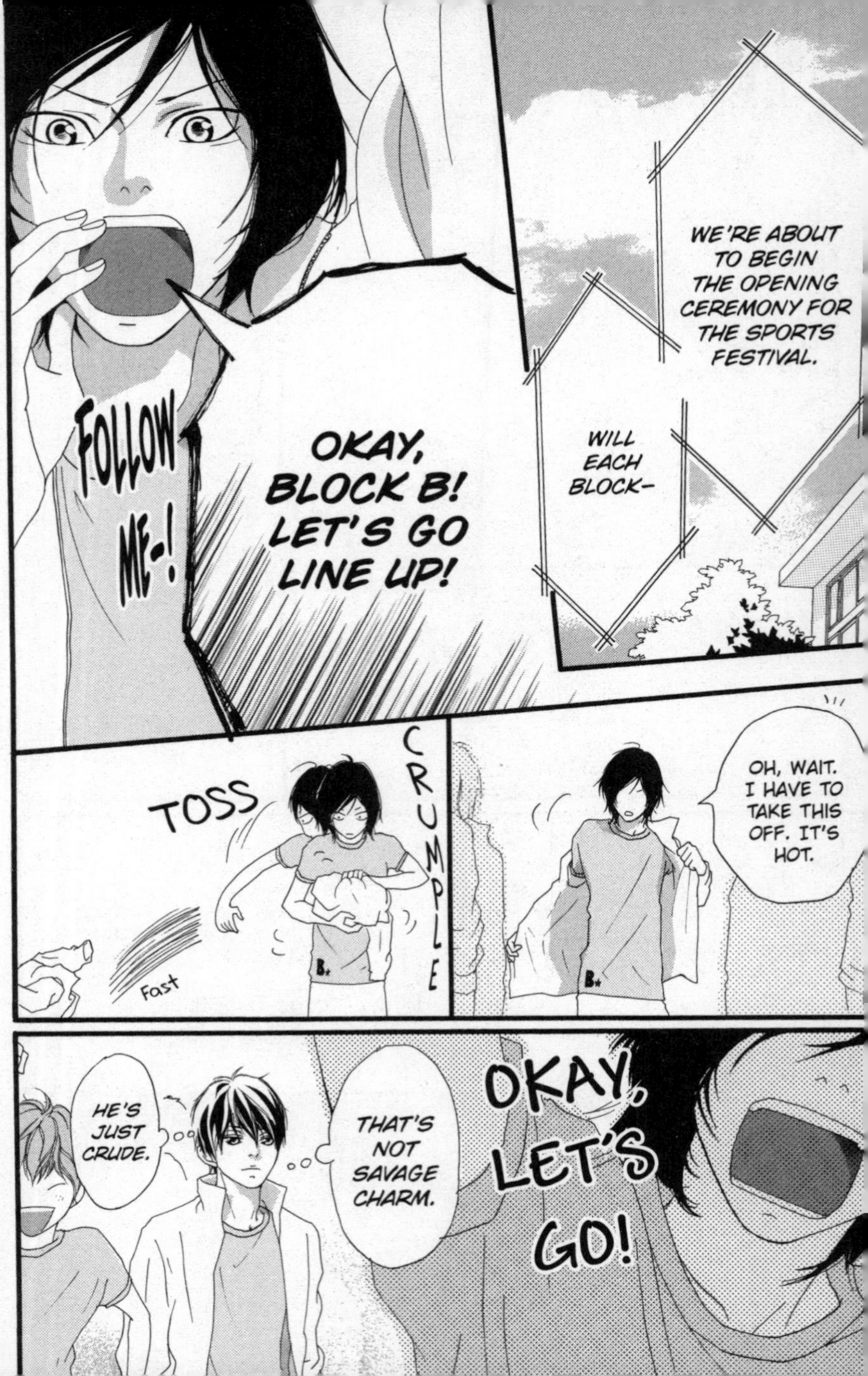
WE'RE ABOUT TO BEGIN THE OPENING CEREMONY FOR THE SPORTS FESTIVAL.
WILL EACH BLOCK-
OKAY, BLOCK B! LET'S GO LINE UP!
FOLLOW ME--!
OH, WAIT. I HAVE TO TAKE THIS OFF. IT'S HOT.
CRUMPLE
TOSS
Fast
OKAY, LET'S GO!
THAT'S NOT SAVAGE CHARM.
HE'S JUST CRUDE.

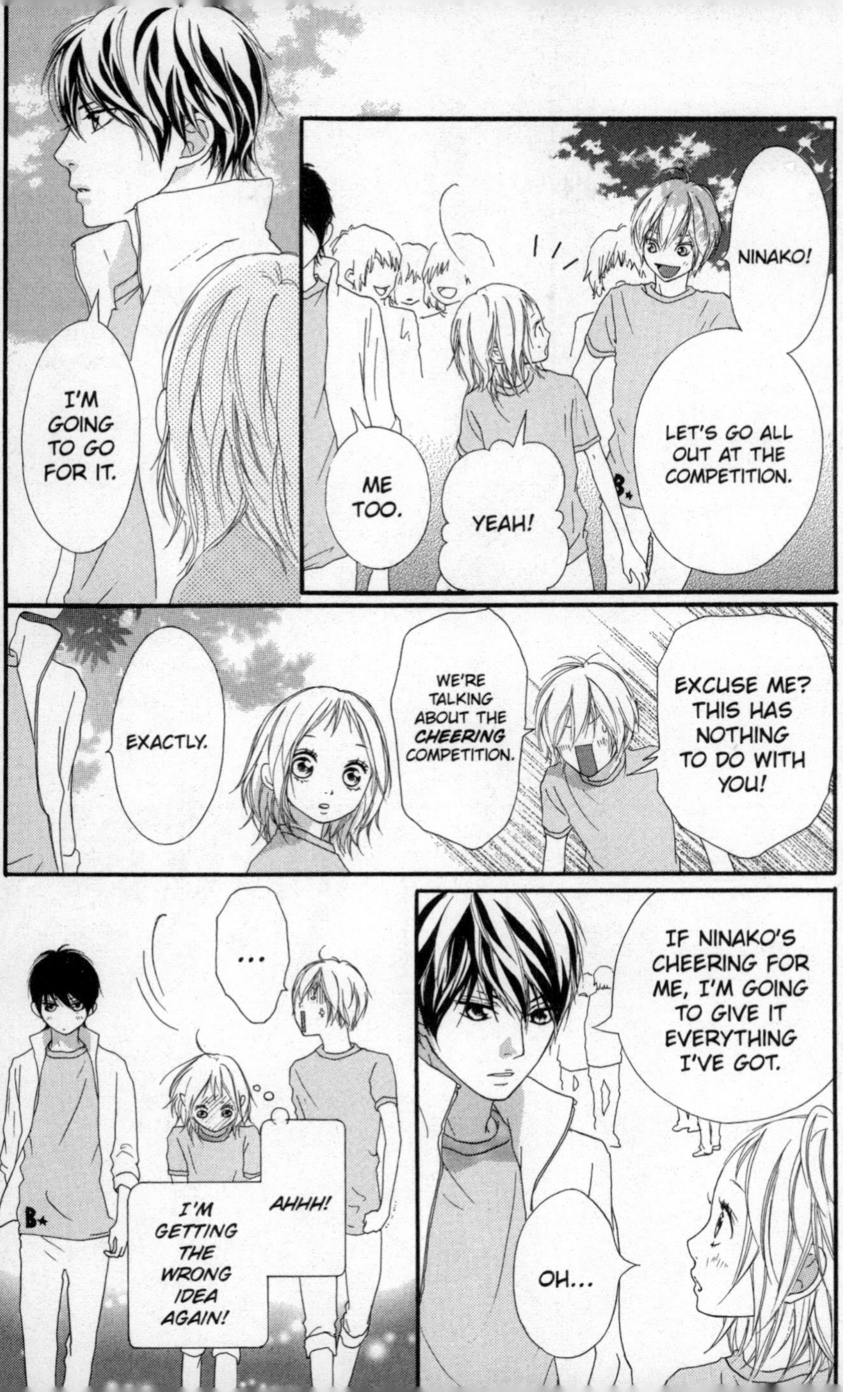
NINAKO!
LET'S GO ALL OUT AT THE COMPETITION.
YEAH!
ME TOO.
I'M GOING TO GO FOR IT.
EXCUSE ME? THIS HAS NOTHING TO DO WITH YOU!
WE'RE TALKING ABOUT THE *CHEERING* COMPETITION.
EXACTLY.
IF NINAKO'S CHEERING FOR ME, I'M GOING TO GIVE IT EVERYTHING I'VE GOT.
OH...
...
AHHH!
I'M GETTING THE WRONG IDEA AGAIN!

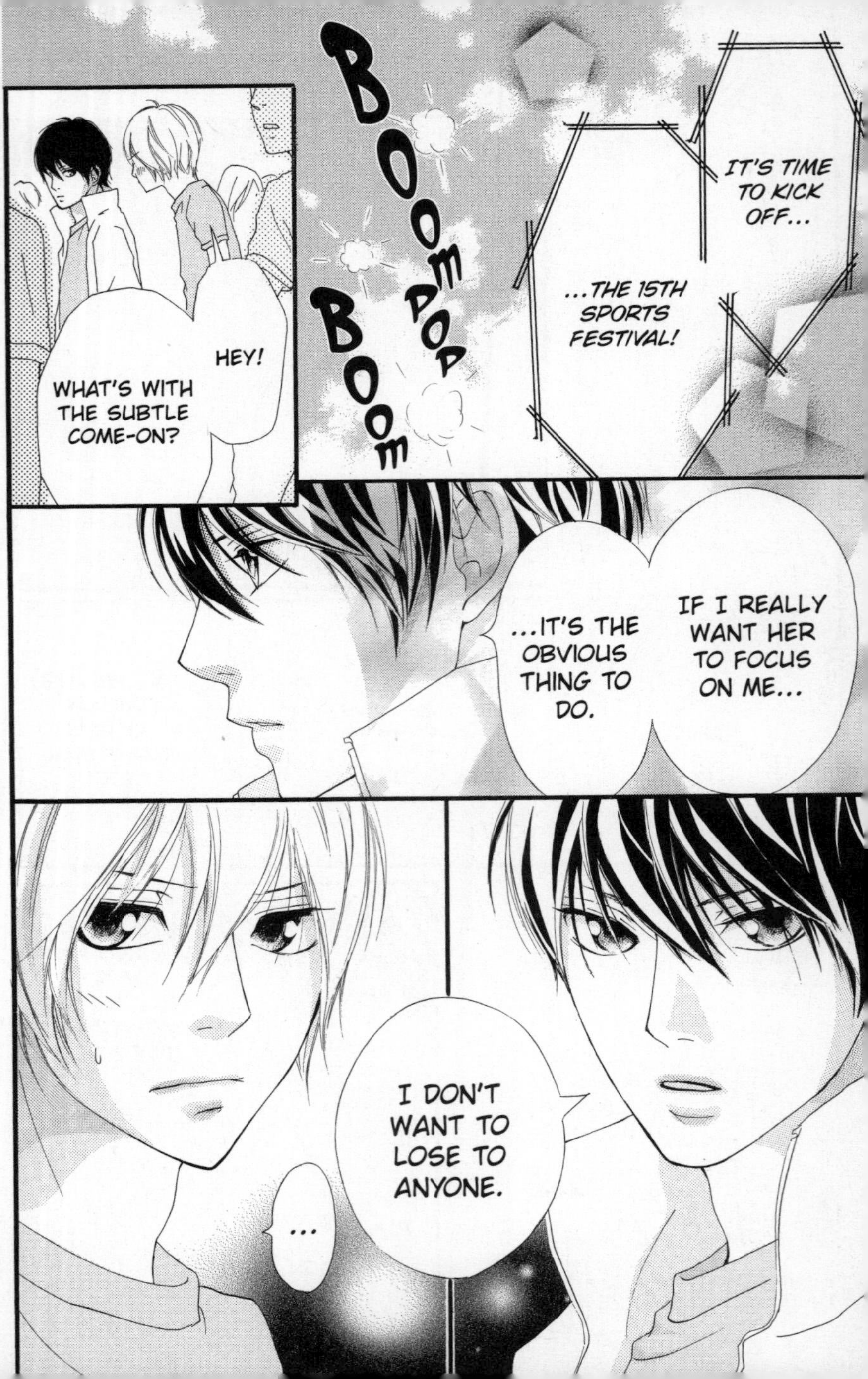
IT'S TIME TO KICK OFF...
...THE 15TH SPORTS FESTIVAL!
BOOM BOOM POP POP
BOOM BOOM
HEY!
WHAT'S WITH THE SUBTLE COME-ON?
IF I REALLY WANT HER TO FOCUS ON ME...
...IT'S THE OBVIOUS THING TO DO.
I DON'T WANT TO LOSE TO ANYONE.
...

One, two!

Daiki, cheer for Block C!

Go, Sayuri!

One, two!

C!

C!

...

B★

B★

SQUEAK
SQUEAK
SQUEAK

BLOCK B!

BLOCK B!

LOOKS LIKE THE MIXED-YEAR RELAY.

WHAT'S YOUR NEXT EVENT, TAKUMI?

OH, AWESOME! THE RELAY'S WORTH A LOT OF POINTS! IT'D BE GREAT IF YOU WON.

PROGRAM

B

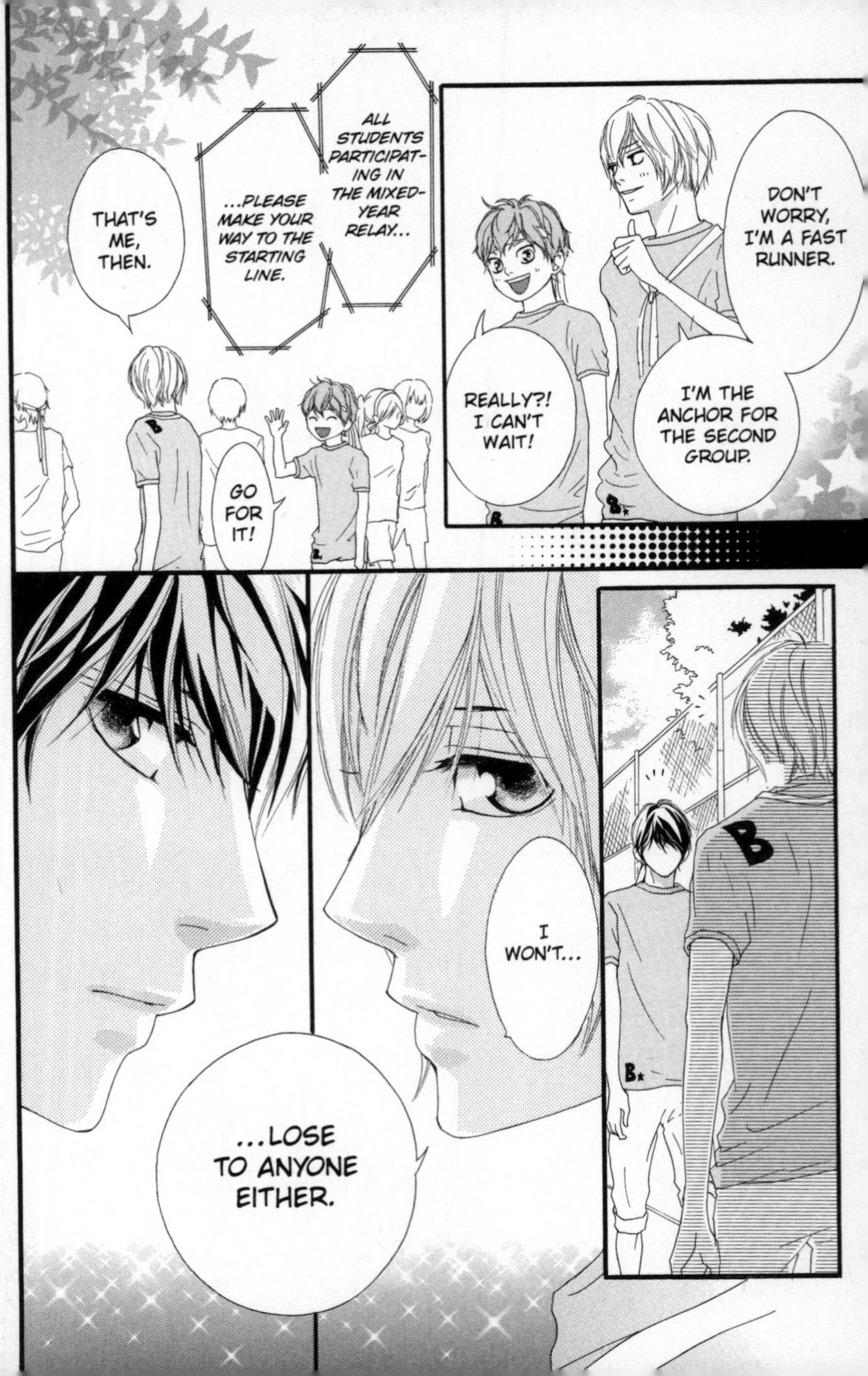
DON'T WORRY, I'M A FAST RUNNER.
I'M THE ANCHOR FOR THE SECOND GROUP.
REALLY?! I CAN'T WAIT!
ALL STUDENTS PARTICIPATING IN THE MIXED-YEAR RELAY...
...PLEASE MAKE YOUR WAY TO THE STARTING LINE.
THAT'S ME, THEN.
GO FOR IT!
I WON'T...
...LOSE TO ANYONE EITHER.

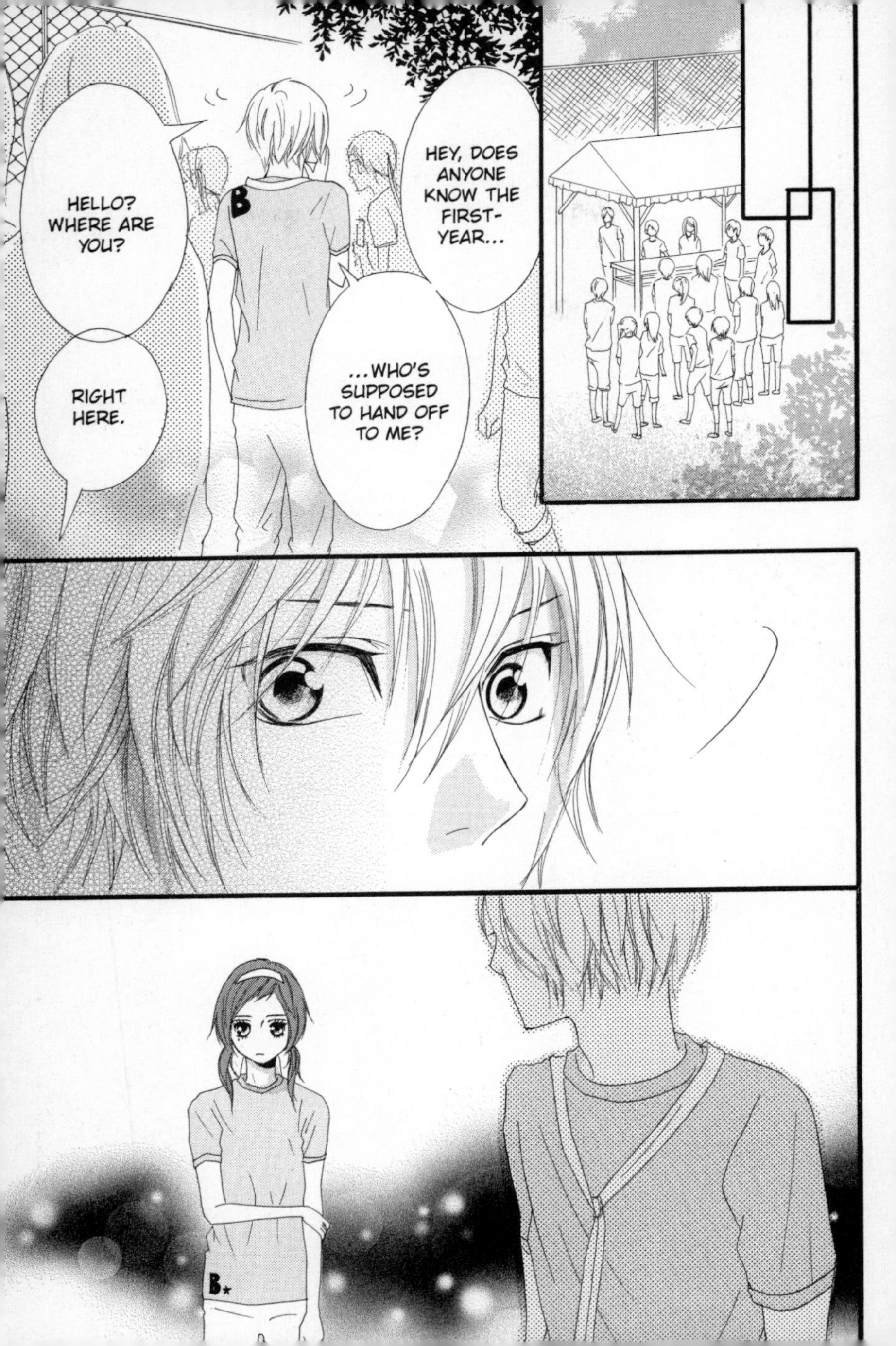
HEY, DOES ANYONE KNOW THE FIRST-YEAR...
...WHO'S SUPPOSED TO HAND OFF TO ME?
HELLO? WHERE ARE YOU?
RIGHT HERE.

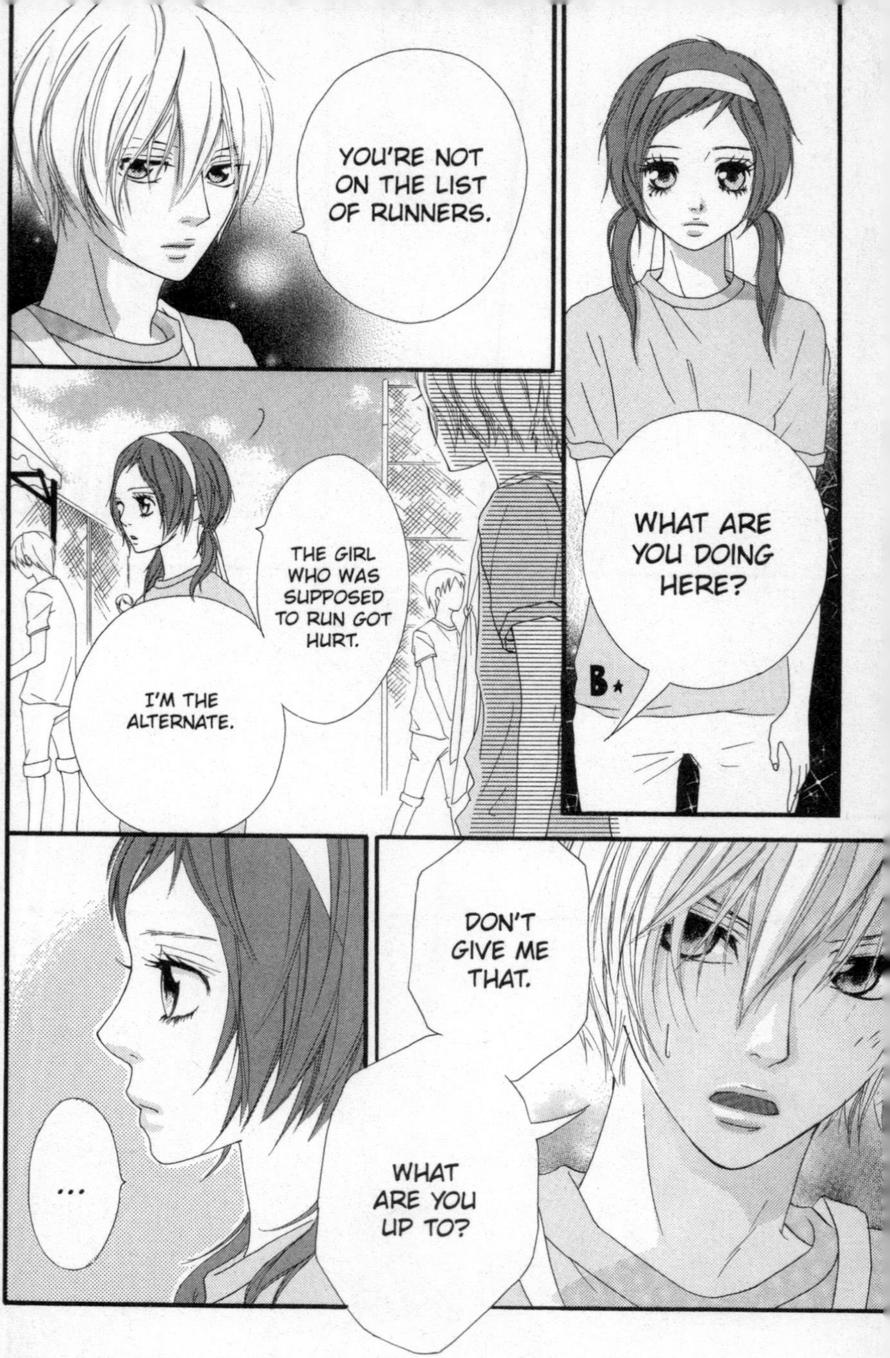
WHAT ARE YOU DOING HERE?
B★
YOU'RE NOT ON THE LIST OF RUNNERS.
THE GIRL WHO WAS SUPPOSED TO RUN GOT HURT.
I'M THE ALTERNATE.
DON'T GIVE ME THAT.
WHAT ARE YOU UP TO?
...

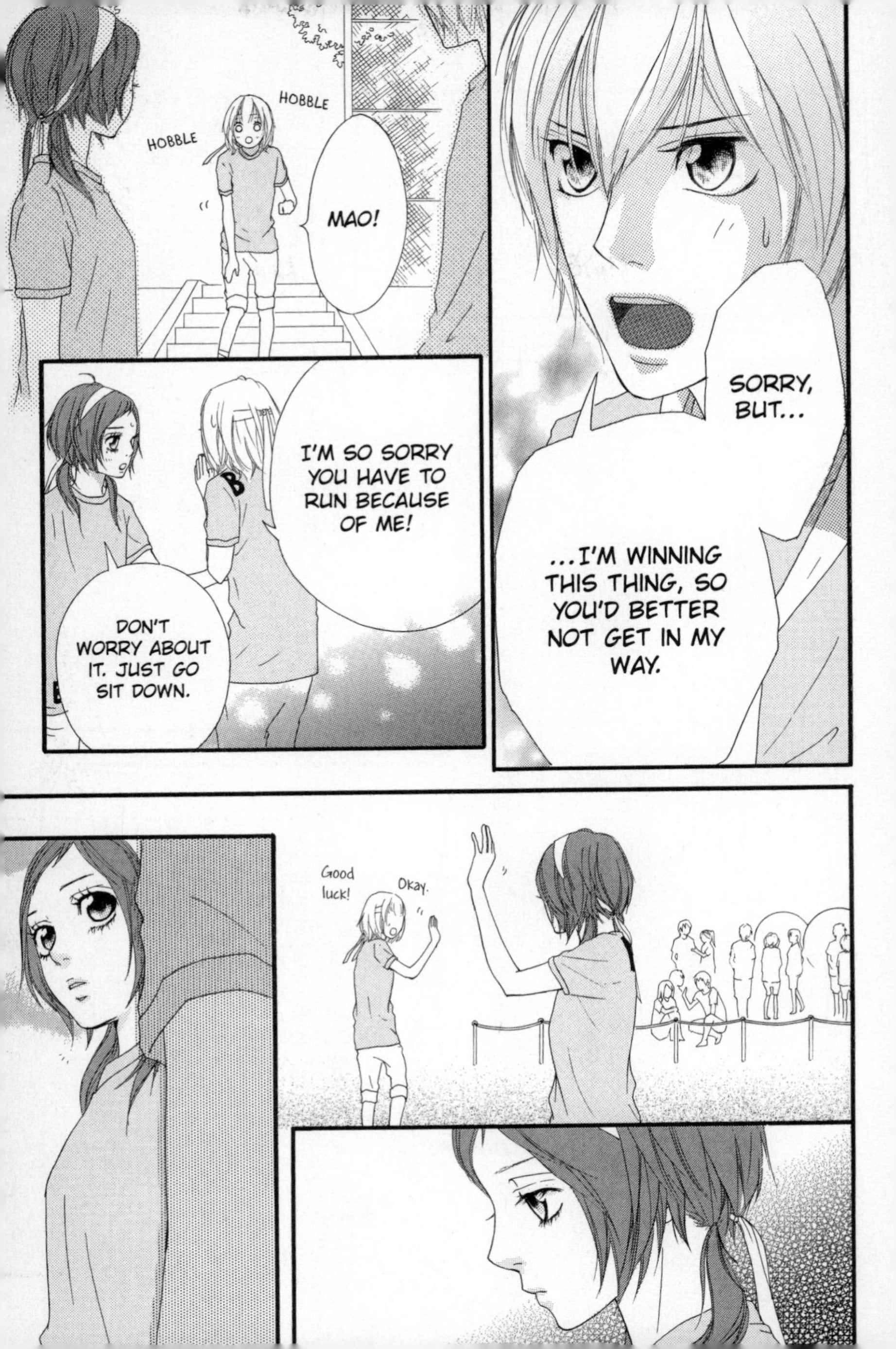
HOBBLE
HOBBLE
MAO!
SORRY, BUT...
...I'M WINNING THIS THING, SO YOU'D BETTER NOT GET IN MY WAY.
I'M SO SORRY YOU HAVE TO RUN BECAUSE OF ME!
DON'T WORRY ABOUT IT. JUST GO SIT DOWN.
Okay.
Good luck!

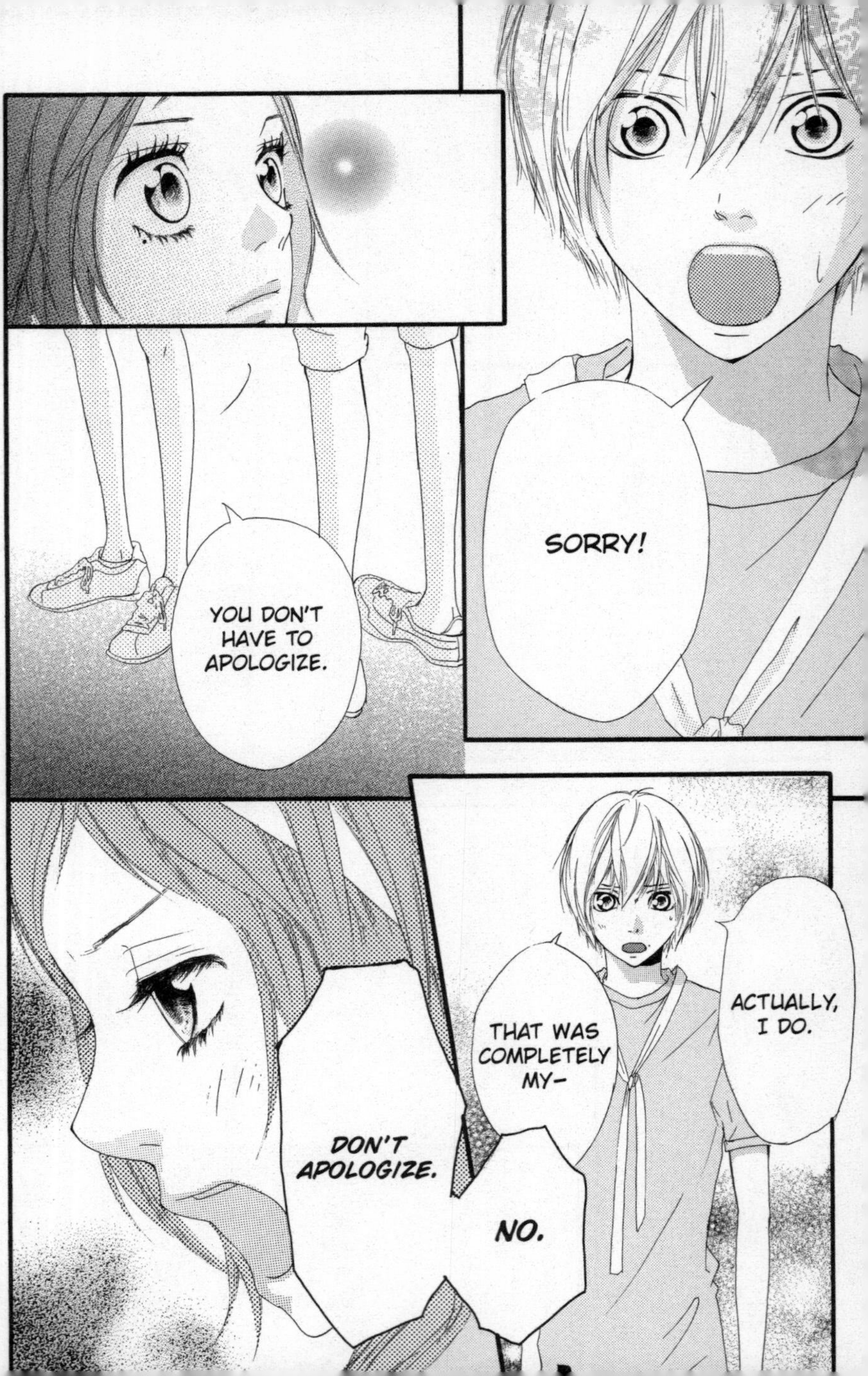
SORRY!
YOU DON'T HAVE TO APOLOGIZE.
ACTUALLY, I DO.
THAT WAS COMPLETELY MY-
NO.
DON'T APOLOGIZE.

WHAT
...

...JUST HAPPENED?

PLEASE TAKE YOUR PLACES.

ANYWAY, DON'T WORRY. I'LL RUN FAST.

BANG!

ON YOUR MARK...

GET SET...

RAH RAH RAH RAH RAH

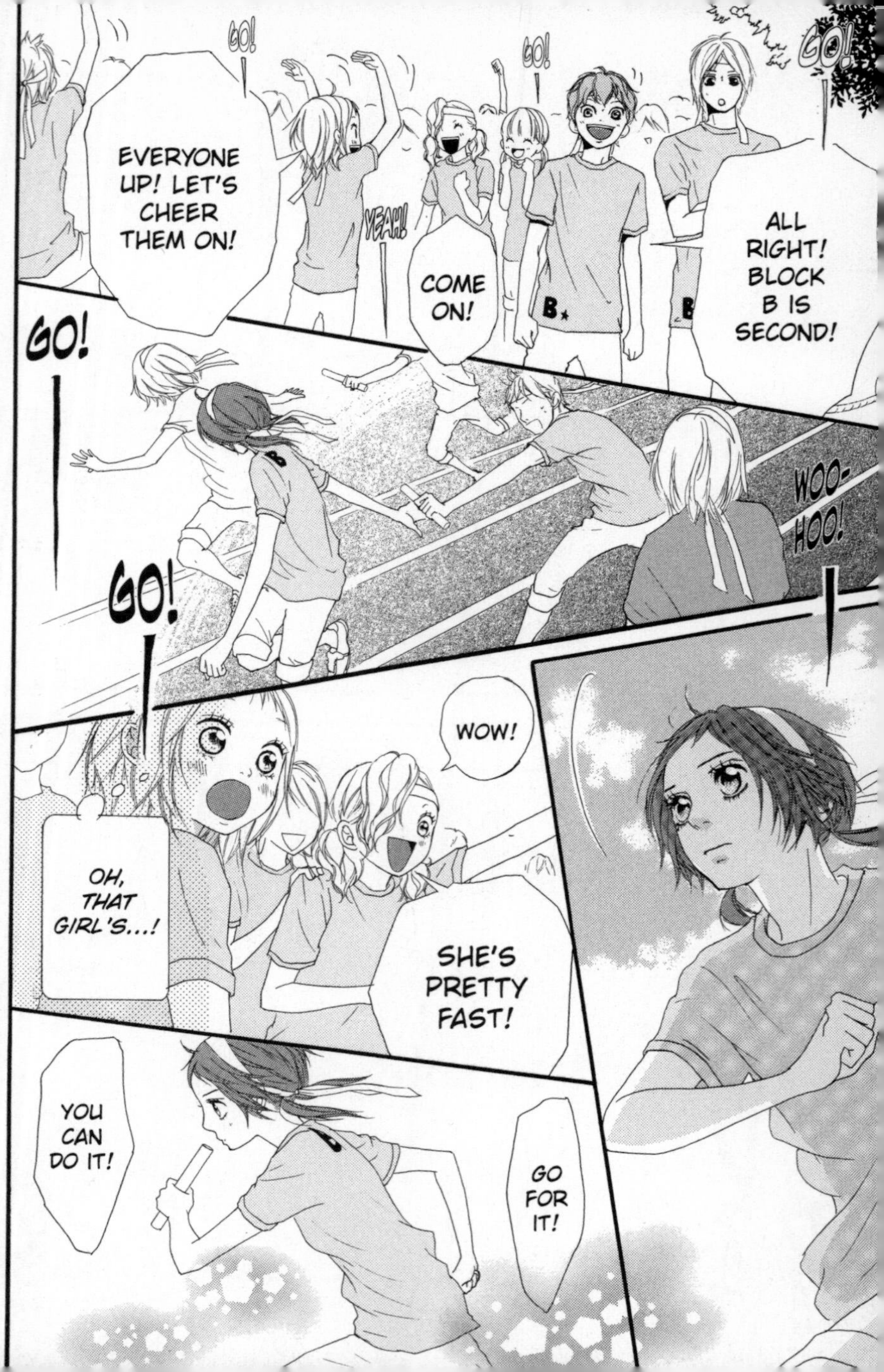
GO!
ALL RIGHT! BLOCK B IS SECOND!
GO!
COME ON!
YEAH!
GO!
EVERYONE UP! LET'S CHEER THEM ON!
WOO-HOO!
GO!
GO!
WOW!
SHE'S PRETTY FAST!
OH, THAT GIRL'S...!
GO FOR IT!
YOU CAN DO IT!

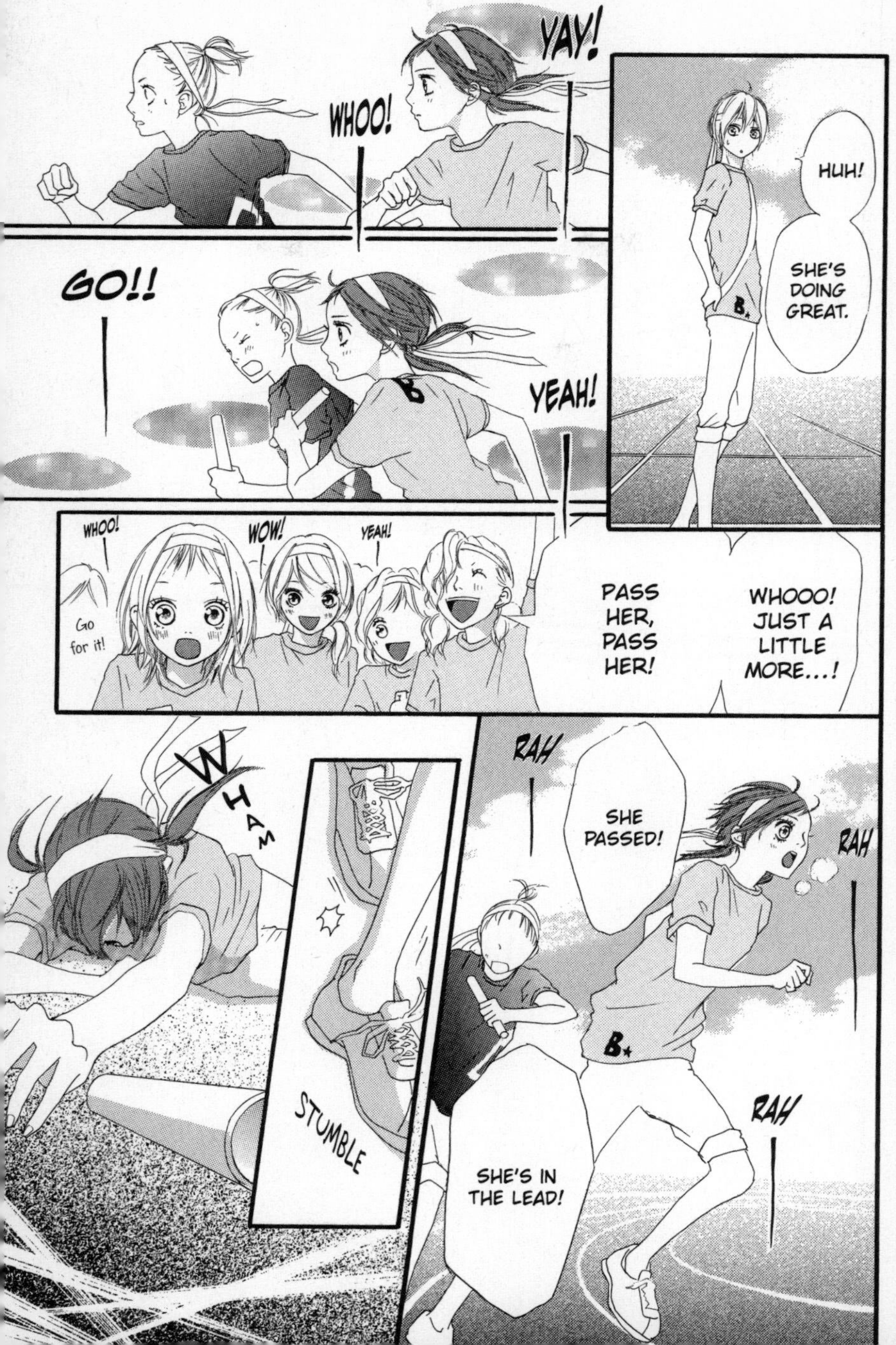
HUH!
SHE'S DOING GREAT.
YAY!
WHOO!
YEAH!
GO!!
WHOOO! JUST A LITTLE MORE...!
PASS HER, PASS HER!
YEAH!
WOW!
WHOO!
Go for it!
RAH
RAH
SHE PASSED!
RAH
SHE'S IN THE LEAD!
STUMBLE
WHAM

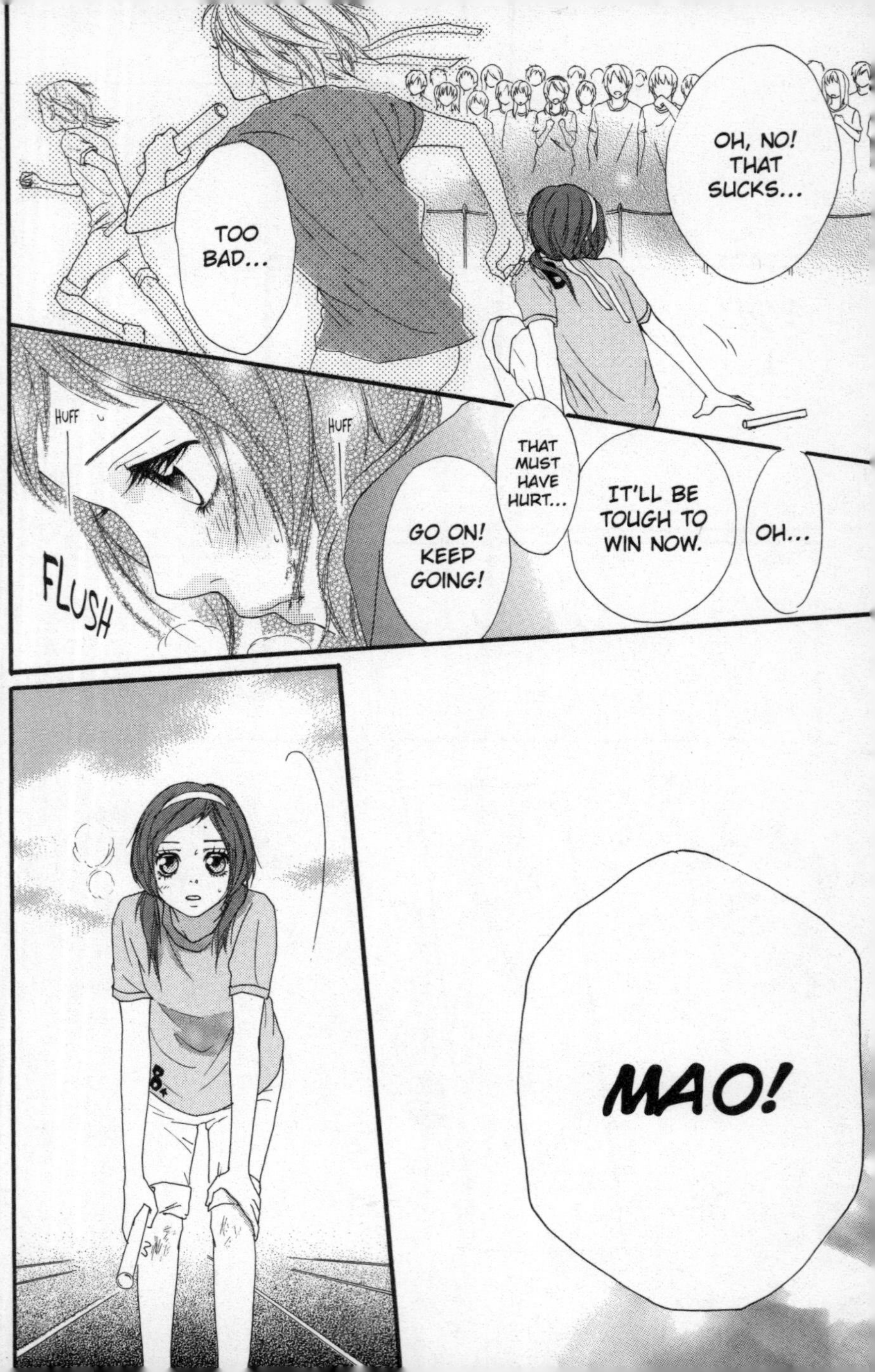
OH, NO! THAT SUCKS...
TOO BAD...
OH...
IT'LL BE TOUGH TO WIN NOW.
THAT MUST HAVE HURT...
GO ON! KEEP GOING!
HUFF
HUFF
FLUSH
MAO!

IT'S JUST
A LITTLE BIT
FARTHER!

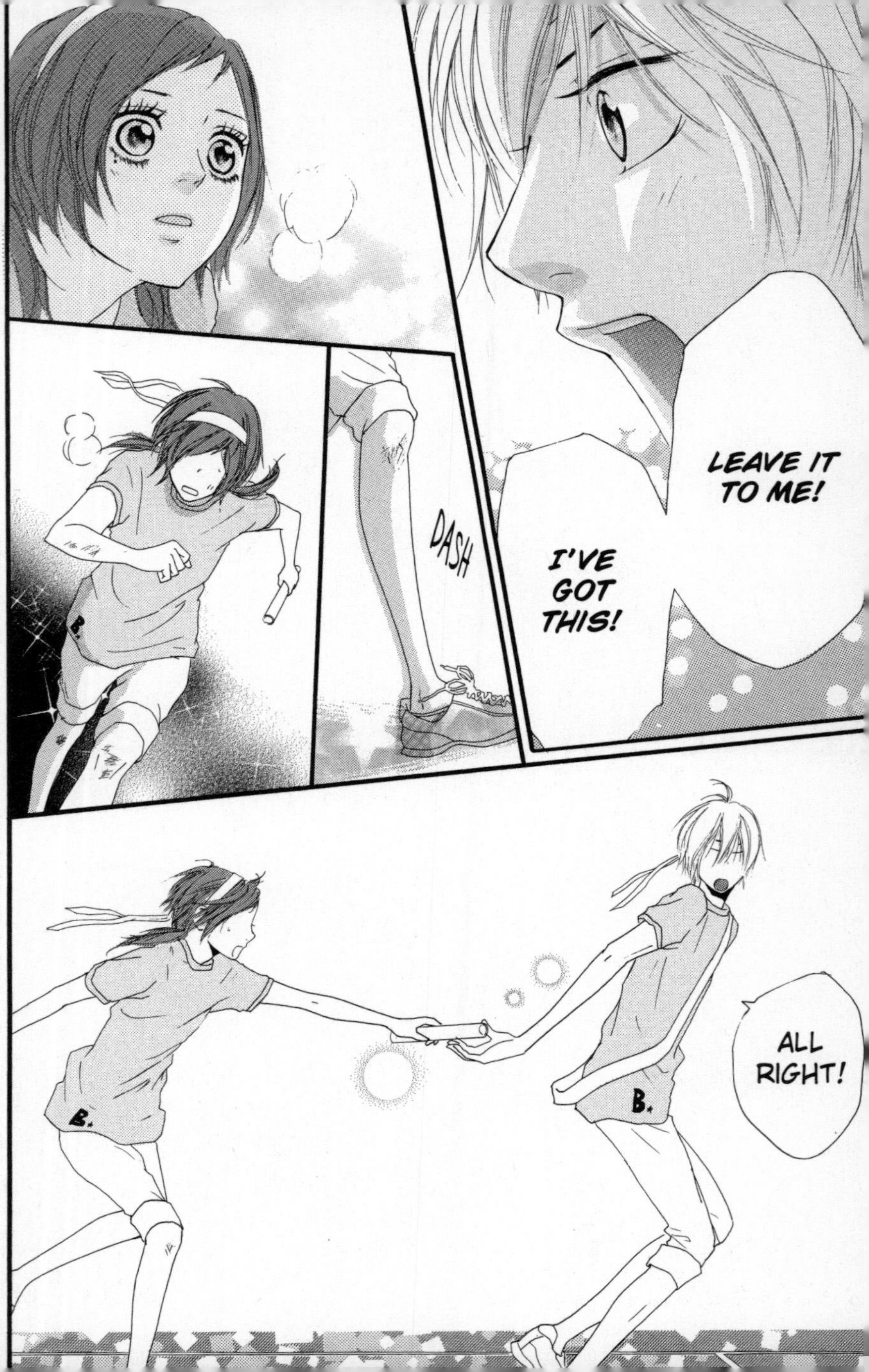
LEAVE IT TO ME!
I'VE GOT THIS!
DASH
ALL RIGHT!

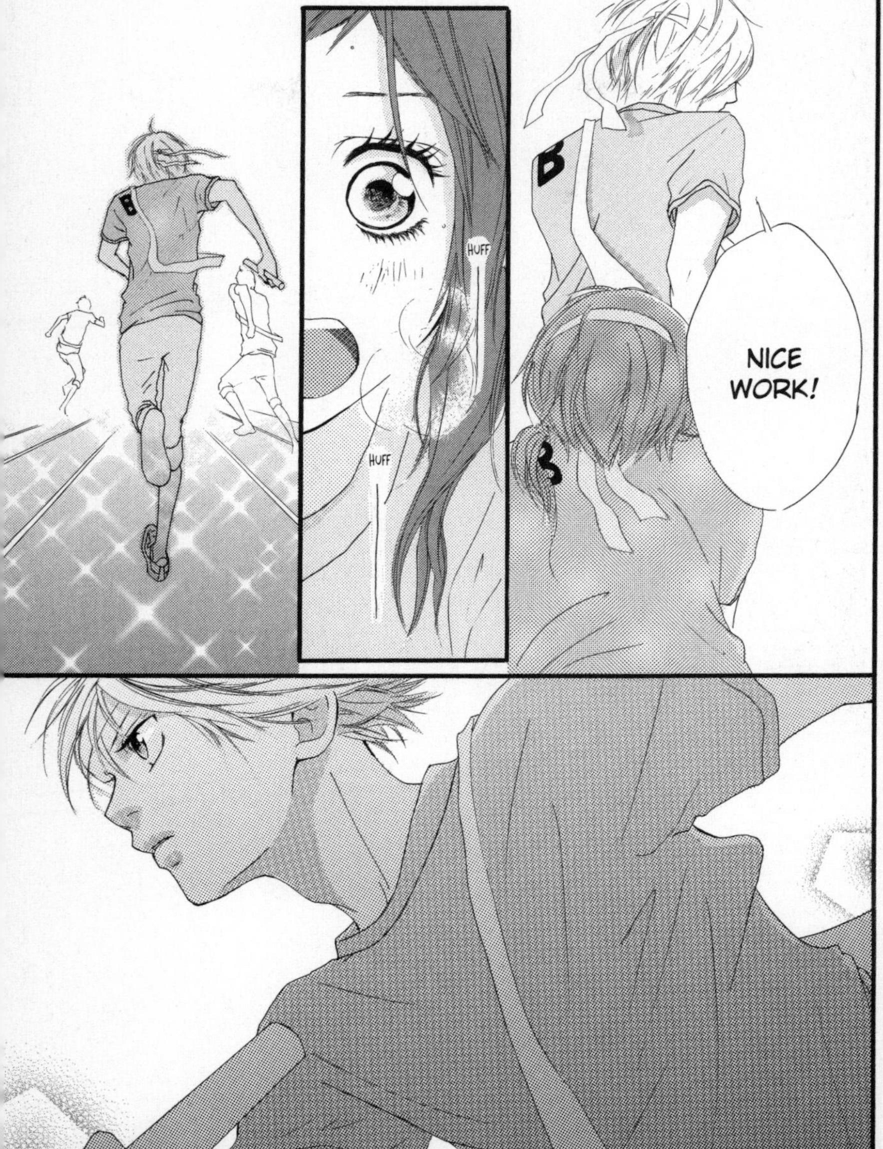
NICE WORK!
HUFF
HUFF

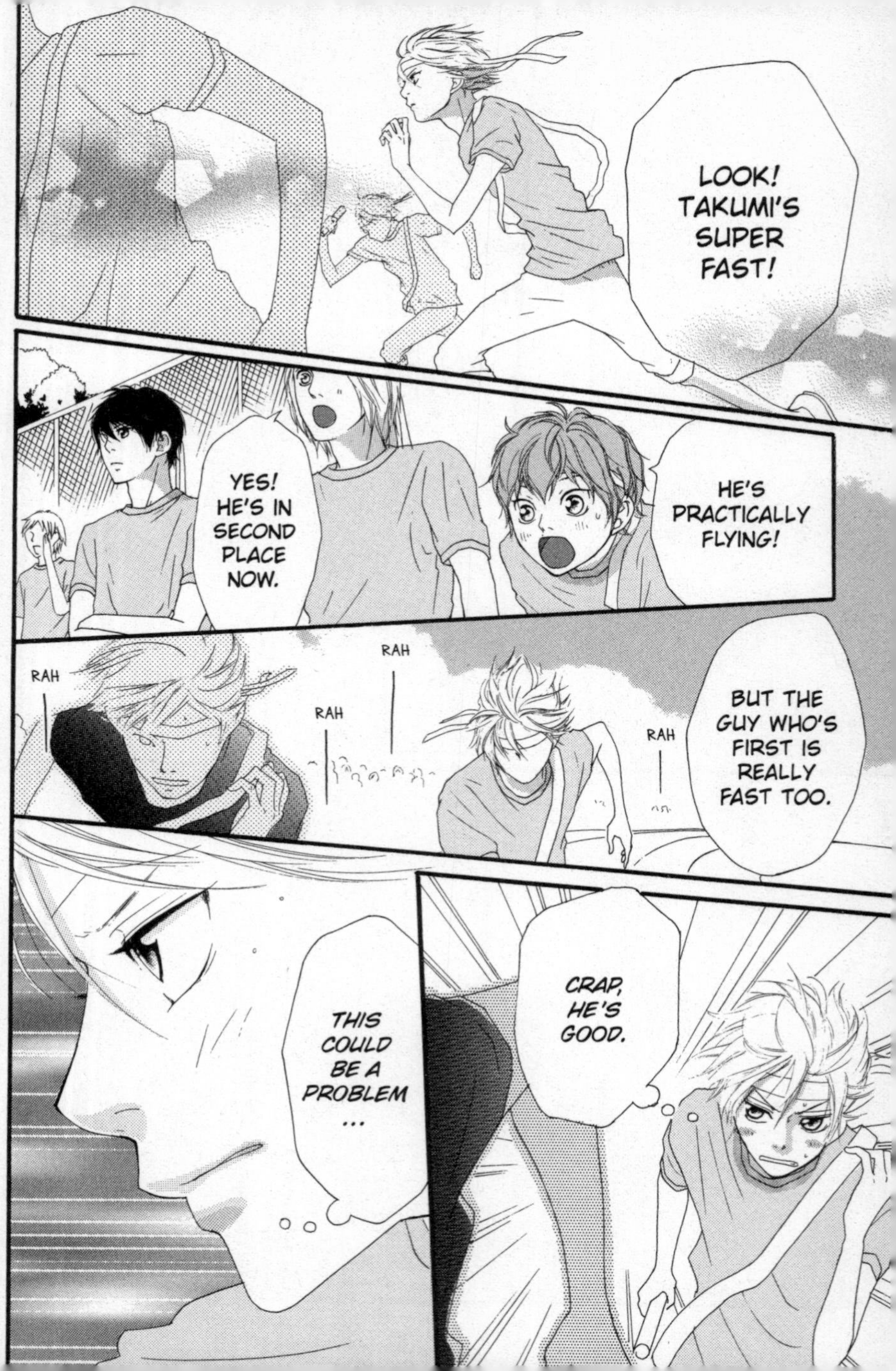

LOOK! TAKUMI'S SUPER FAST!
HE'S PRACTICALLY FLYING!
YES! HE'S IN SECOND PLACE NOW.
BUT THE GUY WHO'S FIRST IS REALLY FAST TOO.
RAH
RAH
RAH
RAH
CRAP, HE'S GOOD.
THIS COULD BE A PROBLEM ...

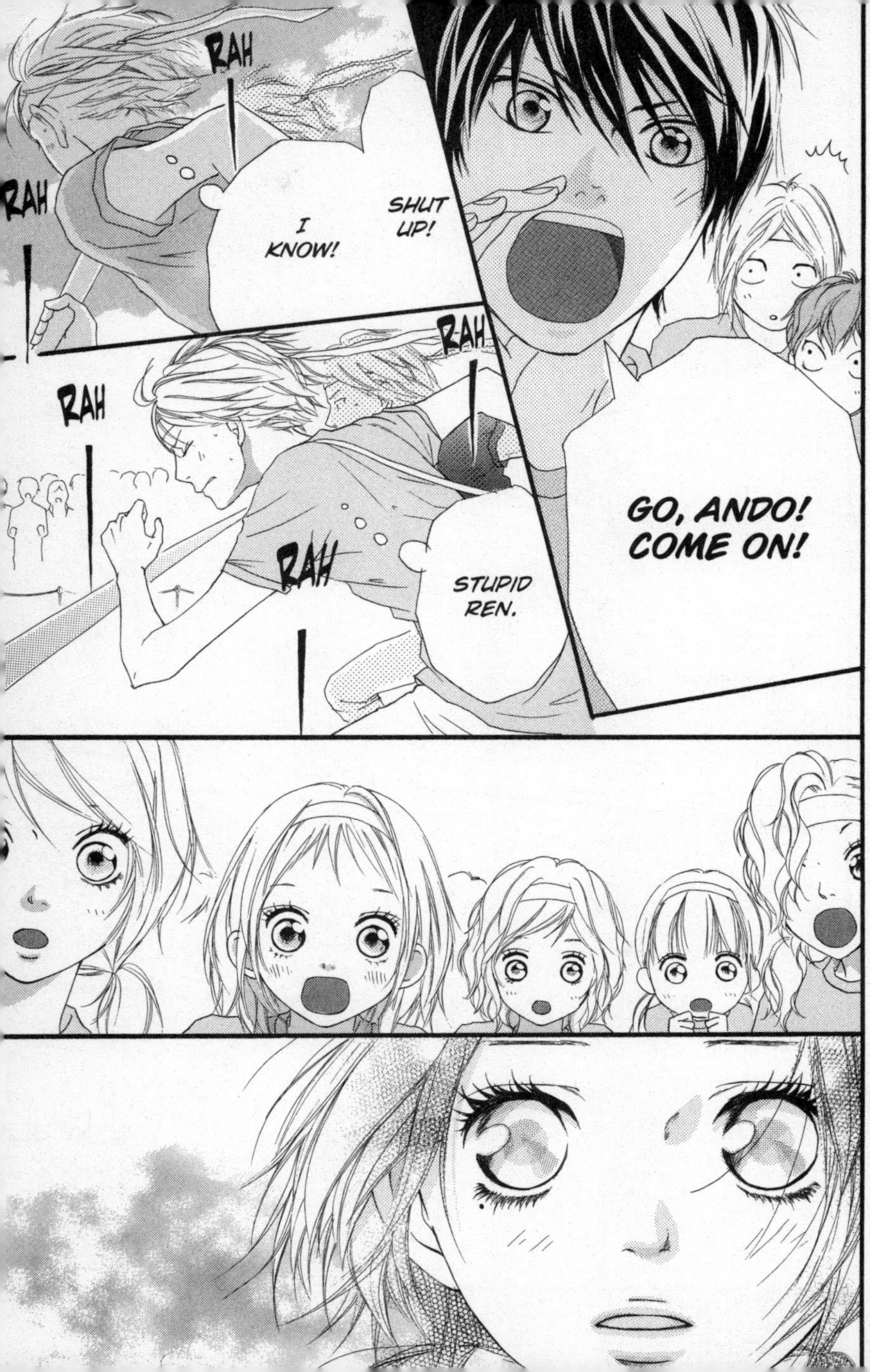
GO, ANDO! COME ON!
SHUT UP!
I KNOW!
RAH
RAH
RAH
RAH
RAH
STUPID REN.

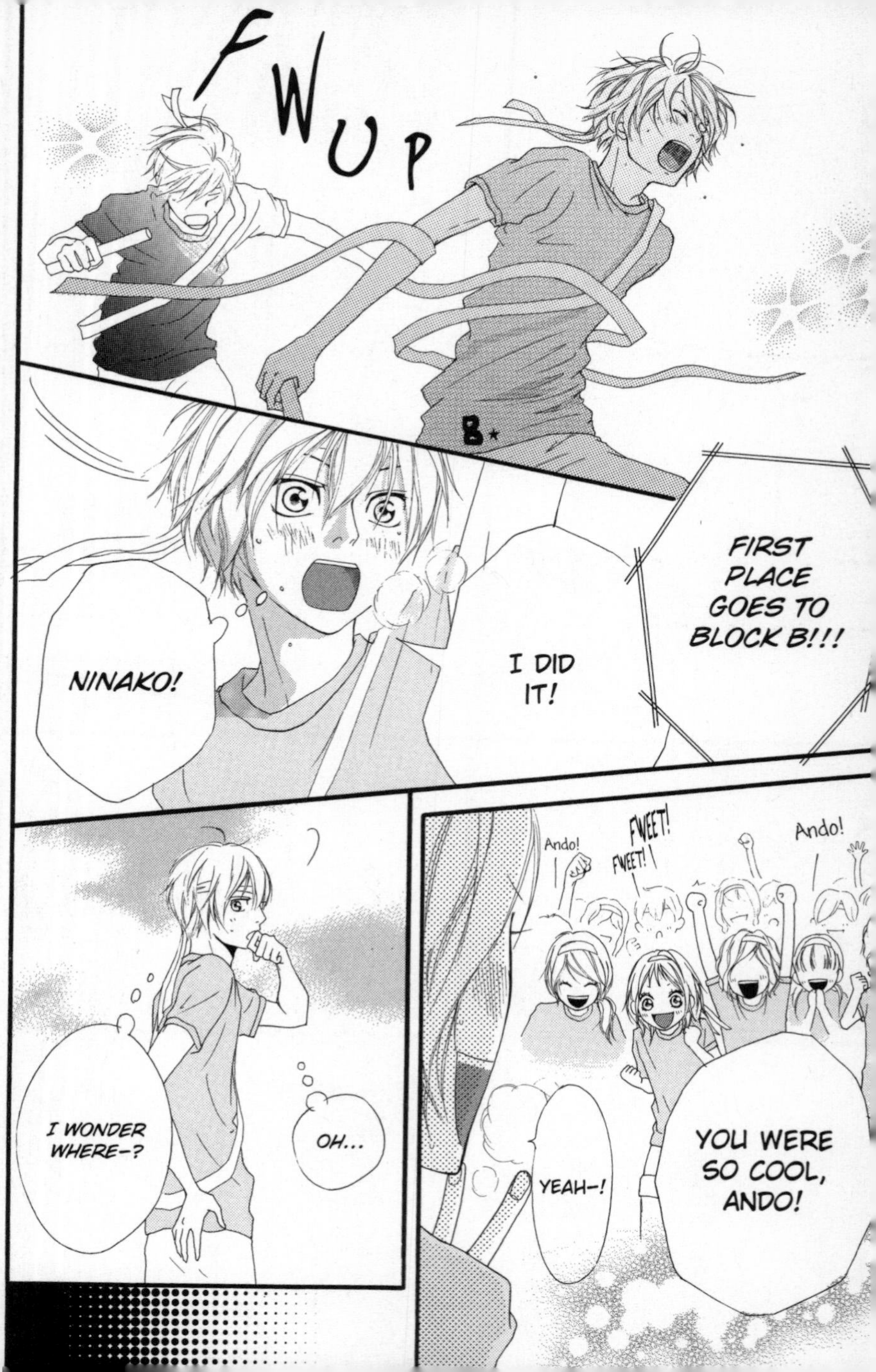
FWUP
FIRST PLACE GOES TO BLOCK B!!!
I DID IT!
NINAKO!
Ando!
FWEET!
FWEET!
Ando!
YOU WERE SO COOL, ANDO!
YEAH-!
OH...
I WONDER WHERE-?

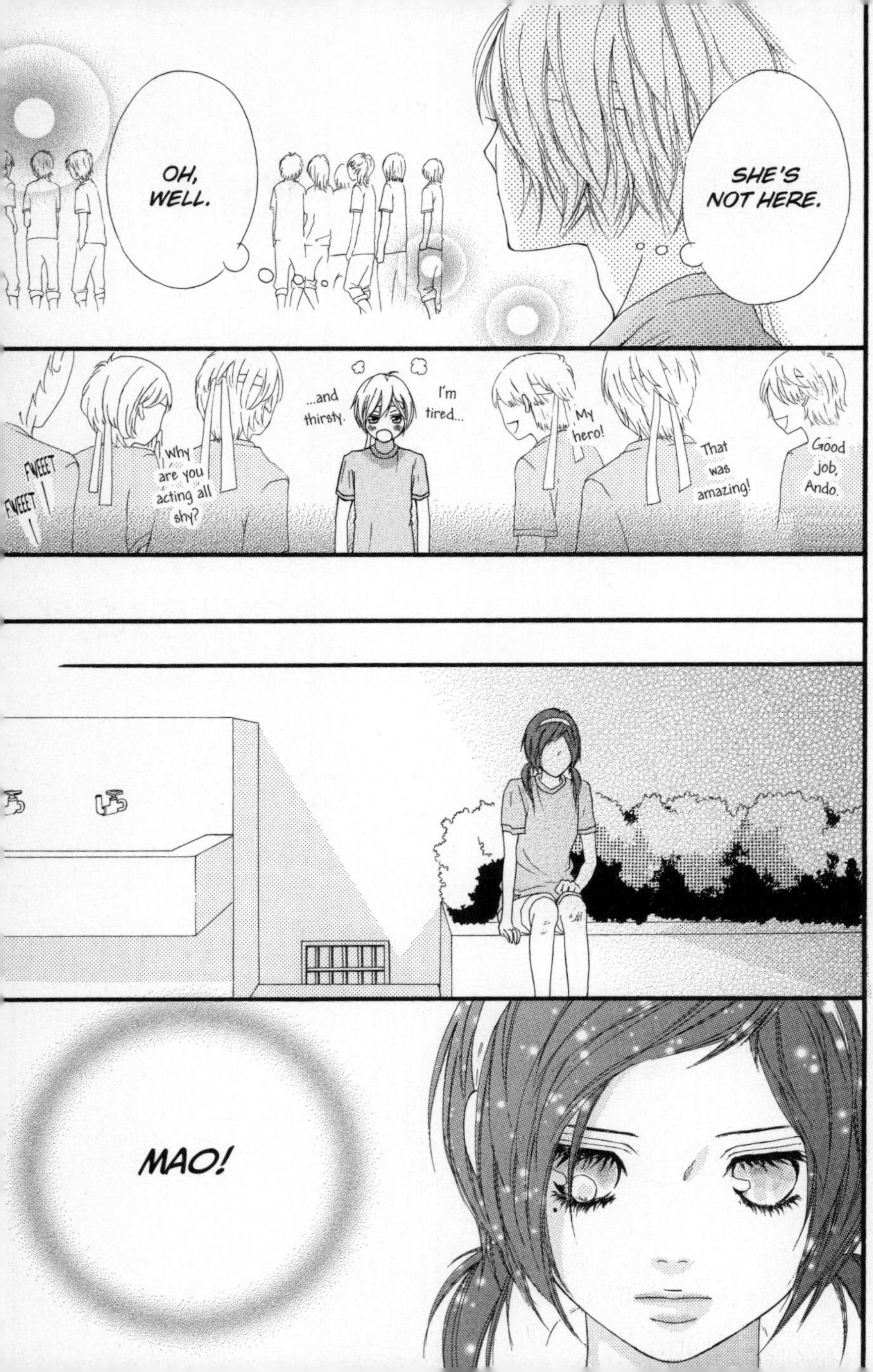
SHE'S NOT HERE.
OH, WELL.
Good job, Ando.
That was amazing!
My hero!
I'm tired...
...and thirsty.
Why are you acting all shy?
FWEEET
FWEEET
MAO!

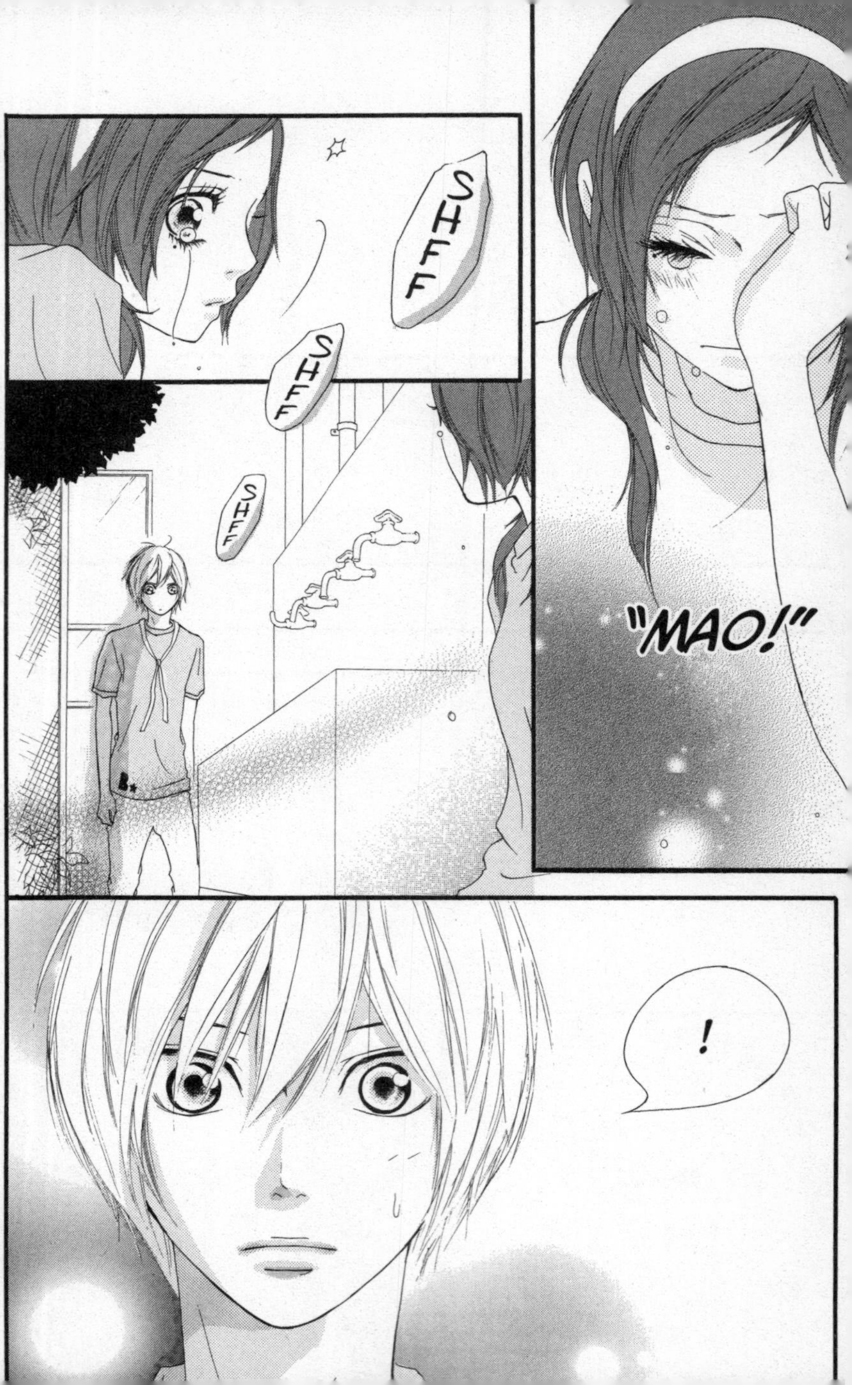
"MAO!"
SHFF
SHFF
SHFF
!

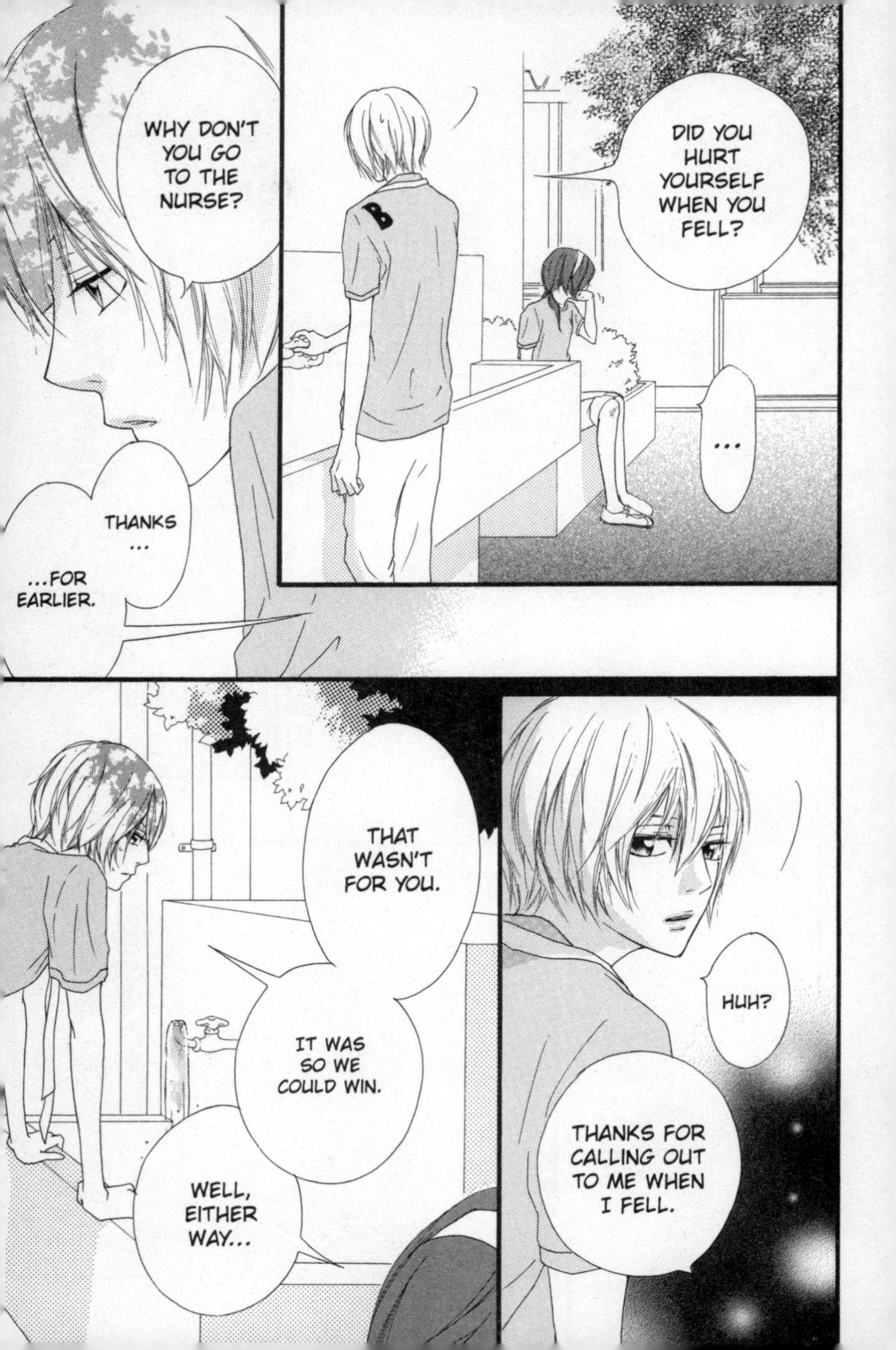
DID YOU HURT YOURSELF WHEN YOU FELL?
...
WHY DON'T YOU GO TO THE NURSE?
THANKS...
...FOR EARLIER.
HUH?
THANKS FOR CALLING OUT TO ME WHEN I FELL.
THAT WASN'T FOR YOU.
IT WAS SO WE COULD WIN.
WELL, EITHER WAY...

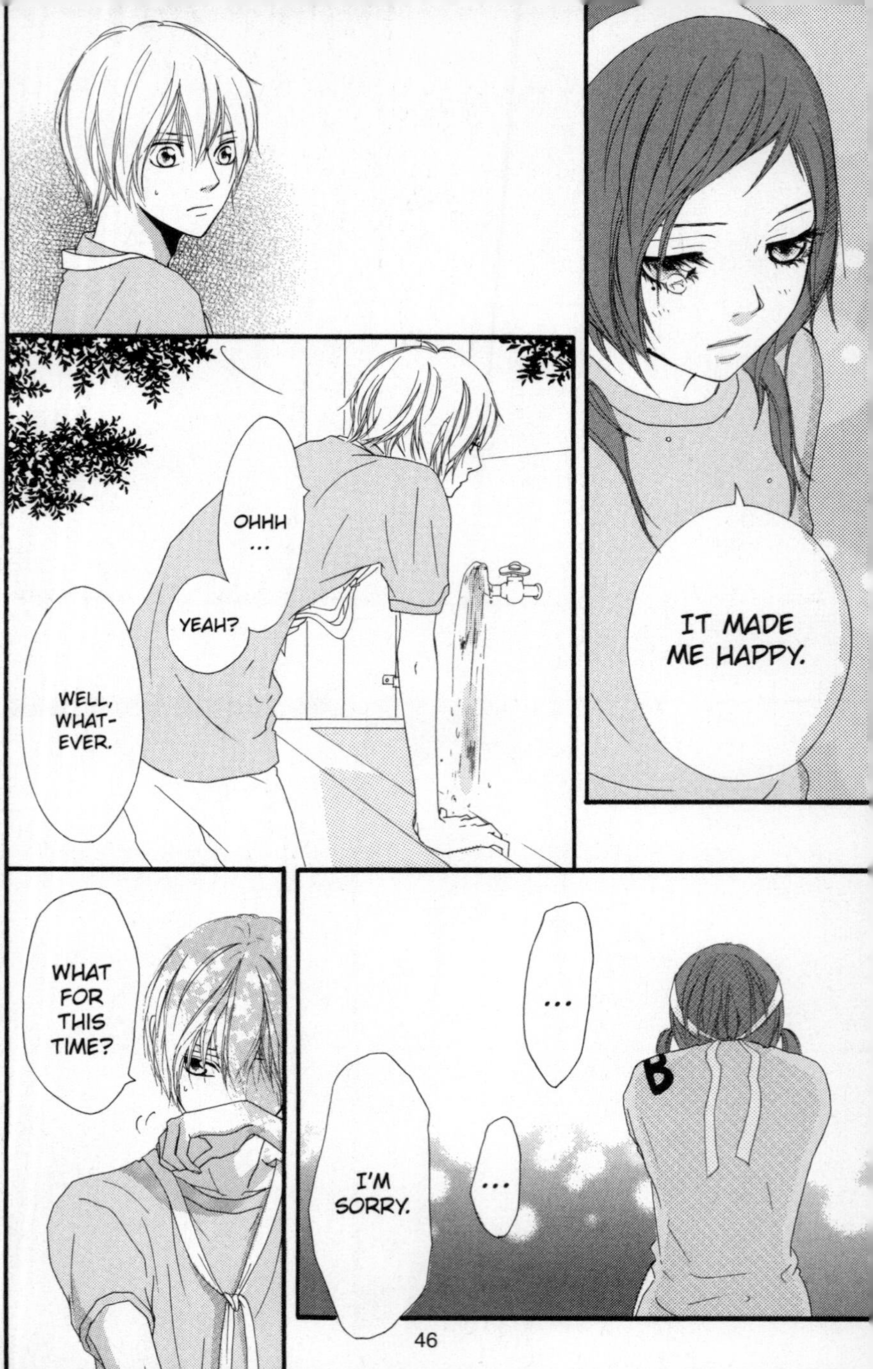
IT MADE ME HAPPY.
OHHH ...
YEAH?
WELL, WHAT-EVER.
...
...
I'M SORRY.
WHAT FOR THIS TIME?

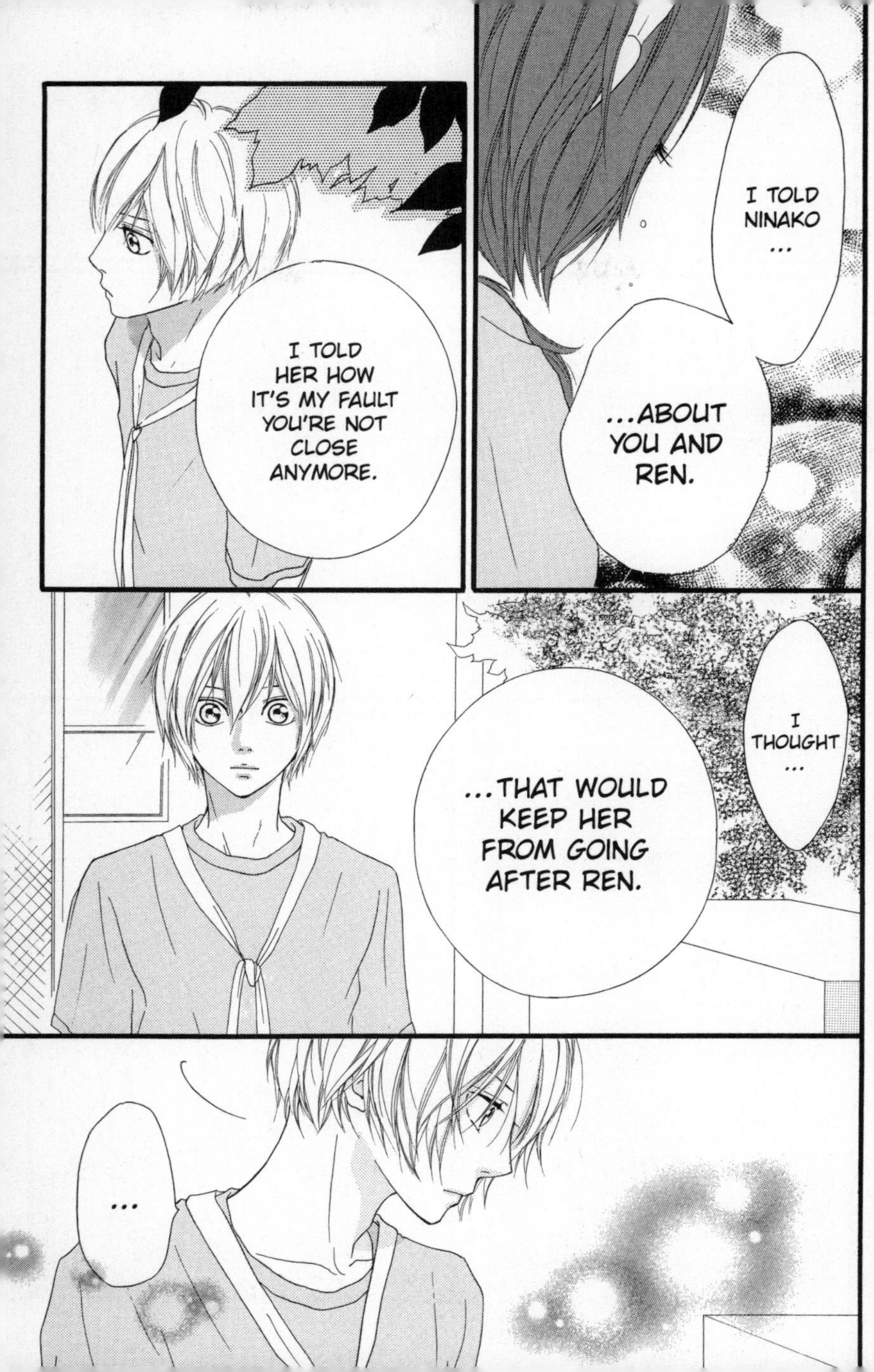
I TOLD NINAKO ...
...ABOUT YOU AND REN.
I TOLD HER HOW IT'S MY FAULT YOU'RE NOT CLOSE ANYMORE.
I THOUGHT ...
...THAT WOULD KEEP HER FROM GOING AFTER REN.
...

I SEE.

"I'M NOT IN LOVE WITH REN ANYMORE."

SO NINAKO DID...

...LIE TO ME.

UGH, THIS IS SO LAME.

EVERYONE'S IN LOVE WITH REN.

PULLING A STUNT LIKE THAT...

THAT'S JUST IDIOTIC.

...WON'T MAKE REN FALL FOR YOU.

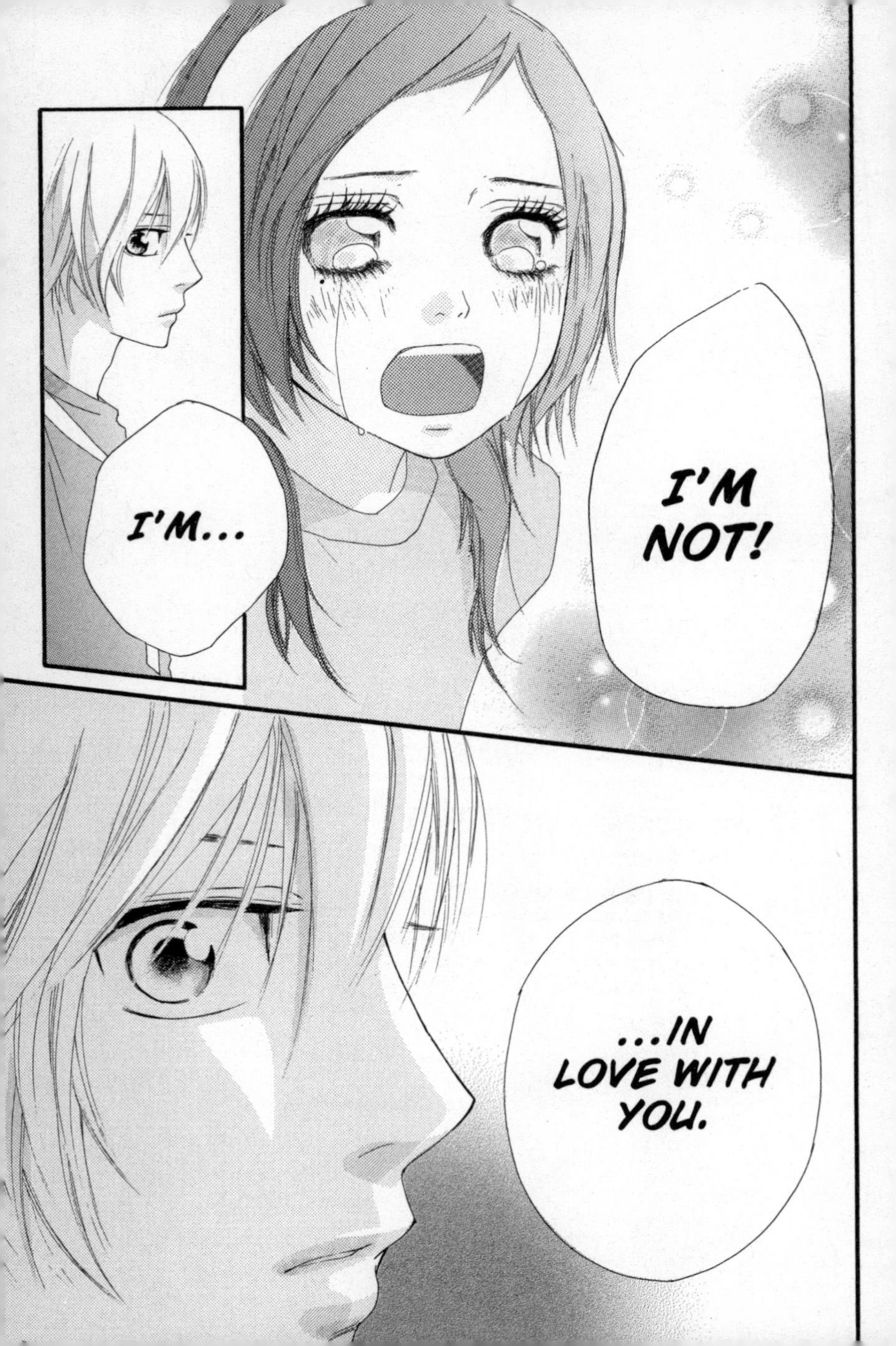
I'M NOT!
I'M...
...IN LOVE WITH YOU.

MY PROFILE

Name: Sayuri Uehara   **Nickname:** Sayu

Birthday: December 6   **Horoscope sign:** Sagittarius   **Blood Type:** A

Height: 5' 4"   **Weight:** 108 pounds

Favorite Food: Gratin   **Favorite Musician:** MEG

Current Obsession: Twitter

THOUGHT CORNER

WRITE IN THE NAME OF THE
PERSON YOU THINK OF!

CUTE/ Noriko	COOL/ Daiki ♡
FUN/ Manabu	MATURE/ Terada
STYLISH/ Ando	ENERGETIC/ Ninako

QUESTION CORNER

- You first fell in love at age (6).

- You've confessed your love before. (Yes)

- Someone has confessed their love for you. (Yes)

- You've had your first kiss. (Yes)

- There is someone you like right now. (Yes)

Once you've filled this out, turn it in to: Sakisaka!

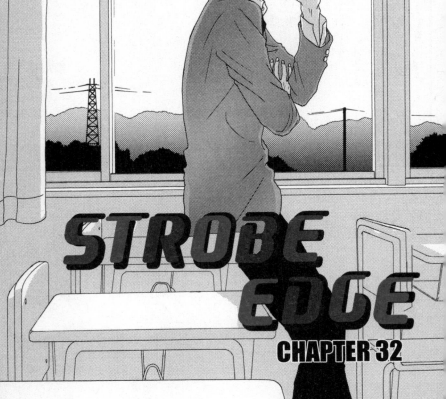

STROBE EDGE

CHAPTER 32

WHAT...?

YOU THINK I'LL FALL FOR THAT AGAIN?

ARE YOU KIDDING ME?

YOU'RE THE ONE...

...I'M IN LOVE WITH, TAKUMI.

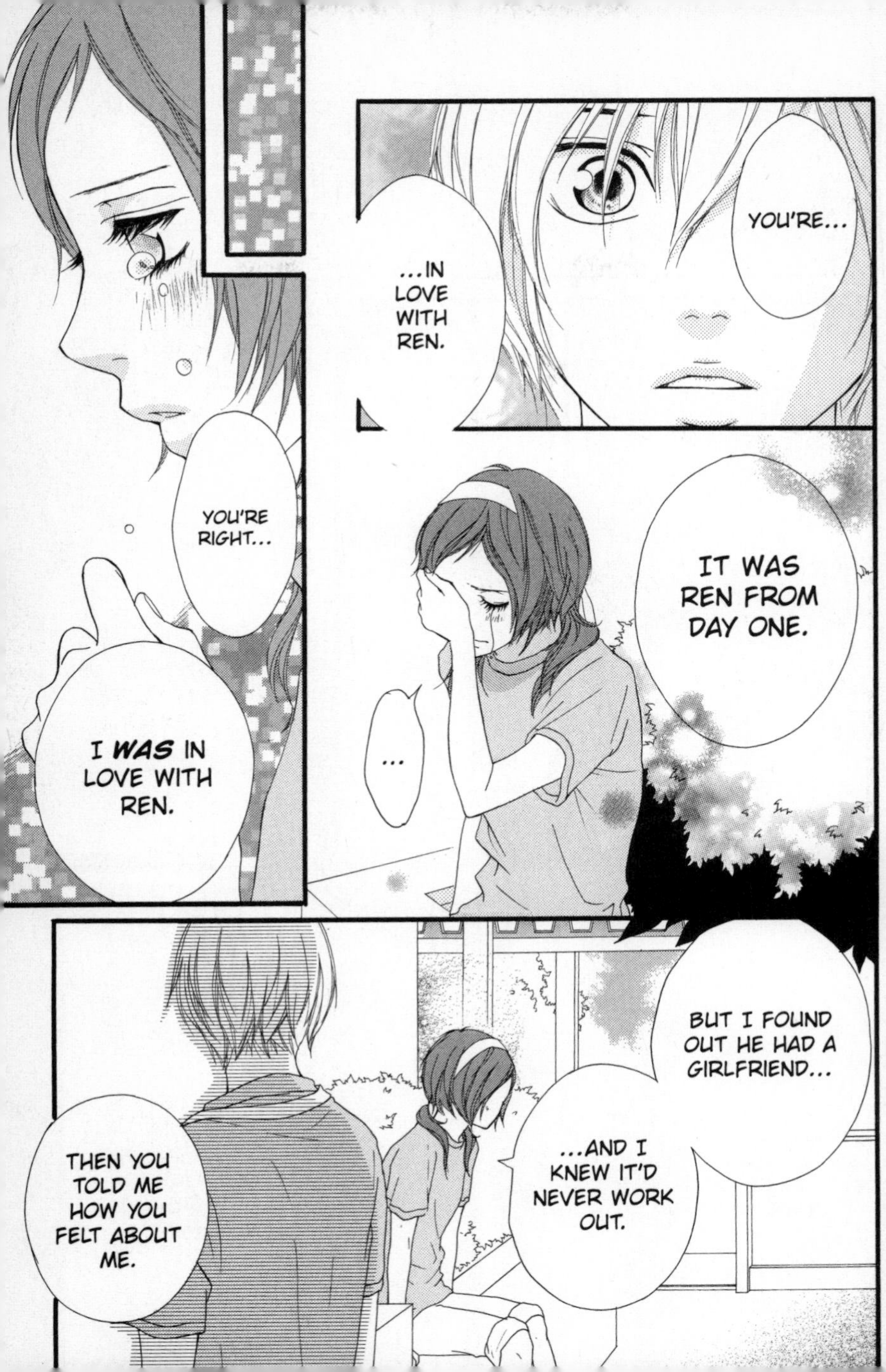
YOU'RE...
...IN LOVE WITH REN.
YOU'RE RIGHT...
I *WAS* IN LOVE WITH REN.
IT WAS REN FROM DAY ONE.
...
BUT I FOUND OUT HE HAD A GIRLFRIEND...
...AND I KNEW IT'D NEVER WORK OUT.
THEN YOU TOLD ME HOW YOU FELT ABOUT ME.

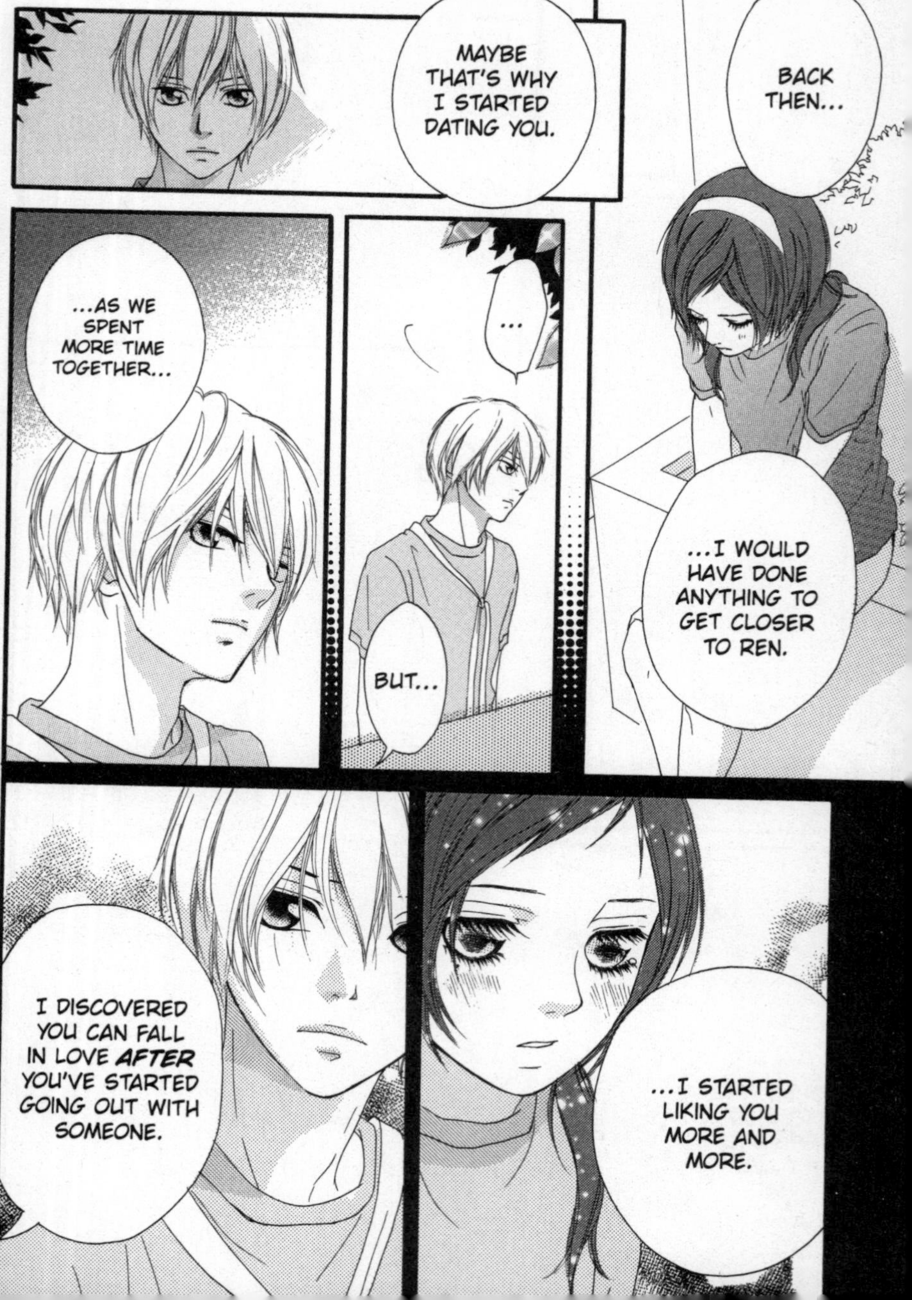
BACK THEN...
MAYBE THAT'S WHY I STARTED DATING YOU.
...I WOULD HAVE DONE ANYTHING TO GET CLOSER TO REN.
...
BUT...
...AS WE SPENT MORE TIME TOGETHER...
...I STARTED LIKING YOU MORE AND MORE.
I DISCOVERED YOU CAN FALL IN LOVE *AFTER* YOU'VE STARTED GOING OUT WITH SOMEONE.

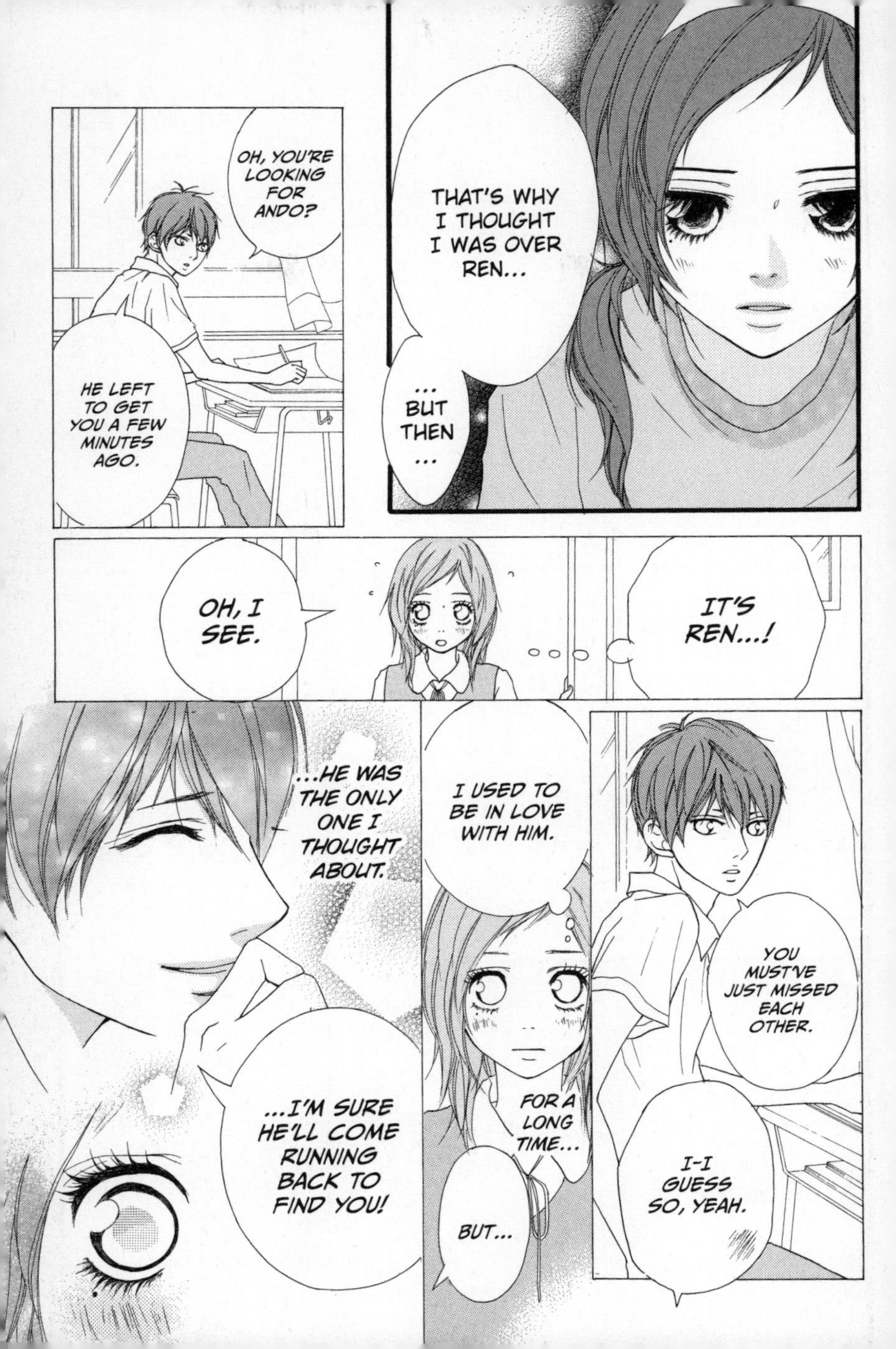
THAT'S WHY I THOUGHT I WAS OVER REN...
...BUT THEN...
OH, YOU'RE LOOKING FOR ANDO?
HE LEFT TO GET YOU A FEW MINUTES AGO.
IT'S REN...!
OH, I SEE.
YOU MUST'VE JUST MISSED EACH OTHER.
I-I GUESS SO, YEAH.
I USED TO BE IN LOVE WITH HIM.
FOR A LONG TIME...
BUT...
...HE WAS THE ONLY ONE I THOUGHT ABOUT.
...I'M SURE HE'LL COME RUNNING BACK TO FIND YOU!

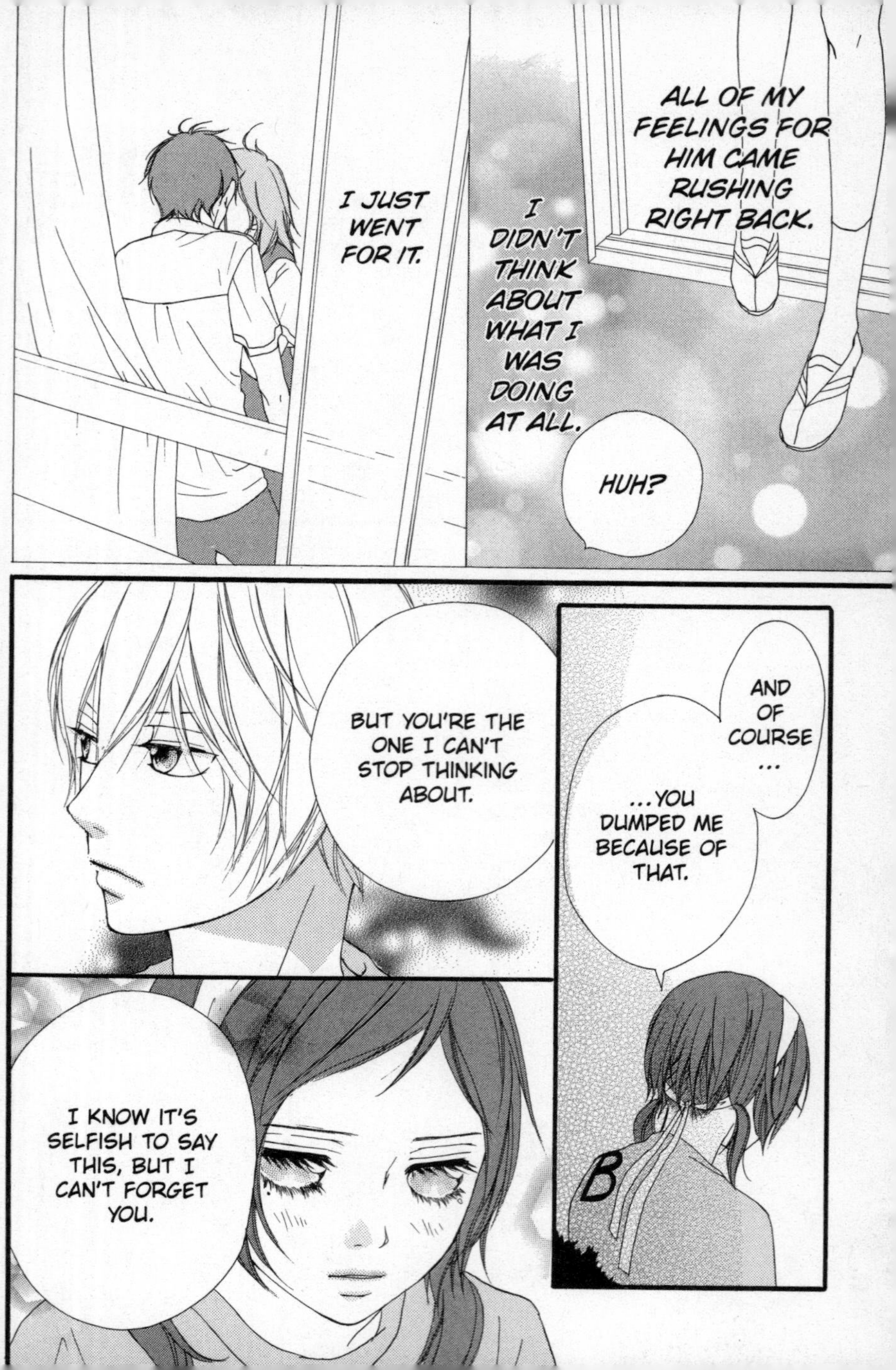
ALL OF MY FEELINGS FOR HIM CAME RUSHING RIGHT BACK.
I DIDN'T THINK ABOUT WHAT I WAS DOING AT ALL.
I JUST WENT FOR IT.
HUH?
AND OF COURSE...
...YOU DUMPED ME BECAUSE OF THAT.
BUT YOU'RE THE ONE I CAN'T STOP THINKING ABOUT.
I KNOW IT'S SELFISH TO SAY THIS, BUT I CAN'T FORGET YOU.

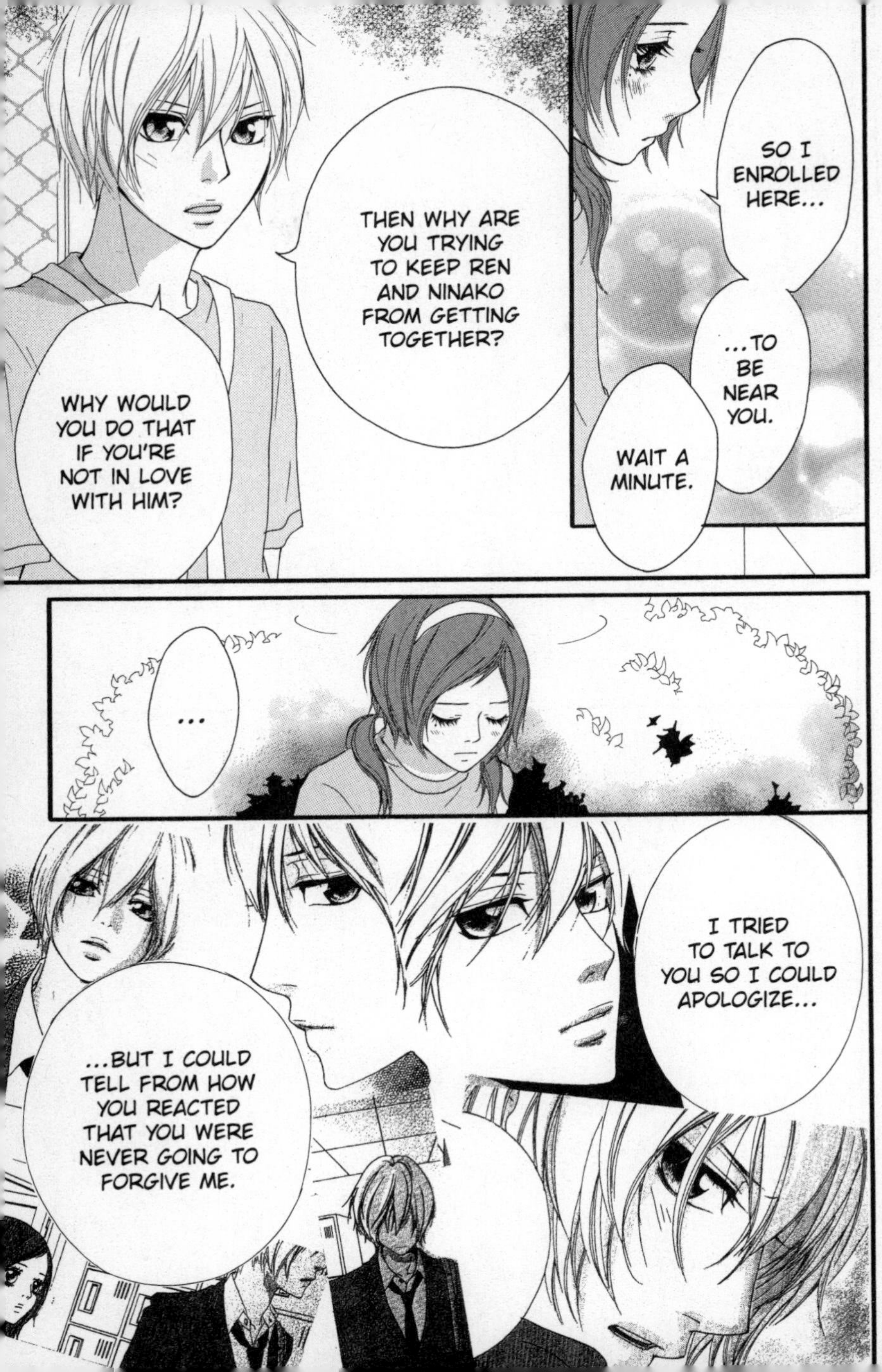
SO I ENROLLED HERE...
...TO BE NEAR YOU.
WAIT A MINUTE.
THEN WHY ARE YOU TRYING TO KEEP REN AND NINAKO FROM GETTING TOGETHER?
WHY WOULD YOU DO THAT IF YOU'RE NOT IN LOVE WITH HIM?
...
I TRIED TO TALK TO YOU SO I COULD APOLOGIZE...
...BUT I COULD TELL FROM HOW YOU REACTED THAT YOU WERE NEVER GOING TO FORGIVE ME.

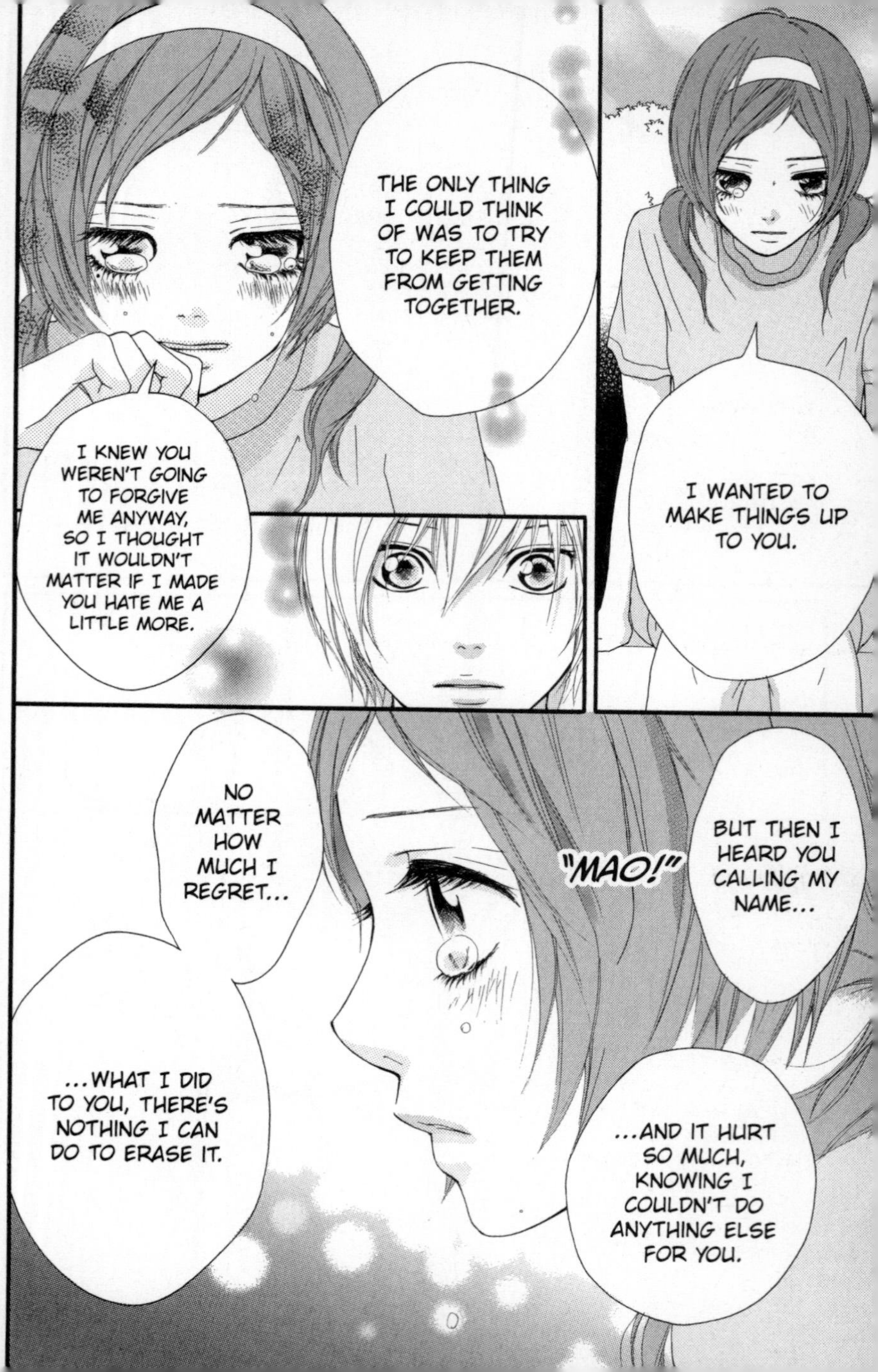
I WANTED TO MAKE THINGS UP TO YOU.
THE ONLY THING I COULD THINK OF WAS TO TRY TO KEEP THEM FROM GETTING TOGETHER.
I KNEW YOU WEREN'T GOING TO FORGIVE ME ANYWAY, SO I THOUGHT IT WOULDN'T MATTER IF I MADE YOU HATE ME A LITTLE MORE.
BUT THEN I HEARD YOU CALLING MY NAME...
"MAO!"
...AND IT HURT SO MUCH, KNOWING I COULDN'T DO ANYTHING ELSE FOR YOU.
NO MATTER HOW MUCH I REGRET...
...WHAT I DID TO YOU, THERE'S NOTHING I CAN DO TO ERASE IT.

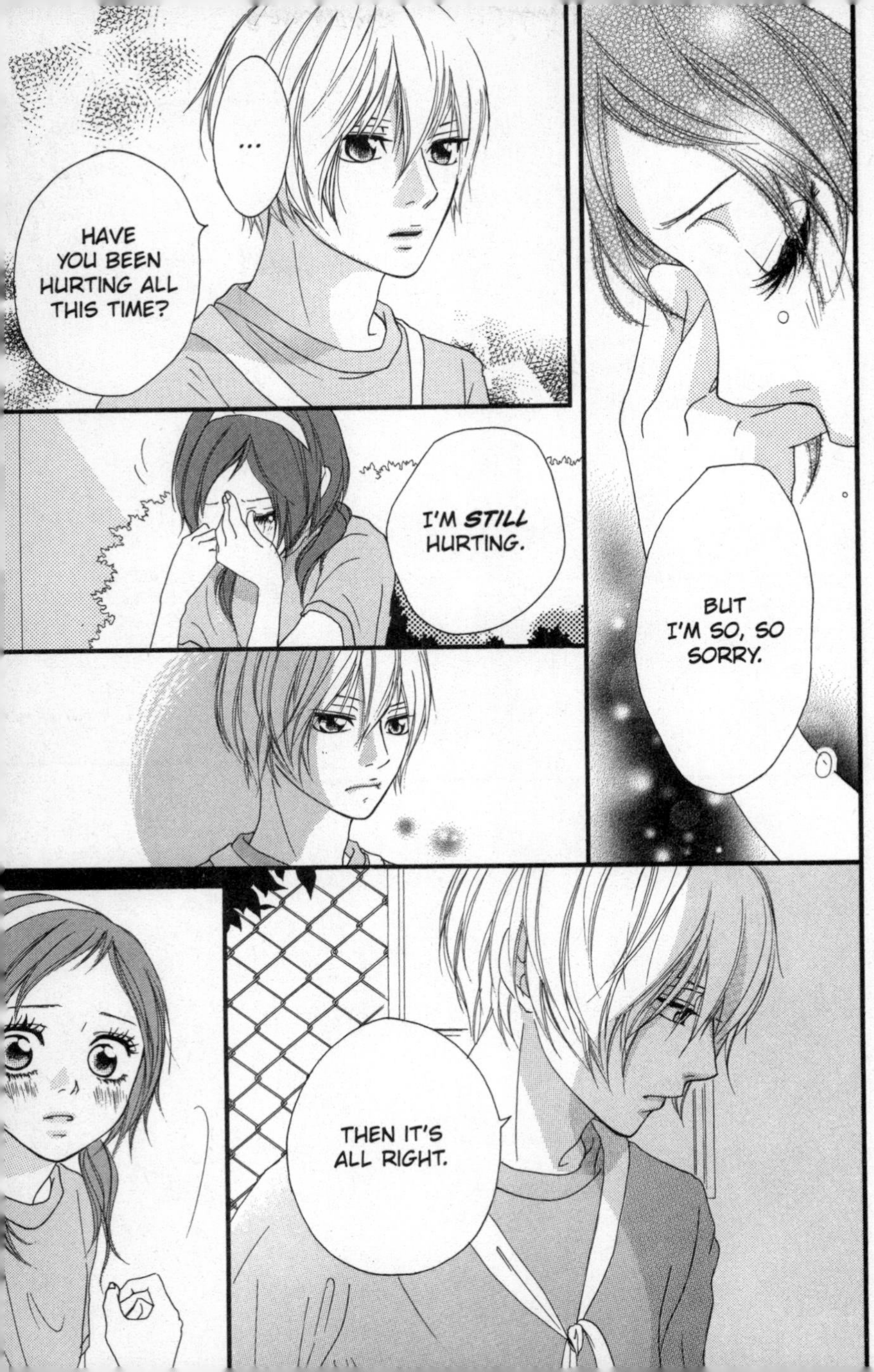
...
HAVE YOU BEEN HURTING ALL THIS TIME?
I'M *STILL* HURTING.
BUT I'M SO, SO SORRY.
THEN IT'S ALL RIGHT.

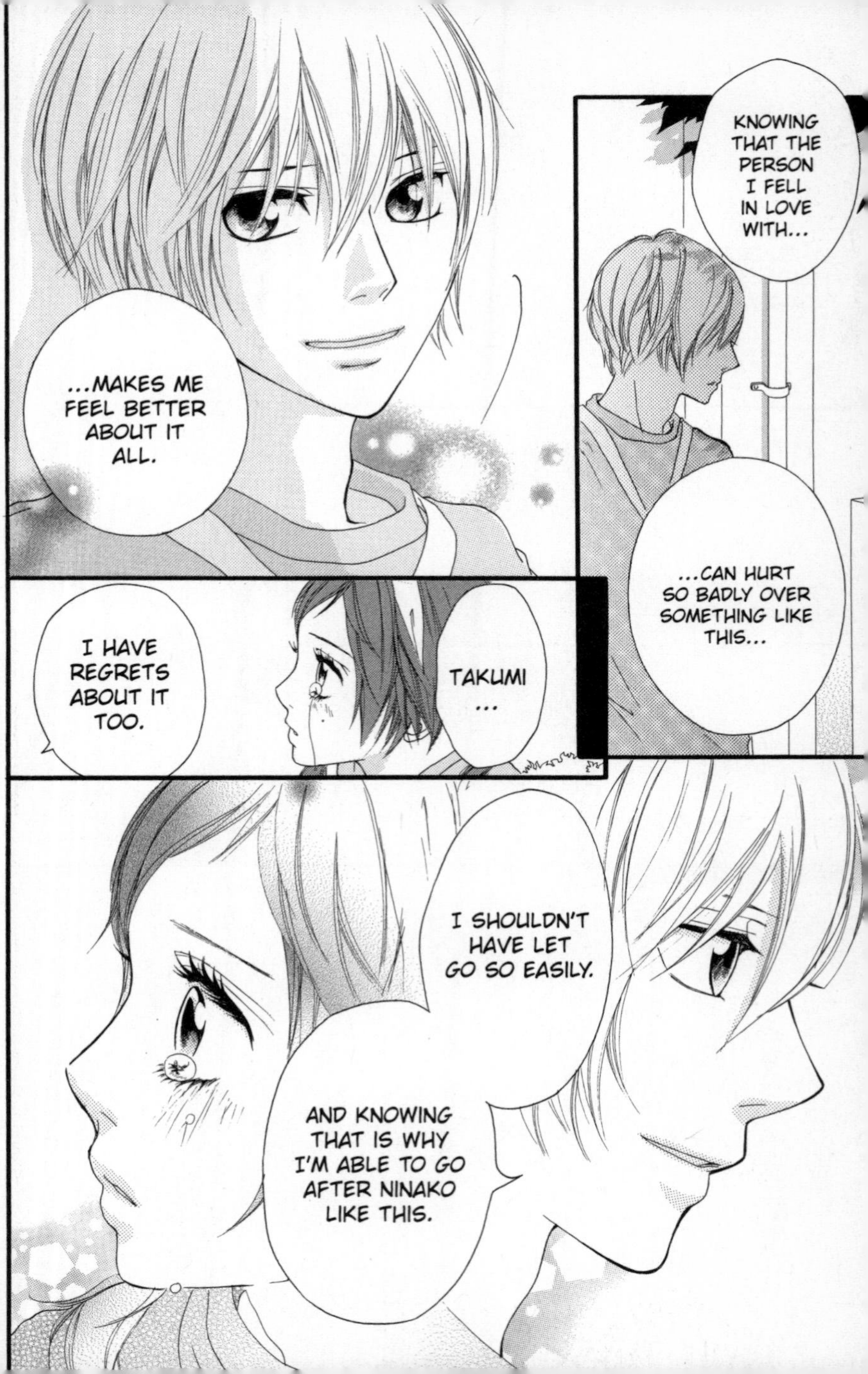
KNOWING THAT THE PERSON I FELL IN LOVE WITH...
...CAN HURT SO BADLY OVER SOMETHING LIKE THIS...
...MAKES ME FEEL BETTER ABOUT IT ALL.
TAKUMI ...
I HAVE REGRETS ABOUT IT TOO.
I SHOULDN'T HAVE LET GO SO EASILY.
AND KNOWING THAT IS WHY I'M ABLE TO GO AFTER NINAKO LIKE THIS.

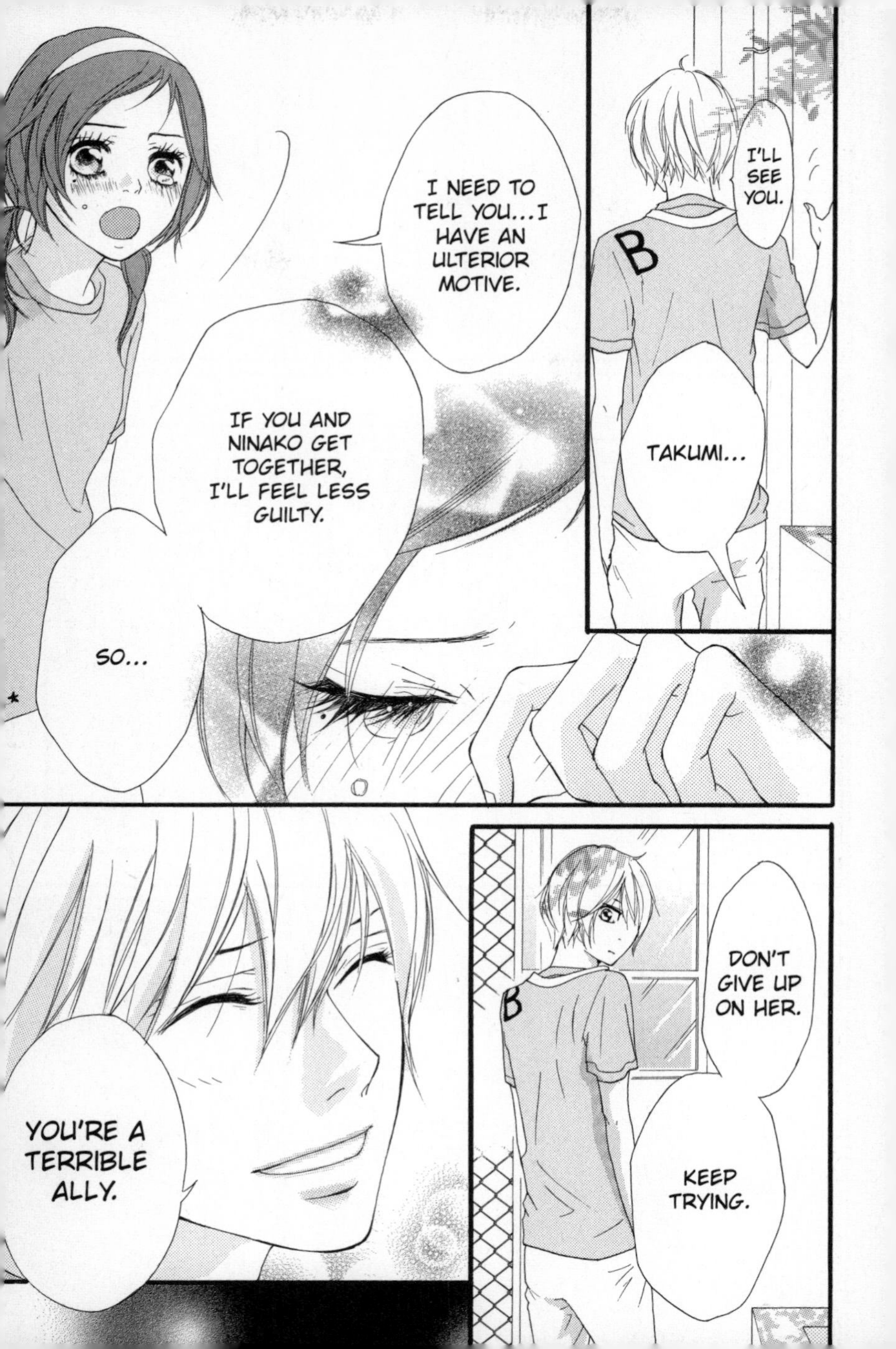
I'LL SEE YOU.
TAKUMI...
I NEED TO TELL YOU...I HAVE AN ULTERIOR MOTIVE.
IF YOU AND NINAKO GET TOGETHER, I'LL FEEL LESS GUILTY.
SO...
DON'T GIVE UP ON HER.
KEEP TRYING.
YOU'RE A TERRIBLE ALLY.

NINAKO STILL—

IT'S NOT OVER YET!

NAH, CUT THAT OUT.

WE'VE JUST CIRCLED BACK TO THE BEGINNING.

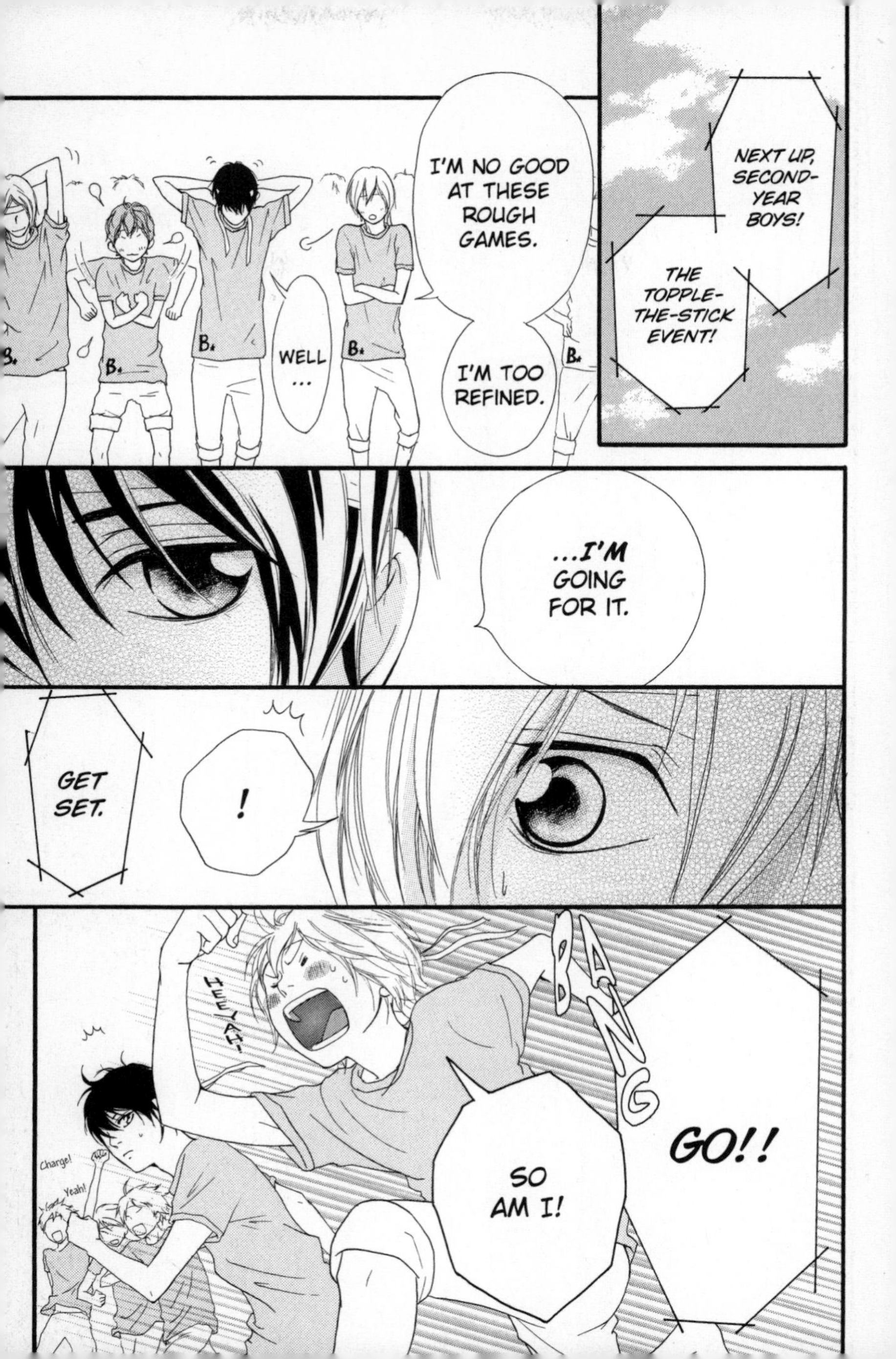
NEXT UP, SECOND-YEAR BOYS!
THE TOPPLE-THE-STICK EVENT!
I'M NO GOOD AT THESE ROUGH GAMES.
I'M TOO REFINED.
WELL ...
B.
...I'M GOING FOR IT.
!
GET SET.
GO!!
BANG
SO AM I!
HEEYAH!
Charge!
Yeah!

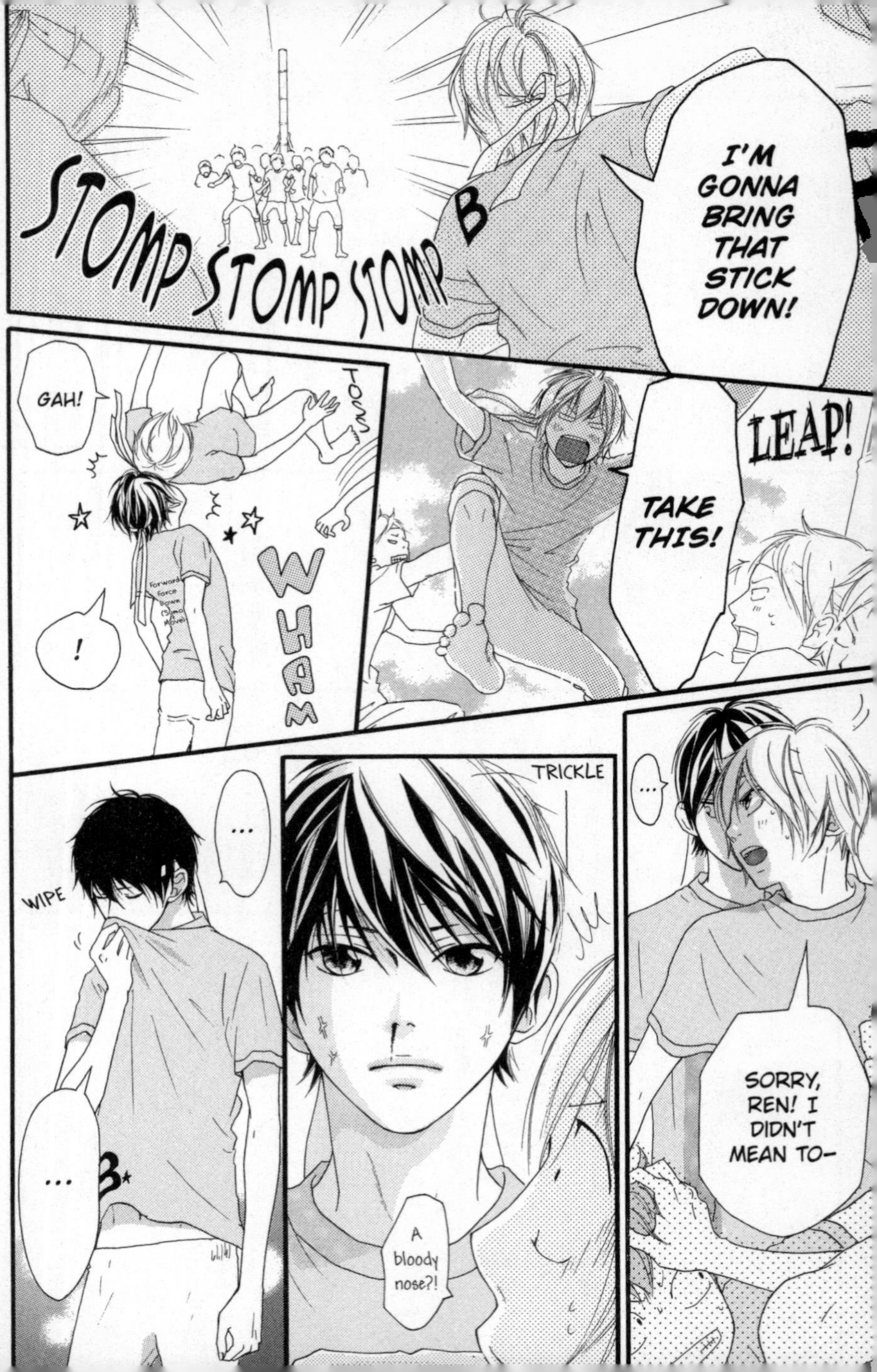
I'M GONNA BRING THAT STICK DOWN!
STOMP STOMP STOMP
B
LEAP!
TAKE THIS!
TOSS
GAH!
WHAM
Forward Force Down (Sumo Move)
!
...
SORRY, REN! I DIDN'T MEAN TO—
TRICKLE
A bloody nose?!
WIPE
...
...

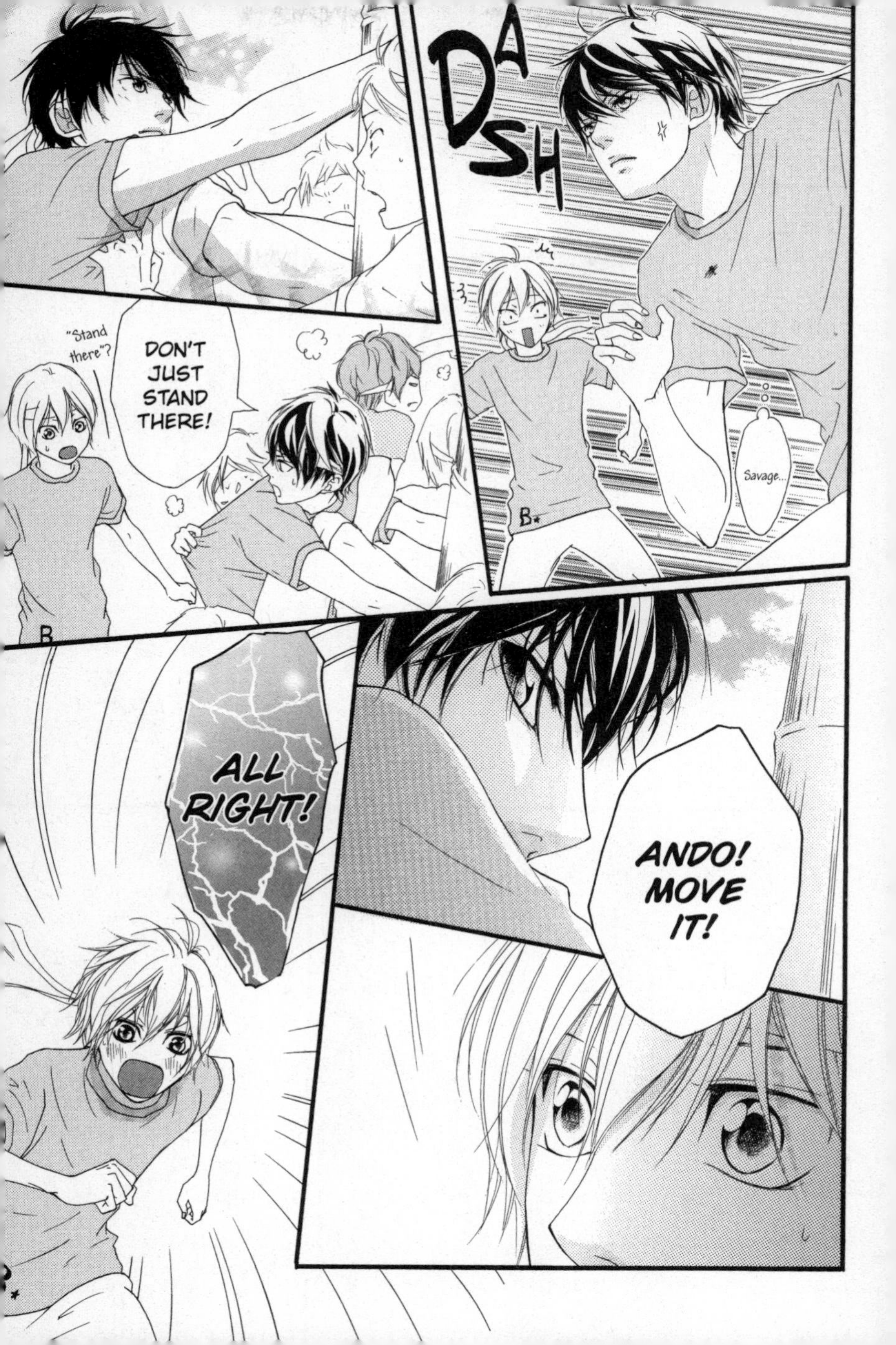
DASH
Savage...
DON'T JUST STAND THERE!
"Stand there"?
ANDO! MOVE IT!
ALL RIGHT!

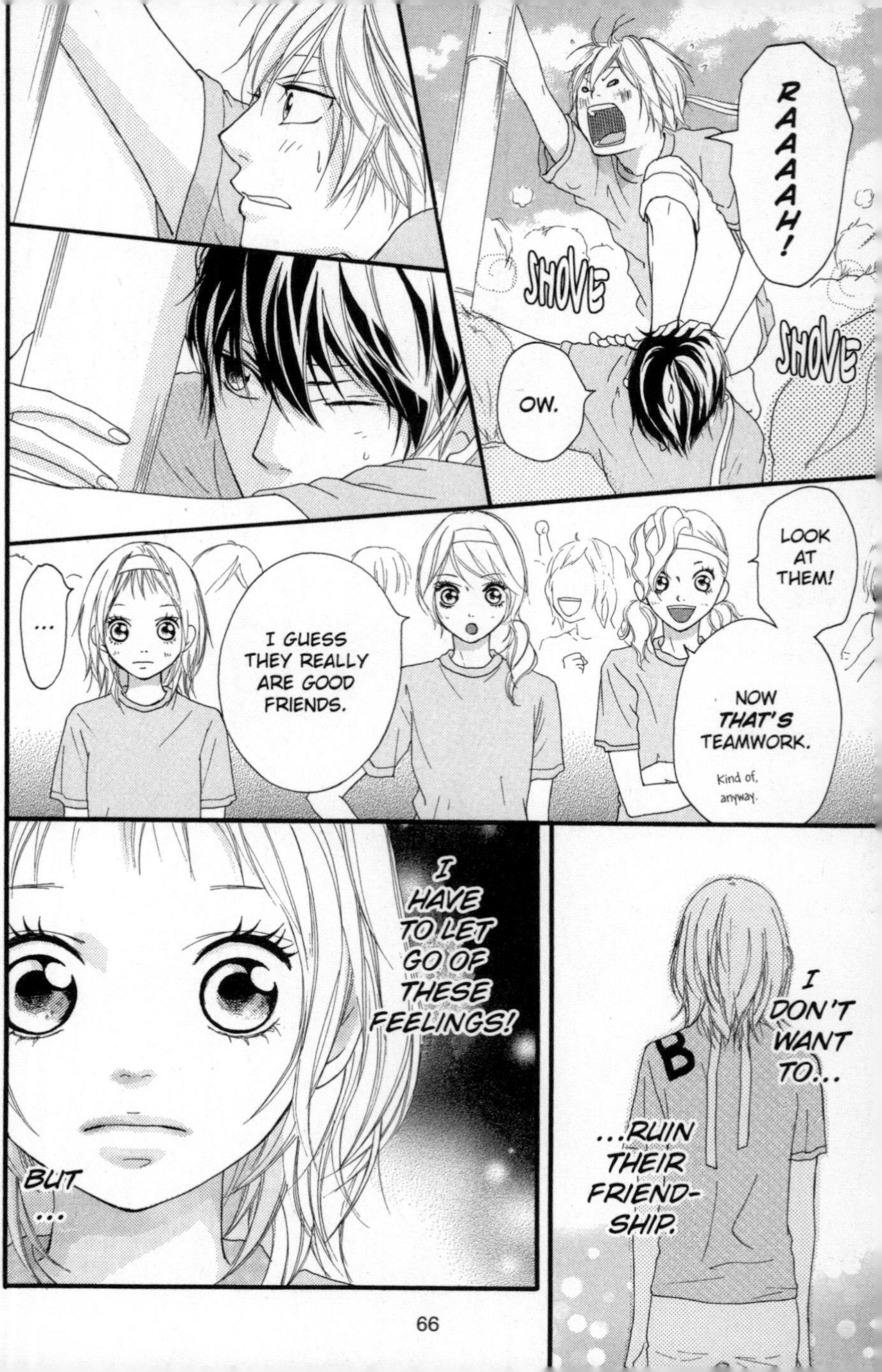
RAAAAH!
SHOVE
SHOVE
OW.
LOOK AT THEM!
NOW THAT'S TEAMWORK.
Kind of, anyway.
I GUESS THEY REALLY ARE GOOD FRIENDS.
...
I DON'T WANT TO...
...RUIN THEIR FRIEND-SHIP.
I HAVE TO LET GO OF THESE FEELINGS!
BUT...

YOU KNOW...

...MY EYES...

...KEEP FOLLOW-ING REN.

...LOVE ISN'T ABOUT WHAT YOUR HEAD THINKS.

IT'S WHAT YOUR HEART *FEELS.*

NORIKO...

...BUT YOU CAN'T JUST FORCE YOUR HEART TO DO THAT.

YOU CAN KEEP TELLING YOURSELF THAT YOU'RE GOING TO LET GO...

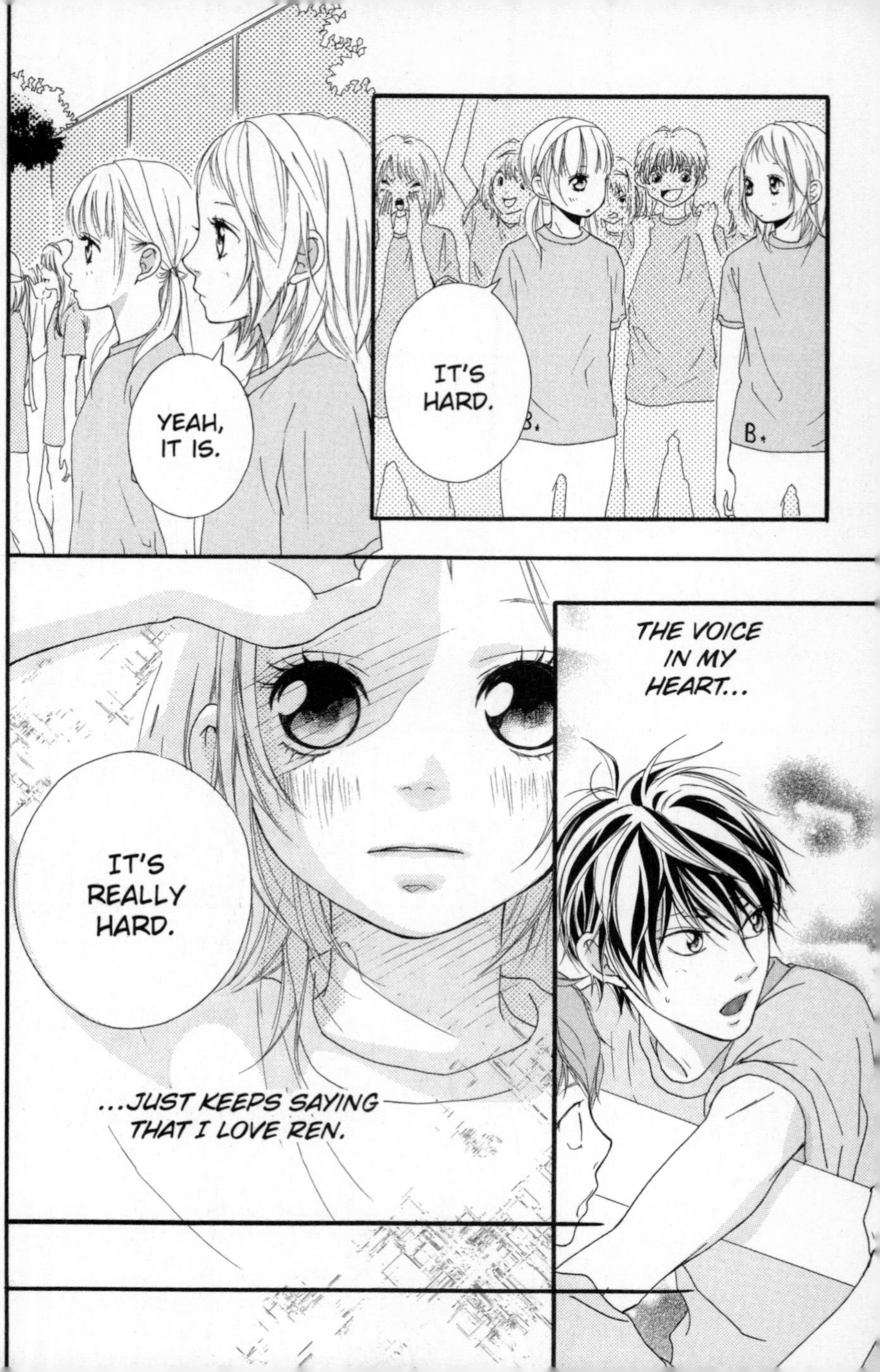
IT'S HARD.
YEAH, IT IS.
THE VOICE IN MY HEART...
IT'S REALLY HARD.
...JUST KEEPS SAYING THAT I LOVE REN.

Questions Part 1

I'd like to answer the questions you've all sent me!

Q: What is the best thing about being a manga artist? How about the worst?

A: The best thing is how much fun my work is. Of course, there are also a lot of challenges, but ultimately, I love the creative process. The worst thing is that my life tends to be a little random. (That said, there are many artists who live much more orderly lives!)

Q: Outside of work, what things make you happiest?

A: Eating delicious food! It's a pleasure, or maybe I should say it's a joy.

Q: How do story developments come to you?

A: In all kinds of ways. Sometimes I won't be thinking about it at all and it just comes to me. Sometimes I sit down and map out a story by thinking through different scenarios. Sometimes when I'm on a deadline and thinking there's no way I can finish on time, the ideas come from sheer panic.

It's a drama every time.

Continued in part 2!

WE'RE NEXT!

BUT...

BLOCK A IS TAKING THE FIELD.

THE CHEER-LEADING COMPETITION IS ABOUT TO BEGIN!

...WHY DO WE HAVE TO WEAR THESE LONG SCHOOL UNIFORMS?

THE OTHER BLOCKS HAVE CHEERLEADER OUTFITS.

WELL, I GUESS THESE ARE MORE DISTINCTIVE...

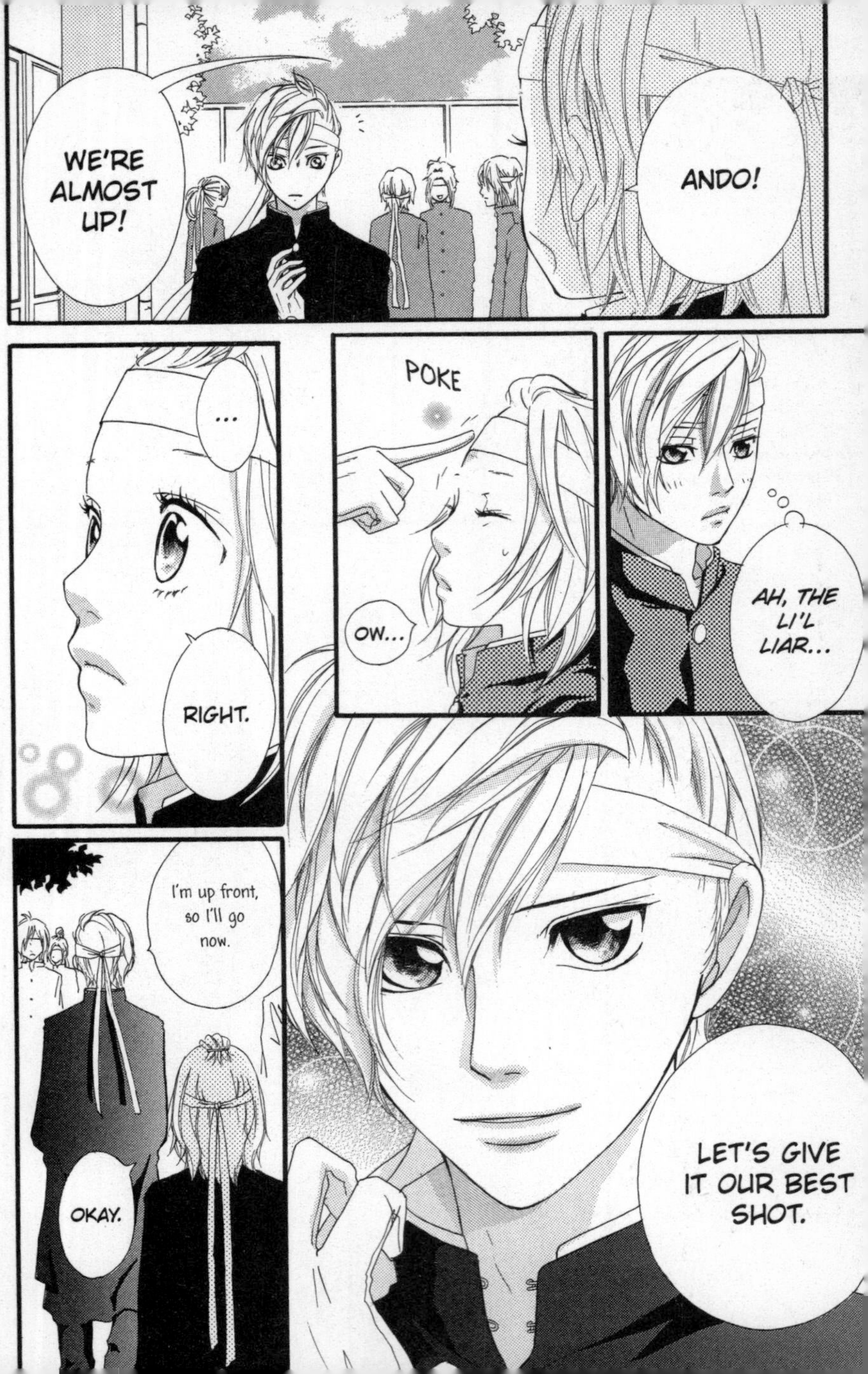
ANDO!
WE'RE ALMOST UP!
AH, THE LI'L LIAR...
POKE
OW...
...
RIGHT.
LET'S GIVE IT OUR BEST SHOT.
I'm up front, so I'll go now.
OKAY.

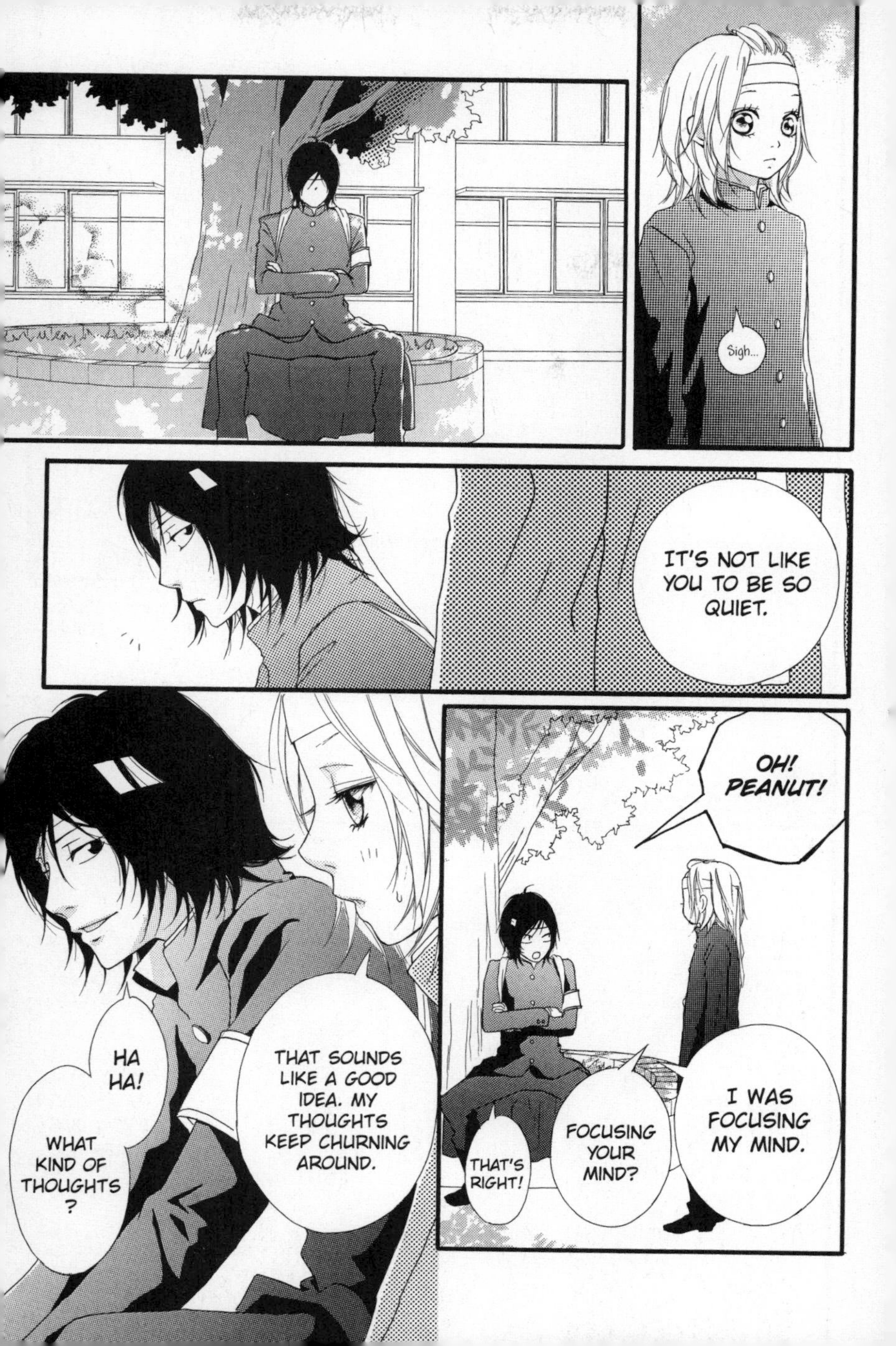
Sigh...
IT'S NOT LIKE YOU TO BE SO QUIET.
OH! PEANUT!
I WAS FOCUSING MY MIND.
FOCUSING YOUR MIND?
THAT'S RIGHT!
THAT SOUNDS LIKE A GOOD IDEA. MY THOUGHTS KEEP CHURNING AROUND.
HA HA!
WHAT KIND OF THOUGHTS?

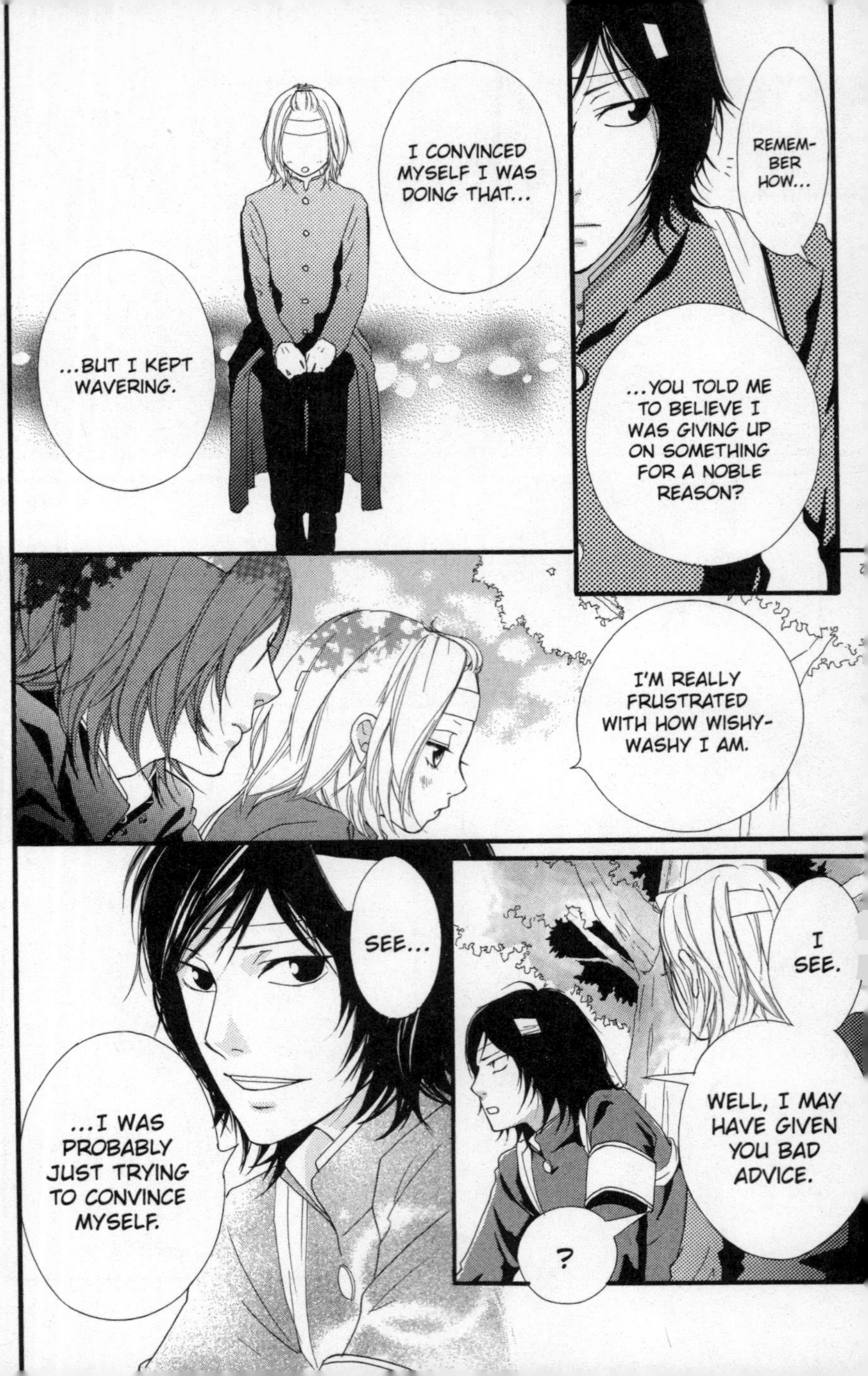
REMEM-
BER
HOW...
...YOU TOLD ME TO BELIEVE I WAS GIVING UP ON SOMETHING FOR A NOBLE REASON?
I CONVINCED MYSELF I WAS DOING THAT...
...BUT I KEPT WAVERING.
I'M REALLY FRUSTRATED WITH HOW WISHY-WASHY I AM.
I SEE.
WELL, I MAY HAVE GIVEN YOU BAD ADVICE.
?
SEE...
...I WAS PROBABLY JUST TRYING TO CONVINCE MYSELF.

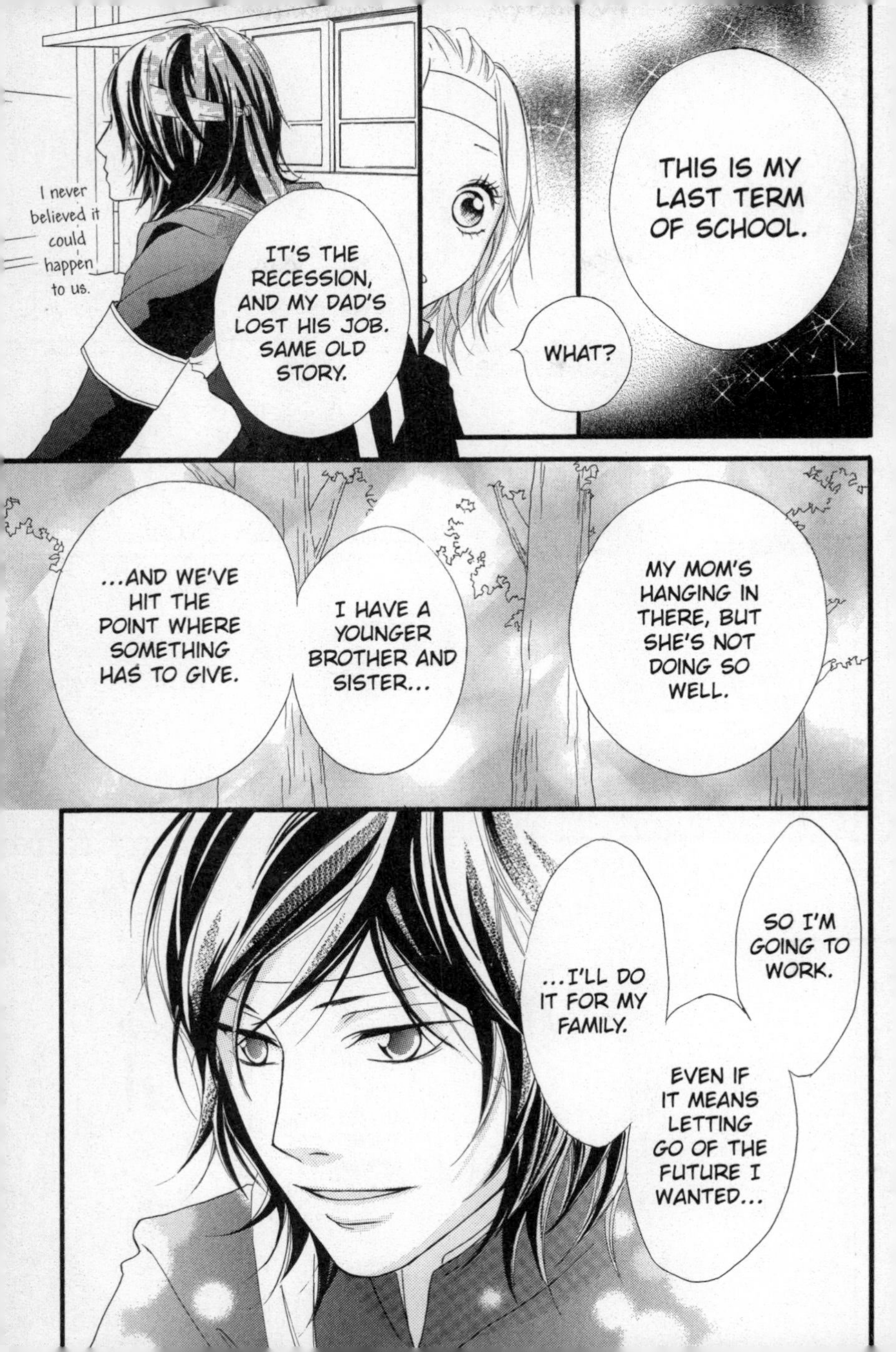
THIS IS MY LAST TERM OF SCHOOL.
WHAT?
IT'S THE RECESSION, AND MY DAD'S LOST HIS JOB. SAME OLD STORY.
I never believed it could happen to us.
MY MOM'S HANGING IN THERE, BUT SHE'S NOT DOING SO WELL.
I HAVE A YOUNGER BROTHER AND SISTER...
...AND WE'VE HIT THE POINT WHERE SOMETHING HAS TO GIVE.
SO I'M GOING TO WORK.
EVEN IF IT MEANS LETTING GO OF THE FUTURE I WANTED...
...I'LL DO IT FOR MY FAMILY.

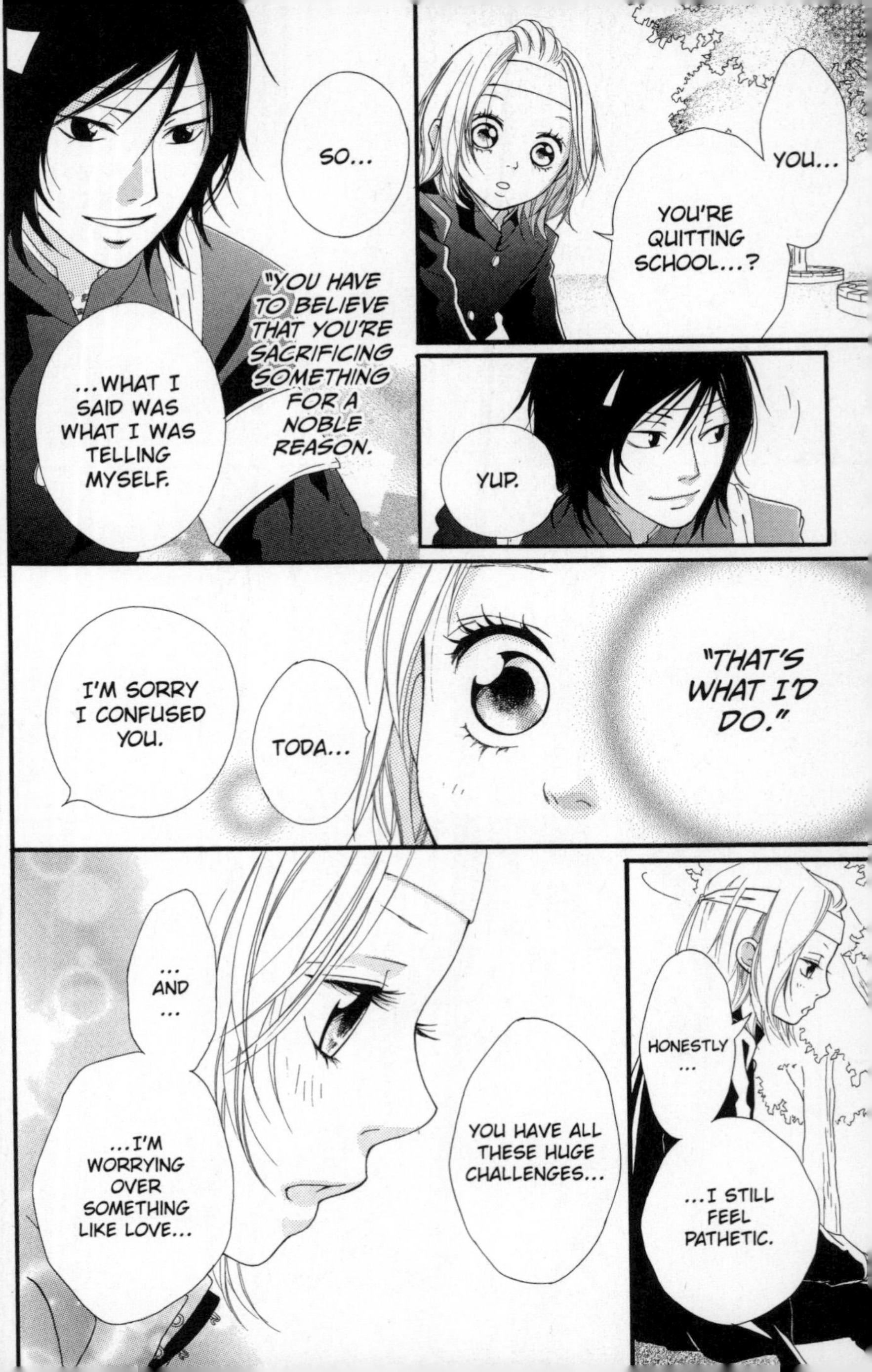
YOU...
YOU'RE QUITTING SCHOOL...?
YUP.
SO...
"YOU HAVE TO BELIEVE THAT YOU'RE SACRIFICING SOMETHING FOR A NOBLE REASON.
...WHAT I SAID WAS WHAT I WAS TELLING MYSELF.
"THAT'S WHAT I'D DO."
TODA...
I'M SORRY I CONFUSED YOU.
HONESTLY...
...I STILL FEEL PATHETIC.
YOU HAVE ALL THESE HUGE CHALLENGES...
...AND...
...I'M WORRYING OVER SOMETHING LIKE LOVE...

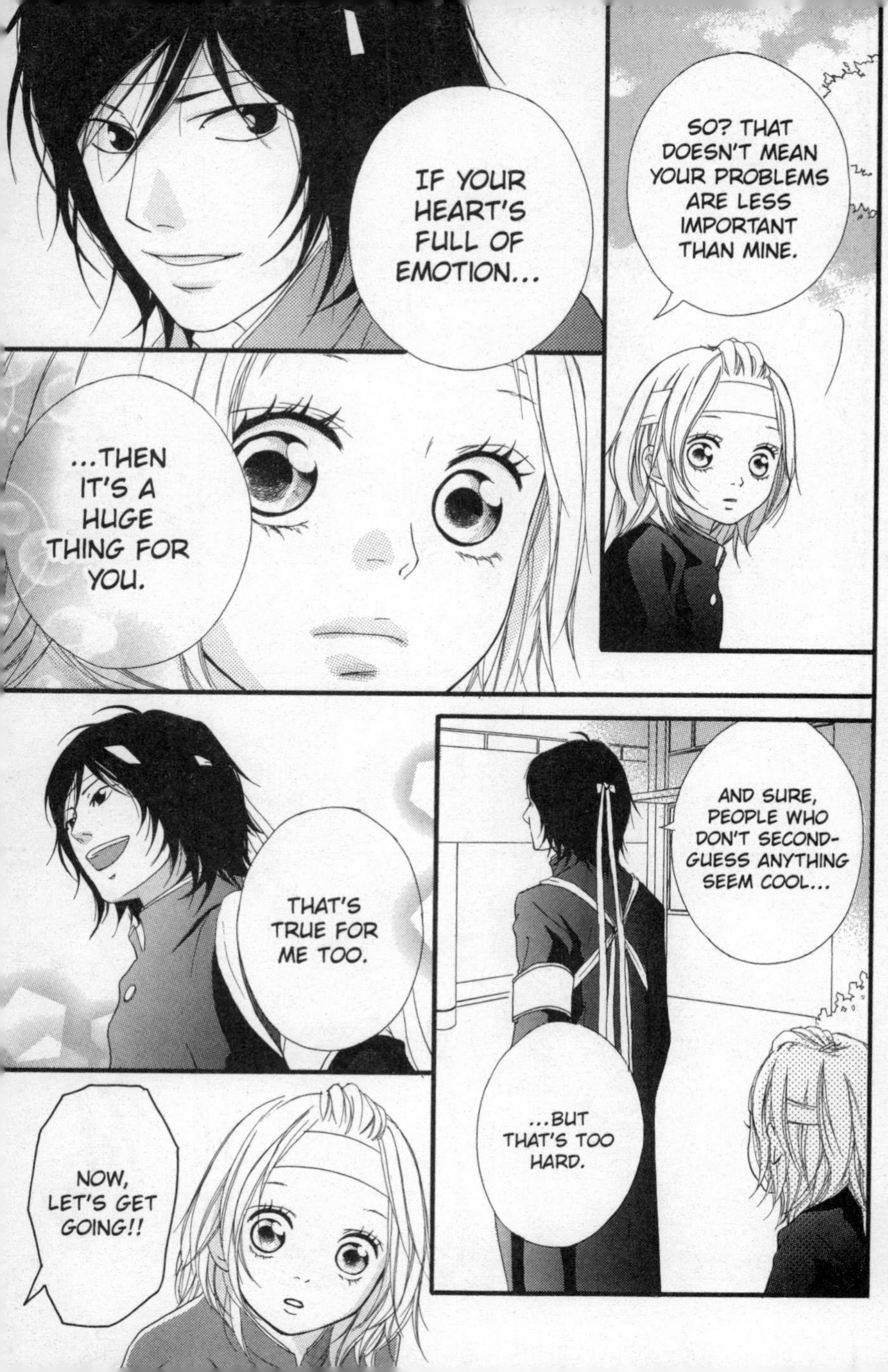
SO? THAT DOESN'T MEAN YOUR PROBLEMS ARE LESS IMPORTANT THAN MINE.
IF YOUR HEART'S FULL OF EMOTION...
...THEN IT'S A HUGE THING FOR YOU.
AND SURE, PEOPLE WHO DON'T SECOND-GUESS ANYTHING SEEM COOL...
...BUT THAT'S TOO HARD.
THAT'S TRUE FOR ME TOO.
NOW, LET'S GET GOING!!

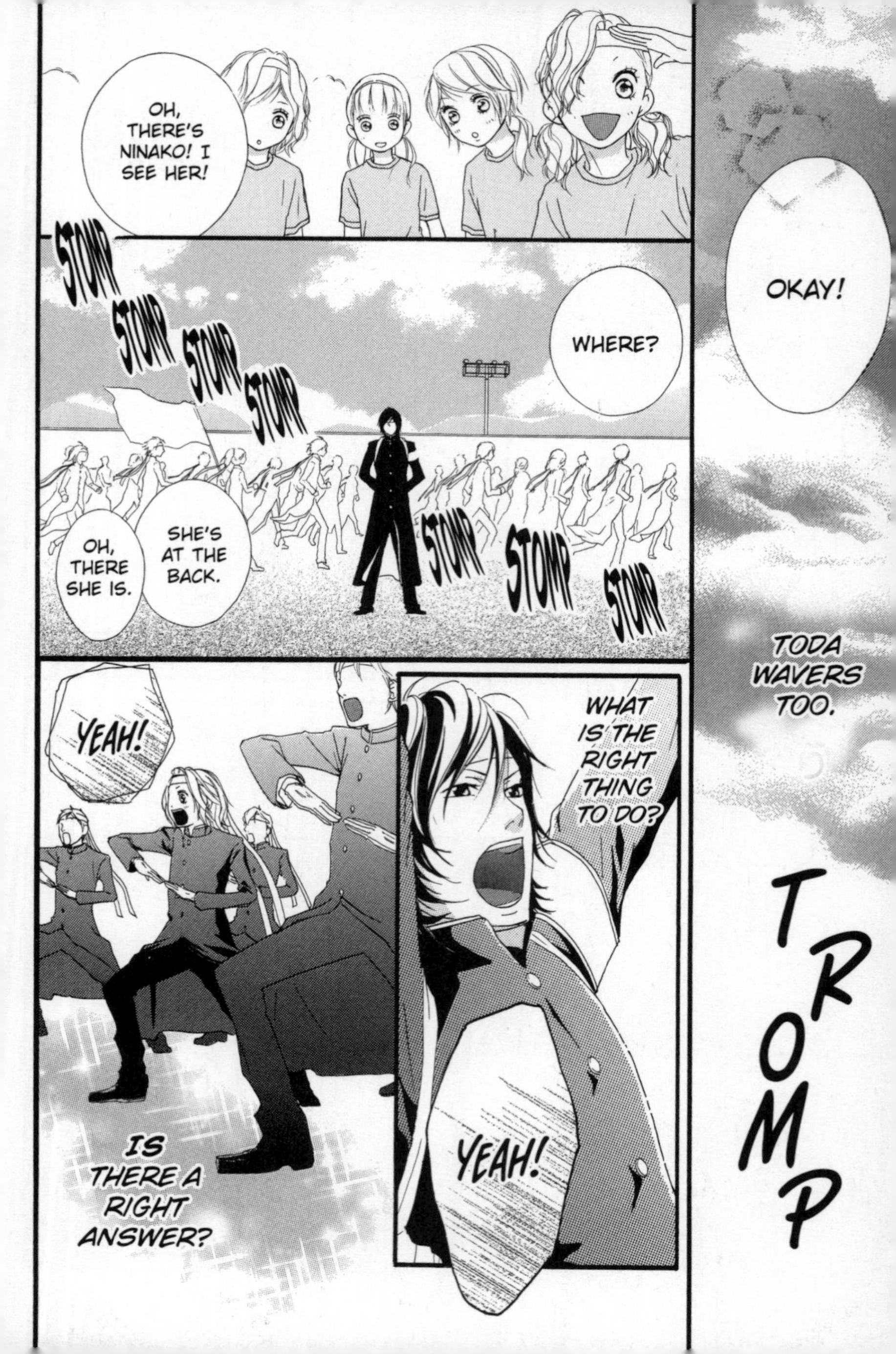
OKAY!
OH, THERE'S NINAKO! I SEE HER!
STOMP STOMP STOMP STOMP
WHERE?
SHE'S AT THE BACK.
OH, THERE SHE IS.
STOMP STOMP STOMP
TODA WAVERS TOO.
TROMP
WHAT IS THE RIGHT THING TO DO?
YEAH!
YEAH!
IS THERE A RIGHT ANSWER?

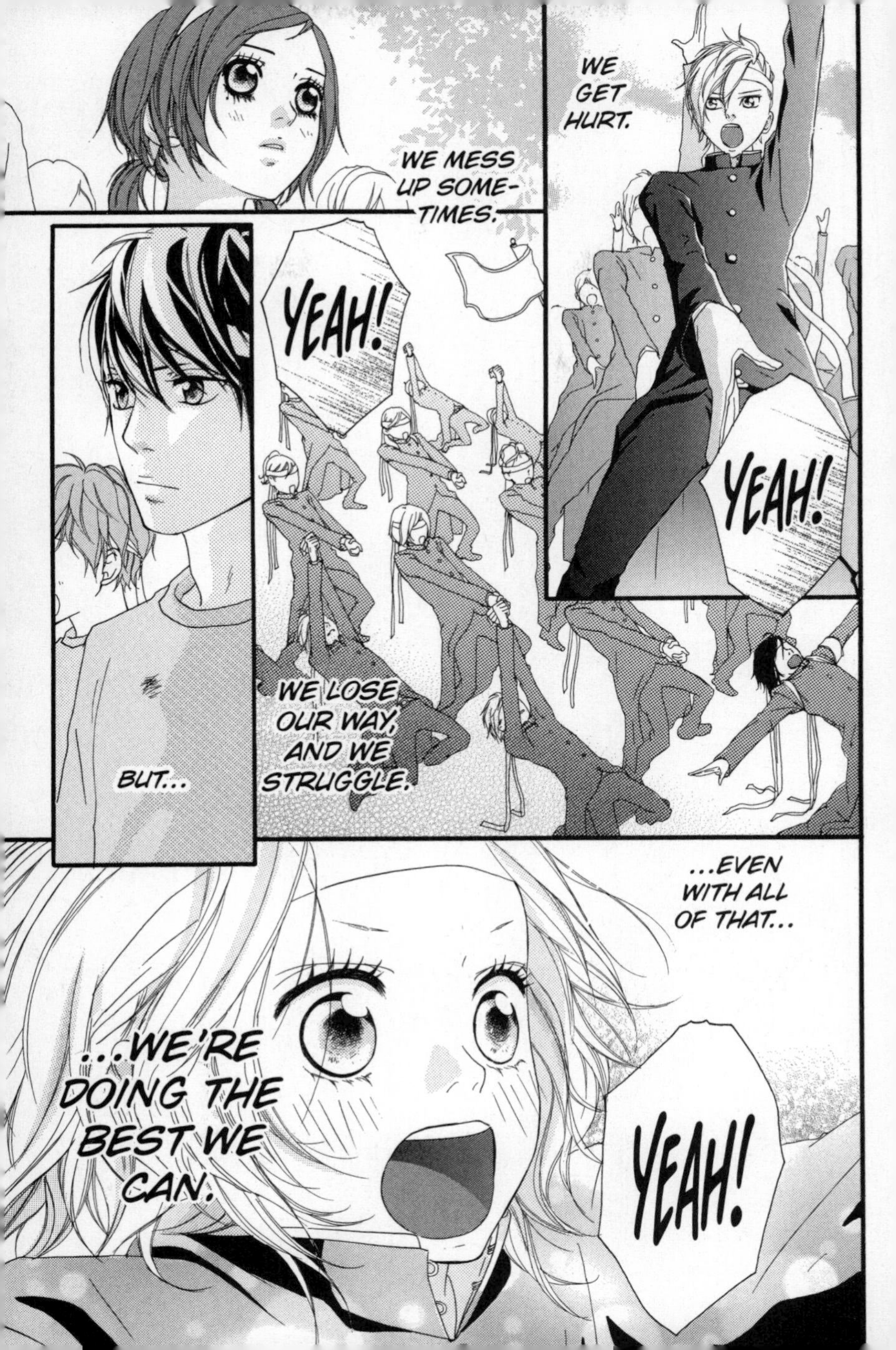
WE GET HURT.
YEAH!
WE MESS UP SOMETIMES.
YEAH!
WE LOSE OUR WAY, AND WE STRUGGLE.
BUT...
...EVEN WITH ALL OF THAT...
YEAH!
...WE'RE DOING THE BEST WE CAN.

THE OVERALL WINNER FOR THE 15TH SPORTS FESTIVAL IS...

...BLOCK D!!!

WOO-HOO!

AND THE CHEER-LEADING PRIZE...

...GOES TO BLOCK A!!

HEY, TODA?

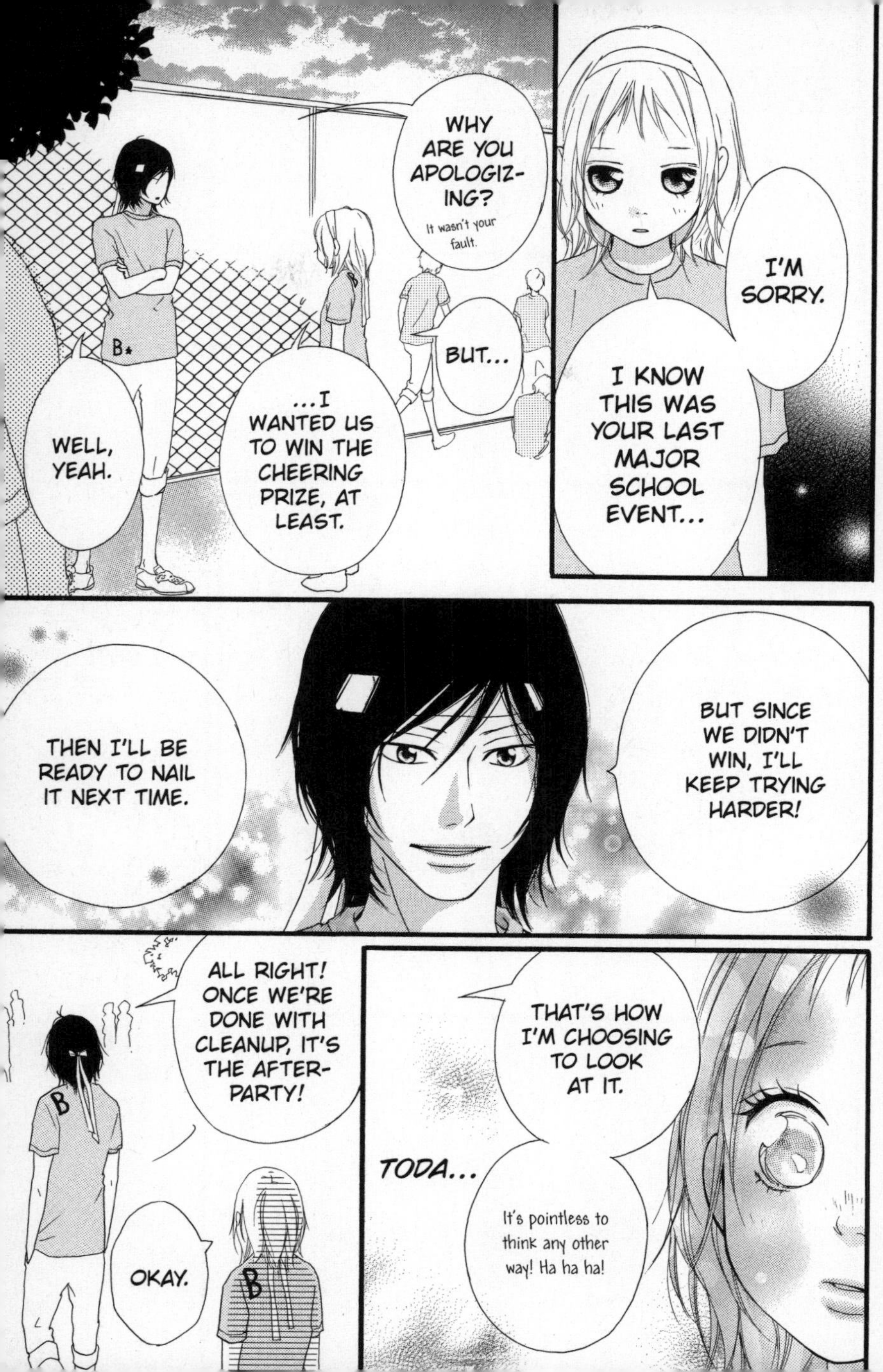
I'M SORRY.
I KNOW THIS WAS YOUR LAST MAJOR SCHOOL EVENT...
WHY ARE YOU APOLOGIZING?
It wasn't your fault.
BUT...
...I WANTED US TO WIN THE CHEERING PRIZE, AT LEAST.
WELL, YEAH.
BUT SINCE WE DIDN'T WIN, I'LL KEEP TRYING HARDER!
THEN I'LL BE READY TO NAIL IT NEXT TIME.
THAT'S HOW I'M CHOOSING TO LOOK AT IT.
It's pointless to think any other way! Ha ha ha!
TODA...
ALL RIGHT! ONCE WE'RE DONE WITH CLEANUP, IT'S THE AFTER-PARTY!
OKAY.

I REALLY WANT...

...TO BE ABLE TO LOOK AT LIFE...

...THE WAY YOU DO.

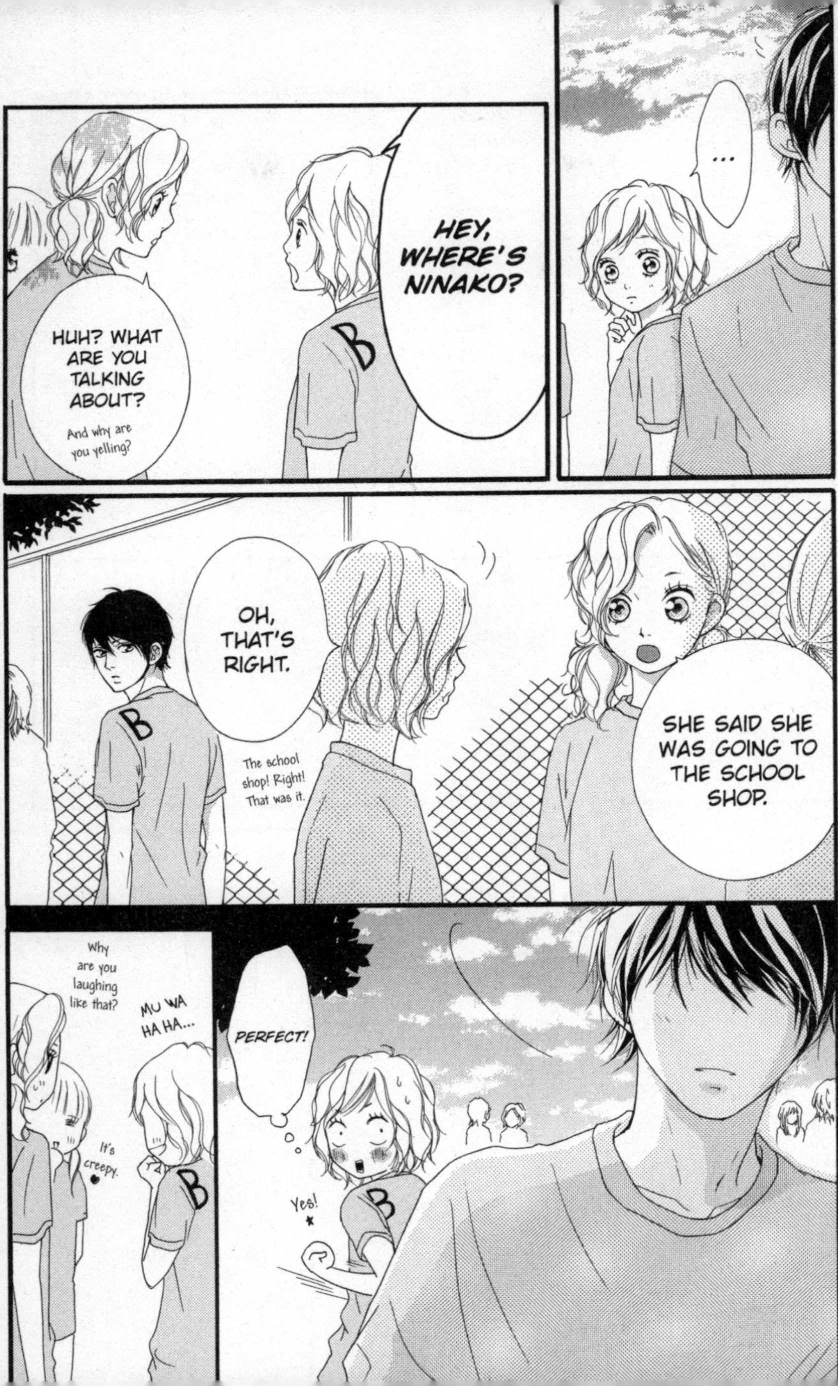
...
HEY, WHERE'S NINAKO?
HUH? WHAT ARE YOU TALKING ABOUT?
And why are you yelling?
SHE SAID SHE WAS GOING TO THE SCHOOL SHOP.
OH, THAT'S RIGHT.
The school shop! Right! That was it.
PERFECT!
Yes!
MU WA HA HA...
Why are you laughing like that?
It's creepy.

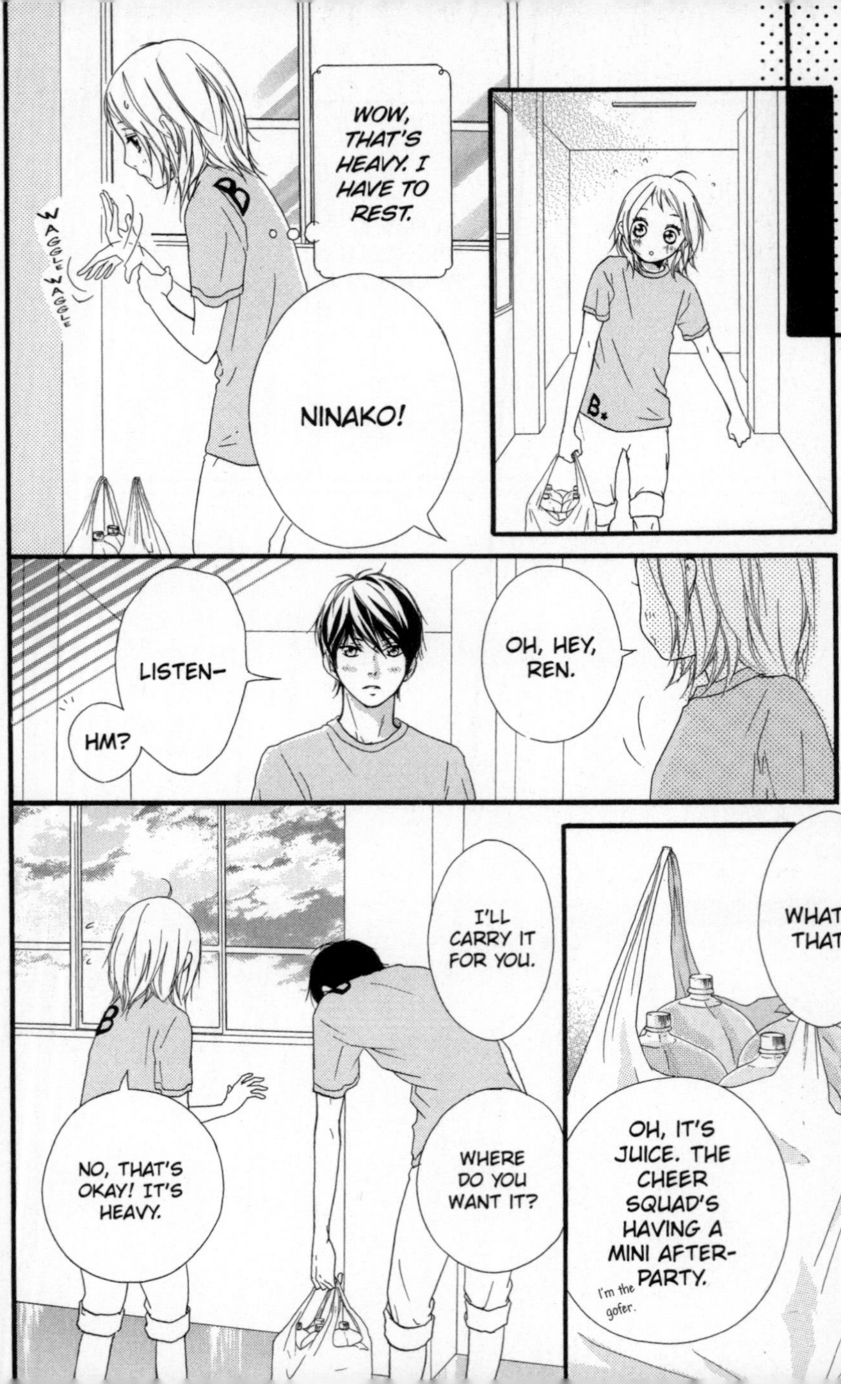
WOW, THAT'S HEAVY. I HAVE TO REST.
WAGGLE WAGGLE
NINAKO!
OH, HEY, REN.
LISTEN—
HM?
WHAT'S THAT?
OH, IT'S JUICE. THE CHEER SQUAD'S HAVING A MINI AFTER-PARTY.
I'm the gofer.
I'LL CARRY IT FOR YOU.
WHERE DO YOU WANT IT?
NO, THAT'S OKAY! IT'S HEAVY.

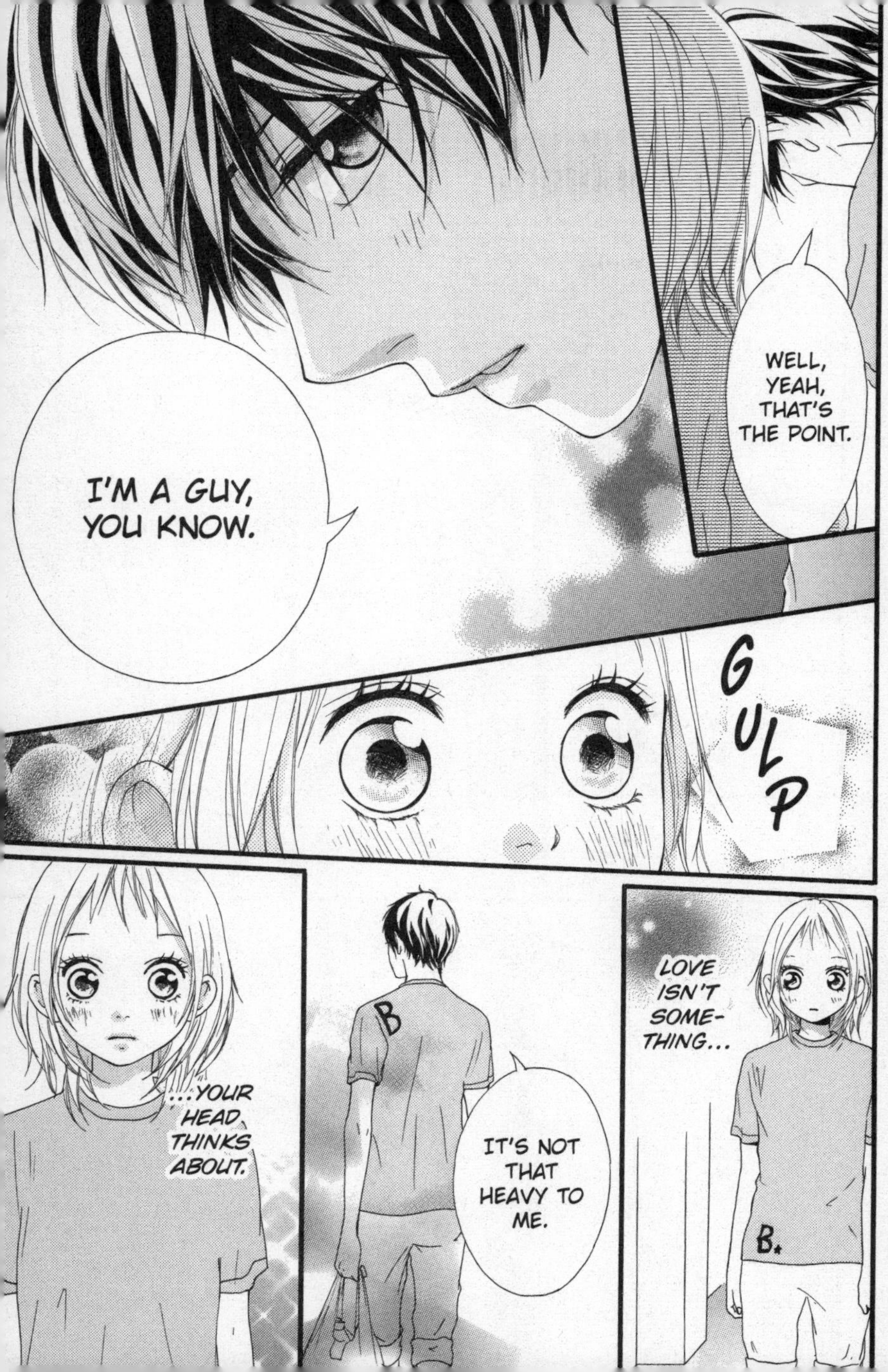
WELL, YEAH, THAT'S THE POINT.
I'M A GUY, YOU KNOW.
GULP
LOVE ISN'T SOME-THING...
IT'S NOT THAT HEAVY TO ME.
...YOUR HEAD THINKS ABOUT.

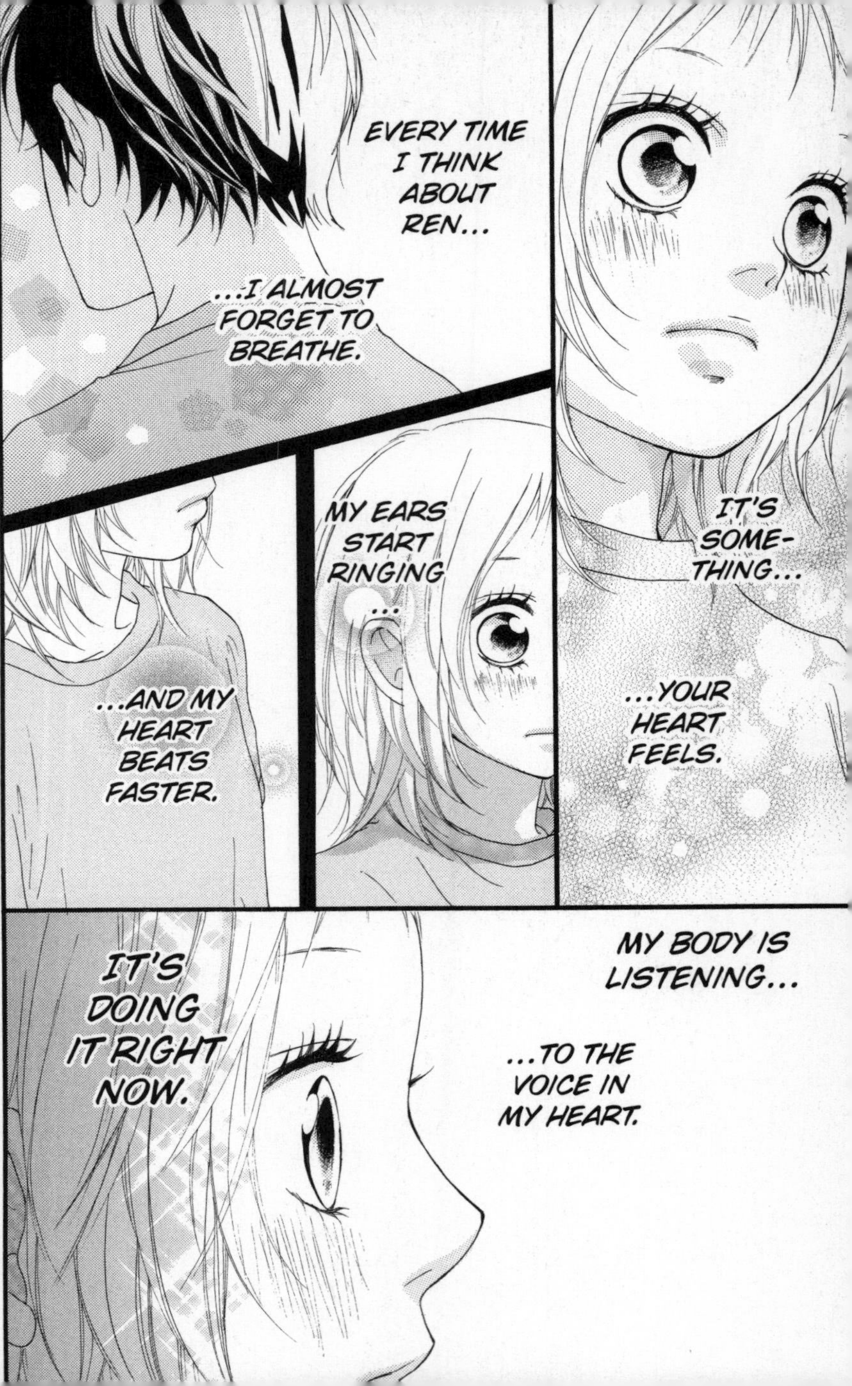
EVERY TIME I THINK ABOUT REN...
...I ALMOST FORGET TO BREATHE.
MY EARS START RINGING ...
...AND MY HEART BEATS FASTER.
IT'S SOME-THING...
...YOUR HEART FEELS.
MY BODY IS LISTENING...
...TO THE VOICE IN MY HEART.
IT'S DOING IT RIGHT NOW.

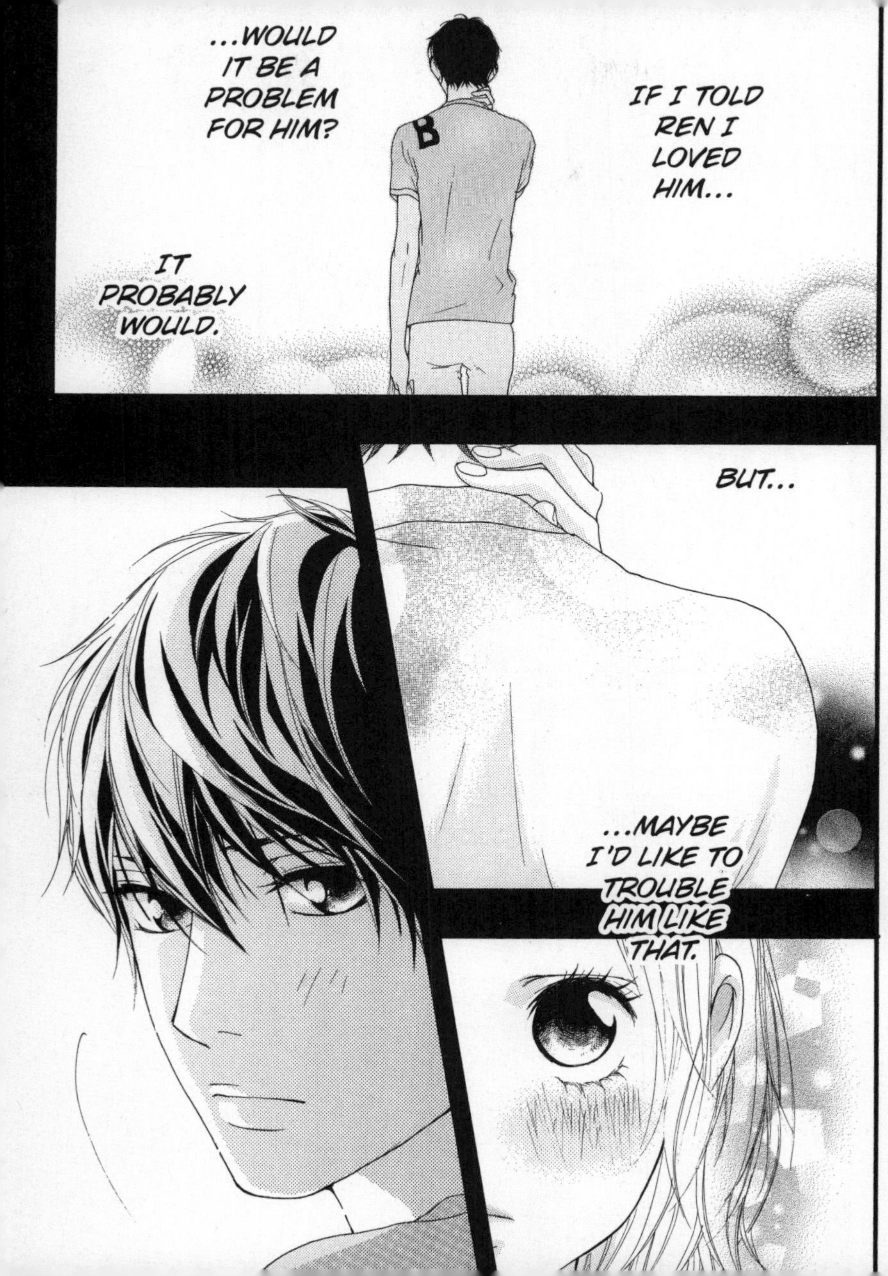
IF I TOLD REN I LOVED HIM...
...WOULD IT BE A PROBLEM FOR HIM?
IT PROBABLY WOULD.
BUT...
...MAYBE I'D LIKE TO TROUBLE HIM LIKE THAT.

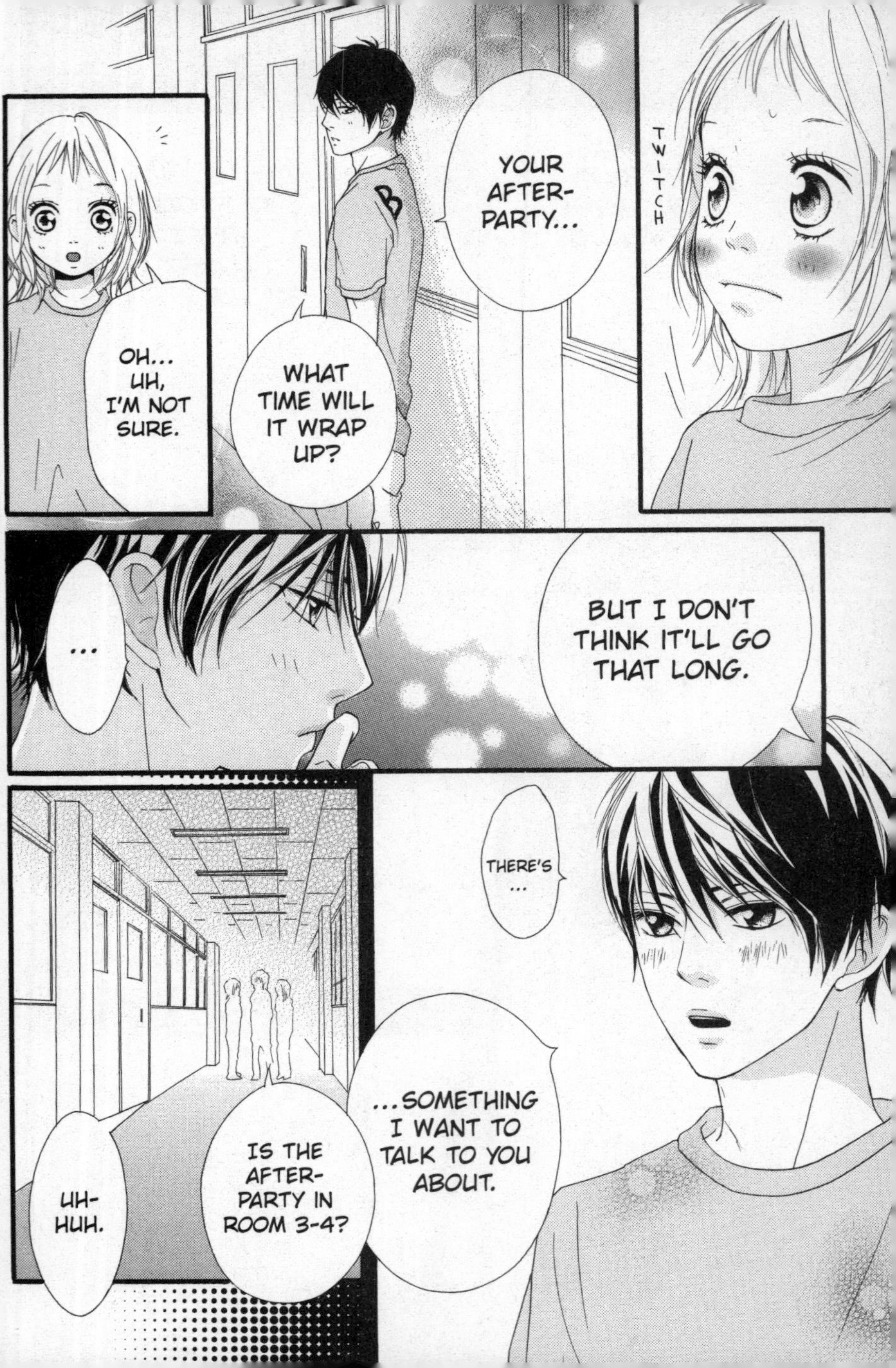
YOUR AFTER-PARTY...
TWITCH
WHAT TIME WILL IT WRAP UP?
OH... UH, I'M NOT SURE.
BUT I DON'T THINK IT'LL GO THAT LONG.
...
THERE'S ...
...SOMETHING I WANT TO TALK TO YOU ABOUT.
IS THE AFTER-PARTY IN ROOM 3-4?
UH-HUH.

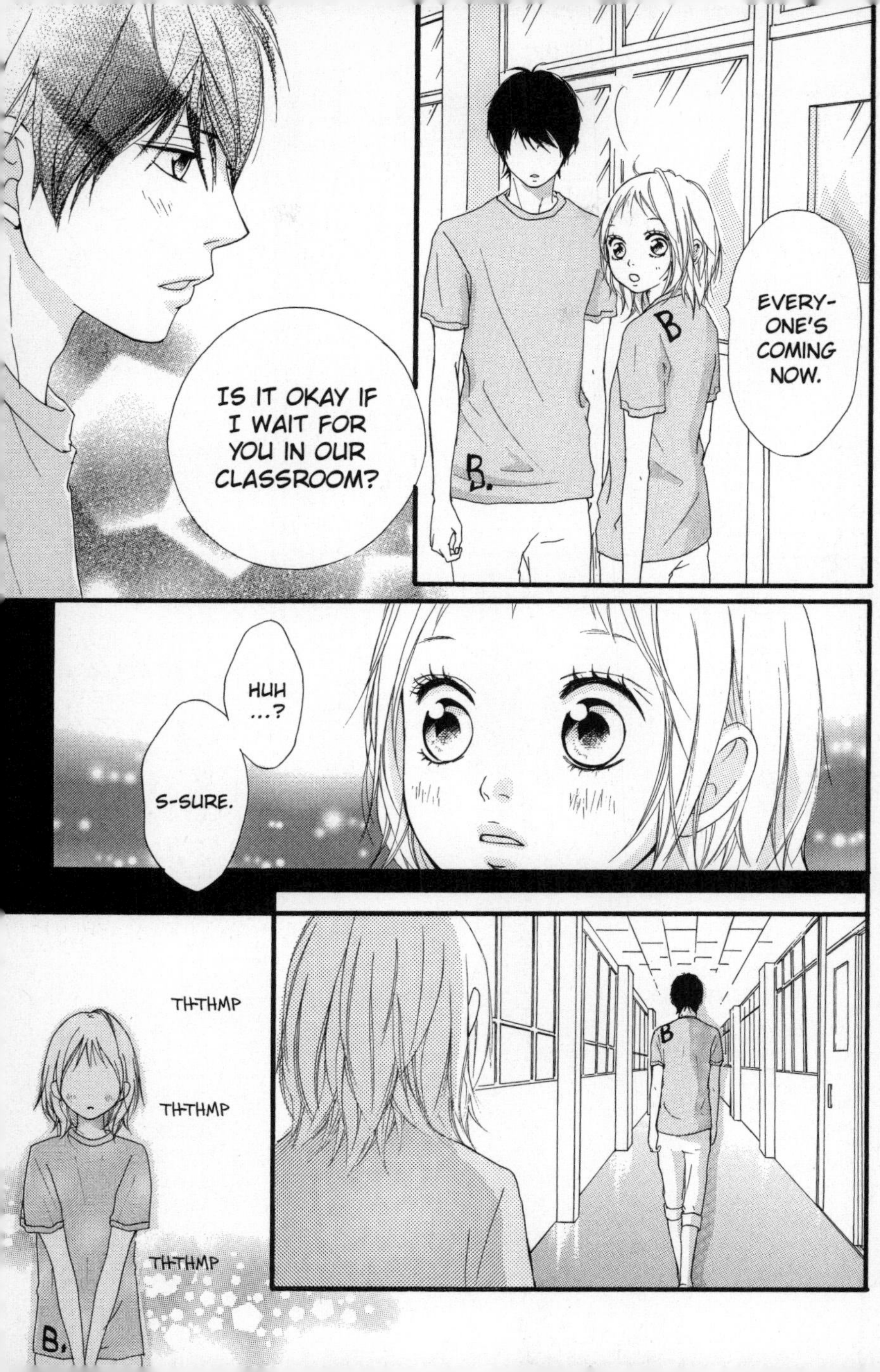
EVERY-ONE'S COMING NOW.
IS IT OKAY IF I WAIT FOR YOU IN OUR CLASSROOM?
HUH ...?
S-SURE.
TH-THMP
TH-THMP
TH-THMP

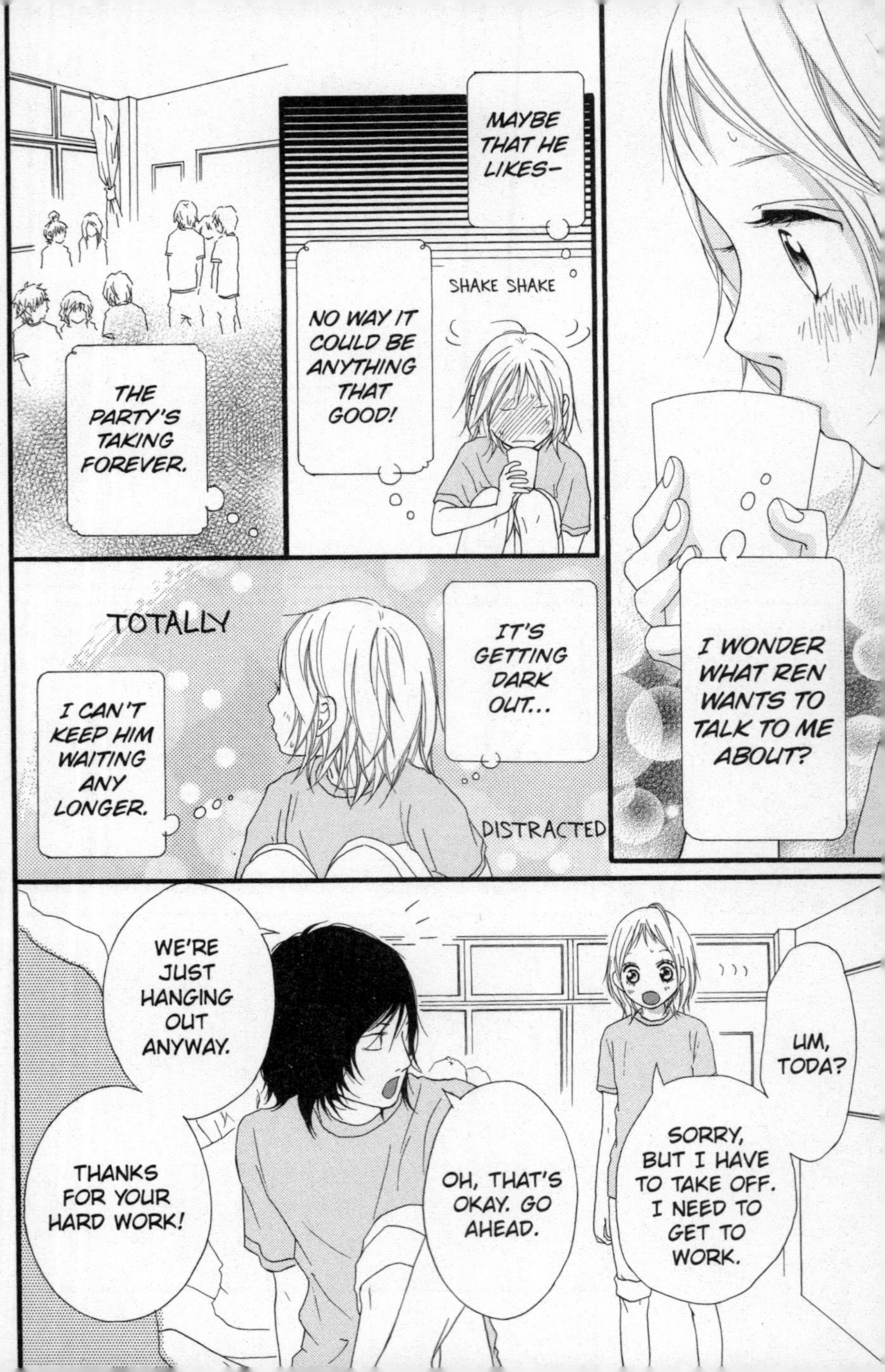
I WONDER WHAT REN WANTS TO TALK TO ME ABOUT?
MAYBE THAT HE LIKES-
SHAKE SHAKE
NO WAY IT COULD BE ANYTHING THAT GOOD!
THE PARTY'S TAKING FOREVER.
IT'S GETTING DARK OUT...
TOTALLY
DISTRACTED
I CAN'T KEEP HIM WAITING ANY LONGER.
UM, TODA?
SORRY, BUT I HAVE TO TAKE OFF. I NEED TO GET TO WORK.
OH, THAT'S OKAY. GO AHEAD.
WE'RE JUST HANGING OUT ANYWAY.
THANKS FOR YOUR HARD WORK!

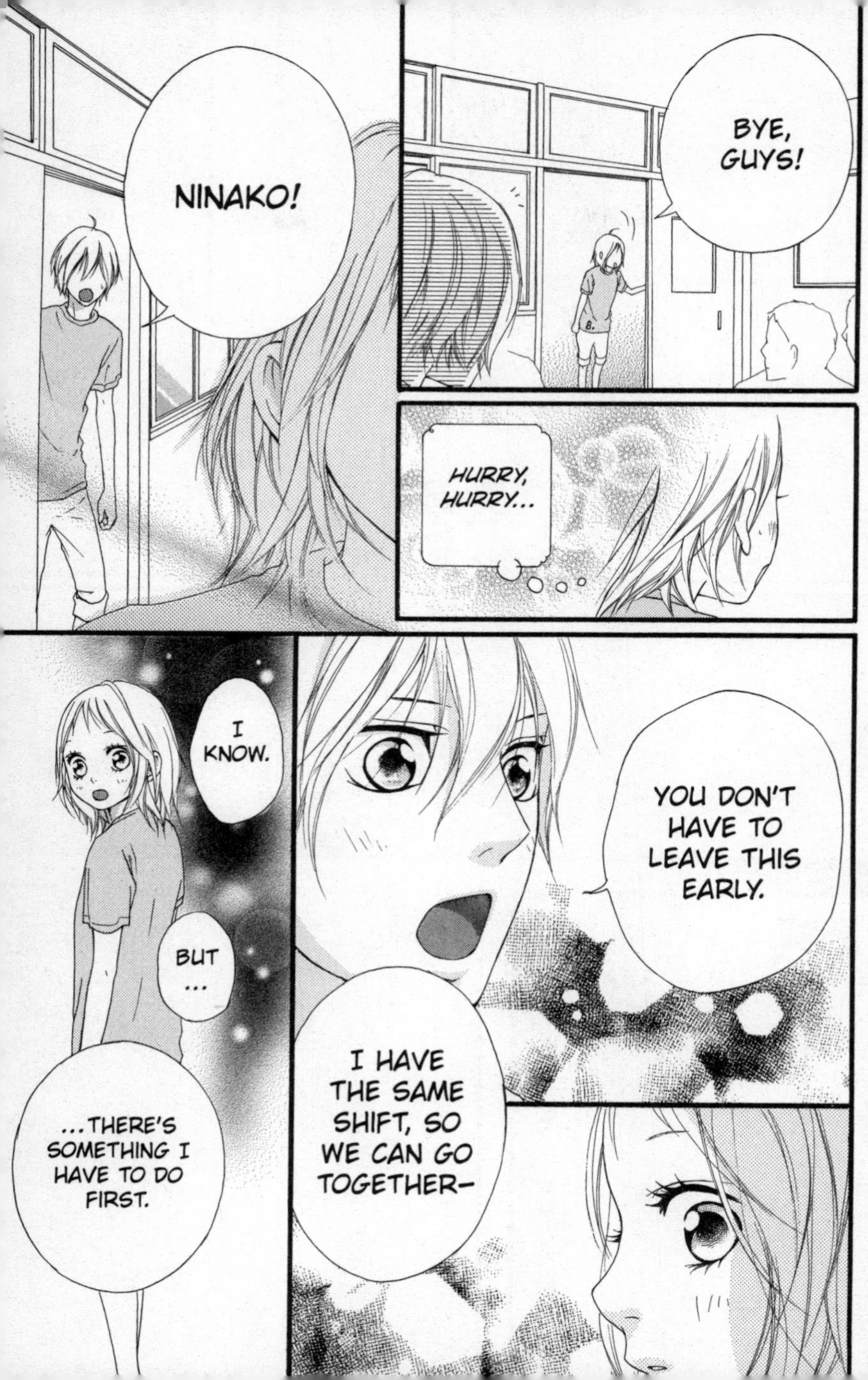
BYE, GUYS!
NINAKO!
HURRY, HURRY...
YOU DON'T HAVE TO LEAVE THIS EARLY.
I HAVE THE SAME SHIFT, SO WE CAN GO TOGETHER–
I KNOW.
BUT ...
...THERE'S SOMETHING I HAVE TO DO FIRST.

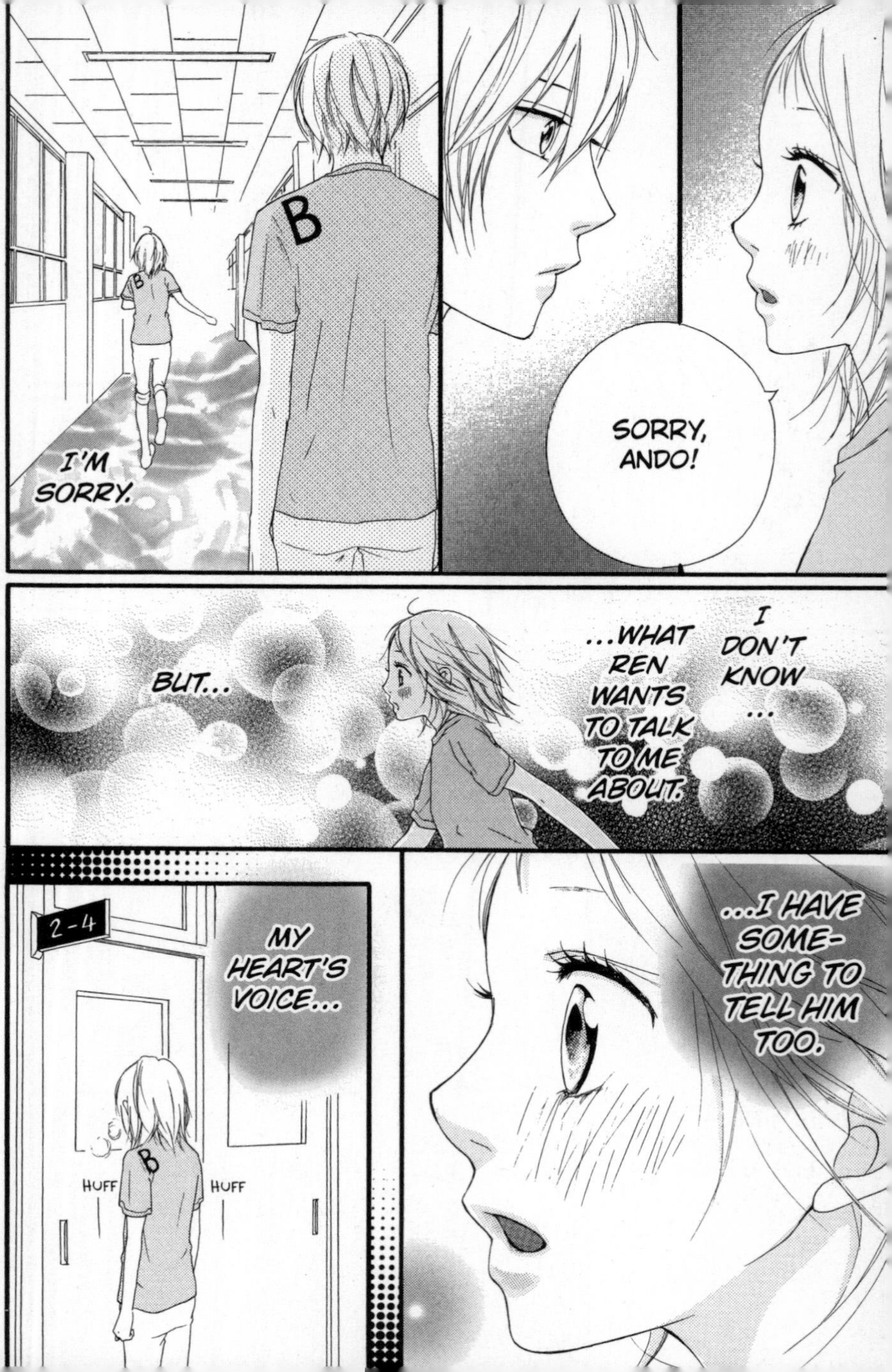
SORRY, ANDO!
I'M SORRY.
I DON'T KNOW...
...WHAT REN WANTS TO TALK TO ME ABOUT.
BUT...
...I HAVE SOME-THING TO TELL HIM TOO.
MY HEART'S VOICE...
2-4
HUFF
HUFF

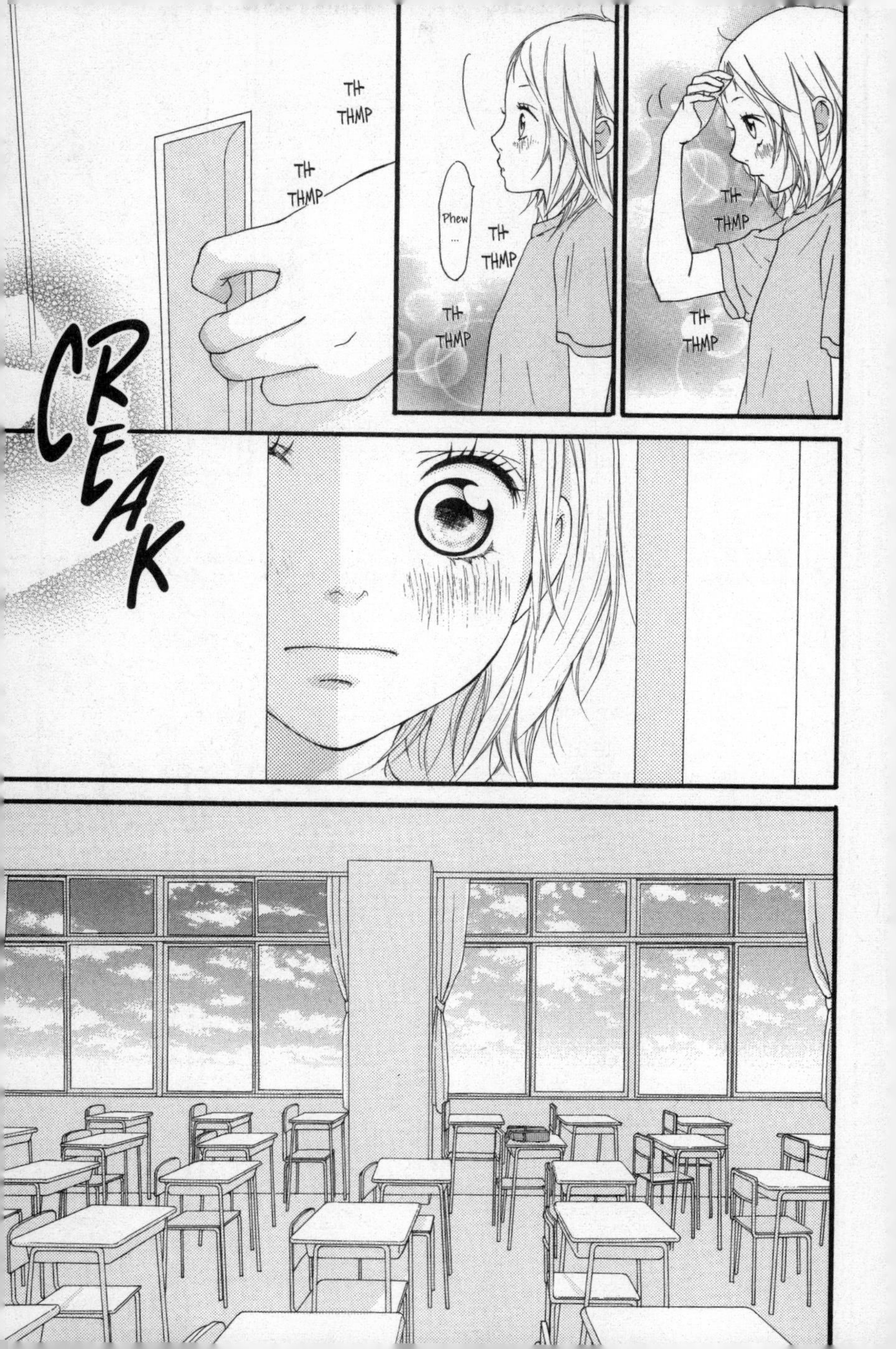
TH THMP
TH THMP
Phew ...
TH THMP
TH THMP
TH THMP
TH THMP
CREAK

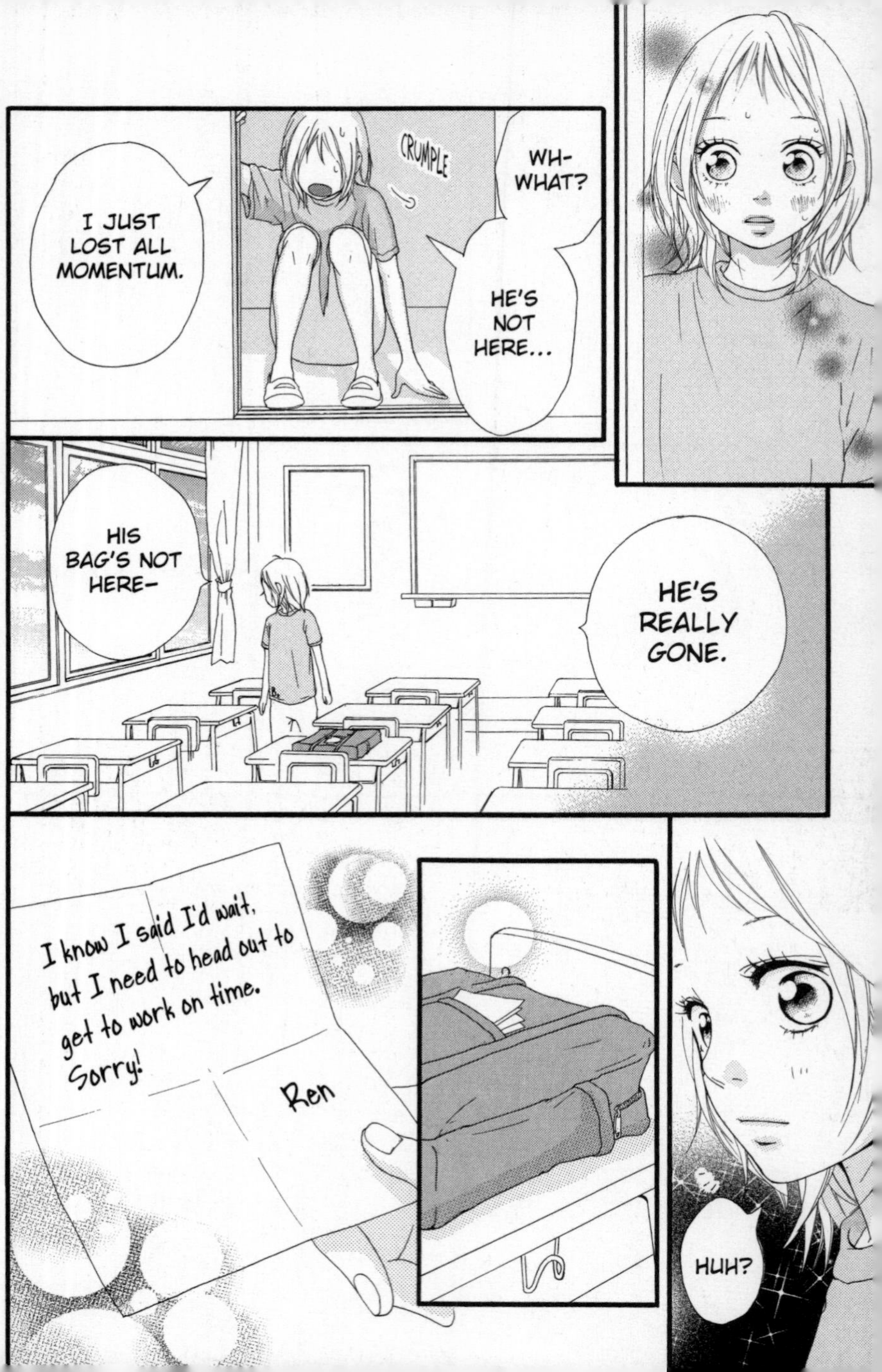
WH- WHAT?
HE'S NOT HERE...
CRUMPLE
I JUST LOST ALL MOMENTUM.
HE'S REALLY GONE.
HIS BAG'S NOT HERE-
HUH?
I know I said I'd wait, but I need to head out to get to work on time. Sorry!
Ren

...

HIS NUMBER...

HE GAVE IT TO ME WHEN WE WORKED TOGETHER.

...

TH THMP

TH THMP

BUT...

RRRING

RRRING

TH THMP

THIS WILL BE THE FIRST TIME...

...I'VE EVER USED IT.

TH THMP

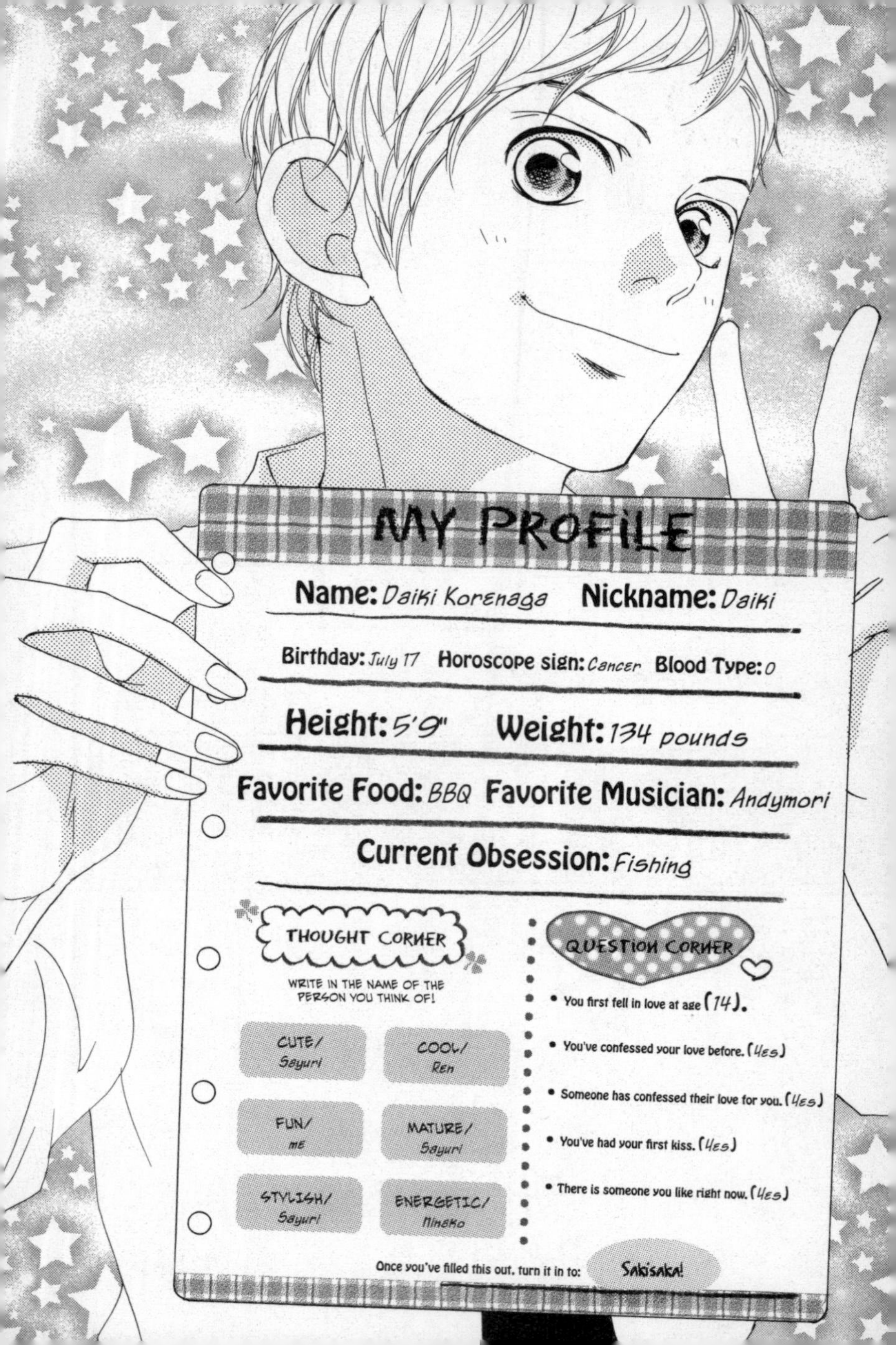
MY PROFILE
Name: Daiki Korenaga Nickname: Daiki
Birthday: July 17 Horoscope sign: Cancer Blood Type: O
Height: 5'9" Weight: 134 pounds
Favorite Food: BBQ Favorite Musician: Andymori
Current Obsession: Fishing
THOUGHT CORNER
WRITE IN THE NAME OF THE PERSON YOU THINK OF!
CUTE/ Sayuri
COOL/ Ren
FUN/ me
MATURE/ Sayuri
STYLISH/ Sayuri
ENERGETIC/ Ninako
QUESTION CORNER
• You first fell in love at age (14).
• You've confessed your love before. (Yes)
• Someone has confessed their love for you. (Yes)
• You've had your first kiss. (Yes)
• There is someone you like right now. (Yes)
Once you've filled this out, turn it in to: Sakisaka!

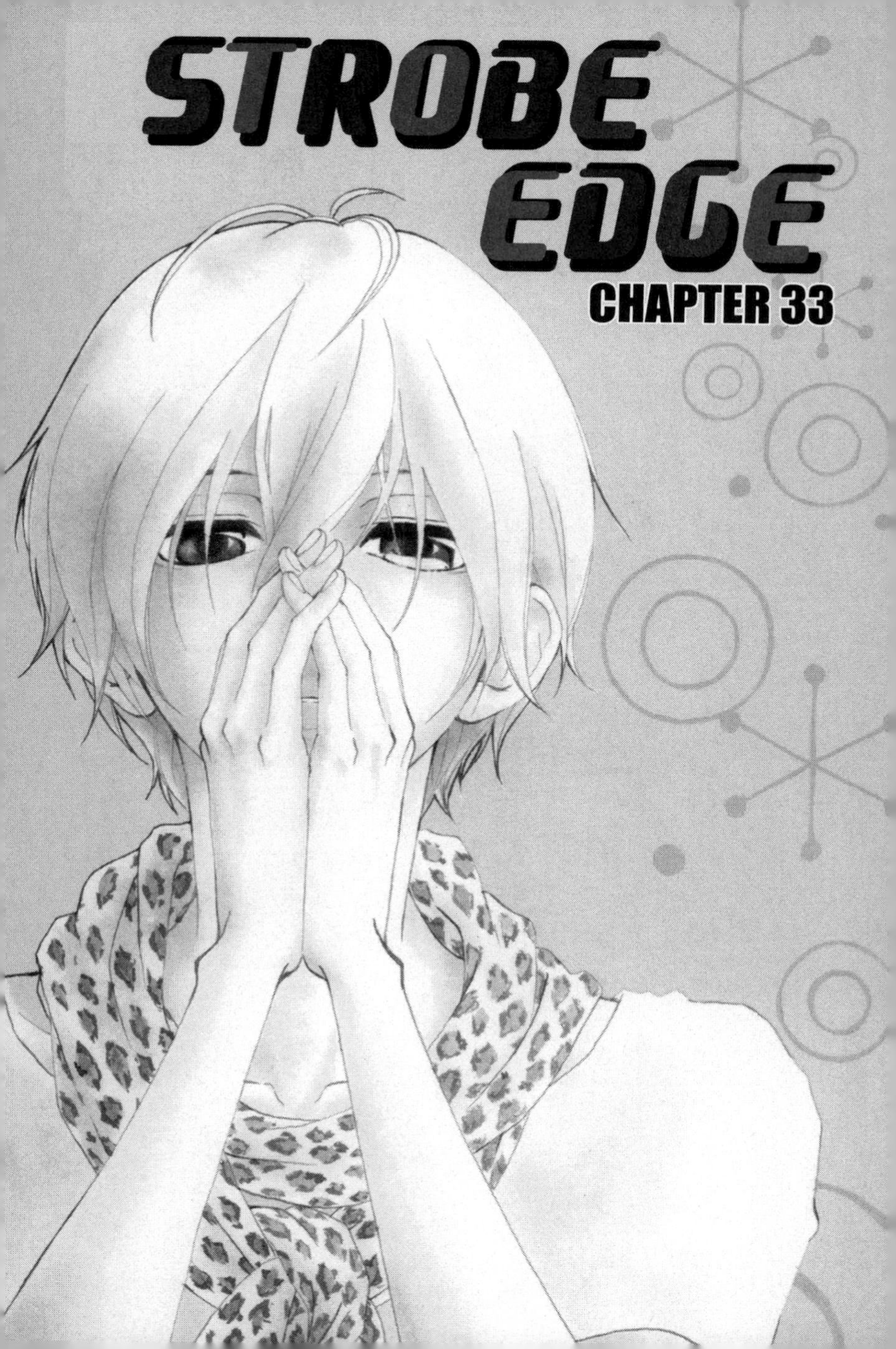
STROBE EDGE
CHAPTER 33

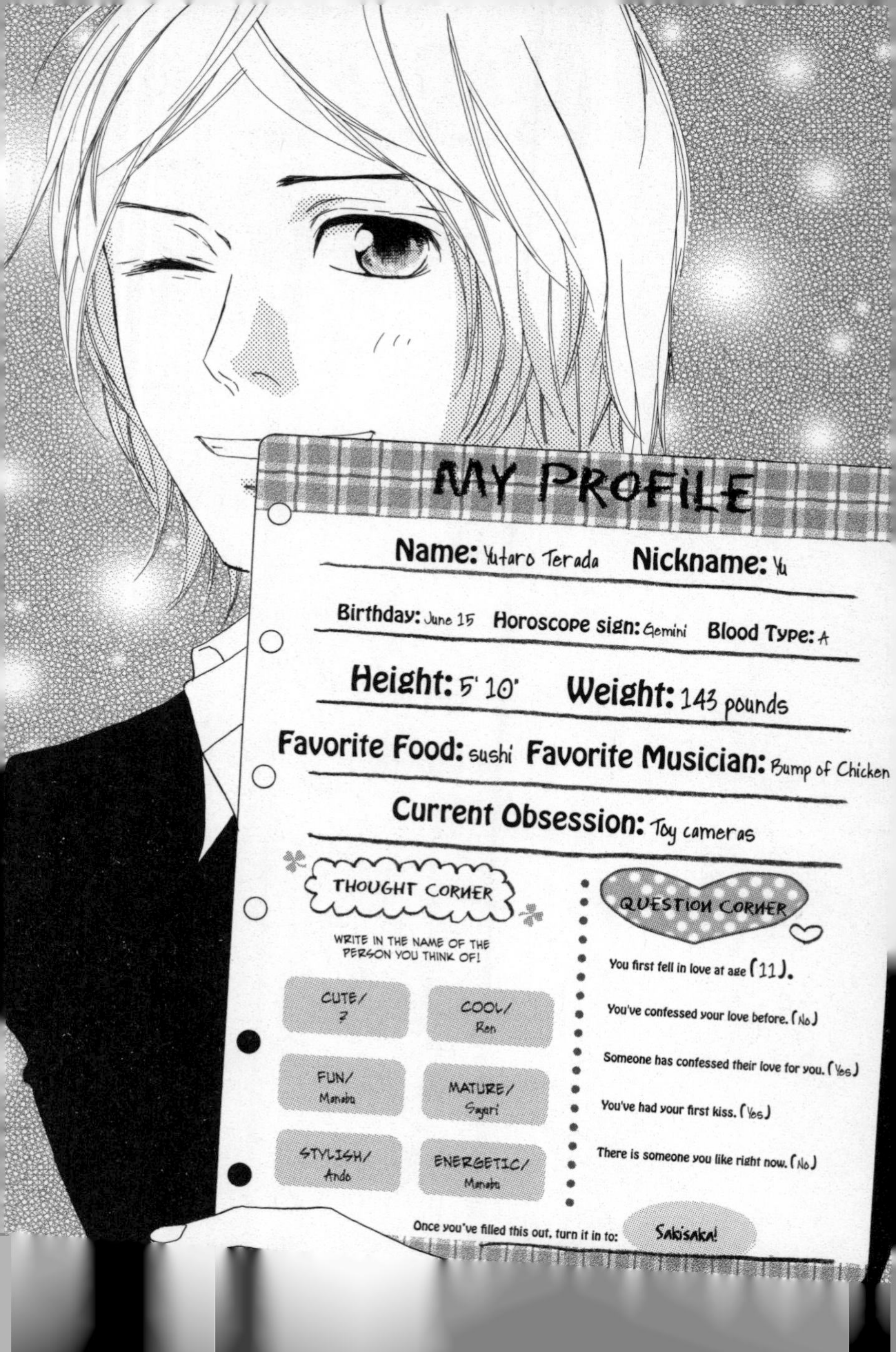

MY PROFILE
Name: Yutaro Terada
Nickname: Yu
Birthday: June 15
Horoscope sign: Gemini
Blood Type: A
Height: 5' 10'
Weight: 143 pounds
Favorite Food: sushi
Favorite Musician: Bump of Chicken
Current Obsession: Toy cameras
THOUGHT CORNER
WRITE IN THE NAME OF THE PERSON YOU THINK OF!
CUTE/ ?
COOL/ Ren
FUN/ Manabu
MATURE/ Sayuri
STYLISH/ Ando
ENERGETIC/ Manabu
QUESTION CORNER
You first fell in love at age (11).
You've confessed your love before. (No)
Someone has confessed their love for you. (Yes)
You've had your first kiss. (Yes)
There is someone you like right now. (No)
Once you've filled this out, turn it in to: Sakisaka!

TH·
THUD

CLICK

RRRING

2-4

TH
THMP

TH
THMP

TH
THMP

RRRING

RRRING

HE
PICKED
UP!

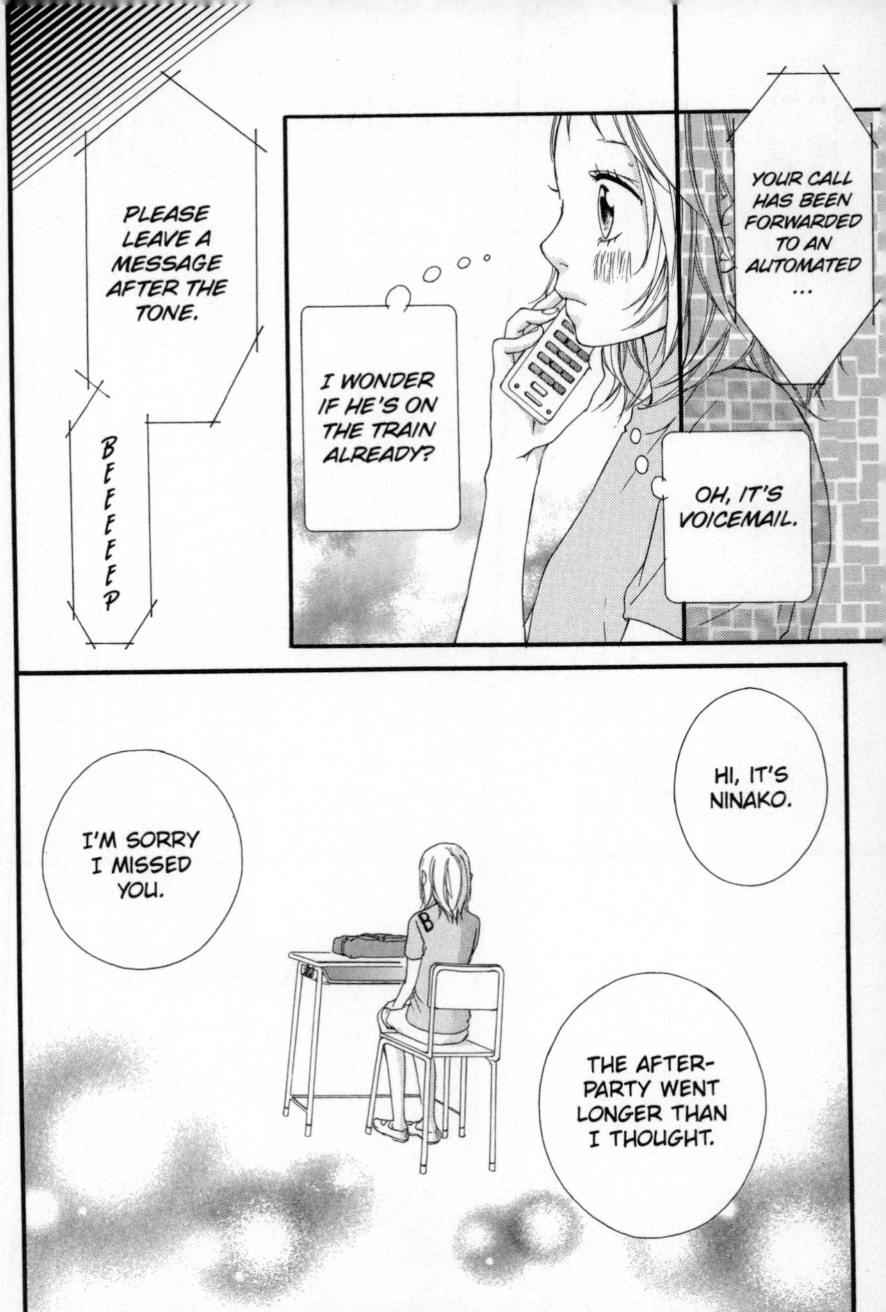
YOUR CALL HAS BEEN FORWARDED TO AN AUTOMATED ...
OH, IT'S VOICEMAIL.
I WONDER IF HE'S ON THE TRAIN ALREADY?
PLEASE LEAVE A MESSAGE AFTER THE TONE.
BEEEEEEP
HI, IT'S NINAKO.
THE AFTER-PARTY WENT LONGER THAN I THOUGHT.
I'M SORRY I MISSED YOU.

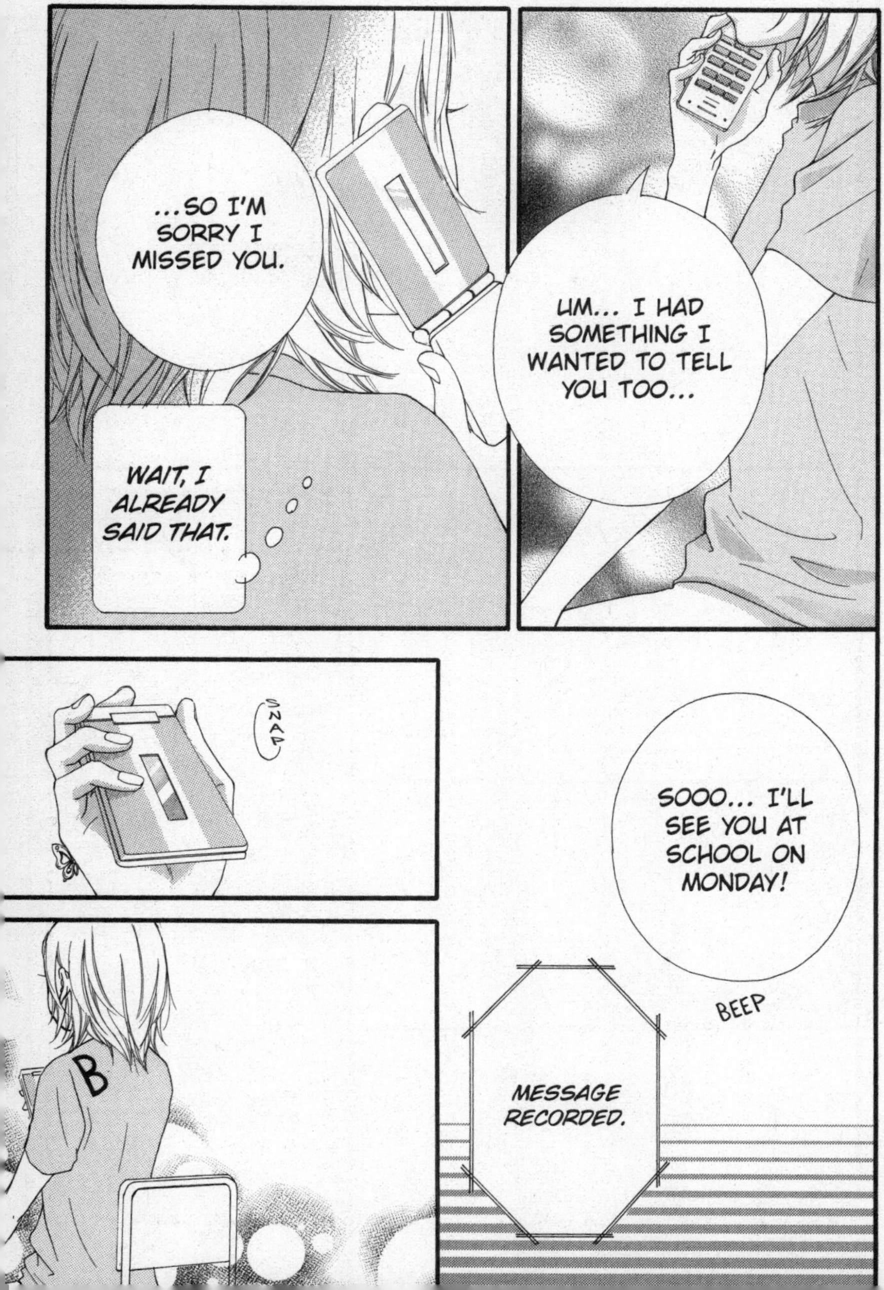
UM... I HAD SOMETHING I WANTED TO TELL YOU TOO...
...SO I'M SORRY I MISSED YOU.
WAIT, I ALREADY SAID THAT.
SOOO... I'LL SEE YOU AT SCHOOL ON MONDAY!
SNAP
BEEP
MESSAGE RECORDED.

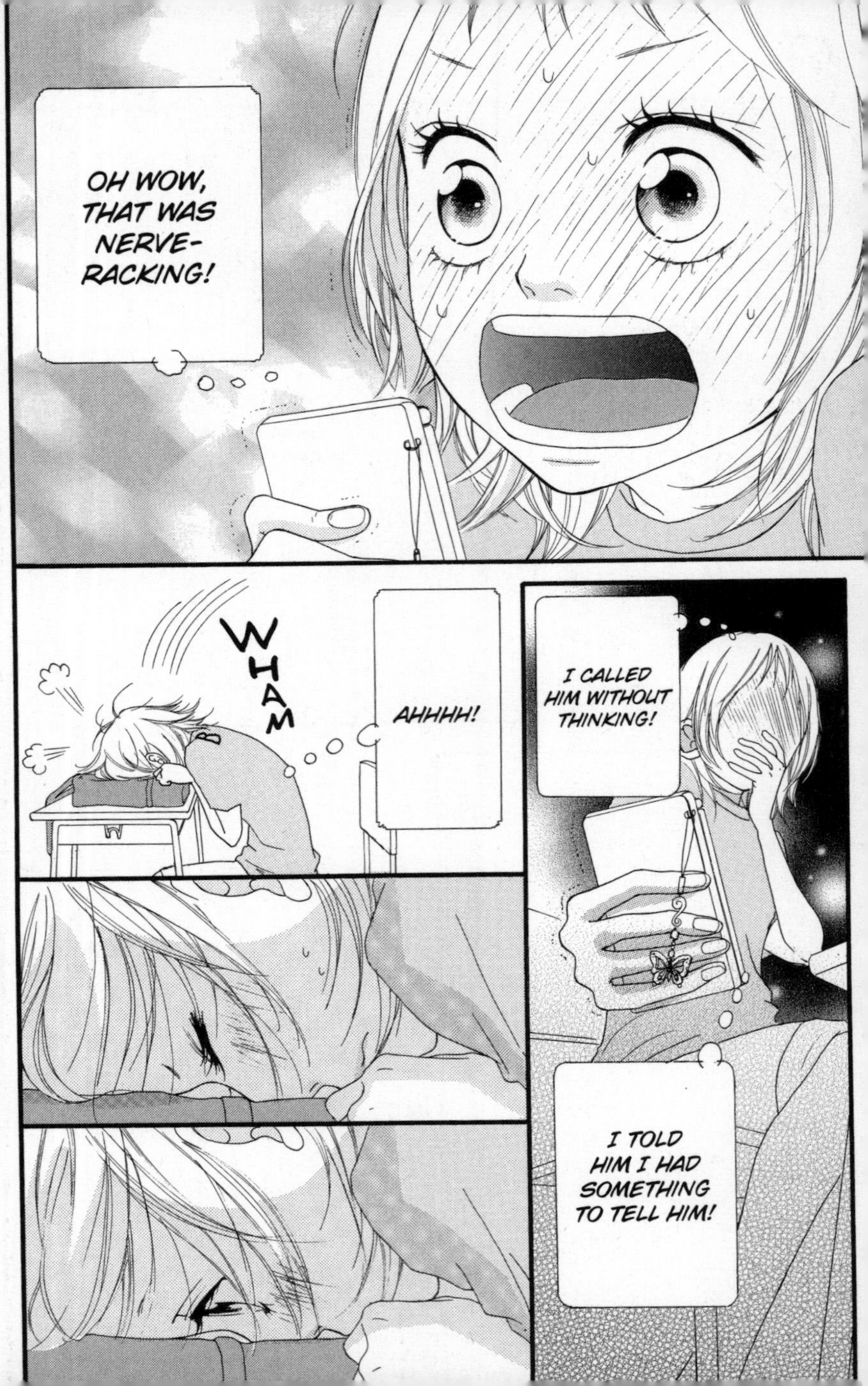
OH WOW, THAT WAS NERVE-RACKING!
I CALLED HIM WITHOUT THINKING!
I TOLD HIM I HAD SOMETHING TO TELL HIM!
WHAM
AHHHH!

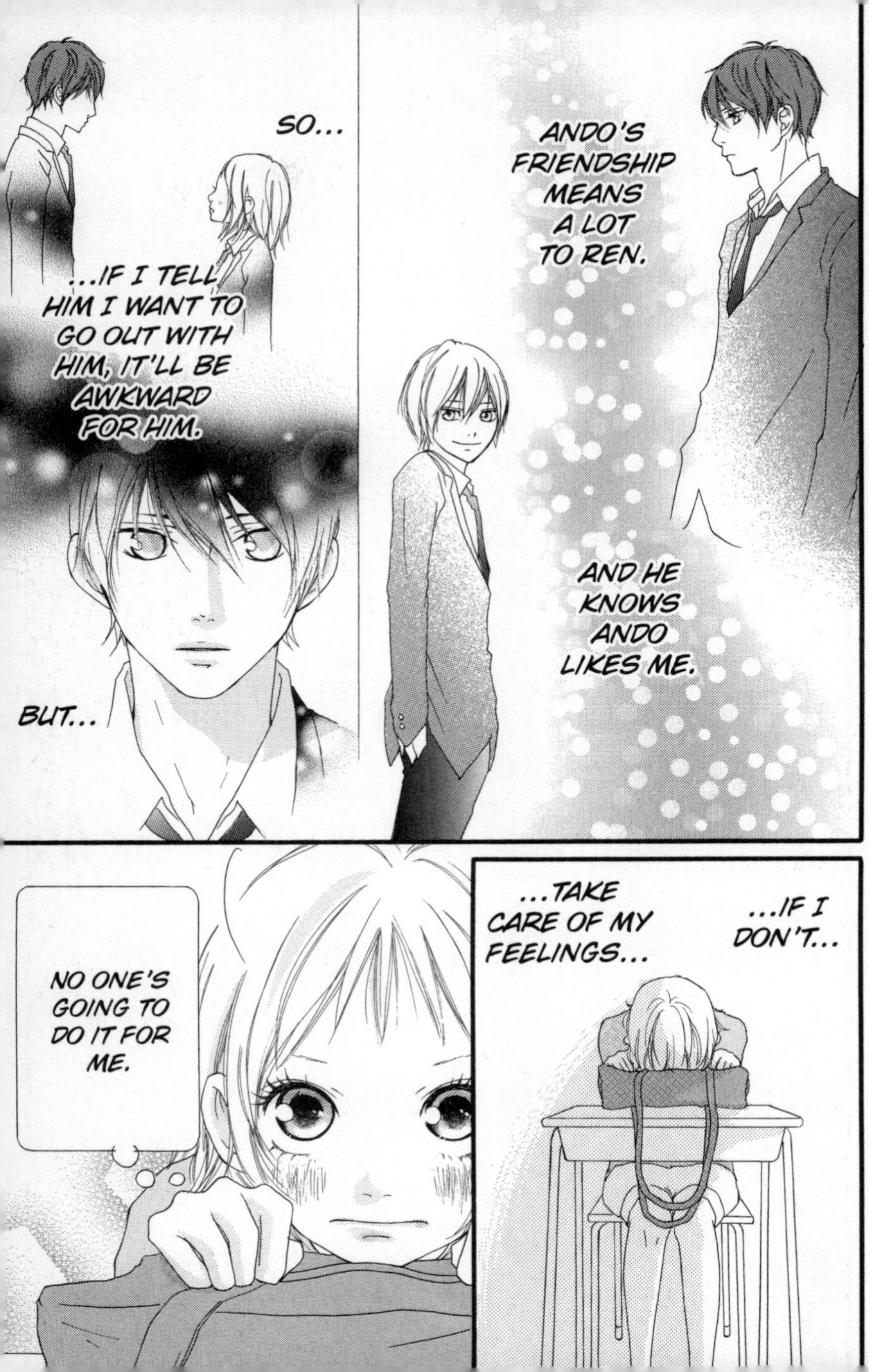
ANDO'S FRIENDSHIP MEANS A LOT TO REN.
AND HE KNOWS ANDO LIKES ME.
SO...
...IF I TELL HIM I WANT TO GO OUT WITH HIM, IT'LL BE AWKWARD FOR HIM.
BUT...
...IF I DON'T...
...TAKE CARE OF MY FEELINGS...
NO ONE'S GOING TO DO IT FOR ME.

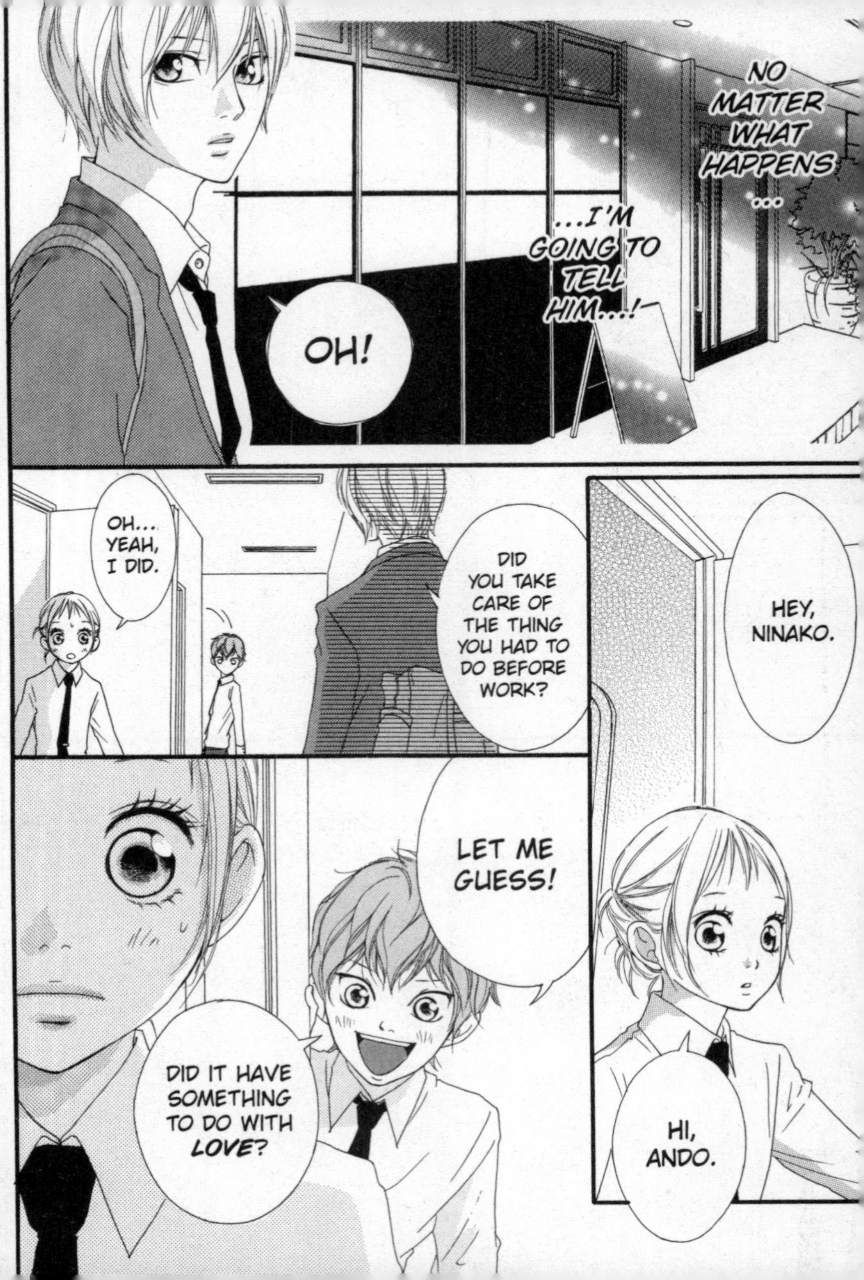
NO MATTER WHAT HAPPENS...
...I'M GOING TO TELL HIM...!
OH!
HEY, NINAKO.
DID YOU TAKE CARE OF THE THING YOU HAD TO DO BEFORE WORK?
OH... YEAH, I DID.
HI, ANDO.
LET ME GUESS!
DID IT HAVE SOMETHING TO DO WITH *LOVE*?

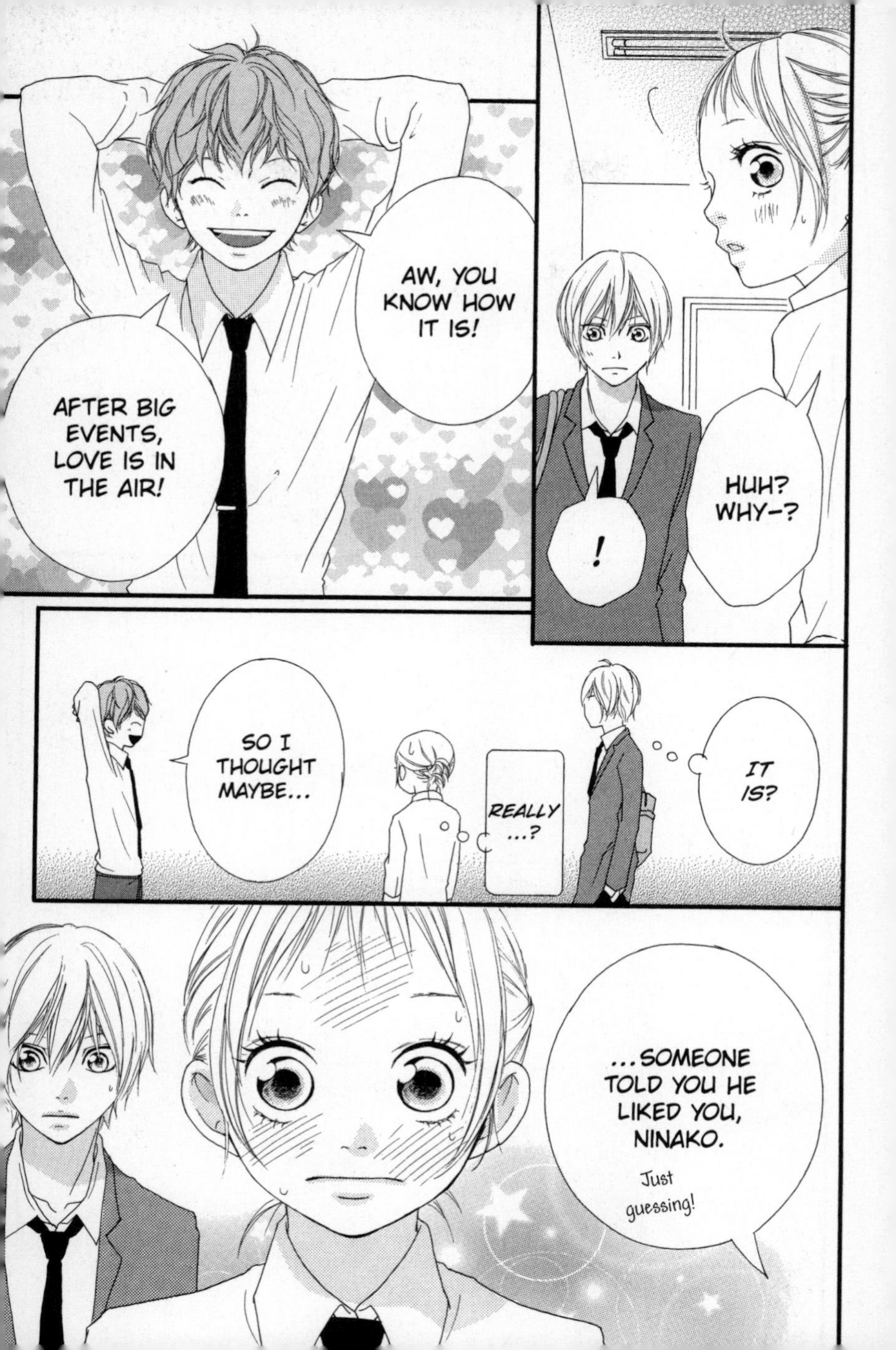
HUH? WHY-?
!
AW, YOU KNOW HOW IT IS!
AFTER BIG EVENTS, LOVE IS IN THE AIR!
IT IS?
REALLY ...?
SO I THOUGHT MAYBE...
...SOMEONE TOLD YOU HE LIKED YOU, NINAKO.
Just guessing!

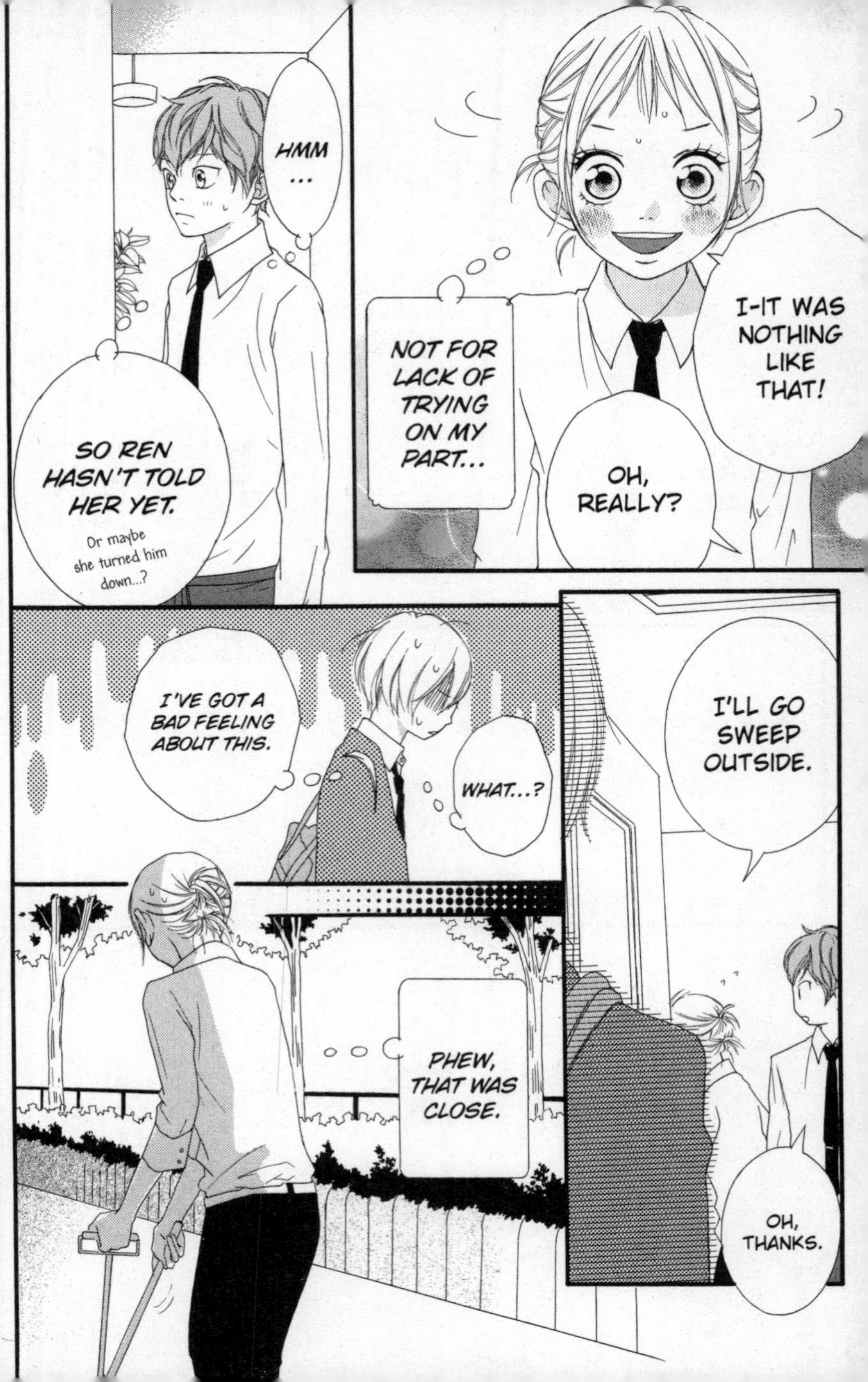
I-IT WAS NOTHING LIKE THAT!
OH, REALLY?
NOT FOR LACK OF TRYING ON MY PART...
HMM ...
SO REN HASN'T TOLD HER YET.
Or maybe she turned him down...?
I'LL GO SWEEP OUTSIDE.
OH, THANKS.
WHAT...?
I'VE GOT A BAD FEELING ABOUT THIS.
PHEW, THAT WAS CLOSE.

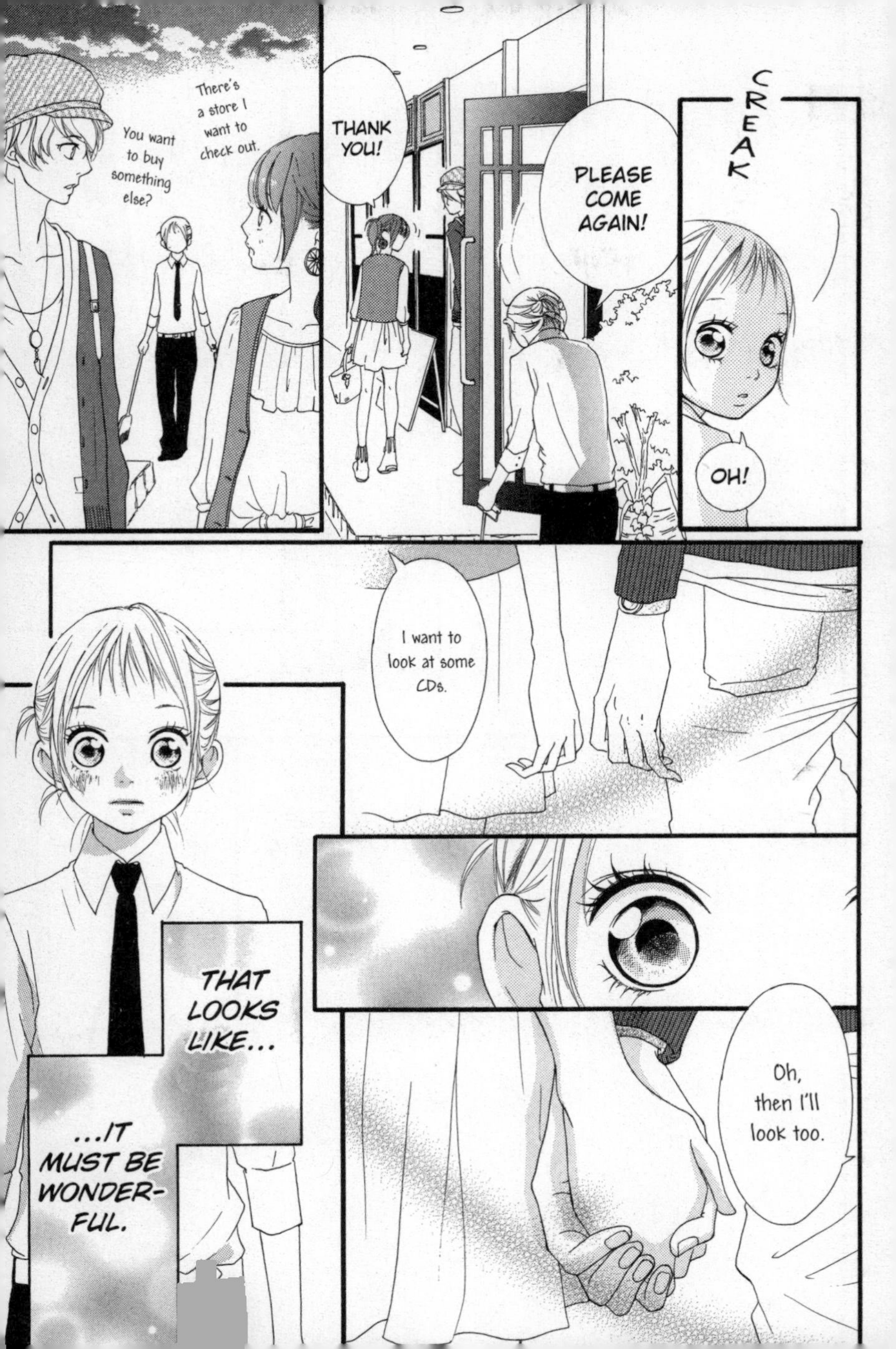
CREAK
OH!
PLEASE COME AGAIN!
THANK YOU!
There's a store I want to check out.
You want to buy something else?
I want to look at some CDs.
Oh, then I'll look too.
THAT LOOKS LIKE...
...IT MUST BE WONDER-FUL.

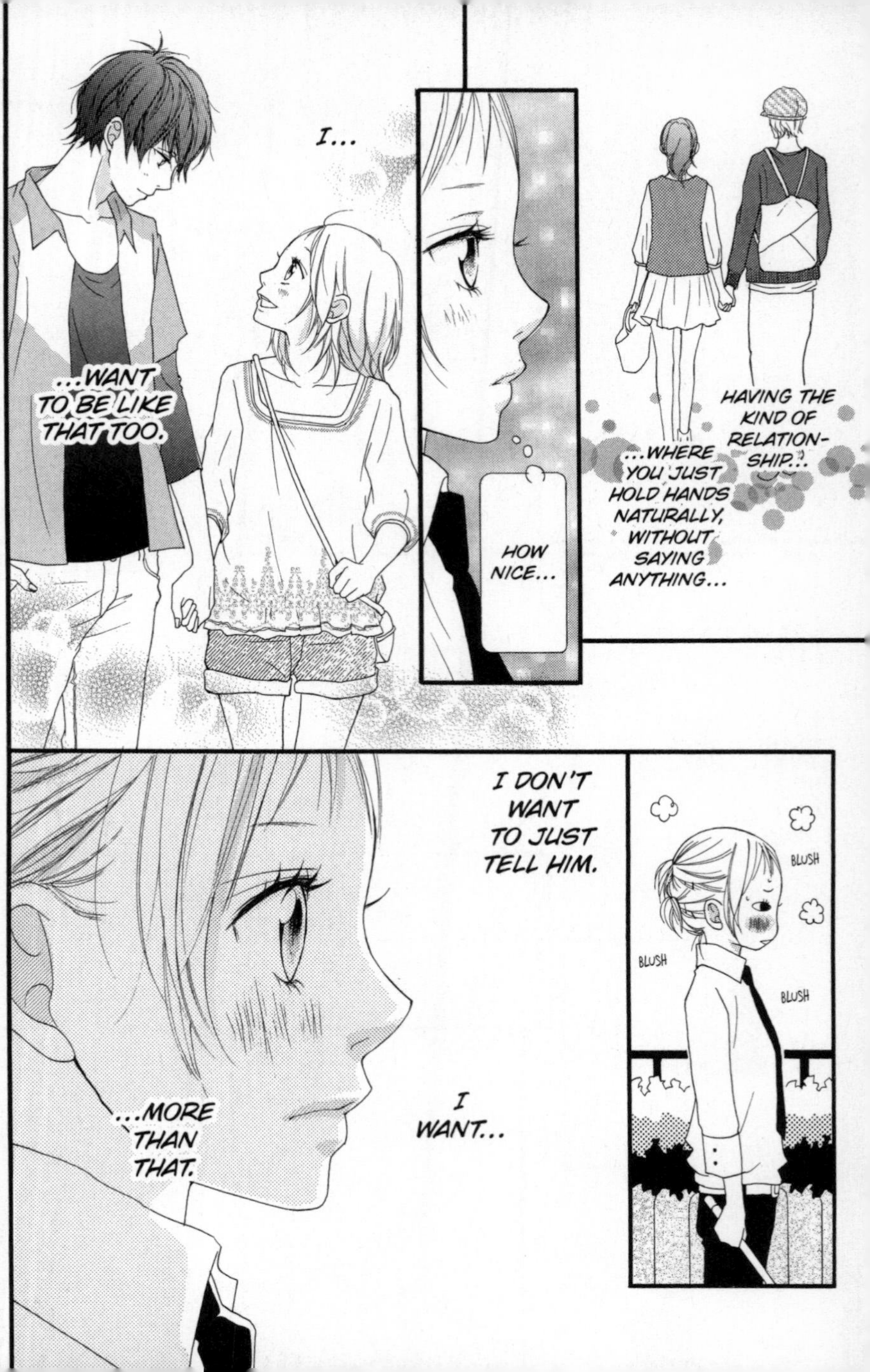

HAVING THE KIND OF RELATION-SHIP...
...WHERE YOU JUST HOLD HANDS NATURALLY, WITHOUT SAYING ANYTHING...
HOW NICE...
I...
...WANT TO BE LIKE THAT TOO.
I DON'T WANT TO JUST TELL HIM.
BLUSH
BLUSH
BLUSH
I WANT...
...MORE THAN THAT.

Questions Part 2

Q. Is *Strobe Edge* based on a true story?
A. No, it is not.

Q. Have you ever loved someone and had to give them up?
A. Yes, I have. I fell in love with someone who had a girlfriend. But as it turns out, when I find out someone's in a relationship, I lose interest for some reason. So I haven't suffered on that front (well, not much, anyway).

Q. What's your favorite manga?
A. *Slam Dunk* and *Gunjou Gakusha*.

Q. What are your favorite words?
A. Freedom, justice, rice.

Q. What club did you belong to in high school?
A. The going-home club! I played with my friends, fell in love, had a job and studied a little. I didn't have time for clubs. But in junior high, I was on the basketball team for three years.

Q. Are bananas a snack?
A. No, they are not! (According to the travel notes of Sakisaka Academy.)
This question was hilarious.

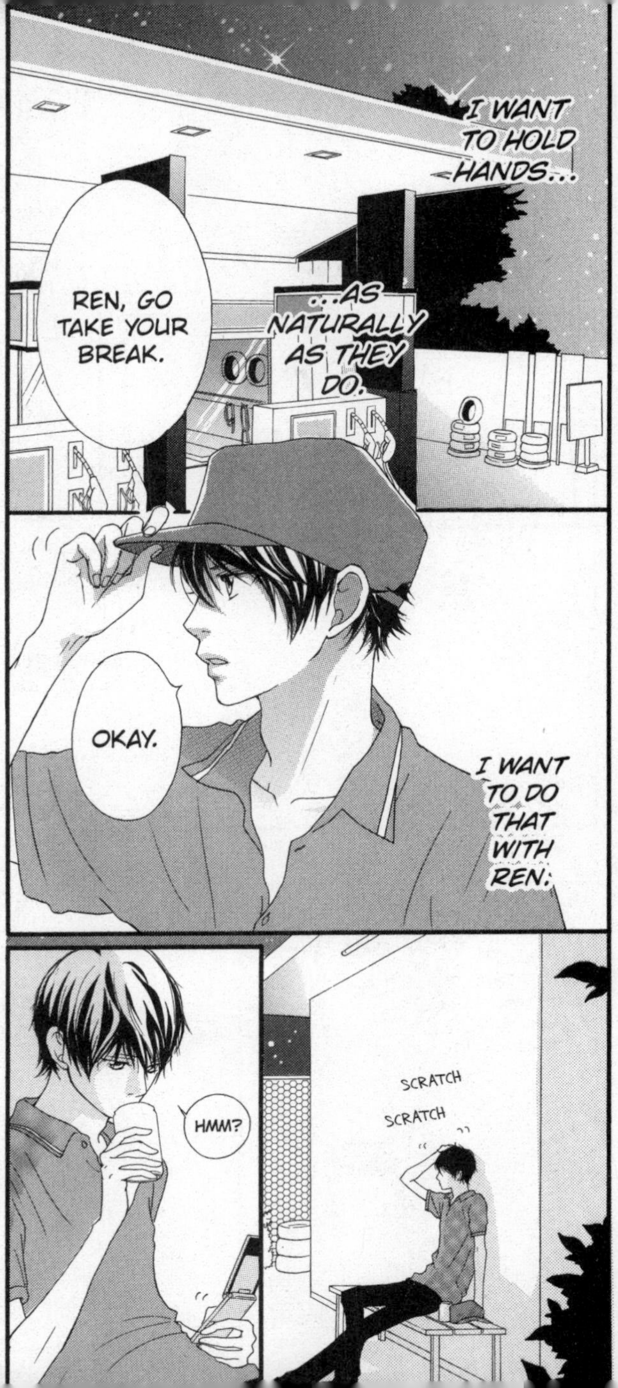
I WANT TO HOLD HANDS...
...AS NATURALLY AS THEY DO.
REN, GO TAKE YOUR BREAK.
I WANT TO DO THAT WITH REN.
OKAY.
SCRATCH
SCRATCH
HMM?

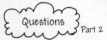

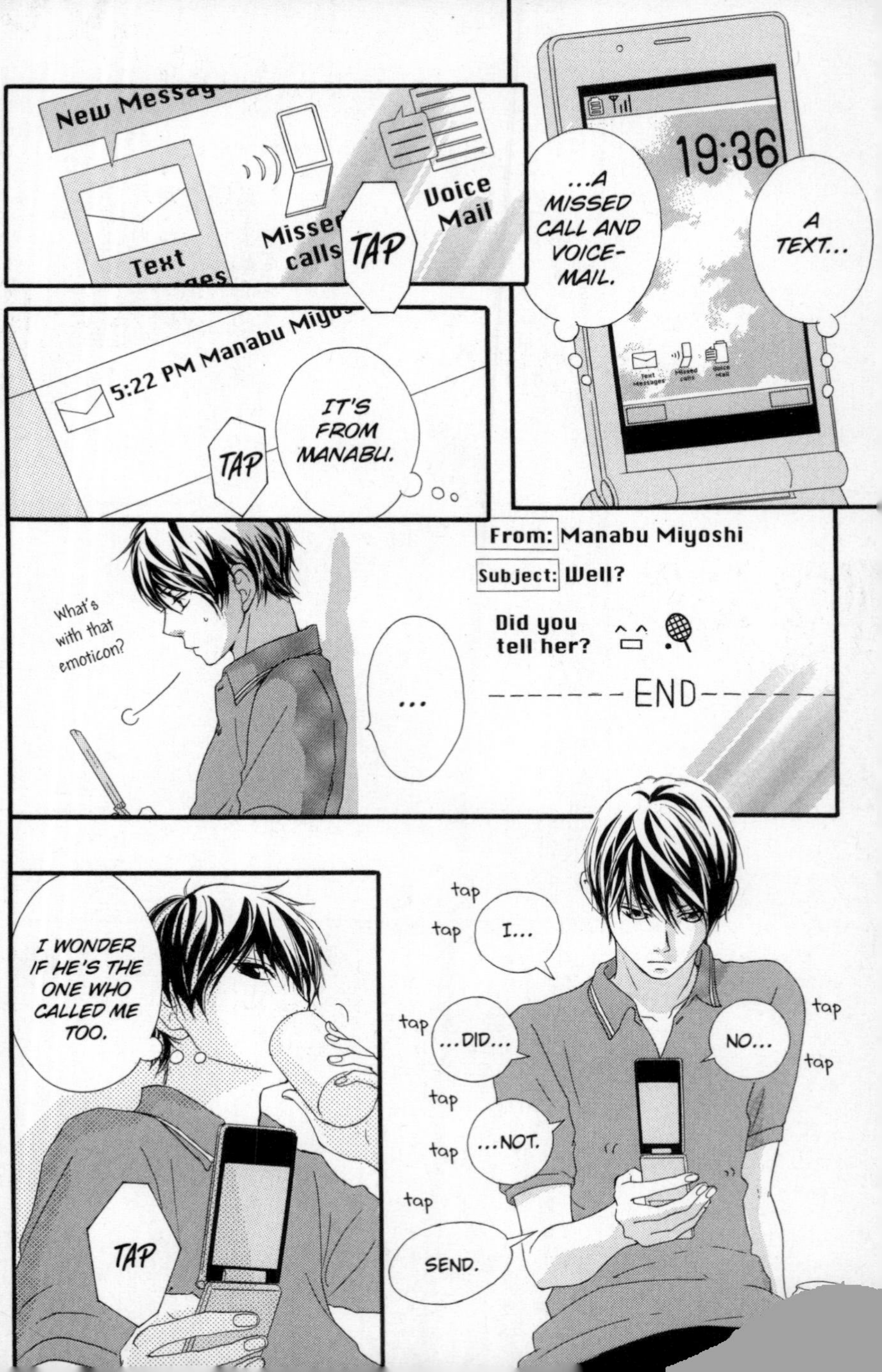
19:36
A TEXT...
...A MISSED CALL AND VOICE-MAIL.
New Messag
Text
Missed calls
Voice Mail
TAP
5:22 PM Manabu Miyo
TAP
IT'S FROM MANABU.
From: Manabu Miyoshi
Subject: Well?
Did you tell her? ^_^
--------END--------
...
What's with that emoticon?
tap
tap
I...
tap
...DID...
tap
tap
NO...
tap
tap
...NOT.
tap
SEND.
I WONDER IF HE'S THE ONE WHO CALLED ME TOO.
TAP

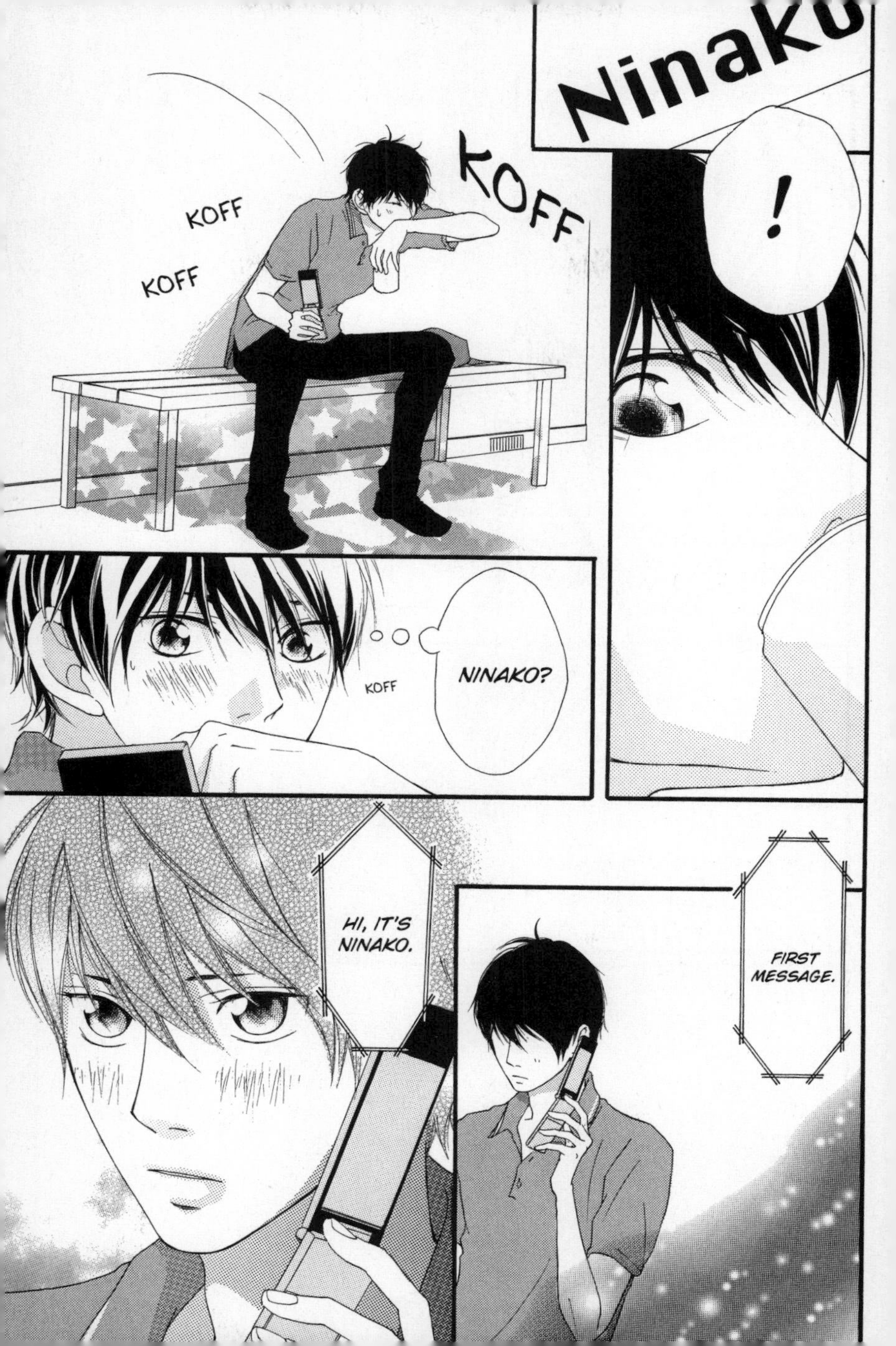

Ninak
!
KOFF
KOFF
KOFF
NINAKO?
KOFF
FIRST MESSAGE.
HI, IT'S NINAKO.

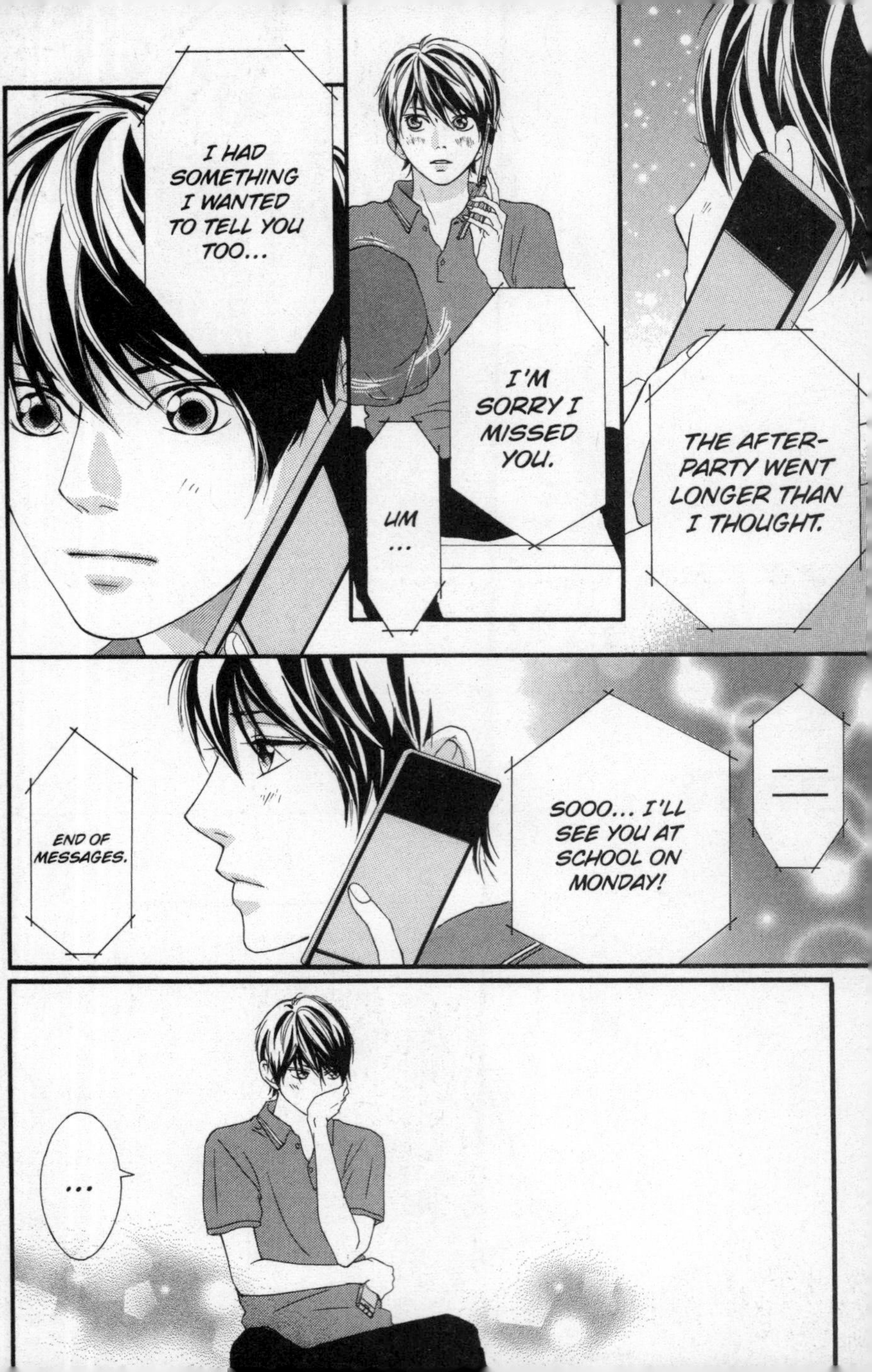
THE AFTER-PARTY WENT LONGER THAN I THOUGHT.
I'M SORRY I MISSED YOU.
UM ...
I HAD SOMETHING I WANTED TO TELL YOU TOO...
——
SOOO... I'LL SEE YOU AT SCHOOL ON MONDAY!
END OF MESSAGES.
...

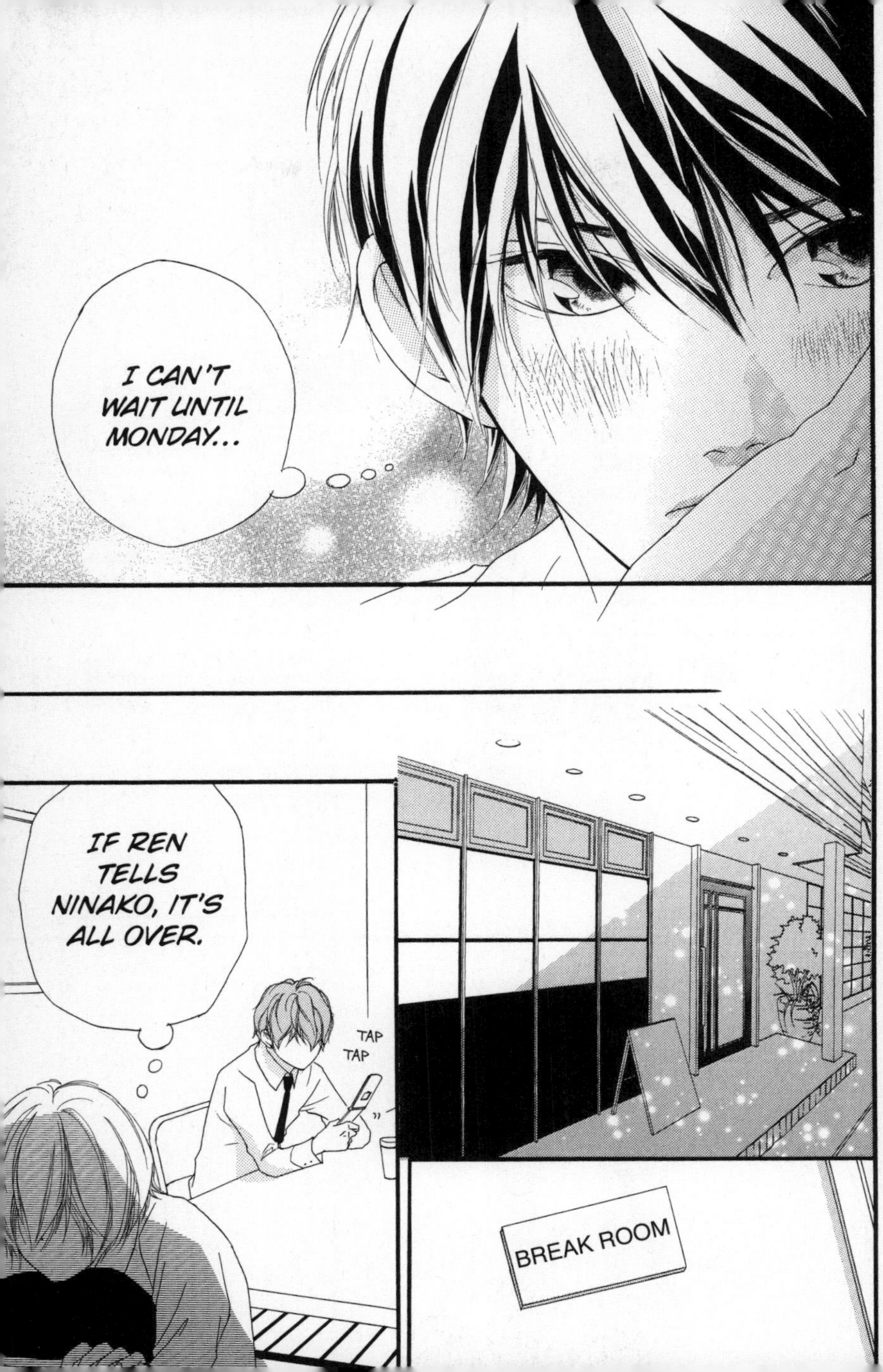
I CAN'T WAIT UNTIL MONDAY...
BREAK ROOM
IF REN TELLS NINAKO, IT'S ALL OVER.
TAP TAP

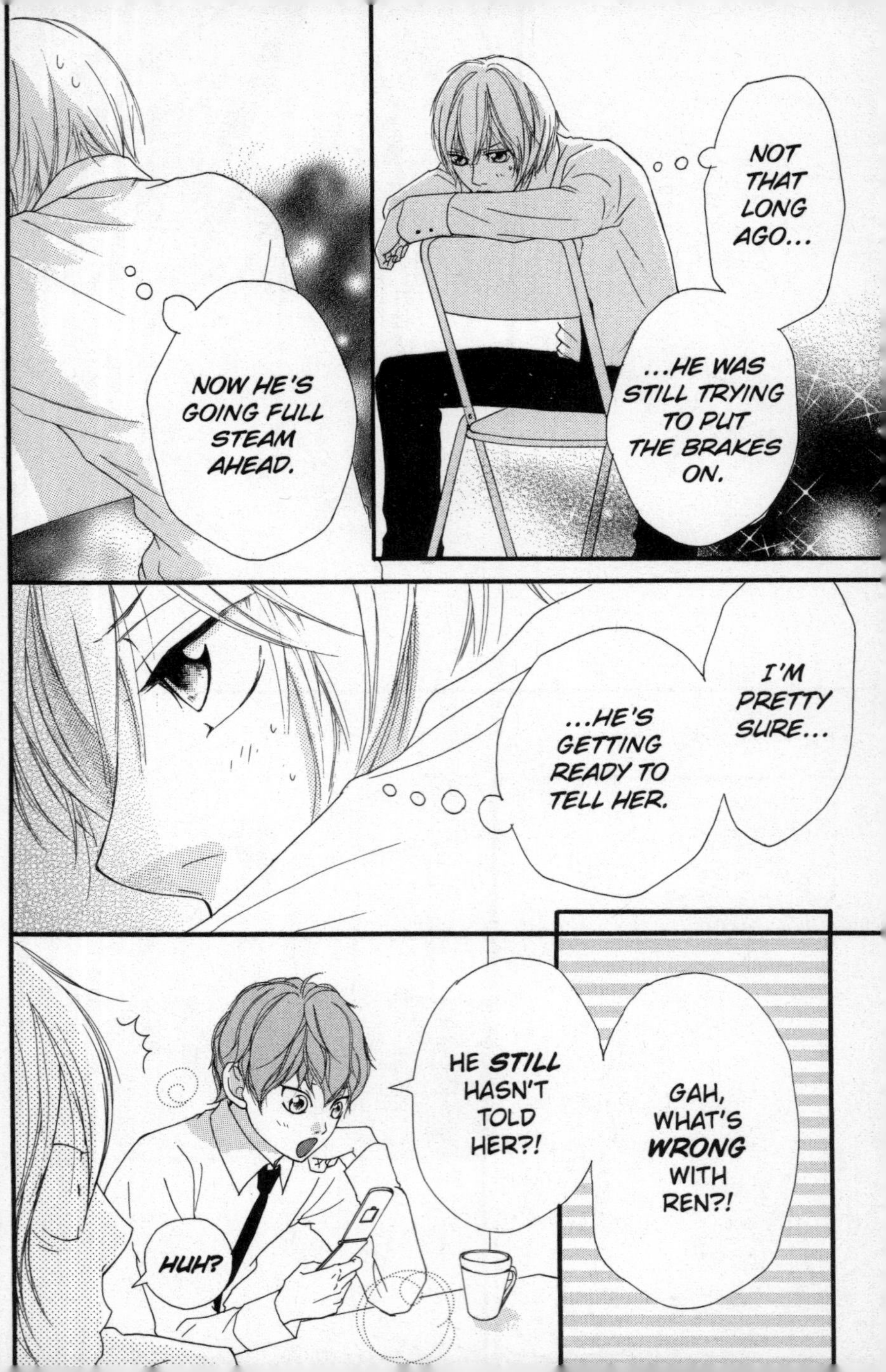
NOT THAT LONG AGO...
...HE WAS STILL TRYING TO PUT THE BRAKES ON.
NOW HE'S GOING FULL STEAM AHEAD.
I'M PRETTY SURE...
...HE'S GETTING READY TO TELL HER.
GAH, WHAT'S WRONG WITH REN?!
HE STILL HASN'T TOLD HER?!
HUH?

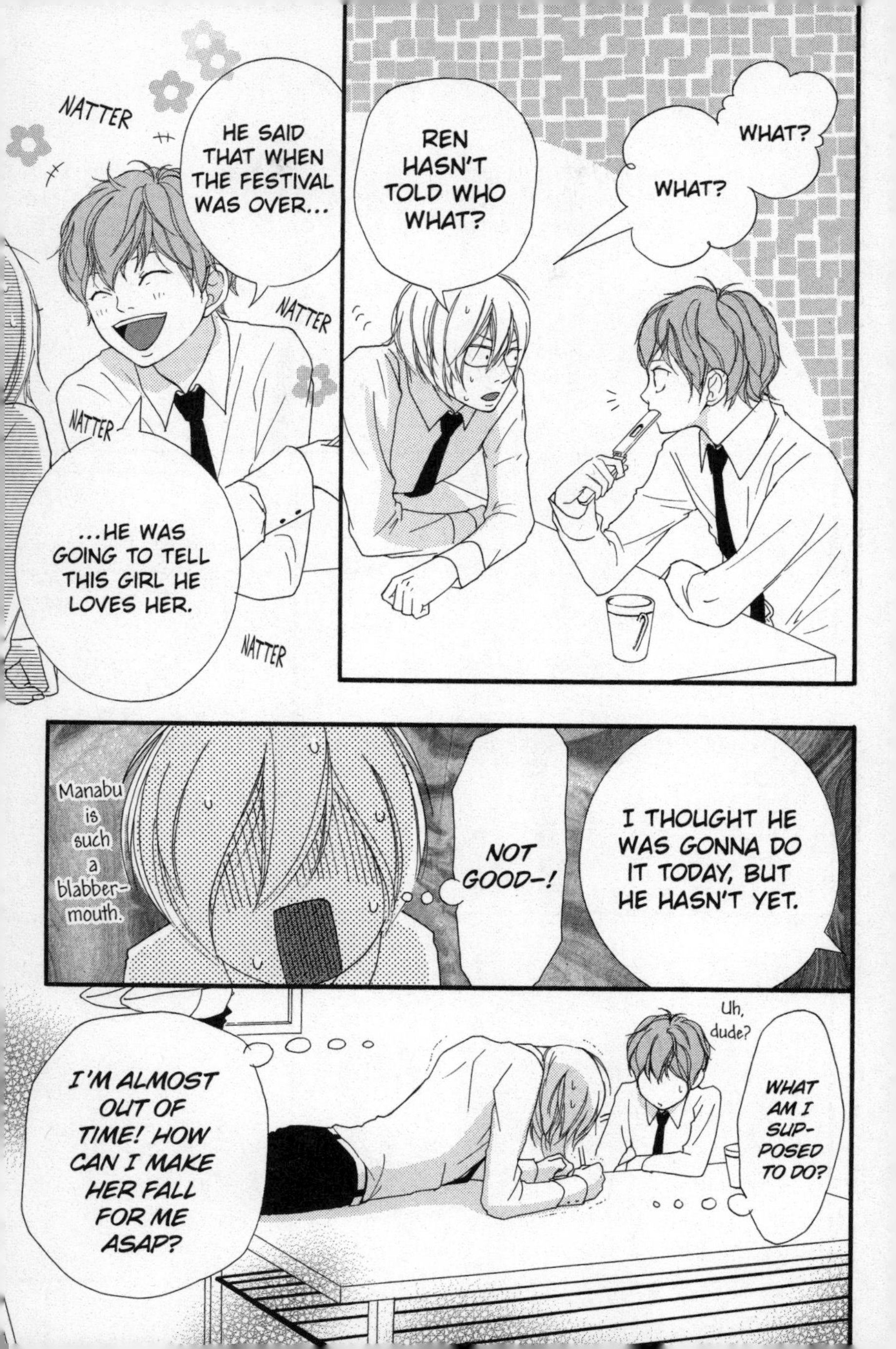
WHAT?
WHAT?
REN HASN'T TOLD WHO WHAT?
HE SAID THAT WHEN THE FESTIVAL WAS OVER...
NATTER
NATTER
NATTER
...HE WAS GOING TO TELL THIS GIRL HE LOVES HER.
NATTER
I THOUGHT HE WAS GONNA DO IT TODAY, BUT HE HASN'T YET.
NOT GOOD-!
Manabu is such a blabber-mouth.
Uh, dude?
WHAT AM I SUP-POSED TO DO?
I'M ALMOST OUT OF TIME! HOW CAN I MAKE HER FALL FOR ME ASAP?

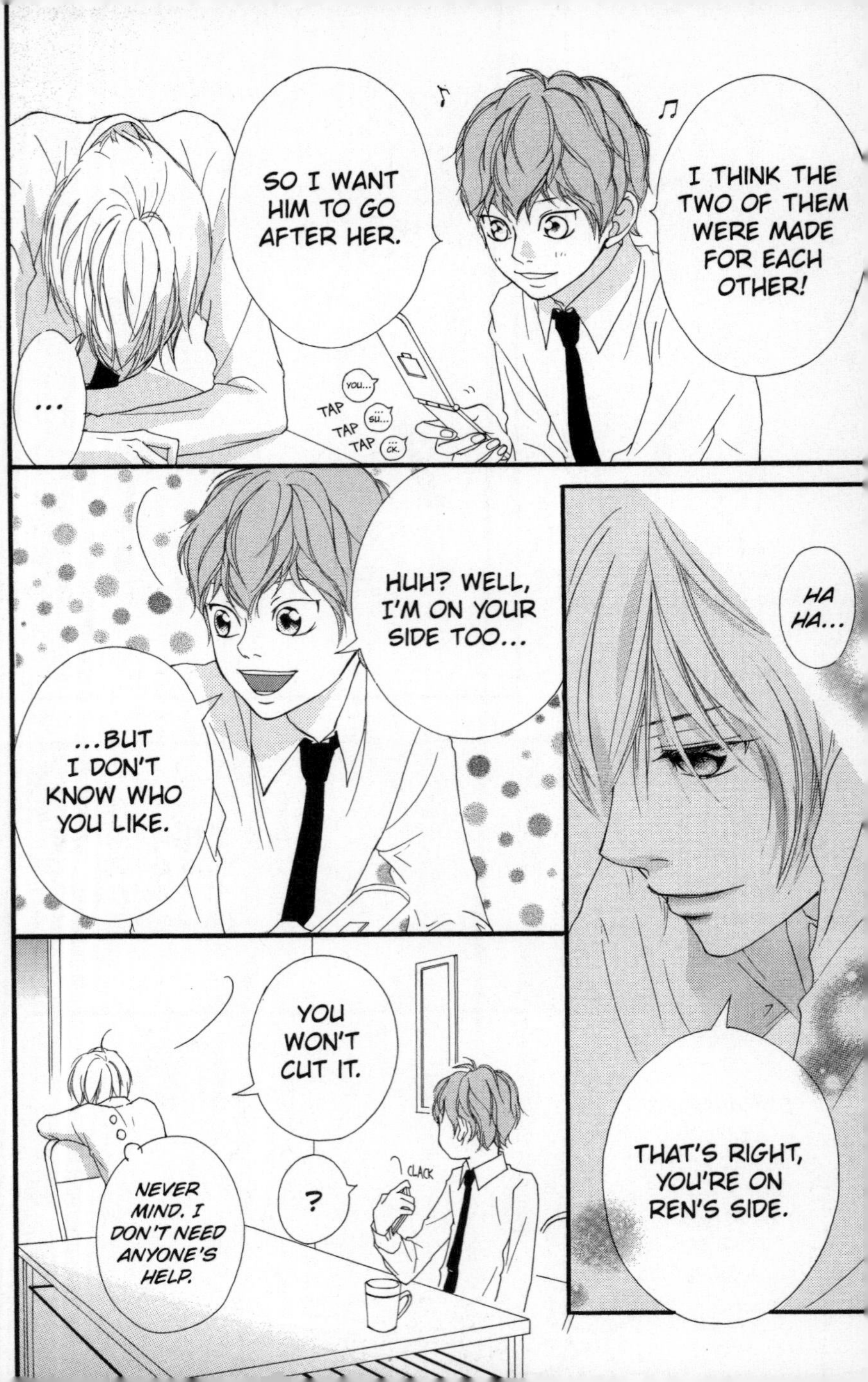
I THINK THE TWO OF THEM WERE MADE FOR EACH OTHER!
SO I WANT HIM TO GO AFTER HER.
YOU...
TAP
...SU...
TAP
...CK.
TAP
...
HA HA...
THAT'S RIGHT, YOU'RE ON REN'S SIDE.
HUH? WELL, I'M ON YOUR SIDE TOO...
...BUT I DON'T KNOW WHO YOU LIKE.
YOU WON'T CUT IT.
?
CLACK
NEVER MIND. I DON'T NEED ANYONE'S HELP.

A BAD ONE.

RIGHT—I DO HAVE AN ALLY.

HMM?

SEE YOU GUYS LATER!

Okay!

ALL RIGHT, YOU GUYS CAN GO NOW.

HUH?

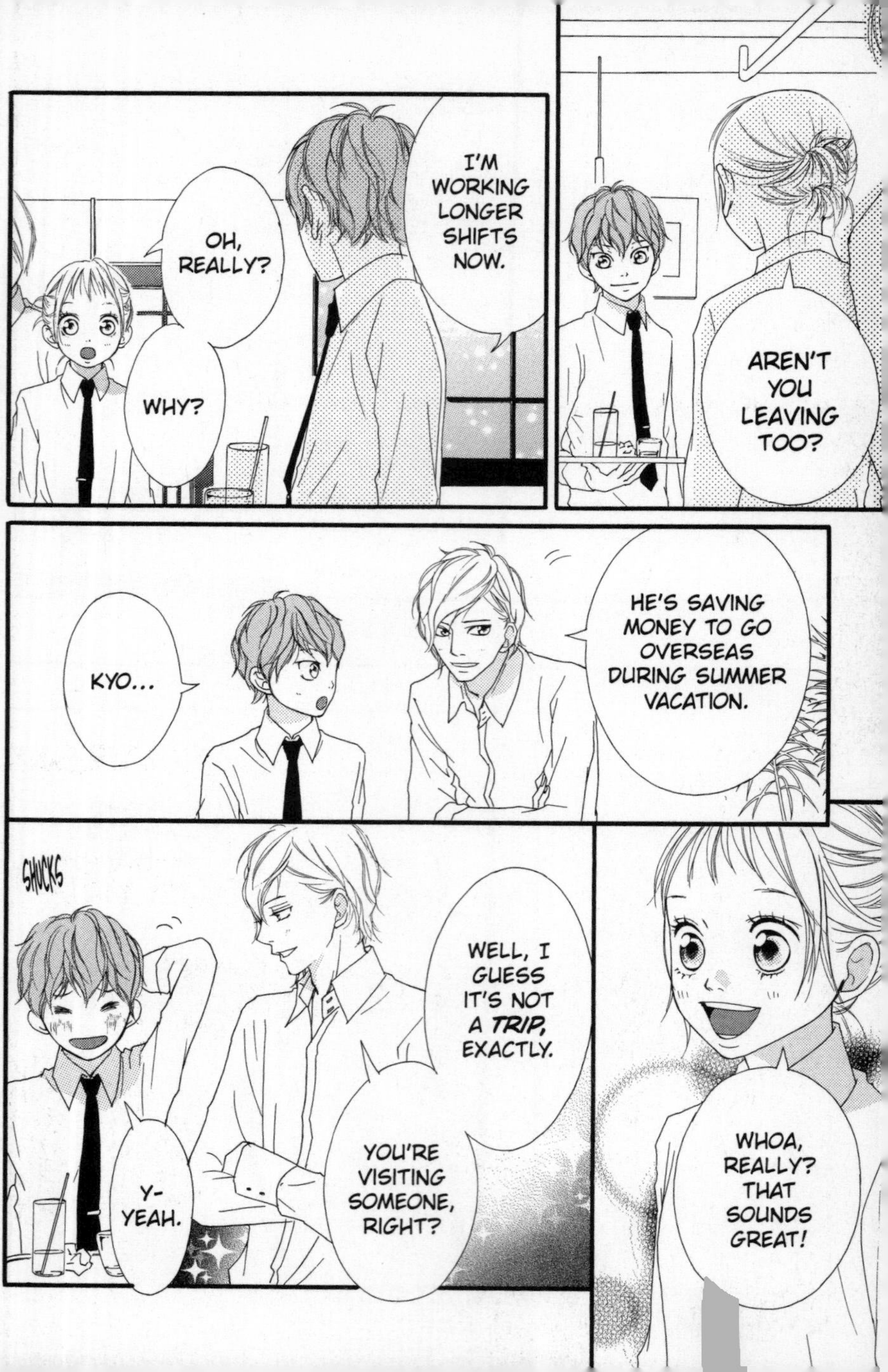
AREN'T YOU LEAVING TOO?
I'M WORKING LONGER SHIFTS NOW.
OH, REALLY?
WHY?
HE'S SAVING MONEY TO GO OVERSEAS DURING SUMMER VACATION.
KYO...
WHOA, REALLY? THAT SOUNDS GREAT!
WELL, I GUESS IT'S NOT A *TRIP*, EXACTLY.
YOU'RE VISITING SOMEONE, RIGHT?
SHUCKS
Y-YEAH.

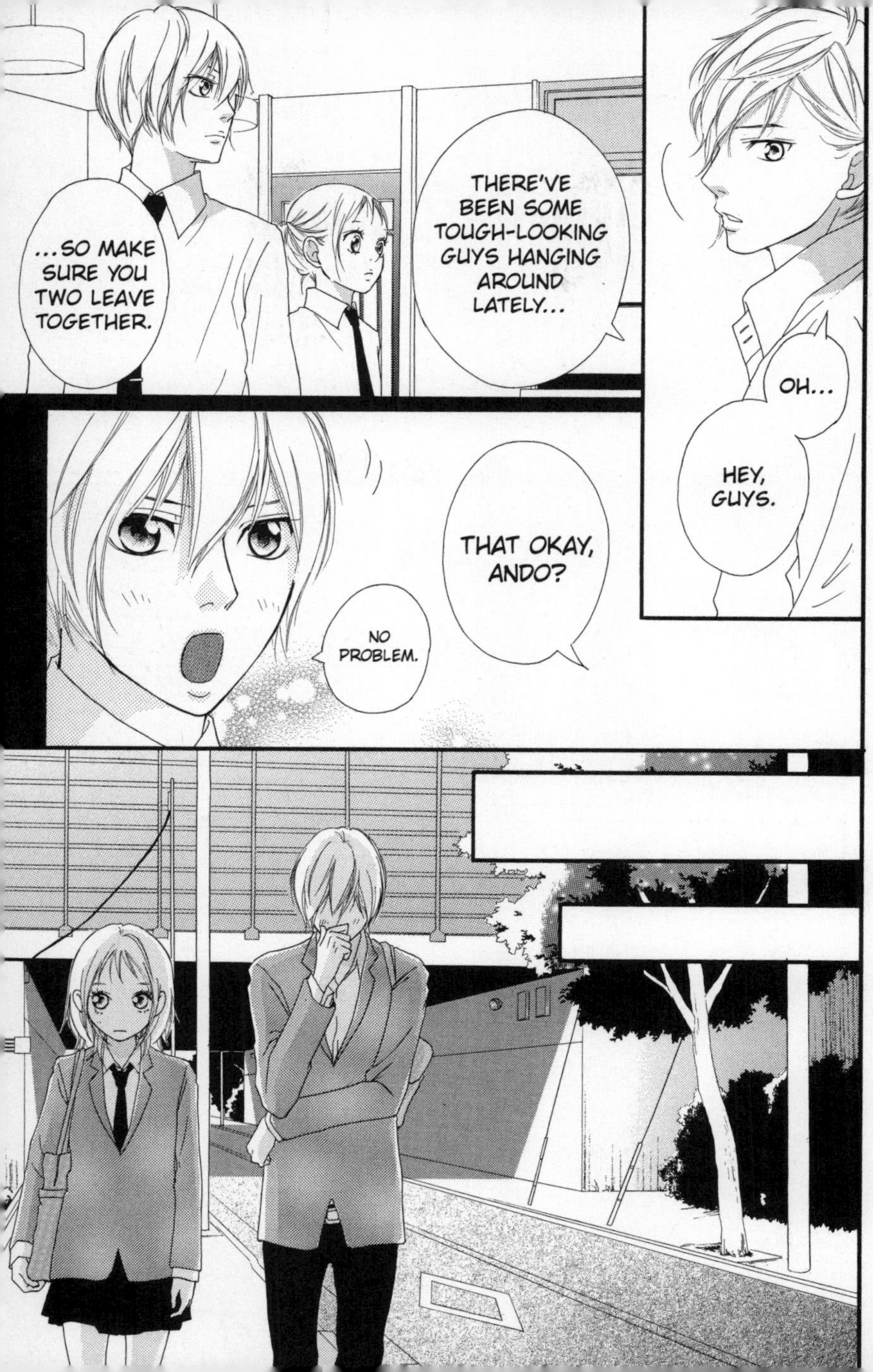
OH...
HEY, GUYS.
THERE'VE BEEN SOME TOUGH-LOOKING GUYS HANGING AROUND LATELY...
...SO MAKE SURE YOU TWO LEAVE TOGETHER.
THAT OKAY, ANDO?
NO PROBLEM.

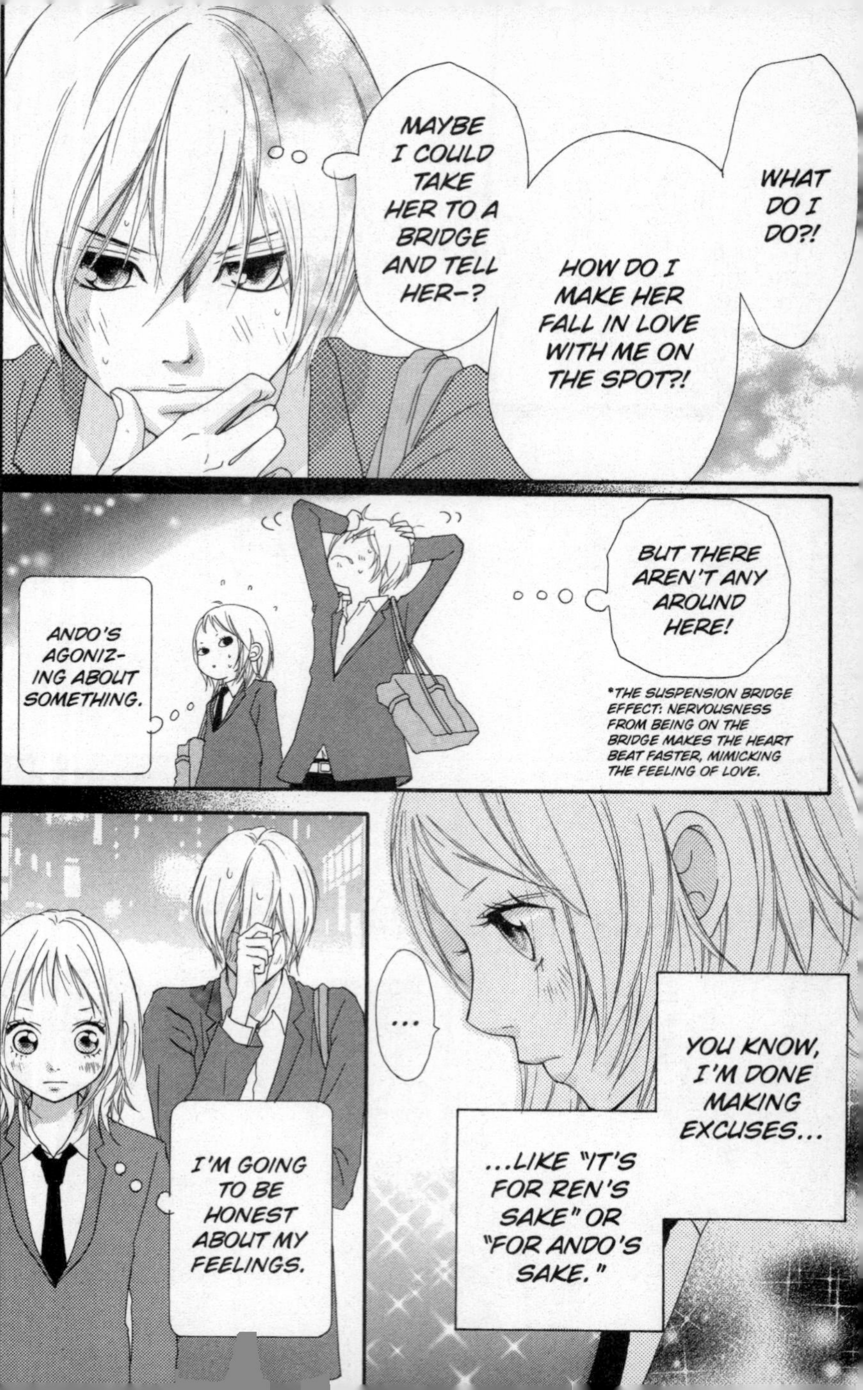
WHAT DO I DO?!
HOW DO I MAKE HER FALL IN LOVE WITH ME ON THE SPOT?!
MAYBE I COULD TAKE HER TO A BRIDGE AND TELL HER-?
BUT THERE AREN'T ANY AROUND HERE!
*THE SUSPENSION BRIDGE EFFECT: NERVOUSNESS FROM BEING ON THE BRIDGE MAKES THE HEART BEAT FASTER, MIMICKING THE FEELING OF LOVE.
ANDO'S AGONIZ-ING ABOUT SOMETHING.
YOU KNOW, I'M DONE MAKING EXCUSES...
...LIKE "IT'S FOR REN'S SAKE" OR "FOR ANDO'S SAKE."
...
I'M GOING TO BE HONEST ABOUT MY FEELINGS.

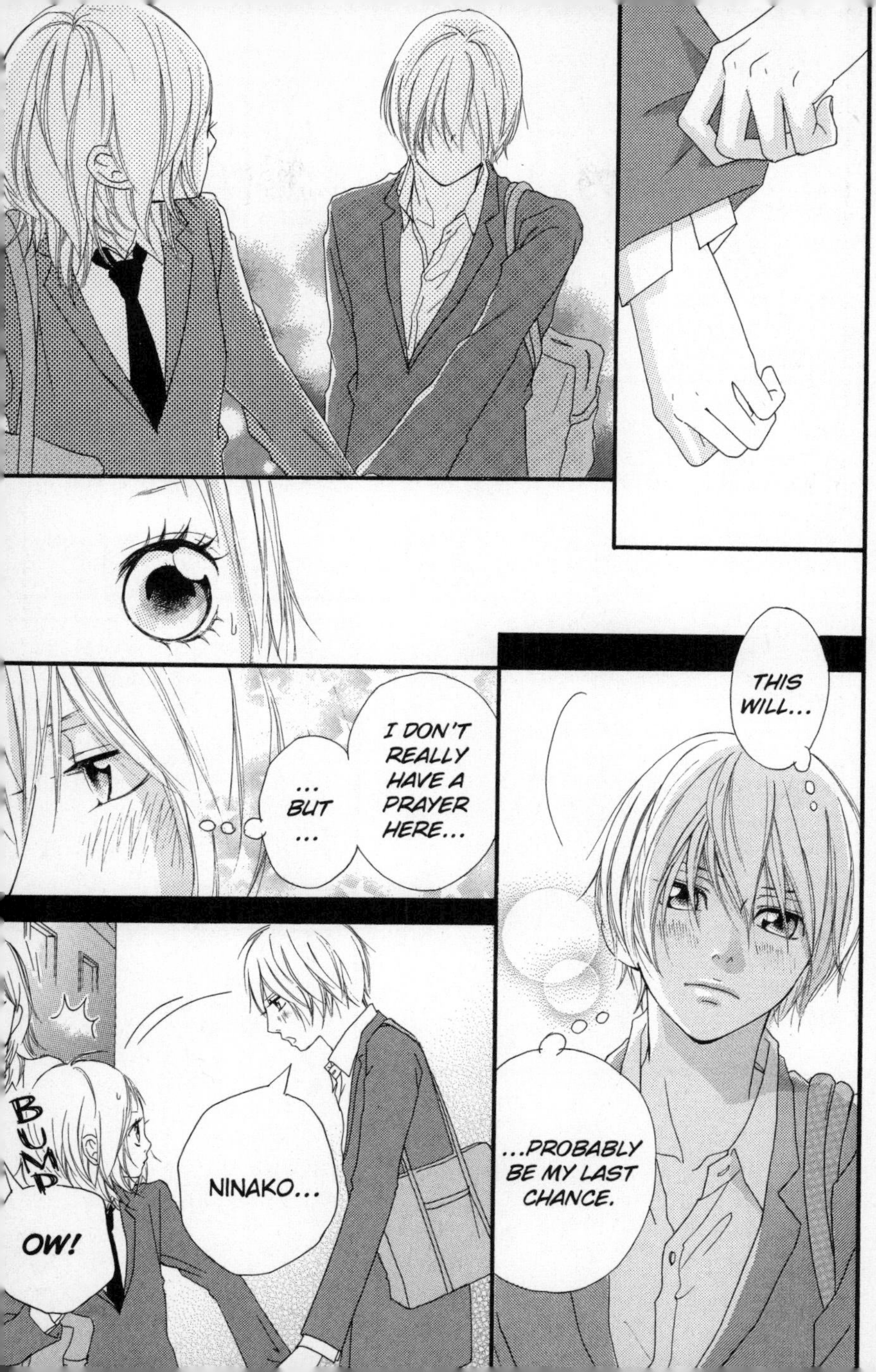
THIS WILL...
...PROBABLY BE MY LAST CHANCE.
I DON'T REALLY HAVE A PRAYER HERE...
...BUT...
NINAKO...
BUMP
OW!

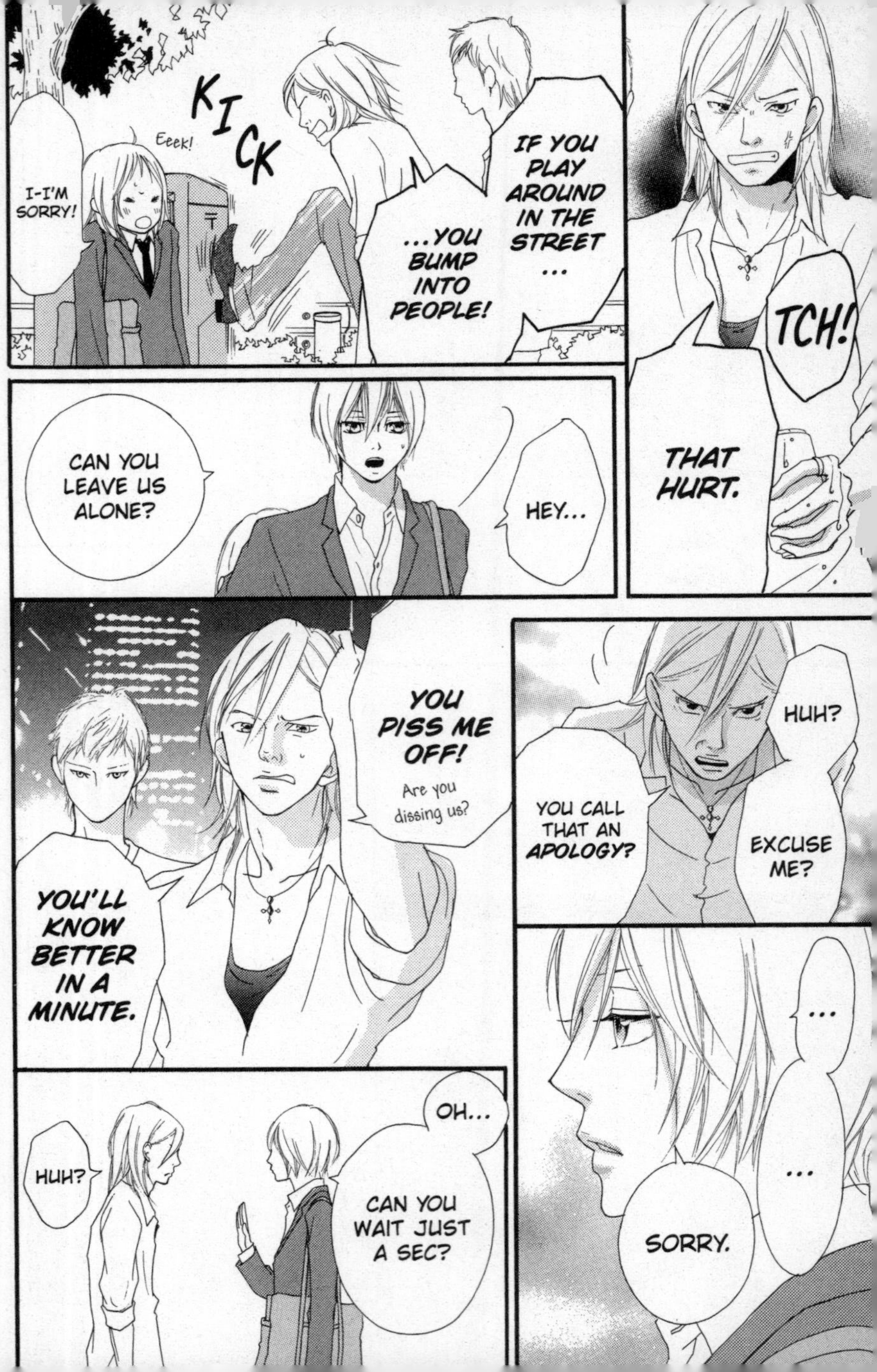
IF YOU PLAY AROUND IN THE STREET...
...YOU BUMP INTO PEOPLE!
KICK
Eeek!
I-I'M SORRY!
TCH!
THAT HURT.
HEY...
CAN YOU LEAVE US ALONE?
HUH?
EXCUSE ME?
YOU CALL THAT AN APOLOGY?
YOU PISS ME OFF!
Are you dissing us?
YOU'LL KNOW BETTER IN A MINUTE.
...
...
SORRY.
OH...
CAN YOU WAIT JUST A SEC?
HUH?

HEY, NINAKO?

THAT AIN'T HAPPENING.

SHE'S GONNA STAND RIGHT THERE...

I'M A TERRIBLE FIGHTER, SO I DON'T WANT YOU TO SEE THIS.

CAN YOU GO ON AHEAD?

...AND WATCH...

ANDO-!

...WHILE I BEAT THE SNOT OUT OF YOU!

HA!

WHAM

THUD

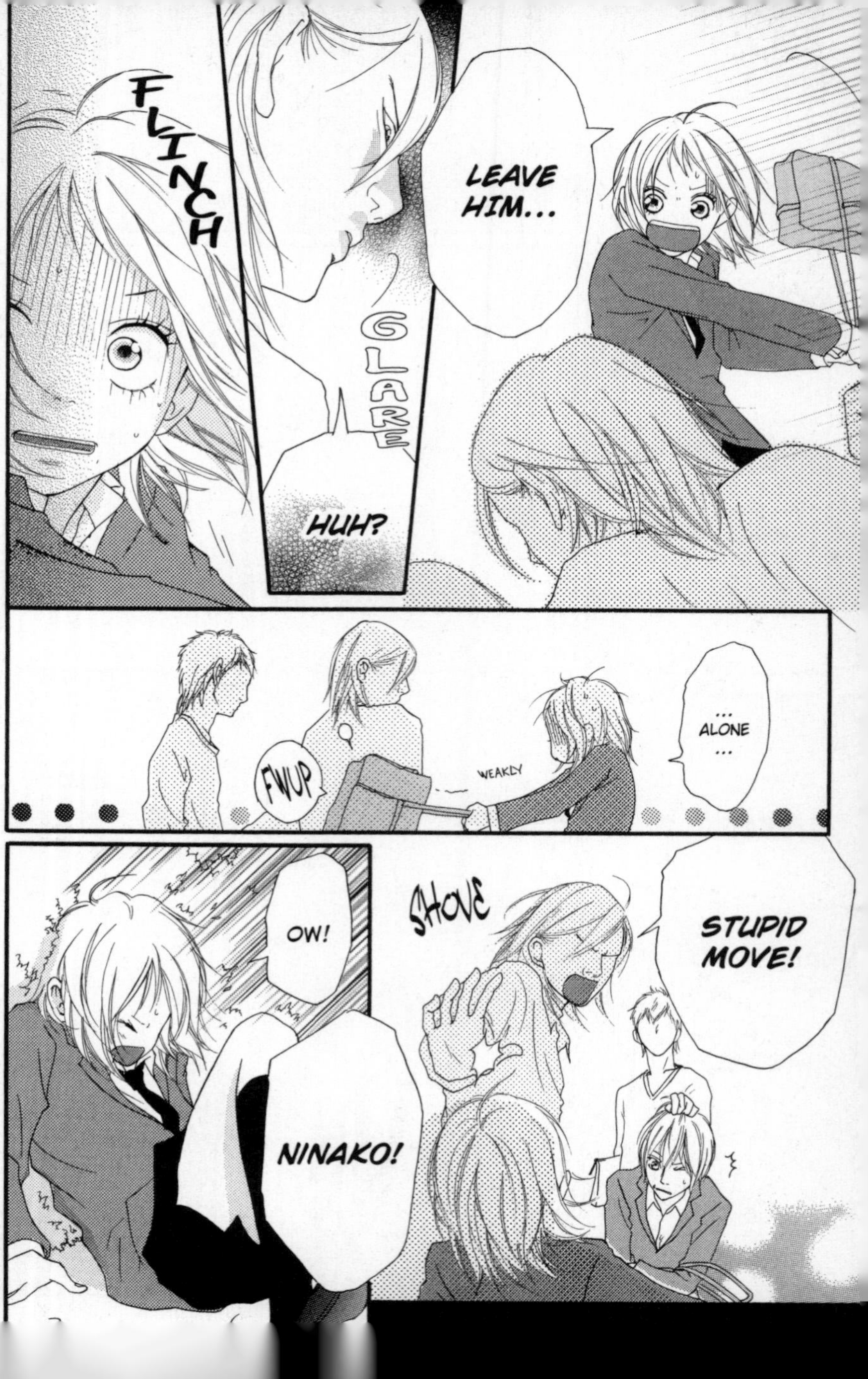
LEAVE HIM...
GLARE
HUH?
FLINCH
...ALONE...
WEAKLY
FWUP
STUPID MOVE!
SHOVE
OW!
NINAKO!

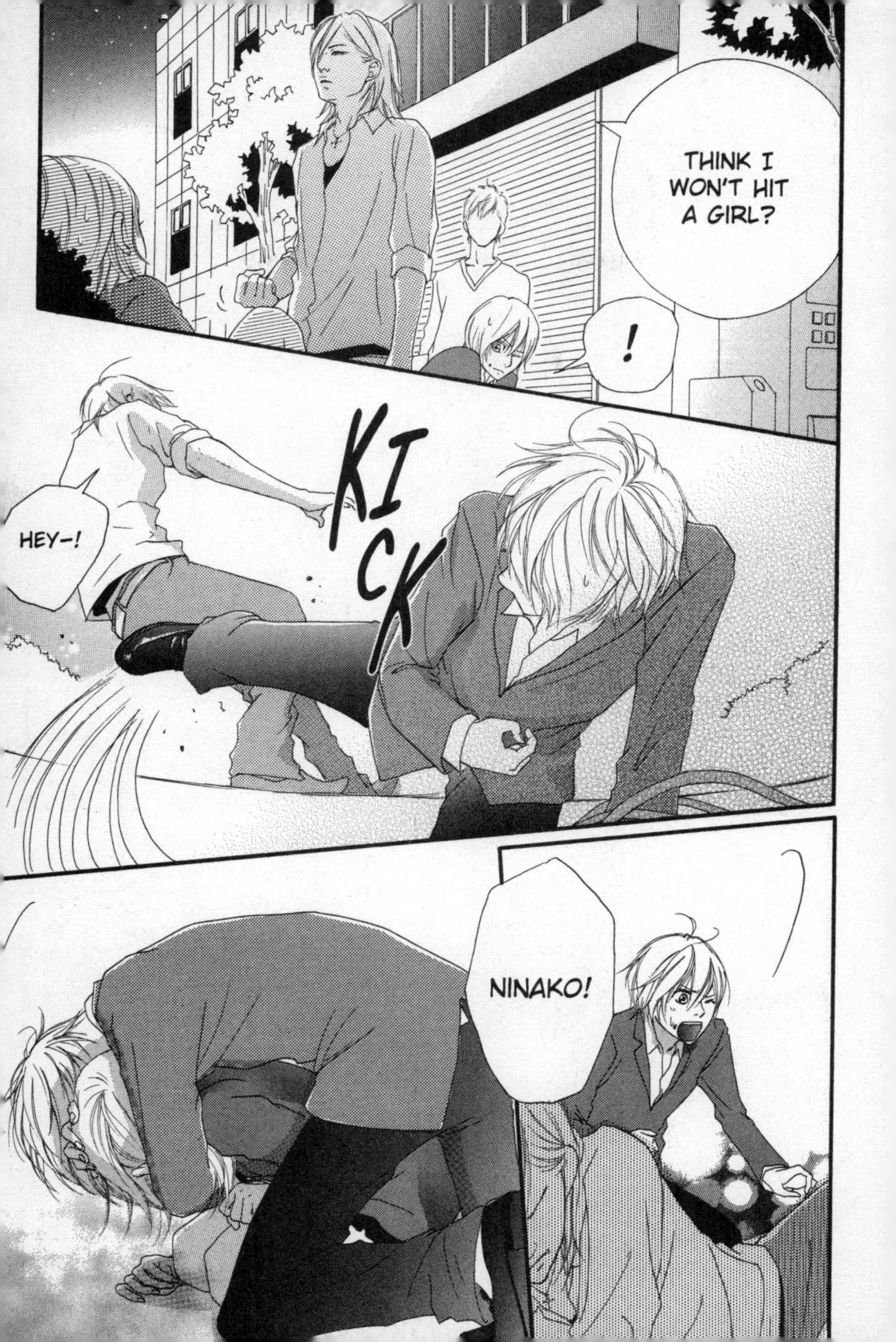
THINK I WON'T HIT A GIRL?
!
KICK
HEY-!
NINAKO!

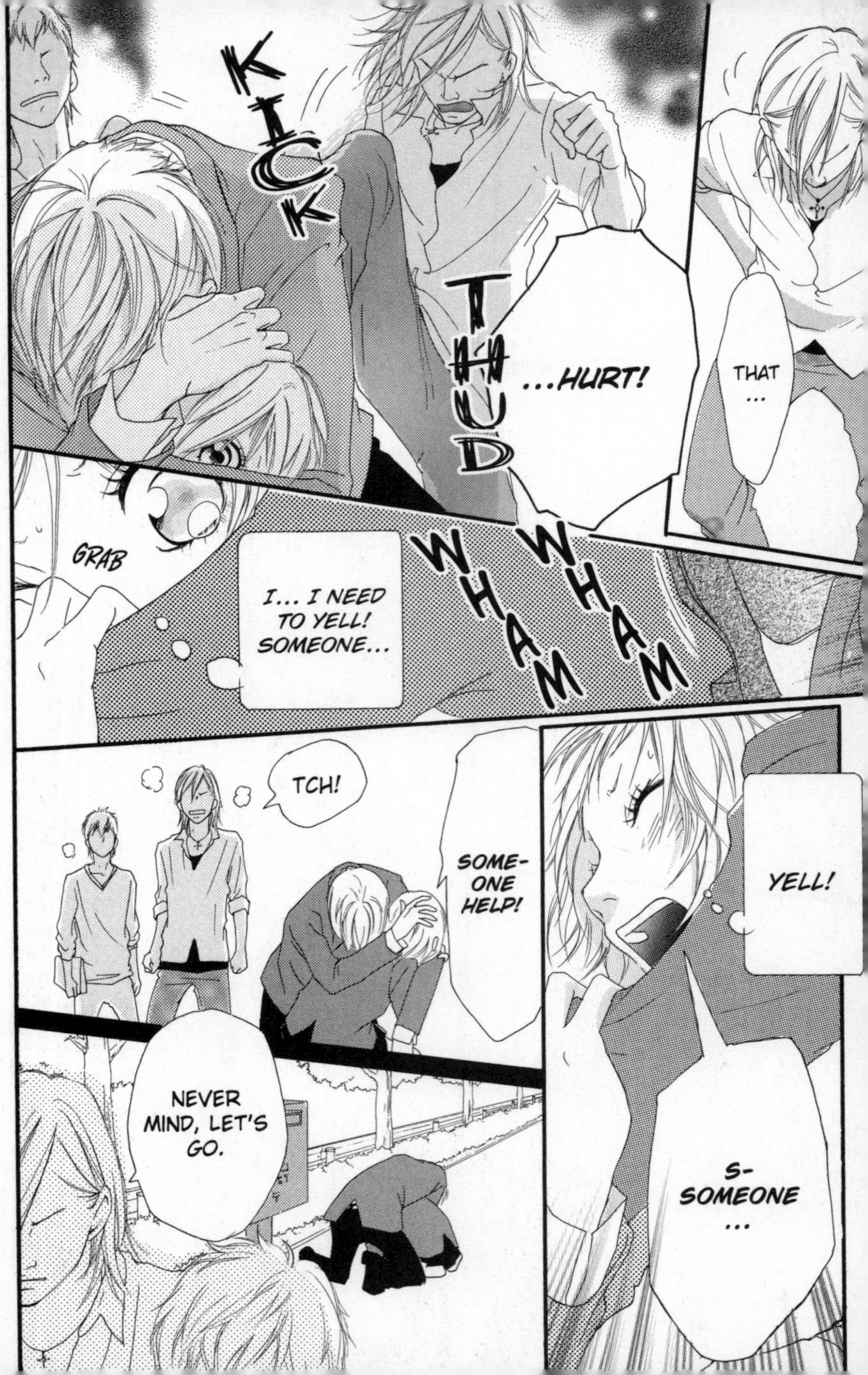
THAT...
KICK
THUD
...HURT!
WHAM WHAM
I... I NEED TO YELL! SOMEONE...
GRAB
YELL!
S-SOMEONE...
SOME-ONE HELP!
TCH!
NEVER MIND, LET'S GO.

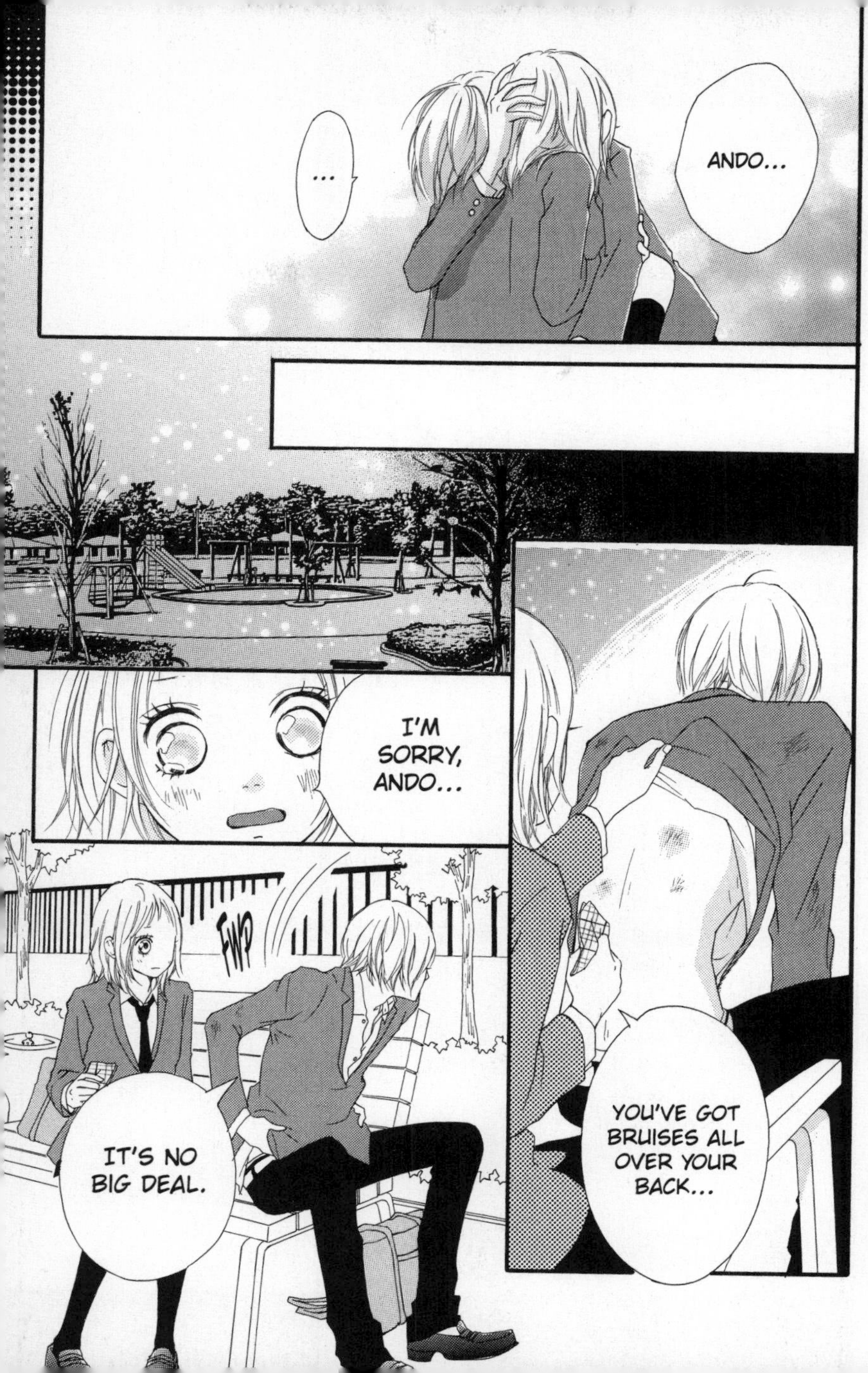
ANDO...
...
I'M SORRY, ANDO...
YOU'VE GOT BRUISES ALL OVER YOUR BACK...
FWP
IT'S NO BIG DEAL.

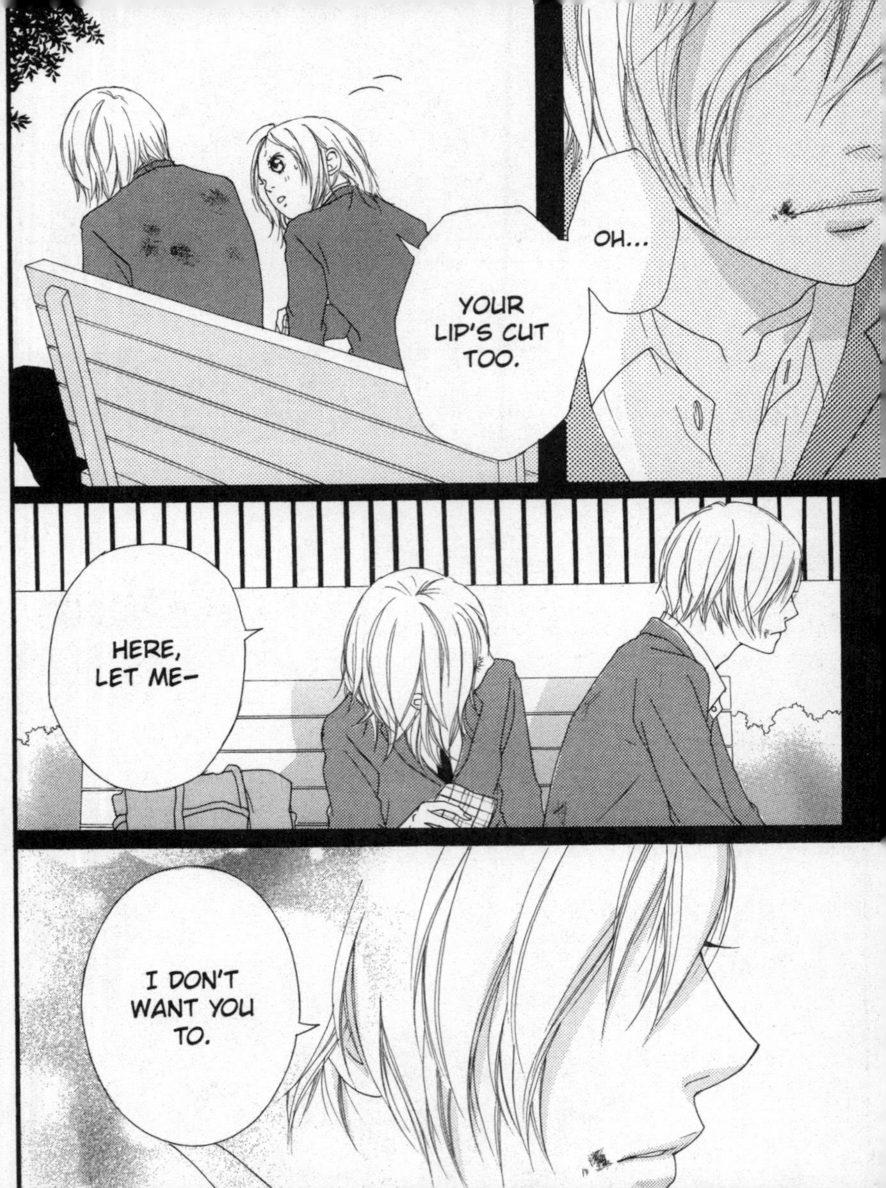
OH...
YOUR LIP'S CUT TOO.
HERE, LET ME–
I DON'T WANT YOU TO.

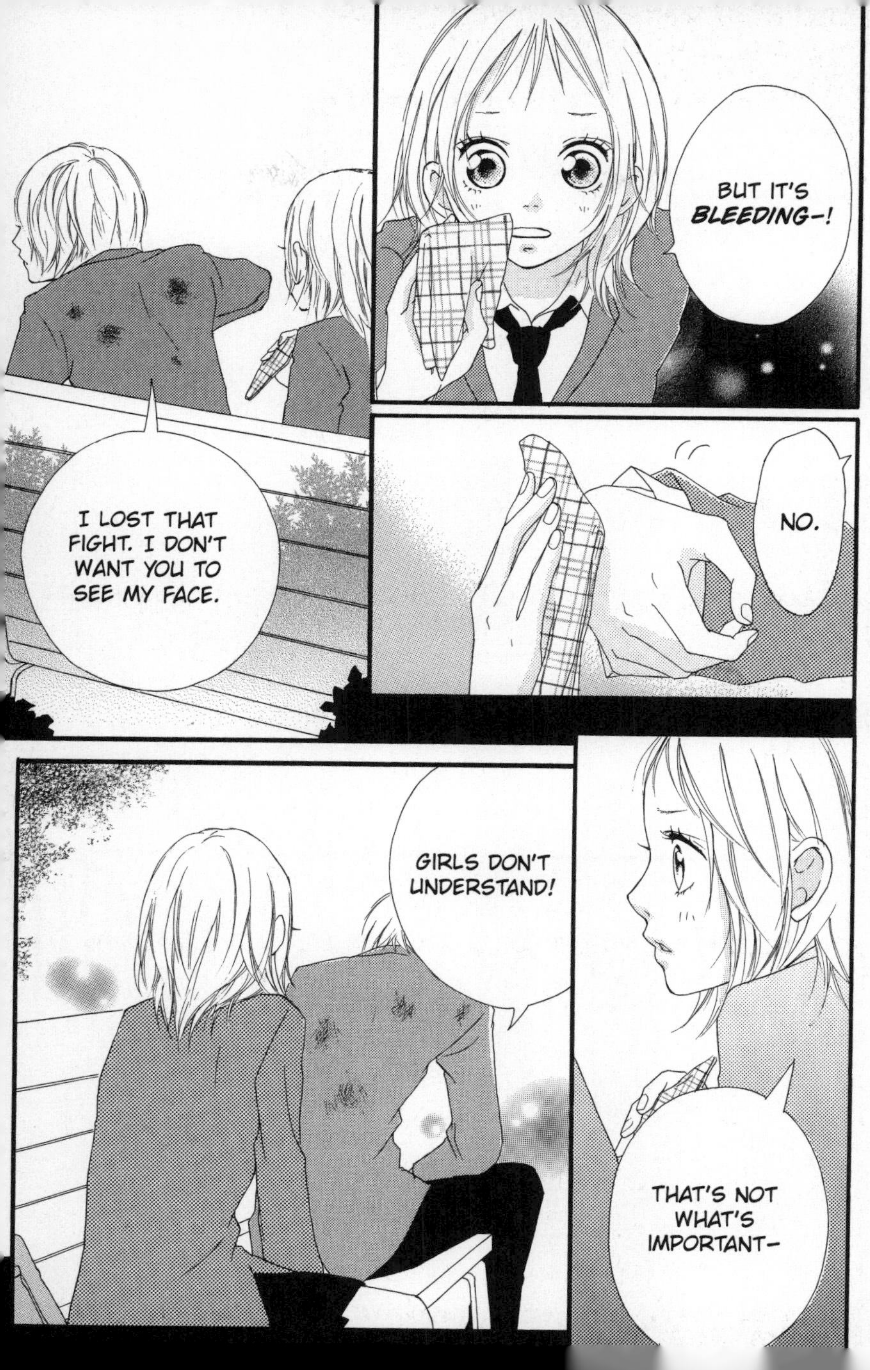
BUT IT'S BLEEDING-!
NO.
I LOST THAT FIGHT. I DON'T WANT YOU TO SEE MY FACE.
GIRLS DON'T UNDERSTAND!
THAT'S NOT WHAT'S IMPORTANT-

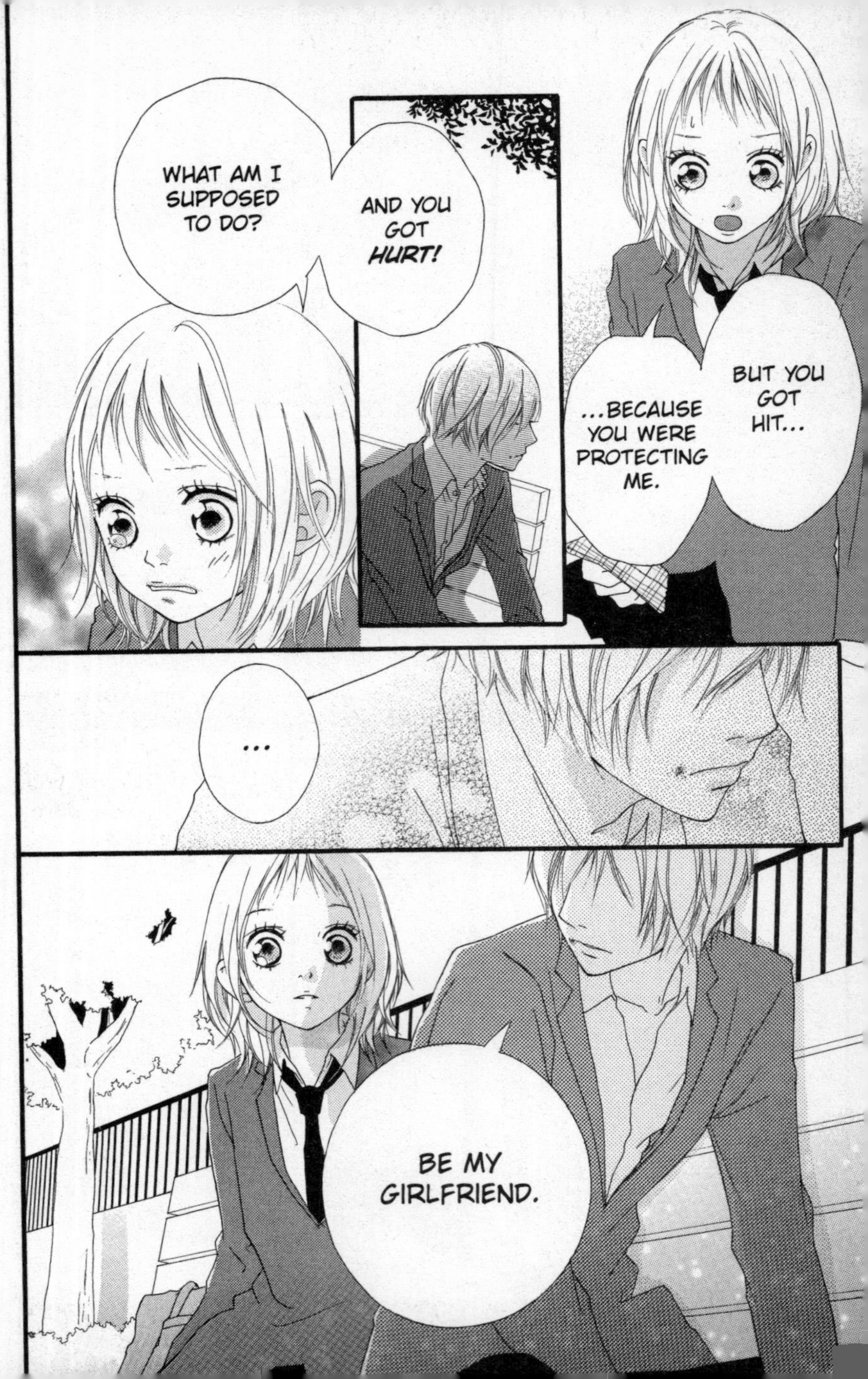
BUT YOU GOT HIT...
...BECAUSE YOU WERE PROTECTING ME.
AND YOU GOT *HURT!*
WHAT AM I SUPPOSED TO DO?
...
BE MY GIRLFRIEND.

AS IF!

JUST KIDDING. IT WAS A JOKE!

HA HA HA!

...

THERE CAN'T BE ANYTHING LESS COOL...

...THAN GETTING BEAT UP IN FRONT OF THE GIRL YOU LOVE.

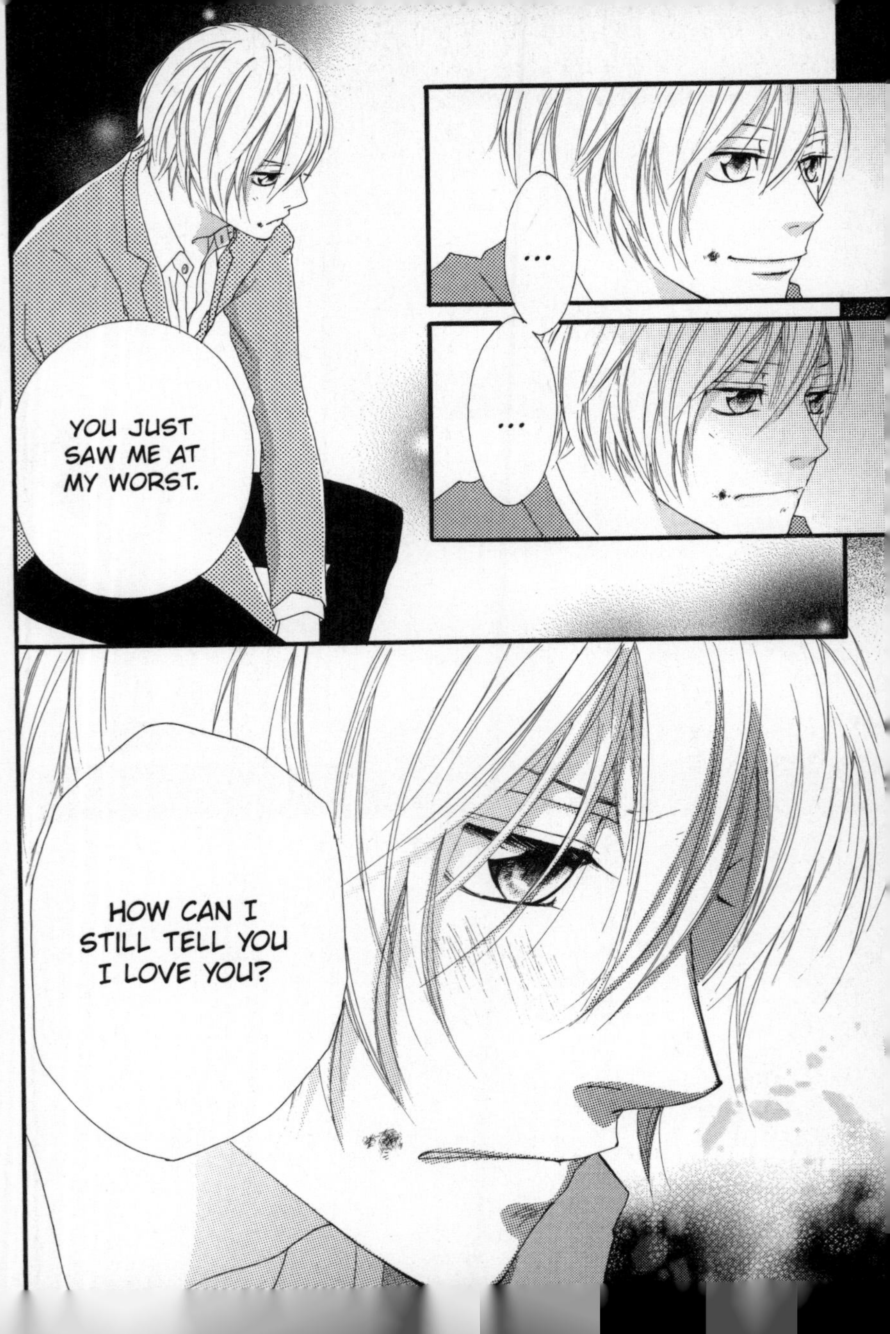
...
...
YOU JUST SAW ME AT MY WORST.
HOW CAN I STILL TELL YOU I LOVE YOU?

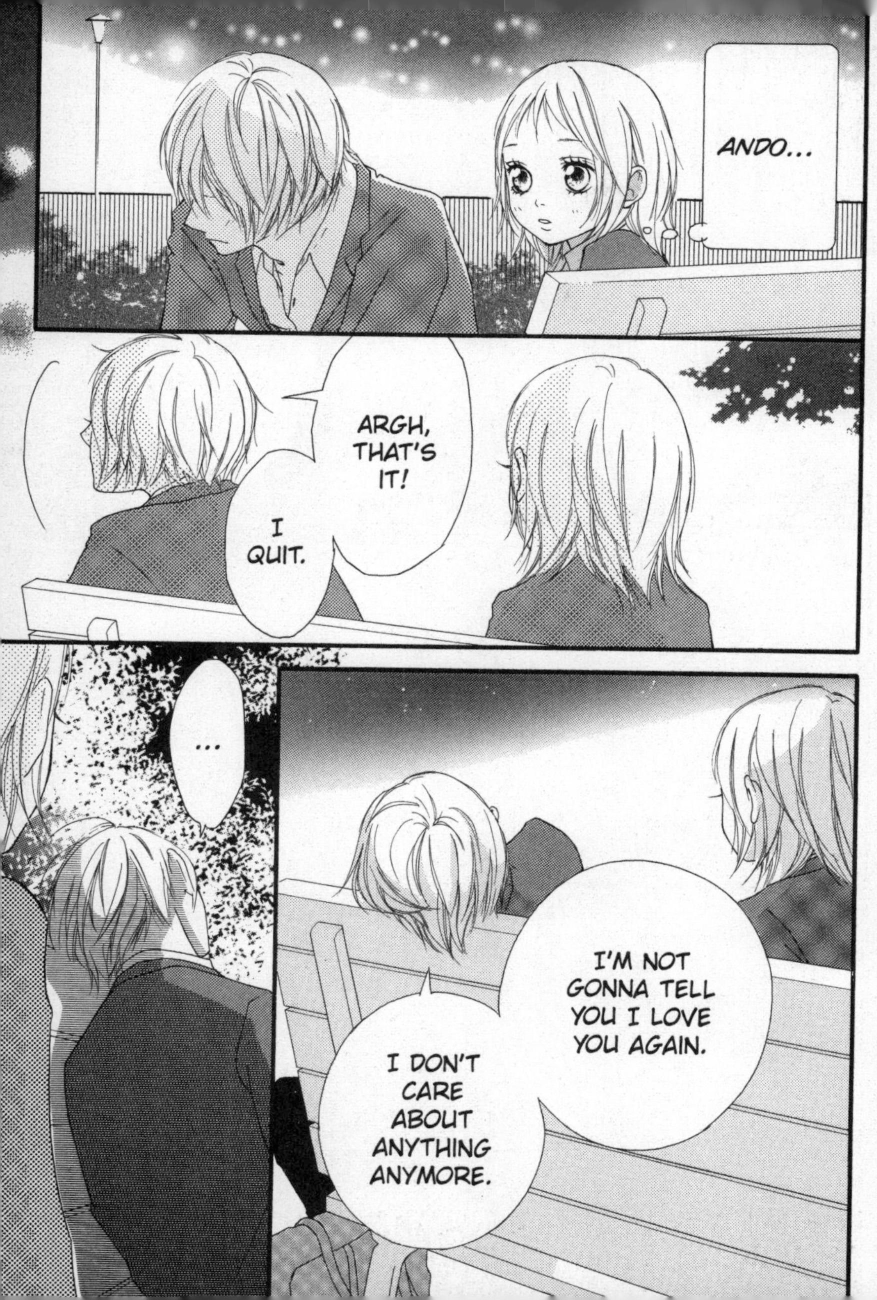
ANDO...
ARGH, THAT'S IT!
I QUIT.
I'M NOT GONNA TELL YOU I LOVE YOU AGAIN.
I DON'T CARE ABOUT ANYTHING ANYMORE.
...

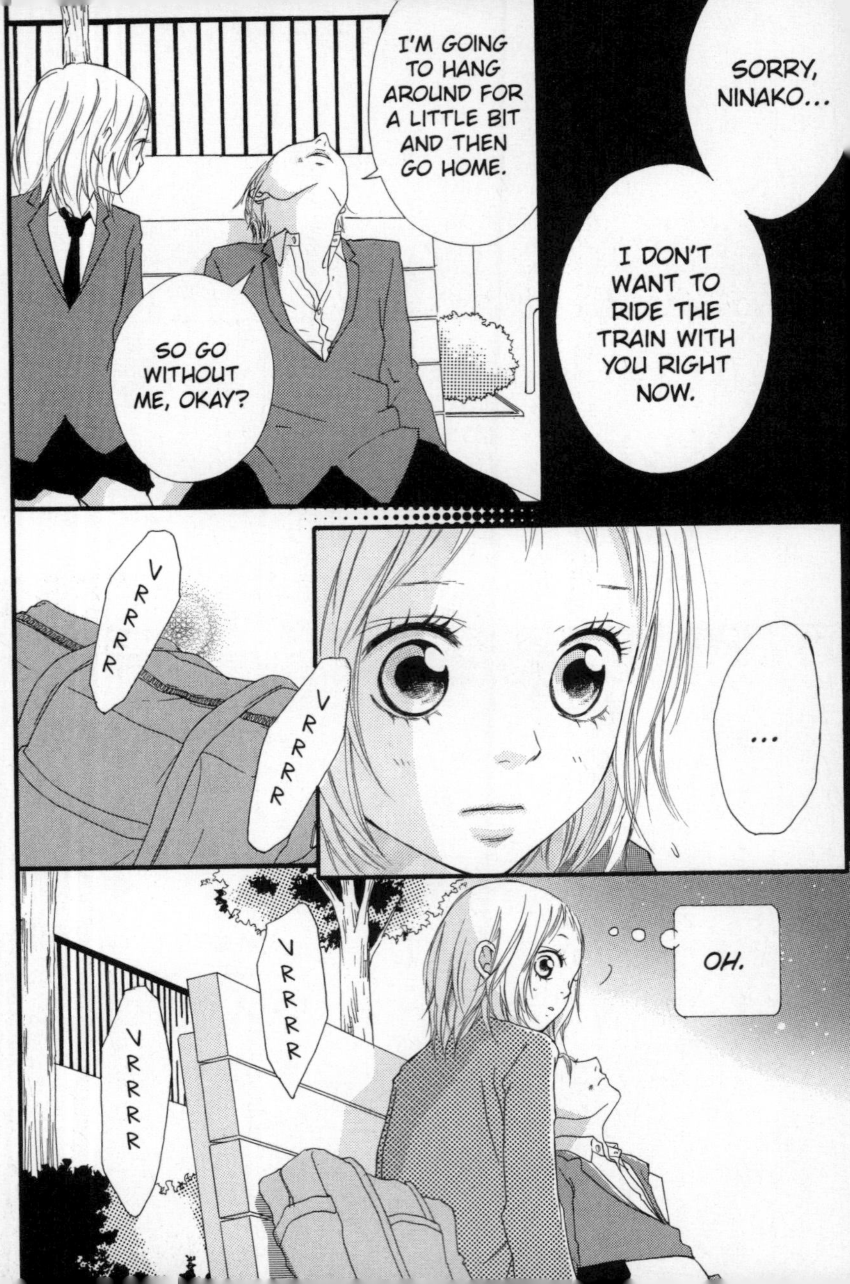
SORRY, NINAKO...
I DON'T WANT TO RIDE THE TRAIN WITH YOU RIGHT NOW.
I'M GOING TO HANG AROUND FOR A LITTLE BIT AND THEN GO HOME.
SO GO WITHOUT ME, OKAY?
...
VRRRR
VRRRR
OH.
VRRRR
VRRRR

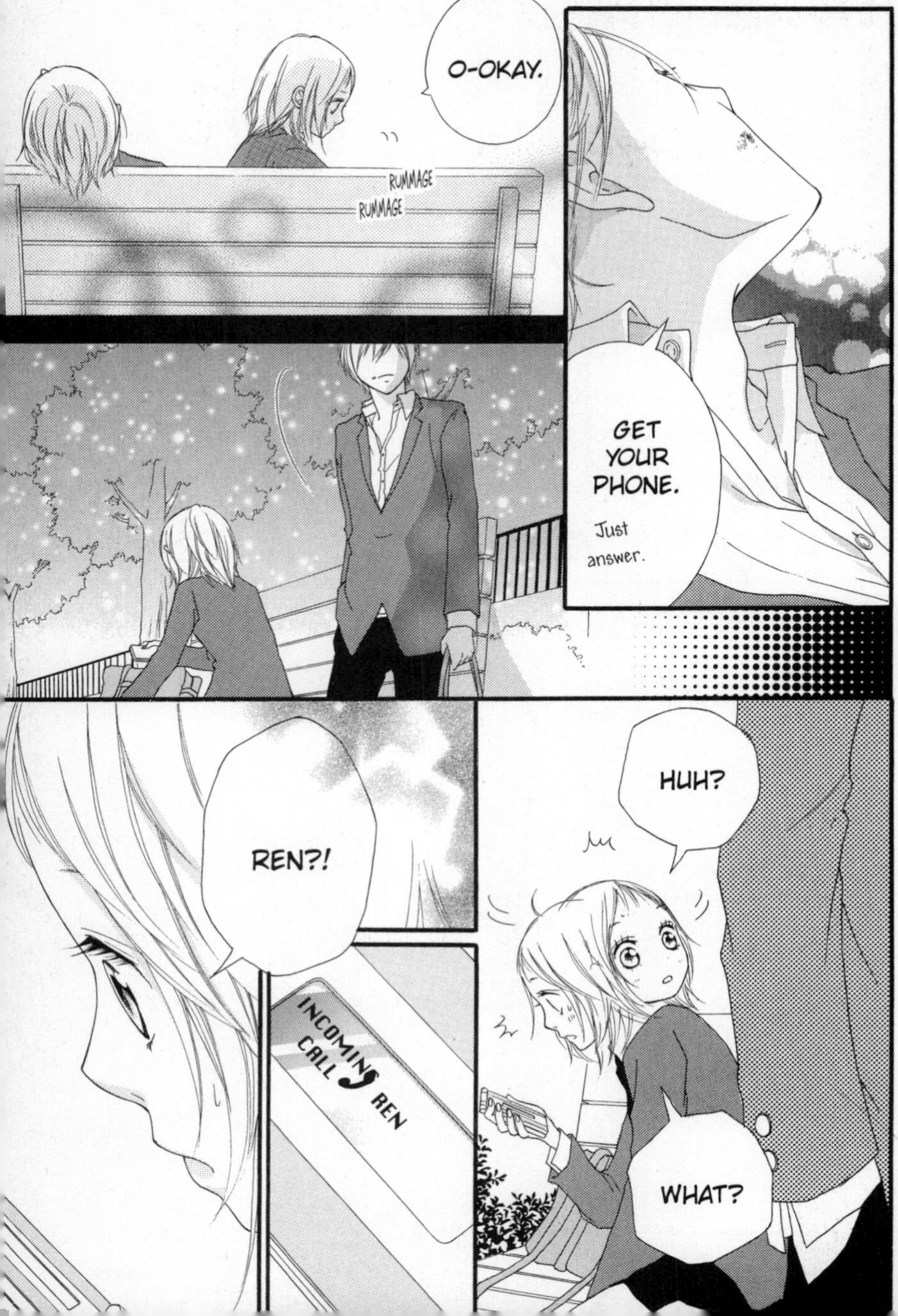
GET YOUR PHONE.
Just answer.
O-OKAY.
RUMMAGE
RUMMAGE
HUH?
WHAT?
REN?!
INCOMING CALL REN

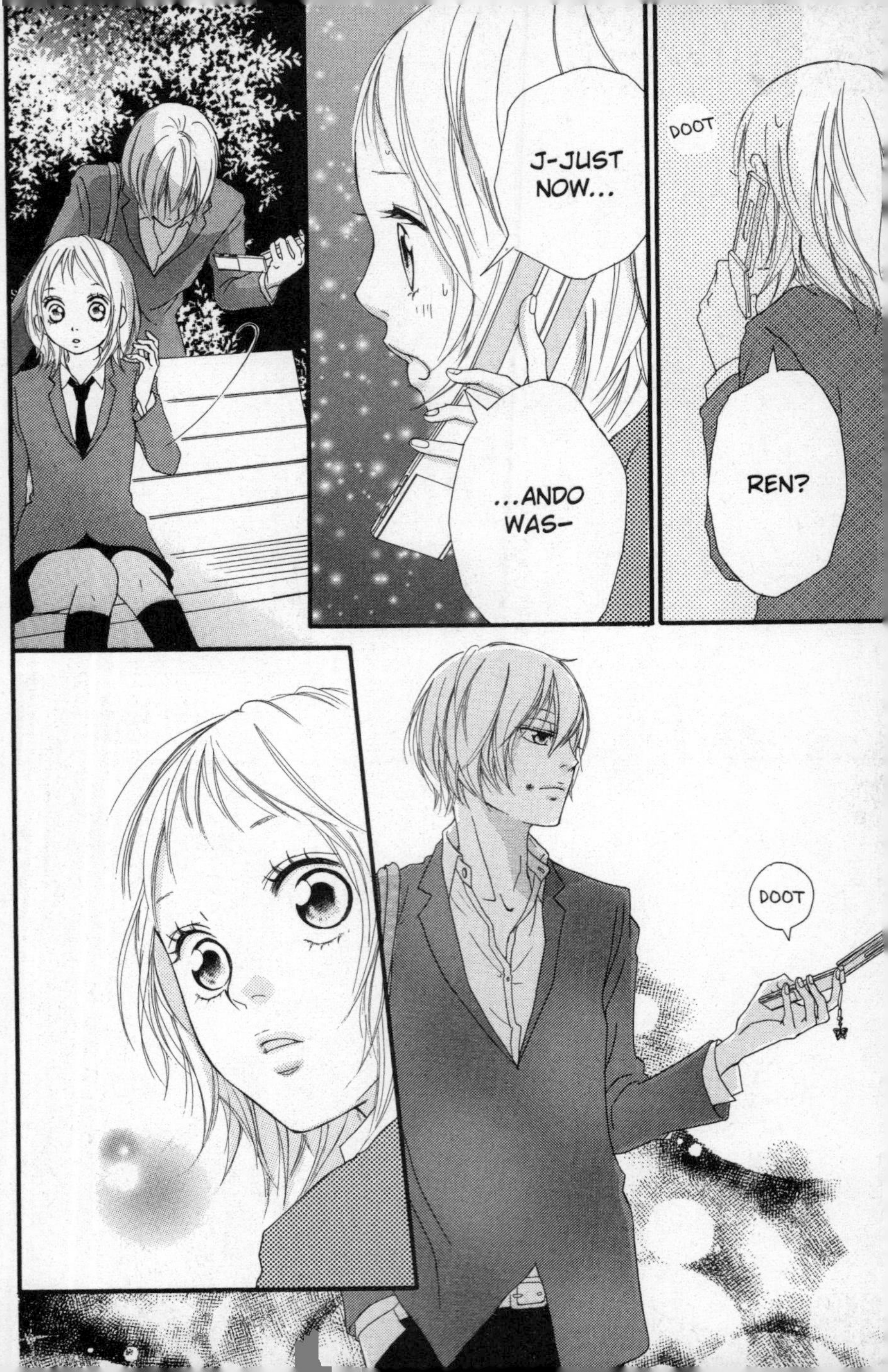
DOOT
REN?
J-JUST NOW...
...ANDO WAS-
DOOT

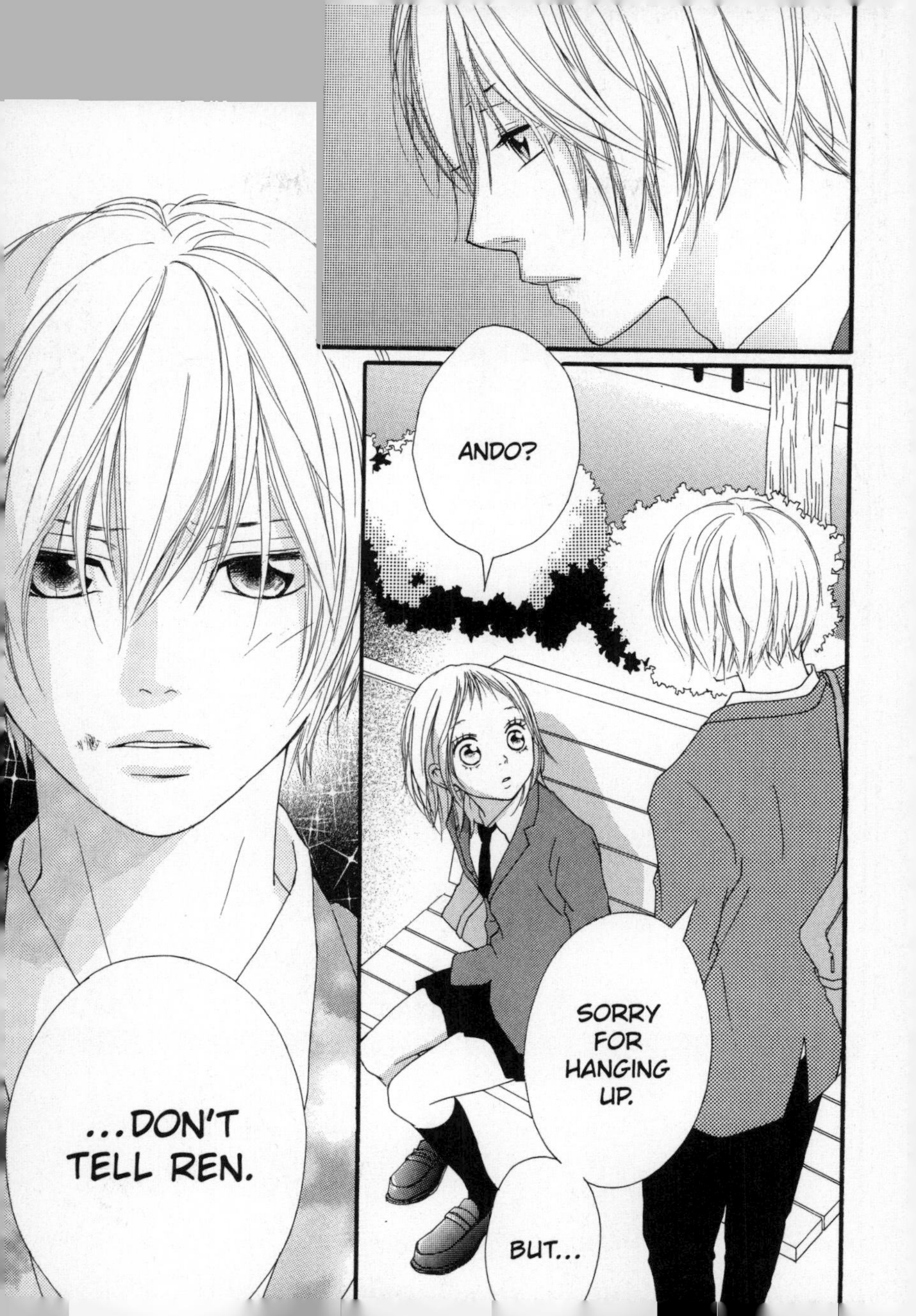
ANDO?
SORRY FOR HANGING UP.
BUT...
...DON'T TELL REN.

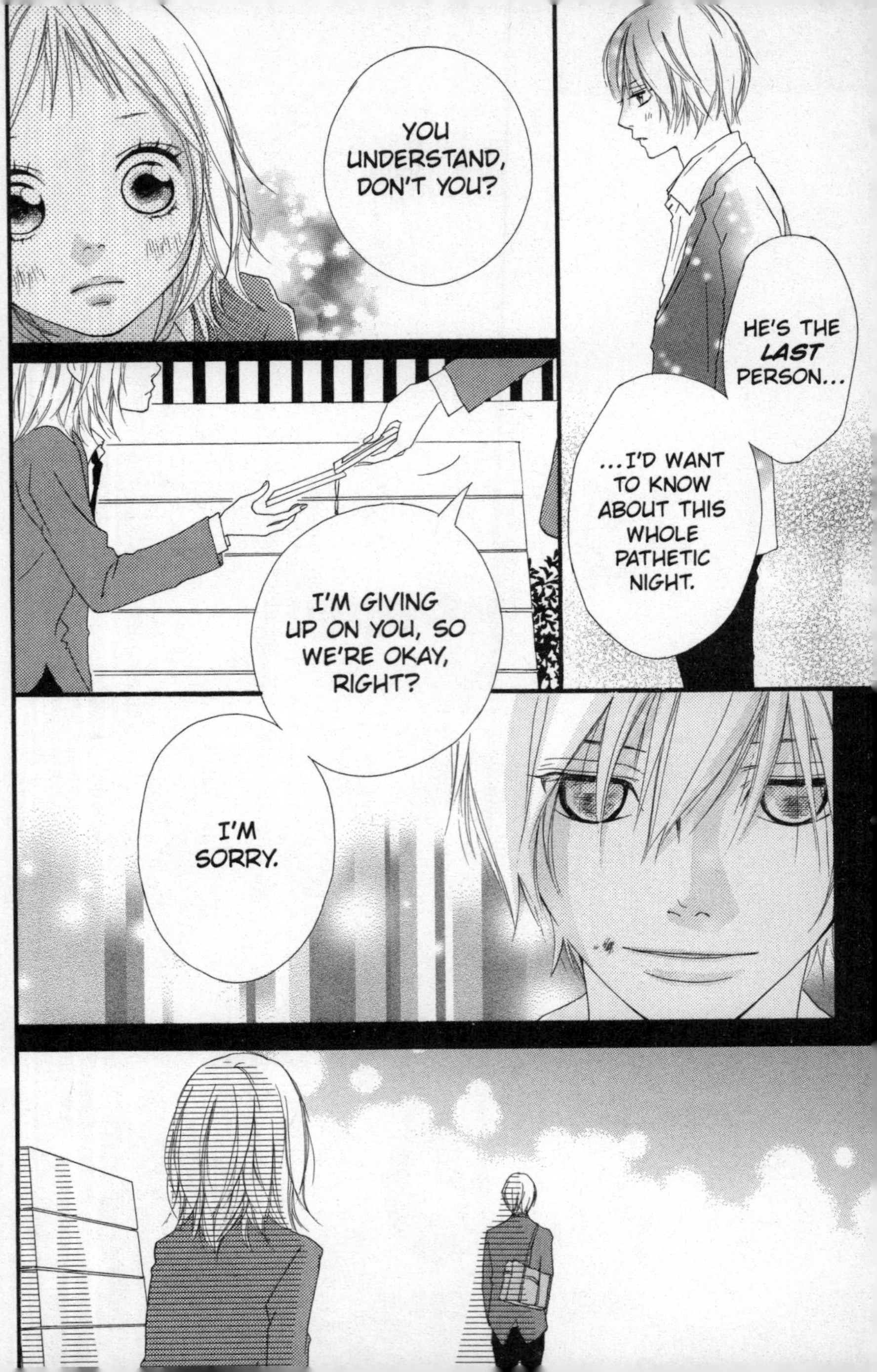
HE'S THE *LAST* PERSON...
...I'D WANT TO KNOW ABOUT THIS WHOLE PATHETIC NIGHT.
YOU UNDERSTAND, DON'T YOU?
I'M GIVING UP ON YOU, SO WE'RE OKAY, RIGHT?
I'M SORRY.

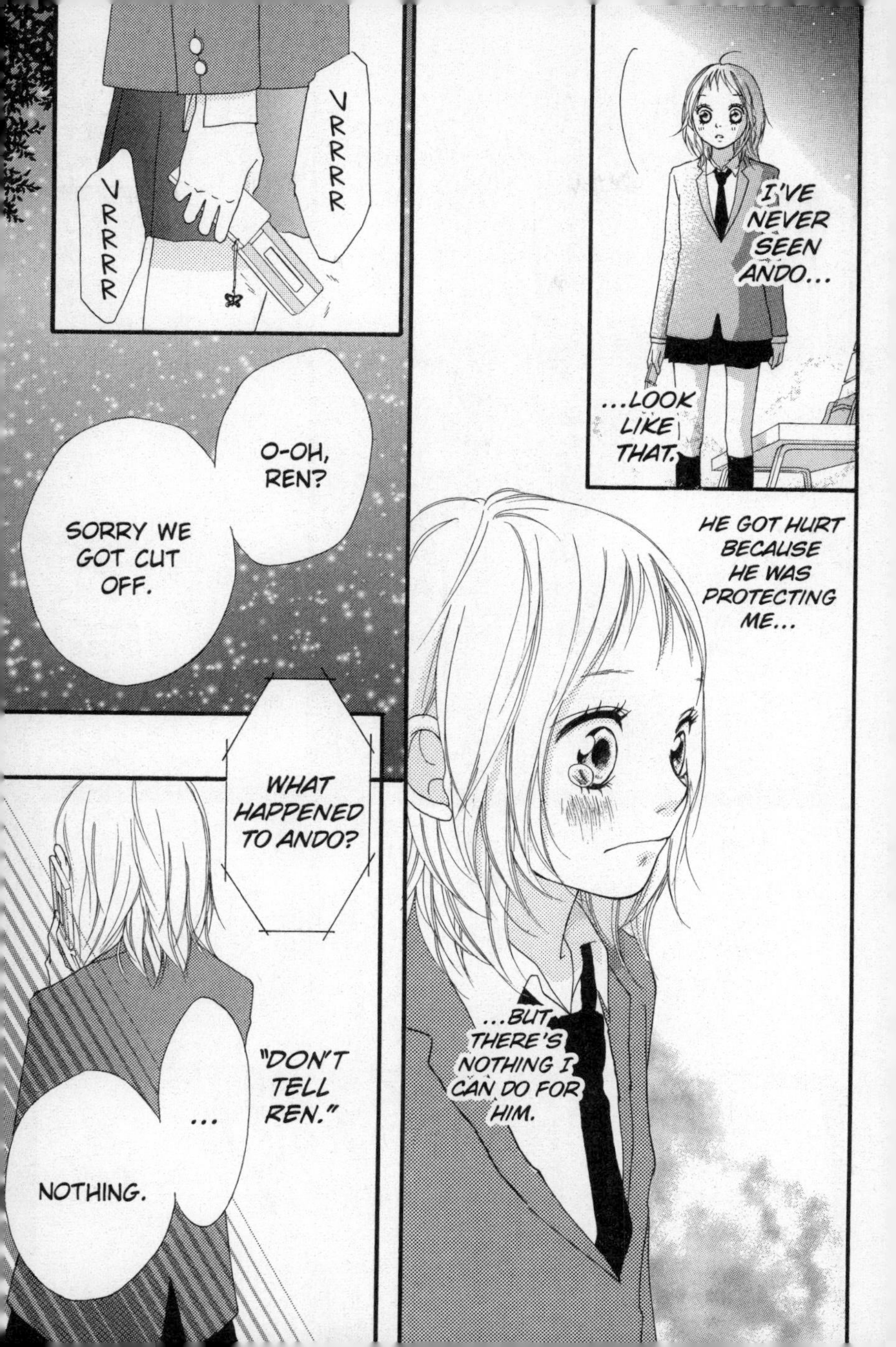

I'VE NEVER SEEN ANDO...
...LOOK LIKE THAT.
VRRRR
VRRRR
O-OH, REN?
SORRY WE GOT CUT OFF.
HE GOT HURT BECAUSE HE WAS PROTECTING ME...
WHAT HAPPENED TO ANDO?
"DON'T TELL REN."
...
NOTHING.
...BUT THERE'S NOTHING I CAN DO FOR HIM.

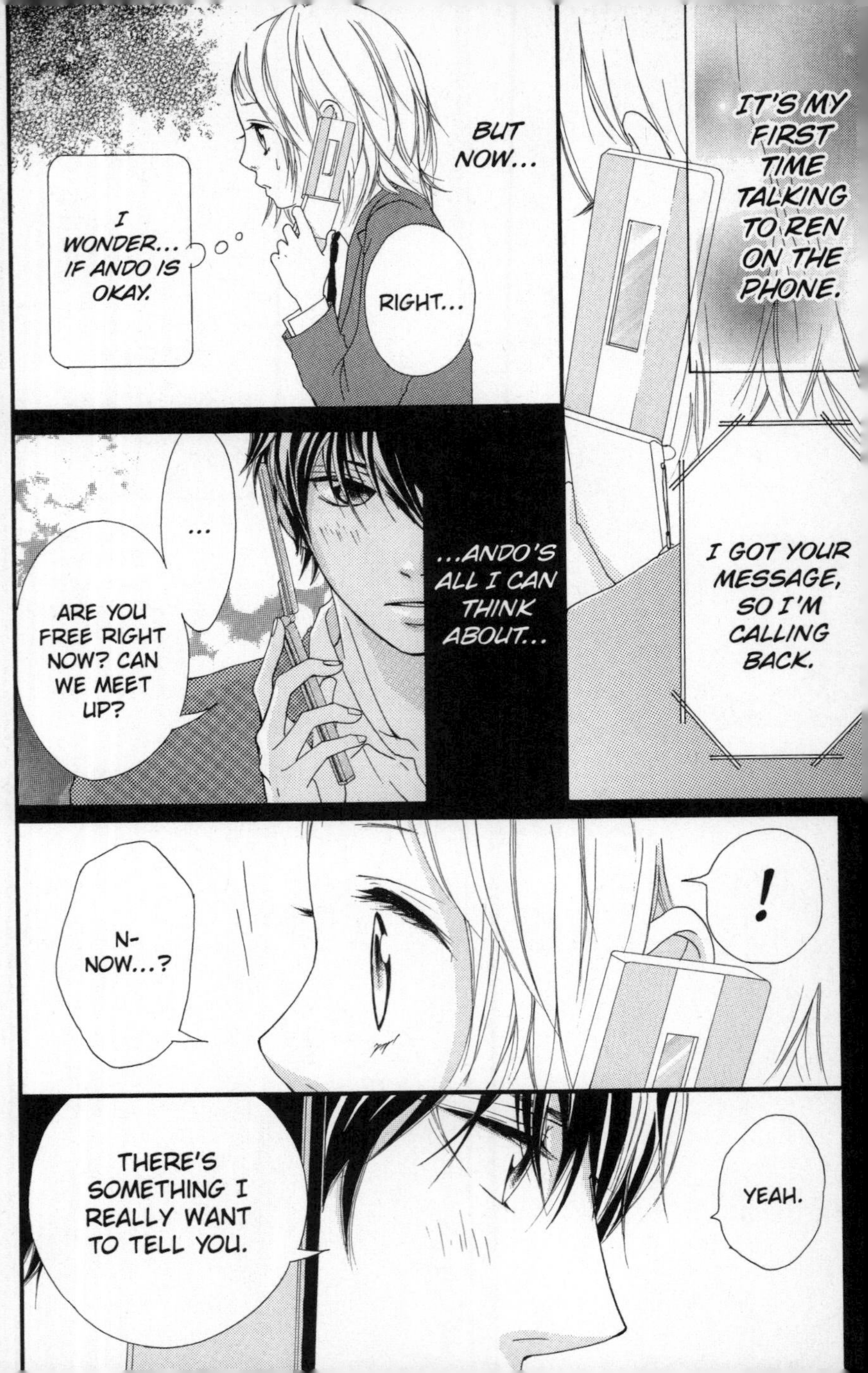
IT'S MY FIRST TIME TALKING TO REN ON THE PHONE.
I GOT YOUR MESSAGE, SO I'M CALLING BACK.
BUT NOW...
RIGHT...
I WONDER... IF ANDO IS OKAY.
...ANDO'S ALL I CAN THINK ABOUT...
...
ARE YOU FREE RIGHT NOW? CAN WE MEET UP?
!
N-NOW...?
YEAH.
THERE'S SOMETHING I REALLY WANT TO TELL YOU.

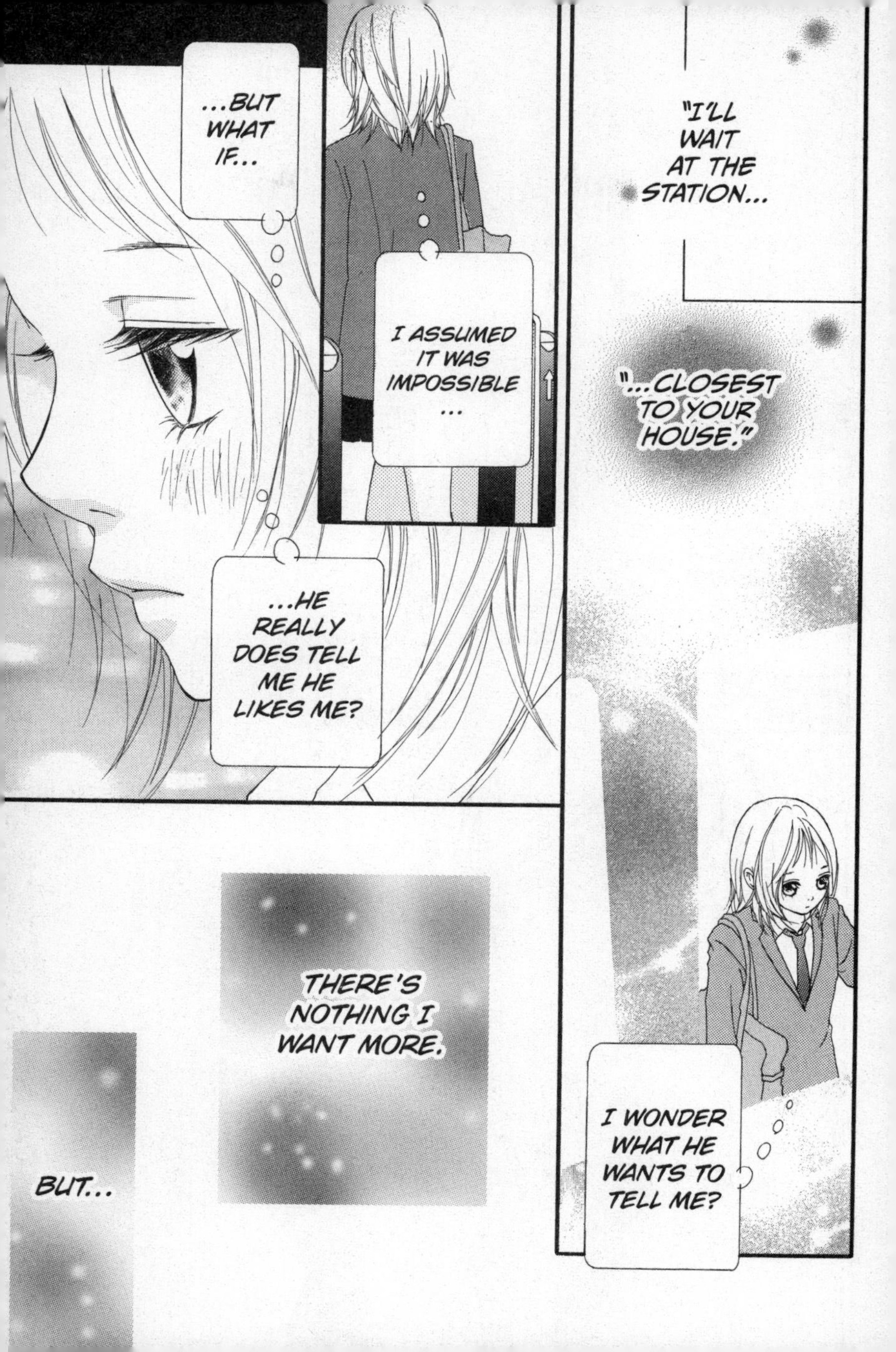
"I'LL WAIT AT THE STATION...
"...CLOSEST TO YOUR HOUSE."
I WONDER WHAT HE WANTS TO TELL ME?
I ASSUMED IT WAS IMPOSSIBLE...
...BUT WHAT IF...
...HE REALLY DOES TELL ME HE LIKES ME?
THERE'S NOTHING I WANT MORE.
BUT...

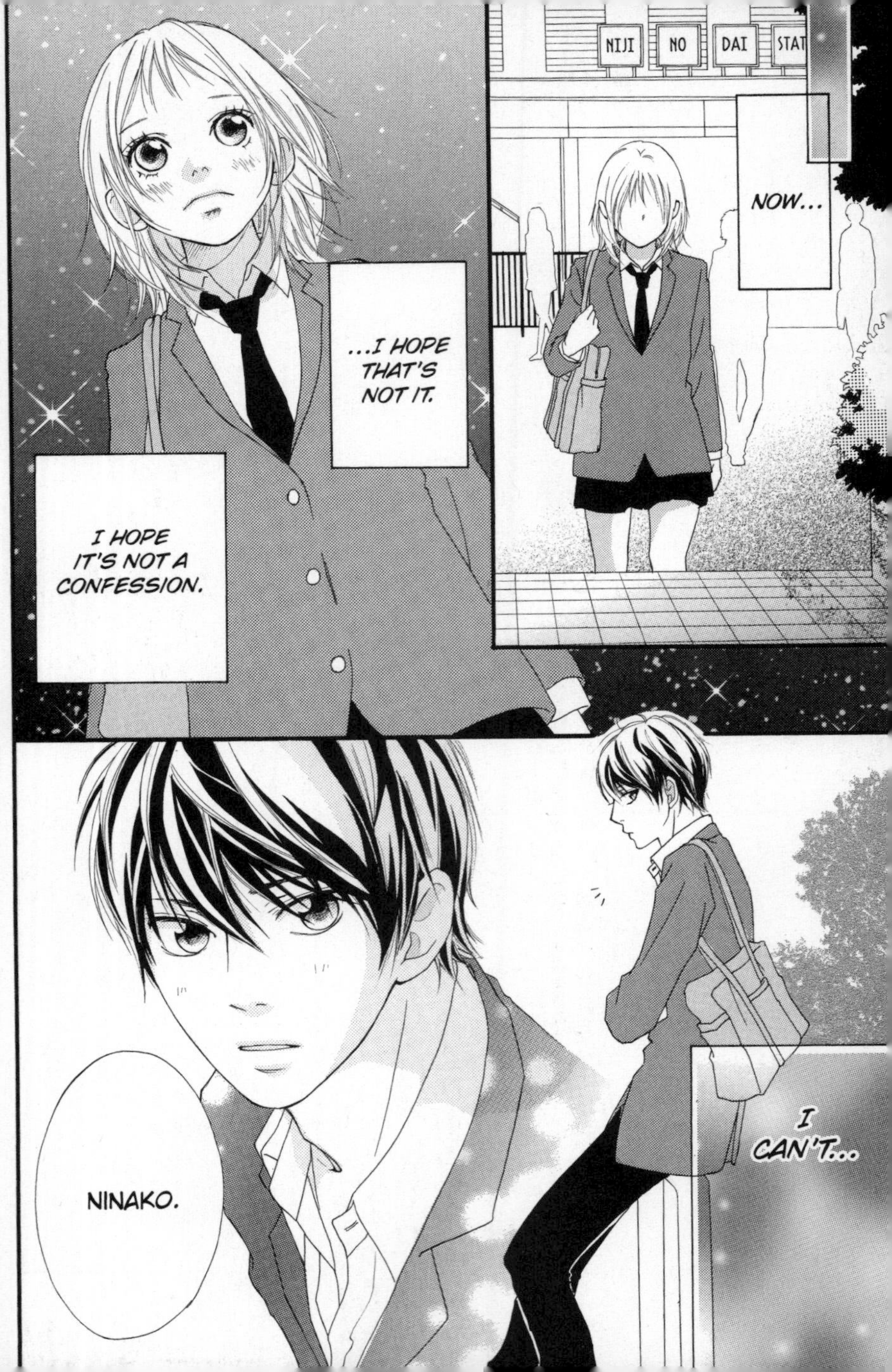
NIJI NO DAI STAT
NOW...
...I HOPE THAT'S NOT IT.
I HOPE IT'S NOT A CONFESSION.
I CAN'T...
NINAKO.

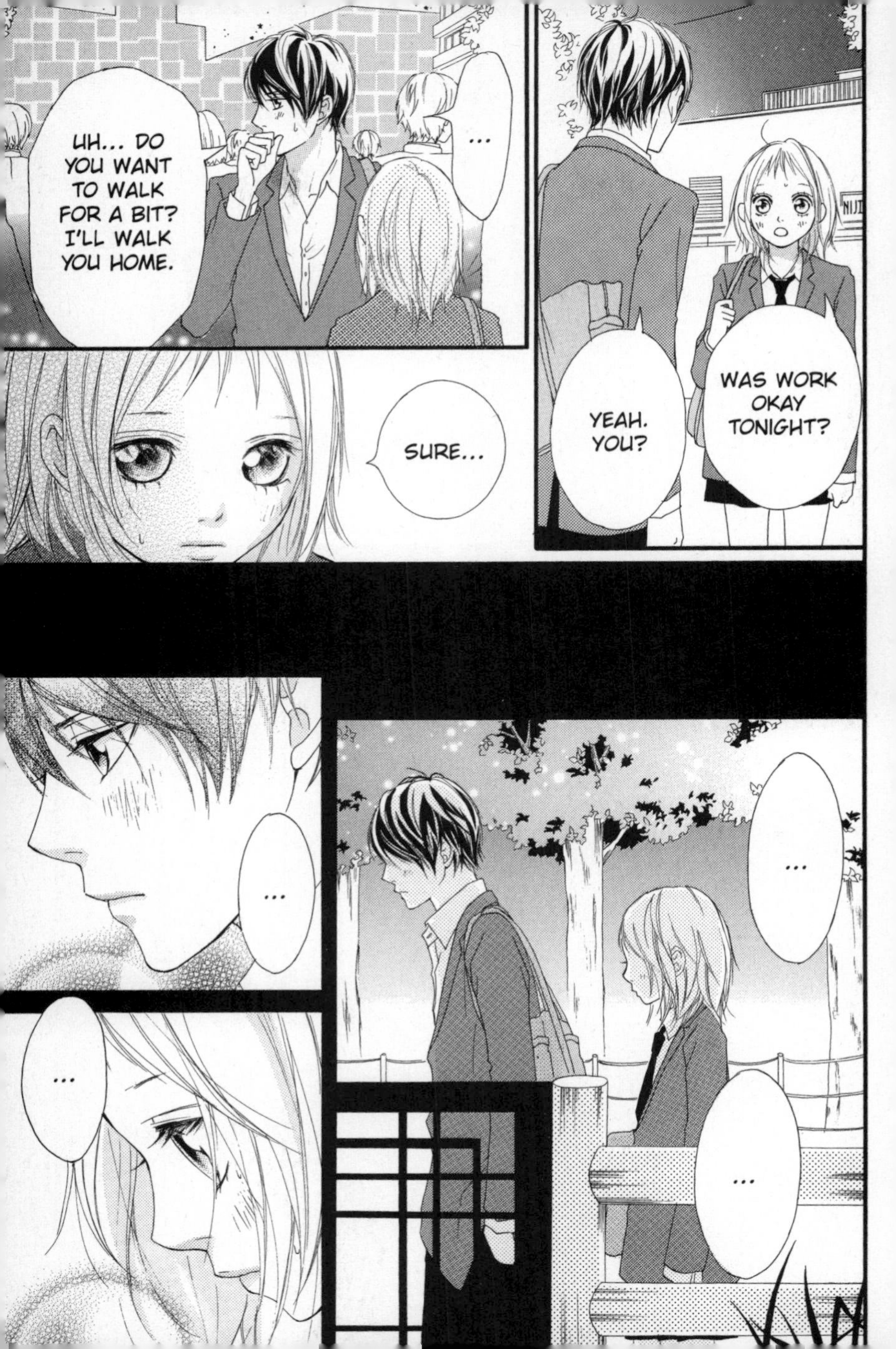
WAS WORK OKAY TONIGHT?
YEAH. YOU?
...
UH... DO YOU WANT TO WALK FOR A BIT? I'LL WALK YOU HOME.
SURE...
...
...
...
...

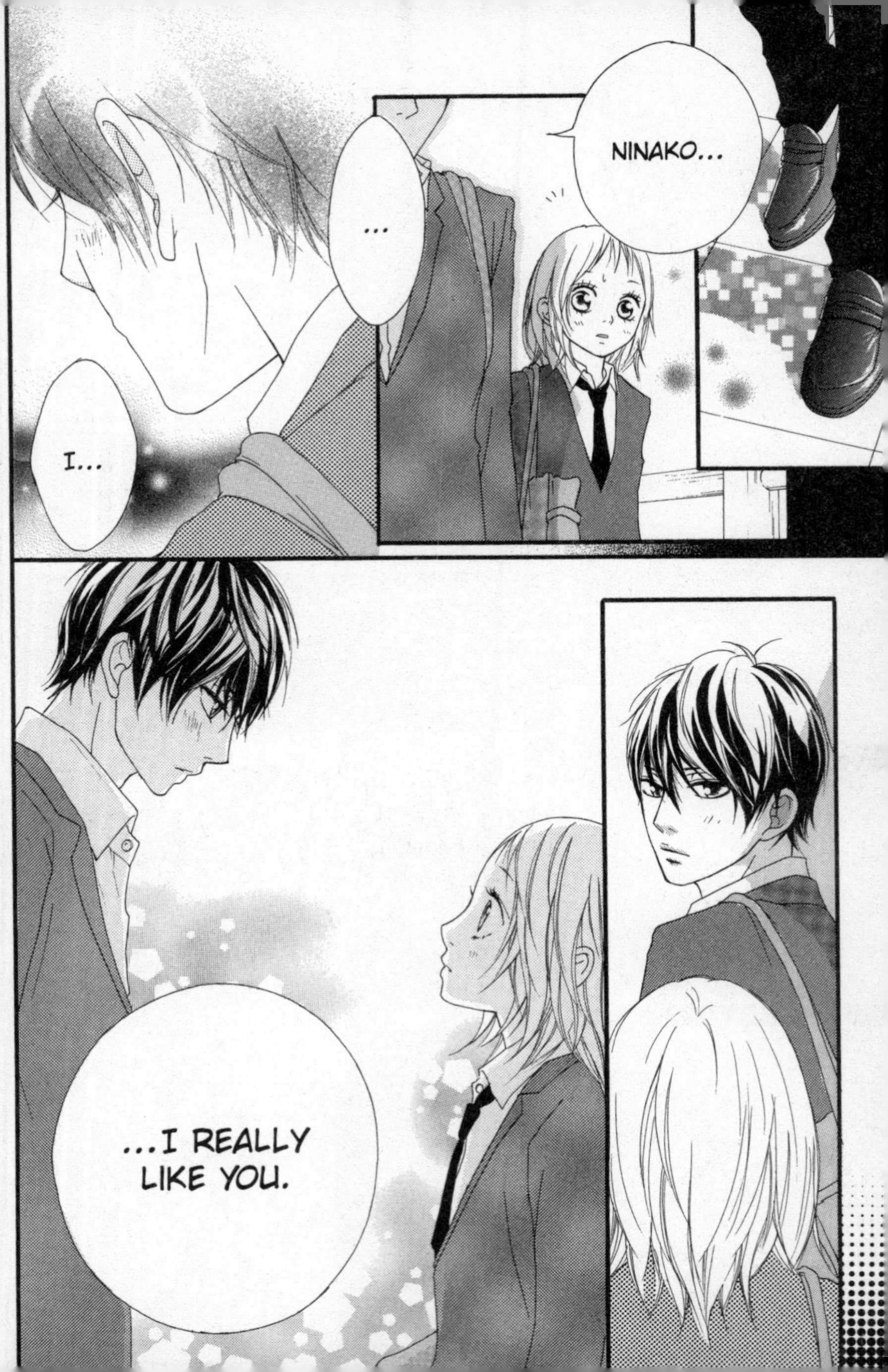
NINAKO...
...
I...
...I REALLY LIKE YOU.

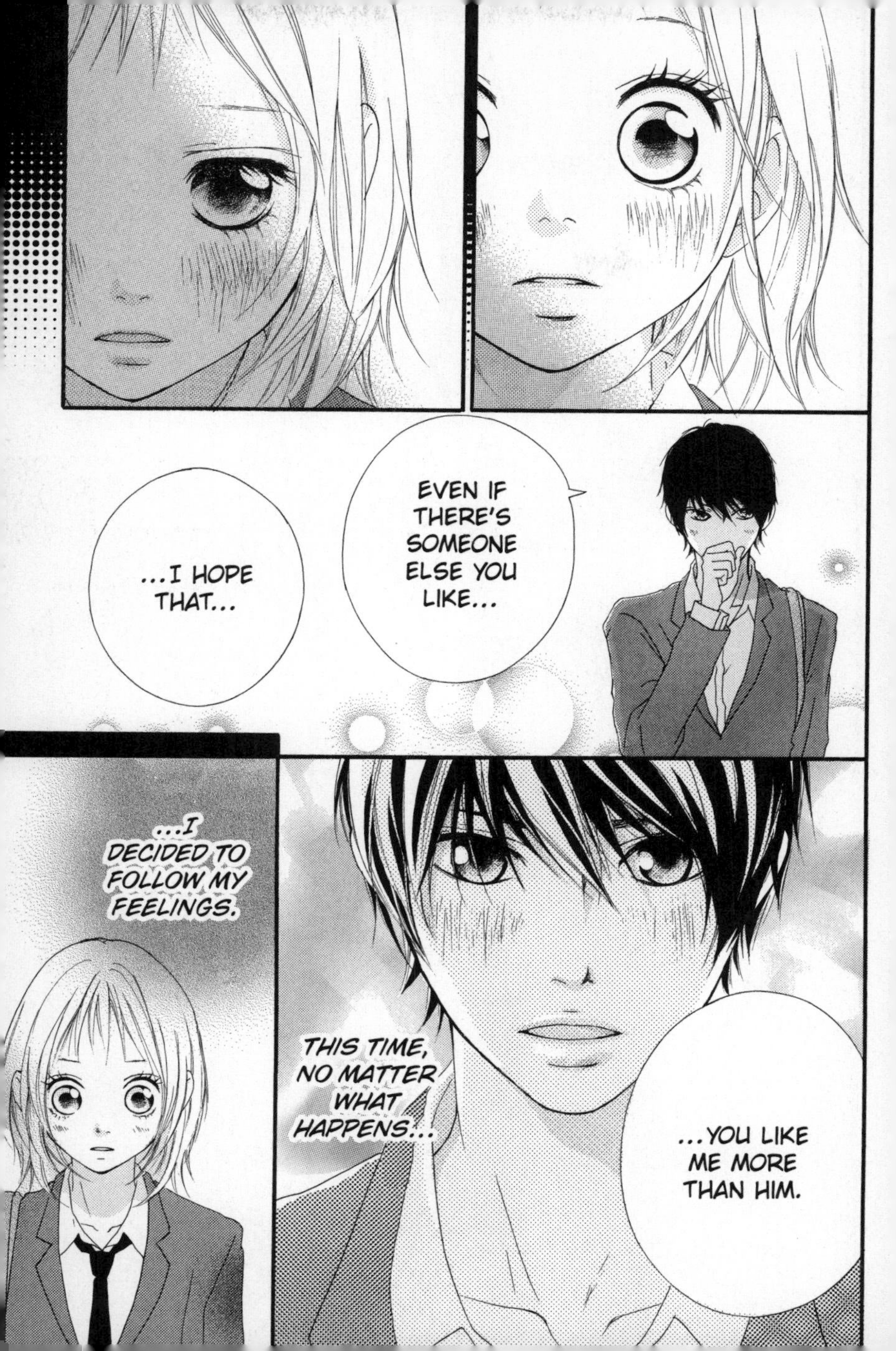
EVEN IF THERE'S SOMEONE ELSE YOU LIKE...
...I HOPE THAT...
...YOU LIKE ME MORE THAN HIM.
THIS TIME, NO MATTER WHAT HAPPENS...
...I DECIDED TO FOLLOW MY FEELINGS.

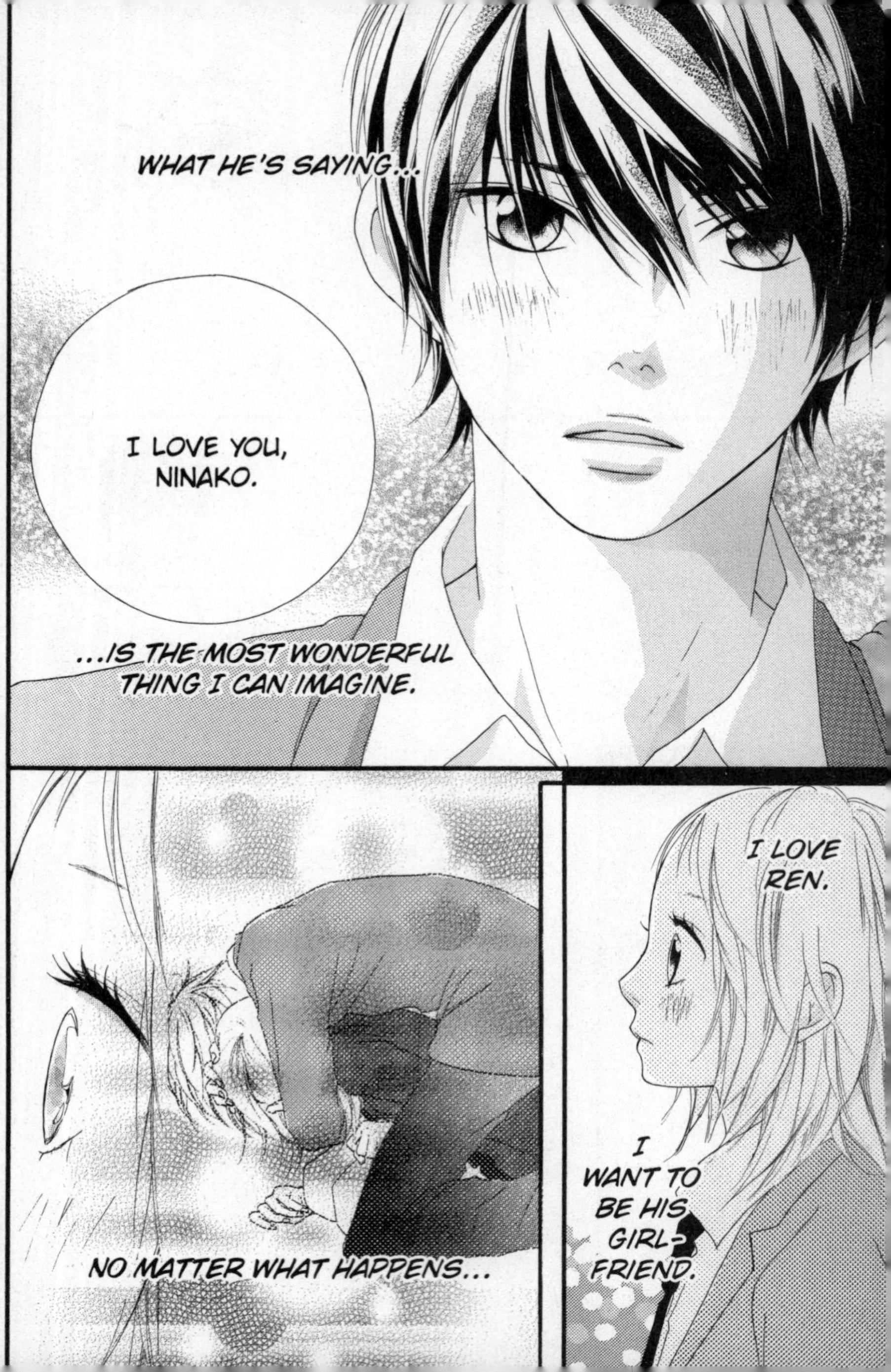
WHAT HE'S SAYING...
I LOVE YOU, NINAKO.
...IS THE MOST WONDERFUL THING I CAN IMAGINE.
I LOVE REN.
I WANT TO BE HIS GIRL-FRIEND.
NO MATTER WHAT HAPPENS...

...I'M GOING TO CHERISH THE VOICE IN MY HEART.

I'M GIVING UP ON YOU, SO WE'RE OKAY, RIGHT?

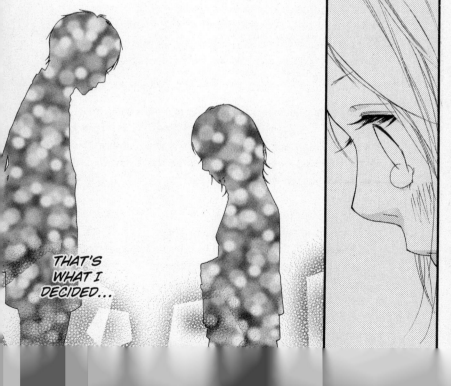

THAT'S WHAT I DECIDED...

Writing a love story about high school students makes me remember my own loves in junior and senior high. Of course, sometimes I'm looking back to remind myself of something for work, or maybe just to wallow in the memories.

But I've realized that there's never been a time in my life when I wasn't in love, after my first love in preschool. There's always someone.

There's no rhyme or reason to the type of guys I fall for, or the situations in which it happens. I don't force it—it just happens! If I had a dream about some guy, I'd abruptly fall head over heels for him (even though I didn't have any feelings for him before that). Don't do what I did.

At my age, though, I seem to have outgrown my instantaneous loves. There was a period of time when I didn't like that trait about myself, because it seemed like I'd fall for anyone, but then I looked on the bright side! I decided it could mean that writing romantic manga for girls was the perfect job for me.

I've had so many experiences with being in love, but I never use them directly in my work. (Instead, I overhaul them so I look at them objectively.) But I still think it's helped a lot as I've developed my stories, so I'll keep on using embarrassing events from my life as manga fodder. And I look forward to your support in the future!

 Io Sakisaka

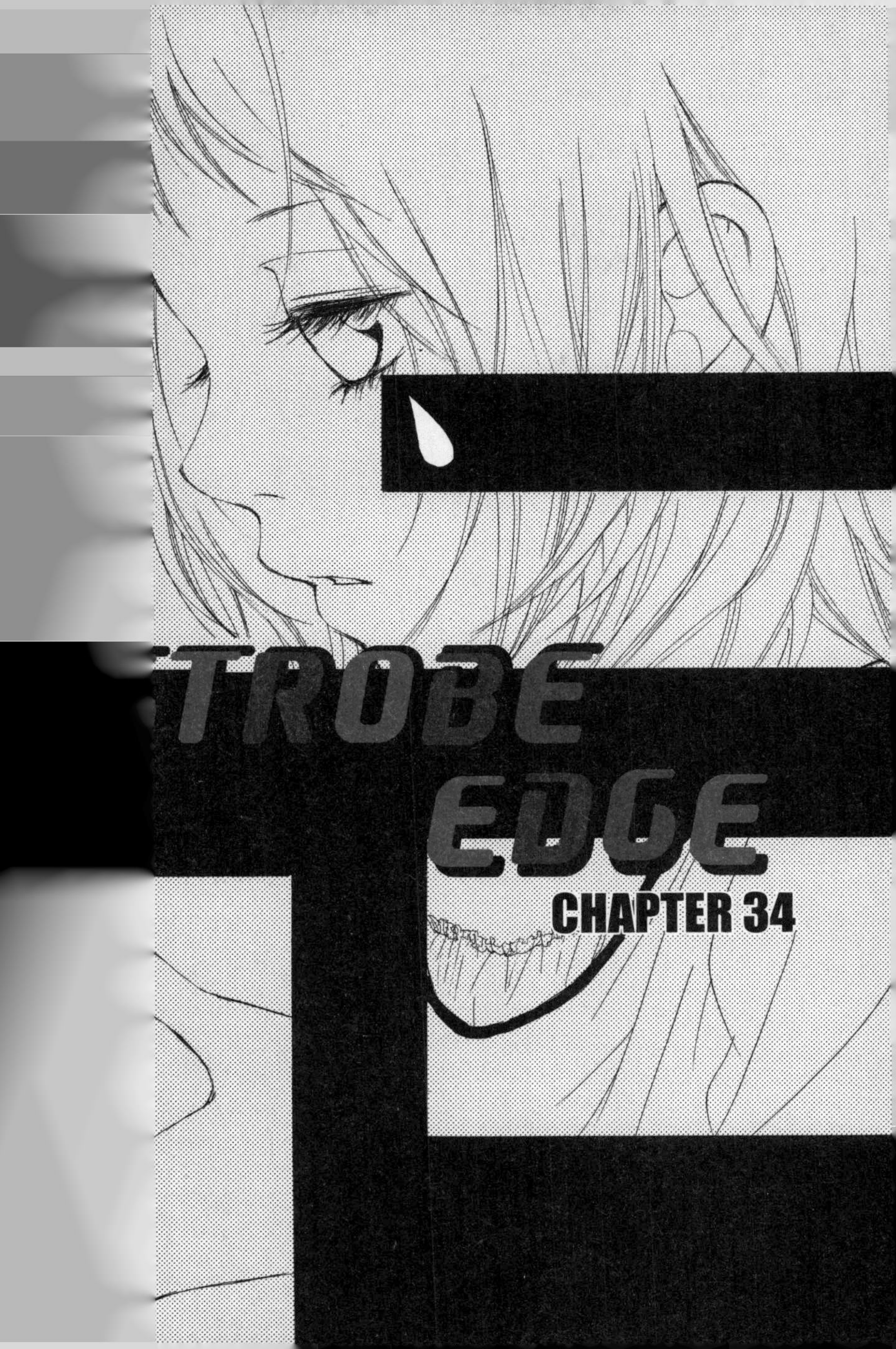
STROBE EDGE
CHAPTER 34

MAYBE THEY'RE OFF SOME- WHERE...

...NINAKO'S CELL PHONE.

REN CALLED...

...TELLING EACH OTHER HOW THEY FEEL...

...AND FINDING OUT IT'S MUTUAL.

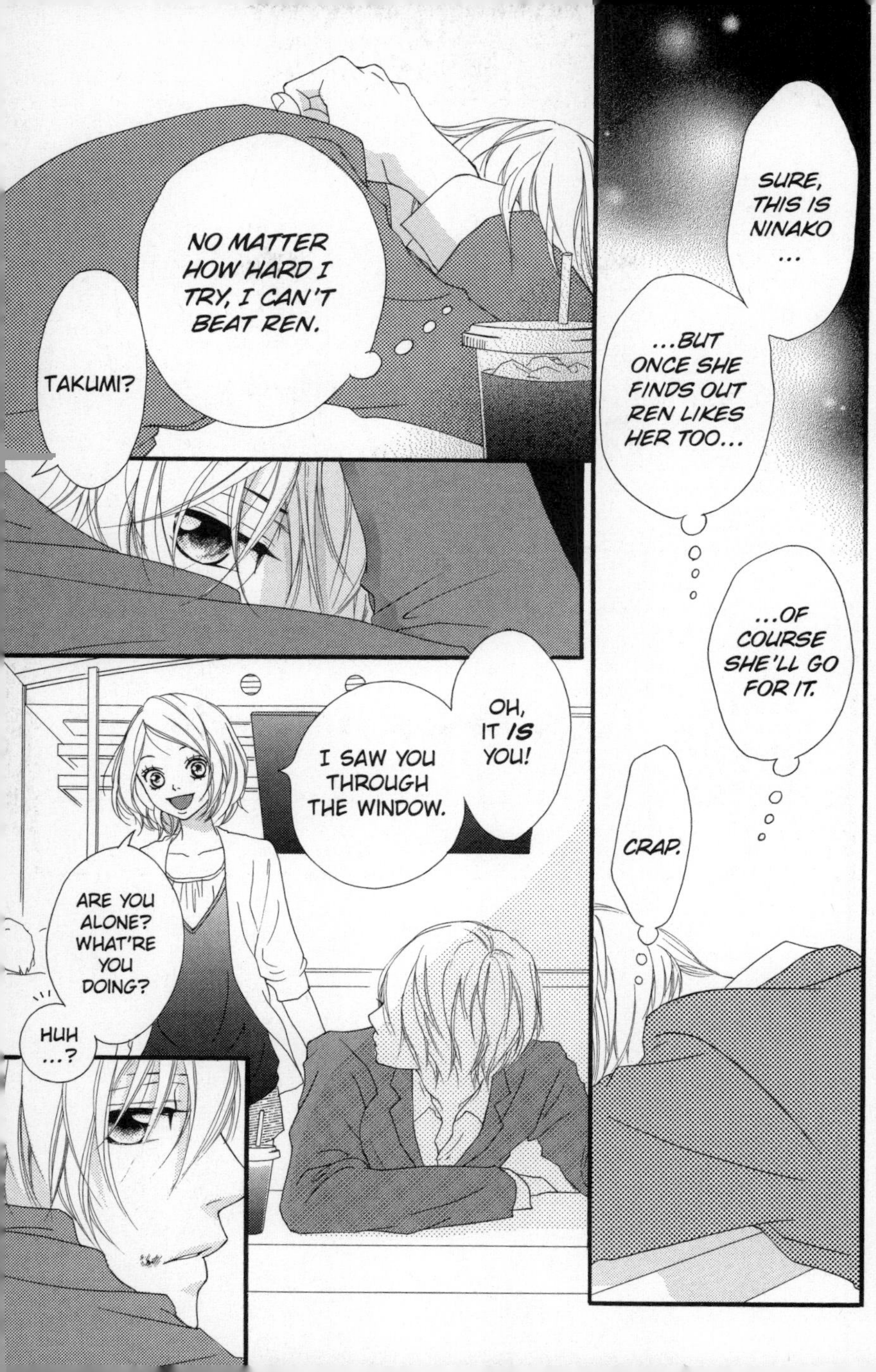
SURE, THIS IS NINAKO ...
...BUT ONCE SHE FINDS OUT REN LIKES HER TOO...
...OF COURSE SHE'LL GO FOR IT.
CRAP.
NO MATTER HOW HARD I TRY, I CAN'T BEAT REN.
TAKUMI?
OH, IT *IS* YOU!
I SAW YOU THROUGH THE WINDOW.
ARE YOU ALONE? WHAT'RE YOU DOING?
HUH ...?

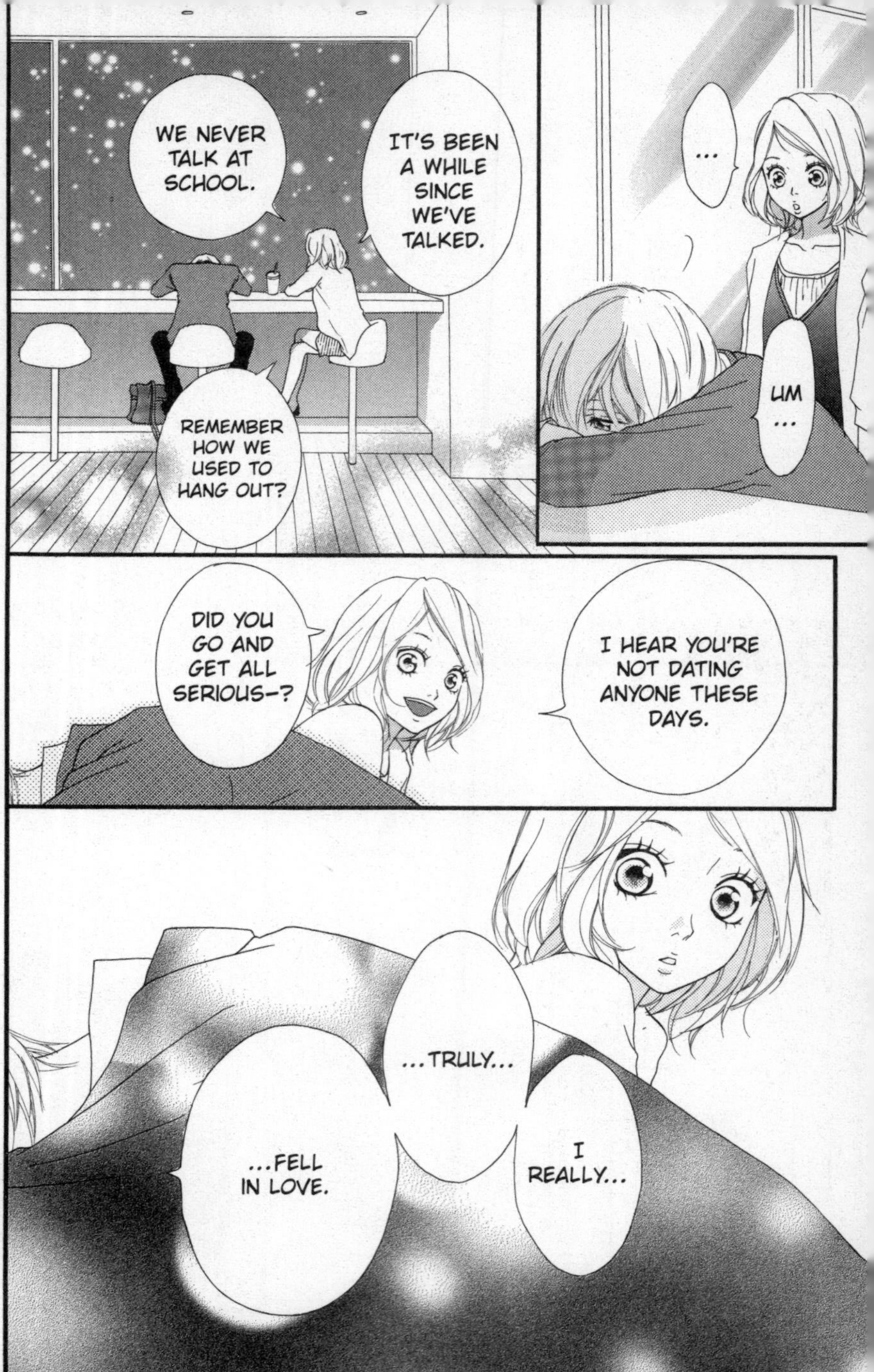
...
UM ...
IT'S BEEN A WHILE SINCE WE'VE TALKED.
WE NEVER TALK AT SCHOOL.
REMEMBER HOW WE USED TO HANG OUT?
I HEAR YOU'RE NOT DATING ANYONE THESE DAYS.
DID YOU GO AND GET ALL SERIOUS-?
I REALLY...
...TRULY...
...FELL IN LOVE.

I WAS GETTING READY TO TELL HER HOW I FELT, ONE LAST TIME.

...AND I GOT THE CRAP BEATEN OUT OF ME.

By some thugs.

REALLY? You?

OH...

THAT'S TERRI-BLE.

OHHH...

I WAS JUST WITH HER...

THEY'RE PROBABLY FIGURING THAT OUT RIGHT ABOUT NOW.

LISTENING TO THIS IS JUST PAINFUL.

...

I PUSHED AS HARD AS I COULD, BUT IT DIDN'T WORK.

SHE LIKES MY FRIEND...

...AND HE LIKES HER TOO.

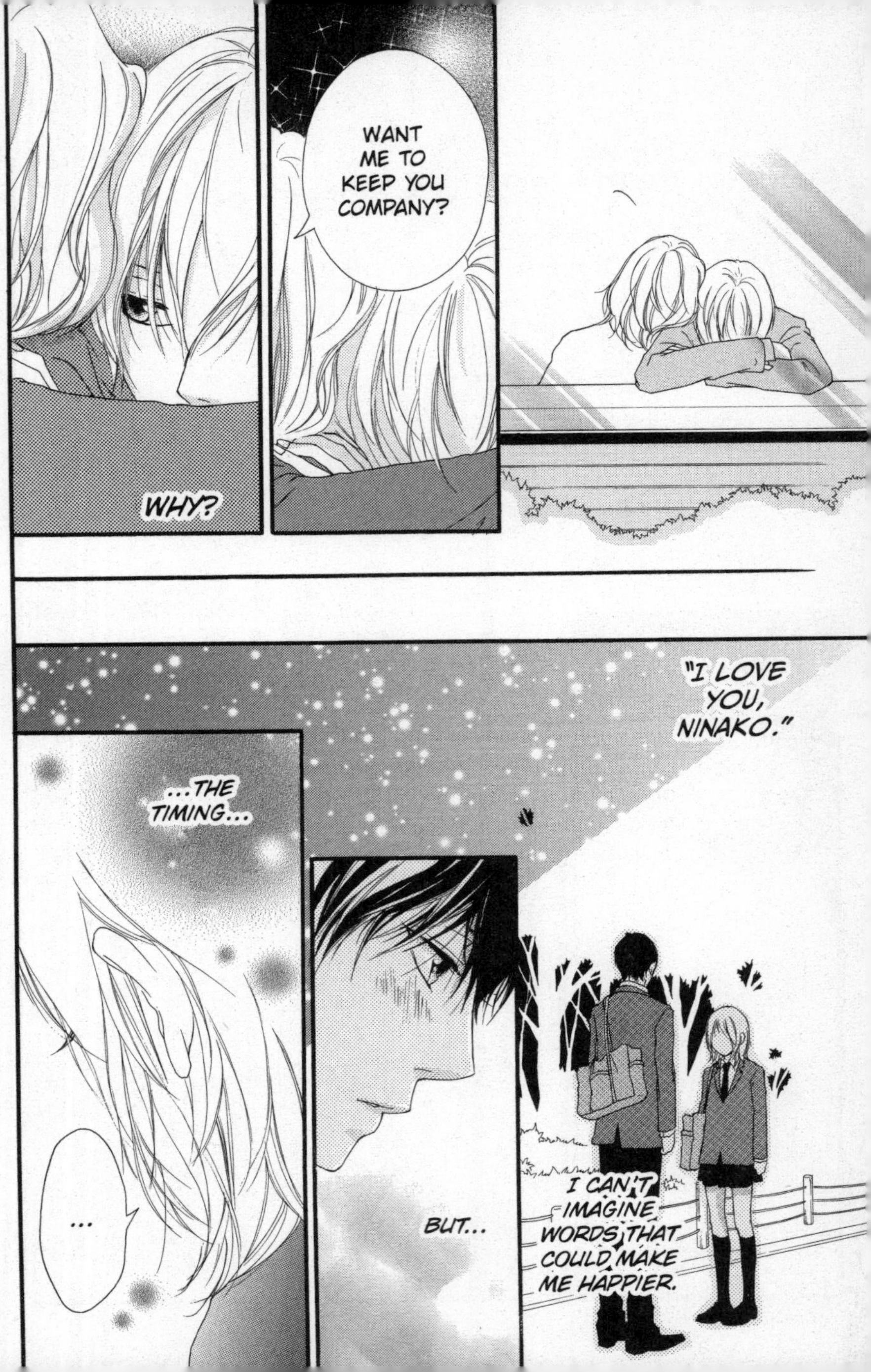
WANT ME TO KEEP YOU COMPANY?
WHY?
"I LOVE YOU, NINAKO."
I CAN'T IMAGINE WORDS THAT COULD MAKE ME HAPPIER.
BUT...
...THE TIMING...
...

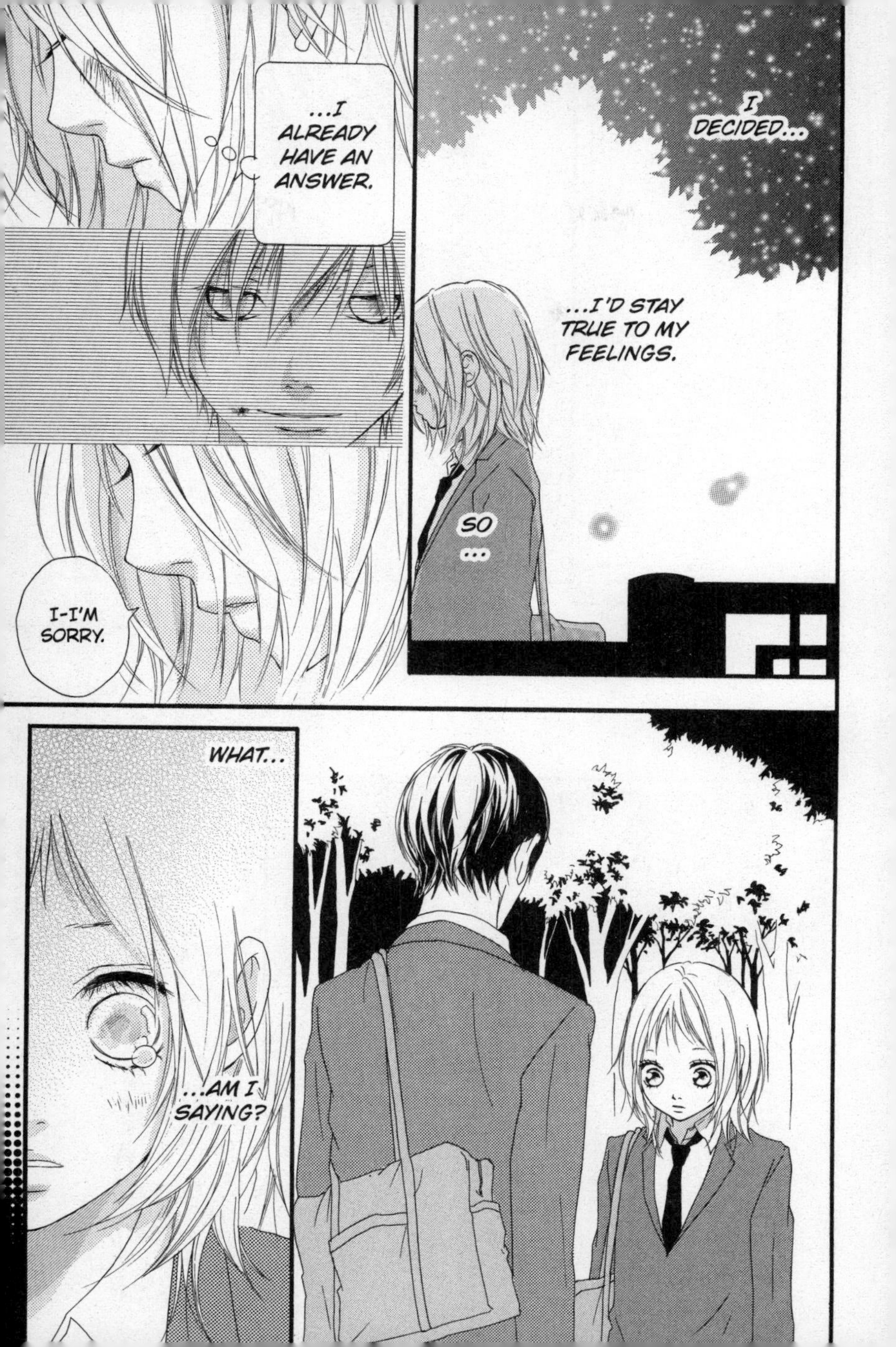
I DECIDED...
...I'D STAY TRUE TO MY FEELINGS.
SO ...
...I ALREADY HAVE AN ANSWER.
I-I'M SORRY.
WHAT...
...AM I SAYING?

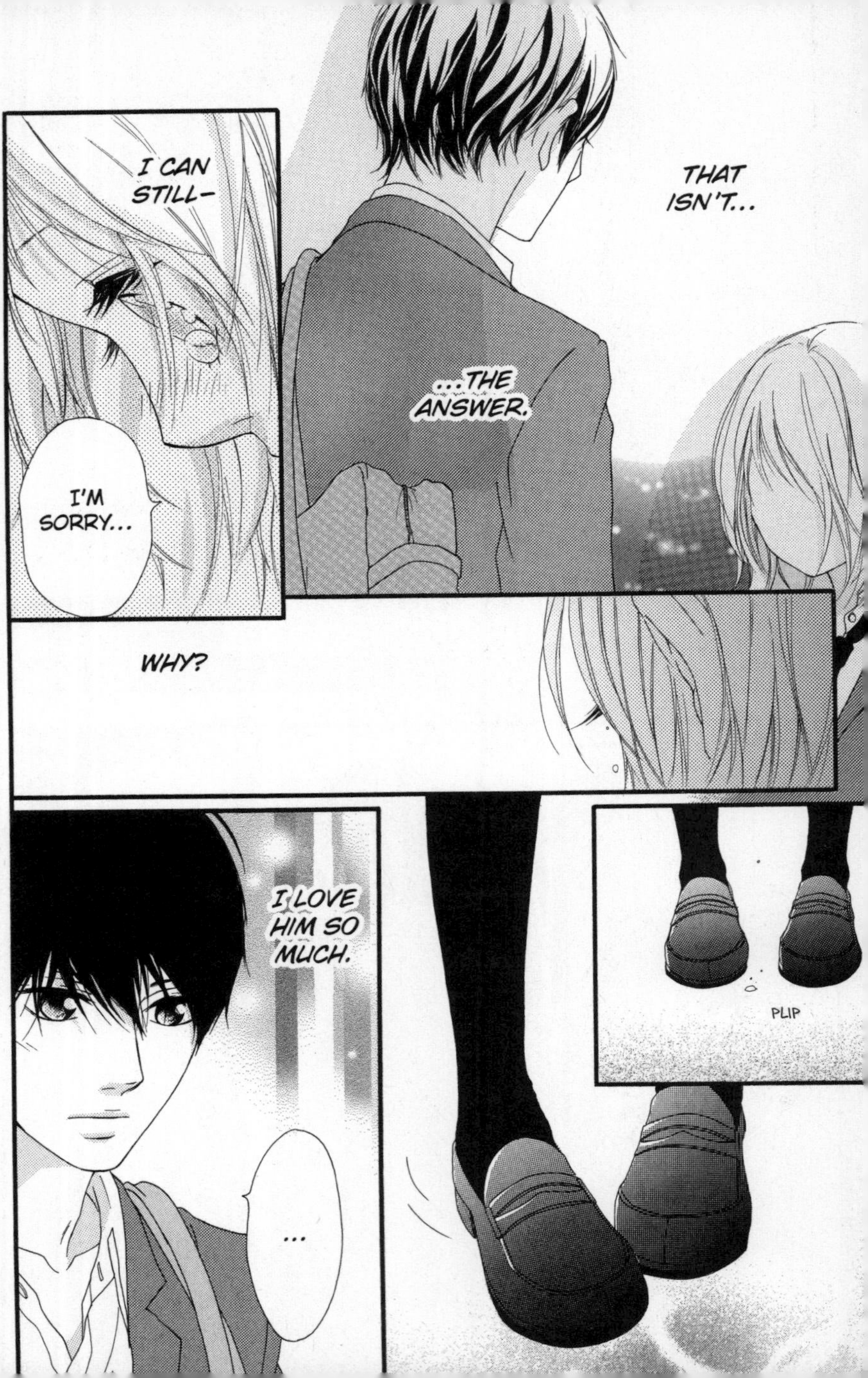
THAT ISN'T...
...THE ANSWER.
I CAN STILL-
I'M SORRY...
WHY?
PLIP
I LOVE HIM SO MUCH.
...

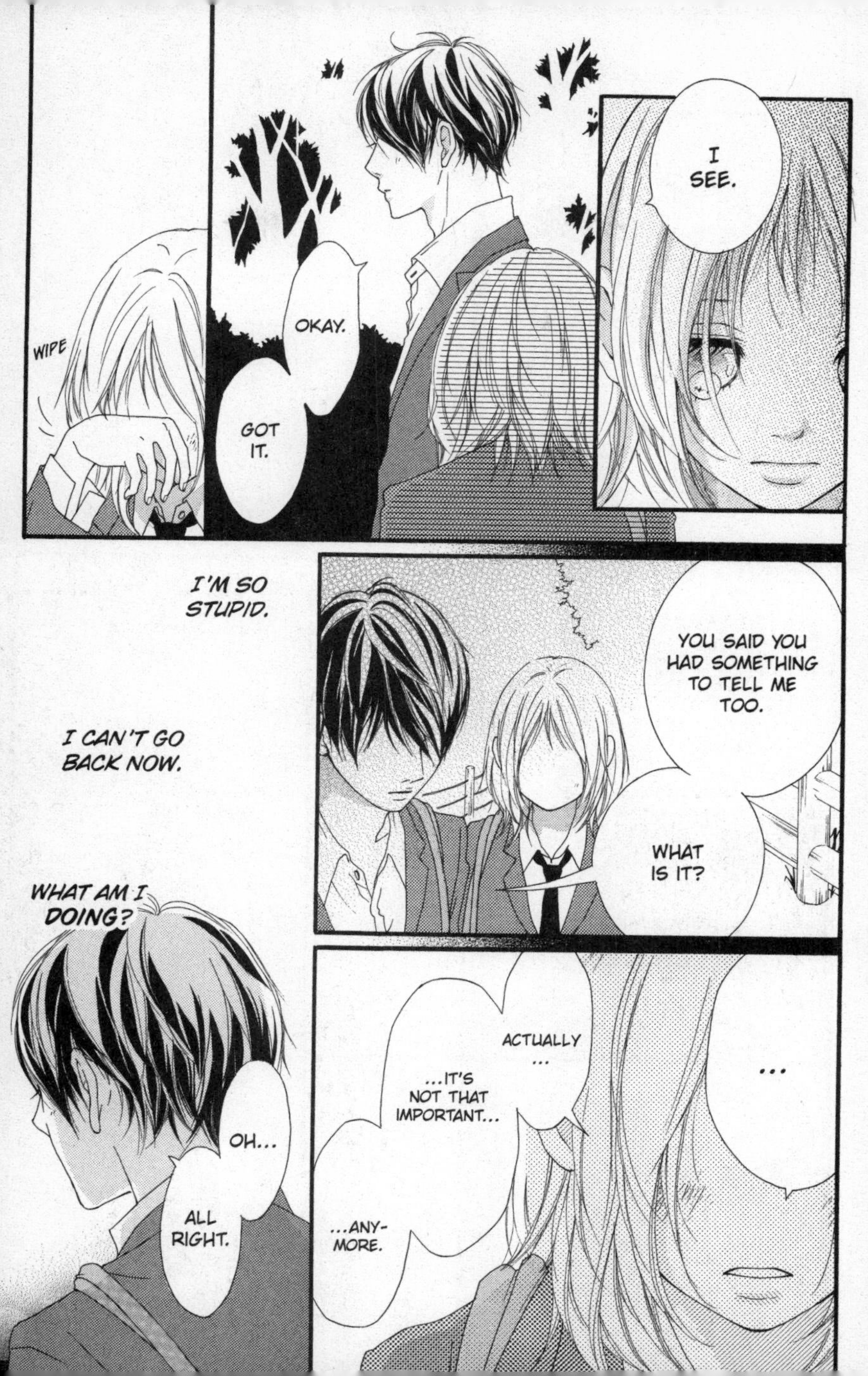
I SEE.
OKAY.
GOT IT.
WIPE
YOU SAID YOU HAD SOMETHING TO TELL ME TOO.
WHAT IS IT?
I'M SO STUPID.
I CAN'T GO BACK NOW.
...
ACTUALLY...
...IT'S NOT THAT IMPORTANT...
...ANY-MORE.
WHAT AM I DOING?
OH...
ALL RIGHT.

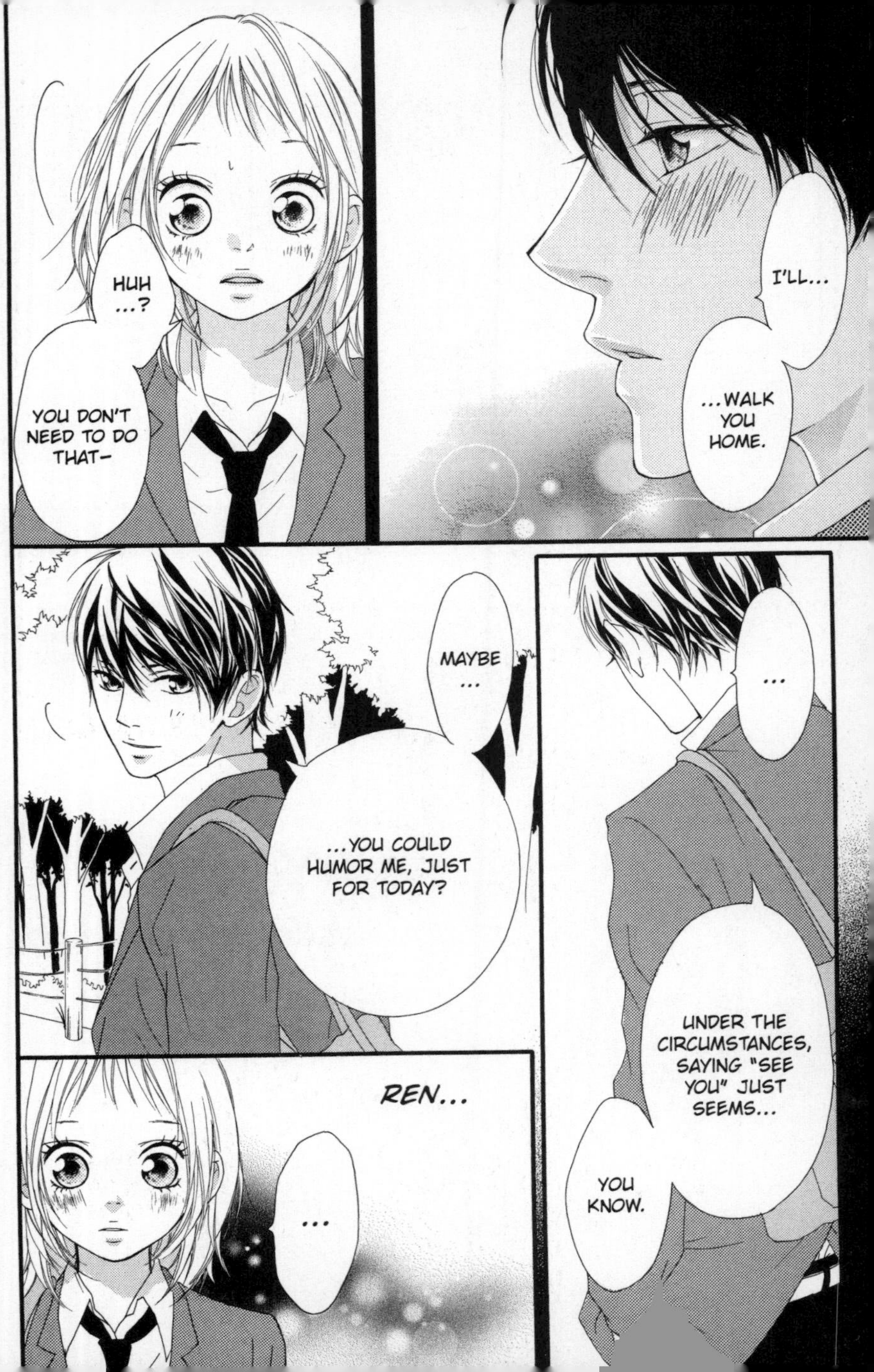
I'LL...
...WALK YOU HOME.
HUH ...?
YOU DON'T NEED TO DO THAT–
...
UNDER THE CIRCUMSTANCES, SAYING "SEE YOU" JUST SEEMS...
YOU KNOW.
MAYBE ...
...YOU COULD HUMOR ME, JUST FOR TODAY?
REN...
...

THE DISTANCE BETWEEN US...

THE SMALL TALK ON THE WAY HOME...

HOW QUICKLY WE WALKED...

WHAT AM I DOING?

WHAT AM I DOING?

ALL OF IT...

BYE, THEN.

...WAS REN BEING THOUGHTFUL.

HOW CAN I STILL TELL YOU I LOVE YOU?

BE MY GIRL-FRIEND.

BUT...

...AFTER SEEING ANDO LIKE THAT...

...I COULDN'T JUST TURN AROUND AND START DATING REN.

WHY DOES EVERY-THING...

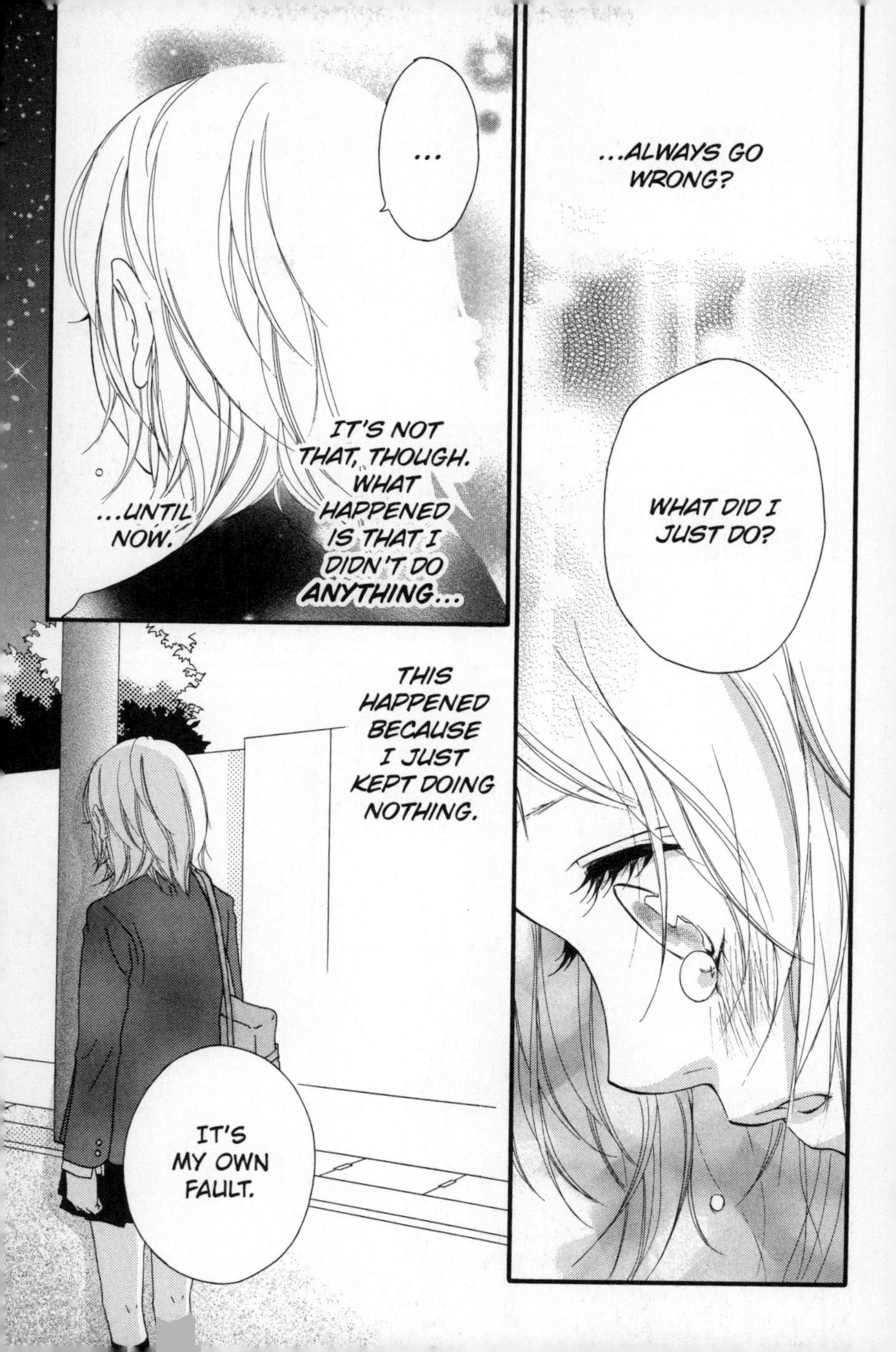
...ALWAYS GO WRONG?
WHAT DID I JUST DO?
...
IT'S NOT THAT, THOUGH. WHAT HAPPENED IS THAT I DIDN'T DO ANYTHING...
...UNTIL NOW.
THIS HAPPENED BECAUSE I JUST KEPT DOING NOTHING.
IT'S MY OWN FAULT.

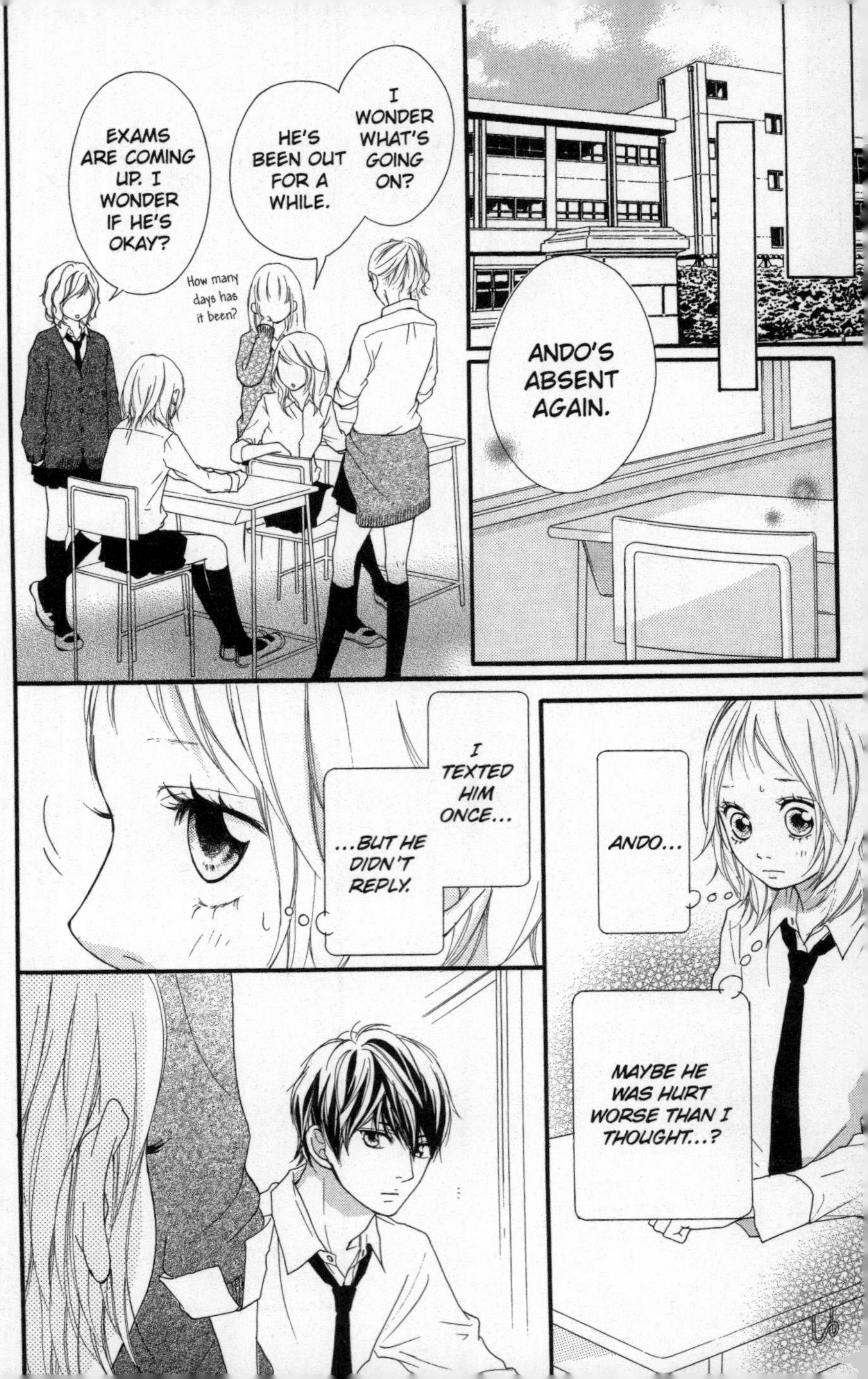

ANDO'S ABSENT AGAIN.
I WONDER WHAT'S GOING ON?
HE'S BEEN OUT FOR A WHILE.
How many days has it been?
EXAMS ARE COMING UP. I WONDER IF HE'S OKAY?
ANDO...
I TEXTED HIM ONCE...
...BUT HE DIDN'T REPLY.
MAYBE HE WAS HURT WORSE THAN I THOUGHT...?

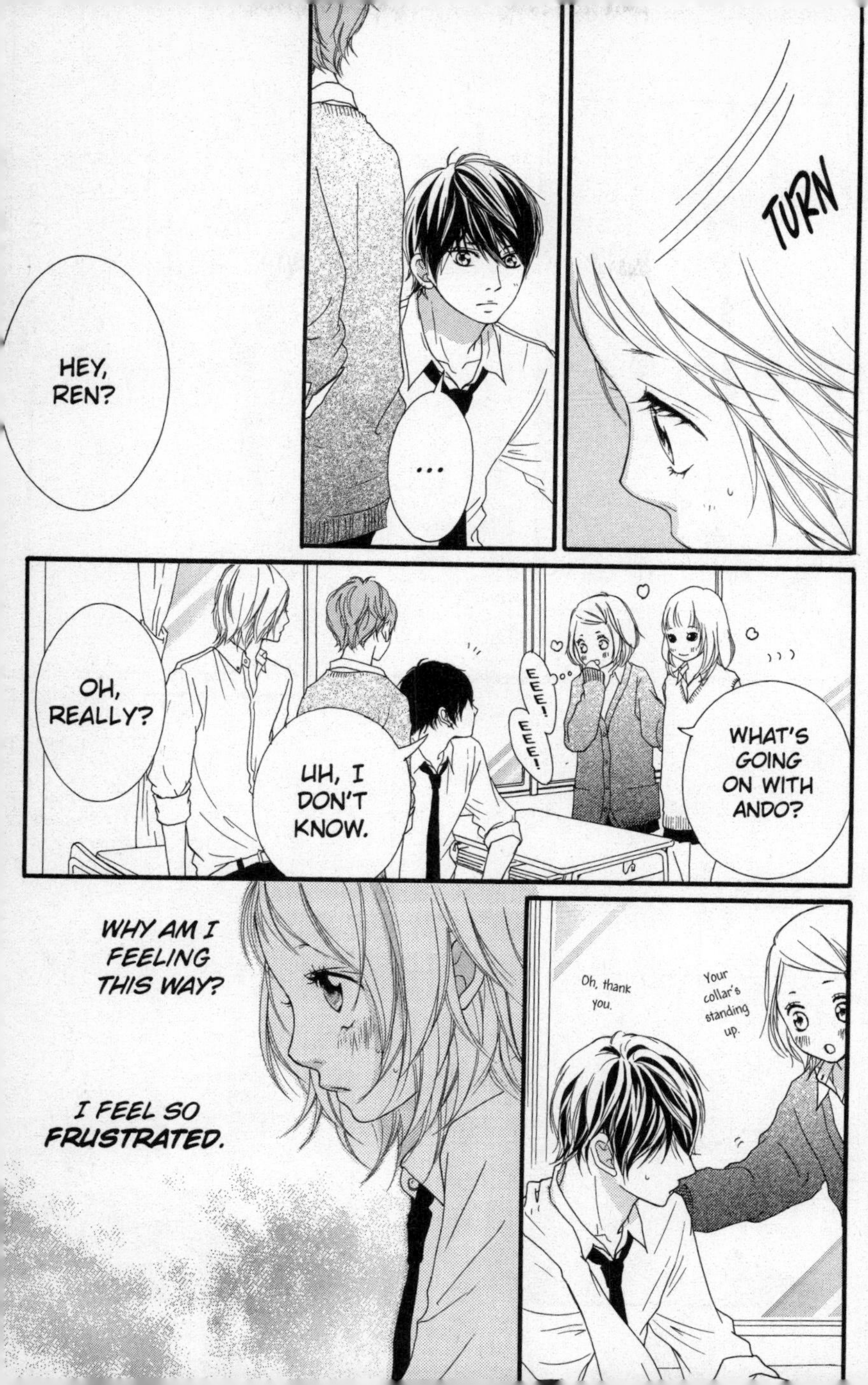

TURN
...
HEY, REN?
WHAT'S GOING ON WITH ANDO?
EEE! EEE! EEE!
UH, I DON'T KNOW.
OH, REALLY?
Your collar's standing up.
Oh, thank you.
WHY AM I FEELING THIS WAY?
I FEEL SO FRUSTRATED.

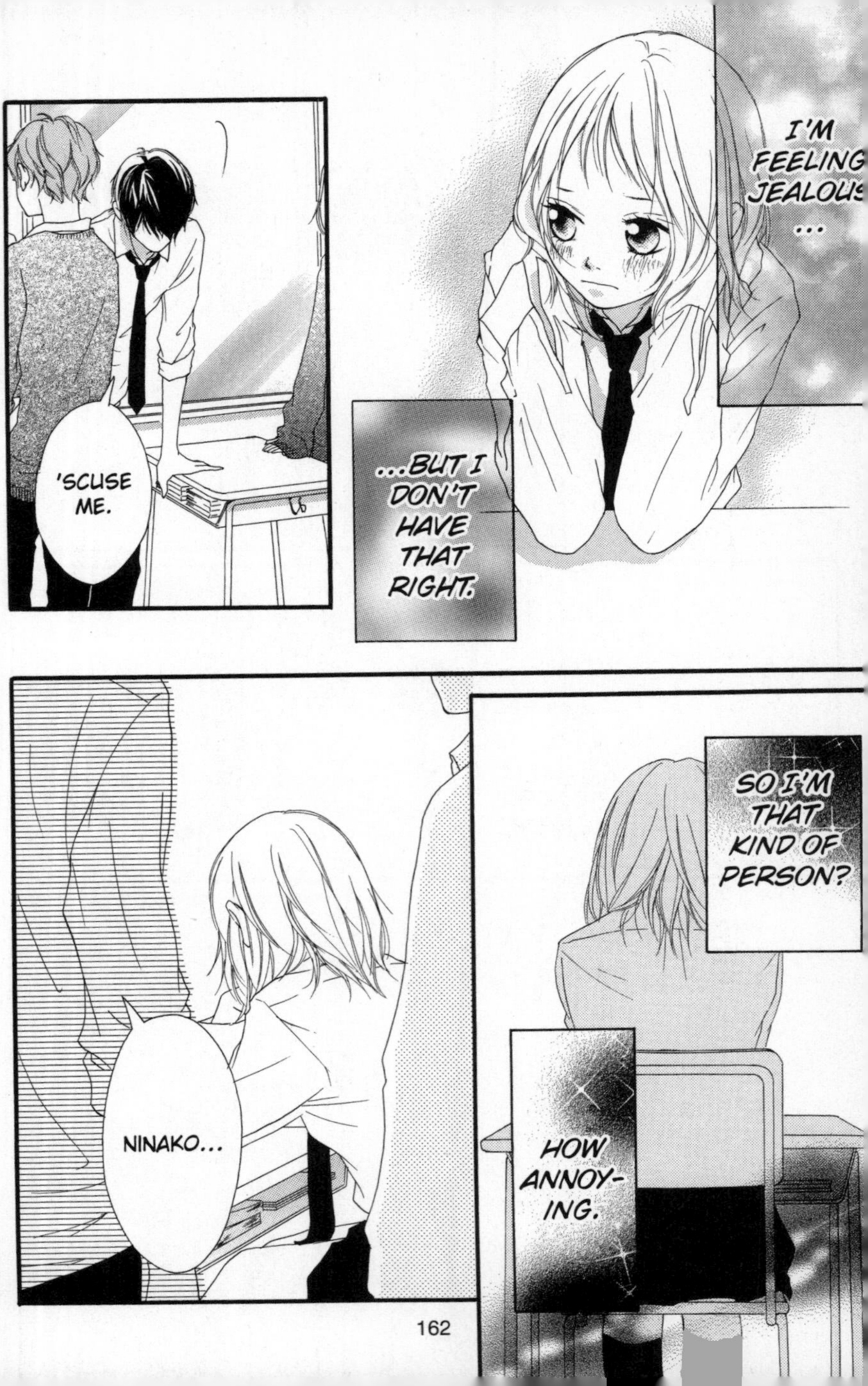
I'M FEELING JEALOUS...
...BUT I DON'T HAVE THAT RIGHT.
'SCUSE ME.
SO I'M THAT KIND OF PERSON?
HOW ANNOY-ING.
NINAKO...

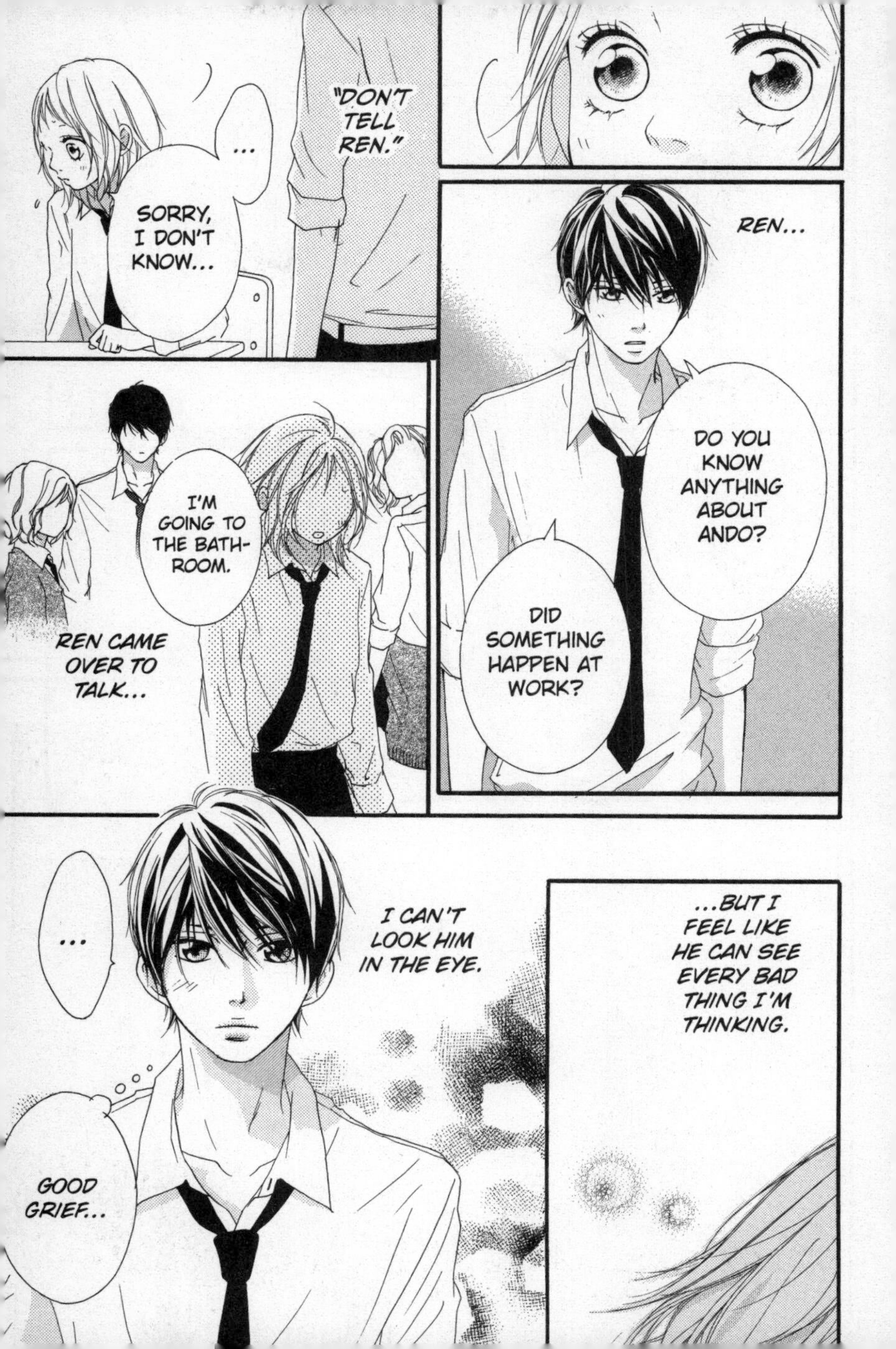
"DON'T TELL REN."
...
SORRY, I DON'T KNOW...
REN...
DO YOU KNOW ANYTHING ABOUT ANDO?
DID SOMETHING HAPPEN AT WORK?
I'M GOING TO THE BATHROOM.
REN CAME OVER TO TALK...
I CAN'T LOOK HIM IN THE EYE.
...BUT I FEEL LIKE HE CAN SEE EVERY BAD THING I'M THINKING.
...
GOOD GRIEF...

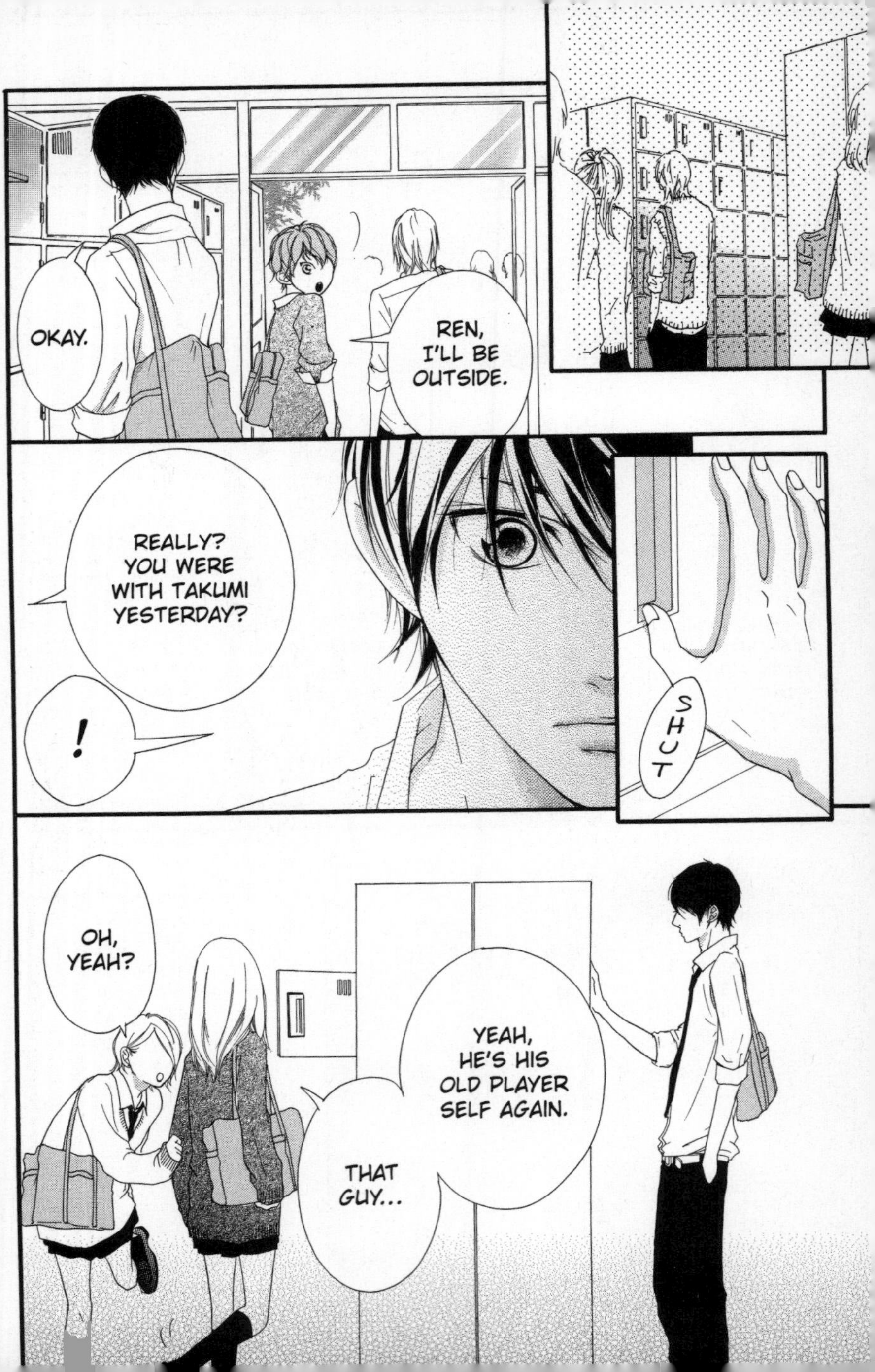
REN, I'LL BE OUTSIDE.
OKAY.
SHUT
REALLY? YOU WERE WITH TAKUMI YESTERDAY?
!
YEAH, HE'S HIS OLD PLAYER SELF AGAIN.
THAT GUY...
OH, YEAH?

★ A mini preview of the ★
next volume!

One thing a lot of you have been asking for is a bonus story about Manabu. Actually, his story was published a while ago in the magazine, but due to publishing constraints, it's been pushed to the next graphic novel volume. So to all the Manabu fans—hang in there! I'll be so happy if you look forward to the next volume!

The angels who helped me out with this manuscript are:

Hanemi Ayase, Runchi Koyama, Satomi Sera, Emi Fujino, Natsumi Kaisaki, Chidan Mizuguchi

Thank you for always helping me!

Saki

It was meant to be a heart, but it looks more like an unagi pie.

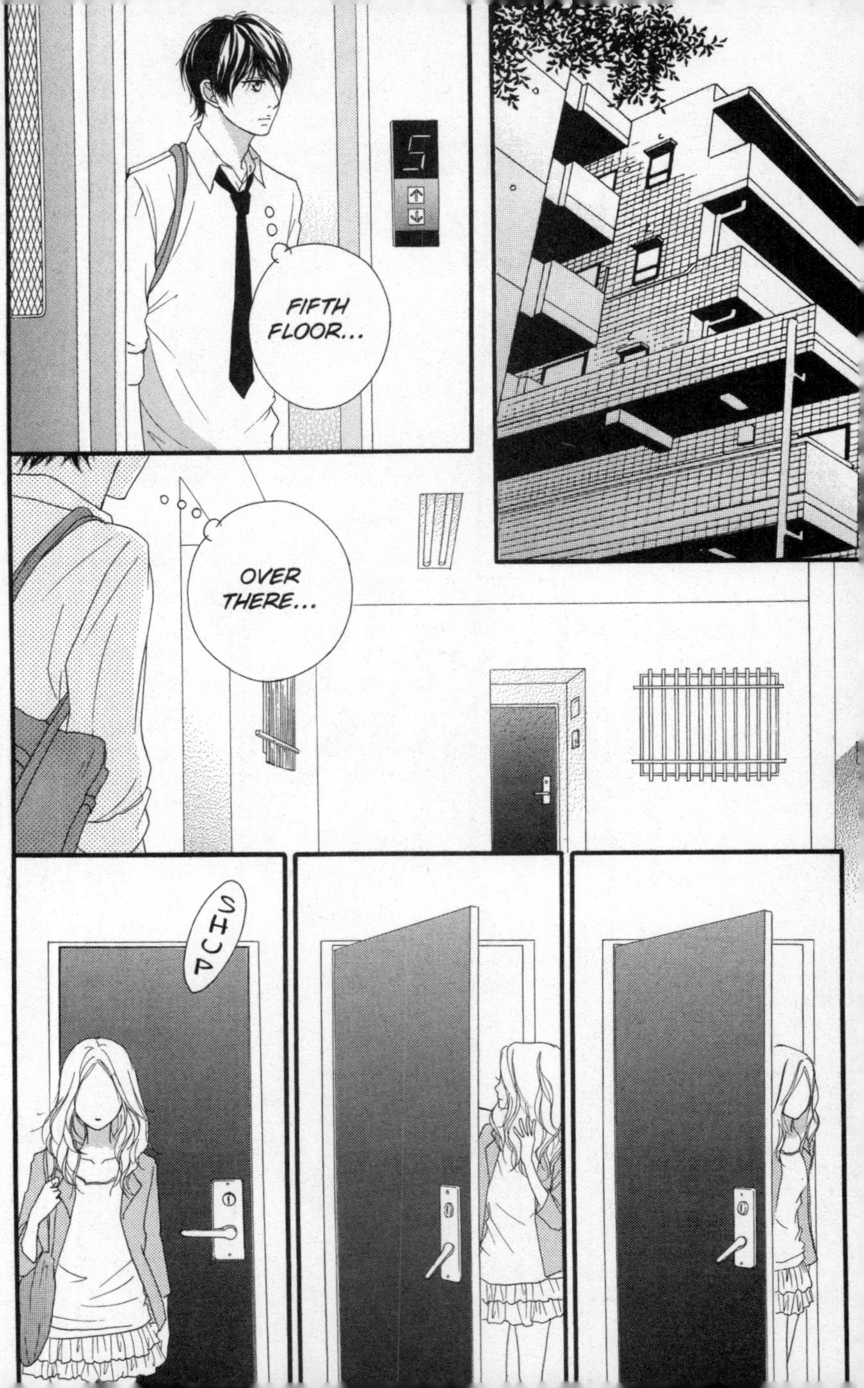
FIFTH FLOOR...
OVER THERE...
SHUP

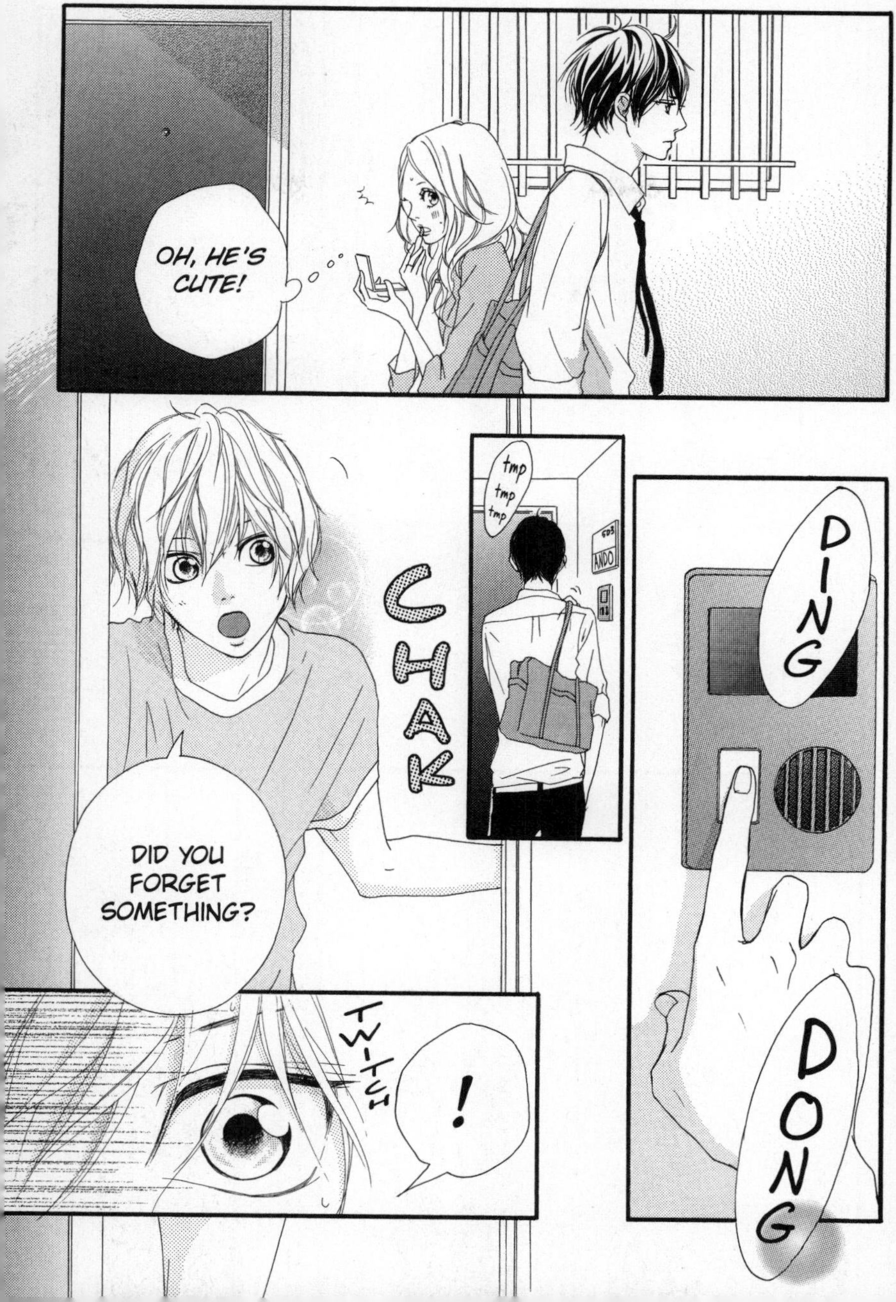
OH, HE'S CUTE!
DING
DONG
tmp
tmp
tmp
ANDO
CHAK
DID YOU FORGET SOMETHING?
TWITCH
!

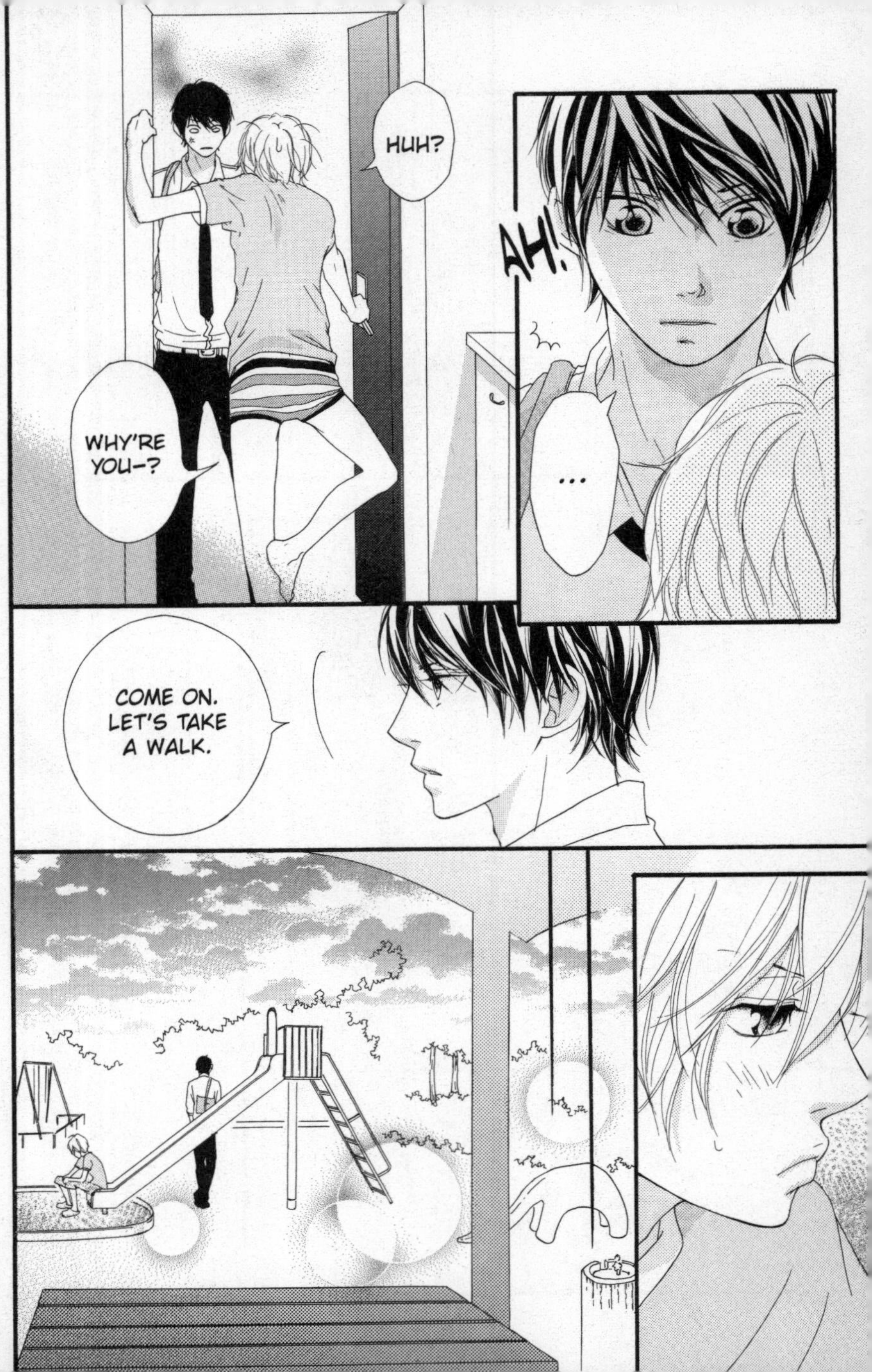
HUH?
WHY'RE YOU-?
AH!
...
COME ON. LET'S TAKE A WALK.

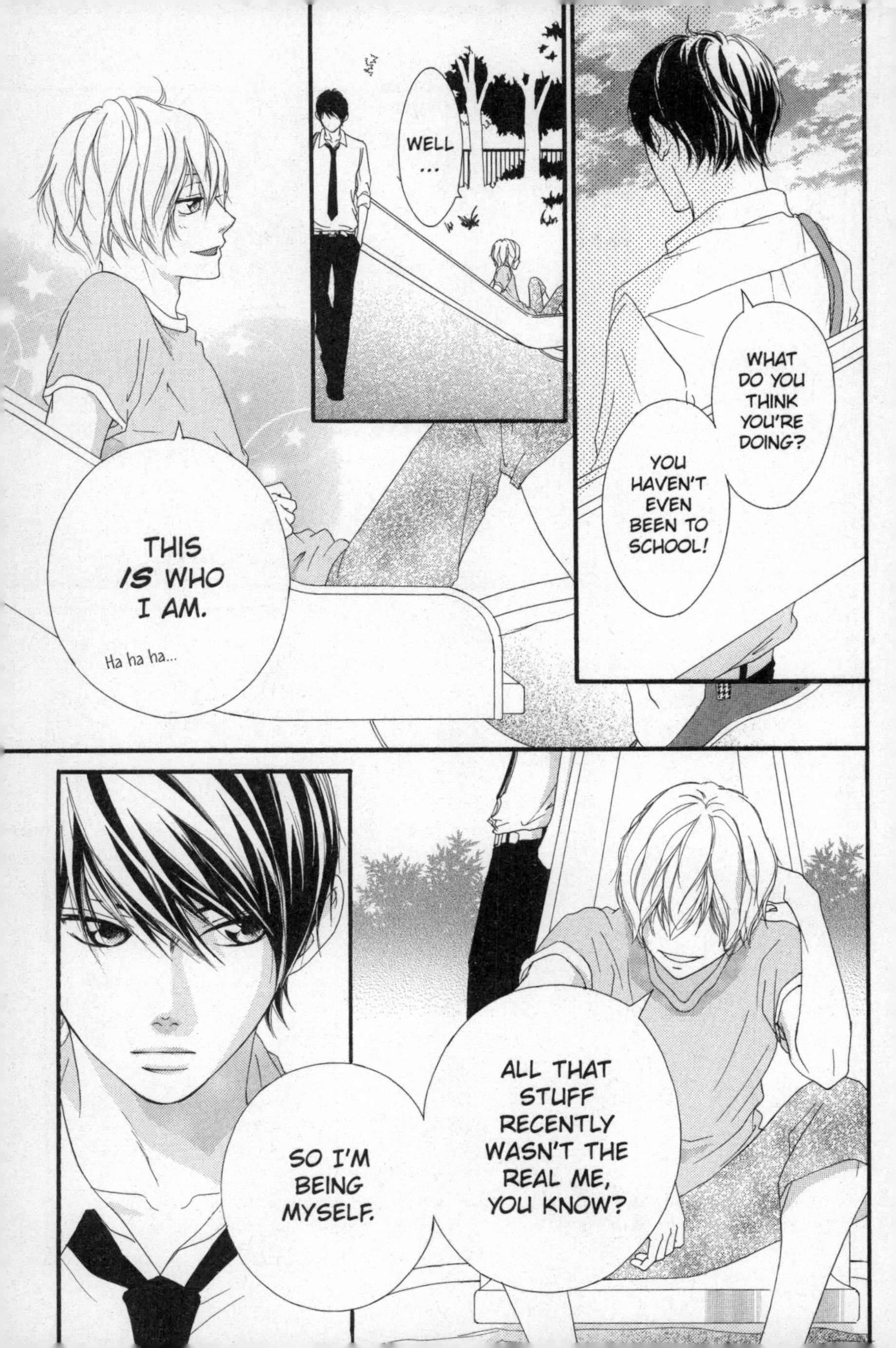
WHAT DO YOU THINK YOU'RE DOING?
YOU HAVEN'T EVEN BEEN TO SCHOOL!
WELL ...
THIS *IS* WHO I AM.
Ha ha ha...
ALL THAT STUFF RECENTLY WASN'T THE REAL ME, YOU KNOW?
SO I'M BEING MYSELF.

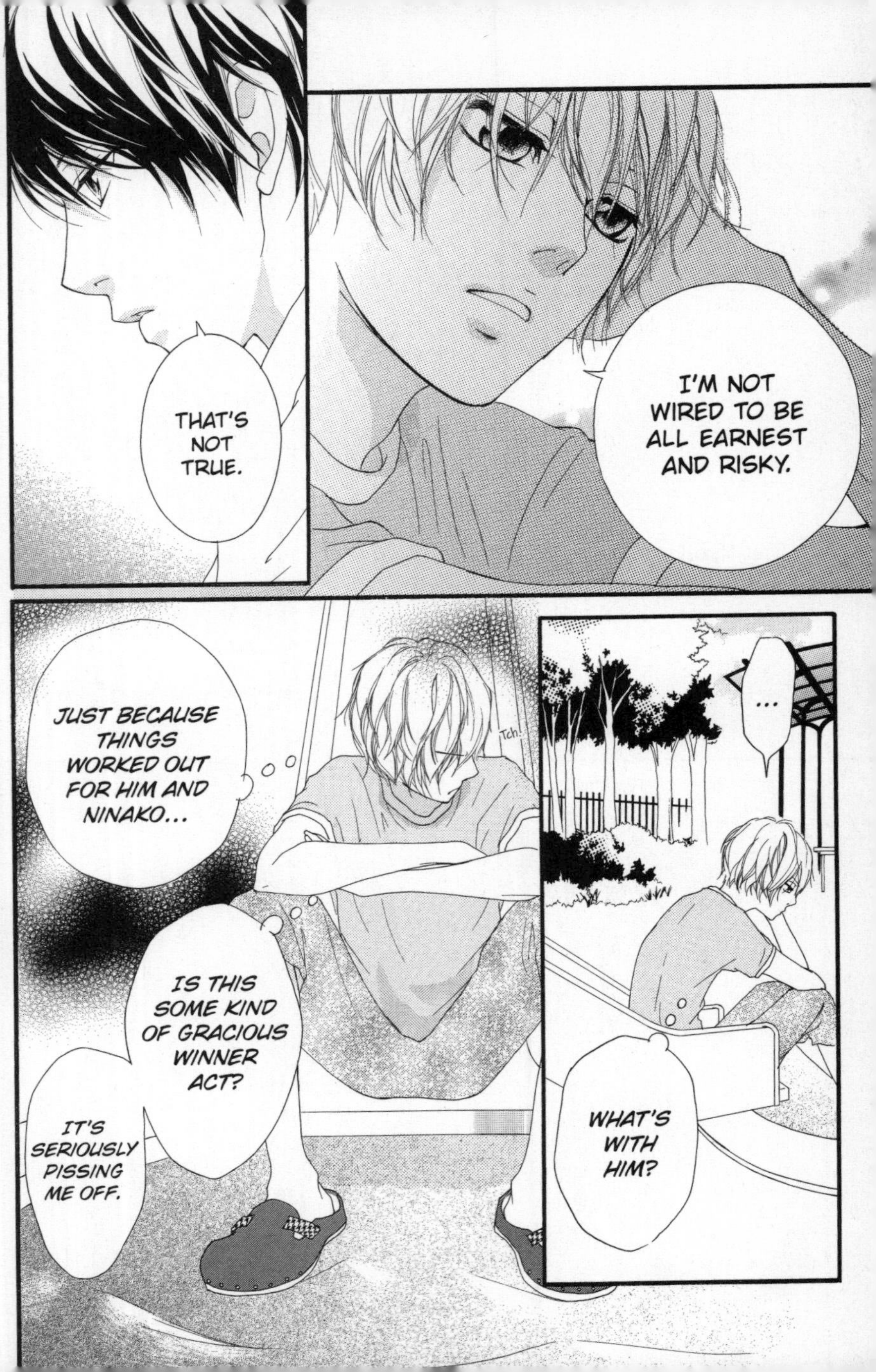
I'M NOT WIRED TO BE ALL EARNEST AND RISKY.
THAT'S NOT TRUE.
...
WHAT'S WITH HIM?
Tch!
JUST BECAUSE THINGS WORKED OUT FOR HIM AND NINAKO...
IS THIS SOME KIND OF GRACIOUS WINNER ACT?
IT'S SERIOUSLY PISSING ME OFF.

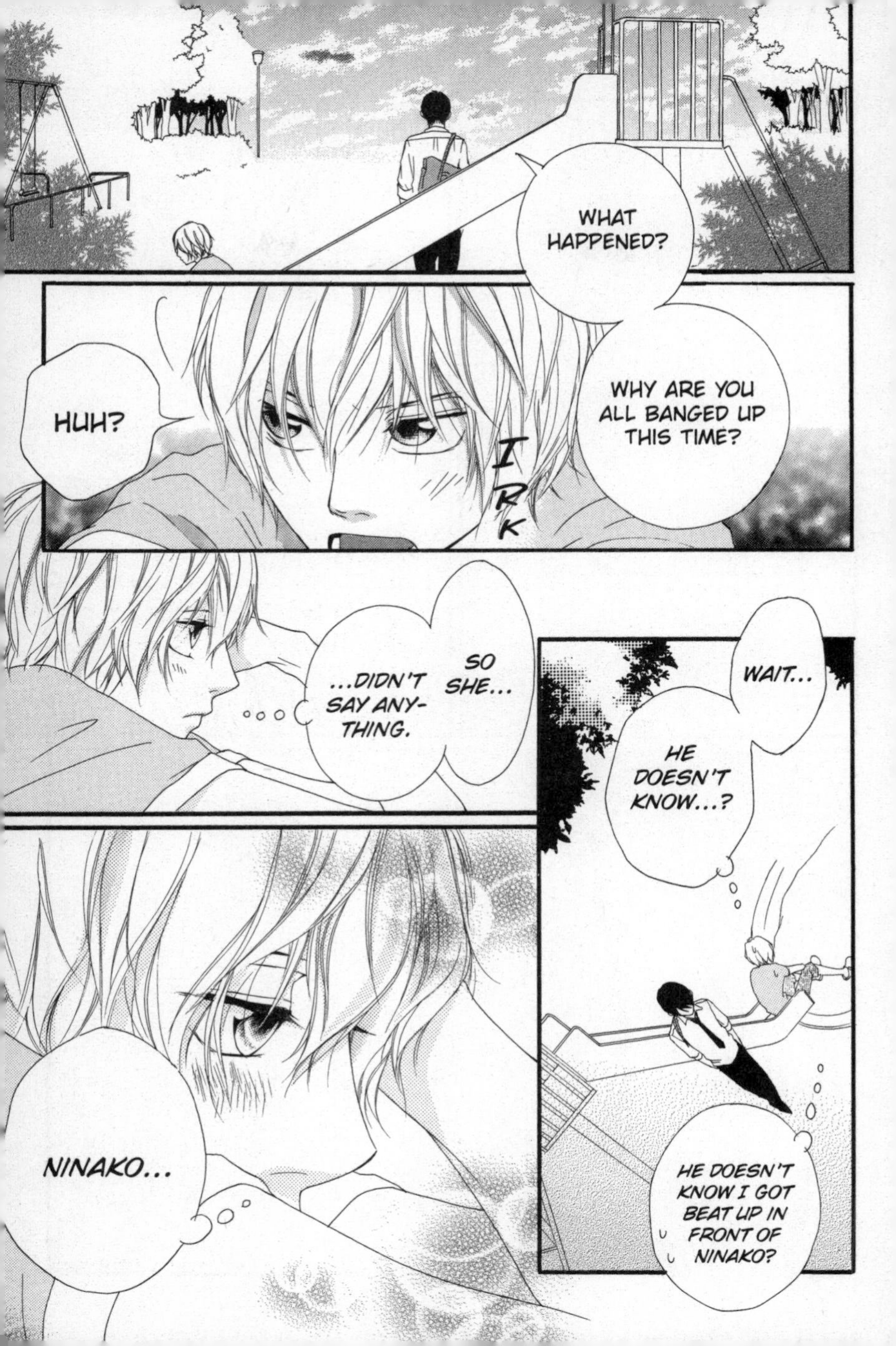
WHAT HAPPENED?
WHY ARE YOU ALL BANGED UP THIS TIME?
IRK
HUH?
WAIT...
HE DOESN'T KNOW...?
HE DOESN'T KNOW I GOT BEAT UP IN FRONT OF NINAKO?
SO SHE...
...DIDN'T SAY ANY-THING.
NINAKO...

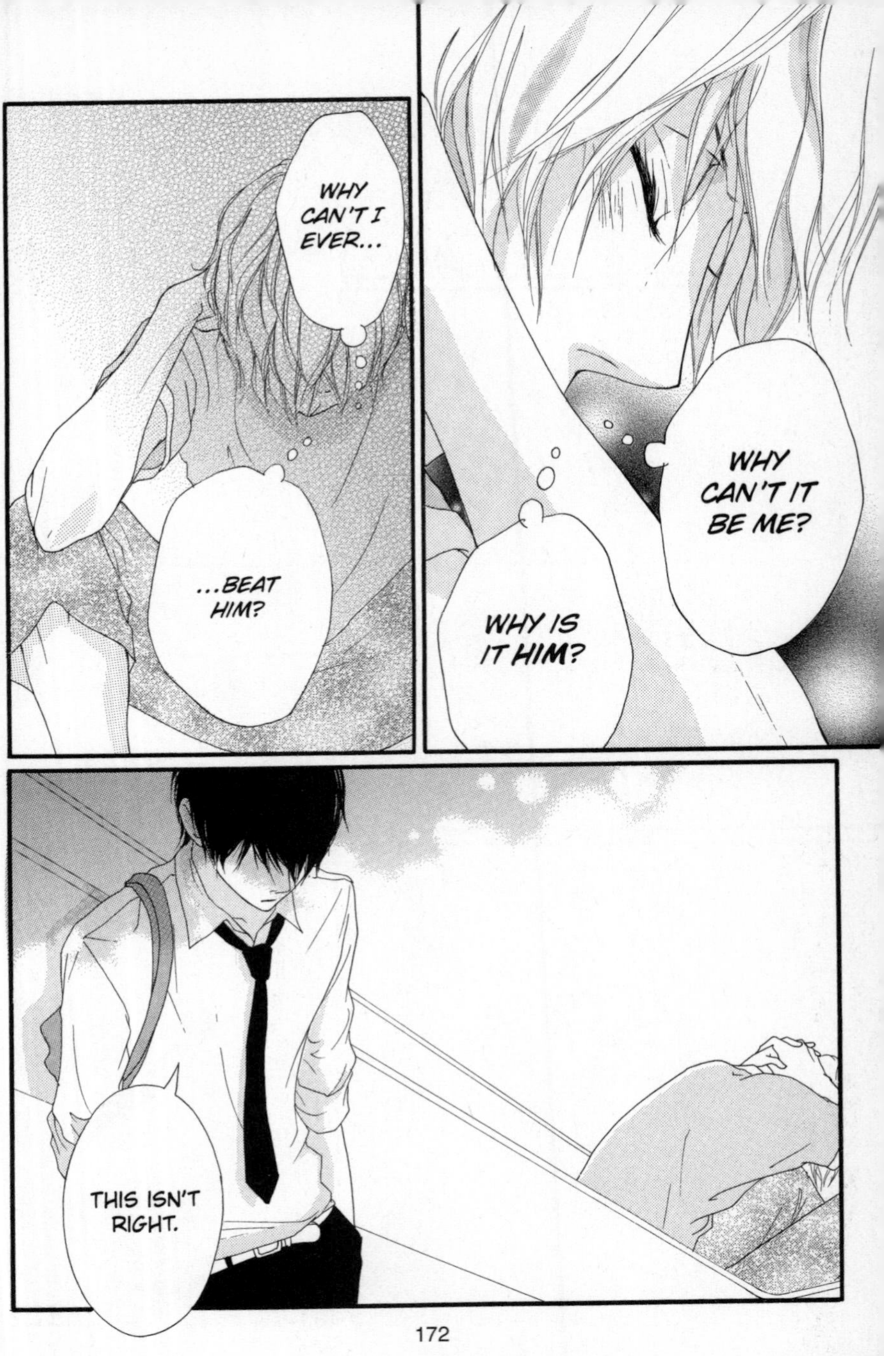
WHY CAN'T IT BE ME?
WHY IS IT HIM?
WHY CAN'T I EVER...
...BEAT HIM?
THIS ISN'T RIGHT.

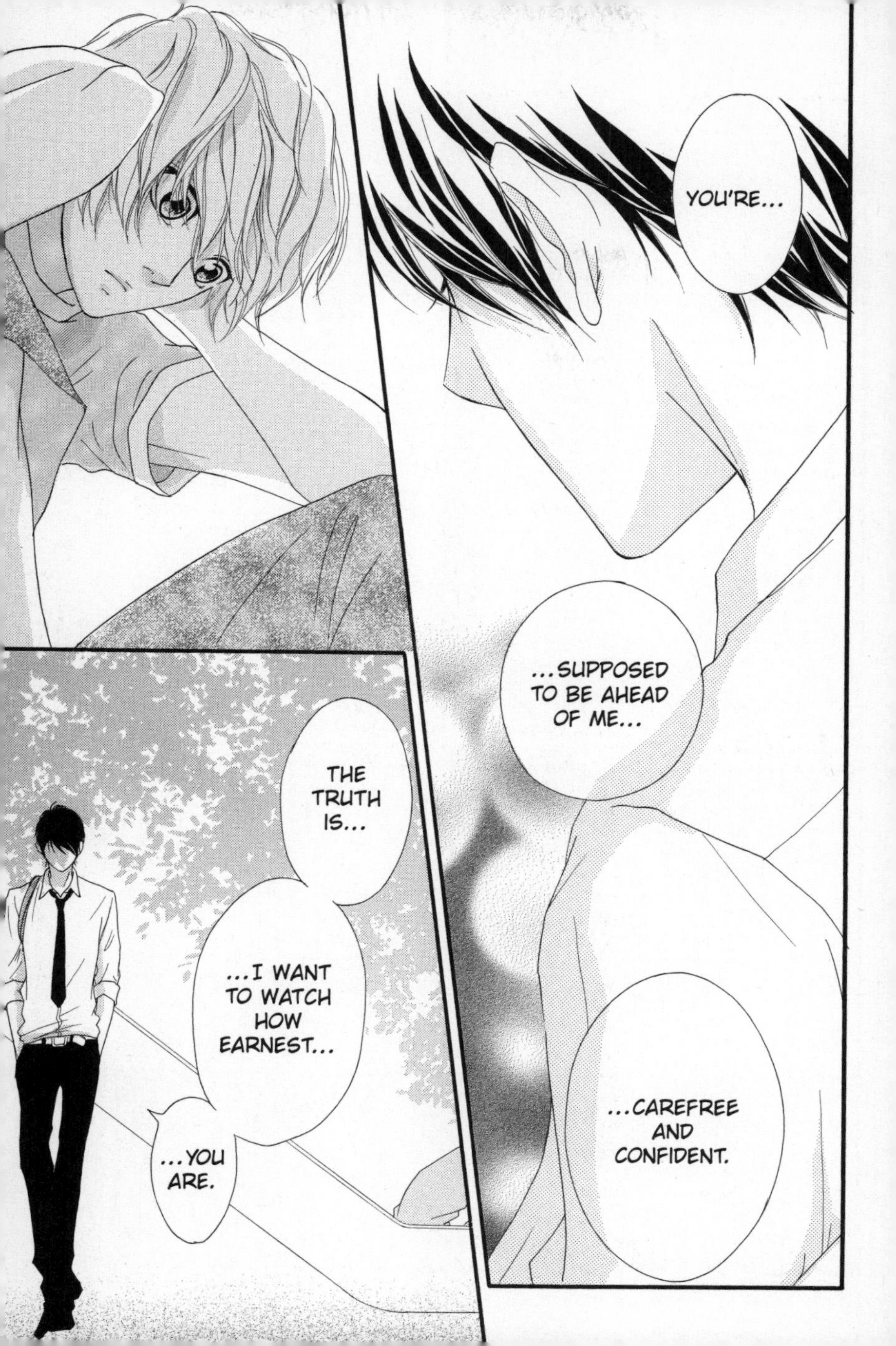
YOU'RE...
...SUPPOSED TO BE AHEAD OF ME...
...CAREFREE AND CONFIDENT.
THE TRUTH IS...
...I WANT TO WATCH HOW EARNEST...
...YOU ARE.

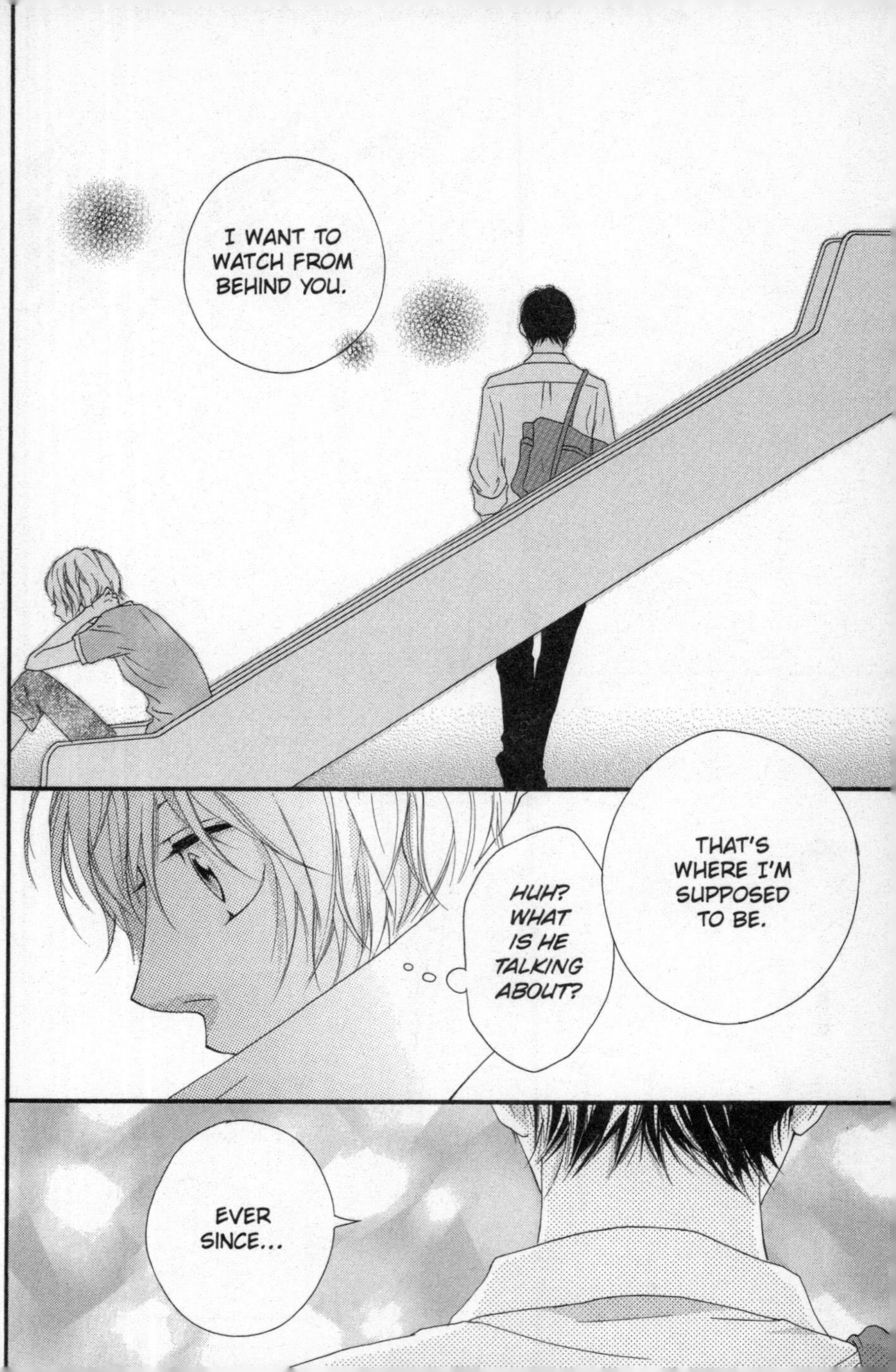
I WANT TO WATCH FROM BEHIND YOU.
THAT'S WHERE I'M SUPPOSED TO BE.
HUH? WHAT IS HE TALKING ABOUT?
EVER SINCE...

...THE FIRST TIME...

...YOU TALKED TO ME...

...THAT'S BEEN MY PLACE.

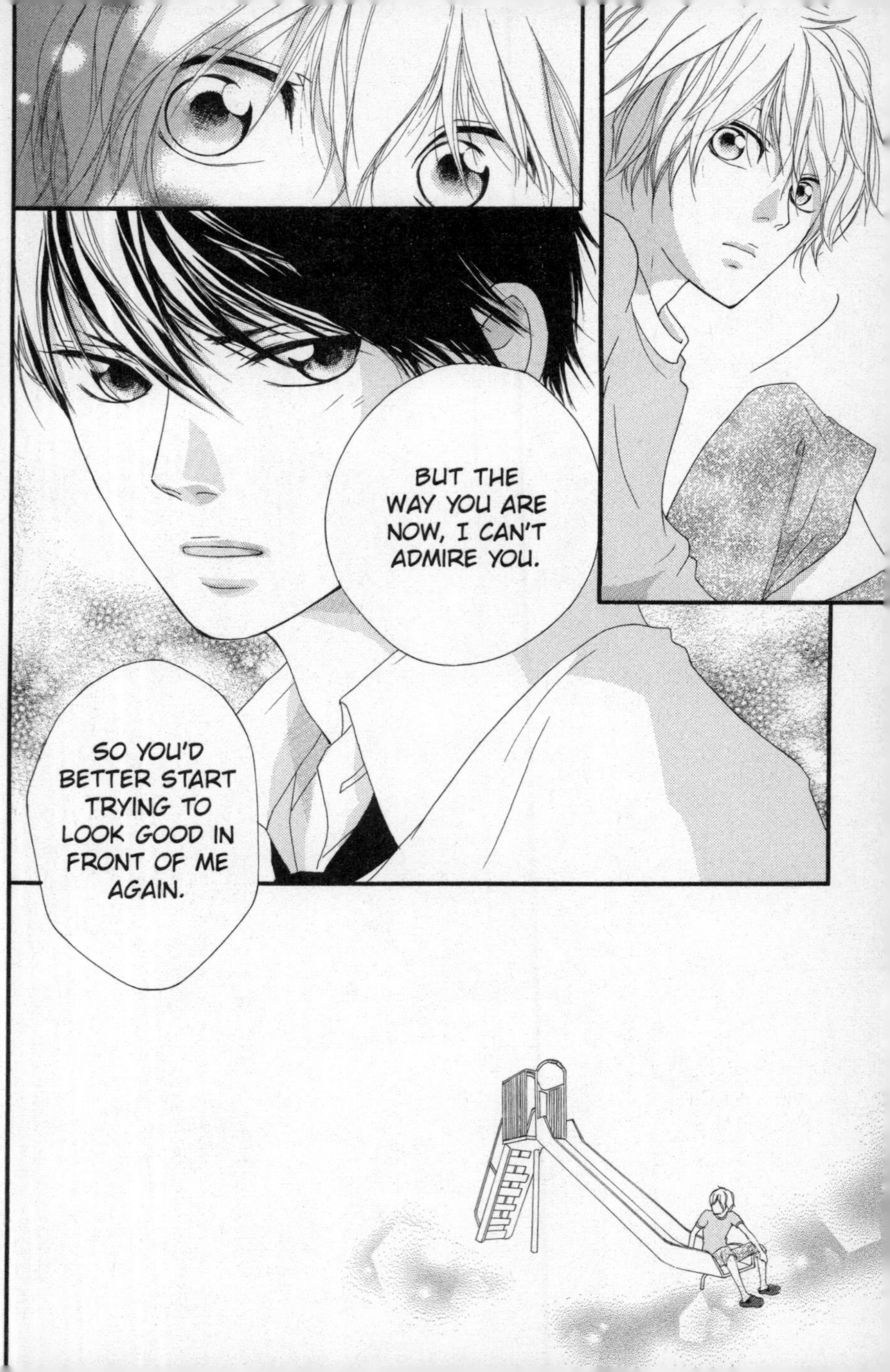
BUT THE WAY YOU ARE NOW, I CAN'T ADMIRE YOU.
SO YOU'D BETTER START TRYING TO LOOK GOOD IN FRONT OF ME AGAIN.

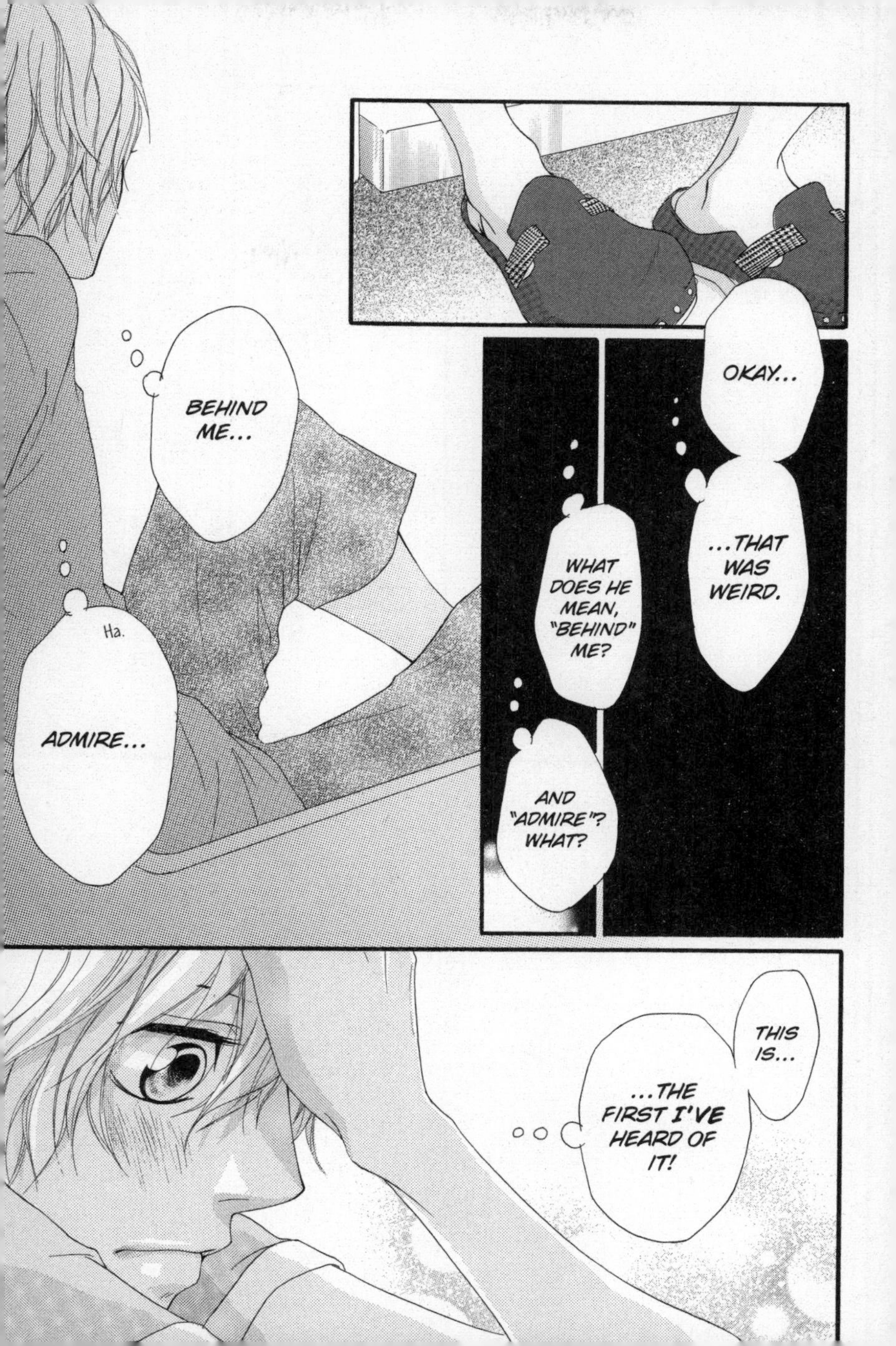
BEHIND ME...
Ha.
ADMIRE...
OKAY...
...THAT WAS WEIRD.
WHAT DOES HE MEAN, "BEHIND" ME?
AND "ADMIRE"? WHAT?
THIS IS...
...THE FIRST I'VE HEARD OF IT!

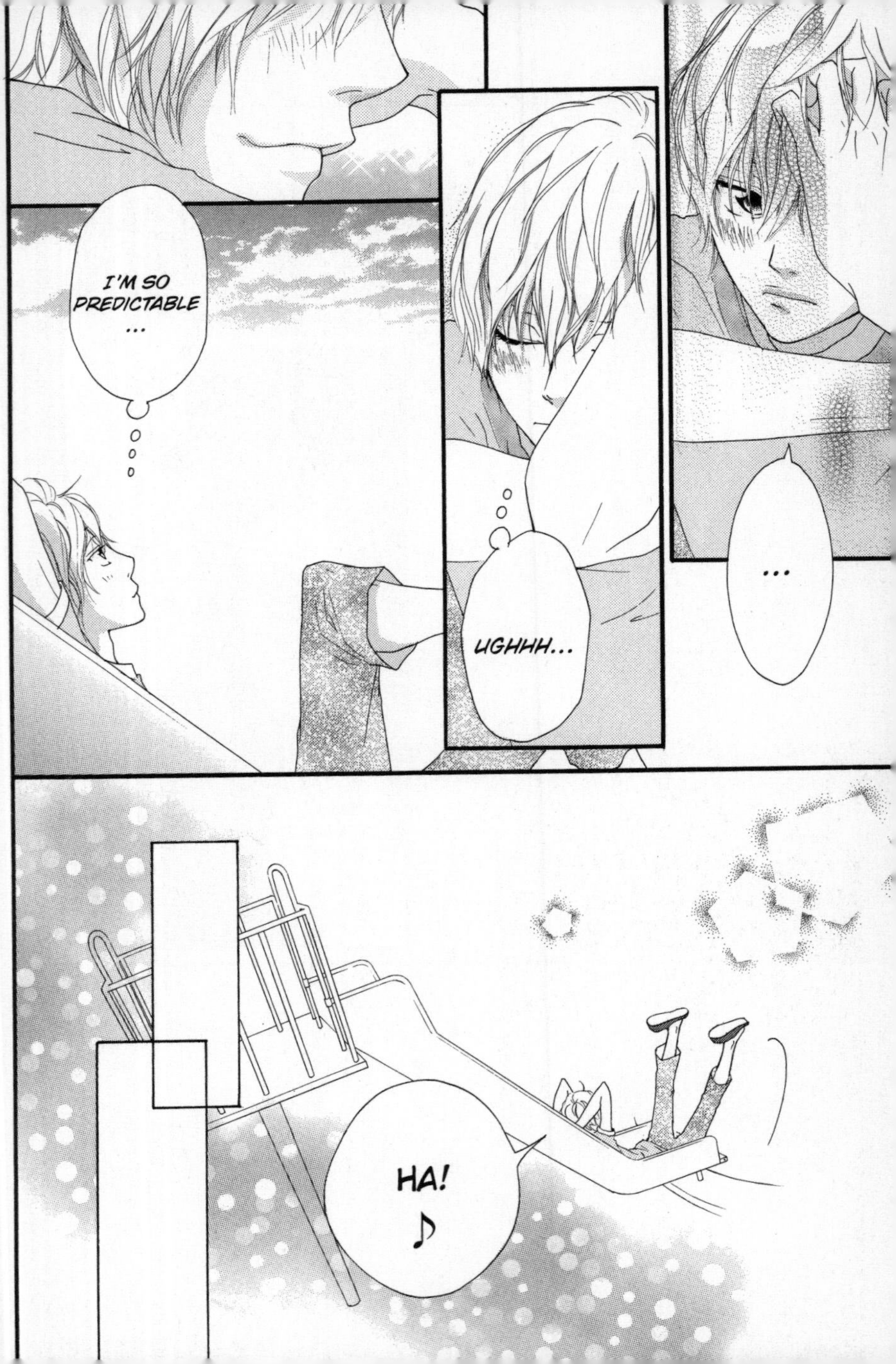
I'M SO PREDICTABLE ...
...
UGHHH...
HA! ♪

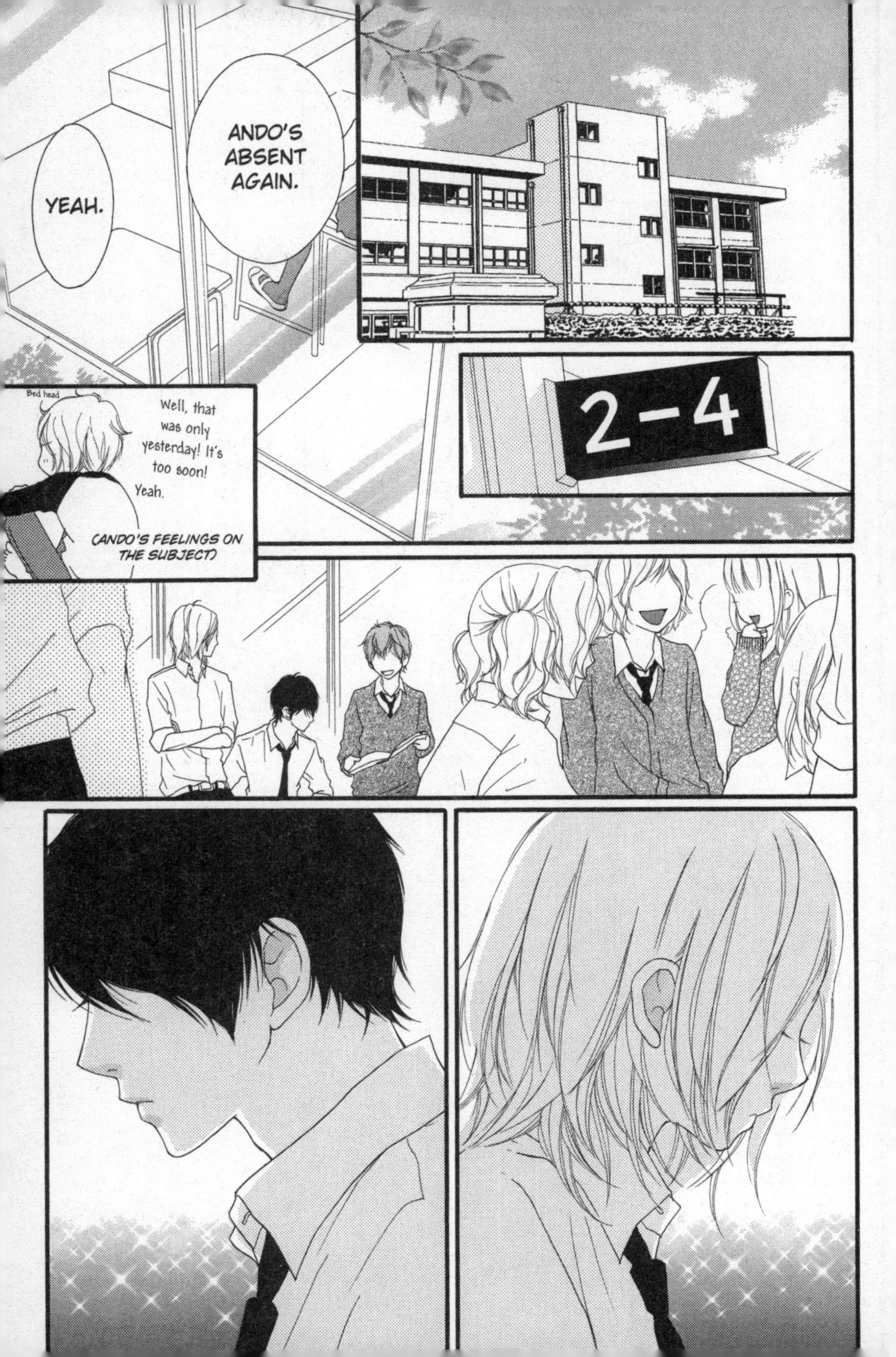
ANDO'S ABSENT AGAIN.
YEAH.
2-4
Bed head
Well, that was only yesterday! It's too soon!
Yeah.
(ANDO'S FEELINGS ON THE SUBJECT)

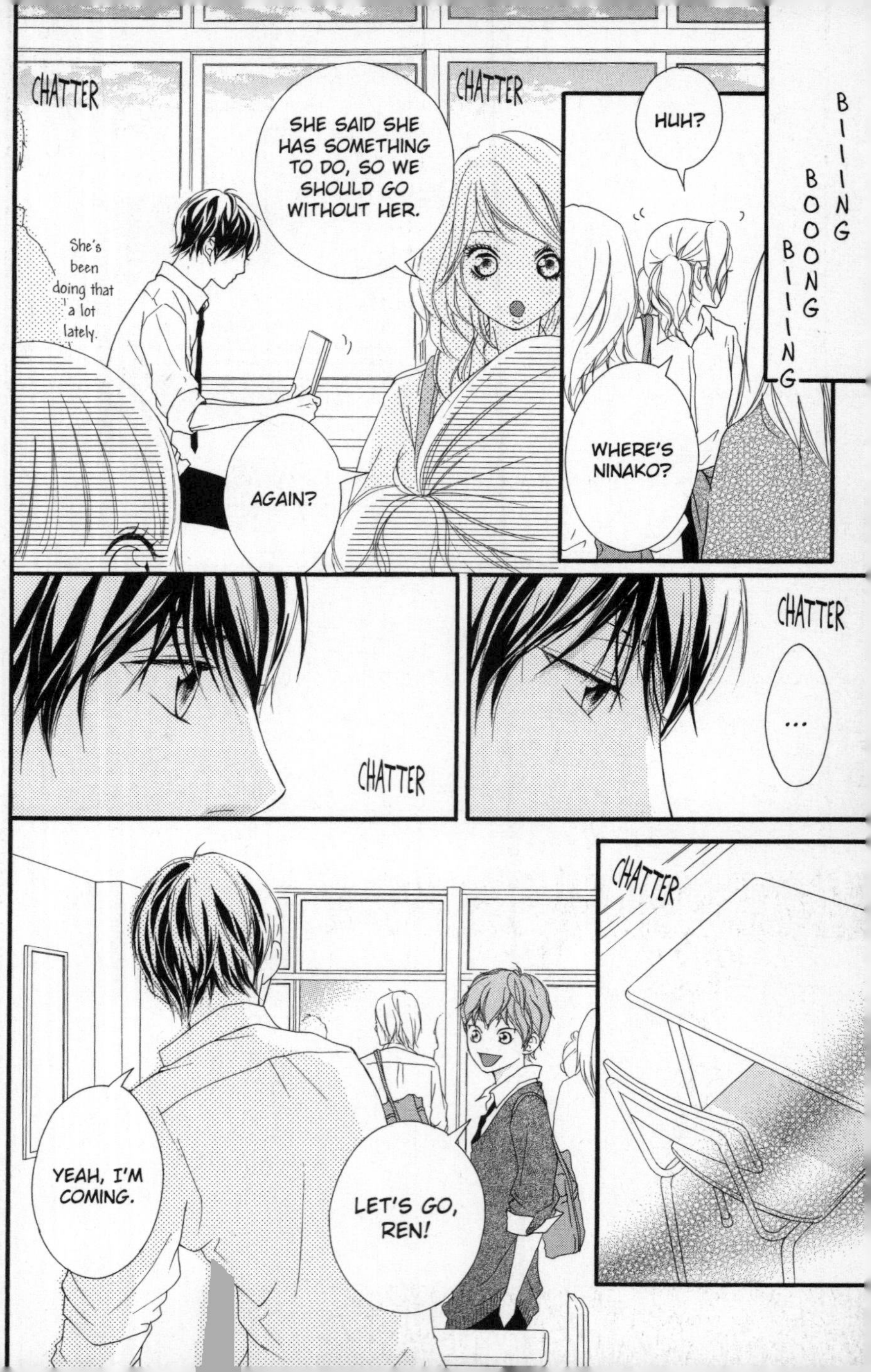
BIIING
BOOONG
BIIING
HUH?
WHERE'S NINAKO?
CHATTER
SHE SAID SHE HAS SOMETHING TO DO, SO WE SHOULD GO WITHOUT HER.
CHATTER
AGAIN?
She's been doing that a lot lately.
CHATTER
...
CHATTER
CHATTER
LET'S GO, REN!
YEAH, I'M COMING.

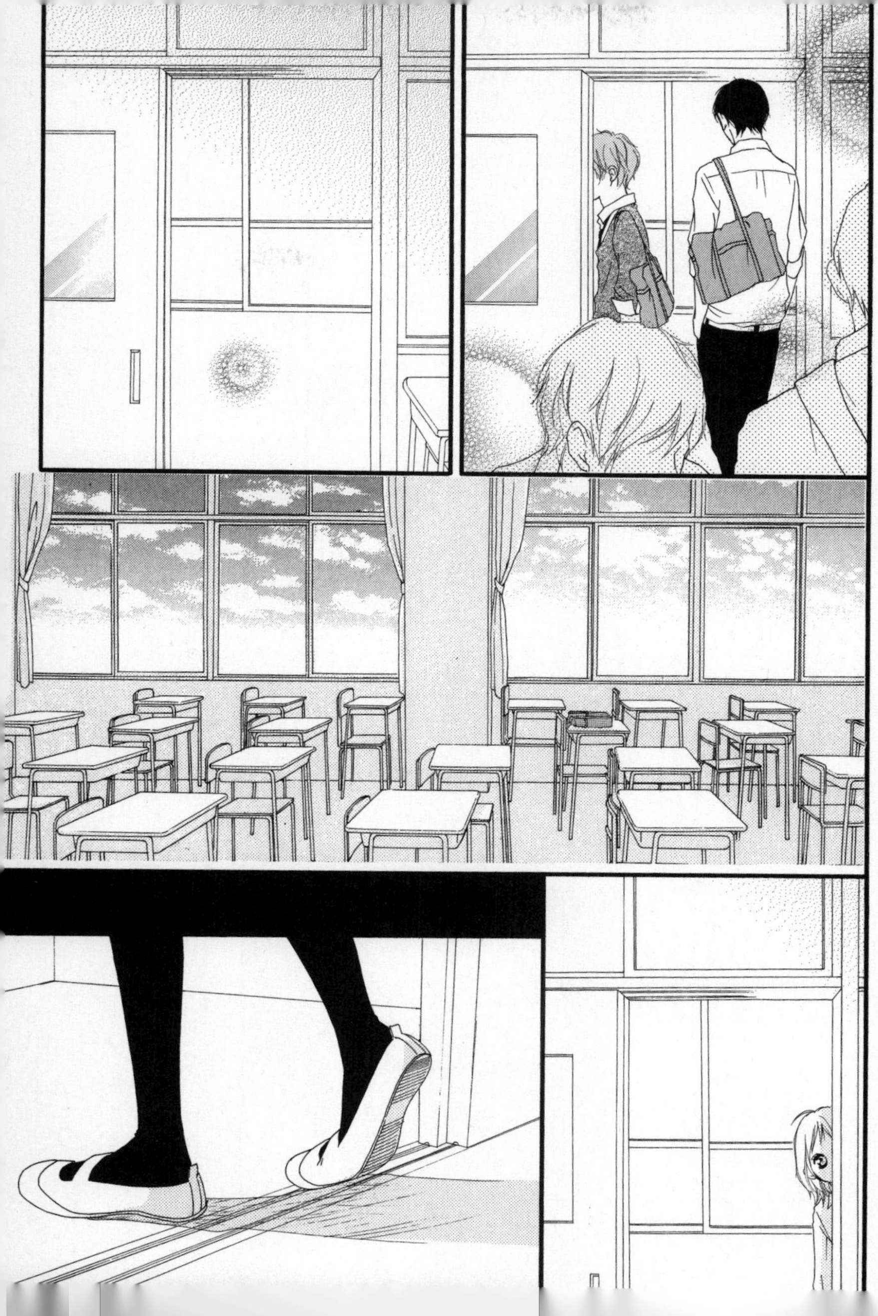

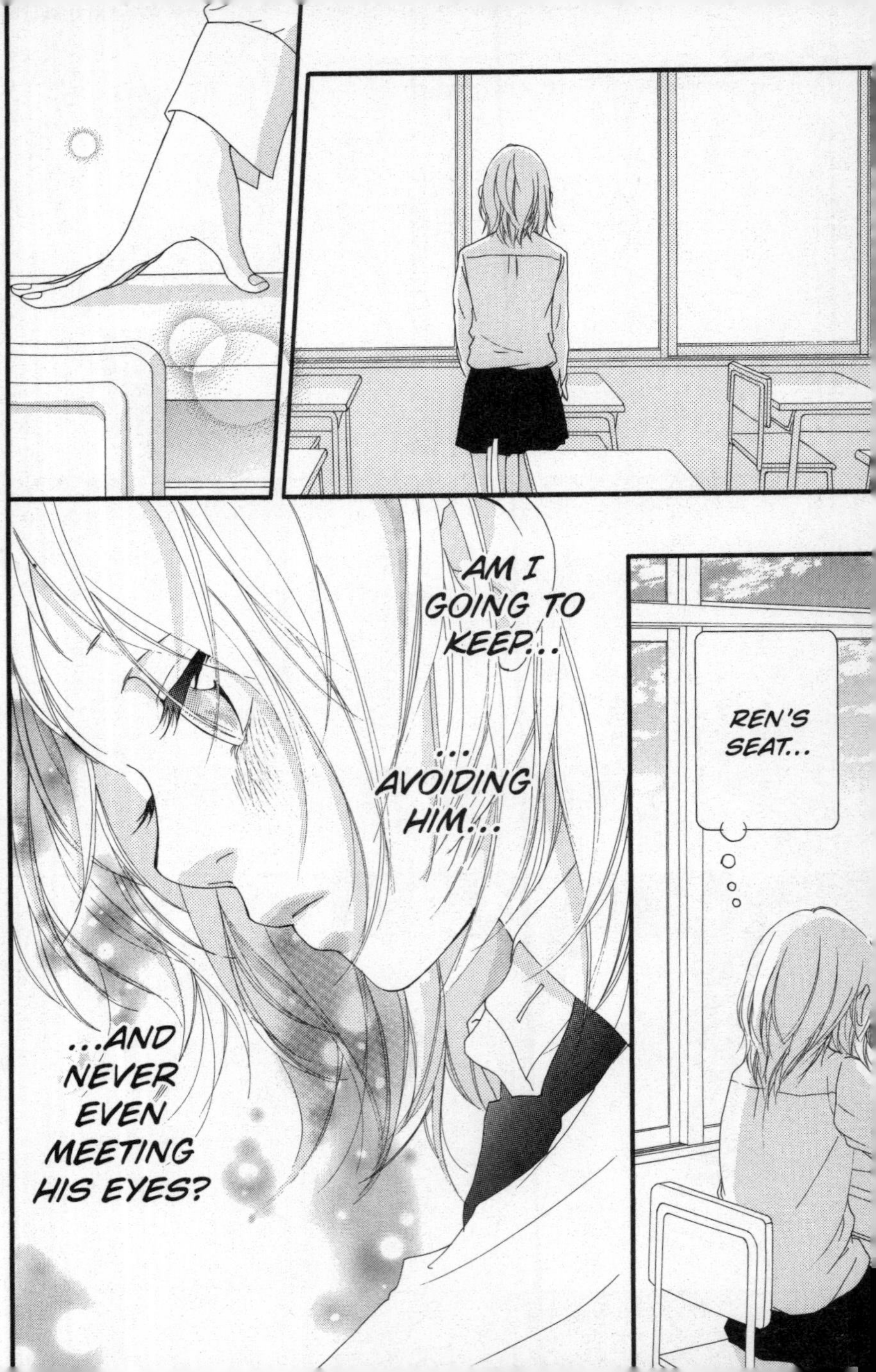
REN'S SEAT...
AM I GOING TO KEEP...
...AVOIDING HIM...
...AND NEVER EVEN MEETING HIS EYES?

WILL IT ALWAYS BE LIKE THIS NOW...?

BANG

I...CAME BACK TO GET SOME- THING...

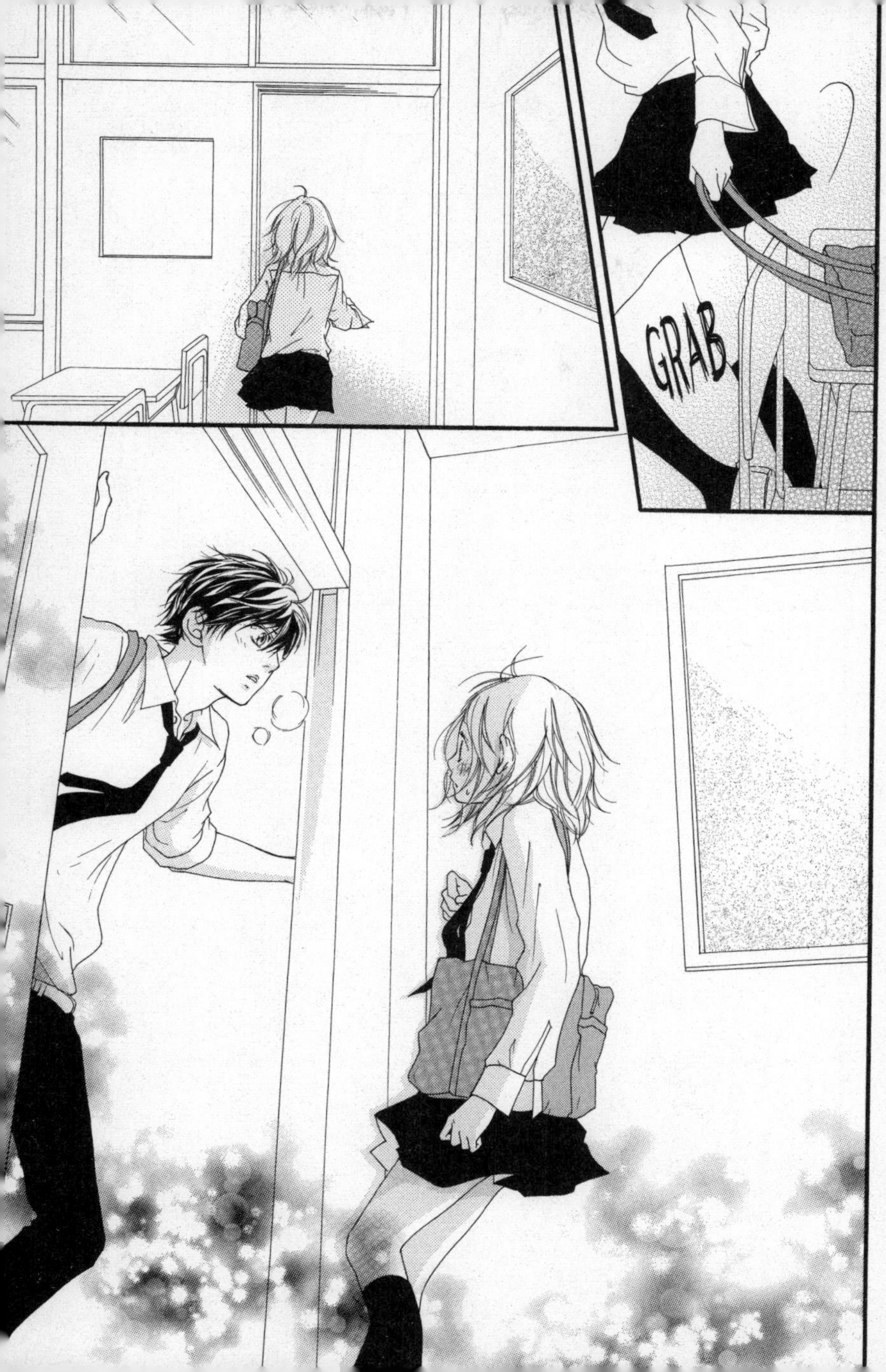
GRAB

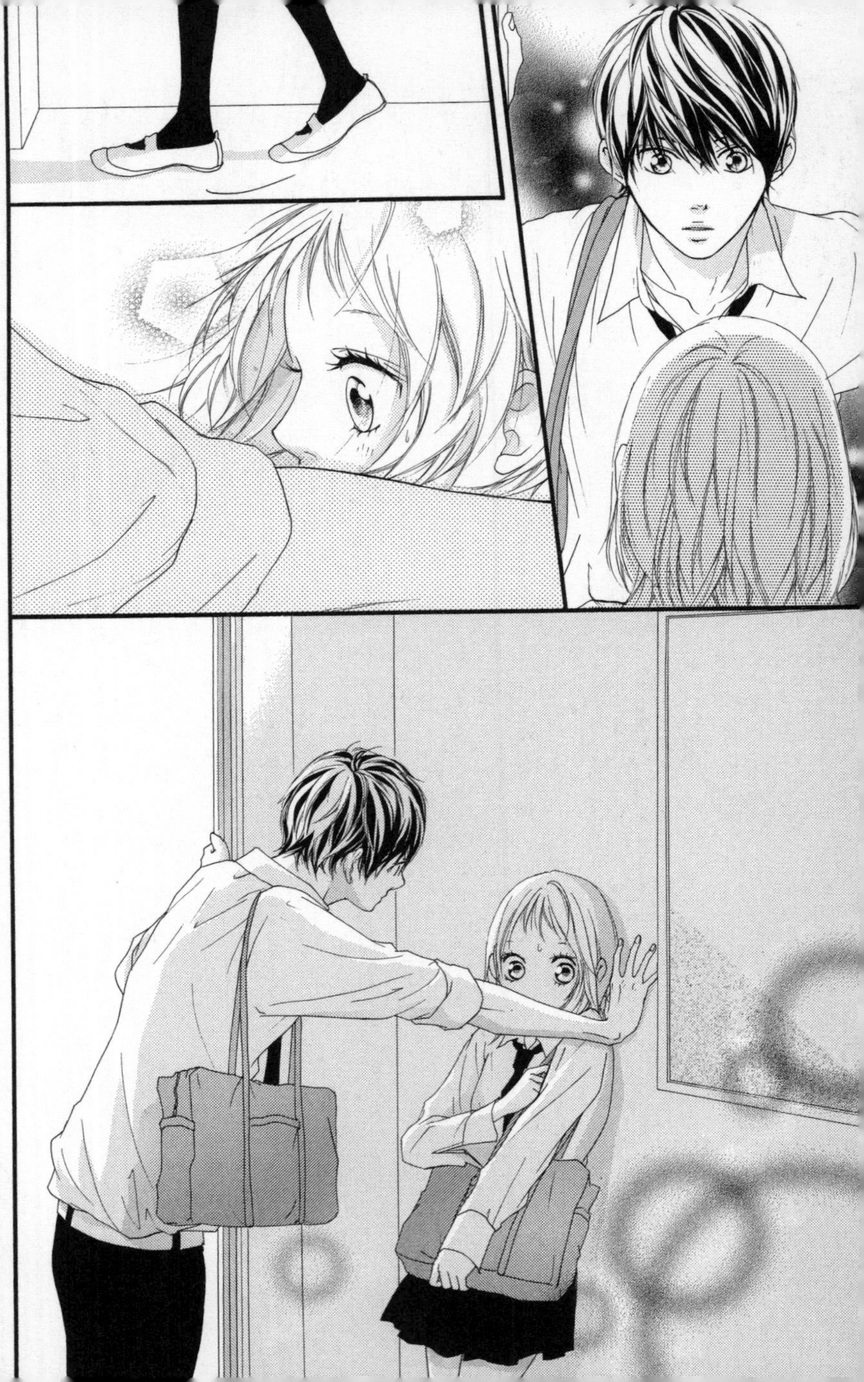

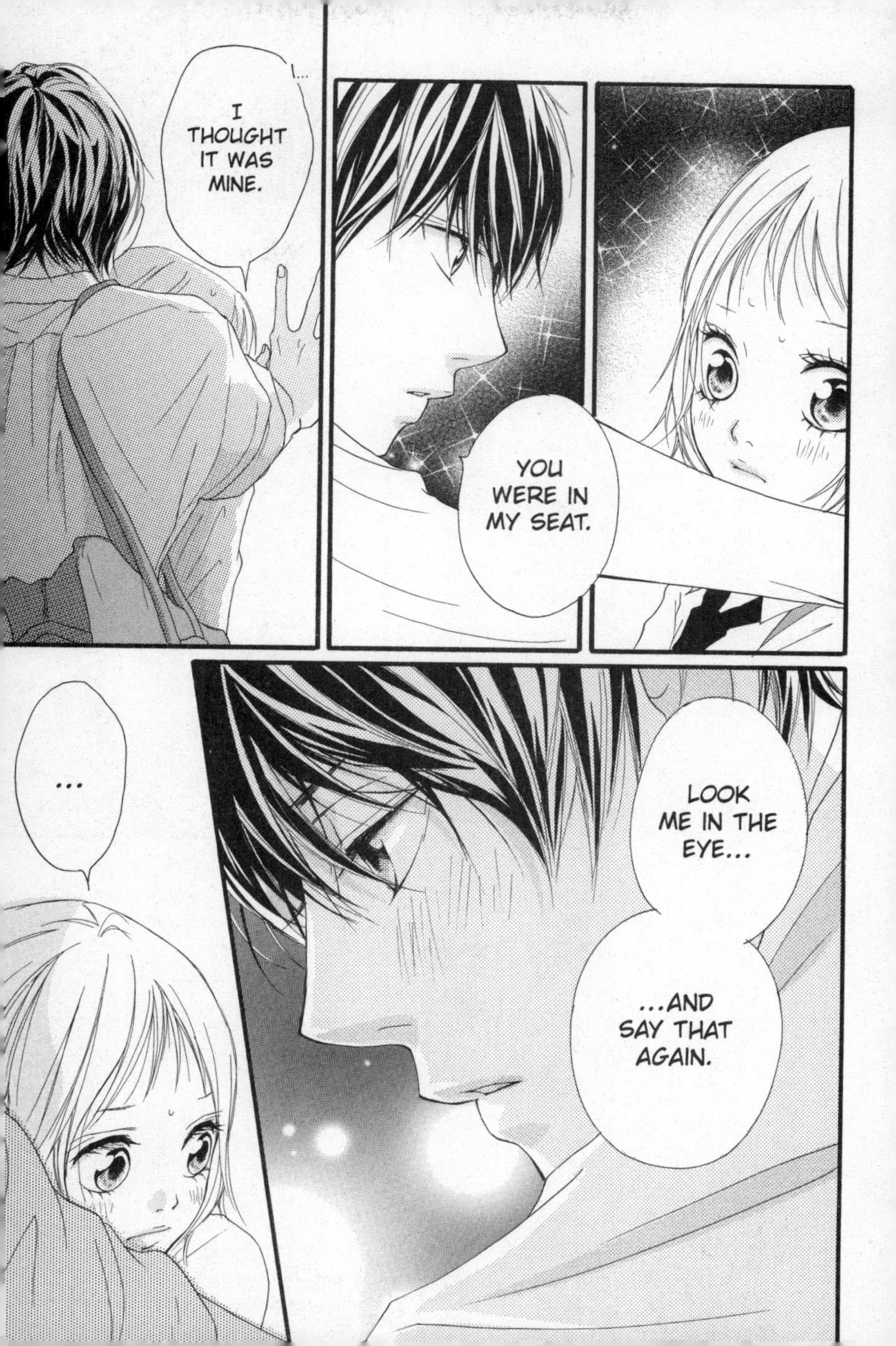
YOU WERE IN MY SEAT.
I... I THOUGHT IT WAS MINE.
LOOK ME IN THE EYE...
...AND SAY THAT AGAIN.
...

BUT YOU TURNED ME DOWN, DIDN'T YOU?

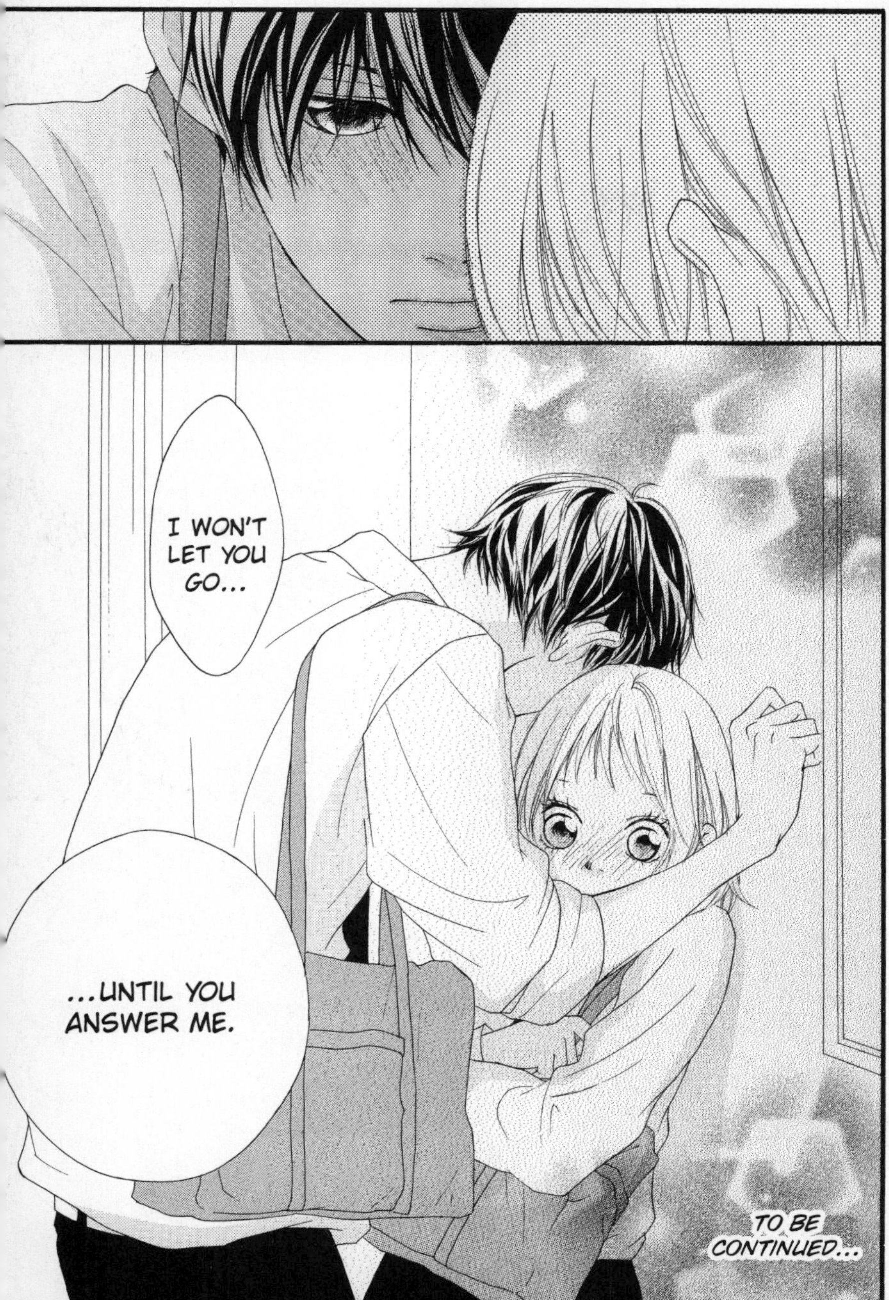
I WON'T LET YOU GO...
...UNTIL YOU ANSWER ME.
TO BE CONTINUED...

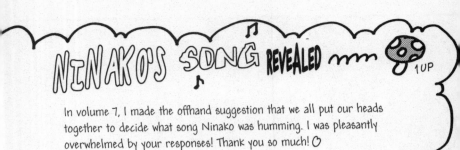

In volume 7, I made the offhand suggestion that we all put our heads together to decide what song Ninako was humming. I was pleasantly overwhelmed by your responses! Thank you so much! ♡

Some of you wrote out the lyrics for me, and that was very helpful for the selection process. I listened to each song and gave it some serious thought!

The criteria were: 1) It had to be something both Ninako and Ren might sing. 2) It couldn't be a sad song. 3) It had to either be a hit or something used in a commercial, so lots of people know it. 4) The lyrics.

Keeping all of that in mind and taking into account the number of votes, I made a decision! Drum roll, please! The song is...

LITTLE LOVE SONG BY MONGOL 800

Yay! Hooray! And to the Mongol 800 members,
sorry for dragging you into this. Whee!

First off, the title is perfect! When I started this project, Yui Niigaki was singing it in a commercial, so it was easy to imagine what it would sound like if someone hummed it. Ninako and Ren would definitely both know this song, and it fits all the criteria, so this was it! It really is a great song! It also had the most votes, but that's not the only reason I picked it. 🜁

So now, when you reread volume 7, imagine this Mongol 800 song, slowed down a little. Come to think of it, a couple of pages before the humming scene, Ren says something that goes perfectly with the song: "Having just one person understand me would be all I need."
I high-fived myself!

It's so much fun to think that everyone who reads this scene is imagining the same song! It's like we're a wonderful team. Well, it really was a lot of fun. Your willingness to go with the flow, plus your kindness, is just the best. Even though we've never met, I feel like we've become very good friends. I'd like to think you all feel that way too. ❀ Love and thanks to everyone who participated in this project!

P.S.
Ikimono-gakari, Arashi and RADWIMPS got lots of votes too. Oh, and a couple of you voted for "The Bear in the Woods"! Very funny! Even something like that can have multiple votes. And there were lots more!!

Thank you ever so much! ☆

★Io sakisaka★

...in volume 10!

To be continued...

My trace table broke while I
was feeling more pressure than
usual due to my work schedule.
"Now?! Now of all times?!"
I screamed in frustration.
I continued working and
comforted myself by saying
something good would happen
later.

I hope something good
happens.

—Io Sakisaka

Born on June 8, Io Sakisaka
made her debut as a manga
creator with *Sakura, Chiru*. Her
works include *Call My Name*,
Gate of Planet, and *Blue*. Her
current series, *Ao Haru Ride*, is
currently running in *Bessatsu
Margaret* magazine. In her spare
time, Sakisaka likes to paint
things and sleep.

STROBE EDGE
Vol. 9
Shojo Beat Edition

STORY AND ART BY
IO SAKISAKA

English Adaptation/Ysabet MacFarlane
Translation/JN Productions
Touch-up Art & Lettering/John Hunt
Design/Yukiko Whitley
Editor/Amy Yu

Printed in Canada

Published by VIZ Media, LLC
P.O. Box 77010
San Francisco, CA 94107

10 9 8 7 6 5 4 3 2 1
First printing, March 2014

www.viz.com   www.shojobeat.com

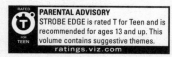

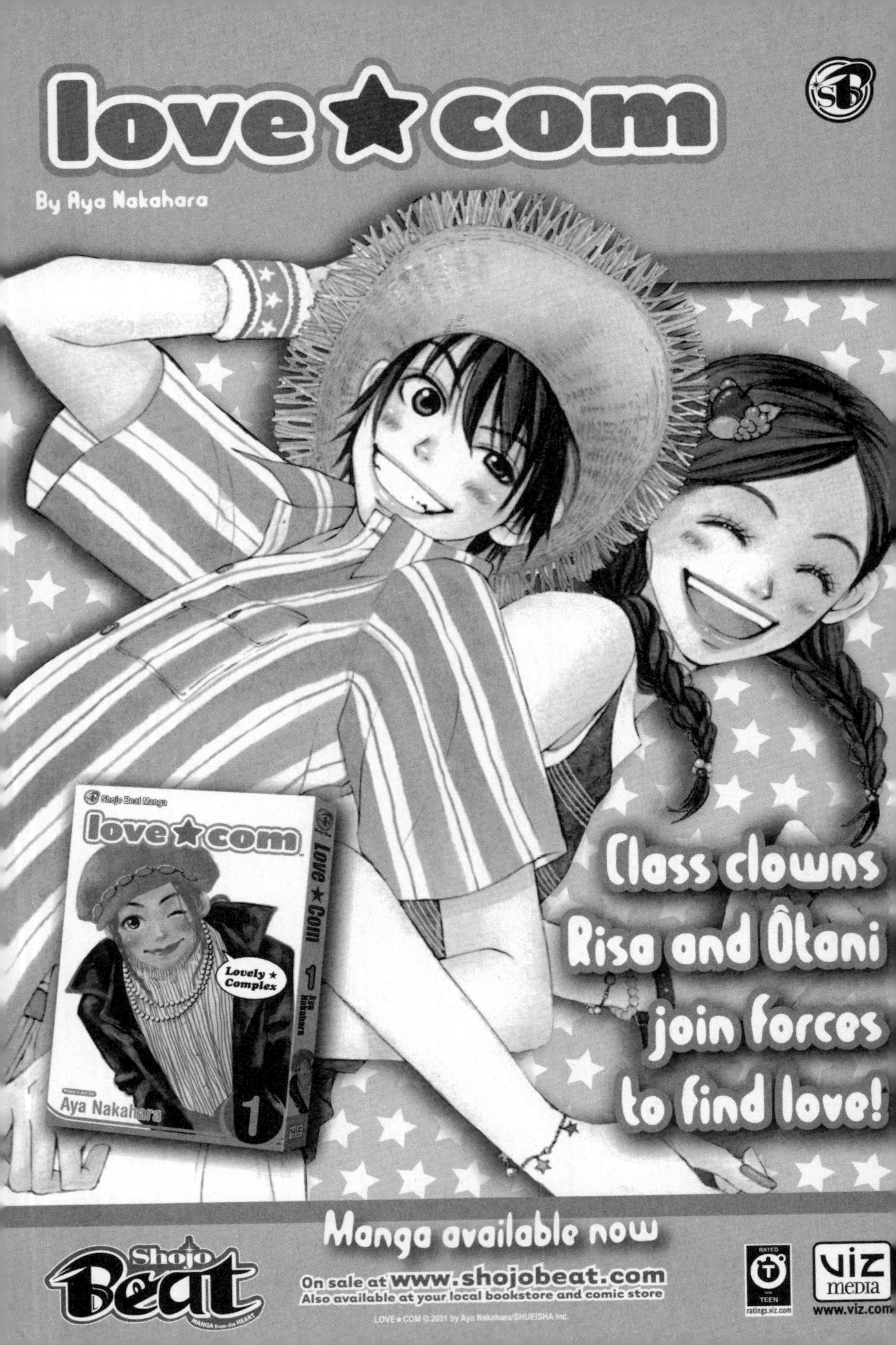
love★com
By Aya Nakahara
Shojo Beat Manga
love★com
Lovely ★ Complex
Love★Com
1
Aya Nakahara
Aya Nakahara
1
Class clowns Risa and Ôtani join forces to find love!
Manga available now
Shojo Beat
MANGA from the HEART
On sale at www.shojobeat.com
Also available at your local bookstore and comic store
RATED T TEEN
ratings.viz.com
VIZ media
www.viz.com
LOVE★COM © 2001 by Aya Nakahara/SHUEISHA Inc.

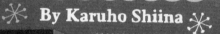

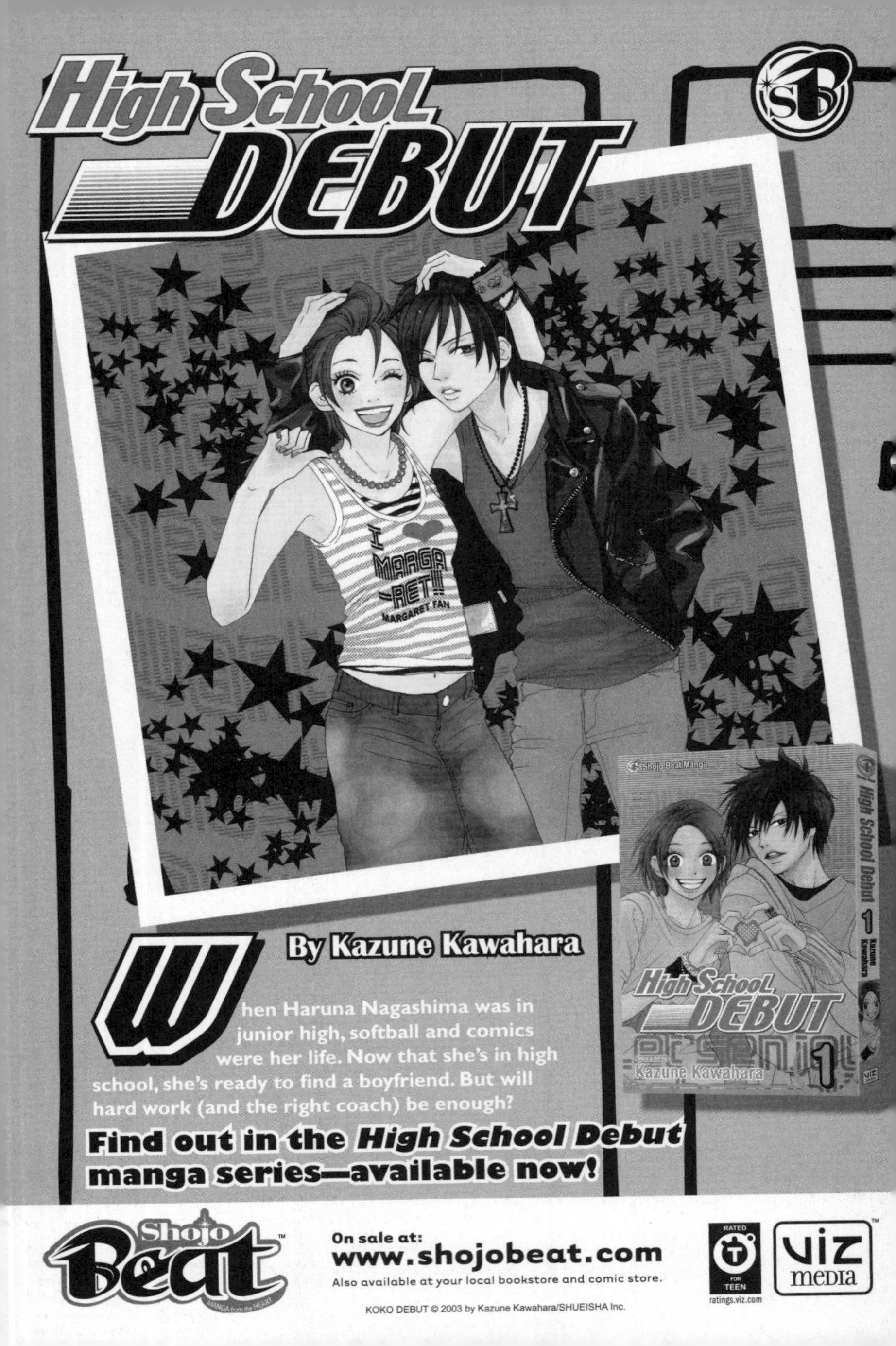
High School DEBUT
I ♥ MARGA-RET!!
MARGARET FAN
Shojo Beat Manga
High School Debut 1 Kazune Kawahara
High School DEBUT
Kazune Kawahara
1
By Kazune Kawahara
When Haruna Nagashima was in junior high, softball and comics were her life. Now that she's in high school, she's ready to find a boyfriend. But will hard work (and the right coach) be enough?
Find out in the High School Debut manga series—available now!
Shojo Beat
MANGA from the HEART
On sale at:
www.shojobeat.com
Also available at your local bookstore and comic store.
RATED T FOR TEEN
ratings.viz.com
VIZ media
KOKO DEBUT © 2003 by Kazune Kawahara/SHUEISHA Inc.

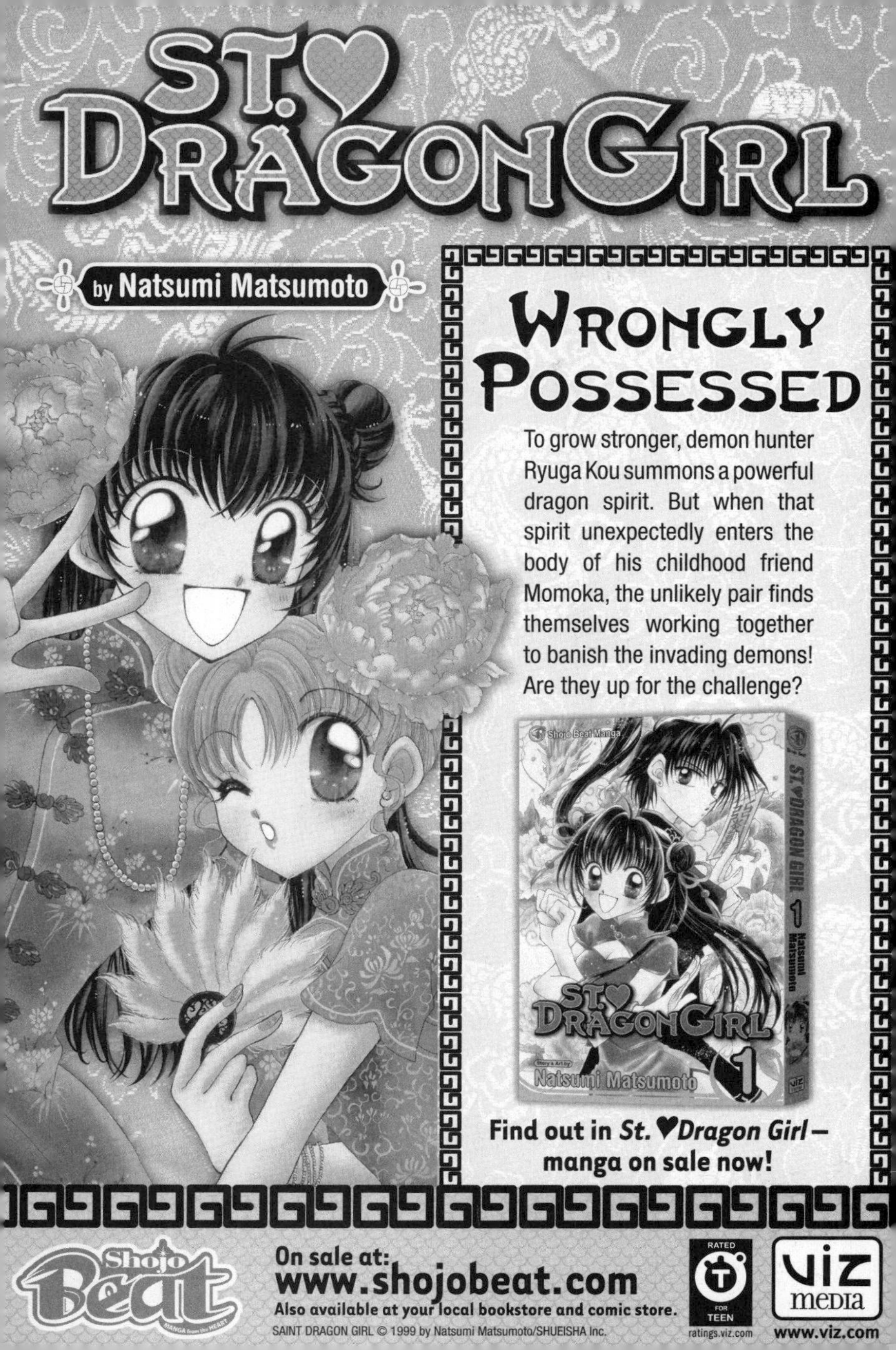

ST.♥ DRAGON GIRL
by Natsumi Matsumoto
WRONGLY POSSESSED
To grow stronger, demon hunter Ryuga Kou summons a powerful dragon spirit. But when that spirit unexpectedly enters the body of his childhood friend Momoka, the unlikely pair finds themselves working together to banish the invading demons! Are they up for the challenge?
Shojo Beat Manga
ST.♥ DRAGON GIRL 1
Story & Art by Natsumi Matsumoto
Find out in St. ♥Dragon Girl— manga on sale now!
Shojo Beat MANGA from the HEART
On sale at:
www.shojobeat.com
Also available at your local bookstore and comic store.
SAINT DRAGON GIRL © 1999 by Natsumi Matsumoto/SHUEISHA Inc.
RATED T FOR TEEN
ratings.viz.com
VIZ media
www.viz.com

Surprise!
You may be reading the wrong way!

It's true: In keeping with the original Japanese comic format, this book reads from right to left—so action, sound effects, and word balloons are completely reversed. This preserves the orientation of the original artwork—plus, it's fun! Check out the diagram shown here to get the hang of things, and then turn to the other side of the book to get started!

"Going, TEACH..."

Commentary on the
Apostolic
Exhortation
Catechesi Tradendae
of John Paul II

"Going, TEACH..."

Commentary on the Apostolic Exhortation *Catechesi Tradendae* of John Paul II

Coordinator: Cesare Bonivento, PIME

Edited by the Institute of Missionary Catechesis
of the Pontifical Urban University

Translated by the Daughters of St. Paul

ST. PAUL EDITIONS

NIHIL OBSTAT:
    Richard V. Lawlor, S.J.
    Censor Deputatus

IMPRIMATUR:
    + Humberto Cardinal Medeiros
    Archbishop of Boston

Original title: *"Andate e predicate"—Commentario all'Esortazione Apostolica "Catechesi Tradendae" di Giovanni Paolo II,* published by Editrice Missionaria Italiana (E.M.I.), Via dell'Arcoveggio 80/7, 40129 Bologna, Italy.

Unless otherwise noted, the Scripture quotations are:

From the Revised Standard Version Bible (modified form), Catholic Edition, copyrighted © 1965 and 1966.

Specified Scripture texts used in this work are taken from the *New American Bible,* copyright © 1970, by the Confraternity of Christian Doctrine, Washington, D.C., and are used by permission of copyright owner. All rights reserved.

The text of *Catechesi tradendae* is reprinted with permission from *L'Osservatore Romano,* English Edition.

16 Documents of Vatican II: NC translation.

Library of Congress Cataloging in Publication Data:
Main entry under title:

"Going, teach..."

        Translation of *"Andate e predicate."*
        Bibliography: p.
        Includes index.
        1. Catholic Church. Pope, 1978-   (John Paul II)
2. Catechetics—Catholic Church—Addresses, essays,
lectures. I. Bonivento, Cesare. II. Catholic Church.
Pope, 1978-   (John Paul II) Catechesi tradendae.
English. 1980. III. Pontificia Universitas Urbaniana.
Institute of Missionary Catechesis.
BX1968.C393A5213   268.'82   80-24211
ISBN 0-8198-3009-7

Cover photos: top—Rev. G. Colton, all others—DSP

Authorized English Edition

Printed in the U.S.A. by the Daughters of St. Paul
50 St. Paul's Ave., Boston, MA 02130

The Daughters of St. Paul are an international congregation of religious women serving the Church with the communications media.

To John Paul II,
who, taking up and continuing the teaching
of Paul VI and of John Paul I,
points out to the whole Church
in catechesis
the path for the evangelization of the world

Presentation

The Institute of Missionary Catechesis of the Pontifical Urban University, born in the climate of the Apostolic Exhortation *Catechesi tradendae,* transparently presents itself to the Church with the clear missionary identity that characterizes Propaganda Fide, which throughout the whole course of its existence has always been concerned about diffusing the Good News among all peoples and rooting it solidly in them.

Notwithstanding the fact that this Institute had been erected mainly for the needs of the missionary Church, concretely, thanks to its particular attributes, it can contribute to the enrichment of catechesis wherever it is carried out. This is shown by this present book, which offers a vast and original commentary on the Apostolic Exhortation of John Paul II, fruit of the Fourth General Assembly of the Synod of Bishops.

Here we have a commentary which from the very opening pages gathers the wealth of traditional catechesis and rejuvenates it in the light of Vatican II, of the General Catechetical Directory issued by Paul VI through the Sacred Congregation for the Clergy, of the International Catechetical Congresses, and lastly of *Evangelii nuntiandi,* which is the Magna Carta of the Missions and of the entire evangelizing work of the Church.

The reader will immediately note that this work of ours develops along two well defined lines: on the one hand, a profound ecclesiality, for it makes constant reference to the pontifical directives, always amply confirmed by the catechetical experience of the entire Church; on the other hand, a great sensitivity to the problems of the various missionary situations, for it not only illustrates the directives mentioned above, but facilitates their application by placing itself within the varying cultural contexts.

It follows that this commentary presents itself almost as an organic and complete treatise on catechesis in our times in the light of the Ecclesiastical Magisterium.

Therefore, I congratulate those who have collaborated in the preparation of this volume—that is, the professors and friends of our Institute of Missionary Catechesis—for their attentive and wise work. I extend my cordial thanks to Father Cesare Bonivento, PIME, director of the same Institute and the soul of this initiative, for the promptness with which this publication has been realized. Translations into other languages are already under way, witnessing to the contemporary relevance of the theme and the originality of its framework.

May this work not only favor the apostolic and missionary formation of future ecclesiastical directors (priests, seminarians, religious and catechists) who are preparing themselves in our Pontifical Urban University, but may it also further the catechetical apostolate in the world according to the spirit of the Church of Christ.

Rome, May 18, 1980
(60th birthday of the Holy Father, John Paul II)

AGNELO CARDINAL ROSSI
Prefect
Sacred Congregation for the Evangelization of Peoples

Introduction

Although amid many difficulties, the Church is living today a providential moment of missionary dynamism which extends all along the ecclesial front. Particularly eloquent witnesses to this are the two Synodal Assemblies of the worldwide Episcopate held in 1974 and in 1977, which treated the subjects of evangelization and catechesis.

The reader will certainly know the new viewpoint with which these themes have been illustrated to the People of God. From being a specific characteristic of mission territories, *evangelization* has been taken up as a primary necessity of the whole Church, to the point of becoming the context and the goal of every ecclesial activity; *catechesis*, set in this new framework, becomes a privileged and decisive stage in evangelization, so as to assume a most important role not only within the Christian community, but also impelling the Christian community itself towards the world which does not believe. Evangelization and catechesis are, therefore, two realities which cannot be separated, under pain of becoming incoherent and inoperative.

It seems to us, then, that the point of arrival and at the same time of departure of this ecclesial maturation has been given by the recent and very beautiful Apostolic Exhortation of John Paul II, *Catechesi tradendae*, which thus comes to complete the teaching of Paul VI, left to us in the historical *Evangelii nuntiandi*. To be convinced of this, it suffices to read no. 18 of the new pontifical document on catechesis. It states: "The Apostolic Exhortation *Evangelii Nuntiandi* of December 8, 1875, on evangelization in the modern world, rightly stressed that evangelization—which has the aim of bringing the Good News to the whole of humanity, so that all may live by it—is a rich, complex and dynamic reality, made up of elements, or one could say moments, that are essential and different from each other, and that must all be kept in view simultaneously. *Catechesis is one of these moments—a very remarkable one—in the whole process of evangelization.*"

The Institute of Missionary Catechesis (ICM), which chronologically represents one of the latest initiatives of the Sacred Congregation for the Evangelization of Peoples (SCEP) and of the Pontifical Urban University (PUU), finds itself in profound harmony with the present ecclesial moment. It was willed with most apt intuition by Propaganda Fide precisely to emphasize the very close relationship between catechesis and universal evangelization. Hence, it is logical that the Institute felt that the responsibility was its own, more than anyone else's, to undertake the task of preparing an ample commentary on the Apostolic Exhortation *Catechesi tradendae,* so as to illustrate the magisterial, catechetical directives of John Paul II in the dynamic missionary context in which he deliberately placed them.

Here, therefore, is the present volume. Through its broad divisions and numerous articles, it endeavors to place in history the great themes of the new document on catechesis and to present them systematically by content. Roughly we have chosen to follow the development of the apostolic exhortation itself. After a first section dedicated to the historical premises which gave rise to *Catechesi tradendae,* we pass to a second which, almost in the manner of a camera flash, describes the role carried on by catechesis in the history of the Church. The central section of the work is constituted by the third and fourth parts, which illustrate, without pretending to be exhaustive, the characteristics of the truly ecclesial catechesis and the wealth of its dynamism, making continual reference to the points set forth in the document of John Paul II. Thus we come to the fifth part, which offers a panorama of the present catechetical effort in the varying cultural areas of the world. At the same time gratitude is given to John Paul II, who in no. 53 of CT confronted and oriented the problem of the "incarnation of the message in the various cultures," and homage is paid to those, above all the missionaries, who courageously find themselves engaged in this work. In this same part we have chosen to give particular service to the reader by offering him a significant panorama of the catechetical initiatives in the principal religious and cultural areas of the world. In the last section, the sixth, we recall, briefly but dutifully, the age-old effort of Propaganda Fide for the growth and improvement of the catechetical apostolate, as the essential means for universal evangelization.

Leafing through these pages, the reader will soon notice that the articles in general are brief and immediately understandable, with critical references reduced to an indispensable minimum. The reason is simple. We wanted this commentary to be of use to catechists especially: that is, to priests, men and women religious, and especially to the laity who have been greatly valued by *Catechesi tradendae.* It is to them that the present publication is directed, in order that in carrying out their catechetical apostolate they will be aided in an essential and profound manner to grasp the true meaning of the orientations of John Paul II.

Another point which the reader cannot help but note regards the "school" and very different origins of the authors of the various articles: a diversity which to someone might seem utterly incoherent. Even here the explanation is very simple. The commentary is supported by the Higher Institute of Missionary Catechesis, but its writing was deliberately not restricted to the members of this Institute. If the commentary had been realized by a team of experts who normally associate with one another and work together, surely the result would have been more homogeneous, but, we believe, also the poorer for it. Instead, we preferred to accept a certain incoherence of method and of contents (quite restricted, however, and inevitable in works of collaboration such as this) to the advantage of greater representation. Thus, the collaborators on this commentary include, besides the professors of the Institute of Missionary Catechesis, professors of the various faculties of the Pontifical Urban University and of the other Universities and Institutes of Rome. Furthermore, it seems necessary for us to emphasize that the commentary was prepared not only by teachers, but also by experts, many of whom are members of the boards of the Roman Curia (their representation highly qualified and numerous), while others work in many catechetical centers of the young Churches.

Thanks to this standard (which could have been much better met, had not some difficulties arisen) the outcome is a work of ample breadth, which offers itself as almost the harmonious echo of the many who, in various roles, are today working for the development and perfecting of the catechetical apostolate. To all of the individual writers of the various articles we extend, therefore, our sincere and cordial thanks.

Permit us also to express our gratitude to those who have made possible, with their encouragement and support, the realization of this publication. First among these is His Eminence, Cardinal Agnelo Rossi, Prefect of the Sacred Congregation for the Evangelization of Peoples, who has been not only the supporter of this initiative but also its very author, for he explicitly promised it in the presence of the Ninth Plenary Assembly of Propaganda Fide, held in October, 1979, in Rome at the very time that *Catechesi tradendae* was released. We thank His Excellency, Bishop Simon Lourdusamy, Secretary of the S.C.E.P., who followed us step by step and with his profound sensitivity helped us to keep in mind the demands of catechesis in the entire missionary world. We also thank all the administrative and teaching staff of the Pontifical Urban University.

Lastly, our thanks to Father Jesus Lopez-Gay, S.J., to Father Domenico Colombo, PIME, and to Doctor Francesco Grasselli of the Editrice Missionaria Italiana (E.M.I.) for their precious editorial assistance.

The present volume has been dedicated to His Holiness, John Paul II, which we find in no. 15 of his Apostolic Exhortation: to express an act of filial gratitude to the reigning Pontiff, whom history must from now on remember as the author of the postconciliar catechetical renewal. It is upon this renewal—we are certain—that the internal solidity of the Church depends, together with her missionary zeal towards the world which anxiously waits to be of Christ. Because of this it is our most lively hope that the whole Church will know how to accept, assimilate and suitably translate into practice the heartfelt words of John Paul II, which we find in no. 15 of his Apostolic Exhortation: "The more the Church, whether on the local or the universal level, gives catechesis priority over other works and undertakings the results of which would be more spectacular, the more she finds in catechesis a strengthening of her internal life as a community of believers and of her external activity as a missionary Church."

CESARE BONIVENTO, PIME

Director
*Institute of Missionary Catechesis
of the Pontifical Urban University*

TABLE OF CONTENTS

COMMENTARY on
Catechesi Tradendae

11   **Presentation**
      Agnelo Cardinal Rossi
      Prefect, Sacred Congregation for the Evangelization of Peoples

13   **Introduction**
      Cesare Bonivento, PIME
      *Director, Institute of Missionary Catechesis of the Pontifical
      Urban University*

23   **List of Authors**

PART ONE

*Continuity of the Evangelizing Magisterium from
Paul VI to John Paul II*

29   **The Council: the Great Catechism of Modern Times**
      Agnelo Cardinal Rossi
      Prefect, Sacred Congregation for the Evangelization of Peoples

38   **Paul VI and Catechesis**
      Sergio Goretti

49   **Catechesis in John Paul I**
      Gino Concetti, O.F.M.

62   **"Redemptor Hominis": A Catechesis for the Man of
      Today**
      Aloysius Bogliolo

75   **From "Evangelii Nuntiandi" to "Catechesi Tradendae":
      Continuity of the Magisterium**
      Most Reverend Lucas Moreira Neves

82   **General Introduction to the Apostolic Exhortation
      "Catechesi Tradendae"**
      Jesús López-Gay, S.J.

PART TWO

"An Experience As Ancient As the Church"
Catechesis in the History of the Church

99   The Catechesis of the Apostles and of the First Christians
     Paolo Giglioni

114   The Catechesis of the Fathers
     Agostino Trapè, O.S.A.

123   Liturgical Catechesis in the Early Church
     Anscar J. Chupungco, O.S.B.

138   The Council of Trent and the Origins of Modern Catechesis
     Giuseppe Cavallotto

168   Contemporary Catechesis from Pius X to Our Own Times
     Giuseppe Cavallotto

PART THREE

The Nature and Spirit
of Authentically Ecclesial Catechesis

191   For a Christocentric Catechesis
     Tommaso Federici

221   The Holy Spirit, the Teacher Within and Inspirer of All Catechetical Work
     José Saraiva-Martins, C.M.F.

235   Liturgical Dimension: Elements of Sacramental Catechesis
     Anscar J. Chupungco, O.S.B.

247   Spiritual Dimension: Marian and Missionary Attitude
     Msgr. Juan Esquerda-Bifet

260   Missionary Dimensions of Catechesis
     Olegario Domínguez, O.M.I.

272   Catechesis in Ecumenical Perspective
     John Long, S.J.

285   Orthodoxy and Orthopraxis
     Bonifacio Honings, O.C.D.

295   Catechesis and Theology
     G. Battista Mondin, S.X.

PART FOUR
The Dynamics of Catechetical Action

311   The Workers of Catechesis in a Community
      All Catechizing and All Catechized
         Duc Dao Dinh
324   The Lay Catechist
         Jesús López-Gay, S.J.
334   The Irreplaceable Role of the Family
         Guzman Carriquiry
347   The Receivers of Catechesis and the Centrality
      of Man
         Silvio Riva, O.F.M.
360   Permanent Catechesis and the Catechumenate
      in Reference to Adults
         Paolo Milan
373   Memorization in Catechetical Teaching
         Ubaldo Giannetto, S.D.B.
380   Popular Devotions and Catechesis
         Msgr. Mario Puccinelli
389   Using the Means of Social Communication
         Piero Gheddo, PIME
402   The Catechetical Office and Missionary Center of the
      Pastoral of Togetherness
         Msgr. Agostino Bonivento

PART FIVE
The Missionary Dynamism of Catechesis
in the Actual Historical Moment

415   The Thought of "Catechesi Tradendae" on the
      Incarnation of the Evangelical Message in Cultures
         Most Reverend D. Simon Lourdusamy
435   Catechesis in a Traditional African Milieu
         Paul Cardinal Zoungrana
446   Some Aspects of Catechetical Renewal in India
         D. S. Amalorpavadass
458   Catechesis in a Buddhist Ambient
         Marcello Zago, O.M.I.
474   Proposals for a Catechesis in a Muslim Ambient
         Maurice Borrmans, P.B.

490   Problems and Characteristics of Catechesis in Oceania
         Henk te Maarssen, S.V.D.

504   Development of Catechesis in North America
         Francis Kelly

513   Catechesis in the Documents of the Church in Latin America
         Emilio Alberich, S.D.B.

528   Significant Moments of the Catechetical Renewal in Europe
         Roberto Giannatelli

546   The Environmental Influence on Catechesis in the Countries of Eastern Europe
         Msgr. Francesco Skoda

PART SIX

The Work of "Propaganda Fide" in the Catechetical Apostolate

559   The Present Action of the Sacred Congregation for the Evangelization of Peoples for the Development of Catechesis in General, with Some References to the Territories of the Asian and African Continents
         Msgr. Tiziano Scalzotto

579   Missionary Catechesis in the Directives of the Sacred Congregation for the Evangelization of Peoples or "De Propaganda Fide" (1622-1980)
         Josef Metzler, O.M.I.

595   1970 Plenary Assembly of the Sacred Congregation for the Evangelization of Peoples (S.C.E.P.) on Catechists
         Msgr. Bernard Jacqueline

602   The World Encounter of Missionary Catechists During the Holy Year, 1975
         Robert Rweyemamu

617   Institute of Missionary Catechesis
         Cesare Bonivento, PIME

TEXT of *Catechesi Tradendae*

Apostolic Exhortation of Pope John Paul II

Introduction

627   Christ's Final Command — 1
627   Paul VI's Solicitude — 2
628   A Fruitful Synod — 3
628   Purpose of This Exhortation — 4

I
We Have But One Teacher, Jesus Christ

630   Putting into Communion With the Person of Christ — 5
630   Transmitting Christ's Teaching — 6
631   Christ the Teacher — 7
632   The One "Teacher" — 8
632   Teaching Through His Life as a Whole — 9

II
An Experience as Old as the Church

634   The Mission of the Apostles — 10
634   Catechesis in the Apostolic Age — 11
635   The Fathers of the Church — 12
636   Councils and Missionary Activity — 13
636   Catechesis as the Church's Right and Duty — 14
637   Priority of This Task — 15
638   Shared but Differentiated Responsibility — 16
638   Continual Balanced Renewal — 17

III
Catechesis in the Church's Pastoral and Missionary Activity

640   Catechesis as a Stage in Evangelization — 18
641   Catechesis and the Initial Proclamation of the Gospel — 19
642   Specific Aim of Catechesis — 20
643   Need for Systematic Catechesis — 21
643   Catechesis and Life Experience — 22
644   Catechesis and Sacraments — 23

645   Catechesis and Ecclesial Community — 24

645   Catechesis in the Wide Sense Necessary for Maturity
         and Strength of Faith — 25

IV
The Whole of the Good News
Drawn from Its Source

647   Content of the Message — 26

647   The Source — 27

648   The Creed, an Exceptionally Important Expression
         of Doctrine — 28

648   Factors that Must Not Be Neglected — 29

650   Integrity of Content — 30

651   By Means of Suitable Pedagogical Methods — 31

652   Ecumenical Dimension of Catechesis — 32

653   Ecumenical Collaboration in the Field of
         Catechesis — 33

654   The Question of Textbooks Dealing with the Various
         Religions — 34

V
Everybody Needs To Be Catechized

655   The Importance of Children and the Young — 35

656   Infants — 36

656   Children — 37

656   Adolescents — 38

657   The Young — 39

658   The Adaptation of Catechesis for Young People
         — 40

659   The Handicapped — 41

659   Young People Without Religious Support — 42

659   Adults — 43

660   Quasi-catechumens — 44

660   Diversified and Complementary Forms of
         Catechesis — 45

VI
Some Ways and Means of Catechesis

662   Communications Media — 46

662   Utilization of Various Places, Occasions
         and Gatherings — 47

663   The Homily — 48
664   Catechetical Literature — 49
665   Catechisms — 50

VII
How To Impart Catechesis

666   Diversity of Methods — 51
666   At the Service of Revelation and Conversion — 52
667   The Message Embodied in Cultures — 53
668   The Contribution of Popular Devotion — 54
669   Memorization — 55

VIII
The Joy of Faith in a Troubled World

671   Affirming Christian Identity — 56
671   In an Indifferent World — 57
672   With the Original Pedagogy of the Faith — 58
672   Language Suited to the Service of the Credo — 59
673   Research and Certainty of Faith — 60
674   Catechesis and Theology — 61

IX
The Task Concerns Us All

676   Encouragement to all Responsible for
        Catechesis — 62
676   Bishops — 63
677   Priests — 64
678   Men and Women Religious — 65
678   Lay Catechists — 66
679   In the Parish — 67
680   In the Family — 68
681   At School — 69
683   Within Organizations — 70
683   Training Institutes — 71

Conclusion

685   The Holy Spirit, the Teacher Within — 72
686   Mary, Mother and Model of the Disciple — 73

693   *INDEX* of the Commentary

LIST OF AUTHORS

His Eminence, Agnelo Cardinal Rossi, Prefect of the Sacred Congregation for the Evangelization of Peoples.

His Eminence, Paul Cardinal Zoungrana, Archbishop of Ouagadougou (Upper Volta).

His Excellency, Most Reverend D. Simon Lourdusamy, Secretary of the Sacred Congregation for the Evangelization of Peoples.

His Excellency, Most Reverend Lucas Moreira Neves, Secretary of the Sacred College of Cardinals and of the Sacred Congregation for Bishops.

Alberich, D. Emilio, S.D.B., professor of fundamental catechetics at the Catechetical Institute of the Pontifical Salesian University of Rome.

Amalorpavadass, D.S., Director of the National Biblical, Catechetical and Liturgical Center of Bangalore, Secretary of the National Catechetical Commission of the Catholic Bishops' Conference of India (CBCI).

Bogliolo, D. Aloysius, S.D.B., professor of Christian anthropology at the Institute of Missionary Catechesis, formerly Magnificent Rector of the Pontifical Urban University (PUU).

Bonivento, Msgr. Agostino, Rector of the Diocesan Seminary of Chioggia (VE), Episcopal Vicar for catechesis and of the means of social communication.

Bonivento, P. Cesare, PIME, Director of the Institute of Missionary Catechesis, professor of missiology at the Faculty of Missiology of the PUU.

Borrmans, P. Maurice, P.B., professor of Islamology at the Pontifical Institute of Arabian Studies of Rome.

Carriquiry, Doctor Guzman, professor of history at the Institute of Missionary Catechesis of the PUU, major official of the Pontifical Council for the Laity.

Cavallotto, D. Giuseppe, professor of the history of catechesis at the Institute of Missionary Catechesis of the PUU.

Chupungco, P. Anscar J., O.S.B., professor of liturgy at the Institute of Missionary Catechesis of the PUU, president of the Pontifical Liturgical Institute of the Pontifical Ateneo of St. Anselm of Rome.

Concetti, P. Gino, O.F.M., editor of *L'Osservatore Romano*.

Dinh, P. Duc Dao, professor of spirituality at the Institute of Missionary Catechesis of the PUU.

Dominguez, P. Olegario, O.M.I., doctor of missiology, vice-librarian of the PUU.

Esquerda-Bifet, Msgr. Juan, professor of spirituality at the Institute of Missionary Catechesis and at the Faculty of Missiology of the PUU.

Federici, Doctor Tommaso, professor of Sacred Scripture at the Theology Faculty of the PUU.

Gheddo, P. Piero, PIME, Director of the missionary magazine "Mondo e Missione" of the Pontifical Institute of Foreign Missions (PIME).

Giannatelli, D. Roberto, Director of the Institute of Catechetics of the Pontifical Salesian University of Rome.

Giannetto, D. Ubaldo, S.D.B., professor of the history of catechesis at the Catechetical Institute of the Pontifical Salesian University of Rome, responsible for the Center of documentations at the Salesian Catechetical Center of Turin.

Giglioni, D. Paolo, professor of Sacred Scripture at the Institute of Missionary Catechesis of the PUU.

Goretti, Msgr. Sergio, Secretary of the International Council for Catechesis, at the Sacred Congregation for the Clergy.

Honings, P. Bonifacio, O.C.D., professor of moral theology at the Institute of Missionary Catechesis of the PUU, Dean of the Faculty of Theology of the Pontifical Lateran University.

Jacqueline, Msgr. Bernard, Under-secretary of the Secretariat for Non-Believers.

Kelly, Rev. Francis, Director of the Department of Religious Education of the National Catholic Educational Association of the United States.

Long, P. John, S.J., department head of the Secretariat for the Union of Christians.

López-Gay, P. Jesús, S.J., professor of missiology at the Faculty of Missiology of the Pontifical Gregorian University.

Maarssen, P. Henk te, S.V.D., Director of the Liturgical Catechetical Institute of Goroka, Papua, New Guinea.

Metzler, P. Josef, O.M.I., professor of history at the Faculty of Missiology of the PUU, archivist of the Sacred Congregation for the Evangelization of Peoples.

Milan, D. Paolo, professor of catechetics at the Institute of Missionary Catechesis of the PUU, national assistant of the "adult" sector of Italian Catholic Action.

Mondin, P. Giovanni Battista, S.X., professor at the Faculty of Philosophy of the PUU, Director of the Higher Institute for the Study of Atheism of the PUU.

Puccinelli, Msgr. Mario, professor of pastoral theology at the Faculty of Theology of the PUU.

Riva, P. Silvio, O.F.M., Dean of the Pontifical Pastoral Institute of the Pontifical Lateran University.

Rweyemamu, D. Robert, professor of catechesis at the Institute of Missionary Catechesis of the PUU, and at the Faculty of Missiology of the PUU.

Saraiva-Martins, P. José, C.M.F., Magnificent Rector of the PUU, professor of sacramentology at the Faculty of Theology of the PUU.

Scalzotto, Msgr. Tiziano, Under-secretary of the Sacred Congregation for the Evangelization of Peoples.

Skoda, Msgr. Francesco, professor of "atheism" at the Faculty of Philosophy of the PUU, officer of the Secretariat for Nonbelievers.

Trapè, P. Agostino, O.S.A., professor of patristics at the Institute of Missionary Catechesis of the PUU, and at the Patristic Institute "Agustinianum" of Rome.

Zago, P. Marcello, O.M.I., professor of missiology at the Faculty of Theology of the Pontifical Lateran University, assistant general of the Oblates of Mary Immaculate (O.M.I.).

PART ONE

Continuity of the Evangelizing Magisterium from Paul VI to John Paul II

"This Exhortation takes up again the reflections that were prepared by *Pope Paul VI*, making abundant use of the documents left by the synod. *Pope John Paul I*, whose zeal and gifts as a catechist amazed us all, had taken them in hand and was preparing to publish them when he was suddenly called to God. To all of us he gave an example of catechesis at once popular and concentrated on the essential, one made up of simple words and actions that were able to touch the heart. *I am therefore taking up the inheritance of these two Popes* in response to the request which was expressly formulated by the Bishops at the end of the fourth general assembly of the synod and which was welcomed by Pope Paul VI in his closing speech. I am also doing so in order to fulfill one of the chief duties of my apostolic charge. Catechesis has always been a central care in my ministry as a priest and as a Bishop."
—CT 4

1

The Council: the Great Catechism of Modern Times

With the present chapter we begin the commentary on the Apostolic Exhortation of John Paul II, *Catechesi tradendae*, which sums up, illustrates and perfects the catechetical updating treated by the 1977 Synod of Bishops.

It seems to me very opportune, in order to grasp the whole importance of this new pontifical document, to begin from the Second Vatican Ecumenical Council, which is at the basis of the updating and renewal of all the sectors of the Church, and, therefore, also of catechesis, just as John XXIII desired in the Bull *Humanae salutis*, with which he summoned the Ecumenical Council.

The motive and the origin come to us from *Catechesi tradendae* itself, which in paragraph two recalls the beautiful expression of Paul VI: "The Council is the great catechism of modern times." Certainly this phrase can be understood only in the context of the Pontiff's address. Evidently it does not mean finding in the sixteen documents which come from Vatican Council II an organic exposition of Catholic doctrine, but they are certainly rich in the authentic teaching of the Church, and, therefore, full of doctrinal and also methodological points for an effective catechesis in regard to the man of today. In fact, these documents are the fruit of the solemn Magisterium of the Church and are meant to guard the deposit of faith in an updated form. They are overflowing with wisdom, vigor and confidence, and are, therefore, to be amply utilized to overcome the evils and difficulties of the present times with the vitality of the Church.

I. PERSONAL EXPERIENCE

Permit me to relate my own pastoral experience. Nominated Archbishop of São-Paolo in Brazil during Vatican II, I found myself unexpectedly facing the complex problems of a metropolis which had more than eight million inhabitants. I must admit that I was able to find tranquillity, security and a clear pastoral orientation even in the most painful questions precisely by referring to the conciliar texts. I organized, therefore, sixteen study commissions, made up of priests, religious and laity. They attentively examined the directives of the individual documents of the Council, and were thus able to suggest the best application in the actual situation of the Archdiocese. In this manner we arrived at the elaboration of a pastoral plan of togetherness for the Archdiocese based on the spirit of renewal desired by Pope John XXIII and effected by Paul VI.

Such was my conviction of the doctrinal and pastoral importance of the Council that, when asking the Holy See's permission to ordain as a priest the elderly and praiseworthy President of the St. Vincent de Paul Society—he had become a widower and had always been a true Catholic leader of great religious culture and exemplary piety, besides being the father of a bishop and of religious daughters—I asked and obtained permission that he be examined on the basis of the conciliar documents.

This is sufficient to indicate the importance I have always attributed to the Council, above all in relation to catechesis. The latter has constantly represented my greatest pastoral effort, not only before as Metropolitan Archbishop, but also now as Prefect of the Sacred Congregation for the Evangelization of Peoples and hence entrusted by the conciliar Decree *Ad gentes* to plan and to give dynamism to all missionary activity and cooperation throughout the world, with respect, however, for the right of the Oriental Churches.

II. INDIRECT INDICATIONS OFFERED US BY CONCILIAR CATECHESIS

The theme to be treated is so vast that we find ourselves obliged to pass over very important aspects of the conciliar magisterium, which however we think will be considered in the following chapters. It is therefore almost impossible for us to assure even a panoramic vision of Vatican II in relationship to catechesis. We will try, however, to outline briefly the Council's actuality and its pastoral, spiritual and theological importance.

To this end I would like to pause first of all on the directives which come to us from the conciliar catechesis itself, because this is how the teaching of the Council must be understood. It concerns directives of great importance, because they are obligatory, above all today, for the person who finds himself working in the field of catechesis. It seems to me that they can be summed up as follows. *True catechesis must:*

a) *Be sensitive to the problems of the one being catechized.* The Council willed to speak to the Christian and to the man of the twentieth century, putting itself in tune with him. For this it could not help but take into account the problems which he is experiencing. Therefore, it listened to and perceived both the problematic of the Christian in relation to the Church, to Sacred Scripture, to missionary activity, to ecumenism, to non-Christian religions, to the relationship with earthly realities, etc., as well as the anguishes of man for peace; culture and the cultures; the relation between science and faith; religious freedom; human rights; the family; progress; injustice; poverty; hunger; etc. It is within this framework that the Council willed to place its proclamation, well aware that otherwise it would not have been listened to much less understood.

b) *Present the Gospel in its entirety.* Placing itself in an attitude of listening to man and wanting to dialogue with him, the Council presented a selection of truths, almost proposing to him the truths which are easier to be understood, more acceptable and more attuned to "modern culture." The Council re-proposed to modern man the Gospel of Jesus Christ in all its entirety. Whoever takes up the conciliar documents finds himself almost faced with *a summa theologica*, from which nothing of the Catholic Truth received and transmitted by the Apostles is omitted. The Gospel of Vatican II is the whole Gospel, "a stumbling block to Jews and folly to Gentiles,"[1] and it is presented with the same courage with which the Apostles presented it in Jerusalem, in Athens and in Rome, knowing that for everyone without distinction an act of faith was necessary in order to accept it. I remember that Paul VI said in this regard at the end of the Synod of 1974: "The content of the faith is either Catholic or it is not. We all have received the faith from an uninterrupted and constant tradition; Peter and Paul did not disguise it to adapt it to the ancient Jewish, Greek and Roman world, but they watched over its authenticity, over the truth of the one message, presented in a diversity of languages."[2]

c) *Interpret Catholic doctrine in communion with the whole of Tradition.* The peculiarity of Vatican II, however, consists in having known how to transmit the entirety of the Gospel to the anguished man of today through a theological mediation fully faithful to Tradition. As a witness of this, we cannot help but refer the reader to renewed ecclesiological vision, to the teaching on Revelation, on the episcopate, on the priesthood, on the laity, on the relation of the Christian to earthly realities, on the re-establishment of Catholic unity and on the relation with non-Christian religions. The Council certainly did not present a Gospel different from that of the Apostles, but we must concede that it knew how to place it into the problematic of modern man in a way that could not have been better. This is the reason why its message and its catechesis are found to be completely faithful to God and to man. No one can ever blame Vatican II for having failed the Truth given us by Christ, just as no one can ever affirm that the Church, with the Council, has ignored the requests of man. We have in the conciliar documents a perfect balance which becomes an obligatory pattern for the person who sets out to preach the Word of God today.

d) *Communicate a great pastoral inspiration.* The catechesis of the Council is supported by a great pastoral sensitivity, that is, by an attitude of desiring to understand the questioner and to make itself understood by him in a simpler and more immediate manner. It succeeds, on the one hand, by grasping the problems in their essentials without excessive divergencies, and, on the other hand, by having recourse to solid and profound theology, yes, but always expressed with a terminology of crystalline transparency. It is a common testimony that the conciliar documents can be read and understood by everyone. Consequently, no gap is placed between the Council and those to whom it speaks. The common man feels himself reflected in it, and is, therefore, disposed to enter into dialogue with the Council, which can therefore transmit to him the Christian truth in its essence, with profundity, simplicity, and clarity of language. The comparison with many modern texts of theology comes spontaneously. These were written with the intention of being read by everyone, but they ended up very quickly on library shelves to be consulted only by those "assigned to the works." The conciliar texts, on the other hand, have entered homes, are still read and understood, and have become a point of constant reference for many.

e) *Stimulate an effective evangelizing dynamism.* It is my duty, finally, to point out the concrete and effective missionary dimension which animates all conciliar teaching. Certainly the Council does not treat of only one dimension. We cannot, in fact, forget the dimensions that are liturgical, biblical, ecumenical, etc. But it is also true that the missionary dimension represents one of the most precious aspects of the catechesis of Vatican II, and one of the most providential admonitions for the Church which, today more than ever, finds herself faced with enormous responsibilities of evangelization. If it is true that with *Evangelii nuntiandi* and *Catechesi tradendae* the Church seems to have acquired a rich and profound missionary conscience and dynamism, it is also true that this would not have been possible without a Council which did not confine the missionary problem only to the Decree *Ad gentes,* but has strewn all the Decrees and Constitutions with strong missionary reminders (cf. GS, PO, CD, NA, UR, DH, PC, etc.). And, above all, it willed that the Dogmatic Constitution on the Church should open, develop and conclude in the light of universal evangelization.[3] This is true to such a degree that to speak of the Church today signifies remembering immediately her missionary dimension, following the example of *Ad gentes,* which in no. 2 affirms: "The pilgrim Church is missionary by her very nature." It is from this continual permeation that there comes to us an impelling admonition to see to it that catechesis, wherever it is carried out, expresses first of all and always the missionary vocation of the Church.

To me these seem to be the fundamental characteristics of the catechesis of the Council. Undoubtedly it is a matter of indirect signs, but surely lived and made their own by the Bishops who were the first to be catechized by Vatican II. We owe it to them if these signs came up again in the Synod of 1977 and, hence, in the magisterial Apostolic Exhortation of John Paul II. Vatican II represents, therefore, the great turning point of catechesis, both for the teaching given, as well as for the experience lived by the entire episcopal college.

III. CONCILIAR STATEMENTS ON CATECHESIS

Now we come to the conciliar statements on catechesis. Permit us to recall the principal ones, almost as a listing. Perhaps this might give the impression of an arid succession of citations, but in reality it is an effective way to become acquainted with the Council's wealth of suggestions. It is also an invitation to return to them for a more profound reflection and use.

The statements are contained, above all, in the Decree *Christus Dominus*, which addressed itself to the Bishops, reminding them that their first duty is that of evangelization and catechetical instruction (CD 12-14), but many others are dispersed throughout all the documents. We can put them in topic order in the following manner:

1. *Importance of catechesis.* One of the clearest statements in this regard can be taken from the Declaration on Christian Education, wherein the Council says precisely: "In fulfilling its educational role, the Church, eager to employ all suitable aids, is concerned especially about those which are her very own. Foremost among these is catechetical instruction, which enlightens and strengthens the faith, nourishes life according to the spirit of Christ, leads to intelligent and active participation in the liturgical mystery and gives motivation for apostolic activity" (GE 4). It is clear that this is the educational duty of the family, of the school and of the Church, as we shall soon see.

2. *Essential characteristics.* Catechesis must be biblical, liturgical and based on the Magisterium and the life of the Church (SC 14; DV 24; AG 17, 19), open to missionary problems (AG 39) and to the necessities of the universal Church (PO 11), suited to form seminarians well (OT 19), and also open to the means of social communication (IM 16) in a manner that responds to the problems of the man of today (CD 13).

3. *Principal duty of the Bishops.* Catechetical instruction is prescribed for Bishops in a synthetic but obligatory form: "Bishops should take pains that catechetical instruction—which is intended to make the faith, as illumined by teaching, a vital, explicit and effective force in the lives of men—be given with sedulous care to both children and adolescents, youths and adults. In this instruction a suitable arrangement should be

observed as well as a method suited to the matter that is being treated and to the character, ability, age, and circumstances of the life of the students. Finally, they should see to it that this instruction is based on Sacred Scripture, tradition, the liturgy, magisterium, and the life of the Church" (CD 14).

4. *Duty of pastors.* Afterwards when the same decree speaks of the principal collaborators of the Bishops—the pastors—it prescribes: "In the exercise of their teaching office it is the duty of pastors to preach God's Word to all the Christian people so that, rooted in faith, hope and charity, they will grow in Christ, and as a Christian community bear witness to that charity which the Lord commended. It is also the duty of pastors to bring the faithful to a full knowledge of the mystery of salvation through a catechetical instruction which is consonant with each one's age. In imparting this instruction they should seek not only the assistance of religious but also the cooperation of the laity, establishing also the Confraternity of Christian Doctrine" (CD 30).

5. *Role of the family.* The parents are to be considered the first ones responsible for the Christian education of their children. Regarding this, the Council recalls: "It is particularly in the Christian family, enriched by the grace and office of the sacrament of matrimony, that children should be taught from their early years to have a knowledge of God according to the faith received in Baptism, to worship Him, and to love their neighbor.... Let parents, then, recognize the inestimable importance a truly Christian family has for the life and progress of God's own people" (GE 3).

6. *Role of the school.* The Church holds that catechesis is a duty so irrevocable as to be exacted not only in the Catholic schools, but in the non-Catholic ones as well: "Feeling very keenly the weighty responsibility of diligently caring for the moral and religious education of all her children, the Church must be present with her own special affection and help for the great number who are being trained in schools that are not Catholic" (GE 7).

7. *Respect for non-Christian religions.* It is dutiful to note that the courage of the Church in the carrying out of catechesis is accompanied by a great sense of tact in regard to those who follow other religions. What is affirmed in the Declaration on Non-Christian Religions in regard to the Jewish religion is signifi-

cant: "All should see to it, then, that in catechetical work or in the preaching of the word of God they do not teach anything that does not conform to the truth of the Gospel and the spirit of Christ" (NA 4).

8. *Formation of catechists.* The Council does not fail to mention catechetical centers (AG 31) and the collaboration of lay catechists, especially in mission territories (AG 15), but it dwells at length particularly on the formation of the catechists themselves, with words of encouragement, praise and lively appreciation, which, because of their importance, merit to be quoted entirely:

"Likewise worthy of praise are the ranks of men and women catechists, well deserving of missionary work to the nations. Imbued with the apostolic spirit, they labor much to make an outstanding and altogether necessary contribution to the spread of the Faith and of the Church.

"In our time, when there are so few clerics to preach the Gospel to such great numbers and to exercise the pastoral ministry, the position of catechists is of great importance. Therefore their training must be so accomplished and so adapted to advances on the cultural level that as reliable co-workers of the priestly order, they may perform their task well, though it be weighed down with new and greater burdens.

"There should therefore be an increase in the number of schools, both on the diocesan and on the regional levels, wherein future catechists may study Catholic doctrine, especially in the fields of Scripture and the liturgy, as well as catechetical method and pastoral practice; schools wherein they can develop in themselves a Christian character, and wherein they can devote themselves tirelessly to cultivating piety and sanctity of life. Moreover, conventions or courses should be held in which at certain times catechists could be refreshed in the disciplines and skills useful for their ministry, and in which their spiritual life could be nourished and strengthened. In addition, for those who devote themselves entirely to this work, a decent standard of living should be provided, and social security, by paying them a just wage.

"It would be desirable for the Sacred Congregation for the Propagation of the Faith to provide special funds for the due training and support of catechists. If it seems necessary and fitting, let a special 'Association for Catechists' be founded.

"Moreover, the churches should gratefully acknowledge the noble work being done by auxiliary catechists, whose help they will need. These preside over the prayers in their communities and teach sacred doctrine. Something suitable should be done for their doctrinal and spiritual training. Besides, it is to be hoped that, where it seems opportune, catechists who are duly trained should receive a *missio canonica* in a publicly celebrated liturgical ceremony, so that in the eyes of the people they may serve the Faith with greater authority" (AG 17).

It seems to us that we have outlined succinctly but concretely the task and the importance which Vatican Council II attributes to catechesis, and especially to that of mission territories.

The decree *Christus Dominus* (no. 44) concludes with a general mandate, in which is also prescribed a general catechetical directory of which the following chapter will speak, outlining the rapport between Vatican Council II and the catechetical work of Paul VI.

In conclusion, the Council is a font of crystalline waters, which becomes a river and gives fertility to the earth. Now the providential moment has arrived to plant in the ground prepared by the Synod of Bishops and by the Apostolic Exhortation *Catechesi tradendae* the tree of the catechesis of our times, as was previously done in the history of the Church after the Council of Trent. And the "go ahead" must be given, in the Roman Curia, by the Sacred Congregation for the Clergy.

But the Sacred Congregation for the Evangelization of Peoples, as it will be pointed out in the final part of this book, has not remained inactive in this period. In the field of its competency it has made research and experiments to be able to produce abundant fruits in its mission territories.

Therefore, we salute the anxiously awaited Apostolic Exhortation *Catechesi tradendae* with intense joy and profound thanksgiving. This solicitous commentary is already the initial starting point of Propaganda Fide in this immense field of vital importance for evangelization.

CARDINAL AGNELO ROSSI

FOOTNOTES

1. 1 Cor. 1:23.
2. AAS, MDCCCCLXXIV, pp. 636-637.
3. Cf. LG, nos. 1, 9-17, 69.

2

Paul VI and Catechesis

(Profession of Faith, General Catechetical Directory, Catechetical Congress and International Council)

We do not intend here to give a brief history of catechesis as it was developed during the span of the pontificate of Paul VI. It would be already very risky to attempt conclusions and to dare to synthesize a difficult and complex pontificate, which had the weighty heredity of concluding and applying Vatican Council II. Also to be considered is the fact that every history, no matter how limited and precise, always sinks its roots down into the past, living on what has preceded us. Here we aim only to allude to the publication of a few special documents and magisterial acts, to their motivations, to their significance and to the goals that they had set for themselves, so as to be able to understand the goals which were specified as a stimulus and orientation of catechetical activity.

A Catechetical Council
That Almost Did Not Speak of Catechesis

Vatican II, as is known, had primarily pastoral purposes. It proposed, as John XXIII specified already in his opening speech, to obtain a leap forward through "a more perfect fidelity to ancient doctrine," studied, however, "through the forms of research and of the literary formulation of modern thought."[1] The purposes of Vatican II, therefore, were much more vast than those which concerned catechetical renewal. They touched the whole life of the Church and did not aim at change but at a better understanding. On the one hand, there was "fidelity to ancient doctrine"; on the other, the necessity of scrutinizing it in all its dimensions to be able to propose it effectively to the man of our time. The great prophetic sense of Pope John was that of having noted that such a general reflection could no longer be deferred.

The catechetical world watched the Council with supreme interest and awaited its conclusions with confidence. It understood that from the Council would come such an orientation that it would be possible to solve or at least clarify the more serious problems. Not a few, however, were continuing to act as though nothing or almost nothing were changed, as though one could still speak to the man of today, with all his ebb and flow, in the same manner that one spoke to the man of yesterday. Still, others referred in a static manner to the great inheritance of the Council of Trent. At the time of Trent the world was intrinsically permeated by Christianity, even if in a manner that was more conformist than real. The risk then was constituted not so much by the abandonment of the faith as by falling into heresy. In such a world it was sufficient to present the doctrine with clarity and authenticity and to limit oneself to following those pastoral directives, of which the Council had given a magnificent example with the publication of the *catechismus ad parochos*.[2] For centuries the situation was considered substantially unchanged and hence the model of a "catechism of Christian doctrine" was still used. However, catechesis, which is human mediation at the service of the Word of God, cannot ignore that cultural, social, economic and political situations change, and that, in changing, they create applications and needs which are partly new. Not only the break, but also the difference between faith and culture is ruinous. Culture is, in fact, the human manner of interpreting the world; it is the means which man constructs for himself in order to live his existence; it is the image which man has of himself, his conception of history, of nature and of relationships with others. The wiser part of the catechetical world had taken note of this change and hoped that the Church would have that same strength which she had shown eighteen centuries before when she had succeeded in planting Christianity in the Greco-Roman culture. It was proposed that "from the catechism of doctrine" there should be a movement "towards the catechism for Christian life." In particular, there was an awareness of the need to propose a message rather than a doctrine. Every message implies a doctrine; in fact, the message implies a certain, vital and liberating[3] doctrine. Doctrine and message, however, do not have exactly the same meaning and, above all, they do not imply the same pedagogical procedure. "The message is essentially addressed to someone; it implies, in the one who transmits it, a person-to-person attitude; the message is questioning and is awaiting an answer. Whoever speaks of doctrine speaks of the content of the message, contemplated in itself and for itself as a collection of truth without an equally direct and explicit reference to a person. Now this objective attitude, didactically useful and necessary, is second; the act of catechesis always concerns transmitting a message."[4]

Resolving to reconsider and to renew the Church interiorly and in her activity, Vatican II, as it was said, went beyond the aspirations of catechesis, but was similar to the whole which contains the part. Even if it did not occupy itself directly with catechesis, it concluded by answering all its requests. Catechesis is ever present in all the conciliar documents[5]—in some places more extensively and in some less. To it continual reference is made directly or indirectly, because it is seen as one of the specific instruments for bringing all the wealth of conciliar reflection to fulfillment. The Council was catechetical, because it revealed the importance of living the evangelical message and deeply analyzed the human question and the thirst for God. The power of the Gospel is not an article to be exported. The first task of the Church is that she herself live communitarianly the message which she preserves and proposes. But to live the Gospel also means accepting the plan of God to transform humanity and participating in this plan as intensely as possible. It is the Spirit who works and forms the aspirations of humanity, so that they will meet, through the mediation of the Church, their object, which is Christ, the source and fullness of everything. Even the encounter between human demand and God is the work of the Spirit. But not for this is the human task less necessary and enthusing: the Council has indicated to us how to determine the encounter and render the means accessible that make the encounter possible. The parallelism between the Council and the goal of catechesis is impressive.

Therefore, the Council as a whole was a catechetical happening—which it probably would not have succeeded in being had it treated the theme in an explicit manner. "A simple decree, perhaps even a constitution," says S. Riva, "would have limited catechesis to the cage of a temporary discourse, with short duration of validity and of actuality."[6]

The Council opened perspectives of great interest to catechesis. But how were these to be applied? Were all ready to welcome them with clarity and equilibrium? Sad to say, we have to admit that some found themselves lost and disoriented, not succeeding in knowing how to fuse the past with the new. Others did not hide their irritation for what had happened and were obstinate in repeating traditional models of catechesis and of pastoral care, or of proposing, at the most, some exterior reform. Others, lastly, went beyond the Council and in the name of what, in their opinion, had not been made explicit, arrived at proposing radical and profound changes, confusing aggiornamento and renewal with denunciation, contestation and innovation. Thus catechesis went through a rather delicate period and, even though it had already experienced analogous situations, it found itself lost and uncertain at times. The heavy and new responsibility of orienting and guiding the application of the Council fell upon the Supreme Pontiff, Paul VI, and on the Sacred Congregation for the Clergy, insofar as it is the central organ in charge of catechesis in the world.

The Profession of Faith

The application of the Council and its extension to catechesis was the work of the daily magisterium of Paul VI, who from his very first encyclical, *Ecclesiam suam*, put himself to the task of reviving dialogue with the world in the evangelical sense: "The Church should enter into dialogue with the world in which it exists and labors. The Church has something to say; the Church has a message to deliver; the Church has a communication to offer."[7] In all his acts there was a constant catechetical preoccupation, expressed in the typical form of regular development, of patience, and of constancy, that is, of the certainty of attaining the purpose step by step. He respected the nature of catechesis, the beginning and end of which is God, who manifested His plan of love; the point of reference of which is Christ, in whom this act of love was realized and fully expressed; the seat of which is the Church, in whom and through whom the Word of God is diffused to all the earth and to all fields; the recipient of which is man, the privileged subject of God's attention. To actualize renewal is difficult, because it is a work, above all, of courageous equilibrium. On the one hand, the Pope aimed at safeguarding the patrimony of faith

which the Church has the duty to preserve in its intangible purity; on the other hand, he worked so that the message could be
understandable and persuasive for the man of today. However,
he did not choose the way of the simple dogmatic proposal, but
that of the act of faith. The Pope, first in the Church, realized
that he had to be first also in the humble answer to the gift of
God. This is what occurred the evening of June 30, 1968, in the
Basilica of St. Peter, when at the end of the "year of faith,"
Paul VI pronounced his solemn *Profession of Faith*.[8]

The catechetical goals were evident. Having chosen, from
among so many possibilities, the form of the profession was
already a concrete indication of how the dichotomy between
faith and life could be avoided. Against every fear and every
unilateralism the Pope reaffirmed immutable fidelity to the
deposit of faith. And there was need for this, to recall those who
were failing in this fundamental duty. He confirmed that faith is
not simple adhesion to an abstract truth, but is the substance of
life in the historical situation in which we find ourselves living as
pilgrims in the world. This was also needed to shake up those who
acted as though the Council had not taken place. The profession
of faith, in fact, is much more than a formula or a list of truths. It
is a doxology, it is a recognition of the role of God and of man, it
is a thanksgiving, it is a sign of interior vitality, it is an act of joint
charity and of fraternal communion in the one faith.

The General Catechetical Directory

The most specific document regarding catechetics issued
during the pontificate of Paul VI was the *General Catechetical
Directory*. This instrument, prepared in obedience to a specific
mandate of the Ecumenical Council,[9] proposed to speak a clear
and precise word about the nature, the contents and the goals of
catechesis. For the first time in the history of the universal
Church, the theme of catechesis was treated in an organic and
systematic way. Because it concerns a document, by now known
and diffused, it is sufficient here to limit ourselves to pointing out
a few of its principal characteristics[10]:

a) *Document of general orientation*. The Directory is not
something in itself definite and complete, but it is a document
which postulates and requires, in order to be wholly practical,
other documents more definite in time, in place and in recipients.
The concrete pastoral options and the inquiries about human

situations, which the ministry of the word must clarify and illuminate, cannot but be the specific work of the various episcopates. For this reason the Directory is addressed to the episcopal conferences in a particular way. Furthermore, to say that the Directory is a general document does not at all mean that it is a generic document. What could have been said of catechesis, as a theoretical arrangement, was said. It is general in the sense that it did not make and could not make catechesis concrete, that is, implicating the specifics for the recipient and his conditions of life.

b) *Nature of catechetical action.* Catechesis is conceived as an educative work, mediated by human action, which takes the Christian by the hand and leads him to deepen a living knowledge of God and of His plan of salvation, centered in Christ. It concerns a project which the Christian fulfills by working and acting in the ecclesial community and in the human community. For the Directory catechesis is not a teaching destined exclusively to proposing a patrimony of truths and making them accepted. "With the Directory," wrote K. Tilmann, "the idea is definitely overcome that in catechesis one must communicate a scientific dogma in an abbreviated form or at the most a group of maxims and ready answers. Catechesis, instead, is presented as the mediation of a central event of salvation, which must be considered globally in all its relationships and in all its effects."[11] The encounter of a soul with God and his progress in the life of faith do not occur exclusively through a gift of truth, even if the Word of God is in itself effective. It is a matter of a much more complex encounter, wherein the principal part is mysteriously carried out by God and the very truth proposed is accepted if it is significant and revealing. "Illuminism," wrote F. Paier, "held that clear and distinct ideas would automatically become personal convictions and motivations of behavior. But we asked ourselves rightly: are clear ideas (that is, the cognitive understanding of truth) sufficient to create an interior unity of culture and to educate a mentality and a coherent attitude of life? Without fail psychology answers negatively. And experience confirms it. In fact, simple understanding does not by itself lead to judging and interpreting the happenings and experiences of life. So, if nothing else intervenes, understanding and knowledge remain divided from the mass of events and experiences which intermingle in man's daily state of consciousness."[12]

c) *The problem of the contents.* If, on the one hand, the Directory does not reduce catechesis to the proposing of truths, on the other hand, nevertheless, it could not fail to consider the importance of the contents and hence refuse a few forms of catechesis in which the elevation of man, the interpretation of experience and the permanent state of research and opinion were inculcated to the point of placing in the shadow the fundamental and irrevocable fidelity to the Gospel and the teaching of the Church. There is no pedagogical or didactic reason which could be considered to reduce the fundamental contents. Neither must we minimize the importance of intellectual life. Even if the head is not everything, it is the most important part of man, the decisive place of his choices and also the part which more fully reveals his malice and the intrinsic pristine disturbance and weakness. Catechesis is not a common instruction; rather, it is the teaching of Christ, entrusted to the Church and by her faithfully guarded.

The problem of content was also faced during Vatican II and on that occasion voices were not lacking which powerfully denounced some of the risks and limits of modern catechesis. In reality, the passage from catechesis of doctrine to catechesis for life did not occur without the phenomenon of a few emphasized unilateralisms. As at times happens, in remedying one defect, one falls into the opposite extreme. Now, it is evident that if there is a field in which the obligation to fidelity is essential and total, it is precisely in that of catechesis, which is certainly a proposal of life, but a proposal of life according to the teaching and example of Christ. The Directory, to confirm the importance of this aspect, dedicated the entire third part to the content of— *catechesis*, offering both the criteria for organization as well as a perspective for the life of faith and the hierarchy of truths. "[Catechesis] must take diligent care faithfully to present the entire treasure of the Christian message."[13]

When catechesis alters or mutilates doctrine it incurs the worst of defects. In fact, there is no pedagogical or didactic error which can be compared to this and which can be as harmful as this. It is obvious that there will always be a difference between the servants of the Gospel and the Gospel which they must serve. This must be a stimulus to develop human ingenuity and keen discernment, but it is also a motive for comfort: the Word of God is above every one of us, and each one of us is its servant. The

Church, without adapting herself to the world, must manifest how she was converted, by listening, meditating and celebrating the Word of God, sharing and scrutinizing the questions of men.

d) *Priority of catechesis for adults.* A strange mentality existed and still exists which considers catechesis as an activity directed primarily, if not exclusively, to children and adolescents, almost as a propaedeutics to Christian life, destined to end as soon as man enters maturity. The order of values was changed. The Directory, without limiting catechesis for children—because every plant must be attentively cared for from its very origins—has placed the adult at the center of attention in catechesis: "Catechesis for adults, since it deals with persons who are capable of an adherence that is fully responsible, must be considered the chief form of catechesis. All other forms, which are indeed always necessary, are in some way oriented to it."[14] The motives which impelled the Directory to place the adult at the center of the ministry of the word are many. Without catechesis for adults, the very catechesis for children is destined to become ineffective, because the child breathes and is conditioned by the environment which surrounds him, made and regulated for the most part by adults. It is the adults who have the greatest familial, professional and civic responsibilities, and there is no situation of life which must not be illumined by the Word of God. The crises of identity which the adult experiences in the Church, at times perhaps with greater intensity than in civil society, are often due to the insufficient preparation received and to the imbalance between secular culture and religious culture.[15] The adult needs to discern the various projects and values proposed to him and thus also review the image he has constructed of himself, of history and of society, in such a way that he no longer makes himself the center but places himself by the side of Christ.

The Catechetical Congress and the International Council

These brief points are sufficient for an understanding of how the Directory has put the Council into practice and channeled itself in the path indicated by it. It overcame that easy "catechetical youthfulness" which seemed, in a first moment, to have taken a few impatient spirits, as though the Council had almost buried the past. At the same time the Directory understood that it was urgent, in serenity and without any polemic, to overcome every form of dualism between faith and life. It confirmed the importance of doctrine, avoiding, however, shutting itself up in that doctrinalism which had shown little sensitivity to the authentic biblical and liturgical values and hardly any attention to man. Catechesis rediscovered its original vocation, which was authentically biblical and patristic, and its privileged climate, the liturgical celebration. It was recognized that man—who had been the great forgotten one for a long time, even though catechesis was directed to him—has the right to be considered and treated as a human person, in respect to his age, his psycho-intellectual needs and his needs for faith, and in respect to `his commitments and his historical era. The catechetical vocation was considered like a rediscovery of baptismal commitments, and to the catechist was attributed great dignity. He was considered the "interpreter of the Church among those who are to be instructed"; it is he who "reads the signs of faith and teaches others how to read them. The chief of these signs is the Church herself."[16] The ecclesial community, in fact, gains voice from the men who make it up and who make themselves messengers and witnesses of the Gospel.

The guidelines of the Directory were given a very close examination by representatives from every part of the world during the Second International Catechetical Congress, held in Rome from the 20th to the 25th of September, 1971.[17] Paul VI defined the Congress an "important event for the Church...and an expression ever so significant and consoling of the work of the Church herself after the Council."[18]

During the Congress the basic criteria of the Directory were confirmed. Very interesting in this regard was the unanimity which was attained with notable ease concerning the nature and goals of catechesis. It was repeated that "catechesis is for man.... Announcing the word of God to this man is, therefore, transmitting to him a living word in the total complexity which molds him. In this sense the attention on man is not only a pedagogical means, but a fundamental need of the word itself: since the Incarnation concerns communicating the life of God to the real man. "Even while being much more than a communication of truth, Revelation postulates, however, that catechesis must safeguard "the organization of the Christian message, respecting the hierarchy of the truths which it contains."[19]

For many congress members, the great meeting in Rome was the occasion for rediscovering the role and function of the Holy See at the service of universal catechesis. It was for this reason that on the part of the Congress a request was made for the institution, within the Congregation for the clergy, of "a special organism of authoritative and competent representatives of catechesis."[20] Paul VI welcomed the proposal and instituted the International Council for Catechesis, which has the aim of studying the problems of catechesis, proceeding to a mutual exchange of experiences and of knowledge and proposing suggestions and orientations. The institution, which was added to the other already existing ones, confirmed the sensitivity of the Pope to catechesis and his vivid desire to make the Holy See the place of serene encounter and of sure orientation for a real ecclesial work.

Catechetical activity is so vital that it cannot be cared for with documents, however important, of the ordinary government alone. Paul VI willed that the Synod of Bishops should also dwell on this topic: one time the theme was evangelization, and its fruit was the Exhortation *Evangelii nuntiandi;* another time the theme was catechesis, and its fruit, brought to fulfillment by his successor John Paul II, was the Exhortation *Catechesi tradendae.*

SERGIO GORETTI

FOOTNOTES

1) John XXIII, *Opening Address of the Council,* October 11, 1962.

2) *Il catechismo romano del Concilio di Trento,* Rome 1938; *Catechismo del Concilio di Trento,* ed. Paoline, Rome 1961; Cf. Pio Paschini.

3) Cf. E. Pironio, *Quale liberazione?* LDC, Turin 1973, pp. 30-31.

4) J. Colomb, *Al servizio della Fede,* LDC, Turin 1969, vol. I, p. 16.

5) Cf. *Lumen Gentium,* no. 25; *Christus Dominus,* nos. 12-14; *Optatam Totius,* nos. 14-18; *Gravissimum Educationis,* no. 4; *Apostolicam Actuositatem,* no. 29; *Presbyterorum Ordinis,* no. 4.

6) S. Riva-G. Gatti, *Il movimento catechistico italiano,* EDB, Bologna 1977, p. 29.

7) Paul VI, *Ecclesiam suam,* no. 65.

8) Cf. Paul VI, *Encicliche e discorsi,* ed. Paoline, Rome 1968, pp. 249-261. Cf. also *The Credo of the People of God* (Boston: St. Paul Editions, 1968).

9) Cf. *Christus Dominus,* no. 44.

10) The Directory has been translated and diffused in all the principal languages of the world. Cf. D. Grasso, "Riflessioni sul Direttorio Catechistico Generale," in *La Civiltà Cattolica,* October 1971, pp. 57-64; the entire number of October 1971 of the magazine *Catéchèse;* John Cardinal Wright, "Il nuovo Direttorio Catechistico e l'iniziazione ai sacramenti della Penitenza e dell'Eucharistia," in *Palestra del Clero,* December 1971, pp. 1394-1418; S. Goretti, "Per un'interpretazione del

Direttorio Catechistico Generale," in *Monitor Ecclesiasticus*, I, 1974, pp. 3-17.

11) K. Tilmann, "Il ministero della parola," in *L'Osservatore Romano*, July 12-13, 1971.

12) F. Paier, "Aspetti metodologici della catechesi scolastica e della pastorale giovanile," in *La religione nella scuola*, Ascoli Piceno, 1972, p. 41.

13) General Catechetical Directory (GCD), no. 38.

14) GCD, no. 20.

15) Cf. GCD, nos. 79, 92-94, 96-97.

16) GCD, no. 35.

17) Cf. Sacred Congregation for the Clergy, *Atti del II Congresso Catechistico Internazionale*, Rome 1971.

18) Allocution by Paul VI to over one thousand Congress members during the audience of September 25, 1971.

19) *Atti...Orientamenti conclusivi*, o.c.p., 502, 506.

20) *Atti...Orientamenti conclusivi*, o.c.p., 509.

3

Catechesis in John Paul I

In his thirty-three days of pontificate and in his twenty discourses and messages, John Paul I revealed himself to be an extraordinary catechist of our time and a profound expert in the laws which regulate this evangelical ministry. Only one who hurriedly pretended to make a comparison with the magisterium of Paul VI or of Pius XII interpreted in a very limited way his teaching as that of a "good pastor." John Paul I had behind him the direct experience of a catechist. Before he was a Pope he walked through almost all the intermediary stages. Above all, he was a catechist in the total sense.[1]

"Catechetica in briciole" (Catechism in crumbs)

Father Albino Luciani had, it can be said, catechesis in his blood and the charism of the catechist. He was not satisfied with repeating and making others repeat mechanically or even interpreting the official catechism in the light of the magisterium and of theology. First Pius X[2] and then Pius XI[3] had given a notable impulse to catechesis. But it was necessary to insert into human reality those brief and complete formulas which were memorized and which, in a broad way, constituted the base and at the same time the doctrinal patrimony of the faith of the Christian people.

For his catechists of Belluno he prepared some outlines, and later on collected them in 1949 into one small volume entitled, *Catechetica in briciole* (Catechism in Crumbs). It was a "limpid" and "easy" text for the formation of catechists, at that time called "teachers of Christian doctrine" or simply "teachers of catechism." It was still the climate of the *Provido sane* of Pius XI and there had not been the renewal postulated by Vatican II. The didactic element was predominant: whoever catechized had to know how to teach and to be acquainted with teaching aids and instruments.

49

No one today would dream of considering the little volume as a jewel of diamonds in the catechetical production prior to Vatican II. However, we would not be generous if we were to undervalue it completely. It is not only an effort to offer a valid instrument to future catechists and a compendium of norms for sharing the truths of faith. In its structure and traditional form it also contains a validity and a fluency which reveal the attempt to render easy what is "technically" difficult, credible and understandable what could appear to the simple and to children, complex or matter only for the initiated.

There is a "novelty" which is to be emphasized. The catechism had to be functional. It had to be an aid for learning the truths of faith. Hence, the care and skill of Luciani for endowing the catechism not only with suitable elements, but also opening it to the influences of the active pedagogical movement which in Italy had its most qualified representatives in Mario Casotti, Gesualdo Nosengo, Friar Leone Maria and Friar Anselmo Balocco. The anxiety of the pastor is coupled to a culture, updated and adapted to the needs of the recipients of the Word of God.[4] "A catechist," we read in it, "must not only know or possess knowledge; he must also have the ability to communicate his knowledge to little ones with *didactics*, rather with *catechetical didactics.*"[5]

This presupposes some fundamental requisites. Luciani lists them thus: first of all, the *sense of adaptation*, which consists in "knowing how to proportion what one says to the listener." The form cannot be the same for everyone; it must vary according to age and degree of intelligence. And here Luciani adds a note more than a counsel, an expression of his personality: "Always seek to say easy things and to say difficult things in an easy way. Always present things under a pleasing aspect, in such a way that children will be pleased with them and will love them."

In the second place, *clarity.* Luciani describes it in these terms: "Few ideas, but colorful and incisive; better a few and well understood than many and confused; easy *words*, words which the children already know and understand, concrete and, if possible, accompanied by pictures." Accompany this teaching with concrete examples.

In the third place, *know how to tell a story.* Luciani judges this talent "one of the best resources to succeed with young people who like stories and avidly drink them in if they are narrated with good grace and with details." He also adds a few external qualities, such as a glad and joyful face, serene but vigilant and penetrating gaze, gestures which render words livelier and more attractive, a pleasant tone of voice with proper inflection and, finally, a dignified and amiable exterior comportment.[6]

Wisdom of Heart

Catechetica in briciole (Catechism in Crumbs) is not a complete "codex" of the catechist, nor did Luciani claim to have drafted one. It is, nevertheless, the expression and the manifestation of the personality of an apostle with an uncommon charism and uncommon attitudes. What he evangelically required in teachers of the faith, Luciani possessed himself. But he had not stopped at the initial stage; he had studied and deepened the truths of faith with daily effort; he had refined his learning and his sensitivity to pastoral problems; above all, he had cultivated and intensified his life of communion with God in a progressive impetus which knew no rest or deviations. A profound servant of God and of the Church, he matured first as a priest, then as a Bishop in the various sees to which he was called to carry out the ministry of successor of the apostles and of Vicar of Christ, a singular experience.

For him catechesis was not just that which occurred in the traditional way. He came to the conclusion very soon that it was necessary before a world always more dominated by the instruments of social communication and attacked by materialism to make the message of salvation reach outside the temple's walls. What had his book, *Illustrissimi*,[7] signified if not a perfectly successful attempt to carry out catechesis in a new and original way? "When I preach in St. Mark," he confessed to a journalist, "one hundred, one hundred and fifty, the most two hundred faithful listen to me: half are tourists who do not understand Italian; the other half are adorable, but already convinced, little old ladies."[8] From this came his willingness to collaborate with several newspapers and periodicals which had a wide diffusion.

The Luciani of the pen was not that much different from the Luciani of the proclamation of the word, from Luciani the catechist. A fundamental quality characterized his personality and, by reflection, his episcopal and apostolic ministry: wisdom of heart. Posthumously an expression was pointed out which was noticed by everyone in his presentation immediately after his election as Bishop of Rome and successor of Peter: "I have neither the *wisdom of heart* of Pope John, nor the preparation and culture of Pope Paul, but I am in their place. I must seek to serve the Church."[9]

Every comparison, for a personality like the pope, appears improper, but it would be an injustice to the humility of John Paul I not to recognize in him the possession of these two qualities. If then they were on an equal plane with those of the pontiffs to whom he referred, it is out of place to point it out. An attentive critic like Rigobello did not hesitate to write: "Wisdom of heart *(sapientia cordis)*—Pope Luciani...possessed it. If he had not had it, how would he have been able to interpret the expectation and the intense hope of the multitudes who unexpectedly drew close around him? How would that eruption, that flood of sympathy, of harmony, of affection have been possible without his possession of a profound intuition of the historical moment and of the spiritual situation of his people? If we read his discourses we find many beautiful, devout and opportune considerations, but his fascination was due, in addition to his works, to his presence, a presence in which precisely 'wisdom of heart' was translated into images and became a reminder, an exhortation, a conviction."[10]

The same Rigobello acknowledges in Pope Luciani the second quality also, even though it was different from that of Paul VI. "The profound significance which Pope Luciani represents on the cultural plane," thus writes Rigobello, "consists in his reference to that deep simplicity which popular wisdom knows how to preserve and express in a humble way, but with an intense power of communication. The ancient civilization of his land of origin, the tender and strong Venetian land, knew how to give to his word and his gesture a dignity and a candor, a perfect experience and an open abandonment which make his book a document of a culture between the most splendid and the less literary of Europe. Perhaps we have wandered a bit, but we wanted to emphasize, in John Paul I, a profound and discreet presence of cultural motives which have acted as a support to the intensity of his human communication and to the immediacy with which his message was welcomed. In him the Venetian climate placed itself at the service of a universal fatherhood."[11]

Wisdom of heart and profound and discreet learning constituted in him an inseparable binomial. The catechist, whatever
be his mission, his investiture and his role, must possess both.
How can one communicate the message of God, instruct in the
faith, nourish and help to progress in the knowledge and understanding of the truths to believe and to practice if with one's life
and one's own behavior one does not allow the Spirit to act? If
one hinders His action and influence? And further: how can one
render the message acceptable if one does not know how to
translate it into the existential context of the recipients? But
learning would be insufficient if it were not sublimated and
transformed by the Spirit, who acts in believers, rendering
testimony to the truth itself and to the apostle.

The catechist, as apostle and prophet, is before all else one
sent, one chosen by God. He does not act on his own account, nor
does he carry out an office identifiable with a profession, be it
even the most qualified and honorable. It is to God, to Christ,
from whom he receives strength and authority through the
mediation of the Church, that he must render an account of his
actions and his mission. He must follow the law of the Incarnation. God, without losing anything of His divinity, became man,
assuming in everything the features and the conditions of man,
with the exception of sin. The law of the Incarnation claims an
assumption of responsibility, but also an assumption of human
values, both the interior as well as those which constitute the
valid patrimony of a civilization. In Luciani—it was acutely
pointed out—magisterium illumines the dynamics of the signs of
the times, with directives which consolidate the right doctrine
and the modern life of men[12] who, although overwhelmed by
temporal seductions, do not lose the call to transcendency, to permanent values and to future goods.

His Contribution
to the Synod of Bishops of 1977

In the autumn of 1977 (September 30—October 29) the
Catholic Church celebrated the fourth general assembly of the
Synod of Bishops. Catechesis was its theme. Cardinal Luciani was
a member of the delegation of Italian Bishops. We cannot ignore
his intervention, which was presented in writing. His reflection
was limited to the third part of the *Instrumentum laboris*,[13]
elaborated by the secretariat of the Synod. A few of these points,

he noted, "are expressed in a manner so as to give entrance to un-
due and arbitrary interpretations on the part of one who has
preconceived ideas and such a one could be tempted to bend the
meaning in the direction pleasing to him."[14]

The text spoke of "new places of catechesis," identified in the
parish and the family. Cardinal Luciani observed: "More than
'new places' they can be called 'hinge places,' and they must
be closely connected with the new realities of groups and movements, in which the youth love to gather together: groups of
children, in which the catechist attains a bit the figure of the
father or of the mother who teaches, admonishes and guides";
analogously, in the groups of adolescents. In both cases "the
catechist will present himself, above all, as the friend who accompanies, who imposes himself with the prestige of his goodness and
maturity of faith and who draws with his example."

Interesting are the stresses about witness. "It is necessary to
give a Christian witness," he emphasizes, "because the youth expect it. It is true, but we must not be afraid to say that the Word
of God also requires it from everyone." And he adds: "It seems a
bit excessive to present the witness of the Christian community
(most important, certainly) as *the* sign, *that* sign on which all or
almost all the credibility of the divine message depends. It should
not be forgotten that there is also the Church, with her history
and her saints, her propagation, etc.; there is the Gospel as *virtus
Dei;* there is the Word of God in which much efficacy and power
is inherent to be the support and vigor of the Church *(Dei Verbum,* 21). The catechist with his talents, the community who supports him, etc., have a great influence, but they do not constitute
the sole, or nearly sole, element of credibility."

Firm also is his position on the *status* of catechists, "whose
task goes beyond that of a simple voluntary help to the parish and
the family, to carry out a dutiful ecclesial task, aiming at an all-
catechizing community to be animated dynamically and to be
drawn along." "It is the highest ideal," observes Cardinal Luciani. "There remains to be clarified the manner of reconciling
the magisterial authority of the bishop with the obligation-right
to evangelize which exists in every baptized person by virtue of
the common priesthood."

Realistic is his judgment on the role of the family. He
observes: "It is true that there exist new experiences regarding the
task of the family; they are to be followed and encouraged.

However, we must not generalize a still limited phenomenon. The reality seems to be the following: parents ardently desirous of catechizing their own children are not many, and they usually desire to be better prepared—doctrinally and spiritually—by priests. Their attitude, therefore, is not to be considered almost a vindication, almost a reaction to a supposed invasion of the parish to the detriment of the family. Tepid and negligent parents are much more numerous; in their regard action is necessary to urge them to feel their responsibility, in order to have them give catechism its due consideration, cooperate with the parish catechists, complete their work, never destroying it with bad example, etc. The third case is that of families which are anything but Christian; the catechist has to carry out a very delicate work to neutralize in those being catechized the bad influence of the family environment.

The working document of the secretariat of the Synod insisted on a return to the Bible and in particular to the Gospel, both for content and for method. Cardinal Luciani had precise directives also on this topic. "Christocentricity is an excellent thing," he pointed out, "for it leads children to an encounter with the person of Jesus and not with an arid formula. But perhaps it is a bit exaggerated to affirm that what is not made of the Gospel and according to the Gospel is not catechesis. The doctrine of salvation can be presented through Christian life and its traditional forms, especially the liturgy; through the biblical story, as the history of salvation; through an experience in a systematic form, as a complex of propositions logically connected among themselves. This last form is not to be despised or neglected, because it is useful for answering many current objections and prejudices, and because these truths, verified by solid theological study, are like stones with which a house is built or a street paved. Obviously they must be presented in a manner not overly intellectual, not insisting too much on the negative aspects [prohibitions], but also placing in relief the sentimental and affective values. Religion is not pure sentiment, but neither is it without sentiment. Let us be careful not to rid ourselves indiscriminately of the catechetical tradition of the past, which also produced many good fruits."

The return to the Bible must imply a more profound bond with tradition and the magisterium. They are three pillars about which Cardinal Luciani does not compromise. It pays to follow him in his reflections. "All that is said on the use of Sacred Scripture in catechesis *(plene tradere)* is right if it is practiced gradually, especially where youth and children are concerned, and with caution, considering the difficulties connected with a right interpretation. It is right that the Bible be at the basis of a catechesis set forth preferably in a historical form, since Christianity is not a philosophical system, but rather a historical event inserted in the history of the world.... To be avoided, however, is the danger of letting the importance of the law of God pass unnoticed while insisting that the Word of God in its vastness be read *indiscriminately* by all the faithful. Today many children do not know the commandments, because the Decalogue is undervalued by many theologians and exegetes, whereas traditional catechesis explained it, making it culminate in the great precept of charity." And in addition: "It would be necessary also to better unite Scripture, Tradition and the living magisterium, which today is so much despised." "For the right recognition of the magisterium it is necessary to distinguish—more than the *Instrumentum* does—the *sensus fidei populi Dei* from the magisterium itself, to which the *sensus fidei* remains subjected (*Lumen gentium*, 12). It is excellent to recall the example of the saints; hagiography should be used more in catechesis. Correct also is the suggestion that in catechesis preference should be given to those fonts which are more congenial to the recipients. Congeniality, however, is not to be followed in the selection of the truths to be taught, and if truly of faith, they are all to be equally believed, even if some can be said to be more important than others insofar as these others rest on and are illumined by the first."

His observations about recipients are pointed. Catechesis as evangelization has the poor as its recipients. This term, however, could generate misunderstandings because of the influx of marxist culture. Cardinal Luciani goes back to the evangelical concept, asserting that it is the "poor in both the sociological sense (who enjoy the preferences of the Church) as well as in the moral sense." And he adds: "It is right to make the recipients of catechesis coincide with the poor, provided that a better clarification be made as to who these poor are. It is not easy to distinguish between love of the poor and love of poverty; the very poverty of the Church is difficult to define." But, besides demanding this basic clarification, Cardinal Luciani warns that one must "not pass inadvertently from the field of true and proper catechesis—

which aims at bringing individuals and communities to the maturity of faith and of Christian life—to that of pre-evangelization, as is required in certain cases by a real situation of ignorance on the part of the baptized."

Regarding the socio-political dimension of catechesis, he reveals himself to be an exacting and almost rigid critic. "Where the document speaks of human promotion, peace, justice, etc., it would be necessary to specify better that these remain a second-ary integrating part and not the *essential* part, and not even *the* part or *a* constitutive part, as is read respectively in the English translation and in the Italian one of the Synod Document of 1971. Today many appeal to *Gaudium et spes*, but they forget that this document also speaks of the theology of the cross. Similarly they speak of liberation (rather than of salvation), accentuating too much the aspect of liberation from evil (political and economic) and too little that of entering into communion with God."

He does not show excessive enthusiasm for the section dedicated to the young. "To speak of the greatest readiness of the young to find solutions to problems or to assume the burden of work," he observes, "seems excessively optimistic." With reserva-tion he agrees that this attitude is a "sign of the times." Two dangers, he insists, are to be avoided: "first of all, to take as a norm of what catechesis must or must not say, only or principally the requests and questions of the men of today—young or not—by omitting things which are, perhaps, less pleasing to them. To be avoided also is the risk of presenting a Church continually at the school of the young, to whom she too has much to teach. The second danger to be avoided is the lack of a deepened and con-tinued dutiful effort of adaptation of the message to new situa-tions, being content to repeat the things done and said in other times. Faith is a living thing which grows."

In regard to adaptation to the various forms of culture, Car-dinal Luciani sets forth the essential guidelines in a clear and precise manner. "The problem of cultural mediation," he sus-tains, "has always existed and most of the time it has been re-solved after necessary preparation by entrusting oneself to the power of the Word of God and to grace, which arouses the zeal and the sanctity of the catechists." Presently catechesis finds itself "in a kind of unstable imbalance, and in regard to culture it ex-presses, from time to time irenicism, dialogue, conflict and separa-tion. In every case it requires wisdom and didactic prudence." He insists on avoiding "even the shadow of semi-pelagianism!" The competence of the laity is important "to make known the psychological and spiritual situation of those being catechized. Of much more importance, however, is the genuineness, clarity and certainty of the doctrine transmitted by the catechists, lay or otherwise, in agreement and without confusion."

Catechists are not alone, nor must they act autonomously. Backing them up are "the theologians and the bishops." This bond was very profound in the past. "Today," laments Cardinal Luciani, "in a different manner, catechists and theologians are often bound together by a mass of publications, which are at times neither controlled, nor read and assimilated critically. Bishops are to exercise greater vigilance and make use of theologians, but in a manner that will be of advantage to the Church and to the theologians themselves; they are to recognize the particular charism of theologians, which, however, is usefully explicated only if placed humbly at the service of the bishops, in full respect for the magisterium, without trying to constitute a 'Church of professors' opposed to the shepherds, or which conditions them through pressure groups linked with the publishing industry, universities and theological associations."

To Cardinal Luciani it appeared opportune to insist on *hierarchical communion*, "according to which the first catechist is the Pope; then, together with him and guided by him as the true head come the episcopal college, individual bishops and priests; then come the others, if they do not carry out a private and familial catechesis, but an official and ecclesial one, by assignment of bishops and of pastors." At the same time he shows himself aware of the necessity of "valuing more humble people, people often without culture or special pedagogical ability, but who at times are rich in the gift of the Spirit." He was of the opinion that on "themes of great importance and commitment" the Synod should not work hastily. Rather, it was preferable to transmit to the Pope all the material that had been worked out and which had arisen from the discussion, so that a document analogous to *Evangelii nuntiandi* should be prepared.

Catechesis, Integrating Part of the Missionary Mandate

Not even a year later, Cardinal Luciani was chosen to succeed Paul VI in the See of Peter (August 26, 1978). The Synod had concluded by turning over the material to the Pope, as, with Cardinal Luciani, the Synod Fathers had wished. One of the electors of Pope Luciani, Cardinal Baggio, in an article recalling the event, refers to a popular story which, among other things, affirmed that "on the night after the conclave which has elected the Pope, an angel comes, sent by God, who unscrews the head of the man who up until then had been Cardinal So-and-So, and he screws back on a new one made specially for this purpose."[15] Aside from its näiveté, the story contains a disconcerting truth: whoever is elected Pope ceases to be what he had been before and assumes a new personality proportionate to the responsibility of the office. From the chair and on the chair of Peter events are evaluated with criteria far different from those of a bishop, even one from so prestigious a city as Venice. Even his teaching, carried out through his writings, witness and works, assumes a content and a breath that are different. John Paul I was supremely aware of this. The writer can attest that the Pope did not like his writings as a bishop to be published without his first having gone over them and approved them for publication. This is understandable, both on the human as well as on the purely theological plane. Not all that one said or wrote yesterday is necessarily considered valid for today. Not only that, but not everything that one believed convenient and opportune to say or write as a bishop can be considered convenient or opportune to say or write as a Pope.

Does this norm hold true also for what Luciani wrote regarding catechesis? Undoubtedly—above all, if one takes his booklet *Catechetica in briciole (Catechism in Crumbs)*, so distant in time and so distant from the innovating impulses of Vatican II. Is it valid also for his observations regarding the document of the fourth general assembly of the Synod of Bishops of 1977? Certainly, but with less setting aside. As Pope he did not have the material time to formulate norms on catechesis, nor did he have the honor of promulgating *Catechesi tradendae*,[16] according to the votes of the Synod Fathers. However, he carried out an intelligent and fascinating work of catechesis in his few Wednesday encounters with the overflowing and enthusiastic crowds of the faithful. It is from this and from his writings preceding his pontifical election that his teaching on catechesis must be derived.

Having reached this point we prefer to listen to others. Mario Agnes, President of Catholic Action, affirmed in a testimony: "His catechesis was a supreme service: a singular catechesis,

which cannot be easily filed away.... It was his catechesis—
singular, probing, incisive; a catechesis which has made and
makes history, a catechesis full of pure, authentic values; a
'familiar' catechesis." In one of his interventions, during the
assembly of the CEI [Italian Episcopal Conference] of February 21,
1968, Luciani pointed out that it was necessary "to be clear
and simple," and in regard to his style, Agnes observes: "Certainly his teaching of catechism—which from the first moment
reminded me of St. Pius X (and this is an affirmation about which
I have thought much)—was scintillating with wit; it varied in the
infinite turnings of his prodigious literary memory, nourished by
ancient and recent readings; it was strengthened by a selective
culture and illumined by a reflective and melancholically serene
interiority and by an inviting Franciscan simplicity."[17]

"We are on the path of the best Christian pedagogical tradition," comments Julius Nicolini, "in which notable figures shine:
Francis de Sales, Philip Neri, John Bosco.... In this style and in
this language Luciani constantly applied what we could define as
the genius of his simplicity.... Thus is also completed the image of
the Bishop and Pope as the catechist who speaks to children,
dialogues with them and projects the dialogue to everyone. In
truth, he measured the listening capacity of everyone by the
simplicity of the children, according to the Gospel method."[18]

In the history of catechesis, Pope Luciani will be
remembered as a model of simplicity and clarity—two virtues
which radiate from his authentically evangelical personality.
With teaching and with deeds he proved that the profound truths
of faith, to be understood and pleasing, must be clothed with a
universally accessible language. But simplicity does not mean to
reduce doctrine, which must be proclaimed whole and entire. He
also proved that catechesis is an integrating part of the missionary
mandate, the urgency of which does not suffer any limitations.
Catechesis is now, more than ever, the way for people to grow
and be educated in the faith of the Church as it has been
transmitted by the Apostles.

GINO CONCETTI

FOOTNOTES

(1) For the life, the writings and the personality of Pope Luciani, cf. *Il magistero di Albino Luciani.* Writings and discourses edited by Alfredo Cattabiani, Edizioni Messaggero, Padua 1979; G. Nicolini, *Trentatre giorni un pontificato,* Edizioni Instituto Padano di Arti Grafiche, Rovigo 1979; *Albino Luciani, Giovanni Paolo I. Il dono della chiarezza,* Edizioni Logos, Rome 1979. For the daily news and periodicals, cf. *La rassegna* edited by *Prospettive nel mondo,* no. 43, January 1980, 184-199.

(2) Pius X, *Acerbo nimis,* in *Acta* (1905), II, 69-84.

(3) Sacred Congregation of the Council *Provido sane,* in AAS (1935) 145-152.

(4) Cf. S. Riva, Introduction to *Catechetica in briciole,* in *Albino Luciani, Giovanni Paolo I, Il dono della chiarezza,* 65-67. We will cite this volume in this edition.

(5) *Catechetica in briciole,* 81.

(6) *Catechetica in briciole,* 81.

(7) A. Luciani, *Illustrissimi,* Edizioni Messaggero, Padua 1978.

(8) F.S. Pancheri, *Il giornalista e lo scrittore,* in *Prospettive nel mondo,* no. 43, January 1980, 179.

(9) Allocution from the balcony of the basilica of St. Peter, August 27, 1978.

(10) A. Rigobello, "La 'novita' di Papa Luciani: annuncio il carisma di Giovanni Paolo II," in *Prospettive nel mondo,* no. 43, January 1980, 144.

(11) A. Rigobello, "La 'novita' di Papa Luciani," 145.

(12) G. Nicolini, "Ci ha ridato i valori dell'innocenza," in *Prospettive nel mondo,* no. 43, January 1980, 161.

(13) General Secretariat of the Synod of Bishops, "De catechesi hoc nostro tempore tradenda praesertim pueris atque iuvenibus," in G. Caprile, *Il sinodo dei vescovi 1977,* Edizioni "La Civiltà Cattolica," Rome 1978, 468-522.

(14) The written intervention of Cardinal Luciani is from the cited book of Caprile, *Il sinodo dei vescovi 1977,* 224-228.

(15) S. Baggio, "Un sorriso che non conoscevamo," in *Prospettive nel mondo,* no. 43, January 1980, 147.

(16) this honor instead fell upon John Paul II. The date of promulgation is October 16, 1979. In the introduction the Pontiff renders this testimony of his two predecessors: "in essence, the exhortation (apostolic exhortation) takes up again the reflections that were prepared by Pope Paul VI, making abundant use of the documents left by the synod. Pope John Paul I, whose zeal and gifts as a catechist amazed us all, had taken them in hand and was preparing to publish them when he was suddenly called to God" (*Catechesi tradendae,* no. 4).

(17) M. Agnes, "Ha segnato il cammino verso il duemila," in *Prospettive nel mondo,* no. 43, January 1980, 153.

(18) G. Nicolini, "Ci ha ridato il valori dell'innocenza," 164-165.

4

"Redemptor Hominis": A Catechesis for the Man of Today

Premise

Redemptor hominis (RH) is a catechesis directed to all men.

It is directed to *all Christians* in the first place, because they are obliged by Baptism to build up the Mystical Body of Christ by forming and catechizing themselves; it is directed to all those who profess the Christian faith, because they have the responsibility to attract other men with word and example to Jesus Christ, Way, Truth and Life. The doctrine and life of Christ, as catechesis, has been entrusted to the Church and through her to all Christians—not for them to keep selfishly for themselves as a privilege for their own exclusive advantage, but for them to communicate to all people without exception. This is the Church's reason for being and the meaning of her mission (RH 11, 12, 18ff.).

Catechesis is directed, then, to *all men of good will.* The command of the Savior: "Go into the whole world and preach the gospel to every creature" (Mk. 16:15) is the logical consequence of the truth of the incarnation. The Word became flesh for all men, taking on what is common to every man: human nature. There is something of Jesus Christ in all men, without exception: human nature. "Christ in a certain manner united Himself with every man" is the refrain which underlies almost every page of *Redemptor hominis.* But, precisely in view of the incarnation, of the mystery of God made man, the fact is also derived that in Jesus Christ man is fully revealed to man.

It is the *central idea* of the Encyclical which can be summed up in a few words: Jesus Christ is the revelation of man, the light which illumines his identity, the way every man must follow to fully find himself again, the secret for success in overcoming the dramatic historical moment which humanity is living on the threshold of the year 2,000.

As is evident, the theme has a burning catechetical relevance. But it is necessary to add that the Encyclical, pervaded as it is by a conviction and warmth which become witness, is highly catechetical also in *spirit*. The first gift of an authentic catechesis is faith lived and experienced, faith which makes itself witness. One cannot announce Christ to the world if one does not first live Him in faith and in the love of God and neighbor. The modern world does not need words but deeds. In a certain sense in RH the spirit has more value than the words of the explicit discourse itself, even though these are so profound and persuasive.

For the rest, even the very *method* of the Encyclical, as we will show, has great catechetical value. One of its most outstanding characteristics lies in presenting Christianity in a profoundly integral manner. This unity of its multiple aspects is not, however, artificially imposed from the outside, but flows forth from within, from the very nature of truth and of Christian life.

Perhaps one of the most striking defects of the presentation of ecclesiastical sciences—philosophy, theology, pastoral, catechesis—in these last centuries has been the vivisection of the organic unity which joins truth on the human plane and on the revealed plane. Division into too many treatises, detached from one another, ended up by making divergency prevail over convergency. On one side, anthropology; on the other side, theology; on one side moral theology, on the other side, dogmatic theology; and then, in addition to moral, ascetical and mystical theology also; on one side, reason; on the other, faith; on one part, nature; on the other, grace; and all without a good integration which unites and joins these doctrines among themselves, and unites doctrine with practice. Confusion is a bad thing, but "separation" is much worse. Vivisection of a vital organism is always painful and bloody and can be fatal.

The Encyclical of John Paul II inaugurates a *new manner* of presentation of doctrine and of Christian life, where nothing is separated from the totality and where every thing is duly distinct from every other. Differentiation and distinction are born from the root of identity. Distinction and division are always at the ser-

vice of unity and identity. In this sense RH can constitute a good
lesson of philosophical, theological and catechetical methodology
together.

The new methodology of the Pontiff, which places man at
the center of the attentive love of God and of the Church, carries
forward the spirit of Vatican II. If one can and must speak of an
anthropological turn, the Catholic manner of understanding it,
of proposing it and of carrying it forward is that of RH and of the
other numerous interventions of the Pope in this regard.

Truth about God and Truth about Man

RH brought to full maturity the reconciliation between faith
and reason, which in these last centuries had gradually drifted
apart from one another, entering into artificial conflict. It is
almost as if scientific progress and the philosophies born (and
dead!) during this period were offering only this choice: either
faith or reason. It was almost as though faith were placed beyond
reason, creating a detachment, an irretrievable distance between
them. This mentality entered profoundly into the gamut of
Catholic and ecclesiastical culture itself. An eloquent proof of this
is the fact that not a few ecclesiastical exponents of philosophy
held a "Christian philosophy" impossible; this implies real incompatibility between reason and faith.

The incompatibility of faith and reason is a *prejudice still
universally diffused today*, and it constitutes a difficult obstacle
to the acceptance of Christian truth, even in nations of traditionally Christian culture. Its consequences are felt in every field.

Thus, in these times of acute sensitivity to the freedom of
man and the dignity of the human person, too many think of
Christianity as the negation of liberty and of the sovereign dignity
of the person. We could historically and theoretically affirm the
contrary: sensitivity to the dignity of the person and of liberty has
Christian roots. Unfortunately, what impedes the vision of the
history of Christianity as a history of liberty is an erroneous concept of liberty itself, childishly understood as arbitrariness and
permissiveness without limits.

To illumine the situation, a rapid scan of history would be
useful. We must keep in mind that perhaps because of most ancient platonic prejudices, a certain line of Catholic theology—of
which we find evident traces in some theologies of the thirteenth
century (for example in William d'Auvergne)—was inclined to

depreciate the creature in order to restore appreciation for the Creator, as though what was given to one was taken from the other. In other words: Either God or the creature. This way of thinking implies an erroneous concept of creation. More recently the crisis of the rapport between nature and grace has become more serious in the Lutheran and Calvinist conception of original sin, understood so pessimistically as to annihilate man's intelligence and liberty. Human reason with its powers is judged incapable of any knowledge of God whatsoever, and free activity is judged incapable of performing any good whatsoever by itself. The influence of this doctrine has been reflected both in Jansenism and in certain currents of Catholic theology itself.

For more ample information on the topic of the break and incompatibility between reason and faith, see the work of G. Mora, *La cultura Catolica e il nichilismo contemporaneo* (Catholic Culture and Contemporary Nihilism).

But the magisterium of the Church has always opted for the full appreciation of reason and its reconciliation with faith. Because of this, schools of theology used to start immediately with a treatise on apologetics: in the first place, to defend the faith from the attacks of reason. The methodology of apologetics in the Encyclical of John Paul II becomes that of overcoming from within. .This is proper to a Christian faith, aware that it has lost its inferiority complex in the face of reason and science, in order to offer to all men a truth which contains and surpasses without comparison all the human truths of non-Christian religions, philosophies, ideologies and science. It contains them and surpasses them, not through opposition but through superior inclusiveness.

There can be no conflict between reason and faith when one understands what reason is and what faith is. Faith surpasses reason because it surpasses its contents by containing them; it has no need to defend itself by presenting itself polemically from outside. Faith does not suffocate but rather widens the horizon of reason. It not only takes absolutely nothing away from man, but it also stimulates reason to progress, to a deepening, to a development of all the sciences, adding clarification and precision where reason encounters impassable limits. Reason is more reason with faith than without faith, just as man is more man with grace than without grace, freer in the riverbed of the will of God than outside or against it.

Herein lies the central idea of the modern catechesis of *Redemptor hominis.* Truth about God and truth about man are intimately connected. When one falls, so does the other. We cannot preach the truth as Revelation about God without preaching and communicating the truth as Christian revelation about man. Because of the very fact of the incarnation, the proclamation of Jesus is simultaneously the proclamation of who God is, of what God has done for man and of who we are. Not for nothing is there in Jesus, together with the fullness of divinity, the fullness of humanity. This implies fullness of harmony between reason and faith. It is the logical consequence of the divine and of the human indissolubly united in the divine person of the Word.

Christianity, the Highest Form of Humanism

The full accord between faith and reason, as between nature and grace, needs to be highly proclaimed in the general confusion of ideas which reigns today in the world, not excluding Catholic and even ecclesiastical circles. And this is catechesis, or rather the presupposition of every catechesis. Really, it does not concern accord only, but also manifests that Christianity has the most sublime concept about man and offers everyone the means for the complete fulfillment of the person.

Catechize the world about the *humanity of Christianity:* this is the basic thought of the Papal Encyclical. Christianity is presented by the Pope as the highest form of humanism. Most sensitive to the mentality of today, he places *man* at the foundation of his catechesis for the modern world. The vocation to Christianity is the vocation of every man.

In fact, the Church throughout the centuries has always strenuously defended man. The history of the Ecumenical Councils shows that there is never a defense of the truth about God which is not at the same time a defense of the truth about man. In the first centuries, the Ecumenical Councils strongly and repeatedly reaffirmed the *humanity of Christ*, against all who denied it. Later on, beginning with the Council of Vienna, through the Tridentine Council, to Vatican I and, above all, Vatican II, the Church defends the *humanity of man.* Yesterday, in the face of a conception about original sin that would have destroyed what renders man human, the Church forcefully taught that human nature has been weakened by original sin, but not destroyed. Today, in contrast to the pessimism about man diffused by too many anthropologies, RH brings a fresh wave of healthy optimism into the world upset by restlessness, bewilderment and violence.

It could not be otherwise. The Catholic thought about man is based on two capital truths of Christianity: the creation and the incarnation-redemption.

In this perspective the catechesis of John Paul II links itself not only to the recent Council but also to the entire great tradition of Catholic catechesis as carried out by the most illustrious Popes and the Fathers and Doctors of the Church, both Eastern and Western. It suffices to recall the renowned expression of Saint Irenaeus: "the glory of God is the living man" (Adversus Haereses, IV, 20, c-7; SC, 100, 640-642). St. Gregory the Great, in commenting on the command of Jesus to the Apostles to preach the Gospel to *every creature*, observes that with these words is meant *man*, inasmuch as he is the synthesis of creation. Saint Thomas takes up and develops this concept with the power of his genius in the Prologue to the Third Book of the Commentary on the Sentences of Peter Lombard.

Today a catechesis centered on man, in the light of the Man-God, is more effective and suitable for impressing modern sensitivity than any other. Creation and the incarnation project an extraordinary light on man, made the object of the infinite love of God—not on man in general, but on every single person, who is the purpose and immediate goal of the world and of the care of God and of the Church. If for every single man God does so much, what will He not do for all men together, for all humanity?

The binomial God-man and man-God is the modern and contemporay version of the binomial reason-faith and faith-reason, grace-nature and nature-grace. In reality herein lies the crucial point of a solid catechesis: the harmonious conception of the relationships between the terms of these binomials facilitates catechesis and renders it not only acceptable, but attractive and fascinating. This fascination entirely pervades the encyclical *Redemptor hominis*.

Redemption: Renewed Creation

RH not only affirms in a general manner that Christ "fully reveals man to himself" (no. 8), but also indicates how this occurs in speaking precisely of the capital truths of Christian revelation:

creation as Scripture presents it, and the redeeming incarnation of the Word. The three moments have their *dynamic center* in the redemption, renewed creation. It is the keystone of Christian catechesis which modern man needs. These moments, so closely united in the plan of God, are not to be separated, but each one brings its light on the reality of man as he is revealed in Christ.

The purpose of the creation of the world, in the Christian perspective, is man, made capable of knowing things, of giving them new life in himself, of giving them a consciousness in his own consciousness, a voice in his own voice, a purpose in the purpose of his own life. Things lacking consciousness would have no meaning without man. Man was created not only to dominate the sub-human world, making it an instrument for his own spiritual, intellectual and moral development, but also to give a meaning to the world. For man to give meaning to the world and to himself are one and the same.

More. God created man "to his image and likeness." Even before he was enriched with the gift of grace, man as such appeared immediately the "image of God." And as such, man, among all the creatures, has a *direct rapport with God.* According to the Bible it is impossible to think of man without thinking of God, as it is impossible to see the image without thinking of Him who is represented in the image. It is precisely to man as the image of God, and therefore His representative in the world, that there is entrusted the sub-human world. Man is placed in the world almost as plenipotentiary, minister and representative of the Creator.

Considering all this, it seems difficult to think that, already in the ambit of creation itself, the rapport between God and man is not the same as the rapport between father and son. God, in fact, immediately establishes a pact of friendship and of alliance with Adam, with the sole condition of obedience to Him as recognition of his own position as creature. God immediately treats man as a person and establishes a pact from person to person. It could be said almost that God forgets that He is the Absolute in order to bring Himself as much as possible to the level of man, almost to identify Himself with man. All this will be clarified with the incarnation of the Word.

It is precisely in the incarnation that the meaning of the creation of man made "to the image and likeness of God" shines *in all its splendor.* In Jesus Christ human nature was assumed in all its integrity and fullness and "raised...to a dignity beyond compare" (RH 8). In fact, "by His Incarnation, He, the Son of God, *in a certain way united Himself with each man.* He worked with human hands, He thought with a human mind. He acted with a human will, and with a human heart He loved. Born of the Virgin Mary, He has truly been made one of us, like to us in all things except sin" *(ibid.).*

God Himself, therefore, took care to explain to us, more with deeds than with words, the mysterious and profound significance of the words with which He had created us.

In this setting of the Encyclical the Incarnation is and can only be the redeeming Incarnation. RH closely unites the *Incarnation to the Redemption* and configures them to "a new creation." "In the mystery of the redemption man becomes newly 'expressed' and, in a way, is newly created. He is newly created!" (RH 10) "The man who wishes to understand himself thoroughly ...must, so to speak, enter into Him [Christ] with all his own self; he must 'appropriate' and assimilate the whole of the reality of the Incarnation and Redemption in order to find himself" *(ibid.).*

This is a most well-chosen approach for an effective catechetical action—always, but especially for the world of today. The thought that Christ united Himself in a certain manner to every man is like a precious diamond which sets itself in the admirable fabric of the Encyclical. It is like a musical tune which transforms itself into a symphony and animates the entire catechesis of *Redemptor hominis.*

A great teaching wells up from this: every authentic Christian catechesis must have in Jesus Christ its focal point, the center of irradiation for all other Christian truths, the point of both the departure and arrival of the Gospel message.

Thus from Christology, anthropology and even ecclesiology itself are illumined. "Man in the full truth of his existence, of his personal being and also of his community and social being...this man is the primary route that the Church must travel in fulfilling her mission: *he is the primary and fundamental way for the Church,* the way traced out by Christ Himself, the way that leads invariably through the mystery of the Incarnation and of the Redemption" (RH 14).

The two poles of catechesis on which *Redemptor hominis* hinges are *Jesus* and *man.* From all ages the Church has traveled and travels "this primary and fundamental way," which leads from Jesus Christ to man. It is impossible to separate the way which leads from Christ to man from that which leads from man to Christ; just as it is impossible to separate the divine nature from the human nature in Christ without destroying the fundamental truth of Christianity; just as it is impossible, in the Christian, to separate love for Jesus from love for man, for every man, without any exception, "because man—every man without any exception whatever—has been redeemed by Christ, and because with man—with each man without any exception whatever—Christ is in a way united, even when man is unaware of it..." (ibid., 14).

Human "Nature" and the Human "Situation"

Man does not have only a very precise nature in virtue of which he is man, no matter from what part of the globe, nor from which historical age; but he also has a *situation* because of which he is placed in a determined time and in determined historical circumstances. Even though catechesis has a perennial base in the measure in which human nature is perennial, it must take into account the *historical situations* in which man is inserted from time to time. The history of the Church is interior and not exterior to human history, with all the vicissitudes which accompany and characterize it.

Now, the man of the catechesis of RH is not the de-historized and abstract man, but the man of today with all the historical components which qualify him. The man of today finds himself at a turning point which perhaps has no equal in the entire course of lengthy human history. Even if it remains always true that the evils of humanity have their root first in the fragile human interior, all the dangers and most serious menaces which have threatened man in the past centuries and millennia were or appeared more external than internal. Today it is not so. Man has become his own enemy: the snare and the threat come from products of his own hands, his own intelligence and his own will (cf. RH 15). The man who approaches the third millennium of Christianity, *above all, fears himself.* He fears that the products of his own genius, like a boomerang which turns back upon the one who threw it, will be transformed into the "means and instrument for an unimaginable self-destruction, compared with which all the cataclysms and catastrophes of history known to us seem to fade away" (ibid., 15).

The Pope grasps this dangerous situation which torments the world to place in clear relief the dignity and transcendence of the human person. Man inasmuch as he is principally intelligence, will and liberty is principally spirit.

The most serious evil of the hour is the failure of being conscious about human transcendency, a failure which results in negating man; it is the indifference to the primacy of moral values over all the others. The humanity of man is saved only by saving the primacy of the spirit, which is the principal and fundamental distinction of the person's sovereignty over the cosmos.

The constitutive primacy of the human person must find *its prolongation* in his very way of life and in his individual and social history. Otherwise, not only the failure of man's transcendency over the cosmos will occur, but his very self-destruction. And the Pope warns that "there is already a real perceptible danger" that man will "lose the essential threads" of dominion over things, and that even his humanity will "become subject to manipulation in many ways" (RH 16), rendering man the slave of things, of economic systems, of production and of his own products. "A civilization purely materialistic in outline condemns man to such slavery, even if at times, no doubt, this occurs contrary to the intentions and the very premises of its pioneers" *(ibid.)*.

It is here that the problem becomes acute: who is man? Never before was there an urgent need for a catechesis about the *reality and identity of man*. Man must either recognize, not only theoretically, the emergence of the spirit, the primary distinctive sign of human nature which must find its connatural and logical prolongation in all the organization of personal and communitarian life, or head towards catastrophe, "to self-destruction."

The alternative placed by the Pope's catechesis about man is inescapable: either accept, against all forms of materialism, the primacy of the spirit, that is, the transcendency of man; or resign oneself to slavery and to man's race towards his ruin. And since the transcendency of man would have no meaning without the transcendency of God, the catechesis directed by the Pope to the contemporary world in RH acquires a power and a vigor that is truly extraordinary. Only those who do not want to listen because of having taken a stand, or who do not have at heart the destinies of humanity can remain insensible.

"Appropriate" Christ

If Jesus Christ, as has been seen, is the identity of man, for a person to find himself and his dignity again and to fulfill his own vocation, he has the sure and royal way: to "appropriate" Him (RH 10). This expression of *Redemptor hominis* is as exultant as it is profound. We have already referred to it, but it merits to be studied historically and deeply penetrated.

"Appropriate" has as its contrary "expropriate." One is expropriated when he is deprived of the goods which are due to him. Where there is expropriation, there is *alienation*. Already St. Thomas used the term "alienation" in multiple meanings, not excluding that commonly understood in today's culture. Let us consider this briefly.

In Hegel, alienation is a process in virtue of which what is produced by man, that is, what belongs to his being or is a product of his activity, becomes extraneous to him, something different from himself. Man is emptied of his interiority. The things which he has created, the instruments with which he dominates nature, turn against him and become the negation of the human. Nevertheless, in idealism, alienation becomes reabsorbed and surpassed dialectically in the unity of the Subject.

Feuerbach restricts the concept of alienation to the religious ambit, which becomes the strong point of his atheism. For him, man "alienates" himself by projecting in God his own needs and his own ideals. We "expropriate" ourselves to enrich God. As we can see, we are exactly at the opposite extremes of the Christian concept of creation. For Feuerbach, God does not create man, but, rather, man creates God. This will be the concept which Marx will make his own as an indisputable truth. God becomes the alienation of man. Marx will then go in search of the causes which have led to alienation, and he will find them in the manner of economic production of capitalistic society, in which the products of human work are no longer considered the fulfillment of man, but purely "merchandise."

A few existentialistic currents place under accusation alienation insofar as it is caused by the mechanization of modern civilization. Here we are already close to the denunciation of uncontrolled technology, the threat of the man of today, as stated by RH.

These allusions aid in understanding with what sharpness of perception John Paul II in RH has recourse to a new language, in contrast to the desacrilized one of laicism and of militant atheism intent on uprooting even the idea of God from the heart of man. After the Encyclical places in full light the truth that man finds his identity in Jesus Christ it points out—in this moment of the universal crisis of anti-Christian ideologies directly to all Christians and indirectly to all men of good will—the way to overcome every alienation. Jesus Christ the Redeemer is the true liberator from alienations, the sure way for rediscovering oneself.

The expression, to "appropriate Christ," signifies "knowing Him, living Him, following Him, imitating Him, conforming oneself to Him, clothing oneself with Him..." but it is stronger than all these expressions. There comes to mind the identification of oneself with Christ of which St. Paul speaks: "For me to live is Christ" (Phil. 1:21), or "I have been crucified with Christ" (Gal. 2:20). But "appropriate" is a more dynamic and beautiful term than "follow," more energetic than "imitate," stronger than "conforming." Since the treasure of our personal identity is in Christ, to "appropriate" Him does not mean to reduce one's being, but to become "another Christ," an expression in which the two terms "another" and "Christ" must remain distinct but cannot be separated. When man has appropriated Christ, he becomes much more himself than before, he becomes truly himself. He acquires the fullness of his own identity by really participating in the fullness of Christ's identity.

The Christian religion is *exactly the opposite* of every expropriation. It is the restitution of man to himself. Anything but *alienating,* Christianity is by essence *appropriating,* that is, the giver of identity, of authenticity and of humanity, the font of personal spiritual growth for each man.

But Christianity is not only a doctrine or a method. Rather, it is Christ living and active, the inexhaustible source of life in the Church. Due to this intimate presence of Christ, living and resurrected, the Mystical Body of Christ, the Church, is sacrament, sign and instrument of the intimate union with God and the unity of the entire human race (cf. LG 1). In this light, the Word and the sacraments become the effective means for "appropriating" Christ always more perfectly. Thus, in concluding RH gives light about the Church's mission toward man as a prophetic, priestly and royal service. And among the sacraments, it highlights especially the Eucharist and Penance, which lead us toward an authentic and full appropriation of Christ.

In the background of the catechesis of John Paul II, there rises up at the end the supreme model of both human and Christian fulfillment, the tender and most sublime figure of Mary most holy, to whom each must look who really wants to "appropriate Christ."

ALOYSIUS BOGLIOLO

5

From "Evangelii Nuntiandi" to "Catechesi Tradendae": Continuity of the Magisterium

Whoever asks himself about the values which constitute the wealth of the Pontifical Magisterium will realize that one of these resides in the continuity-discontinuity which is found in the Magisterium itself.

There is absolute full and unshakable continuity in affirming the truths taught and their influence both on the life of every Christian and also on the life of the whole ecclesial community. A Pontiff can certainly carry out and deepen a discourse on faith begun by his Predecessors, but he will never depart from what they have proclaimed.

Discontinuity, instead, is seen in what concerns the clearer vision of certain aspects of the evangelical truths, and, consequently, the greater or lesser importance that these same aspects assume in view of the external changing circumstances. Many times this leads to the deeper study of a thought which at first had been just barely outlined. In this sense, the teaching of a Pope can enrich that of one of his successors or predecessors. It is, therefore, interesting and fruitful to examine the various themes as they appear in the teaching of different Pontiffs in the light of the principle of continuity-discontinuity.

Two Pontiffs within the span of less than four years have treated the subject of catechesis: Paul VI in *Evangelii nuntiandi* (EN) of December 8, 1975, and John Paul II in *Catechesi tradendae* (CT) of October 16, 1979.

A comparative examination of the teachings proposed in the two documents would undoubtedly be precious, but impossible in these pages. Nevertheless, here we can indicate a few points of discontinuity and of continuity present in these documents.

I. ELEMENTS OF DISCONTINUITY

Discontinuity is revealed, first of all, in the fact that Paul VI alludes in a passing and necessarily brief form to catechesis, in a text in which he intended to treat a much broader topic, that is, "Evangelization in the Modern World." John Paul II, instead, dedicates an entire lengthy apostolic exhortation to the topic of catechesis alone and thus can dwell on the very important aspects of this subject, deepening them and enlightening them with many considerations which would be fruitlessly sought for in EN. It goes without saying that the document of John Paul II takes up the rich and profound reflection of an episcopal synod with its three years of preparation and an entire month of synodal assemblies.

The discontinuity is manifested also in the different views of the questions. The two Popes differ from each other in their cultural identity, theological formation and pastoral experience, as well as in style, sensitivity and temperament. Why, therefore, be surprised that they approach the topic of catechesis from different angles?

II. ELEMENTS OF CONTINUITY

However, the elements of continuity seem to us to be more numerous and significant.

1. The first element is *the exceptional importance which the two Pontiffs attribute to catechesis.* For John Paul II, catechesis is a "priority task" of the Church (cf. CT 15), a "sacred duty and an inalienable right" (CT 14). In no. 15 of the same Apostolic Exhortation Pope Wojtyla reminds everyone with trepidation and firmness that "the more the Church, whether on the local or the universal level, gives catechesis priority...the more she finds in catechesis a strengthening of her internal life as a community of believers and of her external activity as a missionary Church."

Even though not directly confronting the problem of catechesis, Paul VI took care to indicate its importance by placing it in the context of evangelization. For Pope Montini, evangelization is a "reality in all its richness, complexity and dynamism" (EN 17), which cannot be reduced to one or the other of its components. But among the ways which serve evangelization, "a way not to be neglected" (cf. EN 33), at the risk of a fatal impoverishment, is precisely that of catechesis.

For the rest *Catechesi tradendae* itself takes up this concept again, both indicating catechesis as a stage of evangelization which cannot be dissociated from the whole, and presenting catechesis as "one of these moments—a very remarkable one—in the whole process of evangelization." Permit me to cite more amply this section, which is very significant for showing the reciprocal harmony and integration between the two pontifical documents: "The Apostolic Exhortation *Evangelii nuntiandi* of December 8, 1975, on evangelization in the modern world, rightly stressed that evangelization—which has the aim of bringing the Good News to the whole of humanity, so that all may live by it—is a rich, complex and dynamic reality, made up of elements, or one could say, of moments, that are essential and different from each other, and that all must be kept in view simultaneously. Catechesis is one of these moments—a very remarkable one—in the whole process of evangelization" (CT 18).

2. The second element of continuity: *the insistence on the necessity of an education in the faith.* Paul VI, already in paragraph 44 of *Evangelii nuntiandi,* does not hesitate to present catechesis as an answer to a "need to learn," felt, above all, by children and adolescents—"to learn...the fundamental teachings, the living content of the truth" revealed by God and transmitted by the Church. The Pope adds that precisely for this reason catechesis must be a "systematic religious education," "a catechetical instruction," he will say, which makes use of "suitable texts, updated with wisdom and competence," one that does not scorn memorization, one that demands good teachers, etc.

John Paul II explains all of catechesis in terms of instruction given and received: the image of Christ the Teacher dominates the entire Apostolic Exhortation (cf. CT 2-5); the mission given to the Apostles to "go and teach" (or, to make disciples, according to other translations) marks, according to the Pope, the beginning of catechesis (CT 10-11); the Church carries out a catechetical activity only because she continues this mission and makes herself, in turn, a teacher (CT 12-17). Having to offer a rather succinct definition of catechesis, John Paul II also says that it "includes especially the teaching of Christian doctrine...in an organic and systematic way" (CT 18).

We say immediately—and here, too, there is continuity—that for both Popes this instruction, far from being an exercise of the mind, as an end in itself, opens up to a "living" instruction, which is, as Paul VI wrote in paragraph 44 of EN, "given to form patterns of Christian living and not to remain only notional." On his part, John Paul II affirms that, yes, catechesis must represent a "deeper and more systematic knowledge of the person and the message of our Lord Jesus Christ" (CT 19), and an "understanding of the mystery of Christ in the light of God's Word" (CT 20), but immediately he takes care to point out its aim, which is this: "so that the whole of a person's humanity is impregnated by that Word" (CT 20). The paragraphs contained in numbers 19 and 23 of CT are all to be read and meditated in this perspective.

3. A third element of continuity—though amply developed in CT and just barely hinted at in EN—is *recalling to mind the various places where catechesis is to be done and the various persons and groups involved in catechesis.* EN refers explicitly not only to the Church (with this word, we mean the parish, the basic community, Bible groups and other ecclesial communities), but also to the school and to the family (EN 44). CT confirms that the "task concerns all of us," and after having recalled the catechetical role of Bishops, priests, religious men and women and lay catechists, it takes up with appropriate comments the places of catechesis foretold by EN: the family, which carries out a special catechetical function, thanks to its particular physiognomy to such a point that "family catechesis precedes, accompanies and enriches all other forms of catechesis" (CT 68); the school, both Catholic and non-sectarian, which "provides catechesis with possibilities that are not to be neglected" (CT 69); and the parish, to which the Pope attributes a privileged role in catechesis, since it almost represents the point of union between the family and the school (cf. CT 67).

It would be necessary at this point to emphasize also the importance of catechists as recognized by EN, be they volunteers, or school teachers who assume the mission of teachers of religion, or parents who are aware of their duty to educate their own children in the faith. "It is necessary to prepare good instructors," emphasized Paul VI, because in a field of such urgency and delicacy on which depends the future of the Church, it is not wise to improvise, nor is good will or right intention sufficient; it is necessary that the instructors be "desirous of perfecting themselves in this superior art, which is indispensable and requires religious instruction" (EN 44).

John Paul II does not neglect this reminder: in a paragraph of CT devoted to them, he proposes in very clear and eloquent terms the great importance of lay catechists. In mission territories, as well as in the already established Churches, the activity of these catechists is, according to the Pope, "an eminent form of the lay apostolate" to be encouraged and promoted (CT 66). I believe that the pressing invitation of EN about *aggiornamento* and about an always more adequate preparation of catechists is to be considered understood in CT. It is convenient, in any case, to keep it in mind when reading the above cited paragraph 66.

4. Another element of continuity is shown by *the perspective of catechesis for youth, young adults and adults*. There is only one sentence in EN on this topic, but it is very significant. No pretext must diminish the interest or question the effectiveness of catechesis for children, it states, and yet contemporary society knows the phenomenon of a vast number of young people and adults who were not even minimally introduced to catechesis as children, and who, having discovered the Lord through the most diverse paths and wanting to adhere to Him, have the urgent need for that "systematic and organic religious instruction" without which their religious impulse would risk becoming transformed into mere sentiment, or would simply fall into strange beliefs, instead of taking refuge in the true faith. Hence, the inescapable necessity of authentic catechumenates (the term is used in EN 44) for young people and adults.

In taking catechesis as a topic, the Synod of 1977 desired to make it clear that it intended to consider "mainly children and young people." One could have feared a narrowing down of the catechetical horizon to these age categories. In reality, even during the course of the Synod, it was seen that many Bishops deliberately widened the perspective, frequently inserting with the most heartfelt terms the subject of catechesis for young adults and adults. The phenomenon of the already well established process of secularization in several European countries and in the United States, and of the same process in an accelerated phase in Latin America (the document of Puebla registers it significantly), which creates growing masses of uncatechized adults, renders the question of their catechetical instruction urgent. CT does not avoid the question, but points it out as "the central problem of catechesis." The document devotes a brief but profound paragraph to it, which does not hesitate to define as "the principal form of catechesis" precisely that which is addressed to adults (CT 43).

A few ideas were the main inspiration for this last paragraph.

The first is given by the affirmation that to catechize adults means to form persons in the faith who often assume the greatest responsibilities in society and who in a certain way manage the world and temporal realities. To form their faith means to help them imbue these realities with faith.

The second idea: by definition adults are those who can live fully a faith which children and adolescents live in a manner that is always very conditioned, that is, limited by their age. It would be truly serious if these adults, who were deprived of catechesis during the age of childhood and adolescence, were not able to find any way to supplement this regrettable void and to receive a suitable catechesis in their maturity.

The third idea is that of the fruitfulness of a permanent catechesis. In the end, "everybody needs to be catechized." This is the suggestive title of Chapter V of CT, and it can be said very well that even a person who as a child or adolescent received a good catechesis for that age, needs, as an adult, to deepen his catechetical instruction in correspondence to his human maturity. CT says with reason that it would be absurd if the catechetical formation "were to stop precisely on the thresholds of the mature age," since it is precisely for adults that it is necessary, even though style, method and contents are to be suitably adjusted.

With these three aspects, CT illumines and immensely enriches the reading of the Apostolic Exhortation of Paul VI.

III. TWO TEXTS THAT COMPLETE EACH OTHER

In regard to the theme of catechesis, EN and CT penetrate each other and in a certain manner complete each other reciprocally. In effect, catechesis is an element of evangelization, one of the more characteristic and hence one of the more relevant, and in this sense all of CT is inserted and grafted perfectly in EN, almost bringing to fulfillment what is found barely outlined in no. 44 and in some other paragraphs of the document of Paul VI. It could be said that something was missing in EN, and that now this has been supplied with the precious developments of CT. On the other hand, the teachings and the pastoral directives on catechesis imparted by John Paul II would remain incomplete if they did not refer to the broader perspectives of EN.

In fact, catechesis does not exhaust itself in itself, but finds its roots and reason for being, as well as its aim and inspiration, in evangelization as presented by the *magna carta* of the magisterium of Paul VI. It is precisely due to viewing its placement within the process of universal evangelization that catechesis feels itself invested with a new dynamism and a universal responsibility. This is just what is recalled to us by no. 25 of CT, which sums up the chapter dedicated to "Catechesis in the Church's Pastoral and Missionary Activity." It is similar to no. 18, in which catechesis is indicated as the moment of evangelization for all strata of humanity: "In the final analysis, catechesis is necessary both for the maturation of the faith of Christians and for their witness in the world: It is aimed at bringing Christians to 'attain to the unity of the faith and of the knowledge of the Son of God, to mature manhood, to the measure of the stature of the fullness of Christ'; it is also aimed at making them prepared to make a defense to anyone who calls them to account for the hope that is in them." Therefore, something would be lacking in CT in regard to its intelligibility and its application if it were not intimately connected with EN.

The two Apostolic Exhortations reciprocally help each other, if they are read in strict relationship to one another. They are symptomatic of the convergence which exists between the documents of the pontifical magisterium, even while keeping in mind the principle of continuity-discontinuity pointed out at the beginning.

The few reflections which precede aim to put into focus this simple reality: if CT (no. 2) sends the reader to EN and to what this apostolic exhortation affirms about catechesis, it is not due to an empty formalism or in order not to lack respect for the custom of citing one's predecessors. It is because the very teaching of CT, far from cancelling that of EN, presupposes it, reclaims it and refers to it.

+ Most Rev. LUCAS MOREIRA NEVES, Archbishop
Secretary of the Sacred College of Cardinals
and of the Sacred Congregation for Bishops

6

General Introduction to the Apostolic Exhortation "Catechesi Tradendae"

The Historical and Doctrinal Premises

Before the Apostolic Exhortation *Catechesi tradendae* can be studied and understood, its special character must be underscored. This is not an original document of the Pope, as was the Encyclical *Redemptor hominis*, in which the Holy Father chose to bequeath to us his most personal thoughts "which then, at the beginning of this new way, were urgent with particular power in my mind, and which without a doubt, already before this had been maturing in me, during the years of my service" (OR, March 12-13, 1979).

The Apostolic Exhortation CT presents itself principally "in response to the request which was expressly formulated by the Bishops at the end of the fourth general assembly of the synod" (no. 4). It concerns, therefore, a *response* to the official requests of the Synodal Fathers. At the same time, it becomes an *inheritance* of the teaching of the Synod and of the two preceding Pontiffs on catechesis: "The theme is extremely vast and the exhortation will keep to only a few of the most topical and decisive aspects of it, as an affirmation of the happy results of the synod. In essence, the Exhortation takes up again the reflections that were prepared by Pope Paul VI, making abundant use of the documents left by the Synod. Pope John Paul I...had taken them in hand and was preparing to publish them" (no. 4). This paragraph reveals to us that the first outline of the exhortation had been drafted by Paul VI, making use of the documents of the Synod, and that John Paul I was preparing it for speedy publication. It is true that there are not lacking, as we shall see, characteristic and personal annotations of Pope John Paul II, which make this exhortation an original document.

In reading CT we find constant references to the Synod of 1977, which it intends to follow faithfully. Let us examine a few cases:

"The fourth general assembly of the Synod of Bishops often stressed the Christocentricity of all authentic catechesis" (no. 5a). This sentence opens the door to the Christological theme which occupies the first chapter of the exhortation.

When the document speaks of the specific character of catechesis it calls to mind the Synodal Assembly, which repeatedly made this problem the object of inquiry "during the preparatory work and throughout the course of the general assembly" (no. 18a).

The social doctrine of the Church is presented among the elements not to be forgotten for catechesis, because: "Many synod fathers rightly insisted that the rich heritage of the Church's social teaching should, in appropriate forms, find a place in the general catechetical education of the faithful" (no. 29 at the end).

The document deals with a few of the concrete problems of catechesis because: "During the synod, a certain number of Bishops drew attention to (them)" (no. 33b).

The document recalls that during the Synodal Assembly and the following two years, the Church shared in the preoccupation for a suitable catechesis for youth: "In this way the synod has been valuable for the whole Church by seeking to trace with the greatest possible precision the complex characteristics of present-day youth" (no. 40a). And in regard to adults: "I cannot fail to emphasize now one of the most constant concerns of the synod fathers" (no. 43).

The Pope intends to treat the subject of "memory" in catechesis, a delicate issue, contested in some quarters today, and he introduces the topic with these words: "The final methodological question, the importance of which should at least be referred to—one that was debated several times in the synod—is that of memorization.... Certain very authoritative voices made themselves heard on the occasion of the fourth general assembly of the synod, calling for the restoration of a judicious balance between reflection...and memory work" (no. 55a; the Synod is also remembered in other texts of CT: 21, 35, 51, 55b, 61a, 63).

At the end of the session, the Synod Fathers addressed a *Message* to the People of God: "We wish to present a report on the major conclusions of our work to the People of God" (Introd.). The Pope also has this message present and he recalls it, for example, when analyzing the wealth of the concept of catechesis "with its three dimensions of word, memorial and witness—doctrine, celebration and commitment in living—which the synod Message to the People of God emphasized" (no. 47b). All the topics of the Message find a place in the pages of the apostolic exhortation, some with special emphasis, such as the difficulties of catechesis in the world of today (Mess. 4; CT 14, 64), catechesis as memory (Mess. 9; CT 55), coresponsibility (Mess. 12ff.; CT 62ff.), etc. Even the new terminology "inculturation"—used by the Synod and accepted in the Message (no. 4)—is not forgotten in CT (no. 53).

Together with the other documents of the Synod, the Fathers presented to the Pope, in a compendium of thirty-four *Propositions*, the result of their labors, asking him to issue a document on catechesis. These Propositions, which offer a summary of the synodal debates, were to serve as the basis of the future apostolic exhortation. A thorough examination of the above-mentioned Propositions has led us to the conclusion that all of them have been incorporated into the text of CT. In fact, a few topics only suggested by the thirty-four Propositions, are developed greatly by CT. Proposition 6 speaks, for example, of the ecumenical dimension of catechesis, avoiding the danger of a false irenicism; CT (nos. 32-34) deepens the topic of ecumenism, but "with a view not to facile irenics" (no. 32d); Proposition 13 presents the rapport between catechesis and theology: this, too, will be better analyzed by CT; Proposition 18 asks that "dichotomies" be overcome, and the same topic is explained in CT with the same terminology: "avoid dichotomies" (CT 52b, 22). It is only in light of the Propositions that many passages of CT can be read and understood.

The Propositions are followed by a list of thirty-eight particular *Topics* which had not found place in the Propositions. These were to have been studied and deepened in view of the future apostolic exhortation. It is easy to discover the presence of these topics, too, in CT. One of them sketches the rapport between catechesis and the sacerdotal-religious vocation (see CT 39b). Another treats catechesis to the mentally handicapped (see CT 41); others speak of the use of Scripture and of liturgy in catechesis (CT 23, 27), or of the catechetical function of the homily (see CT 48), or of the special duty of the priest in catechesis (see CT 64), or of the pedagogy of faith (see CT 58), or of the role of Mary, Help of Christians, in catechesis (see CT 73).

Globally these data show us how *Catechesi tradendae* willed to *respond* to the synodal requests expressed in the Message, in the Propositions and Topics, thus becoming the greatest *heir* of the catechetical doctrine of the Church. In this context we cannot forget how CT gives renewed value to the *General Catechetical Directory*, published by the Sacred Congregation for the Clergy on April 11, 1971, and today forgotten in some quarters, by citing it eight times (nos. 18, 22, 27, 29, 32, 43, 50, almost always in the notes). CT recalls the *Credo* of the People of God of Pope Paul VI (nos. 28, 61), and it follows the doctrine and the terminology of *Evangelii nuntiandi*, which was the fruit of the preceding Synod (nos. 6, 18, 29, 39, 47, 61, 72).

The Pope has chosen to develop this exhortation according to a theme that is always very important, but especially so today: "I am also doing so in order to fulfill one of the chief duties of my apostolic charge" (no. 4a). The Pope does not apply himself coldly to this apostolic task, but with enthusiasm: "Now, beloved brothers and sons and daughters, I would like my words, which are intended as a serious and heartfelt exhortation from me in my ministry as pastor of the universal Church, to set your hearts aflame, like the letter of St. Paul the Apostle..." (no. 62a). The reading of this text reveals to us that the terminology apostolic "exhortation" finds its full meaning in this document of the Pope. He not only teaches but also exhorts as pastor.

Pope John Paul II found himself especially prepared and qualified to draw up this exhortation, first of all because of his pastoral experience, that is, because of the many hours dedicated to the teaching of catechesis during his priestly and episcopal life. Often in CT one hears an echo of this catechetical activity of his. "Catechesis has always been a central care in my ministry as a priest and as a Bishop" (no. 4a). "I may also mention the youth groups that, under varying names and forms but always with the purpose of making Jesus Christ known and of living by the Gospel, are in some areas multiplying and flourishing in a sort of springtime that is very comforting for the Church" (no. 47a). This paragraph makes us think of the plenary Assembly of the

Polish Episcopate (June, 1976), in which pastoral ministry among the youth was treated. In the same context Cardinal Wojtyla, during a pilgrimage to a Marian shrine, had explained how catechesis concerns all ages of man, and he had insisted on the primary duty of the family to denounce the attempts of an atheistic education made in the schools, where full-time teaching hinders religious formation. No. 68 of CT, about the family, seems to take up again those exhortations of his, and the section on the school seems to repeat the same words (no. 69). In fact, in the last few years the Polish Church, under the direction of Cardinal Wojtyla, had witnessed the birth of new forms of catechesis and new centers of education in the faith. University catechesis has attained great development, and the diocese of Krakow today offers us the best example. Cardinal Wojtyla had, therefore, an excellent catechetical experience and practical preparation which rendered him capable of writing this document on catechesis. At the same time, his pastoral experience conferred a personal character on the whole exhortation.

There is another element which has contributed more directly to making Cardinal Wojtyla the person best qualified for the accurate writing of a document on catechesis today. I refer to the active participation which he had in the preparation and development of the synod on catechesis, the origin of CT. The then Cardinal was a part of the *Council* of the General Secretarial Staff of the Synod which in March 1975 discussed the theme of the future Synod. Again he was among the components of a small commission which worked intensely and presented a valid basic document for the *Outlines*. Already during the meetings for the proximate preparation of the Synod, May 7-15, 1977, Cardinal Wojtyla was chairman of the Council when the *Instrumentum laboris* for the synodal discussions was drawn up: the Pope knew perfectly the pre-history of the Synod.

Lastly, Cardinal Wojtyla took active part in the synodal debates. The ideas expressed in his interventions merit our attention. They will find, in fact, a special prominence in CT, where even the very same words will be repeated. All this belongs to the most original and personal aspect of CT.

The first intervention of the prelate was on the occasion of the third General Congregation. He began by presenting a few experiences of the Polish Church. In Poland the withdrawal of public schools from all influence of the Church touches a fundamental point of the right of religious freedom. In this way there would have been created in social life an anti-catechetical complex that violates religious liberty and other human rights. The conscience of the Church must be very sensitive about this. It seems that the Pope takes up the same intervention when in CT he exclaims: "I vigorously raise my voice in union with the synod fathers against all discrimination in the field of catechesis, and at the same time I again make a pressing appeal to those in authority to put a complete end to these constraints on human freedom in general and on religious freedom in particular" (no. 14b). In the second part of his discourse he had then spoken of the parish as the center immediately responsible for catechesis and toward which all catechetical activities are directed (see CT 67). At another intervention in the twelfth general congregation the prelate had presented catechesis as a means for introducing the young into the mystery of Christ through an assent of faith and a vital adhesion: it seems that these same words have passed into the last part of no. 19 of CT, where much stress is laid upon the catechesis which transmits the teaching of the faith and proposes a total adherence to Christ. On that occasion, Cardinal Wojtyla touched on an idea which now he still has at heart—that is, the relationship between catechesis and "vocations," an idea which will be accepted later on by the Topics and by the text of CT (no. 39b).

During the Synod, Cardinal Wojtyla was part of the Italian group together with Cardinal A. Luciani: two future Popes, both great catechists, were working together. As fruit of this work a few pages were distributed containing the presentation of catechesis as "education and initiation"—two words which will not be forgotten in CT—with a return to the theme of parochial catechesis and to the relationship between catechesis and theology, which, in fact, are not identical, but which imply a certain homogeneity because they must offer the integral message of faith without prescinding from the magisterium; the above-mentioned pages also speak of *traditio Symboli* (the handing on of the creeds) and of the hierarchy of truths which must be maintained in every catechesis. These topics, almost in the same words, are to be found in CT.

The facts, the information and the documents set forth until now are necessary for a penetrating and enlightened reading of the apostolic exhortation of Pope John Paul II. Without knowledge of these data it is impossible to understand well the document's contents, its choice of topics and the dimensions of its practical implications.

The Structure of the Exhortation

Let us come to the outline of CT. Besides the introduction and a conclusion, the document contains nine chapters. The order is clearly logical and progressive. From the fundamental principles we go down to the more concrete forms of catechesis. The first part also contains an historical outline. The literary style is direct, almost as though it were a conversation of the Pope with the readers: in reading it one immediately draws near to the Pope's thought and heart. Repetitions, which are expressions proper to a conversation, are not lacking.

— The first chapter wishes, above all, to center the catechetical effort on *Christ*, on His Person. His doctrine is contemporaneously lesson and life. Christ is not only the model of every catechist, but also the object of catechesis itself, an object-Person, hence always alive and up-to-date. Catechesis teaches Christ and leads to a vital encounter with Him.

— The second chapter is rather historical and recalls a few salient points of catechesis in the *history of the Church*. The exhortation derives from Church history a few lessons for the world of today; history is not just a recalling of the past, but has a prophetic characteristic of actuality. The lessons remembered are four: the right and duty of the Church concerning catechesis, the priority which it bears among her other activities, the common and differentiated responsibility, and the continual renewal.

— The third chapter is one of the most important of the exhortation, and it intends to examine the *specifics of catechesis* in connection with other components of evangelization. Catechesis finds a germinal faith in the hearts of men, and then it treats of developing this faith through an education (teaching) and initiation (life) to the faith. Here the theme of the relationship between catechesis and the sacraments finds its place.

— The fourth chapter dwells on the *content* of catechesis; it goes over a few points set forth in the first and third chapters, but after the exposition of the sole font (Scripture and Tradition) of catechesis, it develops theological themes concerning the integrity of the faith and its moral requirements. Into this context enters the ecumenical dimension of catechesis.

—The fifth chapter studies the receivers of catechesis: everybody needs to be catechized. A description follows of the various categories of receivers. As always, the Pope shows a great confidence in youth; he knows their real problems, and contemplates in them the future of the Church. The section dedicated to the catechesis of adults reveals great pastoral richness.

—The sixth chapter enumerates a few *ways and means* for developing a real catechesis. It begins by speaking about the means of social communication, dwells on the description of the homily, and ends by presenting the catechetical tools and catechism texts. It is clear that the Pope desires to see soon a catechism well made, faithful to the contents of revelation, which answers the requirements of Vatican II and the necessities of the world of today.

—The seventh chapter studies *methods* in the light of the practical interference between catechesis and new ideologies, culture and particular devotions. A few dangers of deviations and changes are set forth. Into this context enters the topic of "memorization." It is presented as an *anamnesis* or remembrance actualizing the facts of the history of salvation.

—The eighth chapter deals with the *difficulties* of catechesis in the world of today; difficulties which demand a more attentive use of pedagogical resources, of the adaptation of language, etc. Faith must be presented as a certainty, and this theme leads to the study of the relationships between catechesis and theology.

—The ninth chapter, finally, calls all the members of the People of God to *make themselves responsible* in the work of catechesis. It is to be noted how the parish is the privileged place of catechesis. This is the chapter written with more enthusiasm and hope.

In the conclusion the Holy Spirit as interior Teacher and the Madonna as Mother and model of the disciple are recalled.

Topics and Directive Guidelines

Now it is necessary to dwell on a few of the newer and more characteristic elements of this apostolic exhortation. They will help us understand its doctrine better. They are elements which illuminate the contemporary problematic of catechesis and at the same time offer some avenue of solution. Many of them also reveal the more profound and original thought of Pope Wojtyla.

In the very first chapter, the Pope develops the Christological theme, on which all the Synod Fathers had insisted, but he does it in a truly personal form. He speaks with his heart full of love for the mystery of Christ: He is "the only Teacher" who teaches with all His life. He still lives, speaks, corrects, exhorts and "goes with us day by day on the path of history" (no. 9b). This vocabulary makes us remember a few really personal extracts of *Redemptor hominis,* as when Christ is spoken of as He who "walks with each person the path of life" (RH 13a). Catechesis not only reveals the mystery of Christ, as the object of its teaching, but brings man to communion with Him.

Another aspect that is proposed is the true concept of catechesis: it has to do with a "new" concept as the foundation, new even for having recovered many values neglected in the moments of unsuccessful experiments, and new because it opens to us new paths for carrying out catechesis. Catechesis has a specificity of its own, and it differs from the kerygma or first announcement, from the homily and from theological teaching. It is described with the following vocabulary: first of all, it is an "education" with the significance of the Greek *paideia,* that is, a teaching in the truth which requires, on the one hand, the function of a teacher, and, on the other, a personal commitment to learning on the part of the disciple; "education" does not remain at the level of knowledge, but envelops life. "All in all, it can be taken here that catechesis is an education...in the faith" (18d); "the specific character of catechesis, as distinct from the initial conversion-bringing proclamation of the Gospel, has the twofold objective of maturing the initial faith and of educating the true disciple" (no. 19a); the specific aim of catechesis is "education in the faith" (no. 51a; the term is also used in nos. 22a, 25, 68).

The expression "catechesis as formation" (see no. 24) completes this idea of education. As more specific practical notes concerning education in the faith, CT often recalls the systematic character of catechesis. "It must be systematic [teaching], not improvised but programmed to reach a precise goal" (no. 21c). "It is also quite useless to campaign for the abandonment of serious and orderly study of the message of Christ in the name of a method concentrating on life experience" (no. 22b); faith is deepened "in catechesis...by reflection and systematic study" (no. 26). We are before one of the salvaged values of catechetical teaching. It does not deal with the exclusion of experience and of life—this as we shall see is also a part of catechesis as "education"—but of saving the dimension of a teaching which, thanks to its systematic, organic character, becomes profound. Without doubt the cognitive phase is essential in catechesis, and in order that knowledge be true, a whole systematization is necessary. The initial proclamation was accepted with the "heart," explains the Pope (nos. 25, 26). Catechesis sees to it that this evangelical content passes also to the intellect. And from there, when it is well understood and grasped, it can afterwards penetrate one's existence affecting the whole of life. We are confronted with the journey of faith, which is born in the heart of one who accepts Christ the Savior, is deepened in the intellect through catechesis, and only then will be able to be applied to life. The function of the intellect is essential; we must recognize it. And the intellect penetrates and grasps a doctrine only when it is set forth in an organic and systematic form.

As a complementary notion of "catechesis-education," the Pope presents the concept of "catechesis-initiation." Initiation adds to teaching the character of experience, because every initiation is linked to life and to human existence. "All in all, it can be taken here that catechesis is an education...in the faith, which includes especially the teaching of Christian doctrine imparted, generally speaking, in an organic and systematic way, with a view to initiating the hearers into the fullness of Christian life" (no. 18d). This text shows us the whole process of catechesis-education which begins with a teaching of the doctrine offered in a systematic way, and terminates in initiation into the fullness of Christian life. The Pope theologically explains this tie between initiation and life. First of all, catechesis is an initiation into the Revelation of God, and, in fact, Revelation illumines and envelops human existence. "Authentic catechesis is always an orderly and systematic initiation into the revelation that God has given of Himself to humanity in Christ Jesus.... This revelation is not however isolated from life or artificially juxtaposed to it. It is concerned with the ultimate meaning of life and it illumines the whole of life with the light of the Gospel, to inspire it or to question it" (no. 22c).

Another theological argument, which unites catechesis-initiation with life, we find in the liturgical dimension of catechesis. Every initiation has a ritual character, united to human existence. "Catechesis does not consist merely in the teaching of doctrine: it also means initiating into the whole of Christian life, bringing full participation in the sacraments of the Church" (no. 33a). After the exposition of catechesis as initiation, in the third part of no. 22, the following article continues thus: "Catechesis is intrinsically linked with the whole of liturgical and sacramental activity, for it is in the sacraments, especially in the Eucharist, that Christ Jesus works in fullness for the transformation of human beings" (no. 23a). Catechesis is united to the liturgy, in which Christ transforms the life of men. Thanks to the liturgy, catechesis becomes initiation, and changes men. At the same time, if catechesis is not based on teaching and on doctrine, its union with the sacraments is "ritualistic."

Recently the science of catechesis has made much progress in this direction regarding the character of initiation. The apostolic exhortation does not forget all this progress made, and it structures the various aspects within the notion of catechesis. Thus, catechesis teaches the whole plan of life, and envelops the existence and the conduct of the catechumen, who becomes not only a disciple but also a witness. "In the understanding expounded here, catechesis keeps the entirely pastoral perspective with which the synod viewed it. This broad meaning of catechesis in no way contradicts but rather includes and goes beyond a narrow meaning which was once commonly given to catechesis in didactic expositions, namely, the simple teaching of the formulas that express faith" (no. 25b). In catechesis, not only is the evangelical message deepened through reflection and study, but also "by awareness of its repercussions on one's personal life—an awareness calling for ever greater commitment—and by inserting it into an organic and harmonious whole, namely, Christian living in society and the world" (no. 26). All this conception of catechesis is again set forth in other paragraphs of the exhortation (no. 20c offers a most beautiful synthesis of all that we have said; no. 49c requires that catechetical works be really connected to the concrete life of the generation to which they address themselves, keeping well in mind its anxieties and its questions, its struggles and its hopes). In this light, we cannot understand how some authors hastily denied to CT this "vital" character, of social and human commitment. For the Pope—since catechesis is "education and initiation"—there is no opposition but complementarity and mutual need, between doctrine and life, teaching and experience.

The attentive reading of this description of catechesis, offered us by the present Pontiff, recalls the fidelity of CT to the theological and pastoral doctrine of *Evangelii nuntiandi*, according to which evangelization is not identical with kerygma, but is a process which includes kerygma, catechesis, the sacraments and the formation of the Church as a community (17, 24). This theological setting has been fully accepted by theologians and missionaries.

Another important point of guidance for an in-depth reading of CT, and of light on the whole text, is the insistence upon doctrinal "integrity." The Synod Fathers had already expressed themselves often on this topic. But the originality of the Pope is expressed in the form with which he deals with the theme and in the theological arguments which he uses to explain it. In the second chapter, it becomes, as it were, a lesson taught us by the history of catechesis; a few limitations of certain initiatives are recalled, and "these limitations are particularly serious when they endanger integrity of content" (no. 17). But it is chapter four which pauses to study the theme of doctrinal integrity in cate-chesis. "With regard to the content of catechesis, three important points deserve special attention today. The first point concerns the integrity of the content" (no. 30; see nos. 17, 31, 49, 59). Integrity is not a nostalgic effort to preserve an ancient message, which has only an historical significance. Integrity does not oppose a wise adaptation in the use of new means and methods of transmission of the message (no. 17), nor does it dispense from the organic and hierarchical character of the truths to be taught (no. 31), or from the effort to find a more understandable and suitable language (no. 59). Doctrinal integrity is not foreign to the ecumenical dimension, but seeks it without renouncing an integral presentation of the content of faith (nos. 32, 33). Neither is integrity passive; instead, it presumes cultural dialogue and incarnation, without, however, allowing the Gospel to be altered in its contact with various cultures (no. 53).

Integrity is due to the nature of the message of Christ, who is the bearer of salvation and becomes always present. Catechesis is not a teaching of personal invention, but a transmission of what the Church in her turn has received and faithfully guards. Catechesis as "transmission" is the theological foundation most confirmed by *Catechesi tradendae*; to this the document appeals more often to explain the meaning of "integrity" (nos. 31, 17, 53,

58). The term "transmit, transmission" has a profound biblical and theological significance, as was already pointed out in *Evangelii nuntiandi;* this is recalled in CT (no. 6, footnote 14). This "transmission" means that the message of Christ has a definitive salvific character, which imposes renunciation of the introduction of personal opinions and options, but is fulfilled in terms of fidelity to Christ, and lived as the consequence of the ever-present value of the Gospel. This message has its own originality: that of the faith, which is beyond the results of pedagogical and human techniques. Speaking of a "pedagogy of faith is not a question of transmitting human knowledge, even of the highest kind; it is a question of communicating God's revelation in its entirety.... A technique is of value in catechesis only to the extent that it serves the faith that is to be transmitted and learned; otherwise it is of no value" (no. 58b). Christ Himself used to transmit what He had received, so that His doctrine was not His own but that of the Father (Jn. 8:26, 28; 7:16; see CT 6 at the end).

Pope Wojtyla recalls also as the foundation of "integrity" the right which all men have of receiving the message of Christ totally: "The person who becomes a disciple of Christ has the right to receive the 'word of faith' not in mutilated, falsified or diminished form but whole and entire, in all its rigor and vigor" (no. 30b). The Gospel as salvific message is timely because it always bears fruits "that Christ and the ecclesial community have a right to expect" (no. 30b). To save the doctrinal integrity, the Pope who so greatly defends human rights does not forget the rights of the catechumen, of the Church and also of Christ Himself.

In the preceding pages the theme of "faith" emerged frequently. We must add a note to the concept of faith in CT, which having already appeared in the first paragraph, will be repeated on almost every page. In this concept there are aspects of actuality; at the same time it manifests the spiritual and theological personality of the Pope, who wrote his doctoral thesis on the "concept of faith in St. John of the Cross." The introduction says: "Very soon the name of catechesis was given to the whole of the efforts within the Church to make disciples, to help people to believe that Jesus is the Son of God, so that believing they might have life in His name" (no. 1b). Catechesis, through faith, forms disciples who accept Jesus as the Son of God (doctrinal character) and thus have life. (The mediatorial function of faith, a means of knowing and a means of union, is one of the points emphasized the most in the doctoral thesis of Wojtyla).

The acceptance of Jesus is a knowledge, neither abstract nor obscure, which brings with it the concrete experience of the encounter with Him. Faith has a certitude, because it bases itself on the very Word of God, who does not deceive, and this certitude becomes a clear light, even though *in enigmate* (enigmatic). Faith is light and also darkness, due to the excessive light which originates from God. "It is also one of the aims of catechesis to give young catechumens the simple but solid certainties that will help them to seek to know the Lord more and better" (no. 60d). Temptations are overcome which arise from certain ideologies and theologies that present faith as a search for the absolute, an opening to the infinite and an orientation of the spirit, which, however, never reaches its object (no. 60b). With faith we reach Christ! Other temptations against faith come from the field of pedagogical and experimental research. These temptations want to reduce catechesis to a pedagogical method and limit its content and fruits to a humanly measurable result. But faith has an original pedagogy, which we find in God's form of proceeding in history and in that of Jesus in the Gospel (no. 58). The message is then not diminished for fear that it will not be accepted or will scandalize; but neither are the fruits measured by external results. Faith is not a simple human knowledge. The real pedagogue or teacher is the Holy Spirit (no. 72f).

Conclusion

At one and the same time, CT concludes one stage in the history of catechesis and opens another. It concludes the stage of dichotomies and uncertainties, characteristic of many catechetical experiments of recent years, which thought in an alternative form, setting in opposition teaching and experience, methodology and spontaneity, dogma and practice, memory and compromise. The orientation and content of CT is not "exclusive" (it does not exclude any authentic theological or pedagogical value), but rather integrative: it accepts all the present values of the catechetical movement and integrates them within a clear doctrine, full of certainties. It does not forget the urgent and real problems which catechesis finds today, but it illumines them and orients us as to how to face them. There are certain criteria and certain binding norms, which indicate a direction of march more than a boundary. In the pages of CT there does not appear the temptation of snobbishness, but there is manifest a profound wisdom, and wisdom is always new.

The apostolic exhortation CT initiates a new catechetical stage. Primarily it renders everyone responsible and explains the concrete form of collaboration and catechetical participation which each one in the Church is called to offer. In fact, each one will find in this document a concrete answer to his own vocation of catechist. At the moment of realizing this vocation, CT offers a series of topics which must be the object of further inquiries according to the criteria therein indicated, such as the study of the characteristics of the various categories of hearers of catechesis, or the form of evaluating its privileged places (parish, movements, family).

At the end of the exhortation the Pope recalls the grave difficulties which await us in catechetical work, but paradoxically this chapter is entitled: "The Joy of Faith in a Troubled World." The joy which is always hope is, however, the fruit of the reading of this document. The Pope has obtained what the document asks of Bishops: "to bring about and maintain...a real passion for catechesis, a passion embodied in a pertinent and effective organization, putting into operation the necessary personnel, means and equipment" (no. 63c).

JESÚS LÓPEZ-GAY, S.J.

BIBLIOGRAPHY

C. Caprile, *Il Sinodo dei Vescovi 1977*, Rome, 1978 (a work necessary for knowing the premises of CT: the instruments of work, the synodal debates, the Propositions and Topics.

C. Bissoli, "Guida alla lettura di 'Catechesi Tradendae,' " *Catechesi* 49 (1980) 5-16.

La Catechesi nel nostro tempo: La "Catechesi Tradendae," introduction and commentary by Mario Puccinelli, Rome, 1980.

"Testimonianze sull'esortazione apostolica 'Catechesi Tradendae,' " *L'Osservatore Romano*, January 26, 1980, p. 5 (collaboration by E. Giammancheri, F. Ricci, L. Negri, H. Louette).

"L'Esortazione Apostolica 'Catechesi Tradendae,' " presented by Cardinal Rubin, *Bulletin of the Pontifical Commission for Social Communication.* Press Room of the Holy See, no. 424, October 24, 1979.

"Educazione alla Fede, oggi La 'Catechesi Tradendae.' " Text and commentary by A. Ugenti, Bologna, 1980.

"L'Uomo, via della Chiesa. Riflessioni sul documento 'Catechesi tradendae,' " Pontifical Lateran University, Rome, 1980.

PART TWO

"An Experience As Ancient As the Church"

Catechesis in the History of the Church

"It would be impossible here to recall, even very briefly, the catechesis that gave support to the spread and advance of the Church in the various periods of history, in every continent, and in the widest variety of social and cultural contexts. There was indeed no lack of difficulties. But the word of the Lord completed its course down the centuries; it sped on and triumphed, to use the words of the Apostle Paul."

—CT 12

1

The Catechesis of the Apostles and of the First Christians

It has already been said, also in the preceding contributions, that with his Apostolic Exhortation *Catechesi tradendae*, John Paul II intended to pinpoint the present situation of catechesis in our time, taking up again those more salient and current aspects debated during the fourth general assembly of the Synod of Bishops in 1977.[1]

The development of *Catechesi tradendae* does not depart greatly from the structure which Paul VI had already given to his *Evangelii nuntiandi*. The point of departure necessarily remains the person of Christ. A true catechesis cannot permit itself to walk a way other than that of placing the catechized in communion with the person of Christ, with His mystery, through the explanation of the actions, words and signs worked by Him.

Thus, Christ becomes the sole and indispensable Way to draw near to the love of the Father in the Spirit. He is also the sole Truth which every catechist must transmit into the intellect and heart of the one whom he is catechizing. Therefore, a genuine catechesis must preoccupy itself, not so much with transmitting abstract truths, but rather with communicating the mystery of the living God, the eternal plan of the Father which is fulfilled and revealed in Christ.[2]

As if to confirm these premises, *Catechesi tradendae* offers a model of catechesis; a tested catechesis; a catechesis which has "an experience as ancient as the Church": the catechesis of the Apostles, the catechesis of the first Christians.

Following the numerous biblical citations offered in CT 10 and 11, we will seek to manifest contents and forms of this twofold catechetical experience which is as "ancient as the Church." Thus it will be easier to draw workable conclusions for the catechesis of our time.

I. THE CATECHETICAL EXPERIENCE OF THE APOSTLES

The didactic activity of Jesus as authentic "Teacher" who does what He teaches, must have profoundly impressed not only the crowds, but the Apostles themselves. In fact, He had a manner of teaching particularly all His own, which certainly had nothing in common with the sterile verbosity of the Scribes.[3] What, therefore, did the Apostles learn at the school of Jesus Master?

1. Catechesis Is Mission

The mandate given by Jesus to the Twelve and to the first disciples: "Go..., teach all nations" (Mt. 28:19), oriented their entire life. They understood that Jesus is the true *apóstolos;* that is, the one sent with authority from the Father.[4] Above all, in the fourth Gospel, everything that Jesus did and said is always referred to as having originated from the Father who sent Him. Because Jesus is the only One who knows the Father, it follows that He can also reveal Him: "All that I have heard from my Father I have made known to you" (Jn. 15:15). For this reason whoever loves God will also love Jesus; in fact, the One sent is inseparable from Him who sends Him.

As Jesus is inseparable from the Father, so also those whom Jesus chooses as apostles will have to announce to all peoples the universal salvific will of God, revealed in Christ. They will do so, however, on the condition that they are sent by Him and remain united to Him.

From the totality of the scriptural texts cited in *Catechesi tradendae* concerning the mission of Christ and of the disciples, it appears clear as a consequence that the "mission" of him who is sent to bring the announcement must be a mission which proceeds from an authority. It is not a personal initiative. "You did not choose me, but I chose you" (Jn. 15:16); it is rather an authoritative mission in the sense of delegation of power. This is to say that in the history of salvation the divine initiative has always been dominant: the Son is sent by the Father and the Son in turn has chosen His own disciples, who, with their mission and life continue the work of divine grace.[5] "For this reason He formally conferred on them after the resurrection the mission of making disciples of all nations" (CT 10, with reference to Mt. 28:19).

Only thus can the mission bear abundant and lasting fruit. Catechesis, therefore, presupposes fidelity to the vocation and to the mission received.

2. Catechesis Is Communion

To be faithful to the mission means to maintain a close "communion" with him who sends and with those to whom one is sent. We see, then, that *Catechesi tradendae*, citing the first of the "summaries" reported from the *Acts of the Apostles*,[6] intends to furnish the "permanent image" of a Church which seriously considers the obligation of the mission, forcing herself to live also in her fullness the consequent obligation of "communion."[7]

Thus is described, in Acts 2:42 (NAB), the first Christian Community: "They devoted themselves to the apostles' instruction *(didachê)*, and the communal life *(koinôní)*, to the breaking of bread and the prayers."

We have here, in the lifestyle of the first Christian community,[8] a model of how our communities should be, as they seek to render their catechetical service effective. For a fruitful catechesis—capable, that is, of making the Church be "born and grow"[9]—a fourfold communion is therefore required:

a. "They devoted themselves to the apostles' instruction"

First of all, the faithful find themselves all together and have full awareness of being a *community*.[10] Luke describes this gathering of persons not as the fruit of a casual convergence of intentions, but rather as the sign of a common agreement, sincere harmony and mutual free assistance. He underscores this community's devotion in listening to the teaching of the apostles. It is the apostles, in fact, who, having been formed at length in the school of Jesus,[11] become His qualified witnesses in transmitting the actions and doctrines (cf. Acts 1:1) of the Master, explaining the salvific meaning of His death and resurrection (cf. Acts 2:22-36; 3:12-26, etc.). Devotion in listening leads to profound adhesion to the doctrine of the Apostles and to perseverance in it (cf. Acts 5:12-13).

The Book of the *Acts* also makes evident the particular prestige which Peter enjoyed among the other Twelve.[12] Even Paul feels the need to "get to know" Peter, spending fifteen days in his company (cf. Gal. 1:18). In fact, lack of communion with Peter and with the Apostles leads to this risk: that of running or having run in vain (cf. Gal. 2:1f.).[13] From this "experience as ancient as the Church," we deduce that to have an authentic and effective catechesis there is necessarily required a devout "communion" with the Word of God[14] and communion with Peter, who together with the apostolic college is the authentic interpreter of this Word.

b. "Communal life"

This "communal life" is indicated by the technical term "koinônía,"[15] and it indicates not only the "spiritual" communion of the believers among themselves and with the Apostles, but also a "material" communion through the placing of temporal goods in common.[16] The peak of this communion is obviously had in the "eucharistic" communion which unites the faithful to Christ and among themselves through the sacrament.[17]

The koinônía, meanwhile, makes it possible for the infant Church to realize within itself a total, effective and affective "communion." In Acts 4:32 this "communion" is specified by stating that "those who believed were of one heart and soul."

It may also be deduced that this apostolic experience teaches that to carry out an effective catechesis the catechist must be in "fraternal communion" with the ecclesial community to which he or she belongs. "Every kingdom divided against itself is laid waste" (Mt. 12:25).

c. "The breaking of the bread"

With the technical term of "the breaking of the bread," the Acts of the Apostles (Acts 2:42, 46; 20:7, 11) intends to designate that well-determined meal which produces the messianic and eschatological exultation (agalliasís) and which is celebrated on the first day of the week (Sunday, according to Acts 20:7).

"The breaking of the bread" is, therefore, the first name given to the unique Eucharist celebrated by the community of the new alliance under the guidance of the Apostles, the Twelve tribal heads of the new People of God.[18] Catechesis requires notable spiritual energies. We cannot remain undernourished, either at the table of the Word, the teaching of the Apostles, or at the table of the Eucharistic bread. It will also be remembered that, according to 1 Cor. 11:17-34, "communion" with the Body of Christ must be total: one cannot communicate the Eucharistic Body of Christ if one is not in communion with His ecclesial body.

d. *"Communion in the prayers"*

The primitive community is described by *Luke*, the evangelist of prayer,[19] as a praying community. He speaks of a prayer of praise (Acts 2:47a) and of a prayer of petition (cf. Acts 4:24f.). If, in the meantime, prayer is essentially a "communion" with the Father, through the Son, in the Holy Spirit, it follows that those who carry out "communion in prayers" consolidate their communion with God and, consequently, their communion among themselves because it is the Holy Trinity which consolidates and guarantees the unity of the brethren in the Church.[20]

We have here another important deduction about catechesis as communion: catechesis requires communion with God in prayer. The catechist who does not pray can be certain that his mission is destined to certain failure. "Apart from me you can do nothing." Not little, but "nothing" (Jn. 15:5).

There appears, therefore, the "lasting image of the Church being born of and continually nourished by the word of the Lord, thanks to the teaching of the Apostles, celebrating that word in the Eucharistic Sacrifice and bearing witness to it before the world in the sign of charity" (CT 10).

It is from this model of Church that every Christian community engaged in catechesis should derive inspiration, seeking with every effort to fulfill that fourfold "communion" with the Word, with the brethren, with the Eucharist, and with prayer, as the indispensable conditions for a true and fruitful catechesis.

All this reminds us also that the first catechesis is example, and the first example is "communion." For this reason, in fact, they had "favor with all the people" (Acts 2:47; cf. 4:33; 5:13), and already this fact permitted that "the Lord added to their number day by day those who were being saved" (Acts 2:48).

3. Catechesis Is Indispensable

If mission and communion can be called characteristic *ad intra* of catechesis, indispensability can be considered a condition *ad extra*. We cannot do without catechesis, it is indispensable. We cannot remain silent and at a standstill; it is necessary to go and to bring the announcement received.

In speaking of the catechetical mission of the Apostles, *Catechesi tradendae* presents this characteristic thus: on the one hand, there was the opposition of the adversaries who took offense at the activity of the Apostles and were "annoyed because they were teaching the people" (Acts 4:2). They gave the order not to teach any longer in the name of Jesus (cf. Acts 4:18; 5:28). On the other hand, we see instead the distinct stand of the Apostles who answered thus: "Whether it is right in the sight of God to listen to you rather than to God, you must judge; for we cannot but speak of what we have seen and heard" (Acts 4:19-20). If, therefore, "we must obey God rather than men" (Acts 5:29), this means that no human authority can ever impede what God Himself has commanded to His Church.[21]

The facts, however, are always the same, then as well as today: the Word always finds difficulties, it is opposed, it is hushed up, it is downtrodden, it is forced to grow up among thorns, it is carried away by the devil (cf. Mk. 4:1-9, 13-20: the parable of the sower). He who brings the Word is also ridiculed, as in the case of Paul in the Areopagus of Athens (cf. Acts 17:32). In spite of that, the apostle must be always ready to answer whoever asks him the reason for the hope which he has in himself (cf. 1 Pt. 3:15). Also in Acts 4:33 we find: "With great power the apostles gave their testimony." The path of one who witnesses to the resurrected Jesus is the path of refusal, of suffering, and probably of death (cf. Acts 22:20: the witness-martyrdom of Stephen).[22]

In the footsteps of Christ who witnesses to the truth (Jn. 18:37), His disciples must render testimony to Him in the same manner that the Spirit Paraclete renders testimony to Him (Jn. 15:26-27). Only those who witness to Christ will receive the testimony—that is, will be recognized by God as His own (cf. Heb. 11:2, 4, 5, 39; 12:1).[23]

II. CATECHESIS IN THE APOSTOLIC ERA

The mission entrusted by Christ to the Twelve, "Go...make disciples of all nations" (Mt. 28:19), most certainly did not exhaust itself with the activity of the Apostles. The mission continues. Describing the continuation of this mission, which cannot have limits either of space (cf. Mk. 16:20: "They went forth and preached everywhere"), or of time (cf. Mt. 28:20: "I am with you always, to the close of the age"), *Catechesi tradendae*, no. 11, expresses itself thus:

"The apostles were not slow to share with others the ministry of apostleship (cf. Acts 1:25). They transmitted to their successors the task of teaching."

Just as Jesus, apostle of God (cf. Heb. 3:1), willed to institute a college which multiplies His presence and His Word, so the Twelve communicate to others the exercise of their apostolic mission, maintaining with them a special bond. In this manner the history of salvation continues in the community of faith before the world.

Scripture indicates a few characteristics of this shared apostolate and of the teaching transmitted:

—the *parádosis*, tradition—that is, the act of "passing on from hand to hand" the contents of the Gospel, to which corresponds the *parálepsis*, the act of receiving on the part of the faithful[24];

—the *diadochê*, succession—uninterrupted handing on of the mission and of the necessary powers, by the older to the younger ministers.

From the very beginning of the Christian communities these elements were held to be essential. We intend, later on, to cast more light on them, because from them we must derive teaching in view of the formation of the present communities that carry out catechesis.

In writing to the community of Thessalonica, Paul recommends: "Stand firm and hold to the traditions which you were taught" (2 Thes. 2:15; 3:6). Before dying, the same Paul urges Timothy to entrust what he had heard from him to "faithful men," who in turn will be capable of transmitting it to others (cf. 2 Tm. 2:2). This is, in fact, a fundamental and indispensable duty of the "servants of Christ and stewards of the mysteries of God. Moreover it is required of stewards that they be found trustworthy" (1 Cor. 4:1-2; 7:25; 1 Thes. 2:4; etc.).[25]

With regard to the manner of transmitting uninterruptedly the authentic doctrine of Christ,[26] the New Testament texts speak to us of fidelity (cf. 1 Cor. 4:2), of courage (*parresía*: 1 Thes. 2:2; 2 Cor. 3:12), of crystalline transparency (*eilikrinéia*: 2 Cor. 2:17). The *Acts of the Apostles* ends precisely with these expressions:

Paul "welcomed all who came to him, preaching the kingdom of God and teaching about the Lord Jesus Christ quite openly and unhindered" (Acts 28:30-31).[27]

During the Apostolic age catechesis is, therefore, "shared" between the Apostles and the other ministers. Among these ministers of the Word there are some who receive a specific "institution," as with the Deacons; but there are also many other disciples (cf. Acts 15:35) who, still remaining ordinary Christians, are taken as associates by the Apostles in the task of teaching. This extension of the mission of "teaching" and of spreading the Word of God (cf. Acts 6:8; 8:4) is without doubt one of the most effective New Testament models from which to draw example for the formation and organization of the ministers of catechesis even in our own day. Let us, then, examine more closely how this experience of catechesis was organized in the apostolic age.

1. Deacons and Catechesis

The task of teaching was entrusted by the Apostles to the Deacons from the very beginning of their institution. In the New Testament we find the Deacons named (cf. Phil. 1:1; 1 Tm. 3:8-13) as a specific ministry, as "servants" consecrated for service, as "those entrusted with the *diaconía* of Jesus Christ."[28] They are the "ambassadors" of Christ (2 Cor. 5:20), animators of the community "for the equipment of the saints, for the work of ministry" (Eph. 4:12). While still expressing itself in various ways, the diaconal ministry has nevertheless a pre-eminent service to which to dedicate itself: the *diaconía* of evangelization (cf. Eph. 3:7-8). This is the supreme *diaconía* which permits the transmission "to the whole creation" (Mk. 16:15) of the salvation worked by Christ the Lord. The Deacon, therefore, while neglecting neither the service of the Eucharist nor that of the works of charity, remains principally the one "consecrated to the service" of the Word of God.

This New Testament vision of the Deacon as "consecrated to the service of the Word" in the catechetical activity of the ecclesial community again becomes ever more current today.[29] Nevertheless, the diaconate of today is not due to the lack of priestly vocations, as a few erroneously believe; it has instead a constitutive role of its own which consists in being the "sacramental sign" of service as a following of Christ the servant, within a Church which places service as the central value of her own renewal (cf. LG 8).

We have an example in the *diaconía* of Stephen, who, "full of grace and power," did not cease to teach, moved as he was by the wisdom of the Spirit (cf. Acts 6:8). So, too, we have the example of the Deacon Philip, who catechized the minister of the Queen of Ethiopia (cf. Acts 8:26-40).

2. The Laity and Catechesis

At this point, *Catechesi tradendae*, no. 11, observes: "The Apostles associated 'many others' (Acts 15:35) with themselves in the task of teaching, and even simple Christians scattered by persecution 'went about preaching the word' (Acts 8:4)."

Here appears a Church that is anything but clericalized. The ministry of the apostolate is a ministry shared also by the simple "lay" Christians. The basis of this apostolate is to be sought in the direct action of the Holy Spirit: "You have been anointed by the Holy One, and you all know.... The anointing which you received from him abides in you, and you have no need that anyone should teach you; as his anointing teaches you about everything, and is true, and is no lie, just as it has taught you, abide in him" (1 Jn. 2:20, 27).

We speak of the Holy Spirit given to the Messiah (cf. Is. 11:2; 61:1) and by Him transmitted to the believers (1 Jn. 3:24; 4:13; cf. 2 Cor. 1:21). The Spirit instructs in everything; thanks to Him the words of Jesus are "spirit and life" (Jn. 6:63). Even if, in fact, the simple faithful receive instruction from the Apostles, nevertheless it is always through the grace of the Holy Spirit that the exterior preaching penetrates into souls.

The plant that has been sown possesses its own roots in new and fresh soil; it produces its own fruits.[30]

With a synthetic but effective expression, the *Epistle to Diognetus* expresses thus this new mentality which has created itself within the apostolic community: "Having become a disciple of the Apostles, I become a doctor of the people."[31]

The role of the laity in catechesis is essentially that of preserving and transmitting sound doctrine:

—to conserve it in faithfulness, not only of thought, but also of Christian action; their sense of the faith is nothing other than their Christian fidelity, which conserves what it has received;

—to transmit it through teaching and education, through witness and the profession of faith.

With all this, the faithful exercise a function of "maternity" in the Church, transmitting the deposit of the apostolic faith. Incessantly the Fathers affirm that men are generated by believing and that they in turn, generate by talking and teaching. Better still, they generate by constituting, through the unity of their community, the spiritual and moral environment in which one is formed according to the faith.[32]

This consciousness regarding the condition of the catechetical ministry was, therefore, clear in the apostolic age. *Catechesi tradendae* encourages us to become aware of this perennial spirit of shared ministry and seems to hope that in the Church of our time, too, there can be many persons, even simple Christians, "teaching about the Lord Jesus Christ quite openly" (Acts 28:31).

A Church that wants to seriously consider the mission of diffusing the Word of God cannot, therefore, fail to "share" this ministry also with the laity.[33]

3. The Catechetical Structure of the Gospels

"Before being written down, the Gospels were the expression of an oral teaching passed on to the Christian communities, and they display with varying degrees of clarity a catechetical structure" (CT 11).

Both the *kerygma*—that is, the official proclamation, the announcement of salvation to non-believers—as well as *catechesis*—that is, instruction and the later more detailed development of the announcement—used to be adapted in part according to the listeners and the circumstances.[34] One can discover in Paul diversities of language and of form between the discourse given at Antioch of Pisidia for the Jews (cf. Acts 13:16-41), that given at the Areopagus of Athens for the gentiles (cf. Acts 17:21-31) and that given at Miletus for the Christians (cf. Acts 20:18-35).[35]

It will be noted that the Good News clearly has a common framework within which the individual didactic units which form the material of catechesis are inserted. Thus the words and the facts of the life of Jesus are transmitted according to an "oral style"[36] which keeps in mind mnemonic and catechetical demands, as well as environmental and cultural demands. In a word, oral catechesis, which later on was to flow into the written

Gospels, besides drawing constantly from the person of Jesus, from His word and from His actions, always reflects an environment and a concern: that of bringing the message of salvation in a manner suitable and consonant with the daily demands of life. All this intense work of primitive catechesis, consisting of didactic explanations, of a deepening in faith of applications to diverse circumstances, is developed always under a particular assistance of the Holy Spirit and always finds its ultimate matrix in faith and in the life of the Church. Thus, before the present Gospels were a writing in which the Church fixed a part of itself, they were above all the mirror of a preaching and a life. Their perennial value lies in the fact that they came from a catechesis made in the Church, for the Church and by the Church.

The evident "catechetical structure" (CT 11) of the Gospels was the reason why the account of St. Matthew was called the Gospel of the catechist and that of Mark the Gospel of the catechumen (cf. CT 11). Starting out from the presupposition that every Gospel was born in the ambient of its preaching, many exegetes are inclined to affirm that the work of Matthew had a catechetical destination. "There is a growing belief in the idea that behind the Gospel of Matthew there is the figure of a catechist who argues, instructs, seeks to convince.... It seems that the Gospel of Matthew represents the manual of a theological school, perhaps that of Antioch, destined in the first instance for the catechetical instruction of the protoChristian community."[37]

Conclusion

Wishing to draw conclusions useful for the catechesis of our time, we can ask ourselves a question: with the presentation of an experience as ancient as the Church, what does *Catechesi tradendae* suggest as to the precise nature of the preaching of the Apostles and the catechesis of the first Christian community?

From an over-all view the document seems to us to catalogue the following points:

1. Catechetical activity is not a free initiative of individual Christians, as if it were an undertaking in which each one can apply himself at pleasure according to his own zeal. Catechesis has a structure that is organized hierarchically under the guidance and control of the Apostles, who are responsible for the message and are guarantors of it. Catechesis is consequently a missionary service entrusted by the Bishop to trustworthy persons under his

supervision. It is not, therefore, a phenomenon of euphoric transmission of vague and imprecise news. Communion with the Church, with one's own Bishop, with the Pope, is an indispensable condition for a catechesis to be apostolic and missionary.

2. Catechesis must have a "testimonial" character. A witness is one who, through an immediate personal experience, does not limit himself to teaching a doctrine, but makes known the living person of Christ the Lord. The catechist is not an opportunist, but a person who has assumed the obligation of the mission as a vocation.

3. Catechesis must have an eminently "ecclesial" character. Communion with the Church signifies conserving unaltered the good deposit of the faith; it means living a communion in faith and in charity both with the priests of one's own community, and also with all the other brethren who form one sole people of God. If communion in charity is lacking, the work of catechesis cannot be fruitful, because every kingdom which is divided within itself is destined to perish.

4. Catechesis must have a "supernatural" character. The doctrine which we announce is not ours, nor do we announce ourselves, but solely the work of salvation willed by the Father, fulfilled in Christ and continued by the Holy Spirit. From this stems the necessity of drawing continually from the Word of God and of assimilating it profoundly to the point of making ourselves authentic persons of prayer. The catechist's awareness that his mission goes way beyond his poor human powers must lead him to an intense Eucharistic life, consisting both of participation in the table of the Body and Blood of Christ and of adoration of Him who even after the celebration remains the Emmanuel, that is, the God-with-us.

5. Catechesis must be also "incarnate"; in fact, it is one of the components of the great mystery of the Incarnation. Fidelity to tradition does not exclude an intense work of "inculturation" of catechesis into the individual cultures of the peoples to whom it is addressed. As the apostolic preaching knew how to adapt itself, even without abdicating or attenuating its own message, to both the Jewish and the Graeco-Roman cultural ambients, so also the contemporary catechetical announcement is called to incarnate itself into the different cultures and ambients in which the people of today are found.

These and still other points could be derived from an attentive reading of *Catechesi tradendae*, numbers 10 and 11. However, this already seems sufficient matter to render the catechesis of our time an effective instrument capable of making the Church be born and grow "until we all attain to the unity of the faith and of the knowledge of the Son of God, to mature manhood, to the measure of the stature of the fullness of Christ" (Eph. 4:13).

PAOLO GIGLIONI

FOOTNOTES

1. Cf. *Synodus Episcoporum, De catechesi hoc nostro tempore tradenda praesertim pueris atque iuvenibus; Ad Populum Dei Nuntius*, ed. Civitate Vaticana, 28/10/1977; cf. *L'Osservatore Romano*, October 30, 1977, pp. 3-4.

2. Cf. CT 5-9.

3. Cf. Mk. 1:22; cf. also Mt. 5:2; 11:1; 13:54; 22:16; Mk. 2:13; 4:1; 6:2, 6; Lk. 5:3, 17; Jn. 7:14; 8:2; etc.

4. Cf. L. Cerfaux, "Pour l'histoire du titre 'apostólos' dans le Nouveau Testament," in RSR 48 (1960) 76-92; K. H. Rengstorf, art. *apostéllo*, in GLNT I (1965) 1063-1194, shows that the idea of apostolate implied sending with all the powers; what the apostle does is done by God; his word is the word of God.

5. It is useful to recall the text of *Evangelii nuntiandi*, no. 15, which effectively emphasizes this topic.

6. For an introduction and a study of the *Acts of the Apostles*, refer to C. M. Martini, "Introduzione agli Atti degli Apostoli," in AA.VV., *Il messaggio della salvezza*, 6, Turin-Leumann 1979, pp. 447-466; J. Dupont, *Etudes sur les Actes des Apôtres*, Paris 1967; ital. trans.: *Studi sugli Atti degli Apostoli*, Rome 1971.

7. Cf. F. Hauck, art. *koinós* in GLNT 5 (1969) 671-693; Idem., art. *koinónós*, ivi, pp. 693-724; J. Hamer, "L'Eglise est une Communion," Coll. *Unam Sanctam*, n. 40, Paris 1962 (Ital. trans., "La Chiesa e una comunione, Brescia 1964); S. Cipriani, "La Chiesa come

comunione nel N.T.," in *Presenza Pastorale* 41 (1971) 163-179.

8. L. Cerfaux, "La première communauté chrétienne à Jerusalem," in ETL 16 (1939) 5-31 *(Recueil L. Cerfaux*, II, Gembloux 1954, pp. 125-156); B. Ramazzotti, *Comunità e missione. L'impegno missionario oggi alla luce degli Atti degli Apostoli*, Bologna 1978.

9. J. P. Charlier, *L'Evangile de l'enfance de l'Eglise. Commentaire des Actes 1-2* (Etudes religieuses, 772), Paris 1966; Ph. H. Menoud, *La vie de l'Eglise naissante*, Neuchâtel 1969; ital. trans.: Milan 1970.

10. Cf. C. M. Martini, "La comunitá cristiana primitiva e i problemi della Chiesa del nostro tempo," in *Parole di vita* 14 (1969) 341-356.

11. Cf. P. Franquesa, art. *Apostolato*, in EncBibbia 1(1969)575-582; L. Cerfaux, *Le chrétienne dans la theólogie Paulinienne*, Paris 1962, pp. 98-117.

12. It is Peter who takes the initiative; it is he who speaks in the name of all (cf. Acts 1:15; 2:14, 37f.; 3:4, 6, 12; 4:8; 5:2f.; etc.); it is he who visits all the communities (9:32); it is he who introduces the pagans into the Christian community (10:1-48).
Cf. AA.VV., "Saint Pierre dans le Nouveau Testament," *Lectio divina* 79, Paris 1975.

13. Cf. H. Schlier, *I capitoli 1 e 2 della lettera ai Galati e gli Atti*, in *Lettera ai Galati*, Brescia 1966, pp. 109-122.

14. Regarding devout communion with the Word of God, the expressions of *Jeremiah* could be recalled:

"When I found your words, I devoured them; they became my joy and the happiness of my heart" (Jer. 15:16; cf. also Ezek. 3:1-3; Apoc. 10:9-10).

15. Besides what was said in *footnote* 7, to be cited here is the study of J. Ratzinger, *Die christliche Brüderlichkeit,* München 1960 (Ital. trans.: *Fraternità cristiana,* Rome 1962); H. von Soden, art. *adelfós* in GLNT I (1965) 385-392.

16. Regarding the pooling of material goods in common as a characteristic expression of the *koinônía* of the first Christians, see the classical study of J. Dupont, "La comunità dei beni nei primi tempi della Chiesa," in *Studi sugli Atti degli Apostoli,* Rome 1971, pp. 861-889.

17. Cf. S. Lyonnet, "La 'koinônía' del'Église primitive et la Sainte Eucharistie," in *Atti del XXXV Congresso Eucaristico Internazionale,* I, Barcelona 1953, pp. 511-515.

18. Cf. B. Klappert, art. *Cena del Signore,* in *Dizionario dei concetti biblici del Nuovo Testamento,* Bologna 1976, pp. 224-239; O. Cullman, *Le culte dans l'Eglise primitive,* Paris 1945.

19. In general on the theme of prayer in Luke, cf. A. Drago, *Gesú uomo di preghiera nel vangelo di Luca,* Padua 1975.

20. See S. Cipriani, *La preghiera nel Nuovo Testamento,* Milan 1970.

21. For the whole question, cf. R. R. Williams, *Acts of the Apostles. Nothing Can Stop the Gospel* (Torch Bible Paperbacks), London 1965.

22. Regarding the series of interventions of the Apostles in *Acts,* cf. J. Dupont, "I discorsi missionari degli Atti degli Apostoli, secondo un'opera recente," in Idem. *Studi sugli atti degli Apostoli,* Rome 1971, pp. 227 & 265; C. H. Dodd, *The Apostolic Preaching and Its Developments,* London 1950; Ital. trans.: "La predicazione apostolica e il suo sviluppo," *Studi Biblici,* 21, Brescia 1973.

23. L. Cerfaux, in studying the use of the term "witness" in the *Acts,* clearly showed how the Apostles, rendered courageous by the grace of the Holy Spirit, publicly appear as authentic and qualified witnesses of His works and of His words; the people who are converted accept their testimony, because they know that it rests upon a precise knowledge of the facts; cf. L. Cerfaux, "Témoins du Christ d'après le livre des Actes," in *Angelicum* 20(1943)166-183, (now in—*Recueil Cerfaux,* II, Gembloux 1954, 157-174); cf. also H. Strathmann, art. *mártys* in GLNT 6(1970) 1269-1392.

24. Regarding the term "tradition" cf. L. Cerfaux, "La tradition selon saint Paul," in *La Vie Spirit.,* Supplém., 1953, pp. 176-186, (now in *Recueil Cerfaux,* II, Gembloux 1954, pp. 253-263; F. Büchsel, art. *paradídômi,* in GLNT 2(1966)1120-1190; Y. Congar, *La tradizione e le tradizioni.* I: *Saggio storico,* Rome 1961; II: *Saggio teologico,* Rome 1965.

25. Cf. C. Spicq, "Saint Paul et la loi des dépots," in *Rev. Bibl.* 40(1931) 481-502; Idem. *Les Epitres pastorales,* Paris 1947, pp. 327-335, (= un *excursus* sul "buon deposito").

26. We cite here, as an example, a significant text of Irenaeus: "All these things I have listened to with care, and have conserved them in my memory, not at all on a piece of paper, but in my heart. Through the grace of God, I have always meditated them with love": *Epist. ad Flor.,* in Eusebio, *Hist. eccles.,* 5, 20, 6-7.

27. Cf. H. Schlier, art. *parresia* in GLNT 9(1974)877-932; G. Scarpat, *Parressia, Storia del termine e delle sue traduzioni in latino,* Brescia 1964.

28. Ignatius of Antioch, *Ad Magnesios* 6, in *Patres Apostolici,* ed. F. X. Funk, I. Tubingen 1901, p. 195.

29. For the restoration of the discipline of the diaconate in the Catholic Church, see the *Motu Proprio* of Paul VI, *Ad Pascendum,* in AAS 64 (1972)534-540; for the English language in *The Furrow* 23(1972) 747-751; for the French language in *Documentation Catholique* 69(1972)854-857; for the Spanish language in *Phase* 12(1972)534-541.

For a bibliography see: A. Kerkvoorde, "Elementi per una teologia del diaconato," in *La Chiesa del Vaticano II*, Florence 1965, pp. 896-955; J. Lecuyer, "Les Diacres dans le N.T.," in *Le Diacre*, Paris 1966; AA.VV., *Il diaconato nella Chiesa e nel mondo d'oggi*, Padua 1968.

30. Y. M. Congar, *La tradizione e le tradizioni*, II, Rome 1965, p. 176.

31. *Epistola a Diogneto* 11, 1, in *Patres Apostolici, cit.*, p. 410; see also the compact commentary of H. X. Marrou, "A Diognète,"² *Sources Chrétiennes* 33, Paris 1965, p. 78ff.

32. Cf. Y. M. Congar, *La tradizione e le tradizioni*, cit., p. 179; Idem., *Per una teologia del laicato*, Brescia 1966; H. Rollet, *laïcs de l'histoire*, Paris 1964.

33. One can find very good reflections on the meaning of "mission" in E. Gatti, *Atti degli Apostoli: il libro della missione*, Bologna 1975.

34. Among the recent treatments of this problem we recall: P. Rossano, in *Introduzione alla Bibbia*, IV, Turin 1959, pp. 72-87; L. Randellini *in Introduzione al Nuovo Testamento*, Brescia 1961, pp. 35-138; C. M. Martini, in *Il messaggio della salvezza*, 6, Turin-Leumann 1979, pp. 16-107; for a more specific study, see W. Langer, *Kerygma e catechesi*, Brescia, 1971.

35. For a commentary on these discourses of Paul, cf. B. Stonehouse, *Paul before the Areopagus and other N.T. Studies*, London 1957; J. Dupont, "Le discours de Milet. Testament Pastoral de Saint Paul (Actes 20, 18-36)," *Lectio Divina*, 31, Paris 1962; Ital. trans.: *Il testamento pastorale di San Paolo*, Rome 1967.

36. Cf. J. Schmitt, "Predication apostolique," in DBS 8(1972) 246-273; useful is the article of C. M. Martini, "La primitiva predicazione apostolica e le sue caratteristiche, in *Civiltà Cattolica* 113 (1962) III, 246-255; cf. also AA. VV., *La formation des Evangiles*, Louvain 1957; L. Vaganay, *Le probleme Synoptique*, Tournai 1954, pp. 35ff.; P. Hitz, *L'annonce missionaire de l'Evangile*, Paris 1955.

37. A. Läpple, "Dalla bibbia alla catechesi," 4, EDB, Bologna 1979, p. 110; the specialist K. Stendahl, *The School of St. Matthew and Its Use of the Old Testament*, Uppsala 1954, p. 35, defines, with good reasons, the Gospel of Matthew as "the work of a school for teachers and leaders of communities."

2

The Catechesis of the Fathers

In the Apostolic Exhortation *Catechesi tradendae,* John Paul II writes:

"This mission of teaching that belonged to the apostles and their first fellow workers was continued by the Church. Making herself day after day a disciple of the Lord, she earned the title of 'Mother and Teacher.' From Clement of Rome to Origen, the post-apostolic age saw the birth of remarkable works. Next we see a striking fact: Some of the most impressive Bishops and pastors, especially in the third and fourth centuries considered it an important part of their episcopal ministry to deliver catechetical instructions and write treatises. It was the age of Cyril of Jerusalem and John Chrysostom, of Ambrose and Augustine, the age that saw the flowering, from the pen of numerous Fathers of the Church, or works that are still models for us" (CT 12).

The following pages seek to illustrate these wise words.

With regard to catechesis we can distinguish between the Fathers in this way:

1) those who catechized, and they are all;

2) those who composed catechetical treatises for future catechists, and they are various;

3) those who wrote treatises to teach the manner of catechizing, and there is at least one.

1. Fathers Who Catechized

I intend to use "catechesis" in the proper sense as that part of the ecclesial ministry, distinct from theology and from preaching in general, destined to transmit the basics of the faith. Even in this sense all the Fathers were catechists. In fact, they felt themselves to be such, even though they were often great theologians; in reality, they explained the catechism to the flock entrusted to them—to everyone: learned and unlearned, children and adults. When requested by a deacon of Carthage to give him norms for teaching catechism, St. Augustine politely replied: "If you have so much trust in me as to believe that I can teach you something, come and see how I myself teach catechism: seeing me and listening to me while I put these norms into practice, you might apprehend them better than reading them as dictated by me" *(De Catechizandis Rudibus,* 15, 23).

But not all of the catechetical writings of the Fathers have come down to us. We have those of Cyril of Jerusalem, of John Chrysostom, of Ambrose, of Augustine (the four mentioned explicitly by John Paul II) and of Theodore of Mopsuestia.

The most famous writings, the catecheses of Cyril, constitute one of the most precious treasures of ancient Christianity. There are twenty-four, divided as follows:

—a procatechesis or preliminary discourse;

—eighteen *baptismal catecheses,* addressed to those preparing themselves to receive baptism, the *illuminandi;*

—five *mystagogical catecheses,* directed to the *neophytes* during Easter week.

The procatechesis contained a warm greeting and a paternal admonition concerning the gravity and the conditions (there was much insistence on the *disciplina arcani)* of the step which the candidates were about to take.

The eighteen catecheses successively treated of baptism (1), of penance and temptations (2), of baptism and salvation (3), of Christian doctrine (4), of the nature and origin of faith (5), of the articles of the Creed (6-18). These last twelve were dedicated respectively: four to the Father (6-9), five to the Son (10-15), two to the Holy Spirit (16-17), and one to the resurrection, to the Church and to eternal life (18). The mystagogical catecheses concerned Baptism (19-20), Confirmation (21), the Eucharist (22), and the liturgy of the Mass (23). The studious argue as to whether the mystagogical catecheses, briefer than the others but also more precious, are the work of Cyril or of his successor John or of both together. But it is not necessary to enter into erudite questions: these are not pages of erudition but of information.

Criticism has recently restored to us some—though not all— of the *Baptismal Catecheses* of the great Christian orator, John Chrysostom: we had two, now we have twelve. These enrich our knowledge of the baptismal liturgy of the Fourth Century in Antioch, and they show us the wise clarity with which John used to instruct the *illuminandi* and the neophytes.

Historical studies, furthermore, have discovered and placed at our disposition the precious *Catechetical Homilies* of Theodore of Mopsuestia, precious, I say, above all because of their testimony regarding the sacraments of the Eucharist (real presence and sacrifice) and Penance (auricular confession). They are sixteen, addressed to catechumens and to neophytes, divided as follows: ten on the articles of the Creed of Nicea (1-10), one on the *Our Father* (11), three on the liturgy of Baptism (12-14), and two on the Eucharist (15-16). There is no need to note that they constitute an interesting parallel with the conferences of Cyril of Jerusalem just mentioned.

If we turn from East to West, we can observe that modern critics have rendered other services to our knowledge of the patristic catechesis. I refer in particular to Ambrose and Augustine.

We already had an important work of Ambrose: *On the Mysteries*, which is an accurate re-elaboration of preceding homilies (provided that the homiletic form is nothing but a literary appearance) in which the Bishop addresses the neophytes, speaking to them of the rites of Baptism and of the Eucharist.

But now criticism has positively resolved doubts regarding two other works of Ambrose, written in shorthand, which, it seems, were homilies really given to the neophytes to explain to them the creed and the sacraments of Christian initiation. I allude to *The Exposition of the Symbol to Beginners* and *Upon the Sacraments*. While the first work consists of just one homily, the second contains six of them, respectively on Baptism (1-3), on the Eucharist (4-5) and on Confirmation and the *Our Father* (6).

Criticism has performed the same good services in regard to the *Catechetical Discourses* of Augustine, considerably increasing their number, which, however, always remains much lower than the total of discourses really delivered. We can distinguish three groups:

1) *dogmatic catechesis* or explanation of the Creed: divided into two parts, the consignment or *traditio symboli* and the restitution *redditio symboli;*

2) *moral catechesis*, which comprises the discourses to the "competent" (*ad competentes:* in the etymological meaning of "asking together" for Baptism), that is, to those who had asked to

be baptized during the coming vigil of Easter, who would be instructed on the moral duties which they were assuming with Baptism;

3) *mystagogical catechesis*, which comprises the discourses on the Christian mysteries destined for the neophytes *(ad infantes)*.

They are respectively: the *Discourses* (in the Maurine edition reproduced from Migne) 212; 213 (new critical edition in *Miscellanea Ag.* I, 441-450); 314; 315 (first group); 216 (second group); 225-228; 272 (third group). Other *Discourses* upon the sacraments or *ad infantes* are in *Miscellanea Ag.* I.

In this brief listing of the catechetical discourses of the Fathers the method which they followed and the fundamental points on which they placed emphasis stand out. These were: faith (the Creed), prayer (the *Our Father*), the Christian duties, the Christian mysteries. The Creed was explained, learned by heart and repeated. St. Augustine tells the catechumens: "You must always have it memorized and always repeat it" *(Serm.* 212, 2); and elsewhere: "You have received and have repeated what you must always retain in your mind and in your heart, what you must say in bed, think of in the public squares, and not forget while you eat; regarding this even when you sleep with your body, you will always be vigilant with your spirit" *(Serm.* 215, 1).

Sometimes the Creed would be explained by listing the errors which were to be avoided in order to remain faithful to the truths contained in it. This is the case of the *Christian Combat (De agone christiano)* of Augustine, a kind of circular letter or, if one wishes, a manual of postbaptismal catechesis in which the new bishop admonishes his people (addressing this *"humili sermone"* to everyone, particularly to the more simple, "unlearned in the Latin language,") to preserve faithfully *"regulam fidei et praecepta vivendi,"* by not listening to those who teach doctrines in opposition with the articles of the Creed. And he lists these doctrines, repeating nineteen times the formula: "Let us not listen to those who say..." and summing up each time an error to avoid. In this manner he goes over, in distinct groups, the contents of the Creed and the trinitarian, Christological, ecclesiological and eschatological errors opposing it.

Elsewhere the same doctor observes that in some churches in the catechetical teaching of the "competents" *(in catechismis competentium)* no mention was made of the vice of adultery (not because it was approved but because the exemplary conduct of the Christians rendered it unnecessary), with the consequence that, because it was not spoken of, some on their part began to defend it *(De fide et operibus* 19, 35).

2. Fathers Who Composed Catechetical Treatises

When we pass on from catechetical discourses to catechetical treatises, the panorama becomes restricted and, in a word, confused: restricted, because the Fathers who wrote these treatises (at least, those which remain to us) are few; confused, because it is not always easy to distinguish which of these works are catechetical and which are theological. An example can be the *De principiis (On the principles)* of Origen: the title and the initial pronouncements tend toward the catechetical, but the considerations which the great Alexandrian sets forth in them are such and so many as to make this book a precious manual of theology, one of the most important of the patristic era. Thus, just to give another example, the golden letter or discourse *A Diogneto*, written for one who was preparing himself "to learn the Christian religion" and who asked the unknown author six precise questions about it, is something half-way between catechesis and apologia.

The six questions are:

1) What God do the Christians believe in and how do they venerate Him?

2) Why do they scorn the world and despise death?

3) Why do they not offer worship to the gods of the pagans?

4) Why do they not follow the religion of the Hebrews?

5) Why do they love each other so much?

6) Why did this new sect—that of the Christians—appear in the world now and not before?

I have set down the questions in order to tempt the reader to go and read the answers: the little work which contains them is truly a pearl of ancient Christian literature.

Leaving aside, therefore, the works which are only dubiously classified as catechetical, I will recall only three writings: one from the dawn of Christianity, another of Irenaeus, and a third of Gregory of Nyssa, even though this last, explicitly meant for catechists, is also an important dogmatic work.

The first is the *Didaché*, a simple and plain little work of evident catechetical preceptual character, written, according to the most probable opinion, toward the end of the first century. It sets forth the doctrine of the two ways, the way of life and the way of death, the precepts and the virtues of the one and the vices of the other, liturgy (Baptism, prayer, Eucharist), ecclesial discipline, the liturgy. Both for content and for style it was greatly valued by ancient Christianity. The author remained and remains unknown. It speaks of the duty to accept or not accept catechists according to whether they teach or do not teach the doctrine set forth: "If someone coming among you will teach all that was said before, accept him. But if, distorted, he were to teach another doctrine in order to destroy, do not listen to him" *(Didaché,* 11, 1-2).

The second is the *Exposition of Apostolic Preaching* of Irenaeus of Lyons. We know that this great bishop, who died a martyr in 202-203, wrote a great work against the heresies, the *Adversus haereses,* in five books, a fundamental work for theology.

The *Exposition of Apostolic Preaching* is a brief catechetical treatise, almost a "summary memorial" addressed to a certain Marcianus with the aim of confirming him in the faith: "in order that," he writes to him, "from little you will derive great advantage, and succinctly know all the aspects of the body of truth and have in brief the proofs of the 'divine dogmas,' and, to whoever wishes to know them, you will be able to set forth our reasons with full certainty, in their integrity and purity." Irenaeus, on a clear trinitarian basis, develops in synthesis the fundamental points of the *regula fidei:* the doctrine of the Father, of the Son and of the Holy Spirit (the three articles of the Christian faith), and therefore of the creation, the redemption and the salvation of man.

The third work that we wish to recall, written explicitly for Christian teachers who had to instruct the catechumens, is by Gregory of Nyssa, brother of Basil the Great. Its title is its program: *Oratio catechetica magna.* In the author's intention, therefore, it is a work of catechesis; but because teachers needed "a system in their instructions" (Prologue), the exigencies of being both systematic and profound led the author to compose a doctrinal synthesis of the principal dogmas of Christianity, even defended with rational arguments—a kind of "Summa theologica."

We can see that Gregory demanded much of catechists: they had to know both the content of the Christian faith and the reasons which support it; hence, catechesis and theology together. The work is divided into three parts:

—part I (chs. 1-4) on God and the Trinity,
—part II (chs. 5-32) on the Incarnation of the Word and the redemption,
—part III (chs. 33-40) on sanctification (Baptism and Eucharist).

The central point, as can be seen from the distribution of the chapters alone, is that of man's restoration accomplished by Christ, which includes in turn the doctrine of the nature and destiny of man and of his fall. Even though it contains the Origenian theory of the *apocatastasi*, opposed and condemned by the Church, the work had a vast diffusion in the Eastern Churches.

3. Fathers Who Taught How To Catechize

If from the catechetical treatises we pass to the concrete manner of teaching catechism, the panorama becomes still more restricted. The patristic era has left us only one work of this kind—only one, but very important: it is the *De Catechizandis Rudibus (On the Manner of Catechizing Beginners)* of Augustine. The work was written around the year 400 at the request of the Carthaginian deacon Deogratias, who had asked how he should teach catechism and how he could overcome the boredom which often intruded upon him. In answering, the Bishop of Hippo drew from his own personal experience and pedagogical wisdom, both very rich. He divided the work into two parts, one theoretical and the other practical. The theoretical part was subdivided into three arguments which he expressed with the words: *narratio, cohortatio, hilaritatis comparatio.*

The *narratio*, a technical term of the art of public speaking, implies the exposition of the divine revelation, as it is manifested in the history of salvation, that is, "from the point in which it is said '*In the beginning God created heaven and earth,'* until the present period of the history of the church" *(Ibid.,* 3-5). However, it is not only the facts, but also the truths contained in the facts which must be set forth, and the entire narration must be ordered to the fostering of love in the listeners. Precious is this admonition: "After having proposed to you love as the end to which everything you say is to converge (so writes Augustine to Deogratias and in him to all catechists) whatever thing you set forth, do it in such a manner that the one who hears you, in hearing believes, in believing hopes, and in hoping loves" *(Ibid.*, 4, 8). But for man there is no greater incentive to love than the demonstration of "how much God loves him." The supreme manifestation of this love of God for man is Christ. For this reason all Scripture, for one who knows how to read it, speaks of Christ and recommends love: *Christum narrat et dilectionem movet.* And precisely this is what the catechist must put in relief in narrating the history of salvation.

"Having ended the narration," Augustine continues, "we must infuse hope in the resurrection." This is precisely the central theme of the *cohortatio:* this great, blessed Christian hope, which implies the knowledge and the practice of one's own duties, fear of divine judgment, and expectation of the final destinies of the two cities, of the just and the unjust, of God and the world. The *cohortatio*, by setting forth the last things of Christian eschatology, looks toward the eternal destiny of men in the final judgment, which will be held by God "with goodness toward the good, with severity toward the evil, with truth towards all" *(ibid.*, 7, 11).

Both the *narratio* and the *cohortatio* must have as a necessary ally the *hilaritatis procuratio*, that is, the art of promoting joy, the joy of both speaker and listener. This was the point on which the Carthaginian deacon insisted in turning to the Bishop of Hippo. The Bishop in answering writes most beautiful pages of pedagogy and gives wise counsels. He enumerates the causes of boredom, which he reduces to six, and he indicates the remedy. The reader of the latter should not omit making himself a reader of the former, if he has not already done so. To sum up, without defacing them, is impossible. I will only say that the psychological intuitions and the didactic observations which Augustine sets forth have a common denominator: *love.* He had a particular genius in speaking of love, and here he does it as a great teacher. This is a sample: "If we get bored in repeating often banal things and childish ones, let us also place ourselves on a level with the children with paternal, fraternal and maternal love; and...even to us those things will seem new.... It is the same thing that usually happens when we show to persons who have never seen them magnificent and beautiful places...before which we would usually pass without any delight because we have seen them so often; our delight is renewed through the freshness of the delight of the others" *(Ibid.,* 12, 17).

These are the three arguments which Augustine develops in the first part of the work. But together with them, implicitly, there is a fourth, no less important than the others: the *listener.* The catechist must first of all know whom he has before him in order to adapt himself to him with speech and attitude. "I myself," Augustine writes, "find myself moved in one way or another according to whether I find myself before a learned or an ignorant person to be catechized, a citizen, a foreigner, a rich man, a poor man...." The enumeration continues, and concludes: "According to the various impressions my discourse begins, proceeds and ends." And he gives particular counsels, by way of example, for two categories, that of the scholar and that of the rhetorician. In these cases, as in all the others, those counsels have one sole root: charity: "In fact...charity caresses some, is severe to others, is enemy to no one, *is mother to all" (Ibid.,* 15, 23).

Then before one who is rather hard-headed—a case far from unreal—"we must say many things," Augustine shrewdly observes, "but more to God for him than to him of God" *(Ibid.,* 13, 18).

The book ends with the concrete example of a catechetical discourse, proposed in two forms which emphasize the same plan but vary greatly in length: this is the second part, which certainly does not have the same importance as the first.

In *De Catechizandis Rudibus* the patristic age has left us a work of everlasting value; a work of catechesis and at the same time of pedagogy, which completes in the meantime all the others of that kind, and, so to speak, places the seal on them of the mature experience and genial intuitions of a great teacher: it is truly, to repeat the words of the Holy Father, a model.

AGOSTINO TRAPÈ, O.S.A.

3

Liturgical Catechesis in the Early Church

Introduction

From the beginning the Church's liturgical catechesis has been intimately linked with sacramental celebration. As *Catechesi tradendae*, no. 23, affirms, "Catechesis always has reference to the sacraments." The Fathers of the Church drew spiritual insights for their flock and explained the message of the gospel from the celebration and within its framework. Many of them were great and profound theological thinkers, but when they spoke to their people, their topic and their language were inspired by liturgical experience. Today catechists in their own way are called upon to collaborate with the Church's role of forming the Christian people. Since Christian formation must have liturgical and sacramental dimension, it is incumbent on catechists to know how to draw their catechetical material from the liturgy.

Liturgical catechesis, especially during the fourth and fifth centuries, was primarily mystagogical, that is, an explanation of the mystery which had been celebrated. The newly baptized received spiritual and theological insights on what they experienced during the rite of Christian initiation. For a week the bishop gathered them and explained step by step what the words they heard and the signs they saw signified. It was a reflection and review of the past experience, in order to enter more deeply into it and draw from it the spiritual strength they needed for their new life as Christians.

But while the mystery itself, that is, the liturgical celebration, was not explained to the candidate until after baptism itself, preparatory catechesis was given to him. It consisted of basic

Christian doctrine, imparted through the moral standards of the Church.[1] In other words, liturgical catechesis, in its patristic form as mystagogy, presupposed previous instruction on faith and morals. Indeed the candidate was accepted to the sacraments, only on condition that he had lived the years of catechumenate with fidelity and fervor. The sacramental celebration was the culmination of his conversion to God and initiation into the Church. The mystagogical catechesis that followed looked back to it and pointed out how the future had to be lived.

This practice came about at a time when the Church held strict secrecy regarding her liturgical and sacramental celebrations for fear of being misunderstood and falsely imitated by pagans. It was a *disciplina arcani*, a discipline of secrecy, which was useful during that period, although when needed some Fathers of the Church did not hesitate to break it even before a pagan audience.[2] Today the Church does not insist on such a discipline, because of the immense possibility of modern communication. However, this patristic method of catechesis has still its value today, for it shows that effective liturgical catechesis presupposes an experience or at least a witnessing of sacramental celebrations.

To corroborate these affirmations and provide catechesis with historical models, it is useful to discuss here some patristic data on liturgical catechesis.

Preparatory Catechesis

The anonymous book of the *Didaché*, which speaks of baptism in c. 7, provides the readers with the essential elements of baptism: the formula which is trinitarian, water which should be living, the manner of baptism which is immersion, and the preparatory practices of prayer and fasting.[3] For the history of catechesis the first line of c. 7 is important: "After giving the foregoing instructions, baptize...." Notwithstanding the complex composition of the book, it can be affirmed that the author refers to the foregoing six chapters on the "Two Ways," a Christianized version of Jewish moral instructions to proselytes. For the author it was not so much the question of instruction on doctrinal matters as the observance of moral conduct according to the standards set by the Church.

Another author who speaks of preparatory catechesis is Justin Martyr in his *I Apology*, c. 61.[4] He writes: "Those who are convinced and believe that what we say and teach is the truth, and pledge themselves to be able to live accordingly...." Justin insists on the ability (*dynamis*) of the candidate to live according to the norms of Christian conduct. Indeed the candidate should pledge to observe it. It was not enough to be willing; the early Church, beset by persecutions, required that the candidate be, in fact, able to keep the faith.

From Justin Martyr we pass on to Tertullian who offers an interesting insight on the preparatory catechesis.[5] Referring to the case of St. Paul who "was baptized when he believed," Tertullian makes it clear that sufficient knowledge of the faith should precede the reception of baptism. St. Paul, he writes, "had sufficiently learnt and believed the Nazarene to be the Lord, the Son of God," before he was baptized. He also speaks of the eunuch (Ac 8:26-40) who was "not suddenly seized with an eager desire to be baptized, but after going up to the temple for prayer's sake, being intently engaged on the divine Scripture." Basing himself on Mt 7:7, Tertullian further notes the necessity on the part of the candidates to desire and beg for baptism: "Let them know how to ask for salvation, that you may seem at least to have given to him that asks." The question of infant baptism, raised by Tertullian, need not be discussed here, but the message he hands on in this connection is valid: those who are responsible for baptism should not do so rashly, but should first test parents and godparents on their ability to educate their children in the faith.

It is in the *Apostolic Tradition* of Hippolytus of Rome that for the first time we come across catechumenate as an organized institution in the early Church.[6] According to Hippolytus, the candidates for catechumenate were brought to the teachers (*didáskaloi*, equivalent to our modern-day catechists) who ascertained the motive of the candidates. Patrons or godparents led them to the Church and were responsible for them. For in conscience they were bound to bring to the Church only those who were sincere and able to live up to the demands of the faith. That is why Hippolytus asks that patrons give testimony on the worthiness of their lives before they could be admitted into catechumenate. He, in fact, enumerates various professions which he considered incompatible with being a Christian. With sternness he warns candidates to either give up such professions or face rejection by the Church.

Catechumens, according to Hippolytus, "are to listen to the Word for three years." This was a standard length of time during which the candidate's gradual conversion to the faith could be proven. During this period the teacher or catechist instructed the catechumens on the practice of Christian morality. It was not so much a time for doctrinal information as for moral testing. The doctrinal catechesis, in systematic form, was handled only later, when catechumens were ready for the baptism of Easter night. Hippolytus does not dwell on the detail of the moral catechesis, but we know from his contemporary, Origen, that the catechist read and explained selected passages from the books of Esther, Judith, Tobit and Wisdom which contained suitable moral guidance.[7] Hippolytus indeed defined this period of the catechumenate as zealous and faithful listening to the Word of God in order to derive from it the necessary inspiration for Christian conduct.

Hippolytus mentions certain practices connected with catechetical instruction. Catechumens were told to pray by themselves after each instruction. They were not, however, given the kiss of peace, "for their kiss is not yet holy." Kissing was the early Church's sign of fellowship and communion given only to the baptized. After prayers the catechist, whether cleric or layman, laid his hands on the catechumens as a sign of blessing.

Sometime before Easter Triduum (Lent as such did not yet exist), those who were considered to be sufficiently prepared for baptism were selected and enlisted as the "elect." This time the patron had to testify that the catechumen had lived a worthy life during the time of probation. "Let their conduct be examined, whether they respected the widows, visited the sick and performed every good deed." And to make sure of it, Hippolytus mentions that the bishop himself exorcised the elect one by one. Through the prayer of exorcism the unworthy could be discovered and rejected, "because he did not listen to the word in faith, because it is impossible for a stranger to pretend at all times."

The catechesis received by the elect differed in nature and scope from that received by other catechumens. Hippolytus says that "they should listen to the gospel," but he does not give further specifications on the "gospel." We do know, however, that the catechesis given to the elect in the fourth and fifth centuries consisted of a thorough and systematic exposition of Sacred Scripture and the Apostles' Creed. Cyril of Jerusalem has left us his 18 catechetical instructions on Christian doctrine, which he delivered to the elect sometime before the Easter Triduum of 349.

Certain rites accompanied the formal catechetical instruction of the elect. Daily the catechist exorcised them and laid his hands on them. On Holy Thursday the elect washed themselves, and on Friday and Saturday they observed the paschal fast. Finally on Saturday the bishop convoked them, exhorted them to pray on their knees and laid his hands on them. Then he blew on their faces and signed their foreheads, ears and nostrils with the cross. The whole night was spent in vigil which consisted of Scripture reading, prayers and last-minute instructions. Catechesis was, therefore, not a mere classroom instruction; it was done in the context of prayer and liturgical rites, all of which helped to heighten the experience.

From the data discussed above it can now be seen that in patristic times there were two forms of catechesis preparatory to the celebration of baptism. One was given to simple catechumens during the period of about three years. It was one of instruction on basic Christian faith and on the moral standard required by the Church of her members. From the writings of the Fathers we have examined it appears that the stress was laid on the moral qualification of the catechumen at this stage. Indeed the patrons had to follow up the instructions given by catechists, and at the end of the catechumenate they testified before the Church regarding the life of the candidate. The catechist, on the other hand, played an important role at this phase of conversion. He was indeed a kind of spiritual father who guided the catechumen on the way of Christian conduct, he taught him how to pray and gave him his blessing. His book (or textbook) was the Word of God, as Hippolytus alludes and Origen specifies. Authentic Christian catechesis derived its material and inspiration from the Scripture which the catechist liturgically proclaimed. And the instruction was not a mere classroom affair: it was accompanied by prayer and liturgical blessing. Thus the Word of God was not only assimilated intellectually, but also prayed upon.

The other form of catechesis was given to the elect who was chosen for baptism on the basis of the worthiness of his life as catechumen. This stage initiated the elect into the intellectual illumination which was bestowed on him by the knowledge of revealed truths. Although the period we are discussing did not know of the later Lenten organization of scriptural readings, it is most probable that the theme was Salvation History as unfolded by the readings in the liturgy. Later on the Apostles' Creed was also systematically explained to the elect. The Church furnished this catechetical instruction with liturgical rites and prayers. Systematic instruction, however, did not mean cold and abstract information on doctrinal statements. One has only to read the Catechesis of Cyril of Jerusalem to appreciate the spiritual and practical aspects of doctrinal catechesis.

The culmination of this period of catechetical instruction and spiritual formation was the Easter celebration of baptism, confirmation and Holy Eucharist. Although the candidate was as yet ignorant of the full meaning and every detail of the mystery, he was nevertheless prepared for it. The day after the celebration he would look back to the preceding night's experience, as the bishop explained it and drew spiritual insights from it.

Mystagogical Catechesis

Strictly liturgical catechesis, in the form of mystagogy, was given to the neophytes or the newly baptized. Two classic examples of such a catechesis are those of Ambrose of Milan, *On Mysteries* and *On Sacraments*,[8] and of Cyril of Jerusalem, *Mystagogical Catechesis*.[9] In these works one can see the skill of the Fathers in catechetically leading the neophytes into a profound understanding and appreciation of Christian sacraments. Both authors continually made references to the preceding sacramental celebrations, to their rites, words and signs. Whatever was helpful in grasping the deeper meaning of the sacraments was exploited or at least made into a starting point for spiritual and practical reflection. And as is typical of the Fathers of the Church, the Christian mystery was explained principally under the light of Salvation History. Types or figures from both the Old and New Testaments helped the neophytes to plunge themselves into the stream of God's saving plan. Through such a method the Fathers of the Church were able to impress on the minds of the new members that in the sacraments they celebrated God's salvation which had been realized in them.[10]

In the West the most famous mystagogical catechesis is that of St. Ambrose which is preserved in the two works, *On Mysteries* and *On Sacraments*. Because of the wealth of methodological and thematic materials found in these two works, we shall discuss them in a systematic order, hoping that they can provide today's catechists with method and material.

a. Baptismal Renunciation

When explaining to neophytes what baptismal renunciation meant, Ambrose made an allusion to the preceding night's event. "When you were asked, 'Do you renounce the devil and his works?', what did you reply? 'I do renounce.' 'Do you renounce the world and its pleasures?', what did you reply? 'I do renounce.' " Ambrose then explains the seriousness of their baptismal promise and its consequences on their future lives. "Always remember what you promised, and be prudent."[11]

He also explains the meaning of turning to the East after the rite of renunciation. "Having entered, therefore, that you might recognize your adversary, whom you think you should renounce to his face, you turn toward the East. For he who renounces the devil, turns toward Christ, recognizes him by a direct glance."[12] Although the rite does not exist in the Roman liturgy, it is mentioned here in order to show how Ambrose did not ignore ritual details, especially those with symbolic significance, which illustrated the meaning of the sacrament.

The catechist should note the experiential approach of Ambrose: "When you were asked, what did you reply?" or "Having entered (the baptismal room), you turn toward the East." Ambrose continually reminded the neophytes of their past experience and in so doing clarified the meaning of the mystery and led them to take their new state of life seriously and responsibly.

b. Baptismal Water

Ambrose spoke at great length on the baptismal water. "You entered, you saw the water, you saw the bishop, you saw the deacon. Maybe someone would have said, 'Is this all there is to it?' "[13] With this experiential reference he begins the exposition on baptismal water by citing first of all the types or figures found in Scripture. The first type is the water of creation over which the Spirit hovered: "He who moved over the waters (of creation), did He not also work on the waters (of baptism)?" Just as the Spirit of God gave life to the creatures in the waters at the time of creation, so now He gives life to those who were immersed in the water of baptism. The water of creation is thus the figure of baptismal water. And so was the flood in the time of Noah a type of Christian baptism. Baptismal water not only signifies life; it also signifies remission of sin, for "the water is that in which the flesh is immersed, that all carnal sin may be washed away." Still another figure was the water of the Red Sea: "You notice that in the crossing of the Hebrews the figure of holy baptism even then was prefigured, wherein the Egyptians perished and the Hebrews escaped." This baptismal type was popular among the Fathers, who on the basis of 1 Cor. 10:1-2 viewed baptismal immersion as the Christian's crossing from sin to grace through the water, as the Israelites crossed from slavery to freedom through the waters of the sea. Ambrose also mentions the bitter water in the desert which was made sweet by Moses when he cast wood into it (Ex. 15:23), thereby prefiguring the cross of Christ which turns water into spiritual laver. Another type of baptism is the cleansing of Naaman, the Syrian, from leprosy, by bathing in the waters of the Jordan. Ambrose also speaks of the cure of the paralytic in the pool of Bethsaida (Jn. 5:4) as a New Testament type of Christian baptism.[14]

Through these biblical types Ambrose puts the neophyte in contact with Salvation History. Through baptism man enters into God's plan of salvation, that is to say, he re-experiences in himself the love and power of God. Catechists should carefully take note of this patristic view of the sacraments. They are the realization of God's promise. Those who celebrate them enter, therefore, into Salvation History and receive God's salvation.

Echoing the teaching set in Jn. 3:5 that "a man must be born again of water and the Spirit," Ambrose constantly associates the Holy Spirit with baptismal water and its biblical types. Water has the power to sanctify because of the "operation" or presence of the Holy Spirit in it. As he told his neophytes, "Learn that water cleanses not without the Spirit."[15] Or as he says in the treatise *On Sacraments* I, 5, "Water does not cure unless the Holy Spirit descends and consecrates that water." Comparing the work of the Holy Spirit in the Incarnation of the Word of God in the womb of the Blessed Virgin with His work in the regeneration of Christians in baptism, he says, "If then the Holy Spirit coming upon the Virgin effected conception and effected the work of generation, surely there must be no doubt that the Spirit, coming upon the font, or upon those who obtain baptism, effects the truth of regeneration."[16]

The historical development of sacramental catechesis cannot be treated with justice without reference to the role of the Holy Spirit. Catechists should, therefore, seriously take into account this patristic treatise of the work of the Holy Spirit in Salvation History and in the celebration of the sacraments. Sacramental catechesis is not complete, indeed loses its true meaning, without reference to the Holy Spirit. The Fathers have still much to teach us today regarding the content of our sacramental catechesis.

Another important aspect of Ambrose's catechesis on baptismal water is its connection with the cross of the Lord, prefigured by the wood cast by Moses into the water. "For without the preaching of the cross of the Lord water is to no advantage for future salvation; but when it has been consecrated by the mystery of the saving cross, then it is ordered for the use of the spiritual laver."[17] Or as he further explains, "Just as Moses, that is the prophet, cast wood into that fountain, also into this fountain the priest casts the message of the cross of the Lord and the water becomes sweet for grace." In other words, the prayer used for the blessing of baptismal water must have included a special reference to the cross of the Lord, that is, to his death, as we have it today in the blessing of baptismal water. From this liturgical usage Ambrose concludes, "Behold where you are baptized, whence baptism is, if not from the cross of Christ, from the death of Christ."[18] Here the catechist should note now Ambrose linked baptism with the paschal mystery. He did not do it through abstract language; he alluded to an event in Salvation History and to a liturgical experience. Indeed he offered the neophyte an insight into the paschal dimension of his baptism. It is his passage, his Exodus, from the world to the Father, after the example of Christ's own Exodus through death: "He who passes through this font, that is from the earthly to the heavenly—for there is a passage here, that is Easter which is his passage, the passage from sin to life, from fault to grace, from defilement to sanctification—he who passes through this font does not die but rises."[19]

Thus from the experience of the preceding baptismal liturgy Ambrose unfolded the meaning of baptismal water. By entering into it the Christian entered into Salvation History, he became a part of God's plan, he was born anew by the power of the Holy Spirit who dwelt in the water and sanctified him in it, and as Ambrose tells the neophyte, "When you dip, you take on the likeness of death and burial, you receive the sacrament of that cross, because Christ hung on the cross and his body was transfixed with nails. You then are crucified with him; you cling to Christ, you cling to the nails of the Lord Jesus."[20]

Modern sacramental catechesis should take into account this patristic approach to baptismal water. Ambrose did not speak of it as mere symbol of purification. He spoke of it as a *sacrament*, that is to say, a visible sign of the Holy Spirit's presence in the water in view of the washing away of man's sins and of his regeneration unto grace. Ambrose was very explicit on the sacramental character of baptismal water, that water in which the Holy Spirit dwells and operates. "In this faith you died to the world, you arose to God, and as if buried in that element of the world, dead to sin you were revived to eternal life. Believe, therefore, that these waters are not without power."[21]

Modern catechesis should also note that the patristic approach to sacraments was principally biblical. Although today's catechesis should make allusions to the people's practical use and symbolic understanding of water, it should not ignore its biblical dimension, in order to link it up with the History of Salvation. The catechist will do well to explain the meaning of baptismal water by examining the prayer-text of the blessing of baptismal water, a formula which is at once imbued with biblical figures and enriched by patristic theology.

c. Baptismal Immersion

The early Church ordinarily baptized by immersion. In the tradition of Hippolytus of Rome, of Cyril of Jerusalem and of Ambrose of Milan, it consisted of the triple credal interrogation and triple immersion. This usage has given way to the actual practice of infusion or immersion accompanied by the declaratory formula, "I baptize you...." However, it is useful to consider here how Ambrose treated the ancient mode of baptism in his mystagogical catechesis. "You were asked, 'Do you believe in God the Father Almighty?' You said, 'I believe,' and you dipped, that is, you were buried. Again you were asked, 'Do you believe in our Lord Jesus Christ and in his cross?' You answered, 'I do believe,' and you dipped. So you were buried together with Christ.... A third time you were asked, 'Do you believe also in the Holy Spirit?' You said, 'I do believe.' You dipped a third time."[22] Or as he explains in his work *On Mysteries* 5, 28: "You have descended then (into the water); remember what you replied to the questions, that you believe in the Father, you believe in the Son, you believe in the Holy Spirit. You confess that you believe in the cross of the Lord Jesus alone."

Thus Ambrose catechetically explains the meaning of baptismal immersion as burial with Christ. His explanation is obviously inspired by Rm. 6:4, but it is catechetically supported by the reminiscence of the most solemn act of entering into the pool of water, the "tomb" of the baptismal font, and rising again unto newness of life.

d. Illustrative Rites of Baptism

Ambrose also explained the different illustrative rites of baptism as they existed in his Church. They were the rites of Ephpheta, the pre-baptismal anointing which he compared to the anointing of athletes ("You are anointed as an athlete of Christ, as if to contend in the contest of this world"), the post-baptismal anointing which signified "anointing unto the kingdom of God and unto the priesthood," the washing of the feet (a special rite among Gallican liturgies), and the vesting with white garments which symbolized "the chaste robes of innocence."[23]

Illustrative rites are called thus, because they illustrate or explain the principal rite itself; they explicitate those aspects of the sacrament which are only implicitly present in the celebration. And since many of these illustrative rites originate from the Church's contact with culture, they serve as bridge between the biblical and the non-biblical world. In explaining the illustrative rites of his Church, Ambrose returned to the Scripture or else he invoked the cultural origin of the rite, as in the case of pre-baptismal anointing. But the catechist should note that in any case Ambrose always showed the Christian dimension of these rites.[24]

e. The Spiritual Seal

After baptism the neophytes were confirmed. Ambrose explains this as the bestowal of the spiritual seal which is the Spirit of wisdom and understanding, the Spirit of counsel and power, the Spirit of knowledge and piety, the Spirit of holy fear.[25] At this point Ambrose's exposition becomes more exhortatory and even mystical. He not only reminds neophytes of what they received, the seal of God, but he also leads them to a mystical experience of

God's presence in their hearts through the Holy Spirit. Indeed Ambrose's catechesis takes the form of a dialogue between God and the newly confirmed. But if Ambrose uses this form, it is obviously to inspire them to action: "Let your faith be resplendent in the fullness of the sacrament. And let your work shine and manifest the image of God in whose likeness you have been created." The spiritual seal is both an experience of God and a call to apostolic action.

f. The Solemn Procession

"The cleansed people, rich in these insignia, begin to walk in procession towards the altar of Christ, saying, 'And I shall go unto the altar of God who gives joy to my youth.' "[26] The neophytes in white robes and with candles in their hands walked solemnly towards the altar singing Psalm 42. The sight must have so thoroughly impressed Ambrose that he could exclaim, "There follows your coming to the altar. You began to come; the angels observed: they saw you approaching, and that human condition which before was stained with the shadowy squalor of sins they saw suddenly shining bright."[27]

The historical development of sacramental catechesis has necessarily to take this detail into account. The solemn procession was in itself a most eloquent form of catechesis. Ambrose could speak the way he did, because the experience deeply moved him, as it must have done to both the neophytes and the assembly. It was no common experience; it was impressive and dramatic. And so the catechesis on it was necessarily eloquent. What this shows is that effective catechesis presupposes a fully developed sacramental celebration, where rites are properly performed and signs and symbols truly speak. Catechesis not only leads to the liturgy; it is also nourished by it.

g. The Eucharistic Bread and Wine

"They come then and seeing the sacred altar prepared, exclaim saying: 'Thou hast prepared a table in my sight.' " For the first time the neophytes took part in the celebration of the mysteries; for the first time they were allowed to "see" the sacraments of the altar. "You went, you washed, you came to the altar, you began to see what you had not seen before. That is, through the font of the Lord and the preaching of the Lord's passion, your eyes were then opened."[28] Ambrose here was invoking the patristic concept of baptism as "illumination." It allowed the baptized to have a glimpse of the mysteries laid on the altar. But Ambrose was careful not to give the wrong impression regarding the mysteries. The neophytes, seeing the elements on the altar, might construct unwarranted fantasies: "Indeed you have wondered at the elements themselves; yet they are customary and known."

In explaining the eucharistic species Ambrose stays on the "sacramental" level, that is, on the visible and tangible signs. These are not strange things; there is no need to marvel at them and imagine of what they are composed. They are bread and wine known and familiar to all. But at the eucharistic prayer, and, as Ambrose insists, particularly at the words of consecration, these natural elements are transformed into the body and blood of Christ. "The Lord Jesus Himself declares, 'This is my body.' Before the benediction of the heavenly words another species is mentioned; after the consecration the body is signified. He Himself speaks of His blood. Before the consecration it is mentioned as something else; after the consecration it is called blood."[29]

Once again it should be insisted upon that patristic catechesis on the sacraments was not based on some speculative theology. Ambrose asked the neophytes what they witnessed and heard during the celebration. Thus he developed the doctrine of the eucharistic presence within the context of sacramental liturgy. In other words, the catechist, when explaining the real presence, should not take the tabernacle as his starting point; he should turn to the eucharistic liturgy. Indeed, like Ambrose, he should dwell on the meaning of the eucharistic prayer itself in order to show more clearly the connection between real presence and liturgical action.

Conclusion

The liturgical catechesis in the early Church, especially during the fourth and fifth centuries, has several elements of great interest to modern catechesis on sacraments. From the preceding discussion the following practical conclusions can be drawn:

a. Liturgical catechesis presupposes a process of conversion to the faith through information on basic Christian doctrine and formation in moral behavior according to the standards of the Church. Indeed, the liturgy is not for those who totally ignore the faith or are unfamiliar with the Word of God. Sacraments and their celebration presuppose familiarity with the Scripture and the doctrine of faith.

b. Liturgical catechesis draws its material from the celebration itself, from its signs and words. To a certain extent, every liturgical catechesis should have the quality of a mystagogy. Although today catechumens should already be catechized on the mysteries, the instruction should not be done, as it were, in a vacuum. They should be allowed to witness (though not participate in) the celebration of the sacraments, in order to make catechesis truly effective. On the other hand, those who have already been baptized in infancy should be gathered together to join the community in the celebration of the sacraments as a prerequisite to liturgical catechesis. This should not mean that the celebration itself becomes a demonstration during which the catechist explains each particular rite. Liturgical catechesis should follow rather than accompany sacramental celebrations.

c. Liturgical catechesis is not mere information on the meaning of the sacraments. It is a spiritual formation, a deepening of one's commitment to the faith, a real experience of God in prayerful instruction. That is why it should not be given merely as classroom instruction, but should be accompanied by Scripture reading and prayer. The words of *Catechesi tradendae*, no. 23, have special relevance to this point: "Sacramental life is impoverished and very soon turns into hollow ritualism if it is not based on serious knowledge of the meaning of the sacraments, and catechesis becomes intellectualized if it fails to come alive in sacramental practice."

ANSCAR J. CHUPUNGCO, O.S.B.

FOOTNOTES

1. Cf. J. Danielou: *La Catéchèse aux premiers siècles,* Paris (1968).

2. Justin Martyr, *I Apol. 61* and 65-67, broke the rule in order to correct the misconceptions of pagans regarding the Eucharist and the innocence of Christians in the matter of worship. The new Order of Christian Initiation for Adults, 19, 3, suggests that catechumens, if possible, should not be present in the liturgy of the Eucharist, or at any rate should not actively participate.

3. *Didaché,* ed. J. Audet, Paris (1958).

4. Ed. L. Pautigny, Paris (1904).

5. *De Baptismo,* ed. R. Refoulé, *SCh* 35 (1952).

6. *Traditio Apostolica,* ed. B. Botte, Münster (1963).

7. *Hom. in Num.* 27, 1, ed. A. Méhat, *SCh 29* (1951).

8. *De Mysteriis* and *De Sacramentis,* ed. B. Botte, *SCh 25bis* (1961).

9. Ed. A. Piédagnel, *SCh 126* (1966).

10. Cf. J. Daniélou: *Bible et Liturgie,* Paris (1951).

11. *De Sacr.* I, 2.

12. *De Myst.* 2, 7.

13. *De Sacr.* I, 10.

14. For the biblical types, see: *De Myst.* 3, 9 (water of creation); *Id.* 3, 11 (the great deluge), *Id.* 3, 12 (water of the Red Sea), see also *De Sacr.* I, 6, and *Id.* II, 2 (pool of Bethsaida).

15. *De Myst.* 4, 19.

16. *Id.* 9, 59.

17. *Id.* 3, 14; see also *De Sacr.* II, 4.

18. *De Sacr.* II, 2.

19. *Id.* I, 4.

20. *Id.* I, 7.

21. *De Myst.* 4, 21.

22. *De Sacr.* II, 7.

23. *De Myst.* 7, 34; see *De Sacr.* I, 2 for the type of pre-baptismal anointing; *De Myst.* 7, 34 for the meaning of white vestment; *Id.* 6, 30 for the type of post-baptismal anointing.

24. J. Jungmann: *The Early Liturgy,* trans. A. Brunner, London (1966).

25. *De Myst.* 7, 42.

26. *Id.* 8, 43.

27. *De Sacr.* IV, 2.

28. *De Myst.* 8, 43; see also *De Sacr.* III, 2.

29. *De Myst.* 9, 54; *De Sacr.* IV, 4, 5.

4

The Council of Trent
and the Origins of
Modern Catechesis

The sixteenth century marks a decisive turning point in the history of catechesis and opens a new path. Summoned by the strongly deficient religio-pastoral situation and prompted by the catechetical movement of the Reformation, promoted in particular by Luther and Calvin, the Catholic Church launched, especially in the second half of the sixteenth century, an impressive catechetical action which progressively implicated her principal energies: pastors, theologians, priests, religious and laity.

The catechetical facts which marked this period were many: from the Council of Trent, with its priorities and its catechetical orientations, to the numerous councils and diocesan synods promoted to reorganize catechesis in the parishes; from the compilation of modern catechisms to the parochial and scholastic organization of catechesis; from the promotion of religious instruction of adults to the initiation of the catechesis of children; from the catechetical effort of many priests and laity in the parishes and in the schools to the dedication of numerous religious congregations which, originating in this period, chose as first field of service religious instruction and the education of the young to the faith.

Such catechetical fervor could not help but make an impression on ecclesial, religious and catechetical life. Within the space of a few decades the Church had placed herself in a state of evangelization, rediscovering her high-priority mission of announcer of the Word and educator to the faith. The animation of the catechetical initiatives resulted, as was easily seen in the following century, in a Christianization of the masses, especially those in rural areas. The rich catechetical activity concentrated its effort upon a few aspects which set the pace of catechesis until the beginning of our century: the catechesis of children, Sunday instructions for adults, the centrality given to the catechism as the book of Christian doctrine, parochial and scholastic organization of catechesis.

In order to grasp the catechetical richness of this period in its broad outlines, we will essentially recall the more significant catechetical facts, giving preference to catechesis of youth, which is the new event in the history of catechesis.

RELIGIO-PASTORAL SITUATION

The catechetical initiatives of the sixteenth century were, for the most part, an answer to the pastoral and religious situation of the time, which was particularly deficient. A glance at this situation will help to better understand the catechetical renewal in its priorities and its importance.

At the end of the fifteenth century and at the beginning of the following one, religious life and pastoral action in the Christian communities presented themselves as poor and insufficient. Significant is the lamentation expressed by Luther in the preface to the *Little Catechism,* which came out in 1529: "The lamentable, miserable situation recently known in fulfilling my office of visitor has obliged me to write this catechism of Christian doctrine in a brief and simple form. Good God, how much misery I saw: the man of the people, especially in the villages, knows nothing of Christian doctrine, and sad to say many pastors are almost inept and incapable of teaching. And yet all must call themselves Christians and be baptized and participate in the holy sacraments, but they do not know the Our Father, nor the Creed, nor the Decalogue. They live like the good herds of cattle and the unreasoning pigs."[1]

The features of this spiritual and religious misery of the Christian people can be condensed into a few lines:
— a notable ignorance of the Christian message in general and of the Bible in particular;
— a mentality tending to interpret Christian rites and duties in a magical sense;

—a strong moralism which in many cases impoverished Christian life by viewing it only in terms of duties, of precepts and of practices to be observed;

—a devotionalism which especially concentrated on a great cult of the saints;

—an individualization of the liturgy which, disengaged from life, was lived not as a communitarian celebration of the salvific mystery of the Lord, but mainly as the experience of individual union with God.

Among the factors which were at the root of this religious poverty must be listed the inadequacy of the pastoral action of the time, marked by outstanding voids:

—an episcopate often little interested in the spiritual-pastoral care of the people and, in some cases, more attentive to the cultural sensitivities of the Renaissance than preoccupied with the religious problems of the Christian communities;

—the non-residence of titular pastors, above all, those of the rural parishes, and the development of a clerical proletariat;

—the lack of theological preparation of the clergy, whose formation in some cases did not even provide for the study of the Bible;

—the lives of the clergy and religious, whose moral conduct appeared in some cases questionable and blameworthy;

—the religious instruction of the people, which was for the most part deficient: in the parishes there was no preaching or the preaching was poorly done and the teaching of catechism, when it was done, was limited in content and in time;

—an excessively moralistic teaching in which the morality proposed was disengaged from faith, and attention was insistently directed to detailed lists of vices to avoid and virtues to practice.

In this very serious crisis, which involved the life and pastoral activity of the Christian communities, not even theological studies knew how to offer prospective solutions. Theological reflection occupied itself more with subtleties than with the penetration of the Word of God. Furthermore, gaining always more ground was an ecclesiology which emphasized the juridical-social aspect of the Church over that of the "people of God" and "Body of Christ" and which accentuated the role of the clergy, leaving the responsibility of the laity in the shadow.

At the vigil of the Reformation, notwithstanding the efforts of zealous preachers, such as St. Vincent Ferrer and St. Bernardine of Siena, and despite the intense activity of the mendicant Orders, the spiritual-religious life of the people and of the Christian communities, especially in rural areas, was dragging itself along in a disoriented manner.[2]

THE CATECHISMS OF LUTHER AND OF CALVIN

Beginning with the grave religious situation of the people, Luther and Calvin matured the conviction that the reformation of Christian life would depend fundamentally on the teaching of Christian doctrine. This was the reason for the serious catechetical effort of the two reformers.

Luther and Calvin were not the initiators of catechesis for children nor the inventors, in the absolute sense, of the modern catechisms. Before them many others, in the Protestant and Catholic spheres, had applied themselves to the religious instruction of children and had written catechisms.[3]

Nevertheless, the zeal with which they brought ahead the cause of catechesis and the great influence which their catechisms had among the Protestants and indirectly among Catholics, oblige us to place Luther and Calvin among the pioneers of modern catechesis.

The Catechisms of Martin Luther, 1483-1546

Origin. The idea of a catechism came to Luther from the knowledge of the situation of religious ignorance and poverty, which he noted above all among the Christians of the villages and among the young. Luther himself reveals this in the preface to the *Little Catechism.* Having to organize catechism classes for children, Luther asked some of his disciples to compose a manual. Not satisfied with the various attempts, he decided to write a catechism himself, availing himself of his experience as a preacher and as a catechist.

In 1529 he composed in German first the *Great Catechism* and a few months later the *Little Catechism.*

The Recipients. The "Great" was conceived as the book of the instructor, a manual destined for the preachers and teachers.

The "Little" was composed for children and for the simple faithful, but to be placed in the hand of the pastor or of the catechist for a vivid explanation. The preoccupation was twofold: to promote the spiritual life of the children and of the families and to make Christian doctrine known.

Structure and Contents. The "Great" is written in a discursive, continuous form. In all it contains 140 pages. The "Little" is edited under the form of questions and answers, about thirty in all. In general there was a question for each Commandment, for every article of the Creed, for every petition of the Our Father. The development of the contents of the two catechisms is identical: the Commandments, the Creed, the Our Father, the Sacraments of Baptism and of the Lord's Supper.

From the doctrinal point of view, the two catechisms are substantially faithful to Christian tradition. The heretical aspect is manifested in the thematic setup: the Commandments are presented as the first theme, so that man is made aware of his inability to observe them and, hence, discovers his radical poverty, his impotence and his sin; from this, he arrives at the conclusion that only the mercy of God can save him.

Characteristics. We refer to the *Little Catechism.* Its characteristics can be summed up in a word: it is a *popular* aid, capable of penetrating into the masses in a capillary manner and of catechizing them. It was written in common language, in German, at a time when the greater part of the preceding catechisms had been in Latin, a language incomprehensible to the people. It was explicitly compiled for children and for simple people, whereas previous usage provided only the compilation of a guide for priests and teachers. The language is simple, easy, incisive. The catechism is compiled in question and answer form to facilitate memorization. This expedient had already been attempted by Alcuin and Gerson, but had not been diffused in catechetical practice. The text is centered upon the essential: it limits itself to the central point of doctrine and leaves aside any theological problem whatsoever. There are many biblical citations and examples drawn from Sacred Scripture. One can note a certain catechumenal dimension: the catechesis—centered on the Commandments, the Creed and the Our Father—intends to prepare and initiate the child for Baptism and the Lord's Supper.

All this explains the wide acceptance and diffusion of the Catechism. It has gone through numerous editions and translations. It was diffused throughout the world and was still being utilized in our own century.

The Catechisms of John Calvin, 1509-1564

Origin. The pastoral preoccupation of Calvin was twofold: to put the Church in order and to instruct. For this reason he placed two conditions for his return to the Church of Geneva, from which he had been driven away: the re-establishment of discipline and the organization of catechism. Having re-entered Geneva in 1541, he responded to these two preoccupations by writing in the same year two works: *The Ecclesiastical Ordinances*, on the reorganization of discipline in the Church, and the *Formulary for the Instruction of Young People in Christianity*, a real and proper catechism.

Recipients and Structure of the "Formulary." The catechism is addressed to young people from ten to fifteen years of age, and it consists of 373 questions. All the matter is subdivided into fifty-five parts or lessons, one for every Sunday, according to this structure: articles of faith (the first twenty Sundays), the ten commandments and the two precepts of charity (twenty-first to thirty-third Sunday), prayer and the Our Father (thirty-fourth to forty-fourth Sunday), the Word of God and preaching (forty-fifth Sunday), the sacraments of Baptism and the Supper (forty-sixth to fifty-fifth Sunday).

Contents. The first two points of Christian life are *faith* as trust in God and *penitence* as obedience to the law of God. They are placed on the same plane and considered two absolutes.

The point of departure of the catechism is not the Gospel, but a series of philosophical considerations. The dominant preoccupation, which clearly shows in the catechetical proposal of Calvin, is the formation of young people in respect for laws and in obedience to pastors.

Characteristics of the "Formulary." We recall the principal ones. The catechism was written in a common language, French. It was edited in questions and answers. The text was very ample: 373 questions. The answers were very long and generally not too clear. The vocabulary was difficult and obscure. There predominated a theological-dogmatic language. The catechism was scarcely biblical: the first exposition of the Word was met in the forty-fifth lesson.

Notwithstanding these limitations, the *Formulary* had a notable diffusion, especially in France. This fact was due in a particular manner to the prestige of the author. After the first ample acceptance, however, the catechism of Calvin rapidly disappeared. By the end of the century it had already fallen into disuse. But even though it had a brief life, its influence was determining. In France the *Formulary* of Calvin not only inspired in the Catholic field the compilation of the Catechism of E. Auger, but gave rise to a great catechetical effort in the Reformed Church and in the Catholic Church.

Somewhat schematically we can affirm that the catechisms of Luther and Calvin contributed decisively to the beginning of the new season of catechesis: also thanks to their aid a new interest in the instruction of the people was created; the catechesis of children was begun seriously and zealously; "modern catechisms" were planned, intended as handbooks for children or for others of the faithful; edited in question and answer form, these synthesized Christian doctrine in a simple, essential and complete manner.

THE COUNCIL OF TRENT
AND CATECHETICAL PRIORITIES

In 1545 the Council of Trent began (1545—1563). The principal objectives were two: to present a clarification of Christian doctrine in the face of the spreading Reformation, and to propose solutions for bettering the spiritual and religious life of the Christian people, which was in crisis and strongly decadent.

Regarding this second problem, it was clear that the solution had to be effected through a renewed and deepened instruction of the people. From the very beginning, therefore, the Council gave special priority to preaching and catechesis. Two facts confirm this. Already in the spring of 1546 (April 13), after just a few months of work, the Council discussed and decided upon the compilation of a catechism. On June 17 it enjoined upon the churches the explanation of the Bible by special lecturers.

The catechetical effort of the Council of Trent can be summed up as having taken three directions: the promotion of a biblical formation, the organization of religious instruction, and the proposal of a catechism.

Biblical Formation

Before the Council of Trent, Sacred Scripture occupied a very modest and at times irrelevant place both in the formation of the clergy and in preaching and religious instruction.[4]

Taking note of the patristic tradition of the first centuries, the Council had the intuition that the Christian people should return to nourishing itself abundantly with the Word of God. Hence, the Conciliar priorities.

First of all, in regard to seminaries, the need of a good biblical-liturgical formation of the future priests was presented.[5]

In the second place it was made obligatory to explain Sacred Scripture in the churches where prebends existed. This duty could be carried out directly by the Bishops or by special lecturers. The conciliar decree expressed itself thus: "In order that the treasure of the sacred books will not be set aside, the Holy Synod decreed that, in those churches in which there are prebends for lecturers in sacred theology, the bishops, the archbishops, the primates and the other ordinaries of the place should personally, if they are capable, or by means of a substitute, expound and interpret Sacred Scripture."[6] Lastly, the Council proposed that preaching and catechesis should be profoundly biblical: the preachers and catechists "will explain the divine word and will exert themselves to make it penetrate into hearts."[7] In particular the explanation of the Word of God during the Sunday Mass was restored[8] and the priests were ordered to "announce the Sacred Scripture" every Sunday and at least three times a week during Advent and Lent.[9]

The Organization of Religious Instruction

Among the more workable and more pastoral decisions that were most incisive for the following centuries are to be numbered the conciliar decrees concerning the organization of religious instruction. The prescriptions refer to religious teaching in the schools, to the instruction of the Christian people, and to the catechesis of children.

Religious teaching in the schools. The Council reproposed for the school the same prescriptions already adopted by Lateran Council V. In synthesis it commanded the school teachers to instruct the children not only in the human sciences but also in regard to religion, in particular the divine commandments, the articles of faith and the lives of the saints; on holy days to teach them only what referred to religion and to good customs and to

10. *Going, Teach....*

have the children participate at Mass, at Vespers, at the divine office and at sermons. Furthermore, the Council prescribed a scholastic inspection, asking the Bishop or the Pastor to examine or listen to the examination of religion, to know how much progress the teachers and the students had made in Christian piety.

Instruction to the Christian people. In clear and decisive language the Council carried out a few pastoral priorities which outlined until our own times the religious instruction of adults. In synthesis these were the conciliar directives:

—a Sunday and holy day instruction on the part of pastors: "Those who have care of souls, at least on Sundays and on solemn feasts, should nourish with salutary words the people entrusted to them, teaching what is necessary for salvation, announcing with brevity and ease the vices to be avoided and the virtues to be practiced"[10];

—a sermon on Sacred Scripture and the divine law every Sunday and on all weekdays during Lent and Advent: "At least all Sundays and solemn feast days...and all the days, or at least three days a week, of Lent and of the Advent of the Lord they will announce Sacred Scripture and the divine law"[11];

—a sacramental catechesis done by Bishops and by pastors: "They should explain the power and the use of the sacraments for the understanding of those who receive them...in order that the people will receive the sacraments with greater devotion and reverence"[12];

—a homily during the Sunday Mass on the Word or on the Eucharistic Mystery: "In order that the sheep of Christ will not be hungry, nor the little ones ask for bread and there will be no one to break it for them, the Holy Synod orders pastors and those individuals responsible for the care of the souls frequently during the celebration of the Masses to explain what has been read in the Mass and clarify some aspect of this most holy sacrifice, above all on Sundays and feast days."[13]

Therefore, for the Council of Trent the instruction of the Christian people, especially of adults, had to be based on three forms: a Sunday and daily instruction during Advent and Lent, a sacramental catechesis, and the Sunday homily during Mass.

Catechesis of children. On November 11, 1562, the council decreed the birth of parish catechesis for children: "The Bishops will have care that at least on Sundays and on other feast days, in every parish, the children should be diligently instructed, by those whose duty it is, about the rudiments of the faith and of obedience to God and to parents; if necessary, they will oblige even with ecclesiastical censures. This notwithstanding privileges and varying customs."[14]

Concretely, the Council proposed that the catechesis of children should be organized in every parish. This was to be characterized by an elementary teaching of the faith, carried out regularly on Sunday "by those to whom it pertains." This last expression—*ab iis ad quos spectabit*—is an open formulation: it can mean pastors, teachers, parents, godparents, etc.

Thus, a new chapter in the history of catechesis was opened: now the religious formation of children, for fifteen centuries left to the total responsibility of parents, was being officially aided by a religious instruction promoted by the parish.

Therefore, the Council proposed as a pastoral remedy for the grave religious ignorance the reorganization of religious instruction centered upon a permanent formation of adults and an elementary catechesis for children.

To bring this work to completion, the Council first of all indicated the Bishops as having prime responsibility; then, together with them, the priests, especially the pastors.

"The Catechism of the Council of Trent"

Origin. To make its own contribution to the catechetical renewal more concrete, the Council decided to draw up a catechism. Because of the difficulties encountered, the Council Fathers did not succeed in finishing their project. The *Catechism of the Council of Trent*—also called the *Roman Catechism*—was only conceived by the Council, of which it was a posthumous fruit. The past which led to this result was long.

In 1546 the Council Fathers made the decision to compile, on Luther's example, two catechisms: one for children and one for pastors. But the work was not completed because of the interruption of the Council. Only in 1561, by initiative of the Pope, was a commission of Spanish, French and Belgian theologians entrusted with the writing of the text. The work was suspended because of the lack of agreement among the theologians. In 1562-63 a new commission was constituted which comprised the best theologians and canonists. But the outline developed did not obtain the consensus of the Council Fathers.

On September 11, 1563, the Council Fathers abandoned the initial project and decided to give the catechism the form of a guide, directed to pastors and preachers. The writing of the catechism was begun, but it was not finished at a suitable time for the closing of the Council. In the final session, the Council Fathers approved the plan of the catechism *en bloc* and handed over to the Pope the task of compilation together with the plan and the material developed.

In 1564, after the termination of the Council, Pope Pius IV entrusted the writing up of the catechism to a commission of Bishops and theologians, presided over by Cardinal Charles Borromeo.

The work was brought to completion and placed in the hands of the new Pontiff, Pius V. In 1566, having had the text translated into beautiful Latin, the Pope provided for the publication of the Cathechism both in Latin and Italian under the title: *Catechismus ex decreto Concilio Tridentini ad Parochos Pii V jussu editus* (Catechism for pastors according to the decree of the Council of Trent, issued by order of Pius V). The same Pius V took personal care of the translation into various languages.

Recipients and structure. More than a real and proper catechism—in the sense of an essential and complete text of Christian doctrine to be placed in the hands of children or of adults—this is a pastoral directory, that is, a manual for pastors and Bishops, to offer them a sure guide for preaching, for catechesis and at the same time for pastoral work.[15] The Catechism is divided into four parts: Faith and the Apostles' Creed (Part I), the Sacraments (Part II), the Commandments (Part III), the Our Father (Part IV). The whole, therefore, corresponds to an essential plan: first of all, what God has done and is doing for man (Part I and II); then what man in response must do for God (Part III and IV).

Characteristics and evaluation. The Tridentine Catechism distinctly distinguished itself from the other catechisms of the era not only in regard to its recipients, but especially in several great catechetical and pastoral intuitions.

First of all, it is a catechism addressed to pastors. This is a precise pastoral priority: the renewal of catechesis hinges upon the direct involvement of the pastors, both as the persons chiefly responsible and as the mediators of catechesis.

Furthermore, the Catechism presents itself fundamentally as a pastoral directory. It is not a text of catechesis ready for use, nor

an aid which it suffices to read, explain and assign for memorization. It offers directives, especially in the Preface, regarding cate-
chetical-pastoral activity, and in its four parts it proposes an
ample content which, to be used, must be studied by each pastor
and adapted to the needs of his listeners. This decision is contrary
to the style of many bishops of the time who, resigned to the ignorance of a portion of their clergy, wrote instructions or aids
which the pastors limited themselves to merely reading.

Thus, the Catechism requires an ample adaptation to the recipients. The authors had set themselves the goal of making the
catechism an instrument of work, and they explicitly refused to
furnish a plan of catechesis: "Regarding the manner in which (the
pastors) will treat these things," states the Preface, "they will
choose what will seem to them more suited to the persons and the
topics." Every pastor, therefore, must bring about the due mediation, keeping in mind the needs of the recipients. The Preface
also gives a clear reminder: the pastor in catechizing "must keep
in mind the age of the listeners, their intellectual capacities, their
manner of living and the conditions in which they find
themselves. Above all, the pastor must not imagine that those
committed to his care are all on the same level, so that he can
follow one fixed and unvarying method of instruction to lead all
to knowledge and true piety in the same way."

Particularly significant, then, given the historical moment,
is the recall to a catechesis centered upon a knowledge-following of Christ: "A true teacher of the Church," says the Preface,
"should apply himself first of all to bringing to birth in the souls
of the faithful the desire to know Jesus Christ and to walk in the
footsteps of our Savior."

Departing notably from other contemporary texts, the Catechism emphasizes, although in a form yet elementary, the bond
between catechesis and liturgy. In particular the pastors are invited to "explain as clearly as possible the ceremonies" of the
sacraments, because if "the faithful ignore what they signify, they
cannot in any manner whatsoever be useful to them." Above all,
the Catechism reminds pastors that "they must never be per-
suaded that they have sufficiently instructed their people regarding the sacrament of Baptism," and in the meantime it invites
them to give a baptismal catechesis every "time that they will
have the occasion,"[16] especially when they administer the sacrament.

Rather limited is the theology of the sacraments, which fundamentally are considered as means.

Also in the presentation of the Church, to which the Catechism dedicates special importance, a modest attention is given to the spiritual dimension, whereas notable consideration is given to the visible dimension: society of the faithful, the various components (pastors-faithful; Church militant-triumphant), the distinctive marks of the Church, etc.

Although characterized by a theological foundation, the text is very rich with frequent references to the Bible.

Lastly, one is struck by the tone of the text: a rare serenity is to be noted. The refutation of error is always done with great discretion.

In conclusion, we can say with E. Germain that "this manual constitutes a small masterpiece of doctrinal firmness and prudence."[17] One of the most genial pastoral intuitions of the Tridentine Catechism consists in not offering anything ready made for use either in catechesis or in preaching. The matter is not divided by lessons and by questions. It is left to each pastor to do his best and to select the plan of catechesis most ideal for his listeners. Unfortunately, many would prefer to the Tridentine Catechism much simpler, more practical and less challenging texts.

THE CATHOLIC CATECHISMS

Impressed by the widespread acceptance given to the Protestant catechisms, especially those of Luther and Calvin, and urged by the catechetical priorities of the Council of Trent, the Catholics, too, especially in the second half of the sixteenth century, compiled numerous catechisms, conceived as handbooks of Christian doctrine, and destined directly for children or for the other faithful.

Together with the Tridentine Council these catechisms also contributed to the shaping of the catechetical renewal.

Among the many Catholic catechisms we recall those which had greater acceptance and diffusion.

Catechism of Peter Canisius, 1521-1597

Origin of the catechism. In Germany, already before 1550, some Catholic catechisms had appeared. These did not gain approbation because their language and contents were too intellectual. In the meantime the *Little Catechism* of Luther was being diffused even in the most remote areas. Preoccupied by the spread of the Reformation, King Ferdinand of Austria asked the Jesuit Fathers of Vienna to produce a handbook of Christian doctrine for the use of pastors, preachers and teachers, suitable for refuting the Protestant errors.

The task was entrusted to Fathers Le Jay and Canisius. In 1552 the former died, and the work was continued by Peter Canisius.

The catechism of Canisius was issued anonymously in 1554 under the title of *Summa doctrinae Christianae* ("Summa of Christian Doctrine").

The edict of King Ferdinand constituted a sure springboard: "Let this catechism and no other be proposed, explained and taught to the children in the schools, whether in public or in private, by teachers, tutors and instructors."

Adaptations of the "Summa" to the recipients. The *Summa*, also called the *Great Catechism*, appeared in Latin as a great book. Made up of octaves, it numbered 193 pages with 213 questions, whch in the succeeding editions became 222. It was intended for young students: the book was to be used and explained in school. Given its wealth and vastness, not only did it serve as a text for the students of the higher schools, but also as a guide for the teachers and, in some cases, also as a pastoral manual for pastors and preachers.

Very soon Canisius noted the need not only of translating his *Summa* into German, but also of adapting it to the various age levels. In 1556 there appeared in Latin the *Catechismus Minimus*, called the *Small Catechism*, of 59 questions, for younger children. This was immediately translated into German. In 1558 there was published the *Catechismus Minor*, of 121 questions, meant for young people of secondary schools. In some editions this "Middle Catechism" was to be accompanied by the Sunday Epistles and Gospels or by other books of prayer. The first edition in German was that of 1560. This last catechism was the best one and was to have the greatest success.

During Canisius' lifetime his catechisms were reprinted over two hundred times and were translated into the principal European languages.

Structure and content of the "Summa." The *Summa* is divided into two parts. The first part is dedicated to Wisdom. The themes developed are faith (Creed); hope (Our Father and Hail Mary); charity (commandments and precepts of the Church); the sacraments.

The second part treats of the Christian Justice. There is a detailed examination of the sins to avoid (sin in general, capital sins, the sins of others which we cause and occasion, sins against heaven) and the good to be done (the corporal and spiritual works of mercy, the cardinal virtues, the eight beatitudes, the gifts of the Spirit, the evangelical counsels).

Therefore, the first place is given to the Wisdom of the Christian man, which for Canisius consists in a life of faith, hope and charity, that is, in a theological life.

Christian justice is nothing other than the realization of the theological life in daily situations. It consists in putting off the old man, that is, fleeing from sin, and in putting on the new man, that is, practicing the virtues. At the center, therefore, of the theological vision of Canisius lies the Pauline conception of the Christian, the new man in Christ, called to live according to the newness of life received in Baptism.

Clearly separating himself from Luther, Canisius affirms in accord with Christian tradition that God through Christ communicates His sanctity to man, who thus becomes effectively justified and sanctified. Transformed radically in his being, the Christian man, who with his faith has adhered to Christ, must change his behavior: faith must be translated into works; it must express itself in justice, that is, in avoiding sin and in doing good.

It is evident that at the center of catechesis for Canisius is man saved and justified by Christ, called to live in Wisdom and according to Justice. Because of this, we can affirm with E. Germain that "the whole meaning of the catechesis of Canisius is the edification, the education of the Christian man, the education of man according to the gaze of God."[18]

Characteristics and evaluations. Let us first recall some positive aspects of the Catechisms of Canisius. To be appreciated in the first place is the effort to put out three different aids, to answer the different needs and capabilities of the recipients. At times, then, one has the impression that the catechism had been conceived more as a guide to the Christian life, than as a handbook of formulas to be memorized. To this end a few editions of the Catechisms were enriched with prayers, with the Sunday readings of the Word, with a presentation of the essentials of the liturgical year. Furthermore, the language was concrete, rich with comparisons and biblical images, lacking in terms and expressions which were too technical or abstract. The apologetical preoccupation, even though present, was nonetheless expressed in a tone always calm, dignified and serene. And especially worthy of appreciation is the centrality of the Christian life in the plan of catechesis. Lastly, in the Catechisms of Canisius there is a return to the Bible and to the Fathers. Above all, there are in the *Summa* frequent references to Bible history in order to exemplify the definitions proposed.

However, some limitations are not lacking. First of all, the language is not vivacious enough. In general the answers are too long to be memorized. The very amplitude of the *Summa* is, perhaps, excessive. There is, then, an evident methodological limitation: the edition of the *Little Catechism* and of the *Medium* is nothing other than a reduction of the *Great Catechism*. The result is a concentration of doctrine which is not easily assimilated and little suited to the recipients. This is especially true of the *Little Catechism*. Furthermore, the division into two parts— Wisdom and Justice—risks causing a certain dissociation of the Christian mystery. Lastly, the appreciation of Scripture is questionable, for God's Word is frequently used more as a confirmation or demonstration of the doctrine set forth than as a source of catechesis.

Notwithstanding these limitations, the Catechisms of Peter Canisius remain among the best catechetical works of the modern age. They were the most widely diffused in the schools of the Company of Jesus and in German-speaking countries. Many were the Bishops who had them translated and adapted, at times with some changes, in their dioceses. And all this notwithstanding the presence in the Church of an official Catechism, the Tridentine or Roman one. Often, in the embarrassment of a choice between the two catechisms—that of Canisius or the Roman text—many Bishops gave preference and precedence to that of Canisius. Significant in this regard is the instruction which Cardinal Charles Borromeo used to give his priests: "When the children have assimilated well the Catechism of Canisius, then you can have those who are capable turn to the *Roman Catechism*."

Catechisms of E. Auger, 1515-1591

Origins of the catechisms. It was 1563. In France the period of bloody fighting had begun between Catholics and Protestants to which history gave the title "Wars of Religion" (1562-1598). The Reformation was making always more headway, especially in the south of France, where the Catechism of Calvin was being diffused, especially among the youth. Up until the Council of Trent, the French Bishops had hesitated to compile catechisms to place in the hands of children. In more recent years there had been a few attempts at producing catechisms, but the results had been rather modest and of little success.

The spreading of the Reformation, the diffusion of the *Formulary* of Calvin and the catechetical void in the Catholic sphere were among the principal motives which impelled the Jesuit Edmund Auger to publish his Catechism in 1563.

Recipients and structure. The Catechism of 1563, called simply *Catéchisme* or *Sommaire de la doctrine chrétienne*, is the basic one and the best known. It was directed to youth and to a vaster public. It was enriched by a formulary for the confession of sins for people of all ages and classes: clergy, nobles, jurists, merchants, married people, children, servants, etc.

The author followed up this great Catechism with others for a more restricted group: one for persons without an education, one for children of the lower grades, another for students of the upper grades and for the learned clergy.

The structure of the Catechism was identical with that of Calvin's Formulary: Creed, Commandments, Our Father, Sacraments. The development of the contents also followed that of Calvin step by step. The reason for this parallel development was the purpose which Auger had set for himself: to refute point by point the Catechism of Calvin.

Characteristics and evaluations. We recall the principal characteristics. The catechism was written directly in French, in question and answer form. It is basically too theological, perhaps because the author's objective was to confute the text of Calvin. Moreover, there may be noted a certain leveling of content: fundamental truths and secondary aspects appear to be on the same plane. In general the language is clear, although sometimes it is somewhat emotional and oratorical. The questions are too long.

Finally, it must be acknowledged that the ever-present apologetic preoccupation is never polemical. We may say that the author refutes the affirmation of Calvin, blow by blow, with great respect.

Auger's Catechism was diffused rapidly in France. Between 1563 and 1582 it went through twenty editions. Yet, it disappeared very soon: its life, therefore, was intense but brief.

In France the influence of Auger, as that of Calvin, would have a determining influence on future catechisms, modelled on them, which would be compiled in French, in question and answer form, to be placed directly into the hands of children or of adults. For this, without difficulty, one can accept the evaluation of J. C. Dhotel: "Calvin and Auger can be considered as the inventors of the French catechisms of modern times.[19]

Catechisms of Robert Bellarmine, 1542-1621

Origins and approval. With the exception of Luther, none of the authors mentioned up until now had the idea of writing a catechism for children that was not a summary of a larger one. The first Catholic catechisms for the use of children that were compiled directly for them came into being in Rome through the initiative, first of James Ledesma in 1573[20] and then of Robert Bellarmine in 1597.

The catechisms of Bellarmine are two: *Brief Christian Doctrine* (1597), for children, and *A More Ample Declaration of Christian Doctrine* (1598), a guide for priests and teachers.

These two catechisms are the fruit of the author's long experience as a teacher of theology and as a catechist among the coadjutor brothers of the Company of Jesus.

The first catechism seems to have been expressly willed by Pope Clement III, who solemnly approved it in 1598 and ordered all the Brothers of the Archconfraternity of Christian Doctrine in Rome to make exclusive use of the Bellarmine method.

Furthermore, the Pope exhorted "the venerable Patriarchs, Archbishops, Bishops, Vicars General, Abbots, Pastors and Priests, in every part of the world to apply themselves in every way possible, so that the catechism, written by his orders, should be adopted and followed in their churches, dioceses and parishes." In 1633, Urban VII recommended it for the mission of the Orient. Also Benedict XIV, in 1742, expressed the desire that the catechism of Bellarmine be diffused throughout the world, noting that there existed "nothing more suitable."

No other catechism, except the Catechism of Trent, received such great appreciation and such a universal recommendation. During Vatican Council I the Catechism of Bellarmine was presented as the most authoritative model for the compilation of the universal catechism.

Structure. The plan of development of the catechisms of Bellarmine is analogous to that followed by Canisius in the *Summa:* theological virtues, sacraments, Christian justice. An introductory section treats the name of Christian and the sign of the cross. The central section develops first of all faith (Apostolic Symbol), hope (Our Father and Hail Mary) and charity (the commandments of God and the precepts of the Church), then the sacraments and lastly Christian justice (cardinal virtues, gifts of the Spirit, works of mercy, sins, the evangelical counsels, the last things). A conclusive addition, very practical, comprises three instructions on Confession, Penance and Eucharist, a manner of serving the Mass and a collection of prayers.

The intentions of the author seem clear: the catechism was to be not only a collection of truths to be known but also a kind of vademecum containing the essentials for the daily life of the Christian.

Characteristics and evaluation. We refer in particular to the *Brief Christian Doctrine.* First of all, the Catechism was written directly for children. For the first time children were considered as such and not as adults in miniature. The form used, then, is according to tradition, that of questions and answers. In the *Brief Christian Doctrine* the teacher is the one who asks; in the *More Ample Declaration of Doctrine* it is the youth who places the questions.

Furthermore, the text is didactically successful: it goes to the essentials, eliminating the difficult; the doctrine is set forth in a clear and logical manner; the language is simple and direct, even if some technical terms have remained in it; the questions are brief and the answers, at times long, are always expressed in a clear way so as to be easily memorized. The result is a simple, clear and essential presentation of Christian Doctrine.

To these positive aspects are to be added a few limitations which must not be overlooked. First of all, if the breaking up of Christian Doctrine into questions and answers facilitates understanding and memorization, it nevertheless deprives the child of a view of the whole. Furthermore, every reference to an historical-biblical dimension of salvation is lacking. The references to Sacred Scripture are few. The dominant preoccupation, instead, is that of explaining the various mysteries and the sacraments through questions, images and comparisons drawn from experience.

Notwithstanding these and other limitations, the Catechism of Bellarmine, especially because of its simple, practical development and completeness of contents, had a very wide diffusion: it went through more than 340 editions and was translated into fifty-eight languages. Until the appearance of the catechism of Pius X it was the official text in the Church and one of the most widely used catechisms in the parishes.

Catechisms in Spain and in the Indies

The religious situation in Spain was different from that in the rest of Europe: the Protestant Reformation was absent and in the sixteenth century the Spanish ambient was still profoundly religious. This can explain the order and form of the Spanish catechisms, which present themselves with a character which is essential, abstract, full of listings and very close to the medieval traditions. Together with the principal attempts which arose in Spain, we recall a few catechisms produced in the Spanish colonies of South America, the so-called Kingdom of the Indies, dependent upon the motherland.

The *Syllabus of Christian Doctrine*, a catechism composed in 1651 by the Jesuit Father Jerome Martinez (1532-1618). It was a collection of precise, brief, synthetic formulas, lacking in explanations. It was judged too theological and not easily memorizable.

Christian Doctrine, a catechism completed in 1599 by the Jesuit Gaspare Astete (1537-1607). The text was written in a brief form, for the most part abstract, with an obsessive insistence on numbers. Excessive attention was given to morality. The catechism had a most wide diffusion: around the year 1900 the number of editions had already surpassed 600.

Christian Doctrine and the Catechism for the Instruction of the Indians. This was the first catechism printed in South America. It came out of the typography of Lima in 1583. The author was the Jesuit Father Joseph de Acosta, who compiled the text by will of the provincial council of Lima (1582). Its setup follows that of the Roman Catechism, whereas the text is in the form of questions and answers. The real promoter of this catechism was St. Turibius Alphonse de Mongrovejo (1538-1606), who, because of his catechetical zeal has been called the Saint Charles Borromeo of the lands overseas. As soon as he arrived in Lima in 1581 as bishop, St. Turibius convoked the provincial council which united ecclesiastics from Nicaragua to Chile in order to discuss the methods of applying the conciliar decrees of Trent. During this regional meeting there matured the idea of the compilation of a catechism which Father De Acosta was asked to write.

Later on, the same Turibius ordered the compilation of a *Catechismo Minimo* for children, which was later called *Synodal Catechism*. Very similar to the syllabi of Fathers Ripalda and Astete, this text had a very widespread use.

The Diffusion of Catechisms After the Council of Trent

The catechisms mentioned are the most noted of the sixteenth century. All had great acceptance and almost all an ample diffusion, which extended far beyond their land of origin and the century in which they had appeared. Because of their characteristic setup as easy and essential summaries of Christian doctrine, presented in the vernacular in the form of questions and answers, destined directly for children, these catechisms are to be considered the pioneers of the catechisms of modern history.

Starting especially from the Council of Trent there was in the Church an increasing blossoming and diffusion of catechisms which were to explode into a rich and original proliferation of diocesan or regional texts, especially in the second half of the seventeenth century and the successive eighteenth and nineteenth centuries.

In the individual local churches the flowering of catechisms took three directions of expression: the acceptance and diffusion of the most successful catechisms, the compilation of new texts for Sunday catechism, and the production of new catechisms for the schools and colleges conducted by numerous religious congregations.

THOSE RESPONSIBLE FOR
CATECHETICAL RENEWAL

The renewal of the catechetical pastoral in the sixteenth century was due in part to the decrees of the Council of Trent, to the new catechisms and to the parochial and scholastic organization of catechesis. On the other hand, the most constant source was the activity of many and various individuals who had taken to heart the catechetical reformation at the different levels. We recall simply their various categories.

Bishops and priests. If the decrees of the Council of Trent did not remain a dead letter, this was due not only to the reforming will of the post-conciliar Popes, but in particular to the commitment of numerous Bishops who took a lively interest in the problem of catechesis: they convoked diocesan councils and synods to organize parochial and scholastic catechesis and to recall the priests to the obligation of catechizing[21]; they recommended or proposed this or that catechism, and they intensified their visits to the parishes.

Among these bishops one figure predominates: Charles Borromeo (1538-1584), Bishop of Milan. He was called the "Bishop of the Council of Trent." All his pastoral energies were spent in putting the Tridentine Council into action in his diocese: sermons, visits to parishes, contacts with priests, the opening of the seminary, the convocation of provincial councils and diocesan synods. In all this activity catechesis took first place. Many were his dispositions regarding catechesis. He directed all pastors to teach catechism every Sunday, imposed upon confessors the obligation of questioning their penitents on their knowledge of the fundamental Christian formulas (the Our Father, the Hail Mary, the Creed and the Decalogue), and encouraged the erection in the parishes of the Confraternity of Christian Doctrine. In particular, he promoted the capillary organization of parochial catechesis: at his death, the Sunday schools of catechism for children numbered more than 3,000.

By the will of the Council of Trent and by the choice of the bishops, the priests, especially the pastors, became the pivots of the catechetical activity and hence of the renewal of catechesis. It was a choice which saw the priests as those principally, and at times, solely, responsible for parochial catechesis.

Teachers and catechists. At the side of the priests, many lay persons were involved in the religious instruction of children: teachers in the schools and catechists for Sunday catechism. Their catechetical activity was always carried out under the responsibility and guidance of the priest. At times they exercised secondary roles; at other times, broad responsibilities. Above all in the catechetical congregations—such as, in Italy, the Company of Christian Doctrine in Milan,[22] the Archconfraternity of Christian Doctrine in Rome, the "Vachetoni" in Florence—the lay catechists were able to express a determining contribution to the renewal of catechesis in the parishes.

Religious. Besides the Jesuits, many religious congregations —such as the Barnabites, the Somaschi, the Scolopi, the Oratorians, the Theatines, the Ursulines, the Dottrinari, etc.—made religious instruction and the education of children and of youth the principal aim of their ecclesial service. The greater number of religious congregations of women carried out their own educative action in academies and schools, making them centers of religious instruction. Others offered their contribution to Sunday catechesis in the parishes.

This listing of catechists, even though brief, adequately informs us of the ecclesial amplitude and importance of the catechetical movement which arose in the sixteenth century: it was not the undertaking of only some; progressively it became an ecclesial action which involved the Church's principal energies.

METHOD

In the sixteenth century, along with the organization of catechesis, some methodological orientations began to delineate themselves. Given the variety of catechetical experience, we will limit ourselves to recalling a few aspects of catechesis for children, keeping in mind above all the catechetical Sunday schools.

The Catechist. For the catechesis of children, alongside the pastor, who was the person chiefly responsible, the figure of the lay catechist began to emerge. The catechist's role was at times limited to teaching prayers and hearing lessons; at other times, instead, it was expressed with greater responsibility and initiative. Many qualities were required of the catechist in general. St. Charles Borromeo called for charity, competence and prudence. Others further specified: devotion, zeal, humility, purity, discernment, modesty, spiritual joy, etc.[23] Furthermore, regarding relationship with the children, it was suggested in particular that the catechist attain a certain closeness and familiarity with the pupils.

The children. In the mentality of the time, the psychological conception of the child could be reduced to two dimensions: pliability and intellectual capacity.

According to the first dimension, the children, compared with soft wax, were considered subjects easily permeable and susceptible of taking every form. For this reason childhood was seen as the time in which it was necessary to intervene pedagogically to form the future adult. In this attitude, therefore, a certain adultism is visible: the child was seen in view of the adult of tomorrow.

Emphasis on the other dimension, intellectual capacity, led to viewing the encounter of catechesis essentially as a moment of instruction and a deeper study of truth.

Worthy of attention, then, is the recall to adaptation. In various sectors, in fact, as a guideline, emphasis was given to the need of adapting catechesis to age, sex, situations...to the necessities of the children. In actuality, however, beyond the separation of boys from girls, which was dictated by moral preoccupations, the sole distinction made among the children was by age. In this regard one of the more structural organizations was to be found in the diocese of Milan and precisely in the schools of catechism, promoted by the Company of Christian Doctrine, where provision was made for three classes of children: the little ones, who strove to learn by heart the Our Father, the Hail Mary, the Creed, the Commandments, and the first questions of Bellarmine; the older ones, to whom the Creed was explained word for word and who memorized the remaining questions of Bellarmine; the oldest, who were taught some aspects of the Roman Catechism.

The encounter or catechism lesson. The encounter of catechesis for children used to be held on Sunday in the early afternoon between dinner and vespers. It would last from one to two hours. The lesson, above all in the Sunday catechism schools promoted by the Company of Christian Doctrine, consisted substantially of a four-part development.

At the beginning of the encounter the children were divided into little groups of four or six students, around the teacher, who would teach them the principal prayers, the commandments, and the catechism questions and would listen to recitations.

Then the great moment of discussion would arrive. This was inspired by the contests of the Jesuit schools. At the beginning of the lesson, the prior would name two boys to be entrusted with discussing and competing about a portion of the catechism. At the sound of the bell all the groups of children would suspend their activity and gather together around the two "champions," settling themselves along the sides of the room. Having said a prayer, the two contestants received the blessing of the prior and mounted the dais. They would make the sign of the cross and would debate: out loud the two would question each other reciprocally; then they would question each of those present, selected at random. This was a way of achieving active participation and stimulating everyone to study and memorize.

At the end of the lesson some little gift was distributed: a book of devotions, a rosary, medals, holy images. This was another means of motivating the children to study.

Lastly, the lesson ended with a moment of prayer and hymns.

Didactic-methodological orientations. If we examine the catechetical act more closely, we can easily note the progress of certain didactic and pedagogical choices worthy of attention.

Above all, the model of teaching was fundamentally explicative-deductive: first a text was read, in general a definition or an answer of the catechism; then it was explained word for word. This explanation was followed often by an instruction that would exemplify and apply it. Through an ample use of facts or of examples, often taken from Scripture, from the Fathers and from history, the teacher sought to enlighten the mind, to clarify the explanation of the formulas, and, above all, to "warm" the heart to move the child to action.

Communication, then, was exclusively oral. It rested on the word: the explanation of the teacher, the teacher-student dialogue, the repetition of the formulas, singing and prayer.

In particular, the catechism encounter had as principal objective the knowledge and memorization of the fundamental

Christian truths. This explains the ample time that was given, in the teaching activity, to explanation, to repetition, discussion, contests, and to the use of rewards.

Catechetical instruction, furthermore, was given in small groups: it was recommended that the groups consist only of four or six subjects. In fact, later, these were formed on the basis of the numerical availability of catechisms. In every case this pedagogical intuition, considering the times, remains astonishing.

Another pedagogical fact worthy of attention was the active involvement of the children. The principal activities were dialogue, repetition by the children, discussion, catechetical contests and singing. Their principal limitation was that they relied exclusively on the ear and the word, completely neglecting the use of pictures and the value of sight.

Lastly, if we take a total view of the catechetical practice and concrete methodological priorities, a fact clearly seems to emerge: Under the structural and didactic aspect the catechesis of children drew inspiration, right from the start, from the classroom model. As in the regular school, so in Sunday catechism, there were classrooms, teachers, a book to study, lessons, formulas to memorize, citations, contests, debates...levels of teaching. Probably this fact, too, would contribute, in future centuries, to the emphasis on the study of truths and to the cognitive and mnemonic preoccupation of catechesis.

Naturally the various aspects of the method mentioned above are not to be generalized. Some didactic and pedagogical situations, such as instruction to small groups, the relationship of closeness and familiarity between the catechist and the children, the progressive and articulated presentation of Christian doctrine over several years...would be realized only in some privileged situations. In the majority of cases, above all in the rural world, the catechetical experience was rather modest: the catechetical encounter was limited to a reading and literal explanation of the formulas, followed at times by an exhortation or an application to concrete life through examples, and ending with numerous group recitations of the formulas to foster their memorization.

CONCLUSIVE BALANCE

Catechetical tradition was not born in the sixteenth century. Even without catechisms in the modern sense of the term—understood as "manuals of Christian doctrine, made up of questions and answers, written in the vernacular and destined to be placed in the hands of children"[24]—there existed in the Catholic Church, even with its limitations, a stable tradition of preaching and of religious instruction of the people of God. Its method was exclusively oral and the teaching, done by the pastor, was substantially concentrated on the articles of faith, the Commandments, the Christian prayers, the vices and the virtues.

However, it is necessary to recognize that in the sixteenth century a new chapter in catechetical pastoral was opened: the sixteenth century was the century of the renewal and reflourishing of catechesis. This renewal was not the work of just a few, but of many, and was due to diverse factors: the production and ample diffusion of new texts, that is, of catechisms; the catechetical priorities of the Council of Trent; a serious and concrete effort by many pastors; the generous and decisive contribution of numerous religious congregations at the service of parochial catechesis; the spread in the parishes of the Company and Archconfraternity of Christian Doctrine or analogous associations.

Naturally, as with every realization, the catechetical movement of the sixteenth century also had its limitations, together with its positive aspects. We will attempt a conclusive evaluation.

First of all, the *positive aspects*. We list the principal ones:

—the catechetical renewal, begun by a few, progressively involved the whole Church;

—the reflourishing of catechesis brought with it a reflourishing of Christian life, which would be particularly evident in the following century;

—the catechetical renewal brought about a permanent catechesis, foreseeing that catechesis was to be destined both for adults and for the little ones, both for students and intellectuals and for the simple people.

—in this period catechesis for children was born as a specific, serious service, institutionalized and juridically recognized;

—in this era the modern catechisms came into being as texts which contain Christian teaching in a simple, essential and complete manner—texts which are to be placed directly into the hands of the recipients of catechesis;

—in this century catechetical organization was planned: for the little ones, the Sunday catechism school; for adults, the Sunday instruction; for students, religion taught in the school. Future centuries would do nothing other than to consolidate this organization;

—on the methodological plane several anticipatory intuitions of the modern conquests were developed: the need of a catechetical adaptation corresponding to age, to environmental situations, to the maturity of the subjects...to the concrete needs of the recipients; the necessity of a continually developed teaching; the value of some activities; the instruction of a small group.

Limitations were not lacking. We list the most outstanding:

—at the center of catechesis, rather than the ecclesial community, the Word of God and man, was placed the catechism, as the book to be known, as the synthesis of Christian doctrine. In this manner there was the risk of reducing catechesis to school and instruction;

—a few didactico-methodological choices were somewhat questionable: limited activity centered almost exclusively on the word and the ear; the importance given to competition; the emphasis on memorization; the model of deductive-explicative teaching applied to children;

—contentwise: a limited and instrumental evaluation of the Bible; a reductive presentation of the sacraments and of the liturgy; a vision of the Church which did not stress her mystical dimension; a certain levelling of the Christian truths, due in part to the question and answer form chosen;

—lastly, on the operative pastoral plane serious limitations were present: the family and the parish community were little involved; centered upon catechesis for children, the catechetical effort at times neglected service to the adults; catechesis often became an "affair" of the priest, without an effective and responsible involvement of the laity; at times excessive dependence upon the text relegated the role of the catechist to just a "work" of explaining the book. Thus, there was little room for the catechist's effort of study and of mediation, together with his creative and original contribution as an educator in the faith.

Notwithstanding these deficiencies, the catechetical experience of the sixteenth century represented a milestone in the history of catechesis. On the one hand, catechesis experienced in this time a fervor perhaps never seen in the Church after the experience of the first centuries. On the other hand, the catechetical priorities and accomplishments of this century shaped successive history up until the twentieth century. For this reason the sixteenth century was not only the century of the "new catechisms," but also the century of the new modern catechetical pastoral appeal.

GIUSEPPE CAVALLOTTO

FOOTNOTES

1. From M. Luther, *The Little Catechism*, edited by E. Lessing, Florence, Sansoni, 1942, p. 7.

2. For a deeper study of the life of the Church in these centuries, see H. Daniel-Rops, *L'Église de la Renaissance et de la Reforme*, vol. 2, Paris, 1955.

3. Mangenot lists thirty-nine Protestant catechisms prior to that of Luther. During the same years numerous catechisms were also written in the Catholic field. Cf. E. Mangenot, *Catéchisme*, in D.T.C., coll. 1902-1917.

4. Cf. A. Etchegaray, *Storia della catechesi*, E. P., Rome, 1967, pp. 229-232.

5. Council of Trent, Session XXIII, chap. 18.

6. Council of Trent, Session V, chap. 1.

7. Council of Trent, Session XXIV, chap. 7.

8. Council of Trent, Session XXII, chap. 8.

9. Council of Trent, Session XXIV, chap. 4.

10. Council of Trent, Session V, chap. 2.

11. Council of Trent, Session XXIV, chap. 4.

12. Council of Trent, Session XXIV, chap. 7.

13. Council of Trent, Session XXII, chap. 8.

14. Council of Trent, Session XXIV, chap. 5.

15. The Preface to the Catechism deserves special attention because of its fine pedagogical and pastoral sensitivity. It treats: first of all, the necessity and authority of pastors and catechists; then their functions, their duties and, in particular, guidelines for their teaching; lastly, method and content.

16. From The Catechism of the Council of Trent, *Introduction to the Sacrament of Baptism*.

17. E. Germain, *Langages de la foi a travers l'histoire*, Fayard-Mame, Paris, 1972, p. 46.

18. E. Germain, *op. cit.*, p. 39.

19. Cf. J. C. Dhotel, *op. cit.*, p. 62.

20. The Spanish-born Jesuit, James Ledesma (1519-1575), spent all his life as a religious in Rome as teacher of theology at the Roman College. In 1573 he composed his catechism with the title: *Brief Christian Doctrine to teach in a few days, through a dialogue form of interrogation between teacher and disciple*. It is a small book of about thirty pages, which presents a summary of the essentials of Christian Doctrine according to the plan of the "Summa" of Canisius.

21. An ample list of regional and diocesan councils and synods, applying the Tridentine decrees on catechesis, can be seen in: E. Mangenot, *op. cit.*, coll. 1919-1920.

22. The Company of Christian Doctrine came into being at Milan in 1539 through the efforts of Castellino of Castello. It received a notable impulse from Cardinal Charles Borromeo, and

spread throughout Italy and Europe. In Rome, following the example of the Company of Milan, the Archconfraternity of Christian Doctrine came into being. It was an association of laity and priests, greatly involved religiously, who dedicated themselves to organizing Sunday schools of catechism for children in the parishes.

23. Cf. J. C. Dhotel, *op. cit.*, pp. 123-124.

24. J. C. Dhotel, *op. cit.*, p. 28.

BIBLIOGRAPHICAL REFERENCES

E. Mangenot, *Catéchisme*, in DTC, tom. II, coll. 1907-1925.

L. Csonka, "Storia della Catechesi," in *Educare*, Zürich, Pas-Verlag, 1964, vol. III, pp. 111-134.

A. Etchegaray Cruz, *Storia della catechesi*, E. P., Rome, 1967, pp. 223-288.

J. C. Dhotel, *Les origines du catéchisme moderne*, ed. Aubier, Paris, 1977.

E. Germain, *Langages de la foi a travers l'histoire*, Fayard-Mame, Paris, 1972, pp. 17-107.

U. Giannetto, *L'idea di catechismo nella Storia della Chiesa*, in AA.VV., *Il rinnovamento della catechesi in Italia*, ed. La Scuola, Brescia, 1977, pp. 41-58.

5

Contemporary Catechesis from Pius X to Our Own Times

Even though it has not yet ended, the twentieth century already shows itself to be one of the most lively catechetical periods. Without fear of exaggeration we can affirm that ours is, pastorally, the century of catechesis: a time of a more profound and organic study of pastoral catechetics, a time of reorganization of the service to catechesis at all levels, a time of interest in reflection and catechetical action which progressively involves the whole Church, a time of serious attempts and of decisive changes. Little by little as we approach the years of Vatican Council II, debate around catechesis is intensified, new perspectives for pastoral catechetics are outlined, and undertakings are multiplied. Always more clearly, two very relevant priorities in particular are consolidated on the pastoral plane. First of all, the field of action of catechesis widens out: it becomes always more a permanent deepening of the faith addressed to all ages. Furthermore, there slowly matures a "national or local way" to catechesis: fidelity to man and the demand for an inculturation of the faith urge every nation and every local Church to work out original priorities and mediations in regard to catechesis. Thus we find ourselves in the presence of a surprising variety and multiplicity of catechetical experiences.

Because it is impossible for us to present the catechetical wealth proper to every nation or continent, we will limit ourselves to an essential and general glance at the catechetical movement of the twentieth century: the principal factors in the renewal of catechesis, a few of the more significant catechetical events, the great catechetical changes of this century and, lastly, an indication of some of the tendencies emerging in the pastoral catechetics of our century.

FACTORS IN THE
CATECHETICAL RENEWAL

Save for some exceptions and limited corrections, from the Council of Trent until the beginning of the twentieth century the catechetical movement registered in the whole Church a substantial continuity in its basic priorities regarding organization, content and method. During the twentieth century, instead, we see a continual renewal which invests the aspects of organization, method and content to the point of questioning the very identity of catechesis. The factors in this change are many. We list the principal ones.[1]

Theological studies. From a speculative and abstract theology, slowly, already at the end of the nineteenth century, theological indications that were more biblical and more attentive to the life of man were developing. In particular "positive theology" made itself the promoter of a method of research centered on the direct study of the Fonts, the Bible and Tradition. The current French "théologie nouvelle" has emphasized the necessity of giving a Christian interpretation to the problems of man. "Kerygmatic theology" has proposed that the revealed truths be exposed not in a systematic way but according to historico-salvific development: creation, promise, covenant, Incarnation, death and Resurrection....

These theological trends had their beneficial influence on catechesis, which was asked to present the message in an historico-biblical manner, centered on the person and action of Christ and existentially attentive to the problems and life of man.

Besides these theological currents, it is necessary at least to recall the determining influence on catechesis of both the liturgical renewal and the biblical movement, which contributed not a little to the priorities of Vatican II and of the post-conciliar period.

Trends of Thought

Among the currents of thought particularly influential at the beginning of the century, we are to recall positivism, existentialism and modernism.

For positivism the only valid method is the positive one, based on experience and on experimentation.

For existentialism what is central and valid is the existence of man in his individual moments.

For modernism the individual religious conscience is the judge of revelation. From this stems opposition to every dogmatic teaching and the relativization of every magisterial pronouncement of the Church.

In the Catholic field, above all in the years following the Second World War, the influence of the personalism of E. Mounier and of E. Borne was relevant. Drawing from existentialism, this current tended to dissolve dichotomies in the dynamic synthesis of the existence of the person.

These various currents of thought could not fail to have, directly or indirectly, some influence on catechesis, which would feel itself stimulated to a more attentive analysis of man, of his life and of his environmental conditions, to a greater endeavor to center upon the concrete existence of man with his real problems, and to a pedagogical effort to evaluate the personal initiative of the act of faith.

Socio-cultural context

In this century we have witnessed socio-cultural changes that have been truly profound and radical. These transformations, which at first concerned chiefly the industrialized nations, have extended themselves to the whole world.[2]

Among the more relevant factors that can be listed at the origin of these changes are industrialization, urbanization, internal and external migration, the ever-increasing extent of the mass media, the increased secularization, the multiplication of relationships between men at all levels and the consequent new socialization.

Due to these phenomena always more profound changes have followed both in the traditional local communities—such as patriarchal families, clans, tribes, villages—and in the mentality of mankind. Progressively new conditions and conceptions of life have arisen.

Among the numerous consequences of this socio-cultural transformation some facts are particularly relevant for education to the faith and for catechesis itself:

—the break-up of a unified and monolithic system of values and behavioral norms, replaced by a plurality of scales of diverse and, often, contradictory values;

—the formation of a scientific mentality, which has relied always more extensively and, at times, unconditionally both on the human and positive sciences and on technology. This fact has shaped culture and thought patterns in a new way;

—the decline of the religious fact both as practice and as fundamental value is socially relevant. Not only has the phenomenon of atheism grown, but religion has become, for the majority, a private fact. From a Christian society we have become a secularized society;

—the emergence of a new human and social consciousness: more and more, man refuses to be an agent and feels himself as the protagonist and star of history. A new social, democratic and participative sensitivity has been born within him.

Naturally, these facts and, more globally, the new sociocultural situation, have progressively obliged catechesis to question itself on its own method, on its language, on its recipients and on its very purpose.

New Pedagogical Applications

The twentieth century is the century of the child. Due to the "Active School"—whose founding fathers can be considered John Dewey (1859-1959) for American activism, and the Genevan Adolph Ferriére (1879-1960) for European activism—there has been a real Copernican revolution in pedagogy and in didactics.

In fact, not one but many activisms have arisen. Among these one in particular has exercised its influence on catechesis and education in the faith: the activism which takes its inspiration from personalistic child-centeredness. Its point of departure is the conception of the child as a total result of vital energies and not as a *tabula rasa*. From this comes education understood as a process of the maturation and growth of these energies. Alongside this general affirmation, some pedagogical principles are worthy of note.

First of all, childhood is considered as a stage of life which has value in itself. The child, therefore, is placed at the center of the educational enterprise for what he is today and not for the adult that he will be tomorrow. Against adultism, child-centeredness is affirmed.

Furthermore, precisely because the child, rather than the program, is at the center, the educative endeavor must keep in mind the real development of the subject and of his complete capability. It must set out from the real and global interests of the person: biological, social, spiritual and religious needs. Hence, the rejection of every standardizing undertaking and the option for an individualized procedure.

Lastly, there is the law of activism: the child learns by doing. From this concept arises pedagogical and didactic activism: the educative enterprise must use "activities" suited to the child, capable of involving him fully.

Slowly these pedagogical demands of the "Active School" had an influence upon catechesis, which was asked to review both its conception of the child and its method of transmission and of education in the faith.

Lastly, together with activism, psychology and sociology have influenced catechetical pedagogy. Due to psychology a new light has been cast upon the dynamism of learning, upon the value of motivation...upon moral and religious development. In parallel, sociology has helped to discover the influence of the environment, the value of the group, the sociological conditionings of faith...social pressure.

CATECHETICAL FACTS

The catechetical movement in this twentieth century presents a surprising blossoming of initiatives which concern persons, undertakings and structures: from the reorganization of catechesis to the formation of catechists; from the official interventions of the ecclesial magisterium to the original intuitions of individual catechists; from the development of new methods of catechetical pedagogy to an abundant and diversified production of texts, of aids, and of catechetical means; from encounters and international debates about great problems and the fundamental priorities of catechesis to an explosion of conventions and of local initiatives: days, weeks, permanent schools—for the study, examination and programming of service to catechesis and of concrete itineraries of faith.

The list of these catechetical facts or events would be endless. We limit ourselves to briefly recalling a few from among those which have had a universal repercussion.

Pius X's Contribution to Catechesis

During the pontificate of St. Pius X catechesis enjoyed privileged attention. His particularly significant undertakings were two: the encyclical *Acerbo nimis* of 1905 and the compilation of a catechism.

Acerbo nimis was a milestone in the catechetical movement of this century. In it, above all, the Pope emphasized the primacy of catechesis in the mission of the Church. He reminded expressly that religious instruction is "the first duty of all those who are entrusted in any way with the government of the Church" and that for the pastors and for the priests "there is no duty more grave or obligation more binding than this." Then the Pope passed on to dictate some practical norms derived from tradition:

—in every parish there are to be organized for children Sunday catechism classes, an hour in length;

—a particular instruction is to be carried out for a certain period in preparation for Confession and Confirmation, and another in preparation for Communion;

—the Confraternity of Christian Doctrine is to be erected in every parish;

—special courses of religion are to be organized among students;

—Sunday instructions for adults, in addition to the homily, are to be re-established.

In this manner parochial catechesis was reorganized. Attention was centered on catechism for children and on Sunday instruction for adults. All was entrusted to the care of the pastor, who was to avail himself of the help of priests and devout laity, especially the members of the Confraternity of Christian Doctrine.

These norms of Pius X, later taken up by the Code of Canon Law of 1917, contributed in many nations, particularly in Italy, to a resumption of service to catechesis and to a serious restructuring of catechesis on the parish level.

Not less determining was the influence of the Catechism of Pius X, entitled *Compendium of Christian Doctrine*. The first edition (1905) was a text derived from the Catechism of Casati, compiled in 1765, whereas the second (1912) was a real re-elaboration of its predecessor. Rather than just one catechism, there was a plurality of texts, four to be exact. The most complete was the *Larger Catechism,* which in the second edition comprised more than 400 questions. The structure was traditional: Creed, Commandments, Grace. The set up was an essentially doctrinal and theological one, and the terminology at times too technical. The questions and answers were brief, easy and clear and in the appendix, the Catechism made an explicit reference to sacred history and to the liturgy; with its complete and exact presentation of Christian Doctrine, the text was truly theology (up until then reserved to a few) in familiar language.

The Catechism of Pius X was diffused in many European nations and in those of the missions. In Italy, it became the national text.

For over fifty years the Catechism of Pius X has influenced the history of catechesis, particularly in Italy. In comparison with other catechisms, this text rendered very fruitful service to young people, due to the ease of comprehension and of memorization; for a few generations it was a font of nourishment and of consolidation of the Christian faith; it fostered, at least in Italy, a homogeneity in catechetical practice.[3]

Catechetical Coordination

Not only did Pius XI continue to foster parochial catechetical organization; he advised that catechesis also be promoted and coordinated at all levels through suitable organization. Thus were born the various offices of coordination. In 1923, with the Motu Proprio *Orbem Catholicum*, the Catechetical Office was instituted at the Sacred Congregation of the Council. It had the duty of "promoting and moderating catechetical activity throughout the world." In 1935, with the decree *Provido sane consilio* of the Sacred Congregation of the Council, the erection of diocesan catechetical offices was prescribed. The national offices for the coordination of catechesis would come into being later, at various times and with different titles and functions according to the nation.

With the passing of the years, these organisms would become effective instruments for the promotion and coordination of catechesis at the various ecclesial levels. Furthermore, the establishment of these different organisms of coordination of catechesis revealed a pastoral intuition which became more explicit little by little as the time of Vatican Council II approached: on the one hand, the Church must stimulate and promote an original catechetical experience in every local reality, and, on the otner hand, in parallel, it must favor an organic unity of catechetical priorities among the various local experiences.

The Local Way to Catechesis

At the end of the nineteenth century in one and the same nation one would come across a multiplicity of catechisms. Often each diocese had its own official text. To overcome this catechetical proliferation, a plan for a universal catechism was presented during Vatican Council I. The proposal did not obtain the necessary votes. It returned again, without any outcome, with Pius IX, Pius X and Benedict XV, who even named a special commission. Later on, neither Pius XI, nor Pius XII, nor John XXIII considered the universal catechism, whose hypothesis was shelved with Vatican Council II.[4]

Instead the proposal expressed by Vatican Council I—that each nation have its own official national catechism—was welcomed with greater fervor. Many bishops saw in this proposal a wise solution which, on the one hand, helped to overcome the excessive fragmentation of catechetical initiatives, and, on the other hand, respected the pastoral realities proper to each nation.

In fact, during this century, at various times and in different ways, the episcopates of many nations have applied themselves to the compiling of national catechisms. We recall the principal accomplishments before Vatican Council II: Italy in practice accepted as the national text the Catechism of Pius X; in 1937, France developed its own catechism, which was fundamentally revised in 1947; Germany and Austria brought to completion, after years of work, the writing of their national catechisms, in 1955 and 1960 respectively; Holland, after a first national catechism in question and answer form, written for children in 1948, produced in 1966 a national catechism for adults.

The "national" dimension of catechesis was further perfected in the post-Vatican II period. The difficulties which many local communities found in trying to give importance to a national catechism, the ample emphasis given to the local church by Vatican II, the always more felt need of the inculturation of the faith, led many national episcopal conferences to give priority, more than to national catechisms, to the development of guidelines, orientations and national catechetical plans, capable of guaranteeing a common frame of reference for catechetical activity and, on a parallel plane, capable of respecting and promoting the originality of the different local situations. Thus there arose many pastoral documents, of a national character, for catechesis: "Catechetical Directories," "Basic Documents" for the catechetical renewal, "Fundamental Guidelines" and "Pastoral Orientations" for catechesis.[5]

[Official guidelines for these national documents were set down in the *General Catechetical Directory*, published in 1971 by the Sacred Congregation for the Clergy in accord with a directive of Vatican II (CD 44).]

In this manner a suitable national coordination of pastoral catechetics was assured and local guidelines for catechesis were fostered, involving the parochial and diocesan communities more fully.

National catechisms of Germany and of Holland. Their appearance revealed the new sensitivity, which had by now matured in the catechetical field. *The Catholic Catechism of the Dioceses of Germany* saw the light in 1955, after seventeen years of work. The particularly innovative aspects are two: its biblico-Christocentric setup and the presentation of content as lessons developed in an expository method. After centuries, this was the first officially approved catechism which abandoned the procedure of questions and answers. It was not a matter of irrelevant priorities. By now it was clear that catechesis could not be limited to a doctrinal teaching and that a catechetical method different from the explicative-deductive method, so privileged for a long time, was indeed possible.

In the Church of Holland, in 1957 a commission was constituted and given the task of revising the national catechism of 1948, destined for children. After two years of work, the commission concluded that an official national text for the catechesis of children under the age of twelve was impossible. After deep reflection and having abandoned the project of a national text for children, the Dutch Bishops decided in 1962 to compile a national catechism addressed directly to adults. The text appeared in 1966 with the title *New Catechism*.* Hence, the adults were considered the first recipients of catechesis. This was a sign that a new catechetical sensitivity was maturing in the Church. Later, many official documents oriented themselves in the same direction:

*See Translator's note, p. 533.

without neglecting the catechesis of the younger children, they emphasized that adults are in the full sense the recipients of catechesis.[6]

Catechetical Reflection

Which method must one use in catechizing? Which content? What is catechesis? Before our century, similar questions were reserved to the few who were assigned to catechetical work. By the major part of those involved in catechesis—pastors and catechists—it was taken for granted that their work consisted in explaining the questions of the catechism and assigning them for memorization.

Precisely. in this century there has arisen a catechetical debate-confrontation always more broadened, both with regard to the involvement of persons—scholars, pastors, those actually engaged in catechetical work—and with regard to the problems faced: catechetical organization, the formation of catechists, methods, goals, and the very nature of catechesis.

At the beginning of the century, as an opportunity to reflect on and discuss catechesis, there were many catechetical congresses and conventions, both national and diocesan. For the most part these were held for those involved in catechesis: pastors, teachers of religion, catechists. Among the themes tackled more often were the organization of catechesis, the formation of catechists and method. The first attempt was back in 1889: The National Catechetical Congress of Piacenza. In the vanguard for catechetical encounters of this type there were besides Italy and France also Germany and Austria, with their numerous Congresses of Munich and Vienna.

In the period from the Second World War to our own times, we have witnessed the birth and continual flourishing of centers of pastoral catechetics, of catechetical periodicals and of catechetical institutes. Some have been local, very many have been national and many international.[7] Centers, periodicals and institutes of catechesis have become in our time the "permanent seats" of the study and deepening of catechesis, of the gathering and comparing of experiences and of catechetical promotion and animation.

Finally, in the last twenty years, the catechetical reflection has found new expressions of discussion always more widened.

First of all, there have been "International Weeks of Catechesis," in which researchers of catechesis from all over the world have compared ideas.[8]

In the second place, the Synods of Bishops of 1974 and of 1977 gathered together over three hundred representatives of all the local Churches, to discuss the problem of evangelization in the contemporary world and that of catechesis, especially of children and of youth. These two events have been decisive for the pastoral catechetics of the whole Church, enriched respectively by the two apostolic exhortations—*Evangelii nuntiandi* of Paul VI in 1975 and *Catechesi tradendae* of John Paul II in 1979. Hence, with the passing of the years reflection on catechesis has broadened and intensified. In these last times, then, the whole Church has placed herself in a state of research in regard to catechesis. If, on the one hand, all this can be symptomatic of the always more serious difficulties encountered in catechetical work, on the other, it is certainly a sign of the seriousness of the endeavor to make persons at all levels responsible in catechetical service. This also reveals how catechesis slowly has occupied an always more central place in the pastoral of the Church.

The Formation of Catechists

The catechetical schools which came into existence in the first centuries at Alexandria in Egypt, at Caesarea in Palestine, at Antioch and Edessa, as well as the catechetical formation promoted in the post-Tridentine period by the Company of Christian Doctrine in Milan, by the community-seminaries of St. Nicholas-du-Chardonet and of St. Sulpice in Paris, testify that several times in the history of the Church serious proposals for the formation of catechists have been carried out. Nevertheless, only in our century has the preparation of catechists—laity, religious, priests —become a pastoral priority always more widespread, qualifying and on-going. This formative service has expressed itself in different ways.

Among the most successful initiatives of the first decades of the century we can recall the numerous conventions of catechetical studies, such as the national and diocesan congresses and conventions, especially in the European nations. To this must be added sessions for the formation of catechists and teachers of religion: in Italy a notable influence was exercised by the schools for catechists, which sprang up in the principal cities of the north, as well as by the diocesan "catechetical weeks."[9] In France the "Oeuvre des Catéchisme," founded in Paris in 1884, contributed notably to the preparation of catechists; in Germany and in Austria true cenacles of study, of formation and of catechetical activity were the associations of teachers of religion that sprang up in Munich and Vienna at the end of the nineteenth century. Furthermore, it is also necessary to remember both the permanent formation assured by the associations of catechists, among which emerged the Confraternity of Christian Doctrine, and the work of support and qualification promoted by the first periodicals for catechists, which came into being in this period.[10]

Towards the 'thirties, the study of catechetics was officially introduced in seminaries and in theological faculties: in 1926 the Sacred Congregation for Seminaries and Universities insisted that future priests be given a theoretical and practical catechetical instruction; in 1929 the same Congregation ordered the institution of a catechetical chair in the courses of theology; in 1931, the apostolic constitution *Deus scientiarum Dominus* prescribed that catechetics should be numbered among the special disciplines of the faculty of theology. With this priority, it was indeed recognized that for a serious service of catechesis not only a biblico-theological deepening was necessary, but also a specific catechetical qualification.

From the 'fifties to our own times, the effort for catechetical formation has further broadened and qualified, expressing itself in diversified services. Numerous institutes of catechetics, national and international, have arisen for the preparation of qualified workers in catechesis; there has been a multiplication of catechetical centers, regional and diocesan, with the task not only of stimulating and orienting pastoral catechetics, but also of offering instruments, courses of study and periods of formation for catechists. In these last years catechetical groups, regional and local, for the permanent formation of catechizers have arisen and been intensified. To all this must be added the size, by now imposing, of the catechetical conventions, of specialized periodicals and the theoretical and practical aids for the updating and the qualification of those responsible for catechesis and of its animators. It is by now a common conviction that the renewal of catechesis is closely bound up with the preparation of catechists. In her official documents, the Church explicitly affirms that the formation of catechists has priority over the renewal of texts, that first should be the catechists and then the catechisms.[11]

After this quantity of catechetical information, it remains difficult to make a summary. The listing of facts has been very limited. Among the many catechetical events omitted, a nod of acknowledgement should have been given to the organization of catechesis in parishes and in schools, to the vast catechetical production enriched in these last decades by audiovisual media, to the many attempts at adult catechesis, among which particular attention is merited by catechumenal programs and the catechetical experiences of the *small communities (communautés de base)*, to the involvement of parents in the catechesis of their children, to the serious catechetical endeavors fostered in the young Churches during these last twenty years, and finally to Vatican Council II, which, although it dedicated no document to catechesis, was the most decisive catechetical event of the century and will remain in itself—as Paul VI used to say—the catechism of modern times.

Notwithstanding these lacunae, this recollection of more significant catechetical events has at least served the purpose of helping us to sense the extraordinary richness and vivacity of the catechetical experience that has been continuously maturing in these last eighty years.

Catechetical Trends

Four stages may be distinguished in the history of catechesis in the twentieth century. Each of them is characterized by a prevailing catechetical concern: doctrine, method, biblical content, the life of man.

The doctrinal phase. This embraces an ample period extending from the Council of Trent to the beginning of the twentieth century. Attention was concentrated on Christian doctrine. The chief purpose of catechesis, sometimes the only one, was religious instruction, oriented to the knowledge of both the principal Christian truths and the fundamental duties of the baptized. The catechism, which occupied the central place in catechesis, was the book of knowledge. Written in question and answer form, it provided an extensive list of precise definitions derived from systematic theology, and it consisted in a summary of Christian doctrine. The catechetical method was fundamentally based on a deductive-explicative procedure: from the reading of the formulas to their explanation and memorization.

This model of doctrinal catechesis had the unquestionable advantage of eliminating, to a noteworthy extent, the grave religious ignorance of the Christian people and of permitting even the most simple to have access to the riches of theology.

The inherent limits of this catechetical model were: an intellectual and cognitive dimension of catechesis which—although it valued intelligence—did not speak, however, to the whole man; a leveling in the presentation of truths due to the very question and answer structure of the catechism; and a methodology of little incisiveness, inadequate for the involvement of the children.

The methodological phase. This extended from the first years of the century to the Second World War. During this period attention shifted from doctrinal content to method. During the first decades of the twentieth century, it was noted that religious instruction—especially that of children and young people—could not reduce itself to a simple explanation of definitions and to their memorization. In the meantime the influence of the "Active School" and the didactic renewal in the schools was urging the catechetical pastoral to review its own pedagogy. During this period new pedagogical research was developed in the field of catechetics. New techniques were tried and new methodological procedures elaborated. To be recalled among the more significant contributions are the Munich method and the active pedagogy that was especially promoted in France.

The Munich or Vienna method took its name from two cities in which rational catechetical congresses were held: Vienna (1905, 1912 and 1925); Munich (1905, 1911, 1912 and 1928). In these congresses the Method was thoroughly examined. It consisted in an inductive procedure, characterized by a threefold process: first, the presentation of an event, usually biblical; then, explanation of the same in order to pinpoint the truths contained therein; finally, an application to life of what had been discovered. Clearly we are speaking here of a process much more concrete and much closer to the sensitivities of the child than the preceding catechetical method.

But the new road entered upon left some questions open. Was the content of the faith fully respected? Was the Word of God adequately appreciated? Did the children succeed in identifying the central message of Christianity among all the truths learned?

In France, especially under the influence of the "Active School," interest in catechetical method concretized itself in original attempts. Among these may be recalled:

—the Quinet method.[12] This consisted in an explanation of the catechism based on comparisons and images close to the concrete world of the child.

—the psychological method of Marie Fargues.[13] Very attentive to the life of the child, it made use of sensitive periods and centers of interest.

—the more sociological method of Yvan Daniel, Madeleine Munich and Canon Lanquetin.[14] Their attempt consisted in an adaptation to the mentality and language of the environment in which the child lived.

The numerous methodological attempts of this period signaled a decisive turn in pastoral catechetics: from the explanation of the book a proposal was made to pass to a way that was more concrete, active and faithful to the children. Modern catechetical pedagogy was born.

The kerygmatic phase. This took root during the years 1935-1940 and characterized the catechetical movement up until Vatican II.

The request for a biblical catechesis did not fall from heaven. Already in the seventeenth century with C. Fleury and then, especially in the following century, with the school of Tubingen—particularly with the writings of Sailer, Moehler, and Hirscher—there were serious attempts to place revelation at the center of catechesis and to return to the Gospel. But these intuitions were not welcomed.

The relaunching of biblical catechesis, thanks above all to J. A. Jungmann, H. Rahner, F. X. Arnold and J. Colomb, found an ample following in the next thirty years of our century.

On the one hand, hesitancy on the part of some resulted from the comparison with the methodological direction taken over by catechesis, and, on the other hand, the influence of biblical studies and of the liturgical movement created favorable conditions for kerygmatic catechesis to take root.

Its strong points can be synthesized in a few phrases:

—Catechetical renewal does not come about through methodological adaptation, but through reflection on the content of the faith.

—Christianity is neither a system of truths nor a code of moral laws, but above all a message, a Good News. Catechesis must return to its sources, to the kernel of the Christian message, which is the kerygma.

—At the center of the message is a Person—Jesus Christ, salvation of the world. Catechesis must therefore be Christocentric.

—The principal events in Christ's life are two: His Death and Resurrection. Catechesis must center its message around the paschal mystery.

—Christ is not only a personage of the past; He is the synthesis of all the history of salvation. Catechesis must show that the whole of salvation history leads to Christ and is fulfilled in Him. Because of this the catechetical method will be historico-biblical.

The great merits of kerygmatic catechesis are: its fostering of a renewal of content, its promotion of a return to the Bible, and its recovery of both the centrality of Christ and a vital bond with the liturgy.

The anthropological phase. This has developed during the last twenty years and is characterized by a preponderant attention on man, his life and his problems. It has assumed various names, according to the experimentation done: anthropological catechesis, catechesis of liberation, catechesis of interpretation, vital catechesis, experiential catechesis, etc. Behind each name are verifiable sensitivities and differing priorities. All these attempts, however, are characterized by a common interest—man.

Originally, in 1960-65, the attention to man arose as exigency of the preparation and adaptation of the Christian message: one started from man, from his questions, from his interests—some call this process pre-evangelization—in order gradually to lead the person to be catechized to the explicit announcement of Christ. Subsequently, owing to the contribution of Vatican II and catechetical reflection—a decisive stage was signaled by the International Catechetical Week of Medellin in 1968. There was introduced the consideration of man's life and problems, of the events of history as echoes of the Word of God, etc., and therefore as content of catechesis.

The anthropological priority signaled a new turn in catechesis. According to F. Pajer, the fundamental conditions on which anthropological catechesis is based may be synthesized as follows:

—the point of departure, vehicle and content of catechesis is man, exactly as he is situated in the present historical context;

—anthropology and theology will plumb the depths of man and, together with him, his most vital experiences, in order to discover there the salvific mystery and express it in the light of faith;

—catechesis, then, describes itself as "the action through which a human group interprets, lives and expresses its own situation in the light of the Gospel" (Audinet);

—catechesis cannot, therefore, ignore man's political dimension, in the sense that the Christian interpretation of man and his situation is not possible without a continual "coming and going" dialectic between concrete, daily experience and the typical experience that is accomplished in Christ.[15]

It is difficult to evaluate an experience that is still being lived. Among the effects of anthropological catechesis are to be noted the recovery of the value of man and of history and a more explicit involvement of the Christian in the commitment of liberating the whole man and building up the Kingdom in the present. But equally to be outlined are some question marks: the risk of anthropocentrism, the danger of a limited and instrumental use of the Bible and the difficulty of offering believers a profound and systematic vision of the Christian message.

These four phases alone reveal both the vivacity of the catechetical experience of our century and the effort of the Church committed to mark out a service to the Gospel that is attentive to man and his times. Each of these phases has opened new perspectives. It will be up to catechetical practice wisely to evaluate the unique intuitions present in each of them.[16]

Trends

Besides being premature, a balance sheet of the catechetical movement of this twentieth century would be difficult to draw up. By way of conclusion it seems to us proper to recall some tendencies that have progressively emerged during these eighty years of history. This will be a matter of emphasis rather than synthesis:

—The ecclesial community has recognized its fundamental role in education to the faith. In front of the catechists and specialized workers stand the communities: dioceses, parishes, families...*communautés de base*. And the Church catechizes especially through what she is and lives.

—All in the Church are responsible for the Gospel. Each baptized person is called to announce Christ according to his own gifts and responsibilities.

—Parents are the persons who are first and chiefly responsible for the religious education of their children. This conviction, always present in the magisterium of the Church, was recalled with insistence by Vatican II.

—Catechists are not only teachers, but also educators in the faith. Their role is to walk together with the catechized and guide them to Christ.

The renewal of catechesis takes place through the obligatory formation of catechists. Hence, there should be a serious and qualified spiritual, theological, biblical and pedagogical preparation.

—Everyone in the Church is called to nourish himself on the Word of God and to grow in faith. From an educative proposal for children, catechesis becomes a permanent service directed toward all ages and in a fuller manner to adults.

—The final purpose of catechesis is the maturation of faith. Attention has shifted from the catechism book of knowledge, to man, to his life of faith, to the development of evangelical attitudes.

—The aims of catechesis are broadening. From the transmission of Christian doctrine catechesis characterizes itself as adhesion to Christ, maturation of a mentality of faith, deeper penetration of the Christian message, initiation into the life of the Church, the interpretation of life and of events, education to ecumenism, to dialogue...to witnessing.

—In the catechetical pastoral there is space not for one method only but for a plurality of itineraries of faith. The fundamental criteria for the choice of a method remain fidelity to God and to man.

—Finally, catechesis characterizes itself by its local aspect. Attention to man and to his culture oblige every region, every local Church, to mark out local pastoral projects and ways of catechizing.

Although incomplete, this section on trends presents a considerable catechetical heritage. It is the fruit of long years of reflection and research. It is the patrimony acquired from the pastoral documents of many regions and local Churches.

GIUSEPPE CAVALLOTTO

FOOTNOTES

1. A more analytic presentation of the factors that influenced catechetical renewal at the beginning of the century may be found in: L. Csonka, "Storia della Catechesi" in *Educare* vol. III, Zürich, Pas-Verlag, 1974, pp. 157-163.

2. Vatican II paid particular attention to the profound social and moral-religious changes of our time. Cf. *Gaudium et spes*, 4-7.

3. A more extensive presentation of the Catechism of Pius X may be found in: S. Riva, in AA.VV. "Nuove vie della catechesi in Italia," ed. La Scuola, Brescia, 1970, pp. 9-17.

4. At the conclusion of the Synod of Bishops of 1977, Cardinal J. Villot, then Prefect of the Sacred Congregation of the Council, presented to the synod fathers a communication on the problems of catechesis, in which he silenced the talk that the Holy See would advocate the compilation of a universal catechism, official and unique for the whole Church.

5. Among many contributions we recall the more significant:
—1964: French episcopate, *Directory of Catechetical Pastoral for the Use of the Dioceses of France.*
—1967: Argentine Episcopal Conference: *Directory of Catechesis.*
—1968; CELAM, *Medellin Conclusions.*
—1970: Italian Episcopal Conference: *The Renewal of Catechesis.*
—1971: Sacred Congregation for the Clergy, *General Catechetical Directory.*
—1972: Episcopal Commission of Evangelization and Catechesis, *National Directory for Evangelization and Catechesis in Mexico.*
—1974: National Office of Catechesis, *General Guidelines for Catechesis in Chile.*
—1976: Gemeinsame Synode der Bistümer in der Bundesrepublik Deutschland, *der Religionsunterricht in der Schule.*
—1978: United States Catholic Conference, *Sharing the Light of Faith, National Catechetical Directory for Catholics of the United States.*
—1979: CELAM, *Puebla, Evangelization in the Present and Future of Latin America.*

6. Among the documents may be noted: Italian Episcopal Conference, *Il rinnovamento della catechesi*, E.P.I., Rome, 1970, no. 124; Sacred Congregation for the Clergy, *General Catechetical Directory*, LDC, Turin, 1971, no. 20.

7. The centers and institutes of catechesis number more than a hundred, scattered almost everywhere. Only the higher institutes of catechetics spread throughout the world are more than fifteen. Chronologically speaking, at this date the latest international institute for catechists was set in operation in 1977: it is the Institute of Missionary Catechesis, linked with the Faculty of Missiology of the Pontifical Urban University of Rome.

8. The series of international weeks opened in Nijmegen in 1959 with the theme: "Missions and Liturgy." The second, at Eichsta'c in 1960, had as its topic: "Missions and Catechesis." The third, that of Bangkok in 1962, launched, on a large scale, reflection regarding anthropological catechesis. Among them all, the sixth international week, held at Medellin in 1968, had a particular resonance.

9. The first diocesan catechetical week originated in Parma in 1913. These "weeks" multiplied rapidly: in 1930 the seventieth was held and in 1940 the two hundredth. Each consisted of an entire week of practical catechetical lessons for priestly and lay catechists.

10. Among the principal magazines that came into existence at the end of the nineteenth century and the beginning of the twentieth we may recall: *Catechista cattolico*, founded in 1876; *Le Catechiste*, which came into existence in France in 1919; Cateche-

tische Blätter, official organ of the catechetical movement of Munich.

11. Cf. Sacred Congregation of the Clergy, *General Catechetical Directory*, no. 108; Italian Episcopal Conference, *Il rinnovamento della catechesi*, no. 200.

12. C. Quinet, *Carnets de préparation d'un catéchiste*, 3 vol., Ed. Spes., 1929-1930.

13. M. Fargues, *Le bon Dieu et son enfant*, Ed. du Cerf, 1949; *Dieu aime les hommes*, Ed. du Cerf, 1949.

14. Y. Daniel, *Vivre en chrétien dans mon quartier*, Ed. Ouvrieres, 1949;

Lanquetin-Munich, *Vivre en chrétien dans mon village*, Ed. Ouvrieres, 1948.

15. F. Pajer, "Il metodo nella catechesi oggi," in *Catechisti parrocchiali*, IX, 1972, no. 5, p. 31.

16. For a deeper sounding of this catechetical phase, one may see: L. Erdozain, "L'evolution de la catéchèse," in *Lumen Vitae* XXIV (1969) no. 4, pp. 575-599; F. Pajer, *art. 'cit.*, pp. 27-31.

PART THREE

The Nature and Spirit of Authentically Ecclesial Catechesis

"In order that the sacrificial offering of his or her faith should be perfect, the person who becomes a disciple of Christ has the right to receive 'the word of faith' not in mutilated, falsified or diminished form but whole and entire, in all its rigor and vigor. Unfaithfulness on some point to the integrity of the message means a dangerous weakening of catechesis and putting at risk the results that Christ and the ecclesial community have a right to expect from it. It is certainly not by chance that the final command of Jesus in Matthew's Gospel bears the mark of a certain entireness: 'All authority...has been given to me...make disciples of all nations...teaching them to observe all...I am with you always.' "

—CT 30

1

For a Christocentric Catechesis

PREMISE

The Apostolic Exhortation *Catechesi tradendae* has a lively program in view for renewal of the ecclesial fact "catechesis," already broadly treated by the magisterium of the Church, especially by the Popes, by Vatican Council II, by the work of the Bishops and by the 1977 Bishops' Synod. This renewal program was re-launched in a constant manner by Paul VI, made his own by John Paul I as a constitutive fact, and finally taken up and reorganized, on the basis of all these indications and experiences, by John Paul II.

The aim of the Document, therefore, is not primarily to offer content in a systematic order. For content, reference is continually made to the divine Word, to the Tradition of the Church, to the liturgy of the Church, to the specific documents issued in good number by the authorities, and also to the uninterrupted practice of the universal Church and the local Churches. And these references are found in the Document from number 1 on.

And yet, from the very text of the Document, from the more than rich citations and references to the Scriptures, and from the notes, there emerges a content that is full, historico-salvific, livable, synthetic and global.

Of necessity, therefore, it can be said that throughout the entire seventy-three numbers of the Document, there stands out in the forefront as the originating and central "content," co-extensive with the whole teaching of the Church, the Person of Our Lord, the great God and Savior Jesus Christ, with His titles, His works, His activity in His historical life in the Spirit, His restoration of all to the Father, His rendering of Himself constantly present to the Community of His faithful and also to men in history. Of this history He is the fulfillment, the ultimate meaning, the seal.

It is therefore necessary to show that the realities of Christ can be "read" in this Document, which wants to launch catechesis anew in the Church today. It is evident that the methods of "reading" are different, but not opposed; in fact, they converge toward the whole meaning that Christ always has for us, a meaning which today is deepened even further, scrutinized more, and, if this could be said, is more "significant" for the man of today, whom everyone believes to be in crises: existential crises, crises of identity, crises of meaning, crises of goals, and other real or imaginary crises, analyzed and ideologically revisited. It is as though men in whatsoever part of the world and of history did not ultimately have, as a real condition, the "crisis" which Scripture, in its long uninterrupted "history of salvation," identifies in strict realism with the general situation of sin (cf., for example, Rom. 2-3; 5; 7). But Scripture also points out with healthy optimism the definitive emergence from this crisis: conversion of heart, return to God, to oneself, to one's neighbor, to the world (cf., for example, Rom. 4; 6; 8; 12).

The possible readings, therefore, can go "from God to men and to history," and vice versa "from men and from history to God." But what else is the historical incarnation of Christ if not the first reading? And, for example, what is the Psalter with Psalm 1: "Happy the man..." that opens out to Psalm 150: "Alleluia! Praise the Lord!, " if not the second reading? The problem consists in knowing how to read in global synthesis and in historical progress the saving realities without opposition, but with the method of the Church: continual patient analyses, consequent rich syntheses, and then new analyses and new syntheses, always more comprehensive and rich. But the Churches, in the East and in the West, have always done this. It is up to us to know how to carry out the same method today by the intelligent use of all the means we have at our disposal, which our predecessors did not have, in fact, did not even dream of: for example, the human sciences, the interdisciplinary approach; scientific exegesis; theological and spiritual renewal; the rediscovery of the missionary nature of the Church; the new lived "spirituality," fundamentally biblical and liturgical.

The two readings, descending and ascending, teach us that in the effective "history of salvation" while God became man, by the incarnate God through the gift of the vivifying Spirit, man is brought to live "in the manner of God," as the Fathers say, that is, of the same divine life as the Document precisely notes, and as we will see.

The will to "humanize God, a God of men" is only an ideological sophistry, a waste of words in bad taste, the fruitlessness of solely human efforts. This will is seriously professed even by various forgetful Christians, because Christ had *already* become man to make of us true children of God (cf. 1 Jn. 3:1-2) and, therefore, His true brothers in the Holy Spirit.

Another previous annotation must converge on the fact that the Document, in number 50, reminds us systematically that it and the Synod of Bishops of 1977 did not at all intend to exhaust the contents of catechesis. And, therefore, these must undergo continually a legitimate, in fact, a dutiful integration, with a knowledge of realities that are always new, always vigilant, always dynamic, under the active inspiration of the Spirit of God, in the divine light of the Divine Teacher sent by the Father to mankind.

Therefore, the treatment of Christ the Lord must be articulated according to the many reminders of the Document.

A guide to reading which can be followed from now on suggests, therefore, an arrangement of subject matter according to the following points:

I. CHRIST, THE FATHER, THE SPIRIT

1. The divine Person of Christ.
2. The mystery of Christ.
3. Christ teaches and acts.
4. Christ gives the Holy Spirit for the mission.
5. Christ sends the Apostles.
6. Christocentric catechesis.
   Conclusion.

II. THE CHURCH, FAITHFUL DISCIPLE AND TEACHER

1. The Church in fullness.
2. The bearer of divine wisdom.
3. The Church as announcer.
4. The Church as celebrant.

III. THE EFFECTS WORKED BY CHRIST

"Divinization."

Conclusion.

I. CHRIST, THE FATHER, THE SPIRIT

The catechesis of the Church, in its various degrees—that is, as catechesis proper to the catechumens who prepare for the determining experience of their Baptism and of paschal Confirmation, and as "mystagogical" catechesis (from the Greek *mystêrion*, and the verb *ágô*, permanent, progressive introduction to living the mystery of Christ) for the faithful who have received the baptismal, chrismal and Eucharistic initiation—should always stem from this irrepeatable experience of the Mystery. Catechesis can never omit the experience of the mystery; from it catechesis must develop every form of Christian life in the baptized. *This catechesis of the Church, therefore, must be Christocentric* (CT 5).

The term is not found in the New Testament, but the reality, yes, and richly so, as can be derived from just one text, which is Pauline and important in itself, and which has now also officially entered the Roman Liturgy, where it may be used at the beginning of the Eucharistic celebration:

The grace *(cháris)* of the Lord Jesus Christ
and the love *(agápê)* of God
and the fellowship *(koinônía)* of the Holy Spirit
be with you all (2 Corinthians 13:14).

This transparent reading traces the way that the Fathers call "economical," that is, in regard to the effective carrying out of the work of our salvation:

—the Lord Jesus Christ, when first encountering men, gives His *grace*, the grace of salvation,

—which is the effective way of being able to receive from the Father His *love*, His divine original Charity,

—and which, together with this Charity, produces the permanent condition of salvation, the "communion" worked by the Spirit, existing between Father and Son and Spirit, but bestowed "through grace and love" also to men, to "you *all*."

Hence, from Christ to the Father through the gift of the Spirit.

Christ is the center of reunion for every initiative of divine salvation, the recapitulator of every reality to be led back to the Father (cf. Eph. 1:10), and already the center of the undivided divine life (cf. Col. 1:15-20). This last aspect, according to the language of the Fathers, is not "economical," but "theological"; that is, it concerns the unfathomable and indescribable life of the divine Persons themselves.

The Document treats mainly the first aspect, the economical one, but it also gives important material for the second. The two aspects, economical and theological, in fact, must always be balanced.

The catechesis of the Church, therefore, must not neglect either of these two aspects.

Typical is the way the Document opens (no. 1). The figure of Christ is immediately placed in the perspective of the "economy": having died and risen again, He "returns to the Father" according to His own announcement (cf., for example, Jn. 14:12-13), but He first instructs the Apostles with the definitive mandate: to announce the Gospel to the nations, teaching them to become disciples of the Lord to carry out all His precepts (Mt. 28:19-20).

From this beginning it is possible to analyze the presentation of the Lord in the Document. Starting from the top (the "theological" way) or from the bottom (the "economical" way), aids, therefore, a global understanding.

1. The Divine Person of Christ

Let us begin by delineating the Person of the Lord with the very titles attributed to Jesus Christ by the Apostolic Exhortation.

After two thousand years of history, of evangelization, of catechesis and mystagogical catechesis, of celebration, of social works, and always in obedience to the divine command to "do" what He Himself "did" (a strong, active, dynamic verb), after an uninterrupted liturgical and mystical Christian experience, after a continual school of conversion and of perfection, it is always difficult to speak of our Lord without a precise order, which comes from the texts of Divine Revelation, and to speak of Him, above all, in an exhaustive manner.

This is clear. The infinite possibilities that are given in the biblical texts are inexhaustible, and such that to every generation, with different sensibilities, there will appear in greater evidence, besides a common universality, one or another aspect of the Person of the Savior. This already occurred during the generations of the first Christians, who formed the communities of the New Testament, for example, among the Christians of Hebrew origin and those of pagan-Hellenistic origins. The fact is not new; it is marvelous. Every generation "knows" the same Lord according to the grace that each generation is given by the Lord Himself.

St. Augustine understood this with his usual lucidity and profundity, when in the liturgical homily to his people he tersely admonished: "Let no one believe anything about Christ except what Christ has willed one to believe about Him" *(Sermo* 237, 4; in PL 38, 1124).

We see, then, a few splendid proofs, which emerge from the Document. They will be based on the titles of the Lord and on His works.

a) *Jesus, Son of God* (cf. Jn. 20:31). Christ appears from the beginning of the Document (no. 1) as the fullness of Revelation: the Son of God, who gives life to whoever believes in His divine Name, showing Himself in the history of mankind with all the active "signs" of salvation, valid and effective always, down to our own times. The efficacy of the "signs" worked by Christ extends to the Word which the Church announces to catechumens who, having received the same life of Christ, become His body.

b) *The Lord* (no. 1), or else *"Our Lord."* This does not concern a title of honor, but a qualification of Christ, who in His Resurrection by the work of the Holy Spirit (cf. Rom. 1:1-4; Acts 2:32-33) was manifested by the Father in His divine fullness, and, therefore, was made manifest to us as "Lord and Christ" (Acts 2:36), continually present to His Church, of which, even in this respect, He is Sovereign. But "Lord" in the New Testament translates the divine Name of the Old Testament, which already the Greek Bible had rendered with *Kyrios,* Lord. Therefore, this title manifests the divinity of Christ, who is in unity with the Father and the Spirit. When the Church calls Him Christ the Lord, God of the Covenant, she invokes Him also as *"our* Lord," which is the formula proper to the covenant: "I am your Lord—You are our Lord," with the complement: "You are my people—We are your people."

c) *The Incarnate Word who is the Christ, the Son of God* (no. 6). He is the center of the Church's catechesis. In fact, the Word of God, "the active and dynamic Word of the Father," who exists from all eternity in the Father, the Word who is God, God from God, Light from Light, Life of the world, all-powerful Creator (Jn. 1:1-4), He Himself became flesh, and therefore is true man, taking His flesh from the Virgin Mary, in the history of men, and He pitched His tent among us (cf. Jn. 1:14a), and dwelt among men, fulfilling with them the paschal exodus (the "tents" of the desert) up to the epilogue assigned by the will of the Father: the cross and His resurrection. And for this "we have beheld his glory, glory as of the only Son from the Father, full of grace and of truth" (Jn. 1:14b). The glory of the Only Son, in fact, is the consummation of His historical Incarnation: the death, resurrection and inexhaustible Gift of the Holy Spirit, to be communicated to all mankind.

And this same Word is found in regard to the Father and us in this situation: "No one has ever seen God" (Jn. 1:18a). God, in fact, is the Invisible by definition (Col. 1:15). But His Only-Begotten Son, remaining eternally in the divine bosom of the Father, as the divine See of Divine Wisdom, "has made an exegesis" of the Invisible Father for us, giving a faithful, complete and accessible explanation (Jn. 1:18b), through the visibility of His humanity.

d) *Christ is thus the Revelation that God makes of Himself* (no. 22). This occurs in the history of Christ *(ibid.)*, and is forever deposited, through a continual activity of listening and of vision, in Scripture and in the Tradition of the Church (nos. 22, 27). Therefore, it is necessary that whoever wants to have access to the inexhaustible wealth of this divine Revelation is to be led to it with order and with certainty of motivations and content (no. 22). In fact, it is a matter of a personal Revelation to be received gradually in a personal and personalizing manner.

e) *Christ is the Image of the Father* (no. 60). Here we have an enormous chapter of fundamental importance, one that is basic to our very existence. In fact, Christ is the Icon (Image) of the invisible God (cf. Col. 1:15). This means that whoever wants to see the Father must see His faithful Image. The Father is the divine Prototype; His Icon is consubstantial with Him and hence the only one who can show Him in a faithful and complete manner. In the Holy Spirit, Christ, who is in the bosom of the Father (cf. the text of Jn. cited above 1:18b), nonetheless, without alteration manifests, shows and demonstrates "the visibility of the Father," as the Fathers of the Church say. "He who has seen me has seen the Father" (Jn. 14:9), because "I am in the Father and the Father is in me" (cf. Jn. 14:10): "Knowledge" of God—profound, experiential and personal—occurs through grace, only through the mediation of Christ, especially, however, of His holy humanity. Thus, of Christ it is necessary to know also the dynamism of "Image-Icon": by accepting to become incarnate, the Son of God in His humanity makes Himself totally the will of the Father, the action of the Father. By the work of the Word and of the Spirit His humanity is constituted for men of all times, as the Fathers say, the "privileged place" of the Charity of the Father and of the Son and of the Spirit, the unique divine Charity reflected on the holy Face of the Lord, and which radiates on mankind. This is being the Icon of the Father. It is the Face seen many times by the disciples while He taught, worked wonders, consoled, fed the crowds—seen in a special way while He was transfigured by divine light on the high Mount, while He broke the Bread and distributed the Cup during the Last Supper, while he suffered totally His passion, while, horribly tortured, He fell asleep in the Holy Spirit on the cross, when He was resurrected in the divine glory, when He ascended to the Father. It is the same Face which the anxious disciples of all times await to return "as He ascended to heaven" (Acts 1:11).

Certainly, for now the disciples see all this "in a mirror dimly" (1 Cor. 13:12; cited in no. 60), also because they must never forget that Christ is God, "and dwells always in inaccessible light" (1 Tm. 6:16; cited *ibid.*). But meanwhile the Church and all the disciples must make themselves "faithful images," as their Lord is, of the divine Charity among mankind. They must continue the teaching and the work of their Lord. Especially they must present, the Document insists, their Lord as the Divine Teacher.

f) *The Image of the Teacher* (no. 8). In ancient times the Church often represented with her immediate, significant, communicative art Christ as "Teacher." No. 8 is very full, as we will soon see, in its treatment of Christ as Teacher *(infra.*, no. C).

g) *The Son of God who gives life* (no. 1). The citation of Jn. 20:31 is the first conclusion of the Gospel of John. This Gospel is the collection of the "signs" worked by the Lord, many of which were not written down. Some of them were written—"these" which lead to faith in Jesus, the Christ, the Son of God. Precisely only through this Son of His, the Only-begotten, does the father give life to other faithful children. The Father, therefore, has disposed that the men that He calls (cf. Jn. 4:23-24) should adhere first to His Son and from Him have eternal Life, the Spirit.

h) *The Son of Man* (no. 30). Properly speaking, Christ in His historical life vindicates for Himself this messianic title, and only this one. The motive is central. In fact, "the Son of man" appears in a definitive manner in Daniel (7:1-14, especially 13-14), in a grandiose context of the theology of history. The powerful kingdoms, fruit of only human works, will cease. The Eternal at this time confers His universal power only upon a mysterious figure, who appears in an apocalyptic vision: He is a heavenly Being, who comes from God and comes to God, and from God receives "power and glory and reign" (verse 14), that is, in biblical language, every authority and responsibility of salvation. In fact, biblically speaking, a "king" is he who saves his people. The messianic King is the messianic Savior. But the Son of Man is regal, yet nevertheless "one similar to the son of man." He appears, therefore, as truly man, one who acts among men, in their history, and who among men founds the Kingdom of God, the Kingdom of peace and of perfect salvation.

We understand, then, that while the Lord is ascending again to the side of the Father, where He has always lived but to which He is now transferring His risen humanity as well, He presents Himself for the last time to His disciples as "the Son of Man" in the fullness of His divine and human powers, as man who has shown Himself to be God from God, in the words of Matthew 28:18: "All authority in heaven and on earth has been given to me (that is: the Father has given to me)"; in other words, universally, without any corner of existence being excluded (as Paul affirms in Ephesians 1:18-23: with His ascension Christ fills with divine glory, His glory, every existing space). Therefore, He sends His disciples to make disciples of all peoples and to baptize them in the unique divine Name of the Father and of the Son and of the Holy Spirit (Mt. 28:19-20).

i) *The Son of God, Sole Mediator* (no. 29). By the sovereign disposition of the Father, Christ is invested with the Holy Spirit and with every power of salvation, to accomplish coextensively the perfect worship of the Father and the perfect salvation of mankind. In Him the Father "sums up" every reality of heaven and of earth (cf. Eph. 1:10). Every divine salvation comes to men from Christ; that is, from His person and from His universal work: the gift of the Spirit, the culmination of this work, flows from Him (cf. Acts 2:32-33). And, conversely, whoever consents to approach the living God must consent to "make liturgical entrance" in the Holy Spirit to the Father through Christ (Eph. 2:18). There does not exist "another way" of salvation for men. Every illusion must fall; every human effort, every ideology and every direction which is not within this "Way" is destined to failure, more or less clamorous and ruinous.

j) *"The Way and the Truth and the Life"* (no. 22). At the Last Supper, in an atmosphere filled with content—the washing of the feet, the unique precept of charity, the institution of the Eucharist, the divine promise of the Spirit—and at the same time an atmosphere tense, because of the imminent sacrificial and oblative death of the Son of God, the Incarnate Word, the Lord announces to the disciples, who are still very confused, that now He will go to His Father to prepare "the dwelling places" for them (Jn. 14:1-2), because where He is His disciples would be with Him forever (v. 3). To this mysterious place, the bosom of the Father, He has already indicated the direction, "the way" (v. 4). In response to the uncertain question of Thomas about this "way," which the disciples still do not know, the Lord affirms, "*I am the way, and the truth and the life*" (vv. 5-6). Of the three terms, all important biblical themes, the most decisive is the first: biblically speaking, "way" means "to make a paschal exodus," but even "to conduct oneself in a paschal manner." Christ as the divine Way is such that to walk with Him is already to enter into God, who is the divine Truth and the divine Life, for already in the Son does the Father give His Life, the Spirit.

k) *Christ, divine Truth* (no. 30). The splendid citation is from Ephesians 4:20-21: to have listened to Christ, through the Word announced by His Apostles, is to have been taught by Jesus, who contains the divine Truth and is the divine Truth; it is to be invited to divest oneself of the sinful past and clothe oneself with the "new man," the perfect "image of God" (vv. 22-23). Now, Christ Truth is a great evangelical, Pauline and Johannine theme. Christ Truth is the fullness of the Divinity, indivisibly possessed whole and entire by the Father, and by Him communicated whole and entire to the Son and to the Spirit. "Doing the Truth," "living the Truth," is therefore the realization as faithful disciples of what the Divinity communicates with total love to mankind.

1) *Christ has the Words of eternal Life* (no. 31). After the miraculous multiplication of the loaves and fish (Jn. 6:1-15), the Lord explains at length this "sign," speaking of faith in His Person and in His Word—one unique reality—the true Bread descended from heaven to give divine life to mankind (6:22-40). And He explains that this Bread, divine food, is offered to mankind because it has been sealed by the Spirit of the Father (v. 27). This divine food is "His" flesh and "His" blood, the divine Eucharist (6:41-59). It is evident that, as His very disciples object, "This is a hard saying; who can listen to it?" (6:60) But Christ announces that His Words "are spirit and life" (v. 63). For this He is abandoned (v. 66). To the question whether the few faithful ones want to leave also (v. 67), Peter answers with absolute fidelity: "Lord, to whom shall we go? You have the words of eternal life" (v. 68). In fact, the faith of the Church is expressed by, "We have believed, and have come to know, that you are the Holy One of God" (v. 69)—that is, the holy Supreme Priest, who with Word, Spirit and Sacrifice gives eternal life (cf. Jn. 17:3). Here number 31 also cites Acts 5:20: the Angel of the Lord frees the Apostles from prison and orders them: "Go and stand in the temple and speak to the people *all* the words of this Life." And also 7:38: Stephen in his long discourse to the Sanhedrin recalls that already Moses had received from the Angel of God the living Words, "to give to us."

Having delineated the Person of the Lord with reference to the Document, we can now see how the Document itself insists profoundly on the mystery of Christ.

2. The Mystery of Christ

The term *mystêrion, mysterium*, is to be understood only in the biblical Pauline sense, that is, as the divine plan of salvation, hidden throughout the centuries in God, and now, in the last ages, made manifest in Christ to all mankind through the power of His preaching, which becomes the preaching of the Church, who announces it to herself and to all peoples (cf. Col. 1:26; Rom. 16:25; 11:25; Col. 2:2; 4:3; Eph. 3:4; 6:19; 1 Cor. 2:7; 4:1). Christ Himself brings this Mystery and gives it: Mk. 4:11; Mt. 13:11. "Mystery" is His very Person, bearer in the Spirit of the Kingdom of God.

Most precisely the Latin Fathers translated "mystery" with *sacramentum:* instrument, sign and concrete celebration of salvation starting with the Word of Christ, the Word of Mystery, the fullness, therefore, of Revelation, with its center in the celebration of the Church and especially, however, Christian initiation: Baptism, Confirmation, the divine Eucharist. Thus, even the liturgy of the Church is mystery-sacrament. And the catechesis of the Church constitutes a substantial part of this mystery sacrament.

a) The mystery of Christ causes joy in the communities (no. 4). In fact, it is the fullness of announcement, of preaching, of celebration, of paschal life, of the gift of the Spirit, and, therefore, of Christian joy.

b) The mystery of Christ is a full gift (no. 29). Its content is discussed at length and minutely by St. Paul, for example, in Ephesians, cf. 3:3 (the text cited in no. 29). It is the divine Mercy, which now admits to the fullness of the divine Life Hebrews and non-Hebrews, by the power of the Holy Spirit; and the Church must announce this Mystery and make men, the world, the cosmos and even the invisible powers partakers in it (cf. all of Ephesians 3).

This "Mystery," the fullness of *historical* content for mankind, always brings these realities into contact with men in their history (no. 22). And the realities are concentrated around the Word of God Incarnate—"historical," as the Fathers of the Church explain: that is, the Word who, having become flesh, lived His Pasch in its entirety for the salvation of all mankind, and in His death and resurrection through the gift of the Holy Spirit brings to a climax the work of redemption, which now and forevermore has been entrusted to the preaching of the Church, with the consequent catechesis, as the continuation of the same preaching of the Lord and of His "signs" worked with power. All this finds the privileged place of His presence in the sacramental celebration of the Church (no. 29).

But this "Mystery" is such that it is possible to penetrate it in a more profound manner (no. 54). In fact, its contents are like a progressive way of apprehending, of deepening and of living, which because of its admirable complexity requires the whole lifetime of the faithful in order to be globally understood:

—the love and the mercy of God;

—the incarnation of Christ, as an unfathomable, operation of Divine Wisdom;

—the cross, precious instrument of human redemption;

—the resurrection, center and climax of the Mystery;

—the continuous, strong and tender activity of the Holy Spirit in the hearts of the faithful, and in the very bosom of the Church, an activity which is the purpose of the incarnation and the direct consequence, therefore, of the divine resurrection;

—the end, the result, the eternal future of men, disposed by God with admirable sovereignity and goodness and already capable of being contemplated;

—the evangelical virtues, which arise from the divine Word and from the fact of the resurrection which gives them existence and motivation;

—the "social life"—that is, the deportment of Christians in the world, in history, among their brethren, which is, as it were, the extension of the incarnation and the actualization of the power of the resurrection in the life of the world.

The Church celebrates the whole Mystery, especially when she gathers in an hierarchical, praying, paschal assembly, listens to the Word and its preaching, and celebrates the memorial of her dead and risen Lord with the "signs" of Bread and the Cup, adoring the Father and the Son and the Spirit.

3. Christ in His Earthly Life— "Divine Teacher" and "Divine Worker"

The Document gives singular importance to outlining the activity of Christ during His earthly life and then His continuing efficacious presence among His own. And this is understandable: for Christ wills that what He has taught and done His faithful disciples should also teach and do. Because of this, as the Document often recalls (as we shall see), He has given to them His and the Father's all-powerful Spirit.

Besides, the New Testament has already preserved for us the precious testimony of the Apostles who lived with the Lord (cf. Acts 1:4, 21-22; 10:41, fundamental texts). They narrate how, in order to carry out His mission, the Lord Himself was "anointed by the Holy Spirit" in His baptism in the Jordan, and then taken under the divine cloud of glory, the Spirit, in His transfiguration: and this in order to teach and to do, to fulfill the entire plan of the Father, until His oblative death.

Therefore, a twofold reality stands out: Christ Teacher; Christ Do-er. Here we distinguish the two aspects, without separating them. Already the New Testament has accurately noted and distinguished them, but always keeping them together, as in Acts 1:1, "Jesus began to do (*poiéin*) and to teach (*didáskein*)." Thus cites the Document also, no. 7.

a) *The Divine Teacher.* The catechesis of the Church is legitimate because it repeats the teaching of her Master and Lord: she does what He did.

Now in the four Gospels alone, one of the recurring terms is precisely *didáskalos*, "the Teacher," which is said of Jesus. This term occurs about fifty times, in various and important contexts. The verb *didásko*, to teach, with other similar verbs, appears just as often, if not more frequently. The Gospel thus wants to indicate that only Christ is the Teacher, according to His severe words: "But do not you be called '*Rabbî* (teacher); for one is your teacher (*ho didáskalos*, with the article), and all you are brothers" (Mt. 23:8).

The reference is to the ancient prophecy, for one of the concrete "signs" of the New Covenant promised by the Lord is that "no longer shall each man teach his neighbor and each his brother, saying, 'Know the Lord,' for they shall all know me, from the least of them to the greatest, says the Lord!" (Jer. 31:34; cf., moreover, 31:31-34). And regarding this divine Word, the Lord Himself in the "Eucharistic Discourse" already mentioned, refers to another prophet and speaks thus: "It is written in the prophets, 'And they all shall be taught by God' " (Jn. 6:45, citing Is. 54:13, who in turn knew Jer. 31:34).

"Teacher" signifies, therefore, God who teaches. More specifically, it signifies the Divine Wisdom who became incarnate to live in the midst of mankind and to teach men the ways of God (cf. all of Sir. 24). It is the same Divine Wisdom who gives the Spirit, bearer of His doctrine: "But the Counselor, the Holy Spirit, whom the Father will send in my name, He will teach you all things, and bring to your remembrance all that I have said to you" (Jn. 14:26); "When the Spirit of truth comes, he will guide you into all the truth; for he will not speak on his own authority, but whatever he hears he will speak, and he will declare to you the things that are to come" (Jn. 16:13).

Therefore, Christ is the perennial Teacher in His historical life, and still and always in the Church through the power of His and the Father's Spirit. The texts cited here are, in fact, Trinitarian.

As the Teacher both divine and human, God and man, the Lord calls His disciples toward this profound reality. Not out of arrogance does He call Himself "Teacher" (cf. no. 8). In diverse synoptic contexts such as Mt. 10:25; 23:8 already seen; and 26:18; in Johannine texts, such as Jn. 13:13-14 (at the moment of the washing of the feet of the disciples), He tries to make them understand that the unique divine doctrine brought to men can come only from the Teacher (cf. also no. 25). And hence from the Teacher, through the faithful mediation of the disciples, this doctrine—unaltered—must reach the men of all times.

But the disciples, too, even before receiving the Spirit of Pentecost, and, therefore, the Fire of the Word and of Wisdom, in the presence of the imposing personality of Jesus of Nazareth recognize Him as "the Teacher" (no. 8). The texts are numerous: no. 8 cites in this regard Mt. 8:19; Mk. 4:38; 9:38; 10:35; 13:1; Jn. 11:28. But the citations can be multiplied.

Even disciples who are still uncertain, Nicodemus for example, call Him "Teacher" with great respect: Jn. 3:2. Then at the cross Nicodemus will come to the full light. In the meantime he approaches the Lord by night (no. 8).

And even the indifferent, or real adversaries, recognize Him as "Teacher": Mt. 12:38; Lk. 10:25; Mt. 22:16 (no. 8). They ask themselves where He has acquired such wisdom and such authority, He who has attended no authoritative school: thus it is in the beautiful text of Mk. 1:27, right at the beginning of the teaching mission of the One baptized in the Jordan.

b) *The Divine Worker.* It is clear: baptized and transfigured, the Lord accompanies His teaching in the Holy Spirit with His activity in the Holy Spirit, one unique work for the salvation of mankind. It is also clear that, as the Document repeatedly insists, the words and actions of the Lord constitute the matter of the catechesis of the Church to bring men to the celebration of the Mystery. *Dei Verbum*, in nos. 2 and 14, reminds us that the salvation of men is disposed by God in concrete history through *gesta verbaque*, that is, with effective deeds and words.

Number 9 offers a rich, magnificent list of verbs showing the activity of Christ the Lord, which should always be kept before one's eyes:

—the Teacher,

—who reveals God to men,

—and at the same time reveals man to man,

—who protects,

—who sanctifies,

—who directs (the divine Guide),

—who lives,

—who speaks,

—who urges,

—who promotes,

—who corrects,

—who judges,

—who pardons,

—who day by day proceeds together with us along the way of history,

—who comes as Teacher,

—and who as Teacher will return in glory.

The text of number 9 opportunely states that all this increases in us the desire for Christ, an ardent desire, which the contents of the Tradition of the Church continually bring to the faithful.

These verbs outline the greater part of the work of the Lord as Teacher, Prophet, Priest, Servant and glorious King. Throughout the liturgical year a continual memorial of this is celebrated.

4. Christ Gives the Holy Spirit for the Mission of His Disciples

Already in the beginning, in number 1, the Document recalls the central fact that, after His death and resurrection and His ascension to the Father, Christ nevertheless does not at all abandon His faithful disciples, but gives them with an infinite outpouring the Holy Spirit, the Spirit of Easter and of Pentecost, of the resurrection, of divine power, of sanctity, of priesthood, of prayer, of communion and of charity, "so that the disciples will fulfill the mission" to which the Lord Himself has called them as a vocation and for which He has gathered them in a community: the proclamation of salvation to all men.

Now, the Document provides a rich treatment on the Holy Spirit, dispersed throughout, but recapitulated in synthesis in the admirable number 72, which will be outlined here, following the order of the biblical citations.

The Spirit is called, as He must always be called, "the Spirit of the Father and of the Son." As we can see, this has to do with a trinitarian formula, because the catechesis of the Church must be Christological and trinitarian, under pain of no longer being the catechesis of the Church.

The text of number 72 wills to relate the very description of the divine function *(munus)* which the Spirit was to fulfill in the Church, according to the promise of Christ:

—"He will teach you all things, and

—bring to your remembrance all that I have said to you": Jn. 14:26;

—"he is the Spirit of truth,"

—who comes;

—"he will guide you into all the truth,

—and he will declare to you the things that are to come": Jn. 16:13;

—He is the "interior Teacher" who in the existential inner depths of each of the faithful clarifies whatever was still confused. Here number 72 cites an exceptional text of St. Augustine in his great *Commentary on John* 97, 1, in PL 35, 1877:

"Even now the Holy Spirit teaches the faithful in accordance with each one's spiritual capacity. And He sets their hearts aflame with greater desire according as each one progresses in the charity that makes him love what he already knows and desire what he has yet to know."

All this is yet and always the divine work of the Holy Spirit.

—The Spirit transforms the disciples into witnesses of Christ.

—He will bear witness to Christ: Jn. 15:26.

—Thus, the disciples, too, will bear witness to Christ: Jn. 15:27.

—He gives the divine Life, which St. Paul calls "life according to the Spirit": Rom. 8:14-17; Gal. 4:6.

—Only the Spirit makes it possible for us to call upon God as "Father." The essential quotation, filled with yearning, is a word whose sound was in the mouth of the Lord Himself to invoke "His" Father. In the mysterious, secret moments of Christ's existence, the Spirit present in Him would bring Him to total union with the Father, in the sense that while as God He is united consubstantially with the Father, as man He had to show the complete giving of His human will, most holy and life-giving, to form with the will of the Father one sole cooperation ordered to our salvation. Now, the Father called Him: "My Son!" at the Jordan and at the Transfiguration. It is an essential Word for us, revelatory, profound and unfathomable with the intimacy of God. Christ has to answer Him in the Spirit received at the Jordan and at the Transfiguration: "My Father!"

And when does He do it? When He speaks to the Father in order to praise Him for having revealed the Mystery of the Kingdom only to little ones: Mt. 11:25 (see, moreover, 11:25-30); paralleled in Lk. 10:21, who precisely mentions the Holy Spirit (see also 10:21-24). When He offers thanks to the Father at the resurrection of Lazarus: Jn. 11:41-42. When He uplifts His "Priestly Prayer" to the Father at the Last Supper: Jn. 17:1-26; see here v. 1, the beginning, but then verses 5 and 11 ("Holy Father!"); verses 21, 24, 25 ("Just Father!")—hence six times in only twenty-six verses. When in Gethsemane He must proceed to the total, sacrificial offering of His human will to the will of the Father: Mk. 14:36; Mt. 26:42; Lk. 22:42. Then, finally, when on the cross His last breath is addressed to the Father in the Spirit: Lk. 23:46.

"My Son!" is the offering of the alliance of the Spirit, from the Father to the Son. "My Father!" is the acceptance and cementing in the Spirit of this same alliance, from the Son to the Father.

But only Mark writes the authentic Aramaic sound of the term "Father": *Abbà!* This word signifies, more than the severe "father," the most loving, trusting, confiding, praising, asking, interceding, sorrowful and at the same time joyful "my Daddy"! It is the invocation which towards a divine "Daddy" only a divine Son can have who with the Father in the Holy Spirit forms total unity and communion. But it is also the invocation of the Christ man, who, cementing the new Covenant in the Spirit with His blood, is now uplifted to live "the manner of the divinity," as the Fathers of the Church say. And only a Little One, an Infant who enjoys the complete love of the Father, who rests His whole life in the Father, can, and knows how to, call Him *"Abbà!,* my Daddy!" Our translations, which try to render *"Abbà"* with "Father," lose the important interior significance of the most momentous Word which Christ pronounced in the New Testament, the central, nodal, fundamental, basic word of the whole divine "economy" of our salvation.

In fact, in Galatians 4:6, and then a few months later (in the year 57) in Rom. 8:15, St. Paul shows how the same Spirit of the divine sonship of Christ is now poured forth within us. It cries out in us, and makes us cry out together with Christ, because of Christ, in Christ, to the Father: "Abbà!" Here the translation "Father" is equally weak, because it should be "our Daddy!" It is evident that if in our assemblies we were to pray the "Our Father" as "Our Daddy," many would feel ill at ease. But the mystagogical catechesis of the Church must finally make us understand that we are elevated as the Man Jesus to being able to pray as He did, *"Abbà!"* St. John repeats this when he says to his communities: God loved us very much—He has made us His true children, not only in words, but in deed! We still do not know what we will be. But we are certain that we will see Him as He is—because we will be as He is (cf. 1 Jn. 3:1-2). It is a formidable text: "We will see Him as He is—we will be as He is!" And it concerns the Father, God, the invisible one!

This is, therefore, the work of the Holy Spirit, given to us by the Risen Lord.

—In fact, without the Holy Spirit no one can pray, "Jesus is Lord!": 1 Cor. 12:3. This fundamental text should not pass unnoticed in the catechesis of the Church, for it is an ancient baptismal formula of the ancient Church, that of the Apostles, in Aramaic; a clear cut and complex formula: because "Lord" (in Greek, *Kyrios)* is God, the God of the Old Testament, as already has been said; "Jesus" is the man seen by the Apostles. Now, in Baptism it was recognized that "this Jesus, who is risen, has shown and proven Himself the God of the Old Testament," together with the Father and the Spirit, the divine Spirit who inspires this historical faith. The formula is also a testimony, for the persecutors used to oblige one to say "Caesar is Lord (God)!" at the pain of shedding one's blood, as the Hebrew martyrs and later the Christian martyrs knew well.

This formula must not be set in opposition to the classic one of Mt. 28:19, "in the Name of the Father and of the Son and of the Holy Spirit," because both are ancient, both are apostolic, both come from Christ, both are sacramental, both are inspired by the Spirit, both are trinitarian, both wonderfully complete each other, for in both of them the same baptismal Spirit is at work.

—The Spirit with His "gratuitous gifts, the *charísmata,"* is forever building up His Church: 1 Cor. 12:4-11. Note the contiguity of the text with the preceding baptismal one. The "charisms" come to the Church not from the clouds of the air, but from the Holy Spirit in Baptism and Confirmation, and from this celebrative sacramental initiation they develop *ad infinitum*, there where they find correspondence in the community and in the individual faithful.

—The Spirit is the divine fullness: Eph. 5:18. A magnificent text! The context is above all baptismal, and so are the effects: vv. 14-17. Then follows—as is revealed well in the comments of the Fathers and the best modern commentaries—the violent opposition of the idolatrous cult, whose sacrificial libations used to lead to dissolute orgies (v. 18a), against the divine fullness of the Spirit (v. 18b), which comes from the Eucharistic Cup. Lastly, the context speaks of the Eucharist: because of the Eucharistic Cup the Community is able to render perennial thanks to God the Father through Christ in the joy of the Community: vv. 19-20. Thus, the divine fullness of the Spirit that is given by the Father through the Son is the continual Eucharistic and Baptismal Pentecost of the praying Church.

The Spirit gives us the gift of believing and acting. This is a famous text of St. Augustine, *Retractationum liber* 1, 23, 2, which goes thus:

"Both the facts (that is, 'believing' and 'acting')...are proper to us because of the decision of (our) will: and, nevertheless, both are given (by God) through the Spirit of faith and of charity."

The text is explained thus: before we believe and before we act, God gives us His Spirit, who produces faith and charity in us. This is the true Christian impulse to belief and action. It is a matter of pure grace, without merits, which comes from God and "works through superabundance." Therefore, the Spirit is the Divine Agent of our Christian life, which is faith—our response of love to God who calls our response of love, for Him and for the brethren—and charity, a communion of love and of goodness towards God and our neighbor. And yet this faith, this charity, this divine life which we possess in our Christian intimacy must be made our own by a free act of our total will. (To avoid the equivocations of our modern languages, we may translate *arbitrium*, this free act, as "deciding oneself.") Otherwise, faith and charity remain dead letters.

—The Spirit, therefore, carries out the catechesis of the Church, precisely insofar as this is a maturation toward the fullness of faith and of charity in the Church. Only the Spirit can inspire and sustain this work in the Church of God.

—Other texts of the New Testament, not cited by the Document, are alluded to by it, and to these we must constantly be sent, because the catechesis of the Church is not an explanation of books and of treatises, no matter how good, but of the Word of God.

—When the Church catechizes, she knows that she is and must be the living, docile instrument of the Spirit and that, in consequence, she must act accordingly.

—In the teaching Church and for every catechist, the Spirit must be the constant goal, the end to strive for. Here three verbs are to be considered:

a) Invoke the Spirit always. The *epiclesis* is the invocation of the total presence of the Spirit: "Father, send us Your Spirit and that of Your Son," or else: "Come, Holy Spirit!" This prayer must be a habitual, constant, and glorifying fact.

b) Communicate always with the Spirit of the Father and of Christ, for only He, divine *Koinônía*, Communion of the Father and of the Son, is also Divine Communion for us among ourselves, and for us communicating with Him, with the Father and with the Son. Here two fundamental texts are to be cited: 2 Cor. 13:13, already seen, in which the Grace of Christ and the Love of the Father are the Communion of the Spirit for us; and 1 Jn. 1:1-4, in which everything that the Apostles have heard, seen and touched of the Word of Life they announce to us so that our Communion, which is the Spirit, will be with the Father and with His Son Jesus Christ—and our joy will be made full by God.

c) Docilely accept, therefore, the "motions," impulses, urgings and inspirations which with extraordinarily abundant outpourings the Spirit continually brings about in the Church and in the faithful.

Thus, from the Father through the Risen Son in the Spirit, the divine mission of the Church continues to act in the world among the brethren, for the sole glory of God, for the sole good of mankind.

5. Christ Sends the Apostles

Number 1 states anew and strongly the fact that Christ gathers, prepares and disposes the Apostles, and gives them the Father's Spirit and His, so that they may go into the whole world to announce at last all that they have heard, contemplated and touched of the Word of Life. The text cited is that of which we have recently spoken: 1 Jn. 1:1-4.

6. "Christocentric" Catechesis

Now, with this enormous amount of material, we can turn to see in which sense the catechesis of the Church must be "Christocentric," and at the same time, as we have noted in detail, "Christocentric-trinitarian."

Only a few lines are needed to summarize what has already been set forth.

According to nos. 5 and 35 we must treat:

a) the divine Person of the Lord:

—His Mystery: Eph. 3:9, 18-19;

—the Divine Counsel;

—the Kingdom of God;

—"the gestures, the words, the signs": cf. again DV 2, 14;

—the divine Communion;

—the full, active participation in the divine Life of the Holy Trinity, the Life of the Father, and of the Son and of the Holy Spirit;

—the universal vocation to this Life;

—the eternal life, the future of the promise, which today is customarily called, in biblical and patristic language, "eschatology," the final destiny of all men.

Therefore, catechesis concerns all the realities deriving from the presence and activity of Christ in the world.

b) the faithful teachings of Christ: no. 6:

—about Him as the only Way and Truth and Life: Jn. 14:6;

—about the one, global object of His teaching, which cannot in any manner be altered to vague nonessentials nor proposed in a reduced manner;

—about the only, but entire, Word of God, read in the Church.

A concrete example of this Christocentricity of catechesis is given in no. 38 in relation to young people.

These have the right, in reality, to receive Christ, presented in His totality:

—as Friend, and unique true Friend,

—as Guide of life,

—as formidable Example to be reproduced,

—as He who with His full announcement brings young people the answer to their vital questions in our time; clearly this does not have to do with ready formulas, but with a life to be lived,

—as Bearer of the entire divine Counsel,

—as Bearer of the divine Counsel of love with goodness, as Christ the universal Savior,

—as the unique Former and Reformer of unity among men, painfully felt as a stringent necessity and yet never attained with ways, plans, methods, techniques, or activities other than those of the Gospel,

—as the center of the mystery of the passion and resurrection; as the center of faith, hope and the certainty of all men.

Conclusions

Catechesis, therefore, is fullness—
fullness of divine and human content.

It is the operative presence of the Father through the Son in the Spirit.

It is the maternal love and solicitude of the Church,

wherein the Church, as is still to be seen, shows herself truly mother and teacher and disciple of her Lord.

II. THE CHURCH, FAITHFUL DISCIPLE AND TEACHER

The treatment here can be given according to the following points, which recall other specific treatments.

1. The Church in Fullness

The Document insists on the living and operative Church. She is at once a series of realities.

She is the beloved Bride of her Spouse and Lord. Therefore, she is the *locus* of full communion, and community and communality of divine life with her Spouse, and because of her Spouse with all her children.

She is the "image and likeness" of her Spouse, the perfect image of God, the invisible one (cf. Col. 1:15). In their teaching and in their pastoral work, the Fathers of the Church have insisted much upon the Church, the praying paschal assembly, baptized and confirmed, who celebrates her Lord in His salvific events, as "the image and likeness of God," ruined by sin but never lost, now in fact restored by the work of the Spirit, particularly starting from the Word listened to, preached and celebrated, and from the consequent Christian initiation.

She is the living body, gathered member for member by the Spouse and by the Spirit (cf. Eph. 5:20-33, emblematic text!) to form a new living person, Head and Body.

She is the faithful disciple of her Lord and Spouse and Teacher, in a state of continual listening, in a colloquy that is uninterrupted, adoring and ineffable.

She is the Mother and Teacher, rendered such by her Spouse and Teacher with the permanent, inconsumable gift of the Holy Spirit.

She is, therefore, "the Catechist" of the *mirabilia Dei*, of the admirable works performed by God in the world.

She is, therefore, in the Mystery of Christ a Community of Charity, a Mystery of communion and of salvation.

She is the Church in fullness.

2. The Bearer of Divine Wisdom

Number 30, which cites the magnificent text of Philippians 3:8, shows that the Church is, by the merciful disposition of God, the bearer—because already she lives of it intensely—of the eminent knowledge of Christ Jesus. St. Paul explains here that every other reality is worth nothing in the presence of this divine Knowledge—a *gnôsis*, that is, a "knowledge" lived, experiential and vital, which centers upon Christ Jesus inasmuch as He is "*my* Lord," the God of the new Covenant. With a vehement expression the Apostle declares that he counts every other reality as "repugnant refuse," and he detaches himself from all, "to earn, to gain Christ," for the purpose of "being found (by God) in Him" (v. 9).

3. The Announcing Church

Number 25 shows, as the chief consequence of Christ's teaching and power, that the Church is launched into the world to "announce."

This concerns the evangelical announcement of the Kingdom, which the New Testament calls *kêrygma*, the first proclamation, made by the herald (verb *kêryssein*), to people who still do not know "the joyful news," the Gospel of God.

This first announcement must be followed by normal preaching, which leads to the celebration of the Mystery that has been proclaimed.

And all this means a continual, constant, minute, accurate explanation, which should introduce believers always more fully into the Mystery celebrated—that which is called "mystagogical" catechesis. We have explained it above.

4. The Celebrating Church

Number 48 is rich with liturgical material. The Church is by her nature an announcing and celebrating Community; she is a liturgy in action. The conciliar text recalled in the rich *Sacrosanctum concilium*, no. 7, a classic passage on the "active presence" of Christ in His Church and in all her life.

In fact, a Church which would not come into contact with the Lord and would not bring the faithful to celebrate Him would not attain her goal.

For the liturgy of the Church is the "summit and font" to which all her action attains, and from which every power of her activity derives: cf. 10.

In particular, however, explains number 23, the celebration of Baptism, with the gift of the Spirit, and the Eucharistic Celebration show the privileged "space-time" of the Church in prayer. Mystagogical catechesis, therefore, must constantly go back to the baptismal and Eucharistic realities.

Thus, the Church shows herself to God and to the world as truly the faithful disciple of the Lord, and the qualified and loving mother and teacher of all men.

III. THE EFFECTS WROUGHT BY CHRIST

Here, too, schematically, are indicated the principal effects that Christ the Lord brings about with the gift of the Spirit in His Church and in His individual faithful disciples who accept in Him the Father's plan of goodness.

"Divinization"

The term and the reality that the word "divinization" brings is in itself the center of the historical work intended by the divine plan. The Scriptures of the Old Testament treat of this often. But the Scriptures of the New Testament, which together with the Old form the sole Word of God revealed to men, make this reality the pivot of the divine activity regarding men. The Fathers of the Church have transmitted an intense, extensive, oft-repeated, time-honored treatment of this subject. And the liturgy of the Churches, in the East as in the West, re-proposes it—one can say—in every moment of the celebration of the Eucharist and of the sacraments, of the hours and of the liturgical year, with limitlessly varied terminology.

In any case, what is strange is that this reality has still not been rediscovered on the level of theological and spiritual studies, and hence on the level of the pastoral apostolate among the people of God, whose supreme aim it should be: and this, not because of caprice in the original foundation, but because of the very plan of God. In this regard, the Fathers, at least from St. Irenaeus (second half of the second century), have formulated a true axiom, so evident as to be held proven and not to be subsequently rediscussed. He precisely states the plan, the activity, the effect and the aim of divine salvation:

> The God who is infinite by nature and eternal
>> became Man, finite by nature and temporal,
> in order that
> every man, finite by nature and temporal,
>> may become God by grace.

Certainly, the prospect is little known. In catechesis, then, it is wholly absent. To restore it, an almost unimaginable effort would be needed: to change the old mentality and "spirituality," to take on that which is biblical, Christocentric and trinitarian.

Nonetheless how can the very biblical texts which speak of it be ignored?

Here let us limit ourselves to two very clear ones.

a) Christ Himself says, in a polemic regarding the incomprehension obstinately directed against Him:

> "Is it not written in your law (teaching):
> 'I said, you are gods'? (Ps. 81:6)

If he (God) called them gods
to whom the Word of God came
(and scripture cannot be broken),
do you say of him whom the Father consecrated
and sent into the world,
'You are blaspheming,'
because I said, 'I am the Son of God'?"
(Jn. 10:34-36)

b) The Apostle Peter tells us (even if the attribution of this writing to him is no longer sustained):

"His divine power has granted to us all things
that pertain to life and godliness,
through the knowledge of him
who called us to his own glory and excellence,
by which he has granted to us his precious and very great
    promises,
that through these you may...*become partakers of the divine
nature...*" (2 Pet. 1:3-4).

Now, with differing terminology, the Document in number 52 shows how against every political and social ideology, against every reductive and deforming personal option, the process begun by the preaching of the Church, and hence the process to which the catechesis of the Church must bring an essential contribution, is developed through these phases:

—God, creator and universal redeemer;
—His Son, who comes into the world among men;
—who actually assumes human flesh;
—who enters into the life of each one;
—who really inserts Himself into history;
—who becomes the center of each one and of history;
—and who changes the existence of mankind in its very structure.

Men are led, therefore, to live "another" existence, which, as we have seen above, is the very life of the divine Trinity.

Number 23, in particular, shows how Christ transforms men through the liturgy lived.

Number 29 shows this efficacious transformation, which is already "living in Christ," and which according to the theology of the Apostle Paul is:

—newness of life: Rom. 6:4; note the catechetical and baptismal context, centered on the death and resurrection of the Lord;

—the new creation: 2 Cor. 5:17;

—being or living Christ: *ibid.;*

—eternal life in Jesus Christ: Rom. 6:23.

All this can be summed up in evangelical terms as follows:

—It is already the life in this world,

—which, however, is lived according to the evangelical beatitudes,

—and according to a final tension,

—and is destined "to the transfiguration in heaven."

This last term, in Greek *metamórphôsis*, in Latin *transfiguratio*, is precisely the language of what the Fathers have called the "divinization" of man by the work of the Holy Spirit given by the Father and by the Son, and which restores to every man the divine sonship, the perfect "image and likeness of God," the participation in the divine nature.

Divinization, therefore, is the important, decisive material of our catechesis. The Document launches it anew in full.

Conclusion

Properly speaking, we must not conclude. On the contrary, the discourse, as the Document postulates, must begin, if it has not already done so, and it must proceed in growth if it is already begun.

However, a few points can be indicated as an outline that will enrich the reading of the Pontifical Document.

We have set down some points for a great discourse on Christ our Lord. These can be listed in a certain order:

1. The Primacy of Christ

This concerns His primacy in every order:

—in the love of the Father,

—in the possession of the Spirit,

—in the work of salvation,

—in the Church,

—in the divinized life.

2. The Trinitarian Life

The very fact that we must catechize about Christ, Son of God and Giver of the Spirit, recalls the unfathomable Mystery of the trinitarian life—vivifying, divine and divinizing.

This life calls us to participate in it totally. Christ, at the center of our expectations, leads us back to live this life, from which we are distant both by nature and by sin. Therefore, innately this is a call to continual conversion, which is a condition for the effectiveness of the Church's preaching and catechesis.

3. A Personalizing Person

Christ, sent by the Father to make us adhere to Him, to give us the Spirit and to bring us back to the Father, is the divine Person incarnate, who lived also in the manner of men, sharing in our experiences and sufferings.

He works in such wise as to re-establish the persons of men in the ultimate depths of their existence. He incorporates us into His Body, and makes this His Bride—this is personal, personalistic language. With the gift of the Spirit, He makes each one of us a true and real "son of God," to whom the Father can speak the last Word: "*You*, too, are my son, the beloved. In *you*, too, have I been pleased."

The Church teaches this to all mankind.

4. The Community of Integral Exchange

Catechesis is one of the most distinctive moments of the exchange of life which occurs within the Community of the Lord.

As is said in another part, the Church Community is both a great Teacher of catechesis, and a great Receiver of the same catechesis. The exchange thus occurs in the same interior: the catechist must feel himself to be the perennial catechized. And he must feel himself to be the perennial catechizer of the brethren.

5. To Announce, To Celebrate

To announce the Word means to preach the Word by right, to explain it, to make catechesis of it and to make continual mystagogy of it. The objective goal is to bring the recipients to the full communitarian, personal celebration of the Mystery of Christ.

It is not possible to approach the Word and make ever new brothers approach it, without celebrating it. To read it and study it is already to enter into its historical realities, to assimilate them and to live them. Therefore, together with Christ the Teacher, Lord and Priest, we celebrate it in the Holy Spirit, in the perfect worship of the Father, and for the sanctification of mankind.

6. *Liturgical Life, Social Life*

Thus understood, catechesis which brings one to the liturgical life has an intense influence upon "social" life, in the sense that it inserts the faithful always more and always better into their personal responsibilities and community commitments.

7. *To Transform the World*

Christ did not come to bring an "nth morality," however sublime and noble. He came to bring us a law of existence based on the transformation, the "transfiguration" of men, in order to give them the divine life, divinization.

But none of this can be done without at the same time proceeding to transform the whole world.

Catechesis is, therefore, very interested in this, and must work in this direction, always more effectively.

8. *The Last End*

When treating of Christ God, the divine Alpha and Omega, the First and the Last, before whom and after whom nothing exists, we necessarily arrive at the catechesis of the ultimate ends of man.

This does not involve starting out from ideological exigencies, which the Pontifical Document frankly and continually rejects. For the ideologies of today, so much in vogue even for those who monstrously profess to have exorcised them all, bring with them their own death and that of the others.

It is only a matter of starting out from God's plan for man, of working, with God, according to the divine plan for man, of realizing this divine plan in its entirety for man and becoming a part of it forever with all mankind.

This is why Christ continually pours forth the Spirit of the Father upon His Church and upon mankind.

TOMMASO FEDERICI

2

The Holy Spirit, the Teacher within and Inspirer of All Catechetical Work

Toward the end (no. 72) of the Apostolic Exhortation *Catechesi tradendae,* John Paul II turns his pastoral gaze toward the Holy Spirit, in order to emphasize clearly and forcefully, His essential and, therefore, irreplaceable role, both in the Church in general and in the field of catechesis in particular. Let us dwell for a while on each of these points, in order to set forth, even though succinctly, the rich content of the pontifical document in this regard.

I. THE HOLY SPIRIT AND THE CHURCH

Regarding the action of the Spirit in the Church, the Apostolic Exhortation, in perfect harmony with the best theological tradition, makes a few extremely important affirmations which merit to be studied more deeply. The Spirit of Christ is: 1) the Teacher within the Church; 2) He who transforms the disciples into witnesses of the Lord; 3) the principle from whom come all the charisms which build the Church as Community of salvation in the midst of men.

1. The Holy Spirit, "Teacher Within"

The Paraclete is, first of all, the Teacher within the Church, and, as such, exercises in her a real magisterial and directive activity. This is the first key affirmation of the present Pontiff in his Exhortation on catechesis. In making it, he simply recalls one of the fundamental truths of the Christian Faith, which has always seen the Spirit of the Father and of the Son as the One who continuously illumines and guides the new Messianic People which, while a pilgrim in time, is waiting for its Lord.

The biblical texts are very clear in describing this function of the Spirit in the bosom of the ecclesial Community. The teaching contained in them is very explicit.

To the saddened disciples, Jesus promises the sending by the Father in His name of another Consoler, who will remain with them and in them forever, in a permanent and definitive manner.[1] The purpose of the sending of the Paraclete upon the Twelve is explicitly indicated by Jesus Himself: the Consoler, the Holy Spirit whom the Father will send in His name, "will teach you all things, and bring to your remembrance all that I have said to you"[2]; He "will guide you into all the truth...and he will declare to you the things that are to come."[3] The mission of the Spirit will be, therefore, according to the very words of Christ, that of teaching, of reminding, of guiding toward the truth, that is, the mission of Teacher.

The Paraclete began to carry out this mission in a visible and extraordinary manner on the day of Pentecost when, according to the promise, He actually descended upon the Twelve, filling them with His gifts. Indeed, after having received the Spirit, they were completely transformed. Before, they had been obtuse and slow in understanding the words of Christ and the mystery of His life and of the Kingdom He had established. Now, they showed that they had penetrated both the real meaning of the former and also the true nature of the latter. Before, all had been obscure for them; now, all became clear. They had received the Spirit of truth[4] who with His light has illumined their minds, erasing from them every doubt.

This same magisterial function continues to be carried out by the Spirit of the Lord in the Church and in each one of her members. "The Spirit is thus promised to the Church and to each Christian as a teacher within, who, in the secret of the conscience and the heart, makes one understand what one has heard but was not capable of grasping."[5]

To understand the role of the Teacher within, which the Paraclete carries out in the Church, it is necessary to consider it in the light of the essentially pneumatological conception of the ecclesial Community offered to us by patristics and taken up again by the Second Vatican Ecumenical Council, a concept which we find expressed, no less categorically, in those documents of the post-conciliar magisterium which treat of our topic.[6]

For the Fathers, the Church is, as Christ is, full of the Holy Spirit, "led by the Spirit."[7] He dwells in her as in His temple. "The Spirit of the Son," "the Spirit of the Lord,"[8] is also "the Spirit of the Church," the principle of her very life. The Paraclete is for the Church of Christ, even if analogously, as is obvious, what the soul is for the human body—its vital and dynamic principle.

This is what St. Augustine says clearly: "the Holy Spirit is in regard to the members of Christ, to the Body of Christ, which is the Church, what our spirit, that is, our soul, is in respect to our members."[9] Identical is the thought of Chrysostom when he affirms that "as in the body there is one spirit, which contains all the members and forms a single organism out of the different organs of which it is composed, so it is in the Church. The Holy Spirit, in fact, was given so that He would unite in one body the different members, distinct among themselves as to race, culture, customs, and traditions."[10]

This is also the ecclesiological conception of the Council. Following the Fathers, it has brightly illuminated the pneumatic dimension of the new People of God. Numerous are the passages in the conciliar documents in which this dimension is highlighted along with the Christological one. It has been said that the Second Vatican Council was "the Council of the Spirit."[11] We say that the Church of the Council is truly "the Church of the Spirit," viewed, that is, in a spiritual dimension.[12]

The patristic and conciliar teaching is confirmed, with no less vigor, by the Apostolic Exhortation, *Evangelii nuntiandi*, of Paul VI. Not few are the texts of this Pauline document which allude, directly or indirectly, to the presence and action of the Spirit in the Church. But it is above all in number 75 that the topic in question is treated in a more profound and organic manner. Here the Church is defined as a Community which develops "full of the consolation of the Holy Spirit."[13] According to EN, the presence of the Paraclete in the midst of His people is particularly tangible today; thus, one can affirm that the Church is living a privileged moment of the Spirit.[14]

What we have said of the rapport between the Holy Spirit and the Church goes for the relationship between the Holy Spirit and the individual faithful. To say that the Spirit of the Father and of the Son lives in the Church is to say that He lives in each one of her members. Paul insists in a special way upon the indwelling of the Spirit in individual believers.[15] Didymus of Alexandria will say in his turn in perfect adherence to the Pauline thought that the one and undivided Spirit of God "is present in everyone and in each individual; all participate of Him and all possess Him."[16] Obviously, "to the members He is present and assists them in proportion to their various duties and offices, and the greater or less degree of spiritual health which they enjoy."[17]

The origin of the indwelling of the Spirit in the individual faithful is to be sought in the sacraments of Christian initiation. Already in Baptism, believers begin to be dwellings of the Spirit. The same Spirit, in fact, who descended upon Jesus of Nazareth while He was being baptized in the Jordan, descends also upon believers in the very moment in which they are regenerated with the baptismal water. The Baptism of Christians is, as was that of Christ, a real Baptism *ex aqua et Spiritu.*[18] Confirmation, the complement of Baptism not only from the liturgical standpoint but also from the theological one, will render the presence of the Spirit in the hearts of the faithful more intense and, hence, more perfect. Such is the effect proper to the second sacrament of Christian initiation.

The presence of the Holy Spirit in the Church and in each of the faithful is essentially dynamic. He is present in the ecclesial Community to unify it in communion, and in the ministry to rejuvenate it and renew it with the power of the Gospel, to adorn it with His fruits, to instruct it and direct it with various hierarchical and charismatic gifts, and in this way to lead it to perfect union with her Spouse.[19] As interior and invisible Teacher of the Church, the Spirit guards in her the Word of salvation brought to us by Christ, assuring its right interpretation and proclamation to men. The infallibility of the People of God has no other foundation than the presence and the action in it of the Spirit of Truth who vivifies and illuminates it.

The Paraclete performs this same role as the Teacher within, directly in each of the baptized, uninterruptedly guiding them in the ways of faith and making them understand, not only conceptually but also, and above all, vitally, faith's salvific content, which is centered in the mystery of Christ. This constitutes the primary object of catechesis.[20] Paul says in this regard that the believers "are led by the Spirit of God,"[21] and, following the same line of thought, John adds, in turn, that they know everything that concerns the faith, because they have received the anointing from the Holy One.[22] This is what Augustine will set forth much later, most suitably cited in this regard by the Pope in *Catechesi tradendae:* ..." 'Even now the Holy Spirit teaches the faithful,' says the Bishop of Hippo, 'in accordance with each one's spiritual capacity. And He sets their hearts aflame with greater desire according as each one progesses in the charity that makes him love what he already knows and desire what he has yet to know.' "[23]

2. He Who Transforms the Disciples of Christ into Witnesses

The Apostolic Exhortation points out that besides being the interior Teacher of the Church the Holy Spirit is also the Spirit of witness. There are two principal reasons on which the Supreme Pontiff bases himself in formulating this second statement on the role of the Paraclete within the People of God.

First of all, when the Spirit will come, it will be He Himself who will witness to Christ. The Lord says to the Twelve, "When the Counselor comes, whom I shall send to you from the Father, the Spirit of truth, who proceeds from the Father, he will bear witness to me."[24] That is, He will make known to men the mysteries of the life of Christ and of the Kingdom of God established by Christ with His coming, His life, His death and His resurrection.

Witness to Christ, the Paraclete is also witness to all who have been incorporated into Christ with Baptism. He dwells in them not only to sanctify them, but also to testify that they are truly children of God. In this regard Paul affirms that "it is the Spirit himself bearing witness with our spirit that we are children of God."[25] It is He, the Spirit of adoption, who, present in us and addressing Himself to God, calls Him: "Father."[26] The Paraclete is, therefore, the witness, the agent and, so to speak, the pledge of our state as children of God.

Secondly, the Spirit of the Son is the Spirit of witness insofar as He has, in particular, the mission "to transform the disciples into witnesses to Christ."[27]

As for the Apostles, their transformation into witnesses to the death and resurrection of the Lord, through the work of the Holy Spirit, appears clearly in the Acts. At first timid and cowardly, the Twelve become, after Pentecost, bold, intrepid heralds of that Jesus of Nazareth whom previously they denied or abandoned through fear. They do not even hesitate to give their lives for Him. They have received "power from above," the Spirit of fortitude. With His gifts, the Paraclete has wrought in them a profound transformation, not only on the intellectual plane but also on the moral level. In the days following Pentecost, the Apostles are clearly seen to be under the irresistible influence of the Spirit who descended upon them in the Cenacle.

Even if no longer so spectacularly as at Pentecost, the Spirit of the Lord continues to work the same transformation in those who have been called to succeed the Apostles, the bishops. As were the Twelve, also their immediate successors in the ministry are obliged to be, with word and with life, authentic witnesses to Christ, whom they incarnate and sacramentalize in the midst of those for whom they carry out their pastoral ministry. This task of being witnesses to Christ within the orbit of their ministry is entrusted to shepherds in the episcopal consecration. With the imposition of hands, they also receive the power to be able to carry out this task effectively. The same holds true for priests, the immediate collaborators of the bishops. Consequently, presbyterial and episcopal ordination is a true consecration on the level of ministerial priesthood to the mission of being witnesses to Christ. The gift of the Spirit given in ordination transforms those who receive it into witnesses to the Lord before the world exactly as it did at Pentecost, in regard to the Apostles.

What we have said is valid also, *servatis servandis*, for the laity. In Baptism they, too, have been constituted by the Spirit as witnesses to Christ within the sphere of action proper to the lay life. In their own orbit, therefore, the laity, no less than their shepherds, are obliged to bear witness to that mystery of salvation in which they have been given a share and of which they are bearers in order to communicate it to the brethren. Christian existence has a dimension essentially dynamic, apostolic and missionary. The believer, vitally incorporated into Christ, who was sent by the Father, and into the Church, which is sent by Christ, necessarily becomes an apostle, an envoy, a witness, a *martyr* of Christ and of His Mystical Body, the Church.

But besides transforming the disciples into witnesses to Christ, the Spirit of the Father fills them with the abundance of His messianic gifts—wisdom, understanding, counsel, fortitude, knowledge, reverence and holy fear—of which the prophet Isaiah speaks,[28] in order that they will remain faithful to their task, even in the midst of the greatest difficulties. The "robur," the strength of the Spirit, is indispensable for this purpose. In fact, only supported by Him can the Church always and everywhere bear witness to her Lord before men.

3. The Spirit, Fountainhead of All Charisms

But there is more. The Paraclete does not limit Himself to guiding the Church and to transforming the disciples into witnesses to the Lord. His action is much more vast. It extends to the whole life of the ecclesial Community and to that of each of its members.

The pontifical document recalls, first of all, that the Christian existence itself has a strong pneumatic dimension. In fact, according to St. Paul, who sums up the thought of the whole New Testament, the new life born in Baptism is a life according to the Spirit.[29] The Christian lives so much under the influence of the Spirit that, without Him, he could not even say: "Jesus is Lord."[30] The very fact of believing and of acting, "is ours because of the choice of our will, and yet both are gifts from the Spirit of faith and charity."[31] The Christian is, therefore, from his very birth, wholly penetrated by the Spirit, who illumines him and promotes his development until he attains the fullness of the stature of Christ.

It is from the Spirit, furthermore, that there "come all the charisms that build up the Church, the community of Christians."[32] He is, therefore, the sole font of the same, and to Him, consequently, are attributed the fruits which they produce in the pilgrim Church.

The Pauline doctrine on charisms is well known.[33] The Council takes it up and makes it its own in these words: "It is not only through the sacraments and the ministries of the Church that the Holy Spirit sanctifies and leads the People of God and enriches it with virtues, but...He distributes *special graces* among the faithful of every rank. By these gifts He makes them fit and ready to undertake the various tasks and offices which contribute toward the renewal and building up of the Church.... These charisms, whether they be the more outstanding or the more simple and widely diffused, are to be received with thanksgiving and consolation for they are perfectly suited to and useful for the needs of the Church.[34]

The Council distinguishes, therefore, three kinds of gifts or charisms: "gifts of the ministries" (also called 'hierarchical gifts' or 'institutional gifts'); "special graces," and "extraordinary gifts." Basically, this relates to the threefold Pauline division, to which the conciliar fathers chose to remain faithful.

Not rarely have some chosen to see a kind of opposition among these various classes of gifts, almost as though contrary and antagonistic forces were involved. Such counterposition is not compatible with the genuine Pauline thought reaffirmed by
• the text of *Lumen gentium* just cited. Both for Paul and for the Council, the above-mentioned gifts given by the Spirit to His Church are very closely connected. Not only do they not oppose one another; rather, they complement one another reciprocally. Nor could it be otherwise, because of the sole source from which they spring. Paul says, "There are varieties of gifts, but the same Spirit.... All these are inspired by one and the same Spirit, who apportions to each one individually as he wills."[35]

Regarding the purpose of the charisms, the Apostolic Exhortation is very explicit in affirming that it is ecclesial. They are given by the Spirit to the faithful for the good of the Church, for her upbuilding: "To each is given the manifestation of the Spirit for the common good."[36] They are a real gift of the Paraclete to the new Messianic People.

In fact, it is through these charisms (in addition to the sacraments and the ministries) that the Holy Spirit sanctifies and guides the People of God while it crosses the desert of this world toward the Parousia. It is also through these special graces that the Paraclete irresistibly impels this People ceaselessly to renew itself, so that, having removed every obstacle, it can fulfill its mission more effectively. It is still through these above-mentioned gifts grafted into the organism of the Church that the Spirit makes of all the believers a true *koinonía*. Referring to this last point, *Lumen gentium* expresses itself thus: the Holy Spirit, "Lord and Life-giver...brings together the whole Church and each and every one of those who believe, and...is the wellspring of their unity in the teaching of the apostles and in fellowship, in the breaking of bread and in prayer."[37] Finally, it is by incessantly infusing His gifts into the body of the Church that the Spirit of the Lord makes her overcome all those difficulties that stem from the deficiencies, omissions, and possible resistance of her members.

This is how, with His marvelous gifts, the Spirit of the Father and of the Son builds up the Church, the community of Christians, and leads her to carry out, without delay and with evangelical courage, her irreplaceable mission of salvation among the men who succeed one another in time and in history.

II. THE HOLY SPIRIT, INSPIRER OF ALL CATECHETICAL ACTIVITY

As the vivifying and animating principle of the Church, the Holy Spirit cannot but be also the font of the Church's every activity, in particular of evangelization and catechesis. Referring to the latter, the Apostolic Exhortation cannot be more explicit and categorical: "Catechesis, which is growth in faith and the maturing of Christian life towards its fullness, is...a work of the Holy Spirit, a work that He alone can initiate and sustain in the Church."[38] In other words, the Paraclete is the principal agent of the Church's catechizing activity, as He is of her evangelizing activity.

1. The Church, Living Instrument of the Spirit

From what was said before, it follows that the Church, in carrying out her mission of catechizing, always acts as a "living, docile instrument" of the Spirit, as an organ which He uses to fulfill His plan of salvation.[39] This concept must be stressed as *Catechesi tradendae* does, because we consider it extremely important for a precise conception of catechetical activity on the part of those engaged in it. The catechist must be aware that he does not act in his own name, but as the instrument of the Spirit of Christ.

To be effective, however, the instrument must be docile. Instrumentality and docility are, in reality, two terms and two concepts that are intimately united. It is unlikely that an instrument which is not docile would achieve the purpose which the principal agent pre-established in choosing it. Only a Church as docile to the breath of the Spirit as Christ was, can as a consequence effectively carry out her mission of leading men, through catechesis, to the always more perfect knowledge of the mystery of Christ, in order that they may be always the more profoundly impregnated by it.[40]

Many and of supreme transcendence are the consequences for the life of the Church which stem from her being the instrument of the holy and sanctifying Spirit.

First of all, the awareness of being an instrument of the Paraclete urges the Church ceaselessly to call upon Him to make her catechetical activity fruitful. The catechizing Church is, therefore, a *praying* Church, as is the evangelizing one, with which she obviously identifies herself. Of maximum importance in the work of announcing the Gospel, prayer, in the same measure and for the same reasons, is equally important in the work of catechesis. Let it not be forgotten that catechesis constitutes a privileged moment in the whole process of evangelization.[41]

Furthermore, the Church whose activity is catechesis must be an apostolic Community in intimate communion with the Spirit. This means that her own life and that of each one of her members develops, in every dimension and sector, under the influence of the Paraclete. The Church of catechesis, as that of the Gospel, must be a Church full of the Spirit, as were Christ and the Apostles.

The Church engaged in catechetical work will thus be led to "know the authentic inspirations" of the Spirit,[42] to listen to His voice, and to follow His directives regarding the most suitable ways to follow and the more efficacious methods to use in carrying out her mission of catechizing. And since the Spirit often speaks through the "signs of the times," the Church, in order to be docile and faithful to him, cannot leave off scrutinizing them attentively, seeking to discover in them everything that He wishes to reveal to her.

Hence, an attitude of docility to the Spirit, of prayer and of listening—this must be the attitude of the Church and of every catechist who, in her bosom, acts in her name.

2. A Catechetical Awakening

The attitude of docility and of abandonment to the Holy Spirit must be such as to arouse in the Church a true catechetical awakening,[43] that is, to create in her members an always greater sensitivity toward the vast and complex problems of catechesis, and to lead an ever growing number to consecrate themselves to catechetical activity, both in the so-called mission countries and in those of ancient Christendom.

In reality, we have witnessed in these last years a renewed interest in catechesis in the various sectors of the ecclesial Community. Always more numerous are those who have acquired a clear awareness of the decisive importance and urgency of catechesis for the future of the Church, above all in specific strata of contemporary society. A catechetical *forma mentis*, has been progressively developing in the Church, becoming always more common among clergy, religious and laity.

An expression of this phenomenon, full of promise for the future, is the always greater frequency with which problems concerning catechesis are studied in various localities within the ambit of the Church. Within this context is to be viewed, for example, the Institute of Missionary Catechesis created in the Urban University, which proposes to collaborate with the Bishops in the formation of the catechetical leaders of local Churches.

It is not difficult to see in this catechetical awakening the invisible but effective action of the Spirit, who arouses it in believers in order that the Church can fulfill her mission of proclaiming the Good News and of bringing to fullness the lives of those who accept it. This awakening is, therefore, a tangible sign of the presence of the Spirit in the Church. Paul VI in *Evangelii nuntiandi* said, "We live in the Church at a privileged moment of the Spirit."[44] The catechetical awakening which we are witnessing is the most convincing proof of this.

The growing interest in catechesis very soon brought about the need for a thoroughgoing catechetical renewal, especially regarding methods, language and the utilization of new means for the transmission of the Christian message. It was a renewal begun and carried forward with great courage, notwithstanding enormous difficulties, everywhere in the Church, especially after the Second Vatican Council.[45] Even this desire to renew catechesis, to adapt it to the men of our time and in this way to make it more incisive, is to be attributed to the influence of the Spirit. This fact was recognized by the catechetical synod, as the Pope reminds us in his Apostolic Exhortation: "It (the synod) saw in catechetical renewal a precious gift from the Holy Spirit to the

Church of today, a gift to which the Christian communities at all levels throughout the world are responding with a generosity and inventive dedication that win admiration."[46]

3. A Catechesis Inspired by the Spirit

The Paraclete does not confine Himself to giving life and nourishment to catechesis and to promoting catechetical renewal. His action accompanies all who are engaged in this work, so that they will bring it to conclusion with coherence and courage, according to the directives of the Bishops.

In fact, it is the Spirit of truth, present and active in the Church, who interiorly illuminates catechists, so that in the exercise of their mission they may remain indefectibly faithful to the message which they transmit. Only in this manner will the "word of faith"[47] be received by those to whom it is announced, "not in mutilated, falsified or diminished form but whole and entire, in all its rigor and vigor."[48] The hearers of the Word which saves have the full right to receive from the one who pronounces it, not only fragments of truth, but rather the *whole* truth. To betray in some respect the integrity of the message would also be, as CT notes, a dangerous emptying of catechesis itself and a compromising of the fruits that the Community expects from it.[49]

Furthermore, it is the Holy Spirit, acting in the hearts of catechists, who leads them to overcome the temptation—very strong at times, especially in certain social situations—"to mix catechetical teaching unduly with overt or masked ideological views, especially political and social ones, or with personal political options."[50] To yield to such temptations would signify: radical distortion of catechesis; forgetfulness of catechesis' transcendence of the necessarily limited and restricted horizon of the various socio-political conceptions; and lack of consideration of the reality that catechesis transcends all "messianisms" of a social and political character to reach man in his totality and in the very depths of his heart.[51]

It is again the Spirit who constitutes the foundation of the *testimonium vitae*, inseparable from evangelization and, hence, also from catechesis.[52] "This witnessing to be given to the world does not base itself on human elements of experience, of learning, of acquired knowledge, but on the power of the Holy Spirit, who helps to transmit the very witnessing of Christ, who was and remains the only faithful witness."[53] The teaching contained in these words of the then Cardinal Karol Wojtyla in the Synod of 1974 we find reaffirmed and set forth again in an authoritative form both in EN and CT.[54]

It is equally the Spirit who, in the actual context in which Catholics live always more in contact with the followers of other religions, both Christian and non-Christian, and with non-believers, makes us understand more clearly the need for catechesis to assume today a dimension truly ecumenical and missionary. Nor could it be otherwise, because it is the Holy Spirit who is at the origin both of the ecumenical movement and of the mission.

It is also the Spirit who leads the believers engaged in catechesis *to acculturate* the evangelical message—that is, to incarnate it in the various cultures of the peoples. It is the Spirit, too, who indicates to them the criteria to be followed in order that this work of rendering the Gospel indigenous will take place without the slightest alteration of the same. It is necessary that the power of the Good News be brought into the hearts of cultures, but without weakening the one or mutilating the other. Otherwise, there would no longer be true catechesis.[55]

Lastly, it is the Spirit who leads catechists to discover in the various religio-cultural traditions of the peoples the "seeds of the Word," that is, the human, moral and religious values which they contain, to consider these as many other rays of the divine Wisdom, and to use them as providential means for bringing men to Christ and to the fullness of Revelation.[56]

Here, in conclusion, is the role of the Holy Spirit in catechetical work, according to the Apostolic Exhortation *Catechesi tradendae* of John Paul II. As the fountainhead of every salvific activity of the Church, and in particular as Teacher within and inspirer of all catechetical work, He is the principal agent of the catechesis of the Church.

May the Paraclete grant to His Church, pilgrim on earth, a still greater zeal in the catechetical work which is essential to her, as is that of evangelization. Only then, the pontifical document notes, will the Church effectively fulfill, in this time of grace, the mandate received from the Lord to announce the Gospel to all nations.[57]

JOSÉ SARAIVA-MARTINS, C.M.F.

FOOTNOTES

1. Jn. 14:16.
2. Jn. 14:26.
3. Jn. 16:13.
4. Jn. 14:17; 14:26.
5. John Paul II, Apost. Exh. *Catechesi tradendae* (= CT) 72c.
6. Cf., v.g., LG 4; EN 75.
7. Cf. Mt. 4:1; Lk. 4:18-19, 21.
8. Gal. 4:6; 2 Cor. 3:17.
9. Augustine, St., *Sermo* 268,2; PL 38:1232.
10. Chrysostom, J., *In Eph., Hom.* 9,3; PG 62, 72.
11. Urs Von Balthasar, H. *Spiritus Creator,* Morcelliana, Brescia 1972, 209.
12. Cf., for example, LG 4.
13. EN 75.
14. Ibidem.
15. Cf. Rom. 8:1-27.
16. Didymus of Alexandria, *Trinit.* 2,1; PG 39:449.
17. Pius XII, Enc. Letter *Mystici Corporis,* no. 57; in AAS 35:1943, 219-220.
18. Jn. 3:5.
19. Cf. LG 4.
20. CT 5.
21. Rom. 8:14.
22. 1 Jn. 2:20, 27.
23. Augustine, *In Ioan. Evangelium tractatus,* 97; PL 35:1877; cf. CT 72c.
24. Jn. 15:26.
25. Rom. 8:15-16.
26. Gal. 4:6.
27. CT 72d.

28. Is. 11:2.
29. Rom. 8:14-17; Gal. 4:6.
30. 1 Cor. 12:3.
31. Augustine, *Tractationum lib I,* 23,2; PL 32:621.
32. CT 72e.
33. 1 Cor. 12:4-11.
34. LG 12.
35. 1 Cor. 12:4, 11.
36. 1 Cor. 12:7.
37. LG 13; cf. Acts 2:42.
38. CT 72f.
39. CT 72g.
40. CT 5 and 20.
41. CT 18.
42. CT 72g.
43. CT 72h.
44. EN 75.
45. Cf. Caprile, G., *Il Sinodo dei vescovi 1977,* Ed. La Civiltà Cat., Rome 1978, 573.
46. CT 3.
47. Rom. 10:8.
48. CT 30.
49. Ibidem.
50. CT 52.
51. Ibidem.
52. Cf. EN 21; CT 22.
53. *Relatio in qua themata quaedam theologica cum experientiis connexa clarificantur,* Typis Pol. Vat. 1974, p. 8.
54. Cf. EN 21; CT 22.
55. CT 53.
56. Ibidem.
57. CT 73.

3

Liturgical Dimension: Elements of Sacramental Catechesis

Introduction

The Apostolic Exhortation, *Catechesi tradendae*, no. 23, of Pope John Paul II is explicit on the connection between liturgy and catechesis: "Catechesis is intrinsically linked with the whole of liturgical and sacramental activity, for it is in the sacraments, especially in the Eucharist, that Christ Jesus works in fullness for the transformation of human beings." If the aim of catechesis, as CT 20 says, is to give growth to the seed of faith sown by the Holy Spirit through the initial proclamation of the gospel and effectively transmitted by baptism, it is clear that it has to be done within the framework of the liturgy. That is why CT 23 affirms that "catechesis always has reference to the sacraments." And this in two ways. First, by preparing for their celebration, or as the same CT 23 expresses it, "every form of catechesis necessarily leads to the sacraments of faith." This echoes the Constitution on the Liturgy (SC), arts. 9-11, which states that the Church must prepare the faithful for the sacraments, and lead them to "come together to praise God in the midst of His Church, to take part in the sacrifice, and to eat the Lord's Supper." In order to be enriched by the liturgical celebration, it is obviously necessary that the faithful should come with the proper disposition. Catechesis has this role of instructing the faithful in the meaning of the celebration and of imbuing them with the right spirit of the liturgy. The other way whereby catechesis is related to the liturgy is in the fact that "authentic practice of the sacraments is bound to have a catechetical aspect." Once again CT reaffirms SC, which in art. 33 speaks of the catechetical dimension of the liturgy where "God speaks to his people and Christ is still proclaiming His gospel."

Catechesis, therefore, should draw its material from the liturgical and sacramental activity of the Church. It is not enough to propose and clarify doctrinal and moral statements; it is necessary to illustrate as well how the Church lives her faith through the celebration of the liturgy. Indeed the liturgy with its proclamation of God's Word, its prayer texts and signs offers catechesis an eminent and valuable material for understanding the faith of the Church. For the liturgy celebrates and experientially expresses the faith transmitted by tradition and expounded by the Church. Hence, the liturgy is the living interpretation of what the Church received from the Apostles. Catechesis has thus to draw its didactic elements from it.

In explaining the meaning of the liturgy, especially of the sacraments, the catechist should consider primarily the liturgical texts and signs. Indeed these should be the starting point of every liturgical catechesis. Abstract theological concepts regarding the liturgy and sacraments certainly have their own value in the intellectual formation of a Christian, but the aim of catechesis can only be realized within the context of sacramental experience. It is through such an experience that the Christian enters more profoundly in contact with the mystery of Christ and the Church. The role of catechesis is to lead him to encounter this mystery through an understanding of its expressions in texts and signs. Thus true sacramental catechesis can never be a mere abstract doctrinal information, but an experiential unfolding of the faith which the liturgy celebrates. As CT 23 rightly puts it, "Sacramental life is impoverished and very soon turns into hollow ritualism if it is not based on serious knowledge of the meaning of the sacraments, and catechesis becomes intellectualized if it fails to come alive in sacramental practice."

The elements of sacramental catechesis can be classified under theological, historical and pastoral perspectives. Catechesis has to be totally in accord with sound theology; it should be supported by historical research on the authentic liturgical tradition of the Church; and it should be relevant to Christian life.

Theological Perspective of Sacramental Catechesis

The theological perspective of sacramental catechesis is to be drawn from the liturgical texts and scriptural readings for each sacramental celebration. The *Praenotanda* or Introduction of the rituals serves as guide in correctly interpreting the texts and readings and in formulating the theology of the sacraments. In other words, the right approach should not be abstract. It is not enough to take the Introduction and explain it point by point; the starting point should be the liturgical celebration itself, although within the theological framework of the Introduction.

The Order of Infant Baptism, for example, offers rich theological elements of baptismal catechesis. Already in the rite of welcoming the children the catechist can draw the ecclesial dimension of the sacrament. One has to know how to utilize the ritual. Indeed the introductory rite of receiving children for baptism intends to elicit from parents and godparents the desire to have the children baptized and their assurance that these will be brought up in the knowledge of the faith, the observance of God's commandments and the practice of Christian love.[1] Only after this desire has been expressed and the assurance elicited are the children welcomed into the Christian community. The act of welcoming is also the act of claiming the children for Christ. This is done by tracing the sign of the cross on their forehead. The words of the rite are impressive: "The Christian community welcomes you with great joy. In its name I claim you for Christ our Savior by the sign of the cross."[2] Since parents and godparents represent the community, they also trace the sign of the cross on the forehead of their children. From this rite alone the catechist can begin to develop the meaning of baptism as entry into the Christian community which the parents and godparents represent. To formulate this doctrine the catechist can then turn to the Introduction which states that children are baptized in the faith of the Church. This faith is proclaimed by parents and godparents who represent the local Church as well as the assembly of all the saints and believers, that is, the universal Church.[3]

The same procedure should be followed with regard to the other parts of the baptismal liturgy. The themes of the various Scriptural readings, the prayer formulas, especially the blessing of the baptismal water, and the allocutions should all be carefully analyzed, in order to show the different theological dimensions of baptism. For the sake of systematic exposition the catechist can refer to the Introduction, both general and particular.[4]

To give another example at random the formula of absolution in the rite of reconciliation of penitents can be cited.[5] The catechist should note that the reconciliation of penitents is the initiative of God, "the Father of mercies." This initiative He manifested through the death and resurrection of His Son. Or as the Introduction puts it, "The Father showed His mercy by reconciling the world to Himself in Christ, making peace with everything on earth and in heaven through the blood of the cross."[6] The effect of Christ's paschal mystery was the bestowal of the Holy Spirit for the forgiveness of sins, as the formula further states. In other words, in the sacrament of reconciliation the Church commemorates the mercy of the Father who reconciled man to Himself through the mediation of His Son. The seal of reconciliation is blood and its effect is the outpouring of the Holy Spirit in the heart of the reconciled person. But as the formula further insinuates, the sacrament is celebrated through the ministry of the Church who is herself holy and at the same time in constant need of purification in her members. Once again for the sake of systematic exposition the catechist should refer to the Introduction which speaks of the virtue of penance in the life and the liturgy of the Church and of the ecclesial dimension of this sacrament. The Introduction, in fact, echoes the formula of absolution when it says that "penance always brings about reconciliation with the brethren."[7] As one can observe, the text is very rich in theological doctrine: it expresses how the sacrament actualizes and makes present to the penitent that once-for-all act of reconciliation effected by Christ on the cross. It shows furthermore that reconciliation with God necessarily implies reconciliation with and in the Church. Here, therefore, the catechist touches the basic theological elements of catechesis on the sacrament of penance.

Still another example, this time on the use of scriptural readings, can be given on the sacrament of anointing of the sick. The ritual offers a choice of readings with the indication of the theme of each one. From the gospel readings the catechist can find sufficient theological material on the sacrament. For these readings express the concern Jesus had for the sick: indeed, He took our own infirmities upon Himself. They also speak of the command of Christ to His disciples to continue His work of healing the total person in body and spirit through this sacrament. And they indicate the response of faith and the spirit of gratitude the sick person should assume. Finally the gospel readings exhort the sick and the whole assembly to be vigilant through prayer and good work.[8] These theological thoughts can be corroborated by the systematic exposition of the meaning of human sickness, especially in the context of Salvation History, as developed in nos. 1-4 of the Introduction.

It should be kept in mind that in the liturgy the Church proclaims the Word of God according to a theological perspective which is in consonance with patristic and liturgical tradition. Thus, the readings indicated by the ritual should be interpreted in the context of sacramental celebration. Indeed as SC 23 has affirmed, "in the liturgy God speaks to His people and Christ is still proclaiming His gospel." The Word of God in the liturgy has a sacramental character, that is, it is an audible sign (for it is proclaimed) of God's presence among His people. In the sacrament of the anointing of the sick the Word of God assumes a special reference to the relationship of Christ and His Church with the sick person. The same principle can be applied to other sacramental celebrations. Hence, catechesis should not overlook the role of God's Word in sacramental life, and consequently in sacramental catechesis.[9]

Historical Perspective of Sacramental Catechesis

Sacramental catechesis does not deal with texts and readings alone, but also with signs and symbols. These express the interior meaning of sacraments. They manifest visibly the presence of Christ and His mystery to the celebrating community or its response to God's initiative. In sacramental celebrations signs may belong to the very nature of the sacrament itself, like water, bread and wine, oil, laying on of hands. These are the elements around which the sacramental action revolves. Or they may serve as illustration of the sacrament, as in the case of the explanatory rites.[10] As illustration liturgical signs may often take the quality of symbol. Thus, lighted candles symbolize the faith which the newly baptized are to keep burning through their lives. But if signs constitute the external form of the sacraments themselves, they belong strictly to the category of sacramental signs, that is to say, visible signs of God's presence among His people. The Fathers of the Church, basing themselves on liturgical theology, speak of the presence of the Holy Spirit in baptismal water, as we would speak of the real presence of Christ in His Word that is proclaimed in the liturgical assembly. Thus it is imperative that catechesis take signs and symbols into account, for these belong to either the nature or the integrity of sacramental celebrations.

Signs and symbols, however, have to be treated within the framework of sacramental celebrations. This means that they should be explained from the perspective of the text that accompanies them. For in the liturgy the signs are usually clarified by words. In the case of the explanatory rites of baptism, for example, the post-baptismal anointing with chrism is explained by the accompanying formula as the incorporation of the baptized into the priestly, prophetic and kingly office of Christ. The white vestment, on the other hand, is "the sign of the dignity" of Christians, a dignity to be kept immaculate unto eternal life.[11] Thus, the liturgy itself offers, in these and several other cases, the meaning of the signs and symbols it uses.

But to understand more fully the meaning of these signs, it is important to view them from the perspective of historical development. Especially in the missions or in cultures which have no Greco-Roman influence, questions will necessarily arise regarding the use of such signs. The Greco-Roman culture has a very pronounced influence on the Roman liturgy, just as the Jewish has on the entire Christian form of worship. Why water for baptism? Why oil for the sick? Why the laying on of hands? Or why bread and wine for the Eucharist? All these questions require answers that are based on a good knowledge of biblical tradition. On the other hand, why the oil of catechumens, the use of white vestments, or the marriage ring? These have to be answered from the cultural perspective of ancient Greece and Rome.[12]

For a people, therefore, that does not in any way associate such elements with their own culture, the catechist will have to have recourse to history. Where water, for example, is not linked with the concept of initiation rite, the catechist has to invoke the biblical culture in which it originated. In the case of bread and wine a historical background of the paschal meal of the Jews is necessary. White vestment in baptism has to be explained from the contact of the Church at the time of Constantine with the initiation practice of Mithraic religion or of Roman citizens' use of white clothes to express their dignity. In many cultures white is not necessarily the color that signifies dignity.

In a number of cases, however, the liturgical text itself does not provide a clear explanation of the meaning of signs and symbols. Thus, the formula for the commingling of eucharistic bread and wine after the breaking of the bread offers no cue as to the real meaning of the rite. All it says is that the commingling of the Body and Blood of the Lord brings everlasting life to those who receive them. In this particular case only history can enlighten the catechist. Originally it was the rite performed by priests in the Roman parishes with the particle of consecrated host from the papal Mass. It expressed the unity of parish Eucharist with the bishop's.[13] Although the bishop no longer sends the particle or *fermentum* to parishes, the rite of commingling is still done, and should still be explained as a sign, even if less expressive than before because the particle is taken from the priest's host. As sign it means the assembly's eucharistic communion with the local Church presided over by the bishop. The catechist should avoid any mystical interpretation, such as the resurrection of Christ. Such an explanation is facile and may be even attractive to people, but it is not coherent with theology and liturgical tradition.

Even in some cases where the liturgical text offers a clear interpretation, history can be very useful for a deeper appreciation of signs. For example, the washing of hands at the preparation of eucharistic gifts is explained as the desire for interior purification before the eucharistic prayer.[14] The prayer that accompanies this rite clearly expresses it. But we know from history that the Roman Mass did not give it such a symbolic meaning, but considered it rather as a hygienic practice after the celebrant received the eucharistic gifts from the people. With this added historical perspective the washing of hands can be done more truthfully rather than merely symbolically, by a true washing of hands, complete with soap and towel, not only of the priest but also of the other ministers, especially those who distribute holy Communion.

It is especially in the case of liturgical signs and symbols that the catechist should beware of easy mystical interpretation. He should, first of all, take the accompanying liturgical formula into account, and if possible, also the historical and traditional background of the rite. In a number of cases the liturgical text alone will not suffice to clarify the meaning of signs and symbols.

16. *Going, Teach....*

Recourse to history is thus imperative. The historical perspective can even enrich the meaning of the rite by inducing a more truthful sign. Liturgy should not be satisfied with token symbols. But a mystical interpretation can prove dangerous, since it can distort the meaning of the sign and eventually of the sacrament itself.

Pastoral Perspective
of Sacramental Catechesis

Sacramental catechesis has also its pastoral aspect. This means that its language should be adapted to the circumstances of the listeners. The method used by the Fathers of the Church in their mystagogical catechesis can be considered as an excellent example of a catechesis within the reach of the people. The meaning of the celebration and its elements were explained in simple words and illustrated with many examples taken from Scripture and the culture of the period.

But an effective pastoral approach to sacramental catechesis is possible only if the listeners have had an experience of the sacrament being discussed, either as the recipient themselves or as witnesses. In both cases they should be provided with model celebrations which can serve as meaningful experiences and hence as point of reference in the catechetical instruction. To explain signs, symbols and texts to one who never saw nor heard them before will have little or no benefit. And, pastorally speaking, the sacramental catechesis based on a poorly prepared and clumsily performed celebration is bound to cause a loss of interest for the sacrament itself. In other words, catechesis on sacraments requires an experience of model celebrations in order to be effective. Exemplary liturgy is the task of the entire community, but especially of the ministers and catechists themselves. It will be an easier and more fruitful endeavor for the catechist to explain the meaning of baptism as initiation into the Christian community, if there is really a community present at baptism. Catechesis on the reception of children at baptism can assume a truly and authentically human dimension, if there is warmth and a sense of hospitality on the part of the ministers towards the child and its parents and godparents.[15]

Pastoral approach, however, should not be limited to practical points. It should also enrich the spiritual life of the listeners by offering them insights which will nourish their faith. Once again it is necessary to turn to the example of the Fathers of the Church who always drew food for the heart and spirit from sacramental celebrations. Suffice it to cite here a very moving and spiritually rich address of Ambrose of Milan to his neophytes, as he explained to them the meaning of baptismal immersion: "Just as Christ died, so you also taste of death; just as Christ died to sin and lives unto God, so you too died to the former allurements of sins through the sacrament of baptism and rose again through the grace of Christ. So death is, but not in the reality of corporal death but in likeness. For when you dip, you take on the likeness of death and burial, you receive the sacrament of that cross, because Christ hung on the cross and His body was transfixed with nails. You then are crucified with Him; you cling to Christ, you cling to the nails of our Lord Jesus Christ, lest the devil be able to take you from Him."[16]

In this text the catechist will note that Ambrose began his talk by recalling the experience of baptismal immersion and explaining its meaning as burial and resurrection with Christ. Then he shifted his attention to the spiritual consequences of baptism as death to sin, as being nailed with Christ on the cross and remaining faithful to that cross; otherwise, the neophyte could be won over by the devil. In very moving language Ambrose told the neophyte that fidelity to Christ implied fidelity to the cross by never abandoning it but ever staying nailed to it. As one can see, sacramental catechesis among the Fathers of the Church was not mere instruction on the faith by communicating doctrinal information. The catechist played the role of a spiritual father who helped form the heart and mind of the listeners according to the values of Christianity.

Besides the practical and spiritual aspects of sacramental catechesis, there is also the liturgical dimension which lays down certain catechetical principles. Sacramental catechesis should center on the essential elements of the celebration rather than on other elements which may be interesting but have only a secondary value in the celebration. Often the faithful are carried away by the more dramatic, though unessential, ceremonies, and completely ignore the basic and essential elements of the celebration.

Thus, sacramental catechesis on holy orders should not ignore the gesture of laying on of hands by the bishop on the head of the candidate and the prayer immediately following it. These are, in fact, the primary elements of the ordination rite and hence should be the starting point of catechesis. All other signs and symbols should revolve around the primary elements. The simplicity of the essential signs often result in lack of proper appreciation; the catechist should underline such a simplicity and lead the faithful to see solemnity even in simplicity. Thus, the dramatic prostration of the candidate should be viewed within the context of the essential laying on of hands and the prayer of ordination.

In this connection it should be remembered that explanatory rites revolve around the essential rite; they explain or illustrate these, and exist in view of explicitating through signs and words what the essential element only implicitly contains. It should be noted that basic sacramental signs are usually simple and direct. What could be simpler than water, bread, wine, oil, laying on of hands? What could be simpler than immersion or infusion? And yet these are the signs of God's presence in the Church. Tertullian already criticized the complexity of pagan rituals and praised the simplicity of Christian baptism: "With so great simplicity, without pomp, without any considerable novelty of preparation, finally without expense, a man is dipped in water and washed amid the utterance of some few words."[17] Sacramental catechesis should be able to discern what is essential from what is explanatory. The right catechetical approach to the sacraments is, therefore, necessarily liturgical.

Such a liturgical approach should be applied to all other sacraments. The catechist should be sufficiently trained and formed in the knowledge of sacramental celebrations, so that he can distinguish the center of the sacramental action. He should be aware, for example, that introductory rites have a preparatory character and should not be given excessive attention. Explanatory rites, on the other hand, flow from the essential and should consequently be made to refer back to it. Although the introductory and explanatory rites may be more impressive, colorful and dramatic than the essential rite itself, they have an accessory character and exist within the framework of the more simple, less colorful and less dramatic but essential rite of the celebration.

Conclusion

In this study on the relationship between catechesis and the sacraments, we have stressed some very important aspects of catechesis. The catechist should, following the appeal of the papal exhortation, *Catechesi tradendae*, seriously consider the nature and consequences of such a relationship. To conclude we can indicate some practical considerations.

1. Catechesis is essentially related to the liturgical and sacramental activity of the Church. It should lead to the sacraments and draw its material from them. And when one speaks of liturgy and sacraments, one has to keep in mind that they are primarily celebrations, rather than abstract concepts. Hence, sacramental catechesis must be done strictly within the framework of the celebration, of its texts and scriptural readings, of its gestures, signs and symbols. To aid the catechist in correctly interpreting these liturgical elements the rituals usually offer a systematic exposition of the meaning of the celebration in the Introduction.

2. Sacramental catechesis has three perspectives: theological, historical and pastoral. The catechist has to be, in his own way, a theologian who is able to transmit to his particular group of listeners sound theological reflections on sacramental life. He has to know sufficiently well the historical background and the tradition of sacramental signs and symbols. And he has to have a pastoral spirit whereby, like a spiritual father, he can lead his listeners to a more profound appreciation of the sacraments. For the catechist does not only give information; he also helps the Church in forming the heart and mind of the faithful.

3. Sacramental catechesis is, therefore, a most delicate task which requires considerable preparation on the part of catechists. It is not without serious reason that *Catechesi tradendae* insists on the formation of catechists. And it is not without reason that Vatican II has encouraged serious study of the liturgy under its theological, historical and pastoral aspects. Indeed, because of the task of catechists in the sacramental life of the Church, it is imperative that they should be formed according to the authentic liturgical spirit, that they should return to the sources of liturgical life and tradition, and that they should have a deep spiritual life based on the liturgy of the Church.

ANSCAR J. CHUPUNGCO, O.S.B.

FOOTNOTES

1. *Ordo Baptismi Parvulorum* (OBP), ed. typ. altera, no. 39. Cf. B. Neunheuser: *Baptism and Confirmation*, New York (1964); J. P. Schanz: *The Sacraments of Life and Worship*, London (1967); J. D. Crichton: *Christian Celebration: The Sacraments*, New York (1976).

2. *OBP*, 41. The text cited above is the translation of ICEL.

3. *OBP*, Praenotanda 2.

4. *OBP*, Praen. Gen. 3-6.

5. *Ordo Paenitentiae* (OP), ed. typica, no. 46. Cf. B. Poschmann: *Penance and the Anointing of the Sick*, New York (1964); C. Vogel: *Il peccatore e la penitenza nella Chiesa antica*, Turin (1967); J. Ramos-Regidor: *Il Sacramento della Penitenza*, Turin (1970).

6. *OP*, Praenotanda, 1.

7. *Id.* 5.

8. *Ordo Unctionis Infirmorum eorumque Pastoralis Curae* (OUI), ed. typica, nos. 204-99; cf. C. Ortemann: *Il Sacramento degli infermi*, Turin (1971); AAVV: *Il Sacramento dei malati*, Turin (1975).

9. Cf. A. Verheul: *Introduction to the Liturgy*, London (1968) 149-72; see also the treatise of S. Marsili in *Anamnesis I*, Casale (1974) 101-02.

10. Cf. A. Martimort, "Les Signes," *L'Eglise en prière*, Paris (1961) 150-83.

11. *OBP* 62, 63. Cf. A. Chupungco, "Greco-Roman Culture and Liturgical Adaptation," *Notitiae* 153 (1979) 202-18.

12. See: A. Martimort, *l'Eglise en prière*, op. cit.; J. Danielou, *Bible et Liturgie*, Paris (1960); J. Jungmann, *The Early Liturgy*, trans. F. Brunner, London (1966); for quick reference, see also the *Dictionnaire d'Archéologie chrétienne et Liturgie* (DACL), ed. F. Cabrol and H. Leclercq, from 1907-53 in 30 volumes.

13. J. Jungmann, *Missarum Solemnia*, trans. F. Brunner, New York (1959) 475-79).

14. *Inst. Gen. Missalis Romani*, no. 52; J. Jungmann, *Missarum Solemnia*, op. cit. pp. 349-52.

15. See: *OBP* 75 which exhorts priests to greet the parents and godparents before the celebration of baptism in order to show the human dimension of the celebration. The possibility of using one's own words during allocutions also makes it clear to priests that there is a human angle in the liturgy which should be taken into account.

16. *De Sacramentis II*, 7, ed. B. Botte, *SCh* 25bis (1961).

17. *De Baptismo*, ed. R. Refoulé, *SCh* 35 (1952).

4

Spiritual Dimension: Marian and Missionary Attitude

"Mary, Mother and Model of the Disciple"

1. Introduction: Marian and Missionary Attitude in Catechesis

The last part of the Apostolic Exhortation *Catechesi tradendae* is a resumé of the *interior attitudes* which form the basis of the *spirituality of catechesis,* that is, of the Marian and ecclesial attitudes of listening to the Word of God, under the action of the Holy Spirit, that are necessary to allow Jesus to be born and grow in every Christian. In this context, Mary is the Virgin of Nazareth and of Pentecost (73).

Mary collaborated in the growth of Jesus at Nazareth; it was a growth "in wisdom and in stature, and in favor" (Lk. 2:52). Jesus "was formed by her in human knowledge of the Scriptures and of the history of God's plan for His people, and in adoration of the Father" (CT 73). At the same time, Mary received everything from Jesus; therefore, she "was the first of His disciples" in her attitude of contemplating the lessons that she kept in her heart (cf. Lk. 2:51). Mary was, therefore, "both mother and disciple" (St. Augustine, *Sermo* 25, 7, cited in CT 73, note 137).

This attitude of listening, of answering and of collaborating causes Mary to become "a living catechism" and the "mother and model of catechists" (CT 73). Hers is precisely the attitude which constitutes the prophetic and missionary nature of the Church.

With the presence, affection, example and intercession of Mary, the Church becomes faithful to "the catechetical work that is essential for her," and in this manner, the Church "will effectively carry out, at this moment of grace, her inalienable and universal mission, the mission given her by her Teacher: 'Go...and make disciples of all nations' (Mt. 28:19)" (CT 73).

The marian and ecclesial attitude of listening to the Word, following the inspirations of the Holy Spirit, constitutes the whole process of *Christian perfection* and embraces the entire dynamic of *apostolic action*. This attitude of fidelity becomes maternity: it allows Jesus to be born in the spiritual and apostolic life. The maternity of Mary and of the Church intersect; they need one another (LG 63-65).

As a consequence of this marian and ecclesial reality, the apostle, especially the one dedicated to the prophetic service of catechesis, must possess an apostolic zeal in order to be qualified for "maternal love": "The Virgin in her own life lived an example of that maternal love, by which it behooves that all should be animated who cooperate in the apostolic mission of the Church for the regeneration of men" (LG 65). In this marian and ecclesial attitude of the apostle all the spirituality of catechesis is summed up.

In this perspective, the "follow me" of Jesus, calling one to be with Him and to evangelize, acquires the marian accent of "behold, your Mother" (Jn. 19:27). At the same time, Mary receives the mission of continuing as Mother to form Christ in the apostle: "behold, your son" (Jn. 19:26).

Through this fidelity to the Word of God, in the process of sanctification and in prophetic and catechetical service, the two maternities, that of Mary and that of the Church, unite and manifest themselves in one sole attitude: " 'Who are my mother and my brethren?' And looking around on those who sat about him, he said: 'Here are my mother and my brethren. Whoever does the will of God is my brother, and sister, and mother' " (Mk. 3:33-35); "My mother and my brethren are those who hear the word of God and do it" (Lk. 8:21).

2. From the Annunciation to Pentecost

The basic attitudes of the Virgin Mary, which are the model of the Church's prophetic and catechetical attitudes, appear clearly throughout the period of Jesus' infancy (Lk.1:29; 2:19; 2:50-51), beginning from the Annunciation.

These attitudes constitute a "yes" to the Word of God, a yes which indicates total openness, contemplation and a transparency of life that allows Christ to shine through in the sight of everyone. This marian attitude of "annunciation" stands out in the key moments of the life of Mary, that is, at Cana and beneath the Cross.

With this attitude of fidelity, of contemplation and of mission, Mary enters actively into the mystery of the "hour" of Jesus (Jn. 2:4; 13:1); this "hour" will occur when the Lord communicates the Holy Spirit as the fruit of His death and resurrection (Jn. 7:39; 19:34; 20:22).

Through this attitude of "yes" to the Word of God, under the action of the Holy Spirit, Mary becomes the personification, model and type of the Church, which begins this same maternal process at Pentecost. Therefore, the presence of Mary among the apostles, while waiting for the coming of the Holy Spirit, is a salvific and permanent reality. Mary is "the Virgin of Pentecost" (CT 73).

Every historical era of the Church is a new Pentecost in which we find *Mary always present.*

Today the Church feels herself in "a privileged moment of the Spirit" (EN 75). We are living in "a time particularly hungry for the Spirit" (RH 18). In the field of catechesis, the catechetical renewal is a precious gift of the Holy Spirit to the contemporary Church (cf. CT 72).

The spirituality of catechesis, therefore, draws inspiration from the active presence of Mary, from the Virgin of Pentecost, who helps the Church to become mother in receiving the Word of God under the action of the Holy Spirit, with an attitude of contemplation, of discernment and of fidelity. The Church feels herself a mother, especially through catechetical and evangelizing activity. It is precisely because of this that she "has need of a Mother" (RH 22).

The interior attitude or spirituality of the catechist is, therefore, an attitude of response, which manifests itself in convictions and decisions similar to the "yes" of Mary: humanity began its return to God from the moment of the Madonna's "fiat" *(Marialis cultus,* no. 28).

So that the renewal of Pentecost in catechetical and evangelizing activity may be a reality, it is necessary to make a pledge to imitate the "yes" of Mary in the Annunciation. Ecclesial, conciliar and postconciliar texts often place the Annunciation and

Pentecost in relation to each other to make us see the vital rapport between Mary and the Church in every moment of the Church's history (LG 59; AG 4; EN 82; RH 22).

3. Marian and Ecclesial Maternity

The maternal action of Mary cannot be restricted only to the time of generating, carrying in the womb, and giving birth to Jesus. Mary being "virgin in body and in spirit" (according to patristic affirmation), remains associated to Jesus in a continual and permanent process of maternity in respect to the Mystical Jesus.

In His infancy Jesus was to some degree dependent upon Mary: "As He sat on her lap and later as He listened to her throughout the hidden life at Nazareth, this Son, who was 'the only Son from the Father,' 'full of grace and truth,' was formed by her in human knowledge of the Scriptures and of the history of God's plan for His people, and in adoration of the Father" (CT 73).

This maternal action of Mary continues in the Church: "This maternity of Mary in the order of grace began with the consent which she gave in faith at the Annunciation and which she sustained without wavering beneath the cross, and lasts until the eternal fulfillment of all the elect" (LG 62). However, this marian maternity is also ecclesial at the same time: "Mary and the Church are one mother and many mothers.... Both are mothers of Christ; however neither gives birth without the other" (Bl. Isaac da Stella, sermon 51).

Ecclesial maternity is expressed through ministerial signs, among which emerges the service of the Word: "The Church indeed, contemplating her (Mary's) hidden sanctity, imitating her charity and faithfully fulfilling the Father's will, by receiving the word of God in faith becomes herself a mother. By her preaching she brings forth to a new and immortal life the sons who are born to her in baptism, conceived of the Holy Spirit and born of God" (LG 64).

There is a particular fact that is common both to marian and to ecclesial maternity: Annunciation of the Word and evangelization are generally accompanied by *suffering*. It is precisely here that we find the heart of ecclesial maternity, which transforms suffering into love and, consequently, into apostolic fruitfulness.

This is why Jesus compares the apostles to a mother who suffers to give birth to a son (Jn. 16:20-22). The grain of wheat—and also the preacher and the catechist—must "die" in the furrow to be able to produce much fruit (Jn. 12:24).

St. Paul manifests himself in this evangelizing and prophetic process, which is the process of ecclesial maternity: "My dear children, with whom I am in labor again, until Christ is formed in you!" (Gal. 4:19). This Pauline affirmation is made in the frame or context of marian maternity (Gal. 4:4) and of ecclesial maternity (Gal. 4:26).

The evangelizing zeal of the catechist, therefore, has the characteristic of maternal love, which reflects, at the same time, the maternity of Mary and of the Church: "What is this love? It is much more than that of a teacher; it is the love of a father; and again, it is the love of a mother. It is this love that the Lord expects from every preacher of the Gospel, from every builder of the Church" (EN 79).

When the Church follows the example of Mary, she becomes mother like her: "Making herself day after day a disciple of the Lord, she earned the title of 'Mother and Teacher' " (CT 12). "The Church is 'mother' because by baptism she unceasingly begets new children and increases God's family; she is 'teacher' because she makes her children grow in the grace of their baptism by nourishing their *sensus fidei* through instruction in the truths of faith" (CT note 40, citing *Mater et Magistra* of John XXIII).

By means of catechesis and evangelization in general, this missionary and ecclesial maternity leads through moments of suffering toward the joy of fruitfulness. Then the apostle or catechist presents the joy of the Good News or of Christian hope, which rests on the Risen Christ, who is present. It is "the delightful and comforting joy of evangelizing, even when it is in tears that we must sow" (EN 80). It is the "paschal joy" which today's world needs to see in the evangelizers, who cannot reflect sadness, discouragement or doubt, but must rather reflect "the joy of Christ" (*ibid.*).

The catechetical action of the Church "contributes" to spreading "among the communities the joy of bringing the mystery of Christ to the world" (CT 4). Every apostle and every community, precisely by becoming involved in the work of evangelization, sense the fact that they are mother Church, like Mary and with Mary's help. It is a maternity without boundaries. If boundaries are erected in the horizons of the community, the ecclesial maternity cannot be missionary and hence cannot even be maternity. The "total Christ" (His Mystical Body) must embrace all mankind, in order to avoid becoming a "ghetto."

4. Contemplation of the Word

Mary influenced the formation of Jesus and meanwhile she was the "first of His disciples" (CT 73). She was the first to believe (Lk. 1:45), but also the one who opened to the disciples the path of faith in Jesus (Jn. 2:11). Therefore, in regard to faith, she was the first in time, the first in depth, and the first in representation. In her, from the moment of the Annunciation, the Church had already said "yes" to the fullness of God's saving plans in Jesus Christ.

Like Mary, the Church is "the great giver as well as the great receiver of catechesis" (CT 45). The Church, which by her very nature is an evangelizer, "begins by being evangelized herself... by constant conversion and renewal, in order to evangelize the world with credibility" (EN 15).

Mary becomes the disciple of Christ, who is the personal Word of God, by means of a process of *contemplation* of this same Word, because "she received from Him lessons that she kept in her heart" (CT 73).

The contemplative attitude in regard to the Word is a painful process of entering into the cloud of *faith* (Lk. 1:29), of *adoring* the saving plans of God (Lk. 2:19), of lovingly *admiring* these plans to the point of incurring the same lot as "spouse" of Christ (Lk. 2:33-35). This means *hiding ourselves* in Christ, in His mystery of the redeeming and liberating incarnation and also in the "Nazareth" of ordinary life, which becomes a continual immolation (Lk. 2:48-51).

The in-depth formation of the evangelizer and of the catechist is a slow process which transcends ordinary intellectual and moral formation. It treats precisely of attuning ourselves to the criteria of Christ, to His scale of values and to His attitudes of decision and of action.

The process of catechizing is a process of faith (to think as Jesus thinks), of hope (to give things the same value that He gives them), of charity (to love as He loves).

The action of the Holy Spirit causes the evangelizer and the evangelized to enter always more into the interior of the mystery of Christ by means of a progressive communication of gifts and of charisms, which arouses and demands an attitude of adoration of the Word of God, of admiration and of silence, of fullness and of friendship in Christ.

It is from this contemplative attitude that the apostolic zeal of St. Francis of Assisi, of St. Francis Xavier or of St. Thérèse of Lisieux springs forth. One feels the need of "loving and making Love loved," of "becoming love in the heart of the Church" (St. Thérèse of Lisieux).

Through contemplation, which is a relationship of friendship with and simple affection for God, one arrives at the vital conviction that "love is not loved" (St. Francis of Assisi). From this is born untiring zeal, which is at once respect and dialogue.

The catechist who has learned to listen to God in the painful and joyful process of contemplation also knows how to listen to every brother without impatience. The capability of contemplative silence becomes the capability of listening to the voice of God in the heart of every culture, of every people, and of every person. Then one hears the strong and perturbing call to be evangelized which is born from the most intimate depths of every situation and of every human heart.

Announced by the catechist, the Word of God first of all engraves itself in the announcer himself, molding him by means of a process of configuration with Christ. Mary received this Word with a total openness which made her become the Mother and transmitter par excellence of this same Word. This marian and ecclesial process of openness to the Word is awareness of one's own "poverty"—"he has regarded the low estate of his handmaiden" (Lk. 1:48)—but at the same time, of his own election to communicate this Word to others—"he who is mighty has done great things for me" (Lk. 1:49).

The Word of God transcends our poor reflections and explanations. It is infinite and efficacious in itself, even if it acts by means of the apostle, a "living instrument."

The contemplative attitude helps the catechist not to manipulate the Word, nor to use it for his own interests nor for the excessive support of his own "opinions." Therefore, the catechist continually reflects on the doctrine of the Church, on the liturgy and on the lives of the saints, who are the most authentic commentary of the Word contained in Scripture and in Tradition and taught by the Church. This humility of the contemplative apostle becomes authenticity and lets Jesus shine through.

5. Letting the Word Shine

Mary is "a living catechism" (CT 73). She is not only the *continual* transparency of Christ because she does not retain anything for herself, but she is also the transparency of the *entire* mystery of the Lord.

Taken together, the marian titles and feasts constitute a resumé of the history of salvation and of the message of Jesus Christ; in fact, they show forth the various aspects of the paschal mystery or of the victory of the risen Jesus over sin (Immaculate Conception) and over death (Assumption). The virginity and divine maternity of Mary indicate the divinity and humanity of Jesus the Redeemer. What God has worked in her is the type of that configuration with Christ to which all humanity tends.

In a few marian images or pictures we find a catechetical synthesis which embraces all dogmatic and moral teaching, together with the sacramental life. Two examples are the Madonna of Guadalupe (Mexico) and the Madonna of Ambato (Equador). Through careful analysis, it may be noted that, when the initial evangelization of a people is made with a marian catechetical perspective (Latin America, southeastern India, southern Japan, etc.), Christianity reaches the heart of the people and remains permanently within it throughout the subsequent centuries.

Mary is the transparency of Jesus; therefore, she is the instrument of the epiphany of the Word made man for John the Baptist (Lk. 1:41-44) and for the disciples (Jn. 2:11). This salvific reality is maternal (Jn. 19:25-27) and permanent throughout the history of the Church (Acts 1:14; Rev. 12:1).

The Church looks at Mary as "the living catechism," so that she herself may also become *like* and *with* Mary, a transparency of Jesus Christ for all peoples. This presupposes an evangelizing action of announcement, of witnessing and of donation. *Announcement* means communicating the Word of God, the Word made our brother, as He is in His entirety, to all peoples, to every person in his own circumstances and with his concrete problems. *Witnessing* presupposes the effort of fidelity to the Word translated into sanctity and works of charity. *Donation* means not only communication of words and of things, but also dedication of the person, as was the maternal donation of Mary at the cross: "grieving exceedingly with her only begotten Son, uniting herself with a maternal heart with His sacrifice, and lovingly consenting to the immolation of this Victim which she herself had brought forth. Finally, she was given by the same Christ Jesus dying on the cross as a mother to His disciple..." (LG 58).

This transparency is the evangelizing mission accomplished mainly through catechesis or the vital and binding announcement of the Word. Therefore, the spirituality of catechesis has a significance of totality, because it conditions the person with all that he is and all that he has.

The preaching of the message "merits having the apostle consecrate to it all his time and all his energies, and to sacrifice for it, if necessary, his own life" (EN 5). From this attitude of dedication, "courage, hope and enthusiasm" spring forth (CT 62). Then the catechist, as a member of the Church, places himself *"in statu missionis"* (RH 20).

6. Mother and Model of the Catechist

In 1977 the synod fathers gave Mary the title which Pope John Paul II cites in *Catechesi tradendae* (73): "mother and model of catechists."

Mary is model because she collaborated in the formation of Jesus and because she is the first of His disciples, as has already been emphasized.

Mary is *mother* of catechists because every person is entrusted to Mary according to his own charism and vocation. In the case of the catechist, the words of Jesus, "behold, your son" (Jn. 19:26) signify that Mary exercises her maternity also with regard to this disciple who has received the duty of following Christ and of announcing the Gospel.

In Mary we find the basic attitude of the catechist, which is that of pointing out Christ as the goal: "Do whatever he tells you" (Jn. 2:5). And this is also the attitude of the Precursor: "He must increase, but I must decrease" (Jn. 3:30).

It would be an error with unforeseeable consequences to make catechesis consist only in the teaching of a culture or of an ideology. Human ideas and culture are channels and means, but they are not the message of Jesus.

Catechesis must be centered in the very person of Jesus, Son of God and our brother, who died and rose, is present among us, and calls us to encounter and configuration with Himself through a process of conversion and of "Baptism."

Consequently, "the definitive aim of catechesis is to put people not only in touch but in communion, in intimacy, with Jesus Christ" (CT 5). To catechize also means to teach how to dialogue with God. Christian truths, which are assimilated in the dialogue of prayer, remain rooted in the most profound of convictions.

The interest of the catechist and evangelizer is not to form disciples who are enthusiastic about an "idea," but rather to form followers of Jesus, of His person and of His message or doctrine, to the point that they truly live of Him, "in spirit and truth" (Jn. 4:23), in a style of new life which is being born "of water and the Spirit" (Jn. 3:5). "It is in fact a matter of giving growth, at the level of knowledge and in life, to the seed of faith sown by the Holy Spirit with the initial proclamation and effectively transmitted by Baptism" (CT 20).

In this profound formation of the catechist, Mary's role is indispensable. Her maternal love becomes attention, intercession, stimulus, encouragement and presence. The simple, humble and unshakeable faith of Mary must also throb in the heart of the catechist. Therefore, it is not only a matter of learning or of pedagogical and intellectual formation, but also principally of a formation of "interior attitudes" (EN 74): fidelity to the Holy Spirit, authenticity or experience of God, ecclesial communion, devotion to the truth, apostolic zeal, detachment, joy.... Therefore, "the most valuable gift that the Church can offer to the bewildered and restless world of our time is to form within it Christians who are confirmed in what is essential and who are humbly joyful in their faith" (CT 61).

7. Conclusion: Missionary Dimension of the Marian Attitude of the Catechist

The conclusion of *Catechesi tradendae* (no. 73) makes us live Pentecost anew, with the presence of Mary, for an evangelization without frontiers: "May the presence of the Holy Spirit, through the prayers of Mary, grant the Church unprecedented enthusiasm in the catechetical work that is essential for her!"

This invitation is similar to that of Paul VI in *Evangelii nuntiandi* (no. 82): "On the morning of Pentecost she watched over with her prayer the beginning of evangelization prompted by the Holy Spirit: may she be the Star of the evangelization ever renewed which the Church, docile to her Lord's command, must promote and accomplish, especially in these times which are difficult but full of hope!"

This is also the invitation which John Paul II made in his first encyclical *Redemptor hominis* (no. 22): "Accordingly, as I end this meditation with a warm and humble call to prayer, I wish the Church to devote herself to this prayer, together with Mary the Mother of Jesus, as the apostles and disciples of the Lord did in the Upper Room in Jerusalem after His ascension. Above all, I implore Mary, the heavenly Mother of the Church, to be so good as to devote herself to this prayer of humanity's new advent, together with us who make up the Church, that is to say, the Mystical Body of her only Son. I hope that through this prayer we shall be able to receive the Holy Spirit coming upon us and thus become Christ's witnesses 'to the end of the earth,' like those who went forth from the Upper Room in Jerusalem on the day of Pentecost."

The spirituality of catechesis is a marian and ecclesial attitude of a prayerful and committed fidelity toward the new graces of the Holy Spirit, according to the different epochs of the progress of evangelization. In this ecclesial progress, Mary is "a great sign" (Rev. 12:1) which points to eternity.

In effect, the Word or message announced by the catechist is only an anticipation of the vision and possession, which will be a reality only in the definitive encounter with Christ. Mary, as Type and Mother of the Church, has already reached the goal; now with her presence she sustains the hope and eschatological tension of the Church; but this hope has its source in Christ, the Lamb immolated and present in the Eucharist.

Catechetical service is part of the "sacramentality" of the Church, which is the "universal sacrament of salvation" (AG 1). This prophetic service leads to the Eucharistic and sacramental celebration of the mystery of the Christ who is announced and to a personal and communitarian obligation. Thus, the maternity of the Church becomes a reality in every human community through the "implantation" or building up of the Church, establishing the permanent signs of the presence and of the action of the risen Jesus.

The spirituality of catechesis is, therefore, availability without frontiers, because catechesis must be "open to missionary dynamism" (CT 24).

The apostle called to this catechetical service is inserted into the reality of the maternity of the Church, which, as Mary and in union with Mary, is permanent and universal: "This maternity of Mary in the order of grace began with the consent which she gave in faith at the Annunciation and which she sustained without wavering beneath the cross, and lasts until the eternal fulfillment of all the elect. Taken up to heaven she did not lay aside this salvific duty, but by her constant intercession continued to bring us the gifts of eternal salvation. By her maternal charity, she cares for the brethren of her Son, who still journey on earth surrounded by dangers and difficulties, until they are led into the happiness of their true home" (LG 62).

Through catechetical and sacramental action, the Church remains united to this maternal action of Mary: "The Church ...becomes herself a Mother. By her preaching she brings forth to a new and immortal life the sons who are born to her in baptism, conceived of the Holy Spirit and born of God" (LG 64).

The spirituality of the catechist can, therefore, be summed up in these attitudes of fidelity (virginity) and of instrumentality (maternity) which characterize Mary and the Church: "Hence the Church, in her apostolic work also, justly looks to her, who, conceived of the Holy Spirit, brought forth Christ, who was born of the Virgin that through the Church He may be born and may increase in the hearts of the faithful also" (LG 65).

If this marian and ecclesial spirituality of catechesis becomes a reality, the Church thus will "effectively carry out, at this moment of grace, her inalienable and universal mission, the mission given her by her Teacher: 'Go therefore and make disciples of all nations' (Mt. 28:19)" (CT 73). This missionary mandate of Jesus is united with the "follow me" of the vocation and with the invitation extended from the cross: "Behold, your Mother" (Jn. 19:27).

The evangelizing catechist imitates the disciple "whom Jesus loved" (Jn. 13:23), by listening to the sentiments of the Word made man and by becoming His friend. Of this reality, Mary is the most perfect model: "Here are my mother and my brethren!

Whoever does the will of God is my brother, and sister, and mother" (Mk. 3:34-35). The spirituality of catechesis is, therefore, the marian attitude of listening to the Word of God and of giving a concrete response in the spiritual life, in the apostolic life and in the transmission of this Word to everyone (Lk. 1:45; 2:19, 51; 11:27-28).

JUAN ESQUERDA-BIFET

BIBLIOGRAPHY

O. Domínguez, "María, modelo de la espiritualidad misionera de la Iglesia," *Omnis Terra* (1979) no. 86, 226-241.

J. Esquerda-Bifet, *Spiritualità e animazione missionaria*, Pont. Urban University, Rome 1977; *Comunita in cammino*, Rome, Rogate 1978; *Testimoni della speranza*, Bologna, EMI 1959 (translation in Spanish, French, English).

J. Galot, "Marie, Type et modéle de l'Eglise," in *L'Eglise du Vatican II, vol. 2,* Paris 1966.

I. Lecuyer, "Marie et l'Eglise comme Mère et Epouse du Christ," *Etudes Mariales* (1952), 23-41.

S. Meo, "Maria stella dell'evangelizzazione," in *L'Annunzio del Vangelo oggi,* Pont. Urban University, Rome 1977, 763-778.

See a few studies in *Seminarium* (1975) no. 1.

Abbreviations used in this chapter: LG (Lumen gentium), AG (Ad gentes), EN (Evangelii nuntiandi), RH (Redemptor hominis), CT (Catechesi tradendae).

5

Missionary Dimensions of Catechesis

Significantly, the Exhortation *Catechesi tradendae* opens and closes with a reference to the missionary mandate: "Go...and make disciples of all nations" (Mt. 28:19). The mandate to announce or to proclaim the Gospel to every creature in this account of Matthew takes on a definite sense of authoritative teaching, of universal magisterium: "Teach all nations," or else "Make disciples of all peoples." From the above we see that teaching or catechesis is to be considered an essential function or decisive moment in the universal mission of the Church. The announcement of the Gospel cannot be conceived and fulfilled without involving the functional element of the instruction and teaching of the people. Therefore, there is no true evangelization without catechesis.

Speaking generically and globally, the area of evangelization and that of teaching or of catechesis largely coincide. This can be seen from the very mandate of Christ, which sends the Church into the world: "Make disciples of all nations" in the most explicit text of Matthew (28:19), corresponding in Mark to "Preach the gospel to the whole creation" (Mk. 16:15), and in Luke to: "You shall be my witnesses...to the end of the earth" (Acts 1:8; cf. Lk. 24:47-48). Preaching, announcing, witnessing, authoritative instructing—all are either true catechesis, or they imply catechesis as an essential component.

So as not to remain on the surface of the topic, but to understand the meaning and content of CT, we must endeavor to state with precision the specific concept of catechesis, in its deepest relations with evangelization and, in particular, with that evangelization which in a more restricted meaning bears the name of "missionary."

Therefore, we wish to set forth *the missionary dimension* of catechesis, according to CT, or, better said, since the relationships between the two realities are multiple, *the missionary dimensions* of catechesis.

The principal dimensions which are pointed out in the document are these three:

a) *Catechesis in the missions:* as a function or dynamic moment in the *plantatio Ecclesiae;*

b) *Catechesis in the "missionary" situations* of the churches, whether they be missionary churches or those already established;

c) *Catechesis for the missions,* that is, the content and missionary orientation of every catechesis.

As can be seen, in all three cases one can speak of "missionary catechesis"; however, the adjective can take on different meanings. In the first, it takes on a fully functional sense; in the second, it has an extended functional sense; in the third, it acquires the ultimate sense of a perspective. In the first case, catechesis is a constitutive factor of the mission; in the second, a complementary element of the same; in the third, a motive, a spiritual source, an education which inspires and stimulates missionary zeal.

1. Catechesis in the Missions

"The missions are also," says CT, "a special area for the application of catechesis" (CT 13). They are a *special area,* because, in fact, the work carried out in the formation of new churches implies a special attention to the *catechumenal stage.* In this stage the faith of the new converts finds its first and fundamental development, which prepares them and initiates their incorporation into the Church through Baptism. Thus, in the missions the practice of the catechumenate has been regularly carried out, whereas in the churches of ancient tradition that practice as such has disappeared, because Baptism is administered to infants, and the care of their Christian formation is left up to the family, to the school and to various forms of pastoral instruction.

The catechumenate, seen as the novitiate to Christian life, was brought into focus by the Council, which required that throughout the whole Church "the catechumenate for adults...is to be restored" (SC 64), in order to provide for the essential development of the faith. The decree on the missions then confirmed the need for the catechumenal period, in which the "progressive change of outlook and morals" (AG 13), is brought about, and described it as a real "training period in the whole Christian life...during which disciples are joined to Christ their Teacher" (AG 14). The Exhortation CT notes with joy that throughout the Church today the catechumenate is experiencing "a renewal...and is abundantly practiced in the young missionary Churches" (CT 23).

The catechumenate, therefore, is the progressive passage from the initial faith aroused by the kerygma or "first announcement" of Christ, to that Christian formation which permits the fruitful reception of Baptism in the awareness of the obligations it implies. This stage, between conversion and Baptism, is a privileged period of catechesis, on which depends substantially and in considerable measure the *plantatio Ecclesiae* in every region. As is obvious, catechesis will continue, after the catechumenal stage, to further deepen the faith and the Christian life.

Here we can grasp the original and specific meaning of catechesis as a dynamic moment of evangelization. Our Document explains this significant point thus: "The specific character of catechesis, as distinct from the initial conversion-bringing proclamation of the Gospel, has the twofold objective of maturing the initial faith and of educating the true disciple of Christ by means of a deeper and more systematic knowledge of the person and the message of our Lord Jesus Christ" (CT 19). "The specific aim of catechesis is to develop, with God's help, an as yet initial faith, and to advance in fullness and to nourish day by day the Christian life of the faithful..." (CT 20).

Education, formation, development, maturation of the faith on the levels of doctrine and of life—this is the specific task of catechesis. In the strictly missionary activity of the Church this task has its time and its established method. And it ever conserves a precise and characteristic importance. The first announcement stimulates the universal option of faith (the initial conversion to Christ); catechesis prolongs this evangelizing action, bringing one's personal adhesion to the message of Christ to maturity.

In missionary action catechesis, therefore, is clearly seen as a necessary and typical function of evangelization, a function which, on the one hand, is vitally bound to the kerygma, whose normal projection and development it is, while, on the other hand, it strains ahead toward full participation in the ecclesial life. The all-embracing choice, the maturing of the faith and the final deepening of an already-mature faith, are dynamic moments of one and the same process, that of evangelization. They are different moments, even though intimately and vitally connected in the normal formation and development of a Christian community.

In nos. 19 and 20 the Exhortation CT explains with clarity and depth the essential connection of catechesis to the kerygmatic proclamation: catechesis directs itself to "maturing the initial faith," developing "an as yet initial faith," "developing understanding of the mystery of Christ." Now, what precise activity does this education and development of faith in Christ imply? How is this process of Christian maturing concretely actualized?

This involves offering man, already attracted by the splendor of the mystery of Christ, the possibility of penetrating the meaning and requirements of the evangelical message and becoming imbued with it. "The Christian thus sets himself to follow Christ and learns more and more...to think like Him, to judge like Him, to act in conformity with His commandments, and to hope as He invites us to" (CT 20). We are speaking, therefore, of *making into disciples* of Jesus Master, in the strictest sense of the word, those who had been converted to Him with a total, general adhesion. Catechetical formation resembles the doctrinal and moral initiation by means of which certain groups of disciples of old used to imbue themselves with the teaching and essential attitudes of their teachers. In this way the initial adhesion becomes progressively clearer, more profound, more convinced and more heartfelt, implying a new way of seeing and of living, in affective and effective harmony with the master that each man has chosen. Thus "the Gospel kerygma...is gradually deepened, developed in its implicit consequences, explained in language that includes an appeal to reason, and channelled towards Christian practice in the Church and in the world" (CT 25).

The object of this progressive study is fundamentally the very person of the Teacher—center of His own message and center of the faith which accepts Him—and then His work and His religious doctrine with the moral requirements which it implies. The Exhortation states that in the catechetical phase the believer, "having accepted by faith the person of Jesus Christ as the one Lord and having given Him complete adherence by sincere conversion of heart, endeavors to know better this Jesus to whom he has entrusted himself: to know His 'mystery,' the kingdom of God proclaimed by Him, the requirements and promises contained in His Gospel message, and the paths that He has laid down for anyone who wishes to follow Him" (CT 20).

If conversion already constitutes a "yes" given to Jesus, Savior and Teacher, catechesis leads to an intensification of that "yes," that is, to a mature and total "yes" which embraces the whole existence of those who follow Jesus and remain in His school (cf. *ibid.*). As CT indicated at the beginning: "the definitive aim of catechesis is to put people not only in touch but in communion, in intimacy, with Jesus Christ" (CT 5).

In the missions, therefore, catechesis in its most characteristic stage—the catechumenate—marks a fundamental step in the process of establishing a new local Church. It prepares the catechumens—already united to the Church through their initial faith (LG 9; AG 14)—for a mature and responsible entrance into the Christian community. In the churches of ancient tradition, instead, the entrance already effected in Baptism will have to achieve maturity and awareness in future catechesis. Therefore, the council's summons to universal restoration of the catechumenate for adults (SC 64) is in itself an invitation to do something equivalent with regard to the baptized whose Christian life is not yet mature. This is precisely the aim of the neo-catechumenal communities which are springing up here and there. The institution of the missionary catechumenate is hence a motive of inspiration and of reference for the general catechesis of the Church.

An essential aspect of mission catechesis is *the incarnation of the message in the cultures,* a task inherent in the evangelizing action in all its phases and forms. "We can say of catechesis, as well as of evangelization in general, that it is called to bring the power of the Gospel into the very heart of culture and cultures.... In this manner it will be able to offer these cultures the knowledge of the hidden mystery and help them to bring forth from their own living tradition original expressions of Christian life, celebration and thought" (CT 53).

This mode of procedure, which particularly distinguishes missionary activity, requires from the catechists of the young churches a notable effort of study and of discernment, in order that they may grasp those elements "that form part of the cultural heritage of a human group and use them to help its members to understand better the whole of the Christian mystery" (CT 53). However, such an effort will be of value not only in facilitating the entrance of groups into the Christian life, but above all in constituting an authentic native church with its peculiar physiognomy. Acculturation will also bring about the enrichment of the same cultures, "by helping them to go beyond the defective or even inhuman features in them, and by communicating to their legitimate values the fullness of Christ" (CT 53).

2. Catechesis in Particular Missionary Situations

Besides the specific catechumenal discipline, which has a sufficiently definite field of its own and its characteristic methods, there are certain more or less abnormal situations which call for particular catechetical activity, missionary in nature. These situations are found everywhere in today's world, invaded in many quarters by secularism and de-Christianization, while at the same time the population is so subject to migrations and displacements. This is sometimes true in the mission lands themselves but above all in secularized countries, whether non-Christian or Christian. At any rate, this concerns situations which can be called *missionary*, if not always in the more strict sense of the term (because the Church is established in the region), at least through a clear relationship of analogy. The Exhortation CT expressly refers to this in no. 19:

a) The first case to be considered is that of *baptized children not initiated into the faith,* not evangelized: "A certain number of children baptized in infancy come for catechesis in the parish without receiving any other initiation into the faith and still without any explicit personal attachment to Jesus Christ; they only have the capacity to believe placed within them by Baptism...." And this situation often becomes more critical because coupled with it are the "prejudices of their non-Christian family background or of the positivist spirit of their education."

It is evident that these children need a catechesis that will function as a supplement to the initial evangelization. They need a "kerygmatic" catechesis which stimulates personal adherence to Christ and the explicit orientation of their lives toward Him. At times this catechesis should also be propaedeutic to the faith or apologetical, in order to eliminate the obstacles which existentially interpose themselves between the baptized youth and the profession of faith which his Baptism implies and essentially requires.

b) A similar case is offered by *unbaptized children who attend the course of ordinary catechesis,* that is, who are catechized together with the baptized who have already made the total option of the Christian faith. "In addition, there are other children who have not been baptized and whose parents agree only at a later date to religious education: for practical reasons, the catechumenal stage of these children will often be carried out largely in the course of the ordinary catechesis" (CT 19). Even in this case—whenever circumstances do not counsel or permit the specific fulfillment of the various tasks—catechesis should be *missionary,* that is, directed to arousing the initial conversion through the kerygma, and furthermore it should fulfill the task proper to the catechumenal stage preparatory to Baptism.

Since concrete situations are so diverse, it is impossible to indicate the precise manner of carrying out the supplementary missionary task. The wise catechist will know how to find the methods, times and places more suitable, according to the cases. The Exhortation intends only to render the pastors and catechists attentive to the problem and aware of this missionary obligation.

c) The third abnormal situation considered is that of *baptized adolescents who are hesitant in their adherence to Christ:* "Many pre-adolescents and adolescents who have been baptized and been given a systematic catechesis and the sacraments still remain hesitant for a long time about committing their whole lives to Jesus Christ—if, moreover, they do not attempt to avoid religious education in the name of their freedom" (CT 19). The phenomenon is well known and widespread, especially in certain scholastic environments and social groups. The climate of rationalistic criticism, overflowing naturalism, various types of prejudices, and the intrinsic difficulty of making a definitive option which seems to imprison liberty—all these favor this situation of internal resistance, which for some will consist in *delaying* personal adherence, not as yet given, for others in *doubting* the value and meaning of the option already made, and for still others in outrightly *refusing* all religious formation and implicitly the faith itself.

All these young people also need a *missionary* catechesis in which they are offered the announcement of Jesus in such a way as to overcome psychological and environmental resistances and to arouse or re-arouse fundamental adhesion to the faith.

In no. 44, the Exhortation explains in detail the various forms which can be used in the situation of adults who need catechesis or are even "quasi-catechumens": "Our pastoral missionary concern is directed to those who were born and reared in areas not yet Christianized, and who have never been able to study deeply the Christian teaching that the circumstances of life have at a certain moment caused them to come across. It is also directed to those who in childhood received a catechesis suited to their age but who later drifted away from all religious practice and as adults find themselves with religious knowledge of a rather childish kind. It is likewise directed to those who feel the effects of a catechesis received early in life but badly imparted or badly assimilated. It is directed to those who, although they were born in a Christan country or in sociologically Christian surroundings, have never been educated in their faith and, as adults, are really catechumens."

In regard to all these persons it will again be a matter of offering a catechesis that suitably takes kerygmatic and apologetic factors into account in order to awaken or reawaken the total option of the Christian faith, which then will be helped to mature. Keeping in mind the presence of men in similar situations, in the normal programs of religious formation the typically evangelizing or missionary function will not be neglected.

d) Then there are *adults in crises of faith:* "Even adults are not safe from temptations to doubt or to abandon their faith, especially as a result of their unbelieving surroundings" (CT 19).

Having set forth these various situations of immature faith or of faith in crisis or of faith entirely lost, the Exhortation concludes with this wise invitation to a catechesis in which, keeping in mind these situations, sufficient attention is given to the fundamental task of arousing total adherence to Christ. Catechesis, as part of the developmental process, cannot separate itself from the general perspective of the mission of the Church; and even though it has its specific task, it cannot help but take on supplementarily those functions without which its work would be useless or impossible. "This means that 'catechesis' must often concern itself not only with nourishing and teaching the faith, but also with arousing it unceasingly with the help of grace, with opening the heart, with converting, and with preparing total adherence to Jesus

Christ on the part of those who are still on the threshold of faith. This concern will in part decide the tone, the language and the method of catechesis" (CT 19).

It seems unnecessary to add anything to such a clear and logical affirmation. Wherever "missionary" situations exist, therefore, catechesis must not forget its kerygmatic and missionary function, and will adapt to this its manner, its form and its methods.

3. Catechesis, Molder of the Missionary Conscience

Catechesis has not only a task in *missionary action* as such, but also another one, much more extensive (one likewise decisive for missionary action). This task is the *missionary formation* of the People of God. In fact, the integral formation of the disciple of Jesus belongs to catechesis. The missionary spirit and conscience are essential components of this formation.

CT affirms, "Catechesis is likewise *open to missionary dynamism*. If catechesis is done well, Christians will be eager to bear witness to their faith, to hand it on to their children, to make it known to others, and to serve the human community in every way" (CT 24). Then speaking of the parish as "the pre-eminent place for catechesis," in which "the bread of good doctrine and the Eucharistic Bread" are broken in abundance, the document continues that from the parish the faithful "are sent out day by day to their apostolic mission in all the centers of activity of the life of the world" (CT 67).

The theme of the essentially missionary nature of Christian life and hence of the necessary missionary projection of catechesis is not new. The insistent and pressing appeals of the Pontiffs in the great missionary encyclicals, which had a singularly luminous and dramatic expression in *Fidei Donum*, found again in the Council a solemn and manifold reconfirmation.

In fact, Vatican II not only enunciates the great directive principle, "the whole Church is missionary" (AG 2, 35), but it expressly sets forth the consequences, both in regard to all the faithful, who must have "a vivid awareness of their own responsibility for spreading the Gospel...(and) do their share in missionary work among the nations" (AG 35), and in regard to the shepherds, who must arouse among the faithful "a zeal for the evangelization of the world, by instructing them in sermons and *in Christian doctrine courses* about the Church's task of announcing Christ to all nations" (AG 39). The Council also recommends, in reference to pastoral concern for vocations: "In sermons, *in catechetical instructions*, in written articles, priests should set forth the needs of the Church both locally and universally..." (PO 11).

Clear is the theology upon which these appeals are based, and equally clear is the logical consequence which they express. The theology of the Church as People of God, which "is to be spread throughout the whole world" (LG 13), as Body of Christ which must grow to recapitulate all in Him (LG 7) and as "universal sacrament of salvation" (LG 48), points out that all the faithful are essentially involved in missionary work, and therefore that all must cultivate the missionary spirit. "As members of the living Christ...all the faithful are duty-bound to cooperate in the expansion and spreading out of His Body.... Therefore, all sons of the Church should have a lively awareness of their responsibility to the world; they should foster in themselves a truly catholic spirit; they should spend their forces in the work of evangelization" (AG 36).

Therefore, the missionary dimension cannot be missing from normal catechesis. If catechesis were to forget this aspect, it would fail in its essential function of bringing the faithful to true Christian maturity. If in the past this dimension was not sufficiently fostered, today—in the midst of so many and such powerful appeals from the Church, in the midst of so many and such clear signs of the times—to neglect it would be inexcusable.

Furthermore, the essential structure of catechesis itself implies the missionary projection and insists on it in a decisive manner. The object, the content and the aim of catechesis bear an unmistakable missionary imprint.

In regard to the merely formal and doctrinal *content*, which is "the whole of the Good News drawn from its source"—as the title of section 4 of CT expresses itself—we find missionary references, in the consideration of the *saving plan of God*, in the attention to the "*mystery of Christ*," Savior of the world—center of the evangelical perspective—in the contemplation of *the Church with her universal mission*, and finally in the reflection upon *man's own vocation* to share the divine life through Christ in His Church.

But catechesis is much more than a pure teaching of truth: it is a permeation of the whole person by the "mystery of Christ" in such a manner that Christ illumines, directs and pervades the whole life of the disciple. "Catechizing is," says our Document, "...to lead a person to study this mystery in all its dimensions.... It is, therefore, to reveal in the Person of Christ the whole of God's eternal design reaching fulfillment in that Person. ...Accordingly, the definitive aim of catechesis is to put people not only in touch but in communion, in intimacy, with Jesus Christ" (CT 5). This stupendous *aim* of catechetical action illumines the profound meaning of catechesis and reveals its missionary irradiation.

To enter into contact and communion with Jesus, Teacher of truth and of life, means to enter into His perspectives as universal Mediator and Redeemer, who gave Himself in sacrifice for the salvation of the world. It also means to share in His sentiments and attitudes of merciful love reaching out toward the regeneration of all humanity, His compassion for the crowds which were exhausted like sheep without a shepherd and for the ripe harvests waiting for the reaper, His solicitude as Good Shepherd toward the lost sheep, His thirst for souls which has, throughout the centuries, aroused much missionary heroism....

This normal outlet of catechesis is expressly indicated in the conciliar decree on the missions, which requires that the catechumens "should learn to cooperate wholeheartedly...in the spread of the Gospel and in the building up of the Church" (AG 14), and shows as the fruit and sign of real evangelization and catechetical formation "that the young churches should participate as soon as possible in the universal missionary work of the Church" (AG 20). It also affirms that "the grace of renewal cannot grow in communities unless each of these extends the range of its charity to the ends of the earth" (AG 37).

Thus we can appreciate how the great mandate of Jesus to "make disciples of all peoples" by its very nature involves the disciples themselves in extending the magisterium of Jesus to the very ends of the earth....

Conclusion

The previous considerations highlight the truth that "catechesis is intimately bound up with the whole of the Church's life," particularly whatever regards "her geographical extension and numerical increase," that is, her missionary expansion (CT 13). This expansion is always accompanied by an "inner growth," because both are manifestations of the same inner vitality, the same zeal of love engendered by the Spirit of Jesus.

It is especially to catechesis that the missionary Church owes the normal development of the new Christian communities to that degree of growth and maturity which will make possible their functional insertion into the community of churches, with reciprocal exchange of goods and services. The catechetical task of the missionaries, the task of the catechists in particular and the task of the catechumenal institution have prime value not only for the Christian education and Christian growth of new converts, but also for the formation of the particular native churches, which "endowed with their own maturity and vital forces... should make their contribution to the good of the whole Church" (AG 6).

This missionary dimension of catechesis is to be extended to every situation in which, because of lack of evangelization or difficulties that have arisen in the progress of the faith, men are found who have not knowingly crossed the threshold of Christian life. Catechesis regularly carried out in the Church must keep these situations in mind and assume forms and tasks proper to missionary activity, directed to arousing the faith and to preparing the recipients for personal conversion to Christ.

Finally, the missionary dynamism of the Church is profoundly indebted to catechesis as the molder of Christian consciousness. The truly and completely Christian consciousness is a Catholic consciousness, a missionary consciousness. And from this awareness arise missionary vocations and the spirit that stimulates all the people of God to pray for the missions and to cooperate in all the forms of diffusion of the Gospel as far as the ends of the earth.

These missionary functions or dimensions of catechesis invite us to give it the fundamental, high-priority task that belongs to it within the totality of pastoral works and initiatives. For, as CT affirms, the more the Church "gives catechesis priority...the more she *finds in catechesis a strengthening* of her internal life as a community of believers and *of her external activity as a missionary Church*" (CT 15).

P. OLEGARIO DOMÍNGUEZ, O.M.I.

6

Catechesis in Ecumenical Perspective

INTRODUCTION

To work for the restoration of Christian unity according to the will of Christ is one of the principal tasks of the Catholic Church, reaffirmed in the Second Vatican Council and corresponding to the needs of the Church herself and of her members.

The Council spoke of the need for Christians to be ecumenically minded and to know and understand each other[1]; it encouraged cooperation of many kinds between Christians of different traditions and, as far as possible, "a common profession of faith in God and Jesus Christ."[2]

Several documents of the Secretariat for Christian Unity have insisted that ecumenical progress demands renewal in religious training.[3] In the Apostolic Exhortation *Evangelii nuntiandi*, Pope Paul VI stressed how important for evangelization is the overcoming of Christian divisions, and repeated the call of the Third Synod of Bishops for an "even greater common witness" to Christ.[4] Most recently, in the Apostolic Exhortation *Catechesi tradendae*, Pope John Paul II clearly stated: "Catechesis cannot remain aloof from this ecumenical dimension, since all the faithful are called to share, according to their capacity and place in the Church, in the movement towards unity."[5]

The following reflections are based on studies which have been made over the years in the Vatican Secretariat for Promoting Christian Unity. They remain, however, the exclusive responsibility of the author, who has already expressed them previously in public.

I. THE ECUMENICAL DIMENSION OF CATHOLIC CATECHESIS

At the very outset, a question may be asked: can Catholic catechesis be given an "ecumenical dimension" without prejudicing the integrity of Catholic witness? Or better, more positively, can Catholic catechesis be simultaneously a process of maturing in faith and life and a process of reconciliation between Christians? Moreover, can it be such while facing fully the challenges we will describe further on?

An Ecumenical Dimension: Motives and Characteristics

Ecumenism aims at re-establishing, concretely and visibly, that "catholic unity" of which the Council speaks in the Constitution on the Church.[6] It aims at taking up and manifesting the fullness and richness of the mystery of truth and grace which Christ has given to His Church. Now, one of the chief aims of catechesis within the Catholic Church should be to lead Christians to a faith which is not only conscious but expresses itself as fully as possible in their lives.

This faith is integral not only because it means complete abandonment to God and His word, but also because it embraces the whole content of the Gospel, the Truth which God has communicated and which the believer possesses. Some still mistakenly believe that ecumenism threatens this integrity by "reduction" in doctrine, impoverishment of faith, "minimalism." On the contrary, ecumenism fosters integrity by inspiring the believer to penetrate the Word of God more deeply and draw out all its richness.[7]

Catholic catechesis helps to open the way to full Christian unity when it sets out to bring to the believer the entire Christian truth. Catechesis, and especially catechisms have at times marred this integrity not only by piecemeal structure lacking organization and centrality, but also by a cramping apologetic and controversial bias which narrowed the horizons of truth, often being content to define the Catholic by his differences from other Christians.[8] On the other hand, a catechesis which fosters a mature faith drawing on all the riches of the Gospel will be also an ecumenical catechesis.

A mature faith is dynamic: it is capable, while maintaining its integrity, of growing, though not without vicissitudes, and making vital contact with other faiths and even with contemporary ideologies. The risk for many believers is that they seem able to keep integrity only by being carefully protected from such contacts. Such anxiety as this may lead to ecumenism being seen as no more than creating a neutral zone where peace is gained by armistice or disarmament. Mature faith thrives on activity inspired by further gifts of the Spirit and supported by brothers within the community of the Church: it prefers dialogue and contact to neutrality and indifference.

The Catholic Church believes that it is endowed with the fullness of the Gospel committed to it by Christ.[9] When it enters into dialogue with others, Christians or not, it possesses essentially the life and dynamism which comes from Christ. But as the Decree on Ecumenism states, the fullness existing in the Catholic Church cannot be completely expressed and lived apart from the restoration of unity among all Christians.[10] Thus the Church must be constantly open to those "truly Christian endowments from our common heritage" which are to be found outside its own visible boundaries, and recognize "the riches of Christ and virtuous works" in the lives of others, whether individuals or communities, who are bearing witness to Christ. Whatever is wrought by the Holy Spirit within them can contribute to the building up of the Church, to a broader realization of the mystery of Christ. Whatever is truly Christian never conflicts with the genuine interests of the faith. Indeed as the Council further says: "these elements of sanctification and of truth...are forces impelling toward catholic unity."[11]

Catholics who possess this understanding of true maturity of faith will communicate it in their catechetical work.

An Ecumenical Dimension: Principles

1) An ecumenical approach to catechesis will distinguish the content of faith from the cultural forms in which this content has found expression in history.[12] This distinction is one help towards discerning those non-theological factors (psychological, social,

linguistic, etc.) which have contributed to divisions among Christians and may still be helping to maintain them. Ecumenism asks that catechesis help in removing a wide variety of obstacles which are rooted in a wrong understanding of confessional identity and loyalty. Suspicion, fear, inertia, rigid traditionalism which fails to distinguish the essential from the secondary or even from the distorted and exaggerated, all these impede the action of the Holy Spirit and the growth of mutual understanding.

2) But to remove or avoid creating such barriers is not the only task. The Word of God is incarnated in many historical cultures, and ecumenical catechesis not only enlarges the believing community's understanding of this process, but itself contributes to the process and helps maintain continuity with creative variety.

The ecumenical aim is not dilution but profounder comprehension of the riches of the Word manifested in the history of salvation: manifest especially in the Bible,[13] in spite of the problems raised by certain ways of interpreting it. Catechesis must take up and manifest all these riches, and so help the Catholic not only to understand the plurality of forms in which the Catholic tradition has manifested itself, but to appreciate the traditions of the other Christians in theology, liturgy, and spiritual life which, according to the Second Vatican Council, derive their efficacy from the fullness of grace and truth entrusted to the Catholic Church.[14]

All concerned with catechesis need to realize fully the ecumenical importance of the christocentric, theocentric, trinitarian character of Christian teaching.[15] Again, while recognizing that all revealed truths demand the same assent of faith, they must understand and respect the hierarchy of truths within the one Christ-centered message of salvation.[16] Such an approach helps to bring out and define the shared elements in the Christian heritage, its deep common roots. It does not obscure the doctrinal divisions which remain to challenge ecumenical convergence and prevent the full acceptance of other traditions, but it does create a positive and sympathetic climate in which differences can be tackled.

The teaching and practice of other Churches should be presented in catechesis fairly and objectively. This will normally call for the cooperation in some form of those who belong to the tradition being presented. It is especially important to define and evaluate carefully both the reality and the limits of those convergences with the Catholic tradition which result from ecumenical dialogue. In all this the possibilities will of course vary with the different stages of catechesis.

Because there is envisioned that restoration of unity among Christians which will advance the proclamation of the Gospel and the unity of mankind, catechesis is not only concerned with the past and the present history of salvation. It must also help to lay foundations for an ecumenical future, taking account of what Christians and Churches already experience in their partial and growing communion. Hence, in addition to maintaining an ecumenical dimension throughout its work, catechesis can also give attention to particular elements of the ecumenical movement as time and circumstances suggest.[17]

II. THE GROUNDS FOR COOPERATION BETWEEN CATHOLICS AND OTHER CHRISTIANS IN CATECHESIS

A Common Challenge

Proclamation of God's mighty acts both glorifies Christ and brings salvation to men. But in practice, in the contemporary world, this proclamation presents problems, and these problems are not peculiar to any Church but are common to all who are committed to the fundamental Christian vocation of witness and, in particular, to those charged with forming people to a mature Christian faith and life.

All Christians can agree in recognizing that we live no longer in a world where the sense of God is strong and prompt to manifest itself, or where the Christian message of salvation is received unambiguously. Though some manifest in various ways the desire for God, the Augustinian "restlessness," there is equally a confident secularism[18] which finds all its values in this life, or even in the name of philosophical analysis rejects religious discourse as meaningless. Each Christian community is called to respond to this situation, not in a defensive manner but by searching more deeply into the richness and the depth of the mystery of Christ. Therefore, each must search more deeply into the meaning of the "hierarchy of truths" already mentioned, seeing the concept not merely as a convenient instrument of ecumenical maneuver but as a recall to fundamentals, a guide to a true scale of Christian values for all.

The richer and the more embracing the Christian message is seen to be in relation to human living, both personal and social, and the more it is seen as concerned with great human issues óf justice, development, peace, family life, reverence for creation, the stronger becomes the demand for common Christian witness and hence the need to explore a catechesis which can prepare people for this witness and, at the same time, be an effective example of it.

These are practical concerns of every Christian catechist; but underlying them all is a great question: what is the place of "the one visible Church of God, a Church truly universal and sent forth to the whole world that the world may be converted to the Gospel and so be saved, to the glory of God,"[19] the Church that, as the Council says, almost everyone, though in different ways, longs for?[20] The Church is not something that stands outside humanity—it is the embodiment of the faith and charity of living Christians. Even where there are deep differences in understanding the nature and structures of the Church, Christians and Churches are being forced to face crucial questions of fidelity— to Christ, to man, to the Church herself. This question cannot be treated merely by defining by differences, by seeing oneself as something which others are not. More satisfactory answers to these questions require common Christian reflection, the results of which will undoubtedly influence the future training of Christians.

Reference has been made already to surviving prejudices, suspicions, and fears, even distorted understanding of our own beliefs, which are still obstacles to brotherhood in Christ and certainly to common witness to Christ. These obstacles Christians must break down by ecumenical reflection and action. Then, in looking outwards together and witnessing to the world at large, they will see the need for varying emphases as the Gospel is expressed in life.

Possibilities and Necessity of Common Catechesis

The differences between Christian Churches and communities are not merely institutional or cultural. There are real differences of faith. And yet as Christians begin to confront together the situations described above, they are coming to a clearer understanding of the faith and Christian life of the other and to a deeper understanding and appreciation of their own faith.

It is important to recognize those fundamental truths of the Christian faith which are common to all Christians: the existence of God our heavenly Father, the creator of all, and our ability to communicate with Him in prayer; the person of Jesus, His Son, who was born of the Virgin Mary and became one of us, and by this has given new meaning to the world and its history; His life and teaching as recorded in the Gospels; His call to men to become His by faith and Baptism and Christian living; His saving death, resurrection and ascension; the Holy Spirit who is the bond of communion with Jesus and the Father; the dwelling of the Holy Spirit within those who love Him, and who thus is the bond of our own communion with God and each other, so that we may grow into the body of Christ, which is the Church, and which is to witness to Him to the end of time.

Christians of different traditions establish the extent and limits of such common faith by dialogue, in which each responds to the call to "give an account of the hope that is in us" (1 Pt. 3:15).

They may begin with distorted or inadequate views of each other's faith. Beliefs which at first seem opposed may prove after discussion to be legitimate though mutually unfamiliar expressions of the same shared faith. But this can only be seen if each tradition speaks for itself and is listened to with patience and charity.

In such dialogue and joint work Catholics not only understand other traditions better, but grow in knowledge of their own faith. For example in joint Bible study and in shared work for translating and distributing the Scriptures they have learned to love the word of God more and to draw more spiritual profit from it. The benefits of dialogue (which are, of course, reciprocal) appear in a better grasp of fundamental Christian truths such as the sacramental life, the nature of mission of the Church, the role of the successor of St. Peter in the Church, the foundations of Christian moral life and in their more effective proclamation. These benefits have already shown themselves in dialogues at many levels.

At the same time dialogue will establish more precisely the limits of common profession of faith and so of common catechesis. As long as Christians are conscientiously divided on matters of faith and Christian living they cannot give adequate training by common catechesis alone: each Church must continue to discharge its own responsibility. But dialogue will securely establish what can be done in common and what must be done separately. Thus, even if serious differences do exist among Christians, dialogue and common witness to what we believe contribute so much and are so intimately related to our own understanding of God as He has revealed Himself in Christ, that they must be considered an essential part of evangelization. It is for this reason that Pope Paul VI, in recognizing "the sign of unity among all Christians as the way and instrument of evangelization," made his own the desire expressed by the Third General Synod of Bishops "for a collaboration marked by greater commitment with the Christian brethren with whom we are not yet united in perfect unity, taking as a basis the foundation of Baptism and the patrimony of faith which is common to us. By doing this we can already give a greater common witness to Christ before the world in the very work of evangelization. Christ's command urges us to do this: the duty of preaching and of giving witness to the Gospel requires this" (*Evangelii nuntiandi*, no. 77).

III. COMMON ACTIVITY THROUGH CATECHESIS: PRACTICAL CONSIDERATIONS

We have seen that catechesis is not simply concerned with teaching children in schools, and that it must be exercised in many different situations. Relations between Christian Churches vary very much in different regions. This serves to emphasize that it is impossible to formulate general rules or give detailed guidance, applicable everywhere. The documents mentioned in the introduction all recognize this and indicate how important it is that whatever initiatives may be taken should correspond to the reality of the local situation.

Joint work in catechesis does not necessarily call for the creation of new structures. Serious thought should be given to promoting the use and development of those which already exist. The document *Ecumenical Collaboration at the Regional, National and Local Levels,* says something of practical possibilities, methods of cooperation and the responsibility of Church authorities. [21] Attention should also be given to initiatives undertaken by informal groups under the conditions mentioned in the same document.[22]

Catechesis naturally gives importance, though not exclusively, to the intellectual aspects of the faith—to doctrine, instruction. At the same time, there is need more than ever today to stress the other demands of the Christian life which, as we have seen, are met by a complete catechesis. Ecumenical catechesis helps to meet these demands, impelling Christians to prayer, to conscious effort to overcome divisions, to mutual forgiveness, to repentance and spiritual renewal.[23]

Catechesis can reflect the progress which is taking place in dialogue and ecumenical cooperation. Convergences and agreements matured between responsible theological commissions and accepted for reflection by the Churches, still more those made between Church authorities, should be reflected in common catechetical programs at the appropriate levels; otherwise, the value of ecumenical theological dialogue will seem very limited and be called into question.

Yet we must recognize realistically the limits of these common efforts. Where real differences continue to exist, they must be acknowledged sincerely and humbly. Catholics cannot let those doctrines of their faith which other Christians conscientiously do not share be treated as if they were secondary or marginal. In all catechesis, whether done jointly with other Christians or not, they must give effective witness to their own faith in its entirety and see that their fellow-Catholics receive a training in it which will be intellectually and spiritually sufficient.

Furthermore, because catechesis includes not only training in doctrine but also in Christian life, especially through developing the sacramental life and participation in the total life of the ecclesial community, common catechesis remains essentially limited, and must be integrated with Catholic catechesis.[24]

Who can contribute to common catechesis?

Faculties of theology, through research, symposia, seminars, etc., can help to define and bring out the essentials of the Christian message. They can advance understanding of the concept of a "hierarchy of truths" and its application to the understanding of the faith. Laying scientific foundations for any program of common catechesis calls for cooperation among theologians of many Christian Churches and communities.

Historical studies need to go beyond ecclesiastical institutions and policies to spiritual movements, thought and worship. General or regional Church histories, in which scholars of different traditions have collaborated to present all traditions fairly and adequately, will benefit catechesis.

International or regional educational associations can organize work which will promote common witness and help common catechesis. Attention is drawn to the various institutions mentioned in the Ecumenical Directory, Part II, and to the roles these can play in laying the proper foundations for common catechesis.[25]

Institutes for theoretical or applied catechetics can promote joint preparations of texts, audiovisual aids and other catechetical materials. As far as method is concerned, joint inquiry should be further developed into the most effective methods of presenting Christian doctrine to those of various age groups and cultural backgrounds, e.g., in some of the younger Churches, applied cultural anthropology is a useful aid. Joint reflection will also be valuable on ways of maintaining that relation of doctrine to life-in-the-Church which have been emphasized throughout these reflections. Furthermore, there should be cooperation to ensure that both what is common and what remains divergent is fairly and accurately set out in teaching programs and syllabi.

Religious teachers and catechists can be trained to take common witness more seriously, avoiding an indifferentist, relativist attitude to doctrine but equally rejecting superficial, polemical apologetics.

The new interconfessional or common Bible translations being produced in many languages can be important catechetical instruments. Catholic cooperation with the Bible Societies, in promoting still wider circulation of these texts, is a basic act of evangelization and ecumenism, but the use of these texts in programs of training at various levels can also contribute to the progress of ecumenism.

Particular attention should be given to pastoral ministry to special groups. The document *Ecumenical Collaboration at the Regional, National and Local Levels* has already indicated ways and means of fruitful cooperation among Christians.[26] This cooperation is not merely a means of giving common witness in a broad sense but also of forming and strengthening the knowledge and practice of the faith. According to circumstances this strengthening of the faith can express itself in formal teaching, common prayers, informal meetings and discussions. Some examples may be cited:

The development of huge urban and industrial complexes has meant the uprooting of many people from their traditional ways of life. They find themselves living without the support of a believing community and are almost in anonymity. Catechesis to these people where they are and taking account of the circumstances in which they live is a pressing problem for all Christian Churches and can certainly offer opportunities for cooperation in Christian training.

The problems mentioned earlier concerning the search for God are sometimes particularly acute in universities. Christians divided among themselves have difficulties bearing witness whether before professors or students. Common catechesis by those who take into account present currents of ideas and who are familiar with research in scientific, historical and theological fields, may be valuable here, and help research to be faithful to past traditions as well as to profit by present currents and spiritual progress.

Some governments impose common religious programs in schools. Others offer them as an opportunity for Christians to avail themselves of state resources. Elsewhere economic pressures strongly suggest common programs. Whatever the circumstances may be, these circumstances offer opportunities for common witness which should be exploited as fully as possible, even when keeping in mind the essential limitations of such programs.[27]

An important branch of common catechesis being developed in some places is that for children of mixed marriages. This should be encouraged and furthered. It does not wholly ensure the adequate religious formation of the children but it does present a wide field of cooperation which can help to diminish the tension inevitable in mixed marriage situations, especially where both parties are convinced and practicing Christians.[28]

Today young people often inhabit, temporarily at least, a world of their own with its own language and culture. There can be cooperation in interpreting this situation and keeping contacts with young people. Here assistance and guidance should be available in the classroom, based above all on accumulated and shared experience.

Increasing numbers of people are on the move today. The Churches can link their efforts so that the Good News may reach these moving populations: expatriate workers, political or religious refugees, people in the armed forces, international agencies, holidaymakers.... They may be so circumstanced that a common catechesis is the only way the Gospel reaches them.

Finally, it is necessary to stress how important pastoral leadership is both for the ecumenical dimension in Catholic catechesis and for common catechesis. Bishops and others responsible for the pastoral care of individuals and communities have a particular role to play. They can fulfill this by encouraging close cooperation between those responsible for catechetical and ecumenical work. Furthermore, they should maintain regular contacts with their colleagues from other Churches to discuss common pastoral problems, review existing programs, suggest improvements and deal with difficulties which may have arisen.

Conclusion

The Fathers of the Second Vatican Council, promulgating their Decree on Ecumenism, proclaimed "we confidently look to the future," realizing that "this holy purpose—the reconciliation of all Christians in the unity of the one and only Church of Christ —transcends human powers and gifts."[29] It is in that same spirit that the present reflections are offered. In the years since the Council spoke, the movement for unity among Christians has been blessed by God; at the same time experience has made it steadily clearer that the leadership of pastors and the dedication of faithful people everywhere is essential to true and lasting progress. This leadership and this dedication can only be assured for the long journey ahead if catechesis, the maturing of Christians, is at once deeply Catholic and ecumenical. The Apostolic Exhortation *Catechesi tradendae* is a new encouragement to continue along this way.

JOHN F. LONG, S.J.

FOOTNOTES

1. *Unitatis redintegratio*, nos. 4, 5, 9, 10. *Ad gentes*, no. 16.
2. *Ad gentes*, no. 15.
3. *Ecumenical Directory*, Part I, AAS 59 (1967), pp. 574-592; (English Translation in Secretariat for Promoting Christian Unity *Information Service*, no. 2 (1967) p. 5.

Ecumenical Directory, Part II, AAS 62 (1970) pp. 705-724; (English Translation in Secretariat for Promoting Christian Unity *Information Service*, no. 10, June 1970; cf. especially nos. 68, 72, 74).

Reflections and suggestions concerning ecumenical Dialogue, Secretariat for Promoting Christian Unity *Information Service*, no. 12 (December 1970).

Common Witness and Proselytism (with World Council of Churches) Secretariat for Promoting Christian Unity *Information Service*, no. 14, April 1971, p. 18.

Ecumenical Collaboration on the Regional, National and Local Levels, Secretariat for Promoting Christian Unity *Information Service*, no. 26, 1975.

4. *Evangelii nuntiandi*, no. 77.
5. *Catechesi tradendae*, no. 32.
6. *Lumen gentium*, no. 13.
7. Cf. *Unitatis redintegratio*, no. 11.

8. *Reflections and suggestions concerning Ecumenical Dialogue*, no. 12.
9. Cf. *Unitatis redintegratio*, no. 4.
10. *Ibid.*
11. *Lumen gentium*, no. 8; *Catechesi tradendae*, no. 32.
12. Cf. *Catechesi tradendae*, no. 53.
13. Cf. *Dei Verbum*, no. 24.
14. *Unitatis redintegratio*, no. 3.
15. *General Catechetical Directory*, nos. 40, 41, 50-54.
16. *Ibid.*, no. 43. Cf. also *Reflections and suggestions concerning Ecumenical Dialogue*, IV, 4b and *Misterium Ecclesiae*, AAS 65 (1973), p. 402.
17. Cf. *Ecumenical Directory*, Part II, no. 75.
18. Cf. *Gaudium et spes*, no. 55.
19. *Unitatis redintegratio*, no. 1.
20. *Ibid.*
21. Cf. *op. cit.*, chap. 6, a) to e) *Pastoral and Practical Reflections for Local Ecumenical Action*.
22. *Ibid.*, chap. 7.
23. Cf. *Unitatis redintegratio*, nos. 6-8.
24. Cf. *Catechesi tradendae*, no. 33.
25. *The Ecumenical Directory*, Part II, nos. 86 and 87.
26. Cf. chap. 3.
27. Cf. *Catechesi tradendae*, no. 33.
28. Cf. *Evangelii nuntiandi*, no. 71.
29. Cf. *Unitatis redintegratio*, no. 24.

7

Orthodoxy and Orthopraxis

The Fathers of Vatican II, following in the footsteps of Trent and of Vatican I, intended "to set forth authentic doctrine on divine revelation and how it is handed on, so that by hearing the message of salvation the whole world may believe, by believing it may hope, and by hoping it may love."[1] By revealing Himself, the invisible God speaks to all men as to friends to invite and admit them to communion of life with Himself. By proposing the mystery of God's saving will, the Church has done nothing other than continue the Johannine mission: We "proclaim to you the eternal life which was with the Father and was made manifest to us—that which we have seen and heard we proclaim also to you, so that you may have fellowship with us; and our fellowship is with the Father and with his Son Jesus Christ" (1 Jn. 1:2-3).

Now, this "plan of revelation is realized by deeds and words having an inner unity: the deeds wrought by God in the history of salvation manifest and confirm the teaching and realities signified by the words, while the words proclaim the deeds and clarify the mystery contained in them. By this revelation then, the deepest truth about God and the salvation of man shines out for our sake in Christ, who is both the mediator and the fullness of all revelation."[2]

This explains why the fourth general assembly of the synod of Bishops insisted that Christocentricity is necessary for catechesis to be authentic. John Paul II made it explicit in *Catechesi tradendae:* "In the first place, it is intended to stress that at the heart of catechesis we find, in essence, a Person, the Person of Jesus of Nazareth.... The primary and essential object of catechesis is, to use an expression dear to St. Paul and also to contemporary theology, 'the mystery of Christ.' Catechizing is in a way to lead a person to study this mystery in all its dimensions.... It is, therefore, to reveal in the Person of Christ the whole of God's eternal design reaching fulfillment in that Person. It is to seek to understand the meaning of Christ's actions and words and of the signs worked by Him, for they simultaneously hide and reveal His mystery.... Only He can lead us to the love of the Father in the Spirit and make us share in the life of the Holy Trinity" (CT 5).[3] In other words, in catechesis it is Christ, Incarnate Word and Son of God, who is taught; not only that—and this is of the greatest importance to our topic—Christ is also the One who teaches. It is precisely this that causes the Apostle to say: "For I received from the Lord what I also delivered to you" (1 Cor. 11:23). Meanwhile, Christ as subject and object of Revelation renders vain every attempt to contrapose orthopraxis to orthodoxy; in fact, as Way, Truth and Life, He vindicates orthodoxy's primacy in order to attain a relationship of fruitful symbiosis with orthopraxis. It seems to me that these are the ideas that carry through the Apostolic Exhortation on catechesis in our time, in regard to orthodoxy and orthopraxis.

1. Futility of Methodological Contraposition

The first reason that a dichotomy is uncalled for may be found in the very nature of Christianity, which is inseparably both orthodoxy and orthopraxis. The teachings of Christ, whether one is considering His words or His actions, can never be separated from His life; moreover, they are an expression of His very being: the Word of God Incarnate. In this sense, "the whole of Christ's life was a continual teaching: His silences, His miracles, His gestures, His prayer, His love for people, His special affection for the little and the poor, His acceptance of the total sacrifice on the cross for the redemption of the world, and His resurrection are the actualization of His Word and the fulfillment of Revelation" (CT 9). This is why St. John could write: "That which was from the beginning, which we have heard, which we have seen with our eyes, which we have looked upon and touched with our hands, concerning the word of life...we proclaim also to you"; and then logically he added: "This is the message we have heard from him and proclaim to you, that God is light and in him there is no darkness at all. If we say we have fellowship with him while we walk in darkness, we lie and do not live according to the truth; but if we walk in the light, as he is in the light, we have fellowship with one another, and the blood of Jesus his Son cleanses us from all sin" (1 Jn. 1:1-8). To be Christian means, therefore, to walk in the light of God, who appeared in our midst in human form. For this the Christian allows himself to be illuminated by the Light-Truth, so that he can walk on the way of Life. In the measure with which the Christian participates in the truth, his journey becomes life. Now, this interaction of truth, which urges us to walk in the light, and of journey, which incites us to seek always more the truth, renders useless every catechesis which contraposes orthopraxis to orthodoxy. Precisely in this regard John Paul II states: "Firm and well-thought-out convictions lead to courageous and upright action; the endeavor to educate the faithful to live as disciples of Christ today calls for and facilitates a discovery in depth of the mystery of Christ in the history of salvation" (CT 22).

Another reason which renders untenable the abandonment of a more theoretical method in favor of a more practical one lies in the inexhaustible wealth of the integral truth. In fact, no matter how profound it can be, no individual life experience will ever succeed in adequately expressing the prismatic value of the message of Christ. The situational nature of experience restricts and, hence, renders particular the essential universality of Christ—Way, Truth and Life. With reason CT 22 cites a pertinent thought of Paul VI: "No one can attain to integral truth with a simple private experience, that is, without an adequate explanation of the message of Christ, who is Way, Truth, and Life."[4] The fullness of revelation contained in the words and actions of Christ is, certainly, destined to be shared in by the vital experience of every person, but this does not mean that the experience can replace, and even oppose itself to, a serious and systematic study of the message of salvation—just the contrary.

John Paul II also says: "Nor is any opposition to be set up between a catechesis taking life as its point of departure and a traditional doctrinal and systematic catechesis" (CT 22). Catechesis distinguishes itself precisely from the kerygma insofar as it tends toward "the twofold objective of maturing the initial faith and of educating the true disciple of Christ by means of a deeper and more systematic knowledge of the person and the message of Our Lord Jesus Christ" (CT 19). It is what St. Paul asks of the Father in his beautiful prayer on behalf of the Ephesians: "...I bow my knees before the Father...that according to the riches of his glory he may grant you to be strengthened with might through his Spirit in the inner man, and that Christ may dwell in your hearts through faith; that you, being rooted and grounded in love, may have power to comprehend with all the saints what is the breadth and length and height and depth, and to know the love of Christ which surpasses knowledge, that you may be filled with all the fullness of God" (Eph. 3:14-19). Not only cannot the immense wealth of Truth and Life of the Person and message of Christ be adequately expressed in a life experience, but it precisely calls for an orderly and systematic initiation "into the revelation that God has given of Himself to humanity in Christ Jesus, a revelation stored in the depths of the Church's memory and in Sacred Scripture, and constantly communicated from one generation to the next by a living, active *traditio*" (CT 22).

An authentic catechesis, precisely because it must always place the converted person in communion with the Person and life of Christ, has as much need of orthodoxy as of orthopraxis; every opposition of one to the other is completely futile; rather, it would mean altering the nature of catechesis in its center: *Christ: Way, Truth, Life.*

2. Primacy of Orthodoxy

If Christianity teaches men to walk in the light of God, catechesis is first of all and above all the deepened announcement of the truths of faith and of morals. In the course of the centuries, in fact, "an important element of catechesis was constituted by the *traditio Symboli* (transmission of the summary of the faith)— followed by the transmission of the Lord's Prayer" (CT 28). This transmission of a summary of the essential truths to be believed was a very important stage in the life of the disciple of Christ. The knowledge of the essential elements was the point of departure for an always more profound and more committed following of Christ. In *Evangelii nuntiandi* Paul VI says: "The intelligence, especially that of children and young people, needs to learn through systematic religious instruction the fundamental teachings, the living content of the truth which God has wished to convey to us and which the Church has sought to express in an ever richer fashion during the course of her long history" (EN 44). There is no doubt that a profound knowledge of God greatly serves to give a religious meaning to everyday life; so, too, it is clear that the knowledge of Christ working in our midst does much to give an orientation of hope to daily existence. The Pope writes: "It is important to explain that the history of the human race, marked as it is by grace and sin, greatness and misery, is taken up by God in His Son Jesus, 'foreshadowing in some way the age which is to come' " (CT 29). All the good fruits of human industry and of nature, such as human dignity, brotherhood, liberty, justice and peace, diffused upon the earth in the Spirit of Christ, "...we will find them again, but freed of stain, burnished and transfigured, when Christ hands over to the Father: 'a kingdom eternal and universal....' On this earth that Kingdom is already present in mystery. When the Lord returns it will be brought into full flower."[5]

It is precisely the true religious sense of life and the prophetic announcement of a transcendental and eschatological salvation history that reveal the ultimate reason for everything that exists and comes into being.

Orthodoxy with regard to God and with regard to Christ His Son discerns practice by illuminating it and inspires practice by animating it, because orthodoxy reveals "man's profound and definitive calling, in both continuity and discontinuity with the present situation: beyond time and history, beyond the transient reality of this world, and beyond the things of this world, of which a hidden dimension will one day be revealed—beyond man himself, whose true destiny is not restricted to his temporal aspect but will be revealed in the future life" (EN 28).

This is the sense in which orthodoxy must indisputably take its place: *the first*. Only thus can the reductions and ambiguities of the various practices, both of advancement and of liberation, be avoided. Paul VI wrote: "We must not ignore the fact that many, even generous Christians who are sensitive to the dramatic questions involved in the problem of liberation, in their wish to commit the Church to the liberation effort are frequently tempted to reduce her mission to the dimensions of a simple temporal project. They would reduce her aims to a man-centered goal; the salvation of which she is the messenger would be reduced to material well-being. Her activity, forgetful of all spiritual and religious preoccupation, would become initiatives of the political or social order. But if this were so, the Church would lose her fundamental meaning. Her message of liberation would no longer have any originality and would easily be open to monopolization and manipulation by ideological systems and political parties. She would have no more authority to proclaim freedom as in the name of God" (EN 32).

As a deepened transmission of the Credo of the People of God through reflection and organic and systematic study, catechesis is hence faithful to its primary and fundamental function only in the measure to which it is "attached to a view of man which it can never sacrifice to the needs of any strategy, practice or short-term efficiency" (EN 33).

It is to be noted that this anthropological orthodoxy is intrinsically connected with the announcement of the truth about Christ and His Church. The primacy of orthodoxy thus implies a twofold conviction: first, that it concerns a truth which comes from God; second, that only by its light can one discover true freedom and authentic, integral liberation. It was precisely this twofold conviction which guided the great assembly of the Latin-American Episcopate at Puebla from January 27 to February 13, 1979. In order first to evaluate the reality of Latin America, then to rectify or integrate many inadequate visions, and finally to contribute to the upbuilding of a society more Christian and meanwhile more human, the Latin-American Bishops proposed, both in the light of faith and in the light of reason, a Christian vision of man. As is obvious, I do not intend to go into the Puebla thematic which thus illuminates the primacy of orthodoxy with regard to man; however, I permit myself two citations: "On her part, the Church has the right and the duty to announce to all the peoples the *Christian vision* of the person, because she knows that men need it to illumine their own identity and the meaning of life, and because it declares that every affront to the dignity of man is at the same time an affront to God Himself, whose image man is. Consequently, evangelization in the present and in the future of Latin America demands from the Church a clear word about the dignity of man."[6] "It is certain that the mystery of man can be perfectly illuminated *only* by faith in Jesus Christ, which faith has been for Latin America the historical font of this anxiety for dignity which today becomes an always more stabbing pain to our believing and suffering people. *Only* the acceptance and the following of Jesus Christ open us to the most comforting certainties and to the most exacting demands of human dignity. This dignity is, in fact, rooted in the gratuitous calling to life which the Heavenly Father makes us hear in a new way through the struggles and hopes of history."[7]

To avoid misunderstanding, I emphasize that the primacy of orthodoxy in catechesis, does not exclude a commitment to life in its concrete, historical existence; rather, such commitment is explicitly required. In fact, revelation concerns "the ultimate meaning of life and it illumines the whole of life with the light of the Gospel, to inspire it or to question it" (CT 22). Catechesis must educate to Christian maturity—that is to say, to the capacity of knowing how to discern natural exigencies and the will of God in major or minor events. The mature Christian knows that he cannot live egotistically, but that he must commit himself to the benefit of others in the measure of the graces received. In this way each one, on his own account, and everyone all together, fulfill in a Christian manner their manifold obligations in the human community, both civil and ecclesial.[8] The Holy Father points out "the importance in catechesis of personal moral commitments in keeping with the Gospel and of Christian attitudes, whether heroic or very simple, to life and the world—what we call the Christian or evangelical virtues. Hence also, in its endeavor to educate faith, the concern of catechesis will be not to omit but to clarify properly realities such as man's activity for his integral liberation, the search for a society with greater solidarity and fraternity, the fight for justice and the building of peace.... Many synod fathers rightly insisted that the rich heritage of the Church's social teaching should, in appropriate forms, find a place in the general catechetical education of the faithful" (CT 29).

What has been set forth to this point is more than enough to enable us to say that the primacy of catechetical orthodoxy can, and indeed must, coincide with an orthopraxis in daily life.

3. A Profound Symbiotic Relationship

At this point I would like to point out that there is in the field of orthopraxis an important distinction which derives from orthodoxy. I mean that it is necessary to distinguish between a practice of a rather *cultic* character and that of a rather *cultural* character. Even if the two practices derive from the harmonious and systematic announcement of the creed and of morals and, hence, are inseparable, the fact remains that practice in relation to God is an *essential* dimension of orthodox catechesis, whereas practice in relation to commitment in the world is an *integrating* dimension of it.

Because it is primarily a clear and in-depth proclamation of salvation in Christ offered to each man who comes into this world, catechesis implies an intrinsic connection "with the whole of liturgical and sacramental activity, for it is in the sacraments, especially in the Eucharist, that Christ Jesus works in fullness for the transformation of human beings" (CT 23). Catechesis teaches that the Son of God, through the paschal mystery, has transferred us into the kingdom of the Father precisely so that we would accomplish "the work of salvation...by means of sacrifice and sacraments, around which the entire liturgical life revolves."[9] In other words, we must continue until the very end of time what occurred on the day of Pentecost, when the Church manifested herself to the world by means of those who accepted the word of Peter and were baptized. "From that time onwards the Church has never failed to come together to celebrate the paschal mystery: reading those things 'which were in all the scriptures concerning Him,' celebrating the eucharist in which 'the victory and triumph of His death are again made present,' and at the same time giving thanks 'to God for His unspeakable gift' in Christ Jesus, 'in praise of His glory,' through the power of the Holy Spirit."[10]

Thus, orthodoxy and orthopraxis render one another reciprocally vital, avoiding that the first become a steril intellectualism and the second an empty ritualism. Very realistically the Apostolic Exhortation notes: "...sacramental life is impoverished and very soon turns into hollow ritualism if it is not based on serious knowledge of the meaning of the sacraments, and catechesis becomes intellectualized if it fails to come alive in the sacramental practice" (CT 2). It is precisely in virtue of this profound symbiotic relationship, intrinsic to every authentic catechesis, that both the sacred character and the organic structure of the Church, understood as a priestly community, are realized. "Incorporated into the Church through baptism, the faithful are destined by the baptismal character for the worship of the Christian religion; reborn as sons of God they must confess before men the faith which they have received from God through the Church.... Taking part in the eucharistic sacrifice, which is the fount and apex of the whole Christian life, they offer the Divine

Victim to God, and offer themselves along with It. Thus both by reason of the offering and through Holy Communion all take part in this liturgical service, not indeed all in the same way but each in that way which is proper to himself. Strengthened in Holy Communion by the Body of Christ, they then manifest in a concrete way that unity of the people of God which is suitably signified and wondrously brought about by this most august sacrament."[11] From this it is clear how integral catechesis renews man in Christ and places him in communion with God and with everyone else participating in the privileged signs of the Christian faith: *the sacraments.*

Nevertheless, the cultic community would not be the one willed by Christ if it would not take part in the upbuilding of an authentic cultural or "political" community. The Episcopal Conference of Puebla states this unequivocally, drawing inspiration from the guidelines of *Evangelii nuntiandi.* In the field of concrete priorities it has developed two concepts: communion and participation. "In the text there is given a precise and sure interpretation of the nature and of the mission of the Church: however, in giving this attentive presentation of the orthodoxy of faith, there has been a constant concern to relate it to the social and pastoral situation of the continent. That is, we set out from that reality in which the Latin-American lives...and then verify whether this reality is in conformity with the teaching of Christ, seeking to give an answer which, in the light of faith, can orient the believer in his action within society."[12] In other words, the symbiotic relationship between orthodoxy and orthopraxis means that catechesis involves the whole life of every man, of all men. The organic and systematic study of the creed and of morality must keep in mind the reciprocal appeal which exists between it and life. For this reason, the believer who has matured in the faith and lived it in the liturgy must, consequently, also apply himself for the coming of a world worthy of the human dignity of every man.

In speaking of catechesis not only is there no room for a futile contraposition of method, but not even for a theoretical polemic about the primacy of the one or of the other; if there is a primacy, and there is, it is only because liturgical practice and the practice of daily life are to be truly in conformity with the dignity of man: son of God and human person.

A catechesis which knows how to conserve the first place for orthodoxy, in order to relate it continually to the practical demands of ecclesial and social life, carries out its task of service. Studying deeply the central truths of revelation in a harmonious and systematic manner, it illumines, inspires and discerns what the practice should be.

This catechesis is that of "a creating and redeeming God, whose Son has come among us in our flesh and enters not only into each individual's personal history but into human history itself, becoming its center...." This catechesis is accordingly that of "the radical change of man and the universe, of all that makes up the web of human life under the influence of the Good News of Jesus Christ. If conceived in this way, catechesis goes beyond every form of formalistic moralism, although it will include true Christian moral teaching. Chiefly, it goes beyond any kind of temporal, social or political 'messianism.' It seeks to arrive at man's innermost being" (CT 52).

BONIFACIO HONINGS, O.C.D.

FOOTNOTES

1. "Dogmatic Constitution on Divine Revelation," *Dei Verbum*, no. 1.
2. *Ibid.*, no. 2.
3. John Paul II, Apostolic Exhortation *Catechesi tradendae*.
4. Paul VI, *Discourse at the Closing of the Synod* (October 29, 1977), AAS 69, 1977, p. 634.
5. "Pastoral Constitution on the Church in the Modern World," *Gaudium et spes*, no. 39.
6. Puebla, *Il messaggio della speranza*, Universal Christian Library directed by L. Castiglione, Ed. Logos, 1979, p. 155, no. 203.
7. Puebla, p. 159, no. 216; underlining mine.
8. Cf. "Decree on the Ministry and Life of Priests," *Presbyterium Ordinis*, no. 6.
9. "Constitution on the Sacred Liturgy," *Sacrosanctum Concilium*, no. 6.
10. *Ibid.*
11. "Dogmatic Constitution on the Church," *Lumen gentium*, no. 11.
12. Puebla, p. 57.

8

Catechesis and Theology

The Apostolic Exhortation *Catechesi tradendae* explicitly deals with the topic "catechesis and theology" only in number 61. However, thanks to the inevitable similarity of the greater part of the thematic and problematic that involve both activities (catechetical and theological), the treatise which the Holy Father develops in regard to catechesis presents frequent links with and references to theology.

In my contribution, therefore, I will not limit myself to commenting on number 61 but will attempt to illustrate the relationships which occur between catechesis and theology, keeping in mind all the significant texts in which the treatise on catechesis involves some rapport with theology.

Before dealing with the problem of rapport, allow me to recall a few fundamental concepts which concern the nature, the tasks and the characteristics of catechesis and of theology, because only if we have clear concepts in this regard is it possible to derive valid indications about the respective relationships.

1. Definitions and Tasks of Theology and of Catechesis

There is a general definition of theology upon which we all agree: theology is essentially *fides quaerens intellectum*, a deepening of the understanding of the faith, carried out with rigorous methods and in a systematic form. The Word of God is the object of many disciplines: history, exegesis, preaching, pastoral care, catechesis, liturgy, etc. What characterizes the theological discipline is its scientific nature. The theologian approaches the Word of God with the intention of assuring and guaranteeing to it a certain scientific accuracy, a certain rigor and objectivity.[1] Its objective is "to conserve, penetrate always more profoundly, set forth, teach and defend the sacred deposit of Revelation; that is, to illuminate the life of the Church and of mankind through the divine truth."[2]

For catechesis the Apostolic Exhortation proposes the following definition: it "is an education of children, young people and adults in the faith, which includes especially the teaching of Christian doctrine imparted, generally speaking, in an organic and systematic way, with a view to initiating the hearers into the fullness of Christian life" (no. 18).

Both theology and catechesis pursue a finality essentially and primarily theoretical: that is, they draw near to the revealed truth for the truth itself and not in view of other objectives, but they do so in different ways and from this their specific differences result. In theology the believer seeks to obtain for himself (and not for others) a deeper and more systematic knowledge of the truth. In catechesis the believer who is already in possession of revealed truth seeks to make it known better, more completely and more systematically, to one who knows it only imperfectly. Theology is exquisitely speculative, whereas catechesis is essentially pedagogical. Catechesis is a training in the truth; it is *paideia*, education.

However, neither theology nor catechesis are exclusively theoretical activities: both have as their goal orthopraxis; that is, through a better knowledge of truth they intend to favor a more dedicated and generous following of Jesus, a more fervent and intense Christian life. The orthopraxic objective in theology first of all invests him who dedicates himself to the theological activity, whereas in catechesis the aim is to better the Christian practice of the catechized. Catechesis proposes "giving growth, at the level of knowledge and in life, to the seed of faith sown by the Holy Spirit with the initial proclamation and effectively transmitted by Baptism. Catechesis aims, therefore, at developing understanding of the mystery of Christ in the light of God's Word, so that the whole of a person's humanity is impregnated by that Word" (CT 20).

Nevertheless, both in catechesis and in theology the theoretical objective precedes the orthopraxic one. To this point *Catechesi tradendae* returns with insistence (nos. 20, 25, 26, 33, etc.) and it does so with good reason, in view of the very strong tendency even among Catholic theologians and catechists to favor orthopraxis over orthodoxy.

Theology and catechesis differ not only in regard to their recipients but also in regard to the cultivators of the respective disciplines. To cultivate theology (I refer to specialized theology not to the "ordinary" study which all the faithful are obliged to pursue) only a few experts are called, who are supplied with an uncommon cultural store of information: theology is the work of a few specialists. Instead, according to varying levels and forms, all Christians are called to cultivate and to practice catechesis. "Catechesis always has been and always will be a work for which the whole Church must feel responsible and must wish to be responsible. But the Church's members have different responsibilities, derived from each one's mission. Because of their charge, pastors have, at differing levels, the chief responsibility for fostering, guiding and coordinating catechesis.... On another level, parents have a unique responsibility. Teachers, the various ministers of the Church, catechists, and also organizers of social communications, all have in various degrees very precise responsibilities in this education of the believing conscience, an education that is important for the life of the Church and affects the life of society as such" (CT 16). Not all Christians can be theologians by profession, whereas all must be catechists when they have attained a certain physical, intellectual and spiritual maturity.

2. Characteristics of Theology and of Catechesis

Theology is a rational, systematic, profound, critical, exhaustive, intelligible, updated, edifying, ecumenical reflection on the history of salvation, on the Word of God, on the Christian message. For lack of space, I will not dwell on the illustration of every element of this rather long list of the principal characteristics of theology; furthermore, the adjectives which I used are clear enough and eloquent in themselves.

Almost all the characteristics of theology are ascribed to catechesis by CT. Number 21 prescribes that catechesis be systematic, based on the essentials ("without any claim to tackle all disputed questions or to transform itself into theological research or scientific exegesis"), complete, open to all the components of Christian life. In number 32 the ecumenical character is emphasized; in number 49 updating is recommended ("showing close acquaintance with the anxieties and questionings, struggles and hopes" of the generations to which it addresses itself), completeness (making a point "of giving the whole message of Christ and His Church, without neglecting or distorting anything"), intelligibility ("they must try to speak a language comprehensible to the generation in question"), edification ("they must really aim to give to those who use them a better knowledge of the mysteries of Christ, aimed at true conversion and a life more in conformity with God's will").

If we confront the list of the properties which CT attributes to catechesis with what I have presented for theology, it can be noted that there is an almost total coincidence, and in effect there are cases (for example, the teaching of theology imparted to the laity at certain levels) in which no difference is registered for any of the characteristics listed above. However, as a matter of principle and also on the basis of what CT teaches, it seems to me that the above-mentioned characteristics do not always relate to catechesis and to theology in the same way. Thus, for example, theology requires a greater completeness (it should deal with all disputed questions), a more scientific nature, a more critical attitude, and more profundity. In regard to aggiornamento, to clarity and to intelligibility, on the other hand, we can be more demanding with catechesis than with theology.

Of all the properties which catechesis must possess, that to which the Apostolic Exhortation returns with greater insistence is integrity and fidelity to the ecclesiastical magisterium. It recommends avoiding all arbitrary and reductive selections: "The person who becomes a disciple of Christ has the right to receive 'the word of faith' not in mutilated, falsified or diminished form but whole and entire, in all its rigor and vigor. Unfaithfulness on some point to the integrity of the message means a dangerous weakening of catechesis and putting at risk the results that Christ and the ecclesial community have a right to expect from it" (no. 30). Therefore, the catechist "will not seek to keep directed towards himself and his personal opinions and attitudes the attention and the consent of the mind and heart of the person he is catechizing. Above all, he will not try to inculcate his personal opinions and options as if they express Christ's teaching and the lessons of His life" (no. 6).

In effect, integrity and fidelity to the magisterium, properties so essential for theological and catechetical activity, are those against which catechists and theologians have sinned more often and more seriously in the decade of "doctrinal permissiveness" following Vatican Council II. During this period in which theologians and catechists have been able to utilize an unlimited freedom of research and of teaching, they have circulated interpretations so personal, so extravagant and, at times, so aberrant as to profoundly confuse the hearts and minds of the simple faithful. In a heartbroken discourse to the international theological commission, the late-lamented Paul VI sadly pointed out: "Today the very principles of the objective moral order are contested. The outcome is that contemporary man is disconcerted. He no longer knows what is good and what is bad, nor to which criteria he can entrust himself; and a certain number of Christians share this doubt, having lost confidence both in a concept of natural morality and in the positive teachings of Revelation and of the magisterium."[3]

CT denounces all the deviations which wound integrity and fidelity to the magisterium—whether in the conservative or in the progressive sense. Conservative deviation, by repulsing every change, "leads to stagnation, lethargy and eventual paralysis" (no. 17); whereas progressive deviation "with its readiness for any venture...begets confusion on the part of those being given catechesis...; it also begets all kinds of deviations, and the fracturing and eventually the complete destruction of unity" (no. 17).

3. Sources and Contents of Catechesis and of Theology

The sources and contents of catechesis and of theology are substantially the same. The principal fonts for both are Tradition, Sacred Scripture, the Fathers of the Church and the ecclesiastical Magisterium.

For the teaching of dogmatic theology (but valid also for theological research) Vatican II gives the following directives: "these biblical themes should be proposed first of all. Next there should be opened up to the students what the Fathers of the Eastern and Western Church have contributed to the faithful transmission and development of the individual truths of Revelation. The further history of dogma should also be presented, account being taken of its relation to the general history of the Church. Next, in order that they may illumine the mysteries of salvation as completely as possible, the students should learn to penetrate them more deeply with the help of speculation, under the guidance of St. Thomas, and to perceive their interconnections" *(Optatam totius,* no. 16).

Having affirmed the principle that catechesis draws its content from the living font of the Word of God, transmitted by Tradition and by Scripture, CT adds: "To speak of Tradition and Scripture as the source of catechesis is to draw attention to the fact that catechesis must be impregnated and penetrated by the thought, the spirit and the outlook of the Bible and the Gospels through assiduous contact with the texts themselves; but it is also a reminder that catechesis will be all the richer and more effective for reading the texts with the intelligence and the heart of the Church and for drawing inspiration from the 2,000 years of the Church's reflection and life. The Church's teaching, liturgy and life spring from the source and lead back to it, under the guidance of the pastors and, in particular, of the doctrinal magisterium entrusted to them by the Lord" (no. 27).

With reference to the essential contents, CT enumerates four: God, Christ, the Church and Christian existence (anthropology) (no. 29). These are undoubtedly also the essential contents of theology, insofar as they are the fundamental themes of the Word of God and the chief actors in the history of salvation.

Of these four themes the one that occupies the first place both in theology and in catechesis is Christ. "The primary and essential object of catechesis is...'the mystery of Christ.' Catechizing is in a way to lead a person to study this mystery in all its dimensions" (CT 5). In effect Christ is the fullness of the Revelation of the Father, the fulfillment of the history of salvation, the first fruit and the anticipation of the Reign of God, the new man (the "new creature"), the head of the mystical body, the Church. Therefore, "Christ is the true *methodos* of all theological research, because He is 'the way' (cf. Jn. 14:16) by which God came to us and by which we can reach Him."[4]

It is especially in relation to Christ that the new theology and the new catechesis have sinned by reductionism, making of Him a simple man, even if the best, most just, most generous, most free: a real model for all men and the greatest model for humanity, who initiated a process of liberation from the manifold forms of oppression which afflict humanity, a process which Christians have the responsibility of bringing to fulfillment.

Already denounced by Paul VI in *Evangelii nuntiandi* (no. 35), these most serious Christological errors have also been condemned several times by John Paul II. Against those theologians who claim to show that Jesus was politically committed, that He struggled against Roman domination and against the powerful, indeed, was involved in class warfare—in his programmatic discourse at Puebla, the Holy Father decisively reaffirmed the Christological faith of the Church: "Jesus Christ, Word and Son of God, became man in order to draw near to man and to offer him, with the power of His mystery, salvation, the great gift of God." Therefore, the perspective from which Jesus' mission stems is much more profound than that attributed to Him by secular theologians, theologians of hope, theologians of liberation, etc.: "It consists in integral salvation through a transforming, pacifying love, a love of pardon and of reconciliation." In CT John Paul II recommends that the catechist be careful "not to reduce Christ to His humanity alone or His message to a no more than earthly dimension" (no. 29).

4. The Acculturation of the Christian Message in Catechesis and in Theology

Recently even Catholic philosophers and theologians have taken cognizance of the importance and significance that the cultural dimension has for man. Culture is understood by them as an essential, rather than accidental, structure of the human condition. Man is not simply a natural being, prefabricated and fully finished off by nature itself. Rather, he is largely entrusted to his own initiative, to his own work, to his own development. Man is essentially a cultural being—a formula which, without taking anything away from the celebrated Aristotelian definition (" 'rational' being or animal"), better expresses what sets man apart from nature and from all other living beings. However, culture, which is a product of man and which reflects on man, modifying and perfecting him, assumes many forms: every social group creates a culture of its own, with languages, techniques, customs and different values.[5] The culture of the Egyptians is one, that of the Babylonians another, still others are the cultures of the Greeks, of the Romans, of the Chinese, etc. This cultural diversity, at times very great and profound, gives rise to considerable problems whenever persons or groups of differing cultures encounter one another in order to establish contact or dialogue. These problems intimately affect catechesis and theology also; frequently these must occupy themselves with the transmission of the Word of God and of the Christian message from one culture to another.

The question of the relationship between the Word of God and culture is considered by John Paul II both in the Apostolic Constitution *Sapientia Christiana* and in the Apostolic Exhortation *Catechesi tradendae*. In the first, addressing himself to theologians, the Holy Father declares that "it is necessary that the whole of human culture be steeped in the Gospel. The cultural atmosphere in which a human being lives has a great influence upon his or her way of thinking and, thus, of acting. Therefore, a division between faith and culture is more than a small impediment to evangelization, while a culture penetrated with the Christian spirit is an instrument that favors the spreading of the Good News. Furthermore, the Gospel is intended for all peoples of every age and land and is not bound exclusively to any particular culture. It is valid for pervading all cultures so as to illumine them with the light of divine revelation and to purify human conduct, renewing them in Christ" (Foreword). From these considerations of John Paul II derive two norms for theology: 1) its exposition of revealed Truth "is to be such that, without any change of the truth, there is adaptation to the nature and character of every culture, taking special account of the philosophy and the wisdom of various people. However, all syncretism and every kind of false particularism are to be excluded. 2) The positive values in the various cultures and philosophies are to be sought out, carefully examined, and taken up. However, systems and methods incompatible with Christian faith must not be accepted" (art. 68).

In CT, addressing catechists, the Holy Father affirms that they are called to bring through their teaching "the power of the Gospel into the very heart of culture and cultures. For this purpose, catechesis will seek to know these cultures and their essential components; it will learn their most significant expressions; it will respect their particular values and riches. In this manner it will be able to offer these cultures the knowledge of the hidden mystery and help them to bring forth from their own living tradition original expressions of Christian life, celebration and thought" (no. 53). However, the Holy Father adds immediately, that in this difficult work it is necessary to keep two points in mind. First of all, it is not possible totally to isolate the evangelical message from the cultures (Hebrew and Graeco-Roman) in which it was initially inserted and formulated. Even though it is said that culture is the form of a society and that the

Judaic-Hellenistic culture is the form of the New Testament, in neither of the two cases are accidental forms meant, which could easily be taken away and replaced by others. In the second place, "the power of the Gospel everywhere transforms and regenerates. When that power enters into a culture, it is no surprise that it rectifies many of its elements. There would be no catechesis if it were the Gospel that had to change when it came into contact with the cultures" (CT 53).

The illumined and illuminating directives in regard to the acculturation of Christianity which the Holy Father imparts to theologians and catechists in these two solemn documents respond to a genuine need. In the past, theologians and catechists, still bound to a fixed and immobile conception of culture, almost always sinned through lack of acculturation of the Christian message. This is what almost always happened in mission territories, where not only were the cultures of primitive peoples never valued, but not even those of the Chinese, Indians, or Japanese, who had reached very high cultural levels. But the theologians of the European continent during the modern epoch have also sinned by hardly acculturating the Christian message, the authentic cultural values of which they did not know how to understand, appreciate and adopt with critical vigilance.

Today, sensitized to the historicity and mutability of culture and to cultural pluralism, theologians and catechists often fall into the opposite error—an excessive acculturation of the Christian message. At times the message is poured into wineskins of other cultures too small or worn out to collect all of it or to conserve it integrally. Marxist, existentialist, personalistic, African, Chinese, Cuban, etc., acculturations of the Gospel are effected without consideration of the exigencies which the Gospel promotes in regard to every man and his culture, exigencies which ultimately ask of man not only an interior conversion but also a total conversion, which, therefore, embraces also a cultural conversion.

Against the errors of acculturation in which theologians and catechists of our time frequently let themselves be trapped John Paul II directed the central portion of his discourse of December 15, 1979, to the Pontifical Gregorian University. Among other things we read: "Theology must select its own 'allies' according to the criteria dictated by the methodology which is proper to it. There are currents of thought which, either because of their fundamental attitude or because of other developments given them by their authors, do not present the requisites necessary for entering usefully into collaboration with theological research. In such cases, it will be indispensable to give proof of a lucid, critical sense in evaluating the contributions offered by one or the other philosophic or scientific system, accepting whatever can be helpful to the progress of theological knowledge, and refusing instead whatever opposes such progress. St. Paul's precept: *omnia probate, quod bonum est tenete* (1 Thes. 5:21) is valid even here. There are, in fact, optics, visuals and philosophical languages that are decisively deficient; there are scientific systems so poor and closed as to render a satisfactory translation and interpretation of the Word of God impossible. To take these systems as allies in a non-critical manner would mean a self-inflicted wound for theology and exposure to irreparable mutilation. The history of the deviating developments followed by certain theological tendencies during the last decades is instructive."

5. Relationships Between Catechesis and Theology

CT affirms the existence of a "profound and vital link" between catechesis and theology as something evident, but in the end the Document does not explain in what this link effectively consists. We are able to do so, by keeping in mind what was said before in regard to the nature, properties, sources and objectives which characterize catechesis and theology. As a result of our analysis, we find ourselves faced by two sister disciplines, so similar to one another that they may appear to be twins, but, in effect, theology, insofar as it possesses the Word of God in depth, is the firstborn, whereas catechesis, insofar as it instructs and forms to the Word of God, is the second child.

We have already seen that the catechist is a teacher of the Word of God. This presupposes that he is in possession of a sufficiently deep knowledge of this Word; that is to say, in a more or less elevated degree, he must first of all be a theologian: only thus could he also be a teacher.

We are accustomed to consider theology and catechesis as two distinct specializations, to the point of assigning their study not only to different professors but even to distinct institutes of faculties. To us it seems sufficiently difficult for the same person to carry out both activities, theological and catechetical. However, in the past, all the great theologians were also eminent catechists: from Clement of Alexandria to St. Basil, from Saint Augustine to St. Thomas himself. Nevertheless, even though the distinction between the two specializations is kept, we absolutely must not ignore the very close link which unites one to the other.

As Bernard Lonergan[6] has testified, the communication of the Word of God that is catechesis represents the point of arrival, the final goal of theology. According to the outline of Lonergan, catechesis is the eighth functional specialization of theology. It studies "the transpositions which theological thought must develop in order that (Christian) religion preserve its identity, but at the same time find access into the minds and hearts of men of all cultures and classes," and, even more, it makes "the necessary adaptations to employ in a full and appropriate manner the various means of communication available in different places and times."[7]

Therefore, the catechetical purpose is not secondary but essential to theology. In effect, the work of the theologian is not an investigation of the faith simply for personal use, but for common and social use: it is an investigation carried out for the good of the community. Theology is a service which the researcher of the Word of God renders to the Truth; it is a service which he carries out for the Church, in particular for the teachers of the Word of God, the catechists.

"Aware of the influence that their research and their statements have on catechetical instruction, theologians and exegetes have a duty to take great care that people do not take for a certainty what on the contrary belongs to the area of questions of opinion or of discussion among experts" (CT 61).

Also the choice of methodology and of language as well as the actual acculturation of the Christian message accomplished by the theologian must correspond to the exigencies of catechesis: first of all and above all, the integrity of the Christian message must be safeguarded. This is valid even for theologians who seek to develop new interpretations and new theological systems; whereas the critical vigilance of those who work "second hand"— that is, who adopt theological constructions effected by others in order to diffuse them in their own surroundings—must be twofold. First, they must test whether the new system is valid in itself, that is, whether it is a faithful interpretation of the Word of God. Secondly, they must verify whether it corresponds to the needs of their own environment. One of the most frequent and serious errors committed by many "new theologians" is to have indiscriminately taken up interpretations of the Word of God developed in a quite restricted cultural context and transferred them whole and entire to their own nation, as though they were universally valid. This is what happened with the "theology of the death of God" (an intrinsically erroneous interpretation of the Word of God which had a meaning only in the Anglo-American cultural context, whereas it turned out to be absolutely incomprehensible in Latin countries), with the "theology of hope," with the "theology of liberation," etc.

A problem that is very difficult (especially today, because there is no longer found a theology peacefully shared by everyone) is that of the utilization of the new theologies by catechists for themselves and in their catechetical activities. The essential guidelines for the solution of this problem are as follows:

1. The catechist must be up to date; that is, he must acquire a knowledge of the new theologies, a knowledge which will be more or less broad and deep according to the level of catechesis which he is called to carry out. For one who teaches catechism in elementary and secondary schools, a simple smattering will suffice, the reading of some popular article will be enough; whereas for one who is in charge of teaching Christian religion in college or of giving courses to adult and educated laity, it will be necessary to have much more.

2. CT recommends that catechists have "the wisdom to pick from the field of theological research those points that can provide light for their own reflection and their teaching, drawing, like the theologians, from the true sources, in the light of the magisterium" (no. 61).

3. The catechist must seek to adapt the reflection of the theologian to the needs of catechesis, to his particular audience's capacity for understanding (which will vary, obviously, according to age and culture). This adaptation concerns themes (since not everything that the theologian says is of interest to catechesis) as well as language (which in the case of catechesis need not be as precise, rigorous or scientific as in theology). In particular, in making use of theological research, the catechist must refrain from troubling "the minds of the children and young people, at this stage of their catechesis, with outlandish theories, useless questions and unproductive discussions, things that St. Paul often condemned in his pastoral letters" (no. 61).

As valid as the golden rule, both for theology and for catechesis, is the statement at the end of CT 61: "The most valuable gift that the Church can offer to the bewildered and restless world of our time is to form within it Christians who are confirmed in what is essential and who are humbly joyful in their faith." The complete and faithful exposition of the Word of God will be of advantage to catechetical and theological activity itself.

One last observation before concluding: For all subjects which have an affinity of theme and of objectives, interdisciplinary work is recommended with insistence today. This is undoubtedly valid even for theology and catechesis. Interdisciplinary work is helpful to both. Catechesis can learn from theology that critical vigilance which helps it to control the intelligibility, clarity, systematization and integrity of its own teaching. Meanwhile, contact with catechesis helps theology not to fall into abstractions, and to make its own reflection upon the Word of God "orthopractical."

G. BATTISTA MONDIN, S.X.

FOOTNOTES

1. On the concept of science applicable to theology, cf. E. Agazzi, "Analogicita del concetto di scienza. Il problema del rigore e della oggettività nelle scienze umane," in AA. VV., *Epistemologia e scienze umane,* Massimo, Milan, 1979, pp. 57-76.

2. Paul VI, *Discorso al Congresso Internazionale della Teologia del Concilio Vaticano II,* Oct. 1, 1966; AAS 58 (1966) p. 891.

3. *L'Osservatore Romano,* Dec. 18, 1974, p. 2.

4. Discorso di Giovanni Paolo II alla Gregoriana, *Oss. Rom.* Dec. 17-18, 1979, p. 2.

5. On the concept of culture and its essential constitutive elements; cf. B. Mondin, *Cultura, marxismo e cristianesimo,* Massimo, Milan, 1979.

6. B. Lonergan, *Il metodo in teologia,* Queriniana, Brescia, 1975.

7. Lonergan, *op. cit.,* p. 152.

PART FOUR

The Dynamics of Catechetical Action

"Catechesis always has been and always will be a work for which the whole Church must feel responsible and must wish to be responsible. But the Church's members have different responsibilities, derived from each one's mission. Because of their charge, pastors have, at differing levels, the chief responsibility for fostering, guiding and coordinating catechesis. For his part, the Pope has a lively awareness of the primary responsibility that rests on him in this field.... Priests and religious have in catechesis a pre-eminent field for their apostolate. On another level, parents have a unique responsibility. Teachers, the various ministers of the Church, catechists, and also organizers of social communications, all have in various degrees very precise responsibilities in this education of the believing conscience.... It would be one of the best results of the general assembly of the synod that was entirely devoted to catechesis if it stirred up in the Church as a whole and in each sector of the Church a lively and active awareness of this differentiated but shared responsibility."

—CT 16

1

The Workers of Catechesis in a Community All Catechizing and All Catechized

Catechesis is "the whole of the efforts within the Church to make disciples, to help people to believe that Jesus is the Son of God, so that believing they might have life in His name (cf. Jn. 20:31), and to educate and instruct them in this life and thus build up the Body of Christ" (CT 1).

At all times the Church has always considered this obligation one of her fundamental duties (cf. CT 1). We must, however, point out a new awareness of today's Church in regard to this task.

Until now, even though catechesis has always been considered one of the fundamental tasks of the Church, this obligation has normally been considered exclusive to bishops, priests and religious. The presence of lay catechists has been viewed, therefore, in relation to the shortage of priests and religious; thus, lay catechists have served rather to make up for this shortage in some way. We further observe that catechesis has often been reduced to the so-called "catechism," that is, to the religious instruction of children.

In the vision of *Catechesi tradendae* these limitations are definitively overcome. On the one hand, this Document clearly affirms that catechesis is the duty of the whole Church (cf. CT 16), hence, of all members of the Church, both pastors and faithful; on the other hand, the Document declares without equivocation that "nobody in the Church of Jesus Christ should feel excused from receiving catechesis" (CT 45), because the Church is "the great giver as well as the great receiver of catechesis" *(ibid.)*.

This vast and dynamic vision of *Catechesi tradendae* arouses, however, a series of questions which we now seek to examine.

I. THE WHOLE CHURCH IS CATECHIST

"Catechesis is intimately bound up with the whole of the Church's life. Not only her geographical extension and numerical increase, but even more, her inner growth and correspondence with God's plan depend essentially on catechesis" (CT 13). For this reason, it is necessary that the Church of our time pay special attention to catechesis and consecrate to it her best resources of men and of means (cf. CT 15).

The question which we want to consider here concerns, therefore, the performers of this great and immense task, and a question rises spontaneously: who is called to dedicate himself to this work of catechizing? According to the Apostolic Exhortation *Catechesi tradendae*, the whole Church must feel responsible for catechesis and everyone must apply himself in this work (cf. CT 16). Hence, *all**** the members of the Church, pastors and faithful, are catechetical personnel and are called to apply themselves to catechizing.

Such a perspective offers a great reason for hope because it presents the Church as a community in which every member is a zealous bearer of the mystery of Christ. Hence, the Church will be a community full of life and of joy. To achieve this goal of reawakening a lively and active awareness of this responsibility and joy in the whole Church and in each one of her sectors and members, it is, however, necessary to rediscover the theological foundation. To say that catechesis is a fundamental duty of the pastors in the Church is, by now, an obvious truth, whereas to affirm that catechesis is also the duty of every member of the faithful is certainly a new aspect. Hence, to involve the faithful in the work of catechesis, it is necessary to reflect upon the theological foundation of this obligation.

*In the course of this chapter, italics are used only to emphasize a few words.

The Practice of the Church

What seems a novelty to many of the faithful today was, instead, a common practice at the time of the Apostles and throughout the history of the missions.

The Apostles always considered the catechetical obligation a fundamental responsibility. This was why when the number of disciples began to increase greatly, the Twelve made a decision: "It is not right that we should give up preaching the word of God to serve tables. Therefore, brethren, pick out from among you seven men of good repute, full of the Spirit and of wisdom, whom we may appoint to this duty. But we will devote ourselves to prayer and to the ministry of the word" (Acts 6:2-4).

Although the responsibility of catechesis was always alive in the Apostles' awareness and considered as the fundamental duty of their mission, they did not, however, regard it as their exclusive task. Very soon, in fact, the Apostles entrusted the task of teaching to their successors, to the deacons and to many other disciples (cf. Acts 15:35). Thus, the simple Christians, scattered after the persecution, "went about preaching the word" of God (Acts 8:4).

This practice, begun in the time of the Apostles, continued in the Church, particularly in the mission lands. In our time, the presence of lay catechists in the missionary field has again been confirmed and highly valued by Vatican Council II (AG 17) and by the present Apostolic Exhortation *Catechesi tradendae* (cf. CT 66).

Theological Foundation

This manner of acting of the Apostles and of the Church is not the result of circumstances, but is certainly founded on a theological reason. Before returning to the Father, Christ gave the Apostles a mandate: to make disciples of all peoples and to teach them to observe everything He had taught (cf. Mt. 28:18-20). This last command of Christ is at the origin of all apostolic catechetical work. This mandate entrusted to the Apostles has never been limited only to the hierarchy, that is, to the sole successors of the Apostles in the guidance of the Church, but has always been considered a mandate left to the whole Church, insofar as even before being the hierarchy of the Church, the

Apostles were the founders upon whom the Church was built and inaugurated. The Apostles, therefore, represent at one and the same time the hierarchy and the People of God; they are the first pastors of the Church, but also its first members.

In the Message to the People of God, the 1977 Synod of Bishops founded the catechetical responsibility of every one of the faithful upon the sacraments of Baptism and of Confirmation: "Catechesis is a task of vital importance for *all* the Church. *All Christians,* according to the circumstances of their own lives and their special gifts or charisms, are really involved in it. Indeed all Christians, by virtue of *Baptism* and *Confirmation,* are called to transmit the Gospel and to be concerned about the faith of their brothers in Christ" (Message of the Synod 1977, no. 12).

To be baptized means to be incorporated into Christ; this incorporation is strengthened and brought to full maturity by Confirmation. Hence, through Baptism and Confirmation, the Christian participates in the life of Christ and is called to continue His same mission: "As the Father has sent me, even so I send you" (Jn. 20:21). In this manner, the catechetical responsibility of the Christian is based precisely on his life in Christ. By participating in the life of Christ, the Christian participates also in His anxiety to announce the Gospel and to bring the brethren to full communion with the Father.

Seen both from the command left by Christ to the Apostles and from shared life with Christ communicated to the Christian in Baptism and in Confirmation, the work of catechesis shows us that it is entrusted to all the members of the Church. Nevertheless, at this point, it is necessary to note that the responsibility is not identical for everyone, but that all participate in the work "according to the circumstances of their own lives and their special gifts or charisms" (Message of the Synod 1977, no. 12).

II. THE CHURCH— CATECHIST AND CATECHIZED

The Church is the great catechist and at the same time the great "catechized." These two aspects are linked by a profound bond which renders them inseparable. A good example of this is found in the life of the primitive Church. According to the testimony of the Acts of the Apostles, the primitive Church was a community vibrant in zeal to spread the Word of God (cf. Acts 8:4-5), but at the same time, it was also a community devoted to listening to "the apostles' teaching and fellowship, to the breaking of bread and the prayers" (Acts 2:42).

This bond is born precisely from the inner life of the Church. Indeed, the Church to whom Jesus entrusted the mission of teaching and of making all nations His disciples was born from the catechetical action of Jesus and then grew because of the catechetical action of the Apostles and of the succeeding generations. While engaged in catechesis, the Church, being immersed in the world, is often tempted by idols and, therefore, always needs to hear "the mighty works of God" proclaimed (Acts 2:11) and to hear again the message to renew faith and hope and to confirm herself on the path of love (cf. EN 15).

The bond between these two aspects, "Church catechist and Church catechized," is based, moreover, on the nature of catechesis itself. "Catechizing is in a way to lead a person to study this mystery in all its dimensions...to put people not only in touch but in communion, in intimacy, with Jesus Christ: only He can lead us to the love of the Father in the Spirit and make us share in the life of the Holy Trinity" (CT 5). In this sense, catechesis does not concern a theory to be acquired, but rather a life to be lived and made to grow. It is a process of continual and unceasing growth. Therefore, in leading to intimacy with Jesus, the Church must enter always even more into depth of communion with Him.

The reality of the Church, in being simultaneously catechist and catechized, implies a very concrete consequence: "Nobody in the Church of Jesus Christ should feel excused from receiving catechesis" (CT 45). This does not concern only children and youth, but also adults; not only the simple faithful, but also seminarians, religious and "all those called to the task of being pastors and catechists" (CT 45). All in the Church are workers and at the same time subjects of catechesis. Each catechist always has a need to be catechized if he wants to conserve freshness, zeal and strength in catechetical effort (cf. EN 15). The effort and the fervor of the Church in catechesis depend upon catechesis itself. "The more the Church, whether on the local or the universal level, gives catechesis priority over other works and undertakings the results of which would be more spectacular, the more she finds in catechesis a strengthening of her internal life as a community of believers and of her external activity as a missionary Church" (CT 15).

III. COMMUNITY, THE PLACE AND WORKERS OF CATECHESIS

"Catechesis always has been and always will be a work for which the whole Church must feel responsible" (CT 16). As a consequence, the catechetical task must truly involve all the faithful (cf. Message of the Synod, 1977, no. 12), that is, everyone in the Church must become a "catechizer," even though in a different manner and with different responsibility. Nevertheless, at present catechesis is still considered the task of a few, while for the majority of the faithful it remains always something extraneous to them. Consequently, a question is raised: How can the members of the Church participate in the great work of catechesis?

Community, the Place of Catechesis

To make the vision of the Church as catechist and catechized a reality, it is necessary greatly to esteem the small communities. Both the Synod of Bishops of 1977 as well as the Apostolic Exhortation *Catechesi tradendae* spoke of this and gave it particular attention (cf. Message of the Synod, 1977, no. 13; CT 24, 70) insofar as the community is the environment in which all the members know one another and thus favors and makes possible an exchange of experience of the faith among all the members. This is why every Christian can become in community not only an active worker of catechesis, but also a receiver of catechesis through the experience and communication of the faith of the others. In this manner, the Church, catechist and catechized, will not be only a beautiful idea, but a reality.

The community is furthermore a dynamic exigency of catechesis. "A person who has given adherence to Jesus Christ by faith and is endeavoring to consolidate that faith by catechesis needs to live in communion with those who have taken the same step" (CT 24). Therefore, catechesis risks becoming sterile and stagnant if it does not foster a community of faith which welcomes the catechumen and helps Christians grow always more in the mystery of Christ.

Community, the Worker of Catechesis

In the community as a favorable environment for exchange of experience of faith, the members are catechists one to another. This, however, is only one activity within the community; therefore, the dynamic tension of the Christian's catechetical responsibility cannot be exhausted in this, inasmuch as every Christian and all Christians must feel "eager to bear witness to their faith, to hand it on to their children, to make it known to others, and to serve the human community in every way" (CT 24). Hence, the catechetical responsibility of the Christian cannot limit itself solely to the environment of the community, but must transcend these confines to reach others—all humanity; it must be "open to missionary dynamism" (CT 24).

To be open to missionary dynamism, the community cannot remain passive; that is, it cannot be merely a place favorable to catechesis, but it—the community itself—must be the worker of catechesis. This corresponds perfectly to the vision of the Synod of Bishops of 1977, according to which "catechesis is not simply an individual task; it is carried out in the Christian community" (Message of the Synod, 1977, no. 13). Hence, we must not conceive the agent of catechesis only in reference to Christians as individuals, but also in reference to community.

The methods by which the community can be active in the process of catechesis are varied:

—Be leaven in the mass and in the world to transform it by being a clear sign of the unity of the Church, of mutual charity and of communion (cf. Message of the Synod, 1977, no. 13).

—Offer the members an atmosphere of faith in which they can live in the fullest manner what they have learned in catechesis. And more, the community must take care to provide for its members a religious formation always more profound, in such wise as to arouse and to foster in the members themselves a more explicit involvement in catechesis. In this way, the whole community participates in the catechetical tension which spreads beyond the limits of the community itself.

From all this it clearly follows that the community has to be valued and strengthened, but at the same time two questions arise: to what type of community must we address ourselves? What criteria determine the ecclesial and catechetical character of the community?

Forms of Community

All are in agreement as to the role and importance of the community in the work of catechesis, but of which community are we speaking? Aside from the parish as a fundamental form of community, we normally intend to speak of spontaneous groups, such as prayer groups, study clubs, movements of renewal, youth associations, communities of catechumens, etc.

According to Msgr. McSanda, in the African mentality the community in question would be a familial community, a community of the village or neighborhood. It must be noted, however, that according to the African mentality the community of the family does not limit itself to the fundamental nucleus of parents and children, but embraces the larger family which includes several generations.

Hence, in the present manifestations, the community exists under various forms and depends upon situations, upon individual cultures and upon the mentality of the various peoples. In any case, in all its forms of existence, the community always has the following characteristics: all the members know one another, and hence there exists a certain circulation and exchange of help and of personal and direct communication. Furthermore, all participate actively in the decisions and common activities of the community.

These elements are important for the life of the community. However, they still do not determine the good functioning of the community in the work of catechesis. Therefore, it is necessary to examine which of the ecclesial criteria of the community are truly determining.

Ecclesial Criteria of the Community

To be a place where its own members can be catechists to one another and hence agents of catechesis, the community must keep alive in its life the following elements:[1]

1. Clear awareness of a special and original relationship with the Father, through Christ, in the Spirit.

2. Acceptance of the Word of God in order to know always better the plan of God for men.

3. The celebration of the faith, particularly in the sacraments.

4. Communion with the bishop, the source of the unity of the local Church, and, through the bishop, communion with the successor of Peter, who assures the ministry of unity of the entire Church.

5. Communitarian and individual prayer in the light of the Word of God and as a response to this Word.

6. Brotherhood in love.

7. Awareness of the universal mission.

8. Recognition of the community's own limitations; hence, the necessity of opening itself to other communities for a necessary complement.

IV. DIRECT WORKERS OF CATECHESIS

The whole Church must have care for catechesis and hence for the need of awakening "in the Church as a whole and in each sector of the Church a lively and active awareness of this ...responsibility" (CT 16). This does not mean to ignore the fact that there are some members of the Church who involve themselves in catechizing in a more direct manner. We wish, therefore, to focus our attention on these direct workers of catechesis.

Catechesis, Ecclesial Act

"Before Christ ascended to His Father after His resurrection, He gave the Apostles a final command—to make disciples of all nations and to teach them to observe all that He had commanded (cf. Mt. 28:19ff.)" (CT 1). This last command of the Lord, which is the origin of the entire catechetical work, is to be conceived not as a command given to the Apostles as individuals, but to the whole Church. From this conviction springs forth the conclusion that the whole Church is catechist and catechized at one and the same time.

Even if the workers of catechesis are called to involve themselves in the work personally, catechesis is never a purely individual and private task (cf. Message of the Synod, 1977, no. 13), but it is the undertaking of the whole Church and is realized always in the dimension of the Church. Hence, it follows that this is always a properly ecclesial act. A similar observation leads to two important conclusions for every direct agent of catechesis.

On the one hand, the catechetical involvement of every catechist, even of the most obscure in the remotest place on earth, always participates in the immense catechetical commitment of the whole Church. Every act of his is an act of the Church because "his action is certainly attached to the evangelizing activity of the whole Church by institutional relationships, but also by profound invisible links in the order of grace" (EN 60). On the other hand, if catechesis is not an individual and private act but the work of the whole Church, if the involvement of every catechist is not an isolated act, but a participation in the vast catechetical task of the whole Church, no catechist will be the absolute master of his own catechetical action, "with a discretionary power to carry it out in accordance with individualistic criteria and perspectives; he acts in communion with the Church and her pastors" (EN 60).

To be in communion with the Church means to be faithful to the message of faith entrusted to the Church in order to present it with integrity. This quality is especially necessary for every catechist in the delicate effort to adapt language to the diverse cultural environments and in the actual situation where one feels the need of attracting the attention of people who are often indifferent to this message. In such a delicate context, it is necessary that every catechist avoid either a categorical refusal of every change, or a change that is hasty and inconsiderate. Habitual repetition which resists every change "leads to stagnation, lethargy and eventual paralysis. Improvisation begets confusion on the part of those being given catechesis and, when these are children, on the part of their parents; it also begets all kinds of deviations, and the fracturing and eventually the complete destruction of unity" (CT 17). Instead, the ecclesial sense of catechesis requires that the catechist courageously seek new ways and prospects for catechetical instruction, undertaken, however, with wisdom and fidelity, in communion with the Church (cf. CT 17).

Distinct and Complementary Responsibilities

Even though the whole Church is catechist and hence everyone in the Church is responsible in the work of catechesis, in reality some members of the Church are called to involve themselves in a more direct and explicit way. The question which we then ask is: Who can be called to direct involvement in catechesis?

Catechesi tradendae has given a clear answer to this question.

After having affirmed that the whole Church is responsible for catechesis, the Exhortation becomes more concrete and lists: the Pope, the bishops, priests, men and women religious, parents teachers, the various ministers of the Church, catechists, responsible persons in social communications—all have clearly precise responsibilities in catechesis (cf. CT 16, 63, 64, 65, 66, 68, 69). From this it follows that everyone in the Church, pastors and faithful, can be and is called to direct involvement in catechesis and all merit the great title of "catechist."

The vision is broad; nevertheless, for various reasons, it can give rise to tensions and confusion. Therefore, it is necessary to promote good harmony among the workers of catechesis. Essentially, this harmony requires, on the one hand, a clear idea about the responsibilities of the various persons involved in catechesis, and, on the other hand, the center of unity.

In regard to the responsibilities of the workers of catechesis, it is necessary to say that although all are called to work in catechesis, responsibilities and functions are not identical for all, because "the Church's members have different responsibilities, derived from each one's mission" (CT 16). The responsibility of every worker of catechesis depends upon his role in the Church and in the particular ecclesial community. All are catechists, but the responsibility of a priest catechist is different from that of a lay catechist.

The fact that the members of the Church have distinct responsibilities implies two consequences.

First: precisely because the catechetical responsibilities of the various members are distinct, they are also complementary. Only with difficulty can the priest fulfill his task of catechist without the collaboration of parents and teachers. In fact, "No one can accomplish the task (of catechizing) by himself, since it demands the energies of many. Each one, according to his or her function and charism, contributes to the same mission: the bishop with his priests, deacons, parents, catechists and animators of Christian communities...consecrated persons" (Message of the Synod 1977, no. 14).

Secondly: a communication of the "Fides" Agency, indicates that in the territories dependent upon the Sacred Congregation for the Evangelization of Peoples, there are 108,000 catechists in Asia, Africa and Oceania (cf. *Mondo e Missione*, January 1, 1979, p. 19). This information is truly a source of hope for the Church, and we hope that the number of catechists will still increase. However, this does not absolutely dispense priests and men and women religious from their responsibility in catechesis.

On the contrary, the large number of lay catechists stimulates and challenges priests and men and women religious. The priest, besides being a zealous catechist, an educator in the faith (cf. PO 6), must also form the souls of the catechists, his collaborators in the community (cf. CT 65). Men and women religious, in view of their religious consecration, must render themselves still more available in the service of the Church and prepare themselves for the catechetical task in the best way possible, according to the charism proper to the Institute and the needs of the missions (cf. CT 66).

Simply a clear idea of the various responsibilities, however, is not enough to harmonize the involvement of all the agents of catechesis; it is necessary to find the focal point of catechesis. Both *Catechesi tradendae* (cf. CT 63) and the Message of the Synod to the People of God (Message of the Synod, 1977, no. 14) see the bishop as the focal point of the local Church; through him we reach the Pope as the center of unity for the whole Church in catechetical involvement.

Consequently, it is indispensable that all in the work of catechists must relate themselves to the bishop. He "has the primary role in the catechetical activity of the local Church" (Message of the Synod, 1977, no. 14), and he shares with the Pope "in the spirit of episcopal collegiality" and has "charge of catechesis throughout the Church" (CT 63). This demands that the bishop personally involve himself in catechesis and take the initiative to arouse and maintain an authentic passion for catechesis, to denounce deviations, correct errors and defend the integrity of the message (cf. CT 63). To fulfill this difficult task, the bishop must be the first catechist, not only by right but also by fact; thus, he becomes the sign and center of the ecclesial community, all catechizing and, at the same time, all catechized.

Permanent Formation of Catechists

If the Church is "the great giver as well as the great receiver of catechesis" (CT 45), it is necessary that each catechist be this also. As we have already mentioned, there is an intimate bond between the two aspects: Church catechist and Church catechized. In order that the catechetical task be carried out suitably, it is necessary to "be carefully prepared" (CT 71). To be a good catechist one must first be well catechized.

Initial formation is indispensable, but not less necessary is permanent formation. Every catechist always needs a deeper formation, conversion and continual renewal, if he wants to retain freshness, zeal and power in the task of catechizing (cf. EN 15). To this end it is necessary to organize appropriate centers and institutes (cf. CT 71). Presently there are forty-five national or regional centers for the formation of catechists in the territories dependent upon the Sacred Congregation for the Evangelization of Peoples.

Conclusion

In affirming that the whole Church is "the great giver as well as the great receiver" (CT 45), *Catechesi tradendae* has pointed out to the whole Church the journey to be made in this stage of history and at the same time has indicated clear paths for the direct workers of catechesis. Now it awaits from the Pastors concrete initiatives to awaken the awareness of the faithful and to infuse catechetical zeal into the whole Church. It also awaits from every member of the faithful openness of spirit and personal commitment in order that the whole Church may be renewed in the new impetus of penetrating and diffusing the unsearchable mystery of Christ.

P. DINH DUC DAO

FOOTNOTE

1. Cf. R. Coffy, "Synode-Catéchèse," in *La Documentation catholique,* 59 (1977) 1036, and A. Marranzini, *"La catechesi per il nostro tempo: the IV Synod of Bishops, in Rassegna di Teologia,* 18 (1977) 537.

2

The Lay Catechist

Throughout the present Apostolic Exhortation, the Pope fulfills his "ministry as Pastor of the universal Church" (no. 62), presenting the various persons' responsibilities for catechesis. What we take into consideration here is perhaps the part of the document in which resound the most ardent and courageous words which aim to "set your hearts aflame." Here the Document speaks of "passion for catechesis" (no. 63), and of "courage, hope and enthusiasm" (no. 62). The Holy Father even declares, "I wholeheartedly exhort you" (no. 65), etc.

In the text, the Pontiff indicates as responsible for catechesis: ordained ministers first of all (no. 63), other ministers (no. 64), and, after a number dedicated to men and women religious (no. 65), he dwells on the "lay teachers of catechesis" (no. 66). Under this title are included all those laity—"the men and the still more numerous women"—who throughout the world dedicate themselves to catechesis and to religious education. The Pope begins with words of thanks which he addresses in the name of the whole Church to those who fulfill this "eminent form of the lay apostolate." And as happens in other pages of the Apostolic Exhortation, he presents a personal remembrance: "How many of us have received from people like you our first notions of catechism and our preparation for the sacrament of Penance, for our First Communion and Confirmation!" (CT 66)

Speaking directly to these lay catechists, John Paul II recalls: "The fourth general assembly of the synod did not forget you." In fact, in the *Instrumentum laboris* or basic document for the use of the synod fathers, treating of the renewal of catechesis (Part I, chap. 3, no. 15), catechists appear in the limelight. There is a clear reference to the numerical growth of the catechists, and the "diverse ministries of the Church" are presented "in relationship with catechesis." The synod is asked to study such a theme, and further on the same document returns to the function proper to the catechists (Part III, chap. 5, no. 48). The *Report* which was read in the second general congregation of the synod, as an introduction to the study of the *Instrumentum laboris*, presents three questions regarding lay catechists: "Can we speak in the Church of a particular vocation to the catechetical ministry? What is the importance of this ministry in the Church today? Is it necessary that the work of catechists become a special ministry in the Church?" During the synod, almost all the contributions of the fathers spoke of the catechists with expressions of esteem and asked for a new re-evaluation of their task. In the end, the summary *Report* of the synod's work read by Cardinal Lorscheider explains that the synod fathers insisted on the function proper to catechists, on their formation in special centers, on the witness which must spring forth from their spirit of prayer, on their doctrine, which must not be personal but truly ecclesial. Some fathers, states the *Report*, asked for the institutionalization of the "ministry of the catechists" in some manner.

In the *Propositions* which the fathers presented to the Pope as material for a future document on catechesis, two are dedicated to catechists: the first informs about the talents of the catechist (Prop. no. 31), the second refers to his formation (Prop. no. 32). The first insists that the catechist, not only in setting forth his arguments but also in his conduct and in his methods is to ever irradiate the ecclesial character of catechesis.

It follows that catechists must keep themselves in full communion with the Church. When in the act of catechesis dialogue arises spontaneously, when there is prayer in common, when one reads and meditates Scripture, then in some way one transmits the image of the Church. As is evident, the characteristic note of the catechist is "ecclesiality," and this note has been explained very well by the Pope in the Exhortation *Catechesi tradendae*, when he speaks of the "awareness" of ecclesial responsibility proper to the catechist (no. 16), of his union with and obedience to the bishop (no. 70b), and of his fidelity to the doctrine of the Church (no. 30). The second Proposition on catechists insists on their formation, which must precede every other attempt at renewal of methods, of instruments, etc. Preparation and continual updating are of vital importance. It is the duty of diocesan bishops to provide for the formation of the catechists, without sparing effort and expense.

The above-mentioned proposition on the formation of lay catechists was accepted by the Pope with special interest. He, in the number of the Apostolic Exhortation on which we are commenting (CT 66), does not forget this theme: "I rejoice at the efforts made by the Sacred Congregation for the Evangelization of Peoples to improve more and more the training of these catechists." We believe that this paragraph is a clear and stimulating allusion to the *Institute of Missionary Catechesis*, founded recently in Rome by the Sacred Congregation for Evangelization, about which Cardinal A. Rossi had presented information to the synod. In addition to this brief paragraph, the Pope dedicates an entire number of the Apostolic Exhortation to the theme of the formation of catechists: "These lay catechists must be carefully prepared for what is, if not a formally instituted ministry, at the very least a function of great importance in the Church. Their preparation calls on us to organize special centers and institutes, which are to be given assiduous attention by the bishops" (no. 71). Continuing, the Pope recalls the need for inter-diocesan, rather, national, cooperation within this sector.

Besides the Propositions, the synod fathers made a list of *Topics* deserving of study, which they had not been able to find space for in the Propositions. The Topics numbered thirty-eight, divided into six groups. The first topic of the sixth group concerns the status of the catechist in the Church of today, and the Pope also treats this topic, as we shall see. At the end of the synod, the synod fathers sent a *Message* to the world, number 14 of which states: "In many countries, catechists share with the priests in the function of directing the Christian community. In union with the bishops, they assume responsibility for transmitting the faith. The synod reaffirms to all the importance of their mission, and voices the hope that all will receive the help and understanding they need. The synod asks that this ministry or office should not be assumed without prior formation. This formation must be true to the double goal or dimension of catechesis: fidelity to God and fidelity to man. This demands a formation in the sacred sciences, as well as a knowledge of the human person, adapted according to the needs of nations and environments, and including knowledge of the human sciences." Again these themes have appeared: the function of the catechist as responsible for the vitality of the Church by transmitting the faith in union with the bishop, and theological and human formation founded on fidelity to the Church and to man.

Having set forth the premises necessary for being able to understand the text of the Apostolic Exhortation, we return to the number which is the object of our commentary (CT 66). Clearly the text is divided into two parts: the first speaks of lay catechists in Christian environments or in areas previously evangelized; the second presents lay catechists in mission territories as those who especially merit the title of "catechist."

We know that the term "catechist" began to be applied to the laity in the sixteenth century, with the beginning of the great missionary age. St. Francis Xavier himself wrote an "Instruction for Catechists" (Letter 53), and from that time the term catechist entered into missionary vocabulary to denote especially laity who were working in the missions. Many of them were born in Christian families, the Pope explains; others were converted to Christianity at some point. In the missions there is a well-known phenomenon of neo-converts, full of fervor, who want to dedicate themselves to the work of evangelization under the concrete form of catechesis. Lastly, the Pope recalls how many of these catechists have been "raised to the glory of the altars."

Types of Lay Catechists, According to "Catechesi Tradendae"

By using the very words of the Exhortation, we can present types of catechists in the following outline:

—collaborators in the life of the Church (builders of the Church),

—parochial catechists,

—catechists dedicated to religious education,

—catechists of children and youth,

—catechists of adults,

—catechists dedicated to preparation for the sacraments of Christian initiation and of reconciliation.

The first type listed is generic. It presents us with the catechist as an authentic collaborator, necessary for the birth and life of the Church. The sentence which illustrates the qualities of "vital collaboration" of the catechist closes the first part of the number which we are examining and opens the discourse on the missionary catechist. In fact, the Pope recognizes that historically "Churches that are flourishing today would not have been built up without them." Throughout the New Testament the verb "build" has a missionary character, and it means to lay the first foundations and help to form a new community. St. Paul used to recall that the churches had been built "upon the foundation of the apostles and prophets" (Eph. 2:20); as fruit of the first Pauline mission, "the Church...was built up" (Acts 9:31). The term means a communitarian and personal more than a material "up-building." The Old Testament rather uses the verb "build up" to speak of the communication of life and of the formation of a family (Gn. 2:22; Ruth 4:11; Is. 9:6; etc.). In the Christian mission it is the "word" which has a special power for building up (Acts 20:22; cf. Jer. 1:10).

At the time of the formation of a Church, the lay catechist collaborates especially through the word: he calls, teaches, exhorts. He does not carry out an office of substitution, but of necessary complementarity. The catechist is not called to work at the building up of the Church because priests are lacking, but because as a lay person he has a specific role to carry out in the building up of the community. Within this type, the "missionary" catechist finds his place first of all: a frontier catechist, always available to begin new works, to go where the missionary has not yet gone, to make the first contacts, and at the same time to remain completely dedicated to the formation of the neophytes. We know that each of the most flourishing churches in the history of the missions counted upon a group of lay catechists. Often these catechists were recognized with names proper to the cultural and religious traditions of the nation: in India in the sixteenth century there appear the "kanakkapillei"; the first conversion of Japan was due, in great part, to the "dôjuku" (the term is Buddhist); in the Philippines and in Latin America from 1523 the married lay natives who dedicated themselves full-time to catechetical instruction were called "fiscales" (later on, Councils such as those of Tucumán valued this image); in seventeenth-century Indochina the "thay" or teachers were the great catechists, bound by a vow of chastity and of dedication to the ministry. Mainly in Africa, from the nineteenth century, women have formed part of the ranks of lay catechists. Thinking of all these collaborators, we can understand the fruit obtained.

The second type of catechists is more specific. These are the so-called *parish catechists*. Today, the parish has once again become a privileged place of catechesis, as the next number in *Catechesi tradendae* explains (no. 67). It is true that the parish has passed through a crisis, but the Pope has complete confidence in the parish, and he hopes that it can be renewed by more adequate structures so as to remain a point of constant ecclesial reference.

Not only is the parish catechist present in nations previously evangelized, but he also works in mission countries, where, as we shall see, the parish has an irreplaceable function. The work of the parochial catechist is manifold. His most characteristic note is responsibility for parochial catechesis, that is, for that catechesis which has the parish as its center and is developed in a well-organized way both on weekdays and principally on Sundays. The basic comportment of the parish catechist is his or her "welcome" to each of those who come to the parish seeking light and truth. This is a rather urban type of catechist, who becomes the immediate collaborator of the diocesan clergy. But in the missions, it is often the catechist who takes on the responsibility of a parish which the priest can visit only once or twice a month. This full-time parish catechist is necessary mainly when the pastor is a foreigner. Not only does he make himself responsible for parochial catechesis, but he can and must visit the sick and continue their Christian formation. He also distinguishes himself as animator of the liturgy. In his functions he does not act as though he were a priest, but conserves always a "lay" role in the service of the Christian community.

The lay parochial catechist can also become an animator of pastoral care, for example, by organizing programs for the radio, by occupying himself with the translation and adaptation of liturgical texts, by coordinating programs for a continual and seasonal catechetical formation. His close rapport with the small communities which compose the parish is necessary; at the same time it can have the character of an aid and guide, for example, for study groups, for ecclesial *communautés de base* or for prayer groups. It is true that this type of lay catechist is still the object of research, for many new possibilities are opening up to his role.

Then we have the catechist dedicated to *religious education*. This type of catechist seems clearly to refer to the professor catechist of religion in the schools. The school is one of the privileged places for the catechesis of children and of youth. In every school, religious teaching must be integrated into the education of the pupils. The Pope encourages the laity to commit themselves to forming and sustaining the faith of the pupils (CT 69c).

In the churches of the Third World, this type of lay catechist has gained special importance. Today, it often happens that the Church cannot have her own schools, because the State has taken them away from her. In this context, the lay catechist teacher can be more easily accepted in the public school as a professor of religion or of ethics, during school hours. In Catholic schools, the lay catechist has a specific function to carry out. In this case, it is not necessary that he belong to the faculty of the school: he works in the school in the name of the Church. But he must always accompany his doctrine with the witness of life, because example has a decisive influence upon children and youth. His teaching will not remain on an abstract level; rather, it will come down to practical life, without forgetting the moral requisites of catechesis. This type of catechist must be in possession of pedagogical talents and at the same time must prepare himself to use audiovisuals and other modern means, with which education becomes ever more complete today.

The last type of catechist presents himself to us characterized by his/her preparatory work for the proper admission to the sacraments, especially to those of Christian initiation (Baptism, Confirmation, Eucharist) and to that of reconciliation (Penance). In the missions, in fact, catechists have been the ones to prepare almost all the neophytes for Baptism. This preparation has never remained at the cognitive level only: it has always unfolded within a new experience of Christian brotherhood, consequently unforgettable for these new Christians, many of whom choose to take the Christian "name" of their catechist. In preparation for the sacrament of Confirmation, the catechist finds an appropriate way to form the catechized to a sense of ecclesial responsibility and to the apostolate, which must characterize Christian existence. Many new Christians, and not a few old ones, having today drifted away from the sacramental life, have found in the lay catechist the closest of confidants to prepare themselves for the sacrament of reconciliation. In this office, women catechists have a special capability for opening the path towards this sacrament to women and to girls, whereas men open themselves and prepare themselves more easily with the help of men catechists.

Within these categories of catechists, we can include the animators of the sacramental liturgy, who today more than ever play a very important role in the missions, principally during the period of liturgical adaptation and acculturation. It is this catechist who remains in contact with the people, who knows their customs, usages and rites, and can, therefore, easily discern which rites, once purified, can be accepted inside the Christian sacramental line. Coming to the concrete, during the catechumenate the catechist can organize the rites (the new name, the change of clothes, the *traditio*, etc.) which must mark the itinerary of Christian initiation. The native lay catechist also knows all the values of popular non-Christian religiosity which can become the point of departure for catechesis and can later be integrated into the popular piety that is also present in Christianity.

The "Ministry" of the Lay Catechist

Now we must take up a new theme in order to answer the following question: in *Catechesi tradendae* does the Pope speak of "the ministry" of the lay catechist? In 1975, Paul VI instituted the "International Council for Catechesis," which immediately spoke of a "ministry proper to catechists." We have seen that, in the *Instrument of work* prepared for the synod on catechesis, and in the *Report* which presented the *Instrument* in the Synod hall, a "ministry" belonging to the lay catechists was clearly spoken of, and that the fathers were being asked to study this theme in the discussions. A few synodal interventions dealt with this particular theme, but the majority insisted on the importance of lay catechists in the Church and studied the tasks, so vast and varied, to which many of the laity commit themselves. It seems that the synod fathers did not want so important a theme to remain limited only to a concrete problem, such as that of "ministries." In fact, in the *Propositions* and *Topics* proposed to the Pope no mention is made of the ministries of catechists. The final *Message* of the synod recalls the ministries or catechetical tasks (cf. no. 14c), without forgetting the theme of ministry or restricting all the problematic about catechists to this.

The attitude and doctrine of the Pope in *Catechesi tradendae* follow this direction of the synod and of the Message of the synod fathers. The Holy Father does not forget the "ministry" of the catechists, for example, when he says: "These lay catechists must be carefully prepared for what is, if not a formally instituted ministry, at the very least a function of great importance in the Church" (no. 71a). The Pope, therefore, accepts and recognizes the "formally instituted ministry" of the catechists. But number 66, the object of our commentary, is a generic text, which introduces other themes, such as the family, the school, and certain movements, where many, many laity, even without instituted ministry, want to dedicate part of their lives to a "function of very great importance in the Church"; for this reason he does not dwell on the study of the "ministry" properly so-called, but generically presents the lay catechist's work as "an eminent form of the lay apostolate" (no. 66a).

What does the "formally instituted ministry," which the Pope does not forget to present, add to the life and to the tasks of the lay catechist?

Evangelii nuntiandi (no. 73) makes a clear distinction between "ordained ministries" (bishop, priest, deacon) and "lay ministries" or those entrusted to the laity; among these it recalls a few that have already been officially instituted (acolyte, lector), and others which can be created, according to the needs of the Church; first among these latter is the ministry of catechists. Ordained ministers exercise their office in virtue of the sacrament of Holy Orders; lay ministers, thanks to the sacraments of Baptism and Confirmation, which give the capability of receiving a mandate from the Church to fulfill a specific task in her name and service.

The notes which distinguish the "ministry" from a simple lay task are: first of all, a sense of stability in the particular service to the Church; second, the mandate of the Church, of the ecclesial community presided over by the bishop, to fulfill a specific service—in our case, that of catechesis. Thus it can be affirmed that the "minister" works with a greater ecclesial responsibility and a greater ontological and existential union with the community and its pastors. Radically the ministry is fruit of a charism or special grace, originating from the Holy Spirit, who freely distributes these gifts and charisms for the upbuilding of the Church (1 Cor. 12:7, 11; Eph. 4:7-16; AA 3dc). Even though in number 66 of

Catechesi tradendae, the Pope—for the reasons set forth—does not speak of the work of the catechist as an "instituted ministry," he does present his image with a few expressions which in some manner give the impression that he has a real ministry before his eyes. On the one hand, the Pope says that the catechists "consecrate their lives, year after year" to this mission, thus indicating the stability proper to ministries; on the other hand, the goal of their vocation and grace seems to be "the upbuilding of the Church," which in Pauline vocabulary is the purpose of every charism. In other texts he recalls how the work of the lay catechist is especially bound to the bishops (no. 70b).

To conclude, we must cite the last sentences of the Pope in number 66 of *Catechesi tradendae:* "I wholeheartedly encourage those engaged in the work. I express the wish that many others may succeed them and that they may increase in numbers for a task so necessary for the mission." The work of catechists is necessary, because it becomes a work of life or death for the mission, necessary not only for conversions, but also for the formation of an authentic Church. We cannot fail to remember that phrase uttered by Pius XII during the International Congress on the Apostolate of the Laity: "A missionary accompanied by six catechists accomplishes more than seven missionaries" (AAS, 49, 1957, 937).

JESÚS LÓPEZ-GAY, S.J.

BIBLIOGRAPHY

Sacred Congregation for the Evangelization of Peoples, or Propaganda Fide. Commission for Catechesis and for Catechists, *The training of catechists. Situations, efforts, experiences, in Asia, Africa and Oceania,* Rome 1974 (edition also in French).

The Catechist According to the Council. International Study Week, Aachen, 1968.

"Catéchistes?" *Missi,* no. 347 (1971) 79-110.

E. Cuppens, "La personalité du catéchiste," *Lumen Vitae,* 29(1974) 119-148; 270-296. (In the English edition: pp. 429-452).

G. Guarda, "Notas sobre el apostolado seglar en América Española," *Teología y Vida,* 13(1972) 66-78.

J. Kempenners, "Les Catéchistes au service des communautés chrétiennes," *Eglises et Mission,* no. 181(1971) 15-22.

S. Riva, "Il Catechista educatore e animatore. L'apporto delle scienze umane," *Seminarium,* no. 1(1975) 192-208.

_____, *Una nuova tipologia del catechista per la catechesi del nostro tempo,* Turin, 1977.

3

The Irreplaceable Role of the Family

Between Synods

When the 1977 Synod was treating of "Catechesis in Our Times"...there were frequent and forceful references to the family as subject and receiver of an activity that is essential to the life and mission of the Church. Outstanding among various interventions of the synod fathers on this subject was that of Cardinal Francisco Primatesta, Archbishop of Cordova, one of the three prelates chosen personally by Paul VI for the actual council of the general secretariat of the synod. He insisted that "the family is the 'normal way' of living the lay vocation as a Christian experience of faith and apostolate." Taken up again during the discussions and developed in some of the *circules minores*, the family was presented by the synod fathers in their final message as "one of the catechetical *loci*, as was mentioned, in fact, in the Apostolic Exhortation *Catechesi tradendae* itself. It is no surprise, then, that number 68 of the Apostolic Exhortation opens with a clear affirmation: "The family's catechetical activity has a special character, which is in a sense irreplaceable." John Paul II, in *Redemptor hominis*, no. 19, went a step further in his consideration of "family catechesis" as the "fundamental field" which, with other fields of catechesis "should give evidence of the universal sharing by the whole people of God in the prophetic role of Christ Himself."

To refer to family catechesis as "the fundamental field" presupposes the existence, vocation and commitment of a "Christian family." Hence, CT 68 already launches us into one of the fundamental perspectives of the coming bishops' synod, which will deal with "the mission of the Christian family in the modern world," connecting up and clearly expressing themes treated in preceding synods.

Ecclesial Tradition and Critical Actuality of the Theme of the Family

The family has received from God the mission to be the first and vital cell of society (cf. AA II). As the narrower and more permanent circle of social ties and interpersonal relationships, the family is the primary, basic and irreplaceable human community.

At Puebla John Paul II explained: "Our God in His deepest mystery is not a solitude, but a family, for He has in Himself fatherhood, sonship and the essence of the family, which is love." This makes us understand "much more deeply Paul's affirmation: 'the Father, from whom every family in heaven and on earth takes its name' " (Eph. 3:15) *(La familia a la luz de Puebla,* CELAM, Bogotà 1980). Because the married nucleus—the basis of the family—acquires the fullness of its meaning in God's salvific plan and is recreated as a sacrament, it is an effective sign of God's love for men and is changed into "a reflection of the loving covenant uniting Christ with the Church" (GS 48).

Here it is not necessary to enlarge on a permanent and repeated ecclesial tradition in this sense, a tradition which was brought out particularly in Vatican II. But it should be noted that this tradition—which operates as one of the fundamental bases and models of the centuries-old civilizing process of humanity—is today faced with the challenges and demands of "complex and difficult times" in which "immense and insuperable phenomena have produced confusion in families: industrialization, urbanization, cultural progress, internationalization of relationships, affective instability and intellectual precocity" (John Paul II, allocution 5/15/79). Because of the coming global diffusion of urban-industrial civilization that has continued at different rhythms to provoke profound transformations in the living, acting and working patterns of men and peoples, this primary and most sensitive cell of the whole social organism has received the impact of a multitude of stimuli and reactions. Among other things, in the last decades, it has become commonplace to note tendencies to modify inter-family relationships and their social functions, accompanied by much greater physical, moral and spiritual disintegration of the family-community, growing separation of the sexuality-communication from its essential pro-creative function, the lowering of the birth-rate and the revin-dication of new "rights" that go to the alarming extreme of the "right" to kill the unborn life in the mother's womb. In this new context, and in the economic, cultural and spiritual socialization, the condition of family life and the family itself imposes the con-sideration of different "contemporary" variables, such as the new image and the human and social projection of woman; increasing problems connected with the transition of youth from the "domus" to the "polis"; cultural gulfs widening between genera-tions; the crisis of traditional educational systems; the invading impact of the mass-media; and different living, working, produc-ing and consuming conditions in the family and its members in the agitated, distracting and anonymous milieu of the big cities, etc. Above all, there are the idols of wealth, power and pleasure on the various platforms of secular materialism and, in addition, the refusal of paternity, the break-up of the father-son relation-ship, selfish utilitarian and pleasure-loving egoism, and the threats that menace every form of conjugal and fraternal com-munion. From these new conditions come answers that question family integrity and put it in crisis, in regard to both its essence and its mission. A crisis in a civilization almost necessarily attacks these three essentials—life, love and death—that are the very roots of humanity, "the deepest human problems that concern the family" (John Paul II, 1/9/79). In the face of challenges and at-tacks of such vast proportions, nostalgic lamentation and mythical idealization of the past are useless. Nor is it enough to denounce and condemn, though there are plenty of good reasons for doing so, those called "not to model (themselves) on the pres-ent age" but to stand as a "sign of contradiction" against every-thing that goes contrary to natural reason and revelation in the question of matrimony and the family. It is more important and urgent that Christian families should gather up the human and Christian wisdom of our heritage in the life of men, families and peoples, and make use of the best and widest possibilities and desires of human dignity, liberty and communion expressed at the heart of new social conditions. They should thus become clear-cut models that summarize, witness to, and illuminate the Church's tradition about the family for the "contemporary world."

In the framework of this general perspective, the challenge and irreplaceable task of the family as subject and receiver of ecclesial catechesis stands out in all its actuality and urgency.

The Domestic Church and Catechetical Ministry

"At different moments in the Church's history and also in the Second Vatican Council, the family has well deserved the beautiful name of 'domestic Church' " (Apost. Exhort. *Evangelii nuntiandi*, no. 71); it is an "authentic cell of the Church, basic and germinal, and the smallest cell doubtless, but at the same time the most basic of ecclesial organisms" (Paul VI, allocution 5-4-71). Sealed in the sacrament of Matrimony, the family actualizes and reflects in a little space the mystery of the Church as God's family (including the trinitarian riches of this expression). And as such it is itself a sacrament of salvation. This is its deepest identity. Such a title is deserved only if the family confesses by its faith, life and works that Christ is the Lord, as the whole Church professes. It is a milieu created by God the Father, redeemed and sanctified by God the Son, and inhabited and animated by God the Holy Spirit. In it, as the domestic Church, must be found the various aspects of the life and mission of the whole Church, among which catechesis is fundamental as an intrinsic function of the married couple who participate with all the People of God— and, in particular, with the apostolate of the laity—in the prophetic mission Christ gave the Church.

Hence, if parents are, on the one hand, the "first and principal educators of their children"—a "natural right" that comes from procreation and the very special and original relationships that are created intimately in the family—*(Gravissimum educationis*, 3)—at the same time, they are also their first catechists. Personal formation and education in the faith are the vital and theological part of the experience and mission of the Christian family, because "to educate Christian persons means to make them in the likeness of Christ, who is at one and the same time wholly man and wholly God" (CELAM, *op. cit.*). Not for nothing did the Council call the family the school of the richest, integral, Christian humanism.

When the couple become father and mother, they discover at the baptismal font that their child is henceforth a son of God and that he has been given to them to be cared for most certainly in his moral and physical growth, but also in the unfolding and manifestation of the "new man" (Eph. 4:24).

For this reason the Council associates the procreative and educative function with the mystery of the fruitfulness and maternity of the Church. Father and mother are "witnesses and cooperators with the Church's fruitfulness" (LG 41). Applied to education, this image of fruitfulness includes and transcends the purely biological and human significance to bring out the spiritual and religious as well. Just as the Church is fruitful, forever engendering new sons for God through the evangelization of the Word, sacramental life and the witness of charity, so also the family is an image of and participation in this mysterious fruitfulness. "The sublime mission of paternity and maternity," of the "priests" of the home—St. John Chrysostom goes on to describe their role—is similar to that of the bishop in the Church; that is, they are teachers of faith within the charity and unity of the family.

Hence, the family will be, and very much so, the "fundamental subject" and "main locus" of catechetical action (John Paul II, allocution to the council of the synod, 1-21-79).

Various Levels and Requirements of Family Catechesis

In the Apostolic Exhortation *Catechesi tradendae*, no. 68, there is a presentation of various levels and requirements of catechetical action in family life, in a series of forms and times that are interconnected and inseparable: Christian witness in daily life according to the Gospel, more intense and explicit catechesis at peak-points of family life, and further methodical and systematic Christian formation at home, in harmony and in communion with what is imparted in other "ecclesial places."

As for what we could call a *first essential level*, CT notes that "education in the faith by parents...is already being given when the members of a family help each other to grow in faith through the witness of their Christian lives, a witness that is often without words but which perseveres throughout a day-to-day life lived in accordance with the Gospel." In this sense, the family is, and should be, primarily a place of basic human experiences— predominantly of faith and love—which each and every member needs for personal and communitarian growth. Family living, the foundation of these experiences—with its continuity, frequency and affective intensity in the original atmosphere that permeates and animates it—constitutes a permanent "non-verbal language" through which Gospel values and behavioral models filter. Far more important at this level than catechetical techniques is the lifestyle of the family with its intangible ethical and religious realities that go to the heart of each person and stamp them radically at every level—sensitivity, will and intelligence. These are a privileged reality-sign, because inter-family relationships are far more indelibly centered in the very being of the person than in what each separate component has, or can produce, however much they may be threatened by depersonalizing or merely functional tendencies.

Each simple family activity—meals, prayer, work, recreation or rest, holidays and Sunday outings, the home atmosphere, receiving friends and relatives, being present as a family in church and every daily gesture and attitude from showing affection to playing, sitting around a common table, tensions and pardons, expression and thanks, blessings and the goodbye embrace, shared worries, joys and projects, and at times inevitable tensions and conflict—all this woof of shared living can become the background of vital existential signs and an introduction to the catechetical dialogue between parents and children.

In this sense, the family experience in its fullest meaning will communicate a "savory knowledge," a wisdom about life impregnated with evangelical values and evocative of the most radical "religious" reality.

Experiences of love will be fundamental, particularly in early childhood. The "four faces of love" (Puebla 583)—fatherhood, marriage, sonship and fraternity—will be learned in the family circle. Not for nothing "the great contents of the evangelical message are expressed in familiar language...: a God-family who is Father, Son and Love, who sends the Son to be integrated as the spouse of the Church so as to change her into our Mother and Family, whence men may become sons, brothers and friends."

It would not be possible to speak of love, pardon and mercy in the family, not to mention authority and justice, providence and God's salvation, unless the children were able to refer to images and behavior concretely lived at home, especially in relation to parents. Attitudes of trust and consolation, docility and obedience, and love and respect of children for their parents can increase the feeling for, and requirements of their baptismal sonship. The mystery of the domestic Church begins to come alive in the mutual fidelity, love, unity and fruitfulness of the married couple. The children, feeling themselves sons of the same parents, will show their mutual love in that Christian fraternity that goes beyond the limitations of blood.

The convergence of these relationships goes to form a milieu whose "atmosphere" permeates the family and its members by osmosis and vital contagion. Its influence is primordial. All the qualities of charity in the Pauline hymn (1 Cor. 1:13)—patience, service, generosity, detachment, serenity, joy, discretion, gratuity, goodness, justice, sincerity, truth, pardon, mutual acceptance, respect, perseverance, hope—all these are tried out in the family circle so that such a life experience may be an evangelical sign of catechetical initiation and growth in faith.

On the other hand, to start out on this catechetical level would be useless if the family did not give itself a minimum of vital space and time for recollection, so as to create an authentic web of living relationships to form a real community among its members.

Obviously, it is impossible to ignore the increasing objective difficulties that are obstacles to such family living, which often make the house more of a transit station than a real home. But if there is no periodical renewal of perspective and a common will to attain family living insofar as it is possible, there is a real risk of physical and spiritual dispersion and even disintegration, with the consequent loss of all the human riches that come from healthy and harmonious living together.

To this "life teaching" in the family must be added the "teaching of the word," above all, in the irreplaceable personal catechetical dialogue between parents and their children. Although very often this unceasing exchange of witnessing to Christian living in the family takes place in silence, at the same time, verbal communication of the faith is necessary—communication in familiar language, closely related to the background of common life. For the parents it will mean reflecting with their children on shared experiences from the standpoint of faith. At this level, explicit religious communication will have an existential, spontaneous, occasional but frequent character, not arising from some previous didactic programming, but capturing favorable moments, times of greater intensity in family relationships, in order to inject a presentation of faith, answer children's questions, spark off a catechetical dialogue, inspire an intensifying affectionate exchange between members of the family, and from there move to union with God.

Here it becomes apparent that family prayer—silent or in dialogue with the Lord, biblical reading, the rosary, examination of conscience—all become a true catechetical reality of the greatest importance, because from them the children discover how their parents pray and discern daily events before God. From this, personal prayer and introduction to the liturgy of the Church will arise.

In this conjugal and family life there will be moments of more intense communitarian experience, in which God's interventions are felt with particular strength. This is the *second level* of family catechesis, which, according to *Catechesi tradendae*, no. 68, becomes "more incisive when, in the course of family events...care is taken to explain in the home the Christian or religious content of these events." These are "those moments full of salvific grace that occur in the couple and with the family: engagement, marriage, fatherhood, education of children, anniversaries, baptisms, first communions, family feasts and celebrations, not to mention crises in the family, times of sorrow, illness and death" (Puebla, 597). The special union of the whole family at such happenings, particularly important experiences, is a very good moment for catechetical action. On the level of faith the celebration of certain sacraments (Baptism, First Communion and Confirmation—or the anniversary of others—Marriage, Baptism) should bring out special commitment and solemnity: "they constitute the great stages of the history of salvation" lived by each domestic Church. Just as the great family of God celebrates the Pasch of the Lord each Sunday, the Christian family should remember gratefully the times in which the strength of the Pasch entered into its own life" (CELAM, *op. cit.*, 56).

At this level it is essential that parents assume their role in an "eminently catechetical form," that is, in preparation for the sacraments, especially those of Christian initiation of their children. The whole family participates and grows in faith while the children are being introduced into ecclesial life. The parents themselves listen while they announce, and learn while they teach. In the family, too, the child will learn religious symbolism in its ordinary forms—gestures, signs, prayer formulas, images. At the same time he continues to gather in the human depth of the sacramental signs, the existential and symbolic meaning attached to things and gestures. If sacramental practice is the climax of catechetical initiation, it is also the source of greater growth and education in the faith at the heart of the Christian family, "for it is in the sacraments, especially in the Eucharist, that Christ Jesus works in fullness for the transformation of human beings" (CT 23). Conjugal and family living will then be expressed as a lived eucharist, communion prolonged in dialogue, love and prayer in the family, capacity for pardon, patience and mercy in the face of weaknesses and each other's limitations, etc. This way of living the sacraments is fundamental and the center of the life of the domestic Church as a personal, familiar and communitarian encounter with the Risen Christ. Within the sacramental "intensity" of the Christian family, between parents and children, catechesis will certainly become more incisive and fruitful.

The *third level* presented in the Apostolic Exhortation on family catechesis (CT 68), demands that we go further: "Christian parents must strive to follow and repeat, within the setting of family life, the more methodical teaching received elsewhere." This is the catechetical level properly and completely so-called, as number 18 of the Exhortation affirms when it points out that "catechesis is an education of children, young people and adults in the faith, which includes especially the teaching of Christian doctrine imparted, generally speaking, in an organic and systematic way, with a view to initiating the hearers into the fullness of Christian life." This had already been pointed out in *Evangelii nuntiandi*, when it refers to catechesis, stressing that "the intelligence, especially that of children and young people, needs to learn through systematic religious instruction the fundamental teachings, the living content of the truth which God has wished to convey to us and which the Church has sought to express in an ever richer fashion during the course of her long history" (no. 44).

Clearly, "the methods must be adapted to the age, culture and aptitude of the persons concerned; they must seek always to fix in the memory, intelligence and heart the essential truths that must impregnate all of life" (no. 44). As John Paul II insists, parents are called to contribute to this "more systematic and organic" catechetical formation. However important the witness of Christian life in the family, it would be "quite useless to campaign for the abandonment of serious and orderly study of the message of Christ in the name of a method concentrating on life experience" (CT 22). Neither will it do to be satisfied with a family contribution through occasional, improvised and fragmentary catechesis, limited to expecting organic systematization and deepening to be given in other, extra-familial settings. While cooperating with these, the parents should also offer a planned and more qualified level of catechetics with the characteristics noted in CT 21.

The three levels referred to above are interconnected in a crescendo of catechetical commitment in the Christian family. In this way it is possible "to influence the children in a decisive way for life" (CT 68).

It is certainly not easy today to affirm that a Christian family will necessarily engender Christian children. But it is certain that the religious witness of the parents in example and word is the most authentic matrix of the religious attitude of the children. Although it is true that children spend most of their time outside their homes, we cannot ignore that sociologists and educators continue to attribute to parents and to the family the primary influence, not only for the capital importance of the first years of life but also for the so-called "principle of intense relationship" that acts most strongly on the development of the personality, both human and religious. On the other hand, given that "in a catechetical dialogue of this sort each individual both receives and gives, "the parents themselves grow in faith as they catechize, sharing in the Christian maturation of the whole family.

For all these reasons, before all the Bishops of Latin America, John Paul II pointed out the priority of family pastoral action, "with the certainty that in the future, evangelization depends to a great extent on the domestic Church" (Puebla, Jan. 24, 1979). And in his own country he begged the Polish family "never to cease being strong with the strength of God," because, he said, "what the family is, the nation will be, and such will man be too " (Allocutions at Jasna Gora and Krakow, June 7 and 8, 1979).

The Family as a Recipient of Ecclesial Catechesis

From the original and specific character of catechesis in the Christian family, we infer that "it precedes, accompanies and enriches all other forms of catechesis." This gives us the measure of the irreplaceable role of the Christian family as subject of catechesis. This irreplaceable role is accentuated in regard to "those places where anti-religious legislation endeavors even to prevent education in the faith," or where "widespread unbelief or invasive secularism makes real religious growth practically impossible...." In such situations, " 'the church of the home' remains the one place where children and young people can receive an authentic catechesis" (CT 68). The former Cardinal Karol Wojtyla pointed this out at the last synod when speaking of an "anti-catechesis" in society that imposed greater responsibilities on the Christian family.

The family is not only the fundamental subject, but also the receiver of ecclesial catechesis.

However, the Christian family is not the Church. It is part of her indeed, but not exhaustively so. Nevertheless, the family can in no way be self-sufficient either spiritually or doctrinally. It must go outside the walls of its house if it is not to asphyxiate. It has to open itself to the ecclesial community and live in her, nourishing itself on her life, sacraments and teachings. The Church evangelizes and catechizes the family so that it may be continually renewed as evangelizer and catechist. Hence the need to meet others, the numerous Christian families among the People of God within His great family; the need, also, for those brothers who renounce their own families to follow God totally, because the Christian family is unthinkable without Christ, His priesthood and His sacrifice. And what greater gift could God give than the priestly or religious vocation to the children of those parents who have known how to be teachers of faith and have prayed perseveringly for this grace!

Besides this, in the field of education and socialization regarding children, there have been notable transformations. Not only has there been a broadening and extension of the concept of education but also a multiplication of extra-scholastic activities— sports, recreations and scientific as well as Christian-life experiences. Then there is the powerful effect of the mass-media through ever more perfected cultural models and incisive techniques, not to mention the tricky problem of television in the home. More than ever before, family catechesis needs the basic collaboration and integrating contribution of many other Christian education centers. Multiplying places, groups, times, milieus, educative possibilities, in a plurality of settings and situations where a person may deepen his religious experience, the Church possesses a network of catechetical occasions singularly enriched by complementary factors. There are two important conditions. On the one hand, this diversity of catechetical places and openings—family, school, parish, apostolic movements, youth centers, spiritual retreats, etc.—is to "really converge on the same confession of faith, on the same membership of the Church, and on commitments in society lived in the same Gospel spirit: 'one Lord, one faith, one baptism, one God and Father' " (CT 67). On the other hand, there must be a pastoral plan that respects and supports the original and unrepeatable contribution of each catechetical undertaking.

In this sense, just as it would be absurd to claim catechetical monopoly for the family, the greater risk today is that parents delegate or discharge their prior specific and unavoidable responsibility on other centers of Christian formation. Parents are called, on the contrary, to follow up the development in faith of their children given through parochial or scholastic catechesis not merely as benevolent onlookers from outside, but from within, as living members of the parish and educative communities.

Before all, Christian parents need to be helped in their efforts to prepare for this catechetical ministry to their own children so as to exercise it with untiring zeal.... This is an apprenticeship parents should undertake, with God's grace, first of all, by strengthening their own moral and religious convictions, and likewise reflecting on their own experiences, by themselves or with other parents, expert educators or priests" (John Paul II, allocution, October 30, 1978).

For this reason CT 68 continues: "Encouragement must also be given to the individuals or institutions that, through person-to-person contacts, through meetings, and through all kinds of pedagogical means, help parents to perform their task: The service they are doing to catechesis is beyond price." Not to mention the help so often given by relatives (how many times a grandmother, grandfather, or aunt supports and at times assumes the catechetical role of parents!) or by those godparents who take their baptismal commitment seriously.

The Church's basic service will always be to proclaim the "good news" of the family, defending and promoting the integrity of its existence and mission, while sustaining and animating Christian families and couples with her teaching and sacramental grace on their path to sanctification. Parishes and catechetical centers, family associations and other apostolic movements, marriage and family guidance, preparation for the sacraments, days and seminars for spiritual formation, etc.—every form and instrument coordinated, each according to its kind, for "family pastoral practice"—all these will be attentive to the preparation of young people for marriage, especially engaged couples. They will support and strengthen the Christian growth of married couples—and, in particular, conjugal spirituality—with delicate pastoral attention during moments of crisis; they will be attentive to the education of the spouses to "responsible parenthood" according to the Church's teaching; they will awaken the religious sense of so many married couples who have been absorbed by inertia and indifference and a "non-practicing" Christian life; they will call the attention of Christian couples to their inescapable catechetical vocation and trace out its demands and perspectives; they will help them "remain clear and consistent in their faith, to affirm serenely their Christian and Catholic identity, to 'see him who is invisible' and to adhere so firmly to the absoluteness of God that they can be witnesses to Him in a materialistic civilization that denies Him" (CT 57). Thus parents will bear this witness to their children. These programs will also help couples to live a simple, evangelical life in a family where the members grow in the spirit of the Beatitudes. There is to be a well-grounded biblical, theological and Christian pedagogical formation for parents, based on the truths of the Catholic Faith, to meet the demands and challenges of their children's catechesis. They will be urged to base, permeate and nourish this ministry on an intense spiritual and sacramental life of ecclesial communion, projected and prolonged in family prayer and in offering to God their family's entire life and activity.

GUZMAN CARRIQUIRY

4

The Receivers of Catechesis and the Centrality of Man

The pontificate of John Paul II initiated in the ecclesial community a "rediscovery" of man as a person, an image of God, redeemed by Christ, brother of other men, with whom he shares life, destiny, love, pain, joy, and death, which will have its epilogue in the resurrection.

Catechesi tradendae in Chapter 5 does not hesitate to affirm authoritatively that "everybody needs to be catechized," and, indeed, the pastoral history of the Church documents the fact that, in the origin of the community of faith, catechesis was begun for adults who, coming from Judaism, Hellenism, or idolatry, aspired to and asked for Baptism. Later on, with the formation of Christian families, the need of sharing the parents' faith with the children was felt: catechesis thus descended from the adult level to that of the child.

The pontifical Document again takes up the dictate of the preliminary instrument of the synod, and declares the importance of catechesis to children and youth. In fact, man, from the moment of conception in his mother's womb, lives and carries out a whole process of growth, development and human maturation. His human formation follows a long course: "the increase in the number of young people is without doubt a fact charged with hope and at the same time with anxiety for a large part of the contemporary world" (CT 35).

This is nothing other than an admission of a concrete and disturbing fact. But we ask ourselves: in what terms does the pastoral-catechetical problem present itself? The Document asks: "How are we to reveal Jesus Christ, God made man, to this multitude of children and young people, reveal Him not just in the fascination of a first fleeting encounter but through an acquaintance, growing deeper and clearer daily, with Him, His message, the plan of God that He has revealed...to each person...? (CT 35)

Suitably, therefore, the Document begins with the children who, in this era of ours, seem to be the determining and absolute future of the world of tomorrow and, in our regard, of the ecclesial community itself, in its promises and foreshadowings. If historically and in the Church's pastoral activity of these last four centuries, from Trent to Vatican II, catechesis has meant the *plenum* for school-age children, today we are beginning to speak of cultivating the religious sense and the sense of God in small children.

Infants Are Not To Be "Excluded"

Pedagogy and catechesis for young children (0-9 years) open a new page in education to the faith, or, better, in Christian initiation. A beginning points to and requires a continuation, but everything is conditioned by a concrete, respectful and illumined start. It must be said that the education of little ones to the faith begins in the maternal womb, when the new life, united to and yet distinct from that of the mother, breathes the interior climate and vitality of the maternal, and, in a certain sense, also the paternal, faith. The family's life of faith is essential for the birth and the growth of the yet unborn infant, so that, upon the opening of his eyes to the light, if he will receive with the gift of life also the gift of divine sonship in Baptism, he will find himself already situated and placed in the cradle of his Christian "being."

The Document acknowledges that from his parents the infant receives the first elements of catechesis, which perhaps will be nothing but a simple revelation of the heavenly Father, good and provident, toward whom he learns to lift up his heart (cf. CT 36). But it immediately states that often this catechesis also consists of very short prayers, and, delving deeper into the pontifical text, it may further be said that there should be simple, delicate and respectful conversation about the person of Jesus, in His typically human moments, which are the most accessible to this age, and are open to a subsequent, more global, vision of Jesus, of His Gospel, of His community of faith and life.

Often, even today, psychology disputes whether the religious sense is innate in the infant or rather is "environmental," resulting from education, from patterns observed, from family customs. It is to be noted that, in regard to baptized infants, infused theological faith precedes the religious sense, but is dormant and awaits activation. Education to the religious sense, which in this case has a "Catholic" specificity, has an initial and basic coefficient: it is a matter of method, of the capacity to dialogue and converse, of a gradualness that avoids haste and impatience, but, on the other hand, also disengagement, inertia and fear. A catechetical document of a national episcopal conference rightly acknowledges that infants have an openness and an availability to the religious sense, excluding discriminations and absolutisms, but conserving an openness to a pastoral of integration.

The problem is to sensitize the parents to the fundamental role of this first announcement, which is above all pre-verbal, that is, before the infant gives his own vocal response, because it is constituted by that "simple and true presentation of the Christian faith" (CT 36) which is offered to the observation of the little ones by what is before their eyes: the life of the adults in the family in their relationship with God. Urgent would be the discussion of nursery schools which are to be the continuation and integration of the educational work of the family, a first experience of social life, the beginning of the human phenomenon of communion, which, subsequently made more aware, becomes ecclesial consciousness.

Children "Dictate" a Method of Catechesis

Children, in the most accepted meaning of the term, are the subjects of basic schooling, and, even more, of the sacraments of Christian initiation, the Eucharist and Confirmation. Psychology defines childhood as a stable age, from the viewpoint of physical, psychic and intellectual development, in the sense that it does not involve jumps, and growth proceeds normally. It is an age in which "memory" and "sentiment" are fertile, and going to school is the most accepted fact everywhere, accepted both by the community and by the children themselves. The process of socialization is favored by the faith and school communities. Contact with culture and science, even if in a purely elementary degree, refine the intelligence and orient it not so much to perceiving, which does take place too, but also to the first forms of research and of documentation.

From the pastoral point of view, children can be considered to have four different origins: 1) children coming from seriously Christian families, and, hence, with a first announcement of Jesus, from an environment that breathes faith; 2) children coming from nominally Christian families, with little religious practice and some rudimentary and confused catechetical notions; 3) children coming from non-believing, indifferent or hostile families, with very little or no serious education to the faith; 4) children without a family due to the death or unworthiness of their parents, who have been gathered into institutions in order to promote their human qualities and develop their religious dimension.

From this empirical classification, it is possible to understand how their concrete situation and condition of life determine the characteristic signs of catechesis, which no type of educator can ignore.

After alluding to the structures of the school, parish, Catholic academy or state school, the Document outlines the categories of catechesis to children: didactic catechesis, but aimed at witnessing; initial catechesis, which reveals the principal mysteries of the faith and their influences on the child's human behavior; and catechesis directed to awareness of the sacraments received or to be received, "a catechesis that gives meaning to the sacraments, but at the same time it receives from the experience of the sacraments a living dimension that keeps it from remaining merely doctrinal, and it communicates to the child the joy of being a witness to Christ in ordinary life" (CT 37).

At a certain point, *Catechesi tradendae* states that catechesis concerns inserting the child "organically into the life of the Church, a moment that includes an immediate preparation for the celebration of the sacraments" (CT 37). The global context of the Document, however, insists upon the pedagogy of faith, for every age of man, and the child is not excluded. For a religious education which acts as the basis for all Christian life, the education to the faith has a primary role: in fact, the sacraments themselves, in the most common language, are called the "sacraments of faith," and the essential and ordinary educative element to lead to the faith, after the first announcement, is catechesis. But catechesis, which is reading, listening, reflecting on and responding to the Word of God, transmitted in catechesis, virtually leads to the sacrament; it completes and actualizes itself in the liturgical celebration.

Having specified that Christian initiation is the aim of the catechesis of children, we must outline the fundamental goals to which catechesis itself tends. First of all, it presents itself as a true and proper "catechumenate," framed within the dimensions of the person's age, his degree of education, and his insertion into a community of faith. As a catechumenate, it follows a gradual but progressive dynamic of its own, according to essential goals, from which then branch out other goals on the basis of special needs of the local churches and of the communities of faith.

The right and need of all children to have a permanent education in the faith must be defended, for the sacraments presume of this age not only the beginning of a true and active faith, not only potential faith, but dynamic faith and perfectible faith.

Faith is not taught to children, because it is unteachable, but the revealed data of the faith are proposed, insofar as they can be perceived and explained. The faith of children requires an uninterrupted response to the continual "calls" of God: herein lies the task of catechesis. Education to the faith is not a problem of the sacramental moment alone, but of one's whole existence.

Not to be undervalued is the initiation into the liturgical-sacramental life, because catechesis as a simple communication of the evangelical message does not stop at the cognitive moment, but leads to the moment that can be and is lived, which is actualized in the liturgy. Some catechetical and pedagogical points are worthy of note. Catechesis brings about a small catechumenate of Baptism, whether already received or to be received, undertaking a retrospective or preliminary and introductory journey. It gives a first sense of Penance, by pointing out the need for continual purification and proof of what is evil. As a fundamental stage in the journey of faith, the Eucharist is to be presented not only as food-communion, but also as personal communion and community communion. The role of the Holy Mass does not conceal the fact that one finds himself together with his brethren, around the same altar-table, as church which forms itself and lives and the instruction about the Mass is not to ignore a first announcement of the "sacrifice" of Jesus. In catechesis,

Confirmation takes on the function of a natural and supernatural verification and ratification of the process of development and growth of the person, of faith, of grace, of incorporation into the Church, and of the conscious beginning of the witnessing of Christian life, which is possible for children.

The present liturgy for children, with the recent "children's missal" and the corresponding lectionary, facilitates the entrance of the little ones into the liturgical world and the Christian mystery.

Sometimes we seem to note, in educative circles, a certain silence regarding moral catechesis, with the exception of the repetition of the slogan: "Life is love." All this is true, but the children's age and degree of intellectual and affective development cannot but require an explanation, an orientation. The principle that the education of conscience is to be preferred to a systematic collection of cases is also acceptable. But the catechesis of children takes up the theme of the first announcement of Jesus to them. The children are shown how to live "by looking" at the behavior, life, person and words of Jesus as the model. This is an announcement which calls for amplification into a true and proper catechesis in order to make it concrete. A synthetic diagram could be set forth as follows:

First: Catechesis prefers to clarify that morality is the law of love, above all the love of Jesus for the children, but also the love of the children for Him and for their own life; it does not cancel out the meaning of "law," which can find a more down-to-earth expression in "rule" or "standard" or "duty." Second: Catechesis on the decalogue, with an evangelical interpretation, according to the explanation given by Jesus, and hence positive in its orientation. Third: Catechesis gives priority to the evangelical norm of charity-love. Fourth: Catechesis chiefly introduces the students to an awareness of the good to be done. Fifth: Catechesis pays attention to the environments in which the children live: house, yard, neighborhood, school, street, fields, faith community (parish). Sixth: Catechesis focuses on the common activities of children today. Seventh: Catechesis aids and guides in the reading of universal events which reveal to the world the presence of good and evil.

It is commonly held that the education of the moral conscience of children is of fundamental importance. This, however, does not justify the evasion of the responsible recognition that the child becomes always more a man, even though with regard to man and human life he grasps only silent patterns of life which multiply uninterrupted questions without answers. Catechesis is a way to give a timely answer to the greatly praised self-made conscience.

Adolescence: Evolving Arch of Questions and Answers

The Document speaks of puberty and adolescence, but does not distinguish preadolescence from adolescence true and proper. The *General Catechetical Directory* of the Sacred Congregation for the Clergy (1971) advises: "National directories should distinguish preadolescence, adolescence, and early adulthood" (art. 83). Taking a universal view of the problem of development, it seems to us that today some characteristics of preadolescence easily penetrate into adolescence, and that a few aspects of adolescence continue from preadolescence. From the pedagogical point of view, in line with psychological findings, it seems that in catechesis a global treatment of the adolescent, prescinding from analyses, adequately directs itself towards one group without ignoring the other. The Document summarily points out some aspects of adolescent development, which can be found in the adolescent or preadolescent of diverse and varied populations and communities: the discovery of self in the new reality, the perception of one's own interior world with its tensions and aspirations, a fascination for projects, the sentiment of love, sexuality, a social sense, enthusiasm and joy.

The Document also points out the profound questions which spring up in his conscience, the anxious and frustrating quests, his withdrawal within himself, his first failures and bitternesses. This is not a psychological paradigm, but a glance at the reality which is common to that age. Catechesis does not transform itself into socio-psychological sessions, but neither can it ignore this vivid image of the adolescent. Childhood faith is subjected to a partially critical revision, often severe and crude. It is the age of choices. What he had previously accepted, more or less maturely and knowingly, is now subjected to an examination, in order that he may make it his own, accept it and personalize it—or reject it.

It is not a summary of knowledge that is examined, but a person—Christ. Catechesis must offer and propose to the adolescent a Christ who knows man, who is fully aware of the burning human problems, who loves man and gives Himself to man. The existential and human reality of Jesus serves as a basis for the adolescent's perception of the divine reality of Jesus.

The adolescent subjects his faith, his "creed," his sacraments, his morality to an examination of the service that they can offer as a solution to his life: "If they are useful to me, I will accept them and make them mine; if they are not useful to me, I won't concern myself with them." Rarely is the adolescent hostile as regards the faith; what strikes one is his indifference, his lack of interest. Often God does not concern him; Christ may be an interesting personage to him, but only on the level of culture and literary preference. Adolescence is a transitional period between two stable ages: childhood and adulthood. As such it is important due to the opening of the spirit and intellect to concrete and functional values; it is also important due to the emphasis on the affective life in the awakening of the sentiments of love and of sexuality in the full and mature meaning of the terms.

Certainly the problem of love is to be placed within the context of his life in a serious and Christian manner, and in this sense the Document proposes the Revelation of Jesus-friend, guide and model, who is to be admired and imitated (no. 38). This friendship with Christ permits him to realize an education in the faith which projects a light upon his first sufferings and those he discovers in the world. It is a catechesis to be re-invented, not only according to the age but also according to individual persons or groups, in fidelity to the message and in an equally important fidelity to this typical moment of human life. It implies a revision of life, to bring to maturation what has been growing in childhood and also to give the proper Christian dimensions to whatever presents itself as new. An adolescent who conquers this age presents the image of a convinced and tenacious Christian adult. Adolescence, with its crises, is not a discomfort for which one bides one's time for it to "pass," but a bridge that must be crossed, which must stimulate educators and pastors of every level and inspiration.

Young People and the Message of Jesus

The pastoral problem of young people preoccupies the Christian community, which asks itself whether youth are really experiencing a religious awakening, or rather a temporary phenomenon that compensates for the human and social voids from which they suffer. Both tendencies find convinced and combative adherents. Our opinion tends rather to believe that the youth of today, suffering from forms cut off from concrete life, from decadent legalisms, from poverty of ideals, really feel and look to the religious fact with confidence, because it is pregnant with certitudes, because transcendency fascinates them in the face of the desolating picture of a life "made in this way."

The Document states a few characteristics of the youth of today: the time of the first decisions, personal responsibilities, fundamental choices of accepting or of rejecting. The Document does not limit itself to these descriptive data, but calls for a catechesis that denounces egoism and asks for: generosity, the awareness of the value of work, of the common good, of justice, of the promotion of man as man, of peace and justice, of liberation from impediments which retard maturation, and especially the sense of human dignity. Catechesis thus becomes the moment in which the Gospel can be presented, understood and accepted as capable of giving a meaning to life (no. 39). In fact, life imposes two demands on young people: First: to accept their own place, to carry out their own task and to be judged on the way in which they carry it out—because the exalting ideal must transform itself into daily fidelity—and to believe that this does not concern only enriching oneself, but risking everything; Second: to choose and to hold to the choice made, rejecting and excluding other possible orientations; it is necessary to assume responsibility for one's own choice and one's own liberty, because youth are on the threshold of adult life, which is always difficult for man and even more so for a Christian.

If one observes the religious situation of today's youth, these premises risk becoming mere rhetoric, but the salvific intention of evangelization and of catechesis does not set any limits to the possibilities of a feasible and effective action of grace and pastoral activity. We must believe in a better future for youth, accept the signs of an awakening of faith, and fuse the experiences of yesterday with the needs of today, while conserving the essentials of the Gospel message. If man is the way for the Church, youth are the way for the Church of tomorrow.

Without touching on the methodological question, it seems nonetheless opportune to explore a few situations in order that the young adults' encounter with Christ will not be transient: faith must free itself from the subjectivism of adolescence; if adolescence, through faith, gave itself wholly to Christ and little to His Kingdom, young people run the risk of seeing only the Kingdom and forgetting Christ. The faith of youth allows for balance, and is not only a recollection of Jesus' life, nor only a discovery of His countenance, but an entrance into His mystery. And in this regard catechesis invokes an option for cultural animation, which does not consist in giving courses of religious instruction, speaking of everything and of nothing; it is a procedure involving study, meetings and reflections, in order to foster in the young persons knowledge and attitudes for resolving all the problems of life and growth in the light of the Gospel.

Catechesis clearly suggests three approaches which are presently under experimentation: group dynamics; the avenue of human problems; the avenue of commitment. It is logical that, in this sense, catechesis is an inquiry into the faith, in meetings which have human and religious problems as an object, almost in the structure of "week-reco," in which the Bible, the liturgy, Tradition, and the very life of the Church are taken up as incentives for deep excavations, free and oriented by the lived experience of the Christian communities that are more faithful to the original sources. Catechesis, hence, does not come to a standstill at a simple moment of this age, but necessarily becomes a permanent, progressive and continued form of various contacts—always richer and more influential—with the Gospel and with the thought of the Church.

We cannot ignore the problem of youth without religious support, who at present are not few for various reasons, and who do not refuse attention to the problem of Christian faith in one way or another. Catechesis must seek ways of access to their mentality and situations. The truth is not halted by difficulties; it is diffusive and convincing, if, in part, it encounters an elementary availability. The question is broad and does not limit itself to a few indications: it suffices to have mentioned it, since it is also noted in the pontifical document.

It seems that we can conclude that the major application is this: to give to youth the whole Bible, to introduce them to a serious and adult study, to bring about the recognition of the truths of faith in the light of the Word of God, and not to avoid the use of a certain dimension of biblical typology. Youth have a hunger and thirst for God, who presents Himself to them in His Word, contained in Scripture and in Tradition.

The Central Problem of Catechesis to Adults

Reflecting the thought of the synod, the pontifical Document defines adult catechesis as "one of the most constant concerns... imposed with vigor and urgency by present experiences throughout the world" also because "this is the principal form of catechesis, because it is addressed to persons who have the greatest responsibilities and the capacity to live the Christian message in its fully developed form" (CT 43).

In effect, in the Christian communities of every continent and race, in countries already traditionally evangelized or in countries in progress toward the faith, adults live in a heated tension to apply the nuclei of the evangelical message to the convulsive problems of contemporary existence, in the balance between secularization and the interior call to fidelity to God, to His Word and to His community which is the Church. Entering into the problem and making it more acute are "catechisms" for adults, publications of a high theological level that are diffused among the People of God, who are not always prepared to distinguish what is certain and proven from what is only an opinion, or is still in an embryonic stage, or is erroneous. The experiences mentioned in the Document are not of ancient date; they come from the post-conciliar years, and, particularly, with more intensity, from these last years. The question is not simple: to define today's adult is a venturesome enterprise, because of the variety of types, of cultures, of social extractions, and of traditions. One fact seems certain: the adult of today is generally an authentic adult, made such by the mountain of easy information, by the rapidity of international and continental encounters and contacts, by commercial pressures and industrial interchanges, by a certain expansion and diffusion of the missionary action of ancient religions and of the various Christian confessions. Except for a small proportion of human beings, the adult man of today has become aware of himself, of his human rights, of his dignity, of his need for liberty, for free choice, for justice, for peace, for material sufficiency and for participation in the world of culture.

The Christ of infancy and of youth always remains a precious conquest, but He is entreated to intervene and to resolve the indefinable gamut of questions which social, political, cultural, scientific, and productive life create without interruption, and especially to propose guidelines for solution to the too numerous problems which swarm in every corner of the world and of life. Much is asked, everything is asked, because adults feel themselves responsible and able workers "to pervade the temporal realities" (CT 43). This is not to mention the serious fact that youth watch adults to see "how" and "how much" faith really serves to insert one into life, to qualify it as the answer to the tremendous finalistic questions of man's existence. Catechesis, which came into existence for adults at the very beginning of the Church and then became the instrument for the faith of children and of youth, now takes up again, as never before, its "adult" dimension: adults are the catechists; the parents, the first educators of their children to the faith; the pastors of souls; the professors and teachers; those who, in various ways, have an extensive experience of life and do not lack responsibilities toward others.

The difficulty which seems to present itself in the present situation is the frequent absence of the conviction that catechesis is not an ecclesial act for the non-adults (children and infants) but for every person of every age and condition, as long as he lives. A beginning could be made by employing the homily in the celebration of the Eucharist and of the sacraments; this, however, does not exhaust the catechetical need, but it does become a prominent form of catechesis. It is not impossible to pass on from the homily to the catechesis of families, of groups and of communities. This is not to mention the efficacy of the instruments of communication—press, religious publications, radio and TV, audio-visual instruments—which "catechize" at home; together with other members of the family, they offer the possibility of comments and of dialogue. These are adult forms of our times which undoubtedly have lagged and have suffered from a certain lack of concern, but arouse an exceptional interest today.

The mass form or method of catechesis for adults seems inefficient, whereas the attention and desire for catechesis for little family groups or catechumens is being intensified. The problem is alive in the world: all that remains is to contribute more trust, and also more effort.

Conclusion

Taken in general, the receivers of catechesis belong to different classes and categories, but it is necessary to attest that the recipient is one: it is *man*. It is this man who is problematic, upset, confused, open, and yet still available to God, to the mysterious and invisible operation of grace, in search of supports and props for his insecurity. Catechesis, which, at first sight, seems far from his burning reality, is instead always a road open and rich in resources, because it maintains its pristine vocation of evoking the signs of the presence and of the action of God in man, rendering these visible and credible. And, not to end, but to begin, catechesis is the vehicle which transports man toward Christ and the mediation with which Christ goes towards man to save him.

This consideration would suffice to bring catechesis back to its native and sublime source.

SILVIO RIVA, O.F.M.

SELECTED BIBLIOGRAPHY

Coudreau, F., *L'enfant et le probleme de la foi*, Paris, 1961.
Colomb, J., *Al servizio della fede*, LDC, Turin-Leuman, 1969.
Riva, S., *L'educazione religiosa del fanciullo*, EDB, 1978.
Babin, P., *Les jeunes et la foi*, Lyons, 1961.
Vergote, A., *Psicologia religiosa*, Borla, Turin, 1967.
Brien, A., *Le cheminement de la foi*, Paris, 1964.

5

Permanent Catechesis and the Catechumenate in Reference to Adults

Premise

Catechesi tradendae is the document that synthesizes the experience of catechetical renewal that the local churches have carried out in the first post-conciliar period. This Apostolic Exhortation has an authority which derives, among other things, from its expression of an ample consultation and of living experiences conducted by the Church in these years. It is a document of programming, because, in the synthesis, it causes the most fruitful, significant and promising intuitions to emerge, marked out for the future.

In fact, *Catechesi tradendae* makes the effort to introduce into the Christian community one of the most fruitful acquisitions of modern pedagogy: that of a permanent education as a requisite of "apprendre à être,"[1] which, in the Christian experience, assumes the characteristics of permanent formation and has one of its most significant expressions in a catechesis addressed to man in his own situation, to the whole man, in every age. Thus, catechesis is an essential component of that process of growth which leads the Christian and the Christian community to live the faith as a continual conversion. As a disciple of the Word, it is necessary to place oneself in the following of the Master to the point of realizing the adult image of Christ in us.

In this perspective we confront here a reflection regarding the catechesis of adults—a catechesis modelled on the catechumenate.

1. THE CATECHESIS OF ADULTS: "CENTRAL PROBLEM"

The central problem of catechesis, according to the indications of *Catechesi tradendae*, concerns adults. In Christian communities, with the growth of religious indifference and of a form of practical atheism, we note an always more accentuated preoccupation over the adult generation, both as regards propositions of faith, which are questioned at this age, and as regards adults' presence in the community, in the moments of planning and carrying out its pastoral effort.

We see the risk of finding ourselves with a Church of children and of old people; we are aware of the absence of adults from the life of the community not only in formative moments, but at every moment, thus reducing to insignificance the experience of a reality which has nothing to say to the life of a person in the fullness of maturity.

This preoccupation, confronted in explicit terms by various documents of the Church, has imposed itself in an always more extensive manner on pastoral workers as well. These have come to the conclusion that the catechesis of adults is a problem, "the central problem" of catechesis, as the Pope calls it. The moment of more explicit awareness and of statement of this problem was the last synod of Bishops (autumn 1977). Committed to treating the "catechesis of our time, with particular reference to the catechesis of children and of youth," it concluded by debating the problem of adult catechesis as a fundamental pastoral problem.[2]

As a consequence a series of initiatives was born, very diverse in structure, methods and contents, yet all preoccupied in once again involving the adults in a dialogue of faith and in religious inquiry.[3]

This is not the place to make an inventory of the existing initiatives, or to evaluate them. Here it is urgent to recall the continual arising of experiences which are, in our opinion, expressions at one and the same time of an availability and of a question on the part of the adult world; and also, and above all, expressions of the reactions and preoccupations of pastoral workers in the face of a crisis situation.

The centrality of adult catechesis, however, does not find its justification only in the deChristianized socio-cultural situation and environment, or in a situation not yet Christianized, but rather in a program of the Church. A Church without adults condemns itself to clericalism, because inevitably the priests become the only persons responsible for pastoral action; it deprives itself of the missionary possibility, because it lacks those persons who witness to the faith amid temporal realities, such as the family, the world of work, culture, etc., which are relative to the experience of the laity.

A church without adults is a church which deprives itself of the charism of maturity and of the other charisms and ministries which are connected to it, thus decisively impoverishing its own life and the possibilities of realizing its mission.[4]

The Christian community is aware of the need of the presence of adults for the knowledge of its own vocation and mission. Adults render possible the fulfillment and expression of the Church's originality in regard to culture and the surrounding environment. This originality of life is gathered around the fundamental gifts of the Lord: the Word, the liturgy, charity.

Catechesis is one of the moments of listening to and of deepening the Word; hence, it is an essential and necessary moment in view of the maturation of Christian life even for adults. In fact, the faith of adults cannot be mature and authentic if, of the three goods of the Christian community, only the liturgy and charity are lived. Always, at every age of life, faith must be nourished by listening to the Word in order to grow and to animate life. The Word, in fact, is not only a complexity of ideas to learn, but a living reality, which engenders life and growth because it provokes one to a continual conversion; because, in hope and in the announcement of a love which is manifested in every situation, it creates and regenerates the existence of the disciple of the Lord.

Basically, if it were a question only of communicating a system of ideas, it would suffice to teach them to children and "have them go over them" at some points in life. Only a Christian community that knows how to offer to every age of life the possibility of regenerating one's own existence, by confronting it with the vitality of the Word, shows its belief that it is a living reality.

Recalling the centrality of adult catechesis, *Catechesi tradendae* especially points out motivations of an ecclesial nature, which emphasize the necessity of the presence of adults so that the Christian community can be what it should be.

Adults are called to be leaders in the journey of growth in the faith proposed by the community, insofar as they have a responsibility toward the new generations, who will live in the world prepared by the adults, that is, in a civilization inspired by the values in which the adult world has believed and for which it has known how to spend itself consistently. *Catechesi tradendae* says: "The world, in which the young are called to live and to give witness to the faith which catechesis seeks to deepen and strengthen, is governed by adults. The faith of these adults too should continually be enlightened, stimulated and renewed, so that it may pervade the temporal realities in their charge."[5]

We could say that if it is true that today's world looks more willingly at witnesses than at teachers,[6] it believes in a faith that knows how to manifest values, which it incarnates in practice, a faith that knows how to express itself in a lifestyle adhering to the most profound questions of man's heart, a faith that knows that it is relevant in daily life and in the surroundings in which it is lived.

Only the adult, because of his psychological maturity, which gives him the capacity to integrate the element of faith into daily living, and because of his responsibilities on the social, civil and ecclesial levels, can carry out this role in regard to the new generations.[7]

For this reason the Pope affirms that "the Christian community cannot carry out a permanent catechesis without the direct and skilled participation of adults, whether as receivers or as promoters of catechetical activity."[8]

The responsible and active presence of adults in the catechetical itinerary is the presupposition of a missionary church. A church of children cannot be missionary. She needs adult laity who will witness in their daily life to the vitality of the Word in which they believe and with which they continually confront themselves through listening and deepening. This does not mean that the child cannot be missionary-minded, but is a potentiality that cannot express itself in all its fullness if it cannot have reference to a living and witnessing community of adults.

2. CATECHESIS TO ADULTS IN THE SOCIAL AND ECCLESIAL REALITY OF TODAY

To the reflections developed above, in view of the ecclesial motives which demand a permanent plan for an itinerary of faith for adults, it is necessary to add others relative to the cultural context in which this faith is called to develop and manifest itself and still others related to the response which the Christian community today is giving to these exigencies in its pastoral planning.

Catechesi tradendae individualizes a few diverse categories of persons who require varied attentions in order to grow in the faith, making reference to the complex reactions which such growth develops when it encounters a culture or certain customs of life. It speaks of those who have met the faith without being able to develop it, because they live in nations still unchristianized; of those whose religious formation stopped at what they had "learned" in childhood; of those who received a very poor catechesis; of those who, even though they received the sacraments, in practice have never been explicitly educated to live the mystery which they have accepted in their hearts.[9]

This is the list of all the most difficult conditions, those, in fact, which require a catechesis that is at the same time a proclamation and which is capable of placing one face to face with the essentials of a faith that has never been known or deepened. This catechesis is needed by the greater number of today's Christian adults, who for the most part find themselves in the conditions indicated by the Pope. Even in their diversity, these conditions are reducible to one series of root causes, to be sought in the secularized cultural context. The influence of various atheistic, materialistic and at the same time messianic ideologies; the spread of a mode of life which sets aside the religious fact and values; the growing sense of autonomy which has taken possession of contemporary man, hypnotized by scientific research and by the results of technology—all these have given life to a society that is in reality pagan, imbued with criteria and values that are totally human, lay, and immanent.

Many nations have "to be evangelized," either because they have never been able to hear the Christian proclamation or because they have to be scraped free of the encrustations which time and patterns of thinking and of living had deposited, rendering the faith a "tired habit" without any relevance in life,[10] all this aggravated by the fading away of that Christian environment and homogeneous cultural context which up to a certain point used to permeate the traditions and customs of peoples.

The response of the Christian community to the renewed needs of the adult world has not always been adequate and timely; among the secularized realities, it has been and may be noted that it is difficult to replace the preceding rhythm of life of the parish or of associations with new plans and ways of forming to the faith.

Thus, if, on the one hand, there is an almost spontaneous affirmation of forms of catechesis for adults, it can be said that almost nowhere is there a proposal that comes from the community as such to express its preoccupation about consigning the treasure of faith and of maternally guiding its children in its growth. For the Sunday catechesis and the associative catechetical encounters, promoted by various apostolic movements, almost nothing has been substituted; for the endeavor to convoke the adults of the parish for systematic and organic itinerary of faith, there has been substituted some sporadic encounter in the family, when the children prepare for the sacraments or in some other rare circumstance; the dialogue of faith is restricted to a few, even though significant, events in life!

In many cases we still delude ourselves that, in the impossibility of reviving a dialogue of faith with the adults, we can start out from the children, with the illusory hypothesis that tomorrow these, who today do not find an adult community which they can take as a point of reference, tomorrow will be mature Christians who will give life again to renewed parishes and communities....

A catechesis of adults adequate to the present needs must rely on a community which places itself in a state of evangelization and knows that it must turn to the adults and renew the proclamation, for nothing can be taken for granted and presupposed. On the other hand, the experience of faith always and anyway demands this possibility of regenerating oneself in the acceptance of the message of Christ: "Even fervent Christians always need to listen to the announcement of the truth and of basic facts of salvation and to know their root meaning, which is the joyful news of the love of God."[11]

3. CATECHESIS WITH A CATECHUMENAL DIMENSION

Adults catechesis must, therefore, revive a kerygmatic and catechumenal dimension, so as to bring about a journey of faith and conversion which introduces the adult anew "into the mystery of Christ and into the life of the Church."[12]

Such catechesis recalls the ancient experience of the catechumenate, intended for the preparation of converts for Baptism and for their insertion into the Christian community. From the totality of the testimonies and documents which have come down to us from the first centuries of Christianity, we can gather the fundamental elements of the catechumenal process. These are:

—the *Word of God* proclaimed by the Church, accepted in faith, source of faith, of conversion and of new life;

—the *liturgical-sacramental celebration*, in which, through concrete signs and gestures, the believer lives the experience of the paschal life always more profoundly;

—*commitment and witness* to the Risen Christ in the world;

—*the Church* as the environment in which this process is to be carried out; she goes to meet man and, with word and witness, announces the Lord to him; the Church welcomes the catechumen, evaluates his availability, helps and sustains him, inserts him into the mystery of Christ, and sends him out into the world as a witness.

The journey of faith-conversion, therefore, takes place in and through the Church. In this regard, a few observations capable of concretizing this discussion are appropriate. *Historically* it has resulted that the whole ecclesial community concretely incarnates itself in the local Church to take care of the catechumen. The *Apostolic Tradition of Hypolitus Romanus* is the first document which gives us information in this regard; the catechumenate is carried out in the care of the community, particularly the *sponsores* (sponsors) and *doctores:* the former with the task of remaining close to the candidates as adult Christians, witnesses to the Lord, guarantors and educators of the faith and qualified representatives of the entire community; the latter (catechists, deacons, priests, bishops), to instruct in the faith and to celebrate the liturgical-sacramental moments.

Theologically this action of the Church has its own broad foundation. In fact, in the today of time, that is, from the Ascension until the return (Parousia) of the Lord, it is the Church who concretely mediates the encounter, the dialogue and the communion between God and man in Jesus Christ. And this corresponds to a precise fulfillment of that "law of incarnation" which presides over the whole history of salvation. From the moment that God, adapting Himself to man, selected the way of involvement in history to reveal Himself and communicate Himself to man, it is impossible to encounter Him except through sacramental mediation: yesterday it was the humanity of Christ; today it is the Church, with her word and her sacraments, who prolongs His presence and His mission. The Church, therefore, is called to exercise a real and proper mediating and maternal action in the catechumenate: it is the Church who generates the Church (Saint Augustine). This theme is amply developed by Vatican Council II and by the following reflection.[13]

This communitarian dimension of the catechumenate witnessed by the Church of the first centuries opens several problems:

First of all, the necessity for *every community* to listen faithfully to the Word of God and be docilely attentive to the problems of man, *as a credible sign of communion and of service*. The primitive catechumenate flourished as long as this witness was living and authentic. Therefore, the problem is to create and form authentic communities in which the faith-conversion process is visible in a life of dialogue, of reciprocal communion, of poverty, of joy and of love. Then it is necessary to overcome a mass pastoral which remains anonymous, indeterminate and easily repetitive, for the sake of a pastoral which penetrates into concrete realities and involves every person in groups, movements and basic communities, [14] which become the vital nuclei of every larger community, be it parish or diocese.

The community should become co-responsible in the itinerary of faith of the very young and of the poor, above all in view of the celebration of the sacraments (the task of the animators of catechesis, of parents, of the parish community...). The ancient catechumenate would have been inconceivable without this communitarian co-responsibility.

Finally, *the community must participate as much as possible in the same sacramental moment*, giving concrete proof of its own faith, thus demonstrating what fruits were and are produced in it by the action of the Holy Spirit. It is not to be forgotten that the sacramental moment is privileged for the formation of a true and adult community: in fact, not only is it true that the Church makes the sacraments, but it is also true that the sacraments make the Church. This communitarian awareness which finds its summit and its expressive font in the liturgical-sacramental action, had its fullest experimentation in the third and fourth centuries, that is, during the most flourishing season of the catechumenate. The loss or lessening of this profound sense of church has negatively conditioned the working, witnessing and evangelizing capability of the Church.

The ways and forms of realization of the primitive catechumenate, lastly, urge us to recover this experience in its entirety and its full formative significance. For us, today, it becomes the occasion for a few fundamental rediscoveries:

—*The catechumenate is a permanent itinerary of faith,*[15] which gradually follows the Christian from infancy through the successive phases of life; through it, all of existence must be considered as a gradual and progressive insertion into the mystery of salvation (a dynamic conception of the Christian life). In this perspective, the celebration of the sacraments is to be seen as a strong moment in this journey.

—However, we can foresee *particular catechumenal itineraries:* for baptized adults who ask to receive Confirmation or to celebrate Matrimony; for adults (parents) who ask the sacraments for their children and thus make themselves witnesses and guarantors of the faith; for baptized children who prepare themselves for their First Communion Mass; for young people who dispose themselves to receive Confirmation.

It is urgent that the catechumenal itinerary not be exhausted with the celebration of the sacrament, but that it continue and follow those who have received the gift and the aids to insert themselves always more responsibly into the Church and to assume the task of witnessing amid their own surroundings. Thus will be avoided those "lacunae" that are so injurious and, unfortunately, are present in contemporary pastoral practice.

—*The catechumenate is not a simple preparation for the sacraments.* In general, catechesis is carried out in view of the sacraments, according to criteria of pre-established and set dates, not on the basis of maturation of the faith. The realization of a permanent catechumenate will permit the overcoming of pastoral difficulties and problems which come up in this regard.

— *The motives which justify a vigorous resumption of the catechumenate*, not as an institute or structure of the past, but as a pastoral duty of the present, are manifold: a growth of the person and of the community and hence the necessity of not performing actions that do not spring from intimate conviction with maturity as their basis; the passage from a social Christianity, secured by institutions to a personal and responsible Christianity; promotion of the pastoral action of the priest, not considered as an automatic distributor of sacraments, but as an educator in the faith and an animator of authentic communities; finally, the responsible growth of the Christian communities, called to involve themselves directly in this educative work.

The catechumenate is not a pastoral recipe, or a methodological expedient, to free us from the shoals on which our pastoral has run aground and is drowning; it is rather a vigorous effort which requires of the pastoral workers a mentality of new faith. Only thus will we be able to emerge from an anonymous and social type of Christianity and enter into the dynamism of an authentic faith and of a serious Christian commitment. Only thus will the foundations be laid so that our communities will become missionary, capable of an effective and original proclamation of the Gospel today.

4. A JOURNEY OF FAITH WITH LITURGICAL RHYTHM

A reconsideration of the itinerary of the formation of adults to the faith highlights the fact that today's catechumenate is not to be understood as a reproduction of the ancient experience, but as a reliving of its spirit and its fundamental inspiration, giving especial value to the two common moments of the life of the Christian community.

Sunday, Pasch of the Christian

Christians know that they have been generated by the Easter of the Lord, whose celebration every Sunday takes on an exceptional value. This weekly rhythm of celebration leads back to

Easter, as the unique event, celebrated in this unique feast. To Christians Easter suffices as an event and Sunday as a feast. So rich a fact, however, asks for an on-going acceptance by the Christian consciousness and by the pastoral practice of the communities.

The Liturgical Year, Journey of Popular Faith

The liturgical year is the plan to live a journey of faith within the Church to celebrate the mystery of Christ in time.

Under what conditions can it be a journey of maturation for personal faith and that of the community?

First of all, its significance is to be grasped. It is not to be considered as a succession of anniversaries, celebrated in rites that are without soul and meaning. Throughout the year the unique and indivisible mystery of Christ is celebrated, in the totality of its richness: from the redeeming incarnation up until the return on the last day. This unique mystery is celebrated under various aspects which gradually illumine all its richness.

Thus, the celebration of the incarnation on Christmas particularly illumines the reality of God's condescension, His becoming one of us and His sharing of human vicissitudes. The celebration of Easter illumines the reality of Christ's emptying Himself through the folly of the Cross, which defeats the wisdom of the world. He is the grain of wheat which only by dying under the earth succeeds in bringing forth fruit. Pentecost illumines the reality of life according to the Spirit, the definitive gift of Christ, who makes the rereading of the entire Christian life possible in terms of the progressive experience of the Spirit.

In this journey, Lent has a typical significance, and presents with particular intensity the characteristic demands of the whole year's progress. It is the time dominated by the invitation to conversion and return. This is expresssed through two fundamental appeals: to listen to the Word, in silence and in the "desert"; to express through penitence, in the newness of a life redeemed by the event of Jesus Christ, the whole superabundant wealth of the Gospel.

Lent is time of fasting but also of good works, signs among our brothers of the love of God, real fruits of the Spirit.

Then, throughout the whole year, through the reading of the Gospel, we meet the Churches of Luke, of Matthew and of Mark; it is a challenge to think over one's own journey of faith.

During this journey the feasts of the Virgin and of the saints present ways of living the faith in Christ: in the availability of the Virgin Mary or in the courage of the radicalism of the saints. Thus, these feasts lose their devotionalistic character or legendary tones, to become celebrations of the unique mystery of Christ, who is presented to us through the exemplary lives of the saints. The journey of faith which chooses the liturgical year as its own rhythm has its culminating and almost typical moment in Lent and in Easter, but then continues in the same style for the rest of the year, in a commitment which is a personal effort of growth and witness before the world, a witness which shows that even fraternal love is a gift, a sign of a love which has burst forth into history.

Thus, an adult catechesis of catechumenal dimension highlights the exigencies of the formation of the whole Christian community: to center itself continually on the essential, in the Easter of the Lord, so that through the contemplation of the mystery and immersion in it the capability of daily converting ourselves may mature.

The liturgical year, then, becomes the model of every catechesis of a catechumenal and missionary dimension; even more, it could be truly considered the permanent catechumenal journey of the whole Christian people.

PAOLO MILAN

FOOTNOTES

1. *Rapporto sulle strategia dell'educazione,* by E. Faure, Armando, Rome.

2. The intervention of Cardinal G. B. Benelli, in *Il Sinodo dei Vescovi 1977,* by G. Caprile, pp. 109-110, Ed. "La Civiltà Cattolica," Rome 1978. During the Synod, there were over sixty interventions regarding this problem.

3. E. Alberich, "Catechesis of Adults," in *Catechesi,* 3, (1979) pp. 3-17. In this article the author attempts an analytical reading of the experiences of adult catechesis, offers an abundant bibliography and notes that many pastoral experiences, on their own not qualified in a strictly catechetical sense, are bearers of a catechetical dimension (p. 3).

4. "The catechesis of children and of youth," writes a catechist in this regard, "is always compromised when these become aware that adults are no longer catechized, that catechesis is a thing for children and that the faith seems unable to sustain confrontation with the intellect and to illuminate the diverse human problems which present themselves to the adult.... A Church in which the adults in particular are not catechized cannot be a Church humanly adult." J. Colomb, "Un luogo actuale della catechesi degli adulti nell'insieme della Chiesa," in *Concilium,* 3 (1970), p. 35.

5. CT 43; EN 70, 73.

6. EN 41.

7. CEI, *Il rinnovamento della catechesi*, Rome, 1970, no. 124.

8. CT 43.

9. CT 44.

10. CEI, *Evangelizzazione e promozione umana*, preparatory document to the ecclesial convention of 1976, nos. 11-12.

11. CEI, *Il rinnovamento..., op. cit.*, no. 25.

12. CEI, *Evangelizzazione e sacramenti*, 1973. "The most binding document promulgated by the Church during the last years is without a doubt the *Ordo initiationis christianae adultorum*, of January 6, 1972. This document was preceded by various interventions of the Council. We recall a few: the Constitution on the Sacred Liturgy, SC no. 64; that on the Church, LG no. 14 and 17; the Decree on the Pastoral Office of Bishops, CD no. 14; that on the Ministry and Life of Priests, PO no. 5; lastly the decree on the Mission Activity of the Church, AG nos. 10-18. The Council arrived at these orientations in response to the desire of many bishops who, beginning in 1950, especially in France, had experienced the pastoral validity of the rediscovery of the ancient catechumenate.

The Ordo is presented in Italy as the *Rito dell'iniziazione cristiana degli adulti*, official translation of the CEI, Rome, 1977. It was preceded by *Evangelizzazione e sacramenti*, a document of the Bishops for the initiation of the latest pastoral plan, which in nos. 82-85 treats explicitly of the catechumenate and of itineraries of faith.

13. *Presbyterorum Ordinis*, nos. 5-6.

14. EN 58.

15. CEI, *Evangelizzazione e sacramenti, op. cit.*, no. 82.

6

Memorization in Catechetical Teaching[1]

When many readers of *Catechesi tradendae* reach number 55, they feel that they are making an unexpected leap. From the broad visions of culture, of the evangelization of peoples, etc., we find ourselves led back in number 55 to the small catechism classroom and to a very small problem of insignificant didactics: must we or must we not have the children memorize something of the catechism?

We do not wholly share this impression. Even in this case the horizon can become much more vast, if the question is viewed from the historical and pedagogical-catechetical perspective.

Memorization in the History of Catechesis

In the first place we have to remember that it is precisely in this regard that the most radical turning point in the methodology of catechetical teaching has been witnessed during these last ten years.

For a few centuries, and up until very recent times, the teaching of catechism consisted in having students memorize the official question-and-answer catechism in detail (and at times in very great detail).

Centuries ago, catechetical formulas were few, and they explained the articles of the Creed, the petitions of the Our Father and of the Hail Mary, the individual commandments, the sacraments and, at times, a few other well-known formulas.

Then, in the last 150 years, the content became always more theologico-systematic and the questions-answers always more numerous. In diocesan catechisms diffused on a national scale in this century there has been an average of 400-600 to 700-800 questions for children twelve to fourteen years of age.

Until ten years ago, the episcopates have never approved (except on rare occasions, and only for children six to ten and sometimes nine to eleven) official catechisms which did not exclusively consist of questions and answers.

The catechism of the Austrian Pichler, which contained developed lessons which ended with questions and answers, was blackballed by the episcopate of his country at the beginning of the 1930's, and adopted only by the diocese of Bressanone, in Italy.

The catechism of Quinet-Boyer of 1938 caused a sensation because it published the official French text of 1937 with the introduction of some biblical texts and prayers.

The first official catechism in a non-question-and-answer form and famous precisely for this, was the famous German Catechism of 1955 for children ten to fourteen years of age. It followed the model of Pichler, and its compilers had taken courage from the example of the innovations of Quinet-Boyer, not officially approved, but neither condemned, by the Episcopate concerned.

But this catechism still contained 248 doctrinal questions-answers, even though they had been rendered easier and were viewed as a point of arrival of the lesson and not as a direct and primary text of study.

Only in the 1960's and '70's did a "rejection" of memory come about, followed by a counter-reaction: there had been a passage from one extreme to the other.

The Problem of "Memory" at the Synod of 1977

Methodologically and historically, therefore, the question has not been minor, and both the *Outlines of study for the preparation of the Synod*,[2] and the *Instrumentum laboris* given to the synod fathers expressly stated the problem of the *role of the memory*, together with that of the formulas of faith. In the introductory report to the Synod, Cardinal Lorscheider added an interesting development: What relationship is there between our faculty of memory and the very "memory of faith," the "memory of the People of God?"[3]

Of the fifteen interventions of the fathers in the hall, of the three presented in writing by the episcopal conferences, of the eight *circuli minores* which touch on this topic,[4] *not one* asks for a return to a memorization as *analytic* and *extensive* as was *prescribed* everywhere until the early 1960's. In the ten *Propositions* (from the list of thirty-four in which the synod fathers sought to synthesize some of the more important points of their discussions) there is reference to the integrity of the faith, which is transmitted "especially through the symbols of faith, which contain the fundamental nucleus: the inscrutable mystery of God one and triune, and that of the Son of God, become incarnate for the salvation of all and ever living in His Church," and this dwelling on the essentials is stressed.

Intensive or Extensive Method?

"This *intensive* method of transmitting the Gospel (= the Sacred Scriptures), which has in its favor the most qualified ecclesiastical tradition, distinguishes itself from the other method of catechizing, which transmits the *whole* message of Christian revelation according to a criterion of completeness (*extensive, explicit or analytic*); according to this second current, it would be necessary to present to those being catechized almost everything that the ecumenical councils and magisterial interventions of the Roman Pontiffs have defined (in the strict sense) concerning faith and morals from the beginning of the history of the Church. Such a complex of doctrine certainly has to be investigated and studied by theologians, but it does not necessarily have to be learned by all the faithful, unless there is the danger that some truths may be denied or forgotten" (*Proposition*, no. 10).

Memorize: What and Why?

In general the interventions of the fathers dwell on memorizing a few essential *formulas* taken from the Bible, from the liturgy, from doctrinal formulations, and from habitual prayers. They must serve as *points of reference* (Cardinal Suenens: cf. G. Caprile, *op. cit.*, p. 103). "It is necessary, in one way or another—says the *French Group A*—that the divine announcement remain fixed in the memory of the Christians" (*Ibidem*, p. 270). The *French Group B* proposes memorization of texts which "strengthen the faith" (*Ibidem*, p. 275). The *Portuguese Group A* insists on a "revision of life in small groups and the exercise of the memory to maintain continual union with the Gospel and with the person of Christ, something that engages the life of faith and realizes unity of life, of Christian life" (*Ibidem*, p. 291). The *Latin Group* insists that formulas and essentials are to be "interiorized" and not just memorized (*Ibidem*, p. 321). But the *English Group C* also stresses personal formulations of the faith, considering catechism formulas as being often abstract and "too impersonal to have a permanent effect, even if remembered later on. Now it is necessary that the formulas to be memorized *have Christ at their center*, attract, and mean something real for the situation and the mental capacity of the different ages of those who are catechized" (*Ibidem*, p. 266).

The *Italian group* (to which Cardinal Karol Wojtyla had adhered) proposed as a workable choice "*to make the evangelical announcement of the mystery of Christ the center about which to harmoniously develop the totality of the contents of the faith, as if with concentric circles.* In immediate conjunction with this choice there has appeared the problem of the formulations of the faith and the problem of catechetical texts." And the proposal added: "Regarding the formulations, it is desired that the synod pronounce itself expressly on a fundamental formulary of truths to be believed and to be lived after they have also been memorized, at least with 'the memory of the heart' " (*Ibidem*, p. 315).

The Most Profound Motivations

These positions were coherent with the *Basic Document* of 1970 for the renewal of catechesis in Italy. For an effective catechesis, which forms in the Christian "a mature mentality of faith" and renders "his faith certain, explicit, active, it is necessary that the faithful accept the revealed message, ordering it about a living center, well assimilated and active.... Called to grow among many difficulties and vicissitudes, the Christian needs to accept this seed within himself, this seed capable of providing for all successive developments" (RdC 56). Now "the living center of faith is Jesus Christ. Only through Him can men be saved; from Him they receive the foundation and the synthesis of all truth; in Him they find "the key, the focal point and the goal of man, as well as of all human history" (GS 10).... As it clearly appears from the book of the Acts, from evangelical traditions, from the letters of St. Paul and of St. John, the good news of every catechesis is Jesus (RdC 57).

It is in this light that the *Basic Document* views the problem of *formulas*, which are declared a "fundamental element of catechetical methodology" under various aspects, not only that of memorization, and are called "almost a moment of personal synthesis and of spiritual respite, which concludes a stage of the itinerary of faith and spurs on to further conquests" (RdC 177).

In its footnote this number refers to many others, which explain its various aspects (RdC 16, 39, 54, 58, 76, 111, 117).

We could cite still many others, for example: number 164 on "familiarity with the texts of divine Revelation," in order to emphasize the convergence of the *Basic Document* with the synod and, even more, its wealth of suggestions regarding the topic.

Memorization and Christian "Memory"

Regarding one point it can be said that the synod added something new: the relationship between memorization and the "memory" of the people of God.

Proposition 19 states: "The synod fathers desire that in catechetical action there be cultivated a wholesome balance between the exercise of memory and the memory of faith itself; that is, the memory of the people of God, the 'memorial' that renders the wonder worked by God ever present and celebrates them in the liturgy."

This, for example, can be concretized in the "traditio" and "redditio symboli," as a "sign of communion and of union among the diverse communities and groups of the faithful" and through "also knowing by heart the principal truths and basic prayers" *(Proposition 14, c)*.

More broadly, the point is treated in number 9 of the *Message of the Synod of Bishops to the People of God*, of which we quote here only a few phrases:

"This is another primary aspect of the action of the Church: to recall, commemorate, and celebrate the sacrifice in memory of the Lord Jesus—to carry out the 'anamnesis'.... Catechesis is the manifestation in our day of the 'mystery which was hidden in God before all times' (cf. Col. 1:26). This is why the first language of catechesis must be Sacred Scripture and the

Creeds.... Normally, certain things should be memorized as part of formation: such as biblical texts especially from the New Testament, certain liturgical formulae which are the privileged expression of these texts, and other common prayers. Believers should also make their own those expressions of faith, the living fruit of the reflection of Christians over the centuries, which have been gathered in the Creeds and the principal documents of the Church. Thus to be a Christian means to enter into a living tradition; a tradition which, through the history of humankind reveals how in Jesus Christ the Word of God took on human nature."

Number 55 of "Catechesi tradendae"

In number 55, *Catechesi tradendae* recalls a portion of these reflections. Having recalled the long tradition of mnemonic learning—carried out in various forms throughout the centuries (whether those of the primarily oral civilization, or those of the civilization of the press) which ceased almost abruptly in our time—it invites the "restoration of a judicious balance between reflection and spontaneity, between dialogue and silence, between written work and memory work."

Then it leans for support on secular pedagogy itself, which in various countries is rediscovering the value of memory. With this meaning the episcopal conferences of Canada and the United States, had expressed themselves in the synod with a written intervention, which had affirmed: "The modern catechetical renewal demands a clear and complete presentation of the content of the faith to children (six to twelve years of age); a solid presentation, expressed in comprehensible and familiar terms. This facilitates *memorization, which constitutes an important component of education* and which, if integrated well into a program, gives the child a sense of completeness and of mastery, disposes him to be a part of the community of adults by participating in prayer in the family and in the parish, strengthens his identity as a Catholic, and constitutes a reserve of material upon which to fall back on in the future" (G. Caprile, *op. cit.*, pp. 175-176; the underlining is ours).

Catechesi tradendae then takes up again the role of memorization in the "memory" of the great events of the history of salvation and concludes by exemplifying: "A certain memorization of the words of Jesus, of important Bible passages, of the Ten Commandments, of the formulas of profession of the faith, of the liturgical texts, of the essential prayers, of key doctrinal ideas...far from being opposed to the dignity of young Christians, or constituting an obstacle to personal dialogue with the Lord, is a real need, as the synod fathers forcefully recalled.... What is essential is that the texts that are memorized must at the same time be taken in and gradually understood in depth, in order to become a source of Christian life on the personal level and the community level."

In this regard it would be interesting to do research regarding the lives *of the saints and of great Christians.* It is not without significance to note, for example, that—during a summer vacation as a young cleric—St. John Bosco memorized the greater part of the New Testament in Greek, or that, at the age of fifteen, St. Thérèse of the Child Jesus knew whole chapters of the *Imitation of Christ* by heart.

Conclusion

Our discourse could continue on related topics, which also have methodological relevance—such as the problem of teaching *systematically,* of the relationship between *teaching and experience,* or of the *adaptation of language,* and still others, touched on in the various sections of *Catechesi tradendae*—following the same path: from the Italian and worldwide catechetical movement, to the synod of Bishops, to the exhortation of the Pope, to our renewal of mentality in this regard, to practical realization. But it suffices that we have pointed out a path of reflection which, in these moments of syntheses and of operative decisions (CT 15), can reveal itself very fruitful for "education to the faith in our time."

UBALDO GIANNETTO

FOOTNOTES

1. This article has been graciously granted to us by the periodical *Catechesi,* where it appeared in the month of April 1980, pp. 60-64.

2. Cf. LDC, series "Servizio dell' unità," no. 9, Elle Di Ci, Leumann-Turin.

3. Cf. G. Caprile, *Il Sinodo dei Vescovi, Quarta assemblea generale* (September 30—October 29, 1977), Ed. La Civiltà Cattolica, Rome, p. 530.

4. Cf. G. Caprile, *op. cit.,* pp. 19, 25, 49, 53, 56, 69, 72, 76, 86, 103, 114, 122, 123, 155, 157, 176, 182, 204, 260, 266, 270, 275, 285, 291, 315, 321, (the pages *in italics* refer to the interventions which seem more significant to us).

7

Popular Devotions and Catechesis

In these last years, "popular religiosity" has been the object of a kind of "rediscovery" in the Catholic field, especially following a few official stands on the part of both national and regional episcopal conferences,[1] as well as departments of the Holy See,[2] and especially after the synods of Bishops of 1974 and 1977.

Certainly the pastoral visual angle will impose itself even more when knowledge will increase and there will be a growth in the study of what was written about "popular religiosity" by Paul VI in the Apostolic Exhortation *Evangelii nuntiandi* and by John Paul II in the Apostolic Exhortation *Catechesi tradendae:* something which, in our modest opinion, has not yet been done, notwithstanding a few praiseworthy encounters which have given rise to publications that have been exemplary under various aspects.

Our task is not to fill the lamented void because, among other things, there is definite limitation of space. We could, at the most, give a path to be followed in subsequent detailed developments.

Referring to number 54 of the Apostolic Exhortation *Catechesi tradendae*—which is the precise task entrusted to us—we believe it useful to attempt some indication of framework, almost to point out the probable necessary points for the outline which we have indicated.

I. POPULAR RELIGIOSITY AND THE 1974 SYNOD

There is a jargon, now accepted and consolidated, which, even in regard to "popular religiosity," insists on speaking of "approaches." We use it, too, to clarify that we intend to carry out here neither a "sociological approach," nor an "anthropological approach," nor an "historical approach" nor a "political" one. But more simply, the circle of our interest is restricted and finalized to the *pastoral approach* and, more precisely, to the *catechetical approach.* We omit, therefore, all discussions and problematics and scientific work itself. To understand one another, we take as a *point of departure*, which in another way can be also considered a *point of arrival*, the necessity of rendering "popular devotion" a "way of evangelization," as Paul VI classified it, and a "contribution to catechesis," as John Paul II classified it.

Paul VI, in EN had restricted the expression "popular religiosity" and also specified it as "popular piety"; John Paul II restricts and specifies even more, confining in CT "popular piety" to what pertains to "popular devotions." Is this *reductive action* an expression of narrowness or of will of restoration—as has been said—or, rather, is it not a sense of pastoral realism which renders a precise intervention easier?

We incline towards this last hypothesis and will seek to demonstrate it.

In the 1974 Synod of Bishops, which dealt with evangelization in our time, the topic of "popular religiosity" practically made its entrance into the assembly without having waited its turn. There had been no trace of it in the preparatory document of the synod *(lineamente)*, nor in the basic document *(documentum laboris)*, nor in the panorama of the situation of the Church in the world. Aside from the previous report of the Bishops of Latin America, there had been some indications of this theme in the elaboration of the *Consilium de Laicis* sent as a "contribution" without, however, clarifying the terms well, but leaving a certain ambiguity. In fact, this seemed to contribute to distinguishing between a more knowledgeable, elitist religiosity and a popular religiosity, even if it had the merit of declaring that all were to be evangelized.[3]

In the second general congregation of the synod, the theme came to claim attention through the report of the then President of *CELAM, Cardinal Pironio,* with the description which has remained rightly famous: *"By 'popular devotion' we mean the manner with which Christianity becomes incarnated in the various cultures and ethnic situations and is lived and manifested in the people."*[4]

In the Synod of 1974 the topic was taken up again in other interventions, even though in a more fleeting manner through the action of a few fathers.[5] It came to have an important place not only in the syntheses of the interventions held at the end of the first part of the work, but also "in the specific questions made for the discussion of the *circuli minores*,[6] which yielded interesting answers; in the replies of the fathers after the reports of the same *circuli* and prior to the conclusions, and lastly in the final synthesis and, hence, in the 'propositions' presented to the Holy Father."[7]

In the 1974 synodal *Iter* "popular religiosity" finds a landfall of its own in the Apostolic Constitution *Evangelii nuntiandi* of Paul VI in the chapter dedicated to the "methods of evangelization."[8]

I believe that the placement of this topic should be noted not only in a study of *Evangelii nuntiandi* in particular, but also as regards the relationship that this placement gives "popular piety" with catechesis in general and with the Constitution *Catechesi tradendae*[9] in particular, in order to have a precise framing. And the placement must not limit itself to some observations of a semantic character, but must derive its essentiality, even in regard to the terminological choice which has been made.

In no. 48 of EN we can see two parts: the first part which indicates "popular religiosity" in its phenomenology, as it was presented to the synod, and the second part which, in fact, places it among the "methods of evangelization," for whatever positive values it can represent. We note that only in this "second part" did Paul VI call it no longer "popular religiosity," but "popular piety."

The expression "popular piety" in the same "Christian area did not have a great following," notes Vincent Bo, in a valuable work written with wisdom.[10] Proof of this is that not even all the interventions of the fathers in the synod on catechesis adjusted themselves to it.[11] However, I would like to point out that John Paul II takes it up again in *Catechesi tradendae* even though immediately changing the theme to "popular devotions," and that the terminology "popular piety" has been revived, perhaps carelessly, in some article or pious exhortation, without any critical meaning.... But I do not believe that the expression is bound, as Bo says, "to secular dualism...between official, institutionalized liturgy and what in the better cases has been tolerated." Rather, it seems to me that the preference of Paul VI —and hence the choice of a precise terminology—is made by "seen reasons."[12] "Popular piety" seems almost to express positive possibilities for evangelization: whereas, to repeat the phrase of EN, "popular religiosity," purified and vivified, is well oriented....

Certainly this choice of field is reductive in comparison with what is meant by the term "popular religiosity" (a term already less ambiguous than "popular religion" or "Christianity" or "popular Catholicism" as some prefer, not without hidden meaning, precisely because it wants to highlight what can, practically and pastorally, become *a way of evangelization!*

II. "POPULAR PIETY"
IN THE SYNOD OF 1977

During the 1977 synod on catechesis in today's world, there were various interventions in regard to "religiosity" or "popular piety." Some indications are in the preparatory document,[13] some in the document presented by the Congregation for the Evangelization of Peoples, especially referring to the missionary reality, in which was shown the importance of "popular piety" in catechesis and in the catechumenate[14] and in relation to the very Church of silence.[15] The report of the secretary itself spoke of the felt need for a return to forms of popular piety that are at times set aside (such as the Rosary, the Way of the Cross, etc.).[16] Many fathers referred to this: from *Cardinal A. Rossi,* who spoke about the plenary congress of the Congregation ·for the Evangelization of Peoples held on this theme,[17] to *Bishop Bellido of Cajamarca* in Peru, who pointed out that in his country popular piety is closely bound to Christian life and, duly corrected, is a valid element of catechesis,[18] to the *Bishop of Villarrica* in Paraguay,[19] to the *Auxiliary Bishop of Buenos Aires,* who saw in it a "starter for catechesis."[20] Important were the declarations of *Cardinal Jaime L. Sin di Manila,*[21] of *His Excellency, Obeso Rivera, Coadjutor Bishop* of Jalapa (Mexico)[22] and of *Cardinal Primatesta.*[23]

The episcopal conferences of the USA and of Canada insisted on the necessity of encouraging popular Marian piety,[24] as also did other fathers, including *Francisco Borja of Stelipe* (Chile),[25] *Cahal Brendan Daly* of Ardagh (Ireland)[26] and *Father Agostoni, FSCJ*.[27]

Three *circuli minores* in particular insisted on this point: *Group C of the English language* spoke of inculturation and of the necessity of guiding popular religiosity in new directions, without destroying it[28]; the *Spanish-Portuguese Group B* asked new esteem for popular piety, stressing its reasons of prayer and catechesis[29]; whereas the *Spanish-Portuguese Group C* recommended not to consider popular piety in a negative manner as had been done, for in this neglect the group saw a reason for the abandonment of catechesis. Many values, the group's report maintains, should be retained because in this manner the people manifest their faith, whereas deformations are admitted (syncretisms, superstitions, magic, abuses, etc.), and these are to be corrected.[30]

More or less similar were the requests made in other interventions comprising some amendments to the propositions.

To these references may be added a few more specific recommendations concerning devotion to the Sacred Heart, to the Blessed Virgin (much more numerous), and to the saints. In the final propositions the report continues with a recommendation: not "to be neglected is popular religiosity and the popular piety that renders it an authentic expression of personal and communitarian faith and a precious Christian witness."[31]

III. THE CONTRIBUTION OF "CATECHESI TRADENDAE"

At the appearance of *Catechesi tradendae* there was a widely diffused delusion—perhaps too hurriedly people spoke of a reductive criterion.

Let us look closely at number 54, which is part of Chapter VII, which, not in the Latin text, but in the texts of various languages translated by Vatican Polyglot, bears the significant title "How To Impart Catechesis." Having said that the variety of methods is "a sign of life and a resource" of catechesis at the service of revelation and of conversion, and having treated of the incarnation of the message in cultures, it speaks precisely of the *"contribution* (to catechesis) *of popular devotions."*

In order to first see the passages, we proceed by examining the various sentences of the text (we will quote them in italics).

1. The first sentence consists in a general affirmation which presents as a question of method whatever in popular piety is to be seen "positively": *"Another question of method concerns the utilization in catechetical instruction of valid elements in popular piety"* (CT 54).

The Pope does not stop at opinions, nor enter into the problematic, nor does he want to annul questions, however complex, regarding the acceptation, limits and extent of "popular devotion." The preoccupation goes directly to the reality which is incumbent and which is, it can never be forgotten, the *primary duty* of the Church to catechize.[32] "The transition to number 54 [the passage that precisely concerns popular religiosity included in the methodological part of catechesis] is most logical: it treats, in fact, of a method of Christianity incarnating itself in the various cultures and of the consequent expressiveness of this incarnation that has taken place—for catechetical methodology—and it is presented in a positive form...." Thus we wrote in a commentary of ours on *Catechesi tradendae.*[33] If sociology, anthropology, ethnology, and theology itself have reasons for discussions and proper research, catechesis has precise practical necessities. Herein, then, lies the necessity of highlighting the *valid elements* of popular piety as points—as *loci* of catechesis, to express ourselves in terminology dear to the synod of 1977.

2. It is necessary forcefully to accent and to recall attention to that expression *valid elements.* It had already been said that Paul VI had had a certain optimism regarding *popular piety.* Still more has been said about optimism in examining *Catechesi tradendae* of John Paul II.

3. There are three sentences in which John Paul II gives, so to speak, a testimony containing examples. Here is the first: *"I have in mind devotions practiced by the faithful in certain regions with moving fervor and purity of intention, even if the faith underlying them needs to be purified or rectified in many aspects"* (CT 54). Two observations may be made: the first concerns the appreciation of the *subjective* aspect, whose value the document recognizes; the second concerns the *objective* aspect. *Catechesi tradendae* requires not only a purification of the ways with which these devotions are practiced, but indeed even of the *faith underlying them.*

And here are the other two sentences, always in the form of a testimony: *"I have in mind certain easily understood prayers that many simple people are fond of repeating. I have in mind certain acts of piety practiced with a sincere desire to do penance or to please the Lord."*

4. At this point comes the confirmation of what we have said above: speaking of "popular devotions" was not a "reduction" of the theme of popular piety. The "document" has made a choice in view of catechesis and in line with what was said from the introduction—and especially in the first chapter—to the final conclusion. And this is clarified by what is said immediately after the words quoted: *"Underlying most of these prayers and practices, besides elements that should be discarded* [note the evidence of the "realistic" vision of the Apostolic Exhortation], *there are other elements which, if they were properly used, could serve very well to help people advance towards knowledge of the mystery of Christ and of His message: the love and mercy of God, the Incarnation of Christ, His redeeming cross and resurrection, the activity of the Spirit in each Christian and in the Church, the mystery of the hereafter, the evangelical virtues to be practiced, the presence of the Christian in the world, etc."* (CT 54).

"To catechize" popular devotions (from prayers to acts, to "practices") concretely means not to halt at an *action of restoration*, as we often hear it said, but to thrust the action deeper down.

Practically speaking, the presentation of what John Paul II recalls proposes what is to be believed and practiced in answer to the vocation to faith and to the Christian life, through that zeal which the sense of "devotion" involves, even terminologically speaking.

5. The last sentence rings thus: *"And why should we appeal to non-Christian or even anti-Christian elements refusing to build on elements which, even if they need to be revised or improved, have something Christian at their root?"* (CT 54)

To what does this question refer? Certainly not to a refusal to take into account "cultures" and the exigencies which these involve; it suffices to reread the preceding number, which places in the right light the two conditions established by the Pope.

Is it, perhaps, hazardous to consider those attempts to shake off the contribution of the Gospel as spurious for a pure and simple return to pre-existent cultures or to consider so-called philosophical (or pseudo-philosophical), sociological or cultural "exigencies" as data that cannot be renounced because they are incarnate in one or in another *manner of life*, proper to certain peoples? Is it hazardous to think that this question is an indirect, but precise, condemnation of certain propositions cloaked by theological "conquests" or, worse, presented as "social conquests"?

Conclusions

In its search for positive contributions to Christian formation which truly lead to the personal encounter of individual persons, families and groups with Christ, catechesis can find a particular impetus precisely in the mainstream of *popular devotions*. However, there must be the understanding—and this is the *leitmotif* of the entire Exhortation *Catechesi tradendae*—that catechesis be taken in its genuine and proper sense in its dynamic impetus to constitute a true and personal encounter with Christ, "way, truth and life," and not only as an indoctrination at various levels.

At this point permit us to express desires that this paragraph of *Catechesi tradendae* not only invite everyone to reflect personally and to make the fruit of the reflection pass on from personal conviction to pastoral, apostolic and missionary programming, but that it be, together with number 48 of EN, a valid motive and point of departure for a *reading again* in pastoral-catechetical terms of "religiosity" or "popular piety," freeing ourselves, without human respect, from every tie, open or understood, with sociological theories of any kind whatsoever regarding this so delicate area.

There is truly a need for this....

MSGR. MARIO PUCCINELLI

FOOTNOTES

1. We refer particularly to the Conference of the Latin American Episcopate in a general meeting, as well as to individual national episcopal conferences. As points of reference, see: Willi Henkel: "La pietà popolare come via all'Evangelizzazione," in L'annuncio del Vangelo oggi, Rome, PUU, 1977, p. 525ff. with bibliography.
For an update, see Puebla: comunione e partecipazione, edited by P. Vanzan—Ed. AVE, Rome, 1978, passim—(analytical index, pp. 907-8).

2. Cf. "Sacred Congregation for the Evangelization of Peoples," Annuario 1979, p. 163ff. It is very interesting for our specific topic.

3. Cf. Mario Puccinelli: "Aspetti Pastorali della religiosità popolare," in Orientamenti Sociali Nuova Serie, 1978, no. 3, p. 7 (231)—18 (242) and no. 5, p. 40 (496)ff. Cf. the same in Carlo Prandi, "Sulla religione e sul populare," in Testimonianze, 1978, nos. 209-210, pages 735-761. Also Gustavo Guizzardi, "Popolare, populismo, Chiesa Cattolica," in Rivista di Teologia Morale, 42, 1979.

4. For the references to the Synod of the Bishops of 1974 cf. Giovanni Caprile, S.J., Il Sinodo dei Vescovi 1974, Ed. Civiltà Cattolica, 1975 (from here on, referred to as GC 74), and M. Puccinelli, art. cit., in OS, no. 3, p. 9 for the particular citation.

5. Cf. M. Puccinelli, art. cit., p. 9.

6. As is known, circuli minores are those linguistic groups which come together, with spontaneous adhesions, to treat of synodal topics outside of the Regional Congregations.

7. Cf. in this regard GC 74 under the particular term.

8. The Apostolic Exhortation of Paul VI, Evangelii nuntiandi, is indicated by EN.

9. The Apostolic Exhortation Catechesi tradendae is indicated by CT.

10. Vincenzo Bo, La religiosità popolare, Editrice Cittadella, Assisi, 1979.

11. For the 1977 Synod cf. Giovanni Caprile, S.J., Ed. Civiltà Cattolica, 1978: Il Sinodo dei Vescovi 1977, from here on indicated by GC 77. Cf. also Mario Puccinelli, "Dossier: il Sinodo dei Vescovi sulla Catechesi," in Orientamenti Sociali N.S., 1978, no. 1, pp. 53ff.

12. Cf. M. Puccinelli, art. cit. OS, no. 2.

13. Cf. GC 77, p. 13. The reference is to page 4, no. 46.

14. Cf. GC 77, p. 18. This refers to the Plenary Congregation of 1976.

15. Cf. GC 77, page 32. It is the title of a conference of the Secretary General.

16. Cf. GC 77, pp. 45-46, from Panorama, read in the Hall by His Excellency, J. J. Degenhardt, Archbishop of Paderborn.

17. Cf. GC 77, loc. cit.

18. Cf. GC 77, p. 78.

19. Cf. GC 77, p. 85: Bishop Felipe Santiago Benitez Avalos.

20. Cf. GC 77, p. 86: Bishop Horacio Alberto Bozzoli.

21. Cf. GC 77, pp. 104-105.

22. Cf. GC 77, p. 122. This concerns a very articulate intervention which refers explicitly to no. 48 of EN.

23. Cf. GC 77, p. 134. Cardinal Raùl Primatesta, Archbishop of Còrdoba, Argentina. This, too, was an articulate intervention, and the P.R. was placed, in a certain manner, as following the family-catechesis problematic.

24. Cf. GC 77, pp. 172 and 188. This concerns interventions given only in writing.

25. Cf. GC 77, p. 199.

26. Cf. GC 77, p. 223.

27. Cf. GC 77, p. 234.

28. Cf. GC 77, p. 265.

29. Cf. GC 77, p. 296.

30. Cf. GC 77, p. 306.

31. Cf. GC 77, p. 376.

32. Cf. CT introd. and passim.

33. M. Puccinelli: "La catechesi nel nostro tempo," Quaderni CENAC, no. 4, Ed. AVE, Rome, 1980, p. 122.

8

Using the Means of Social Communication

"According to us communists, you Catholic priests in India are at least two hundred years behind the times. You ignore all the modern means of diffusing ideas. With money you build institutions; we print books and newspapers. You open schools and teach children how to read and write, but then you give them nothing to read. We give everything, from wall posters to newspapers, from books to pamphlets, suitable for every age and situation. You print much pious material, but very few ideas. You have typographies, but you make them function for profit above all; we, for propaganda. You distribute powdered milk; we, ideas. You worry about filling the stomach; we, the mind. You say that it is ideas which govern the world, but then you do not diffuse them. The battle of ideas has already been lost by you in the whole world and also in India. On the plane of ideas we communists have beaten you, because we form public opinion, whereas you are incapable. You should spend a hundred times more on the press, on motion pictures, on radio and TV, to print books, posters, pamphlets, newspapers, discussion outlines, periodicals of all types whatsoever: to help those who want to study and those who dedicate themselves to the formation of public opinion. My advice is worth a thousand gold crowns. And I deserve to be expelled from the Party for having given it to you."

Little Consideration for the Mass Media

This is a letter which a director of the communist party in India wrote to a few Catholic priests with whom he had come in contact.[1] I believe it synthesizes very well everything that can be said of the relationship between the means of social communication and evangelization. (The term "catechesis" is ambiguous enough, because it usually is understood as "teaching catechism." We mean it, according to the indication of no. 18 of *Catechesi tradendae*, as a moment of evangelization and hence, in practice, almost as one of its synonyms.)

In the theme that we want to develop it is superfluous to report on the numerous exhortations of Vatican II (*Inter mirifica*) or of the recent Pontiffs and episcopal synods, urging evangelizers to make use of the means of social communication in their apostolates. Neither does it serve to demonstrate "the natural fitness of the instruments of social communication as vehicles of catechesis," as an author knowledgeable in this matter writes.[2] Neither does it serve to insist on the utility and indispensability of these instruments (press, motion pictures, radio, TV, posters, pamphlets, audio-visuals, etc.) for the diffusion of the message of Christ.

It does not serve, I repeat, for at least two good reasons: first, because by now we are all convinced of how effective the means of social communication are in the modern world for the formation of man and of public opinion (everything else is only a consequence); second, because many and profound studies are already available regarding these preliminary themes. Therefore, anyone who would be interested in the theoretical aspects of our problem has ample possibilities for reading.[3]

Instead, it is useful to ask ourselves why, going back to the points contained in the letter of the Indian communist, we Catholics believe so little in the means of social communication and are often ineffective in using them. This theme has not been faced in the official documents of the Church, which are of a rather theoretical and exhortative character. We must recall, however, that John Paul II, for example—to cite one text among many—told the bishops of Venezuela received for the *ad limina* visit (November 15, 1979) that pastoral priority is to concentrate all efforts "in a systematic catechetical action, exercised in depth"; and he added: "In this task, and to give it the breadth not permitted by the scarcity of qualified agents of the pastoral, make the most possible use of the instruments of social communication, capable of multiplying your voices as evangelizers."[4] On the other hand, in number 46 of *Catechesi tradendae* we read: "I think immediately of the great possibilities offered by the means of social communication and the means of group communication: television, radio, the press, records, tape recordings—the whole series of audio-visual means. The achievements in these spheres are such as to encourage the greatest hope...."

The first problem which should be dealt with in the Church is precisely this: few efforts are made in this sector because, notwithstanding all the documents of the Church in this regard other instruments of Christian formation are favored and the mass media are generally left up to the good will of individuals or at least enter into the pastoral program only in a very secondary position. If a portion of all the human efforts and financial means used in different initiatives were destined for the mass media..... But this is an impossible dream. One could think of the hundreds of religious orders of men and women which were born for the Catholic schools, whereas for the press and the mass media I know of none founded precisely for this other than the Congregations of Father Alberione.

Let us take a concrete case: the Church of Kenya. According to a missionary of the Consolata who lives there and applies himself in working for a press at the service of evangelization, catechesis for children is well organized in Kenya, but as for youth and adults they are neglected completely: books are lacking; newspapers and periodicals are lacking; initiatives for radio, films and audio-visuals do not exist. Everything is limited to the printing of catechetical texts for the schools and parishes. In all of Kenya, where the most learned and progressive youth are Christian, there is not even a Catholic leaflet for them, whereas the missionary writes: "The passion for reading is very strong among African youth." What reading material do we give to these young men and women whom we have baptized and catechized in the churches and the Catholic schools? Nothing! Then we complain if, in reading other printed matter, they end up by estranging themselves from the Church, reading Marxist books and those by anarchical philosophers. This missionary, Father Giovanni Tebaldi,[5] wanted to found a magazine for the youth, but he was unable to obtain the means to begin, that is, about ten million lire and a few rooms. However, he told me, if he would have asked for money to build a church, a sanctuary, a hospital, or a seminary he would most certainly have found the necessary means and permissions. "If then I would have wanted to help the lepers, I would have had no further financial problems...."

Kenya is just one case among many. Nations such as Uganda and Tanzania, with a flourishing and fully-developed Christianity, do not yet have a Catholic weekly. In all Africa there are only two Catholic weeklies of some importance: *Afrique Nouvelle* (at Dakar) and *The Southern Cross* (of Capetown: this is diffused, however, almost only in South Africa). The U.C.I.P. *(International Catholic Union of the Press)*, in its last two international Congresses at Vienna (1977) and at Rome (1980) has centered its attention on the Catholic press in the third world, hurling out a cry of alarm and semi-desperate appeals to the young Churches: in the third world, too, we Catholics are losing the battle of ideas!

Let us think of the case, for me serious, of the Indian Church, which is solidly founded, with local personnel, who certainly do not lack the means (with many subsidies from outside and good financial foundations locally), with a considerable burden in Indian society because of the imposing numbers of Catholic universities (about eighty colleges at the university level), high schools, elementary schools, hospitals, lepersaria, etc., and because of its assistance to tribal peoples, to outcasts and to the underprivileged of all kinds. Well then, the Catholics of India do not yet have, I do not say a daily—(and yet India is a nation of great journalistic traditions; notwithstanding the poverty, it has superior newspapers)—but not even one weekly on a national level which is read outside of the narrow circle of "practicing" Catholics! There are five or six weeklies (the *Examiner* of Bombay, the *New Leader* of Bangalore, the *Catholic Herald* of Calcutta and two in local language in Kerala), but all on the parish-bulletin style. Among the monthlies only *Home Life* (the *Famiglia Cristiana* of the Paulines in India) and *Social Action* (of the Jesuit institute of social studies in Delhi) have a certain national value (excluding the periodicals of theology). Thus, the influence of the Church in the mass media is almost nothing, certainly inferior to that of the Protestants.

Two years ago I visited the *Amruthavani* center of Hyderabad, founded a few years ago in the capital of Andhra for the production of newpapers, filmstrips, radio and TV programs, posters, liturgical leaflets and catechetical texts, mainly in Telegu language (the language of the state of Andhra, where my confreres of P.I.M.E. work). After having admired this work, in traveling about in the state of Andhra to visit the missions, I only heard criticism in regard to the *Amruthavani:* too large a building, which employs too many persons and uses too many means, etc. Such criticisms are the evident sign of what little value is given to the importance of the mass media in evangelization. Naturally this is not only in India.

In the Church
There is No Public Opinion

In the third world the young Churches are repeating the very errors of the old Churches of the nations of the west: they neglect information, culture, audio-visuals, the press, the radio and the publishing industry, to dedicate greater attention to other pastoral instruments of more immediate contact between evangelizers and evangelized (parish, school, associations, preaching, popular devotion, etc.). It suffices to see, for example, the space which the documents of Puebla dedicate to the mass media and to other pastoral instruments—the difference of quantity and of tone is immediately evident. With sincerity Puebla affirms[6]: "There is an insufficient utilization of the opportunities for communication which are given to the Church through the media of others, besides an incomplete utilization of the media that are our own or influenced by us; where, then, such media exist, they are not united among themselves nor with the pastoral of togetherness" (no. 1076). And further: "Save for rare exceptions, there still does not exist in the Church of Latin America a real concern for forming the people of God to social communication" (no. 1077).

Puebla itself gives the beginning of an explanation for this situation: "In these last years the Church of Latin America has made many efforts for a greater internal communication. Nevertheless, in many cases, what has been accomplished up until now does not respond fully to the exigencies of the moment. The circulation of experiences and of legitimate opinions, as the public expression of opinions within the Church, is reduced to manifestations that are sporadic, and hence insufficient; these exercise little influence on the ecclesial community as a whole" (no. 1079).

In practice, there does not exist a public opinion formed within the Church, there is insufficient communication of news and of experiences, insufficient discussion and participation. The basic problem of the relationship between us Catholics and the means of social communication is this: we believe that we already possess the whole truth and that all we have to do is live it and apply it to the concrete situations of life. There is no room for many debates on the level of ideas; our tendency is to go directly to the action, to the doing. In his "ashram" of Kullitalai in south India, the Benedictine Bede Griffiths told me that we Catholics are so sure of having God with us that we no longer preoccupy ourselves with searching for Him in our life, whereas the Hindus who have not received Revelation make the search for God the fundamental aim of their very existence.[7] Our formation leads us to regard as perfect a situation that is secure, established with clarity once and for always, whereas any means whatsoever of social communication thrives on debate, on novelty, on movement.

The Second Vatican Council set in motion debate within the Church, which immediately won the interest even of external public opinion (debate means dialogue, experimentation, pluralism, comparison with other cultural and religious worlds). On the other hand, evangelization is dialogue with man, proposal, and exchange, after the example of Jesus.

The pastoral instruction, *Communio et progressio,* on the means of social communication[8] developed these concepts well; however, they are not felt within the Church. Since the instruction is very little known, it is useful to cite a few passages fundamental to a right understanding of the Church-mass media relationship.

"The Church looks for ways of multiplying and strengthening the bonds of union between her members. For this reason, communication and dialogue among Catholics are indispensable. The Church lives her life in the midst of the whole community of man. She must, therefore, maintain contacts and lines of communication in order to keep a relationship with the whole human race. This is done both by giving information and by listening carefully to public opinion inside and outside the Church. Finally, by holding a continuous discussion with the contemporary world, she tries to help in solving the problems that men face at the present time" (no. 114).

"Since the Church is a living body, she needs public opinion in order to sustain a giving and taking between her members..." (no. 115). "Catholics should be fully aware of the real freedom to speak their minds which stems from a 'feeling for the Faith' and from love.... Those who exercise authority in the Church will take care to ensure that there is responsible exchange of freely held and expressed opinion among the people of God. More than this, they will set up norms and conditions for this to take place" (no. 116). "There is an enormous area where members of the Church can express their views on domestic issues.... This free dialogue within the Church does no injury to her unity and solidarity. It nurtures concord and the meeting of minds by permitting the free play of the variations of public opinion. But in order that this dialogue may go in the right direction it is essential that charity is in command even when there are differing views. Everyone in this dialogue should be animated by the desire to serve and to consolidate unity and cooperation. There should be a desire to build, not to destroy. There should be a deep love for the Church..." (no. 117).

Also most beautiful are these paragraphs about the right to information:

"...individual Catholics have the right to all the information they need to play their active role in the life of the Church" (no. 119). "...the spiritual riches which are an essential attribute of the Church demand that the news she gives out of her intentions as well as of her works be distinguished by integrity, truth and openness.... Secrecy should, therefore, be restricted to matters that involve the good name of individuals or that touch upon the rights of people whether singly or collectively" (no. 121). "By virtue of a divine command and by the right to knowledge possessed by the people whose lot she shares on earth, the Church is in duty bound publicly to communicate her belief and her way of life" (no. 122). "It is the mission of those with responsible positions in the Church to announce without fail or pause the full truth by means of social communication, so as to give a true picture of the Church and her life.... On her part, the Church is consequently bound in duty to give complete and entirely accurate information to the news agencies so that they, in their turn, can carry out their task" (no. 123). "What was contained above where commentaries on the news were discussed retains its full force here where Church news is under consideration. Responsible leaders in the Church then should try in advance to be ready to deal with a difficult situation and should not abandon the initiative" (no. 124).

Pardon me for the length of these citations, but they seem to me fundamental for an honest discourse on the relationship between mass media and evangelization, while often they are

almost totally ignored. It seems to me proper to point out that today in the Catholic press there are too many silences, while service
to the truth demands that information be serious and sufficiently
complete. In the dioceses and parishes there do not exist regular
and permanent structures of communication for the exchange of
experiences, of opinions, of ecclesial sensibilities; in other words,
communication too often is unilateral, that is, only from above to
below.

Father Chevalier said to the congress of the UCIP in Vienna
already cited, "Catholic journalists have the important mission of
helping the Church present herself to the modern world and of
making the Church discover the mentality and interests of contemporary man." But this can come about when there is sufficient
freedom of expression within ecclesial life, so that one can understand where the Christian community is going, and what its
problems and anxieties are. In other words, journalists must help
to create a dialogue within the community of believers (local
Church of a nation, diocese, parish), and the hierarchy must accept and foster this dialogue, which is indispensable for the formation of that knowledgeable public opinion in the Church of
which Pius XII already spoke in 1950! Without this public opinion
there cannot be a correct and effective rapport between evangelization and mass media; not only this, but the faithful themselves
will continue to be passive elements in the Church, who only
receive and do not give, while the Church today, all over the
world, needs active laity, engaged especially in the evangelization of those far away.

Evangelize the Culture of the Mass Media

When we speak of the use of the means of social communication in evangelization, we always treat the utility of these means
and the technique of how to use them. For example, today audio-
visuals are indispensable to catechesis for such and such reasons;
what technical norms must be respected to use them effectively?
And so on for all the other instruments of social communication
(posters, filmstrips, pamphlets, books, newspapers, radio, etc...).
Without doubt such points are useful, but specialized publications already exist, and to these we refer the readers.[9] The basic
theme, however, is another one besides that already noted (that
neither true public opinion nor complete information exist in the

Church). Paul VI pointed to it when he said: "The split between the Gospel and culture is without a doubt the drama of our time, just as it was of other times. Therefore, every effort must be made to ensure a full evangelization of culture, or more correctly of cultures. They have to be regenerated by an encounter with the Gospel. But this encounter will not take place if the Gospel is not proclaimed."[10]

It seems to me that we can derive two conclusions from this text:

1) Evangelization is not to be understood solely as the formation and conversion of the individual, but as the Christianization of culture, of the common mentality of a determined people. Now, the almost exclusive choices that the Church makes of formative instruments on the level of the individual or of a small group (catechesis, preparation for the sacraments, Catholic school, homily, spiritual direction, devout books diffused only among the "practicing"), appears to me not to be a very missionary choice; it is addressed only to "conserving" the "practicing" faithful, but is hardly at all incisive in regard to national culture and public opinion. A recent inquiry promoted by Catholic Action in Italy[11] regarding catechesis (understood in the sense of teaching catechism, of giving specific religious instruction) says: "Among the data cited, those regarding adult catechesis were decidedly preoccupying. Catechesis reaches only 0,8% of young adults, 1,2% of the adults, 0,7% of the old*; in 50% of the cases this is accomplished in the associated groups of Catholic Action." In other words, we put forth almost all our efforts to reach one or two percent of Italian adults and we neglect the rest.

2) The culture in which we live in our western world—but this is becoming always more true in the world of the poor as well—is a culture formed in great part by the mass media. At the International Catechetical Congress of 1971 it was admitted that "the Church must carry out her mission in the midst of a new humanity, shaped by the means of social communication."[12]

We cannot go too deeply into this study here: we are anxious only to give the reader the idea of the extent and difficulty of a treatise on the "means of social communication at the service of catechesis." On the theoretical plane, this treatise has already been developed, beginning with *Vigilanti cura* by Pius XI (1936), and continuing up until *Communio et progressio* (1971), and *Evangelii nuntiandi* (1975) by Paul VI, passing through the two discourses of Pius XII on "the ideal film" (June 21 and October 28, 1955), *Miranda prorsus* (1957), the conciliar decree *Inter mirifica* (1963) and many other papal discourses and documents (to speak only of these!) on the mass media (see the volume of E. Baragli cited in footnote no. 8). But sadly enough this discourse on evangelizing the modern culture that is being shaped by the mass media has not yet penetrated into the mentality of the evangelizers, much less into the pastoral structures of the universal Church and of the local Churches. As often happens in the Catholic field, the official texts shine with doctrine and prophetic intuitions, while the ecclesial body continues on in its customary journey, traveling on the traditional tracks. The means of social communication continue to be considered only as passive instruments which amplify the voice of the evangelizers and not instead as creators of a "new civilization" which overturns the language and techniques of communication to which we are accustomed. (Just to give an example, one could reflect on all the forms of oratorical style so dear to us ecclesiastics which have been decisively superseded today but continue to be used: abstract reasoning, courtly language, pompous or high-sounding oratory, paternalistic moralism, etc.).

Thus it happens that, not having entered as evangelizers into the civilization of the mass media (apart from rare exceptions), we cannot even pretend to influence it in depth, and we lose the battle of information, of ideas, of culture, of spectacles of current debate, even in nations for the most part Catholic. We evangelize individuals, families, small groups of the faithful and children, but we lose the capability of creating a Christian culture in the era of the mass media.

I cited the cases of Kenya and of India. Another seriously indicative case is that of Brazil, where during the last twenty years the rate of literacy has climbed from 37% to 78% and students of high schools and universities have increased more than tenfold. At the International Congress of the UCIP in Vienna in 1977, dizzying figures were cited regarding growth of the press, radio and TV in Brazil: practically in these twenty years the "civilization of the mass media" has developed in a tumultuous manner even in that great "Catholic" nation. But the organized presence of Catholics in all this dazzling progress is almost nothing. There is not even one single Catholic daily nor even one weekly on a national level, nor does there exist even one cultural periodical that is also read outside ecclesial environments and which forms opinions. The Church and the various missionary institutes that carry out their apostolate in Brazil have given priority to evangelizing the Indians and the Caboclos, to permeating the whole vast territory with chapels and small Catholic schools, to aiding the lepers, but without expressing one single initiative in the field of mass media on the national level. *("Radio educadoras*—educational radio" has been developed in the more primitive regions, to give a basic education, but this is not an initiative which sufficiently influences the culture and information.)

On the other hand, why go outside of our own house? In Italy what have we done for the press, culture and information during the period of economic and cultural boom? We, dioceses and religious institutes, built hundreds of very large seminaries and novitiates, which today we sell to the highest bidder; we built new churches and oratories, but, meanwhile, only three now remain of the eight Catholic dailies which existed in 1959, and the great mass media (press, publishing houses, films, RAI-TV, cultural debates, etc.) form a new civilization among the masses which is anything but Christian. I permit myself to cite two concrete facts as indices of a general situation. Three years ago, at the RAI-TV of Milan they were taking on new personnel for program development and the founding of a third television network. The Catholics had the right for about ten of their journalists to be employed; but in Milan and all of Lombardy there were not found ten Catholics who were prepared for those positions. As had already happened in the past, they ended up by giving the positions to journalist friends who then turned out to be anything but Christian.

Here is a second fact. Two years ago I went to a large city in south Italy to give a conference at the local university. The auditorium was full and the highest civic authorities were also present. At supper I was the guest of a religious institute for men, which runs a high school-college with about 2,000 students. At table there were about thirty priests of that institute, who told me: "Thank you for having come way down here into the deep south to give this conference; it is one of the few Catholic cultural events in this city, while the Marxists, radicals and lay groups hold debates and give conferences, and establish opinion groups...." I asked: "But is it possible that I have to come from Milan to give a conference? You are about thirty priests with degrees. What do you do to animate your city culturally?" The answers can easily be imagined: "I am a teacher of mathematics; I teach history; I am the bursar of the college; I am the dean; I teach twenty hours of classes a week; I am in charge of discipline and the spiritual life...." They were almost all young, culturally prepared, lively in ideas and in interests, but they do not form opinions in that metropolis of the south. Then we complain that others make the culture, that they impose the themes of debates, the choices of the groups involved....

A "Cultural Revolution" in the Church

Concretely, what must be done? To answer a question of this kind, a few pages would not suffice. On the other hand, precise, concrete indications already exist in the pontifical texts (in particular in *Communio et progressio*) and in the congresses of the UCIP, of the OCIC, and of UNDA (the international Catholic organisms for the coordination of the ecclesial initiatives of press, motion pictures and radio-television). Suffice it to say that there should be a "cultural revolution" in the Church in regard to the use of the mass media in evangelization, up until now outlined in documents and congresses, but not yet felt on the basic ecclesial level.

This "cultural revolution" must at least take cognizance of what St. Pius X affirmed in 1908[13]: "The characteristic sign of our era is that for whatever concerns the manner of thinking and of living men ordinarily draw inspiration from the press." Today we would have to enlarge this affirmation, by also adding the other means of social communication, at least films, radio and television.

The consequences of this assessment of the "new civilization shaped by the mass media" are or should be clear, and they would precisely represent a "cultural revolution" in the Church, if they were to be applied to evangelization: the formation of Christians (and in particular of the evangelizers, of the clergy) to the new language and to the use of the means of social communication, the personal effort of the evangelizers in the use of these instruments, the effective·pastoral of togetherness of the mass media with the employment of the best energies and of adequate financial means, etc.; in synthesis, the conviction that the journalist, the producer, the promoter of a mass culture, the writer, are the teachers of our time and hence that the Christian (or the priest) dedicated to these professions is a real evangelizer, if naturally he carries out his work with missionary spirit.

Years ago, Giovanni Papini published a treatise entitled *Lo scrittore come maestro*, which aroused a lively controversy, but Paul VI said even more when he affirmed that the religious informer is a "prophetic voice." "Your task," he added,[14] "is not so much that of information, but rather of the formation.... Be teachers of life, not only reporters; not only those who give pleasure by means of curiosity or through the exceptional nature of the news...I repeat, formers, that is, persons who bring consolation, persons who draw out moral energies and bring them to birth." The Catholic journalist..."is a preacher who speaks through a printed sheet, a prophet who wants to direct his listeners on the ways of good."

PIERO GHEDDO, PIME

FOOTNOTES

1. Letter printed by the periodical for the clergy of India, *Vidyajoti,* and translated by *Mondo e Missione,* 1975, 430.

2. Pignatiello, L., "Gli strumenti della comunicazione sociale a servizio della catechesi," in the volume of various authors, *La Chiesa e i mass media,* Ed. Paoline, Rome, 1968, pp. 45-92.

3. See the two articles by E. Baragli, "L'istruzione pastorale 'Comunio et Progressio,'" in *La Civiltà Cattolica,* 1979, IV, pp. 39-48, 235-253; with the ample bibliography in the notes. Father Baragli marks out also in *La Civiltà Cattolica* all the important bibliographical news in this field.

4. Cited in *La Civiltà Cattolica,* May 3, 1980, p. 272.

5. Tebaldi, G., "La situazione catechetica in Kenya," in *Mondo e Missione,* 1977, pp. 603-605.

6. See the official translation of the texts in *Puebla—Documenti,* EMI, Bologna, 1979.

7. The discourse with Father Griffiths is naturally more complex. See *Mondo e Missione,* 1978, pp. 231-253.

8. The instruction bears the date of May 23, 1971, Fifth World Day of Social Communications. Regarding this problem see the fundamental volume of E. Baragli, *Comunicazione e pastorale,* Roman Studio of Social Communication, Rome, 1974, p. 566.

9. We cite the periodical *Catechesi* edited by the Salesian Catechetical Center (L.D.C., Turin) and *Lumen Vitae* of the Centre International d'Etudes pour la Formation Religieuse of Brussels. Naturally periodicals of this type abound.

10. *Evangelii nuntiandi,* no. 20.

11. Cited in *Presenza Pastorale,* October-November 1979, p. 71, article by Father Bignardi, "Animatori per la catechesi degli adulti."

*Editor's note: these figures are reproduced here as given in the Italian original.

12. Cited in *Lumen Vitae,* Brussels, 1971, p. 666.

13. In a letter to the Archbishop of Quebec, A.A.S., 1908, p. 193: "...est ingenium aetatis ut quae ad vivendi cogitandique rationem pertinent, vulgo e diariis quaquaversus illatis derivent."

14. Discourse of July 9, 1977, to the FISC *(Federazione Italiana Settimanali Cattolici,* Federation of Italian Catholic Weeklies), cit. in *Bollettino* FISC, October, 1977.

9

The Catechetical Office and Missionary Center of the Pastoral of Togetherness

1. A Catechetical Pastoral

This reflection is not of a theological nature, even if reasons and conclusions of a theological order cannot be absent. It frames itself in the pastoral plan of a diocese and precisely in that conception of the pastoral of togetherness, unfortunately long disregarded, from which concrete pastoral plans derive.

It has to be said from the very beginning that without an adequate diocesan programming, worked out communitarianly, it is impossible today to escape from improvisation and to find the method for channeling the message in a context that is always more in need of orderly standards and of an appropriate reading on a socio-religious plane. And this is not to give in to the postulates of efficiency, many times refuted, but to outline a pastoral efficacy which favors the announcement of the Word and renders a local Church wholly evangelizing. For this we are convinced that a great part of the organic pastoral should be under the sign of catechesis and in function of catechesis, saving in the comprehensive vision of a diocese exigencies and times of partial growth; a pastoral which submits common objectives to everyone, setting up forms of mediation and help which are possible only within the radius of a diocese.

The commitment of catechesis, which consists of "an ordered and progressive education in the faith," as is affirmed at the beginning of the Message of the Synod of Bishops for Catechesis (no. 1), aims at a global growth in which the whole People of God is involved. The catechetical pastoral signifies the transmission of the datum of faith to the individual and to the community, aiming for a permanent catechesis, faithful to man and to God, communitarian and "lay," which means stimulating the laity to evangelization. With this premise one easily understands that to the pastoral plan there must correspond a series of commitments, roles and objectives which, if they demand co-participation, also require directive guidelines and directional responsibilities. We call attention especially to these, deriving our observations, however, from the complex of the present situation and from *Catechesi tradendae*, which to us seems to give much more than an indication on the topic we are treating.

We will begin from an inductive type of consideration. That is, our activity sets out from the real situations in which catechesis must develop, to remind ourselves that a sense of concreteness and of practicality requires not superficiality and improvisation, but orderliness and directional interventions to give a meaning to the very pluralistic fermentations of the experiences.

The concrete application of the directives contained in *Catechesi tradendae* is entrusted, as is known, to precise "places" of catechesis—first among all the parish, "major point of reference for the Christian people," which "must continue to be the prime mover and pre-eminent place for catechesis."[1] This is the first fundamental affirmation; it requires a convergence of energies and of projects and clears the ground from hasty liquidations of the essential role of the parish community. This is, indeed, the first basic structure in which the people of God finds itself and in which the announcement of the Word is clothed with a biblical sense and with a universal dimension, because it is precisely in the midst of His people that God makes Himself present and addresses Himself to everyone. In the parish is studied and carried out that general animation which is facilitated by a series of motives, such as direct contact and the experience of the pastors of souls, an animation which is to be given back to the parish so that it may remain a "point of reference" for all decentralized catechetical action.

Naturally realism and common sense—the Document notes—lead one to keep in mind other "catechetical channels" which are constituted by a vast range of realities around which associated and religious life gravitate: family, school, movements, youth centers, weekly encounters of formation, and other forms of approach which, inspired or articulating themselves in the interior of a local Church, cannot prescind from the fundamental catechetical moment. It is precisely this plurality of "channels," besides the fundamental structure of a diocese, which leads us to a reflection which is of an organizational-pastoral type, yes, but finalized to grasp the manner of placing itself at the summit of the organizations, and in their service, discovering in the meantime, a true interdependence of roles between catechetical office and missionary center in the heart of the same diocesan pastoral. Above them, as well as over and in the community, stands the primary responsibility of the Bishops.

It is natural that the orderly and conscious development of catechesis cannot be entrusted to spontaneity or to imagination or to the responsible commitment of individual pastoral workers, but belongs to the irreplaceable role of the Bishops, to whom *Catechesi tradendae* recommends: "let the concern to foster active and effective catechesis yield to no other care whatever in any way!"[2] *Catechesi tradendae* asks the Bishops to "assume" according to a precise duty which is to be adapted to the programs of the respective episcopal conferences "the chief management of catechesis," in order "to bring about and maintain in your Churches"—it affirms—"a real passion for catechesis, a passion embodied in a pertinent and effective organization, putting into operation the necessary personnel, means, and equipment, and also financial resources."[3] The invitation is directed to an organic vision of catechetical pastoral which aims at planning with intelligence, and at the same time upholds, increases and stabilizes the adequate forms, having kept in mind general directives and the needs of the place. Catechesis, that is, needs suitable organization and proportionate means, and it cannot be entrusted to common sense or, worse, to chance.

The organizational need is not new. It was already part of the general norm, of the Church, which foresaw in every parish the *sodalitium doctrinae christianae* (can. 711, par. 2) as an expression of the serious task of the Bishops to take care of catechetical education (cf. canons 1336 and 1329, which speak of the *proprium* = irreplaceable and *gravissimum* = principal *officium* of the pastors of souls).

In regard to Italy, from 1929 a diocesan catechetical office had been instituted in each diocese under the direct responsibility of the Ordinary as the higher organ of stimulus and control of catechetical teaching both in the parishes and in the schools. With its central organization of director and directive council and peripheral organization of zonal commissions of catechesis; with its regional and national ties, it could be affirmed that "in practically every diocese the diocesan catechetical office is the directive center that promotes all pastoral life."[4]

Undoubtedly the merit of having attempted a unified pastoral setup, thus anticipating many conclusions of Vatican II, is to be attributed precisely to the catechetical office and to the animation that in this sense was carried out for many long years by Catholic associations, especially by the Italian Catholic Action with its annual courses of religious culture.

Outside of Italy, especially in the young Churches, the sharpening of sensibilities in view of evangelization led to a plurality of experiences and to the forming of a network of catechists which has ultimately made them active, authentic and united. From this stemmed the urgency of centers of catechesis and of institutes of catechetical formation, in the general conviction that the primacy of evangelization granted absolute precedence to this type of organization in the local Churches.

The Council and post-Conciliar reflection accelerated in this direction. In particular Vatican II with its ecclesiological renewal favored a review of catechetical experience spurred on to methods and pastoral structures in harmony with a more organic vision of the Church and of her mystery. In its turn the missionary dimension of *Lumen gentium* could not but penetrate into the actuality of the dioceses; the diocesan offices or missionary centers made themselves its mouthpieces and pressed for a universalistic opening, transformed into a flowering of initiatives toward the Third World, especially with the birth of cooperation among the Churches in the spirit of communion.

Lastly the need to restore a more pastoral and less bureaucratic spirit to the central diocesan organisms themselves[5] has outlined even better the characteristics of the catechetical office and of the missionary center. Because of innate characteristics, they have immediately appeared as co-essential expressions of that pastoral office which has the responsibility of general coordination and orientation, through the organisms of participation. Catechesis and evangelization do not constitute two poles of a centralized bureaucracy, but express in a new manner the pastoral quality of a local Church in its attitude toward the proclamation of the Word. From their integrating function derive opportune pastoral choices in harmony with the spirit of

Catechesi tradendae. Hence it is necessary to notice the reciprocal contributions and the specific values which they imply, so that their integration will not be haphazard but motivated. Among other things this clarification avoids falling into the error of a theologically inexact exclusivism which reduces the first to the pastoral of preservation and directs the second solely to announcing "ad gentes." And this, furthermore would be unjust and reductive.

2. An Evangelizing Catechesis

Numbers 18, 19, and 20 of *Catechesi tradendae* establish the rapport between evangelization and catechesis within the same pastoral commitment. In pinpointing the specificity of catechesis, which constitutes one of the moments of the entire evangelizing process, the pontifical Document affirms: "The specific character of catechesis, as distinct from the initial conversion-bringing proclamation of the Gospel, has the twofold objective of maturing the initial faith and of educating the true disciple of Christ by means of a deeper and more systematic knowledge of the person and the message of our Lord Jesus Christ."[6] The passage is derived from the Apostolic Exhortation *Evangelii nuntiandi,* which in its turn points out the extension of the concept of evangelization and makes it include "a rich, complex and dynamic reality, made up of elements, or one could say moments, that are essential and different from each other, and that must *all be kept in view simultaneously.*"[7] The rapport between initial announcement and catechesis, far from being contradicted or only redimensioned, results in being strictly and profoundly integrated, to the point of a reciprocal interdependence. Still characterized by theological and pastoral peculiarities and by a semantic range differing although akin, evangelization and catechesis find themselves in the pastoral unity of the local Church. To determine this unitarian confluence there is, besides all else, the present day situation itself, which calls for it. Number 19 presents a descriptive panorama of the real picture of a local Church today, in whose catechumenal itinerary, rediscovery of Christian truth, response to the recurring temptations to abandon the faith which spring from "unbelieving surroundings," visualize a new frontier for the catechetical task, called to make itself attentive to the problems of a man who is born and lives in a secularized society, in need of certitude and frequently fleeing from it.

Catechizing is precisely the revelation, the manifestation, of truth to the man of today. In a word it seeks to give an appropriate answer to the scepticism or the anguish of the man of our time concretely proceeding toward the complete formation of a Christian personality. In this vision catechesis becomes receptive of "a certain number of elements" which are to be found in the general mission of the Church, insofar as they either contain a catechetical aspect or prepare for catechesis or constitute a consequence of it. *Catechesi tradendae* lists them thus, by a way of giving examples: "the initial proclamation of the Gospel or missionary preaching through the kerygma to arouse faith, apologetics or examination of the reasons for belief, experience of Christian living, celebration of the sacraments, integration into the ecclesial community, and apostolic and missionary witness."[8] There is affirmed the complementarity in practice of elements bound to the initial announcement and of typical stimuli of catechetical pastoral, with the result that they are seen to be joined in the Christian actuality of announcement. We cannot deny that a sense of *realpolitik* invests the document on catechesis and rescues it from ambiguity and contrasts between catechesis and evangelization which would have been nothing other than mere forms; rather, it integrates the contributions in a vision of togetherness which touches the world and the individual local Churches. Among other things it is a matter of perceiving that such a realistic manner of setting up catechesis finds remarkable points of contact between the Latin-American Churches and those of Europe, in which the initial announcement is assuming such a depth as to put in crisis the supposition of a catechetical form considered as the development of a faith that has been taken for granted.

The most successful result, in this tormented picture, is the discovery of a new education to the faith, more universalistic, more global and aiming more at involving all the baptized of the same local Church and making them responsible. This is one of the most fruitful intuitions, destined to multiply itself tomorrow on the plane of response to the faith; it is precisely this fusion of catechetical pastoral and missionary zeal that will be able to realize what is hoped for in these years—the opening to the universal dimension which becomes a paradigm for the life of the local Church. Catechesis becomes missionary as vocation "to the others," and the Churches of ancient Christianity may learn from the young Churches both the liberating and charismatic power of announcement and the institution of non-burdensome pastoral structures relative to the dynamism of that announcement.

Evangelization and catechesis find themselves, in fact, in the same pastoral project. The local Churches, even those favored by glorious traditions of faith, today move amid types of situations that are no longer compact and often contradictory; these constitute the truthful picture within which they operate. It can be truly said that the historical fact involves the directives of both *Evangelii nuntiandi* and *Catechesi tradendae* in the catechetical pastoral. These documents receive their more attentive and consequential reading within the central organs of the diocese, represented by the catechetical office and by the missionary center, which together are called to meditate on the reality to be evangelized and to reaffirm jointly the centrality of the Word of God in the progress of the Christian community, at whose service they are.

3. A Common Commitment

What we have said up until now offers us a series of elements which favor a certain manner of thinking regarding an organizational setup for catechesis; at the same time it makes us reflect on transformations slowly worked in time, even if only on a conceptual plane. In any case, it is clear that the evangelization-catechesis rapport must have other consequences on the catechetical plane, in particular for adults, who are the recipients of the Christian message in the most complete sense.[9] All else notwithstanding, they are the truer mirror of the request and acceptance of a present-day catechesis of the Christian people. And up until now we have noted that there no longer exists a clear line of demarcation between the acceptance of the message and the successive process of growth.

Already at Medellin the document on catechesis of the Latin-American conference affirmed: "Our catechesis possesses a point in common with all environments: it must be eminently evangelizing, without too easily presupposing a reality of faith." At Puebla the integration between evangelization and catechesis was outrightly taken for granted, placing on catechesis and its particularized application the historical obligation of evangelization: "The work of evangelization, which is *realized* in catechesis, demands communion on the part of everyone (799).... It demands the collaboration of all the members of the Church, each one according to his ministry and charism, without eluding apostolic and missionary responsibilities, because *in catechesis* the Church builds the Church (EN 13-14). The Church is always evangelized and evangelizer."[10] There is one sole obligation, towards which converge missionary action and catechetical pastoral.

It is at this point that we ask ourselves the fundamental question of all this reflection of ours. In what measure can the diocesan missionary center contribute to the catechetical commitment directed by the competent office? We know that the task of the diocesan missionary center is that of promoting and coordinating effectively all the missionary activity of the diocese, of serving as the point of encounter for the various organisms of missionary activity or for those outrightly linked with the missions which work in the diocese, arousing reciprocal collaboration and increasing it in the missionary pastoral of togetherness. At the foundation of this is the conviction that it is the task of the whole Church, "her missionary nature,"[11] to commit herself to the missions and consequently of every local Church to keep alive the dimension of missionarity which is common to the universal Church. For this reason "a priest should be appointed in each diocese for the effective promotion of missionary undertakings, and he should be a member of the pastoral council of the diocese."[12]

The diocesan Missionary Center obviously must avoid falling into two opposite excesses: that of thinking that the mission of the Church exhausts itself solely in the mission to non-Christians; and that of believing, with equal exclusivism, that the mission of the Church is exhausted in the pastoral care of the non-practicing. Instead, there are two activities which compose the sole mission of the Church, and hence neither of the two, the missionary nor the pastoral, can exist alone and alone realize the whole "mission" of the Church. For every diocese incarnates and lives the whole mystery of the Church as a reality of communion-mission; and so also does every parish and every other Christian community.

The typical character of the missionary center is precisely that of furnishing to catechetical pastoral that missionary tension and that experience which the young Churches are able to give in this matter. It is a new chapter of missionarity. One must also learn to receive. And today the moment has arrived to know how

to receive, not material means, but approved forms of evangelization, catechetical organization and indications of method which
in intra-ecclesial exchange enter very well into the dynamic of
communion.

Give, therefore, to catechesis a fundamental missionarity,
and in the meantime invest it with the more authentically missionary and variously articulated zeal. In effect what is lacking to
the effectiveness of our Churches, more than the theological content, is adequately formed personnel and a burst of apostolic zeal
that transcends the central organicity itself, without overcoming
it. Behind these words we read the urgency of the prophetic
charism which to us does not yet appear sufficiently "liberated"
in function of the ecclesial announcement of the Word of God.
We allude to Gospel groups, to the personal or communitarian
encounters with differentiated social strata from which arise
diverse religious questions, to parochial schools of catechism, to
sacramental catechesis (before, during and after), to groups, to
movements, to individual families or groups of them; to difficult
environments: places of work, schools, universities, centers of administrative and associated life. It is logical that for each one of
these "places" of catechesis or of human encounter, a wholesome
programming of proclamation is necessary, but all will be rendered useless if the power of the charism will be defective. And
this, which is a gift of the Holy Spirit, can be aroused by an opportune integration of the missionary centers with the
catechetical office.

At this point, it is natural to think of the schools for catechists
and the happy new phenomenon of courses of theology for the laity, from which we must remove the sense of cultural updating for
one's personal benefit in order to make them become factories of
apostles of the Word. On the other hand, if dioceses and parishes
want to be true evangelizing communities, they must found the
formation of catechists on a missionary basis. Only thus can they
respond to the new demands which increase with particular
gravity even because of the scarcity of vocations. Missionary
center and catechetical office, in the meantime, must work for an
increase of vocations and for the preparation of laymen—they too
sent "as Church," by virtue of Baptism, to those who do not
believe or who must become mature in the faith. Broad must
become the concept of permanent catechesis, always more centered on reflection on the Word of God and interpersonal com-

munion with Christ. That is, a suitable catechetical pastoral will tend toward always more vast involvements and toward studied sensitizations which make the Christian people become evangelized and evangelizing, without there being a break between these two moments. And it is missionary dynamism which will be able to confer on the baptized this charge of apostolate that is already radically present within them.

It will be necessary, then, that together with the study of content and of the most commonly indicated methods for groups, there be a preliminary concern to remove the optional character from the apostolate, and to call attention to it as an essential duty of every Christian. The central organisms of the diocese are thus placed on the top of a design that is more theological than operative, and they make of their commitment the animator of a passion for souls which gives no rest. And it is the real manner of maturing the people in "hearing of the Word of God with reverence,"[13] and making them partakers of the "ministry of the Word."[14] Bind it to the mystery of *Mater Ecclesia* which generates to the faith: "He who is brother and sister of Christ in the faith becomes His mother in preaching; it can be said, in reality, that he generates the Lord whom he has infused in the hearts of his audience, and becomes mother through his preaching, if with his words, the love of the Lord is generated in the soul of his neighbor."[15] Christ is generated in the brethren!

In point of fact the integration between missionary center and catechetical office will lead to new forms of proclamation and will be a spur to understanding more fully the situation of our Churches in a state of mission, but beyond techniques and methods it will give rise to a new spirit, that of the mature and pioneering Christian, a "sent one" and a witness who serves the Word by which he has been conquered.

MSGR. AGOSTINO BONIVENTO

FOOTNOTES

1. *Catechesi tradendae* (CT) 67.
2. CT 63.
3. *Ibid.;* cf. *Christus Dominus,* nos. 13-14.
4. Cf. *La catechesi in Italia,* Turin-Leumann, 1971, p. 9.
5. *Christus Dominus,* no. 27: "The diocesan curia should be so-organized that it is an appropriate instrument for the bishop, not only for administering the diocese but also for carrying out the works of the apostolate."

6. CT 19.
7. CT 18.
8. *Ibid.*
9. *Rinnovamento della Catechesi,* 124.
10. *Puebla documenti,* Bologna, 1979, p. 302 (799-800).
11. *Ad gentes,* no. 2; *Lumen gentium,* no. 17.
12. *Ecclesiae sanctae,* Part III, no. 4.
13. *Dei Verbum,* no. 1.
14. Acts 6:4.
15. St. Gregory, *hom. III in Evang.*

BIBLIOGRAPHY

CEI, *Il rinnovamento della catechesi,* Rome, 1970.

Medellin documents. La Chiesa nella attuale trasformazione dell' America Latina alla luce del Concilio Vaticano II, Bologna, 1969.

Puebla documenti, EMI, Bologna, 1979.

Hoger Katechetisch Institut, *Linee fondamentali per una nuova catechesi,* Turin-Leumann, 1969.

Direttorio di Pastorale Catechistica ad uso delle Diocesi di Francia, Turin-Leumann, 1965.

V. Schurr, *Cura d'anime in un mondo nuovo,* Rome, 1960.

AA.VV., *La Chiesa locale* (studi di teologia pastorale diretti da K. Rahner), Brescia 1970.

Card. L. Suenens, *La Chiesa in stato di missione,* Rome, 1958.

A. Turck, "A propos de la paroisse missionnaire," in *Paroisse et Liturgie,* 1964, 46.

PART FIVE

The Missionary Dynamism of Catechesis in the Actual Historical Moment

" 'The term *acculturation* or *inculturation* may be a neologism, but it expresses very well one factor of the great mystery of the Incarnation.' We can say of catechesis, as well as of evangelization in general, that it is called to bring the power of the Gospel into the very heart of culture and cultures. For this purpose, catechesis will seek to know these cultures and their essential components; it will learn their most significant expressions; it will respect their particular values and riches. In this manner it will be able to offer these cultures the knowledge of the hidden mystery and help them to bring forth from their own living tradition original expressions of Christian life, celebration and thought."

—CT 53

1

The Thought of "Catechesi Tradendae" on the Incarnation of the Evangelical Message in Cultures

"The split between the Gospel and culture is without a doubt the drama of our time, just as it was of other times" (EN 20). With this intense sentence, Paul VI in 1975 made himself the spokesman of what the 1974 Synod of Bishops had said about evangelization in the contemporary world.[1]

Three years later, the fourth synod of Bishops returned to the argument by occupying itself with the transmission of catechesis in our time.[2] Taking up again a few of "the most topical and decisive aspects" (CT 4) of the Synod, the Apostolic Exhortation *Catechesi tradendae* of John Paul II turns to speak of the incarnation of the message in cultures with expressions that are no less incisive. Among other things we read: "The Gospel message cannot be purely and simply isolated from the culture in which it was first inserted...nor, without serious loss, from the cultures in which it has already been expressed down the centuries" (CT 53).

The problem with which we are occupying ourselves is, therefore, very contemporary, even if not exclusive to our age, for from the very beginning the Church has had to face dialogue with the various cultures with which she came in contact.

Omitting to enter into detailed historical analysis about this topic (there already exists an abundant bibliography to which I refer you),[3] we will rather develop three principal questions: a description of the phenomenon of these last years; the work of Propaganda Fide and the doctrinal synthesis of Vatican II; a comparative reading of *Evangelii nuntiandi* and *Catechesi tradendae*. Thus we will be able to arrive at workable conclusions.

I. THE DIALOGUE BETWEEN THE GOSPEL AND CULTURES: CONTEMPORARY NATURE OF THE PROBLEM

We live in an age in which the awareness of the cultural identity of individual peoples is more acute than ever. The new political relations among nations who are freeing themselves from centuries of colonial hegemony, the rebirth of national ideologies and cultures, the renewed appreciation of traditional religious cultures, the awareness in many particular Churches of their own cultural identity, constitute a new ferment in this our time, so much so that the Church cannot ignore it, or disassociate herself from it or permit that it follow a parallel progress of its own. Using an apt expression of Paul VI, we must say that "every effort must be made to ensure a full evangelization of culture, or more correctly, of cultures."[4]

The Church meanwhile cannot remain aside in the face of the urgency of such pressures as are placed on her by the contemporary world. Nor are we to believe that this phenomenon concerns only mission countries; it also involves the Churches of ancient Christian tradition.[5] In the face of the urgency of these phenomena, the Church must rather make every effort to realize an authentic insertion of life and of the Gospel message into the cultures of humanity, so that the Gospel of Christ can become leaven and light in the development of the nations toward the Kingdom which Christ preached and rendered present in truth and in justice.

In this regard it will be useful to give a summary of information regarding the sensitivity with which the Church of our days gives due consideration to the dialogue between the Gospel and cultures, dedicating herself to it with commitment for a "full evangelization...of cultures" (EN 20). We will first speak of the activity of the Missionary Dicastery which devotes itself specifically to the evangelization of peoples; then we will offer a synthesis of the proposals of Vatican II regarding the dialogue between the Gospel and cultures.

II. PROPAGANDA FIDE AND THE DIALOGUE WITH CULTURES

The attitude of Propaganda Fide in respecting and in appreciating the different cultures of peoples as fertile ground predisposed by Divine Providence to welcome the seeds of the Gospel[6] may be considered almost centuries old and constant.

Already in 1659 in an instruction to the Vicars Apostolic of China and of Indochina we read: "Do not make any attempts, nor seek in any way to persuade those people to change their customs, their manner of living, their habits, when these are not openly contrary to religion and to morality. There is nothing more absurd than to want to bring France, or Spain, or Italy, or any other part of Europe into China. Not all this, but rather the Faith must you bring, the Faith which does not reject or offend the manner of living and the habits of any people, when they do not involve wicked matters; in fact, it wants such things to be conserved and protected."[7]

To come to more recent times, a letter of the Prefect of the Sacred Congregation to the Apostolic Delegate in China, said thus in regard to the Church-culture rapport:

"The Catholic Church does not have imperialistic ends, but is respectful of everything that is good in all civilizations....

"This is the constant tradition of Catholicism, which being the true, and therefore universal, religion, is not bound to any particular form of culture and appreciates, respects and seeks to sanctify all that is good which every civilization knows how to produce" (July 15, 1931).[8]

Also in 1936 on the occasion of an exposition of Congolese sacred art organized by the Orders of the Belgian Congo (today Zaire) in Leopoldville (today Kinshasa), the Sacred Congregation extended these congratulations regarding the initiative:

"The Catholic Church is neither Belgian, nor French, nor English, nor Italian, nor American: she is Catholic. Hence she is Belgian in Belgium, French in France, English in England. In the Congo, she must be Congolese."[9]

Along these lines, there exist various other interventions which it would take too long to report here. Willingly, however, I recall an episode concerning my illustrious predecessor, Bishop Celso Costantini, who, as Secretary of Propaganda Fide, when receiving in 1937 a few representatives of the missionary institutes in preparation for the exposition of native Christian missionary art, insisted on the necessity of a character "purely and totally native in every sector: painting, sculpture and architecture, without paying attention to the degree of development, from the most primitive and spontaneous, to the most elaborate and solemn."[10]

To those who pointed out to him that those people were semi-savages and lacking in any artistic expression whatsoever, he answered: Christianity has the virtue of enabling peoples to grow from infancy, and with the affection of a mother it must know how to look lovingly at the first marks that her child makes.

In this constant care of hers, the Sacred Congregation of Propaganda Fide has always vibrated in harmony with the teachings and concerns of the Supreme Pontiffs. We will make only a few limited references to the more recent Popes.

In the encyclical *Summi Pontificatus* (1939) Pius XII said in addressing himself to missionaries: "Guard yourselves well against transporting into mission countries, as one would transport a tree, the cultural forms of European peoples," because the young peoples, proud of their cultures, are to receive nothing else but the Gospel.[11] In the missionary encyclical *Evangelii praecones* of 1951, Pius XII also wrote: "The Church does not act as one who, respecting nothing, cuts down, plunders, and ruins a luxuriant forest; rather, she imitates the gardener who accomplishes a quality graft onto a wild tree to assure that one day it will produce tastier and sweeter fruits."[12]

On April 2, 1959, in speaking to the participants in a Congress organized by the Société Africaine de Culture, John XXIII encouraged the study and development of a Negro-African culture, and expressed himself thus: "The Church appreciates, respects and encourages such an undertaking of research and reflection which aims at bringing to light the original riches of every culture"; and further on: "The Church is disposed to recognize, to welcome, and also to animate everything that is esteemed by the intelligence and the heart of man in every part of the world, even outside of the Mediterranean basin, which was also the providential fold of Christianity."[13]

As regards Paul VI, the Pope who spoke of the theme of evangelization and culture more than any other, we limit ourselves to some of his contributions which we consider particularly effective:

a) The message *Africae terrarum* of October 29, 1967:

"It is a duty to respect the heritage (of moral and religious tradition) as a cultural patrimony of the past....

"The Church considers the moral and religious values of African tradition with much respect, not only because of their significance, but also because she sees in them the providential foundation upon which to transmit the evangelical message and begin the construction of the new society in Christ."[14]

b) The discourse to the Symposium of the African Episcopate in Kampala on July 31, 1969.

In answer to the question as to whether the Church must be African, Paul VI expressed himself thus:

"This seems a difficult problem, and in practice may be so, indeed. But the solution is rapid, with two replies. First, your Church must be first of all Catholic.... Granted this first reply, however, we now come to the second. The expression, that is, the language and mode of manifesting this one faith, may be manifold; hence, it may be original—suited to the tongue, the style, the character, the genius, and the culture of the one who professes this one faith. From this point of view, a certain pluralism is not only legitimate but desirable.... And in this sense you may, and you must, have an African Christianity. Indeed, you possess human values and characteristic forms of culture which can rise up to perfection, such as to find in Christianity and for Christianity a true superior fullness, and prove to be capable of a richness of expression all its own and genuinely African.... If you are able to avoid the possible dangers of religious pluralism..., you will be able to remain sincerely African even in your own interpretation of the Christian life; you will be able to formulate Catholicism in terms congenial to your own culture; you will be capable of bringing to the Catholic Church the precious and original contribution of 'negritude' which she needs particularly in this historical hour."[15]

c) In the discourse given during the Symposium of the Episcopate of the Far East in Manila, on November 28, 1970, Paul VI was not afraid to say that insufficient knowledge of the riches of Asiatic cultures had in the past impeded the expansion of Christianity in Asia, because the Church had assumed, as a consequence, the aspect of a foreigner.[16]

d) In the discourse addressed to the participants of the IV Symposium of the Episcopal Conferences of Africa and of Madagascar, Paul VI encouraged the Bishops to "integrate the traditional cultural values of your peoples (into the Church), by perfecting them with prudence and wisdom. He added that it is necessary "to dedicate oneself to a studied investigation of cultural traditions of the various populations."[17]

e) We must not forget what the same Pontiff said at the closing of the 1974 Synod:

> "Such adaptation is, of course, necessary if evangelization is to be realistic and effective. But it is neither safe nor devoid of dangers to speak of theologies being as numerous and diversified as the continents and cultures of the world. For the faith is either universal, or it has ceased to exist. Moreover, all of us have received the faith by way of unbroken and constant tradition. Peter and Paul did not give the faith a garb that was foreign to it in order to adapt it to the ancient world of Jews, Greeks and Romans; rather they were most careful that the faith should remain authentic, that is, that one and the same message be kept unchanged presented in the diverse languages."[18]

Beautiful discourses are certainly not enough to allow us to say that we have done everything possible to deal with such an urgent and difficult problem. To the interventions mentioned above we must add two other initiatives—very concrete ones promoted by Propaganda Fide as a tangible sign of its daily interest to facilitate a fruitful encounter between the Gospel and cultures.

We refer to the first International Congress of Missiology, which took place in October, 1975, at the Pontifical Urban University, on the theme "Evangelization and Cultures."[19] As a precious fruit of this Congress, the Congregation of Propaganda Fide instituted a specific office called "Evangelization and Cultures," which has the task of studying and following this intense phenomenon in view of an always better insertion of Christianity into the different cultures of peoples.[20]

We were saying that the dialogue between the Gospel and cultures is anything but easy. It requires seriousness, authenticity and discernment, in order not to reduce this effective sign of the times into an instrument of destruction of the authentic values of Christian Tradition.

This is why there must be a continual confrontation with the suggestions that come to us from Vatican Council II, which, several times, has occupied itself with the encounter of the Church and of the Gospel with cultures.

III. THE SYNTHESIS OF VATICAN II ON THE DIALOGUE BETWEEN THE GOSPEL AND CULTURES

Without doubt, it was Vatican Council II which laid the theological foundations for a reflection, later on always more broadened and deepened, regarding the rapport between evangelization and cultures or, if we wish, regarding an evangelization of cultures. To facilitate the presentation of the numerous points made by the Council,[21] we will sum up under general titles "the many ties between the message of salvation and human culture" (GS 58).

a. The Rapport Between Church and Culture

"Many ties...exist between the message of salvation and human culture" (GS 58), based upon the great law of the Incarnation, according to which both the Son of God and the Church communicate themselves to mankind by inserting themselves in the type of culture proper to the various historical eras. Between Church and culture is set up a communion which enriches both the Church and the various cultures. Through the work of the Church, "whatever good is in the minds and hearts of men, whatever good lies latent in the religious practices and cultures of diverse peoples, is not only saved from destruction but also cleansed, raised up and perfected unto the glory of God" (LG 17).

"The Catholic Church rejects nothing that is true and holy in these religions. She regards with sincere reverence those ways of conduct and of life, those precepts and teachings which...reflect a ray of that Truth which enlightens all men" (NAE 2). She respects and esteems them because they are the living expression of the soul of vast human groups, and they are all impregnated with countless "seeds of the Word" (cf. AG 11; EN 53).

The Church makes use of the different cultures:

—to diffuse and explain the Christian message to all peoples;

—to study and deepen this message;

—to express the message better in the liturgical life and in the life of the manifold communities of the faithful.

Nevertheless, the Church:

—does not bind herself with an exclusive and indissoluble bond to any one culture;

—renews the cultures of fallen man through the preaching of the Gospel; combats and removes errors and evils; purifies and elevates the morality of peoples; fortifies, completes and restores the qualities and talents of each people.

Harmony between culture and Christian formation, however, is not achieved without difficulties (cf. GS 62).

b. The Church Promotes Cultures

In the economy of the Incarnation, the new Churches have the wonderful capability of absorbing all the riches of the nations, which precisely have been assigned to Christ as an inheritance. "They borrow from the customs and traditions of their people, from their wisdom and their learning, from their arts and disciplines, all those things which can contribute to the glory of their Creator, or manifest the grace of their Savior, or dispose Christian life the way it should be" (AG 22; cf. LG 13).

"The Church (in establishing the Kingdom of God) takes nothing away from the temporal welfare of the people. On the contrary, it fosters and takes to itself, insofar as they are good, the ability, riches and customs in which the genius of each people expresses itself. Taking them to herself she purifies, strengthens, elevates and ennobles them" (LG 13).

To be capable of the task which they must carry out, missionaries must gain an adequate formation of general knowledge regarding peoples, civilizations and religious; they must know in depth the history, social structures and customs of the various peoples; they must penetrate the moral order, the religious norms and the most profound ideas which, on the basis of their traditions, these peoples already have about God, the world and man (cf. AG 26).

c. Cultures: Places of Encounter Between God and Man

"So also His disciples, profoundly penetrated by the Spirit of Christ, should know the people among whom they live, and should converse with them, that they themselves may learn by sincere and patient dialogue what treasures a generous God has distributed among the nations of the earth. But at the same time, let them try to furbish these treasures, set them free, and bring them under the dominion of God their Savior" (AG 11).

"And so, whatever good is found to be sown in the hearts and minds of men, or in the rites and cultures peculiar to various peoples, not only is not lost, but is healed, uplifted, and perfected for the glory of God" (AG 9).

Cultures, therefore, are not an obstacle to the proclamation of the Gospel but become a precious point of encounter between Christ and men. The Church should take up these new realities and let herself be taken up by them if she wants to incarnate Christianity in every culture and make sure that all men understand the Word of God and make it their own lifeblood.

At this point, having made a synthetic acquaintance with what Vatican II says about the rapport between evangelization and cultures, it is possible to enter into the specific object of our study: the thought of *Catechesi tradendae* about the incarnation of the evangelical message in cultures (CT 53).

IV. "CATECHESI TRADENDAE" AND CULTURES

As the Apostolic Exhortation *Evangelii nuntiandi* of Paul VI crowned the works of the third general assembly of the Synod of Bishops of 1974 regarding evangelization in the modern world (cf. EN 2, 4), so, too, the Apostolic Exhortation *Catechesi tradendae* of John Paul II is meant to consolidate the happy results of the fourth general assembly of the Synod of Bishops of 1977 regarding catechesis in our time (cf. CT 3, 4).

In both documents a specific number is dedicated to the existing relationship between evangelization and cultures (EN 20; CT 53). But while the contribution of Paul VI was the beginning of a work which had to give to the Church "a fresh forward impulse, capable of creating...a new period of evangelization" (EN 2), that of the present Pontiff, instead, has been a work of consolidation and of deepening which "should" strengthen the solidity of the faith and of Christian living, should give fresh vigor to the initiatives in hand, should stimulate creativity—with the required vigilance—and should help to spread among the communities the joy of bringing the mystery of Christ to the world" (CT 4).

John Paul II has chosen to give his Apostolic Exhortation a very precise "meaning." Among other things we read in it: "The theme is extremely vast (catechesis in our time) and the Exhortation will keep to only a few of the most topical and decisive aspects of it, as an affirmation of the happy results of the synod. In essence, the Exhortation takes up again the reflections that were prepared by Pope Paul VI, making abundant use of the document left by the synod.... I am therefore taking up the inheritance..." (CT 4).

This is why we prefer to read *Catechesi tradendae* according to a "synoptic" criterion, keeping an eye on what had been said by Paul VI in *Evangelii nuntiandi*. In fact, it is not difficult to see the continuity of thought between the two pontifical documents, as well as a few interesting points which in the present theological context serve us as a clear basis for proceeding with assurance in the difficult encounter between evangelization and cultures.

Catechesi tradendae, in number 53, seems to indicate a threefold path of work: it suggests the instruments of dialogue (to know, to learn, to respect); it indicates the conditions needed for this dialogue to be real and effective (a true incarnation, without alterations, abdications or attenuations); and lastly it lets us foresee a few goals as the fruit of such dialogue.

1. The Instruments of Dialogue Between Catechesis and Cultures

Catechesis cannot disregard cultures, because they too must know the hidden mystery, and they too can give valid contributions for the knowledge and expression of this mystery. The relationship existing between catechesis and cultures can, consequently, be summed up in a "mutual give and take." In this regard LG 17 says: "Between Church and culture there is set up thus a communion which enriches both the Church as well as the various cultures." Catechesis, therefore, is not only "called to bring the power of the Gospel into the very heart of culture and cultures" (CT 53), that is, to exercise an active role, but catechesis itself must feel enriched by cultures when it employs them "to help (persons) to understand better the whole of the Christian mystery" (CT 53), that is, to be receptive in regard to cultures.

Catechesi tradendae points out these principal means of dialogue between catechesis and cultures:

a.1: "*to know* these cultures and their essential components."

To be able patiently to track down the *semina Verbi* predestined by Providence for the building up of the truth, patient research and profound study are needed, so as to avoid every form of superficiality, subjectivism, and improvisation. Consequently, catechesis must be preceded by attentive theological research, which must penetrate into the subsoil of the cultures to sample their vital treasures and receptivity. Therefore, we must praise all those institutions which set themselves the goal of studying cultures, thus permitting the discernment of the values contained in them and the capability of bringing through them the unique salvation of Christ and of His message. No value can be disregarded or suppressed: all must be fostered and received (cf. LG 13).

a.2: "*to learn* their most significant expressions."

Between the Church and cultures a sincere and comprehensive dialogue must arise (cf. AG 11), in such wise that, according to the economy of the Incarnation, it will be possible to absorb all the treasures of customs, of traditions, of knowledge, of culture, of arts, and of sciences assigned as an inheritance to Christ the Lord (cf. AG 22). If catechesis wants to be truly effective, it must see to it that all the good found sown in the hearts and minds of men or in the rites and cultures proper to each people, not only not be lost, but that it be purified, elevated and perfected to the glory of God (cf. LG 17). The Gospel and the work of evangelization cannot fail to take into consideration those cultural expressions to which the men who are to be catechized are particularly bound (cf. EN 20).

a.3: "*to respect* their particular values and riches."

Not only must the children of the Church know well the national and religious traditions of others; they must also be ready to respect those seeds of the Word which are hidden in them. For example, to be avoided is the systematic consideration of the religious forms of a determined culture as "pagan" simply because the culture is not Christian. Catechesis must be open to everything that is valid and useful in other cultures, making the effort to discover the God hidden in everything authentically human (cf. Acts 17:22ff.). Only thus is room opened for a purifying and constructive collaboration for the present and for the future, without pre-established exclusions, without suspicions, without limitations of the action of the Spirit.

After having proposed these three principal means of dialogue between catechesis and cultures, *Catechesi tradendae* draws the following conclusions: "In this manner it (catechesis) will be able to offer these cultures the knowledge of the hidden mystery (cf. Rom. 16:25; Eph. 3:5) and help them to bring forth from their own living tradition original expressions of Christian life, celebration and thought" (CT 53).

2. For a True and Effective Dialogue Between Catechesis and Cultures

In order that dialogue between catechesis and cultures may be true and effective, *Catechesi tradendae* invites us to keep two points in mind:

a. The Gospel message cannot be isolated from culture. With this expression we mean to affirm that even the message of salvation has had a full incarnation in what is called "the biblical universe," in the same way in which the incarnation of Christ occurred in a determined "cultural ambient." We would, therefore, go against the law of the incarnation if we would want purely and simply to isolate the Gospel message from the culture in which it inserted itself from the beginning and in which it has expressed itself throughout the centuries. The apostolic dialogue itself has inevitably inserted itself into a certain dialogue of culture.

b. The power of the Gospel transforms and regenerates. We return here to express that particular dialectic which binds catechesis and cultures in the sense of a "mutual give and take." The intrinsic power of the Word of God[22] enables it, once announced, not to simply juxtapose itself to the cultures with which it comes into contact (this would be the concept of "acculturation"), but rather to work an intense "inculturation," because with its intrinsic power it is capable of transforming cultures and regenerating them.[23]

Catechesi tradendae, therefore, wants to say that, excluding the risk of its being the Gospel that will have to undergo alterations in its encounter with the cultures, and overcoming also the conception of a peaceful coexistence between the Word of God and the cultures, almost as though the interior energies of the two were equal, the Document affirms with determination that there must be no cause for wonder (and how could it be otherwise if the Word of God spoke, "and it was so," Gn. 1:7), when the power of the Gospel in penetrating a culture rectifies not a few elements, transforming and regenerating that cultural "humus" in which "it incarnates itself."[24]

By way of conclusion and to reinforce what has been said about the necessity of keeping in mind certain modalities in the process of the incarnation of catechesis in cultures, *Catechesi tradendae* affirms: "To forget this would simply amount to what St. Paul very forcefully calls 'emptying the cross of Christ of its power' (1 Cor. 1:17)" (CT 53).

c. A catechesis impoverishes itself by abdicating or attenuating its message.

The process of incarnation of catechesis in the cultures can also follow this method: "to take...certain elements, religious or otherwise, that form part of the cultural heritage of a human group and use them to help the members to understand better the whole of the Christian mystery" (CT 53).

We must note, however, that this method has to be used with "wise discernment." In fact, not only is this required by the very nature of catechesis (which is not the proprietor of the Gospel, so as to be able to dispose of it as it wills, but is the minister to transmit it with extreme faithfulness; cf. EN 15), but it is also required by those to whom catechesis is addressed. Those adaptations, even of language, or eventual concessions in matters of faith or of morals, which would compromise "the good deposit" of the faith (cf. 2 Tm. 1:14), would force catechesis to such an impoverishment as to render it unrecognizable. The people of today, and in particular the youth, demand a "true catechesis," without abdications or attenuations of the message which it communicates. They are convinced that only a true catechesis can enrich the cultures of such diverse peoples: on the one hand, helping them to overcome the defective features present in their cultures; and on the other hand, communicating the fullness of Christ (cf. Jn. 1:16; Eph. 1:10) to those legitimate values which are also present in the cultures of the peoples (cf. CT 53).

Here, in *Catechesi tradendae*, we again hear what had been said, with as much energy, in *Evangelii nuntiandi:* "This message is indeed necessary. It is unique. It cannot be replaced. It does not permit either indifference, syncretism or accommodation. It is a question of people's salvation.... It brings with it a wisdom that is not of this world" (EN 5). The message of catechesis is to be proposed without reduction or ambiguity (cf. EN 32). Incumbent upon us, stated Paul VI, is a grave responsibility "of preserving unaltered the content of the Catholic Faith which the Lord entrusted to the Apostles: While being translated into all expressions, this content must be neither impaired nor mutilated. While being clothed with the outward forms proper to each people, and made explicit by theological expression which takes account of differing cultural, social and even racial milieu, it must remain the content of the Catholic faith just exactly as the ecclesial magisterium has received it and transmits it" (EN 65).

3. The Goals of the Dialogue Between Catechesis and Cultures

The dialogue between catechesis and cultures must not be simply a matter of dilettantism; rather, according to *Catechesi tradendae*, it must aim at very precise goals. Let us see some.

a. To bring the power of the Gospel into the heart of cultures.

The Church has the duty of extending the ever-new proposal of the hidden mystery to every man, to every culture. This, the irreplaceable aim of catechesis, is clearly given priority by the Apostolic Exhortation. In fact, we must note that sometimes, in the enthusiasm of the moment, we see values turned topsy-turvy and the simple means which catechesis uses are exchanged for the end for which it must strive.

At the present stage of research we cannot suspend evangelizing activity simply because we are seeking a new language suited to individual cultures.

Nor can we discriminate regarding the Word of God by presenting only those aspects of Christianity which are accessible to the respective cultures, or congenial or pleasing, at the expense of other aspects. The power of the Gospel is such that it must be faithfully presented in its own vigorous entirety, in its original and proper contents, without mutilating its integrity and purity.

Cultures cannot be taken as the yardstick of evangelization. In certain cases we witness an absolutization of one's own cultural values so great that it seems that the only valid forms of catechesis are those which sprout from local "creativity," with "received" catechesis being refused on principle simply because it was imported by others. We refer also to certain hasty enthusiasms in introducing into Christian worship elements which stem from other non-Christian religious traditions. To us it seems that at the root of these intemperances there is a certain lack of confidence in the action of the power of the Gospel, seeing that the need is felt to borrow cultural forms born in other ambients. *Catechesi tradendae* justly reminds us that: "In this manner it (catechesis) will be able to offer these cultures the knowledge of the hidden mystery and help them to bring forth from their living tradition original expressions of Christian life, celebration and thought" (CT. 53).

b. To maintain the unity and Catholicity of the Church.

To the particular Churches appertains the task of assimilating the essential of the evangelical message and of transfusing it, without the slightest alteration of its fundamental truth, into the language understood by their own faithful, and hence of announcing it in the same language. Even in this case those values which would be to the detriment of other values would not be authentic. Catechesis would lose its own soul if, for example, in translating the evangelical message into the local context, it would lose the awareness of its own universality. A Church devoid of this universality becomes a nationalistic and regional Church. In fact, either the content of catechesis is "Catholic," or else it is destined to vanish; either it favors communion and unity within the individual particular Churches, or else it will end up in arid isolation and disintegration. This thought is found well expressed in *Lumen gentium*, number 13, which says that such differences are not to hinder unity but rather to contribute toward it.

The principal goals to which missionary catechesis must tend are, therefore, announcing to the peoples the message of salvation and seeing to it that this message, well incarnated in the cultures of the peoples to whom it is addressed, produces genuine fruits of Christian life.

V. OPERATIVE SUGGESTIONS

Speaking of the incarnation of the Gospel message in cultures, *Catechesi tradendae* continually gives operative suggestions in order that, in this area too, catechesis will help the men of our time better to understand the integrity of the Christian mystery. To enable these suggestions to be effective and put into practice, it seems important to us to suggest a few practical resolutions.

1. The Promotion of the Study of Cultures in Universities and Specialized Centers

It is impossible to respect what is unknown, or to learn fruitfully without first having examined the value of what one intends to assume. To avoid every form of harmful cultural or religious syncretism, before assimilating possible elements into the catechetical or liturgical tradition of a particular Church, careful analysis in the search for true values is required.[25]

The privileged place for this type of attentive investigation is principally the Catholic university or other cultural centers duly instituted for this. This research should be authentically scientific and have a pastoral and missionary orientation.[26]

2. The Formation of the Local Clergy

It is upon the proper formation of priests that correct inculturation chiefly depends. The local clergy should deepen the knowledge of its own culture[27] and make every effort to individualize and grasp those elements which would be particularly useful to render catechetical activity effective. In fact, who better than the native clergy is capable of expressing faith and adhesion to Christ according to methods and forms authentically incarnated in a determined culture? Instead, on the part of the non-native clergy the humble role of the Samaritan woman should be followed: "It is no longer because of your words that we believe, for we have heard for ourselves, and we know that this is indeed the Savior of the world" (Jn. 4:42).

3. The Importance of Catechetical Centers

For the formation of the laity, besides that of the clergy, *Catechesi tradendae,* number 71, urges the organization of appropriate centers or institutes. This is an area in which diocesan, inter-diocesan, and, better yet, national collaboration reveals itself to be fecund and fruitful.[28]

4. Ecumenical Sensitivity

This sector of catechetical activity must also have a particular ecumenical sensitivity. The other Christian Churches, too, find themselves in the same necessity of a correct inculturation of the Gospel in local cultures. Communion and cooperation with these Churches will facilitate study and research into those manifold points of encounter between the Gospel and cultures in order that the Word of God may truly be incarnated in the peoples to whom it is announced.

CONCLUSION

In concluding these observations on the thought of the Apostolic Exhortation of John Paul II, *Catechesi tradendae*, about the incarnation of the evangelical message in the cultures of the various peoples, it seems to us that we can say that today the Church follows this problem, which daily becomes ever more urgent, with great interest. One notes the sense of prudence that is so necessary in connection with giving life to a relatively new practice, as well as the stimulus to a creativity capable of finding new and adequate forms of bringing the mystery of Christ to the world.

Without facile enthusiasm, but also with due realism, we have sought to give a rather vast panorama of the phenomenon of the so-called inculturation, understood as the effort which the catechesis of our time must make to bring the power of the Gospel into the heart of cultures.

We close these reflections of ours with a Gospel reference. Looking at the eschatological character of her own mission, the Church, which lives in an attitude of pilgrimaging toward the Kingdom, is called to join to her ranks the peoples and the cultures she meets, offering them the message and the life of the Risen Lord (cf. Lk. 24:13-35: Jesus and the disciples of Emmaus). In offering her own message, the Church must also be ready to take up the values of the peoples and of their cultures. From this marvelous exchange, which is the continuation of the *admirabile commercium* begun with the Incarnation of Christ, the culture and cultures of the peoples will be purified, consolidated and elevated, while the Church will find herself enriched with all the treasures of the nations which have been assigned to Christ as an inheritance (cf. AG 22).

MOST REVEREND D. SIMON LOURDUSAMY

FOOTNOTES

1. Episcopal Synod, *Declaratio Patrum synodalium (exeunte Synod 1974 adprobata)*, Vatican Polyglot Press 1974; cf. Paul VI, Apostolic Exhortation *Evangelii nuntiandi*, 2, 4.

2. Episcopal Synod, *De catechesi hoc nostro tempore tradenda praesertim pueris atque iuvenibus; Ad Populum Dei Nuntius*, cf. "L'Osservatore Romano" (October 30, 1977), pp. 3-4.
Cf. John Paul II, Apostolic Exhortation *Catechesi tradendae*, 3.4.

3. Cf. R. Cantalamessa, "Cristianesimo e cultura nella Chiesa antica," in AA.VV., *Cristianesimo e cultura*, ed. Vita e Pensiero, Milan 1976, pp. 126-145; G. Leonardi, "Cristiani e cultura nel Medioevo," *ibid.*, pp. 146-163. M. Sina, "Illuminismo e cultural cristiana," *ibid.*, pp. 164-176.
Biblical tradition, too, found itself faced with this problem; in this regard, see the interesting study of Beda Rigaux, "Bible et culture," in *Evangelizzazione e culture*, I, Acts of the International Scientific Congress on Missiology, Pontifical Urban University, Rome 1976, pp. 3-24.

4. EN 20. It is to be noted that both in *Evangelii nuntiandi*, no. 20, as well in *Catechesi tradendae*, no. 53, recourse is always made to the distinction between "culture" and "cultures." We follow the following twofold understanding of the terms:
—"Culture": "The word 'culture' in its general sense indicates everything whereby man develops and perfects his many bodily and spiritual qualities; he strives by his knowledge and his labor, to bring the world itself under his control. He renders social life more human both in the family

and the civic community, through improvement of customs and institutions. Throughout the course of time he expresses, communicates and conserves in his works great spiritual experiences and desires, that they might be of advantage to the progress of many, even of the whole human family" *(Gaudium et spes*, no. 53).
—"Cultures": indicates the totality of all the forms of human living—working, transforming, acting, knowing—socially integrated, in a given environment.
In this sense "cultures" would be the concrete result of the developments of the "culture" in a determined social context; they would be synonymous with "civilization" and they would comprise the totality of beliefs, arts, moral law, customs and any other capability and habit acquired by man as a member of a society.
By "cultures" could also be understood the product of the reactions and activities of individuals and of groups in relationship to their own social-cultural environment.
Accepting the difference of meaning between the two terms (culture-cultures) and recognizing the continuity—not the separation—between the two, we can justly observe that "evangelization...is called to bring the power of the Gospel into the very heart of culture and cultures" (CT 53).
For further profound study about the question, see A. Bausola, "Analisi critica del concetto di cultura," in AA.VV., "Cristianesimo e Cultura," cit., pp. 16-35; P. Rossi (ed.), "Il concetto di cultura," ed. Einaudi, Turin

1972; A. L. Kroeber—C. Kluckhohn, *Culture. A Critical Review of Concepts and Definitions,* Cambridge, Massachusetts 1952 (Italian ed., *Il Mulino,* Bologna).

5. Cf. J. Schasching, "Inculturazione nel mondo occidentale," in AA.VV., *Inculturazione. Concetti, problemi, orientamenti,* ed. Centrum Ignatianum Spiritualitatis, Rome 1979.

6. Broader and more detailed news can be found in J. Metzler, "Il nuovo corso missionario iniziato con la fondazione della Sacra Congregazione de Propaganda Fide nei confronti delle culture locali," in *Evangelizzazione e culture,* II, cit., pp. 374-400; M. Kayitakibga, "Le Saint-Siege el les Religions Africaines," in *Religions Africaines et Christianisme,* Acts of the Colloque International de Kinshasa, Faculté de Theologie Catholique de Kinshasa 1979, pp. 139-156 (published also in *Bulletin,* Secretariat for non-Christians, 1978-XIII/2, Vatican City, pp. 94-113).

7. Cf. *Collectanea S.C. de Propaganda Fide,* I, p. 42, n. 135.

8. Reported in the article of J. Metzler, cit., p. 393.

9. Cf. *L'Osservatore Romano,* October 4-5, 1937, p.l.

10. Cf. *L'Osservatore Romano,* November 18, 1937, p. 1, and December 2, 1937, p. 1.

11. In AAS 31(1939), p. 429.

12. In AAS 43 (1951), pp. 521-528.

13. In AAS 51(1959), pp. 259-260. This attention and interest of John XXIII towards the cultures of peoples will be then found with very similar expressions in the pages of Vatican Council II dedicated to the evangelization of cultures. See in particular: LG 13, 17; AG 9, 11, 22, 26; GS 60-62; NAE, 2.

14. In AAS 59(1967), pp. 1073-1097.

15. In AAS 61(1969), pp. 573-578.

16. In AAS 63(1971), pp. 21-27.

17. In *L'Osservatore Romano,* September 27, 1975.

18. Cf. Paul VI, Discourse at the closing of the Third General Assembly of the Synod of Bishops (October 26, 1974), in AAS 66(1974), pp. 634-635.

The point of arrival for the intense reflection of Paul VI on the urgency of a constructive dialogue between the Gospel and cultures remains his Apostolic Exhortation *Evangelii nuntiandi* of December 8, 1975.

19. Cf. *Acts of the International Scientific Congress on Missiology,* I, II, III, held in Rome from October 5-12, 1975, through the initiative of the Pontifical Urban University, on the theme "Evangelization and Cultures" (Ed. Alma Mater, Urban University Press, Rome 1976).

20. The Office "Evangelization and Cultures," founded in 1977 through the initiative of the Sacred Congregation for the Evangelization of Peoples and inserted in the "campus" of the Pontifical Urban University, has the goal of promoting the study of the different cultures and of following this complex phenomenon in view of an ever better insertion of the Gospel in the cultures of peoples.

21. The principal places in which the Vatican II Ecumenical Council speaks of cultures and of their relationship with the Gospel are *Lumen gentium:* 13, 16, 17, 23, 35; *Gaudium et spes:* 44, 53-57; 58-62; *Ad gentes:* 11, 13, 19, 22, 36, 38, 41; *Apostolicam actuositatem:* 7, 13, 16, 19, 26.

Precisely in these days His Holiness, John Paul II, has recalled the centrality of the message of Vatican II with these expressions: "We believe that the Vatican Council II has become for our era the theme and the privileged place thanks to which the Holy Spirit, the Spirit of Christ, 'has spoken' to all the Church and has guided her toward the complete truth, and therefore also toward this truth of the existence 'in the contemporary world,' of the existence just as it appears to us through 'the signs of the times' " (from *L'Osservatore Romano,* February 1, 1980, p. 1).

22. The Word of God is, in biblical language, *dābār,* that is, action, creation, worker of salvation in the history of man. See in this regard the interesting work of H. Schlier, *La parola di Dio,* Rome 1963 (Ital. transl.).

23. *Catechesi tradendae,* no. 53, reports both terms and says: "The term 'acculturation' or 'inculturation' may be a neologism...." The two terms would seem to be cited here as synonyms, which is not exact. The term *"acculturation"* appears already long before Vatican Council II and indicates a certain encounter between the Church and cultures. It would indicate an agreement, a reciprocal exchange between two or more cultures. It would be the exchange which one culture makes with another (if only one culture were to give or take to the detriment of the other we would have to speak of "colonialization" of a culture and not of "acculturation").

Speaking of evangelization, the term "acculturation" is not used very much because it does not translate well the significance of "incarnation" which lies at the base of the dialogue between Gospel and cultures.

The term *"inculturation,"* instead, is rather recent, as far as we can see, and it appears in magazines of missiology around the year 1972. A distinction between these terms can be found in the report of Y. Congar, "Christianisme comme foi et comme culture," in *Evangelizzazione e culture,* Acts of the Congress on Missiology, cit., pp. 83-103; in the same volume one can also read the intervention of P. Rossano, "Acculturazione dell'Evangelo," pp. 104-116.

At present the theological research about this whole question has been notably defined. A good synthesis can be found in J. Lopez-Gay, "Pensiers attuale della Chiesa sull'inculturazione," in AA.VV., *Inculturazione. Concetti, problemi, orientamenti,* Centrum Ignatianum Spiritualitatis, Rome 1979, pp. 9-35; in the same volume is also found the study of A. A. Roest Crollius, "Per una teologia pratica dell'inculturazione," pp. 36-53.

24. It is obligatory here to recall a few expressions of *Evangelii nuntiandi,* no. 20, which, even though not using the term "incarnation" (it uses instead the term "impregnate"), nevertheless speaks very effectively: "The Gospel and therefore evangelization, are certainly not identical with culture, and they are independent in regard to all cultures. Nevertheless, the kingdom which the Gospel proclaims is lived by men who are profoundly linked to a culture, and the building up of the kingdom cannot avoid borrowing the elements of human culture or cultures. Though independent of cultures, the Gospel and evangelization are not necessarily incompatible with them; rather they are capable of permeating them all without becoming subject to any one of them."

25. Already for several years we have had the opportunity of pinpointing the importance and delicateness of this problem in our study: D. S. Lourdusamy, *The Liturgy and Adaptation,* St. Mary's Press, Bangalore 1965; Id., *The Liturgy and the Missionary Apostolate.*

26. Recently, on the occasion of the inauguration of the *Vidya Jyoti Residence* in New Delhi in India, I had the opportunity of insisting on these concepts which must be acquired by the Catholic universities in mission countries.

27. See the importance of this norm given by the conciliar document *Optatam Totius,* no. 16, regarding the formation of priests in our time.

28. From the time of its plenary assembly in 1970, the Sacred Congregation for the Evangelization of Peoples has discussed the problem of fostering the institution of centers of catechesis for the formation of qualified persons who would take care also of the catechesis-cultures relationship. The following year, the Sacred Congregation for the Clergy prepared the *General Catechetical Directory* (March 18, 1971) in which these catechetical centers were expressly recommended. Already for two years now, the *Institute of Missionary Catechesis* has existed in the Pontifical Urban University; the aim of this Institute is to collaborate with the local Churches in the missionary formation of those responsible for diocesan catechesis.

2

Catechesis in a Traditional African Milieu[1]

Introduction

The aim of this report is to give an account of a catechetical and liturgical experience lived through in our diocese of Ouagadougou, Upper Volta.

The members of the ethnic group concerned are called Moose (plural) and Moaga (singular), by far the largest ethnic group among the Voltaic peoples. So this experience extended beyond our own diocese where the same ethnic group lives.

Similar attempts have been made and carried out in other Voltaic dioceses, so that the national catechetical commission has been able to draw up a common plan-framework. That is, our report, which concerns a particular experience in the concrete, at the same time seeks to reflect the whole of our Voltaic Church, searching for a catechesis incarnate in the mentality and spirit of our populations.

This paper has two sections:

I. A sketch of the main orientations of our catechesis.

II. Applications to catechumenal stages and the liturgy.

1. This chapter was presented as a written documentation at the ninth Plenary Assembly of the Sacred Congregation for the Evangelization of Peoples, held in Rome in October, 1979. Although its theme is not presented in a theoretical manner, it clearly indicates the general problematic which catechesis faces in its relationship with traditional African religions. Due to this, it seemed advisable to publish it in this context, having obtained the gracious permission of the Author.

I. MAIN ORIENTATIONS

1. Place Christ within the parental or ancestral circuit.

All the baptismal initiation is then conceived as participation in Christ's parentage or family lineage; the "Doogo," by new birth into the family that is the Church.

2. Avoid making catechism and catechesis in general simply a transmission of teaching. Christianity must absolutely become like an ancestral custom with all its realism, vitality and life lived.

Catechesis becomes the living handing down of an ancestral custom. In this way we go out from the circuit "karemsaaba and karembiiga" (master-pupil), *transmission of ideas*, to enter the circuit of "saamba-saambiiga" (Ancestor-Son of ancestor) *transmission of life*.

3. Avoid making the catechism merely theological teaching. It is less a scientific way to God than a vital undertaking. It is perpetually based on the ground of concrete existence of each man and each people. Its aim is, then, to be the proof of the existence Christ brought us all: from the smallest to the greatest.

II. APPLICATIONS TO CATECHUMENAL AND LITURGICAL STAGES

A. Pre-Catechesis

1. Doctrinal Content

At this point, "seekers for God" discover in Christ the answer to man's basic aspirations: life, happiness, family, survival, etc.

First global presentation of the life of Christ will be given to the "seekers for God."

They will also be given initiation into the main prayers of the Church.

2. Catechetical Expression

The message is conveyed through the Moaga thought-patterns.

In particular:

—Proverbs: condensed popular wisdom, these express a life experience deeply bound up in very concrete situations which are also universal. Men describe their experience of joy, suffering, love and hate. The Gospel of Jesus and God's wisdom comes and throws them into full light.

—Songs: these are bound up with every important moment of life: joy, death, etc. The main stages of the life of Christ are thus bound up with songs as the "griots" sing the lives of great men and life itself.

—Narratives: narratives from the Gospel are told in the way people like to tell legends, stories, calling on every resource of the memory, imagination, intelligence, heart, etc.

3. *Liturgical Expression*

This is the celebration of the first stage that leads into the entry to the catechumenate. Rites used are similar to those of the Roman ritual, but placed in the context and milieu of Moaga *hospitality*.

There is no need to explain that hospitality is one of the basic values of our African populations. The ceremony of welcome takes place within the framework of this vital reality.

We have there all the main elements of hospitality. Thus:

—The communitarian aspect: The stranger is welcomed by the whole community. Hence, this first stage takes place in the presence of the whole Christian community gathered around the parish priest, representative of the head of the family who is the bishop.

—The aspect of progressive integration: the stranger who arrives should progressively adapt his lifestyle to that of the community who welcomes him. But this cannot be done without the tacit agreement and support of the members of the community. The catechumens know this, and as soon as they come into the churchyard they express the desire for integration by an appropriate song.

From this moment everything will be set in motion to make them feel at home (water of welcome), and they will be instructed in the community customs (entry dialogue and basic catechesis).

—The sacral aspect: Hospitality is always carried out under the protection of God and the ancestors. This is signified in our Christian ritual:

—by exorcism and invocation of the efficacious Word of God.

—by the rite of salt: hospitality and alliance.

—by the giving of a name.

—by the imposition of hands: sign of adoption and divine protection.

B. Catechumenate: First Year

1. Doctrinal Content

This first year, called "Epiphanic," is centered on the manifestation of God and His plan of salvation in Jesus Christ, true God and true Man, first-born of every creature, Great-Brother of humanity and head of the great family, the Church.

2. Catechetical Expression

All this doctrinal content is presented to the catechumens through a basic concept of Moaga thought; that of birth "Doge," (to be born).

"Doge" (to be born), a word of the vocabulary of the language which carries within it, and makes clearer, the inexhaustible concept of sanctifying grace and all the privileges of a child of the family that go with it. This verb, to be born = "doge," which gives the word "Dogom," is practically untranslatable by the single word "birth." In itself it contains the meaning of: family, parents, fecundity, birth, blood and parental ties, life in communion. It is the vital link, so precious that nothing could bring more happiness and, at the same time, suffering.

The link of parentage, "dogem," says a proverb, is like a drop of hot pap that burns and makes a big wound. So here is God Himself undertaking to let Himself be burned by this drop, and He will be the first to be led to supreme joys and to the worst of sufferings.

The second word derived from "doge"—"dogem" is "Doogo": house, home, little house, paternal lineage. Doogo is not only the little piece of land that shelters all those who were born there, from the same strain, but in the figure of speech that uses the container for the contained, it also applies to the group of persons living in the same family compound, related to each other by direct descendance from father to son, passing on to each other in direct line the same and unique life capital.

The catechumens are invited to discover with wonder the mystery of God expressed in a deeply lived reality. For God Himself is "dogem"; that is, family, Father, Son and Holy Spirit.

We know this truth through His Son, who henceforth makes us participate in God's Dogem, God's family.

Hence, the presentation of the life of Christ.

Christ, God among His own.

Christ, God with us.

Christ, who reveals a God-family.

Christ, First-born of all creatures, etc.

3. Liturgical Expression

At the end of this first year, there is the rite of *scrutiny* and the *transmission* of the Bible, the Creed and the Our Father.

The Christian community assembles in the inside courtyard of the Church, in a wide semicircle around the bench where the parish priest (head of the family) and his attendants will take their places.

All eyes are on the entrance of the Zaka where the catechumens are standing. These last face the Christian community. Their godparents are with them. During this ceremony the family tradition is transmitted to them.

The Bible, rock from which living water flows, the source of all our customs.

The Creed, abridged formula of our customs.

The Our Father, the custom given to us by Christ, eldest brother of the family.

C. Catechumenate: Second Year

1. Doctrinal Content

Paschal catechesis centered on the *Passage*, following after Christ, from the world of satan and sin to the world of God and holiness (insertion into the Will of God through a life of faith and hope. Charity, by observance of the ten commandments, life according to the Beatitudes...thanks to the three sacraments of Baptism, Penance and the Eucharist).

2. Catechetical Expression

In this second year the doctrinal teaching is based on a notion very close to "dogem" (birth), which is, "dogem-miki": custom.

Custom is nothing else but the transmission of "dogem" (life in communion).

Dogom-miki, dogom-mikri means literally: "find from birth," "to be born and to find"—two similar expressions that signify custom—what everyone finds at birth, the memory of the family, the previously accumulated capital of life.

Starting out from this notion, Christian life is called to go beyond a certain moralizing aspect. The renowned commandments appear more in the light of a demanding life-experience.

Having received this Custom at the end of their first year of catechesis, the catechumens should then experience the content of this custom with all that it implies: a new life corresponding with the newness of the dogem-miki (custom), that is, a conversion.

There is no need to point out that the dogem-miki we transmit has nothing stiff or dead about it. As we have said, it is a capital of accumulated life that is ever-active.

Hence the proposed themes:

By Christ we live with God;

By Christ we lean on God;

By Christ we learn to love God;

By Christ we fight against satan.

In short, we are to live our ancestry, letting ourselves be burnt like God by the burning mark of parentage. So, then, sin is not simply "yelwende" as it was translated up to now, and which means something like astonishing, something bad; but it becomes the act that goes against dogom-miki, deteriorating the "doogo," the family lineage of God that is also ours. Sin takes on more the typical sense of "wiibdo" (something incongruous, inadmissible, an omen of evil), because it is contrary to life, life-destroying, dilapidating the capital of life. Sin becomes what is called "kisgu" (something deserving hate, hateful).

3. Liturgical Expression

At the end of the second catechumenal year we celebrate the rite of the transmission of the Creed and the Our Father, with a personal undertaking in view of the inscription for baptism.

During the same solemn ceremony is the renunciation of satan and attachment to Christ the light. Here the liturgy takes on a marked spatial symbolism of great expression: the East or Orient = the rising sun. There the catechumens will face the light to profess their faith in the risen Christ.

—The West, the setting sun, domain of death and satan. It is in that direction that the catechumens will face to renounce satan.

D. Catechumenate: Third Year

1. Doctrinal Content

"Pentecostal" catechesis, centered on the centuries-old action of the Spirit of God in the heart of the People of God, from the time of Abraham to Pentecost and to the end of time (sacraments of confirmation, order and marriage...).

2. Catechetical Expression

The basic notion here is the family = "buudu." The family, the social matrix of life, is very imperfectly translated by this word that evokes the Western nuclear family (father, mother, children), whereas the word "buudu" is of quite a different nature and has much wider connotations. It refers to several clusters of houses, or a district, or a whole village. It is patrilinear, that is, a lineage built up by "men, from father to son."

In this context the daughter is called "Saana," stranger, because she will necessarily be married into another "buudu" (family), and give birth to children belonging to the "buudu" of her husband.

There is the "buud-kasma," eldest of the family: the first or senior of the lineage, always an old man, the eldest by birth.

The buud-kasma is responsible for the capital of life inherited from the ancestors and intimately bound up with the land on which they lived and in which they rest. All that has to do with the transmission of life is very particularly his concern. For the baptized members, to live the Church like the "buudu," the "roogo" of Christ means to bear responsibility for its growth and development.

The whole Christian community exercises this responsibility first of all towards newly-aggregated members. Hence it is involved in the voting for or against the admission to baptism of new members. But directly concerned are the godparents.

In fact, the name they are given is full of meaning: "soob-ba"—"soob-ma," or (father of baptism—mother of baptism).

During the first ceremony in this stage, the head of the family (parish priest) had spoken in these words: "You, fathers and mothers of baptism, are givers of faith; it is an authentic birth 'rogom.' You who will lead them to baptism, know what it is that baptism is—a true birth; you are going to give birth to your children for Christ." In this way they are given their official charge of godparents, like a mission.

The catechumens themselves will now begin to play a more active part in family life, by taking on responsibilities in the district, parish and nation. Hence, the themes proposed:

The Spirit of Christ sends us to transform the world.

The Spirit of Christ sends us to be the salt of the earth, etc.

3. *Liturgical Expression*

At the end of the third catechumenate year, the catechumens are baptized. The celebration of baptism and the first Communion of the newly-baptized takes place—often at Easter, but in some places at Christmas, a better time since epidemics frequently occur around Eastertide.

The baptism ceremony marks the peak-point of the whole setting of "dogom" (parentage), and "buudu" (the family) that had already marked the other stages and their celebrations.

Indeed, during this celebration another dimension of the family, the vertical, will emerge. Assuredly, the family is not made up only of its actual members, but also of those who went before us, our ancestors.

Here we see the importance of the ancestor cult which is a capital point of the traditional "Moaga" religion.

Their place in the Christian family is brought out in the celebration of baptism. Just before the blessing of the baptismal water, the family invokes their intervention with the litany of the saints: "Let us call on our 'yaab-ramba' (grand-parents), and our 'saamba-damba' (maternal great-uncles) ancestors of the buudu, in heaven, so that they may join us and receive the newly-born."

But the saints are not the first ancestors under whose protection we live: the first is Jesus Christ, and the deep "Moaga" vision of the "buudu" (family) puts the paschal mystery in Pauline perspectives.

Christ, our "buud-kasma" (head of the family), the genealogical senior of the whole family, first son of Adam, first-born of all creation, began by raising Himself, so as then to raise up His younger brothers, through the power and love of the parentage "rogom."

On the Paschal night, the celebration of baptism places in a particularly moving light the solidarity of the whole Christian family around its head, Christ.

THE CEREMONY CONSISTS OF FOUR PARTS:

A. OPENING CELEBRATION

The entire Christian Community gathers in a vast courtyard in the open air. This is a topographical symbolism with a significant orientation of space.

—Towards the West: the great Cross, Christ facing West, the place of death.

—Towards the East: the tomb of Christ dug in the ground in circular form, a tomb destined for the old chief of the family.

It is there the catechumens go to die and rise with Christ in the waters of baptism.

—Towards the North: the Paschal Candle representing the Risen Christ.

—Towards the South: the altar.

The ceremony revolves around these four points which mark the various stages of man's life in the Paschal experience, in a way proper to the "moose": The Christian way towards God, starting necessarily and absolutely by the Cross, followed by the burial in the tomb, then the passage from death to resurrection symbolized by the solemn procession towards the Paschal Candle, and finally, the climb up to the Altar, the Eucharist, the last stage to union with God.

B. LITURGY OF THE WORD

The family re-lives its own history while it listens attentively to the reading of the Biblical texts: the Creation, passage through the Red Sea, etc.

C. LITURGY OF LIGHT

which includes:

1. *The Blessing of the New Fire*
2. *Proclamation of Assumed Names* of Christ, and blessing of the Paschal Candle—symbol of the resurrection. The assumed (given) names "zab-yuiya" are programmatic names that every

Moaga chief assumes when he comes to power. By this name he indicates to his people the direction he intends to give to his reign.

The victorious and risen Christ is thus acclaimed like a chief being enthroned. The president calls out an assumed name, the drum beats it out in a drum-language. Immediately, the herald proclaims it aloud and ends by applause (Kaasgo) which is taken up by the crowd. After a third repetition there is a salvo.

3. Christ's Procession to His Throne

When the guns have given a third salvo, the crowd begins a processional entry in rhythm with the drum beats; the procession sets off towards the place prepared to receive the Paschal Candle.

The movement is slow, the Candle isolated in the midst of the cortege. The bearers take three long steps forward and two backward. Three times, while the singing goes on, the procession stops, and the herald turns towards the Candle that the bearers raise as high as they can, brandishes his spear and cries: "Light of the World" and shouts an acclamation.

4. Christ Enthroned

At the place chosen, the procession stops.

The Candle is raised on a pedestal.

Incensing-Proclamation of the Paschal message:

As soon as the Proclamation is over, a group of about 30 to 40 young men and women advance in a row accompanied by the drums.

They go forward dancing (Warba) towards the leader of the drummers who comes to the head of the row and evolves around the Paschal Candle. After one or two rounds all retire in the same order.

D. BAPTISMAL LITURGY

It follows more or less the Roman Ritual in its sobriety and content.

Note, however, that those to be baptized descend into Christ's tomb (death) to come out again transformed (life) by the baptismal waters.

It should also be noted that the atmosphere created by the "rogom" (parentage) and the "buudu," with their ensuing context, allows for a certain amount of spontaneity and liberty of expression of feeling during the relatively long celebration.

From the moment this spirit of liberty exists, the liturgical gesture or word runs no risk of remaining static and turning into a rite emptied of all vitality: it is constantly being renewed.

A sign of this liberty is the prayer of the body marked by the rhythm of the drums. Often the singing is accompanied by a spontaneous clapping of hands here or there; when it accompanies a procession it gives rise spontaneously to a quiet dance step.

The acclamations of the crowd (the children join in with total abandon), stress the culminating moments of the praise of Christ by the community of which He is the Chief.

PAUL CARDINAL ZOUNGRANA
Archbishop of Ouagadougou
Upper Volta

3

Some Aspects of Catechetical Renewal in India

Introduction

The Word of God becomes meaningful to men and becomes a message for them when it emerges from a concrete situation—human and social, cultural and religious, and when it interprets man's life and gives orientation to the future. Indeed the content of the Word of God is important; but the milieus within which that Word resounds, and the situation which interprets it for men and women living in concrete situations should be equally attended to. Just as the Bible is both God's Word and man's Word, and the human word serves as the medium of the divine, so also catechesis which communicates and interprets God's Word has also to be a meaningful and relevant human word. The context or the milieu—cultural and religious tradition in particular —contributes to its interpretation and relevance.

It is with this understanding that we shall now briefly highlight a few aspects of the catechetical renewal in India.

I. BACKGROUND OF THE CATECHETICAL RENEWAL MOVEMENT IN INDIA

The ministry of the Word in various parts of India can be traced back to the different periods and agents.

The different phases of the world-wide catechetical movement and their trends had their counterparts in the Indian Church too.

Pre-Vatican (II) Efforts

The pioneer, promoter and original expression of the first stage of catechetical movement in India was Fr. Thomas Gavan Duffy, founder and Director of the Catechetical Center of Tindivanam (1921) in the Archdiocese of Pondicherry.

The benefits of the second stage of the catechetical movement—the kerygmatic approach—reached India through the participation of Indian Bishops and priests at the International Catechetical Study Week of Munich in 1960, the publication of the then famous German Catechism and the world-wide lecture tours of Fr. Johannes Hofinger, S.J.

An important event in the life of the Church in Independent India was the First Plenary Council of India held in Bangalore in January, 1950, at which the entire hierarchy met together for the first time after Independence (1947) to re-think the mission of the Church in the changed context of the country. Among its acts and decrees there is a chapter on catechists and another on the preaching of God's Word, especially on catechetical instruction. *(Acta et Decreta Primi Councilii Plenarii Indiae,* 1950, nos. 176-180, 199-207). Its main recommendations bear on the dignity and training of catechists, catechists' schools to be founded, specialized courses to be given for adult education, catechetical office to be set up in every diocese and a catechetical commission to be set up within the Catholic Bishops' Conference of India (CBCI). In keeping with its recommendations a section for catechetics was established at once. Its scope was limited—its initial effort consisted especially in the annual surveys it conducted on one or another aspect of catechetical problems.

Post-Vatican Catechetical Renewal in India

However, it was not until the post-conciliar era that a planned catechetical renewal at all levels of the Church in India was to take place. The Bishops of India, gathered in ordinary General Meeting in Delhi in October, 1966, explored ways to spread and communicate the spirit of the Council and to implement its renewal program in every area of the Church's life in the country. They stated it to be "the pastoral policy of the Church in India to place the liturgical and catechetical apostolate at the very center of its activities, giving them prime importance in its care and preoccupations" (Report, p. 11). One of the decisions which the

Bishops took in this regard was to found a National Catechetical Center at Bangalore to animate, foster and coordinate catechetical renewal on a national level. This center came into being in February, 1967, and Fr. D. S. Amalorpavadass was appointed Director.

The third stage of the catechetical movement corresponds more or less to the post-Vatican renewal in India and the comprehensive, all-round and all-level catechetical renewal program launched and implemented by the National Catechetical Center in collaboration with regional and diocesan structures.

II. PREPARATORY MEASURES AND INDISPENSABLE BASES

When the National Catechetical Center of India was founded, one of the first services clamored for from us was the publication of up-to-date catechisms adapted to the living conditions of our people in India and graded for the different age-groups and classes in schools and parishes. However important and urgent catechisms may be, they had to be situated in the overall and long-term renewal program of the Center and ranked in the order of priorities, according to the strategy adopted for launching a successful renewal movement. Composition of original catechisms for India aimed at a certain quality and high standard, which is an exigency of maturity, authenticity and catholicity of the local Church, implied facilities and called for much preliminary and indispensable work. It supposes basically a renewed Christian community, though catechesis itself can be an instrument of its renewal.

The Spirit Is Primary and Supreme

At the initial stage our main concern was to discover and foster the spirit that should animate our activities and guide our orientations. Conscious of the dangers of institutionalism, the Center wanted to capture, keep alive, incarnate and spread the spirit that inspired the foundation of the new institution. The spirit is expressed in a triptych: all-India and national, ecclesial and pastoral, diaconal and relevant. Now we can say that this spirit influenced effectively the shaping of the policy of the Center, the planning and implementation of its program of renewal.

Vision, Planning and Program

The next concern of the Center was to have a global vision of the Lord's designs for His Church in India in the next decades, to make a master-plan, to draw a long-term program of renewal for the whole country in the fields of the Bible, Catechetics and the Liturgy, convinced that the unit of renewal in the Church is one generation or a span of twenty-five years. The comprehensive vision was not to remain a dream, the long-range policy a wishful thinking, and the overall planning a dead letter. But they were to be translated into reality by implementing at all cost a short-term program of activities taking into account the concrete and urgent needs of the hour, according to an order or priority.

Minimum Structures of Organization and Animation

Next came the task of establishing an effective organizational setup, with minimum structures of operation and collaboration; creating channels of communication and organs of dialogue and offering means of renewal; formation of the CBCI Commission for Catechetics with the appointment of a large panel of forty Consultors; the nomination of the Diocesan Director of Catechetics in over one hundred dioceses of India; making efforts to set up regional catechetical centers for each of the twelve regions into which we had divided India for practical purposes; co-ordination and creation of all catechists' training schools; making contact with the members of the Conference of Religious of India (CRI) at all levels, and with the professors of catechetics in all the twenty-eight Major Seminaries and Scholasticates; maintenance of ecumenical contact and cooperation from the beginning in various ways; realization of pastoral integration and international liaison with about ninety institutes and centers all over the world.

III. OVERALL RENEWAL OF THE CHURCH AND CATECHETICAL TRAINING OF ALL SECTIONS OF THE CHURCH

Even the important catechetical tasks like the composition of catechisms had to be situated in the overall efforts made by the Church in India to renew herself in the spirit of Vatican II. In 1967 we were just at the beginning of the renewal era after the conclusion of the Council. It was a bit too early to undertake this work as the dynamics of change and renewal had not yet begun to be operated in the Indian Church and as aspects, trends, dimensions and emphases of renewal had not yet been clarified and articulated, accepted and lived by the Church at large.

The Center drew up a long-range program which was to be implemented by short-term programs to meet the concrete and urgent needs of the hour. This implementation required a few structures.

At the National, Regional and Diocesan Levels

The catechetical movement is animated and guided at a national level by the CBCI Commission for Catechetics. The Commission is assisted by consultors from all over the country. The National Catechetical Center has an adequate and trained staff to conduct its planned and phased program of catechetical renewal.

Likewise at the regional level, Regional Centers or Regional Commissions have been set up.

Then in every diocese there is a Diocesan Director of catechetics, usually trained. Indeed, one-fifth of all dioceses have such full-time directors. Some dioceses have a diocesan catechetical center and/or commission. Moreover, there are at present ten Catechists' Schools to train full-time catechists.

These various categories of leaders participate in a triennial All-India Catechetical Consultation convened by the CBCI Commission for Catechetics. During the consultation they evaluate their efforts, attempt to identify the trends of renewal in the country, assess the progress made and plan further courses of action.

The Bishops study their recommendations and make relevant decisions.

Focus on Formation

In India the catechetical renewal has been mainly achieved through a very systematic formation.

During the last decade the focus of attention and the greatest efforts have been directed towards the formation of all those who have a catechetical ministry, viz., all sections of the Church. Renewal in general or in any special sphere calls for dedicated people, transformed in spirit and vision, in mentality and attitude, in relationships and values. Catechetical renewal supposes also that we have at every level, and in every institution, a team of competent people who have undergone a process of conversion and received technical and professional training in modern catechetics. These people should have the benefit of actual practical experience of catechizing and should live the incarnational spirituality. That is why the concentration over these past thirteen years has been on the overall formation and catechetical training of all those who do a catechetical ministry whether priests, religious or lay.

Numerous seminars and courses of varying duration for various groups and categories of people have been organized all over the country by the National Center, Bangalore, as well as by Regional Diocesan agencies and by religious orders. The National Catechetical Center of Bangalore alone has offered training programs and refresher courses to approximately 20,000 people, including many major religious superiors and Bishops. The Regional Centers of Tindivanam, Cochin, Hyderabad, Goa, Bombay, Baroda, Patna and Imphal are active and growing. They will be increasingly meeting the wider needs of their dioceses and regions.

IV. CONTEXT OF ALL CATECHESIS: THE REALITY OF TODAY'S INDIA

Our comprehensive vision and orientation of catechetical renewal in the past decade led us always to situate catechetics within the socio-religious-cultural reality of India. Three important realities of Indian society: Social inequality, religious pluralism and cultural heritage have been given increasing emphases in our catechetical approach. Hence the challenges before the catechist and the catechized are:

—The challenge of poverty and the need for liberation;
—and the challenge of religious pluralism and the need for fruitful dialogue with such living reality;
—the challenge of the cultural pluralism and the need for inculturation of all aspects of the Church's life.

New Urban Challenges

Industrialized cities and townships pose new pastoral challenges for our Church. The working class in general is characterized by a life of insecurity, unemployment, exploitation and anonymity. It is harassed by pseudo-politicians and money-lenders. The people suffering from such injustices are not served effectively by the normal ministry of the Church. Workers in new industrial centers, whose number is increasing every day, are by and large coming from traditional rural communities. They are scarcely prepared to meet the demoralizing influence of an industrial society. In these circumstances men become dehumanized. To industrial workers and their families the Church's institutions often appear rich and privileged.

The Changing Village Setting

To be sure, since independence, winds of change have been blowing in our villages: electrification, new roads, bridges, new means of transportation and communication—all bringing new opportunities to India's five hundred thousand villages. Nevertheless, many developmental projects—e.g., public health, education and improved agricultural methods—are also accompanied by problems and changes to which villagers cannot always adapt and from which they cannot profit. Another cause for concern is that the leaders and the educated class migrate from the villages to the cities, thus depriving their communities of leadership.

Bitter Realities

In our country today the number of those living on and under "the poverty line" is increasing steadily from 40% in 1960 to 60% in 1970. The number of those living in destitution is also increasing. There are tens of millions, for instance, living on less than one rupee a day. Degrading poverty deprives 360 million people in our country from necessary food, shelter, clothing, and education. We are also aware that the basic rights of man to work, without which he cannot have dignity nor can he grow as a person, are denied him. We are aware that the number of unemployed is also soaring (between 1960 and 1970 the number rose from 16 to 36 million). Then there is the rapid increase of population (the decade between 1950 and 1960 had an increase of 78 million, and the decade between 1960 and 1970 saw an increase of 128 million). True, a too rapid increase in population hampers a harmonious economic growth, but is that the chief factor of our poverty? Will destitution be eradicated with control of population? How long will it take to control population? Will we permit 60 million children below the age of 6 to suffer from malnutrition until the population is brought under control? These are only some of the questions one could raise about our socio-economic situation. A catechesis which is Christian cannot ignore these realities or pass them over superficially with some shallow moralizing.

Rich Traditions and Discernment

The many rich cultures and religious traditions of our land provide solace amid crises and seasons for celebrations. More attention and appreciation is to be paid to this rich heritage of catechetics. However, it is also true that certain religious customs are not infrequently obstacles to progress, health and growth of solid religion, because of superstitions and a fatalistic mentality which is fostered by them. Catechesis must help sift the good from the bad to uncover the "semina verbi" placed there by the Lord Himself.

In the formation of catechetical personnel and in the composition of catechisms for school, these above dimensions have been very much in focus. Efforts are still under way in the same line to make catechesis an instrument of inculturation and liberation.

V. COMPOSITION OF CATECHISMS FOR INDIA

Having outlined the phases of the catechetical movement in India, indicated the role played by the National Catechetical Center in this renewal in collaboration with regional and diocesan agencies, and ensured the catechetical formation of all those who teach catechesis and finally situating catechesis in the total context of today's India, we are now in a position to share with our readers the efforts made by the Church in India to compose and publish catechisms for all age-groups as an invaluable instrument of catechetical formation.

"God-with-Us" Series

The National Catechetical Center of Bangalore with the encouragement of the Catholic Bishops' Conference of India set about in 1971 to compose and publish original catechisms for India. We appointed teams drawn from among the thousands of people trained at our Center. Within a period of four years we managed to compose graded catechisms, consisting of four cycles and meant for the ten years of primary and secondary schools for children and youth.

The series composed and published by the National Center is called "God-with-Us" Series. For each class there is a student's text and a teacher's text. The series has been translated and adapted to various regional languages of India. Additional series have been composed in some dioceses and regions. Before these new books are introduced teachers are given initiation and training. This entire work is continually evaluated. It is revised every time it is reprinted. This year a third volume "a Companion Volume" has been added to each class: called "Family Catechesis." Thus catechesis has become triangular in dimension: children and youth benefit by the faith-formation of 1) the school, 2) the parish and 3) the home. This family catechesis is primarily parents' catechesis overflowing as children's catechesis at home.

For the university youth we have also composed three series of catechetical themes for the three years of bachelor's degree course. Here too for each class we have a teacher's guide and the student's text ("To Set the Downtrodden Free," "Called To Be Free" and "Marriage").

In this way India has had its own program and approach to catechetical renewal. Thereby it has also in various ways contributed its share to the catechetical movement at world level.

The Process and Approach of Catechesis

India is using the human (incarnational) approach adapted to the conditions of our people in India.

The catechetical pedagogy followed in India can be briefly summed up as consisting of three stages:

a) The evocation of an aspect of human experience, reflection on it and interpretation of its human significance.

b) The interpretation and discovery of its fuller meaning, its ultimate fulfillment in the light of God's Word proclaimed.

c) The discovery of the relevance of this Word to life, a response to the Gospel message and a re-living of the human experience in full consonance with faith.

VI. THE SPECIFICALLY INDIAN CHARACTER OF OUR CATECHISMS

Though India has something in common with the rest of the world regarding the modern catechetical pedagogy and approach, one cannot but be impressed by the *originality of our catechisms and their specifically Indian character*.

First of all, these catechisms have been composed by people working in India, who have had their training in the Indian National Catechetical Institute, Bangalore, who have had several years of catechizing Indian children in Indian milieus and who are conversant with various aspects and problems of life in India. In a word, they have done this work in an Indian context.

Secondly, the approach followed in these catechisms is the human approach; it is an incarnational, environmental, experimental pedagogy. According to this, we start from the human experience of the group; we evoke that experience; analyze it, reflect on it, interpret it in the light of the Gospel, and relive it in faith. We discover God's designs in the heart of the world, in the course of our history and in the midst of our life-situations which are all Indian. The milieu in which we discover God and in which faith becomes relevant and vital is our Indian society, the cultural and religious universe of India, chiefly influenced by Hinduism, but not excluding other religions.

Thirdly, it is Indian because our human experience includes also the religious experience of our countrymen which we share daily in various ways. Adaptation to Indian culture and religious situation in our catechesis does not mean that we merely go back to the past or to the purely Hindu Vedic literature, but that we also relate ourselves with the present situation and move towards the future.

However, in order to make them more Indian we have lately tried to initiate people to Indian forms of prayer and meditation: Yoga, dhyana, Bhajan and nam jap. Aspects of Indian spirituality are incorporated every time we revise the text.

The students' books are illustrated. We invited some Indian artists to draw the pictures. They not only depicted Indian scenes but followed Indian art and used a lot of Indian religious and cultural symbols. Besides these illustrations, we have also printed a series of 140 wall pictures or wall posters covering the whole history of salvation (Bible) but which are painted in Indian art. 5,000 copies were published and widely distributed all over India. This is indeed an original artistic series very helpful for catechesis in Indian context.

Some more of the Indian means and forms of prayer could be integrated. More references could be made to Indian religious literature of the past and the present, especially of other religions. More indologists could be consulted and their contribution obtained, etc. That is why they are revised periodically with the perusal, comments, constructive criticism and positive suggestions of various experts and of catechists from all over India.

The Indian cultural character and Hindu religious dimensions are more evident in the three volumes we have composed for university college catechisms, and in the five volumes of family catechisms.

Conclusion

To conclude, we want to recall with joy some of the recent events which have given a boost to the catechetical movement, set an official seal on our theological understanding and pedagogical approach of catechetics and given recognition and encouragement to our efforts of nearly two decades. They are: the communication on catechetics to the Synod by the Catholic Bishops' Conference of India, the event of the Synod of Bishops in Rome on Catechetics in 1977. Finally there came as a crown and confirmation the Apostolic Letter of our Holy Father, Pope John Paul II, *Catechesi tradendae*. It is indeed a source of inspiration and a clear orientation for the future course of the renewal movement and for our remaining program of catechetical apostolate.

D. S. AMALORPAVADASS

4

Catechesis in a Buddhist Ambient

Catechesis in a Buddhist environment constitutes a particular problem for inculturation. Especially in southeast Asian nations of Theravada tradition, culture and Buddhism are identical with one another. Buddhism has so greatly influenced culture as to reshape it, to transform its fundamental values, its vision of reality, and especially the words used in connection with spiritual things. Hence in such environments it is impossible to separate culture and religion, and the process of catechetical inculturation must necessarily keep this in mind.

Having already treated elsewhere of global evangelization in a Buddhist ambient,[1] and of initial evangelizations to Buddhists,[2] here I limit myself to treating catechesis as "an education of children, young people and adults in the faith, which includes especially the teaching of Christian doctrine imparted, generally speaking, in an organic and systematic way, with a view to initiating the fullness of Christian life," as *Catechesi tradendae* (no. 18) expresses itself. In the first part I will examine the situation of catechesis in countries of Buddhist tradition; in a second, I will point out some paths to be followed for the realization of what the magisterium suggests in general terms.

I. THE SITUATION

Catechetical Inculturation in the Past

The great missionaries of the sixteenth and seventeenth centuries sought to adapt not only their lifestyle and methodology, but also their catechesis, at times composing original texts.

In China, the first Jesuits—Ruggeri, Gomes and Ricci—aided by a group of learned men, composed a catechism, printed in Chinese in 1584 and in Latin in 1590,[3] in which they refer to the literature and religion of the nation, and adopt the style and methodology of Confucianism. After an introduction regarding the Chinese virtues, the "Doctrine" treats in the first part: the existence of God, creation, transmigration and retribution, and the answers regarding these truths as given by the various Chinese religions; the second part treats the threefold promulgation of the law, in hearts, in the tablets of Moses, and in Christ; lastly, the third part presents Christ as the Legislator who proposes the truths to believe and the commandments to follow; one is introduced into His community through Baptism.

In 1593, with the help of a few learned men, the Dominican, Cobo, composed another catechism for China, based on the natural sciences that had been discovered by the occidentals and also by the Chinese.[4]

In Japan, with the collaboration of several wise men, Father Valignano wrote a catechism which drew inspiration from the salvific categories of Amidistic Buddhism. Printed in Japanese in 1580, the book was also printed in Latin six years later in Lisbon.[5]

In Vietnam, in 1629, Father Rhodes composed a catechism with the help of his catechists. Religions are presented as having positive elements, such as sacrifice offered to heaven; however, they have fundamentally lost, in the confusion of languages, the real knowledge of God and true rapport with Him. In a Buddhist perspective, Christ is presented as the physician.[6]

All these catechisms have certain common characteristics which deserve emphasis:

—There is an apologetic section and a kerygmatic one. The apologetic part is based on reason, to introduce the Christian message.

—There is sympathy for local culture, in particular for literature and philosophy, to which abundant recourse is had.

—The religions are considered differently. Confucianism, regarded as a philosophy, is viewed positively.[7] Buddhism, instead, is judged negatively because of experiences had and because of the doctrinal differences.[8] The religions and their doctrines and practices are considered, in order to present almost by contrast the Christian message, which is thus "historicized." Valignano has a soteriological approach as in the Japanese Amidism; Rhodes, a "medical" approach as in Buddhism; Ruggeri, an approach of order and law as in Confucianism. It would be impossible to understand these catechisms without knowing the religions of the place.

—There is common theological vision in regard to these religions, which are considered false or incomplete and incapable of transmitting salvation. There is the desire to adopt the culture, but at the same time the religions are refused and condemned. This attitude and theological vision would have blocked inculturation, even if a dispute over rites had not arisen.

In fact, in 1632, to foster unity and avoid diatribes among missionary groups, Msgr. Ingoli, Secretary of Propaganda, imposed on the Japanese missions the adoption of the Roman catechism of Bellarmine.[9] This "non-historical" catechism was rapidly diffused in Asia, and it fostered the deepening of the psychological as well as the social ghetto of the Christian communities of that continent. From that time on, catechisms were literal translations of texts thought out for other cultural situations. Instead, apologetical books were composed which pointed out the errors of Buddhism and the truth of Christianity.[10] In general the presentation of Buddhism was well done, but then everything used to be systematically demolished, without grasping the religion's profound meaning or recognizing its values. Nevertheless, the method fostered neither conversions,[11] nor the integration of Christians into the respective culture.

Recent Catechetical Inculturation

The churches in Buddhist countries have benefited from the catechetical renewal, and, even more than can be seen, from the examination of texts published in this period. Three stages can be distinguished[12]: the renewal of catechetical pedagogy, preoccupied as to how to catechize; the renewal of contents, preoccupied with the essence of the Christian message; and the anthropological renewal, desirous of bringing about impact of the Gospel in the life of persons and of society.

The methodological period influenced the formation of catechists and the way of teaching. Correspondence courses for non-Christians were born in Japan, Korea, Singapore, and Thailand. The course of Father Ulliana, for example, [13] comprises thirty-two lessons and is divided into four parts: the foundation of the religions and of Catholicism, the principal elements of the faith, the commandments of the Creator, the instruments and means offered by the Church. It is presented under the form of a dialogue between a Catholic priest and a lay Thai Buddhist. The apologetical approach is full of respect for the local culture, but avoids speaking of Buddhism.[14] Catechisms for adults have also been composed or translated[15]; usually these have an introduction that is apologetical in character and keeps in mind the local and cultural context. Even though no mention is made of particular religions, indications are given of universal spiritual needs and the common attitudes and ideas which underlie all religious systems and religious quest.

The kerygmatic renewal has had a greater influence. Almost all the countries of Buddhist culture have translated the German catechism.[16] Korea published its manual to introduce the knowledge of the Bible. The introduction recalls the origin of the Korean Christian community when some wise men, dissatisfied with the answers of Buddhists, Confucianists and Taoists, found satisfaction by reading those of Christians in Chinese books.[17] The China of Formosa has published a catechism for adults prevalently biblical and structured according to the history of salvation.[18] The introduction proposes to foster an encounter between the Chinese person and God. The traditional structure is abandoned; in the first part Christ reveals the Father to us and in the second Christ leads us to the heavenly dwelling. While recognizing the need for inculturation, the commission abstained from adaptations, because it felt "incapable of expressing the revealed truth by using our method of thinking" and because "more profound study and research would be required." In this biblical discovery, however, they noted that the Asiatic of Buddhist tradition needs a special introduction, having to do with an intellectual and spiritual journey, in order to become sensitive to the biblical kerygma. This introductory stage has been called preevangelization[19]; in certain countries discussions about its nature and necessity have been more important than its pastoral use.

The anthropological renewal took the human situation as its point of departure, giving it a Christian interpretation and in this context transmitting the message to nourish the faith. Positive examples in this sense are the catechisms of Singapore, a cosmopolitan and industrialized city,[20] of Sri Lanka,[21] and particularly of India, which is not, however, in the Buddhist area.[22] After a cursory look we ask ourselves whether the biblical dimension is sufficiently present and whether the surrounding religious fact is sufficiently considered. Even the more recent catechetical texts of Buddhist countries have not solved the language problem and do not take Buddhist realities and values into account, thus risking the perpetuation of the religious-cultural ghetto of the Christians and the prolongation of the impression that Christianity is not a serious religious phenomenon. The dialogue with the Buddhists helps to overcome these difficulties, but its practice is still restricted to individuals and groups without in-depth involvement of the churches in their totality.[23]

Catechetical Inculturation and the Asiatic Bishops

During the last ten years the Bishops of Asia have clearly expressed the urgent need for catechetical inculturation. The episcopal conferences of the Buddhist nations had the first opportunity to express themselves in the inquiry made by the Sacred Congregation for the Clergy, in view of the Second International Catechetical Congress of 1971. According to the synthesis presented by Bishop Lourdusamy,[24] the first necessity and priority lies in research for a new approach. "A new Asiatic man has been born, for whom the traditional approach is no longer relevant." Among the elements of this new approach are suggested: 1. "A catechesis which reflects the religious and cultural patrimony of the peoples to be evangelized"; 2. "An ambiental catechesis which gives meaning to the human realities in which men are involved"; 3. "A catechesis concerned about attitudes, which is not only suitable for school, but also for the community, meant not only for children but also for adults."

The requests of three Buddhist countries are revealing: "Whenever the Christians of Thailand will have reflected on the data of Revelation and will have re-formulated their faith in harmony with the kind of thought which is proper to them, when there will be Thai theologians and a catechism that will be something more than a simple translation or adaptation of catechisms composed in the perspective of occidental catechetical pedagogy, regardless of how rich and elastic this pedagogy may be, only then will catechesis in Thailand become a digestible food for baptized souls and not just simple, memorized notionalistic knowledge." And the conference of Laos affirms: "The catechumens, who come from animism, need a catechesis that respects their religious past and culture. Even if dissatisfied with their ancient religions, they remain strongly influenced by them and are grateful to us when we recognize and respect the true values which they contained." And Sri Lanka adds: "Catechesis should aim at forming Christians who recognize the work of the Spirit in the environment and in the events of their existence, as well as in the minds and hearts of persons of different religions with whom they live; nevertheless, they must remain convinced and committed in the unique faith which they have received from the God of salvation whom they adore."[25]

In the 1974 synod for evangelization the Asiatic Bishops articulated this urgent need for inculturation in a broader framework. In order for the Church to be incarnated in Asia, it must draw near to the local culture and to the spiritual traditions of the non-Christians and assimilate their values[26]; it must make use of the thought of the philosophers and of the sages, while avoiding syncretism.[27] If for some "indigenization" is a means and a garb to foster the acceptance of Christian truth,[28] for others it is a necessity in order to render the Church incarnate and catholic.[29] This concerns a vital and progressive process which calls for the purification, assumption and assimilation of values.[30] Dialogue with the religions and with the entire human community round about is a way of adapting dynamically: "Only in a sincere dialogue with the religions can we discover the *semina Verbi* hidden in them."[31]

From the 1977 synod on catechesis more precise contributions from the Bishops of Buddhist nations were expected; however, because of the new situations in Indochina, the representatives of Laos and Cambodia were not present, and those of Vietnam had new preoccupations. Bishop Ek of Thailand recalled the usefulness of following the example of Buddhist initiation, inviting youth to spend a period of time in the monastic life.[32] "It is time that the very great attention owed to orthodoxy yield a little to the more positive concern of constructing a living faith.... Even the catechisms must be adapted to the exigencies of the different cultures in the way and in the extent of explaining certain truths, while always conserving the substantial integrity of the whole...."[33] The spiritual initiation must be as important as the cognitive one.[34] Bishop Kuo of Formosa pointed to the liturgy as the goal and font of catechesis and recalled the suitability of Christianizing civil and family celebrations and anniversaries.[35] Bishop Chan of Malaysia insisted on the ecumenical aspect, also including in it dialogue with Asiatic religions,[36] and stressed the importance of knowing in depth the language, traditions, culture, faith and superstitions of the people to be catechized.[37] For Bishop Deogupillai of Sri Lanka catechesis must be personal, centered upon the sources, incarnated in the world and oriented to action.[38] Other fathers emphasized formation in justice[39] and the nature of catechesis.[40]

The first seminar on the missionary apostolate organized by the FABC pointed to inculturation and dialogue as the priority tasks of the Church in Asia.[41] The Manila congress on missiology focused on and articulated the various themes under the same point of view,[42] even if it did not suggest concrete ways for catechesis.

From this brief survey it may clearly be seen that inculturation is perceived as urgent for the incarnation of the Churches in Asia, but the specifications remain general both because they have to be formulated elsewhere and also perhaps because their realizations are still limited and uncertain.

Orientations of John Paul II in "Catechesi Tradendae"

The principal preoccupation of the document is to assure fidelity to the message and its valid and authentic transmission, in order that the faith of the Christian may grow to full maturity in Christ. In this context the Pope recognizes the validity of inculturation and points out conditions in number 53. Catechesis, he affirms, "is called to bring the power of the Gospel into the very heart of culture and cultures," re-echoing the magisterial indications of Paul VI on the purpose of evangelization.[43] "Genuine catechists know that catechesis 'takes flesh' in the various cultures and milieus." In this process of inculturation the Pope points out a few conditions: 1. The message cannot be "purely and simply isolated" from biblical culture and from the successive historical enrichments. 2. "The power of the Gospel everywhere transforms and regenerates.... There would be no catechesis if it were the Gospel that had to change when it came in contact with the cultures." 3. Catechesis cannot be impoverished "through a renunciation or obscuring of its message, by adaptations, even in language, that would endanger the 'precious deposit' of the faith, or by concessions in matters of faith or morals."

At the same time the document points to some positive orientations. "Catechesis will seek to know these cultures and their essential components; it will learn their most significant expressions; it will respect their particular values and riches. In this manner it will be able to offer these cultures the knowledge of the hidden mystery and help them to bring forth from their own living tradition original expressions of Christian life, celebration and thought." It also recognizes the method which will take with wise discernment, certain elements, religious or otherwise, that form part of the cultural heritage of a human group and use them to help its members to understand better the whole of the Christian mystery."

Number 59 recognizes that "there is no doubt that the question of language is of the first order," but "catechesis cannot admit any language that would result in altering the substance of the content of the Creed," or that deceives or seduces. Instead, it must state or communicate the entire doctrinal content more easily, without any alteration. The search for a suitable language is a part of the continual renewal of catechesis (CT 17). An appeal to non-Christian elements is not excluded, even though, *a fortiori*, the use of popular Christian devotion is to be favored where this exists (CT 54). Courses on religions given in certain schools are useful, but insufficient for formation in the faith (CT 34).

The orientations of John Paul II are rich enough for a serious effort to inculturate catechesis in a Buddhist ambient. The existential and personalistic categories used by him in the encyclical *Redemptor hominis* are still more enlightening. It is necessary to be faithful to Christ and faithful to the concrete man. The concrete man is the first path of the mission of the Church (RH 13, 14, 18, etc.); the task of the Church is to help each man to find himself in Christ (RH 11) or to find Christ, so that Christ can with each one walk the path of life (RH 13), and that each one may find in Christ his own fullness (RH 8, 11) and freedom (RH 12)....
In these documents we must not seek the immediate answers to the particular problems of inculturation, but great guidelines for a work to be carried out in discernment and in ecclesial communion.

II. PROSPECTS

Inculturation and Catechesis

Inculturation is the global process which makes a particular church the sign and sacrament of Christ and of His salvation in the living culture in which it finds itself. It is realized through a deep study of the ecclesial life in Christ in a determined context, so as to give rise to adequate expressions. It is not only or especially a matter of technique, but of a life in Christ which is concretely deepened and manifested as a result. It does not deal with such particular and disconnected aspects as the integration of Christians, the adaptation of undertakings, the inculturation of liturgy and catechesis, etc. Inculturation is all this, and even more it is the incarnation of the communitarian experience in a determined cultural context, so as to be able to express itself in a new, comprehensive and challenging manner to all men of good will.

In the process of inculturation, catechesis has a particular role, precisely because it helps the Christian to live and to witness to his own faith in the concrete context of life. In order that catechesis may have this role in the maturation of the faith of Christians who live in a Buddhist ambient, the following elements must be given due consideration in teaching and in the compilation of the respective texts.

1. Experience must have priority over formulation, and formulation must lead to correct experience. Thus can the Gospel transform and regenerate persons and cultures. This twofold exigency coincides with the Buddhist tradition, in which the lived is more important than the known, and language is in function of experience. For this reason schools of catechesis must be moments of launching and of examining the total Christian experience. The observations of Bishop Ek to the synod on catechesis find their whole importance in this perspective.

2. Language must state and communicate the message, without deforming it. In Buddhism language has a very great importance, to the point of becoming the instrument of spiritual progress and not just an expressive means adapted to the comprehension and spiritual level of the listener. Because of the inadequacy of the language used by the Christian communities, often living in ghetto situations, an examination of terms is necessary. The Church has the right and the need to have a

language of her own, creating new terms and giving a new meaning to ancient terms, as is shown in the history of Christianity. However, the new meaning must be clear and must be pointed out; otherwise, the cultural-religious ambient of the majority will take advantage and foster syncretism rather than incarnation. From research which I carried out in Laos, it appears clear that wherever the dominant cultural religion, such as Buddhism or animism, is ignored, syncretism tends to gain the upper hand.

Examples could be very numerous. We will mention only a few. To translate "heaven" the term *Savama* (sky) is used, which has a very precise significance in the traditional Buddhist cosmology. To use it in catechesis one must at least indicate the Christian sense, thus helping to overcome not only the inherent anthropomorphism but also to point to a definitive and authentic salvation which transcends the wheel of re-incarnation *(samsara)*. Often used for God are generic terms such as Lord (in Thai, *Phra Chao)*, which indicate the traditional animistic divinities, but are transferred to a lower class by Buddhism and inserted into its vision. Hence it is necessary to point out that such a type of being is not meant when we speak of God.[44] For the incarnation of Christ terms and expressions are used which recall the samsaric incarnation of the divinities and the salvific incarnation of Vishnu. To avoid distortions, it is necessary to refer to this need of having the Absolute close and as a savior and at the same time point out the distinctiveness of Christ: God-man forever. The crucifixion is always a scandal, but especially in the perspective of the immanent and individual causality of human action *(karma)*. Therefore, it is necessary to emphasize human solidarity, represented also by certain symbolic figures such as the bodhisattva and in certain ritual practices of Buddhism lived as the transmission of merits.[45]

3. The anthropological approach so fundamental in Buddhism can be respected, at least as a point of departure. The problems of man, the fundamental characteristics of every existence (misery, impermanence and inconsistency), and, more simply, the experience of suffering, open the way to the search for true salvation. But above all it must appear clear that in Christianity man is not alienated, that his responsibility and his effort are not short-circuited. For this reason modern anthropological catechesis and the teaching of John Paul II find points of contact with the Buddhist tradition.

4. It is necessary to recognize and indicate the meaning of the search of the Buddhist way, and the compatible convergences of this with the Christian way; in particular it is necessary to emphasize the importance of the search for true and definitive salvation, which transcends contingent customs and categories, the importance of right intention as the radical choice. of the very salvation which qualifies every consequent act, the need of constant spiritual progress and of personal application to realize it, etc. It is necessary not only to recognize the meaning which the Buddhists give to their life, but also to indicate the meaning which the Christians discover in their search: here enters the discourse on the salvific presence of Christ for every man and in human and religious history.

5. Suitable categories and methods can be taken from Buddhism or at least can be indicated as valid; for example, the five precepts which correspond to the commandments without the first three, the four altruistic virtues *(Brahma-cariya)*, certain methods of spiritual progress commonly called meditation, especially to foster interior attitudes and detachment from self and from everything that is contingent, etc.

6. It is necessary to keep in mind all the dimensions of religion lived by a particular people. Some have the tendency of favoring the religion about which they are specialists and with which they have preferential relationships of dialogue; for example, they may look positively only at canonical Buddhism. In a Buddhist ambient one cannot *a priori* scorn animistic forms or popular Buddhism, which can at times manifest a profound inquiry and need of the religious man. For example, among the peoples of southeast Asia, the cult of animistic divinities manifests the need for interpersonal and communitarian relationships, and the transmission of merit demonstrates interdependence on the way of salvation. But clearly this attention to the religion lived by the masses must not let us forget the values indicated by canonical Buddhism and by the mystics. Catechetical inculturation in a Buddhist environment cannot be single-faceted, for there are different Buddhist ways *(Hinayana, Mahayana, Tantrayana*, etc.), and each way is lived in an original manner within each people.[46]

7. All human dimensions in their developmental dynamism must be considered, because catechesis addresses itself to concrete communities and persons. Today, especially, Buddhism is not the sole unifying value of culture, as, moreover, it almost never was

in the area of the Chinese. Secularism, materialism and atheism have their influence, and so, too, do other social pressures, and catechesis must take them into account.[47]

8. Recourse to the Bible is necessary both in nations where its diffusion is popular and in those where it is unknown. It is necessary, however, to point out its meaning and the progressive revelation, so that it will become an open and evangelizing book. For example, the anthropomorphisms about God must be explained, as also certain attitudes and cultural aspects.

9. It is especially necessary to point out the newness of Christianity. Christ is not only the paradigm of our journey toward total liberation, nor is He only One who points out the way He walked first; He enters into our life and into our actions without supplanting us. A respectful comparison between the affirmations of Christ and of Buddha, between their roles and their respective persons is itself a revealer of the differences. Even though expressed in human language, God is not a being like the gods; He is the ultimate end but also our beginning; He is the Absolute and at the same time personal; He is the unspeakable who revealed Himself. In regard to merit and grace, it is necessary to indicate their originality in comparison with the canonical and popular Buddhist categories, and to correct the prejudices borrowed from the Hindu context. The originality and importance of charity must be developed, because of Buddhist sensitivity to this and because of its centrality in the Christian life. The Church is not only constituted by the elect or by the religious-priestly community: it is a united and diaconal people. Prayer is not only a spiritual action[48] in view of personal progress; it is a communion with God, a recognition of Him....

10. The integrity of the message must not be mutilated under the pretext of inculturation. Certain presentations would be acceptable to the Buddhists,[49] but with difficulty do they seem reconcilable with the message, which must be transmitted in its entirety and in an incarnate manner. Inculturation cannot ignore either the biblical formulations or the enrichments of understanding of the Christian mystery. It must, however, focus upon the essential, making the hierarchy of truths stand out according to their importance and giving an order which takes into account cultural sensitivities. The order of the Chinese catechism is preferable to that of the traditional Roman catechism; in any case, it should not be begun with the creation.

Dialogue, Theology and Catechesis

Dialogue is the means through which the Church is actively present in the world; it is a way of communicating with persons and movements in a manner of give and take, of collaboration and commitment, of leavening and questioning. Inculturation is impossible without dialogue, because the Church cannot incarnate herself by living in a ghetto situation, without being questioned and enriched by a constant osmosis and without continually being sent back to the essential experience of the gift of God humbly received and constantly deepened. Inter-religious dialogue, then, has a particular place, because it permits the perception of the spiritual progress of a people, especially when the religious factor is important in the culture. The lack of dialogue explains for the greater part the ghetto situation in which so many churches of Asia find themselves, their little relevance in the respective cultures and the limited irradiation and diffusion of the Christian message in the continent. To be leaven, witness and interrogation, the Church must be in dialogue with Christ in ever more profound fidelity.

John Paul II has asked that youth, especially, be formed to dialogue.[50] To accomplish this it is necessary to focus on two means: a progressive and incarnate Christian formation and a communitarian discernment of the Christian experience. To form to dialogue, an exhortatory and erratic method is insufficient. This concern must be present in all Christian formation, especially through catechesis, which must help one to understand, to live and to witness to one's own faith in the concrete environment in which the Christian finds himself. The Christian message must be situated and compared with the vision and values of the environment, so that it can be seen in its originality and in its total fullness. And since this is a slow process, it is necessary to have a communitarian discernment under the guidance of those whom the Lord has given as teachers of the faith.

Adapted theology has an important role in the process of inculturation. In a Buddhist ambient there are crucial aspects to be studied deeply, such as the salvific value of the religions and of Buddhism in particular, and Christian specificity in comparison with Buddhism itself, which, as Guardini affirms,[51] is Christianity's greatest challenge. In Asia this theology is still in its first steps, searching for suitable ways and methods. It needs verification and cannot pass to catechesis without discernment. Catechesis and theology are at the service of lived faith; they presuppose the deepening of the Christian experience, and a knowledge of Buddhism not only as a doctrine but also as a reality lived in the totality of modern life.

MARCELLO ZAGO, O.M.I.

FOOTNOTES

1. Zago, M., "L'evangelizzazione in ambiente religioso asiatico," in *Concilium* XIV, 4 (1978), pp. 117-132 (682-698).

"Evangelization in the Religious Situation of Asia," in Greinacker & Müller: *Evangelization in the World Today*, 1979, pp. 72-84.

2. Zago, M., "L'evangelizzazione ai buddhisti," in *Communio*, XV (May 1974) pp. 53-67 (939-953).

(The Proclamation of the Christian Message in a Buddhist Environment. FABC Papers 5, Hong Kong 1977.)

3. *Vera et brevis divinarum rerum expositio,* in Tacchi-Venturi, *Opera Storiche II* (Macerata 1915) pp. 498-540. For the bibliography, cf. Streit R., *Bibliotheca Missionum,* IV (Aachen 1928) no. 1937.

4. Cf. bibliography in Streit R., *Bibliotheca Missionum,* IV (Aachen 1928) no. 1748.

5. *Catechismus Christianae Fidei,* in quo veritas nostrae religionis ostenditur et sectae Japonenses confutantur. Editus a Patre Alexandro Valignano, Societatis Jesu. Olyssipone, Excudebat Antonius Riberius, 1586, cf. Streit R., *Bibliotheca Missionum,* IV (Aachen 1928) no. 984.

6. Catechismus pro ijs qui volunt suscipere Baptismum in Octo dies divisus. Rome in 1651. The last edition made in Saigon was in 1961. Cf. Streit R., *Bibliotheca Missionum,* V (Aachen 1929) no. 1640.

7. Even today the Churches of the Chinese area (China, Korea, Vietnam) prefer adaptation to Confucianism, because it is more important in culture and easier for inculturation.

8. The first missionary approach to Buddhism was positive, both in Japan as well as in China. The contacts with the Buddhist world became difficult little by little. We became aware of the profound differences between the two religions and of the little esteem which the bonzi enjoyed among the higher classes. Cf. DeLubac, *Buddhismo e Occidente,* Milan, 1958.

9. Decretum S. Congregationis de Propaganda Fide, Rome, 1932; in *Pagès, Histoire de la Religion Chrétienne au Japon II,* Paris 1870, pp. 382-388. However, the same Propaganda continued to print other catechisms, such as that of Rhodes in 1651.

10. One of these, published in Thai at the end of the last century (Bangkok, 1897), was reprinted at the end of the 1950's, arousing a real national controversy and causing the closing of the Catholic typography of Bangkok for a few months. There exists an Italian translation of a Birman text by Mantegazza, G., *Dialoghi tra un Kien selvaggio ed un Siamese ex Talapoino.* 1785, Manuscript, in the Borgia Apartment of Vatican Library. Cf. Streit, R., *Bibliotheca Missionum VI* (1931) no. 754.

11. Zago, M., "La conversion en milieu bouddhiste," in Masson J. (ed.), *Chemins de la conversion,* Louvain 1975, pp. 54-77.

12. Amalorpavadass, D.S., *Converging Trends of the Catechetical Movement and Guidelines of Official Documents,* Bangalore 1979.

13. Ulliana, J., Course of Christian Religion (in Thai) 1961, 2nd ed.

14. In the synod of 1977 Bishop Chan of Malaysia emphasized the importance of correspondence courses in the Asiatic context. Written intervention in Caprile *Il Sinodo dei Vescovi 1977*, Rome 1978, p. 209.

15. The two catechisms of Father B. F. Mayer were diffused in various nations of the Chinese area: *The Way to Happiness. A Missionary Manual of Catholic Doctrine*, Hong Kong, 1958. *Two Lives. The Intelligent Man's Manual of the Catholic Religion*, Tai Chung, 1960.

16. Cf. *Guida alla catechesi nel mondo*, by the Sacred Congregation for the Clergy, Rome, 1971, pp. 117-140.

17. *Catholic Doctrine Book* (Kyo Ri Se), Bishop's Catechetical Committee, Seoul, 1968.

Sambae J., *Confucius et Jésus Christ. La première théologie chrétienne en Corée, d'apres l'oeuvre de Yi Piek*, lettré coreen. Paris, 1979.

18. Chad, A., "The New Chinese Catechism," in *Teaching All Nations*, VIII (Manila, 1971) pp. 10-24.

19. Nebrada, A.M., *Kerygma in Crisis*, Chicago, 1965.

Nebrada, A.M., "Preevangelización, primer estadio en el dialogo de salvación," in *Misiones Extranjeras*, XV (Burgos 1968) pp. 1-15.

20. The series of scholastic catechisms of Singapore: Focus on Life Publication.

21. In 1972 the government of Sri Lanka asked all the religions to prepare books of religious initiation to be used in the schools. As a consequence of this, a Catholic commission was entrusted with the work, which was accomplished within a few years. "Sixth standard book, reflecting the man of the twentieth century, reflecting also religious culture of the Sri Lankan which had existed for nearly 2,500 years, was introduced after much deliberation and discussion. Buddhist background, customs and rituals purified of pagan elements, and the mentality of Sri Lankan, was reflected in the book. A chapter on the life and works of Lord Buddha was introduced, which was written by an eminent Buddhist monk himself." Letter of Fraccid Anthony Fernando, O.M.I., one of the authors with Fr. Sylvester (1980). Under pressure from the government what the Synod of Colombo had desired was carried out. Cf. Acts of the Second Provincial Synod of Colombo in Ceylon 1968-1969, Colombo, 1970, pp. 35-49.

22. The "God With Us" series comprises ten volumes for the students with just as many guides for the teachers; it is published by the National Center of Catechesis of Bangalore, 1975, with the approval of the CBCI.

23. Zago, M., "Il dialogo fra cristiani e buddhisti nel sud est asiatico," *Concilium* XIV, 6 (1978) pp. 160-167.

Enomoya-Lasalle, H., "Il dialogo tra buddhisti e cristiani in Giappone," ibid., 168-174.

24. Lourdusamy, S., "La catechesi in Asia: le necessità e le priorità stabilite dai vescovi in Asia," in *Acts of the II International Catechetical Congress, Rome, September, 1971*, by the Sacred Congregation for the Clergy, Rome, 1972, pp. 342-360.

"Needs and Priorities Set by the Asian Bishops Conferences," in *Teaching All Nations*, XX (Manila 1972) pp. 6-22.

25. *Ibid.*, pp. 347-348.

26. Parecattil, III Congress, in Caprile, G., *Il Sinodo dei Vescovi 1974*, Rome 1975, pp. 180-181.

27. Kuo, IV Congress, *ibid.*, p. 205.

28. Kuo, IV Congress and X, *ibid.*, 205, 417-418.

29. Dien, written intervention, *ibid.*, 528-529.

30. Dien, *ibid.*

31. Hadisumarta, XIII Congress, *ibid.*, 450-451.

32. Ek, III Congress, in Caprile, G., *Il Sinodo dei Vescovi 1977*, Rome 1978, pp. 82-83.

33. Ek, written intervention, *ibid.*, 210-211.

34. Ek, XIX Congress, 327.

35. Kuo, III Congress, 33-84.

36. Chan, XII Congress, 331.

37. Chan, VIII Congress, 137.

38. Deogupillai, VII Congress, 125-126.

39. Kim, XII Congress, 328; Kuo, XIII Congress, 352.

40. Satowaki, VI Congress, III; and written intervention 214-215.

41. The First Bishops' Institute for Missionary Apostolate of the Federation of Asian Bishops' Conference. FEBAC Papers, no. 19, Hong Kong, 1979.

42. Zago, M., "Primo Congreso on missiologico d'Asia," in *Missioni OMI*, LIX, Rome (March 1980) pp. 40-44. (English in *Eastern Pastoral Institute Review)*

43. *Evangelii nuntiandi*, nos. 18-20.

44. Zago, M., "L'equivalente di Dio in Buddhismo," in *Esperienza di Dio nelle religioni*, by the Institute of Asian Studies, Bologna, 1980.

45. Zago, M., *Rites et Cérémonies en milieu bouddhiste lao*, Rome 1972, pp. 118-128.

46. *Ibid.*, pp. 377-389.

47. Zago, M., "L'indifferenza religiosa nel buddhismo contemporaneo," in *L'indifferenza religiosa*, by the Secretariat for Non-believers, Rome 1978, pp. 233-257.

48. Zago, M., "La preghiera nel buddhismo theravada lao," in *Studia Missionalia*, XIV (Rome 1975) pp. 127-140.

49. Labarriere, P. J., "Dieu sans Christ et Christ sans Dieu," in *Christus*, 25 (Paris, 1978) pp. 146-158; cf. Galot, J., "Christologie et expérience," in *Esprit et Vie* (Paris 1980-1) pp. 2-12.

50. Discourse to the members of the Secretariat for Non-Christians, April 27, 1979.

51. Guardini, R., *The Lord*, Chicago, 1954, p. 305.

5

Proposals for a Catechesis in a Muslim Ambient

Faithful in presenting the whole mystery of Christ to the Christian young people whom she must educate to the Faith as well as to the catechumens, the adolescents or the adults, whom she prepares to the same faith by admission to Baptism, the Church which lives in a Muslim environment must absolutely propose to both the one and the other a Christian message and an evangelical life which are in "close relationship" with everything that is believed and lived by the Muslims, who at times are their relatives, or else their friends or neighbors. Therefore, what situations must catechesis take into consideration, what can be its problematic dialogue, and what, finally, would be its pedagogical perspectives, properly so-called? These are the directions to be taken by a reflection which has as its aim gradually to express various observations and diverse suggestions, whose perhaps too generic character and too hasty elaboration necessarily require a complement, that is, their interpretation and application in view of the very diversity of the local situations, of the particular churches and of the socio-cultural contexts.

I. THE VARIOUS SITUATIONS TO BE CONSIDERED

If, by now, Christian communities exist all over the world, so, too, are Muslims to be found present to some extent everywhere, because a religious diaspora constituted by aliens has developed both in Islamic nations and in societies of Christian tradition. Hence, *no catechesis should ever be developed which does not keep in mind the religious life of the non-Christians*, and more particularly of the faith of the Muslims. Are there not eight hundred million of them in the world today?

1. First of all, *there are societies that are chiefly Muslim,* where Islamism shapes almost everything, to the point of including the juridical and political scene (as, for example, in the Arab nations, except for Lebanon and Pakistan): as a minority, the Christians are then "protected" by the "pact of *dhimma*" (and hence "controlled") and they cannot promote the public expression of their faith in all the sectors of life. In such a case, culture—be it Arabian, Perisan, Turkish or Urdu—is so impregnated by Islamic values besides the nationalistic ones that catechesis should take this fact into absolute account in setting down its content and in renewing its methods. In this environment, it can happen that Christian children of the place have to learn the Koran and Muslim doctrine when they attend state schools. In this case, although they do not run the risk of not knowing what Islamism is, they are, however, tempted to minimize or forget the specific importance of their faith. On the other hand—that is, when they are completely surrounded by a "confessionalistic system" of teaching and of education, which nourishes and safeguards their Christian faith—it can often occur that they remain profoundly or totally ignorant of the Muslim context in which they are called by God to live and to give witness.

2. Fortunately, there are also *many societies where the total national culture does not have this great Islamic imprint,* even though the majority of the population consists of fervent Muslims (as, for example, Indonesia and many nations of black Africa). In these nations, Christians still represent a small minority, yet, they exercise in reality a great cultural influence, so that the different faiths can express themselves outside of their direct political and institutional implications; yet a very great danger of mutual ignorance always remains, for many other reasons. The lay character of the state and the more or less pluralistic organization of society permit then the Christian faith to develop and express itself on both the personal and communitarian levels. But it is hoped that, for its good, the Christian faith will still take into account that of the Muslims and the religious inquiry of those who follow other religious traditions.

3. It happens, lastly, that in some nations of Asia and of Africa, *the Muslims constitute a local minority,* and that in various nations of Europe and of America they are multiplying in such wise as to constitute *small diasporas* which are in the process

of a more or less swift integration. In this case, it is the Muslims who are called upon to participate in the prevalently Christian national culture. The majority of the population, constituted by Christians, runs the risk of forgetting the presence of the Muslim minority, since a catechesis of the so-called "institutionalized Christianity" could remain more or less silent in regard to non-Christian believers. Would it not be proper, however, for all to keep this minority religion in mind and take some interest in these "other believers," more or less distant, whose faith could be accepted as a challenge and, who, through emulation, force catechists to renew their methods and their witnessing?

These, then, described very briefly and without many details, are *the three situations of the Islamic-Christian context,* in which contemporary catechesis has the duty of assuming a specific attitude, that is, *to consider the essential dimensions of the Muslim faith in order to adapt, as a consequence, the instruction and education of Christians to such a socio-cultural context.* It is necessary to remember, however, that the two latter situations represent the greater part of the national contexts that are lived by Christians today and that, in two sufficiently diverse ways, they express the very effort for pluralistic coexistence being made by the various religious communities. In these contexts, catechesis would have, as a specific task, the preparation of Christians, not only *to understand profoundly the faith of the Muslims* and see to it that they can adequately *render an account of their own faith* among these latter, but even more *to witness to Christ,* in His fullness, among the other "searchers for God." Without ever forgetting this second aspect of things (in the so-called "triangular" situations), however, it is appropriate to dwell at greater length on *how today's catechesis can better its adaptation to the Muslim context* in which or beside which it is called to educate in the faith tomorrow's Christians, whether they be young or old!

II. SPECIFIC PROBLEMATIC FOR A "COMPREHENSIVE CATECHESIS"

Notwithstanding the very great diversity of situations, due to the many variations of the geographical, historical and cultural contexts, it still remains possible to envision for everyone a similar, or else analogical, manner of adapting catechesis to the Muslim context in its own manifestations of content and of method. First of all, we must remember in this regard that education in the faith, as is meant by the word "catechesis," refers, in this inquiry, both *to all the methods of exercising the "ministry of the word"* and *to all the methods of educating the faith of the "ones being catechized."* In fact, *in the carrying out of Christian worship,* it is useful always to remember this presence (possible or actual) of Muslims at the great ceremonies in the lives of their Christian friends (be it Baptism, first Communion, Matrimony or a funeral!) and also at some more or less festive Eucharistic Celebration (especially at Christmas and Easter!). The very choice of the texts of Holy Scripture, the preparation of the homily to be expounded to everyone and the writing up of the general intercessions could be done in such a way that Christians will receive everything they have a right to receive for their faith, while at the same time to the Muslims are proposed a teaching and a witness such that it can first be received by them, then enjoyed, and, lastly, understood. Thus, in church, they would feel themselves to be guests who were expected and are, in fact, respected in such a manner that we think we can share with them a few truths and many values. The same should be said for everything that is transmittted by *"the means of social communication."* Whether in articles in a newspaper, conferences on the radio and/or participation in civic (or Muslim religious) celebrations, Christians should constantly remember that their words, as well as their actions, are equally awaited, received and evaluated by the multitude of Muslims; for this reason, therefore, it would be useful that their language and style be adapted to these unexpected recipients. Also *"mixed marriages"* should not be forgotten where, usually, a Muslim man and a Christian woman have decided to share their love and also their parenthood. The Christian wife should be helped in order that she may express her own faith, living it in a manner that will be well accepted and then respectfully evaluated by the Muslim husband and by their children, who would thus be encouraged in their search for the God "of their parents."

It remains evident, however, that the *catechist,* whoever he be (priest, sister, layman or laywoman), *must keep in mind the Muslim context* in which everyone must live and give witness, when his task leads him to guarantee to the Christians their education to the faith, as autonomous persons and constituted communities. This concerns, therefore, helping everyone on the particular level of his Christian education, personal and communitarian, in order that the faith will be reinterpreted and then newly expressed, in the most uncompromising fidelity to its specific contents and also to the specifically Christian mysteries which concretize it. Consequently, the reflections which will be proposed presume a *twofold level of action*, that of the catechist and that of the catechumen (the catechized). The *catechist* has the right and also the duty, in fact, of receiving a more profound formation and, at the same time, more documented information, whereas the *catechumen* merits to receive from him statements that are explained simply and clearly and also to learn from him the behavior and attitudes that profoundly signify his state of "being a Christian."

However, and primarily, for both of them there is a unity of general principles which it would be proper to point out before entering into the particulars of their application. Christians should be educated, first of all, to *benevolence of intellect* and *generosity of heart* when it concerns understanding and loving their Muslim interlocutors. On the one hand, controversies have been so numerous, and often so acute and harsh, in the past! They should disappear forever! On the other hand, prejudices and errors have not been lacking in the same past; in fact, sad to say, they still exist, with their train of misunderstandings and conflicts which continue, up until now, to confuse the relationships between Christians and Muslims in many nations. It would, therefore, be advantageous to combat ignorance and suppress the complexes and fears that are either their causes or their results. The fact is that there are still unfair competitions, useless rivalries and unworthy clashes. It is necessary to be aware of this and, at the same time, convinced and decisive in having recourse to dialogue or sometimes to compromise in order always to save civil peace and find new ways for coexistence and collaboration! Hence, let there be proposed and effectively guaranteed *better information* at all levels of the education of Christians to the faith, in order that they will no longer consider Islam a "taboo" not to be touched, nor the Muslims as "special" beings to be ignored and not approached! Even more, it is precisely in seriously accepting the spiritual challenge that is addressed to Christians by Muslim faith and practice that the Christian will find himself responsibly capable of understanding and overcoming the various problems of the encounter between the two religions. By doing this, the disciples of Jesus would find themselves invited to abandon their "false security," to which often correspond hasty affirmations of superiority and simplistic conclusions of self-sufficiency!

At first, it would be opportune *to concentrate on the "common patrimony"* which is shared by all monotheists in regard to truths of faith and values of life. This is precisely what *Vatican Council II* did in its Declaration "Nostra Aetate" on the Relation of the Church to Non-Christian Religions. Simultaneously, Christians would discover that, subjectively, the Muslims know a religious experience, develop some spiritual sentiments and express some moral behavior analogous to everything that Christians already live or have been trying to do for a long time. Could not these analogies, perhaps, be considered as possible religious convergences, even while remembering the obligation of authenticity and of fidelity that both have and also the irreducible differences between their respective religious traditions? It is only after this first stage of *partial resemblance*, which reveals itself especially in the subjectivity of the experience of the believers, that the Christian would have access, in a better way, to the mystery of the *fundamental dissimilarity*, precisely at the point where he is no longer a simple believer as are the Hebrews and the Muslims, but a "Christian" who finds himself alone, dramatically invited to imitate in everything his unique "model," Jesus Christ, to be always more conformed to Him and, consequently, to witness a little better to His Gospel. The paradox, therefore, would be found precisely there—that is, in the fact that the very effort of a maximum adaptation of catechesis to the Muslim context leads this very catechesis to emphasize in the Christian what differentiates him from all other believers and forces the catechist to reach this "break-off point" of the Christian being!

To be brief, *the Christian is not a "Christian" because* he believes in God, the Creator and future Judge of the living and of the dead; because he accepts the model and message of the prophets; because he professes the oneness of God; because he prays, fasts, gives alms and makes a pilgrimage: Muslims and Hebrews do the same, and also very well, since all this constitutes the "common patrimony" of all monotheists. *Where the Christian finds himself truly "Christian"* is precisely when he consents to call God "Father," to imitate the perfect Son who became man (the Incarnate Word) and also to live in the Spirit who guarantees him the development of this wholly new life where love of one's enemies, the redeeming death and the "recreative" resurrection constitute the essential elements of the "Christian destiny." These would be the more salient points which every catechesis should indicate and gradually develop in nations of Muslim tradition. From this point of view, it would be more than suitable to refuse for Christians the title of "People of the Book" which the Muslims very willingly concede to them, to then remind with force and conviction that, if the Hebrews are and remain effectively "People of the Book" and the Muslims "People of the Koran," *Christians consider themselves* first of all, and not without theological reason, the *"People of Jesus Christ,"* the eternal Word who became flesh and blood, death and life!

Because of these very pedagogical stages in affirming the similarity and discovering the dissimilarity, since for the Christian it is a matter of a superior and wholly gratuitous call (a call to be made similar in all to Jesus Christ through grace alone!), catechesis should be very careful to incessantly recall *the values of divine transcendence and of human humility, of the believer's submission and abandonment, of the human person's personal responsibility and moral autonomy,* in order that the Christian may feel and know himself to be so in agreement with the Muslims (and also with the Hebrews) as to then live these same values with them—and perhaps better than they do. Catechesis could not forget, however, that its task lies precisely in bringing the Christian beyond this stage, to discover finally both the interior treasure of the unique God, Father, Son and Spirit, as well as the *marvels of the immanence* of the grace which totally transforms the condition of human creatures: do these not become, perhaps, "sons and daughters who are adopted by the Father" in the unique and perfect Son, the first-born Brother of a multitude of brothers and sisters, joined with all of them in sacrifice, in death and in resurrection? Paradoxically, Christians who live in a Muslim ambient thus need that all catechesis invite them constantly *to live,* at one and the same time, *a profound spiritual emulation* with their Muslim questioners on the very level of the religious values which both seem to share in full and also *to humbly and uncompromisingly differentiate themselves* because of these mysteries of the Trinity, of the Incarnation and of the Redemption which must be lived by them as transcendent realities which transform the Christian being in his more profound dimensions.

III. A FEW PEDAGOGICAL PERSPECTIVES

Therefore, catechesis in a Muslim context should guarantee both to the catechist as well as to the catechumen, *genuine, open and sympathetic information* about the Islamism that is lived by the Muslims, its fundamental religious values, and also the particular gaze (and willing "reducer") which the very same Islamism projects on Christianity and all Christians. Secondly, in the education of the Christian being of the catechumen, catechesis would be invited to *insist on certain articles of the Creed, a few important aspects of the liturgical cult and various decisive chapters of Christian doctrine.* Lastly, it would be necessary to have the catechumen discover *the inevitable human collaborations* and *hoped-for religious convergences* which coexistence and dialogue with the Muslims gradually allow to be glimpsed, in total coherence with the exigencies of the Gospel message.

1. Know Who the Muslims Are and What They Want To Be

It is hoped that the catechist will have first studied somewhat the history of Islamic-Christian relationships (at least in his local framework!) then will have done some reflecting on the causes and consequences of the misunderstandings and conflicts, and finally will have attempted to imagine and single out what *types of Muslim inquirers* his catechumens could approach in their daily life: Muslims of the common classes, whose faith is almost "biblical," Muslims of Arab culture (traditionalists or reformists), modern Muslims of a twofold culture (and hence more or less westernized), and modern fundamentalist or else integralist Muslims. It would also be useful if he were able to analyze with all of them the characteristics of the local Muslim ambient and then in what measure these correspond to the fundamental or undifferentiated religious human values which all would already have in common according to their earthly condition.

By means of special strictly scientific information, the catechist should, furthermore, *be adequately brought up to date regarding the exact contents of Muslim beliefs and of the moral requirements of Islam,* in order that he can synthesize them for the Christians and the Christians to be catechized, so that thus gradual emphasis will be given to everything that they must evaluate positively in the religious experience of the Muslims as in that of the Hebrews: submission to God, meditation of a Book (considered as the Word of God), imitation of a prophetic model (here, Abraham, Moses and Jesus seem to be for everyone more or less common models, only in their prophetic condition!), solidarity or a community of believers, voluntarily exteriorized faith in the transcendence of God, adoration courageously affirmed by means of an unadorned cult, obedience and fidelity to the prescriptions of the (divine) Law, ascetical and mystical quests which tend to surpass common legalism!

In all this, Christians should, therefore, be educated to evaluate the religious experience of the Muslims positively, and they should become accustomed to speaking of it with respect and sympathy. It would also be advantageous for them to be enabled to find the right words, from the Christian point of view and in the spirit of dialogue, to speak to their Muslim friends about the realities that stand at the very center of the faith of Islam, and that is the text of the Koran and the person of Mohammed, the prophet of the Muslims. At this point the catechist cannot help but have some ideas, more or less in summary form, of the various contemporary tendencies of Christian theology in evaluating the non-Christian religions, and more particularly Islamism, so close and at the same time so far away.

It is precisely by means of this information and of this reflection that the catechist would gradually be able to help his Christians *free themselves from their most notable prejudices in regard to Muslims.* Then, it would thus be easier for him to lead them to redimension the accusations which too often are addressed against Islamism on the part of non-Muslims. Therefore, he would be able to rectify the judgment of his catechumens so that they will not continue to repeat that Islamism is "fatalism," "juridicism," "laxism," "fanaticism," "immobilism," "a religion of fear or of timidity," etc., because these are temptations which all believers experience, whoever they may be, even if they are

Christians. Thus restored to a more evangelical vigilance, through a very demanding examination of conscience, the Christians would perhaps be given a special assignment to help their Muslim inquirers, in order that they will not be the victims of these very common temptations, and to praise everything in their religious tradition that could be of help to greater endurance!

In any case, in the name of the realism required by the dialogue itself, the catechist would still have *to explain to his catechumens what the Muslims think and say about Christianity and about Christians.* When he will have explained to them extensively: why these believers consider the Scriptures of the Christians falsified and changed (preferring to their Gospels the so-called Gospel of Barnabas!); why they judge the Christian mysteries unacceptable, irrational, and useless; why they think that the monotheism of the Christians is stained by "a subtle polytheism, veiled or hidden"; why they see in the Church only a "terrestrial and profane power"; and why they believe that the Christians have been more or less unfaithful to the message of Jesus; then this catechist will be in a position to undertake their *specific instruction,* emphasizing to his catechumens *the most salient points of their faith.* They are to dwell upon the historicity of the Gospels and, therefore, of Christ (especially His death and resurrection), be very clear in the proper use of the words which designate the divine Persons, witness openly and intelligently to their fundamental monotheism, irradiate the mystery of a Church which is at "the service of the poor" and reveals beforehand the "kingdom of God" on earth, and imitate Jesus Christ always more fully, to live His message completely and coherently.

2. Employ to Advantage Certain Aspects of the Creed, Doctrine and Liturgy

In this context, it would be advantageous, both to catechists and to the catechized, *to dwell in a special way on the articles of the Creed that have some correspondence with the faith of the Muslims:* one unique God, creator of heaven and earth, of all things visible and invisible, "light from light," who spoke to men and who demands of everyone submission to His mysterious decrees, who will come to judge the living and the dead! Let all, therefore, be thus prepared to proclaim the greatness of God, to witness to the honor that is His due, and to admit that everything depends upon His total and free initiative (be it arbitrary or loving!). Let the Christians, then, be more aware than ever of being filled by the light of God Himself in all this "common patrimony" of the monotheists. Therefore, they must believe and then live to the maximum all these positive values which they discover also in their Muslim inquirers, especially because *this is the absolutely necessary condition for bringing out and highlighting these marvels* which are called in turn the Revelation of the divine Fatherhood, the Incarnation of the eternal Word, and the universal Redemption earned by Jesus Christ. As a consequence, the Christian should not be in too much of a hurry in speaking of the Son (an ambiguous word for the Muslim) and he should be *disposed to meditate and express at length the mystery of the eternal Word,* the most faithful Image of the Father, the Word from eternity and forever emitted and expressed, before confessing, in the end, that the Incarnation consists precisely in the gratuitous coming of this admirable Word into the midst of men, in the name of a Mercy and of a Love which witness exactly to the very Fatherhood of God and open to everyone the way that leads to filial adoption! It is really God Who comes to encounter men, to make them similar to Him—*and thus His transcendence is broadened!*—and it is never man who lifts and promotes himself to the point of reaching God to become His equal. Consequently, Christians should be attentive in a particular way to the mysteries of the suffering, death and resurrection of Jesus Christ. It is necessary, then, to know the historic proofs, derive the moral exigencies and describe at length the eschatological perspectives. Lastly, it would be appropriate to give special stress to the role and intervention of the Spirit "who has spoken by means of the prophets" and also to the mission and ministry of the Church as "the communion of saints" and guarantee of the "Kingdom that is to come."

In regard to "doctrine" itself, the catechist should be most convinced of the *"Christian newness"* in history and hence be capable of *making it emerge and irradiate his teaching.* Certainly, Christ did not come to destroy, but rather to bring all things to their fulfillment. Nevertheless, because of the extreme similarity of the Koranic message with so many passages from the Old Testament (especially the Torah, that is, the Pentateuch, and then the

Psalms), it appears so much more useful and necessary to reveal to Christians that all this belongs to the Old Testament, that is to say, to this "ancient world that has passed away": are they not perhaps new creatures in Jesus Christ? The Koran and the Old Testament are, therefore, superseded, and the catechist has the duty of *emphasizing the points of departure and of replacement,* so that the "newness of the Gospel and of the New Testament" can appear in full clarity; in fact, there is no longer room for a "Judaizing" Christianity of simple "believers"! From this point of view, one is instantly invited *to highlight* the historical value of the books of the New Testament, the normative character of the canonical texts, and the complementary value of the apocryphal texts of the Gospels (even while yet insisting on their fundamental difference from the canonical texts, because the Koran, objectively, refers much to their chapters, especially for the infancy of Jesus!). It is recommended, however, that a *presentation of Jesus as "perfect prophet"* be developed, utilizing for this the very method of St. Matthew: it is Jesus who brings all preceding prophecies to their fulfillment and fully realizes all the requisites of the true and perfect prophet. Christians should, therefore, know that this fullness of prophecy (and then its fulfillment in the very person of Jesus) corresponds to criteria and proofs which differ greatly and almost contrast according to whether one is a disciple of Christ or a follower of Islamism. Consequently, the catechist finds himself forced or, at least, led *to place at the center of his teaching this revelation of the "filial life" which the Christian must realize with Christ and in Christ:* "you are no longer slaves, but children!" (cf. Gal. 4:7) It is precisely in living "as children" under the gaze of the Father, in praying filially to the Lord and in fraternally loving all men that Christians *can demonstrate the "vital" importance of the Mysteries* of which they are freely made the confidants and beneficiaries. Therefore, the Christian must know that all his dignity lies precisely in this and that everything else comes as a consequence. In fact, does not perhaps the superior value of monogamous and indissoluble marriage stem from its mission to reflect "sacramentally" this unique love which God has for each one of His creatures? By simultaneously refusing every form of too facile syncretism and every type of exclusivism more or less egoistic, the Christian has, therefore, the obligation of being educated in such a manner that he will be capable of recognizing that the Muslim of good faith has all the "minimum of what is required for salvation" and to understand, at the same time, that he is lacking precisely this approach to and participation in "the fullness of God" of which he, the Christian, is beneficiary, solely through grace, and that he must be its witness by living and expressing it in a language which is comprehensible to the Muslims, that is, which corresponds to their intimate and secret religious aspirations.

May all of the Christian's rites of adoration, of intercession, and of thanksgiving, at home or in church, in private or in public, be thus impregnated by this "superior sense of the sacred," wherein is given proof that all creation participates in the very greatness of God, because of Jesus Christ! And since the Muslims are very sensitive to bodily gestures and exterior manifestations, should it not perhaps be hoped that Christians will know how *to intelligently take advantage of the treasures of their own liturgy?* Hence, let the places of worship (churches, sanctuaries, and chapels) always be clean, worthily adorned, and assiduously frequented by Christians; let the prayer and Eucharist of these Christians be always carried out there with great simplicity and much attention; and let Holy Scripture always find in them a place of honor (and let the Most Blessed Sacrament also have permanently in these places Its silent visitors and contemplative witnesses!). In a few words, *let the whole Christian cult* (Mass, sacraments, etc...) *be lived personally and communitarianly with dignity, authenticity and truth.* Furthermore, the feasts could furnish occasions for exchanges of gifts, wishes, visits, invitations, blessings, etc. Alms, fasts and pilgrimages would themselves also be enriched by concrete gestures of a "lived" offering and of assemblies of "sharing," where the Christian communities would give witness to their sense of God and of their fraternal solidarity. Catechesis could then have recourse to special forms of invocations and to popular kinds of literature where faith and prayer would be expressed in the local cultures and according to the specific character of the place: thus, the professions of faith, the festive hymns and blessings for many circumstances of life would find themselves clarified and reinforced by daily prayer intentions, by the litanies of the beautiful names of God and of Jesus and by meditation of the mysteries of the Rosary. In this case, the inquirers and the Muslim friends would find in these various expressions of the Christian faith the echo, more or less faithful and true, of many of their traditional religious expressions!

3. Necessary Collaboration and Possible Convergences

At this point, catechists and catechumens could develop *the various applications of the precepts of Christian charity*—love of God and love of the brethren being for them the one and only commandment entrusted to them by Christ. It is precisely the effectiveness of their actions that gives Christians their credibility and their faith its authenticity. The catechism should insist, as *Vatican Council II (Gaudium et spes)* reminded us, on the fundamental obligation of the Christian, and that is: *"to bring creation to its fulfillment"* through work, culture and "sharing," in total respect for creation itself (by means of a technology which respects "nature"); to *be wholly "at the service of all men, his brethren,"* because of their fundamental dignity (are they not all created to the image of their Creator?); and to *"organize a just and fraternal society,"* where the will of God—Who is love— would be realized in many concrete ways: the dignity of marriage and of the family (with the prevailing insistence on the rights of woman and child), promotion of the arts and sciences (with a special effort to harmonize faith and reason), economic and social balance (with generalized justice and no discrimination whatsoever), harmony of political societies (in a climate of pluralism which guarantees the peaceful coexistence of everyone) and the civil living together of all nations (through the affirmation, in hearts and minds, of the values of peace and of reconciliation).

Beyond these necessary collaborations, catechists would be invited furthermore to continue their efforts to explore and perhaps guess the *"possible religious convergences"* in which Christians and Muslims could dialogue at length and reciprocally enrich themselves (expressing always in this regard both their "common" experiences as well as their "specific" differences). They could: have the courage to speak together of the mystery of God; courageously attempt some exchange on the importance of the Word of God; make the effort to evaluate to the greatest extent the extraordinary mission of the prophets; appreciate together the importance of the support of the religious Community for the faith of believers; confidentially communicate the secret discoveries made by one and the other in authentic prayer; and finally, share the demands of sanctity which God reveals to men and women of lively faith! Even while always reminding the catechumens wherein *their own Christian characteristics* are to be found in all these experiences, the catechists would still have the duty of encouraging everyone to practice an honest discernment and thus *to discover the manifestations of the intervention of the Spirit of God* in the religious life of their Muslim questioners.

In other words, it is a matter of accustoming the catechists themselves to practice always more the various demands of the *"spirit of dialogue,"* so that the "Christian plenitude," all of whose specific aspects catechesis endeavors to have the catechized discover, will not be considered as a togetherness of truths "already possessed and treasured" nor even as a "treasure of which they would be the legitimate proprietors"; on the contrary, should not *this "Christian plenitude" be considered as a marvelous gift* which generates in the Christian himself a generosity and renewed benevolence toward those who still ignore it without any fault on their part? Hence catechists must be convinced more than ever of the merits and advantages of dialogue, because the Gospel itself makes it the best catechetical method (it is enough, in this regard, to refer to the dialogues of Christ in the various canonical Gospels). To dialogue means precisely to accept one another, to understand each other reciprocally, to attempt and to risk two converging discourses in which we know very well that the Spirit of God will know how to intervene, to convert one another, personally, to the new demands of the Lord and to share together the better part of the gifts received from God, in the certainty that the Holy Spirit will bring everything to its complete fulfillment.

These are the first reflections and a few proposals that can suggest the development of a catechesis for Christians who live in a Muslim context. In the same measure in which this context creates a specific situation where the Islamic imprint of the global society intervenes more or less heavily, one can and must imagine a catechetical education which will be capable of *"integrating"* *this very situation,* by then developing its adaptation in two very precise directions, and that is to *specify which is the common patrimony* so as to be able to share it to the maximum, and, at the same time, to *emphasize wherein lies the specific "Christian plenitude,"* in order that it may be lived totally and knowingly. By so doing, catechesis might prepare the Christian for dialogue with the Muslims (insofar as there is similarity) and lead him back to his profound identity (wherein precisely lies the dissimilarity). With the Muslims, must not Christians recognize themselves equally as men and women who believe, pray, fast, give alms and fulfill their pilgrimage? And among themselves, do not Christians have the duty of penetrating into their common condition as "adopted sons and daughters of God," henceforth conformed to the perfect Son, that is, Jesus Christ? In Christian education to the faith, and in preparing Christians for necessary human collaborations and possible religious convergences, a catechesis of this kind must, therefore, give ample information to the Christians about what the Muslims are and what they want to be; and it must stress in a particular manner certain aspects of the Creed, of doctrine and of liturgy. Thus, for the Christians there would be guaranteed and enriched a fidelity more necessary than ever before, and also an unexpected hope, and that is *to know how to understand and then love their Muslim friends* so that they can approach, with them, the mystery of God Himself and, when it is necessary, render an account to them "of the hope which lies in them" (cf. 1 Pt. 3:15).

MAURICE BORRMANS, P.B.

BRIEF BIBLIOGRAPHY

First of all, we recommend the theological commentary, the *Declaration "Nostra aetate" on the Relation of the Church to Non-Christian Religions of Vatican II,* by R. Caspar, "La religion musulmane" (pp. 201-236), in *Les relations de' l'Eglise avec les religions non chrétiennes,* Paris, Cerf, "Unam sanctam," no. 61, 1966, p. 325.

One could read a few of the documents and books of the *Secretariat for Non-Christians* (Via dell'Erba, Rome):

—*L'esperance qui est en nous: brève présentation de la foi catholique,* 1967, 38 p.

—*Le grandi religioni del mondo,* Rome, Ed. Paoline, 1977, 177 p.

—*Cristiani e Musulmani: Orientamenti per il dialogo fra Cristiani e Musulmani,* Rome, Ancora, 1971, 120 p. (A new edition, entirely corrected and particularly enriched, should be released soon.)

—*Religions, thèmes fondamentaux pour une connaissance dialogique,* Rome, Ancora, 1970, 611 p.

Also to be added in a partiuclar way is:

—*Recherches fraternelles: Pour vivre en amitié entre croyants,* Rome, S.T.I., s.d., 88 p. M. Borrmans, "Le dialogue islamo-chrétien des dix dernières années, Brussels, *Pro Mundi Vita,* 1978, no. 74, 60 p.

Madelaine De Morlaine e Anne-Marie Medous, *Un seul Dieu, tous frères,* Lyon Chalet, 1976.

6

Problems and Characteristics of Catechesis in Oceania

SITUATION

Oceania (the South Pacific) is a unique part of the world, quite different from any other. It sees itself also as being very much different from other developing or Third World countries. To accentuate this it often calls itself the *fourth world*, that is, the world of small island communities, scattered over the large area of the Pacific Ocean.

Isolated by long distances or rough seas, often overlooked and ignored because of the small number of inhabitants, lacking natural resources on the land and lacking funds and technology to exploit the resources in the ocean around, the countries of Oceania are faced with huge problems of communication.

On the few large islands—Papua, New Guinea, the Solomon Islands and Fiji—forests, mountains and swamps also isolate villages from each other. This isolation has resulted in the creation of an extraordinary number of mini-cultures and languages. With a total population of only four and a half million Oceania is the home of some 1,200 languages, about a quarter of all languages in the world.

On the positive side this isolation and diversity have given the Pacific communities—islands, villages, clans, and on the larger islands provinces or districts—a pronounced sense of identity and community. And Pacific Islanders are very keen to maintain this identity and see it recognized by others.

Despite the great distances and cultural differences there is intensive cooperation in political, socio-economic and religious fields.

In this chapter the terms Oceania and South Pacific refer to the islands extending from Papua, New Guinea, in the West to French Oceania in the East. Culturally Oceania is divided into three areas: Polynesia in the east (Tonga, Samoa, French Polynesia, Cook Islands, Wallis and Futuna, Tuvalu); Melanesia in the West (Fiji, New Hebrides, New Caledonia, Solomon Islands and Papua, New Guinea); and Micronesia just north of the equator (Kiribati—formerly Gilbert Islands—Nauru, Carolines, Marshalls, Guam and Marianas). New Zealand also has a substantial Polynesian population, but is not specifically considered in this chapter.

Predominantly Christian

Nearly all the countries in the region are predominantly Christian with percentages ranging from 70 to 100. Fiji is the only exception with a low 49% Christians, due to the big Indian immigrant population who make up slightly more than half the population.

Catholics, however, are a minority in most countries since most countries were evangelized by other Christian churches first before Catholics appeared on the scene, e.g., Papua, New Guinea, 31% Catholic; Fiji, 8% Catholic. The French Territories and Guam (evangelized by the Spanish), however, are predominantly Catholic.

The small population of the island countries (e.g., Cook Islands, 20,000) and furthermore the small size of the Catholic population (New Hebrides, 15,000 Catholics out of a population of 97,000) are a big handicap for developing effective structures and resources for catechetics or any other field.

Papua, New Guinea with a Catholic population of 804,000, 31% of the total of 3 million (2/3 of the total population of the Pacific), is in a much better position than any of the other countries. It is trying to make its resources available to the other countries, especially its high school religious education program, visual aids and "Controlled English" publications.

Ecumenical Cooperation

There is very good ecumenical cooperation on the national and international level. The Catholic Bishops' Conference of

Papua, New Guinea, and the Solomon Islands is a member of the Melanesian Council of Churches, and the Diocese of Tonga belongs to the Pacific Conference of Churches.

In the field of social communications Catholic organizations take part in the Pacific Regional Association of the World Association for Christian Communication (WACC). In Papua, New Guinea, the Churches Council for Media Coordination stimulates and streamlines all media efforts of the Churches, and in the Solomon Islands the Solomon Islands Christian Association (SICA) unfolds activities covering such areas as Christian education, family life, adult education, development and community building. However, on the local level, there is less ecumenical fervor, and traditional rivalries, misunderstandings, historical suspicion or personal differences often get in the way.

The Pacific area is organized in two Bishops' Conferences, the Catholic Bishops' Conference of Papua, New Guinea, and The Episcopal Conference of the Solomon Islands of the Pacific (CEPAC). There is a loose association with the Bishops' Conferences of Australia and New Zealand. The four Conferences meet once every three years, but the cooperation focuses mainly on development programs. In pastoral areas the deliberations touch on broad issues only.

The overall ratio of priests to Catholics is very high by world standards (in 50% of the dioceses 1,000 or less) but great distances, isolation and small communities put a limitation on pastoral activity. On the other hand, in the densely populated highlands of Papua, New Guinea, each priest in the diocese of Goroka has the care of 4,320 Catholics.

The author of this chapter writes from the Papua, New Guinean scene. Most of the material for this chapter was collected in Papua, New Guinea, and the Solomon Islands. I use the general term "Melanesia" to refer to these countries. In general lines it reflects the situation in the other Pacific Islands as well.

PROBLEMS FACING CATECHETICS

Hierarchical Image of the Church in Melanesia

In Melanesia catechetics is carried out mainly by priests, religious, catechists and teachers, the "official church." This situation has arisen because of the methods and structure of evangelization in the past. Missionary activity was, and nowadays pastoral activity still is, to a large extent centered around well developed parish stations, with church, school, parish hall, priest's house, often sisters' house, health center, etc. The priest mostly lives alone, and he uses his station as the base from which to work and to direct the work of catechists, and more recently of parish leaders. The Catholic Church has a very strong hierarchical image. But as a result of "The Self-study of the Catholic Church in Papua, New Guinea (1972-1975)" people slowly start to realize that "We are the church." But it is a very slow process indeed.

Role of Catechists

Most of the catechetical work is done by catechists. In recent years, great emphasis has been placed on in-service training of the village catechists. This has given them a much-needed morale boost, although it often appears difficult to raise the professional quality of the older catechists. Courses have also been given to parish leaders and a variety of other community leaders in pastoral training centers throughout the country. However, efforts to train catechists of a higher academic level have been successful in only a couple of places. Ten years ago already it was considered an urgent need, but most places still continue with the old type of lowly qualified if dedicated catechists.

Inadequate Christian Formation of Adults

Participation of the Christian community in catechesis is minimal in most places. Parents hardly contribute anything to the catechetical formation of their own children. They don't feel "capable" of providing a faith education even for their own children. This may partly be because the Gospel hasn't sufficiently touched their lives. But the major factor is a cultural one. In traditional culture, functions in the community are carried out by the person qualified for this. One is the orator, another peacemaker, fight leader, bridge builder, housebuilder, hunter, medicine man, instructor of initiation candidates, etc. The community relies on this expert. The hierarchical and sacramental church structure of the Catholic Church has re-enforced this cultural pattern. As a result Christian formation has been seen as the responsibility of the "official" church workers and it takes time to change this mentality. But the community is very adaptable. Priest shortage may already be enough to motivate the community to assume responsibility. It is reported from one diocese (Kieta, Bougainville, where in a short time a dozen parishes have been left without a priest) that in many places the Christian Community is coming alive and carrying out the tasks needed by the community.

The inadequate Christian formation of most Catholic adults is the basic problem facing the Church. In this regard the majority can best be described as quasi-catechumens, "who have never been able to study deeply the Christian teaching" (CT 44).

Christian Formation of Children

With regard to pre-school children the general attitude is often that "they are too young to learn." There are very few parents who would even teach the simple prayers or tell a simple story about God, our loving Father, or Christ our Savior to their children.

Once children go to school, they are very soon allowed to make their own decisions. And the parents really are at a loss as to how to educate their older children. Traditionally, in most communities, initiation was the first time that strict control was exercised over the youngsters. Otherwise, children were pretty much free to do what they liked. If ever the Pacific was a tropical paradise, it was a children's paradise. With the rapid changes of the modern time and all the outside influences even this little control has disappeared and parents often feel powerless.

Weak Christian Environment

The parents and the community generally fail to create a Christian environment. Traditional beliefs in spirits, evil forces and taboos are an inherent part of life, and the child grows up with them, and believes in them together with everybody else. The child doesn't get the same experience of the presence of God and of the saving power of Christ. Other factors, like payback, sorcery, tribal fights, are much more a part of life and prove stronger than any Christian teaching.

Failure To Christianize Traditional Values

The Church has failed to Christianize traditional values. But it is too simple to put all the blame on missionaries for this. According to anthropologist Crocombe *(Catalyst* 2, 1, p. 11), "when Pacific Islanders were converted to Christianity, they consciously set out to reject everything associated with traditional religions." This seems to be characteristic of the first stages of evangelization in many cultures, and is mentioned by many missionaries in writing of their efforts to Christianize traditional cultural values (see, e.g., Nilles, *Catalyst* 7, 3 p. 168: Simbu ancestors and Christian Worship).

However, it is necessary for Christians to come to terms with their traditional cultural values. Without them they will be a people without roots. Visiting Ghanaian theologian, Gottfried Osei-Mensah, declared at the National Seminar on Evangelism at Lae (1976): "The recovery and development of distinctive traditional virtues are our responsibility as national Christians both to develop and to use both for the enrichment of our worship and for the dignity of our people."

"Examples from Africa teach us that after a few years of Western contact tribal societies come to various forms of a renaissance of their traditional expressions and values. This can be observed already in some parts of Papua, New Guinea.... A revitalization of traditional concepts may be painful...but it can, if properly guided, lead to a very fruitful incorporation of traditional Melanesian values into the modern life of the people.

"It is a common experience, proved by sociologists and psychologists alike, that nobody—and no society—can live with a peaceful mind unless he has settled his past" (Hermann Janssen, *Tolai Myths of Origin,* 1973).

And this is also the mind of the Lord. "The Church is universal by vocation and mission, but when she puts down her roots in a variety of cultural, social and human terrains, she takes on different external expressions and appearances" *(Evangelii nuntiandi,* no. 62).

Torn Between Two Worlds

For the time being society is subject to great tensions, "torn between two worlds"—the world of tradition and modern Western ways with "freedom," permissiveness, massive drinking problem, materialism, greed, individualism, enslavement to money, marriage breakdown. In short, a clash between traditional and Western culture.

Materialism and individualism have taken hold even of some central values and institutions of traditional culture, such as clan-solidarity, brideprice, compensation, etc., and made a caricature of them.

Rapid change has caused turmoil. There are new laws, new beliefs, new customs, new occupations, new cash crops, new celebrations, new leaders. Nothing is familiar any more, nothing is predictable.

This unleashes reactionary forces especially in the religious sphere. Where everything falls apart, people want religious beliefs and practices to provide an anchor of stability. They see religion as the last stable element in their life. But where Christian teaching is poor and very rudimentary, it is grasped only in a superficial and often misguided manner, and so fails to provide this anchor.

THE CHURCH'S ANSWER

The Church has been very active, and in many cases imaginative in its efforts to answer this situation, and to strengthen the life of the community of believers.

Traditional Value of "Community"

There is, first of all, the traditional sense of "community," with all its mutual bonds and community obligations, and the security it offers individuals. This community sense draws people to their "One Talk," their clan brother, when in difficulties or when in a new environment, e.g., when they move to town.

This community sense can help people see the Church as the "clan of God." In the "Self-study of the Catholic Church in Papua, New Guinea (1972-1975)" the realization that *"we are the Church"* became the main focusing point. This has remained a stimulus for further reflection and an incentive for action over recent years.

In the diocese of Tonga an Education in Christian Living team made up of priests and religious, trained at the East Asian

Pastoral Institute, Manila, has given courses to 800 adult lay persons. These adults, in turn, are responsible in the villages for the teaching of children and adults in small groups. The program takes into account all aspects of Christian living, including the socio-economic. The highly successful Credit Union program in Fiji now forms part of the program in Tonga (G. Arbuckle, *The Church in the South Pacific*).

This Tonga program shows how the cultural value of a strong community sense can overcome the limitations imposed by isolation, small numbers and limited resources. Some areas in Solomon Islands and Papua, New Guinea, have adopted a similar approach on a local scale.

Basic Christian Communities

Also on a local scale a very promising development of Basic Christian Communities is taking place. In November, 1978, a consultation for pastors and leaders involved in these small Christian communities was held at Goroka. It was realized that in Pacific societies, both rural and urban, many natural bases exist on which to build local Christian communities—kinship groups, clan groups, "One Talk" groups, settlement groups. These natural groupings have long been self-dependent and accustomed to rely on local resourcefulness for the solution of problems. This history disposes a small Christian community's will to confront the challenge of transforming the life of their community according to the Word of God.

It also can dispose them to confront materialism and threats of socio-economic dependence imposed by the coming of modern economic and technological influences to this area. This latter affects in particular resource rich countries like Papua, New Guinea.

Basic Christian Communities as Locus of Christian Formation

Within these small Christian communities leaders and individuals in varying ways have taken care of Christian formation of their members and especially children and young people. Liturgies, prayer groups and Bible study groups have also grown well in these surroundings. Services of the Word have gained a permanent and prominent place in the life of these communities. However, the absence of Eucharistic Celebration in most communities is keenly felt. And many times calls are made for the ordination of Eucharistic Ministers to take away the anomaly of a Christian Community deprived of its "source and summit," the Eucharist.

When talking about small Christian communities in the Pacific it must be stressed that they are not copies of the basic Christian communities in Latin America or Africa. Noticeable is the absence in the Pacific of oppressive structures and extreme poverty. Pacific communities make it clear that they want to develop along their own patterns.

Life-Centered Catechesis

Recent catechetical efforts, even where not based exclusively on small Christian communities, have tried to be life-centered. This is especially true of the high school programs and the adult Christian education books. These programs emphasize that it is in the ordinary life experience of each man that he is to find God and establish a relationship with God, with Christ and with his fellow believers.

Communion With the Person of Christ

"At the heart of catechesis we find the Person of Jesus Christ" (CT 5). These programs are Christ-centered. They accompany young persons on their journey to get to know Christ as the Revelation of God the Father, with whom we relate in our life and with whom we enter into communion through prayer and the Sacraments.

Christianity—a Way of Life

Christianity then is a way of life, and not just a set of doctrines and a few religious rites and obligations. This catechesis deals with the problems facing young people and the society— responsibility for self and others, Christian love, boy/girl relationships, preparation for marriage, development, dignity of work. It equips them to cope with life in a rapidly changing society, and how to reappropriate traditional values and practices, and give these values a deeper sense in Christ.

Christian Fellowship

Prayer groups, Bible study groups and discussion groups are increasing. Young people and also adults feel a great need for fellowship. There is a growing openness to learn from other churches and adopt Bible camps, weekends, Easter camps and other fellowships more freely, and without feeling threatened.

However, quite a few young Catholics have left the Church and joined evangelical or charismatic groups. They say that they were not touched by the catechesis they received in primary and high school, that they didn't know Christ and were not able to pray to Him in a personal way. But recently a change is noticeable. Better catechetical methods and programs and better training of the teachers, together with the development in many communities towards a more committed Christian way of life, are in many ways responding to this challenge.

Christian Message and Ideals of Young People

In a number of areas the Christian message and young people are really on the same wave length, more so than the leading forces—political economical and social—of modern society. These common themes are: knowing Christ as a person, who cares for us as persons; the new sense of unity and community; the "soul" of our culture; stress on full human development and not just some material gains and pleasures and comfort; true freedom and mutual respect; equality of all; and concern for social justice. In all these areas the Church often speaks out as the conscience of the nation.

Catechetical Structures and Organization

It is realized that catechetical commissions, programs, materials and training courses are just resources. They are services enabling the believing community to meet the challenges. But the fact that programs and materials were locally developed and not imported from other places has contributed to their effectiveness. Compared to some five or ten years ago one now hears many remarks like "children and students are enjoying Christian education and getting better understanding and a greater interiorization." However, there are complaints of insufficient factual knowledge, and this often troubles parents and pastors. But here, too, are indications that Catholics are taking up the challenge of the proselytizing evangelical groupings with their ready knowledge of selected Bible texts, and are showing greater appreciation of factual knowledge and memorization of Scripture and Catholic teaching.

Social Communications and Catechesis

In Pacific countries great emphasis is placed on means of social communications. Radio is easily the most influential means of communication, bridging the vast distances. The churches are putting a high priority in manpower and resources in spreading the Christian message through the radio. Very effective are also the group media, especially sound-slide series. Other churches have developed an extensive "cassette ministry," but among Catholics this hasn't caught on as yet, maybe because we are not as Word-oriented as the other Christian churches. However, locally produced biblical wallcharts have made a big contribution to the spreading of the Gospel message and to the effectiveness of preaching. The same can be said of several good hymnbooks with authentic local hymns. A program to publish "Controlled English" editions of Vatican II Documents, other Church documents and books for religious formation (undertaken by the Mixed Commission of the Catholic Bishops' Conference together with men and women religious of Papua, New Guinea, and Solomon Islands) is making essential literature accessible to religious and educated laity who speak English as their second language. This program has been a great success and could serve as a model for other parts of the globe where many millions are depending on a second language for their training and information.

Ministries

To serve the needs of the Christian communities new ministries are developing and old ministries are being adapted or strengthened. The catechist is developing into a more mature minister. He is no longer the substitute for the faraway priest. In basic Christian communities a variety of leaders are emerging. And since people in the Pacific are comfortable with having natural leaders to guide and control the community, in many places these leaders are seeing to it that all community needs are met: teaching the Christian message to children and adults, leading prayers, counselling, mediating in disputes, visiting and helping the needy, etc. However, this encouraging development is limited to only a few places. It is a pity, that by and large the potential of these natural leaders in the believing community are not more actively fostered.

Absence of Overall Pastoral Policy

Many of these communities feel that the time is ripe for dioceses or Bishops' Conferences to coordinate pastoral policy and bring unity in these many isolated efforts. But apart from three or four dioceses this has not been done as yet.

SOME SHORTCOMINGS

Poor State of Adult Catechesis in Most Places

Despite the fact that all recent documents stress that "catechesis of adults is the principal form of catechesis" (CT 43) this is an often neglected area. It has matured only in the context of small Christian communities. Sure enough, in most places "catechetical moments" are being utilized, e.g., instructions of the parents when they bring children for baptism, marriage instructions. Many catechists visit family groups at night and pray, discuss and teach with them. But the teaching generally stays on the surface, and often has become a bit of a routine.

A few dioceses announced a theme for the year, e.g., Reconciliation, Eucharist or Family, and introduced parish missions and parish retreats. The first one or two years this was a great success. But after that many places reported a slackening off. This seems to point to the fact that "we have developed programs and not community" (Consultation in Christian Education, Suva, Fiji, 1977). Truly, we never get anywhere without community.

Failure To Minister to the Leaders

It has been said above that the Pacific area is predominantly Christian. Countries consider themselves Christian. In Papua,

New Guinea, this even has been laid down in the Constitution: "We, the people of Papua, New Guinea, pledge ourselves to guard and pass on...our noble traditions and the Christian principles..." (Preamble of the Papua, New Guinea Constitution).

It has been pointed out how central the place of leaders is in the Pacific communities. Most political leaders consider themselves active Christians, even if the relation to their own church is only lukewarm at times. Many former seminarians and priests are in government or public service. And a number of active priests are leaders in national or provincial government. It appears that their theological training has given them a strong commitment to dedicate their life to "full human development." However, the pastoral guidance of people in positions of leadership or potential leadership (political, academic or professional) is almost nonexistent. Several resolutions have been made, and a few attempts to carry them out, but without making much headway. Like the higher training of catechists this area seems to be eluding us, maybe because it needs a coordinated effort on a higher level, e.g., through the Bishops' Conference. It is clearly a matter of getting our priorities straight.

Conclusion

If one were to try to identify some characteristics of the Catholic Church in the Pacific, these would be:

The sense of community, natural communities as the basis of Christian communities and as locus of Christian formation.

The importance of dedicated leaders.

Self-reliance or self-dependence, despite lack of resources or small numbers.

Importance of good communications to cope with the demands of a modern technological world.

Importance of communicating on a level adapted to the community, e.g., by the use of "Controlled English."

May this contribution of a Church small in numbers be an inspiration to the universal Church.

FR. HENK TE MAARSSEN, S.V.D.

SELECTED BIBLIOGRAPHY

The Fourth World Meets, The Report of the Pacific Conference of Churches Assembly, Davuilevu, Fiji, May 1-14, 1971. PCC, Box 208, Suva, Fiji.

The Church Looks at Itself. National Assembly, May 1975. Self-study of the Catholic Church in Papua, New Guinea. Self-study Secretariat, Melanesian Institute, Box 571. Goroka.

Our Major Concerns, Self-study of the Catholic Church in Papua, New Guinea, Self-study Secretariat, Melanesian Institute, Box 571, Goroka.

"A Church Self-study in Papua, New Guinea," *Pro Mundi Vita* Dossiers. May 1976. Pro Mundi Vita, Rue de la Limite 6, B-1030 Brussels, Belgium.

"Simbu Ancestors and Christian Worship, Fr. John Nilles, SVD, in *Catalyst,* (1977) Vol. 7, no. 3, pp. 163-190. Melanesian Institute, Box 571, Goroka.

"Which Way for Christian Education?" Roxanna Coop, in *Catalyst* (1977) Vol. 7, no. 2, pp. 127-146. Melanesian Institute, Box 571, Goroka.

"The Church in the South Pacific," Fr. Gerald Arbuckle, *Pro Mundi Vita* Dossiers. Sept-October, 1978.

"Consultation on Basic Christian Communities," held and the Melanesian Institute, Goroka, Nov. 20-25, 1978, *Catalyst* (1979) Vol. 9, no. 2, pp. 121-146.

Christian Education in Papua, New Guinea, and the Solomon Islands. A Survey. April 1977. Liturgical Catechetical Institute, Box 347, Goroka.

Not To Destroy but To Fulfill, Fr. Kevin Barr, MSC, 1979, Chevalier, Press, Kensington. Australia.

Christ in Melanesia, Exploring Theological Issues, 1977, Melanesian Institute, Box 571, Goroka.

7

Development of Catechesis in North America

The mission of transmitting and teaching the faith is an essential part of the Church's life at every period of history and in every geographical location. Missionaries from Europe in the sixteenth century engaged in a catechetical ministry for the first Catholic settlers in Quebec and the Spanish-ruled provinces of American South and West. Not only the Catholics but the native Indian inhabitants were the objects of this ministry.

The Jesuit martyrs of North America gave their lives in the midst of their efforts to catechize the Huron Indians. One of the outstanding fruits of their catechizing was the Indian maiden, Catherine Tegahkouita, who became such a model of Christian fervor and virtue. The Franciscan missionaries of the California area succeeded in peacefully establishing mission centers all down the Pacific Coast where the faith was taught to the natives.

In the early American colonies founded largely by the British the number of Catholics was small and there was a strong anti-Catholic prejudice. Catholics were prohibited by law from having their own schools and discouraged from religious practice by the Protestant Puritans. The Quebec Act of 1774 granted religious freedom to the Catholics of Canada, and the French influence in that province made religious instruction and practice develop quickly.

In the American colonies the public school system was totally dominated by a Protestant influence with Reformation-style hymns and reading of the King James Bible a regular part of the daily school schedule. Often the schools were centers of Protestant evangelization.

For these reasons, religious instruction for the early Catholic colonists had to be given primarily at home. Priests were very few and outside of a few cities Catholics would be lucky to see a priest and have Mass and formal instruction two or three times a year.

Father John Carroll, Superior of the American Missions (later to be the first American bishop), lamented in a report to the Propaganda Fide in Rome on March 1, 1785, that his Catholic flock showed "...a general lack of care in instructing their children and especially the negro slaves in their religion."

In the nineteenth century the American bishops promoted the establishment of separate Catholic schools as the best means of ensuring religious instruction and moral training. The First and Second Plenary Councils of Baltimore in 1852 and 1866 passed legislation promoting the construction of such schools and urging parents to utilize them. The bishops also commissioned the writing of a uniform catechism to be used in all Catholic schools and catechetical programs. It became known as the Baltimore Catechism and was the standard catechetical text up until the Second Vatican Council. The result was a remarkable uniformity of faith expression among all Catholics in the country.

As the number of Catholic schools grew, legislation was passed insisting that Catholic parents place their children in such schools for the ideal kind of religious instruction. Many communities of religious women and men came to America to staff these schools, and a native order was established by St. Elizabeth Seton.

The concern of the Holy See for proper religious education at this period is evidenced in an Instruction sent to the American bishops by Propaganda Fide decreeing that:

Before a child can be conscientiously placed at a public school, provision must be made for giving it the necessary Christian training and instruction, at least out of school hours. Hence parish priests and missionaries in the United States should spare no labor to give children thorough catechetical instructions, dwelling particularly on those truths of faith and morals which are called most in question by Protestants and unbelievers.

The latter part of the nineteenth century and the first part of the twentieth were characterized by a great influx of immigrants from every nation in Europe to the United States and an ever Westward movement of peoples across the plains of the United States to the West Coast. Remarkably, the Church kept pace with this expansion and Catholic schools were multiplied, and where they were lacking, catechetical programs were developed for the religious instruction of the children.

The content of the instruction tended to be theological in tone, and memorization was a major catechetical strategy. Frequently pastors would come to the school or religion class to hear the children recite the answers memorized from the Baltimore Catechism. The whole approach was characterized by stability and a marked national uniformity.

The past twenty years (1960-1980), in contrast to the preceding years, have been a period of extraordinary development and change in the catechetical apostolate in North America. At the same time it has been a period of some contestation and polarization in the area of religious education. This period has come to a climax in the promulgation of the National Catechetical Directory, sponsored by the American bishops and approved by the Holy See.

Certain major changes began in this period:

1. Those doing the formal catechizing up to this point were almost exclusively priests and religious. In the 50's parish units of the Confraternity of Christian Doctrine were erected and a growing number of volunteer lay persons became involved in the teaching especially of young people who were not enrolled in Catholic schools. These lay volunteers were zealous but sometimes not adequately prepared for their important task. Presently dioceses have begun programs of certification for these volunteers to give them the needed doctrinal and methodological training.

2. A gradual decline in the number of Catholic schools ended the dream of having every Catholic child receive religious instruction in the setting of a Catholic school. The American government and Courts have been very restrictive about any form of aid either to Catholic schools directly or to the parents by tax relief. Thus, Catholic parents who send their children to Catholic schools are doubly taxed—they must support the public schools and also pay an increasingly larger tuition to send their children to a Catholic school. The result is that now the majority of Catholic children must receive their religious instruction in non-school parish programs on their own free time.

Canada has been fortunate to be able to have a government-funded separate school system in which Catholic children may receive a school education under full Catholic influence. Large numbers of laity teach religion in these schools, and constant attention is given by the Canadian Church to ensure that they are adequately prepared for this part of their responsibility.

3. Changes in catechetical technique have been widely introduced and this has been the reason for no little contestation and polarization. The Baltimore Catechism in the United States emphasized a largely question and answer approach and a theological style that was not influenced by the scriptural, liturgical and theological movements of the twentieth century. For this reason alternative catechetical texts began to be published by commercial publishers.

These newer texts employ a more experiential approach and seek to adopt the content to the psychological and learning stage of the student. The primary grade materials, for example, seek to arouse in the child basic religious attitudes of adoration, wonder, trust and thanksgiving towards God. The programs emphasize direct parental involvement in the catechesis and often include special parent books to go along with the children's texts.

The textbook publishing for the Church in the United States is done by commercial publishers. There are about ten different total programs for grades one to eight to choose from. They represent varied emphases—some are more content-oriented while others are more experience-oriented.

The Canadian Church in 1966 decided on a National Catechism for all of Canada sponsored by the hierarchy. This program, known as *Come to the Father* (grades 1-4 and 7-8) and *Born of the Spirit* (grades 5 and 6), is available in both French and English-speaking versions and is published by the Canadian Catholic Conference in Ottawa. It is currently being revised. It employs a Trinitarian orientation in the younger grades and a methodology that emphasizes the experiential and developmental.

There has been some controversy and even polarization in North America as a result of the newer approaches to catechetics. To some there appears to be less doctrinal content and substance in the textbooks and programs. They fear that there has been an overemphasis on pedagogy to the detriment of doctrinal substance.

One result of this controversy is the American bishops' document entitled *Basic Teachings for Catholic Education*, in which the bishops list those doctrinal and moral truths which should be transmitted in catechetical programs.

4. A very significant development in North America has been the emergence of full-time, professionally trained parish coordinators or directors of religious education. This role, which is an American version of the catechist in the mission countries, is often held by religious or lay persons who have completed a Masters Degree program in catechetics in a University. While it is only about fifteen years old there are now thousands of these full-time parish workers.

The role descriptions for coordinators/DRE's differ somewhat from place to place but generally they include a combination of administrative responsibility for designing and organizing a parish program and catechetical responsibility for training the teachers, preparing the sacramental programs and even doing adult education—at least with the parents of the children involved in the program.

The rapidity with which such personnel have been introduced indicates the need that was felt in parishes to have someone qualified devoting full-time attention to the catechetical programs. What is especially significant is the large number of lay persons who have assumed this role.

As the number of parish coordinators/DRE's has increased, diocesan religious education offices developed processes for screening, evaluating and placing qualified candidates in parishes. Programs for the in-service training and ongoing education of coordinators/DRE's have been developed in many dioceses and there is now a National Association of Parish Coordinators/Directors of Religious Education centered at the National Catholic Educational Association in Washington, D.C.

There are problems with this development which still need to be addressed, e.g., the clear identity of the role, proper support systems, professional development and financial considerations. A study of parish coordinators/DRE's was done by the United States Catholic Conference in 1978. It revealed a wide disparity of educational and theological background in those fulfilling the role and much variety in terms of job expectations and roles. While much needs to be done for the further development of this role there is no doubt that its existence is a hopeful and promising factor for parish catechetics in North America.

5. A more recent development that is very significant for catechetics in North America is the emergence of newer models for programming. These models transcend the school and class-

room model which until now has been dominant and involve more direct participation in the process of religious learning by the parents and even by the whole family together.

The principles utilized by advocates of these models are solid. They note that faith is not primarily the learning of doctrinal concepts but a whole way of life based on Revelation. This way of life is above all communicated and absorbed by exposure to a believing community. The family should be a "miniature Church," a living cell of the wider parish community. Both groups are the primary nurturers of faith.

The school/classroom model of catechetics tends to isolate the child's religious learning from these communities. Too often parents felt their duty to rear their children in faith was accomplished by merely sending the child to religion classes.

The more family-oriented models of religious instruction have been most widely used in North America in connection with the preparation of children for the sacraments. On the occasion of Baptism, first Eucharist, first Penance and Confirmation parents are obliged to participate in catechetical sessions at which they are presented on an adult level with the same concepts and truths being presented to their children on a more elementary level. They are also shown ways in which they can reinforce this learning and formation process at home.

More advanced models of family sacramental catechesis involve the entire family coming to the parish together. For instance one popular program for preparing children for first Communion involves nine three-hour sessions for the whole family together—often on a Sunday afternoon. Each session deals with a theme related to the Eucharist. Children are divided up by age levels and parents meet together. All study the theme at their level. Then the whole family comes together and works on an activity or project that expresses the meaning of the theme. Finally, a liturgical or para-liturgical celebration for all the families together culminates the experience.

Some classroom and peer group religious instruction will always be necessary but the growth of unified family learning is a very promising development in North American catechetics.

The Apostolic Exhortation of Pope John Paul II, *Catechesi tradendae,* comes at an opportune moment and will be a valuable yardstick against which catechetical efforts can be measured for some time to come. For religious educators in the United States it comes closely after the promulgation of the National Catechetical Directory, entitled *Sharing the Light of Faith*. This document is the end product of a lengthy process that began not long after the promulgation of the *General Catechetical Directory* in 1971.

The National Catechetical Directory was prepared in dialogue with hundreds of thousands of persons in the United States through three extensive consultations whose results were computerized and analyzed by a coordinating committee of bishops, religious education experts and knowledgeable laypersons. It consists of eleven chapters:

Chapter I: Cultural and Religious Characteristics Affecting Catechesis in the United States
Chapter II: The Catechetical Ministry of the Church
Chapter III: Revelation, Faith and Catechesis
Chapter IV: The Church and Catechesis
Chapter V: Principal Elements of the Christian Message for Catechesis
Chapter VI: Catechesis for a Worshiping Community
Chapter VII: Catechesis for Social Ministry
Chapter VIII: Catechesis Toward Maturity in Faith
Chapter IX: Catechetical Personnel
Chapter X: Organization for Catechesis
Chapter XI: Catechetical Resources

The Directory is very comprehensive in its scope and represents the most significant publication for American catechetics since the Baltimore Catechism. Its directives are now being applied to diocesan and parish programs across the country, and it is intended that approximately five years after its approval by the Holy See it be submitted to an evaluation and review by the National Conference of Catholic Bishops.

Catechesi tradendae reinforces many of the directives of the National Catechetical Directory and gives them the further authority of Papal approbation. The tone of the Apostolic Exhortation is less technical and more obviously pastoral than that of the National Catechetical Directory. For these reasons it is likely to have an extensive and appreciative audience in North America. It also has a strong and distinctive Christocentric spiritual flavor throughout that will be very inspiring to catechists.

At a moment when—in the United States especially—pastoral priorities are being reviewed, there is a regrettable decline of

Catholic schools, and financial and personnel resources are becoming scarce, the Holy Father's clear words are most timely:

"As the 20th century draws to a close, the Church is bidden by God and by events—each of them a call from Him—to renew her trust in catechetical activity as a prime aspect of her mission. She is bidden to offer catechesis her best resources in people and energy, without sparing effort, toil or material means, in order to organize it better and to train qualified personnel. This is no mere human calculation; it is an attitude of faith. And an attitude of faith always has reference to the faithfulness of God, who never fails to respond" (CT 15).

The Pontiff's balanced handling of the difficult pastoral issue of content versus method will be very helpful to catechists in North America as they strive to achieve this balance. He draws attention to the need for a systematic and programmed presentation of doctrinal content that deals with all the essentials and does not stop short at only the kerygma (no. 21). At the same time he recognizes that many young people who were baptized and come to our programs have no real personal commitment to Jesus Christ or His Church (no. 19) and, therefore, cannot be given a catechesis that is "isolated from life or artificially juxtaposed to it" (no. 22).

Especially relevant to the North American scene, which is characterized by religious pluralism, is the Holy Father's treatment of the ecumenical dimension of catechesis (nos. 32, 33). He notes that our religious education programs must "prepare Catholic children and young people, as well as adults, for living in contact with non-Catholics, affirming their Catholic identity while respecting the faith of others." The Pontiff even envisions "experiences of collaboration in the field of catechesis between Catholics and other Christians, complementing the normal catechesis."

As North American religious educators focus more and more on adult religious education they will be heartened by Pope John Paul's statement that "this is the principal form of catechesis" (no. 43). Many initiatives and experiments with adult education are taking place at the present time. They meet with mixed success. Yet, the catechesis of children depends in no small degree for its effectiveness on the quality of faith of the adult community which witnesses to it.

In his treatment of means of catechesis the Pope draws attention to "the great possibilities offered by the means of social communication and the means of group communication: television, radio, the press, records, tape recordings—the whole series of audio-visual means" (no. 46). The invention of printing and the publication of the Bible in the sixteenth century marked an enormous advance for the work of evangelization. The Church has yet to adequately exploit the potential for evangelization in the media possibilities offered by recent technology. Because of its access to this technology North America has a special obligation to heed the Pope's exhortation and make a greater effort in this direction.

The catechetical mission of the Church is perennial and yet in each age it needs to be renewed by the fresh impulses of the Spirit. As one looks back over three hundred years of catechetical activity on the North American continent, enormous growth and development is obvious. Strengthened by the pastoral wisdom of Pope John Paul II and confident of the abiding presence of the Spirit, religious educators can with serene confidence continue their preaching and teaching of the mystery of Jesus Christ.

REV. FRANCIS KELLY

8

Catechesis in the Documents of the Church in Latin America

The Extraordinary Latin-American Postconcilium

To speak of catechesis in Latin America means first of all to refer in a wholly particular way to the period of the last fifteen years, which saw the beginning and the affirmation of a Latin-American pastoral conscience and the assumption of operative directives of enormous ecclesial importance. Two well-known episcopal assemblies, Medellin (1968) and Puebla (1979), are the emerging peaks of a vast movement of reflection and action which not only chose to "apply" to the Latin-American continent the innovating directives of Vatican Council II, but succeeded in re-creating the Council within the concrete historical and cultural coordinates of Latin America, especially by means of a courageous awareness of the profound socio-cultural transformations of the continent and of the decision to incarnate the witness of the Gospel into the real historical adventure of the Latin-American people.

With regard to catechesis, the postconciliar movement of renewal expresses itself especially, even if not exclusively, in a few emerging facts of great significance. To be remembered first of all is the *International Week of Catechesis* of Medellin, of August, 1968,[1] which marked an important turning point in the world-wide catechetical movement, but which especially represented for Latin America a decisive leap forward toward the full inculturation of the educative dynamism of faith. Celebrated a few days later, the Episcopal Assembly of Medellin made extensive use of the results of the Week, elaborating the eighth document of its conclusions, dedicated to *catechesis*—a brief, essential document, but packed with content and with a decisive bearing on the opening of a new catechetical era in Latin America.[2] The ten years separating Medellin from Puebla will be characterized by the progressive assimilation and maturation of the priorities of Medellin, not without tensions, perplexities and polemics, provoked understandably by a newness of catechetical presentation which found many unprepared and others too daring. The recent Assembly of Puebla, which in general represented a calmer reflection and consolidation of the directives of Medellin, represents also for catechesis an ecclesial and magisterial *locus* of prime importance, and this not so much, or not only, because of the articles of the final document dedicated to catechesis,[3] but more because of the general priorities concerning evangelization, which open new and significant perspectives for the carrying out of catechesis.[4]

The Latin-American Way of Pastoral Renewal

Before entering into the merit of the Latin-American catechetical situation, it seems necessary to emphasize those operative peculiarities which constitute the "Latin-American way" of pastoral renewal, those characteristics, that is, having to do with both method and content, without which it is impossible adequately to understand the significance of the pastoral choices made. Concretely I would like to refer to these points:

1. In Latin America it has become proverbial, already from the time of Medellin, to elaborate pastoral documents according to a three-part outline which characterizes the procedure followed. That is, one begins with a description and analysis of the *situation*, then proceeds to a *theological interpretative reading* of the same, without forgetting the search for the causes (even structural) of that situation, and one concludes with *pastoral orientations* of a practical nature. Such a methodology guarantees a strong adherence to concrete historical reality. It prevents the classical defect of pastoral deductivism, and makes it possible for the Latin-American documents to be so relative to the local situations as not to be able to be estimated and applied to other regions of the world without remaking them. Furthermore, another important pastoral consequence follows: the consecration of

pluralism as an exigency of pastoral realism, even in the interior of the diverse Latin-American regions, precisely in homage to the general principle of respect for concrete historical situations.

2. In Latin America *"reflection on practice"* is often spoken of as a basic method for theological elaboration. Speaking in general terms, and beyond possible epistemological specifications which the problem would call for, there emerges the fact that theological and pastoral *reflection* unravels itself beginning from ecclesial *action* in its various manifestations. Therefore, it is a theology eminently "pastoral" in all its expressions, matured in action and oriented to action.

3. The great stands of the Latin-American Church, and especially the documents of Puebla, are the result of. a *vast collaboration among the different levels of ecclesial reality:* basic communities, local churches, experts, national episcopates, etc. Differing from many other episcopal assemblies or documents in other parts of the world, it can be said that the works of Puebla are for the greater part the result of the reflection and action of the *whole* Latin-American Church.

4. An unequivocal attitude of the pastoral orientation of Latin America—already clearly affirmed at Medellin—is the *decisive assumption of the Latin-American reality and of its historical process* as a *locus* for the realization of the mystery of salvation which the Church must proclaim and witness. Continuing the dynamics of the *ecclesiology of service* matured in Vatican II, especially in *Gaudium et spes*, the Latin-American Church intends to rediscover her mission in the historical reality of the Latin-American people, a reality subjected to an accelerated transformation and characterized by a situation of injustice in a certain sense institutionalized.

5. Consequently, we can say that, starting with Medellin, the Latin-American Church has acquired *an awareness of her originality* in the great concert of the universal Church.•If at first the theological and pastoral formulas present in the continent were simple assumptions or adaptations of the European experience, today Latin America has decisively set out on the path of searching for ways of its own, more in harmony and correspondence with its own cultural and historical genius.

All of these characteristics and methodological applications also have repercussions in the field of catechesis and of catechetical reflection. In this sense we can say that Latin America has already taken notable steps forward in that process of the "inculturation" of education to the faith of which the last synod of bishops spoke.

The Great Options of the Latin-American Pastoral

Catechesis is found in the heart of the pastoral action of the Church. As such, it constitutes the primary factor in ecclesial renewal and is conditioned at the same time by the global pastoral context into which it is inserted. It is for this reason that it seems appropriate to have before us the horizon of the pastoral options that have matured during the last years in Latin America. It is not a matter of trying to give a complete picture, but only of recalling those characteristic priorities that can especially influence the physiognomy and function of catechesis. In a very schematic listing they can be synthesized thus:

1. *Option for evangelization.* The rediscovery of evangelization as the essential mission of the Church and central axis of her action forms part of the Latin-American ecclesial conscience, as the general theme of the Assembly of Puebla attests: "Evangelization in the present and in the future of Latin America." It is difficult to exaggerate the pastoral importance of this fundamental choice: it means we must no longer apply ourselves only in the moral and liturgical-sacramental fields, but also and above all in the process of reawakening the faith and bringing it to maturity with an extensive work of missionary evangelization.

2. *Option for the poor.* Repeating the words of the Pope in Mexico, the Assembly of Puebla confirmed the will of the Church to want to keep herself free from all connivance or enslavement to be able to "opt only for man" (Puebla 551). And then it explains this choice in the *preferential option for the poor,* in continuity with the decisions of Medellin: "We affirm the necessity of the conversion of the whole Church to a preferential choice in favor of the poor, for the purpose of achieving their integral liberation" (Puebla 1134).

3. *Option for liberation.* We know how much significance the Medellin choice for the *integral liberation* of man had and has for Latin America, as also the difficulties and controversy which the liberating practice encounters. Now, Puebla chose to confirm the liberating option, even with the preoccupation of working out a clarification and a discernment of the authentic in-

tegral liberation of man in the light of the gospel (Puebla 470-506). In the light of the centrality of evangelization, the liberating option becomes a priority for a *liberating evangelization:* "The best service to our brother is evangelization, which disposes him to realize himself as a son of God, frees him from injustices and develops him totally" (Puebla 1145).

4. *Option for popular religiosity.* Overcoming the temptation to become closed up in a pastoral elite of small groups or specialized movements, Latin America has become aware, throughout the entire postconciliar period, of the importance of popular religiosity, and of the necessity of discerning its inherent values and of distinguishing these from the alienating traits hidden therein. It is in this perspective that the pastoral task *of evangelizing popular religiosity* is advocated (Puebla 457-459), by daring to undertake a work "of pastoral pedagogy, in which popular Catholicism is accepted, purified, completed and dynamized through the Gospel" (Puebla 457).

5. *Option for the evangelization of culture.* This is the process of assumption and of purification, of incarnation and of conversion which the proclamation of the Gospel must work in the historical framework of the Latin-American cultures, in such a way as to overcome the defects of imported pastoral and certain eclecticisms unworthy of the Gospel. Puebla makes itself the promoter of an evangelization which seeks to "reach the roots of culture, the zone of its fundamental values, awakening a conversion which can be the foundation and guarantee of the transformation of structures and of the social ambient" (Puebla 388).

6. *Option for youth.* In a continent where young people constitute the vast majority of the population, the Church is aware of their pastoral importance, not only as the object of pastoral action but also as leaders in it: "The youth must feel that they are Church, by experiencing her as a place of communion and participation" (Puebla 1184). The result is a solemn and clear pastoral choice: "The Church trusts in youth. They are her hope. The Church sees in the youth of Latin America a real potential for the present and the future of her evangelization. Seeing in them truly a wellspring of dynamism for the social body, and especially for the ecclesial body, the Church makes a preferential choice for youth, in view of her evangelizing mission in Latin America" (Puebla 1186).

7. *Option for basic ecclesial communities and for new ministries.* The basic ecclesial communities ("communautés de base"), original creation of the Latin-American Church, are by now a reality of decisive importance in the reconstruction of the ecclesial fabric of Latin America. Notwithstanding the numerous problems connected with their presence and activities, Puebla saw in them a reason for joy and hope, recognizing that in a short time they have become a fulcrum for evangelization and works of liberation and of development (Puebla 96). The Latin-American bishops do not limit themselves to affirming their validity, but they make them the object of pastoral choice: "As pastors, we decisively want to promote, orient and accompany the Basic Ecclesial Communities, according to the spirit of Medellin and the criteria of *Evangelii nuntiandi*, number 58" (Puebla 648). Related, although not exclusively, to the development of the basic communities, there is also a *flowering of new ministries*, especially of laity, which represent a significant and very promising aspect of Latin-American pastoral action.

8. *Option for communion and participation.* This is the theme of the third part of the Puebla Document, and in a way it sums up the pastoral ideal of a Church which wants to put herself at the service of God's unifying plan, not in an abstract manner, but in the knowledge of having to battle to remove the structural and individual causes which impede real communion and participation, in society and in the Church. In this sense, it is a global option which is to be organically bound with the exigencies of evangelization and of liberation. As a Latin-American theologian sums up well: "A priority mission of the Church and of her evangelizing action is to create communion and participation in all human and divine goods through a process of liberation *from* everything that impedes progress towards this end, and a process of liberation *for* what opens the way to the attainment of this goal."[5]

The picture of pastoral options which has been presented is certainly not complete, nor does its skeletal form permit an adequate grasp of its contents and values, but I believe it sufficient to define the *humus pastorale*, in which Latin-American catechesis flourishes and matures. It is in the light of the evangelizing and liberating dynamism of Latin-American pastoral action and in the heart of its lucid priorities that the identity and originality of the catechetical renewal can be grasped.

The Identity of Latin-American Catechesis

If one were asked what traits or dimensions characterize—at least in a synthetic approximation—the new face of Latin-American catechesis, perhaps one would not be far from the truth if one listed the following characteristics: "situational," liberating, evangelizing, Christocentric, biblico-existential, communitarian, permanent. We will seek briefly to explain the significance of these features.

1. *"Situational" catechesis.* This is the most notable feature and great novelty of the catechetical document of Medellin, the most original aspect of the Latin-American catechetical renewal, the qualitative change which then aroused the enthusiasm of many in its realization but also provoked the trepidation of not a few. "Situational" catechesis—also called "prophetic" catechesis—means not only that attention is directed to the "man in his situation" as the object of catechesis, not only that catechesis must be faithful "to the Latin-American man" (Puebla 996),[6] but also that the situation—that is, the concrete problems, needs and hopes of men—must become the *content* of catechesis. Medellin has expressed this exigency in unforgettable terms:

> Present catechesis must totally take up the anxieties and hopes of the man of today to offer him the possibilities of a complete liberation: the treasures of an integral salvation in Christ the Lord. Therefore, it must be faithful to the transmission not only of the biblical message in its intellectual content, but also to its vital reality incarnate in the events of the life of the man of today. *Historical situations* and authentically human aspirations are an indispensable part of the content of catechesis (Medellin 8, 6).

Certainly, it is necessary to recognize that concrete practice has not always known how to avoid the danger of unilateralism and improper reductionism, as even the very document of Puebla[7] admits. But the solution does not lie in counterposing a catechesis of situation to a catechesis of message, a catechesis as an illumination of life to a doctrinal catechesis, but in overcoming every dualism and false antithesis. Word for word, the document of Puebla says:

> One often falls into dichotomies and false antitheses, like that between sacramental catechesis and the catechesis of

practical life; situational catechesis and doctrinal catechesis. Not finding a right balance, some have fallen into the
cult of pure formulas, others into life experience without the
presentation of doctrine, and still others have gone from
memorization to the total absence of memory (Puebla 988).

2. *Liberating catechesis.* Because it is faithful to man in his
situation, catechesis necessarily takes on his state of injustice and
of oppression to become an instrument of integral liberation.
Here, too, Medellin pronounced words of great incisiveness:

> Today Latin America is living a historic moment which
> catechesis cannot ignore: the process of social transforma-
> tion, demanded by the present situation of *need and injus-
> tice*, in which vast segments of society find themselves
> 'marginalized.' It is up to catechesis to help the integral
> evolution of man by giving him its authentic Christian
> meaning, by promoting its motivation in the baptized, and
> by orienting it toward fidelity to the Gospel (Medel-
> lin 8,7).

Even while taking into consideration the tensions and problems which this priority creates, Puebla has confirmed it, considering that the situation not only continues to be dramatic
(Puebla 27-50) but has outrightly become worse (Puebla 46). In
this context, liberating evangelization is the necessary response to
the "challenge" of the situation (Puebla 90), the answer to the
"cry of a people which suffers and which asks for justice, liberty
and respect for the fundamental rights of man and of peoples"
(Puebla 87).

3. *Evangelizing catechesis.* This expression (rather unusual
at that time) already appears in the catechetical document of
Medellin, which states that catechesis "must be eminently
evangelizing without presupposing a reality of faith except after
appropriate verification" (Medellin 8,9). And immediately
thereafter, the pastoral motivation is offered:

> Already the fact of baptizing infants, trusting in the
> faith of the family, makes it necessary to have 'an evan-
> gelization of the baptized,' as a stage in their education in
> the faith. And this necessity is more urgent if we consider
> the disintegration which the family is undergoing in many
> regions, the religious ignorance of adults, and the scarcity of
> basic Christian communities (*ibid*).

The option is clearly reconfirmed at Puebla, which speaks of catechesis as an "evangelizing work" (Puebla, 992) and includes *conversion* among the objectives of the permanent process of catechesis (1007).

4. *Christocentric catechesis.* The necessity of Christocentricity, which belongs to the general history of the catechetical renewal, takes on a special significance in Latin America, insofar as it not only tends to assure fidelity to the unifying heart of the Christian message, but also sees in Christ that perfect synthesis of the human and the divine, of history and eternity, of the immanent and the transcendent, which permits catechesis to find its point of convergence and overcome the traditional dualisms of an easily disincarnated if not outrightly alienating religiosity. It seems that here, too, we are obliged to refer to the noted expressions of Medellin:

> Without falling into confusion or into simplistic identifications, we must always express the profound unity which exists between the divine plan of salvation realized in Christ, and the aspirations of man; between the history of salvation and human history; between the Church, the people of God, and temporal communities; between the renewing action of God and the experience of man; between the supernatural gifts and charisms and human values.
>
> Thus excluding every dichotomy or dualism in Christianity, catechesis prepares for the progressive realization of the people of God up until its eschatological fulfillment, which now has its expression in the Liturgy (Medellin 8,4).

As Puebla amply developed in the central part of the final document, fidelity to Christ as the image of the Father and as revealer of the dignity and destiny of man and as Lord of history must confer on the whole evangelizing effort the guarantee of unity and integrity, and fidelity to the plan of integral liberation.

5. *Biblico-existential catechesis.* The Bible's encounter with the existential reality of the Latin-American man appears as the substantial answer to one of the most felt needs in today's catechetical problem: the question of *language*. In Latin America the effort of reconciling the people to the reading of Sacred Scripture has been greatly strengthened, as is attested by the noted edition of the "Latin-American Bible." Having taken into consideration the existence of "a more profound love for Sacred

Scripture as the principal font of catechesis" (Puebla 981), the document of Puebla then confirms *the primacy of the Bible as the font of catechesis* in the pastoral recommendations (1001). But on the other hand there is also an awareness of the necessity of incarnating the language into the existential categories of the men of today, "giving the word to the people of God"[8] and incarnating it in their culture: "Fidelity to the Latin-American man requires that catechesis penetrate, assume and purify the values of its culture and that as a consequence it apply itself in the use and adaptation of catechetical language" (Puebla 996).

Puebla re-echoes and continues an appeal already strongly felt at Medellin, where the problem of language was perceived to be much more than a simple matter of words—as a condition needed so that the message of the Church will appear to everyone as the word of life, as good news for man in his situation. Because of this, it is not enough simply to repeat or explain the message: "On the contrary, it is necessary to incessantly re-express the Gospel in a new way, in relationship with the forms of man's existence, considering ethnic and cultural human ambients and *always conserving fidelity to the revealed word"* (Medellin 8,15).

6. *Communitarian and ecclesial catechesis.* In Latin America, the renewal of catechesis has progressed at the same pace as the effort and general reflection to promote ecclesial awareness and the formation of new forms of communities. Because of this, the documents concerning catechesis place the *communitarian dimension* of catechesis and the exigencies of *fidelity to ecclesial communion* in the forefront (cf. Medellin 8,10). In particular, Puebla, so sensitive to the theme of "communion and participation," effectively emphasized the various aspects of this fidelity:

—Insofar as it is a work of the Church, catechesis *is the responsibility of everyone* in the Church. Puebla regards as a positive fact in the sphere of the development of catechesis the "rediscovery of its communitarian dimension, in such a manner that the ecclesial community is becoming responsible for catechesis at all its levels: family, parish, basic ecclesial community, scholastic community and also diocesan and national organization" (983).

—Therefore, there is insistence on the necessary collaboration of all, "each one according to his ministry and charism, without eluding apostolic and missionary responsibilities, because in catechesis the Church builds the Church" (993). And in fact, experiences of familial catechesis, as in Chile, or the promotion of lay ministries, or the life of the basic communities are concrete examples which demonstrate that truly we are overcoming the mentality of the "delegation" of catechetical responsibility to a few "professionals" of catechesis.

—Catechesis has as its aim *the building of the ecclesial community*, and, therefore, it requires communitarian sensitivity among all the community's members:

> The work of evangelization which is realized in catechesis demands the communion of everyone: it requires that divisions be absent and that persons find themselves in an adult faith and in an evangelical love. One of the objectives of catechesis is precisely the building up of the community (Puebla 992).

—The root need of catechesis is *fidelity to the Church* and *communion with the Church.* Thus is recalled the great principle of the ecclesiality of catechesis as proclamation and witness, which has meaning only if done in the name of the Church and as an expression of the ecclesial sign in its totality. It is to be kept in mind, therefore, that whoever catechizes "with his effort continually builds the community and transmits the image of the Church," and that he must consequently act in union with the bishops (Puebla 995).

7. *Permanent catechesis*. Finally, Puebla emphasizes the character of a permanent and dynamic process of catechesis as a feature which, according to a Latin-American expert,[9] possesses a strong character of novelty:

> Every catechesis must lead to a process of conversion and of permanent and progressive growth in the faith (Puebla 998).

The *permanent* character of catechesis is a conquest of the contemporary catechetical movement which involves overcoming infantile polarization and the almost exclusive character of certain ambients, especially the school and the parish, as places of catechesis. In Latin America an awareness has developed that catechesis, as a permanent process

—must accompany *all ages of life*, from infancy to old age (Puebla 1011);

—must secure *all the stages and moments* of the growth of faith: conversion, faith in Christ, community life, sacramental life and apostolic effort (Puebla 1007);

—must create an *organic coordination,* a "reciprocal integration of the communities or institutions which catechize; that is, family, school, parish, movements, community and different groups" (Puebla 1011).

It is not difficult to imagine the consequent renewal in pastoral mentality and in the concrete exercise of catechetical action which these statements imply.

Agents, Places and Instruments of Catechesis

After having considered the essential coordinates of the Latin-American catechetical reality, we should now view the different elements that characterize the functioning process of catechesis: agents, places, structures, contents, methods, instruments, etc. The Latin-American documents and the very practice of catechesis in Latin America are very rich in achievements and meaningful proposals, capable even of stimulating pastoral research in other parts of the world. To remain within the limits of these global reflections, however, we will indicate only a few more typical elements of the Latin-American experience, so as to complete and enrich the picture which we are sketching.

1. With regard to the *agents and those responsible* for catechesis, to be remembered first of all is the rediscovered catechetical role of the *bishop* as "first evangelizer" and "first catechist" (Puebla 687), but with the backdrop of a pastoral style that profoundly transforms the traditional figure of the bishop, much closer to the people and identified with them, with greater simplicity and poverty, more open to dialogue and to co-responsibility (Puebla 666). Along the same lines of drawing nearer to the people—together with the role of the family and of the basic community, which we will mention later on—the Latin-American pastoral makes itself the promoter of popular *catechists,* that is, of persons profoundly attuned to the popular reality in which they share and to which they belong, "indigenous and diversified pastoral workers, who satisfy the right which our peoples and our poor have of not being left in ignorance or in rudimentary formation in the faith" (Puebla 439).

2. As *places* and structures of catechesis, at least two are pointed out which enjoy a pastoral preference in the present Latin-American moment: the family and the basic ecclesial community. The Assembly of Puebla dedicated a wholly particular attention to the theme of the *family* (nos. 568-616), aware of its importance, and it confirmed the priority of familial pastoral within the organic pastoral of Latin America (590). In this context stress is placed on the conviction that the family is to be valued "as the irreplaceable active subject of evangelization and as the foundation of the communion of society" (602).

Regarding the *basic ecclesial communities,* whose pastoral importance we have already mentioned above, we now underline the significance which they assume as *privileged places of evangelization and of catechesis.* The widespread experience of the basic communities is the most eloquent testimony of unpublicized possibilities for catechesis, which has been able to develop in new forms of *familial* catechesis and of the education of *adults* to the faith (cf. Puebla 629), assuming new accents in the rediscovering of the Word of God, and new experiential dimensions, in the fruitful contact of the Christian message with the real problems of life. Thus we can speak of a "new catechesis," as the document of Puebla has recognized:

> With these groups, the Church shows herself in the full process of the renewal of parochial and diocesan life, by means of a new catechesis, not only in its methodology and in the use of modern means, but also in the presentation of contents which are vigorously oriented to introduce into life the evangelical motivations for growth in Christ (Puebla 100).

3. A last point merits to be emphasized: the importance given to the *means of social communication* as place, language and instruments of catechesis. In the global and complex reality of the Latin-American continent, the mass media constitute one of the most decisive factors on the socio-cultural transformations and at the same time a limitless field of educative and pastoral possibilities. The attention paid by Puebla (cf. nos. 1063-1095) to this fact and the pastoral conclusions which derive from it are a clear index of the importance that the theme also merits in the ecclesial field, above all in reference to the evangelizing and catechetical mission. An important specification is to be under-

lined: the preferential option for the so-called *"group media,"* which are held to be more suitable to the task of catechesis, both because they are poorer and more popular means (cf. Puebla 1235), and especially because "they offer the possibility of dialogue and are more suited to person-to-person evangelization, capable of arousing participation and a truly personal effort" (Puebla 1090).

In concluding this brief panorama, we can note that a complete picture has not been presented, because we were led by the preoccupation of selecting the more original and the more positive elements. This, however, does not mean to ignore the problematic and also negative aspects of such a complex reality, where certainly difficulties are not lacking and the open problems, the tensions are still unsolved. In order to characterize the Latin-American situation some authors spoke of catechesis as "in conflict."[10] But this takes away neither value nor significance from a catechetical experience which, well beyond Latin-American boundaries, offers lessons and suggestions capable of stimulating the pastoral practice of the whole Church.

EMILIO ALBERICH, S.D.B.

FOOTNOTES

1. Cf. the volume: *Catequesis y promocion humana,* cit. in bibliography.
2. The edition is cited *Medellin Documenti. La Chiesa nella attuale trasformazione dell'America Latina alla luce del conc. Vaticano II,* Bologna, Ediz. Dehoniane, 1969, pp. 75-80 (= Medellin 8).
3. Puebla 977-1011. The Italian definitive text is cited: *Puebla, L'evangelizzazione nel presente e nel futuro dell'America Latina,* Bologna, Editrice Missionaria Italiana, 1979.
4. It must be kept in mind that in the Latin-American documents the terms "evangelization" and "catechesis" cover a substantially equivalent meaning. For example, thus does the document of CELAM for the 1977 Synod express itself: "Respecting the classical distinction between catechesis

and evangelization, we opt in Latin America—a continent of the baptized —for giving to the word evangelization the meaning of an *evangelizing catechesis which is equivalent to a re-evangelization* in the terms of the conclusions of Medellin: *Catequesis para America Latina* (cited in the bibliography), p. 24.

5. L. Boff, "Puebla: logros, avances, interrogantes," in L. Boff and others, *Estudios sobre Puebla,* Bogota, Indo-American Press Service, 1979, p. 20. A similar formula is presented by E. Garcia Ahumada as a central theological and pastoral orientation: "to promote a liberation for communion by means of participation": "Puebla: une catechese prophetique, *Lumen Vitae* 34(1979)3, 202.

6. The Latin-American "situational" covers in part what in Europe is generally called "anthropological," but with a more explicit reference to man *in his historical concreteness*. It is significant that where other documents speak of "fidelity to man" (cf., for example, the basic document of catechesis in Italy, *Il rinnovamento della catechesi*, [Rome, Ediz. Pastorali Italiane, 1970] no. 160), in Latin America, "fidelity to the Latin-American man" is preferred (Puebla, 996).

7. Cf. Puebla, 988, and the articles cited in the bibliography.

8. Cf. R. Viola, *Siete anos despues de Medellin*, loc. cit., p. 398.

9. Cf. M. Borello, loc. cit., p. 122.

10. Cf. C. De Lora, art. cit.

BIBLIOGRAPHY

Besides the documents cited in the footnotes, we point out a few studies more directly dedicated to the theme of catechesis:

Andres Vela, Jesus, *Catequesis Evangelizadora*, Bogota, Indo-American Press Service, 1976.

Borello, Mario, "La catequesis de Medellin a Puebla," *Medellín* 5(1979)17-18, 115-129.

CELAM (Consejo Episcopal Latinoamericano), *Catequesis para América Latina*, Documento de trabajo del CELAM para el Sinodo de 1977, Bogota, Secretariado General del Celam, 1977.

CELAM (Secretariado General del CELAM), "El documento catequístico de Medellín. Sus ideas inspiradoras, sus resonancias, sus lagunas y sus proyecciones," in: ID (Ed.), *Medellín. Reflexiones en el CELAM*, Madrid, BAC, 1977, pp. 101-118.

CLAR (Confederacion Latinoamericana de Religiosos), *Información teológica y pastoral sobre America Latina*, Bogota, Secretariado General de la CLAR, 1974.

De Lora, Cecilio, "Precisions sur la catéchèse en Amerique Latine depuis Medellín" (1968-1975), *Lumen Vitae* 30(1975)3-4, 360-376.

De Vos, Franz, "Puebla y la catequesis," *Didascalia* 33(1979)7, 401-444.

Galilea, Segundo, *Adónde va la pastoral?, En los cinco años de la conferencia de Medellín*, Bogota, Edic. Paulinas, 1974.

Garcia Ahumada, Enrique, "Puebla: una catequesis profética," *Sinite* 20(1979)61, 267-285.

Garcia Ortiz, Jaime, "Las opciones de la catequesis latinoamericana," in: *Medellín, Reflexiones en el CELAM*, l.c., pp. 377-391.

Semana Internacional De Catequesis, *Catequesis y promoción humana, Medellín 11-18 de agosto de 1968*, Salamanca, Edic. Sigueme, 1969.

Spoletini, Benito, "De Medellín a Puebla. De la catequesis situacional y liberadora a la catequesis de comunion y participación," *Catequesis Latino-americana* 10(1979)40, 40-51.

Viola, Roberto, "Siete anos despues de Medellín," in *Medellín, Reflexiones en el CELAM*, l.c., pp. 393-400.

9

Significant Moments
of the Catechetical Renewal
in Europe

At the beginning of *Catechesi tradendae* (CT), the Pope acknowledges that he is exercising his own discernment regarding a "reality that is very much alive," "a precious gift from the Holy Spirit to the Church of today" (no. 3).

This acknowledgement is certainly valid for the catechetical movement in Europe, which, after the Second World War, lived a season particularly rich in ideas, initiatives and persons.

Now it would be meàningful and stimulating to reconstruct the "map" of catechesis in Europe, especially with regard to this movement of ideas and persons.

We should remember the catechetical periodicals (*Lumen Vitae, Catéchèse, Actualidad catequetica...*), the Catechetical Institutes founded in that epoch (Paris, Brussels, Nijmegen, Munich, Rome, Madrid...), the catechisms and national catechetical directories which marked a historical turn for catechesis on a worldwide scale (the German catechism of 1955, the Dutch catechism of 1966, the Italian basic Document of 1970...).

It would also be necessary to present the pioneers and protagonists of catechetical renewal in Europe; men who not only developed new ideas, but who dedicated themselves to their task with a great effort of witnessing: for the Low Countries: Delcuve, Bless, Ramvelt...; for Austria and Germany: Hofinger, Jungmann, Tilmann...; for France: Boyer, Colomb, Liègé, besides the group of lay persons, M. Fargues, E. Lubienska de Lenval, F. Derkenne...; for Spain: Llorente, Estepa...; for Italy: Casotti, Nosengo, Riva....

And this a movement which has not yet stopped, notwithstanding the difficulties of adjustment of the postconciliar period. For Europe, too, the prophetic expressions of the synod are valid: "in all parts of the world, catechesis has become a primary source of vitality leading to a fruitful renewal of the entire community of the Church" (Message of the Synod to the People of God, no. 4).

It would, therefore, be interesting and useful attentively to reconstruct catechesis in Europe over the last thirty years. But here we will stop to consider only the peaks of the iceberg. They are significant moments. These certainly reveal the presence of an immense subterranean mass, but they are always "peaks" which send one back to a more extensive and profound knowledge of the movement which has expressed them.

1955: The New "German Catechism" and the Kerygmatic Renewal of Catechesis

Edited in 1955 for German children of ten to thirteen years of age, translated into over thirty languages, the "Katholischer Katechismus"[1] marks a "Copernican" revolution in the history of catechesis for two reasons: methodology and content.

It represents the most mature fruit of the kerygmatic renewal of catechesis. Its influence in the catechetical movement was enormous.

There was a "revolution" of *method*, first of all. It was the first official catechism of *lessons explained* in *an expository way*, arranged according to a didactic itinerary, while each lesson also contained doctrinal formulations of a traditional type: 248 in all.

The catechism now becomes a "school book," which takes into account the psychological laws of learning and not only doctrinal requirements. The lesson is of the *inductive* type: it starts out from the interests of the student and from the biblical event which is at the root of the theme of the lesson, explains its doctrinal content, synthesizes it in the formula to be memorized, arouses the activity of assimilation and of deepening, and engages the student in moral consistency.

These moments of learning have a name. They are the so-called "formal degrees" of presentation, explanation and application.

The German Catechism of 1955 makes its own the "Munich method" formulated by German catechists at the beginning of the century. Not understood then, and rejected, it is now authoritatively proposed by the episcopate as the "suitable" method for the catechesis of German children of the 1950's.

Such, therefore, is the "revolution" of method, but no less profound is that of *content*. We find ourselves in the presence of the first catechism of the modern era which decisively overcomes "the impoverishment of catechetical exposition which the image of God, of Christ, of the Holy Spirit and of the Church, the treatment of the sacraments, etc., have undergone in the course of the historical evolution of the catechism.... Up until now it is the most meditated catechism from the theological point of view" (H. Fischer).

With the German Catechism of 1955, the "kerygmatic current" of theology officially made its entrance into catechesis: the content is centered upon the *history of salvation;* Christianity is presented not as a system of truths nor a codex of precepts, but as a *message,* as the "Good News" (eu-angelion) for man; at the center of this message there is *a person:* Jesus Christ and His paschal mystery of death and resurrection; the catechism makes ample recourse to biblical, ecclesial and liturgical fonts.

Taking up the principles of the kerygmatic movement, the catechism gains enormously in theological solidity, in internal cohesion (the beginning of "concentration" around the person of Jesus Christ), in vital strength ("the truths of faith must be presented to the young in a living personality"). The authors, who worked on this book for more than seventeen years (1937-1955), have illustrated the *advantages* of the new catechism as follows:

—for the catechist:

a) The closeness of language to Scripture and to the character of the message that is proper to Christian doctrine will have a beneficial influence on living catechesis and on all preaching.

b) The catechist who has no experience or has little time to prepare himself will receive greater help than he would have received from formulas alone, through the certainty and clarity of the ideas expressed.

c) The proposals of activities for the children that are contained in the catechism will help the tired catechist to rest a little while the children work.

d) The parent-catechist will have a greater field of intervention than simply listening to the rote repetition of answers: the catechism will now become a domestic religious manual for religious instruction in the families.

—for the children:

a) They will have a book closer to modern school texts.

b) They will derive from it an incentive to mental activity, through which they will assure themselves of an important heritage of concrete religious facts.

c) They will receive from it an appeal not only to the mind, but to all the faculties and capacities of the person.

d) They will receive help for remembering, because each lesson develops only one theme, in a unified manner.

e) They will find greater connection between all the Christian truths, ordered in a living and vital synthesis: no longer "pills," but "food adequate and tasty."

—for the whole pastoral:

From the new catechism we hope for a renewal of all pastoral activity, of which it should constitute the central point of reference.

1966: The New Dutch Catechism for Adults and the Anthropological Approach

The German catechism of 1955, which seemed to have been made to challenge the generations (as the preceding catechisms of Canisius, of Deharbe, of Mönnichs...had done), soon became the object of discussion.

In this regard Bruno Dreher writes: "It is one of the most impressive facts of the catechetical history of our century that a catechism so valid, which seemed to have opened a new age-long era for catechisms and which expressed the data of the more important theological currents in the Catholic Church from the time of the First World War—and that is the kerygmatic, biblical and liturgical movement—a catechism which had aroused worldwide interest and seemed made for diverse generations, should now have been outdated by the Council. It will have to be rewritten in the spirit of conciliar theology, the expression of today's formulation of the faith of the Church."

What, therefore, had put in crisis this "most solid" catechism for German children? First of all, the event of Vatican Council II. The new understanding of the Church's existence in the world expressed by the Council called for not so many partial touch-ups, but rather a reformulation of the whole catechism.

In the second place, the profound changes taking place in society: the increasing standard of living ("one example suffices: in 1955, when the catechism appeared, about 3,000 German families owned a television..., whereas in 1969 one German out of four, and hence practically every family, owns a television set"); the spread of secularization and the new religious situation created in the schools ("there will be in each group of children some who believe, others who are inclined to believe, others indifferent or contrary or strangers to the faith"); the climate of growing contestation and of the questioning of authority which would find its acute expression in the youth revolt of 1968.

Also the didactics which inspired the teaching in the schools underwent profound transformations: the expository method was replaced by a method more sensitive to group work, to research, to the objectives of teaching, to that rationalization of learning which goes under the name "curricular theory." In this new context, the function of the school book is redimensioned. The remade German Catechism (which appeared in 1969) no longer bore the name "catechism," but a more modest and functional one: "work book" *(Arbeitstext)*.

But in the provocation of this subsequent "revolution" in the catechetical movement, the *new Dutch catechism for adults* of 1966[2] was not extraneous.

For a long time Holland had been dominated by the catechisms of Canisius (of the mid-sixteenth century) and of Malines (of early seventeenth century), and lastly by the catechisms inspired by neo-scholasticism.

After the publication of the German Catechism of 1955, it was still more evident that to continue to adopt these catechisms was impossible. (The last, that of 1948, although renewed in methodological aspects, in substance remained bound to the traditional form.)

The episcopate then gave the mandate to the Catechetical Institute of Nijmegen to develop a new catechism for Holland.

The first report of the work commission, in 1958, concluded that to have only one catechism for all the faithful of the dioceses of Holland, from children to adults, would be inappropriate, or better, impossible. The decisive development, however, occurred in the meeting of the European Equipe of Catechesis held in London in 1961. On that occasion a few members referred to the preparatory work for Vatican Council II and how in the outlines prepared (which in the end were not discussed by the Council) the stress fell on the fact that a real and mature announcement of the faith is proper to adults and that every other catechesis is not complete in itself, but tends to the adult's maturity in the faith towards which it must constantly direct itself. It then appeared clear to the Dutch group that a renewal of catechesis for children necessarily had to be inserted into a global renewal of catechesis, which reaches man at all ages, in a progressive path of permanent formation.

Thus it was that in July, 1962, the bishops decided: "There will appear a new Dutch catechism for the adult faithful. It will contain doctrine in the first place, but it also plans to give suggestions for living the faith better in the present times, for realizing a real contact with Scripture and for participating better in the liturgical celebration."

The New Catechism, * published in 1966 under the form of a book for adults with about 600 pages of development, constituted a "first" in European catechesis for two reasons:

a) It was the first official catechism of the modern era for adults. It proposed an ecclesial priority which would be made its own by the *General Catechetical Directory* of 1971 (no. 92); that is, the *priority of catechesis for adults*. This pastoral principle would influence all other forms of catechesis. From then on catechesis for children, adolescents, and youth would be considered as a catechesis oriented to the catechesis for adults, and, therefore, no longer preoccupied with giving "all" prematurely, but referring to complete material proper to the adult age.

b) It was the first official catechism that clearly took up the *anthropological development* of Vatican Council II. Conse-

---

Translator's note: The author of this chapter makes no reference to the Commission that was set up by His Holiness, Pope Paul VI, to analyze the deficiencies of the *New Catechism* (Dutch catechism) which proposed corrections to be made in its text.

quently, catechesis no longer presented itself as an abstract and synthesized doctrine in short formulas, nor as a kerygma which was proclaimed without excessive preoccupations about the man who listened to it. Catechesis was now understood as "the process of illumination of human existence as the salvific intervention of God, in which the mystery of Christ is witnessed to in the form of the announcement of the word for the purpose of awakening and of nourishing the faith and leading to its realization in life."[3]

Man had become the "didactic principle" of the new catechesis (B. Dreher).

The Dutch Catechism carries out its "anthropological option" in a multiplicity of concrete realizations:

—*Technical terms* are avoided, both those in current use among the authors (anthropology, secularization, fundamental option...) and those of traditional philosophy and theology (the "procession" in the Trinity; the philosophical terms of person, substance and nature...), because the authors hold that catechesis is addressed to everyone and not to a restricted circle of faithful.

—The *meaning for life* of the Christian truths is explained. Rather than with "proving," the catechism is concerned with "setting forth," and "narrating," deepening each time the life significance of the topics treated.

—It wants *the adults "to think" about the faith.* The faithful person is not considered only as "one who listens," but as "one who thinks" together with the authors of the catechism. Noteworthy in this regard are the difficult questions left open, the admissions of ignorance, the "we do not know." Besides respect for the mystery, besides the seriousness with which problems are confronted, not admitting solutions which are too easy and superficial, one of the motives is precisely this: to leave space for personal reflection.

—An example is offered of what *sensibility and modern language* mean. This results in attention to man, love for life, solidarity with the entire material universe and the effort to concretize salvation in the simplicity of daily living and of commitment in the world. Hence the attempt to translate into modern categories, closer to the man of today, the announcement of the faith transmitted through mental concepts proper to the Bible or to philosophies and theologies of the past centuries.

As we shall see further on, in a critical evaluation, such an undertaking is accompanied by not a few difficulties and risks.

1968: Medellin and the Political Phase of Catechesis

The anthropological development of catechesis did not stop at the personalistic and existential demands of the Dutch Catechism for adults. This time the impulse came from the rediscovery of the "political" in relationship with human and Christian existence from new urgencies in the Christian effort to confront the injustices of the world, from the unrest of 1968, from the slogans which vindicated the "participation" of everyone in the construction of the earthly city, and lastly from the influence of Latin-American catechesis, considered also in Europe as a new "prophecy" for the catechesis of the new times. The catechists of Latin America defined their options during the sixth international week of Catechesis, promoted at Medellin (Colombia) by Fr. Hofinger.

On that occasion, this continent—formed by young populations in violent ferment, wherein more than elsewhere exploitations and injustices were manifested simultaneously with the struggle for personal development—clamored in a loud voice for an indigenous catechesis, liberated from European influence and capable of responding to the exigencies of its own people. It was not to be abstract and deductive (whether doctrinal or kerygmatic or anthropological), but in profound solidarity with the man to whom it was addressed, a catechesis bound to life and oriented to action. This "liberation catechesis" is defined as "the action by which a human group interprets its own situation, lives it and expresses it in the light of the Gospel." From now on three key words will be the constitutive moments of every pastoral or catechetical action: analysis of the situation, interpretation, and planning.

a) *Man in his situation.* "The problem proposed to catechesis consists in assumption of the past and insertion into the present, with the gaze on the future. It is impossible to ignore the wealth of four centuries and of Christian tradition. On the other hand, we cannot stop at the forms of the past: some of these forms appear ambiguous; because of historical changes, others manifest themselves inadequate and even harmful. In effect the Latin-

American continent today is subjected to profound and rapid changes: economical, demographic, social and cultural."[4]

The first task of catechesis will be that of incarnating itself in human situations and assuming the anxieties and hopes of the modern man. It would be senseless to present a message of salvation if the salvation were not to begin here and now, on this earth, precisely liberating man from injustice and oppression.

b) *Interpret the situation.* The theological option taken on at Medellin is explicit on this point: it does not tolerate schism between the world beyond and the present world. Catechesis will always have to manifest the profound unity that exists between "the saving plan of God realized in Christ and the aspirations of man; between the history of salvation and human history; between the Church as people of God and the earthly communities; between the revealing action of God and the experience of man; between the gifts or supernatural charisms and human values; between the progressive realization of Christianity in time and its eschatological fulfillment. Unity—complex, differentiated and dynamic. On the one hand, every dichotomy, separation and dualism is excluded; and on the other, every confusion, every monistic or simplistic identification."[5]

c) *Catechesis as action.* "To understand the total meaning of human realities, it is necessary to live fully with the men of our times. Thus we will be able progressively and seriously to interpret these realities in their actual context, in the light of the experiences lived by the people of Israel, by Christ-man and by the sacramental ecclesial community in which the Spirit of the risen Christ lives and acts continually."[6]

For *liberation catechesis* "to evangelize means to sow signs of liberation, to face the problems and necessities of the poor in order to solve them together. In this action of liberation, catechesis is the reflection which permits the grasping of these signs of liberation as signs of the presence and the saving action of God, as signs of resurrection. Catechesis is, therefore, born from action, is developed in action and is in view of an action always more effective."

As has been recalled, the Latin-American catechesis of liberation had a great influence in Europe. It is enough for us to remember the so-called "catechism of Isolotto" and the political catecheses of the basic communities.[7]

1970-1971: The Basic Document for Catechesis in Italy and the General Catechetical Directory

During the years of the Council and after the Council, various national catechetical directories were published in the European nations.

We recall: the "directory of pastoral catechetics" for the dioceses of France (1964), the "fundamental guidelines for a renewed scholastic catechesis" in Holland (1964), Italy's *Il rinnovamento della catechesi* ("renewal of catechesis") (1970) and the "General Catechetical Directory" (1971), prepared by the Sacred Congregation for the Clergy according to the norms of the conciliar dispositions (Decree *Christus Dominus*, 44).

In other nations they are proceeding to develop new orientations for catechesis, such as the "Rahmenplan" or law framework for the teaching of the faith in Germany (1967), or the "programas de enseñanza religiosa" in Spain (1968), etc. There have also been synods on catechesis and on the teaching of religion, such as the German one which produced an excellent document, the most up-to-date until now, on scholastic catechesis.[8]

The objective to which all these interventions are aimed is a *change of mentality*. Only secondarily are dispositions of a disciplinary and organizational type given. In fact, the Council had entreated all the people of God to be converted and to place catechesis in step with the spirit of the new times.

The Italian basic document[9] represents a classic of this "aggiornamento" according to the guidelines of the Council. Having developed step by step alongside the *General Catechetical Directory*, it possesses in relationship with the latter an exceptional harmony in regard to "the interior eschatological vision and similarity—when it is not outrightly identical—of the pastoral proposals" (Msgr. A. Del Monte).

The conciliar ideas continually appear in the paragraphs of "Il rinnovamento della catechesi" and in the GCD. *Which ideas?*

1. The primacy of the Word of God in the building up of the Church.

2. A rich definition of catechesis, understood as Word, memory and witness.

3. The ecclesial community as subject and recipient of catechesis.

4. The catechumenal itinerary as a permanent school of education in the faith.

5. The centrality of Jesus Christ in the message to be announced.

6. Fidelity to God and to man as the inspiring principle of catechetical methodology.

7. The invitation to have recourse to the human sciences, but never to the detriment of the originality of catechetical pedagogy, whose animator is the Holy Spirit.

8. The will to solve the new problems facing catechesis: language, the impact of modern culture, the Word of God and the history of men....

As we can see, the catechetical directories touch upon the great themes already faced by the Council, and in particular they refer to the new understanding of the Church (*Lumen gentium*), to the significance of Revelation and the primacy of the Word of God (*Dei verbum*), to the rapport of the Church with the world and with history (*Gaudium et spes*).

Upon contact with the conciliar perspectives the catechetical practice is enriched and assumes new tasks. It is no longer a simple preparation for the sacraments. It is much more: it is a continual progress in the discovery of the faith, where the sacraments are the principal causes of development and maturation.

The "Word made flesh" is the name of Christ (RdC, 55).

The new catechesis, too, is Word which reaches man where he is found, illuminating and transforming his whole life. Witness, life of charity, human development, are the new levels of post-conciliar catechesis.

"Not simply knowing more, but living more, directly being co-involved, together with the Word, the sacraments and the conversion of life in charity" (Msgr. A. Del Monte).

1974-1977: The Synods of Bishops on Evangelization and Catechesis

The Synods of 1974 and of 1977 reaffirmed the priority task of the Church in our time: evangelization and catechesis. They required a vast documentation from the particular churches and carried out a very studied debate, which will remain for the next ten years the reference point and an effective stimulus for the development of catechesis.

Both synods offered the Pope rich and significant material, from which sprang the Apostolic Exhortations *Evangelii nuntiandi* of Paul VI (of 12/8/1975) and *Catechesi tradendae* of John Paul II (of 10/16/1979).

Evangelii nuntiandi is truly a "pearl" among ecclesial documents. It takes up again the great objective of the Council: "to make the Church of the twentieth century ever better fitted for proclaiming the Gospel to the people of the twentieth century" (EN 2). EN accepts the challenge of modern times: "The conditions of society oblige us all to review methods, to seek with every means to study how to bring to modern man the Christian message in which, alone, he can find the answers to his questions and the strength for his effort of human solidarity" (Paul VI, discourse of 6/22/1973).

And this is to be done in twofold fidelity to God and man: "This fidelity both to a message whose servants we are and to the people to whom we must transmit it living and intact is the central axis of evangelization" (EN 4).

EN intends to answer "three burning questions" which the Synod of 1974 had addressed to itself:

—In our day, what has happened to that hidden energy of the Good News, which is able to have a powerful effect on man's conscience?

—To what extent and in what way is that evangelical force capable of really transforming the people of this century?

—What methods should be followed in order that the power of the Gospel may have its effect? (cf. EN 4)

Catechesi tradendae manifests the same passion for service to the Word of God ("offer catechesis her best resources in people and energy," no. 15; "bring about and maintain...a real passion for catechesis," no. 63), but it proposes to itself a task less complex in respect to EN, that of exercising "discernment" regarding realities "very much alive" in the catechetical movement, which it approves and encourages globally.

The discernment of the Pope emphasizes the mystical and historical roots of catechesis, the necessary ecclesial co-involvement, the safeguarding of the originality and identity of the catechetical act, the "truthful" aspect of catechesis, that is, the truth and organization of its contents.

EN and CT both treat the problem of the *impact of the Gospel on the culture of our time*.

"What matters is to evangelize man's culture and cultures" (EN 20).

"Catechesis...is called to bring the power of the Gospel into the very heart of culture and cultures...and help them to bring forth from their own living tradition original expressions of Christian life, celebration and thought" (CT 53).

Will not this be the great task of the catechetical movement which goes to meet the year 2000, in order that finally there will be overcome that "split between the Gospel and culture (which) is without a doubt the drama of our time" (EN 20)?

The Catechetical Movement in Europe— Its Balance Sheet and Its Prospects

During the last thirty years Europe has been a formidable center for the generation of ideas and a promoter of catechetical initiatives in every part of the world. Ideas have given rise to new ideas, experiences have been succeeded by new experiences.

The limit of such a rapid and disquieting evolution is that it has lacked compensations. For every new dimension of catechesis which has been discovered, there has been a tendency to absolutize it unilaterally, forgetting the others.

Kerygmatic catechesis had the great merit of proposing a new way for catechesis, when the doctrinal formulations of questions and answers, thought up in a society of strong Christian traditions, showed themselves absolutely inadequate to meet the challenge of secularization. It restored to catechesis the freshness and enthusiasm of the beginnings, of the evangelical message as it used to be rediscovered in the biblical and liturgical fonts.

Nevertheless, kerygmatic catechesis ended up by ignoring the other dimensions of catechesis: both the doctrinal, by often rejecting everything that could have appeared notional and abstract, and the anthropological-experiential.

Kerygmatic catechesis did not keep in mind the socio-cultural context in which the subject is found. Faced with the crisis of society, which affirmed itself with acute tones about the year 1968, this catechesis seemed too optimistic and sure of itself, still too deductive and closed up in itself, to be capable of grasping the new religious demands of the young, their real problems, the aspirations and anxieties of our time (cf. GS 1).

Anthropological or experiential catechesis put man "back into the game." It effectively underlined the psychological and sociological situation of the subject, rediscovered the creatural and human dimensions of the Christian event. Catechists generally found themselves at ease with this method of catechizing, and they scored not a few successes, especially among adolescents and young adults.

To traverse the ways of man was often gratifying both for the catechists and for the young people. Furthermore, this was the directive that had come from the Council. Had not Paul VI proclaimed that "it is necessary to know man in order to know God; it is necessary to love man to love God"? (discourse of 12/7/1965)

At that time the catechists, as the Church, felt themselves to be "experts in humanity." But not even this new phase of catechesis was without drawbacks. We witnessed a cultural devaluation which expressed itself in a spontaneistic pedagogy without methods or instruments. The hour of catechism was often transformed into more of an hour of free discussion than of a time for learning and application. We fell into moralism, intent on proposing values, it is true, but without a corresponding foundation in the "professio fidei," "as though catechesis could promote a generous moral life inspired by the Gospel, while leaving the pupils in great religious ignorance, in a void containing no 'theological' rigor capable of eliciting or of strengthening the profession of faith."[10]

Even the much deprecated dichotomy between faith and life, categorically denounced in doctrinal and kerygmatic catechesis, did not find a satisfying solution in anthropological catechesis. The Gospel continues to appear to youth as something "parachuted" from on high, and the interest aroused by the impact with human experiences is soon extinguished once the sacred book is taken in hand.

The dangers of horizontalism and of reductionism, often denounced by the magisterium in regard to anthropological catechesis, have become more evident in the so-called *political or liberation catechesis.*

Without a doubt these catecheses have had the great merit of considering man in his situation and of overcoming an individualistic and disincarnate anthropology. Recalling man to his unavoidable tasks in the face of the future of the world and of society, they redeemed catechesis from "aseptic," "chemically pure" discourses.

Nevertheless, the risk of pushing adaptation to the point of mixture with temporal messianisms and to the point of making catechesis forget its service to the Word has not been theoretical only.

The reminder of *Catechesi tradendae* not to confuse *salvation* with *salvations* and not to "mix catechetical teaching unduly with...ideological views" (no. 52) certainly refers to this type of catechesis.

In proposition 14, the synod fathers had recommended both the insertion of catechesis into the different cultures and social situations, so that "the Gospel can evaluate, purify and transform them" and the education and development of "a critical sense toward ideologies, so that it will appear clear that the Gospel is not conditioned by them, but remains the supreme criterion for every critical evaluation."

The kerygmatic, anthropological and political phases of catechesis mark, therefore, the journey of the European catechetical movement during the last thirty years. These terms also indicate the exaggerations, the one-sidedness and the absolutizations which catechists encountered, especially those who were less prepared.

Now, after the period of effervescent creativity, there seem to have come years of greater calm, desirous of creating a *new synthesis*.

The invitation to the "synthesis" comes authoritatively from the fourth general assembly of the synod of Bishops: "Catechesis must overcome the dichotomies which are often present in catechetical methods, so as to avoid making the Gospel appear almost divided in itself. Some methods insist only on the doctrinal dimension; others only on existential fact or anthropological guidelines; still others are preoccupied only about political problems or temporal efforts, or only about the spiritual aspects of faith. Such polarization is to the detriment of the Gospel proclamation. These dichotomies are to be overcome not with compromise, but with a dialectical tension between the two poles, in order that they may reciprocally enrich one another. Such synthesis will be a creative work, capable of arousing new styles of catechesis, much more faithful to the profound demands of the Gospel. The theological criterion that underlies this synthesis of varying aspects is the mystery of the incarnate Word, who takes up the human condition in His divine person" (Proposition 18).

The task of the "new synthesis" is, therefore, that of explaining on the level of catechesis the theological criterion manifested by the "mystery of the incarnate Word." The synod thus indicated the conceptual picture which can be used in the construction of the new catechetical synthesis.

"The Christian message must find its roots in human cultures and also transform these cultures. In this sense we can say that catechesis is an instrument of 'inculturation.' This means that catechesis develops and at the same time enlightens from within the way of life of those to whom it is addressed. Through catechesis the Christian faith must become incarnate in all cultures. A true 'incarnation' of faith through catechesis supposes not only a process of 'giving' but also of 'receiving' " (Message of the Synod, 5).

The Pope himself acknowledges: "The term 'acculturation' or 'inculturation' may be a neologism, but it expresses very well one factor of the great mystery of the Incarnation" (CT 53).

To be treated, then, is a deepening of what is *inculturation in catechesis.*

Father Arrupe did this to the synod in clear and essential language:

> It is practical corollary of that ideological principle according to which Christ is the unique savior, and nothing can save itself outside of Him, whence the necessity of assuming in His body—the Church—all cultures, of purifying them from what is contrary to His spirit and thus saving them without destroying them; it is the penetration of the faith into the deepest strata of man's life, to the point of influencing his manner of thinking, of feeling, of acting under the animating action of the Spirit of God; it is offering to all human values the same possibility of placing themselves at the service of the Gospel; it is a continual dialogue between the Word of God and the countless ways which man has of expressing himself. Thus it makes us capable of speaking not only *to the* men of our time, but *with* them, and of interpreting better their problems, hopes and aspirations and making them ours.[11]

The *catechesis of inculturation* will avoid the one-sidedness of the preceding catechesis, if it will keep constantly in mind the components of "apostolic dialogue" with the cultures (CT 53): the "giving," the "receiving," the "giving back," or the "expressing."

Catechesis of the "giving" in the first place, of the biblical and post-biblical Tradition. Is not perhaps the situation of the catechist and of the catechized that of being "preceded" by other persons who have lived and written in the past? To recognize the gift, the "given," the "others," history..., is to be fully human beings and Christians.

"One of the challenges of the catechesis of the coming ten years will consist in knowing how to de-codify, with the young, in a rigorous theological manner, the specificity of the Christian faith. It will be a matter of analyzing, with them, in an objective manner and without seeking for immediate applications *per se*, what refers to this original manner of speaking and living that constitutes Christianity."[12]

Catechesis of "receiving"—that is, of dialogue with contemporary culture. It will, therefore, be a catechesis *open* to the profound dimension of human culture which is contained in philosophy, literature, art, and the research of the sciences of man.

This catechesis should be *open* to the man who works, who suffers, who loves and who seeks spaces of contemplation and of hope in his daily life; to the man who questions himself and asks questions about the ultimate significance of his destiny; to the man who is the "great way" walked by Christ and by the Church (*Redemptor hominis*, no. 11ff.).

Deep down the dilemma of contemporary man is this:

To accept faith, Christ and the Church *or* to accept man?
"To avoid this false dilemma catechesis must in an imperative manner encounter *contemporary rationalities* and make use of the instruments, methods and categories of culture to speak today according to the 'rules' of the Christian confession."[13]

Catechesis of "giving back," of expressing, of producing or "catechesis of the scripture," as the Belgian A. Fossión proposes with a rather unusual expression.

"By 'catechesis of the scripture,' we mean a journey which leads the pupils to write (or to speak) in turn according to the rules of the Christian confession in alliance with the culture of their time. It is a matter of asking the pupils to write their own text,* starting out from other Christian scriptures, utilizing the instruments, the methods, the categories and the means of expression of their time."[14]

It is a catechesis, therefore, of creativity, of codification, of production of a "confession of faith" incultured in our century.

Behold, therefore, a line of development and of synthesis for catechesis: "give," "receive," "give back."

Is not the project of inculturating catechesis in our time perhaps stimulating?

Is not human existence itself a "giving back" what one has "received" from life, from history, from others?

ROBERTO GIANNATELLI

FOOTNOTES

1. Italian translation: *Catechismo della dottrina cattolica,* Milan-Rome, Ancora-Herder, 1957.

2. Italian translation: *Il nuovo catechismo olandese,* Leumann (TO), LDC, 1969.

3. *Linee fondamentali per una nuova catechesi,* Leumann (TO), LDC, 1969, p. 40. This concerns the Dutch Catechetical Directory.

4. *Documento finale di Medellin,* nos. 2-3. The acts of the international catechetical week were partially published in the periodical *Catequesis Latinoamericana,* 1969, no. 1.

5. *Ibid.,* no. 12.   6. *Ibid.,* no. 11.

7. Cf. F. Perrenchio, *Bibbia e Comunità di Base in Italia,* Rome, LAS, 1980.

8. Italian translation: *Scuola e insegnamento della religione,* Leumann (TO), LDC, 1977.

9. Italian Episcopal Conference, *Il rinnovamento della catechesi,* Rome, EPI, 1970; Sacred Congregation for the Clergy, *General Catechetical Directory,* USCC, Washington, D.C.

10. A. Fossion, "La catéchèse scolaire d'hier á demain," *Nouvelle Revue Thévlogique,* 1980, no. 1, p. 13.

11. In G. Caprile, *Il Sinodo dei Vescovi 1977,* Rome, La Civiltà Cattolica, 1978, p. 147.

12. A. Fossion, *art. cit.,* p. 17.

13. *Ibid.,* p. 18.

14. *Ibid.,* p. 19.

ESSENTIAL BIBLIOGRAPHY

A. Etchegaray, Storia della catechesi, Rome, EP, 1965.

L. Erdozain, "L'evolution de la catechese," *Lumen Vitae,* 24(1969)4, pp. 575-599.

U. Gianetto, "Orientamenti Generali del rinnovamento della catechesi del nostro secolo," in Facolta teologica dell'Italia settentrionale, *Il rinnovamento della catechesi in Italia,* Brescia, La Scuola, 1977, pp. 59-94.

Translator's note: It is difficult to perceive any positive relationship of this thought and approach with that which the Holy See has expressed—for example, in CT 21, which states that catechesis "must be systematic, not improvised but programmed to reach a precise goal; it must deal with essentials...it must nevertheless be sufficiently complete, not stopping short at the initial proclamation of the Christian mystery...I am stressing the need for organic and systematic Christian instruction, because of the tendency in various quarters to minimize its importance." In the light of these words of CT, it is clear that the content of catechesis cannot come from the children.

10

The Environmental Influence on Catechesis in the Countries of Eastern Europe

It is not our intention to describe in this short article how, and in what measure, catechesis is taught in the communist countries of Eastern Europe. The Bishops of Eastern Europe, present at the Synod of Bishops of 1977, presented written interventions on this topic, which everyone can consult and study.[1] Our aim is to sketch briefly the principal characteristics of the ambient in communist countries and their negative influence on youth and on catechesis. By ambient we especially mean the socio-political order founded on the principles of historical and dialectical materialism, particularly in the USSR and in the so-called satellite nations.[2] The constitutional laws, substantially identical in all the nations of Eastern Europe, limit religious freedom, the rights of the Church and the family to educate youth, and the rights to diffuse the truths of faith; they impose an atheistic education in the schools at all levels. With regard to the limitation in practice of the educational rights of the Church and family, there are notable differences among the individual socialistic nations, which cannot be treated in a suitable or exhaustive manner in an article such as ours. Let us begin in the meantime by describing the socio-political order.

The Socio-political Order

Dialectical and historical materialism, on which the socio-political communist order bases itself, constitutes a conception of the world, of man and of society. In this conception religion is considered a phenomenon wholly negative and hence to be eliminated both by means of a change of the structure of production (nationalization of the means of production and dictatorship of the proletariat), and by means of the ideological battle and administrative measures.

From the definitions of religion as given by the founders of Marxism-Leninism, only grave consequences can result with regard to the communist interpretation of liberty of conscience and of religion. In fact, if religion is something wholly negative, a false vision of the world, an alienation to be overcome, it follows that true human liberty will not be obtained except by freeing oneself from religion.

And this, in effect, is the thought of Marx, expressed in *Critica al programma di Gotha* of 1975: "(Bourgeois) liberty of conscience is only correspondent to free bourgeois competition and is only tolerance in respect to all possible religions, whereas the worker must free his own conscience from the specter of religion."[3]

And Engels on his part, in the writing: *"In criticism of the plan for the program of the social-democratic party"* of 1891, augurs the complete separation of the Church from the State: "All the religious communities, without exception, should be treated by the State as private associations. They lose every public subsidy and every influence in the public schools," and he adds: "However, they cannot be forbidden from founding with their own means their own schools and from teaching in them their absurdities."[4]

In these affirmations of Marx and of Engels are included a few principles that the communist States in their attitude toward the Church and religions have made their own.

For example, Ju. Girman in the book, *"In what does liberty of conscience consist?"* writes: "The soviet State...cannot be indifferent in regard to religion. It is interested in the liberation of men from religious prejudices.... The soviet State, directed by the PC, dedicates much attention to the diffusion among the masses of scientific-atheistic knowledge."[5]

Regarding the separation of the school from the Church the same soviet author writes: "Liberty of conscience in the USSR is also guaranteed by the complete separation of the school from the Church, which means that the intervention of the clergy in the instruction and education of the youth is not permitted. The teaching of religious doctrines and the carrying out of religious worship in the schools is not permitted. The soviet school forms in the students a vision of the world that is scientific-materialistic, and hence atheistic, irreconcilable with religious ideology."[6]

It is according to the principles expressed above that we must understand the liberty of conscience and of religion sanctioned by the soviet Constitution, which serves as a model for the constitutions of the other socialist States, such as Czechoslovakia, for example.

The Soviet Constitution and That of Czechoslovakia

The new soviet Constitution is the fourth in the history of the USSR. It was approved by the Supreme Soviet of the USSR on October 4, 1977. The new soviet law changes the formulation of art. 124 of the Stalin Constitution. Art. 52 of the new Constitutions reads: "To the citizens of the USSR is guaranteed liberty of conscience; that is, the right to profess any religion whatsoever or not to profess any, to practice religious worship and to carry out atheistic propaganda. It is forbidden to incite to enmity and to hatred in relation to religious beliefs.

"The Church in the USSR is separated from the State, and the school is separated from the Church."[7]

Art. 52 modifies the expression "*liberty of practicing religious worship*" contained in art. 124 of the Stalin Constitution: that is, it guarantees not only freedom of worship, but also that of profession of any religion whatsoever.

It is undeniable that in the concept of religious profession greater and broader freedoms enter in, than with regard to participation in worship. But it is clear that the Constitution denies the right of religious propaganda and affirms only the right of atheistic propaganda.

In art. 52, the soviet Constitution reaffirms the separation between Church and State. Nevertheless, we must point out that the concept of separation assumes a particular content in the USSR (as also in the other communist States), different from that established in the western area. In fact, in the USSR (and in the other communist States) the fundamental premises of separation, as it is understood in the free world, are lacking. Lacking, that is, are the freedom of the citizen to profess and to manifest his own religious faith, the recognition of the sovereignty of the Church

in its own sphere, and the affirmation of the principle of eman-
cipation of ecclesiastical activity from the interference of the
State.

The right to religious freedom is, therefore, to be
understood—both in the USSR and in the other countries which
have the USSR as a model—in accordance with the ideological
premises from which the communist State draws inspiration.
Such premises compromise the right of freedom of conscience
and/or religious profession, so much the more if we consider that
in the new Constitution there is repeated insistence on the absolute necessity of an integral adhesion of all the citizens to the
Marxist-Leninist ideology, on the ruling function of the party and
on the partisanship of culture.[8]

How liberty of religion is to be understood in daily practice
was explained by V.A. Kuroedov, President of the Council for
Religious Affairs, at the Council of Ministries of the USSR, in a
book published in Moscow in 1974: "Religious associations do not
have the right to occupy themselves with beneficence, with
creating cooperatives, mutual-assistance funds, sanatoriums or
rest homes, cultural institutions, hospitals, sports organizations,
etc., since such activities are not related to the carrying out of
worship."[9]

Now we pass on to consider the Czechoslovakian Constitution, as an exemplification of the other communist constitutions
which follow the soviet model. The Constitution of Czechoslovakia of November 7, 1960, says in art. 32: "Religious
freedom is guaranteed. Every individual can profess himself in
any religious faith whatsoever or else not have any religious belief; he can participate in religious functions, as long as this is not
against the law."

As is evident, the religious freedom contemplated by the
Constitution, is extended to religious functions, which, however,
are bound by the condition: "as long as this is not against the
law."

Art. 32 on religious freedom is, however, subordinate to
art. 16: "In Czechoslovakia, all political culture, the development of instruction and of teaching are carried forward in the
spirit of the scientific vision of the world, Marxism-Leninism, and
in close union with the life and the work of the people."

If, on the one hand, one sole ideology is proclaimed, and,
on the other, religious freedom is guaranteed, we have to ask

ourselves: what is meant by religion and religious freedom? To privilege an ideology by means of a Constitution constitutes evident discrimination and does not leave room for real religious freedom.

The state is not authorized to decide which vision of the world is scientific; it is not authorized to make an ideology become the valid and obligatory sole vision of the world; it is not authorized to establish at what point religion does or does not go against the scientific vision of the world.

So much for the Constitutions. But how do the Czech and Slovak rulers and party directors understand religious freedom in daily practice?

On October 28, 1975, a few days before the Federal Assembly of Czechoslovakia approved the International Pacts on civil and political rights, Professor Tomas Travnicek, Vice-President of the CC of the National Front of Czechoslovakia, pronounced these words: "The Churches can undertake only those initiatives which directly concern religious worship, and this in the first place within those ecclesiastical edifices which the Churches have at their disposition for this purpose."

In the interpretation of the laws there is, therefore, on the one hand formal recognition of religious freedom, while on the other the necessity of re-educating the people to atheism stands out. There is a contradiction between the idea that religion is eliminated by the betterment of the level of life and the necessity of conducting an uncompromising ideological battle.

The faithful are invited to participate in the building up of the socialist society, but at the same time they are assured that they will be implacably fought. The proclamation of religious liberty reveals itself, therefore, as a propagandistic maneuver and not as a pledge which the State should keep according to the spirit and the letter.[10]

Administrative Measures

The lack of true religious freedom is aggravated by state control of the activity of the Church, of the Bishops and of the priests. This control is entrusted to the specific State offices for religious affairs, set up in all communist countries. It is evident that the existence and activity of such offices, central and peripheral, constitute the gravest violation of the constitutional article on separation of State from the Church, a separation guaranteed in all the communist constitutions.

We believe it useful to illustrate, as an example, the State Office for the Churches (ÁEH-Állami Egyházügyi Hivatal) instituted in Hungary in 1951. In this country, where, as a result of the agreements between the Hungarian State and the Holy See, there is an Episcopate whole and entire, with Cardinal L. Lékai at the head of the Hungarian Episcopal Conference, the State Office for the Churches has a capillary and most efficient structure. The Churches in some other communist States are controlled more or less as in Hungary; for example, in Czechoslovakia and even more so in the USSR; in other States, instead, as for example in Poland and Yugoslavia, the episcopate enjoys a greater and relative freedom.

The President of the State Office for the Churches is a member of the CC of the POSU (Unified Socialist Workers' Party) and of the Security Service of the Hungarian State.

This Office has the duty of nominating the Chancellor of the Bishop's Curia and the Bishop's Secretary.

The Chancellors of the individual dioceses (who in Hungary carry out almost the office of Vicars General) are bound to inform, orally or in writing, the State Office about all diocesan occurrences, about the plans of the Bishop, about visits made to them and even about their correspondence. In regard to the State Office, the Secretary of the Bishop has the same obligations of the Chancellor. In addition, he has to give information about the Chancellor himself. The notification of the Chancellor and of the Secretary regarding their nomination is made by the State Office and confirmed by the diocesan Bishop, to give the impression that the nomination had been made in accord with canonical norms.

The Pastors of the dioceses are watched over so carefully by the Chancellor and by the Secretary, as to literally be unable to move or act or make any decision without the State Office being informed.

In the individual parishes and deaneries the so-called local secretaries, belonging to the State Offices and to the Service of Public Security of the State, gather information about each individual priest, his customs, work, guests, free time, personal contacts, relationship with the Bishop, etc. They also censor the parish and diocesan bulletins. Catechists cannot exercise their ministry without the permission of the local secretaries, which has to be renewed every year.

The diocesan Bishops also depend on the State Office for the nomination of archdeacons, deans, pastors, rectors and professors of seminaries and of ecclesiastical faculties.

The catechesis of children, which is presently carried out in the churches and in parish halls, is regulated and controlled (limited), by a state disposition of January 15, 1975.[11]

In the year 1974-1975, only 6.8% of the total number of children aged seven to twelve attended catechetical instruction, which at the time was still taught by priests in the public schools after the other scholastic subjects.[12]

Nor does the situation of catechesis for children seem to be better in Czechoslovakia.[13] There are intimidations, limitations and state control. Only the Churches in Poland and in Yugoslavia have the possibility of reaching almost all the Catholic youth through catechesis.

Atheistic Indoctrination

The communist State (the USSR and other countries of Eastern Europe) has assumed the education of the citizens as one of its principal tasks and has attributed to the school a primary role in this regard, limiting the educative rights of the Church and of the Christian family. The State has reserved to itself the monopoly of instruction according to the scientific-atheistic vision of the world, in various ways forcing the parents to collaborate in the communistic education of society and of the school.

Scientific-atheistic education represents the most specific part of communist education. Atheism is considered progress, insofar as man, no longer exploited, is no longer obliged to imagine a *"god"* or a *"paradise"* for himself. Atheistic education would free man from religious prejudices, and authentic freedom of conscience would consist in this.

Marxist-Leninist atheism comprises the philosophical critique of all the religions, their critique from the viewpoint of the natural sciences and from history; the latter unveils a real picture of the origin and development of religious beliefs on the bases of the data of history, of archeology, of ethnology and of other sciences.

Such a critique bases itself on three prejudices: the first is that religion is only the work of the imagination and is equivalent to superstition. The second is that science is the enemy of religion. The third sees in all the religions an obstacle to the realization of a just society—free, that is, from exploitation.[14]

Dangers for the Faith

According to communist legislation, the school has the task of forming in the students a scientific—that is, materialistic and atheistic—vision of the world. The contrast between the teaching received at school and religious teaching received from parents or from priests can provoke, and, in fact, does provoke, in youth a crisis of faith or indifference in regard to religion. But even when one does not reach the point of a crisis of faith, the fear of manifesting one's religiousness can often lead to a distortion of character and duplicity of attitude, to a kind of contrast between intimate faith and adaptation to the environment that is atheistic and hostile to religion.

Furthermore, one must think of the grave problem that the lack of books, of manuals and of the Catholic press represents for youth (seminarians included) and for postconciliar updating. Parents in general are not in a position to give answers to the objections made in school against religion; and of priests, who are capable of doing it, there are always still fewer.

In communist countries catechetical activity is carried out amid various obstacles and in very unfavorable circumstances: access to the mass-media and to the appropriate instruments is lacking. The right of catechizing is violated—as John Paul II says in the Apostolic Exhortation *Catechesi tradendae*—by numerous States (the communist ones especially), "even to the point that imparting catechesis, having it imparted, and receiving it become punishable offenses."[15]

Evangelization and catechizing are also rendered very difficult by the fact that the atheistic governments of the East seek to force the Bishops and clergy to support the communist program in economics and in politics. In future circumstances, more favorable to the freedom of catechetical teaching, the explanation of the social doctrine of the Church, an integral part of Christian morality, will be extremely necessary and timely.

How To Teach Religion in Communist Countries?

This problem was presented by His Excellency, Most Reverend Frane Franiĉ, Bishop of Spalato (Yugoslavia) in his book *Putovi Dialoga* (The Paths of Dialogue).[16] In his opinion, it is necessary to develop a new method of teaching religion in communist countries. In explaining the truths, it would be necessary to keep in mind the following points:

1) the rationality of the act of faith (fides quaerens intellectum—intellectus quaerens fidem);

2) the freedom of the act of faith (atheism can be also the result of an option—religious tendency and sentiment must be cultivated—by himself man does not arrive at the Christian religion—fides ex auditu);

3) the presence in man of the natural moral law;

4) the presence of God in the world and in man;

5) the importance of Christian practice and of the witness of faith;

6) faith in man and love of man;

7) do not make a frontal attack on Marxism but in doctrine and in life show the superiority of religion (spirit of dialogue).

Conclusions

We have sought to outline the difficulties which catechesis meets in communist ambients, taking into consideration the constitutional laws concerning freedom of conscience and of religion, substantially identical in the countries of Eastern Europe. As we have seen, such laws aim not to guarantee, but to limit the religious freedom of the Catholics who constitute the majority of the population in Lithuania,[17] Poland,[18] Czechoslovakia[19] and Hungary,[20] but are the minority in the USSR (considered as a whole),[21] in Bulgaria,[22] in the German Democratic Republic,[23] in Rumania,[24] and in Yugoslavia[25] (considered as a whole). Albania has declared itself the first atheistic State in the world, closing all the churches and forbidding every religious manifestation.[26] But also in other communist countries of Eastern Europe, religion is considered a survival from the past, to be eliminated through the progressive building up of the so-called socialism, through atheistic instruction in the schools of every kind and through the limitation of the rights of the Church and family to educate. And precisely in view of the limitation in practice of the educative rights of the Church and family there are notable differences between the individual socialist countries.[27] Our intention has been to delineate the common characteristics of the communist ambients of nine States of Eastern Europe

In each of the above-mentioned countries, there is in act, as we have sought to demonstrate, an atheistic indoctrination which cannot help but leave profound traces in the mentality of youth. Many experts in communism, however, see the great danger for the future of the faith in communist countries not so much in this atheistic, primitive and subtle propaganda, as rather in the limitation of the rights of the Church to announce the Gospel.

The Catholics of the communist States, living in the environmental conditions described above, need much courage and at times true and proper heroism, to profess their faith and to diffuse the Good News. They constitute an important portion of the universal Church (the Suffering Church) and have a right to the understanding, material and spiritual help of all believers.

With its limitations imposed on the announcing of the Gospel and on catechizing, atheistic communism has wrought and will work enormous harm to the faith, but we are certain that the Church, in virtue of the promise of the Savior, will emerge from this trial victorious and will one day find conditions suitable for the diffusion of the faith, for catechesis, which has always been considered—as we read in the Apostolic Exhortation *Catechesi tradendae*—one of her fundamental duties.

MSGR. FRANCESCO SKODA

FOOTNOTES

1. See *Il Sinodo dei Vescovi 1977*, Fourth General Assembly, Civiltà Cattolica, ed., Rome, p. 640.

2. Yugoslavia and Albania do not belong to the so-called Soviet block, even though they organized their States by drawing inspiration from Marxism (from Stalinism in the case of Albania) and they have elevated Marxist atheism to an obligatory subject to be taught in the public schools.

3. Cf. K. Marx—F. Engels, *Opere Scelte*, Riuniti Publishers, Rome, 1966, p. 973.

4. Cf. K. Marx, *Critica al programma di Gotha*, Riuniti Publishers, Rome, 1978, p. 104 (for the critique of the programmed project of the social-democratic party, pp. 89-105).

5. See *V čem suščnosť svobody sovesti?* Mysl, Moscow, 1966, p. 68.

6. *Ibid.*

7. Cf. *La nuova Costituzione sovietica*, Riuniti Publishers, Rome, 1977, p. 48.

8. Cf. Giovanni Codevilla, *Le comunità religiose nell'URSS*, Milan, 1978, pp. 103-113.

9. See AA.VV, o naučnom ateizme i ateističeskom vospitanii (Scientific atheism and atheistic education) Moscow, 1974, p. 29.

10. Cf. "Documenti produtti da gruppi cattolici di Praga," in *CSEO-Documentazione*, Year 11, no. 123.

For the Constitutions of the other States of Eastern Europe we refer to the work of Giovanni Barberini, "Stati Socialisti e confessioni religiose," Milan, Doctor A. Giuffrè, Editor, 1973, p. 537.
For the situation in the socialist countries see Trevor Beeson, *Prudence et courage*. "La situatioǹ religieuse en Russie et en Europe de l'Est," Paris, 1975, p. 328.

11. Cf. Morel-András, *Handbuch des ungarischen Katholizismus*, Ungarisches Kirchensoziologisches Institut (UKI), Wien 1975, pp. 161-162. See also Ernö Eperjes, "Religionsfreiheit in Ungarn?" in *Informationsdienst des katholischen Arbeitskreises fur zeitgeschichtliche Frage* E.V., no. 99, 1979, pp. 52-61.
E. András, S.J., "L'enseignement religieux et l'evangelisation en Hongrie," in *Documentation sur l'Europe Central*, no. 3, vol. XVI, 1978, pp. 167-176.

12. See UKI-Pressedienst, no. 8 (December 1977).

13. See Andrea Rebichini, *Chiesa, società, stato in Cecoslovacchia, II*. 1968-78, Padua, Ceseo-Liviana, 1979, p. 84.
See *Situation der katholischen Kirche in der Tschechoslowakei, Dokumente, Berichte*, Herausgegeben von der Schweizerischen National-Kommission Iustitia et Pax, Bern 1976, p. 150; French translation 1976.

14. See F. Skoda, *La critica della religione nell'URSS*, LDC Turin, 1968, p. 179. G. A. Wetter, "Critica marxista-leninista della religione," in *Ateismo contemporaneo* (Enciclopedia del l'ateismo) SEI, vol. II, 1968, 175-204.

15. See CT 14.

16. See Frane Franiĉ, "Marksitiĉka misaonost i naši mladi u sadasnjem casu" (Marxist thought and our youth of today), in the book *Putovi dialoga*, Split, 1973, pp. 125-144.

17. See Andrè Martin, *Lituania, terra di fede, terra delli croci*, Edizione Paoline, Bari 1977, p. 228.

18. See Andrè Martin, *La Polonia difende la sua anima*, Edizione Paoline, Rome, 1979, p. 351.

19. See footnote 13.

20. See footnotes 11 and 12.

21. See "I cattolici latini in URSS," in *Russia Cristiana*, Anno IV, January-February, 1979, 1 (163), pp. 3-33.

22. See Joachim Härtel, "Religion im Lande Schiwkows" (Bulgarien), in *Informationen un Berichte*, Königstein, no. 11/1979, pp. 1-8.

23. See Peeters Marcel, "Libertè de religion et tolerance en Republique democratique allemande," in *Documentation sur l'Europe Central*, Louvain, vol. XVII, 2, 1979, pp. 99-114.
Herbert Prauss, "30 Jahre DDR-Zur Situation der Kirchen," in *Herder-Korrespondenz*, 33. Jahrg., Nov. 1979, pp. 580-583.

24. See "The Church in Romania," in *Pro Mundi Vita Dossiers*, Nov.-Dec. 1978, Brussels, Belgium.
L. G., "Katholiken im Lande Ceausecus," in: *Informationen und Berichte*, Königstein, no. 7/1979, pp. 8-12.

25. See Yugoslavia, "La difficile libertà della Chiesa nel socialismo." An interview with the Secretary of the CC of the Slovene Communist League, in *CSEO-Documentazione 142*, Anno XIII, Sept. 1979, pp. 377-381.
"La nouvelle loi concernent la religion en Croatie," in *Documentation sur l'Europe Central*, vol. XVI, no. 3, 1978, pp. 227-228.

26. See P. G., (Albania) "The First Atheistic State in the World" (Excerpt from Kana 1979/4), in *Ateismo e dialogo*, Bulletin of the Secretariat for Non-believers, Vatican City, no. 4, 1979, pp. 186-187.

27. For this topic see the legislation and situation present in all the States of Eastern Europe, *Das Recht des Kindes, sich zu einer Religion zu bekennen. Die Kirche als Beschutzerin der Kinder: Der Staatsanspruch auf die Erziehung-Weltanschauliche Manipulation;* in Galube der 2. Welt. Zeitschrift üger Religion, Atheismus und Menschenrechte in kommunistisch regierten Landern. Zollikon, Switzerland, 1979, (7.Jahrg.) no. 11-12, pp. 1-24.
Francesco Skoda, "L'evangelizazione di fronte all'ateismo marxista," in *L'annuncio del Vangelo oggi*, Rome, PUU 1977, pp. 655-672.

PART SIX

The Work
of *Propaganda Fide*
in the
Catechetical Apostolate

"The term 'catechists' belongs above all to the catechists in mission lands. Born of families that are already Christian or converted at some time to Christianity and instructed by missionaries or by another catechist, they then consecrate their lives, year after year, to catechizing children and adults in their own country. Churches that are flourishing today would not have been built up without them. *I rejoice at the efforts made by the Sacred Congregation for the Evangelization of Peoples to improve more and more the training of these catechists.* I gratefully recall the memory of those whom the Lord has already called to Himself. I beg the intercession of those whom my predecessors have raised to the glory of the altars. I wholeheartedly encourage those engaged in the work. I express the wish that many others may succeed them and that they may increase in numbers for a task so necessary for the mission." —CT 66

1

*The Present Action
of the Sacred Congregation
for the Evangelization of Peoples
for the Development
of Catechesis in General,
With Some References
to the Territories
of the Asian
and African Continents*

I. THE COMPETENCE OF THE SACRED CONGREGATION OF "PROPAGANDA FIDE"

The particular identity and function of the Sacred Congregation for the Evangelization of Peoples have been clearly determined and defined in the conciliar decree *Ad gentes divinitus*, which affirms: "For all missions and for the whole of missionary activity, there should be only one competent office, namely that of the "Propagation of the Faith," which should direct and coordinate, throughout the world, both missionary work itself and missionary cooperation. However, the law of the Oriental Churches is to remain untouched."

And moreover:

"This office must be both an instrument of administration and an organ of dynamic direction, which makes use of scientific methods and means suited to the conditions of modern times, always taking into consideration present-day research in matters of theology, of methodology and missionary pastoral procedure."[1]

Further descriptions and clarifications of this declaration are authoritatively expressed in two other conciliar documents and precisely in the two "Motu Proprio": *Ecclesiae sanctae* and *Regimini Ecclesiae Universae:*

"The Congregation for the Evangelization of Peoples, or for the Propagation of the Faith, presided over by the Cardinal Prefect, aided by the Secretary and Under-Secretary, has competence over those matters which concern all the missions established for the spread of Christ's kingdom, and therefore over the assigning and changing of the necessary ministers and of the ecclesiastical jurisdictions; in proposing persons to govern them; in promoting in the most efficient manner a native clergy, to whom gradually the higher offices and government are entrusted; in directing and coordinating all the missionary activity in all parts of the world, in regard to both the heralds of the Gospel themselves and the missionary cooperation of the faithful."[2]

"This Congregation gives missionary impulses, promotes the missionary vocation and spirituality; offers interest in and prayers for the mission, and furnishes authentic and suitable information about them; it equally fulfills with care the duty of educating youth and of forming clerics; it takes an interest in what regards the celebration of synods and of episcopal assemblies or conferences, and reviews, according to the prescriptions of canon law, what is established and decreed by them; it arranges visitations at the pre-established times, by means of which a deeper knowledge about the necessities of the regions and about the more serious problems may be obtained."[3]

The Motu Proprio *Ecclesiae sanctae* also contains a special declaration about the tasks and goals of the Missionary *Dicasterium*, with explicit reference to the task of the promotion of catechesis in agreement with the individual episcopal conferences:

"Because it is desirable that episcopal conferences in the missions be united in organic groups according to the so-called socio-cultural areas, the Sacred Congregation for the Propagation of the Faith should promote such coordinations of episcopal conferences.

"It is the function of these conferences, in collaboration with the Sacred Congregation of the Propagation of the Faith:

"1) To explore methods, even new ones, by which the faithful and the missionary institutes by uniting forces must incorporate themselves into the peoples or groups with whom they live or to whom they are sent, and with whom they must undertake the dialogue of salvation;

"2) To establish study groups to investigate peoples' ways of thinking about the universe, man and his attitude towards God, and to give theological consideration to whatever is good and true.

"Such theological study should provide the necessary foundation for the adaptations which must be made, and which the study groups should investigate. These adaptations should among other things give attention to methods of preaching the Gospel, liturgical forms, the religious life and ecclesiastical legislation.

"With regard to perfecting methods of evangelization and catechesis, the Sacred Congregation for the Propagation of the Faith should promote close cooperation among the higher institutes of pastoral studies."[4]

As is recalled in another section of the present volume, the Sacred *Dicasterium* aware of this, has taken the most suitable initiatives, treating of important themes regarding catechesis in some of its aspects, in the Plenary Congregations according to what is disposed by the General Regulation of the Roman Curia.

"The plenary meetings of the individual Sacred Congregations are composed of the Cardinal members and a certain number of Bishops, according to the norm of the Motu Proprio *Pro comperto sane*, of August 6, 1967, and they take place, except under special circumstances, once a year, in periods to be set by the Congregations themselves; instead, when the opportunities present themselves the other ordinary meetings are held, composed of only the Cardinal members with the participation of the Bishop members who happen to be present in Rome"[5]; this norm refers to Chapter IX of the cited *Regimini Ecclesiae universae* in no. 83, par. 2: "To then treat of problems of greater importance and of a general character, there can participate in the plenary Congregations, as if they were Members, also with deliberative vote if it so pleases the Supreme Pontiff, both Bishops of the Missions named by the Supreme Pontiff himself, and representatives of the Superiors of the Institutes and of the Pontifical Works; it must be seen that persons to set forth the necessities of the so-called 'young' or 'autochthonous' Churches are not missing."[6]

In view of this work, therefore, it will suffice for motives of clarity to present in brief the themes treated in a few of the Plenary Conferences held until now:

Third Plenary Congregation, Year 1970
(April 14-17, 1970)

Theme: *Catechists*

1) The *present situation of Catechists*
   Reporter: His Eminence, Cardinal Stephan Sou Hwan Kim, Archbishop of Seoul (Korea)

2) Problems of the Institution
   Reporter: His Excellency, Jean Zoa, Archbishop of Yaounde (Cameroun)

3) Plan for the Future of Catechists and their Financing
   Reporter: His Eminence, Cardinal Julius Döpfner, Archbishop of Munich

The text was published of the *Deliberations* concerning:

I-II: The Catechist
II: The Formation of Catechists
III: Financing of Catechists
IV: Conclusions.[7]

Fifth Plenary Congregation, Year 1972
(October 17-18-19, 1972)

   Two Reports:
1. "The Present State of Evangelization," given by His Excellency Joseph Cordeiro, Archbishop of Karachi;
2. "The Personnel and Means Assigned to Missionary Activity," by Cardinal Paul Leger (Cameroun).

The Pamphlet *Activité et Coopération Missionnaires dans le Monde* was *published.* Pro Manuscripto, Rome, 1973 (also in English).

Ninth Plenary Congregation, Year 1979
(October, 23-26, 1979)

Proceeding: "Missionary Catechesis Today with Special
Reference to Popular Religiosity."

Reporter: Jésus Lopez-Gay, S.J., Consultor and Expert of
the Sacred Congregation for the Propagation of
the Faith.

II. FUNCTIONS
IN THE CATECHETICAL FIELD

From the foregoing, we note: not only has the Missionary *Dicasterium* not exhausted its office in the field of catechesis, but it makes itself eager to "walk with the times," in harmony with the preoccupations and progammatical vision of the beloved Paul VI, who chose to entrust to the Synod of Bishops the present and urgent theme of catechesis in our time, and in consequent obedience to what came forth from the above-mentioned Synod in the thought of the Synod Fathers and more recently in a pontifical document of universal value, that is, the Apostolic Exhortation *Catechesi tradendae.*

Hence the Congregation feels that principally it must take up its own responsibilities, regarding what is within its competence while also having it in mind to carry out with discretion, *iuxta opportunitatem,* and when the circumstances, gravity and urgency of the problems call for it, works of vigilance, of encouragement, of counsel and of orientation.

In this vision, there is illustrated in a rather essential manner, and with a view to priorities what can be the work of Propaganda Fide for the development of catechesis in each one's territory in general, with a few accentuations in regard to the Asian and African continents.

1. Trusting Attention

The first duty is that *of trusting attention.* At the Second Vatican Council, there was for the first time in the history of the Church and in particular of the missionary Church, participation in the various Sessions by all the Prelates coming from Mission territories. (In the preceding Vatican Council I—for reasons then historically reasonable—such participation was not taken into consideration, rather was not held to be necessary and suitable.)

After this beginning—"a new sign of the times"—when, later on, the synods were held, the participation of missionary prelates was significant, valued and useful for the carrying out of the works and for their conclusions.

Also at the last synod, held in 1977, the presence of missionary Bishops was relevant and gave a valid and positive contribution, as may be seen from the data referred to here.

At the synod, in which 204 fathers took part as representatives of ninety-three episcopal conferences of the whole world, there participated sixty-three synod fathers coming from the territories of Propaganda Fide: thirty-six from Africa, seventeen from Asia, four from Oceania, three from America, three from Europe. Among these there were: seven cardinals: besides Cardinal A. Rossi, Prefect; six residential Archbishops: three from Africa, among whom Cardinal Thiandoum was one of the three presidents of the synod itself, and three from Asia; fifteen Archbishops, of whom one (Bishop Mataca) had been named by the Pope: seven Africans, six Asians, one Antillian, one Fijiian; thirty-nine Bishops: of whom two (Bishop Cavallera and Bishop Bududira) were pontifical nominees: twenty-six from Africa, nine from Asia, two from Oceania, two from America. Among the Superiors General, two were dependent on Propaganda Fide: Father Tarcisius Agostoni of the *Cambonian* Missionaries and Father Joseph Hardy of the Society of the African Missions.

From the varied range of the participants it is easy to deduce how well the Sacred Congregation for the Evangelization of Peoples was represented and how precious was the contribution of the various interventions, as the account of the synodal activity bears witness; and this constitutes a valuable patrimony, considering the interest for such a particular sector of the evangelizing activity of the *Dicasterium* and of the various local Churches.

There is thus a well-founded reason for holding that always in this field both the individual prelates, in their specific responsibilities, and the episcopal conferences, on the basis of their functions, according to the conciliar and post-conciliar recommendations and directives, know and want to carry out their "munus" in the spirit of what is particularly affirmed in the

Decree *Christus Dominus: de Pastorali Episcoporum munere in Ecclesia*, from which we believe it appropriate to quote salient phrases:

The Bishops "should take pains that catechetical instruction—which is intended to make the faith, as illumined by teaching, a vital, explicit and effective force in the lives of men—be given with sedulous care to both children and adolescents, youths and adults. In this instruction a suitable arrangement should be observed as well as a method suited to the matter.... They should see to it that this instruction is based on Sacred Scripture, tradition, the liturgy, magisterium, and life of the Church...(and corresponds) to the character, ability, age and circumstances of life of the students.

"Moreover, they should take care that catechists be properly trained for their function so that they will be thoroughly acquainted with the doctrine of the Church and will have both a theoretical and a practical knowledge of the laws of psychology and of pedagogical methods."

Lastly, "Bishops should also strive to renew or at least adapt in a better way the instruction of adult catechumens."[8]

In regard to this special office, it can be useful and pleasant to refer here to the thought of the then Patriarch of Venice, Cardinal Albino Luciani, who later became Pope John Paul I, expressed in a written intervention given to the Secretary General during the 1977 Synod of Bishops, concerning one of his comments, with reflections, remarks and questions, about the instrument of work developed by the same synod:

In that text the authoritative Author recalls the pre-eminent responsibility of the Bishops in the field of catechesis.[9]

This thought found a most valid and authoritative confirmation in the Apostolic Exhortation *Catechesi tradendae*, in which the Pope affirms in regard to the above-mentioned responsibilities:

"You are beyond all others the ones primarily responsible for catechesis, the catechists par excellence.... Your principal role will be to bring about and maintain in your Churches a real passion for catechesis."[10]

As a parallel, for the renewal of catechesis he warns that for an effective catechetical action the guidance and the responsibility of the Bishop is needed; because every catechesis must be upheld by solidarity with the Bishop.

2. Concerned Awareness

The second duty is one of concerned awareness. Also valid for the Missionary *Dicasterium* in a right and proportionate application, is the wise reflection of beloved Paul VI of venerable memory, contained in the "Motu Proprio," *De Muneribus legatorum Romani Pontifici,* which emphasizes the necessity of an intense exchange of relations between the Pope and his brothers in the Episcopacy:

"The exercise of this manifold mission of ours imposes an intense exchange of relationships among us and our brethren in the episcopacy and the local Churches entrusted to them: relationships which cannot be kept only by means of correspondence, but which are developed through the visit of the bishops *ad limina apostolorum.*[11]

In the following terms, the same document also gives the reason for the Constitution of the Synod of the Bishops:

"Wishing to correspond to the requests of the Church we have constituted the Synod of Bishops, who, responding to our invitation, come to offer us the help of their wise counsels and that of their brethren whom they represent and also to inform us about the state and conditions of the individual Churches."[12]

From this situation we deduce that the Missionary *Dicasterium* is today more than ever aided in regard to timely information about the various and complex problems which the beginning, development and the consolidation of evangelization involve, and in particular as regards the topic under discussion, that is, the state of organization and efficiency of all catechetical activity in the various nations under its competence.

This, however, does not dispense from the duty of proceeding to an always greater specific and concrete knowledge of the catechetical reality in its various aspects, taking advantage of encounters with prelates, of missionary journeys in the various regions, of documentation opportunely requested and studied, and lastly, of conventions arranged with the participation of experts and qualified learned persons.

3. Development

The third duty is one of development. This task springs:

a) from a "vision" of the problem which we can very well define as historical. This affirmation is illustrated with his usual competence by the Very Reverend Father Josef Metzler, O.M.I., our appreciated historical Archivist, in the article published in this volume.[13]

b) from the "experience of its interventions," which through the ages—it can well be said—have permitted the Congregation to test in practice initiatives concerning the various problems of personnel, of methods, of places and of institutions inherent to catechetical activity.

c) from the "global evaluation" of the missionary reality, under the catechetical point of view; and when we say global, the reference is to the multiple and multiform situations of the various local churches which number about 900, constituted or in the process of development, in various contexts: ethnic, sociological, cultural, religious, etc.

d) and lastly from the "singular perception" which arises from its central position in the Church, near the See of Peter, the base of unity and the worldwide point of reference; from the responsibility which arises from its specific competence and mission, and also from the special light which it derives from the Apostolic Mandate and hence from a superior providential plan.

4. Attention to Some Specific Problems

To attain its efficacy, however, such development must always draw inspiration from an incisive awareness of the importance—always, but "specific" in our time—of teaching Catholic doctrine.

This capital importance is not mere opinion, but the voice and thesis of the Vatican II Ecumenical Council, which expresses itself thus:

"...preaching and catechetical instruction which always hold the first place."[14]

The profound and, as far as possible, complete perception of the special problems which catechesis, even missionary catechesis, is called to face today has its fundamental contribution of orientation in the 1977 Synod of Bishops and, hence, in the Apostolic Exhortation *Catechesi tradendae*, which John Paul II made public as fruit of the synodal reflection.

Catechesis does suffer all the problems of the Church to some extent, yet there are some specific ones which the Missionary *Dicasterium* must be attentive to grasp and vigilant to point out.

These specific problems which I repeat, also interest the missionary Church, are fundamentally two:

A) first of all, the problem of content, to which the cited Apostolic Exhortation *Catechesi tradendae* calls attention strongly and repeatedly;

B) then the problem of the relationship of catechesis to the culture of today.

A. *The problem of content*

Regarding this problem, Pope John Paul II insists from the beginning to the end of the cited document that it is necessary to be faithful to the teaching which Christ gave us.

Why does this problem exist? During the past centuries, after the Council of Trent, we have had a primarily doctrinal catechesis. Because of the historical events in which the Church has been involved, with all their repercussions, the problem of fidelity to content has imposed itself in a pre-eminent manner.

For this reason, we have had a strictly doctrinal catechesis for a long time.

Now, this aspect which has been so very fruitful in the past, today no longer appears sufficient to our society in this sense. It is not that the contents were considered less, but it was seen that to speak to the man of today and to be listened to by him, it was not enough to present a doctrine; a life teaching was necessary; that is, a doctrine that would also answer all of his problems, which are somewhat indirect, or implicit, or analogous, or tied in with the problems of faith.

Therefore, catechesis had to take a step forward: from doctrinal catechesis the passage was made to pedagogical catechesis. And, in the name of pedagogy, of human problems, of language and of other related factors, the matter of content ended up somewhat in the shade.

Now, it is urgent and necessary, without forgetting the pedagogical dimension, to recover clarity of content.

Our *Dicasterium*, and all the hierarchical missionary Church, has, therefore, the obligation of examining with precision what points of Catholic doctrine are most contested today, where these are encountered with more frequency and which are the erroneous or unilateral forms used in the exposition of the truths.

In a general picture the principal errors can be grouped under these three aspects:

—regarding ecclesiology
—regarding the Eucharist
—regarding moral life.

In connection with the first, the ecumenical council used various expressions and showed in perspective diverse visions of the Church: the Church, people of God; the Church, mystical body; the Church, community of faith; the Church, community of hope.

These models or images accentuate now one, now the other, aspect.

Sadly enough, however, sometimes in current catechesis one of these images is taken and its exposition and role are amplified, often to the loss or the detriment of the others.

One ends up, therefore, with unilateral forms in which the Church is seen as being detached from reality, as a community animated by the Holy Spirit in a too uniform and equalitarian manner, because of which the Catholic hierarchy, a fundamental fact that must never be renounced, is placed in the shadows.

It is, therefore, a matter of regaining in catechesis these images of the Church in all their values and of proposing them in an organic and connected manner, so as to grasp faithfully and fully this great mystery which is the Church.

With regard to the sacramental life, undoubtedly and indisputably errors are circulating which concern the Eucharist in particular. Certainly, to propose to the man of today the terminology of transubstantiation can objectively present some difficulties. However, other attempts made have ended up by proposing visions not in conformity with the thought and doctrine of the Church.

It is the task of catechesis to proclaim the reality of the eucharistic mystery with clarity and integrity.

The Sacred *Dicasterium* will not let occasions be lacking for doing this in the most ideal and effective manner.

Also in this period we encounter errors of omission or else lack of precision regarding the real nature of original sin. At times attempts are made to reduce original sin to the undetermined and impersonal existence of the first fault. It is clear that authentic catechesis cannot do this, but must rather be most faithful to revelation and to the magisterium of the Church.

Other errors concern further aspects of the moral life. In the name of love, through an exaggerated reaction to a past which perhaps classified sins somewhat too strictly, today there is an attempt to propose an adulterated life, with the risk that later the genuine knowledge of the experience of love in the light of evangelical teaching will be diminished.

The principles of the moral life are a part of the content of the faith. Christ has not only taught us but has given us an example of life which we must imitate. And every time that one speaks of difference between ideology and message it is precisely the moral line that is placed in danger.

Here, too, there is a need for vigilance, for timely intervention and for responsible directives to be carried out in harmony with the wise declarations of the Pope and to support the various stands of the young Churches.

B. The Problem of the Catechesis-Culture Relationship

Another important problem concerns the relationship of catechesis with today's culture.

There is an affirmation in *Catechesi tradendae* which should be taken into full consideration:

"Catechesis...is called to bring the power of the Gospel into the very heart of culture and cultures"; therefore, "genuine catechists know that catechesis 'takes flesh' in the various cultures and milieus." [15]

Christianity is history; the Church lives in history. In the twentieth century the Church is held to do something analogous to what happened in the first centuries when Christianity was implanted in Greek and Roman culture.

It was a marvelous transplant. Today Christianity is called to transplant itself, at least in a good part of the world, into a culture which has some values but also gross limitations.

Therefore, this transplant requires that there be an appropriate language in catechesis; and that at the same time catechesis habituate one to the critical analysis of culture, in such a way as to see its positive aspects but also its limitations.

The currents of contemporary thought have cut their way into the contemporary culture of the whole world; therefore, catechesis is obliged to approach these currents with much frankness and honesty. It is sufficient to allude to Marxism, which catechesis must subject to a serious and critical analysis so as to make clear the absolute incompatibility between that ideology and the Catholic faith.

In addition to problems of a general character, there are two specific problems for the mission territories: one concerns the relationship with local cultures; the other, the relationship with other religions.

A wealth of local cultures exists. In the mission nations, in the nations of the Third World, Christians live in an immense cultural tradition that poses some very important problems. Now, the inculturation of which *Catechesi tradendae* speaks means that catechesis must know these cultures, and must also present them because Christians live in that world and must be citizens of that world. But it must present them with an education that aids in understanding their values and in clearly seeing their limitations, in such a way that one can proceed truly to an animation from within, even if the Christians are a minority, so as to be able to transform these cultures and even have them be assimilated by Christianity.

Valuable in this regard is this competent and authoritative testimony:

"Finally, in catechesis, the great law of psychological and cultural adaptation is of extreme importance. In the manner of presenting catechesis it will be necessary to bear in mind the formation acquired, the psychology, the cultural environment, the problems and life orientations of the listeners, in order to foster the best in-depth assimilation of Christian doctrine; and a constructive confrontation with the beliefs and religious behavior prior to conversion will be necessary in order that the new Christian life will be solid and enlightened, so as to avoid all unacceptable syncretism and conserve all the ancient pre-Christian religious values. In this regard, W. Bühlmann noted: 'We believe that there is not necessarily a greater danger of syncretism when one leads pagans to Christianity without making a sharp break, than when one implants Christianity in their consciousness simply as something entirely new; that the use of a pagan term is not more dangerous than the use of a foreign word—just the contrary.'

"In the first case, one is obliged to make a very clear confrontation with paganism; in the second, there is the danger that one will plant the new within the old, without 'grafting,' and that the two religions will continue to live independently side by side."[16]

C. The Relationship with the Religions

Another contemporary problem is that of the relationship with other religions. In the mission countries, Christians are often a minority or at least are not the greater majority, as in the countries of ancient Christian tradition. Now, catechesis is called upon, here again, for motives of concrete living in the environment, to explain these other religions so that the Christian will know them and be able to evaluate them, and also to say why he has not followed them and has instead chosen the Christian religion and believes in it fully and firmly. But catechesis must also do this out of a motive of respect and esteem for whoever believes in God and seeks Him.

The Christian is a witness to his faith; hence, he must be able to know how to speak to anyone who does not have the same faith or who follows another. Hence, he must be capable of knowing the thought of the others, of knowing how to see points that are different, so that he can act on these and thus be a witness and herald of the Gospel.

This delicate, important and most timely problem, which had such a pre-eminent place in the Council and which constituted one of the most salient efforts of the most recent Pontiffs, from John XXIII to Paul VI, from John Paul I (it suffices to read the message he delivered at the beginning of his pontificate) to John Paul II, demands the whole effort of the missionary Church.

The Sacred *Dicasterium* which attentively follows the reality of the young Churches even under this aspect (which involves not a few implications), will make itself, within the sphere of its competence, always more the promoter of a proper interpretation of the ecumenical spirit and of a positive application of all the initiatives directed to fostering the development without prejudice to the freedom and efficacy of the announcement of the Gospel that is to be realized through preaching and through catechesis.

In time wise norms were set up to apply the conciliar directives through the Ecumenical Directory, of which the first part was published in 1967 and the second in 1970.

Now, both the first and second parts contain precise directives regarding the pastoral responsibility of the Bishops and the method of teaching in general and of catechesis in particular; the application of these should foster an authentic relationship of true ecumenism.[17]

Special Situations

To realize such relationships in an organic and incisive manner, it is necessary to keep ethnic realities always in mind, as well as the religious and structural reality of our territories.

Consequently, in this second part there are presented a few outlines to clarify the "status," in the meaning set forth above, of two great missionary areas: Asia and Africa, with a few consequent suggestions for action.

1) Asia

The Asiatic world has always drawn the full attention of the Missionary *Dicasterium* from the very beginning of its establishment.

Today the reality of that continent, characterized by the constitution of thirty-four nations, has very particular aspects:

Asia is the largest continent in the world; it contains 57 % of the world's population; it has the major young population; 67 % of the inhabitants are not over twenty-five years of age, which indicates what expectations, what problems and what hopes this demographic reality envisages (recently it was announced that in 1979 the world's population had reached the total of four and a half billion).

Asia is the most religious continent in the world. All the great religions, including Christianity, have had their cradle there; however, we are confronted with a continent less Christian than all the others. In fact, excluding the "Catholic Island" of the Philippines, Asia is only 1.5 % Christian and only 0.9 % Catholic.

By comparison, the other continents have become, more or less, Christian.

Asia, however, is not a "tabula rasa" from a religious point of view; rather, just the contrary: there is instead a most rich and varied religious experience to be recognized, to be purified, to be evaluated and to be integrated[18] (cf. the voluminous work of Professor Wilhelm Schmidt: Origins of the Idea of God—*Ursprung der Gottesidee*).

The fundamental problem of Asia is evangelization. This was the theme of the first Colloquy or Encounter organized by the FABC (Federation of Asian Bishops' Conference) and held in Taipei, on April 22-27, 1974. Around the theme "The Evangelization of Asia Today," the Bishops of that continent reflected on the problems and the perspectives of the Church in Asia. Among the more urgent problems of evangelization today is enumerated the formation of true particular Churches with their own Asiatic identity, Churches which at the same time become missionary and responsible for the total development of their human nuclei.

This project of the Asiatic Federation of Episcopal Conferences is identified with the program of the Sacred Congregation for the Evangelization of Peoples. It would be very important if the contacts between the Sacred *Dicasterium* and this Federation were to become more real and continual. In its plan of formation and distribution of missionary forces, the Sacred Congregation can effectively aid in the formation of these particular Churches. On the other hand, they will be authentic Churches insofar as they remain open to catholicity and united to the universal Church and guard the heritage of the one Church of Christ.[19]

Today in all of Asia there are very successful experiments in the field of pastoral and missionary catechesis. A more united action, however, a more attentive mutual collaboration, is lacking, because there is an imbalance of power, and at times a multiplicity not clearly necessary. The Sacred *Dicasterium* has the duty to inaugurate a more united and effective action in the field of mass media, TV, radio, press, news agencies, films, etc. It must make contacts with the pastoral centers and make the successful experiments known to others.

The theme of the mass media is an element of vital efficacy in the missions in general and, concretely, in those of Asia.

Today, dialogue and inculturation are the two themes that have acquired a new special prominence in the Church in Asia. This means interreligious dialogue, because we cannot forget that in the thirty-four nations which today form Asia the great religions of the world—Hinduism, Buddhism and Islamism—are alive and active.

In her daily encounter with the world the missionary Church cannot forget the need for dialogue, which cannot replace the announcement of Christ, but must enrich it, a dialogue which cannot be maintained on a particular or private level.

The Sacred *Dicasterium*, which is intimately united with the Secretariat for Non-Christians, also feels this fundamental problem and must follow all the efforts that are made in this field.

The IX Plenary Session treated of non-Christian popular religiosity and its relationship with catechesis; thus, there was an opportunity to receive all this problematic directly from the Bishops of mission territories. As it enters upon its duty, the *Dicasterium* will certainly be attentive to obtain positive applications from these inquiries and from the conclusions drawn.

2) Africa

A special overall look at the reality of the Church in Africa, happily defined by Pope Paul VI of venerable memory as the *nova patria Christi* permits from the catechetical point of view a general evaluation that is fairly comforting, even if catechesis in Africa, and elsewhere, for that matter, must be further intensified.

In the presence of this specific reality the Missionary *Dicasterium* can take into consideration a few tasks oriented to consolidating what already exists, to promoting what must be started, and to perfecting what already functions:

a) "Realize" a comparative picture of the situation in the various zones of Africa and what has to be faced there. This can be done after becoming familiar with the free and responsible favorable thought of the various episcopal conferences, from the Symposium of the African Bishops (SECAM) through its specific executive offices. This comparative picture should aim at identifying the actual state of catechetical organization and the progress attained by it, both on the national and diocesan levels, with regard to centers, personnel, methods and environmental needs. It is necessary to remember here what *Catechesi tradendae* recommends to the episcopal conferences, and that is to prepare for the individual territories new catechism texts which respect full fidelity to the message of Christ and in their contents are such as to result in being truly joined to the concrete life of the generation to which they are addressed, having well in mind its anxieties, its questions, its struggles and its hopes.[20] In this field it will also be useful for the various episcopal conferences to refer to the *General Catechetical Directory*, as the cited Apostolic Exhortation insists.[21]

Previously, when treating of local organization in mission territories and of the specific responsibility of the episcopal conferences, the Decree *Ad gentes* provided a precious recommendation regarding the usefulness of coordinating initiatives in the pastoral and catechetical fields.

"Episcopal conferences should take common counsel to deal with weightier questions and urgent problems, without however neglecting local differences. Lest the already insufficient supply of men and means be further dissipated, or lest projects be multiplied without necessity, it is recommended that they pool their resources to found projects which will serve the good of all: as for instance, seminaries, technical schools and schools of higher learning; pastoral, catechetical, and liturgical centers; as well as the means of social communication.

"Such cooperation, when indicated, should also be initiated between several different episcopal conferences."[22]

b) Make progress in the methods of a catechesis that has pointedly been defined by the Pope in his cited Apostolic Exhortation, as "systematic"; a catechesis which is to have an organic foundation, not an improvised one, so as to provide a logical picture of the entire Catholic doctrine and of all its implications.[23]

c) Give the proper evaluation to popular religiosity, according to the indications of the Plenary Congregation of the *Dicasterium*, as a particularly ideal instrumer.t for whoever is animated by the pastoral preoccupation of bringing the traditional teaching of the Church into the specific environmental situations which constitute the field of evangelization.

d) Seek out the difficulties emerging today from very real causes, such as can be the widespread nationalization of Catholic schools, the advance of secularization and the lesser availability of teachers.

e) Propose models of centers for the formation of catechists making use of the wonderful experiences already being carried out in the various missionary territories, to this end promoting encounters, exchanges of ideas, reciprocal information and also, within the bounds of possibilities, visits from one center to another to see *de visu* what experience enlightened by grace can have suggested.

f) Emphasize what today is commonly called the missionary approach in pre-Christian ambients where the population is still for the greater part a field of evangelization. There comes to the fore here, on the one hand, the true role of the more committed catechist and, on the other hand, the promotional effort of the evangelizing community.

g) The Sacred *Dicasterium* could also consider sending out an appeal to the religious institutes, already very praiseworthy, so that after the solemn and committed interest shown by the hierarchy in the field of catechesis, especially through the synod of Bishops, the Apostolic Exhortation and previously the *General Catechetical Directory*, they can increase their effort in the field of catechesis with their availability in all those initiatives which the hierarchy (episcopal conferences and individual Bishops with the collaboration of the pastoral councils) can undertake to proportion missionary catechesis to the necessities of our time and to the recommendations of the Apostolic See.

It can also be suggested to employ to better advantage already-existing catechetical institutes and pastoral catechetical centers, in order that their functions may not be only academic and speculative, but will be always better oriented to giving qualified service to the formation and to the work of catechists and also to the use of all the modern instruments of communication suitable for cooperating in the great work of missionary catechesis in this difficult era.

MSGR. TIZIANO SCALZOTTO

FOOTNOTES

1. Conciliar Decree *Ad gentes* (no. 29, para. 2 and 5), Enchiridion Vaticanum, I, Dehoniane, Bologna 1976, nn. 1192 and 1195.

2. Motu Proprio *Regimini Ecclesiae universae*, op. cit., II, 1977, no. 1622.

3. *Ibid.*, no. 1624.

4. Motu Proprio *Ecclesiae Sanctae*, op. cit., I, nos. 903-905, (Part III, no. 18).

5. General Regulation of the Roman Curia, Part II, Title III, art. 110, op. cit., III, 1977, no. 216.

6. *Regimini Ecclesiae universae*, op. cit., II, no. 1623.

7. Missionary Bibliography, 34 (1970), Quaderno no. 13, pp. 41-44.

8. *Christus Dominus*, op. cit., I, no. 602 (CD 14).

9. *Rivista del Clero Italiano*, 61 (1980) January, pp. 2 and 12.

10. *Catechesi tradendae* (CT) 63.

11. *Sollecitudo omnium Ecclesiarum*, op. cit., III, no. 1295.

12. *Ibid.*, no. 1298.

13. P. Metzler, *Missionary catechesis in the directives of the Sacred Congregation for the Evangelization of Peoples or Propaganda Fide*, present op., following chapter.

14. *Christus Dominus*, op. cit., I, no. 601, (CD 13).

15. CT 53.

16. A. Seumois, OMI, *Theologie Missionniare*, II, Rome 1974, p. 184.

17. "Ad totam Ecclesiam," *Ecumenical Directory* op. cit., II, Part I, p. 1004ff.; Part II, p. 1606ff.

18. Wilhem Schmidt, *Ursprung der Gottesidee*, vol. 12, 1912-1955.

19. *Evangelii nuntiandi*, no. 64.

20. CT 49.

21. General Catechetical Directory, 1971, op. cit., IV, 1978, p. 224ff.

22. *Ad gentes*, op. cit., I, nos. 1201-1202 (AG 31).

23. CT 21-26, 31.

2

Missionary Catechesis in the Directives of the Sacred Congregation for the Evangelization of Peoples or "De Propaganda Fide" (1622-1980)

As already in the Encyclical *Redemptor hominis* and in the other documents, so too in the Apostolic Exhortation *Catechesi tradendae*, Pope John Paul II manifests a clear approbation of the historical dynamic of the Christian faith and its tradition, in the conviction, however, that we must not merely conserve the heritage handed down to us, but rather develop it.[1] Repeatedly the Pontiff alludes to the historicity of human existence as an essential element of catechesis, but such a feeling for tradition is intimately bound up "with a strong courage toward the future."[2] These two elements are and must be characteristics for missionary catechesis. The Pope, therefore, can rightly say that "the missions are also a special area for the application of catechesis." And he continues: "The People of God have thus continued for almost 2,000 years to educate themselves in the faith in ways adapted to the various situations of believers and the many different circumstances in which the Church finds herself."[3]

For more than 350 years the Sacred Congregation for the Evangelization of Peoples or Propaganda Fide, responsible for the spiritual direction and promotion of the missionary activity of the Church, has endeavored to seek the forms suitable for the various territorial, cultural and social conditions so as to give to her missionaries wise directives for effective catechesis. Already in the very first documents of the Missionary *Dicasterium*, in fact, we find valid and surprising elements in this regard. It will certainly be useful to list and analyze them, without any pretense of being exhaustive, limiting ourselves, for now, to documents already published, both in the two volumes of the Collectanea,[4] and in the appendix of the fifth tome of the History of Propaganda Fide.[5] Much other information in this regard is undoubtedly to be found in the seven volumes of the Instructions, in the nine volumes of the Register of the Letters of the Sacred Congregation and in those of the "New Series" of the Archives of the same Missionary *Dicasterium*.[6] Even though we do not yet encounter modern terminology in these, we can discover the nature and diverse aspects of missionary catechesis. All the documents which treat the administration of the sacraments, the erection of schools, popular devotion, the formation of native priests and catechists, liturgical questions, the foundation of confraternities or of similar topics, contain valid elements and suitable directives for missionary catechesis.

Catechize "Through Ways That Are Gentle and Full of Charity"

In his Apostolic Exhortation, Pope John Paul II cautions against every kind of deformation of catechesis through ideologies and against "the danger and the temptation to mix catechetical teaching unduly with overt or masked ideological views, especially political and social ones, or with personal political options."[7] The same thought and same admonition are found in the first encyclical letter which the Sacred Congregation of Propaganda Fide addressed, on January 15, 1622, to all the Apostolic Nunciatures, communicating to them the erection of the new Missionary *Dicasterium*,[8] so that they "will make it known to the princes, or to the republics, or to the rulers of the peoples where they find themselves, in order that, knowing the utility, better yet the necessity, of so great an office, they will always promote it, since it is nothing else than the true office of the apostolate."[9] In it the Sacred Congregation formulates the fundamental rules of its missionary program. It is clearly stated that the establishment of the Sacred Congregation of Propaganda Fide does not aim "to erect tribunals, or to exercise temporal jurisdiction in any place, or to hold to violent or unusual methods; but to apply itself through gentle ways, full of charity, which are proper to the Holy Spirit, to the conversion of the infidels, now by preaching, teaching and debating, and again by admonishing, exhorting and praying, and also to draw them sweetly in the way of salvation with prayer, with fastings, and with alms, and even with disciplines, and with tears shed for them, in the light of the truth, and to administer to them the most holy sacraments, without making any noise and, so to speak with, a gentle silence, because it is more the very refined unction of the divine mercy than human work which produces the effect."[10] Clearly, the norms of the missionaries, whom the *Dicasterium* sends to the territories under its jurisdiction, to evangelize, to instruct and to catechize the peoples, must also be the same.

Exemplary Life of the Catechist

There are two factors that the Sacred Congregation considers absolutely indispensable in catechesis: on the one hand, an exemplary life and good example on the part of those who catechize; and on the other, perfect knowledge of the language. The primitive documents of Propaganda Fide abound in these two fundamental rules. To four Capuchin Fathers who were setting out for the Near East, Msgr. Francesco Ingoli, first Secretary of Propaganda Fide, wrote: "First of all, they must behave in their lives and in their conduct in such a way that not only the Latins but also the Greeks will be moved by their example and will form that opinion which the Capuchins have earned throughout all Christianity where their holy Institute is. Having generated this concept in those peoples, they will gain such esteem that it will bear much fruit with the help of God.

"Convinced that the Greeks will allow themselves to be influenced more by the example of their well-regulated lives, maintained in austerity, than by sermons, just as the Constitutions of the Capuchins prescribe, they should seek to live in conformity with their Constitutions."[11]

In the "Rules for Missionaries" of 1707[12] the Sacred Congregation better develops this thought, supporting it with theological arguments: "First of all, it is necessary to recall that the Apostle, while calling you coadjutors of God, holy temples of God, legates of the Lord Christ, nuncios, preachers of the Holy Gospel, nevertheless exhorts you that this apostolic office does not consist in dominion, in honor and in superiority, with, later on, human vainglory, but in service, burdens and work. He himself exclaims: 'Let us glory in tribulations,' 'As for me, let it never be that I glory in anything else save in the cross of our Lord Jesus Christ.' Hence, because you have been made a spectacle for the world, for the angels and for men, hear the same Apostle exhort you through the mercy of the Almighty God, in order that you may present your bodies as a living and holy sacrifice to God, and not to please men. Begin this holy undertaking, therefore, and what you confess with words, do it with evangelical works, following in the footsteps of the Apostles, in order that your ministry, which is an apostolic ministry, will not be blameworthy."[13]

Formation of the Catechist

Here, the very numerous Decrees, Instructions and Letters of the *Dicasterium* which have as their object the spiritual and intellectual formation of the missionaries would deserve to be cited.[14] With equal vigor it insists on the study of languages as a condition *sine qua non* for good catechesis.[15] The same purpose was to be served and contributed to by the polyglot press of Propaganda, founded in 1626 to print liturgical and devotional books, and grammars, dictionaries, catechisms,[16] etc., in all languages. The printing of all these was a praiseworthy initiative without precedence, which fostered not only the development of catechesis (in that time, in fact, there were very few printing plants in the missionary territories themselves), but also the spiritual and intellectual development of the various peoples.

Two fundamental attitudes characterize the action of the Sacred Congregation for the evangelization—and hence for the catechesis—of Peoples, and the Sacred Congregation insistently enjoined the same attitudes upon its missionaries: 1) energetic refusal to any political activity and any interference whatsoever in political matters, 2) prudent inculturation of Christian doctrine. In regard to the first point, the very famous Instruction of 1659, written for the French missionaries in China and Indochina, contains a clear and peremptory command to keep themselves away "from political matters, from affairs of state," and to pretend "not to understand anything of all that and to lack all capacity for civil administration."[17]

Respect for Cultures

Of particular interest and importance are the directives of Propaganda Fide for the inculturation of Christian doctrine by means of catechesis. We already find the first norms in this regard in the same Instruction of 1659. John Paul II, in the Apostolic Exhortation, fundamentally establishes that catechesis must be based upon Revelation. He says: "This Revelation tells of the radical change of man and the universe, of all that makes up the web of human life under the influence of the Good News of Jesus Christ."[18] From this perspective he then examines the serious and decisive problem of inculturation: "We can say of catechesis, as well as of evangelization in general, that it is called to bring the power of the Gospel into the very heart of culture."[19] In the Instruction of 1659, which was written for the first Vicars Apostolic of Indochina and of China, but has, however, a universal value, Propaganda Fide severely forbids the bringing of Western culture into mission nations; in fact, it forbids every comparative reference between Western culture and local culture, and imposes adaptation upon the missionaries. Here are the clear and far-sighted words of the Instruction: "Do not make any attempt or seek in any way to persuade those peoples to change their customs, their way of living, their habits, when they are not openly contrary to religion and to morality. There is nothing more absurd than to want to bring France or Spain or Italy or another part of Europe into China. The Faith, and not all this, is what you must bring, the Faith which does not reject or offend the way of living and the habits of any people, when these are not depraved; in fact, it wants such things to be preserved and protected. Because it is in perfect harmony with human nature to prefer, honor and love one's own nation and all that is inherent in it, more than others, there is nothing more strange than changing ancestral habits, especially those which have been transmitted from time immemorial or—worse still—replacing them with those of your own nation. Consequently, it is well never to make a comparison between the customs of those peoples and those of Europeans; on the contrary, it is necessary to seek with diligence to become accustomed to their way of life. Admire and praise what merits it; on the contrary, you must not praise in a flattering manner what you do not consider worthy; in such a case, it is up to your prudence not to evaluate it and not to condemn it lightly.

However, what you consider evil, you must cautiously and gradually repel, more with your behavior than with words, and if later you judge that the minds are ready to accept the truth, eradicate it completely."[20]

The Synod of Ajuthia

The Vicars Apostolic took these and the other directives of the Instruction literally (for example, the formation of native clergy). In 1665, as soon as they arrived in the Orient, they held a missionary synod with all their clergy at Ajuthia in Siam (today Thailand). It had special importance for the development of the missionary catechesis of the Sacred Congregation of Propaganda Fide for two reasons: 1) because the synod published an instruction for the missionaries of the Institute of Foreign Missions of Paris, containing detailed rules and norms for missionary catechesis, which later were approved by Propaganda Fide and became the official Manual of the Missionary *Dicasterium* for all its missionaries; 2) because the synod made an attempt at rigorous adaptation to the mentality of the Indochinese people, by founding a religious congregation with norms much more severe than those of the European religious Orders, considering that evangelization would be ineffective if the European missionaries did not follow the same (and perhaps more severe) rule of life as the Buddhist monks; in other words, that the example of the evangelizers is a stimulus for the Chinese and Indochinese people to accept the Christian religion or to refuse it. Consequently, these two initiatives of the Synod of Ajuthia merit a more detailed exposition.

The Instruction[21] is divided into ten chapters and treats practically all the aspects of missionary life: the spiritual life of the missionary, which must be a life of recollection, of prayer, of fasting and sacrifices and of continual studies; it speaks of the preaching of the Word of God, of the catechumenate, of Baptism, of the neophytes and of the catechists. Of interest to us now are, first of all, the rules and norms for catechesis which we encounter principally in chapters IV, V and X. The synod considers the preaching of the Word of God, that is, catechesis, the principal apostolic duty of the missionary and of the catechist; however, it must always be coupled with an irreprehensible *modus vivendi* of the one who sets it forth to the others, insofar as good example (the Synod always adds) is worth more in the eyes of the peoples than eloquence. Furthermore, it recommends that the sermon or catechetical instruction be well prepared and delivered in a convincing manner, and be the fruit of prayer and meditation (Chap. IV).

Missionary and catechist must set forth the Christian truths in a clear and easily intelligible manner, avoiding subtle argumentations. They must study the other religions to discover in them possible points of contact for Christian doctrine and thus be able to demonstrate that it is not something entirely new and that God does not desire religious worship as an end in itself, but for the good of man. Detailed rules follow regarding the attitude of the missionary towards pagan worship, towards local rites and customs, etc. (Chap. V). The last chapter (X) contains the norms for the institution of catechists. The synod points out two necessary reasons for such institution: lack of priests and, consequently, the possibility of ordaining the best catechists as priests. The catechist must be a man of irreprehensible moral life, healthy and without bodily deformities. He must know how to control himself, must not be too loquacious, and must, naturally, be well prepared.

From what was set forth above, the Sacred Congregation of Propaganda Fide made this the official "Manual" for all its missionaries.

The other initiative of the synod, that is, the founding of the "Apostolic Congregation," which, in the intention of the French Bishops, should have been a "living catechesis," encountered great difficulties in Rome on the part of those responsible for the Missionary *Dicasterium*, who nevertheless attributed great importance to it, especially in relationship to the Asiatic ambient. Here is how the reporter in the meeting of the particular assembly that had to decide about the approval or otherwise of the "Apostolic Congregation" explained the need to those present: "First of all, on the part of the infidels, who have no more powerful motive for embracing the faith than holiness of life. And their Talapoini, or Religious, have a very regulated and rigorous exterior. If the infidels do not see in the missionaries and in the ministers of the Gospel the equal and even more the surpassing of their Talapoini, there remains no hope for their conversion. Hence, the said Vicars Apostolic, having the obligation of procuring the conversion of the infidels insofar as they can, and this not being obtained except through rigor of life, believe themselves obliged to embrace hardships and austerities in their conduct and behavior."[22] Propaganda Fide asked for the opinion of a few consultants. The result was rather disappointing. All the consultants, not knowing the real intention of the synodal Bishops and completely ignoring the mentality and profound religiousness of the Asiatic peoples, counselled against the approbation of the "Apostolic Congregation," because its rules seemed too austere and, humanly speaking, impossible of being observed; rather, some of them considered invalid the vows already emitted by the members of the synod itself. The Sacred Congregation adhered to this opinion, denying approval of the "Apostolic Congregation."

Concrete Norms

Generally speaking, the Sacred Congregation of Propaganda Fide gave its directives for missionary catechesis in general terms, leaving up to the superiors of every missionary territory the application in view of the various situations which could be foreseen; when, however, it was opportune or necessary, the Sacred *Dicasterium* was not alien to precisely stating its concrete norms.

Thus, for example, it insisted repeatedly that the missionaries in China should not be silent in their teaching about the mystery of the cross, and this with evident allusion to the method of the Jesuits, who spoke of the passion and death of Christ only when they were certain of the perseverance of the neophytes. In its Decree of October 21, 1636, the Sacred Congregation declared that not even temporarily were they to be silent about the mystery of the cross under the pretext of avoiding giving scandal to the non-believers or for reasons of prudence, but that instead it was necessary to teach and to preach, without blushing, not only the glory of the Lord, but also His passion.[23]

On the other hand, in Muslim nations Propaganda Fide advised the missionaries not to speak publicly about the crucifixion of Christ, insofar as it was forbidden, with most serious sanctions by the Islamic states. This attitude, however, was deemed necessary only with Muslims and not with catechumens or Christians.[24]

Also in the Instruction of February 9, 1760, in which Propaganda Fide condemned the superstitious custom of the so-called "Kurbani," we meet special wise directives for catechesis in the dioceses of Nicopolis and Sofia: "Therefore, the missionaries must...apply themselves wholly in instructing (the faithful) fully in the healthy means which God and the Church offer them to attain those ends, which in vain they hope for from Gentile, or Judaic practices, or those infected with schism.... And here it is opportune to instruct the faithful in the spirit of the Church, which appears in the common prayers established by her and proposed for the common use of her children."[25]

The Question of Rites

Also the whole "cursed"[26] question of the Chinese, Malabar and Japanese rites has to be seen and evaluated under the aspect of catechetical teaching. In its Instruction of 1659 the Sacred Congregation of Propaganda Fide had taken a clear and far-sighted position in regard to the cultural usages of the peoples and their rites. However, concerning questions inherent to the faith, it had to turn to the Holy Office to have an answer for the "doubts" of the missionaries. Now, the Holy Office depended for its decisions on the statements of facts of the missionaries themselves. If these said that superstitious rites were involved, then the answer could only be negative: Christians cannot participate in such rites. If instead, the rites were considered as something purely civil or urban, without any religious meaning, the Holy Office had no difficulty in declaring them licit for the Christians also. Later on, to guarantee uniformity of catechesis, and also because the rumors which attributed a religious meaning to the Chinese rites in honor of Confucius and of ancestors were becoming more insistent, the Holy See forbade the participation of faithful Catholics in such rites.[27]

To Stimulate Vocations

Catechesis concerns all the dimensions of the life of the faithful. One of its most noble aims is to stimulate and form priestly and religious vocations; in fact, it is fundamentally important in this respect. By its nature missionary catechesis must aim at the formation of native ecclesial vocations. The Sacred Congregation of Propaganda Fide saw precisely in the formation of the local clergy its holiest task and duty. Very numerous are the Instructions and Decrees with which Directors of the *Dicasterium* called the attention of the Bishops and of the missionaries to this duty. In an Instruction of 1626 Ingoli ordered the Bishops to teach or to have a priest teach "Christian doctrine and the Latin language to the children so as to then choose the best ones to direct them to the clerical life."[28] In regard to the evangelization of Latin America, Ingoli once wrote that if native priests were not ordained, the Church of that continent would "always be a baby, and will never gain vigor, and because Europe will not be able to meet these many needs, not only will the Church not go forward in preaching the Holy Gospel in the midlands,[29] but the littoral parts already converted will slowly be lost."[30] In the Instruction of 1659, Propaganda Fide wrote: "The main reason why this Sacred Congregation sends you Bishops to those regions[31] is so that you will apply yourselves in every way to instruct the youth in such a manner that the young men will become capable of the priesthood.... Never forget this aim of leading to Holy Orders the greatest possible number of young men...to be able later on to ordain native Bishops as well."[32] Therefore, schools were erected everywhere for "the instruction in Christian doctrine of the youth of those regions, with the greatest diligence and in their own language."[33] No race, no category of men was to be excluded from the priesthood. Ingoli energetically applied himself in order that the American Indians, too,[34] should be admitted, and Propaganda Fide, in its programmatic Instruction of 1845, *Neminem profecto*, which was dedicated almost entirely to the formation of native clergy, expressly prohibits the exclusion of youth of inferior castes from the priesthood.[35]

Catechetical instruction is the indispensable presupposition for the formation of native clergy. Where local priests are lacking, says the Instruction, it is necessary to select "men of good habits and of a totally excellent faith" and to form them as catechists. In this document the Sacred Congregation of Propaganda Fide holds that the "religious and civil" instruction and education of the young is "the most valid thing that can be imagined for the growth, permanence and dignity of the Catholic faith." And it continues: "Therefore, it is necessary to do absolutely everything possible to prepare the teachers in the best way, and to erect schools everywhere." What is interesting about this document is not only that Propaganda Fide gives so much importance to catechetical instruction, but also that it ties it in with civil and artisan education, considering the one, in fact, as an integrating part of the other. As far as we can see, this is the first time that such a thought in such clear and explicit terms is encountered in a document of the Missionary *Dicasterium*.

Just a few years before, answering the question of the Vicar General of Nanking as to whether the catechists had to make the profession of Faith according to the formula of Pius IV, Propaganda Fide had given precise directives for their choice. Contrary to a prior decision of 1797,[36] the *Dicasterium* was of the opinion that this was not necessary; however, it insisted on the wise selection of men and women catechists.[37]

Three Important Instructions

Even though they do not contain many new elements in relation to the preceding documents cited up until now, the three other Instructions of Propaganda Fide of the last century that we now want to analyze under our aspect do have a certain importance because of their insistence on the choice, formation and exemplary moral life of catechists.

In the second half of the past century, when spirits previously agitated by the thorny and at times turbulent and violent question of jurisdiction began to grow calm, the Sacred Congregation of Propaganda Fide chose to give a new impulse to the evangelization of India, with the erection of new apostolic vicariates, the nomination of new Bishops, the erection of the ecclesiastical hierarchy, the sending of missionaries, etc. The two great Instructions of 1863 and of 1893 were to serve this same purpose. In the first,[38] the *Dicasterium* touched on the great missionary problems—then current—of the subcontinent: the government of the missions, the formation of native clergy, the religious institutes, the missionary method, the school question, the erection of printing plants and the publication of books, the evangelization of Buddhists and Muslims, the catechumenate, etc. The Instruction speaks twice of catechesis: a precise order is given to the Vicars Apostolic to publish as soon as possible, if it had not already been done, a catechism for the use of the faithful, and of having care for the uniformity of the catechism and of religious instruction. Propaganda Fide deemed it important and necessary that those who preached and taught Christian doctrine should first study well "the customs and the habits of the region," and that they were not to condemn those rites and usages which had nothing to do with superstition.

The other Instruction for the Church in India dates from March 19, 1893.[39] With this, too, the Sacred Congregation intended to give a new missionary impetus, with the invitation to the missionaries to extend evangelization also to those portions of the population which had been neglected up until then and to erect throughout the territory of the individual dioceses new missions with the exclusive aim of preaching the Word of God. Other themes of the Instruction concerned the selection and formation of foreign missionaries; the formation of native clergy and catechists; schools and colleges; and charitable activity. For the execution of the dispositions of this Instruction, the Sacred Congregation prescribed, with a circular letter of August 28 of the same year, the convocation of regional synods.[40]

With regard to missionary catechesis, the Instruction contains some new and interesting elements. It is necessary to cite the text of the most significant passage. Speaking of the obligation to erect new missions for the evangelization of that part of the population until then "forgotten," and of the choice of missionaries for this sole purpose, the Instruction says: "These (the chosen missionaries) must seek to capture the sympathies of the pagans with works of charity, with their good example and with their teaching, manifesting that dignity, wisdom and holiness which are suited to virtue and to the authority of the doctrine which they teach. In regard to the preaching of the Gospel itself, let them know "that this principal part of the apostolate must not be carried out only publicly and in the churches, but first of all in private homes and families,[41] and let them keep in mind that 'in preaching, not subtlety of language, but evangelical simplicity must be used; that it is necessary to receive all pagans kindly and with those honors which are due to their state and degree, to be indulgent with their weaknesses, and to resolve their doubts in a friendly manner, with clarity and without boasting.' "[42] Further on, where the Instruction treats of the catechists, it equally insists that teaching must be done with dignity and courtesy, that catechists must convince not only with doctrine but also with example, and that, therefore, they must be prepared for their apostolate scientifically and morally.

The Instruction of 1883 to the Vicars Apostolic of China,[43] from which the citations in the preceding document were taken, furnishes us with still other elements of missionary catechesis according to the mind of the Sacred Congregation of Propaganda Fide: the publication of apologetical books, in which Christian doctrine is set forth with clarity and "evangelical simplicity" and with respect for the persons to whom they are destined. The Sacred Congregation also considered such books very useful for the uprooting of prejudices against the Christian religion and the destruction of superstitious rites. Besides these apologetical texts there was to be published, in all the apostolic vicariates of China, a catechism, possibly uniform, for the whole nation. In the editing of such a catechism there were to collaborate "Theologians with a profound knowledge of the Chinese conditions" and chosen from all the provinces, since the situation and conditions of life can vary according to the individual regions.

The question of the translation of theological terms into Chinese has always been particularly important for missionary catechesis in China. Various methods had been adopted by the Jesuits and later on by other missionaries. The first accepted already existing Chinese words and terms—but not everyone agreed as to which were the most suitable—giving them a Christian meaning; the others, instead, preferred to "Chinesize" the technical Latin terms, according to the method already introduced in Japan by St. Francis Xavier. In the present Instruction, Propaganda Fide does not make a decision in this regard, but it advises the Vicars Apostolic to consult theologians who are experts in the matter. For the formation of catechists the Sacred Congregation proposes the erection of special schools.

In an Instruction of 1791 for the Bishops of Ireland (they also belonging to its jurisdiction), the Sacred Congregation repeated that the erection of schools and the instruction of youth were its greatest concern.[44] Already a few years before, and precisely in 1785, it had repeated that the Bishop himself (and, in case of his absence or impediment, the pastor) had to explain the catechism in his cathedral, and that with him, in virtue of the Decree of the Tridentine Council, all the pastors were held to impart such teaching to their faithful.[45] In another Instruction, of 1807, the Sacred Congregation stressed the same topic.[46] No wonder then if in the questionnaires which were sent out to the individual Ordinaries every five years, accurate information was asked about the number of schools and the state of catechetical institution.[47]

Conclusion

At the end of our rapid historical synthesis, we cannot help but recall attention to a document, not of the Missionary

Dicasterium, but rather of the Second Vatican Council, in whose preparation and drafting, however, Propaganda Fide had an important role. This is the Decree *Ad gentes*, on the missionary activity of the Church,[48] which contains very wise directives and norms for missionary catechesis in the modern world, with which it has sanctioned and imposed on everyone authoritatively and obligatorily the principles already contained in the documents previously analyzed, and to whose practical application the Sacred Congregation would dedicate its Plenary Assemblies of 1970 and 1979. They are, first of all, principles of accommodation and of inculturation, of the insertion of the young Churches into the cultural and social life of their nation and liturgical adaptation. Here it will suffice to point out the fundamental themes of missionary catechesis treated by the Council fathers: which extend from the duty of the Bishop, who is "essentially the messenger of faith," to the institution of catechists and their "highest importance"; from the spiritual and moral formation of the "messengers of the Gospel" to their spiritual life; from the inculturation of the Christian message to the liturgy "responding to the character of the people" as an important means of catechesis; from the obligation of the episcopal conferences to found catechetical centers to the contribution of catechesis in the formation of the particular Church and for priestly and religious vocations.

The Sacred Congregation of Propaganda Fide has as its task the evangelization of peoples; that is, the territorial expansion of the Kingdom of God on earth and the founding of new particular Churches. It has always known that "catechesis is intimately bound up with the whole of the Church's life," that "not only her geographical extension and numerical increase, but even more, her inner growth and correspondence with God's plan depend essentially on catechesis."[49]

In the documents of the Missionary *Dicasterium* we will discover in a surprising way the three fundamental dimensions which have characterized the discussions of the 1977 Synod of Bishops,[50] and which are mirrored in the Apostolic Exhortation *Catechesi tradendae:* to announce, celebrate and live; that is: catechetical teaching, liturgical celebration and convincing testimony of the Christian life.

JOSEF METZLER, O.M.I.

FOOTNOTES

1. Cf. Zur Freude des Glaubens hinführen. Apostolisches Schreiben über die Katechese heute Papst Johannes Pauls II. Mit einem Kommentar von Adolf Exeler (Herder, Freiburg 1980) 129.
2. *Ibid.*
3. *Catechesi tradendae*, no. 13.
4. Collectanea S. Congregationis de Propaganda Fide seu Decreta, Instructiones, Rescripta pro Apostolicis Missionibus ex Tabulario eiusdem Sacrae Congregationis deprompta (Rome 1893) (2ª ed. 1907: 2 vol.).
5. Sacrae Congregationis de Propaganda Fide *Memoria rerum*. 350 years at the service of the Missions. Vol. III/2 (Herder, Freiburg 1976) pp. 655-840.
6. In regard to the individual funds of this Archive, cf. N. Kowalsky, OMI, Inventory of the historical Archive of the Sacred Congregation of Propaganda Fide. In: Neue Zeitschrift für Missionswissenschaft XVII (Schoneck 1961) 9-23, 109-117, 191-200 (as Extract in Schriftenreihe der Neuen Zeitschrift für Missionswissenschaft no. XVII).
7. CT 52.
8. Erected by Gregory XV on January 6, 1622.
9. Collectanea S. Congregationis de Propaganda Fide, vol. I, p. 2.
10. *Ibid.*
11. Archive of the Sacred Congregation of Propaganda Fide: Various Instructions (1623-1638) fol. 12^{rv}. Published in Sacrae Congregationis de Propaganda Fide *Memoria rerum*. Vol. III/2, p. 674.
12. Archive of the Sacred Congregation of Propaganda Fide: Writings referred to in the Congresses. Missions. Miscellanee, vol. 2 fol. 359-379. Published in Sacrae Congregationis de Propaganda Fide *Memoria rerum*. Vol. III/2, pp. 705-712.
13. *Ibid.*, p. 705.
14. It is sufficient to mention the first volume of *Memoria rerum*.

15. Cf. *Memoria rerum*, vol. I/1, passim.
16. The first catechisms printed in the typography of Propaganda Fide: 1630: Armenian; 1631: Ethiopian; 1633: Chaldean; 1642: Arabian; Syrian; 1650: Kikongo (Congo); 1651: Annamitic (Vietnam); 1658: Hebrew; 1661: Illyrian; 1664: Albanian; 1665: Chaldean; 1667: Vallacian; 1668: Arabian; 1680: English; 1741: Georgian; 1772: Malabarian; 1780: Malgascian.
17. *Memoria rerum*, vol. III/2, p. 702.
18. CT 52.
19. CT 53.
20. *Memoria rerum*, vol. III/2, pp. 702-703.
21. Instructiones ad munera Apostolica rite obeunda perutiles Missionibus Chinae, Tunchini, Cochinchinae, atque Siami accommodatae, a Missionariis S. Congregationis de Propaganda Fide, Juthiae Regia Siami congregatis Anno Domini 1665, concinatae...Romae 1669. —There exist at least ten editions, up until the year 1930, which have as their title: "Monita ad Missionarios."
22. Archive of the Sacred Congregation of Propaganda Fide: Acta CP vol. 1A fol. 168^{rv}.
23. Collectanea S. Congregationis de Propaganda Fide, vol. I, p. 25, no. 87.
24. Cf. the Rules for Missionaries of 1707: *Memoria rerum*, vol. III/2, p. 710, rule 32.
25. Collectanea S. Congregationis de Propaganda Fide, vol. I, pp. 271-276, no. 424.
26. Pius XI in a private audience: Periodica de re morali 35 (Rome 1946) 258.
27. Regarding the result upon the end of the question of the Chinese and Japanese rites, cf. *Memoria rerum*, vol. III/2, pp. 472-476, 483-487.
28. *Memoria rerum*, vol. III/2, p. 676.
29. In the interior parts of the continent.
30. *Memoria rerum*, vol. III/2, p. 695.
31. Of China and Indochina.

32. *Memoria rerum,* vol. III/2, p. 700.

33. *Ibid.,* p. 704.

34. Cf. J. Metzler, OMI, "Francesco Ingoli und die Indianerweihen. Ein Dokumentarbericht," in *Neue Zeitschrift für Missionsweissenschaft,* XXV (Schoneck 1969) pp. 262-272.

35. *Memoria rerum,* vol. III/2, pp. 736-737; Collectanea S. Congregationis de Propaganda Fide, vol. I, pp. 541-545. In the Instruction itself there are cited all the more important documents of Propaganda Fide in favor of the formation of native clergy.

36. Collectanea S. Congregationis de Propaganda Fide, vol. I, p. 391, no. 638.

37. *Ibid.,* pp. 491-492, no. 846. Instruction of February 29, 1836.

38. *Ibid.,* vol. II, pp. 21-28; *Memoria rerum,* vol. III/2, pp. 750-759.

39. *Ibid.,* pp. 286-290; *Memoria rerum,* vol. III/2, pp. 763-769; ASS 25 (1892/83) pp. 513-524.

40. Collectanea S. Congregationis de Propaganda Fide, vol. II, pp. 296-297. In 1894, in fact, there were celebrated Provincial Synods in Agra, Calcutta, Goa, Madras, Pondichery and Verapoly. And already in 1893 the Provincial Synod of Bombay had been celebrated.

41. These words are taken from the Instruction of Propaganda Fide to the Vicars Apostolic of China, of whom we will speak later on.

42. From the same Instruction.

43. Collectanae. S. Congregationis de Propaganda Fide, vol. II, pp. 187-196.

44. *Ibid.,* vol. I, pp. 375-379. In a circular letter of 1819 to the Irish episcopate, the Sacred Congregation again insisted upon the erection of schools. *Ibid.,* p. 432.

45. *Ibid.,* p. 366, no. 581.

46. *Ibid.,* pp. 411-414.

47. Cf., for example, the questionnaire of 1937: question 80: "Num, qua ratione et quibus temporibus habeantur institutiones catecheticae et piae exhortationes ad conversos aliosque alumnos nec non ad famulos aut convictores." Sylloge praecipuorum documentorum recentium Summorum Pontificum et S. Congregationis de Propaganda Fide nec non aliarum SS. Congregationum Romanarum (Vatican City, 1939), p. 662.

48. AAS 58 (1965), pp. 947-990.

49. CT 13.

50. Zur Freude des Glaubens hinführen (cf. note 1), p. 117.

3

1970 Plenary Assembly of the Sacred Congregation for the Evangelization of Peoples (S.C.E.P.) on Catechists

At the end of the plenary congregation of the Sacred Congregation for the Evangelization of Peoples or "Propaganda Fide" in 1969 (October 22-25) and following its directives, a document was prepared on the missionary role of the laity which, after being approved by the 1970 (April 14-16) plenary congregation, was addressed to the local Ordinaries.

This document obviously concerns catechists in the first place. In fact, after laying down a certain number of theological principles and surveying the missionary activity of the laity in general in the service of progress and for salvation, whether by life-witness or by the word, or participation in the efforts of the ministerial priesthood, this text deals with the missionary commitment proper to certain laymen—among whom are evidently the catechists—stressing two points in particular: their selection and their formation, whether they are laymen working in their own country or coming from abroad.

The criteria laid down for *selection* are as follows: the sincere intention of serving the mission of Christ and the Church for the salvation of men and the glory of God—generous humanitarian feelings are not enough; good health and human maturity (common sense, good judgment, firmness, perseverance, openness to others, flexible attitude to work, initiative and readiness to cooperate); professional qualifications, "not simply theoretical, but verified in the concrete and as far as possible in contact with life."

As for *formation*, there are two outstanding aspects: spiritual and moral formation which demands especially some theological and ascetical education—acquired above all through participation in liturgical and sacramental life; and a scientific and technical formation according to age, condition and capacities. For laymen from abroad—which is not usually the case with catechists—cultural and ecclesial insertion and coordination of effort is required besides. This document ends with a certain number of reflections on Church support of lay missionary action.

Such Church support for lay catechists was the precise object of the 1970 plenary congregation (April 14-15) dedicated to catechists in mission countries. The congregation was prepared after an inquiry made among the Ordinaries of territories depending on the Sacred Congregation for the Evangelization of Peoples; the number of answers largely outnumbered those usually obtained from this kind of consultation, and a synthesis was later given to each member of the congregation who were thus able to discuss the matter with full knowledge.

On April 14, His Eminence, Cardinal Kim, Archbishop of Seoul, presented a first report on the *situation* of catechists at that time; on the 15th, His Excellency, Bishop Zoa, Archbishop of Yaounde, evoked the *formation* problem, and on the 16th, His Eminence, Cardinal Dopfner, Archbishop of Munich, spoke of *financial aid* needed for their support. The numerous and lively exchanges that followed each paper showed the interest of the subject. The plenary congregation over, the conclusions that had been hammered out during the work were approved. They were stated in three sections: the catechist, formation and financial aid.

A. The report begins with a definition of the catechist: *"The catechist is a layman (or woman) especially charged by the Church according to local needs, to make Christ known, loved and followed by those who do not yet know Him, and by the faithful: he has also to help in the building up of the Christian community by manifesting there Christ's presence."* Upon request of the Pontifical Works for the Propagation of the Faith, the following clarification was added: "Under the name of layman is to be understood...all those Christians who are not in sacred orders or in the religious state." This addition caused some protests, for according to this text, religious women, many of whom are dedicated to catechesis, may nevertheless not be called "catechists," even when there exist, in fact, congregations of catechist sisters. The text of the conclusions of this plenary congregation also emphasizes the importance of the role of catechists: "The historical development of the role of catechists indicates its great importance everywhere within the mission of the Church: from apostolic times, Christian communities came into being in all nations, thanks to the devoted service of the catechists." It is stressed that the catechist does not, and should not substitute the priest, though he may sometimes replace him, "but within the limits that are his." The way the catechists carry out their role is left to the initiative of the particular churches, and the final reflection on the nature of catechists should be noted: "Although they are not catechists in the whole Church, certain Christians (e.g., writers, publishers, teachers, leaders-of workers or rural movements, religious educators, members of the Confraternity of Christian Doctrine...) may sometimes play a role equal to that of catechists by their word, writings and the example of their life."

B. What is said of spiritual *formation* is not particularly original: the stress is simply placed on fidelity to Christ and the Church, prayer, attachment to the community, personal and liturgical prayer, life in conformity with the Gospel so as to transmit it the better, and service of the brethren for the love of Christ.

What is said of doctrinal *formation* is more detailed: "The catechist will nourish himself with the Word of God, assimilated in meditation on Holy Scripture and through the liturgy and the teaching of the Church. Being charged to make known and loved the person of our Lord Jesus Christ, God and man, he will make Him the continual and central object of his doctrinal formation based on the history of salvation. Being charged to make the Church known and loved, he will familiarize himself with her tradition and history and in particular the lives of the saints. He is charged to bring the community to Christian living, so he must know the principles of Christian ethics, particularly the social doctrine of the Church. Since he is charged to proclaim the Gospel among non-Christians, he will take special care to know the religions practiced in his milieu of life."

A few other directives are also given: before all, the catechist is asked to "invite his listeners to prayer so that they may obtain the gift of faith and the grace to live a Christian life." He is also reminded that he should know "the language, mentality, tendencies and problems of his listeners so that he may respond to their needs. Hence, catechists will receive sufficient pedagogical formation." The same aim of efficiency demands that the catechist be inserted into his community and life-milieu, to enable him to dialogue fraternally with everyone, Christians and non-Christians alike.

C. The third section of the conclusions of the 1970 plenary congregation deals with the *financial support* of the catechists.

As is known, the Sacred Congregation for the Evangelization of Peoples or Propaganda Fide and not the Pontifical Works that depend on it (subjecta sunt), is responsible for the coordination of the collection of sufficient resources to be distributed, taking into account the necessity, utility, territorial extent, number of faithful and non-Christians, works, institutes, ministers and missionaries.

This explains the directives given by the 1970 plenary congregation concerning catechists.

a) Where possible, priority should be given to the creation and functioning (bursaries) of means of formation, notably regional, national and international catechetical schools approved by the Bishops' Conferences—to whom it belongs to determine pastoral practice in this field—and offering qualifications officially recognized by the said conferences.

b) Missionary circumscriptions should tend to take over the entire support of their catechists; aid, however, will still be forthcoming, above all for the retribution of a limited number of full-time catechists who have received qualified formation.

c) Subsidies for catechists will continue to be transmitted through the local Ordinaries and not through the Bishops' Conferences.

Considerable sums since granted for catechists by the Pontifical Missionary Works shows that this directive was carried out.

The 1970 plenary conference also recommended that the secretariat should intervene with the Pontifical Commission of "Justice and Peace" and with "Misereor," to obtain some subsidies in favor of catechists since these latter also render service in the development area; it is not known whether this directive has been implemented.

d) The 1970 plenary conference had also foreseen setting up within the Sacred Congregation for the Evangelization of Peoples a "temporary commission charged with fuller investigation, in liaison with the Bishops' Conferences, into problems and requests concerning catechists, especially in view of directives to be given to the Pontifical Missionary Works."

This commission was first set up within the Pontifical Work of the Propagation of the Faith and not, as prescribed, in the Sacred Congregation for the Evangelization of Peoples. Its first president was Msgr. Van Cauwelaert, CICM named by the Secretary, President of the Pontifical Missionary Works.

The situation was rectified later on by the institution, this time within the Congregation itself, of a *Permanent Commission for Catechesis and Catechists* that deals with formation and methods of catechists and catechetical teaching, and is, therefore, no longer in charge of finances. The decree of erection of this commission dates from May 6, 1972; its first president was His Excellency, Most Reverend Lourdusamy and its first secretary, M. l'Abbé-Robert Rweyemanu, from Tanzania, both of whom are still in office.

e) The 1970 plenary conference had also foreseen that "bishops and superiors of missionary institutes and religious, should be informed, by a letter which took up points relating to the definition, formation and financing of catechists, of the conclusions drawn from the abundant documentation they had been kind enough to submit." At the same time they were sent "a copy of the basic report of the plenary conference."

This brought about the publication of an opuscule entitled *Catechists in Africa, Asia and Oceania: Synthetic Study,* published by the Sacred Congregation for the Evangelization of Peoples, prefaced by a letter of December 23, 1972, from Most Reverend Lourdusamy, at the time sub-secretary of the missionary organization. As this letter indicates, the synthetic study is "a compilation made by this commission for catechists when it still had temporary status and the mission confided to it was to make a deeper inquiry, with the Bishops' conferences, into the question of catechists that had already been treated in the 1970 plenary assembly of the Sacred Congregation for the Evangelization of Peoples (April 14-16). Abundant material gathered and already elaborated was given to the commission, in view of a definitive text to be published under its authority." The synthesis was started by Msgr. Van Cauwelaert, CICM, and Father P. Brunner, SJ, later revised by the Sacred Congregation for the Evangelization of Peoples or Propaganda Fide and was finished with the help of M. l'Abbé Rweyemanu, commission secretary. It is a very interesting piece of work that has the advantage of being based on mission experience and not on an elaboration of arm-chair missiologists. This outstanding study is divided into five sections: 1) Catechists' Ministry; 2) Catechists' Formation; 3) Catechists' Support; 4) Subsidies of Pontifical Missionary Works; 5) Conclusions.

According to these conclusions, thanks to the work of the plenary assembly of the Sacred Congregation for the Evangelization of Peoples, April 1970, and the follow-up commission, a good number of bishops' conferences have put on their annual meeting agenda the elaboration of a pastoral plan for catechists, their formation, support, status, relationship with the community, etc. "These conclusions also insisted that the Pontifical Missionary Works should do more to conscientize the Christian people to the problems of catechists," and finally, the conclusions consider that "it would be good to study the possibility of an official recognition of the *missio canonica* (of catechists) as a ministerial order, which would confer faculties for blessing, distributing communion, presiding at Sunday service, etc."

The plenary congregation of 1972 came back to this question of catechists. The relevant text understands by catechesis that "given to the non-baptized, but also the doctrinal formation of baptized Christians, which is not part of missionary activity but pastoral activity aiming at deepening faith, and especially necessary in pagan milieus and among newly-converted Catholics who have often had rather rudimentary catechesis." In 1971 after the plenary conference in 1970, a great effort was made nearly everywhere by the catechetical commissions of the Bishops' Conferences to adapt programs, texts and catechetical methods, taking into account the various kinds of audiences—adult, adolescent, children, as also the cultural milieu. In spite of this, some replies deplored, in 1972, the lack of interest in catechesis shown by teachers in Catholic schools and even some refusals to give religion courses, their poor formation in this subject as well as deficient religious teaching in schools." This may explain another remark made at the time: "There is a serious problem posed by the indifference to the Faith of young people in secondary or university milieus: where courses in religion exist, they appear too often ineffective."

The impetus given by the'1970 plenary congregation, however, has begun to bear fruit, if not always positive: "It is unnecessary to point out the good influence of well-organized specialized catechetical centers on the Apostolate. Yet, today, it is impossible to avoid the risk that here and there the renewal of pastoral practice and catechesis may be looked on as a means of propagating ideas that lead away from and even contradict the faith. Such a possibility shows up the importance of a central catechetical institute in an ecclesiastical territory, which might disseminate error; the bishops and bishops' conferences should attentively supervise the activities of these centers, and put all their efforts into the propagation of authentic faith." The same 1972 plenary congregation, while noting that subsidies had been given to catechists, asked that "the priority of the proclamation of the Word of God should be insisted on to bring about a renewal in catechesis. And that the catechumenate should be given its rightful place with the help of the catechists." Need for "good catechisms" was expressed as well as "well-prepared catechists, faithful to the authentic doctrine of the Church in the spirit of Vatican II, carrying out their functions in line with the instructions in the *General Catechetical Directory* published by the Sacred Congregation for the Clergy."

Many other orientations of this 1972 plenary congregation followed along the lines held in 1969 and 1970; as the 1972 plenary congregation wished, the following Bishops' Synod was to treat of evangelization, and its reflections helped to inspire the Apostolic Exhortation, *Evangelii nuntiandi*, which returns to the question of catechesis, as also did the following synod.

In this respect it may be said that, in the sphere of catechesis the congregations of the S.C. "de Propaganda Fide" in 1969, 1970, 1972 played a stimulating role that was to prove beneficient not only to the missions but to the Church as a whole.

MSGR. BERNARD JACQUELINE

4

The World Encounter
of Missionary Catechists
During the Holy Year, 1975

I. CATECHISTS FOR THE HOLY YEAR

As I am writing today, it is exactly five years since the project "Catechists for the Holy Year" was launched. The very first circular letter signed by His Grace, Archbishop D. S. Lourdusamy, to break the news to the Pontifical Representatives in countries depending on the Sacred Congregation for the Evangelization of Peoples is dated March 12, 1975. I can look back and recollect, picking up in my memory the many small pieces that go to make the history of this event.

Propaganda's Project for the Holy Year

The World Encounter of Catechists from the mission territories can be related very soberly, stripping the story bare to its essentials: in October, 1975, during the Holy Year, the Sacred Congregation for the Evangelization of Peoples invited a considerable number of catechists to Rome both for the Holy Year and for the celebration of World Mission Sunday. There was enthusiastic response from the Episcopal Conferences and the Bishops to this initiative, and some 500 catechists came to Rome. Was it worthwhile, worth all the time, the money, the energy and trouble on the part of Propaganda Fide to do so? And, of all people, why disturb simple village catechists, asking them to expose themselves to the danger of long flights, to unfamiliar climatic and cultural conditions, to the fatigue of exhausting tight programs for a whole week? These good men and women, most of whom had never travelled far enough to even their national capital or regional cities? And the funds "wasted" on air passage, hotel and restaurant bills? Indeed, some even skeptically and critically pointed out that it would have served a better purpose, in the interests of the missionary catechists themselves, if plans had been made to raise their honoraria or their material stand-ards instead of calling them to Europe for sight-seeing. Fears and criticisms were expressed until the day the catechists arrived and were seen at last to be in Rome.

Inauguration Ceremony

On Monday, October 13th, as most of the groups had ar-rived, His Eminence the Cardinal Prefect wanted all of them to be in the main hall of the Urban University for the inauguration of the World Encounter. It was the first meeting. The guests were going to be received by the Superiors of Propaganda, to meet each other and to be introduced to the program of their work in Rome.

They looked visibly moved and somewhat embarrassed at such a reception in their honor by the Cardinal himself. They walked on red carpets; had places assigned to each national group. Each one of these groups was called, and individual names of participants were mentioned. The groups responded to the cheers and applauses of the hall, and rose to bow to the Authorities of the Sacred Congregation. Participants were from 31 countries in Africa, 18 countries in America, mostly South and Central, 13 countries in Asia and 4 in Oceania. Each mission ter-ritory had been given a fixed number according to the total of the ecclesiastical jurisdictions. However, some Episcopal Conferences requested, and obtained having, their quota increased on condi-tion that the Bishops concerned would make financial contribu-tion to cover the additional expenses for the air tickets. Thus Burundi, Cameroun, Ivory Coast, Kenya, Rwanda, Tanzania, Togo and Uganda had a catechist for each diocese.

Equally participating were seven bishops, eleven priests, nine nuns, seven brothers, with the lay catechists numbering 450, thirty of these being women.

A Week's Program

It would be too long to give, even in short, the account of the program that had been prepared for the catechist's stay in the Eternal City for a whole week. In broad outline, the visit was to be a triple experience for them: missionary, spiritual and cultural. The booklet that was published as a souvenir of this World Encounter has the details.

Missionary was the program, in the first place. The participants were from the mission territories, they had the mission background, their role was in the context of the young local Churches growing towards maturity. They represented a variety of missionary experiences which they were able to share and appraise. Being together discussing together their missionary roles, getting to know each other and exchange views was to be a good lesson, a great encouragement, and a source of inspiration. They were at the center and heart of the missionary Dicastery and the atmosphere was missionary-oriented. For this purpose, apart from personal contacts, a symposium was organized so that the catechists could air their views, express their own points and hear the words of the Pope and of the Cardinal and the Archbishops of Propaganda. Visiting the Collegio Urbano, the University and especially the Headquarters at the Piazza di Spagna was a kind of missionary conscientization; they felt the sense of their own belonging to this Church whose main worry is to proclaim the Gospel and to make Christ known to all peoples and nations. They saw that their own vocation was emphasized and stressed.

But any Catholic coming to Rome feels to be on a pilgrimage. It is the joy of being one in a line of an endless tradition of men and women who have had the privilege of visiting the Apostolic Church, and of paying respects to the visible Head of the Catholic Communion. In this way, the program for catechists placed the pilgrimages as top priority: on the very day, they were all led to the Basilicas to gain their Holy Year Indulgences. This was tied up with other spiritual exercises. A common Holy Mass for them with all the members of the Propaganda Family was concelebrated in the Chiesa del Gesú, the church famous for keeping the relic of the great missionary of all times, Saint Francis Xavier. There was another spiritual experience lived together when Archbishop Lourdusamy presided over a liturgical and biblical hour with prayers, hymns and sermon especially adapted as a model for the catechist's own spiritual and apostolic commitment. The last day of solemn pilgrimage and prayer was Mission Sunday itself.

Apart from that, for our catechists being in Rome meant being in the Holy City. Everywhere they admired churches and shrines; they saw pilgrims; they were made to recall to memory the lives of Saints Peter and Paul, of the early martyrs, of the ancient Roman Christian communities, of the Popes. Rome also has the unique sight to offer—namely that of numerous men and women dedicated to religious life. All this, as we remarked while guiding and accompanying the catechists, was a spiritual refreshment and a call to prayer and recollection.

Nevertheless, the catechists enjoyed being in Rome, as being in a different cultural atmosphere. Indeed, it had not been planned to be a congress or seminar, but its benefits were nonetheless great. It was an opportunity for them to broaden their outlook, to get in touch with another world—technically powerful, historically famous and culturally imposing. As they were shown around, they were grateful to know the interesting sites and impressive memorials. They could see themselves among people of other races, colors and cultures. Rome, as center of the world, made impact.

The Last Days

Seven days passed by very quickly. On Saturday, October 18, it was farewell day to Propaganda, to the Cardinal Prefect and practically to one another.

Having all come to see His Eminence and to visit all the Offices of Propaganda Fide, the catechists were once more received by the Superiors of the Sacred Congregation and every one of them was personally embraced by the Cardinal and given a personal souvenir. Then they went on to see the Archbishop Secretaries, as well as the Secretaries-General of the Mission-Aid Societies.

Before that, Cardinal Rossi had pronounced his farewell message in the small chapel of Propaganda, the chapel that had seen many missionaries ordained, consecrated bishops, and canonically sent to the mission field. Here the Cardinal delivered his address that was translated into English, French and Spanish. He poured out his affectionate heart to all these loyal and dedicated men and women; exhorted them to persevere in their noble cause of the mission apostolate; and requested them to keep united to the whole Church, to the Pope, to their Bishops and to Propaganda Fide now better known to them, as their family and home. These words are certainly the climax to the spirit which had prompted the initiative of inviting the catechists to Rome. These words remain hopefully a source of inspiration to them as they read and re-read them in the souvenir book.

World Mission Sunday

No doubt, Propaganda Fide had organized this day to be the specific Mission Day of the Holy Year: the beatification of four missionary heroes of our times; the presence of many Bishops who are members of the Plenary Assembly of the Sacred Congregation for Evangelization; the participation of thousands of missionary priests, nuns and students belonging to the Institutes of the four who were raised to the honors of the altar; the invitation given to retired missionary Bishops to be in Rome for the day; and, last but not least, our catechists. The last mentioned were singled out for reading the Prayers of the Faithful, for offering symbolic gifts to the Pope during Mass, and twelve of them, representing all the continents, for receiving the award of the medal "Pro Ecclesia et Pontifice." This was the crowning moment. The crowds on St. Peter's Square watched attentively as the catechists went up to the Holy Father and had their distinctive insignia pinned on their jackets and dresses. There were endless roars of applause. It was also the closing act of the Mission Sunday celebration. After honoring those who were declared blessed, these lay men and women were also given public tribute in front of the universal Church.

The Pope's Thanks

Everything was now over—the pilgrimage, the encounter and the program of seven days in Rome. With such a magnificent testimony from the Pope's kind gesture, the end could not have been more gratifying.

Pope Paul, who appeared visibly moved, expressed his satisfaction when he turned to Archbishop D. S. Lourdusamy and embraced him, thanking him for the work done by Propaganda and himself. Indeed, it had been Archbishop Lourdusamy who had taken up the full responsibility for the project, not only as Secretary to Propaganda, but also in his double capacity as Chairman of the Holy Year's Mission Committee and President of the Commission for Catechesis and Catechists. He had seen to it that the initiative taken by Cardinal Rossi should be carried out to achieve the desired purpose.

Collaborators chosen by the Archbishop included those in the Offices of Propaganda especially from the National (Italian) Office for the Propagation of the Faith. However, at the other end, it was the collaboration of the papal representatives who assisted very much in channelling information to and from the episcopal conferences. After the catechists' departure from Rome, Archbishop Lourdusamy wrote to express personal thanks to all of them for their help which had been an indispensable service.

II. SIGNIFICANCE OF THE EVENT

In the first part we have tried to give an account of the World Encounter of Missionary Catechists (W.E.M.C.) as a story based on the chronicle. We are aware that events do not make history by just being recorded; they have to be related to deeper perspectives which make them meaningful in an historical context. The chronicler's task is only half done if he only recounts; he also has to interpret.

Now the fact that Propaganda Fide got 500 catechists from the mission territories to Rome for the Holy Year, 1975, will find its place down in history, if accompanied by testimonies and insights that lend more significance to it. This is what we would like to do.

In Line with History

The W.E.M.C. was a great event, but it was not unprecedented. There were representations from the mission territories attending the previous Jubilees celebrated within our immediate memory. In 1925, Pius XI, known up to this day as the "Pope of the Missions," and his immediate successor, Pius XII, in 1950, urgently requested the presence of people from countries depending on Propaganda Fide to be really felt and visibly seen in the Holy Year celebrations. The records of the times tell us about some distinguished personalities and about occasional groups that came to the Eternal City. Scarce and piecemeal as the presence was, it was greatly appreciated and considered to be a remarkable feature of those two Jubilee Years. I do not mention anything about the special Holy Year promulgated by Pius XI in 1933 yet, even then, the missions did not lack envoys and special representatives.

Likewise the Holy Year in 1975 under Paul VI was to have its missionary presence visibly felt. And, as we shall see, this one was characterized by this missionary feature in a way that cannot be compared to the previous ones.

Presence of the Universal Church

As the celebration of the Universal Church, the Holy Year acquires its full meaning in the measure it becomes a clear sign of the whole Catholic communion manifested round the Bishop of Rome, Supreme Pontiff of the universal Church. The gathering of the members of the People of God from the four corners of the earth to the center of Catholicism achieves the specific purpose of the Jubilee Year to which every Catholic is invited. As pilgrims to the tombs of Peter and Paul, at the sources of early tradition, all feel united in the profession of Christian Faith and recognize their membership within the One, Catholic and Apostolic Church, which precisely during the Jubilee Year radiates in her singular and unique prerogative of being the sacrament of universal salvation for all mankind as she dispenses treasures of graces and indulgences to those who come to perform exercises of piety and penance for spiritual reconciliation and renewal.

In 1975, those immense and numberless crowds from the so-called Third World seized the opportunity to come to Rome. Although the Jubilee facilities were to be extended to the Dioceses as well, men and women from Africa, Asia, Latin America and Oceania paid their air tickets, organized group pilgrimages on diocesan and national levels to be present in Rome, to see the Holy Father and join with innumerable other pilgrims and visitors to live this experience of the Holy Year in the warm communion of the one Church which transcends the limits of geographical frontiers and the barriers of ethnic and cultural zones.

Missionary Holy Year

It was natural to have the presence of the catechists in Rome, for this Holy Year was indeed a great missionary Holy Year. The missionary presence was to be in the forefront, as the mark of the Church in our century.

In the span of the last fifty years since 1925, the growth and rise of the young Churches was the great achievement of the period. The growth of the Church in the mission fields far away from the old Christian countries had to find its living and eloquent testimony in the people evangelized, gathered to form new communities of faith, established to be full-fledged members of the universal Church by the heroic and undaunted zeal of the missionary Institutes, supported by the home Churches and successfully directed by Propaganda Fide.

We should note the connection between the missionary activity of the Church among non-Christian peoples and the Holy Year celebrations. The period of intensification was launched by Pius XI's *Rerum Ecclesiae* in 1926, just following the 1925 Jubilee. And the period of consolidation stressed by Pius XII's *Evangelii Praecones* in 1951 echoes the experience of the Holy Year's spiritual vigor in the Church after the Holy Year in 1950. At the close of 1975, Paul VI issued his own Apostolic Exhortation *Evangelii nuntiandi*, aware that all the Church called upon by Vatican II to be missionary was to arouse and maintain this missionary spirit in all the local Churches and in all the communities that must dedicate themselves to the task of evangelization. With this Exhortation the Pope recalled the tenth anniversary of the close of Vatican II, and the promulgation of the Decree *Ad gentes*; but, most specifically, reference was made to the Holy Year 1975 that was soon drawing to a happy conclusion.

Catechists' Presence Was Necessary

Speaking now about the catechists' pilgrimage in particular, we cannot do better than listen to the Superiors of Propaganda Fide tell us why they invited them to Rome.

His Eminence, Cardinal Rossi, in his welcome address to the catechists assembled for the first encounter at the Urban University hall, gave his word to interpret the event as envisaged by the Sacred Congregation for the Evangelization:

39. Going, Teach....

You are the hope and the Spring in your young Churches.... We wish to tell you that the Church is very grateful to you and she encourages and blesses you.

Soon after His Eminence had addressed his guests, His Excellency, Archbishop B. Gantin, at that time Secretary to Propaganda Fide, said, among other things, in his beautiful speech:

We are aware of what you are for the Church in your countries through the witness of your faith, through the task which is yours and through the generous and self-sacrificing efforts. That is why, after the study that has been conducted on the role of the catechists, it was necessary and very desirable to see you here so that you might see and know that you belong to a worldwide community.

Then His Grace, Archbishop D. S. Lourdusamy, explained in clear detail why this presence was necessary and very desirable:

Our purpose in bringing you here is to highlight your role and the importance and the necessity of your ministry in the mission field, to publicly manifest our great pleasure and full satisfaction with your evangelizing activity, rich in spiritual fruits, and to show in a tangible way our love and esteem for you, dedicated workers. We wish also that you experience here in Rome the universality of the Catholic Church, strengthen the bonds of your loyalty and devotion to the Holy Father, the Vicar of Christ on earth, and go back home to the field of your activity, with increased vigor, zeal and enthusiasm, and with a spirit of solidarity with all your brother-catechists all over the world.

Finally it was the Pope's own words that brought out the relevance of the catechists being in Rome for the pilgrimage.

We wish to express our deep affection for all the missionary catechists present here today.We want you to realize the dignity of your role and the importance of your mission in the Church. *We want the whole world to know our esteem for you.* How often we pray for you! And how many times we inquire about you and send you our blessing with your Bishops.

Beloved Catechists, you must always be strong in your faith. You must teach Christ and bring Him to your fellow men by word and example. *The Church loves you, depends on you.* And in His name we bless you once again.

Dear Catechists here present, what a marvelous mission you have in the Church: to present the Gospel to your brothers, to train them in the faith, to bear witness to it by your own lives, to support your Christian communities. You feel yourselves honored to share in the work with the courage and unselfishness that we know so well. We are happy to greet you here and to give you our wholehearted encouragement along with our apostolic blessing.

And so the significance of the Word Encounter of Missionary Catechists is stressed, and its importance and relevance as an event in the Church during the Holy Year is vindicated. We can add no comment to the above declarations which carry the greatest weight and command highest respect not only because of the Authority of the speakers but also because of the self-evident truth they convey. It was necessary for catechists to come to Rome to hear these words for themselves. And many of those who currently debated on the "ecclesial status" or the "recognition of the catechists' ministry," had their disputed questions settled.

Recognition for the Past

Thus the presence of the catechists in the Church was reaffirmed; their visit of Rome justified and everything that was done to make this possible was gratefully appreciated.

That "the *Catholic World should know,*" emphasized the Pope: the whole world had to know and to know from the center, from top level authorities that the catechists play an important role, that their ministry is indispensable because the Church depends also on them and that they deserve esteem and affection. All these men and women, who are selected and set apart as collaborators in the missionary and pastoral sectors of Church life, have their place in the community.

Just as the Second Vatican Council had recognized the lay catechist's ministry and charism, so Propaganda Fide was doing so in a tangible way. Indeed, from the moment they set foot on

Italian ground, the catechists were treated as special guests of the Holy Father and of the Sacred Congregation for the Evangelization of Peoples. Nothing was left undone to convince them by facts, words and feelings that theirs was a privileged status among other pilgrims of the Holy Year.

Encouragement for the Future

Great services have been rendered in the past, and thanks to these the missionary period has been a prosperous one. Catechists can take credit for the fruits of their labors abundantly blessed by Almighty God. Yet the Church remains missionary. The young Churches locally established must grow from strength to strength in extending to all men the benefits of divine redemption to the end of time. The task of a typically pioneer catechist may be less at one time or place, but it develops into new forms of the apostolate and ministry, for which the lay catechist, loyal and zealous as before, is urgently called. The local Churches have to be missionaries to themselves, raising up men and women to the service of evangelization. Thus the vocation of the catechist is to be encouraged.

In all their addresses the Superiors of Propaganda looked forward to increased activity in the future. Cardinal Rossi's farewell message included a statement to this effect: "Go back and take up again your tasks with a more fervent love and remain united with us here at Propaganda." Archbishop Lourdusamy did not overlook the same aspect: "And go back home to the field of your activity with increased vigor, zeal and enthusiasm." His Holiness, the Pope, sending his first message of welcome pointed out: "We encourage them in their resolution to work perseveringly for the preaching of the Gospel message and the spread of Christ's Kingdom in answer to the needs of today."

Witness to the Whole Church

"Your piety, faith, joy and Christian brotherliness have been a source of great edification to us," said the Cardinal Prefect of Propaganda, remarking how the Catechists' presence in Rome had been for a whole week of community life, prayer, visits, meetings and reciprocal acquaintance. Many other people who met the catechists' groups had the same thing to say: they are really people of faith, very pious, very simple, kind and warm-hearted Christians. Those who had the chance to be with these groups in the hotels, during city tours and especially in the churches, have kept the vivid memory of the catechists from the mission territories—people taking their religion seriously, people living by their faith.

Appreciation of the Local Churches

It would be too long to quote here from numerous letters received after the catechists got home, letters which express the appreciation of the Bishops, the Episcopal Conferences, the Papal Representatives. There are letters sent by very many catechists not only to Propaganda Fide and to His Grace, Archbishop Lourdusamy in particular, but also to others who made acquaintances with them here in Rome. Let me just put down some references, picked up at random, but very revealing. A former Bishop in Pakistan wrote:

> Now that the catechists are back from their pilgrimage, I want to tell you my hearty thanks for this great privilege given them. They returned full of joy and enthusiasm, completely satisfied with the treatment received, and still more, with all they had seen, heard and experienced. This is a great landmark in their life, of which also the Christian community they serve will certainly benefit.
>
> The greatest impressions they are pointing out are: the greatness and the catholicity of the Church (so many from every part of the world); the faith and the devotion of all; the unity in such a great variety of nations and races; and then...the sight and the words of the Holy Father.

A catechist from Thailand:

> I realized the dignity of the catechists and their role in the Church today in the work of spreading the Good News. I feel that I am not alone but am one of the many catechists toiling day and night in the different parts of the world. By sharing experiences I came to know more of what we could do as catechists to help our pastors in their ministry.

The Kenya Episcopal Conference:

> We, the Bishops of Kenya, do appreciate very much what the Sacred Congregation for the Evangelization of Peoples did recently to bring our catechists to the Eternal City to see and hear for themselves the Holy Father, the Vicar of Christ. The Bishops of Kenya and Seychelles are indeed grateful for this gesture of great thoughtfulness. The catechists came back home very much strengthened in their Faith. Those remaining at home, those unlucky ones, were consoled by the thought that the Holy Father thinks so highly of the catechists in the apostolate of the Church.

From Papua and New Guinea:

> The one impression I got is that we catechists have also a place in the Church. We in Papua and New Guinea used to think that catechists were only the right hand of the priest.

From the Pacific Islands, (Rarotonga):

> On behalf of the Diocese of Rarotonga, I wish to thank Your Eminence very sincerely for the splendid gesture for the Pacific mission during the Holy Year. It is the very first time a Cook Island Catholic has represented the diocese in Rome, and we are deeply appreciative of the honor done to us.

These testimonies, among so many from every part of the world, are perhaps the most convincing demonstration of the truth that the initiative taken by the Sacred Congregation for the Evangelization of Peoples in the project "Catechists for the Holy Year 1975" was a most welcome gesture to all interested. In their letters the catechists go beyond the words of appreciation for the "gesture"; they stress the fact that the Encounter was a unique opportunity for them to learn many things concerning catechetical work and the problems as well as the experiences of catechists in other countries. A deeper sense of mutual solidarity among them all and a closer link with the Church were the chief benefits of the coming together of missionary catechists at the center of Catholicism.

A Lasting Acknowledgement

In conclusion, let us say that all this affection, esteem, trust and recognition shown to the catechists during their pilgrimage in 1975 has emphasized what the Church has at all times expressed to these dedicated and loyal collaborators, namely a grateful acknowledgement. This was so in the past, it is so at present, and may be it is more so today than ever before.

Within a few months after the inauguration of his Pontificate, Pope John Paul II made public the same acknowledgement in the words we would like to quote here in full:

> I acknowledge with joy and gratitude the very men and women catechists who serve the Church by proclaiming the Word of God and bringing people to the Faith in Christ. These catechists, filled with a great love and a spirit of sacrifice are able to respond to those who have not yet met Christ and are seeking God with a sincere heart. They faithfully do their work in a quiet and humble fashion. Some work freely and others receive a modest compensation. I think, in a special way, of catechists in countries where missionaries and priests have been expelled. In these countries, the catechists become the center of the religious life of the faithful. They assemble the congregation for prayer and the reading of Scripture and strengthen them in the Faith. To all of them and to each one I say a heartfelt, "May God reward you."

The W.E.M.C. was a token of sincere and grateful acknowledgement, the best token which Propaganda Fide could give. It was also acknowledged as such by the whole world. It was a firm acknowledgment that these men and women are in the forefront as builders of the community of the People of God.

In the wake of the young Churches in Africa, Asia, Latin America and Oceania the role of the catechists will be as important in consolidating Christianity as it was in implanting the Church in the pioneer days of the past. There is not the slightest doubt about that. The catechist is emerging as an ecclesial figure. The signs of the times point to that. The Church communities will need him badly.

The Holy Year was, in this regard, a providential opportunity. It called the simple catechist from his humble, modest place to show him to the world. None could have been more concerned about that than Propaganda Fide. To be sure, while the Jubilee Year of 1975 was becoming really characterized by a great participation of the missions, Propaganda Fide highlighted the representation of the young Churches not only by the members of the hierarchy, clergy and the mission institutes but especially so by what made the greatest impact, namely, the World Encounter of Missionary Catechists.

D. ROBERT RWEYEMAMU

5

Institute of Missionary Catechesis

The Institute of Missionary Catechesis is the most recent sign of the attention with which the Sacred Congregation for the Evangelization of Peoples follows and sustains the catechetical apostolate in the young Churches of Africa, Asia and Latin America.

I. CONSTANT SUPPORT
TO ALL LOCAL INITIATIVES
ON THE PART OF PROPAGANDA FIDE

The preceding articles have already shown the interest that Propaganda Fide has always had in the development of catechesis and the support of catechists in mission nations. This interest, we must affirm, was stimulated in the post-conciliar period following the exhortation of Vatican II, in *Ad gentes*, which not only recognizes the most important role of catechists, but also insistently invites them to better their formation with new initiatives on the diocesan and regional levels "wherein," the text states, "future catechists may study Catholic doctrine, especially in the fields of Scripture and the liturgy, as well as catechetical method and pastoral practice,...can develop in themselves a Christian character, and...can devote themselves tirelessly to cultivating piety and sanctity of life."

For one who knows the concrete situation of the young Christian communities, this exhortation seems fully justified: rarely can the local communities of lesser importance, who still need first-rate catechists, have the possibility of securing for them an adequate preparation. This can be realized only by joining efforts, which is possible but not always possible on a diocesan level. Hence the exhortation to multiply not only diocesan schools, but also regional ones, which certainly have a substitutional function when diocesan schools do not exist. When both exist they complete and complement one another, because they assure a more complete formation and allow the comparison and meeting of different mentalities and various initiatives, demonstrating more the catholicity of the Church. Here, in fact, one feels that the whole Church lives the same faith, is a reality which transcends boundaries, and really unites peoples in the unique praise of the Lord. It is here that one arrives more easily at mutual exchange among the Churches, through a concrete and effective communion precisely on the most sacred level, that of catechesis and evangelization.

For this reason the Sacred Congregation for the Evangelization of Peoples has given its concrete support and aid to diocesan, interdiocesan, regional, national and international catechetical centers. Speaking to the Synod Fathers of 1977, Cardinal Agnelo Rossi, Prefect of Propaganda Fide, testified thus to the support of the Missionary *Dicasterium:* "Let there be an increase of national, regional and diocesan centers for the formation of catechists and for the study of problems regarding adaptation to diverse cultures. These higher or diocesan centers are about 230; the catechists who dedicate themselves to this task full time number 14,000; there are 35,000 who dedicate a limited amount of time; 92,000 others offer themselves spontaneously."[1]

These words are much more significant if we keep in mind that they indicate a support that is not only moral, but also economic. In fact, through the Pontifical Work of the Propagation of the Faith, the Sacred Congregation has given a constant and growing contribution; it suffices to think of the figures that represent the last three years: $6,358,010.72 in 1977; $8,143,047.27 in 1978; $10,093,947.85 in 1979!

II. NECESSITY OF AN INITIATIVE UNIVERSAL IN CHARACTER

Pursuing this line, Propaganda Fide has considered that, to make catechesis on the interecclesial plane more dynamic, it would be necessary to add to the various degrees of initiative (diocesan, interdiocesan, regional, national and international) a new and broader initiative which would give to the catechist-leaders and the better prepared of Africa, Asia and Latin America, a deeper sense of the unity, universality and catholicity of the Church. This would be thanks to an "Institute of Missionary Catechesis," arising in Rome near the Pope, which would visibly express convergence in the one, sole Faith, and would be a point of encounter and interecclesial exchange of the catechetical treasures which have matured in the bosom of the local Churches throughout these years on the various continents. This Institute would have then concretely realized that communion among the Churches which the Dogmatic Constitution *Lumen gentium* affirms in no. 13 when it says: "In virtue of this catholicity each individual part contributes through its special gifts to the good of the other parts and of the whole Church. Through the common sharing of gifts and through the common effort to attain fullness in unity, the whole and each of the parts receive increase."

The thought of Propaganda Fide, therefore, was not to give life to an initiative that would replace or impede others that are of a local character already existing, almost as though Rome were to take upon itself the formation of catechists for mission nations. There was, on the contrary, the desire for a catechetical initiative which would function harmoniously with all the others in its own specific role of service. It would be, therefore, an initiative in full harmony with the new missionary times, because it would be based on the recognition of the maturity of recently founded Churches.

This intuition developed especially after the 1970 Plenary Assembly of the S.C.E.P., which worked exclusively with the problem of catechesis and catechists,[2] and it was further strengthened after the world encounter of catechists held during the Holy Year of 1975.[3]

In 1978-1979 the Institute of Missionary Catechesis was effectively established in its present structure at the Pontifical Urban University through the initiative of His Eminence, Cardinal Agnelo Rossi, Prefect of the S.C.E.P., and of His Excellency, Bishop Simon Lourdusamy, Secretary of the same Congregation.

III. INTERNAL STRUCTURE OF THE INSTITUTE OF MISSIONARY CATECHESIS

In the academic year 1978-1979, the Pontifical Urban University (PUU) offered a program especially prepared for the student-catechists who flocked to Rome from the various local

Churches of Africa, Asia and Latin America, and who were presenting themselves, already in that year, in a larger number, in fact, in a surpising number: 65!

We must say first of all that the PUU, being a Roman university specialized in the problems of evangelization, willingly took the occasion to enrich the problematic of catechesis with a missionary dimension and thus offer a service not only to the young Churches, but also to those of ancient origin. It succeeded by giving life to an "Institute of Missionary Catechesis" incorporated into the Faculty of Missiology and authorized to confer the academic degree of Bachelor. As can be noted from the title, it is not an institute of *"catechetics,"* which would denote a prevalent interest in the methodology used to transmit the evangelical content; but an institute of "missionary catechesis." It is, therefore, a matter of an institute which helps the catechist:

a) to know and deepen the contents of truly Catholic catechesis, as a bond of unity for the whole Church;

b) to enrich these same contents and transmit them dynamically with concern for universal evangelization, with respect for the most appropriate cultural methods, which are to be indicated by the local Churches.

To reach this goal the Institute proposes to its students a biennial course of twenty hours weekly, during which two fundamental lines are developed, recalling also the Apostolic Exhortation *Catechesi tradendae:*

1) First of all, the fidelity and integrity with which catechesis must transmit the Revealed Message, thus becoming an element of unity and communion among all the Churches. In other words, during the first year the catechist is helped to identify and refer constantly to the sources of the unity of the Faith, that is, to the catechetical teaching which derives from Sacred Scripture, from the Fathers of the Church, from the Liturgy and from the Magisterium of the Church; from these fonts emerge the data of the Catholic creed that cannot be renounced;

2) Secondly, the attention which catechesis must concretely give its recipient is emphasized. This is the theme of the second year, during which are presented the elements that oblige catechetical teaching to adapt itself to various situations, and therefore to find methodologies more suitable for the presentation of the unique Faith. From this stems the comparison and study of

the missionary catecheses which better harmonize the intangibility of the Revealed Deposit with the missionary dynamism of its transmission.

We have to admit that a project of this nature found itself faced with a particular difficulty: in fact, we have to give the traditional theological content an essential and pastoral style, suitable for pastoral workers who are in direct contact with the people, without reducing the level of the university study. In other words, the university classrooms found themselves welcoming a new type of student, who does require an accurate preparation, but whose needs are different from those of the seminarian and the priest. Some object that this means impairing the scientific level of the university. We can point out, however, that there can also be a scientific dimension in the search for a more effective pastoral character of theological content. In effect this is the answer which many teachers of the Institute (truly well known and among the most esteemed in the Roman university ambient) have given, precisely on the basis of experience within the Institute of Missionary Catechesis. Several times they have affirmed that the new type of student has stimulated them to find a new presentation of the theological science, a preparation which previously they had tended to neglect or had deemed unnecessary.

IV. LOCATION OF THE INSTITUTE: ROME AND CASTEL GANDOLFO

It is perhaps because of this aspect that the students (whether beneficiaries or not of a scholarship from Propaganda Fide) have visibly grown in numbers to the point that, with the academic year 1979-1980, a double section had to be inaugurated, in both of which the academic program of the Institute is carried out completely:

—at Rome, at the traditional location of the PUU, chiefly for the students who do not make use of the scholarship from the S.C.E.P. and who live in the city;

—at Castel Gandolfo, for the students who have received the scholarship from the S.C.E.P. and also for those who live in the area of the "castelli romani."

It is at this second location, most beautiful for its scenery and its position (next to the Pontifical Villa), that the catechist coming from Africa, Asia and Latin America finds particular assistance from the standpoints of study and of community.

1. From the standpoint of study, because the Institute of Missionary Catechesis offers not only the integral academic program and the assistance of various professors, but also important didactic means, even though still in the process of formation, that is:

a) a specialized library on catechesis;

b) a center of catechetical documentation (photo-library, film-library, record-library, posters, various documentation) with materials from every part of the world.

Thanks to all this, the catechist is in a position to fix his gaze on the world panorama of catechesis and thus to acquire from the experience of others what is more useful for improving catechesis in his own nation.

2. At the same location the catechist also finds assistance from the communitarian point of view, which is most important for the desired goals to be attained. This, in fact, is the location of the "Missionary College Mater Ecclesiae," which assures the student a formation that goes beyond the strictly academic program, and concerns the spiritual and liturgical aspects and those of work, of apostolate, of life in common, etc.

Initiatives of this type are numerous throughout the year and continue even during the summer months. Because the catechists have to derive the maximum benefit from their two years of residence in Rome, they are also assisted during this period. It is for this reason that during the months of July, August and September they are the object of a very precise program. A month is reserved for catechetical experiences both with youth groups at various vacation sites and in parishes; the other two months are reserved for intensive courses in nursing, farming, the means of social communication, etc. At the end of this, the student immediately begins the academic year. Thanks to this continued application, we can almost affirm that the biennial of the Institute of Missionary Catechesis corresponds to three years of normal academic study.

Particular emphasis, however, should be given to the aspect of communitarian life which this biennium involves. It is enough to recall that at the "Missionary College Mater Ecclesiae" alone, a good thirty-five nations are represented. If it is indisputable that this provokes difficulties in living together due to diversity of mentalities, habits, tastes, etc., it is just as true that this gives the feeling of Pentecost, that is, the feeling of the universality of the Church, which reaches out to all peoples, while remaining one and undivided. A few months ago a student from central Africa told me: "I had a hard time getting used to living in this context of mentalities so different from one another; I thought I would not succeed. Often I had nostalgia for my country, and I told myself that I could even have learned some of the things that I was being taught here by remaining in my own diocese and attending our national catechetical center. Now I see that I am returning to my community with a concrete vision of the universal Church and with a spiritual and intellectual openness that I did not have before. I did not realize that I was slowly absorbing it here, day by day. Now I feel that it is my specific duty to communicate to others, especially to my fellow catechists, the immense value of the universality of the Church. For this reason I leave Rome with nostalgia."

Re-reading *Catechesi tradendae* now, we are almost tempted to think that the Holy Father must also have had in mind the Institute of Missionary Catechesis of the PUU and the "Missionary College Mater Ecclesiae," when in number 66 he wrote: "I rejoice at the efforts made by the Sacred Congregation for the Evangelization of Peoples to improve more and more the training of these catechists."

CESARE BONIVENTO, PIME

FOOTNOTES

1. Cf. G. Caprile, *Il Sinodo dei Vescovi 1977*, La Civiltà Cattolica, Rome, 1978, p. 56.
2. Cf. *infra.*, pp. 595-601.
3. Cf. *infra.*, pp. 602-616.

Apostolic Exhortation

of His Holiness
Pope John Paul II

Catechesi Tradendae

on Catechesis
in Our Time

INTRODUCTION

Christ's Final Command

1. The Church has always considered catechesis one of her primary tasks, for, before Christ ascended to His Father after His resurrection, He gave the apostles a final command—to make disciples of all nations and to teach them to observe all that He had commanded.[1] He thus entrusted them with the mission and power to proclaim to humanity what they had heard, what they had seen with their eyes, what they had looked upon and touched with their hands, concerning the Word of Life.[2] He also entrusted them with the mission and power to explain with authority what He had taught them, His words and actions, His signs and commandments. And He gave them the Spirit to fulfill this mission.

Very soon the name of catechesis was given to the whole of the efforts within the Church to make disciples, to help people to believe that Jesus is the Son of God, so that believing they might have life in His name,[3] and to educate and instruct them in this life and thus build up the Body of Christ. The Church has not ceased to devote her energy to this task.

Paul VI's Solicitude

2. The most recent Popes gave catechesis a place of eminence in their pastoral solicitude. Through his gestures, his preaching, his authoritative interpretation of the Second Vatican Council (considered by him the great catechism of modern times), and through the whole of his life, my venerated predecessor Paul VI served the Church's catechesis in a particularly exemplary fashion. On March 18, 1971, he approved the General Catechetical Directory prepared by the Sacred Congregation for the Clergy, a directory that is still the basic document for encouraging and guiding catechetical renewal throughout the Church. He set up the International Council for Catechesis in 1975. He defined in masterly fashion the role and significance of catechesis in the life and mission of

the Church when he addressed the participants in the first International Catechetical Congress on September 25, 1971,[4] and he returned explicitly to the subject in his Apostolic Exhortation *Evangelii nuntiandi.*[5] He decided that catechesis, especially that meant for children and young people, should be the theme of the fourth general assembly of the synod of Bishops,[6] which was held in October 1977 and which I myself had the joy of taking part in.

A Fruitful Synod

3. At the end of that synod the fathers·presented the Pope with a very rich documentation, consisting of the various interventions during the assembly, the conclusions of the working groups, the message that they had with his consent sent to the People of God,[7] and especially the imposing list of "propositions" in which they expressed their views on a very large number of aspects of present-day catechesis.

The Synod worked in an exceptional atmosphere of thanksgiving and hope. It saw in catechetical renewal a precious gift from the Holy Spirit to the Church of today, a gift to which the Christian communities at all levels throughout the world are responding with a generosity and inventive dedication that win admiration. The requisite discernment could then be brought to bear on a reality that is very much alive and it could benefit from great openness among the People of God to the grace of the Lord and the directives of the magisterium.

Purpose of This Exhortation

4. It is in the same climate of faith and hope that I am today addressing this apostolic exhortation to you, venerable brothers and dear sons and daughters. The theme is extremely vast and the exhortation will keep to only a few of the most topical and decisive aspects of it, as an affirmation of the happy results of the synod. In essence, the exhortation takes up again the reflections that were prepared by Pope Paul VI, making abundant use of the documents left by the synod. Pope John Paul I, whose zeal and gifts as a catechist amazed us all, had

taken them in hand and was preparing to publish them when he was suddenly called to God. To all of us he gave an example of catechesis at once popular and concentrated on the essential, one made up of simple words and actions that were able to touch the heart. I am therefore taking up the inheritance of these two Popes in response to the request which was expressly formulated by the Bishops at the end of the fourth general assembly of the synod and which was welcomed by Pope Paul VI in his closing speech.[8] I am also doing so in order to fulfill one of the chief duties of my apostolic charge. Catechesis has always been a central care in my ministry as a priest and as a Bishop.

I ardently desire that this apostolic exhortation to the whole Church should strengthen the solidity of the faith and of Christian living, should give fresh vigor to the initiatives in hand, should stimulate creativity—with the required vigilance—and should help to spread among the communities the joy of bringing the mystery of Christ to the world.

I. WE HAVE BUT ONE TEACHER, JESUS CHRIST

Putting Into Communion With the Person of Christ

5. The fourth general assembly of the synod of Bishops often stressed the Christocentricity of all authentic catechesis. We can here use the word "Christocentricity" in both its meanings, which are not opposed to each other or mutually exclusive, but each of which rather demands and completes the other.

In the first place, it is intended to stress that at the heart of catechesis we find, in essence, a Person, the Person of Jesus of Nazareth, "the only Son from the Father...full of grace and truth,"[9] who suffered and died for us and who now, after rising, is living with us forever. It is Jesus who is "the way, and the truth, and the life,"[10] and Christian living consists in following Christ, the *sequela Christi*.

The primary and essential object of catechesis is, to use an expression dear to St. Paul and also to contemporary theology, "the mystery of Christ." Catechizing is in a way to lead a person to study this mystery in all its dimensions: "to make all men see what is the plan of the mystery...comprehend with all the saints what is the breadth and length and height and depth ...know the love of Christ which surpasses knowledge...(and be filled) with all the fullness of God."[11] It is therefore to reveal in the Person of Christ the whole of God's eternal design reaching fulfillment in that Person. It is to seek to understand the meaning of Christ's actions and words and of the signs worked by Him, for they simultaneously hide and reveal His mystery. Accordingly, the definitive aim of catechesis is to put people not only in touch but in communion, in intimacy, with Jesus Christ: only He can lead us to the love of the Father in the Spirit and make us share in the life of the Holy Trinity.

Transmitting Christ's Teaching

6. Christocentricity in catechesis also means the intention to transmit not one's own teaching or that of some other

master, but the teaching of Jesus Christ, the Truth that He communicates or, to put it more precisely, the Truth that He is.[12] We must therefore say that in catechesis it is Christ, the Incarnate Word and Son of God, who is taught—everything else is taught with reference to Him—and it is Christ alone who teaches—anyone else teaches to the extent that he is Christ's spokesman, enabling Christ to teach with his lips. Whatever be the level of his responsibility in the Church, every catechist must constantly endeavor to transmit by his teaching and behavior the teaching and life of Jesus. He will not seek to keep directed towards himself and his personal opinions and attitudes the attention and the consent of the mind and heart of the person he is catechizing. Above all, he will not try to inculcate his personal opinions and options as if they expressed Christ's teaching and the lessons of His life. Every catechist should be able to apply to himself the mysterious words of Jesus: "My teaching is not mine, but his who sent me."[13] St. Paul did this when he was dealing with a question of prime importance: "I received from the Lord what I also delivered to you."[14] What assiduous study of the word of God transmitted by the Church's magisterium, what profound familiarity with Christ and with the Father, what a spirit of prayer, what detachment from self must a catechist have in order that he can say: "My teaching is not mine!"

Christ the Teacher

7. This teaching is not a body of abstract truths. It is the communication of the living mystery of God. The Person teaching it in the Gospel is altogether superior in excellence to the "masters" in Israel, and the nature of His doctrine surpasses theirs in every way because of the unique link between what He says, what He does and what He is. Nevertheless, the Gospels clearly relate occasions when Jesus "taught." "Jesus began to do and teach"[15]—with these two verbs, placed at the beginning of the book of the Acts, St. Luke links and at the same time distinguishes two poles in Christ's mission.

Jesus taught. It is the witness that He gives of Himself: "Day after day I sat in the temple teaching."[16] It is the admiring observation of the evangelists, surprised to see Him teaching everywhere and at all times, teaching in a manner and with an authority previously unknown: "Crowds gathered to him again; and again, as his custom was, he taught them"[17]; "and they were astonished at his teaching, for he taught them as one who had authority."[18] It is also what His enemies note for the purpose of drawing from it grounds for accusation and condemnation: "He stirs up the people, teaching throughout all Judaea, from Galilee even to this place."[19]

The One "Teacher"

8. One who teaches in this way has a unique title to the name of "Teacher." Throughout the New Testament, especially in the Gospels, how many times is He given this title of Teacher![20] Of course the Twelve, the other disciples, and the crowds of listeners call Him "Teacher" in tones of admiration, trust and tenderness.[21] Even the Pharisees and the Sadducees, the doctors of the law, and the Jews in general do not refuse Him the title: "Teacher, we wish to see a sign from you"[22]; "Teacher, what shall I do to inherit eternal life?"[23] But above all, Jesus Himself at particularly solemn and highly significant moments calls Himself Teacher: "You call me teacher and Lord; and you are right, for so I am"[24]; and He proclaims the singularity, the uniqueness of His character as teacher: "You have one teacher,"[25] the Christ. One can understand why people of every kind, race and nation have for 2,000 years in all the languages of the earth given Him this title with veneration, repeating in their own ways the exclamation of Nicodemus: "We know that you are a teacher come from God."[26]

This image of Christ the Teacher is at once majestic and familiar, impressive and reassuring. It comes from the pen of the evangelists and it has often been evoked subsequently in iconography since earliest Christian times,[27] so captivating is it. And I am pleased to evoke it in my turn at the beginning of these considerations on catechesis in the modern world.

Teaching Through His Life as a Whole

9. In doing so, I am not forgetful that the majesty of Christ the Teacher and the unique consistency and persuasive-

ness of His teaching can only be explained by the fact that His words, His parables and His arguments are never separable from His life and His very being. Accordingly, the whole of Christ's life was a continual teaching: His silences, His miracles, His gestures, His prayer, His love for people, His special affection for the little and the poor, His acceptance of the total sacrifice on the cross for the redemption of the world, and His resurrection are the actualization of His word and the fulfillment of revelation. Hence for Christians the crucifix is one of the most sublime and popular images of Christ the Teacher.

These considerations follow in the wake of the great traditions of the Church and they all strengthen our fervor with regard to Christ, the Teacher who reveals God to man and man to himself, the Teacher who saves, sanctifies and guides, who lives, who speaks, rouses, moves, redresses, judges, forgives, and goes with us day by day on the path of history, the Teacher who comes and will come in glory.

Only in deep communion with Him will catechists find light and strength for an authentic, desirable renewal of catechesis.

II. AN EXPERIENCE AS OLD
AS THE CHURCH

The Mission of the Apostles

10. The image of Christ the Teacher was stamped on the spirit of the Twelve and of the first disciples, and the command "Go...and make disciples of all nations"[28] set the course for the whole of their lives. St. John bears witness to this in his Gospel when he reports the words of Jesus: "No longer do I call you servants, for the servant does not know what his master is doing; but I have called you friends, for all that I have heard from my Father I have made known to you."[29] It was not they who chose to follow Jesus; it was Jesus who chose them, kept them with Him, and appointed them even before His Passover, that they should go and bear fruit and that their fruit should remain.[30] For this reason He formally conferred on them after the resurrection the mission of making disciples of all nations.

The whole of the book of the Acts of the Apostles is a witness that they were faithful to their vocation and to the mission they had received. The members of the first Christian community are seen in it as "devoted to the apostles' teaching and fellowship, to the breaking of bread and the prayers."[31] Without any doubt we find in that a lasting image of the Church being born of and continually nourished by the word of the Lord, thanks to the teaching of the apostles, celebrating that word in the Eucharistic Sacrifice and bearing witness to it before the world in the sign of charity.

When those who opposed the apostles took offense at their activity, it was because they were "annoyed because (the apostles) were teaching the people"[32] and the order they gave them was not to teach at all in the name of Jesus.[33] But we know that the apostles considered it right to listen to God rather than to men on this very matter.[34]

Catechesis in the Apostolic Age

11. The apostles were not slow to share with others the ministry of apostleship.[35] They transmitted to their successors

the task of teaching. They entrusted it also to the deacons from the moment of their institution: Stephen, "full of grace and power," taught unceasingly, moved by the wisdom of the Spirit.[36] The apostles associated "many others" with themselves in the task of teaching,[37] and even simple Christians scattered by persecution "went about preaching the word."[38] St. Paul was in a pre-eminent way the herald of this preaching, from Antioch to Rome, where the last picture of him that we have in Acts is that of a person "teaching about the Lord Jesus Christ quite openly."[39] His numerous letters continue and give greater depth to his teaching. The letters of Peter, John, James and Jude are also, in every case, evidence of catechesis in the apostolic age.

Before being written down, the Gospels were the expression of an oral teaching passed on to the Christian communities, and they display with varying degrees of clarity a catechetical structure. St. Matthew's account has indeed been called the catechist's Gospel, and St. Mark's the catechumen's Gospel.

The Fathers of the Church

12. This mission of teaching that belonged to the apostles and their first fellow workers was continued by the Church. Making herself day after day a disciple of the Lord, she earned the title of "Mother and Teacher."[40] From Clement of Rome to Origen,[41] the post-apostolic age saw the birth of remarkable works. Next we see a striking fact: Some of the most impressive Bishops and pastors, especially in the third and fourth centuries considered it an important part of their espiscopal ministry to deliver catechetical instructions and write treatises. It was the age of Cyril of Jerusalem and John Chrysostom, of Ambrose and Augustine, the age that saw the flowering, from the pen of numerous Fathers of the Church, of works that are still models for us.

It would be impossible here to recall, even very briefly, the catechesis that gave support to the spread and advance of the Church in the various periods of history, in every continent, and in the widest variety of social and cultural contexts.

There was indeed no lack of difficulties. But the word of the Lord completed its course down the centuries; it sped on and triumphed, to use the words of the Apostle Paul.[42]

Councils and Missionary Activity

13. The ministry of catechesis draws ever fresh energy from the councils. The Council of Trent is a noteworthy example of this. It gave catechesis priority in its constitutions and decrees. It lies at the origin of the Roman Catechism, which is also known by the name of that council and which is a work of the first rank as a summary of Christian teaching and traditional theology for use by priests. It gave rise to a remarkable organization of catechesis in the Church. It aroused the clergy to their duty of giving catechetical instruction. Thanks to the work of holy theologians such as St. Charles Borromeo, St. Robert Bellarmine and St. Peter Canisius, it involved the publication of catechisms that were real models for that period. May the Second Vatican Council stir up in our time a like enthusiasm and similar activity.

The missions are also a special area for the application of catechesis. The People of God have thus continued for almost 2,000 years to educate themselves in the faith in ways adapted to the various situations of believers and the many different circumstances in which the Church finds herself.

Catechesis is intimately bound up with the whole of the Church's life. Not only her geographical extension and numerical increase, but even more, her inner growth and correspondence with God's plan depend essentially on catechesis. It is worthwhile pointing out some of the many lessons to be drawn from the experiences in Church history that we have just recalled.

Catechesis as the Church's Right and Duty

14. To begin with, it is clear that the Church has always looked on catechesis as a sacred duty and an inalienable right. On the one hand, it is certainly a duty springing from a command given by the Lord and resting above all on those who in the new covenant receive the call to the ministry of being

pastors. On the other hand, one can likewise speak of a right: from the theological point of view every baptized person, precisely by reason of being baptized, has the right to receive from the Church instruction and education enabling him or her to enter on a truly Christian life; and from the viewpoint of human rights, every human being has the right to seek religious truth and adhere to it freely, that is to say, "without coercion on the part of individuals or of social groups and any human power," in such a way that in this matter of religion, "no one is to be forced to act against his or her conscience or prevented from acting in conformity to it."[43]

That is why catechetical activity should be able to be carried out in favorable circumstances of time and place, and should have access to the mass media and suitable equipment, without discrimination against parents, those receiving catechesis or those imparting it. At present this right is admittedly being given growing recognition, at least on the level of its main principles, as is shown by international declarations and conventions in which, whatever their limitations, one can recognize the desires of the consciences of many people today.[44] But the right is being violated by many States, even to the point that imparting catechesis, having it imparted, and receiving it become punishable offenses. I vigorously raise my voice in union with the synod fathers against all discrimination in the field of catechesis, and at the same time I again make a pressing appeal to those in authority to put a complete end to these constraints on human freedom in general and on religious freedom in particular.

Priority of This Task

15. The second lesson concerns the place of catechesis in the Church's pastoral programs. The more the Church, whether on the local or the universal level, gives catechesis priority over other works and undertakings the results of which would be more spectacular, the more she finds in catechesis a strengthening of her internal life as a community of believers and of her external activity as a missionary Church. As the 20th century draws to a close, the Church is bidden by God

and by events—each of them a call from Him—to renew her trust in catechetical activity as a prime aspect of her mission. She is bidden to offer catechesis her best resources in people and energy, without sparing effort, toil or material means, in order to organize it better and to train qualified personnel. This is no mere human calculation; it is an attitude of faith. And an attitude of faith always has reference to the faithfulness of God, who never fails to respond.

Shared But Differentiated Responsibility

16. The third lesson is that catechesis always has been and always will be a work for which the whole Church must feel responsible and must wish to be responsible. But the Church's members have different responsibilities, derived from each one's mission. Because of their charge, pastors have, at differing levels, the chief responsibility for fostering, guiding and coordinating catechesis. For his part, the Pope has a lively awareness of the primary responsibility that rests on him in this field: In this he finds reasons for pastoral concern but principally a source of joy and hope. Priests and religious have in catechesis a pre-eminent field for their apostolate. On another level, parents have a unique responsibility. Teachers, the various ministers of the Church, catechists, and also organizers of social communications, all have in various degrees very precise responsibilities in this education of the believing conscience, an education that is important for the life of the Church and affects the life of society as such. It would be one of the best results of the general assembly of the synod that was entirely devoted to catechesis if it stirred up in the Church as a whole and in each sector of the Church a lively and active awareness of this differentiated but shared responsibility.

Continual Balanced Renewal

17. Finally, catechesis needs to be continually renewed by a certain broadening of its concept, by the revision of its methods, by the search for suitable language, and by the utilization of new means of transmitting the message. Renewal is sometimes unequal in value; the synod fathers realistically

recognized, not only an undeniable advance in the vitality of catechetical activity and promising initiatives, but also the limitations or even "deficiencies" in what has been achieved to date.[45] These limitations are particularly serious when they endanger integrity of content. The message to the People of God rightly stressed that "routine, with its refusal to accept any change, and improvisation, with its readiness for any venture, are equally dangerous" for catechesis.[46] Routine leads to stagnation, lethargy and eventual paralysis. Improvisation begets confusion on the part of those being given catechesis and, when these are children, on the part of their parents; it also begets all kinds of deviations, and the fracturing and eventually the complete destruction of unity. It is important for the Church to give proof today, as she has done at other periods of her history, of evangelical wisdom, courage and fidelity in seeking out and putting into operation new methods and new prospects for catechetical instruction.

III. CATECHESIS IN THE CHURCH'S PASTORAL AND MISSIONARY ACTIVITY

Catechesis as a Stage in Evangelization

18. Catechesis cannot be dissociated from the Church's pastoral and missionary activity as a whole. Nevertheless it has a specific character which was repeatedly the object of inquiry during the preparatory work and throughout the course of the fourth general assembly of the synod of Bishops. The question also interests the public both within and outside the Church.

This is not the place for giving a rigorous formal definition of catechesis, which has been sufficiently explained in the General Catechetical Directory.[47] It is for specialists to clarify more and more its concept and divisions.

In view of uncertainties in practice, let us simply recall the essential landmarks—they are already solidly established in Church documents—that are essential for an exact understanding of catechesis and without which there is a risk of failing to grasp its full meaning and import.

All in all, it can be taken here that catechesis is an education of children, young people and adults in the faith, which includes especially the teaching of Christian doctrine imparted, generally speaking, in an organic and systematic way, with a view to initiating the hearers into the fullness of Christian life. Accordingly, while not being formally identified with them, catechesis is built on a certain number of elements of the Church's pastoral mission that have a catechetical aspect, that prepare for catechesis, or that spring from it. These elements are: the initial proclamation of the Gospel or missionary preaching through the *kerygma* to arouse faith, apologetics or examination of the reasons for belief, experience of Christian living, celebration of the sacraments, integration into the ecclesial community, and apostolic and missionary witness.

Let us first of all recall that there is no separation or opposition between catechesis and evangelization. Nor can the two be simply identified with each other. Instead, they have close links whereby they integrate and complement each other.

The Apostolic Exhortation *Evangelii nuntiandi* of December 8, 1975, on evangelization in the modern world, rightly stressed that evangelization—which has the aim of bringing the Good News to the whole of humanity, so that all may live by it—is a rich, complex and dynamic reality, made up of elements, or one could say moments, that are essential and different from each other, and that must all be kept in view simultaneously.[48] Catechesis is one of these moments—a very remarkable one—in the whole process of evangelization.

Catechesis and the Initial Proclamation of the Gospel

19. The specific character of catechesis, as distinct from the initial conversion-bringing proclamation of the Gospel, has the twofold objective of maturing the initial faith and of educating the true disciple of Christ by means of a deeper and more systematic knowledge of the person and the message of our Lord Jesus Christ.[49]

But in catechetical practice, this model order must allow for the fact that the initial evangelization has often not taken place. A certain number of children baptized in infancy come for catechesis in the parish without receiving any other initiation into the faith and still without any explicit personal attachment to Jesus Christ; they only have the capacity to believe placed within them by Baptism and the presence of the Holy Spirit; and opposition is quickly created by the prejudices of their non-Christian family background or of the positivist spirit of their education. In addition, there are other children who have not been baptized and whose parents agree only at a later date to religious education: for practical reasons, the catechumenal stage of these children will often be carried out largely in the course of the ordinary catechesis. Again, many pre-adolescents and adolescents who have been baptized and been given a systematic catechesis and the sacraments still remain hesitant for a long time about committing their whole lives to Jesus Christ—if, moreover, they do not attempt to avoid religious education in the name of their freedom. Finally, even adults are not safe from temptations to doubt or to abandon their faith, especially as a result of their unbelieving surroundings. This means that "catechesis" must often concern itself not only with nourishing and teaching the faith, but also with arousing it unceasingly with the help of grace, with opening the heart, with converting, and with preparing total adherence to Jesus Christ on the part of those who are still on the threshold of faith. This concern will in part decide the tone, the language and the method of catechesis.

Specific Aim of Catechesis

20. Nevertheless, the specific aim of catechesis is to develop, with God's help, an as yet initial faith, and to advance in fullness and to nourish day by day the Christian life of the faithful, young and old. It is in fact a matter of giving growth, at the level of knowledge and in life, to the seed of faith sown by the Holy Spirit with the initial proclamation and effectively transmitted by Baptism.

Catechesis aims therefore at developing understanding of the mystery of Christ in the light of God's word, so that the whole of a person's humanity is impregnated by that word. Changed by the working of grace into a new creature, the Christian thus sets himself to follow Christ and learns more and more within the Church to think like Him, to judge like Him, to act in conformity with His commandments, and to hope as He invites us to.

To put it more precisely: within the whole process of evangelization, the aim of catechesis is to be the teaching and maturation stage, that is to say, the period in which the Christian, having accepted by faith the person of Jesus Christ as the one Lord and having given Him complete adherence by sincere conversion of heart, endeavors to know better this Jesus to whom he has entrusted himself: to know His "mystery," the kingdom of God proclaimed by Him, the requirements and promises contained in His Gospel message, and the paths that He has laid down for anyone who wishes to follow Him.

It is true that being a Christian means saying yes" to Jesus Christ, but let us remember that this "yes" has two levels: It consists in surrendering to the word of God and relying on it, but it also means, at a later stage, endeavoring to know better and better the profound meaning of this word.

Need for Systematic Catechesis

21. In his closing speech at the fourth general assembly of the synod, Pope Paul VI rejoiced "to see how everyone drew attention to the absolute need for systematic catechesis, precisely because it is this reflective study of the Christian mystery that fundamentally distinguishes catechesis from all other ways of presenting the word of God."[50]

In view of practical difficulties, attention must be drawn to some of the characteristics of this instruction:

—It must be systematic, not improvised but programmed to reach a precise goal;

—It must deal with essentials, without any claim to tackle all disputed questions or to transform itself into theological research or scientific exegesis;

—It must nevertheless be sufficiently complete, not stopping short at the initial proclamation of the Christian mystery such as we have in the *kerygma;*

—It must be an integral Christian initiation, open to all the other factors of Christian life.

I am not forgetting the interest of the many different occasions for catechesis connected with personal, family, social and ecclesial life—these occasions must be utilized and I shall return to them in Chapter VI—but I am stressing the need for organic and systematic Christian instruction, because of the tendency in various quarters to minimize its importance.

Catechesis and Life Experience

22. It is useless to play off orthopraxis against orthodoxy: Christianity is inseparably both. Firm and well-thought-out convictions lead to courageous and upright action; the endeavor to educate the faithful to live as disciples of Christ today calls for and facilitates a discovery in depth of the mystery of Christ in the history of salvation.

It is also quite useless to campaign for the abandonment of serious and orderly study of the message of Christ in the name of a method concentrating on life experience. "No one can arrive at the whole truth on the basis solely of some simple private experience, that is to say, without an adequate explanation of the message of Christ, who is 'the way, and the truth, and the life' (Jn. 14:6)."[51]

Nor is any opposition to be set up between a catechesis taking life as its point of departure and a traditional doctrinal and systematic catechesis.[52] Authentic catechesis is always an orderly and systematic initiation into the revelation that God has given of Himself to humanity in Christ Jesus, a revelation stored in the depths of the Church's memory· and in Sacred Scripture, and constantly communicated from one generation to the next by a living, active *traditio.* This revelation is not however isolated from life or artificially juxtaposed to it. It is concerned with the ultimate meaning of life and it illumines the whole of life with the light of the Gospel, to inspire it or to question it.

That is why we can apply to catechists an expression used by the Second Vatican Council with special reference to priests: "Instructors (of the human being and his life) in the faith."[53]

Catechesis and Sacraments

23. Catechesis is intrinsically linked with the whole of liturgical and sacramental activity, for it is in the sacraments, especially in the Eucharist, that Christ Jesus works in fullness for the transformation of human beings.

In the early Church, the catechumenate and preparation for the sacraments of Baptism and the Eucharist were the same thing. Although in the countries that have long been Christian the Church has changed her practice in this field, the catechumenate has never been abolished; on the contrary, it is experiencing a renewal in those countries[54] and is abundantly practiced in the young missionary Churches. In any case, catechesis always has reference to the sacraments. On the one hand, the catechesis that prepares for the sacraments is an eminent kind, and every form of catechesis necessarily leads to the sacraments of faith. On the other hand, authentic practice of the sacraments is bound to have a catechetical aspect. In other words, sacramental life is impoverished and very soon turns into hollow ritualism if it is not based on serious knowledge of the meaning of the sacraments, and catechesis becomes intellectualized if it fails to come alive in the sacramental practice.

Catechesis and Ecclesial Community

24. Finally, catechesis is closely linked with the responsible activity of the Church and of Christians in the world. A person who has given adherence to Jesus Christ by faith and is endeavoring to consolidate that faith by catechesis needs to live in communion with those who have taken the same step. Catechesis runs the risk of becoming barren if no community of faith and Christian life takes the catechumen in at a certain stage of his catechesis. That is why the ecclesial community at all levels has a twofold responsibility with regard to catechesis: it has the responsibility of providing for the training of its members, but it also has the responsibility of welcoming them into an environment where they can live as fully as possible what they have learned.

Catechesis is likewise open to missionary dynamism. If catechesis is done well, Christians will be eager to bear witness to their faith, to hand it on to their children, to make it known to others, and to serve the human community in every way.

Catechesis in the Wide Sense Necessary for Maturity and Strength of Faith

25. Thus through catechesis the Gospel *kerygma* (the initial ardent proclamation by which a person is one day overwhelmed and brought to the decision to entrust himself to Jesus Christ by faith) is gradually deepened, developed in its implicit consequences, explained in language that includes an appeal to reason, and channelled towards Christian practice in the Church and the world. All this is no less evangelical than the *kerygma*, in spite of what is said by certain people who consider that catechesis necessarily rationalizes, dries up and eventually kills all that is living, spontaneous and vibrant in the *kerygma*. The truths studied in catechesis are the same truths that touched the person's heart when he heard them for the

first time. Far from blunting or exhausting them, the fact of knowing them better should make them even more challenging and decisive for one's life.

In the understanding expounded here, catechesis keeps the entirely pastoral perspective with which the synod viewed it. This broad meaning of catechesis in no way contradicts but rather includes and goes beyond a narrow meaning which was once commonly given to catechesis in didactic expositions, namely, the simple teaching of the formulas that express faith.

In the final analysis, catechesis is necessary both for the maturation of the faith of Christians and for their witness in the world: It is aimed at bringing Christians to "attain to the unity of the faith and of the knowledge of the Son of God, to mature manhood, to the measure of the stature of the fullness of Christ"[55]; it is also aimed at making them prepared to make a defense to anyone who calls them to account for the hope that is in them.[56]

IV. THE WHOLE OF THE GOOD NEWS DRAWN FROM ITS SOURCE

Content of the Message

26. Since catechesis is a moment or aspect of evangelization, its content cannot be anything else but the content of evangelization as a whole. The one message—the Good News of salvation—that has been heard once or hundreds of times and has been accepted with the heart, is in catechesis probed unceasingly by reflection and systematic study, by awareness of its repercussions on one's personal life—an awareness calling for ever greater commitment—and by inserting it into an organic and harmonious whole, namely, Christian living in society and the world.

The Source

27. Catechesis will always draw its content from the living source of the Word of God transmitted in Tradition and the Scriptures, for "sacred Tradition and Sacred Scripture make up a single sacred deposit of the Word of God, which is entrusted to the Church," as was recalled by the Second Vatican Council, which desired that "the ministry of the word—pastoral preaching, catechetics and all forms of Christian instruction...—(should be) healthily nourished and (should) thrive in holiness through the word of Scripture."[57]

To speak of Tradition and Scripture as the source of catechesis is to draw attention to the fact that catechesis must be impregnated and penetrated by the thought, the spirit and the outlook of the Bible and the Gospels through assiduous contact with the texts themselves; but it is also a reminder that catechesis will be all the richer and more effective for reading the texts with the intelligence and the heart of the Church and for drawing inspiration from the 2,000 years of the Church's reflection and life.

The Church's teaching, liturgy and life spring from this source and lead back to it, under the guidance of the pastors and, in particular, of the doctrinal magisterium entrusted to them by the Lord.

The Creed, an Exceptionally Important Expression of Doctrine

28. An exceptionally important expression of the living heritage placed in the custody of the pastors is found in the Creed or, to put it more concretely, in the Creeds that at crucial moments have summed up the Church's faith in felicitous syntheses. In the course of the centuries an important element of catechesis was constituted by the *traditio Symboli* (transmission of the summary of the faith), followed by the transmission of the Lord's Prayer. This expressive rite has in our time been reintroduced into the initiation of catechumens.[58] Should not greater use be made of an adapted form of it to mark that most important stage at which a new disciple of Jesus Christ accepts with full awareness and courage the content of what will from then on be the object of his earnest study?

In the Creed of the People of God, proclaimed at the close of the 19th centenary of the martyrdom of the Apostles Peter and Paul, my predecessor Paul VI decided to bring together the essential elements of the Catholic Faith, especially those that presented greater difficulty or risked being ignored.[59] This is a sure point of reference for the content of catechesis.

Factors That Must Not Be Neglected

29. In the third chapter of his Apostolic Exhortation *Evangelii nuntiandi*, the same Pope recalled "the essential content, the living substance" of evangelization.[60] Catechesis, too, must keep in mind each of these factors and also the living synthesis of which they are part.[61]

I shall therefore limit myself here simply to recalling one or two points.[62] Anyone can see, for instance, how important it is to make the child, the adolescent, the person advancing in faith understand "what can be known about God"[63]; to be able in a way to tell them: "What you worship as unknown, this I proclaim to you"[64]; to set forth briefly for them[65] the mystery of the Word of God become man and accomplishing man's salvation by His Passover, that is to say, through His death and resurrection, but also by His preaching, by the signs worked by Him, and by the sacraments of His permanent presence in our midst. The synod fathers were indeed inspired when they asked that care should be taken not to reduce Christ to His humanity alone or His message to a no more than earthly dimension, but that He should be recognized as the Son of God, the Mediator giving us in the Spirit free access to the Father.[66]

It is important to display before the eyes of the intelligence and of the heart, in the light of faith, the sacrament of Christ's presence constituted by the mystery of the Church, which is an assembly of human beings who are sinners and yet have at the same time been sanctified and who make up the family of God gathered together by the Lord under the guidance of those whom "the Holy Spirit has made...guardians, to feed the Church of God."[67]

It is important to explain that the history of the human race, marked as it is by grace and sin, greatness and misery, is taken up by God in His Son Jesus, "foreshadowing in some way the age which is to come."[68]

Finally, it is important to reveal frankly the demands—demands that involve self-denial but also joy—made by what the Apostle Paul liked to call "newness of life,"[69] "a new creation,"[70] being in Christ,[71] and "eternal life in Christ Jesus,"[72] which is the same thing as life in the world but lived in accordance with the beatitudes and called to an extension and transfiguration hereafter.

Hence the importance in catechesis of personal moral commitments in keeping with the Gospel and of Christian attitudes, whether heroic or very simple, to life and the world—what we call the Christian or evangelical virtues. Hence also, in its endeavor to educate faith, the concern of catechesis not to omit but to clarify properly realities such as man's activity for his integral liberation,[73] the search for a society with greater solidarity and fraternity, the fight for justice and the building of peace.

Besides, it is not to be thought that this dimension of catechesis is altogether new. As early as the patristic age, St. Ambrose and St. John Chrysostom—to quote only them —gave prominence to the social consequences of the demands made by the Gospel. Close to our own time, the catechism of St. Pius X explicitly listed oppressing the poor and depriving workers of their just wages among the sins that cry to God for vengeance.[74] Since *Rerum novarum* especially, social concern has been actively present in the catechetical teaching of the Popes and the Bishops. Many synod fathers rightly insisted that the rich heritage of the Church's social teaching should, in appropriate forms, find a place in the general catechetical education of the faithful.

Integrity of Content

30. With regard to the content of catechesis, three important points deserve special attention today.

The first point concerns the integrity of the content. In order that the sacrificial offering of his or her faith[75] should be perfect, the person who becomes a disciple of Christ has the right to receive "the word of faith"[76] not in mutilated, falsified or diminished form but whole and entire, in all its rigor and vigor. Unfaithfulness on some point to the integrity of the message means a dangerous weakening of catechesis and putting at risk the results that Christ and the ecclesial community have a right to expect from it. It is certainly not by chance that the final command of Jesus in Matthew's Gospel bears the mark of a certain entireness: "All authority...has been given to me...make disciples of all nations...teaching them to observe all...I am with you always." This is why, when a person first becomes aware of "the surpassing worth of knowing Christ Jesus,"[77] whom he has encountered by faith, and has the perhaps unconscious desire to know Him more extensively and better, "hearing about Him and being taught in Him, as the truth is in Jesus,"[78] there is no valid pretext for refusing Him any part whatever of that knowledge. What kind of catechesis would it be that failed to give their full place to man's creation and sin; to God's plan of redemption and its long, loving preparation and realization; to the incarnation of the Son of God; to Mary, the Immaculate One, the Mother of God, ever Virgin, raised body and soul to the glory of heaven, and to her role in the mystery of salvation; to the mystery of lawlessness at work in our lives[79] and the power of God freeing us from it; to the need for penance and asceticism; to the sacramental and liturgical actions; to the reality of the Eucharistic Presence; to participation in divine life here and hereafter, and so on? Thus, no true catechist can lawfully, on his own initiative, make a selection of what he considers important in the deposit of faith as opposed to what he considers unimportant, so as to teach the one and reject the other.

By Means of Suitable Pedagogical Methods

31. This gives rise to a second remark. It can happen that in the present situation of catechesis reasons of method or pedagogy suggest that the communication of the riches of the content of catechesis should be organized in one way rather than another. Besides, integrity does not dispense from balance and from the organic hierarchical character through which the truths to be taught, the norms to be transmitted, and the ways of Christian life to be indicated will be given the proper importance due to each. It can also happen that a particular sort of language proves preferable for transmitting this content to a particular individual or group. The choice made will be a valid one to the extent that, far from being dictated by more or less subjective theories or prejudices stamped with a certain ideology, it is inspired by the humble concern to stay closer to a content that must remain intact. The method and language used must truly be means for communicating the whole and not just a part of "the words of eternal life"[80] and the "ways of life."[81]

Ecumenical Dimension of Catechesis

32. The great movement, one certainly inspired by the Spirit of Jesus, that has for some years been causing the Catholic Church to seek with other Christian Churches or confessions the restoration of the perfect unity willed by the Lord, brings me to the question of the ecumenical character of catechesis. This movement reached its full prominence in the Second Vatican Council[82] and since then has taken on a new extension within the Church, as is shown concretely by the impressive series of events and initiatives with which everyone is now familiar.

Catechesis cannot remain aloof from this ecumenical dimension, since all the faithful are called to share, according to their capacity and place in the Church, in the movement towards unity.[83]

Catechesis will have an ecumenical dimension if, while not ceasing to teach that the fullness of the revealed truths and of the means of salvation instituted by Christ is found in the Catholic Church,[84] it does so with sincere respect, in words and in deeds, for the ecclesial communities that are not in perfect communion with this Church.

In this context, it is extremely important to give a correct and fair presentation of the other Churches and ecclesial communities that the Spirit of Christ does not refrain from using as means of salvation; "moreover, some, even very many, of the outstanding elements and endowments which together go to build up and give life to the Church herself, can exist outside the visible boundaries of the Catholic Church."[85] Among other things this presentation will help Catholics to have both a deeper understanding of their own faith and a better acquaintance with and esteem for their other Christian brethren, thus facilitating the shared search for the way towards full unity in the whole truth. It should also help non-Catholics to have a better knowledge and appreciation of the Catholic Church and her conviction of being the "universal help toward salvation."

Catechesis will have an ecumenical dimension if, in addition, it creates and fosters a true desire for unity. This will be true all the more if it inspires serious efforts—including the effort of self-purification in the humility and the fervor of the

Spirit in order to clear the ways—with a view not to facile irenics made up of omissions and concessions on the level of doctrine, but to perfect unity, when and by what means the Lord will wish.

Finally, catechesis will have an ecumenical dimension if it tries to prepare Catholic children and young people, as well as adults, for living in contact with non-Catholics, affirming their Catholic identity while respecting the faith of others.

Ecumenical Collaboration in the Field of Catechesis

33. In situations of religious plurality, the Bishops can consider it opportune or even necessary to have certain experiences of collaboration in the field of catechesis between Catholics and other Christians, complementing the normal catechesis that must in any case be given to Catholics. Such experiences have a theological foundation in the elements shared by all Christians.[86] But the communion of faith between Catholics and other Christians is not complete and perfect; in certain cases there are even profound divergences. Consequently, this ecumenical collaboration is by its very nature limited: it must never mean a "reduction" to a common minimum. Furthermore, catechesis does not consist merely in the teaching of doctrine: it also means initiating into the whole of Christian life, bringing full participation in the sacraments of the Church. Therefore, where there is an experience of ecumenical collaboration in the field of catechesis, care must be taken that the education of Catholics in the Catholic Church should be well ensured in matters of doctrine and of Christian living.

During the synod, a certain number of Bishops drew attention to what they referred to as the increasingly frequent cases in which the civil authority or other circumstances impose on the schools in some countries a common instruction in the Christian religion, with common textbooks, class periods, etc., for Catholics and non-Catholics alike. Needless to say, this is not true catechesis. But this teaching also has ecumenical importance when it presents Christian doctrine fairly and honestly. In cases where circumstances impose it, it is important that in addition a specifically Catholic catechesis should be ensured with all the greater care.

The Question of Textbooks Dealing with the Various Religions

34. At this point another observation must be made on the same lines but from a different point of view. State schools sometimes provide their pupils with books that for cultural reasons (history, morals or literature) present the various religions, including the Catholic religion. An objective presentation of historical events, of the different religions and of the various Christian confessions can make a contribution here to better mutual understanding. Care will then be taken that every effort is made to ensure that the presentation is truly objective and free from the distorting influence of ideological and political systems or of prejudices with claims to be scientific. In any case, such schoolbooks can obviously not be considered catechetical works: they lack both the witness of believers stating their faith to other believers and an understanding of the Christian mysteries and of what is specific about Catholicism, as these are understood within the faith.

V. EVERYBODY NEEDS
TO BE CATECHIZED

The Importance of Children and the Young

35. The theme designated by my predecessor Paul VI for the fourth general assembly of the synod of Bishops was: "Catechesis in our time, with special reference to the catechesis of children and young people." The increase in the number of young people is without doubt a fact charged with hope and at the same time with anxiety for a large part of the contemporary world. In certain countries, especially those of the Third World, more than half of the population is under 25 or 30 years of age. This means millions and millions of children and young people preparing for their adult future. And there is more than just the factor of numbers: recent events, as well as the daily news, tell us that, although this countless multitude of young people is here and there dominated by uncertainty and fear, seduced by the escapism of indifference or drugs, or tempted by nihilism and violence, nevertheless it constitutes in its major part the great force that amid many hazards is set on building the civilization of the future.

In our pastoral care we ask ourselves: How are we to reveal Jesus Christ, God made man, to this multitude of children and young people, reveal Him not just in the fascination of a first fleeting encounter but through an acquaintance, growing deeper and clearer daily, with Him, His message, the plan of God that He has revealed, the call He addresses to each person, and the kingdom that He wishes to establish in this world with the "little flock"[87] of those who believe in Him, a kingdom that will be complete only in eternity? How are we to enable them to know the meaning, the import, the fundamental requirements, the law of love, the promises and the hopes of this kingdom?

There are many observations that could be made about the special characteristics that catechesis assumes at the different stages of life.

Infants

36. One moment that is often decisive is the one at which the very young child receives the first elements of catechesis from its parents and the family surroundings. These elements will perhaps be no more than a simple revelation of a good and provident Father in heaven to whom the child learns to turn its heart. The very short prayers that the child learns to lisp will be the start of a loving dialogue with this hidden God whose word it will then begin to hear. I cannot insist too strongly on this early initiation by Christian parents in which the child's faculties are integrated into a living relationship with God. It is a work of prime importance. It demands great love and profound respect for the child who has a right to a simple and true presentation of the Christian faith.

Children

37. For the child there comes soon, at school and in Church, in institutions connected with the parish or with the spiritual care of the Catholic or state school not only an introduction into a wider social circle, but also the moment for a catechesis aimed at inserting him or her organically into the life of the Church, a moment that includes an immediate preparation for the celebration of the sacraments. This catechesis is didactic in character, but is directed towards the giving of witness in the faith. It is an initial catechesis but not a fragmentary one, since it will have to reveal, although in an elementary way, all the principal mysteries of faith and their effects on the child's moral and religious life. It is a catechesis that gives meaning to the sacraments, but at the same time it receives from the experience of the sacraments a living dimension that keeps it from remaining merely doctrinal, and it communicates to the child the joy of being a witness to Christ in ordinary life.

Adolescents

38. Next comes puberty and adolescence, with all the greatness and dangers which that age brings. It is the time of

discovering oneself and one's own inner world, the time of generous plans, the time when the feeling of love awakens, with the biological impulses of sexuality, the time of the desire to be together, the time of a particularly intense joy connected with the exhilarating discovery of life. But often it is also the age of deeper questioning, of anguished or even frustrating searching, of a certain mistrust of others and dangerous introspection, and the age sometimes of the first experiences of setbacks and of disappointments. Catechesis cannot ignore these changeable aspects of this delicate period of life. A catechesis capable of leading the adolescent to reexamine his or her life and to engage in dialogue, a catechesis that does not ignore the adolescent's great questions—self-giving, belief, love and the means of expressing it constituted by sexuality—such a catechesis can be decisive. The revelation of Jesus Christ as a Friend, Guide and Model, capable of being admired but also imitated; the revelation of this message which provides an answer to the fundamental questions; the revelation of the loving plan of Christ the Savior as the incarnation of the only authentic love and as the possibility of uniting the human race—all this can provide the basis for genuine education in faith. Above all, the mysteries of the passion and death of Jesus, through which, according to St. Paul, he merited His glorious resurrection, can speak eloquently to the adolescent's conscience and heart and cast light on his first sufferings and on the suffering of the world that he is discovering.

The Young

39. With youth comes the moment of the first great decisions. Although the young may enjoy the support of the members of their family and their friends, they have to rely on themselves and their own conscience and must ever more frequently and decisively assume responsibility for their destiny. Good and evil, grace and sin, life and death will more and more confront one another within them, not just as moral categories but chiefly as fundamental options which they must accept or reject lucidly, conscious of their own responsibility. It is obvious that a catechesis which denounces selfishness in

the name of generosity, and which without any illusory over-simplification presents the Christian meaning of work, of the common good, of justice and charity, a catechesis on international peace and on the advancement of human dignity, on development, and on liberation, as these are presented in recent documents of the Church,[88] fittingly completes in the minds of the young the good catechesis on strictly religious realities which is never to be neglected. Catechesis then takes on considerable importance, since it is the time when the Gospel can be presented, understood and accepted as capable of giving meaning to life and thus of inspiring attitudes that would have no other explanation, such as self-sacrifice, detachment, forbearance, justice, commitment, reconciliation, a sense of the Absolute and the unseen. All these are traits that distinguish a young person from his or her companions as a disciple of Jesus Christ.

Catechesis thus prepares for the important Christian commitments of adult life. For example, it is certain that many vocations to the priesthood and religious life have their origin during a well-imparted catechesis in infancy and adolescence.

From infancy until the threshold of maturity, catechesis is thus a permanent school of the faith and follows the major stages of life, like a beacon lighting the path of the child, the adolescent and the young person.

The Adaptation of Catechesis for Young People

40. It is reassuring to note that, during the fourth general assembly of the synod and the following years, the Church has widely shared in concern about how to impart catechesis to children and young people. God grant that the attention thus aroused will long endure in the Church's consciousness. In this way the synod has been valuable for the whole Church by seeking to trace with the greatest possible precision the complex characteristics of present-day youth; by showing that these young persons speak a language into which the message of Jesus must be translated with patience and wisdom and without betrayal; by demonstrating that, in spite of appearances, these young people have within them, even though

often in a confused way, not just a readiness or openness, but rather a real desire to know "Jesus...who is called Christ"[89]; and by indicating that if the work of catechesis is to be carried out rigorously and seriously, it is today more difficult and tiring than ever before, because of the obstacles and difficulties of all kinds that it meets; but it is also more consoling, because of the depth of the response it receives from children and young people. This is a treasure which the Church can and should count on in the years ahead.

The Handicapped

41. Children and young people who are physically or mentally handicapped come first to mind. They have a right, like others of their age, to know "the mystery of faith." The greater difficulties that they encounter give greater merit to their efforts and to those of their teachers. It is pleasant to see that Catholic organizations especially dedicated to young handicapped people contributed to the synod a renewed desire to deal better with this important problem. They deserve to be given warm encouragement in this endeavor.

Young People Without Religious Support

42. My thoughts turn next to the ever increasing number of children and young people born and brought up in a non-Christian or at least non-practicing home but who wish to know the Christian faith. They must be ensured a catechesis attuned to them, so that they will be able to grow in faith and live by it more and more, in spite of the lack of support or even the opposition they meet in their surroundings.

Adults

43. To continue the series of receivers of catechesis, I cannot fail to emphasize now one of the most constant concerns of the synod fathers, a concern imposed with vigor and urgency by present experiences throughout the world: I am referring to the central problem of the catechesis of adults. This is the prin-

cipal form of catechesis, because it is addressed to persons
who have the greatest responsibilities and the capacity to live
the Christian message in its fully developed form.[90] The Christian community cannot carry out a permanent catechesis
without the direct and skilled participation of adults, whether
as receivers or as promoters of catechetical activity. The
world, in which the young are called to live and to give witness
to the faith which catechesis seeks to deepen and strengthen, is
governed by adults. The faith of these adults too should continually be enlightened, stimulated and renewed, so that it
may pervade the temporal realities in their charge. Thus, for
catechesis to be effective, it must be permanent, and it would
be quite useless if it stopped short at the threshold of maturity,
since catechesis, admittedly under another form, proves no less
necessary for adults.

Quasi-Catechumens

44. Among the adults who need catechesis, our pastoral
missionary concern is directed to those who were born and
reared in areas not yet Christianized, and who have never been
able to study deeply the Christian teaching that the circumstances of life have at a certain moment caused them to
come across. It is also directed to those who in childhood
received a catechesis suited to their age but who later drifted
away from all religious practice and as adults find themselves
with religious knowledge of a rather childish kind. It is
likewise directed to those who feel the effects of a catechesis
received early in life but badly imparted or badly assimilated.
It is directed to those who, although they were born in a Christian country or in sociologically Christian surroundings, have
never been educated in their faith and, as adults, are really
catechumens.

Diversified and Complementary
Forms of Catechesis

45. Catechesis is therefore for adults of every age, including the elderly—persons who deserve particular attention in
view of their experience and their problems—no less than for

children, adolescents and the young. We should also mention migrants, those who are by-passed by modern developments, those who live in areas of large cities which are often without churches, buildings and suitable organization, and other such groups. It is desirable that initiatives meant to give all these groups a Christian formation, with appropriate means (audio-visual aids, booklets, discussions, lectures), should increase in number, enabling many adults to fill the gap left by an insuffi-cient or deficient catechesis, to complete harmoniously at a higher level their childhood catechesis, or even to prepare themselves enough in this field to be able to help others in a more serious way.

It is important also that the catechesis of children and young people, permanent catechesis, and the catechesis of adults should not be separate watertight compartments. It is even more important that there should be no break between them. On the contrary, their perfect complementarity must be fostered: adults have much to give to young people and children in the field of catechesis, but they can also receive much from them for the growth of their own Christian lives.

It must be restated that nobody in the Church of Jesus Christ should feel excused from receiving catechesis. This is true even of young seminarians and young religious, and of all those called to the task of being pastors and catechists. They will fulfill this task all the better if they are humble pupils of the Church, the great giver as well as the great receiver of catechesis.

VI. SOME WAYS AND MEANS
OF CATECHESIS

Communications Media

46. From the oral teaching by the apostles and the letters circulating among the churches down to the most modern means, catechesis has not ceased to look for the most suitable ways and means for its mission, with the active participation of the communities and at the urging of the pastors. This effort must continue.

I think immediately of the great possibilities offered by the means of social communication and the means of group communication: television, radio, the press, records, tape recordings—the whole series of audio-visual means. The achievements in these spheres are such as to encourage the greatest hope. Experience shows, for example, the effect had by instruction given on radio or television, when it combines a high aesthetic level and rigorous fidelity to the magisterium. The Church now has many opportunities for considering these questions—as, for instance, on Social Communications Days —and it is not necessary to speak of them at length here, in spite of their prime importance.

Utilization of Various Places,
Occasions and Gatherings

47. I am also thinking of various occasions of special value which are exactly suitable for catechesis: for example, diocesan, regional or national pilgrimages, which gain from being centered on some judiciously chosen theme based on the life of Christ, of the Blessed Virgin or of the saints. Then there are the traditional missions, often too hastily dropped but irreplaceable for the periodic and vigorous renewal of Christian life—they should be revived and brought up to date. Again, there are Bible-study groups, which ought to go beyond exegesis and lead their members to live by the Word of God. Yet

other instances are the meetings of ecclesial basic communities, in so far as they correspond to the criteria laid down in the Apostolic Exhortation *Evangelii nuntiandi*.[91] I may also mention the youth groups that, under varying names and forms but always with the purpose of making Jesus Christ known and of living by the Gospel, are in some areas multiplying and flourishing in a sort of springtime that is very comforting for the Church. These include Catholic action groups, charitable groups, prayer groups and Christian meditation groups. These groups are a source of great hope for the Church of tomorrow. But, in the name of Jesus, I exhort the young people who belong to them, their leaders, and the priests who devote the best part of their ministry to them: no matter what it costs, do not allow these groups—which are exceptional occasions for meeting others, and which are blessed with such riches of friendship and solidarity among the young, of joy and enthusiasm, of reflection on events and facts—do not allow them to lack serious study of Christian doctrine. If they do, they will be in danger—a danger that has unfortunately proved only too real—of disappointing their members and also the Church.

The catechetical endeavor that is possible in these various surroundings, and in many others besides, will have all the greater chance of being accepted and bearing fruit if it respects their individual nature. By becoming part of them in the right way, it will achieve the diversity and complementarity of approach that will enable it to develop all the riches of its concept, with its three dimensions of word, memorial and witness —doctrine, celebration and commitment in living—which the synod Message to the People of God emphasized.[92]

The Homily

48. This remark is even more valid for the catechesis given in the setting of the liturgy, especially at the Eucharistic assembly. Respecting the specific nature and proper cadence of this setting, the homily takes up again the journey of faith put forward by catechesis, and brings it to its natural fulfillment.

At the same time it encourages the Lord's disciples to begin anew each day their spiritual journey in truth, adoration and thanksgiving. Accordingly, one can say that catechetical teaching too finds its source and its fulfillment in the Eucharist, within the whole circle of the liturgical year. Preaching, centered upon the Bible texts, must then in its own way make it possible to familiarize the faithful with the whole of the mysteries of the faith and with the norms of Christian living. Much attention must be given to the homily: it should be neither too long nor too short; it should always be carefully prepared, rich in substance and adapted to the hearers, and reserved to ordained ministers. The homily should have its place not only in every Sunday and feast-day Eucharist, but also in the celebration of baptisms, penitential liturgies, marriages and funerals. This is one of the benefits of the liturgical renewal.

Catechetical Literature

49. Among these various ways and means—all the Church's activities have a catechetical dimension—catechetical works, far from losing their essential importance, acquire fresh significance. One of the major features of the renewal of catechetics today is the rewriting and multiplication of catechetical books taking place in many parts of the Church. Numerous very successful works have been produced and are a real treasure in the service of catechetical instruction. But it must be humbly and honestly recognized that this rich flowering has brought with it articles and publications which are ambiguous and harmful to young people and to the life of the Church. In certain places, the desire to find the best forms of expression or to keep up with fashions in pedagogical methods has often enough resulted in certain catechetical works which bewilder the young and even adults, either by deliberately or unconsciously omitting elements essential to the Church's faith, or by attributing excessive importance to certain themes at the expense of others, or, chiefly, by a rather horizontalist overall view out of keeping with the teaching of the Church's magisterium.

Therefore, it is not enough to multiply catechetical works. In order that these works may correspond with their aim, several conditions are essential:

a) they must be linked with the real life of the generation to which they are addressed, showing close acquaintance with its anxieties and questionings, struggles and hopes;

b) they must try to speak a language comprehensible to the generation in question;

c) they must make a point of giving the whole message of Christ and His Church, without neglecting or distorting anything, and in expounding it they will follow a line and structure that highlights what is essential;

d) they must really aim to give to those who use them a better knowledge of the mysteries of Christ, aimed at true conversion and a life more in conformity with God's will.

Catechisms

50. All those who take on the heavy task of preparing these catechetical tools, especially catechism texts, can do so only with the approval of the pastors who have the authority to give it, and taking their inspiration as closely as possible from the General Catechetical Directory, which remains the standard of reference.[93]

In this regard, I must warmly encourage the episcopal conferences of the whole world to undertake, patiently but resolutely, the considerable work to be accomplished in agreement with the Apostolic See in order to prepare genuine catechisms which will be faithful to the essential content of revelation and up to date in method, and which will be capable of educating the Christian generations of the future to a sturdy faith.

This brief mention of ways and means of modern catechetics does not exhaust the wealth of suggestions worked out by the synod fathers. It is comforting to think that at the present time every country is seeing valuable collaboration for a more organic and more secure renewal of these aspects of catechetics. There can be no doubt that the Church will find the experts and the right means for responding, with God's grace, to the complex requirements of communicating with the people of today.

VII. HOW TO IMPART CATECHESIS

Diversity of Methods

51. The age and the intellectual development of Christians, their degree of ecclesial and spiritual maturity and many other personal circumstances demand that catechesis should adopt widely differing methods for the attainment of its specific aim: education in the faith. On a more general level, this variety is also demanded by the social and cultural surrounding in which the Church carries out her catechetical work.

The variety in the methods used is a sign of life and a resource. That is how it was considered by the fathers of the fourth general assembly of the synod, although they also drew attention to the conditions necessary for that variety to be useful and not harmful to the unity of the teaching of the one Faith.

At the Service of Revelation and Conversion

52. The first question of a general kind that presents itself here concerns the danger and the temptation to mix catechetical teaching unduly with overt or masked ideological views, especially political and social ones, or with personal political options. When such views get the better of the central message to be transmitted, to the point of obscuring it and putting it in second place or even using it to further their own ends, catechesis then becomes radically distorted. The synod rightly insisted on the need for catechesis to remain above one-sided divergent trends—to avoid "dichotomies"—even in the field of theological interpretation of such questions. It is on the basis of revelation that catechesis will try to set its course, revelation as transmitted by the universal magisterium of the Church, in its solemn or ordinary form. This revelation tells of a creating and redeeming God, whose Son has come among us in our flesh and enters not only into each individual's personal history but into human history itself, becoming its center. Accordingly, this revelation tells of the radical change of man and the universe,

of all that makes up the web of human life under the influence of the Good News of Jesus Christ. If conceived in this way, catechesis goes beyond every form of formalistic moralism, although it will include true Christian moral teaching. Chiefly, it goes beyond any kind of temporal, social or political "messianism." It seeks to arrive at man's innermost being.

The Message Embodied in Cultures

53. Now a second question. As I said recently to the members of the Biblical Commission: "The term 'acculturation' or 'inculturation' may be a neologism, but it expresses very well one factor of the great mystery of the Incarnation."[94] We can say of catechesis, as well as of evangelization in general, that it is called to bring the power of the Gospel into the very heart of culture and cultures. For this purpose, catechesis will seek to know these cultures and their essential components; it will learn their most significant expressions; it will respect their particular values and riches. In this manner it will be able to offer these cultures the knowledge of the hidden mystery[95] and help them to bring forth from their own living tradition original expressions of Christian life, celebration and thought. Two things must however be kept in mind.

On the one hand the Gospel message cannot be purely and simply isolated from the culture in which it was first inserted (the biblical world or, more concretely, the cultural milieu in which Jesus of Nazareth lived), nor, without serious loss, from the cultures in which it has already been expressed down the centuries; it does not spring spontaneously from any cultural soil; it has always been transmitted by means of an apostolic dialogue which inevitably becomes part of a certain dialogue of cultures.

On the other hand, the power of the Gospel everywhere transforms and regenerates. When that power enters into a culture, it is no surprise that it rectifies many of its elements. There would be no catechesis if it were the Gospel that had to change when it came into contact with the cultures.

To forget this would simply amount to what St. Paul very forcefully calls "emptying the cross of Christ of its power."[96]

It is a different matter to take, with wise discernment, certain elements, religious or otherwise, that form part of the cultural heritage of a human group and use them to help its members to understand better the whole of the Christian mystery. Genuine catechists know that catechesis "takes flesh" in the various cultures and milieux: one has only to think of the peoples with their great differences, of modern youth, of the great variety of circumstances in which people find themselves today. But they refuse to accept an impoverishment of catechesis through a renunciation or obscuring of its message, by adaptations, even in language, that would endanger the "precious deposit" of the faith,[97] or by concessions in matters of faith or morals. They are convinced that true catechesis eventually enriches these cultures by helping them to go beyond the defective or even inhuman features in them, and by communicating to their legitimate values the fullness of Christ.[98]

The Contribution of Popular Devotion

54. Another question of method concerns the utilization in catechetical instruction of valid elements in popular piety. I have in mind devotions practiced by the faithful in certain regions with moving fervor and purity of intention, even if the faith underlying them needs to be purified or rectified in many aspects. I have in mind certain easily understood prayers that many simple people are fond of repeating. I have in mind certain acts of piety practiced with a sincere desire to do penance or to please the Lord. Underlying most of these prayers and practices, besides elements that should be discarded, there are other elements which, if they were properly used, could serve very well to help people advance towards knowledge of the mystery of Christ and of His message: the love and mercy of God, the Incarnation of Christ, His redeeming cross and resurrection, the activity of the Spirit in each Christian and in the Church, the mystery of the hereafter, the evangelical virtues to be practiced, the presence of the Christian in the world, etc. And why should we appeal to non-Christian or even anti-

Christian elements refusing to build on elements which, even if they need to be revised or improved, have something Christian at their root?

Memorization

55. The final methodological question the importance of which should at least be referred to—one that was debated several times in the synod—is that of memorization. In the beginnings of Christian catechesis, which coincided with a civilization that was mainly oral, recourse was had very freely to memorization. Catechesis has since then known a long tradition of learning the principal truths by memorizing. We are all aware that this method can present certain disadvantages, not the least of which is that it lends itself to insufficient or at times almost non-existent assimilation, reducing all knowledge to formulas that are repeated without being properly understood. These disadvantages and the different characteristics of our own civilization have in some places led to the almost complete suppression—according to some, alas, the definitive suppression—of memorization in catechesis. And yet certain very authoritative voices made themselves heard on the occasion of the fourth general assembly of the synod, calling for the restoration of a judicious balance between reflection and spontaneity, between dialogue and silence, between written work and memory work. Moreover certain cultures still set great value on memorization.

At a time when, in non-religious teaching in certain countries, more and more complaints are being made about the unfortunate consequences of disregarding the human faculty of memory, should we not attempt to put this faculty back into use in an intelligent and even an original way in catechesis, all the more since the celebration or "memorial" of the great events of the history of salvation require a precise knowledge of them? A certain memorization of the words of Jesus, of important Bible passages, of the Ten Commandments, of the formulas of profession of the faith, of the liturgical texts, of the essential prayers, of key doctrinal ideas, etc., far from being opposed to the dignity of young Christians, or constituting an obstacle to personal dialogue with the Lord, is a real need, as the synod fathers forcefully recalled. We must be realists. The blossoms, if we may call them that, of faith and piety do not grow in the desert places of a memory-less catechesis. What is essential is that the texts that are memorized must at the same time be taken in and gradually understood in depth, in order to become a source of Christian life on the personal level and the community level.

The plurality of methods in contemporary catechesis can be a sign of vitality and ingenuity. In any case, the method chosen must ultimately be referred to a law that is fundamental for the whole of the Church's life: the law of fidelity to God and of fidelity to man in a single loving attitude.

VIII. THE JOY OF FAITH
IN A TROUBLED WORLD

Affirming Christian Identity

56. We live in a difficult world in which the anguish of seeing the best creations of man slip away from him and turn against him creates a climate of uncertainty.[99] In this world catechesis should help Christians to be, for their own joy and the service of all, "light" and "salt."[100] Undoubtedly this demands that catechesis should strengthen them in their identity and that it should continually separate itself from the surrounding atmosphere of hesitation, uncertainty and insipidity. Among the many difficulties, each of them a challenge for faith, I shall indicate a few in order to assist catechesis in overcoming them.

In an Indifferent World

57. A few years ago, there was much talk of the secularized world, the post-Christian era. Fashion changes, but a profound reality remains. Christians today must be formed to live in a world which largely ignores God or which, in religious matters, in place of an exacting and fraternal dialogue, stimulating for all, too often flounders in a debasing indifferentism, if it does not remain in a scornful attitude of "suspicion" in the name of the progress it has made in the field of scientific "explanations." To "hold on" in this world, to offer to all a "dialogue of salvation"[101] in which each person feels respected in his or her most basic dignity, the dignity of one who is seeking God, we need a catechesis which trains the young people and adults of our communites to remain clear and consistent in their faith, to affirm serenely their Christian and Catholic identity, to "see him who is invisible"[102] and to adhere so firmly to the absoluteness of God that they can be witnesses to Him in a materialistic civilization that denies Him.

671

With the Original Pedagogy of the Faith

58. The irreducible originality of Christian identity has for corollary and condition no less original a pedagogy of the faith. Among the many prestigious sciences of man that are nowadays making immense advances, pedagogy is certainly one of the most important. The attainments of the other sciences—biology, psychology, sociology—are providing it with valuable elements. The science of education and the art of teaching are continually being subjected to review, with a view to making them better adapted or more effective, with varying degrees of success.

There is also a pedagogy of faith, and the good that it can do for catechesis cannot be overstated. In fact, it is natural that techniques perfected and tested for education in general should be adapted for the service of education in the faith. However, account must always be taken of the absolute originality of faith. Pedagogy of faith is not a question of transmitting human knowledge, even of the highest kind; it is a question of communicating God's revelation in its entirety. Throughout sacred history, especially in the Gospel, God Himself used a pedagogy that must continue to be a model for the pedagogy of faith. A technique is of value in catechesis only to the extent that it serves the faith that is to be transmitted and learned; otherwise it is of no value.

Language Suited to the Service of the Credo

59. A problem very close to the preceding one is that of language. This is obviously a burning question today. It is paradoxical to see that, while modern studies, for instance in the field of communication, semantics and symbology, attribute extraordinary importance to language, nevertheless language is being misused today for ideological mystification, for mass conformity in thought and for reducing man to the level of an object.

All this has extensive influence in the field of catechesis. For catechesis has a pressing obligation to speak a language suited to today's children and young people in general and to many other categories of people—the language of students, intellectuals and scientists; the language of the illiterate or of people of simple culture; the language of the handicapped, and so on. St. Augustine encountered this same problem and contributed to its solution for his own time with his well-known work *De Catechizandis Rudibus*. In catechesis as in theology, there is no doubt that the question of language is of the first order. But there is good reason for recalling here that catechesis cannot admit any language that would result in altering the substance of the content of the Creed, under any pretext whatever, even a pretended scientific one. Deceitful or beguiling language is no better. On the contrary, the supreme rule is that the great advances in the science of language must be capable of being placed at the service of catechesis so as to enable it really to "tell" or "communicate" to the child, the adolescent, the young people and adults of today the whole content of doctrine without distortion.

Research and Certainty of Faith

60. A more subtle challenge occasionally comes from the very way of conceiving faith. Certain contemporary philosophical schools, which seem to be exercising a strong influence on some theological currents and, through them, on pastoral practice, like to emphasize that the fundamental human attitude is that of seeking the infinite, a seeking that never attains its object. In theology, this view of things will state very categorically that faith is not certainty but questioning, not clarity but a leap in the dark.

These currents of thought certainly have the advantage of reminding us that faith concerns things not yet in our possession, since they are hoped for; that as yet we see only "in a mirror dimly"[103]; and that God dwells always in inaccessible light.[104] They help us to make the Christian faith not the attitude of one who has already arrived, but a journey forward as with Abraham. For all the more reason one must avoid presenting as certain things which are not.

However, we must not fall into the opposite extreme, as too often happens. The Letter to the Hebrews says that "faith is the assurance of things hoped for, the conviction of things not seen."[105] Although we are not in full possession, we do have an assurance and a conviction. When educating children, adolescents and young people, let us not give them too negative an idea of faith—as if it were absolute non-knowing, a kind of blindness, a world of darkness—but let us show them that the humble yet courageous seeking of the believer, far from having its starting point in nothingness, in plain self-deception, in fallible opinions or in uncertainty, is based on the Word of God who cannot deceive or be deceived, and is unceasingly built on the immovable rock of this Word. It is the search of the Magi under the guidance of a star,[106] the search of which Pascal, taking up a phrase of St. Augustine, wrote so profoundly: "You would not be searching for me, if you had not found me."[107]

It is also one of the aims of catechesis to give young catechumens the simple but solid certainties that will help them to seek to know the Lord more and better.

Catechesis and Theology

61. In this context, it seems important to me that the connection between catechesis and theology should be well understood.

Obviously this connection is profound and vital for those who understand the irreplaceable mission of theology in the service of Faith. Thus it is no surprise that every stirring in the field of theology also has repercussions in that of catechesis. In this period immediately after the Council, the Church is living through an important but hazardous time of theological research. The same must be said of hermeneutics with respect to exegesis.

Synod fathers from all continents dealt with this question in very frank terms: they spoke of the danger of an "unstable balance" passing from theology to catechesis and they stressed the need to do something about this difficulty. Pope Paul VI himself had dealt with the problem in no less frank terms in the introduction to his Solemn Profession of Faith[108] and in the apostolic exhortation marking the fifth anniversary of the close of the Second Vatican Council.[109]

This point must again be insisted on. Aware of the influence that their research and their statements have on catechetical instruction, theologians and exegetes have a duty to take great care that people do not take for a certainty what on the contrary belongs to the area of questions of opinion or of discussion among experts. Catechists for their part must have the wisdom to pick from the field of theological research those points that can provide light for their own reflection and their teaching, drawing, like the theologians, from the true sources, in the light of the magisterium. They must refuse to trouble the minds of the children and young people, at this stage of their catechesis, with outlandish theories, useless questions and unproductive discussions, things that St. Paul often condemned in his pastoral letters.[110]

The most valuable gift that the Church can offer to the bewildered and restless world of our time is to form within it Christians who are confirmed in what is essential and who are humbly joyful in their faith. Catechesis will teach this to them, and it will itself be the first to benefit from it: "The man who wishes to understand himself thoroughly—and not just in accordance with immediate, partial, often superficial, and even illusory standards and measures of his being—must come to Christ with his unrest and uncertainty, and even his weakness and sinfulness, his life and death. He must, so to speak, enter into Christ with all his own self, he must 'appropriate' Christ and assimilate the whole of the reality of the Incarnation and redemption in order to find himself."[111]

IX. THE TASK CONCERNS US ALL

Encouragement to All Responsible for Catechesis

62. Now, beloved brothers and sons and daughters, I would like my words, which are intended as a serious and heartfelt exhortation from me in my ministry as pastor of the universal Church, to set your hearts aflame, like the letters of St. Paul to his companions in the Gospel, Titus and Timothy, or like St. Augustine writing for the deacon Deogratias, when the latter lost heart before his task as a catechist, a real little treatise on the joy of catechizing.[112] Yes, I wish to sow courage, hope and enthusiasm abundantly in the hearts of all those many diverse people who are in charge of religious instruction and training for life in keeping with the Gospel.

Bishops

63. To begin with, I turn to my brother Bishops: The Second Vatican Council has already explicitly reminded you of your task in the catechetical area,[113] and the fathers of the fourth general assembly of the synod have also strongly underlined it.

Dearly beloved brothers, you have here a special mission within your Churches: You are beyond all others the ones primarily responsible for catechesis, the catechists par excellence. Together with the Pope, in the spirit of episcopal collegiality, you too have charge of catechesis throughout the Church. Accept therefore what I say to you from my heart.

I know that your ministry as Bishops is growing daily more complex and overwhelming. A thousand duties call you: from the training of new priests to being actively present within the lay communities, from the living, worthy celebration of the sacraments and acts of worship to concern for human advancement and the defense of human rights. But let the concern to foster active and effective catechesis yield to no other care whatever in any way. This concern will lead you to transmit personally to your faithful the doctrine of life. But it

should also lead you to take on in your diocese, in accordance
with the plans of the episcopal conference to which you
belong, the chief management of catechesis, while at the same
time surrounding yourselves with competent and trustworthy
assistants. Your principal role will be to bring about and maintain in your Churches a real passion for catechesis, a passion
embodied in a pertinent and effective organization, putting
into operation the necessary personnel, means and equipment,
and also financial resources. You can be sure that if catechesis
is done well in your local Churches, everything else will be
easier to do. And needless to say, although your zeal must
sometimes impose upon you the thankless task of denouncing
deviations and correcting errors, it will much more often win
for you the joy and consolation of seeing your Churches flourishing because catechesis is given in them as the Lord wishes.

Priests

64. For your part, priests, here you have a field in which
you are the immediate assistants of your Bishops. The Council
has called you "instructors in the faith"[114]; there is no better
way for you to be such instructors than by devoting your best
efforts to the growth of your communities in the faith.
Whether you are in charge of a parish, or are chaplains to
primary or secondary schools or universities, or have responsibility for pastoral activity at any level, or are leaders of large
or small communities, especially youth groups, the Church expects you to neglect nothing with a view to a well-organized
and well-oriented catechetical effort. The deacons and other
ministers that you may have the good fortune to have with you
are your natural assistants in this. All believers have a right to
catechesis; all pastors have the duty to provide it. I shall
always ask civil leaders to respect the freedom of catechetical
teaching; but with all my strength I beg you, ministers of Jesus
Christ: Do not, for lack of zeal or because of some unfortunate
preconceived idea, leave the faithful without catechesis. Let it
not be said that "the children beg for food, but no one gives to
them."[115]

Men and Women Religious

65. Many religious institutes for men and women came into being for the purpose of giving Christian education to children and young people, especially the most abandoned. Throughout history, men and women religious have been deeply committed to the Church's catechetical activity, doing particularly apposite and effective work. At a time when it is desired that the links between religious and pastors should be accentuated and consequently the active presence of religious communities and their members in the pastoral projects of the local Churches, I wholeheartedly exhort you, whose religious consecration should make you even more readily available for the Church's service, to prepare as well as possible for the task of catechesis according to the differing vocations of your institutes and the missions entrusted to you, and to carry this concern everywhere. Let the communities dedicate as much as possible of what ability and means they have to the specific work of catechesis.

Lay Catechists

66. I am anxious to give thanks in the Church's name to all of you, lay teachers of catechesis in the parishes, the men and the still more numerous women throughout the world, who are devoting yourselves to the religious education of many generations. Your work is often lowly and hidden but it is carried out with ardent and generous zeal, and it is an eminent form of the lay apostolate, a form that is particularly important where for various reasons children and young people do not receive suitable religious training in the home. How many of us have received from people like you our first notions of catechism and our preparation for the sacrament of Penance, for our first Communion and Confirmation! The fourth general assembly of the synod did not forget you. I join with it in encouraging you to continue your collaboration for the life of the Church.

But the term "catechists" belongs above all to the catechists in mission lands. Born of families that are already Christian or converted at some time to Christianity and instructed by missionaries or by another catechist, they then consecrate their lives, year after year, to catechizing children and adults in their own country. Churches that are flourishing today would not have been built up without them. I rejoice at the efforts made by the Sacred Congregation for the Evangelization of Peoples to improve more and more the training of these catechists. I gratefully recall the memory of those whom the Lord has already called to Himself. I beg the intercession of those whom my predecessors have raised to the glory of the altars. I wholeheartedly encourage those engaged in the work. I express the wish that many others may succeed them and that they may increase in numbers for a task so necessary for the missions.

In the Parish

67. I now wish to speak of the actual setting in which all these catechists normally work. I am returning this time, taking a more overall view, to the "places" for catechesis, some of which have already been mentioned in chapter VI: the parish, the family, the school, organizations.

It is true that catechesis can be given anywhere, but I wish to stress, in accordance with the desire of very many Bishops, that the parish community must continue to be the prime mover and pre-eminent place for catechesis. Admittedly, in many countries the parish has been as it were shaken by the phenomenon of urbanization. Perhaps some have too easily accepted that the parish should be considered old-fashioned, if not doomed to disappear, in favor of more pertinent and effective small communities. Whatever one may think, the parish is still a major point of reference for the Christian people, even for the non-practicing. Accordingly, realism and wisdom demand that we continue along the path aiming to restore to the parish, as needed, more adequate structures and, above all, a new impetus through the increasing integration into it of qualified, responsible and generous members. This being said, and taking into account the necessary diversity of places for catechesis (the parish as such, families taking in children and adolescents, chaplaincies for State schools, Catholic educational establishments, apostolic movements that give periods of catechesis, clubs open to youth in general, spiritual formation weekends, etc.), it is supremely important that all these catechetical channels should really converge on the same confession of faith, on the same membership of the Church, and on commitments in society lived in the same Gospel spirit: "one Lord, one faith, one baptism, one God and Father."[116] That is why every big parish or every group of parishes with small numbers has the serious duty to train people completely dedicated to providing catechetical leadership (priests, men and women religious, and lay people), to provide the equipment needed for catechesis under all aspects, to increase and adapt the places for catechesis to the extent that it is possible and useful to do so, and to be watchful about the quality of the religious formation of the various groups and their integration into the ecclesial community.

In short, without monopolizing or enforcing uniformity, the parish remains, as I have said, the pre-eminent place for catechesis. It must rediscover its vocation, which is to be a fraternal and welcoming family home, where those who have been baptized and confirmed become aware of forming the People of God. In that home, the bread of good doctrine and the Eucharistic Bread are broken for them in abundance, in the setting of the one act of worship[117]; from that home they are sent out day by day to their apostolic mission in all the centers of activity of the life of the world.

In the Family

68. The family's catechetical activity has a special character, which is in a sense irreplaceable. This special character has been rightly stressed by the Church, particularly by the Second Vatican Council.[118] Education in the faith by parents, which should begin from the children's tenderest age,[119] is already being given when the members of a family help each other to grow in faith through the witness of their Christian lives, a witness that is often without words but which perseveres throughout a day-to-day life lived in accordance

with the Gospel. This catechesis is more incisive when, in the course of family events (such as the reception of the sacraments, the celebration of great liturgical feasts, the birth of a child, a bereavement) care is taken to explain in the home the Christian or religious content of these events. But that is not enough: Christian parents must strive to follow and repeat, within the setting of family life, the more methodical teaching received elsewhere. The fact that these truths about the main questions of faith and Christian living are thus repeated within a family setting impregnated with love and respect will often make it possible to influence the children in a decisive way for life. The parents themselves profit from the effort that this demands of them, for in a catechetical dialogue of this sort each individual both receives and gives.

Family catechesis therefore precedes, accompanies and enriches all other forms of catechesis. Furthermore, in places where anti-religious legislation endeavors even to prevent education in the faith, and in places where widespread unbelief or invasive secularism makes real religious growth practically impossible, "the church of the home"[120] remains the one place where children and young people can receive an authentic catechesis. Thus there cannot be too great an effort on the part of Christian parents to prepare for this ministry of being their own children's catechists and to carry it out with tireless zeal. Encouragement must also be given to the individuals or institutions that, through person-to-person contacts, through meetings, and through all kinds of pedagogical means, help parents to perform their task: The service they are doing to catechesis is beyond price.

At School

69. Together with and in connection with the family, the school provides catechesis with possibilities that are not to be neglected. In the unfortunately decreasing number of countries in which it is possible to give education in the faith within the school framework, the Church has the duty to do so as well as possible. This of course concerns first and foremost the Catholic school: it would no longer deserve this title if, no matter how much it shone for its high level of teaching in non-

religious matters, there were justification for reproaching it for negligence or deviation in strictly religious education. Let it not be said that such education will always be given implicitly and indirectly. The special character of the Catholic school, the underlying reason for it, the reason why Catholic parents should prefer it, is precisely the quality of the religious instruction integrated into the education of the pupils. While Catholic establishments should respect freedom of conscience, that is to say, avoid burdening consciences from without by exerting physical or moral pressure, especially in the case of the religious activity of adolescents, they still have a grave duty to offer a religious training suited to the often widely varying religious situations of the pupils. They also have a duty to make them understand that, although God's call to serve Him in spirit and truth, in accordance with the Commandments of God and the precepts of the Church, does not apply constraint, it is nevertheless binding in conscience.

But I am also thinking of non-confessional and public schools. I express the fervent wish that, in response to a very clear right of the human person and of the family, and out of respect for everyone's religious freedom, all Catholic pupils may be enabled to advance in their spiritual formation with the aid of a religious instruction dependent on the Church, but which, according to the circumstances of different countries, can be offered either by the school or in the setting of the school, or again within the framework of an agreement with the public authorities regarding school timetables, if catechesis takes place only in the parish or in another pastoral center. In fact, even in places where objective difficulties exist, it should be possible to arrange school timetables in such a way as to enable the Catholics to deepen their faith and religious experience, with qualified teachers, whether priests or lay people.

Admittedly, apart from the school, many other elements of life help in influencing the mentality of the young, for instance, recreation, social background and work surroundings. But those who study are bound to bear the stamp of their studies, to be introduced to cultural or moral values within the atmosphere of the establishment in which they are taught, and to be faced with many ideas met with in school. It is important for catechesis to take full account of this effect of the school on the pupils, if it is to keep in touch with the other elements of the pupil's knowledge and education; thus the Gospel will impregnate the mentality of the pupils in the field of their learning, and the harmonization of their culture will be achieved in the light of faith. Accordingly, I give encouragement to the priests, religious and lay people who are devoting themselves to sustaining these pupils' faith. This is moreover an occasion for me to reaffirm my firm conviction that to show respect for the Catholic faith of the young to the extent of facilitating its education, its implantation, its consolidation, its free profession and practice would certainly be to the honor of any government, whatever be the system on which it is based or the ideology from which it draws its inspiration.

Within Organizations

70. Lastly, encouragement must be given to the lay associations, movements and groups, whether their aim is the practice of piety, the direct apostolate, charity and relief work, or a Christian presence in temporal matters. They will all accomplish their objectives better, and serve the Church better, if they give an important place in their internal organization and their method of action to the serious religious training of their members. In this way every association of the faithful in the Church has by definition the duty to educate in the faith.

This makes more evident the role given to the laity in catechesis today, always under the pastoral direction of their Bishops, as the propositions left by the synod stressed several times.

Training Institutes

71. We must be grateful to the Lord for this contribution by the laity, but it is also a challenge to our responsibility as pastors, since these lay catechists must be carefully prepared for what is, if not a formally instituted ministry, at the very least a function of great importance in the Church. Their preparation calls on us to organize special centers and in-

stitutes, which are to be given assiduous attention by the Bishops. This is a field in which diocesan, interdiocesan or national cooperation proves fertile and fruitful. Here also the material aid provided by the richer Churches to their poor sisters can show the greatest effectiveness, for what better assistance can one Church give to another than to help it to grow as a Church with its own strength?

I would like to recall to all those who are working generously in the service of the Gospel, and to whom I have expressed here my lively encouragement, the instruction given by my venerated predecessor Paul VI: "As evangelizers, we must offer...the image of people who are mature in faith and capable of finding a meeting-point beyond the real tensions, thanks to a shared, sincere and disinterested search for truth. Yes, the destiny of evangelization is certainly bound up with the witness of unity given by the Church. This is a source of responsibility and also of comfort."[121]

CONCLUSION

The Holy Spirit, the Teacher Within

72. At the end of this apostolic exhortation, the gaze of my heart turns to Him who is the principle inspiring all catechetical work and all who do this work—the Spirit of the Father and of the Son, the Holy Spirit.

In describing the mission that this Spirit would have in the Church, Christ used the significant words: "He will teach you all things, and bring to your remembrance all that I have said to you."[122] And He added: "When the Spirit of truth comes, he will guide you into all the truth...he will declare to you the things that are to come."[123]

The Spirit is thus promised to the Church and to each Christian as a teacher within, who, in the secret of the conscience and the heart, makes one understand what one has heard but was not capable of grasping: "Even now the Holy Spirit teaches the faithful," said St. Augustine in this regard, "in accordance with each one's spiritual capacity. And he sets their hearts aflame with greater desire according as each one progresses in the charity that makes him love what he already knows and desire what he has yet to know."[124]

Furthermore, the Spirit's mission is also to transform the disciples into witnesses to Christ: "He will bear witness to me; and you also are witnesses."[125]

But this is not all. For St. Paul, who on this matter synthesizes a theology that is latent throughout the New Testament, it is the whole of one's "being a Christian," the whole of the Christian life, the new life of the children of God, that constitutes a life in accordance with the Spirit.[126] Only the Spirit enables us to say to God: "Abba, Father."[127] Without the Spirit we cannot say: "Jesus is Lord."[128] From the Spirit come all the charisms that build up the Church, the community of Christians.[129]

In keeping with this, St. Paul gives each disciple of Christ the instruction: "Be filled with the Spirit."[130] St. Augustine is

685

very explicit: "Both (our believing and our doing good) are ours because of the choice of our will, and yet both are gifts from the Spirit of faith and charity."[131]

Catechesis, which is growth in faith and the maturing of Christian life towards its fullness, is consequently a work of the Holy Spirit, a work that He alone can initiate and sustain in the Church.

This realization, based on the text quoted above and on many other passages of the New Testament, convinces us of two things.

To begin with, it is clear that, when carrying out her mission of giving catechesis, the Church—and also every individual Christian devoting himself to that mission within the Church and in her name—must be very much aware of acting as a living, pliant instrument of the Holy Spirit. To invoke this Spirit constantly, to be in communion with Him, to endeavor to know His authentic inspirations must be the attitude of the teaching Church and of every catechist.

Secondly, the deep desire to understand better the Spirit's action and to entrust oneself to Him more fully—at a time when "in the Church we are living an exceptionally favorable season of the Spirit," as my predecessor Paul VI remarked in his Apostolic Exhortation *Evangelii nuntiandi*[132]—must bring about a catechetical awakening. For "renewal in the Spirit" will be authentic and will have real fruitfulness in the Church, not so much according as it gives rise to extraordinary charisms, but according as it leads the greatest possible number of the faithful, as they travel their daily paths, to make a humble, patient and persevering effort to know the mystery of Christ better and better, and to bear witness to it.

I invoke on the catechizing Church this Spirit of the Father and the Son, and I beg Him to renew catechetical dynamism in the Church.

Mary, Mother and Model of the Disciple

73. May the Virgin of Pentecost obtain this for us through her intercession. By a unique vocation, she saw her Son Jesus "increase in wisdom and in stature, and in favor."[133] As He sat

on her lap and later as He listened to her throughout the hidden life at Nazareth, this Son, who was "the only Son from the Father," "full of grace and truth," was formed by her in human knowledge of the Scriptures and of the history of God's plan for His people, and in adoration of the Father.[134] She in turn was the first of His disciples. She was the first in time, because even when she found her adolescent Son in the temple she received from Him lessons that she kept in her heart.[135] She was the first disciple above all else because no one has been "taught by God"[136] to such depth. She was "both mother and disciple," as St. Augustine said of her, venturing to add that her discipleship was more important for her than her motherhood.[137] There are good grounds for the statement made in the synod hall that Mary is "a living catechism" and "the mother and model of catechists."

May the presence of the Holy Spirit, through the prayers of Mary, grant the Church unprecedented enthusiasm in the catechetical work that is essential for her. Thus will she effectively carry out, at this moment of grace, her inalienable and universal mission, the mission given her by her Teacher: "Go therefore and make disciples of all nations."[138]

With my apostolic blessing.

Given in Rome, at St. Peter's, on October 16, 1979, the second year of my pontificate.

Joannes Paulus PP. II

FOOTNOTES

1. Cf. Mt. 28:19-20.
2. Cf. 1 Jn. 1:1.
3. Cf. Jn. 20:31.
4. Cf. *AAS* 63 (1971), pp. 758-764.
5. Cf. 44; cf. also 45-48 and 54: *AAS* 68 (1976), pp. 34-35; 35-38; 43.
6. According to the Motu Proprio *Apostolica Sollicitudo* of Sept. 15, 1965, the Synod of Bishops can come together in General Assembly, in extraordinary Assembly or in special assembly. In the present apostolic exhortation the words "synod," "synod fathers" and "synod hall" always refer, unless otherwise indicated, to the fourth general assembly of the Synod of Bishops on catechesis, held in Rome in October 1977.
7. Cf. *Synodus Episcoporum, De catechesi hoc nostro tempore tradenda praesertim pueris atque iuvenibus, Ad Populum Dei Nuntius,* e Civitate Vaticana, 28-X-1977; cf. "L'Osservatore Romano," October 30, 1977, pp. 3-4.
8. Cf. *AAS* 69 (1977), p. 633.
9. Jn. 1:14.
10. Jn. 14:6.
11. Eph. 3:9, 18-19.
12. Cf. Jn. 14:6.
13. Jn. 7:16. This is a theme dear to the fourth Gospel: cf. Jn. 3:34; 8:28; 12:49-50; 14:24; 17:8,14.
14. 1 Cor. 11:23: the word "deliver" employed here by St. Paul was frequently repeated in the Apostolic Exhortation *Evangelii Nuntiandi* to describe the evangelizing activity of the Church, for example 4, 15, 78, 79.
15. Acts 1:1.
16. Mt. 26:55; cf. Jn. 18:20.
17. Mk. 10:1.
18. Mk. 1:22; cf. Mt. 5:2; 11:1; 13:54; 22:16; Mk. 2:13; 4:1; 6:2, 6; Lk. 5:3, 17; Jn. 7:14; 8:2, etc.
19. Lk. 23:5.

20. In nearly 50 places in the four Gospels, this title, inherited from the whole Jewish tradition but here given a new meaning that Christ Himself often seeks to emphasize, is attributed to Jesus.
21. Cf., among others, Mt. 8:19; Mk. 4:38; 9:38; 10:35; 13:1; Jn. 11:28.
22. Mt. 12:38.
23. Lk. 10:25; cf. Mt. 22:16.
24. Jn. 13:13-14; cf. also Mt. 10:25; 26:18 and parallel passages.
25. Mt. 23:8. St. Ignatius of Antioch takes up this affirmation and comments as follows: "We have received the faith; this is why we hold fast, in order to be recognized as disciples of Jesus Christ, our only Teacher" (*Epistola ad Magnesios,* IX, 2 Funk 1, 198).
26. Jn. 3:2.
27. The portrayal of Christ as Teacher goes back as far as the Roman Catacombs. It is frequently used in the mosaics of Romano-Byzantine art of the third and fourth centuries. It was to form a predominant artistic motif in the sculptures of the great Romanesque and Gothic cathedrals of the Middle Ages.
28. Mt. 28:19.
29. Jn. 15:15.
30. Cf. Jn. 15:16.
31. Acts 2:42.
32. Acts 4:2.
33. Cf. Acts 4:18; 5:28.
34. Cf. Acts 4:19.
35. Cf. Acts 1:25.
36. Cf. Acts 6:8ff.; cf. also Philip catechizing the minister of the Queen of the Ethiopians: Acts 8:26ff.
37. Cf. Acts 15:35.
38. Acts 8:4.
39. Acts 28:31.
40. Cf. Pope John XXIII, Encyclical *Mater et Magistra* (*AAS* 53 [1961],

p. 401): the Church is "mother" because by baptism she unceasingly begets new children and increases God's family; she is "teacher" because she makes her children grow in the grace of their baptism by nourishing their *sensus fidei* through instruction in the truths of faith.

41. Cf., for example the letter of Clement of Rome to the Church of Corinth, the *Didache,* the *Epistola Apostolorum,* the writings of Irenaeus of Lyons (*Demonstratio Apostolicae Praedicationis* and *Adversus Haereses*), of Tertullian (*De Baptismo*), of Clement of Alexandria (*Paedagogus*), of Cyprian (*Testimonia ad Quirinum*), of Origen (*Contra Celsum*), etc.

42. Cf. 2 Thes. 3:1.

43. Second Vatican Council, Declaration on Religious Liberty, *Dignitatis Humanae,* 2: *AAS* 58 (1966), p. 930.

44. Cf. The Universal Declaration of Human Rights (UNO), December 10, 1948, Art. 18; The International Pact on Civil and Political Rights (UNO), December 16, 1966, Art. 4; Final Act of the Conference on European Security and Cooperation, Para. VII.

45. Cf. *Synodus Episcoporum, De catechesi hoc nostro tempore tradenda praesertim pueris iuvenibus Ad Populum Dei Nuntius,* 1: *loc. cit.,* pp. 3-4; cf. L'Osservatore Romano, October 30, 1977, p. 3.

46. *Ibid.,* 6: *loc. cit.,* pp. 7-8.

47. Sacred Congregation for the Clergy, *Directorium Catechisticum Generale,* 17-35; *AAS* 64 (1972), pp. 110-118.

48. Cf. 17-24: *AAS* 68 (1976), pp. 17-22.

49. Cf. *Synodus Episcoporum, De catechesi hoc nostro tempore tradenda praesertim pueris atque invenibus, Ad Populum Dei Nuntius,* 1: *loc. cit.,* pp. 3-4; cf. L'Osservatore Romano, October 30, 1977, p. 3.

50. *Concluding Address to the Synod, October 29, 1977: AAS* 69 (1977), p. 634.

51. *Ibid.*

52. *Directorium Catechisticum Generale,* 40 and 46: *AAS* 64 (1972), pp. 121 and 124-125.

53. Cf. Decree on the Ministry and Life of Priests, *Presbyterorum Ordinis,* 6: *AAS* 58 (1966), p. 999.

54. Cf. *Ordo Initiationis Christianae Adultorum.*

55. Eph. 4:13.

56. Cf. 1 Pt. 3:15.

57. Dogmatic Constitution on Divine Revelation *Dei Verbum,* 10 and 24: *AAS* 58 (1966), pp. 822 and 828-829; cf. also Sacred Congregation for the Clergy, *Directorium Catechisticum Generale* 45 (*AAS* 64 [1972], p. 124), where the principal and complementary sources of catechesis are well set out.

58. Cf. *Ordo Initiationis Christianae Adultorum,* 25-26; 183-187.

59. Cf. *AAS* 60 (1968), pp. 436-445. Besides these great professions of faith of the magisterium, note also the popular professions of faith, rooted in the traditional Christian culture of certain countries; cf. what I said to the young people at Gniezno, June 3, 1979, regarding the *Bogurodzica* song-message: "This is not only a song: it is also a profession of faith, a symbol of the Polish Credo, it is a catechesis and also a document of Christian education. The principal truths of Faith and the principles of morality are contained here. This is not only a historical object. It is a document of life. (It has even been called 'the Polish catechism' " [*AAS* 71, 1979], p. 754.)

60. 25: *AAS* 68 (1976), p. 23.

61. *Ibid.,* especially 26-39: *loc. cit.,* pp. 23-25; the "principal elements of the Christian message" are presented in a more systematic fashion in the *Directorium Catechisticum Generale,* 47-69 (*AAS* 64 [1972] pp. 125-141), where one also finds the norm for the essential doctrinal content of catechesis.

62. Consult also on this point the *Directorium Catechisticum Generale,* 37-46 (*loc. cit.,* pp. 120-125).

63. Rom. 1:19.

64. Acts 17:23.

65. Cf. Eph. 3:3.

66. Cf. Eph. 2:18.

67. Acts 20:28.

68. Second Vatican Council, Pastoral Constitution on the Church in the Modern World *Gaudium et Spes,* 39: *AAS* 58 (1966), pp. 1056-1057.

69. Rom. 6:4.

70. 2 Cor. 5:17.

71. Cf. *ibid.*

72. Rom. 6:23.

73. Cf. Pope Paul VI, Apostolic Exhortation, *Evangelii Nuntiandi,* 30-38: *AAS* 68 (1976), pp. 25-30.

74. Cf. *Catechismo Maggiore,* Fifth Part, chap. 6. 965-966.

75. Cf. Phil. 2:17.

76. Rom. 10:8.

77. Phil. 3:8.

78. Cf. Eph. 4:20-21.

79. Cf. 2 Thes. 2:7.

80. Jn. 6:69; cf. Acts 5:20; 7:38.

81. Acts 2:28, quoting Ps. 16:11.

82. Cf. the entire Decree on Ecumenism *Unitatis Redintegratio: AAS* 57 [1965], pp. 90-112.

83. Cf. *ibid.,* 5: *loc. cit.,* p. 96; cf. also Second Vatican Council, Decree on the Missionary Activity of the Church *Ad Gentes,* 15: *AAS* 58 (1966), pp. 963-965; Sacred Congregation for the Clergy, *Directorium Catechisticum Generale* 27: *AAS* 64 (1972), p. 115.

84. Cf. Second Vatican Council, Decree on Ecumenism, *Unitatis Redintegratio,* 3-4: *AAS* 57 (1965), pp. 92-96.

85. *Ibid.,* 3: *loc. cit.,* p. 93.

86. Cf. *ibid.;* cf. also Dogmatic Constitution on the Church *Lumen Gentium,* 15: *AAS* 57 (1965), p. 19.

87. Lk. 12:32.

88. Cf., for example, Second Vatican Council, Pastoral Constitution on the Church in the Modern World *Gaudium et Spes, AAS* 58 (1966), pp. 1025-1120; Pope Paul VI, Encyclical *Populorum Progressio: AAS* 59 (1967), pp. 257-299; Apostolic Letter *Octogesima Adveniens: AAS* 63 (1971), pp. 401-441; Apostolic Exhortation *Evangelii Nuntiandi: AAS* 68 (1976), pp. 5-76.

89. Mt. 1:16.

90. Cf. Second Vatican Council, Decree on the Bishop's Pastoral Office in the Church *Christus Dominus,* 14: *AAS* 58 (1966), p. 679; Decree on the Missionary Activity of the Church *Ad Gentes,* 14: *AAS* 58 (1966), pp. 962-963; Sacred Congregation for the Clergy, *Directorium Catechisticum Generale* 20: *AAS* 64 (1972), p. 112; cf. also *Ordo Initiationis Christianae Adultorum.*

91. Cf. 58: *AAS* 68 (1976), pp. 46-49.

92. Cf. *Synodus Episcoporum, De catechesi hoc nostro tempore tradenda praesertim pueris atque iuvenibus, Ad Populum Dei Nuntius,* 7-10: *loc. cit.,* pp. 9-12; cf. "L'Osservatore Romano," October 30, 1977, p. 3.

93. Cf. Sacred Congregation for the Clergy, *Directorium Catechisticum Generale,* 119-121; 134: *AAS* 64 (1972), pp. 166-167; 172.

94. Cf. *AAS* 71 (1979), p. 607.

95. Cf. Rom. 16:25; Eph. 3:5.

96. 1 Cor. 1:17.

97. Cf. 2 Tm. 1:14.

98. Cf. Jn. 1:16; Eph. 1:10.

99. Cf. Encyclical *Redemptor Hominis,* 15-16: *AAS* 71 (1979), pp. 286-295.

100. Cf. Mt. 5:13-16.

101. Cf. Pope Paul VI, Encyclical *Ecclesiam Suam,* Part Three, *AAS* 56 (1964), pp. 637-659.

102. Cf. Heb. 11:27.

103. 1 Cor. 13:12.

104. Cf. 1 Tm. 6:16.

105. Heb. 11:1.

106. Cf. Mt. 2:1ff.

107. Blaise Pascal, *Le mystère de Jésus: Pensées,* 553.

108. Pope Paul VI, *Sollemnis Professio Fidei,* 4: *AAS* 60 (1968), p. 434.

109. Pope Paul VI, Apostólic Exhortation *Quinque Iam Anni: AAS* 63 (1971), p. 99.

110. Cf. 1 Tm. 1:3ff.; 4:1ff.; 2 Tm. 2:14ff.; 4:1-5; Tit. 1:10-12; cf. also Apostolic Exhortation, *Evangelii Nuntiandi,* 78: *AAS* 68 (1976), p. 70.

111. Encyclical *Redemptor Hominis,* 10: *AAS* 71 (1979), p. 274.

112. *De Catechizandis Rudibus, PL* 40, 310-347.

113. Cf. Decree on the Bishop's Pastoral Office in the Church *Christus Dominus,* 14: *AAS* 58 (1966), p. 679.

114. Decree on the Ministry and Life of Priests, *Presbyterorum Ordinis,* 6: *AAS* 58 (1966), p. 999.

115. Lam. 4:4.

116. Eph. 4:5-6.

117. Cf. Second Vatican Council, Constitution on the Sacred Liturgy *Sacrosanctum Concilium,* 35, 52: *AAS* 56 (1964), pp. 109, 114; cf. also *Institutio Generalis Misalis Romani,* promulgated by a Decree of the Sacred Congregation of Rites on April 6, 1969, 33, and what has been said above in Chapter VI concerning the homily.

118. Since the High Middle Ages, provincial councils have insisted on the responsibility of parents in regard to education in the faith: cf. Sixth Council of Arles (813), Canon 19; Council of Mainz (813), Canons 45, 47; Sixth Council of Paris (829), Book 1, Chapter 7: Mansi, *Sacrorum Conciliorum Nova et Amplissima Collectio,* XIV, 62, 74, 542. Among the more recent documents of the Magisterium, note the Encyclical *Divini illius Magistri* of Pius XI December 31, 1929: *AAS* 22 (1930), pp. 49-86; the many discourses and messages of Pius XII; and above all the texts of the Second Vatican Council: the Dogmatic Constitution on the Church *Lumen Gentium,* 11, 35: *AAS* 57 (1965), pp. 15, 40; the Decree on the Apostolate of the Laity *Apostolicam Actuositatem,* 11, 30: *AAS* 58 (1966), pp. 847, 860; the Pastoral Constitution on the Church in the Modern World *Gaudium et Spes,* n. 52: *AAS* 58 (1966), p. 1073; and especially the Declaration on Christian Education *Gravissimum Educationis,* 3: *AAS* 58 (1966), p. 731.

119. Cf. Second Vatican Council, Declaration on Christian Education *Gravissimum Educationis,* 3: *AAS* 58 (1966), p. 731.

120. Second Vatican Council, Dogmatic Constitution on the Church *Lumen Gentium,* 11: *AAS* 57 (1965), p. 16; cf. Decree on the Apostolate of the Laity *Apostolicam Actuositatem,* 11: *AAS* 58 (1966), p. 848.

121. Apostolic Exhortation *Evangelii Nuntiandi,* 77: *AAS* 68 (1976), p. 69.

122. Jn. 14:26.

123. Jn. 16:13.

124. *In Ioannis Evangelium Tractatus,* 97, 1: *PL* 35, 1877.

125. Jn. 15:26-27.

126. Cf. Rom. 8:14-17; Gal. 4:6.

127. Rom. 8:15.

128. 1 Cor. 12:3.

129. Cf. 1 Cor. 12:4-11.

130. Eph. 5:18.

131. *Retractationum Liber I,* 23, 2: *PL* 32, 621.

132. 75: *AAS* 68 (1976), p. 66.

133. Cf. Lk. 2:52.

134. Cf. Jn. 1:14; Heb. 10:5; *S. Th.,* III, Q. 12, a. 2; a. 3, ad 3.

135. Cf. Lk. 2:51.

136. Cf. Jn. 6:45.

137. Cf. *Sermo* 25, 7: *PL* 46, 937-938.

138. Mt. 28:19.

INDEX
of the Commentary

A Diogneto 118
Abba 208ff.
abortion 336
Abraham 441, 482
absolution
  formula of 238
acceptance
  mutual 340
  of the Word of God 319
Acerbo nimis 173
acculturation 265, 301, 331, 413, 434, 543
  and catechesis 233
  errors of 303-304
acolyte 332
action(s) 210
  catechetical 309ff.
  ecclesial 320
  missionary 268
  motivation for 162
  of Jesus 205, 286, 287
  of Propaganda Fide 579-592
  reflection on ecclesial 515
"Active School" 181; see also *activism*
activity(ies) 165
  apostolic 34
  catechetical 109
  charitable 590
  directives for 149
  family 339
  missionary 493, 595
  of the Congregation for the Evangelization of Peoples 559-577
  of the Holy Spirit 203
  pastoral 600
activism 171-172
Acts of the Apostles 101, 377
Ad gentes 30, 33, 559, 576, 592, 617
Adam 68
adaptation 50, 93, 108, 161, 165, 268, 306, 331, 427, 471, 479, 561, 584
  cultural 571
  in a Muslim ambient 476
  of language 320
  psychological 571
adolescents 34, 54, 77, 80, 266, 353f., 533, 541, 565

adoration 252
  of the Eucharist 110
adult(s) 34, 45, 79, 80, 89, 114, 138, 147, 155, 164, 165, 173, 176, 180, 185, 315, 327, 342, 353, 462, 509, 511, 520, 525, 531ff., 565
  catechesis for 347ff., 501
  catechisms for 461
  catechumenate for 261
  central problem of catechesis to 357f.
  formation of 493, 494
  future 161
  relationship with God of 349
  religious education of 511-512
  young 79, 541
adultery 117f.
adulthood 354
Advent 145, 146
adversaries
  of Jesus 205
affection
  of Jesus 286
Africa 303, 318, 322, 328, 435-445, 475, 498, 559ff., 575ff., 603, 615
  and culture 418-420
  and the media 392
age 161
agent(s)
  of catechesis 320, 524
aggiornamento 41, 79, 298
aid(s)
  financial 596
  visual 491
Ajuthia
  Synod of 584
Albania 554, 555
Alberione, James 391
Alcuin 142
alienation 72, 73
almsgiving 486, 581
Alpha 220
altar 134, 443
ambient 110
  Asiatic 585
  catechesis in a Buddhist 458-471
  in communist countries 546ff.; see also *environment, milieu*

ambiguity 428
Ambrose, St. 116, 128ff., 243
Americas 603
anamnesis 89
ancestors 436, 441
angel(s) 201
animal
  rational 301; see also *human being, man, woman, child*
animism 467
anniversaries 341
announcement 108, 254, 406
  initial 406f.
  pre-verbal 349
Annunciation 248ff., 252, 258
anointing
  baptismal 133
  of the sick 238-239
anonymity 452
anthropology 63, 64, 69, 183-184, 281, 541f.
anthropomorphisms 467, 469
antitheses
  false 519-520
apologetics 65, 118, 155, 281, 459, 590, 591
Apostles (the Twelve) 31, 32, 60, 67, 99, 104, 195, 211ff., 313, 319
  Acts of; see *Acts of the Apostles*
  and catechesis 109f.
  and deacons 106-107
  catechesis of the 99-111
  mission of 104ff.
  successor of the 51; see also *Bishops*
apostle(s) 53, 105, 251, 255
apostolate 412; see also *mission*
  lay 79
Apostolic Tradition of Hypolitus Romanus 366
approach(es) 380-381
  anthropological 460, 461, 467, 531-535
  biblical 132
  catechetical 381
  experiential 129
  human 455
  in catechisms of the Orient 459ff.
  interdisciplinary 192
  kerygmatic 447
  of *Redemptor hominis* 69
  missionary 577
  pastoral 166
  patristic 128ff.
  pedagogical 162
  stability of 506

Archconfraternity of Christian Doctrine 167
armed forces 283
Arnold, F. X. 182
art(s) 425, 487, 544
  native Christian 418
  of India 456
ascension 198, 206, 278, 367
Asia 322, 475, 559ff., 573f., 585, 603, 615
  Bishops of 462
  cultures of 420
  media in 574
assembly
  S.C.E.P. ninth plenary 435
associations
  Catholic 405
  educational 281
  religious 549
  youth 318
Assumption 254
Astete, Gaspare 157
atheism 72, 73, 86, 171, 361, 364, 469, 546-555
attitude(s) 43, 247ff.
  Christian 291, 478
  ecclesial 247
  formation of 256
  in the home 339
  interior 468
  Marian 247
  Muslim 483
  of Jesus 270
  of "yes" 249
  towards God 561
audio-visuals 180, 281, 330, 358, 389ff., 512
Auger, Edmund 144, 154, 155
Augustine, St. 115, 116, 117, 120ff., 210, 305
  on the Holy Spirit 223
Austria 175
authority 37, 53, 199, 339, 532
  of the Bishop 404
  of catechists 166
  of God 104, 204
  of Holy See 47
  of Jesus 100, 205
  of pastors 166
autonomy
  moral 480
awareness 566

Babylonians 301

Baltimore Catechism 505, 506, 507, 510

Baptism 35, 62, 115, 116, 117, 119, 123, 124, 125, 128, 129-135, 142, 143, 149, 152, 194, 199, 202, 210, 235, 237, 242, 243, 244, 246, 251, 256, 258, 261, 262, 265, 278, 296, 314, 330, 332, 337, 340, 341, 347, 348, 351, 366, 410, 439, 441, 442, 459, 474, 509
as "illumination" 135
liturgy of 437-445
of infants 237
of Jesus 203

Baptismal Catechesis 115

baptized 54, 57, 123, 126, 239, 240, 264, 292, 368, 407, 411
evangelization of the 520
in infancy 136
responsibility of the 314

Barnabites 160

Basic Teachings for Catholic Education (U.S.A.) 507

Basil, St. 305

beatification 607

beatitudes 152, 218, 346, 439

behavior 43, 53, 136, 152, 170, 571; see also *conduct*
Christian 478
of the child 350

being
angelic: see *angels, devils*
cultural 301; see also *man*
divine: see *God*
human 302; see also *human being, man, woman, child*

Bellarmine 161; see also *Robert Bellarmine*

belief(s) 196, 210, 571
Muslim 482

believer(s) 76, 231, 237, 273, 296, 378, 555, 579

Benedict XIV, Pope 155

Bible 33, 34, 55, 56, 68, 126, 129, 130, 133, 139, 140, 142, 144, 150, 153, 165, 169, 176, 180, 183, 192, 196, 275, 278, 281, 299, 300, 356, 439, 449, 461, 464, 469, 512, 521-522, 540
and youth 356
events of 529
formulas from 375f.
memorization of passages from 378
study of 499, 500

birth 439-440, 441-442

birthrate 336

Bishop(s) 13, 35, 58, 78, 79, 109f., 114, 117, 127, 128, 145, 147, 148, 149, 153, 155, 159, 175, 244, 311, 321, 322, 332, 366, 412, 510, 524, 551, 553, 561, 565, 566, 576, 591
and catechetical centers 601
as first catechist 322-323
authority of 54
Basic Teachings document of U.S. 507
collaboration with 231
communion with 110, 319
conferences of 600
first duty of 34
irreplaceable role of 404
of Africa 575
of Asia 462
of Canada 507
of India 447ff.
of Latin America 290, 513ff.
of Oceania 492
of the United States 505, 506
unity with 241, 523

Blessed Sacrament 486

Blessed Virgin: see *Mary*

blessings 237, 486

body
healing of 239

books 389ff., 589, 591

boredom 121

Borromeo: see *Charles Borromeo*

boys 161; see also *children, youth*

Brazil
and the media 398-399

bread 239, 240, 244
Eucharistic 240, 241

Brief Christian Doctrine (Bellarmine) 155

brotherhood 277, 289, 319

Buddha 469

Buddhism 458ff., 460, 467, 468, 469
catechesis in an environment of 458-471

Buddhists 589

Bulgaria 554

burial
of Jesus 243

Calvin, John 65, 138, 143f., 144, 150, 154, 155
catechism of 144

Cambodia 463

Cana 249
Canada 504, 506-507
candles 239
  paschal 443, 444
Canisius: see *Peter Canisius*
Capuchins 581
care
  pastoral 295, 329
Caroline Islands 491
Carroll, Bishop John 505
cassette, 500; see also *recordings*
catecheses
  of St. Cyril 115f.
  of St. John Chrysostom 115f.
Catechesi tradendae 13, 14, 15, 37,
  47, 178
  and cultures 415-434
  and *Evangelii nuntiandi* 11, 33, 75ff.,
    77, 80-81, 93, 94, 99, 423, 539f
  and popular devotions 382ff.
  and synodal propositions 84
  complete text of 625-691
  a general introduction to 82-96
  pastoral tone of 510
  structure of 88-89
catechesis
  acculturation and 233
  adaptation and 161
  aim of 185, 256, 270
  ambiental 462
  anthropological 183-184, 527, 540
  apologetics and 118
  Apostles and 99ff.; see also *Apostles*
  apostolic 102, 109
  as communion 101-103
  as deepening of the faith 168ff., 600
  as education 90, 91
  as initiation 91
  as instruction 77
  as mediation 43
  as mission 173
  as systematic religious education 77
  as the teaching of Christ 44
  as transmission 93f.
  as Word, memory, witness 537
  authentic 63, 69, 91, 127, 285, 288,
    292, 344
  baptismal 149
  basic 437
  basis of 232
  biblical 145, 182-183; see also *Bible*
  biblico-existential 521
  Bishops and 565; see also *Bishops*
  catechumenal dimension of 366

center(s) of 186, 256
central organ of 41
characteristics of 297-298
Christocentric 183, 191-220, 288,
  521; see also *Christocentricity*
Church and 109, 311-323
common 279, 280f., 283
comprehensive 476ff.
concept of 84
conciliar 30ff.
conciliar statements on 34ff.
conditions for 579
conscience and 353; see also *conscience*
contemporary 168-187
content of 193, 545; see also *content*
culture and 570ff.
Council of Trent and 138-167
deacons and 106-107
definition of 34, 42
development of 566f.
didactic 350
difficulties of 84, 89; see also *problems*
dimensions of 33
directories for 186
distortion of 232
doctrine and 44, 126, 128, 568
dogmatic 116
dynamics of 309-411
ecclesial 110, 189ff.
ecumenical dimension of 233, 272-283, 511
education and 43; see also *education, teaching*
effective 136
errors in 569f.
essential object of 285
Evangelii nuntiandi and 62-74
evangelization and 13, 14, 406-408
evangelizing 520
experiential 183, 540
family 78, 334-346, 454, 509, 525
fidelity of 258
focal point of 69
good news of 377
historico-biblical 169
history and 579
history of 93, 95, 97f., 138, 165,
  529ff.
the Holy Spirit and 229ff.
identity of Latin-American 519-524
ideologies and 580
importance of 76-77

improvised 343
in Africa 435-445
in a Buddhist ambient 458-471
in China 459
in Church history 97ff.
in context of prayer 127
in Eastern Europe 546-555
in Europe 528-545
in India 446-457
in Latin America 513, 526
in a Muslim ambient 474-489
in North America 504-512
in Oceania 490-502
in the patristic age 127
in rural areas 163
inculturation and 168, 415-434, 543-545
initial 350
inspiration of 249
institutes of 177, 186, 617-623
integral 293
international council of 47
international weeks of 178, 186
irreplaceable role of Bishop in regard to 404
John Paul I and 49-61
John Paul II and 67
kerygmatic 182-183, 366, 540
language and 465, 570; see also *language*
"liberation" 535f., 541
life of Church and 565
limited in time 140
liturgical 123-137
liturgical dimension of sacramental 235-245
liturgy and 149, 565
magisterium and 565
man and 46, 67; see also *man*
Marian attitude in 247
Mary and 247ff.
memorization and 373-379
memory and 84
message and 40, 46, 255
missionary 233, 247, 260-271, 402ff., 429, 577, 579-592
missionary dynamism of 413-555
moral 116f., 126, 352
mystagogical 115, 117, 123, 194, 195, 215, 242
nature of 41
necessity of 103-104
non-Christians and 474
of adolescents 353-354

of adults 45, 79, 80, 146, 147, 164, 180, 357f., 501
of the Apostles 99-111
of children 145, 146f., 164, 358, 371
of the Fathers of the Church 114-122
of the first Christians 99-111
of John Paul I 59f.
of Peter Canisius 152
of *Redemptor hominis* 62-74
of Vatican II 33
of youth 83, 371
on the Holy Spirit 441
oral 108f.
ordinary 266
origins of modern 138-167
organization of 139, 177
parents' involvement in 509
parish and 146f.
parochial 159, 164, 173
paschal 439ff.
pastoral of togetherness and 402-411
patristic 129-135
Paul VI and 38-47
pedagogical 568
permanent 80, 164, 185, 363, 410, 523
places of 54, 78, 79, 96, 316f., 334ff., 403, 410, 524-526
politics and 535-536
popular devotions and 380-387
post-conciliar 538
prayer in 230
preparatory 123-128
primary object of 225
primitive 109
principal agent of 233
priority of 16, 315
problems of 57, 89, 177, 566-569
program of common 281
recipients of 41, 89, 96, 347-359
reduction of 95
renewal of 160, 164, 249
responsibility for 147, 148, 159f., 173, 311-324
Revelation and 583
right to impart 553
rudimentary 600
sacramental 92, 129-135, 146, 235-245, 509
Sacred Scripture and 565
scholastic 537
sensitivity to the problems of 231
"situational" 519, 527

social communication and 525
socio-political dimension of 57
spirituality of 247-259
structure of 109f., 163
suffering and 251
supernatural character of 110
synod on (1977) 53ff.
systematic 90, 119, 126, 294, 576
task of 480
teaching of 307
theology and 295-307
those responsible for 78
to the mentally handicapped 84
Trinitarian 207, 507
true 233, 427
university 86
urgency of 231
use of media of social communication in 389-401, 512
Vatican II and; see Vatican II
vocation and 84
workers of 311-323
Catechetica in briciole 49ff., 59
Catechetical Discourses 116
Catechetical Homilies 116
catechetics 168ff., 179, 449, 451, 492, 508
catechism(s) 39, 50, 89, 114, 138, 139, 141, 149, 155, 159, 165, 166, 179, 180, 273, 311, 324, 528, 530, 575, 589, 601
and memorization 374-379
as a functional tool 50
as guide to the Christian life 152
as a school book 529, 531
Baltimore 505, 506, 507, 510
Catholic 150ff.
diffusion of 158f., 164
for adults 357, 461
French 155
German 461
in Chinese 458-459, 469
in Holland 531-535
in India 448, 453-456
in Vietnamese 459
national 175
of Edmund Auger 144, 154f.
of John Calvin 143, 144
of Martin Luther 141-143
of Pichler 374
of Quinet-Boyer 374
official 175
of Peter Canisius 150ff.
of Pius X 174, 175
printed by Propaganda Fide 593

of Robert Bellarmine 156
Tridentine, 147; see also *Roman Catechism*
uniform 589, 591
universal 175, 186
Catechism of the Council of Trent 147ff.
Catechismus Minimus 151
Catechismus Minor 151
catechist(s) 36, 46, 50, 53, 54, 55, 58, 78, 109, 110, 120, 122, 125, 126, 127, 160, 165, 177, 179, 185, 266, 321, 322, 325, 329, 366, 410, 447, 477f., 530, 557, 577, 585, 587, 590, 595-601
and children 163
and the Church 320ff., 603, 616
and the Holy Spirit 229ff.
and the liturgy 135
and prayer 103
and theologians 304-307
and theology 245
and the whole truth 232
as a spiritual father 243, 245
authority of 166
auxiliary 37
Bellarmine as 155
Church as 312-316
exemplary life of 581
faithfulness of 232
Fathers of the Church as 114
formation of 36, 49, 178-180, 252, 256, 322, 493, 582, 591, 597, 617-623
formation of native 580
funds for 36
guidelines for 120-122
in Christian environments 327
in Latin America 524
in mission territories 327, 596
instrumentality of 258
John Paul I as 49ff.
joy of 251
lay 36, 79, 160, 311, 313, 324-333
men 331
"ministry" of 331ff.
missionary 328, 602ff.
native 331
need to be catechized 315f.
number of 322
opinions of 253
parents as first 337
pastoral plan for 600
1970 Plenary Assembly of S.C.E.P. on 595-601

Pope as 58
prayer of 122
preparation of 323, 601
qualities of 160-161
sanctity of 57
sister 597
teacher of the Word of God 304f.
temptations of 232
types of 327
vocation of 96
volunteer 506
women 331
1975 World Encounter of Missionary 595-616
zeal of 251; see also *zeal*
Catechists in Africa, Asia and Oceania: Synthetic Study 599
catechized 314ff.
catechumen(s) 92, 95, 109, 117,126, 127, 137, 240, 264, 317, 318, 366-369, 478, 565, 586
conduct of 124
patrons of 125, 127
right of 94
catechumenate 79, 125, 331, 351, 360, 366-369, 589, 601
candidates for 125
for adults 261
in Upper Volta (Africa) 435-445
missionary 264
renewal of 262
Catherine Tegahkouita, Blessed 504
Catholic Catechism of the Diocese of Germany 176
Catholicism
and Marxism 571
catholicity 429, 574, 618-619
Catholics 491, 492
and the media of social communication 393-394
and other Christians 272-283
celebration(s) 84, 509
baptismal 442-445
Eucharistic 194, 257
family 341, 464
liturgical 123ff., 366
model liturgical 242
of the sacraments 136, 242, 257, 367-368
centers
catechetical 36, 179, 186, 430, 434, 618ff.
for formation of catechists 326, 576; see also *institutes*
health 493

importance of catechetical 601
missionary 402-411
national catechetical (India) 448ff.
of pastoral catechetics 177
youth 403
centrality
of Christ in catechesis 538; see also *Christocentricity*
of evangelization 517
of man in catechesis 347-359
of the message 530
of the Word of God 408
ceremonies
baptism 442ff.
of African liturgy 437ff.
certainties 95
certitude
need for 406
change(s) 299
rapidity of 496
socio-cultural 170
charisms 209f., 253, 255, 314, 410, 521
and sanctification 228
of institutes 322
of John Paul I 49
Pauline doctrine on 227
purpose of 228
three kinds of 228
charity 35, 42, 56, 103, 121, 143, 152, 156, 160, 200, 206, 207, 210, 270, 277, 317, 338, 439, 469, 581
in the family 338
Pauline qualities of 340
works of 106f.
Charles Borromeo, St. 54, 153, 159, 160f., 166
child 171-172, 363
baptism of the 242
psychological conception of the 161
childhood 161, 267, 349ff., 354, 364
children 34, 35, 50, 54, 55, 56, 60, 77, 79, 80, 114, 121, 125, 138, 139, 142, 145, 146, 154, 155, 156, 159, 160, 161-163, 164, 165, 167, 173, 176, 178, 180, 181, 185, 237, 268, 288, 306, 311, 315, 317, 318, 327, 330, 341, 342, 345, 347ff., 365, 374, 462, 493, 505, 506, 508, 511-512, 530, 533, 545, 565
and Jesus Christ 352
and method 349-353
and parents 339, 343
baptized 265
freedom of 494

of God 193
of mixed marriage 282, 477
parents' education of their 337ff.
unbaptized 266
China 303, 417, 461, 583, 586, 591
catechesis in 458
Chinese 301, 303
chrism 240
Christ 36, 41, 43, 44, 53, 88; see
Jesus Christ
Christian(s) 118, 233, 268, 586
catechesis of the first 99-111
a definition of 156, 287, 378
in a Muslim ambient 475ff.
non-Catholic 272-283
*Christian Doctrine and the Cate-
chism for the Instruction of the
Indians* 157
Christianity 56, 66, 369, 418
and history 64, 570
nature of 286
newness of 469
Christmas 370, 442
Christocentricity 55, 83, 176, 183,
191-220, 275, 285, 376, 510, 521
Christus Dominus 34
Church 16, 31, 32, 34, 40, 46, 53, 54,
57, 58, 60, 66, 67, 76, 78, 94, 96,
103, 108, 114, 115, 138, 150, 152,
164, 165, 179, 192, 196, 213, 218,
277, 292, 300, 325, 367, 375, 469,
493, 538
and catechists 311-323, 598, 603-616
and culture 415-434
and ecumenism 272-283
and evangelization 409
and the family 337, 344, 346
and history 570
and language 466, 467; see also *language*
and liberation 289f.
and Mary 248, 250
and media of social communication
389-401
and public opinion 393ff.
and the sick 239
and State 330, 547ff.
and youth 355, 517; see also *youth*
as catechist 214, 312-316
as disciple 193
as receiver of catechesis 219
as teacher of catechesis 193, 219
catechesis of the 207, 211
catechumenate of the 366-369

catholicity of 429, 618-619; see also
universality
commitment to 511
communion with 523; see also *unity*
diverse visions of the 569
doctrine of 253; see also *doctrine*
documents of 378
domestic 337f., 340
faithfulness to the 523, 570, 597;
see also *fidelity*
family of the 436-445
Fathers of 114-122, 153; see also
Fathers of the Church
history of 88, 375
in imitation of Mary 254
inner life of the 315
instrument of the Holy Spirit 211,
230
life of the 109, 185, 296, 356, 565
liturgical catechesis in the early 123-
137
liturgy of the 215, 236, 245; see also
liturgy
local 178, 231, 408, 409, 429, 515,
567
maternity of 248, 257, 258
members of 312-321
mission of 62, 69, 73, 77, 173, 211,
258, 293, 337, 409, 511, 512
missionary 11, 16, 33, 192, 247ff.,
260-271, 363, 405, 572
nature of 247
Oriental 30
practice of the 313
praying 210
precepts of the 156
problems of the 567ff.
program of 362
rights of 554f.
sacramentality of 257
sacraments of 235ff.
social teaching of 291, 552
status of catechist in the 326
suffering 555
Tradition of the 206, 300, 597
unity of the 317, 322, 618
universality of the 33, 237, 417, 515,
608
upbuilding of the 228, 328
circumstances 108, 282
civilization 53, 71, 363, 378
of the mass media 398-400
urban-industrial 335
clans 170

clarity 50, 58, 60, 115, 298, 307
regarding the Eucharistic Mystery 569
classes
length of 173
Clement III, Pope 155
Clement of Alexandria 305
clergy 140, 145, 231, 362, 547; see also *priests*
formation of 145
native 588, 590
collaboration 96, 515, 522f.
of Christians with Muslims 487ff.
with diocesan clergy 329
college(s) 306, 392, 590
collegiality 105, 322f.
Colomb, J. 182
commandments 56, 142, 143, 148, 152, 154, 156, 161, 162, 164, 174, 237, 263, 439, 461; see also *Decalogue*
commission
for catechesis and catechists 599
commitment 84, 92, 356, 366
faith 136
personal 323
communautés de base 184, 329, 518
communication 52, 124, 452; see also *social communication*
group 390-391
means of social 305, 389-401
media 577
of the faith in the home 340f.
oral 162
use of the means of 389-401
verbal 340
Communio et progressio 394ff.
communion 102, 206, 293
and participation 293, 518
conjugal 336
divine 211
ecclesial 522f.
Eucharistic 102
first 173, 324, 341, 368, 442, 509
fraternal 336
hierarchical 58
holy 241, 293
in charity 110
in the faith 42
of life 101
of love 210
through prayer 103
with Christ 288, 410, 498
with the Church 110, 317, 320, 523
with God 57, 103, 285, 367

with the Word of God 103; see also *Word of God*
communism 389, 546ff.
community(ies) 43, 93, 101, 136, 268, 293, 367, 368, 369, 462, 494, 522f., 524, 597
adult 378
animated by the Holy Spirit 569
apostolic 107, 206
Baptism as introduction to the ecclesial 459
basic 367, 497f., 515, 520, 522, 536
Christian 237, 597, 598
Church 219; see also *Church*
ecclesial 16, 78, 94, 106, 184, 210, 328, 362, 518, 525, 537
familial 318
forms of 318
human 291, 335
insertion into Christian 366; see also *Baptism*
involvement of Christian 437-445
neo-catechumenal 264
of believers 271, 282
of the family 336
parish 403
place of catechesis 316-319
praying 103
present at Baptisms 242
religious 547
scholastic 522
small 180, 316
value of 496f.
Company of Christian Doctrine 161, 166-167
Compendium of Christian Doctrine (Pius X) 173
competence 160
"competent" 116f.
competition 162, 165
completeness
of catechesis 297-298
of message 375
of presentation 378
compromise 95, 232, 427
Conception
Immaculate 254
condition
human 542; see also *man*
conduct 43, 118, 124, 126, 140, 586
Christian 124, 125
of catechists 581f.
of the catechumen 92
conferences
episcopal 560, 561, 564, 600

confession 156, 159
auricular 116
preparation for 173
configuration
with Jesus Christ 69, 73, 253, 254,
256
Confirmation 115, 116, 128, 194,
202, 210, 314, 324, 330, 332, 341
349, 352, 368, 441, 509
preparation for 173
conflict 57
Confucianism 459, 460, 471
confusion 63, 67, 299, 320
confraternities
foundation of 580
**Confraternity of Christian Doc-
trine** 35, 159, 164, 179, 506, 597
congregation(s)
catechetical 160
for the clergy 41
of Father James Alberione 391
religious 158, 164
congress(es)
catechetical 178, 181
International Catechetical 11
on the media 400
conscience 297, 539
and the Holy Spirit 222
and Karl Marx 547
education of 309
examination of 341, 483
missionary 33, 268, 271
self-made 353
consecration
Eucharistic 135
conservatism 299
Constantine 240-241
constitution
soviet 548-550
Constitution on the Sacred Liturgy
235
contemplation 248, 252, 253, 371,
544
content(s) 32, 42, 44, 55, 77, 88, 93f.,
105, 117, 119, 120, 140, 150, 157,
166, 181, 182, 183, 191, 342, 507,
524, 525, 530, 539, 545, 575
and historical situations 519
and method 511
biblical 180
doctrinal 438, 439, 441, 529
essential 300
fullness of 213
of evangelical message 339
of faith 274, 428

of the Gospel 273
of Muslim beliefs 482
problem of 568-570
purely human 95
systematic presentation of doctrinal
511
contestation 41
contests 162, 163
continuity
of the Magisterium 27ff., 75-81
contribution
of popular devotions 384
to the whole Church 271
conventions
of catechetical studies 178
convergences
Christian and Muslim 479
conversation
about God 340-341, 348f.
conversion 90, 124, 127, 192, 195,
219, 252, 256, 262, 264, 267, 271,
298, 303, 333, 360, 362, 366, 367,
371, 406, 440, 451, 517, 521, 523,
581
converts 261, 271, 366, 460, 600
conviction(s) 43
Cook Islands 491
cooperation 280, 405, 490
among Christians 276ff., 280, 282
among higher institutes of pastoral
studies 561
ecumenical 491f.
in the formation of catechists 326
in initiatives 576
coordination
of missionary activity 560
organic 524
coordinators
parish 508
co-responsibility 84, 367, 524
cosmos 71
council 66: see respective names of
the various ecumenical councils
counsel(s)
divine 213
evangelical 156
countries
mission 329; see *missions*
courage 105, 255, 324, 579
courtesy 590
covenant 169, 196
signs of the new 204
creation 67, 68, 119, 120, 129f., 134,
169, 277, 443, 459, 469
creativity 429, 431

Creator 65
creature 65, 67, 68, 69
credibility 54
Credo of the People of God 85, 290
creed(s) 87, 115, 117, 128, 132, 139,
  142, 148, 152, 154, 156, 159, 161,
  174, 291, 293, 378, 439, 440, 465,
  489
  of the Apostles 126
  articles of the 481, 483
  of Nicea 116
  of the People of God 290
crisis(es) 192
  of adolescence 354
  of faith of adults 267
criteria
  individualistic 320
criticism 266
cross 202, 286, 370, 443
  of Jesus Christ 197, 238, 243, 249,
    255, 427
  sign of 156
  teaching about the mystery of 586
  theology of 57
  way of the 383
crucifixion 467, 586
Cubans 303
cult
  ancestor 442
  idolatrous 210
culture(s) 11, 31, 39, 45, 52, 57, 58,
  60, 89, 93, 108, 110, 140, 170, 171,
  185, 233, 240, 253, 255, 264, 265,
  274, 275, 282, 301-304, 349-350,
  357, 362, 385, 396ff., 415-434,
  464, 493, 538, 539f., 542ff.
  and catechesis 570ff.
  and cultures 432
  and the Holy Spirit 223
  and the media 389-401
  Christian 398
  contemporary 570
  dialogue of the Gospel with 415-434
  evangelization of 517
  in India 451ff.
  in Latin America 515, 522
  in Muslim societies 475ff.
  Judaic-Hellenistic 303
  Marxist 56
  occidental 459ff.
  original riches of 418
  respect for 583ff.
  secular 364, 365
  values of 495
  Western 583

curia
  diocesan 412
  Roman 561
custom(s) 425, 439, 585
  and the Holy Spirit 223
  of various peoples 422
  Voltaic ancestral 436ff.
Cyril of Jerusalem, St. 116, 126, 128
  catecheses of 115
Czechoslovakia 548-550, 554

Daniel, Yvan 182
daughter 441
de Acosta, Joseph 157, 158
De agone Christiano 117
De Catechizandis Rudibus 120-122
De principiis 118
deacon(s) 106-107, 322, 332, 366
death 118, 243, 336, 437
  of Jesus 169, 183, 198, 203, 206,
    218, 238, 255, 278, 292, 370, 443,
    530, 586
debates 163, 394f., 581
Decalogue 56, 139, 159, 352
de-Christianization 265
Decree on Ecumenism 274, 283
dedication 255
deeds 63, 69, 126, 285
  of God 205
definition(s) 162
Dei Verbum 538
deportment
  of Christians 203
deposit
  of faith 108, 296, 427, 465
desire 207
  for Christ 206
destiny
  of man 289
detachment 256, 340
development 518
  human 352, 499, 538
  of adolescents 353f.
  of catechesis 566f.
  of the child 349ff.
deviations 299, 320, 322
devil(s) 129, 243; see also *Satan*
devotion(s); see also *religiosity*
  popular 380-387, 580
  to the Sacred Heart 384
Dewey, John 171-172
diaconate 107
diaconia 106
dialogue 32, 41, 57, 60, 163, 185, 253,
  274, 278, 279, 301, 325, 342, 349,

378, 394, 396, 437, 461, 464, 470,
482, 483, 524, 543, 544, 554, 574,
575, 598
between the Gospel and cultures 93,
415-434
between parents and children 339,
340f.
ecumenical 280
"group media" and 526
of faith 365
of salvation 561
teacher-student 162
with Asiatic religions 464
with Buddhists 462
with God 256, 341, 367, 379; see
also *prayer*
with Muslims 474, 484, 487-489
with the religions 463
Dicasterium 580ff.
dichotomy(ies) 84, 95, 286, 519f.,
536, 541, 542
Didachē 118, 119, 124
didactics 50, 109, 163
Didymus of Alexandria 224
differences
between Christian and Muslim 479
of traditions 479
difficulties 178, 229, 576
diffusion
of ideas contradictory to the faith
601
dignity
human 64, 289, 290, 293, 336, 355,
357
diocese(s) 184
catechetical office in a 404
central organs of 408, 411
curia of 412
religious education office of 508
directives
of Propaganda Fide 583ff.
pontifical 11
director(s)
diocesan 449
diocesan catechetical 404
of religious education 508
directory(ies) 176, 186, 528, 537-538
ecumenical 281, 572f.
pastoral 148
U.S. National Catechetical 506, 510
discernment 161, 264, 421, 427, 465,
470, 471, 539
disciple(s) 90, 92, 94, 106, 199, 200,
205, 262, 263, 270, 287

mission of the 206
of all nations 315
discipline 119, 265, 581
discontinuity 75-76
discourse(s)
catechetical 115ff.
religious 276
discretion 150, 340
discrimination 87, 550
discussion 162, 163, 306, 541
disposition(s)
proper 235
Divine Office 146
divinity
of Christ 196; see also *Jesus Christ*
"divinization" 216-218
divisions 275, 280
docility 339
to the Holy Spirit 229-230
doctrine 29, 36, 37, 38, 40, 44, 46, 53,
58, 60, 63, 64, 84, 91, 94, 107, 115,
117, 119, 124, 127, 136, 139, 141,
142, 144, 150, 156, 180-181, 205,
280, 296, 325, 332, 345, 481, 489,
520, 530, 554, 565, 568ff.
and Eucharist 268
and experience 507
and integrity 93-94
and life 91-92, 330
and message 39f.
and practice 63
assimilation of 571
authentic 105, 285, 601
Catholic 36, 567, 576
fidelity to 38; see also *fidelity*
in textbooks and programs 507
Muslim 475, 476, 484ff.
of the Church 253
of the two ways 119
social 83, 553, 597
document(s)
of the Church 378
of the Church on the media 397-398
of Medellin 514ff.
of U.S. Bishops on *Basic Teachings*
507
of Vatican II 29, 372
pontifical 418ff.
postconciliar 372
dogma(s) 95, 119
history of 299
Dominicans 459
doubt(s) 299, 590
doxology 42

drinking 495
dualism 46, 382, 519, 521
Duffy, Fr. Thomas Gavan 447
duties 117, 121, 140
dynamism
    missionary 33, 317, 411

earth 442
Easter 128, 131, 206, 369-370, 371,
    442
    Triduum of 126, 127
    vigil of 117
Ecclesiam suam 41
Ecclesiastical Ordinances, The
    (Calvin) 143
ecclesiology 32, 140
economics 39, 57, 71, 487, 553
Ecumenical Directory 572f.
ecumenism 31, 33, 84, 185, 272-283,
    431, 511, 572f.
edification 298
education 35, 43, 87, 88, 90, 108, 152,
    265, 344, 478, 547, 596
    adult 492, 511-512
    atheistic 86, 552f.
    directors of religious 508
    in the faith 77f., 138, 267, 296, 322,
        342, 492, 575, 579
    in the faith in a Muslim ambient
        474-489
    in the faith with the media 389-401
    information in 478
    of conscience 297
    of the faithful 287
    religious 324, 327, 330, 491, 597
    scientific-atheistic 552f.
    to Christian maturity 291
    unity of principles in 478
educators 343, 345, 354
egoism 291, 336, 355
Egyptians 301
"elect" 126
Elizabeth Seton, St. 505
encounter
    with God 43
    with Jesus Christ 257
encyclical(s)
    missionary 268
    Redemptor hominis 62-74
end
    the last 220
endurance 483
Engels, F. 540
enthusiasm 255, 324

environment 55, 108, 165, 172, 182,
    267, 282, 305, 316, 326, 350, 352,
    362, 365, 406, 408, 452, 455, 463,
    470; see also *ambient, milieu*
    atheistic 553
    Christian 494
    cultural 571
    of the community 317
epiclesis 211
episcopate(s) 43, 290, 515
Epistle to Diognetus 107
equilibrium 41
errors 117, 150, 422, 569
    Christological 300-301
    correction of 322
    dissemination of 601
    regarding ecclesiology 569
    regarding the Eucharist 569
    regarding moral life 569-570
eschatology 121, 156
essentials 156, 275, 297, 280, 307,
    375
    of the faith 364
    of Gospel message 355
eternity 521
    and Mary 257
ethics 330, 597
Eucharist 74, 92, 101, 102, 103, 106,
    110, 115, 116, 119, 128, 134-135,
    137, 146, 156, 198, 201, 202, 210,
    240, 257, 268, 292, 315, 330, 342,
    349, 358, 439, 583
    errors regarding the 569
Europe 417
    catechisms in 528-545
    catechesis in Eastern 546-555
Evangelii nuntiandi 11, 13, 33, 47,
    62, 75ff., 80-81, 178, 223, 272,
    288, 293, 300, 381ff., 423, 539f.
evangelization 13, 14, 33, 34, 56, 76,
    77, 80-81, 93, 138, 178, 195, 260,
    268, 279, 281, 302, 365, 409, 516,
    517, 538ff., 566, 576
    and catechesis 406-408
    and catechesis in Latin America 513-
        527
    and culture 397f., 415ff.
    and the Holy Spirit 229ff.
    and the media 389ff.
    and popular devotions 380ff.
    and social communications 512
    and suffering 250
    and technology 512
    beginning of 257

diaconal ministry of 106f.
in a Buddhist ambient 458ff.
methods of 492-493
of Latin America 290
person-to-person 526
progress of 257
Protestant 504
right to 54
structure of 492-493
evangelizer 252, 253
Evening Prayer 146
event(s) 291
biblical 529
evil 57, 121, 351, 352, 422, 494
examinations
religion 146
examples 50, 330
use of 162
exegesis 192, 295
exegetes 56, 305
existence 69, 91
Christian 300
concrete 291
human 217, 579
law of 220
of God 459
existentialism 169, 170, 303
exodus
paschal 197
exorcism 126, 437
experience(s) 33, 43, 44, 90, 91, 95,
157, 369, 507, 520, 541
and doctrine 507
and language 466
and positivism 169
and teaching 92
basic human 338
Christian 195
human elements of 232
in the family circle 340
life 343
liturgical 127, 129, 437-445
meaningful 242
mystical 133-134
nature of 287
of catechesis in apostolic age 106
in the Church in Upper Volta (Africa) 435ff.
of communion with the Word of
God and with Peter 102
of God 136
of love in early childhood 339
of man 521
of the Mystery 194

of the primitive catechumenate
368f.
of suffering 467
paschal 443-445
plurality of 405
sacramental 236, 350, 437-445
shared 283, 340
experimentation 95
and positivism 169
explanation
adequate 287
based on comparisons and images
182
of a lesson 162
exploitation 452
Exposition of Apostolic Preaching
119
of a lesson 529-531
expression
catechetical 436-437, 438-439, 441
liberty of 444, 445
liturgical 437-438, 439, 440, 443-445
of the faith 505
theological 428

faith 34, 35, 39, 49, 53, 56, 57, 63, 67,
79, 90, 92, 94, 107, 115, 117, 121,
124, 125, 134, 140, 145, 152, 156,
201, 210, 213, 243, 252, 256, 271,
277, 280, 282, 288, 298, 302, 315,
316, 319, 320, 365, 375, 385, 417,
439, 463, 478, 516, 543, 579
act of 170
adults' growth in 360ff.
and life 42, 46
and reason 64, 65, 66
and works 152
articles of 164
assent of 275
attitude of 511
authenticity of 32, 369, 420
Calvinistic 143
children and the 350, 351f.
Christ as object of 95
commitment to the 136
communion in the 110
content of the 93, 181, 182, 274
conversion to the 126
courage needed to profess the 555
crisis of 267, 553
dangers for the 553
deepening of 109, 600
deposit of 29, 42, 110, 465
differences of 277-278

doctrine and life of 136, 509
education in 60, 125, 296, 337, 379, 538
expression of communitarian 384
expressions of the 428
family's life of 338, 341, 348
formation in the 465
formulations of the 376
gift of 597
growth in the 185, 235, 261, 262, 263, 340, 345, 363, 523, 524, 538
ideas contradictory to the 601
indifference to the 600
in Jesus Christ 196, 290
journey of 91, 366ff., 370f.
living 43, 63, 273, 471, 534
maturity of 54, 57, 80, 81, 274, 287, 406, 466, 533
mediatorial function of 95
memory of 377f.
mentality of 185
motive for embracing the 585
of the adolescent 354
of the adult community 512
of Mary 256
of the Muslims 483
of pupils 330
of youth 356, 600
orthodoxy of 285
parents as teachers of 338
patrimony of 41f.
pedagogy of 85, 94, 95, 350
principal elements of 460
profession of the 108, 265, 279, 378, 486, 541
rationality of the act of 554
response of 239
rudiments of 147
sociological conditionings of 172
systems incompatible with 302
totality of the contents of the 376
transmitting the 504; see also *catechesis*
truths of 51, 505, 530
witness to the 317, 362
word of 232
year of (1968) 42
faithful, the 268, 312, 321, 375, 596, 598
formation of 245
responsibility of 269
faithfulness 32, 427; see also *fidelity*
to God 511
family 34, 35, 54f., 78, 86, 96, 165,

184, 261, 277, 362, 365, 403, 520, 522, 524, 525
African 318
as recipient of catechesis 344
catechesis 454
children without a 350
in the catechesis of Upper Volta 436, 438, 441-442
lifestyle of 339, 492
lineage in Upper Volta 436ff.
non-believing 350
prayer 341f., 346, 378
rights of 554
role of the 334-346
unity of the 341
Fargues, Marie 182
fasting 124, 486, 581
father(s) 336, 337f., 338
Father, God the 99, 100, 103, 110, 115, 132, 193, 194-213, 218, 220, 278, 288, 291, 315
Fathers of the Church 108, 114-122, 123, 128, 153, 162, 208, 214, 216, 223, 240, 242, 243
fatherhood 339, 348, 441
fear 70, 121
Ferdinand of Austria 151
Ferrière, Adolph 171-172
fervor 138, 165
Feuerbach 72
fiat 249
Fidei Donum 268
fidelity 38, 44, 94, 105, 107, 117, 248, 298, 320, 325, 478, 538, 539, 575, 597
daily 355
Marian 249
obligation to 44
of catechist 258
to Christian message 521
to Christ's teaching 568
to the Church 523
to deposit of faith 42
to God 326, 357
to the Holy Spirit 257
to man 326
to the revealed word 522
fides quaerens intellectum 295f.
Fiji Islands 490, 491
film(s) 389ff.
ideal 398
filmstrips 392f.
financing
of catechists 599

firmness 595
First Communion 324
Fleury, C. 182
forgiveness 280
  of sins 238
formation 90, 123, 136, 252, 326
    590; see also *training*
  at home 509
  catechetical 450-451
  doctrinal 597
  effective means for human 390
  for parents 346
  in the faith 422, 465
  in justice 464
  intellectual 256
  mission of the journalist 401
  moral 596
  of adult community 368
  of catechetical leaders 231
  of catechists 36, 78, 177, 178-180,
    185, 252, 268, 325, 410, 449, 577,
    582, 591, 595, 598, 599, 617-623
  of Catholics for the media 399-400
  of a Church community 328
  of the community 317
  of evangelizer 252
  of the faithful 245
  of local clergy 430
  of native catechists 580
  of native priests 580
  of priests 145
  of those responsible for diocesan
    catechesis 434
  of the whole Christian community
    371
  poor 600
  spiritual 596, 597
  weekly encounters of 403
Formosa 463
formula(s) 159, 162, 163, 180, 520,
    529
  and memorization 373-379
  "Jesus is Lord!" 209
  liturgical 241
  Trinitarian 207
*Formulary for the Instruction of
    Young People in Christianity*
    (Calvin) 143, 144, 154
France 155, 175, 537, 583,
Francis Xavier, St. 327
  method of 591
Franciscans 504
fraternity 291, 339
freedom 64

  of choice 355, 357
  religious 549f.
  true 290
friendship
  in Jesus Christ 253
  with God 68
  with Jesus Christ 354
fruitfulness
  apostolic 250
Futuna 491
future 579
  for catechists 612

Gaudium et spes 57, 515, 538
General Catechetical Directory 11,
    42ff., 46, 85, 176, 353, 434, 510,
    537-538, 576-577, 601
generosity 340, 355
gentleness 581
German Democratic Republic 554
Germany 175, 176, 537
  catechesis in 529-531
  catechism of 374, 461
Gerson 142
gift(s)
  as a motivation 162
  hierarchical 224
  of the Holy Spirit 193, 209ff., 228
  supernatural 521
Gilbert Islands 491
girls 161; see also *children, adolescents,
    youth*
glory
  of God 211
  of Jesus Christ 197
God 32, 40-41, 43, 62, 66, 72, 77, 110
    118, 120-121, 129-130, 132, 148,
    152, 197, 279, 300, 422, 469, 539,
    541
  and man 67, 293, 359
  as Teacher 204
  belief in 272
  communion with 51, 57, 293
  conversion to 124
  Creator 65
  existence of 278, 459
  experience of 136
  faith, gift of 292
  family of 439
  the Father 193-213, 494
  fidelity to 357
  glory of 211
  grace of 345
  the Holy Spirit 194-213

Incarnation of the Son of 193
Kingdom of 592
knowledge of 35, 65
law of 56; see also *commandments*
love of 63, 67, 365, 494
mystery of 375
obedience to 104
of Revelation 94, 209
one 483
people of 196, 228, 579
plan of 68, 203, 216f., 220, 319, 536, 592
presence of 239, 244, 554
return to 192
Revelation of 91; see also *Revelation*
Son of 207-208, 294, 375; see also *Jesus Christ*
terms for 467
union with 341, 461
way to 436, 440
will of 65, 259, 291, 298, 439
witnesses to 346
Word of 56
godparents 125, 147, 237, 242, 246, 346, 439-442
good(s) 152, 352
common 355
exchange of 271
temporal 102
Good News 11, 13, 77, 108, 183, 231, 269, 283, 294, 302, 377, 530
goodness 54, 210
Gospel(s) 31, 32, 36, 40, 46, 54, 55, 60, 67, 69, 91, 93-95, 108, 123, 126, 143, 151, 182, 184, 185, 213, 233, 262, 268, 279, 283, 291, 300, 302, 314, 348, 356, 369, 370, 397, 493, 539, 541, 542, 583
and catechesis in Africa 437ff.
catechetical structure of 109, 113
dialogue with cultures 415-434, 540
entirety of 428-429
herald of the 572
historicity of the 483
in the home 590
message of the 426
moral values and 233
power of 264, 428-429, 431, 464
right to announce the 555
seeds of 417ff.
servants of 44
the term "teacher" in the 204
grace 35, 57, 63, 65, 67, 68, 100, 174, 194, 198, 210, 211, 228, 267, 273,
275, 289, 291, 320, 345, 469, 480, 597
grandparents 345, 346
gratitude 210, 239
Great Catechism (Canisius) 151
Great Catechism (Luther) 141-142
greed 496
Greeks 301, 420, 581
Gregory the Great, St. 67, 119, 120
group(s) 318, 524
Bible 78
dynamics 356
media 500
prayer 329
small 163, 165, 397, 497, 517
study 499
growth 256
in faith 235; see also *faith*
of the Church 592
spiritual 73, 315
Guam 491
guidance
of the Bishop 565

hagiography 56; see also *saints*
Hail Mary 152, 156, 159, 161
handicapped
mentally 84
hands
laying on of 239, 240, 244
washing of 241
happiness 436
hatred 437
healing 238-239
health
good 595
heart 162, 243, 342, 437
conversion of 264
generosity of 478
memory of the 376
heaven 467
Hebrews 35f., 130, 202, 302, 303
Hegel, G. 72
herald 444
heresy 39
heritage 579
heroism 555
missionary 270
hierarchy 577, 589
of the Church 313, 569
Hinduism 455f.
Hippolytus 125, 126
history 45, 54, 56, 64, 70, 71, 95, 183, 195, 217, 274, 282, 289, 291, 295, 504, 536, 538, 544, 597

and atheism 552f.
and Christianity 570
and Church 570
biblical 443
catechesis in contemporary 413-555
examples from 162
focal point of 376
Lord of 192, 521
of catechesis 97-187
of catechetical movement in India
   447
of Christ 197
of Church 120, 288
of human race 289
of mankind 196
of salvation 121, 128, 130, 169, 174,
   183, 192, 193, 202, 239, 254, 275,
   276, 285, 289, 300, 367, 456, 521,
   530; see also *salvation*
of various peoples 422
Hofinger, S.J., Johannes, 447
Holland 175, 176, 531-535, 537
holy days 145, 146
Holy Orders 244, 332, 441
Holy See 47, 510, 567, 577
   concern for proper religious educa-
      tion 505
Holy Spirit 40, 53, 58, 89, 99, 103,
   107, 109, 110, 115, 130-132, 194,
   204, 213, 218-233, 271, 275, 278,
   292, 296, 315, 332, 368, 370, 410,
   433, 441, 463, 512, 528, 538, 543,
   581
   abandonment to 230
   activity of the 203
   and catechesis 229ff.
   and catechists 229ff.
   and the Church 221
   and the community 223, 569
   and conscience 222
   and ecumenical movement 233
   and evangelization 229ff.
   and evangelizer 252
   and individual 224
   and infallibility 224
   and Mary 249
   and mission of People of God 228f.
   and Pentecost 222
   and the Second Vatican Council 223
   and "signs of the times" 230
   and the teaching of the apostles 228
   as consoler 222
   as teacher 95, 193, 221, 224, 225,
      233
   as transformer 225, 226

   as witness 225, 232f.
   authentic inspirations of 230
   Church as instrument of the 230
   Distributor of special graces 227
   divine fullness 210
   dynamic presence of—, in the Church
      224
   fidelity to 256, 257
   font of charisms 227
   function of the 207
   gifts of the 133, 152, 156, 209, 227,
      228, 274
   in biblical texts 222
   in *Lumen gentium* 228
   in sacraments of Christian initiation
      224
   inspirations of 211
   "interior Teacher" 207
   invocation of 211
   magisterial function of the 222
   work of the 207
Holy Trinity 199; see also *Trinity*
Holy Year, 1975 602ff.
home 340
   catechesis in the 338
   Gospels in the 590
homily 85, 89, 90, 116, 146, 358, 477
hope 35, 121, 152, 156, 255, 257, 289,
   315, 324, 340, 439
horizontalism 541
hospital 391
hospitality 242, 437
host 241
human beings
   transformation of 292
humanism 66, 337
humanity 40, 63, 71, 73, 300, 317,
   541
   cultures of 416ff.
   destinies of 71
   of Jesus Christ 198
   return to God of 249
humility 161, 254, 480
Hungary 551, 554
hymns 162

idea(s) 255, 256
   exchange of 576
   key doctrinal 379
   mass communication of 398f.
   propagation of 389
   transmission of 436ff.
idealism 72
ideology(ies) 65, 89, 95, 217, 255,
   274, 290, 364, 542

and catechesis 580
and error 570
and the message 570
critique of 542
identity 45
as a Catholic 378
confessional 275
crisis of 192
of Christian 479f.
of human being 71, 73
of man 290
idols 315, 336
ignorance 57, 520, 524, 541
elimination of 181
religious 141
illuminism 43
Illustrissimi 51
image of God 200
imagination 437
Imitation of Christ 379
immersion 132f., 244
baptismal 243
immigrants
to the United States 505
immolation 252
improvisation 90, 320
Incarnation 46, 53, 62, 66-69, 110,
120, 130, 169, 192, 197, 198, 202,
203, 367, 370, 467, 480, 538
and culture 413, 415-434
mystery of 252
inculturation 84, 110, 175, 264, 413,
415-434, 452, 453, 460-462 , 464,
543, 571, 574, 582, 583f., 592
and acculturation 434
and catechesis in a Buddhist environment 458ff., 466-469
India 328
and the media 392f.
catechesis in 446-457
Indians 303
of North America 504
Indies 157
indifference 274, 281, 361
of the adolescent 354
to the faith 600
individual
Holy Spirit and the 224
individualism 496
Indochina 328, 417, 463, 475, 583,
584
indoctrination
atheistic 555
induction 529f.
indulgence(s) 604

industrialization 170, 282, 335, 452
inequality
social 451
infallibility 224
infancy 348, 523
information 245, 394ff., 401, 481,
551, 576, 591
in education 478
initiation 87, 88, 91, 92, 194
initiative(s)
availability for 577
ecclesial 400
of Bishops in catechesis 322
injustice 520
innovation 41
inspirations
of the Holy Spirit 193, 211
institute(s) 177, 186, 598
charisms of 322
for catechetics 179, 281, 326, 601
missionary 599
Institute of Missionary Catechesis
11, 12, 14, 15, 186, 231, 326, 434,
617-623
institutionalization 325
instruction 77, 101, 108, 144, 153,
165, 280, 505
adult 139, 146
and the Bible 145
atheistic 554
catechetical 34, 36, 109, 114
daily 146
deficient 140
in the faith 127
in families 531
of children 311
pastoral 261
prayerful 136
preparation of catechetical 585
religious 78, 138, 147, 160, 164, 173,
288, 509
systematic 77, 79, 342
Instruction for Catechists 327
instrumentality
of catechist 258
instruments
of catechesis 524, 525
of social communication 389-401
integrity 94, 119, 193, 273, 274, 298,
307, 463
doctrinal 93f.
of the Christian mystery 430
of the message 189, 320, 322, 469
regarding the Eucharistic mystery
569

intellect 91, 161, 181, 243, 478
intellectualism 292
intelligence 50, 65, 71, 164, 288, 339, 342, 349-350, 437
intelligibility 298, 307; see also *clarity*
intention 595
intercessions
  general 477
interdependence
  between catechetical office and missionary center 402-411
interests
  of man 183
Inter mirifica 390
International Congress of Missiology (1975) 420
International Council for Catechists 331
interpretation 44, 183, 535, 536
  authentic 102
  biblical 56, 224
  faithful 305f.
  mystical 241, 242
involvement
  active 163
  in catechesis 317
Irenaeus, St. 118, 119
irenicism 57, 84
Islam 474-489
  catechesis in an environment of 474-489
  moral requirements of 482
islands 490
isolation 490
Italy 537, 583
  and the media 399

Jansenism 65
Japan 303, 328
  catechesis in 459
Jesuit(s) 151, 153, 157, 160, 458-459
  martyrs of North America 504
Jesus Christ 16, 45, 63, 66-70, 72, 73, 78, 99, 102, 106, 108-110, 120, 121, 129, 131, 132, 152, 183, 191-220, 292, 300, 350, 423, 436, 465, 469, 470, 479, 521, 538
  acceptance of 290
  and adolescents 353-354
  and the Apostles 211ff., 313ff.
  and catechesis in Africa 436ff.
  and children 352

  and the Church 367
  and cultures 302
  and the Father 198
  and man 347ff.
  and Mary 247-259
  and youth 356
  apostle of God 105
  as the "Chief" 445
  ascension of 367
  catechetical action of 315
  center of divine life 195
  commitment to 511
  communion with 410-411
  death of 200; see also *death of Jesus*
  the divine Guide 206
  divine Truth 200
  Divine Worker 203-206
  divinity of 200, 254
  encounter with 256, 257
  essential object of catechesis 300f.
  Eucharistic Victim 293; see also *Eucharist*
  fidelity to 597
  focal point of catechesis 69, 169
  following of 290
  friendship with 253, 354
  fullness of Revelation 196, 197, 285
  God-Man 205, 467
  the good news of every catechesis 377
  Good Shepherd 270
  Holy Spirit as witness to 225
  "hour" of 249
  human will of 207
  humanity of 254
  Image of the Father 197
  imitation of 483
  in catechesis of Upper Volta 436, 438-440
  the Incarnate Word 196, 484, 543
  incorporation into 314
  intimacy with 256, 264, 270, 315
  King 199, 206
  knowledge-following of 149
  Legislator 459
  the Lord 196, 220
  Lord of history 376, 521
  Mediator 238, 270, 359
  message of 93, 94
  mission of 203
  mystery of 201-203, 239, 298, 317, 323, 366, 370f., 431, 512
  Mystical Body of 196, 252, 269
  object of faith 95

paschal mystery of 198, 238, 292, 386, 442ff.
Person of 55, 78, 195-201, 278, 285, 376, 530, 597
personal adhesion to the message of 262
personal attachment to 265
the physician 459
presence of 596
Priest 201, 206, 220
primacy of 218
Prophet 206
Redeemer 270
reductionism of 300-301
Revelation of the Father 498
sacrifice of 351
Savior 91, 199, 264, 269
Servant 206
servants of 105
Son of God 94, 196, 199
spouse of 252
Teacher 77, 100ff., 198, 203-206, 220, 258, 262, 263, 264, 270, 286
transfiguration in 218
true liberator 73
true man 197
unity of Christians in 272-283
Vicar of 51; see also *Pope*
Way, Truth, Life 62, 200, 212, 286, 287, 288, 300
Word of God 378
words of 378
Jews 420, 587
John, St. 286, 377
John Bosco, St. 379
John Chrysostom, St.
on the Holy Spirit 223
John Paul I, Pope 27ff, 49-61, 82, 191
John Paul II, Pope 11, 13, 16, 27ff., 61, 85ff., 191, 347, 382, 512
John XXIII, Pope 29, 30, 38, 39, 175, 418
journalist 399, 400-401
joy 121, 161, 202, 210, 211, 237, 251, 256, 340, 350, 437
jubilee
Holy Year 607f.
judgment 121, 483
good 595
Jungmann, J. A. 182
justice 57, 152, 156, 277, 289, 291, 339, 355, 357, 499, 520
justification 152
Justin, St. 124f.

Katholisher Katechismus 529-531
Kenya 391ff.
kerygma 90, 93, 108, 182-183, 215, 262, 263, 266, 287, 407, 459, 461, 511, 534
Kingdom 199, 289, 356
knowledge 43, 50, 53, 78, 90, 91, 95, 127, 162, 214, 232, 296, 298
human 94
level of 256
of Christ 289
of God 35, 65, 198, 288
of religions 267, 572
of sacraments 136
scientific-atheistic 547
systematic 406
Koinonia 211, 228
Koran 475, 480, 482, 484f.
Korea 461
Kyrios 209

laicism 73
laity 30, 32, 35, 58, 107, 108, 138, 140, 160, 165, 167, 173, 178, 231, 283, 311, 312, 321, 322, 324-333, 337, 363, 396, 403, 410, 477f., 506, 508, 510, 518, 523, 595
as catechists 324-333
missionary role of 595, 596
language(s) 32, 60, 89, 93, 108, 117, 142, 150, 153, 171, 231, 243, 263, 301, 305-306, 420, 427, 429, 462, 464-465, 490-500, 534, 538, 568, 571, 581, 597
adaptation of 320
and media 525f.
catechisms in Occidental 458-460
drum 444
expressions of 428
in Africa 436ff.
in a Buddhist environment 466
in a Muslim ambient 477
Moaga 436-445
"non-verbal" 339
of catechesis 268, 570
of India 454
of the media 400
of men of today 521-522
of *Redemptor hominis* 73
of young people 282
scriptural 530
simplicity of 49ff., 590
study of 582
theological 154
Lanquetin, Canon 182
Laos 462-463

Last Supper 200
"last things" 156; see also *eschatology*
Lateran V 145
Latin 142
Latin America 293, 328, 408, 498, 615
 and the media 393
 catechesis in 513-526
 problems of catechesis in 526
law(s) 143
 and love 352
 divine 146
 natural moral 554
lay apostolate 324; see also *laity*
leaders
 catechetical 501f.
 of workers 597
learning 53, 232, 541; see also *instruction*
 mnemonic 378
 unified family 509
lectionary
 for children 352
lector 332
Ledesma, James 155, 166
legends 437
legislation
 ecclesiastical 561
Lent 126, 145, 146, 371
lesson(s) 163
 catechism 161-162
 explained in an expository way 176, 529-531
 theme of 531; see also *instruction*
liberation 57, 183, 289, 306, 355, 452, 453, 516-520
 and catechesis 530
 authentic 290
 integral 291
 of man 516-517
 theologians of 301
liberty 64, 65, 266, 289, 336, 355, 357
 of conscience, according to communism 547-548
 of man 71
life 34, 39, 53, 76, 77f., 90-92, 296, 554
 according to the beatitudes 439
 according to Christ 44
 according to the Spirit 207, 370
 and catechesis 498
 and doctrine 92, 330
 and faith 46
 and Revelation 91
 application of 181

 attack on 336
 catechesis for all ages of 523
 catechesis oriented to 436-445
 Christian 63, 164, 262, 280, 368
 commitment to 291
 communal 102
 concrete 575
 contact with 595
 divine 193, 269
 effect of catechesis on 293
 eternal 115, 218
 evangelical 474
 experience 343
 experience of paschal 366
 fullness of 91
 future 289
 gift of human 348
 Gospel 597
 holiness of 585
 in the Church 73
 liturgical 220, 351, 596
 maturity of Christian 57, 276
 meaning of 468
 monastic 463
 moral 541, 569, 570; see also *morality*
 nature of Christian 268
 newness of 133, 152, 440
 of charity 538
 of the Christian 156
 of the Church 35, 38, 109
 of communion with God 51
 of faith 273
 of family 492
 of insecurity 452
 of Jesus 286
 of the primitive Church 314f.
 ordinary 252
 orientation of 265
 problems of 525
 religious 561
 revision of 354, 376; see also *conversion*
 sacramental 236, 254, 292, 330, 338, 596; see also *sacraments*
 sin as contrary to 440
 social 220
 source of Christian 379
 spiritual 36, 243, 275
 study of ecclesial 466
 teachers of 401
 testimony of Christian 592
 transmission of 436ff., 441
 Trinitarian 219

unborn 336
way of 71, 498, 499, 509
witness of 330, 595
worthiness of 127
lifestyle
of missionaries 458ff.
light
of God 287
Lima 158
linguistics 275
listener 121, 122; see also *recipient*
listening
Marian attitude of 247
litanies 486
literacy 398
literature 500, 544
Catholic 389ff.
Occidental 459
Vedic 456
Lithuania 554
Little Catechism (Luther) 139, 141,
142, 151
liturgical year 370-371
liturgy 33, 35, 36, 55, 85, 91f., 115,
116, 119, 123ff., 128, 136, 140,
149, 153, 165, 169, 174, 183, 191,
192, 202, 215, 216, 220, 235-245,
253, 275, 292-295, 331, 329, 341f.,
351, 356, 366, 368, 370-371, 375,
377, 382, 422, 449, 463-464, 466,
477, 481, 486, 489, 509, 516, 530,
533, 540, 565, 592, 596
and catechesis in the early Church
123-137
dimensions of 235-246
exemplary 242
for children 352
in Africa 437-445
of the Eucharist 135, 137
Roman 194
study of the 245
locus: see also *places*
of community 213
Lord 209
Lord's Prayer 288; see also *Our Father*
Lourdusamy, Archbishop D. S. 16,
610
love 63, 118, 120, 121, 251, 315, 319,
342, 354, 437
and law 352
and zeal 253
attack on 336
for people 286
fraternal 371

genuine experience of 570
God's plan of 41
in the home 338
maternal 248
of children for parents 340
of God 194, 202, 365
of neighbor 35
practice of Christian 237
response of 210
Luciani, Cardinal Albino 51ff.; see
also *John Paul I*
Luke, St. 103, 370
Lumen gentium 33, 228, 405, 538
Luther, Martin 65, 138-144, 147,
150, 152, 155, 166
catechisms of 141-143

magazines 389ff.
magisterium 11, 34, 35, 41, 49, 53,
55, 56, 58, 65, 75, 81, 87, 260, 298,
299, 300, 306, 375, 428, 458, 541,
570
and catechesis 565
and modernism 170
continuity of 27-96
Holy Spirit and 222
of Jesus 270
man 32, 34, 41, 44, 45, 46, 53, 62, 63,
65, 66, 68, 70, 72, 120, 148, 152,
169, 171, 180, 183, 184, 192, 193,
232, 293, 299, 355, 366, 367, 407,
422, 521, 534, 536, 538, 539, 541,
546, 554, 561, 568
and God's presence 554
and Jesus Christ 197
as creature 67
aspirations of 521
centrality of 347-359
destiny of 203, 289
God and 67
God's plan for 220
history of 197
humanity of 66
identity of 71, 73
in his historical concreteness 436,
527
innermost being of 288, 294
Latin-American 519
open to God 359
Pauline conception of 152
primary way for the Church 69
problems of 170
revelation of God to 205f.
salvation of 285
sanctification of 220

spiritual growth of 73
ultimate ends of 220
mandate
apostolic 195, 260, 313, 319, 567
manipulation 290
manual 151, 163f.
for missionaries 584, 585
for pastors 148
for teachers (Luther) 141-142
of theology 118
Marianas 491
Mark, St. 109, 370
marriage 335ff., 339, 341, 485, 487, 496
mixed 282, 477
preparation for 346
Marshall Islands 491
Martinez, Jerome 157
Marx, Karl 72, 547
marxism 56, 303, 548, 554, 555, 571
Mary 74, 85, 89, 197, 247-259, 278
and apostolic action 248
and catechesis 247ff.
and Christian perfection 248
and the Church 250, 254
and eternity 257
and formation of catechists 256
as disciple 247, 252
as mother 253, 257
as teacher 251
at the Annunciation 252
at Pentecost 249
attitudes of 248
devotion to 383, 384
example of 251
faith of 256
feast of 371
images of 254
in conciliar texts 249
in ecclesial texts 249
in postconciliar texts 249
instrument of the Word 254
"living catechism" 247, 254
maternity of 250, 251, 254, 255
mission of 248
model of catechists 247, 255
mother of catechists 247, 255
Mass 115, 142, 145, 146, 156, 241, 351, 368, 486
mass media 170, 336, 344, 345, 358, 389-401, 553; see also *social communications*
masses 139
materialism 51, 71, 364, 469, 496

dialectical 546ff.
secular 336
maternity 338
apostolic 248, 251
ecclesial 250, 251, 257, 258
of Mary 251, 254, 255
matrimony 35, 335f., 337, 368, 441
Matthew, St. 109, 370
method of 485
maturity 80, 165, 185, 297, 369
and Confirmation 314
human 595
of the adolescent 354
of Christians 283, 291, 362
of faith 263, 274, 276, 538
psychological 363
Medellin 183, 535-536
episcopal assembly of (1968) 513ff.
media 180, 231, 330, 477f., 492, 500, 525f., 553, 577
"group—" 526
in Asia 574
of social communication 51, 389-401
personal 321
mediation
cultural 57; see also *inculturation*
sacramental 367
meditation 468, 585, 597
Melanesia 491ff.
members
of the Church 309, 321ff.
memorization 77, 83, 89, 117, 142, 149, 152, 156, 161, 162, 163, 165. 177, 180, 373-379, 500, 506, 520, 529, 531
memory 83, 84, 95, 342, 437
of the Church 288
of the heart 112
role of the 374ff.
men
catechists 331, 589
religious 321, 322
mentality 597
scientific 171
mercy 339, 342
divine 202
merit(s) 210, 469
message 32, 40, 44, 46, 53, 57, 69, 93, 94, 95, 109, 181, 183, 185, 277, 301, 302, 530, 540
acceptance of Christ's 365
and cultures 301-304, 415-434
and doctrine 39
and ideologies 570

and means 255
authentic transmission of 464
biblical 519
Christian 280, 459, 474
diffusion of 231, 390ff.
evangelical 429
fidelity to 232, 354, 420, 464
Gospel 123, 264, 415ff., 426; see also *Gospel*
integrity of the 189, 322, 469
nature of the 93
necessity of 428
of faith 320
proclamation of paschal 444
responsibility for 109
of salvation 275, 276
whole 375
messianism(s) 232, 294, 364, 542
methodology 29, 95, 164, 165, 181-182, 305, 375, 460, 461, 507, 532, 560
and concrete historical reality 514ff.
and memorization 373-379
anthropological 64
catechetical 538
of Confucianism 459
of German Catechism (1955) 529-531
of the Gospel 60
of John Paul II 65
of missionaries in a Buddhist ambient 458ff.
of *Redemptor hominis* 64
of theology 303-304
patristic 124
method(s) 55, 89, 90, 95, 129, 166, 171, 177, 231, 281, 293, 342, 476, 524, 539, 542, 561, 567
and content 511
historico-biblical 183
Munich 181, 529f.
of catechesis 268
of catechists 599
pedagogical 565
Micronesia 491ff.
migration 170, 265, 283, 496
milieu 464; see also *ambient, environment*
catechesis in an African 435-445
family 340
Moaga 437ff.
pagan 600
mini-cultures 490
ministers 598
assignment of 560

lay 332
ordained 332
·ministry(ies) 332
catechetical 108, 325
diaconal 106f.
episcopal 114
lay 518, 523
of the catechist 500
of the Church 238, 325
of the Word 43
pastoral 281
minorities 475
miracle(s)
of Jesus 196, 201, 286
misery 289
missio canonica
of catechists 600
mission(s) 33, 37, 113, 174, 240, 247ff., 261, 264, 313, 322, 331, 409, 413-555
and the Holy Spirit 233
centers of 402-411
directives of S.C.E.P. for catechesis in 579-592
government of the 589
institute of catechesis for 617-623
of the Apostles 100f.
of the catechist 333
of the Christian 317f.
of the Church 211, 229, 247ff., 258, 260-271, 319
of the disciples 206ff.
of the family 335ff.
of Jesus Christ 203
of the Orient 155
of teaching 114
prayer for the 271
Sunday 602ff.
1975 World Encounter of Catechists from 595-616
missionaries 93, 585, 590, 598
and catechists 333
in a Buddhist ambient 458ff.
in North America 504, 505
life of 584
manual for 584, 585
rules for 581f.
modernism 169, 170
modesty 161
Mohammed 482
money 496
monopolization 290
monotheism 479, 483, 484
moralism 294, 541

morality 124, 126, 140, 157, 220, 233, 291, 293, 294, 299, 354, 375, 422, 427, 465, 505, 507, 516, 553, 583
More Ample Declaration of Christian Doctrine (Bellarmine) 155
Moses 131, 459, 482
motherhood 348
mothers 336, 337f.
motivation(s) 43, 172
movement(s) 96, 403, 524
  catechetical 173
  ecumenical 233, 272-283
  of renewal 318
  spiritual 281
Munich, Madeleine 182
Munich method 181
Muslims 474-489, 586, 589
mutilation 304
Mystagogical Catechesis 128
mystagogy 115, 124, 128, 136, 219
  definition of 123
mystery(ies) 135
  center of the 203
  Christian 117, 128ff., 469
  of the Church 409, 483, 569
  of the Eucharist 146
  of Jesus Christ 213, 239, 264, 270, 276, 285, 287, 298, 300, 317, 323, 366, 474
  of man 290
  of truth and grace 273
  paschal 131, 183, 198, 292, 442-445, 530
  translation of term 201-202
Mystical Body 62, 73, 300
mystics 468

names
  baptismal 443-444
narration 120f.
narratives
  from the Gospel 437
nation(s) 326
  and families 343
National Catechetical Center of Bangalore 446ff.
National Catechetical Directory (in U.S.A.) 506, 510
National Catechism
  in Canada 507
National Catholic Educational Association (U.S.A.) 508
nationalization 576
naturalism 266

nature 63, 65, 67, 71, 289
  divine 218
  divine and human 70
  human 66f., 68f., 219
neighbor 35, 63, 192, 210
neo-converts 324
neophytes 115, 128, 129-135, 243, 328, 330, 586
New Caledonia 491
New Catechism (Dutch) 176, 531-535
New Guinea 490, 491
New Hebrides 491
New Testament 106, 107, 194, 216, 328, 378, 379, 485
New Zealand 491
newspapers 51, 389ff.
Nicodemus 205
Noah 130
nominations 551f.
non-Catholics 505, 511
non-Christians 31, 35f., 233, 409, 460, 463, 474, 597, 598
non-practicing 345, 409
North America
  catechesis in 504-512
Nostra aetate 479

obedience 68, 147, 339-340
  to the bishop 325
obligation
  communitarian 257
  personal 257
obstacles
  to Christian unity 275f.
ocean 490
Oceania 322, 603, 615
  catechesis in 490-502
  French 491
office(s)
  catechetical 402-411
  diocesan catechetical 174, 404
oil 239, 240, 244
Old Testament 216, 328, 484f.
Omega 220
On Mysteries 128ff.
On Sacraments 128ff.
openness 323, 595
  Marian attitude of 248
opinion(s) 44
  personal 94, 253, 298f.
  public 390ff.
optimism 67
  excessive 57
  healthy 192

regarding popular piety 385
options 94
  of the Latin-American pastoral 516-518
  personal 217, 232, 298
Oratio catechetica magna 119
Oratorians 160
Orbem Catholicum 174
ordination 244
organization 161, 165, 174, 177, 180, 273, 499f., 522
Orient
  missions of the 155
orientation(s)
  of catechesis in Upper Volta 436
  of catechetical programs in U.S.A. 507
  pastoral 30, 514, 515
Origen 118, 126
orthodoxy 285-294, 296
orthopraxis 285-294, 296, 307
Our Father 116, 117, 139, 142, 143, 148, 152, 154, 156, 159, 161, 439, 440

Pacific 490, 492, 494
paganism 118, 364, 571-572, 585, 590
paideia 90, 296
Pajer, F. 183
pamphlets 389ff.
Papua 490, 491
parable
  of the sower 104
Paraclete 228, 229; see also *Holy Spirit*
pardon 301, 339, 342
parent(s) 35, 55, 125, 147, 180, 185, 237, 242, 246, 309, 318, 321, 322, 345, 367, 493, 505, 508, 531, 553
  and children 343
  direct participation in catechesis by 509
  first and principal educators 337, 358
  prayer of 341
parenthood 346, 436ff., 477
parish(es) 54, 55, 78, 87, 89, 96, 138, 140, 147, 157, 160, 164, 165, 167, 173, 180, 184, 241, 268, 327, 329, 345, 365, 367, 378, 403, 404, 493, 506, 509, 522, 524
Parousia 228, 367
participation
  and communion 293, 518

catechetical 96
  class 162
  in the divine nature 218
  in the liturgy 34
  in the Mass 292-293
  in the sacraments 92
particularism 302
paschal mystery 238; see also *mystery*
passion
  of Christ 198, 586
pastor(s) 35, 49, 58, 114, 138, 140, 143, 146, 147, 148, 149, 151, 155, 159, 160, 164, 173, 177, 266, 283, 297, 300, 309, 312, 321, 329, 354, 358, 591
  authority of 166
  communion with 320
pastoral of togetherness 402-411
paternity 338
patience 340, 342
patron(s) 125, 126, 127
Paul VI, Pope 11, 27f., 29, 30, 31f., 38, 41, 42, 49, 58, 75, 82, 85, 180, 191, 287, 289, 331, 381, 382, 401, 533, 606-607, 610f.
  and catechesis 38-47
Paul, St. 101f., 104, 105, 228, 251, 285, 287, 328, 377, 420
peace 57, 277, 289, 291, 355, 357
  sign of 126
pedagogy 50, 58, 60, 94, 121, 162-163, 166, 181-182, 250, 348ff., 353, 455, 538, 565, 568
  activism in 171-172
  human 95
  of faith 95, 350
  pastoral 517
  secular 378
  spontaneistic 541
Penance 74, 115-116, 156, 324, 330, 351, 439, 509
  sacrament of 238
  virtue of 238, 370
  Calvinistic 143
penitent(s) 159, 238
Pentecost 205-206, 210, 222, 248ff., 256, 292, 370, 441
people
  dignity of 495
  of God 196, 228, 271, 441; see also *Church*
  of the Book 480
periodicals 51, 177, 179, 186-187, 389ff., 528

permissiveness 64, 495
  doctrinal 298f.
persecutions 125
perseverance 340, 595
person
  consecrated 322
  converted 288
  growth of human 369
  human 71, 293, 326, 347-359; see
    also *man, woman, child*
  of Jesus Christ 212, 219, 270, 285-
    286, 499, 530
  vision of the 290, 531
personalism 170, 303
personality
  development of 343
personnel 567
pessimism 66f.
Peter, St. 101, 278, 420
  communion with 102
  See of 567; see also *Holy See*
  successor of 319; see also *Pope*
Peter Canisius, St. 150ff.
petition 103
Philip, St. 107
Philippines 328
philosophers 301
philosophy 63, 64, 65, 143, 544
  Occidental 459
pictures 50, 163
  motion 389ff.
piety 36
  Marian 383
  popular 331, 381, 383-384
pilgrimage 603ff.
Pius IV, Pope 148
Pius V, Pope 148
Pius IX, Pope 175
Pius X, Pope St. 49, 60, 168ff.,
  173-175, 400
Pius XI, Pope 49, 174-175, 607-608
Pius XII, Pope 49, 175, 333, 418, 607
places
  for catechesis 345
plan
  of God 216f., 220, 269, 592
  of salvation 201
planning 535, 536-537
pleasure 336
pliability 161
pluralism 419, 515
  cultural 303, 452
  religious 451, 452, 511
Poland 551, 554

polarization 506, 507, 542
polemics 281, 514
  lack of 155
politics 39, 57, 184, 217, 232, 290,
  300-301, 475, 487, 502, 553, 582
Polynesia 491ff.
  French 491
polytheism 483
Pontiffs 268; see also *Pope*
Pontifical Urban University 11, 14,
  15, 16, 186
**Pontifical Works for the Propaga-
  tion of the Faith** 596
poor, the 56, 286, 367, 516
Pope 59, 155, 278, 321, 324, 330-332,
  375, 418ff., 566
  as pastor 85
  center of unity 322
  communion with the 110
population 453, 491, 573
positivism 169
posters 389ff.
poverty 56, 253, 452-453
power 336
  divine 206
  of the Gospel 233, 583
  of the Holy Spirit 232
practice 95, 554
  and doctrine 63
  Christian 237, 263
  of the Church 312, 515, 526
  of the faith 285-294, 538
  sacramental 136, 342
prayer(s) 101, 103, 110, 117, 119, 124,
  126-128, 136, 143, 151, 156, 162,
  164, 206, 239, 280, 282, 315, 319,
  325, 342, 348, 375, 378, 469, 486,
  494, 498, 581, 585, 587, 597, 605
  essential 378-379
  Eucharistic 241
  family 341f., 346, 378
  for the missions 560
  for vocations 344
  forms of Indian 456
  formulas 237
  groups 318, 329
  importance of 230
  of the Church 436
  of Jesus 286
  personal 341
preacher(s) 148, 151
  journalist as a 401
preaching 109, 110, 114, 140, 143,
  164, 279, 295, 530, 581, 590

preadolescence 353
pre-catechesis 436-438
precepts 119, 152
pre-evangelization 57, 183, 461
prejudice(s) 55, 64, 265, 266, 277, 478, 482, 504, 591
preparation
of catechist 323
of sermons 585
presentation 181
of doctrine 63, 163
systematic 511
press 51, 358, 389ff., 512, 589
priest(s) 30, 55, 58, 78, 138, 140, 147, 153, 155, 159, 160, 167, 173, 178, 179, 269, 309, 311ff., 321, 322, 328, 332, 344, 345, 366, 401, 477, 492, 493, 500, 502, 504-506, 551, 553, 597
native 580, 588
pastoral action of 369
shortage of 311, 494, 585
priesthood 32, 206, 588, 595
principle
of continuity-discontinuity 75ff.
printing 589
invention of 512
priority(ies) 76
methodological 163
of catechesis 315
of the Word of God 601
pastoral 510-511
problem(s) 31, 32, 95, 356, 525, 534, 567, 598
human 169, 336, 354, 406, 519, 568
in the search for God 282
the media and financial 391
missionary 34, 589
of catechesis 538, 566f.
of catechesis in Latin America 526
of catechesis in Oceania 490-502
of catechesis in U.S.A. 507-511
of contemporary existence 71, 276f. 357, 495f., 544f.
of cultural mediation 57
of human race 395, 396
pastoral 57
religious 140
sensitivity to 231
special 567ff.
process
catechumenal 366-369
procession
baptismal 134, 443, 444

proclamation 108, 411
of paschal message 444; see also *announcement*
procreation 336-338
production
economic 71
profession of faith 108; see also *Creed*
of Paul VI 42
professors 282
of catechetics 449
programs
common religious 282
diocesan 402ff.
parish 506
progress 43, 257
progressivism 299
prohibitions 55
propaganda 548
Propaganda Fide 11, 14, 37, 460, 505, 557-623
and dialogue with cultures 417-421
ninth plenary assembly of 16; see also *Sacred Congregation for Evangelization of Peoples*
prophecy 53, 485
proverbs
African 436-437
providence 339
Provido sane consilio 49, 174
prudence 57, 160, 583, 586
psychology 43, 275, 349, 353, 541, 571
and activism 172
publications 589
publishers 399, 597
of textbooks in U.S.A. 507
Puebla 290, 293, 301, 408
and the media 393
episcopal assembly of (1979) 513ff.
pupils 161, 544f.
and master 436; see also *students*
purification 351; see also *conversion*
purity 161

qualification(s)
catechetical 179
of catechists 595
Quebec Act 504
question-answer form 142, 155, 156, 162, 163f., 165, 174, 176, 373ff., 507
of Calvin's "Formulary" 143
questionnaires 591

questions 57, 358
  of adolescents 213, 353f.
  of man 183, 539
  regarding liturgy 240, 580
Quinet method 182

race 223
radio 329, 358, 389ff., 500, 512
  educational 399
Rahner, H. 182
readings 60
  biblical 136, 237, 341
Real Presence 116, 135
reason 63-67, 120, 263
  and faith 65
receivers
  of catechesis 347-359; see also *recipients*
recipient(s) 43, 53, 56, 105, 108, 120f.,
    149, 165, 171, 176, 219
  family as 344ff.
  man as 359
  of catechesis 41, 315f.
recitations 162
reconciliation 301
  of all Christians 283
  of penitents 238
  sacrament of 331
recordings
  tape 391ff., 512
records 391ff., 512
redemption 67, 68, 69, 70, 119, 120,
    217, 286, 481
  mystery of 252
  promise of 169
Redemptor hominis 62-74, 90
reductionism 300, 428, 541
reflection 83, 90, 92, 356, 378, 515
Reformation 140, 151, 154
refugees 283
regeneration 130
re-incarnation 467
relationship(s)
  among Christians 475
  between Christian and Muslim 478,
    481
  between Christian and non-Christian 479
  among human beings 170
  between orthodoxy and orthopraxis
    293
  between the Pope and the Bishops
    566
  communitarian 468

  inter-family 335, 339
  interpersonal 468
  of Christian message and life 474
  of local ambient to religious values
    481
  with the Trinity 319
  with various religions 571, 572f.
  within the family 340
relativism 281
religion 55, 145, 165, 171, 233, 453,
    463, 468f., 506, 546f., 574, 583
  ancient 357
  and the Church 421f.
  and culture 458
  Christian 118, 292
  courses on 175, 465
  in communist countries 546-555
  knowledge of 572, 597
  non-Christian 35, 65, 482
  Occidental 458-459ff.
  professor of 330
  relationship with 571, 572f.
  respect for 572
religiosity 521
  popular 380-387, 517, 576; see also
    devotion
religious 30, 35, 78, 138, 160, 164,
    178, 231, 309, 321, 322, 324, 449,
    477f., 492, 506, 508, 547, 597
  shortage of 311ff.
Renaissance 140
renewal 16, 30, 41, 49, 139, 148, 160,
    164, 168, 169ff., 179, 182, 185,
    191, 192, 231f., 249, 272, 280, 378,
    446ff., 460ff.
repentance 280
repetition 163, 320
reporter 401; see also *journalist*
research 38, 44, 236, 280, 282, 299,
    300, 304-306, 329, 350, 428, 430,
    431, 524, 532
resistance 266
respect 253, 340, 482
  for cultures 583ff.
  for religions 572f.
  human 104
  in refutation 155
  of children for parents 340
responsibility(ies) 325
  differentiation of 314, 321f.
  for catechesis 160, 173, 178, 279,
    283, 297, 309, 311-323, 324, 367,
    522f.
  for growth of the Church 441

of the Bishop 404, 565; see also
  Bishop
of catechumens 442
of the community 493-494
of the Sacred Congregation for the
  Evangelization of Peoples 563
personal 480
towards new generations 363
restlessness 67, 276
resurrection 115, 121, 169, 183, 196,
  197f., 203, 206, 218, 238, 278, 342,
  366, 431, 443f., 530
retribution 459
Revelation 32, 46, 66, 77, 89, 91, 94,
  120, 195, 197, 202, 205, 233, 285,
  288, 291, 294, 296, 299, 302, 509,
  570, 583
and Modernism 170
fulfillment of 286f.
revision
of life 354
right(s)
human 87, 357, 520
to educate 554f.
to religious freedom 548ff.
rites 123, 128ff., 133, 139, 240, 241,
  244, 331, 437, 439, 486, 587
ritualism 136, 236, 292
ritual(s)
African and Roman 437ff.
introduction to 237
pagan 244
Roman 437
Robert Bellarmine, St. 155f.
Roman Catechism 147, 158, 161, 166;
  see also *Catechism of the Council
  of Trent*
Roman Curia 15
Romans 301, 302, 420
Rome 605ff.
rosary 341, 383, 486
Rossi, Cardinal Agnelo 16, 609f.
rulers 580
Rules for Missionaries 581
Rumania 554

sacrament(s) 73, 92-93, 116, 123-124,
  128ff., 136, 139, 143, 146, 148,
  150, 154, 156-157, 165, 235-245,
  292-293, 319, 327, 330, 341, 350,
  354, 358, 365-369, 439, 486, 498,
  508-509, 516, 538, 581, 596
administration of 580
and catechesis 235ff.

the Church and 73
in life of adults 367-369
of Baptism 129-135
of Christian initiation 224, 349, 435-
  445
sacramentality 257
Sacred Congregation for the Clergy
  11, 47, 537
**Sacred Congregation for the Evan-
  gelization of Peoples** 14, 16, 326;
  see also *Propaganda Fide*
action of 559-577
aim of 580
competence of 559
1970 Plenary Assembly of 595-601
Sacred Congregation of the Council
  174
Sacred Scripture 288, 375-378, 565;
  see also *Scripture*
sacrifice
of Jesus 255, 270, 286
of the Mass 116, 146, 292, 351
Sacrosanctum concilium 215
saints 54, 56, 140, 145, 237, 371
devotion to the 384
litany of 442
lives of 253, 379, 597
salvation 35, 57, 110, 115, 119, 125,
  146, 169, 183, 194, 199, 200, 205,
  218, 229, 270, 292, 339, 365, 368,
  375, 421, 425, 428, 460, 463, 467-
  468, 542, 561, 581, 595
history of 55, 105, 121, 128, 130-131,
  192-193, 202, 239, 254, 275, 276,
  285, 300, 367, 456, 461, 521, 530,
  536, 597
message of 51, 275-276
mysteries of 299
only through Jesus Christ 376
plan of 43, 201, 229
Samoa 491
sanctification 120, 220, 228, 274, 346
sanctity 36, 57, 152, 206
Sapientia Christiana 302
Satan 439-440; see also *devil*
scepticism 407
schism 587
scholars 177
school(s) 34-36, 78, 86f., 138, 145,
  151, 163, 165, 180, 261, 306, 330,
  391, 403-404, 462, 493-494, 524,
  547, 553, 580, 588-590
catechetical 167, 178-179, 598
Catholic 505f., 511, 576, 600
in Canada 506-507

nursery 349
of the Jesuits 153
of Jesus 100ff.
privileged place of catechesis 330
public 505
secondary 491
state 475
science(s) 64-65, 145, 171, 282, 349-
    350, 364, 425, 487
and atheism 552
ecclesiastical 63
human 192, 326, 538, 544
natural 459
sacred 326
Scripture(s) 31, 35-36, 56, 85, 88, 121,
    126-127, 129, 133, 136, 142, 145-
    146, 157, 162, 191-192, 195, 197,
    216, 247, 254, 278, 292, 300, 325,
    356, 483, 521-522, 533, 597
examples from 162
·search 276, 282, 468
Second International Catechetical
    Congress 46
secrecy 395
Secretariat for Christian Unity
    272ff.
secularism 265, 276, 364-365, 406,
    469
secularization 79, 170, 357, 532, 540,
    576
self-destruction 71
semina Verbi ("seeds of the Word")
    425, 453
seminar(s) 280, 451
seminary(ies) 34, 145, 159, 179, 391
semi-pelagianism 58
senses 163, 165
sensitivity 339
ecumenical 431
of the child 181, 182
pastoral 32, 166
sensus fidei 56, 251
sentimentality 79
serenity 150, 340
sermon(s) 146, 159, 268-269, 585; see
    also homily
service(s) 106-107, 160, 271, 294, 340,
    367, 515, 597
sexuality 161, 336, 354
Sharing the Light of Faith 510
sick 126, 238-240, 329
sign(s) 123, 128ff., 134, 203, 239-240,
    286, 366
Eucharistic 135
liturgical 239-241

of catechesis 236
of the cross 156, 162, 237
of faith 293; see also sacraments
of the times 53, 57, 230, 269
sacramental 239, 244-245
silence 253, 286, 378, 581
simplicity 52, 60, 142, 242, 244, 590
sin(s) 53, 142, 152, 154, 156, 192, 219,
    287, 289, 439-440, 570
capital 152
errors regarding original 569f.
forgiveness of 238
original 66
Singapore 461
singing 162, 444-445
sisters 597
situation(s) 57, 161, 165, 289, 474,
    519, 576, 596
analysis of 514ff., 535f.
concrete 436f.
diversity of 476f., 567
ghetto 466, 470
historical 519
missionary 265ff.
slavery 71
Small Catechism (Canisius) 151
social communication 34, 51, 89,
    309, 358, 389-401, 477, 492, 500,
    512, 525-526; see also media
personnel in 321
socialism 554
socialization 170, 336
society(ies) 39, 45, 72, 92, 171, 291,
    406, 475
problems of 496f.
upbuilding of 290, 363
sociology 274, 343, 541
and activism 172
solidarity 291, 467
Solomon Islands 490-491
Sommaire de la doctrine chrétienne
    154
Son
of God 103, 115, 199, 207-208; see
    also Jesus Christ
songs 437
sonship 218, 339
soul(s) 43, 149, 270, 322
sources
of catechesis and theology 299
of the liturgy 245
South Pacific 490-502
Spain 157, 491, 537, 583
spirit(s)
belief in 494

missionary 268-269
  of men 71
spirituality 192, 247-259, 560
sponsors 366
spontaneity 95, 378, 444
Sri Lanka 461-462, 464, 472
stability 496
Stalinism 555
state 330, 475, 547ff.
Stephen, St. 104, 107
stories 50f., 437
structure(s) 269, 499f., 524
  of the Institute of Missionary Cate-
    chesis 619-621
student(s) 35, 146, 151, 163, 164, 165,
    282, 529
study 51, 90, 92, 287, 315, 343, 356
subjectivism 356
suffering 104, 250f., 290, 437, 467,
    581
Summa doctrinae Christianae 151f.
summaries 158
Sunday 102, 146
  catechism classes on 139, 147, 158,
    159, 160, 161, 163, 164-165, 167,
    173, 365, 509
  Mass 145, 146
  Pasch of the Lord 341, 369-370
  World Mission 602
superstition 464, 586, 589, 591
Syllabus of Christian Doctrine 157
sympathy 482
symbolism 341-342, 443
symbols 134, 156, 239-242, 244f.
symposia 280
syncretism 302, 430, 463, 467, 485,
    571
synod(s) 57, 324-325, 440, 564, 584
  diocesan 138, 159
  message of the 1977: 79, 84, 85, 314,
    322, 326, 377f.
  of Bishops 11, 13, 33, 37, 47, 53ff.,
    59, 82, 85, 178, 186, 191, 193,
    231f., 233, 272, 279, 285, 385, 415,
    420, 463f., 538-540, 563, 567, 577
  propositions and topics of 1977: 84,
    375ff.
system(s) 290, 304
systematization 91, 307

tabernacle 135
taboos 494
tabula rasa 171
talents 54, 325, 330

teacher(s) 49, 77, 78, 90, 125, 126,
    145, 146, 147, 151, 160, 162, 163,
    297, 309, 321, 492, 508, 576, 597,
    600
  Jesus Christ as 203-206
  journalist as a 400-401
  of the faith 49ff.
  writer as a 400-401
teaching 29, 33, 34, 43, 44, 77, 85, 90,
    92, 95, 101f., 104, 106, 108, 114,
    140, 146, 163, 164, 166, 212, 254,
    275, 286, 291, 299, 330, 340, 494,
    553, 554, 568, 581, 599, 600
technology 72, 364, 487, 512
television 358, 389ff., 512
temptations 115, 482
  against faith 95, 267
  of catechists 232
ten commandments 378; see also
    commandments
terminology 32, 436ff., 534, 569, 571,
    591
Tertullian 125, 244
texts 89, 281
  apologetical 591
  biblical 216f., 245, 378
  catechetical 77, 236, 376, 507
  catechism 164; see also *catechisms*
  conciliar 33
  liturgical 329, 378-379
  of New Testament 203-204
  pontifical 397-398, 400
Thailand 462, 463
Theatines 160
Theodore of Mopsuestia 116
theologians 56, 58, 93, 138, 147, 155,
    301, 375
  and catechists 304-307
  as catechists 304-305
theology 32, 57, 63, 64, 84, 87, 89, 90,
    95, 114, 120, 140, 142, 145, 169,
    174, 179, 181, 184, 240, 269, 275,
    282, 285, 305, 306, 410, 470-471,
    482, 560
  and catechesis 236, 237-239, 295-
    307
  catechetical purpose essential to 305ff.
theories 306
Thérèse of the Child Jesus, St. 379
Thomas Aquinas, St. 67, 200, 299,
    305
togetherness
  pastoral of 30, 402-411
Tonga 491

totality 189
  of Christianity 313-314
Tradition 32, 35, 55, 56, 88, 169, 191,
    197, 206, 236, 254, 300, 356, 377,
    378, 544, 565, 597
tradition(s) 105, 240, 288
  of non-Catholic Christians 275-276
training
  of catechists 326, 508
  of directors of religious education
    508; see also *formation*
transcendence 53
  divine 480
  of human person 71
transfiguration
  in Christ 218, 220
transformation(s) 92, 225, 292
  of suffering 250
  socio-cultural 170, 513f.
translations 47, 148, 151, 157, 304,
    329, 460, 467
transmigration 459
transportation 452
transubstantiation 135, 569
treatises
  catechetical 114, 118ff.
Trent 39, 138-167, 180, 285
Trinity 103, 110, 115, 119, 120, 194,
    198, 203, 204, 206-207, 209, 211,
    216, 218, 220, 229, 275, 286, 315,
    319, 339, 480
trust 339
truth(s) 31, 32, 43, 44, 50, 53, 57, 60,
    63, 65, 66, 67, 69, 117, 121, 163,
    169, 256, 273, 287, 288, 290, 296,
    305, 365, 375, 376, 394, 396, 429,
    507
  and difficulties 356
  common to all Christians 278
  fullness of 232, 275
  fundamental 162-163, 288
  hierarchy of 44, 46, 87, 93, 275, 281,
    469
  organic unity of 63
Turibius de Mongrovejo, St. 158
Tuvalu 491
"Two Ways" 124

unbelievers 505
unemployment 452, 453
unfaithfulness 298f.
unilateralism 42, 519
union
  with the Bishop 241, 325-326, 565
  with God 73; see also *communion*

United States 504ff.
United States Catholic Conference
    508
unity 32, 108, 272-283, 406, 521, 536
  center of 322
  destruction of 299, 320
  of catechetical priorities 174
  of the Church 103, 317, 319, 322,
    429, 618
  of ecclesiastical sciences 63
  of the family 338, 341
  of the human race 73, 213
universality 33, 287, 319, 429, 495,
    608ff., 618
universe 561
university(ies) 282, 430, 454, 508
Upper Volta 435ff.
Urban VII, Pope 155
urbanization 170, 282, 335, 452
Ursulines 160
U.S.S.R. 546ff.

value(s) 53, 60, 71, 170, 233, 243, 252,
    276, 277, 301, 331, 354, 355, 363,
    364, 428, 429, 463, 521, 571
  cultural 265, 302, 413, 495
  Gospel 94, 233
Vatican II 11, 30, 31f., 38ff., 40, 42,
    49, 59, 89, 156, 168, 174, 175, 180,
    183, 186, 191, 223, 245, 268, 285,
    299, 313, 335ff., 367, 390, 394,
    398, 421-423, 433, 479, 487,
    513ff., 567
  "great catechism of modern times"
    29-37
vernacular 142, 164
vestments 240
vices 119, 140, 146, 164
Vienna method; see *Munich method*
Vietnam 459, 463
vigilance 305, 307, 483, 570
Vincent Ferrer, St. 140
violence 67
virtues 119, 140, 146, 152, 164, 203,
    291, 459
  cardinal 152, 156
  theological 156, 315, 439; see also
    faith, hope, love
vocation(s) 84, 87, 106, 255, 269, 410
  missionary 33, 271, 560
  native 587f.
  of catechist 110
  prayer for 344

Wallis 491
water 29-132, 238, 239, 240, 244

way(s)
of the cross 383
of life and of death 119
wealth 336
week(s)
diocesan catechetical 179
international 186
of catechesis at Medellin 513ff.
widows 126
will 71, 193, 339
decision of the 210
free 65, 210
of God 65, 291
wine 239, 240, 244
wisdom 51, 52, 57, 96, 151, 152, 302,
306, 320, 336
divine 197, 202, 204, 205, 214, 233
of heart 51-53
witness 54, 63, 92, 104, 108, 110, 185,
207, 232, 254, 276, 277, 279, 280,
282, 317, 330, 346, 350, 366, 367,
371, 384, 411, 470, 476, 538, 554,
572
in daily life 338
in the family 343
Wojtyla, Karol Cardinal 86f., 232-
233
dissertation of 95
woman 336; see also *person*
as catechist 331, 589
religious 321, 322
word(s) 50, 63, 69, 123, 162, 163, 285,
446
of Christ 201, 205, 286, 287
Word of the Father 66, 68, 196, 202;
see also *Jesus Christ*
Word of God 32, 35, 36, 39, 41, 43,
45, 46, 54, 57, 78, 95, 102, 104,
106, 108, 110, 126, 127, 138, 140,
143, 145, 146, 153, 165, 181, 185,
211, 219f., 230, 239, 252, 253, 273,
275, 278, 295, 297, 300, 301, 302,
304, 305, 307, 319, 338, 351, 356,
360, 362, 363, 366, 367, 370, 403,
405, 408, 410, 423, 431, 433, 437,
497, 525, 537, 538, 539, 542, 584,
597; see also *Bible, Scriptures*
and inculturation 426; see also *inculturation*
and law of God 56
in the milieu of India 446ff.
interpretation of 224, 304, 305-306
manipulation of 253
response to the 259
sacramental character of 239

seeds of 422, 425
servants of the 44f.
work(s) 271, 362, 378, 598
and faith 152
of charity 106, 590
of God 315
of the Holy Spirit 207
of Jesus Christ 196
of mercy 152, 156
of salvation 194
pontifical 596
Pontifical Missionary 599
social 195
value of 355
worker(s)
catechetical 311-323
expatriate 283
industrial 452
Jesus Christ as 203-206
workbook 532
world 51, 63, 67, 71, 118, 121, 170,
178, 192, 211-212, 218, 286, 289,
315, 363, 422, 538, 546
atheistic vision of the 553
Church in the 214f.
contemporary 71, 548
encounter of missionary catechists
from entire 602ff.
"Fourth" 490
Mission Sunday 602ff.
presence of God in 554
reality of 289
transformation of 220, 442
worship 35, 240, 281, 292, 477, 548,
585
writer(s) 397, 400-401

year
liturgical 206, 370-371
youth(s) 34, 50, 54, 56, 57, 79, 83, 85,
86, 89, 154, 156, 178, 212, 265-
266, 288, 315, 327, 330, 336, 342,
354-357, 367, 368, 427, 463, 498,
499, 511, 517, 541, 546, 553, 555,
565, 600
and dialogue 470
and the media 389, 391ff.
answers for 213
associations of 318
commitment of 511
future of 355
Yugoslavia 551, 554, 555

zeal 16, 57, 161, 251, 253, 256, 261,
268, 323, 407, 410

Daughters of St. Paul

IN MASSACHUSETTS
 50 St. Paul's Ave. Jamaica Plain, Boston, MA 02130;
 617-522-8911; 617-522-0875;
 172 Tremont Street, Boston, MA 02111; **617-426-5464;**
 617-426-4230
IN NEW YORK
 78 Fort Place, Staten Island, NY 10301; **212-447-5071**
 59 East 43rd Street, New York, NY 10017; **212-986-7580**
 7 State Street, New York, NY 10004; **212-447-5071**
 625 East 187th Street, Bronx, NY 10458; **212-584-0440**
 525 Main Street, Buffalo, NY 14203; **716-847-6044**
IN NEW JERSEY
 Hudson Mall — Route 440 and Communipaw Ave.,
 Jersey City, NJ 07304; **201-433-7740**
IN CONNECTICUT
 202 Fairfield Ave., Bridgeport, CT 06604; **203-335-9913**
IN OHIO
 2105 Ontario St. (at Prospect Ave.), Cleveland, OH 44115; **216-621-9427**
 25 E. Eighth Street, Cincinnati, OH 45202; **513-721-4838**
IN PENNSYLVANIA
 1719 Chestnut Street, Philadelphia, PA 19103; **215-568-2638**
IN FLORIDA
 2700 Biscayne Blvd., Miami, FL 33137; **305-573-1618**
IN LOUISIANA
 4403 Veterans Memorial Blvd., Metairie, LA 70002; **504-887-7631;**
 504-887-0113
 1800 South Acadian Thruway, P.O. Box 2028, Baton Rouge, LA 70821
 504-343-4057; 504-343-3814
IN MISSOURI
 1001 Pine Street (at North 10th), St. Louis, MO 63101; **314-621-0346;**
 314-231-1034
IN ILLINOIS
 172 North Michigan Ave., Chicago, IL 60601; **312-346-4228**
IN TEXAS
 114 Main Plaza, San Antonio, TX 78205; **512-224-8101**
IN CALIFORNIA
 1570 Fifth Avenue, San Diego, CA 92101; **714-232-1442**
 46 Geary Street, San Francisco, CA 94108; **415-781-5180**
IN HAWAII
 1143 Bishop Street, Honolulu, HI 96813; **808-521-2731**
IN ALASKA
 750 West 5th Avenue, Anchorage AK 99501; **907-272-8183**
IN CANADA
 3022 Dufferin Street, Toronto 395, Ontario, Canada
IN ENGLAND
 128, Notting Hill Gate, London W11 3QG, England
133 Corporation Street, Birmingham B4 6PH, England
5A-7 Royal Exchange Square, Glasgow G1 3AH, England
82 Bold Street, Liverpool L1 4HR, England
IN AUSTRALIA
 58 Abbotsford Rd., Homebush, N.S.W., Sydney 2140, Australia